KEY TO SOURCE CODES

BrAu	British Authors
BrCA	British Children's Authors
BrWr	British Writers
BroadAu	Broadside Authors and Artists
BusPN	Business People in the News
Cald	Caldecott Medal Books: 1938-1957
CaW	Canada Writes!
CanNov	Canadian Novelists, 1920-1945
CanWW	Canadian Who's Who
CanWr	Canadian Writers
CarSB	The Carolyn Sherwin Bailey Historical Collection of Children's Books
CasWL	Cassell's Encyclopaedia of World Literature
CathA	Catholic Authors
CelCen	Celebrities of the Century
CelR	Celebrity Register
Chambr	Chambers's Cyclopaedia of English Literature
ChiLit	Chicano Literature
ChiSch	Chicano Scholars and Writers
ChhPo	Childhood in Poetry
ChlLR	Children's Literature Review
ChrP	The Children's Poets
ChsFB	The Child's First Books
CivR	Civil Rights
CivRSt	The Civil Rights Struggle: Leaders in Profile
CivWDc	The Civil War Dictionary
ClDMEL	Columbia Dictionary of Modern European Literature
CmCal	A Companion to California
CmMov	A Companion to the Movies
CmScLit	Companion to Scottish Literature
CmpEPM	The Complete Encyclopedia of Popular Music and Jazz
CompSN	Composers since 1900
CpmDNM	Composium Directory of New Music
CnDAL	Concise Dictionary of American Literature
CnE&AP	The Concise Encyclopedia of English and American Poets and Poetry
CnMD	The Concise Encyclopedia of Modern Drama
CnMWL	The Concise Encyclopedia of Modern World Literature
CnThe	A Concise Encyclopedia of the Theatre
CngDr	Congressional Directory
ConAmA	Contemporary American Authors
ConAmC	Contemporary American Composers
ConAmL	Contemporary American Literature
ConAmTC	Contemporary American Theater Critics
ConArch	Contemporary Architects
ConArt	Contemporary Artists
ConAu	Contemporary Authors
ConDes	Contemporary Designers
ConDr	Contemporary Dramatists
ConFLW	Contemporary Foreign Language Writers
ConGrA	Contemporary Graphic Artists
ConICB	Contemporary Illustrators of Children's Books
ConIsC	Contemporary Issues Criticism
ConLC	Contemporary Literary Criticism
ConLCrt	Contemporary Literary Critics
ConNews	Contemporary Newsmakers
ConNov	Contemporary Novelists
ConPhot	Contemporary Photographers
ConP	Contemporary Poets
ConSFA	Contemporary Science Fiction Authors
ConTFT	Contemporary Theatre, Film, and Television
Conv	Conversations
CorpD	Corpus Delicti of Mystery Fiction
CreCan	Creative Canada
CroCAP	Crowell's Handbook of Contemporary American Poetry
CroCD	Crowell's Handbook of Contemporary Drama
CroE&S	Crowell's Handbook of Elizabethan and Stuart Literature
CrtT	The Critical Temper
CurBio	Current Biography Yearbook
CyAG	Cyclopedia of American Government
CyAL	Cyclopaedia of American Literature
CyEd	A Cyclopedia of Education
CyWA	Cyclopedia of World Authors
DcAfL	Dictionary of Afro-Latin American Civilization
DcAmArt	Dictionary of American Art
DcAmAu	Dictionary of American Authors
DcAmB	Dictionary of American Biography
DcAmDH	Dictionary of American Diplomatic History
DcAmLiB	Dictionary of American Library Biography
DcAmMeB	Dictionary of American Medical Biography
DcAmMiB	Dictionary of American Military Biography
DcAmNB	Dictionary of American Negro Biography
DcAmReB	Dictionary of American Religious Biography
DcAmSR	A Dictionary of American Social Reform
DcBiA	A Dictionary of Biographies of Authors Represented in the Authors Digest Series
DcBiPP	A Dictionary of Biography, Past and Present
DcBrAmW	A Dictionary of British and American Women Writers, 1660-1800
DcBrAr	Dictionary of British Artists Working 1900-1950
DcBrBI	The Dictionary of British Book Illustrators and Caricaturists
DcBrWA	The Dictionary of British Watercolour Artists
DcCanB	Dictionary of Canadian Biography
DcCathB	Dictionary of Catholic Biography
DcCAA	A Dictionary of Contemporary American Artists
DcCAr	Dictionary of Contemporary Artists
DcCLAA	A Dictionary of Contemporary Latin American Authors
DcCM	Dictionary of Contemporary Music
DcD&D	Dictionary of Design & Decoration
DcEnA	A Dictionary of English Authors
DcEnL	Dictionary of English Literature
DcEuL	A Dictionary of European Literature
DcFM	Dictionary of Film Makers
DcInB	Dictionary of Indian Biography
DcInv	Dictionary of Inventions & Discoveries
DcIrB	A Dictionary of Irish Biography
DcIrL	Dictionary of Irish Literature
DcIrW	Dictionary of Irish Writers
DcItL	Dictionary of Italian Literature
DcLB	Dictionary of Literary Biography
DcLEL	A Dictionary of Literature in the English Language
DcNaB	The Dictionary of National Biography
DcNiCA	Dictionary of 19th Century Antiques
DcNAA	A Dictionary of North American Authors
DcOrL	Dictionary of Oriental Literatures
DcPol	A Dictionary of Politics
DcRusL	Dictionary of Russian Literature
DcScB	Dictionary of Scientific Biography
DcSeaP	Dictionary of Sea Painters
DcSoc	A Dictionary of Sociology
DcSpL	Dictionary of Spanish Literature
DcVicP	Dictionary of Victorian Painters
DrAP&F	A Directory of American Poets and Fiction Writers
DrAS	Directory of American Scholars
DrBlPA	Directory of Blacks in the Performing Arts
DrInf	The Directory of Infamy
DrLC	Directory of Library Consultants
DrRegL	Directory of Registered Lobbyists and Lobbyist Legislation
Dis&D	Disease and Destiny
Drake	Drake: Dictionary of American Biography
DrmM	Dream Makers
Dun&B	Dun & Bradstreet Reference Book of Corporate Managements
EarABI	Early American Book Illustrators and Wood Engravers
Ebony	The Ebony Success Library

KEY TO SOURCE CODES

EncAAH	Encyclopedia of American Agricultural History
EncAB-A	Encyclopedia of American Biography (American Historical Society)
EncAB-H	Encyclopedia of American Biography (Harper & Row)
EncAJ	The Encyclopedia of American Journalism
EncAR	Encyclopedia of the American Revolution
EncASM	Encyclopedia of American Silver Manufacturers
EncE	Encyclopedia of Espionage
EncFCWM	The Encyclopedia of Folk, Country & Western Music
EncFWF	Encyclopedia of Frontier & Western Fiction
EncJzS	The Encyclopedia of Jazz in the Seventies
EncLatA	Encyclopedia of Latin America
EncMT	Encyclopaedia of the Musical Theatre
EncMys	Encyclopaedia of Mystery and Detection
EncO&P	Encyclopedia of Occultism & Parapsychology
EncPR&S	Encyclopedia of Pop, Rock, and Soul
EncSF	The Encyclopedia of Science Fiction
EncSoA	Encyclopedia of Southern Africa
EncSoB	Encyclopedia of Southern Baptists
EncSoH	The Encyclopedia of Southern History
EncTR	Encyclopedia of the Third Reich
EncTwCJ	Encyclopedia of Twentieth-Century Journalists
EncUrb	Encyclopedia of Urban Planning
EncWL	Encyclopedia of World Literature in the 20th Century
EncWM	The Encyclopedia of World Methodism
EncWT	The Encyclopedia of World Theater
Entr	Entrepreneurs
EuAu	European Authors, 1000-1900
EuWr	European Writers
EvEuW	Everyman's Dictionary of European Writers
EvLB	Everyman's Dictionary of Literary Biography, English and American
FamA&A	Famous Actors and Actresses on the American Stage
FamAIYP	Famous Author-Illustrators for Young People
FamAYP	Famous Authors for Young People
FamMS	Famous Modern Storytellers for Young People
FamPYP	Famous Poets for Young People
FamSYP	Famous Storytellers for Young People
FarE&A	The Far East and Australasia
FemPA	The Female Poets of America
FifBJA	Fifth Book of Junior Authors & Illustrators
FifIDA	Fifth International Directory of Anthropologists
FifCWr	Fifty Caribbean Writers
Film	Filmarama
FilmgC	The Filmgoer's Companion
ForWC	Foremost Women in Communications
ForIL	Forty Illustrators and How They Work
FourBJA	Fourth Book of Junior Authors & Illustrators
Future	The Future: A Guide to Information Sources
GolEC	Golombek's Encyclopedia of Chess
GoodHs	The Good Housekeeping Woman's Almanac
GrEcon	Great Economists since Keynes
GrFLW	Great Foreign Language Writers
GuPsyc	A Guide to Psychologists and Their Concepts
HalFC	Halliwell's Filmgoer's Companion
HanRL	Handbook of Russian Literature
HarEnUS	Harper's Encyclopedia of United States History
HerW	Her Way
HisEWW	The Historical Encyclopedia of World War II
HolP	Hollywood Players
HsB&A	The House of Beadle and Adams and Its Dime and Nickel Novels
ICPEnP	ICP Encyclopedia of Photography
IlBEAAW	The Illustrated Biographical Encyclopedia of Artists of the American West
IlDcG	An Illustrated Dictionary of Glass
IlEncJ	The Illustrated Encyclopedia of Jazz
IlEncMy	An Illustrated Encyclopaedia of Mysticism and the Mystery Religions

IlEncRk	The Illustrated Encyclopedia of Rock
IlrAm	The Illustrator in America
IlsBYP	Illustrators of Books for Young People
IlsCB	Illustrators of Children's Books
InB&W	In Black and White
InSci	Index to Scientists of the World
InWom	Index to Women
IndAu	Indiana Authors and Their Books
IntAu&W	The International Authors and Writers Who's Who
IntDcF	The International Dictionary of Films and Filmmakers
IntDcWB	The International Dictionary of Women's Biography
IntEnSS	International Encyclopedia of the Social Sciences: Biographical Supplement
IntMed	International Medical Who's Who
IntMPA	International Motion Picture Almanac
IntWW	The International Who's Who
IntWWE	International Who's Who in Energy and Nuclear Sciences
IntWWM	International Who's Who in Music and Musicians' Directory
IntWWP	International Who's Who in Poetry
IntYB	The International Year Book and Statesmen's Who's Who
JBA	The Junior Book of Authors
LadLa	The Lady Laureates
LEduc	Leaders in Education
LElec	Leaders in Electronics
LesBEnT	Les Brown's Encyclopedia of Television
LibW	Liberty's Women
LinLib L	The Lincoln Library of Language Arts
LinLib S	The Lincoln Library of Social Studies
LitC	Literature Criticism from 1400 to 1800
LivgBAA	Living Black American Authors
LongCEL	Longman Companion to English Literature
LongCTC	Longman Companion to Twentieth Century Literature
LuthC	Lutheran Cyclopedia
MacBEP	Macmillan Biographical Encyclopedia of Photographic Artists & Innovators
MacDCB	The Macmillan Dictionary of Canadian Biography
MacEA	Macmillan Encyclopedia of Architects
MajMD	Major Modern Dramatists
MakMC	Makers of Modern Culture
MarqDCG	Marquis Who's Who Directory of Computer Graphics
McGDA	McGraw-Hill Dictionary of Art
McGEWB	The McGraw-Hill Encyclopedia of World Biography
McGEWD	McGraw-Hill Encyclopedia of World Drama
McGMS	McGraw-Hill Modern Scientists and Engineers
MedHR	Medal of Honor Recipients, 1863-1978
MemAm	Memorable Americans, 1750-1950
MnBBF	The Men Behind Boys' Fiction
MGM	The MGM Stock Company
MichAu	Michigan Authors
MidE	The Middle East and North Africa
MinnWr	Minnesota Writers
ModAL	Modern American Literature
ModAWP	Modern American Women Poets
ModBlW	Modern Black Writers
ModBrL	Modern British Literature
ModCmwL	Modern Commonwealth Literature
ModFrL	Modern French Literature
ModGL	Modern German Literature
ModLAL	Modern Latin American Literature
ModRL	Modern Romance Literatures
ModSL	Modern Slavic Literatures
ModWD	Modern World Drama
MorBMP	More Books by More People
MorJA	More Junior Authors

WRITERS FOR YOUNG ADULTS:
BIOGRAPHIES
MASTER INDEX

The Gale Biographical Index Series

Biography and Genealogy Master Index
Second Edition, Supplements and Annual Volumes
(GBIS Number 1)

Children's Authors and Illustrators
Fourth Edition
(GBIS Number 2)

Author Biographies Master Index
Third Edition
(GBIS Number 3)

Journalist Biographies Master Index
(GBIS Number 4)

Performing Arts Biography Master Index
Second Edition
(GBIS Number 5)

Writers for Young Adults: Biographies Master Index
Third Edition
(GBIS Number 6)

Historical Biographical Dictionaries Master Index
(GBIS Number 7)

Twentieth-Century Author Biographies Master Index
(GBIS Number 8)

Artist Biographies Master Index
(GBIS Number 9)

Business Biography Master Index
(GBIS Number 10)

Abridged Biography and Genealogy Master Index
(GBIS Number 11)

Gale Biographical Index Series
Number 6

WRITERS FOR YOUNG ADULTS:
BIOGRAPHIES MASTER INDEX

An index to sources of biographical information
about novelists, poets, playwrights, nonfiction writers,
songwriters and lyricists, television and screenwriters
who are of interest to high school students
and to teachers, librarians, and researchers
interested in high school reading materials.

THIRD EDITION

Joyce Nakamura, Editor

Gale Research Inc. • Book Tower • Detroit, Michigan 48226

Editor: Joyce Nakamura
Assistant Editors: Carolyn Chafetz, Laurie Collier
Research Assistants: Shelly Andrews, Kristin R. Dittmeier

Production Manager: Mary Beth Trimper
External Production Assistants: Linda A. Davis, Anthony J. Scolaro

Art Director: Arthur Chartow

Production Supervisor: Laura Bryant
Internal Production Associate: Louise Gagné

Supervisor, Systems and Programming: Diane Belickas
Programmer: Michael A. Hagen

Contents

Introduction

Writers for Young Adults (WYA), now in its third edition, aims to simplify biographical research for high school students and others who have an interest in writers for young adults. This index enables a reader to learn quickly and easily where biographical information can be found for any one of almost 16,000 writers profiled in nearly 600 biographical dictionaries.

Students, teachers, and librarians need not waste valuable time and effort in hit-and-miss searching through many reference books. *Writers for Young Adults* provides one convenient location where the reader can determine how many sources of biographical information exist for a given writer. The reader has the option to compare several sources or to choose the most authoritative or accessible source.

Scope

Writers were chosen for this index on the basis of their appeal to the special reading interests and abilities of high school students. These are the writers that young adults are most likely to encounter when fulfilling class assignments or simply reading for their own pleasure. The range of reading represented here, therefore, is a very broad one. Included here are:

--writers of popular teen-age fiction, like Judy Blume, Ursula K. Le Guin, Richard Peck, S.E. Hinton, Todd Strasser, Cynthia Voigt, and Gary Paulsen;

--writers of adult fiction and nonfiction whose work has been designated as suitable for young adults in book reviews, library cataloging, publishers' classifications, or in recommended reading lists (like that of the National Council of Teachers of English, for example);

--writers of special interest to young adults in media other than books: songwriters and lyricists (like John Lennon, Elton John, and Stevie Wonder), and television and screenwriters (like Steven Spielberg, George Lucas, and Gene Roddenberry).

In *WYA* the editors have included only those writers whose works have been recommended for young adult reading by authorities in the field—librarians, teachers, publishers, book reviewers, or authors themselves. In the absence of authoritative young adult designations for writers in the non-book media, the editors were guided by their own best perception of what screenwriters or lyricists are of interest to young adults.

The biographical sources cited in *WYA* represent a broad range of literary, professional, geographic, and general interest biographical dictionaries. This index has drawn upon all the reference sources contained in Gale's massive *Biography and Genealogy Master Index.* As a result, sources as diverse as the *Directory of American Scholars, Contemporary Authors, The Illustrated Encylopedia of Rock, Who's Who in America,* and *Who's Who in Science Fiction* are cited in *Writers for Young Adults.*

WYA aims to be comprehensive. No attempt was made to select or reject biographical sources on the basis of their content or point of view, or to rate the usefulness of one source against another. Rather, *WYA* includes *all* citations for a given author that occur in *all* the biographical sources researched for this index. Users' needs for information may vary widely; and some sources may be unavailable in some libraries. Therefore, *WYA* attempts to provide the maximum information from which the user can make his or her own best selection.

This index cites only biographical reference books and excludes most material published in journals, magazines, and newspapers, with the exception of periodicals included in *Biography Index.*

Editorial Practices

The third edition of *WYA* retains all material included in the second edition. Thousands of names were added to those listed in the second edition, and all names were computer-matched against the more than one million biographical citations added to the *Biography and Genealogy Master Index* data bank since the previous edition of *WYA*. The computer-generated information was then verified in the original reference sources to ensure that similar names did, in fact, represent the same individual. Names generally appear exactly as they are listed in the source book. Researchers may find biographical sources for the same individual under several listings, such as:

> **Cormier,** Robert 1925-
> **Cormier,** Robert Edmund 1925-

Variations in birth/death dates may also occur.

Cross-references were added as links between "real names" and pseudonyms (or name variants) that often did not exist in the original biographical sources. They have also been used to alert the reader to name variations in sources cited:

> **DeLaMare,** Walter *see also* LaMare, Walter De
> **DeLaMare,** Walter *see also* Mare, Walter DeLa

and to the names of individual members within a group:

> **Beatles,** The *see also* Harrison, George
> **Beatles,** The *see also* Lennon, John
> **Beatles,** The *see also* McCartney, Paul
> **Beatles,** The *see also* Starr, Ringo

Reading a Citation

Each citation gives the writer's name, birth and death dates (if known), and an alphabetically-arranged list of reference sources in which biographical information may be found.

The reference sources cited are given in an abbreviated code form based upon the title of the book. The key to these source codes will be found on the endpapers. Full bibliographic citations, including the codes, begin on page ix.

The abbreviation *[port]* after a source code indicates a portrait or picture of the person appears in the source.

Suggestions for Future Editions

The editors welcome your comments on this edition as well as your suggestions for additional information sources or added features that would be useful in future editions.

Bibliographic Key to Source Codes

Code	Book Indexed
AfSS	*Africa South of the Sahara.* London: Europa Publications, 1978, 1979, 1980, 1981, 1982. Distributed by Gale Research Co., Detroit, Michigan.

AfSS 78	Eighth edition, 1978-1979
AfSS 79	Ninth edition, 1979-1980
AfSS 80	10th edition, 1980-1981
AfSS 81	11th edition, 1981-1982
AfSS 82	12th edition, 1982-1983

Biographies are located in the "Who's Who in Africa South of the Sahara" section in each volume.

AfrA   *African Authors: A Companion to Black African Writing.* Volume I: 1300-1973. By Donald E. Herdeck. Washington, D.C.: Black Orpheus Press, 1973.

AfroAA   *Afro-American Artists.* A bio-bibliographical directory. Compiled and edited by Theresa Dickason Cederholm. Boston: Trustees of the Boston Public Library, 1973.

ALA 80   *The ALA Yearbook.* A review of library events 1979. Volume 5, 1980. Chicago: American Library Association, 1980.

Biographies begin on page 73. The Obituary section, indicated in this index by the code *N*, begins on page 227.

Alli   Allibone, S. Austin. *A Critical Dictionary of English Literature and British and American Authors Living and Deceased from the Earliest Accounts to the Latter Half of the Nineteenth Century.* Containing over 46,000 articles (authors) with 40 indexes of subjects. Three volumes. Philadelphia: J.B. Lippincott & Co., 1858-1871. Reprint. Detroit: Gale Research Co., 1965.

Alli SUP   *A Supplement to Allibone's Critical Dictionary of English Literature and British and American Authors.* Containing over 37,000 articles (authors) and enumerating over 93,000 titles. Two volumes. By John Foster Kirk. Philadelphia: J.B. Lippincott & Co., 1891. Reprint. Detroit: Gale Research Co., 1965.

AlmAP   *The Almanac of American Politics.* The senators, the representatives, the governors--their records, states, and districts. By Michael Barone, Grant Ujifusa, and Douglas Matthews. New York: E.P. Dutton, 1977, 1979.

AlmAP 78	1978 edition, 1977
AlmAP 80	1980 edition, 1979

Use the "Names Index" in each volume to locate biographies.

AlmAP 82   *The Almanac of American Politics 1982.* The president, the senators, the
                  representatives, the governors: their records and election results, their states and
                  districts. By Michael Barone and Grant Ujifusa. Washington, D.C.: Barone & Co.,
                  1981.
                      Use the "Index of Persons" to locate biographies.

AlmAP 84   *The Almanac of American Politics 1984.* The president, the senators, the
                  representatives, the governors: their records and election results, their states and
                  districts. By Michael Barone and Grant Ujifusa. Washington D.C.: National
                  Journal, 1983.
                      Use the "Index of People" to locate biographies.

AmArch 70   *American Architects Directory.* Third edition. Edited by John F. Gane. New York: R.R.
                  Bowker Co. (under the sponsorship of American Institute of Architects), 1970.

AmArt   *American Artists.* An illustrated survey of leading contemporary Americans. Edited by
                  Les Krantz. New York: Facts on File Publications, 1985.

AmAu   *American Authors, 1600-1900: A Biographical Dictionary of American Literature.*
                  Edited by Stanley J. Kunitz and Howard Haycraft. New York: H.W. Wilson Co.,
                  1938.

AmAu&B   *American Authors and Books, 1640 to the Present Day.* Third revised edition. By W.J.
                  Burke and Will D. Howe. Revised by Irving Weiss and Arne Weiss. New York:
                  Crown Publishers, 1972.

AmBench 79   *The American Bench: Judges of the Nation.* Second edition. Edited by Mary Reincke
                  and Nancy Lichterman. Minneapolis: Reginald Bishop Forster & Associates,
                  1979.
                      Use the "Name Index" at the front of the volume to locate biographies.

AmBi   *American Biographies.* By Wheeler Preston. New York: Harper & Brothers Publishers,
                  1940. Reprint. Detroit: Gale Research Co., 1974.

AmCath 80   *The American Catholic Who's Who.* Volume 23, 1980-1981. Edited by Joy Anderson.
                  Washington, D.C.: National Catholic News Service, 1979.

AmComp   *American Composers: A Biographical Dictionary.* By David Ewen. New York: G.P.
                  Putnam's Sons, 1982.

AmEA 74   American Economic Association. *Directory of Members, 1974.* Edited by Rendigs Fels.
                  Published as Volume 64, Number 5 (October, 1974) of *The American Economic
                  Review.*

AmLY   *The American Literary Yearbook.* A biographical and bibliographical dictionary of
                  living North American authors; a record of contemporary literary activity; an
                  authors' manual and students' text book. Volume 1, 1919. Edited by Hamilton
                  Traub. Henning, Minnesota: Paul Traub, 1919. Reprint. Detroit: Gale Research
                  Co., 1968.

                      AmLY   The "Biographical and Bibliographical Dictionary of
                                          Living North American Authors" section begins on page
                                                                                              57.
                      AmLY X   The "Pen-names and Pseudonyms" section begins on page
                                                                                              49.

AmM&WS *American Men and Women of Science.* Edited by Jaques Cattell Press. New York: R.R. Bowker Co., 1971-1973, 1976-1978, 1979, 1982, 1986.

AmM&WS 73P	Physical & Biological Sciences, 12th edition, 1971-1973
AmM&WS 73S	Social & Behavioral Sciences, 12th edition, 1973
AmM&WS 76P	Physical & Biological Sciences, 13th edition, 1976
AmM&WS 78S	Social & Behavioral Sciences, 13th edition, 1978
AmM&WS 79P	Physical & Biological Sciences, 14th edition, 1979
AmM&WS 82P	Physical & Biological Sciences, 15th edition, 1982
AmM&WS 86P	Physical & Biological Sciences, 16th edition, 1986

AmNov *American Novelists of Today.* By Harry R. Warfel. New York: American Book Co., 1951. Reprint. Westport, Connecticut: Greenwood Press, 1976.

The "Index of Married Names and Pseudonyms," indicated in this index by the code *X*, begins on page 477.

AmPB *American Picturebooks from "Noah's Ark" to "The Beast Within."* By Barbara Bader. New York: Macmillan Publishing Co.; London: Collier Macmillan Publishers, 1976.

AmPolW *American Political Women: Contemporary and Historical Profiles.* By Esther Stineman. Littleton, Colorado: Libraries Unlimited, 1980.

AmPolW 80	Profiles
AmPolW 80A	Appendix I: The "Women of the Congress 1917-1980" section begins on page 191.
AmPolW 80B	Appendix II: The "Women Ambassadors of the United States Currently Serving" section begins on page 198.
AmPolW 80C	Appendix III: The "Women Chiefs of Mission 1933-1980" section begins on page 199.
AmPolW 80D	Appendix IV: The "Women Currently Serving as Federal Judges" section begins on page 202.
AmPolW 80E	Appendix V: The "Women Currently Serving in Government in Key Departmental, Agency, and White House Positions" section begins on page 204.

AmPS *American Popular Songs from the Revolutionary War to the Present.* Edited by David Ewen. New York: Random House, 1966.

AmPS	The "American Popular Songs" section begins on page 1.
AmPS A	The "All-Time Best-Selling Popular Recordings" section begins on page 485.
AmPS B	The "Some American Performers of the Past and Present" section begins on page 499.

AmRef *American Reformers.* Edited by Alden Whitman. New York: H.W. Wilson Co., 1985.

AmWom *American Women.* A revised edition of *Woman of the Century,* 1,500 biographies with over 1,400 portraits; a comprehensive encyclopedia of the lives and achievements of American women during the nineteenth century. Two volumes. Edited by Frances E. Willard and Mary A. Livermore. New York: Mast, Crowell & Kirkpatrick, 1897. Reprint. Detroit: Gale Research Co., 1973.

AmWomD *American Women Dramatists of the Twentieth Century.* A bibliography. By Brenda Coven. Metuchen, New Jersey: Scarecrow Press, 1982.

AmWomM *American Women Managers and Administrators.* A selective biographical dictionary of twentieth-century leaders in business, education, and government. By Judith A. Leavitt. Westport, Connecticut: Greenwood Press, 1985.

AmWomWr   *American Women Writers: A Critical Reference Guide from Colonial Times to the Present.* Four volumes. Edited by Lina Mainiero. New York: Frederick Ungar Publishing Co., 1979-1982.

AmWr   *American Writers: A Collection of Literary Biographies.* New York: Charles Scribner's Sons, 1974, 1979, 1981.

AmWr	Volumes I-IV. Edited by Leonard Unger, 1974. Originally published as the *University of Minnesota Pamphlets on American Writers.*
AmWr S1	Supplement I. Two parts. Edited by Leonard Unger, 1979.
AmWr S2	Supplement II. Two parts. Edited by A. Walton Litz, 1981.

AmWrBE   *American Writers before 1800.* A biographical and critical dictionary. Three volumes. Edited by James A. Levernier and Douglas R. Wilmes. Westport, Connecticut: Greenwood Press, 1983.

AnObit   *The Annual Obituary.* New York: St. Martin's Press, 1981, 1982, 1983.

AnObit 1980	*1980*, edited by Roland Turner, 1981.
AnObit 1981	*1981*, edited by Janet Podell, 1982.
AnObit 1982	*1982*, edited by Janet Podell, 1983.

Use the "Alphabetical Index of Entrants" at the front of each volume to locate biographies.

AnObit   *The Annual Obituary.* Chicago: St. James Press, 1984, 1985.

AnObit 1983	*1983*, edited by Elizabeth Devine, 1984.
AnObit 1984	*1984*, edited by Margot Levy, 1985.

Use the "Alphabetical Index of Entrants" at the front of each volume to locate biographies.

AnCL   *Anthology of Children's Literature.* Fourth edition. Edited by Edna Johnson, Evelyn R. Sickels, and Frances Clarke Sayers. Boston: Houghton Mifflin Co., 1970.

Biographies begin on page 1217.

AnMV 1926   *Anthology of Magazine Verse for 1926 and Yearbook of American Poetry.* Edited by William Stanley Braithwaite. New York: G. Sully, 1926. Reprint. Granger Index Reprint Series. Freeport, New York: Books for Libraries Press, 1972.

The "Biographical Dictionary of Poets in the United States" section begins on page 3 of part 4.

AntBDN   *The Antique Buyer's Dictionary of Names.* By A.W. Coysh. Newton Abbot, England: David & Charles, 1970.

AntBDN A	The "Art Nouveau" section begins on page 13.
AntBDN B	The "Book Illustrations and Prints" section begins on page 23.
AntBDN M	The "Pottery and Porcelain" section begins on page 185.
AntBDN Q	The "Silver" section begins on page 250.

ApCAB   *Appleton's Cyclopaedia of American Biography.* Six volumes. Edited by James Grant Wilson and John Fiske. New York: D. Appleton & Co., 1888-1889. Reprint. Detroit: Gale Research Co., 1968.

ApCAB SUP   *Appleton's Cyclopaedia of American Biography.* Volume VII, Supplement. Edited by James Grant Wilson. New York: D. Appleton & Co., 1901. Reprint. Detroit: Gale Research Co., 1968.

ApCAB X　　　*A Supplement to Appleton's Cyclopaedia of American Biography.* Six volumes. Originally published as *The Cyclopaedia of American Biography, Supplementary Edition.* Edited by L.E. Dearborn. New York: Press Association Compilers, 1918-1931.

ArizL　　　*Arizona in Literature: A Collection of the Best Writings of Arizona Authors from Early Spanish Days to the Present Time.* By Mary G. Boyer. Glendale, California: Arthur H. Clark Co., 1935. Reprint. Ann Arbor: Gryphon Books, 1971.

　　　　　Use the Index to locate biographies.

ArtCS　　　*The Art of the Comic Strip.* By Judith O'Sullivan. College Park, Maryland: University of Maryland, Department of Art, 1971.

　　　　　Biographies begin on page 60.

ArtsAmW 1　　　*Artists of the American West.* A biographical dictionary. Volume I. By Doris Ostrander Dawdy. Chicago: Swallow Press; Sage Books, 1974.

ArtsAmW 2　　　*Artists of the American West.* A biographical dictionary. Volume II. By Doris Ostrander Dawdy. Chicago: Swallow Press; Sage Books, 1981.

ArtsAmW 3　　　*Artists of the American West.* A biographical dictionary, artists born before 1900. Volume III. By Doris Ostrander Dawdy. Athens, Ohio: Ohio University Press; Swallow Press, 1985.

ArtsCL　　　*Artists of a Certain Line: A Selection of Illustrators for Children's Books.* By John Ryder. London: The Bodley Head, 1960.

ArtsNiC　　　*Artists of the Nineteenth Century and Their Works.* A handbook containing two thousand and fifty biographical sketches. Revised edition. Two volumes. By Clara Erskine Clement and Laurence Hutton. Boston: J.R. Osgood & Co., 1885. Reprint, two volumes in one. St. Louis: North Point, 1969.

AmSCAP 66　　　*The ASCAP Biographical Dictionary of Composers, Authors and Publishers.* Third edition. Compiled and edited by The Lynn Farnol Group. New York: American Society of Composers, Authors and Publishers, 1966.

AsBiEn　　　*Asimov's Biographical Encyclopedia of Science and Technology.* The lives and achievements of 1,195 great scientists from ancient times to the present, chronologically arranged. New revised edition. By Isaac Asimov. New York: Avon, 1976.

　　　　　Use the "Alphabetic List of Biographical Entries" at the front of the book to locate biographies.

AtlBL　　　*Atlantic Brief Lives: A Biographical Companion to the Arts.* Edited by Louis Kronenberger. Boston: Little, Brown & Co., 1971.

ASpks　　　*The Author Speaks: Selected "PW" Interviews, 1967-1976.* By *Publishers Weekly* editors and contributors. New York: R.R. Bowker Co., 1977.

AuByp　　　*Authors of Books for Young People.* By Martha E. Ward and Dorothy A. Marquardt. Metuchen, New Jersey: Scarecrow Press, 1971, 1979.

AuBYP	Second edition, 1971
AuBYP SUP	Supplement to the second edition, 1975
AuBYP SUPA	Addendum to the Supplement

Au&ICB　　　*Authors and Illustrators of Children's Books: Writings on Their Lives and Works.* By Miriam Hoffman and Eva Samuels. New York: R.R. Bowker Co., 1972.

AuNews   *Authors in the News.* A compiliation of news stories and feature articles from American newspapers and magazines covering writers and other members of the communications media. Two volumes. Edited by Barbara Nykoruk. Detroit: Gale Research Co., 1976.

                 AuNews 1   Volume 1
                 AuNews 2   Volume 2

Au&Wr 71   *The Author's and Writer's Who's Who.* Sixth edition. Darien, Connecticut: Hafner Publishing Co., 1971.

Baker 78   *Baker's Biographical Dictionary of Musicians.* Sixth edition. Revised by Nicolas Slonimsky. New York: Schirmer Books; London: Collier Macmillan Publishers, 1978.

Baker 84   *Baker's Biographical Dictionary of Musicians.* Seventh edition. Revised by Nicolas Slonimsky. New York: Macmillan, Schirmer Books, 1984.

BbD   *The Bibliophile Dictionary.* A biographical record of the great authors, with bibliographical notices of their principal works from the beginning of history. Originally published as Volumes 29 and 30 of *The Bibliophile Library of Literature, Art, and Rare Manuscripts.* Compiled and arranged by Nathan Haskell Dole, Forrest Morgan, and Caroline Ticknor. New York: International Bibliophile Society, 1904. Reprint. Detroit: Gale Research Co., 1966.

BbtC   *Bibliotheca Canadensis: Or, A Manual of Canadian Literature.* By Henry J. Morgan. Ottawa: G.E. Desbarats, 1867. Reprint. Detroit: Gale Research Co., 1968.

BiGAW   *A Bio-Bibliography of German-American Writers, 1670-1970.* By Robert E. Ward. White Plains, New York: Kraus International Publications, 1985.

BiNAW Sup   *A Biobibliography of Native American Writers 1772-1924: A Supplement.* Native American Bibliography Series, No. 5. By Daniel F. Littlefield, Jr. and James W. Parins. Metuchen, New Jersey: Scarecrow Press, 1985.

             BiNAW Sup   "A Bibliography of Native American Writers" section begins on page 1.
             BiNAW SupA   "A Bibliography of Native American Writers Known Only as Pen Names" section begins on page 159.
             BiNAW SupB   The "Biographical Notes" section begins on page 165.

BiAUS   *Biographical Annals of the Civil Government of the United States, during Its First Century.* From original and official sources. By Charles Lanman. Washington, D.C.: James Anglim, 1876. Reprint. Detroit: Gale Research Co., 1976.

        The "Additional Facts" section, indicated in this index by the code *SUP*, begins on page 633.

BiCAW   *The Biographical Cyclopaedia of American Women.* Two volumes. Volume I: Compiled under the supervision of Mabel Ward Cameron. New York: Halvord Publishing Co., 1924. Volume II: Compiled under the supervision of Erma Conkling Lee. New York: Franklin W. Lee Publishing Corp., 1925. Reprint (both volumes). Detroit: Gale Research Co., 1974.

        Use the Index in each volume to locate biographies.

BiDAfM   *Biographical Dictionary of Afro-American and African Musicians.* By Eileen Southern. Westport, Connecticut: Greenwood Press, 1982.

BiDAmBL 83   *Biographical Dictionary of American Business Leaders.* By John N. Ingham. Westport, Connecticut: Greenwood Press, 1983.

        Use the Index to locate biographies.

BiDAmEd *Biographical Dictionary of American Educators.* Three volumes. Edited by John F. Ohles. Westport, Connecticut: Greenwood Press, 1978.

BiDAmL *Biographical Dictionary of American Labor.* Edited by Gary M. Fink. Westport, Connecticut: Greenwood Press, 1984.

  Biographies begin on page 83.

BiDAmLL *Biographical Dictionary of American Labor Leaders.* Edited by Gary M. Fink. Westport, Connecticut: Greenwood Press, 1974.

BiDAmM *Biographical Dictionary of American Music.* By Charles Eugene Claghorn. West Nyack, New York: Parker Publishing Co., 1973.

BiDAmS *Biographical Dictionary of American Science, the Seventeenth through the Nineteenth Centuries.* By Clark A. Elliott. Westport, Connecticut: Greenwood Press, 1979.

BiDBrA *A Biographical Dictionary of British Architects 1600-1840.* By Howard Colvin. New York: Facts on File, 1980.

  "Appendix A," indicated in this index by the code *A*, begins on page 969.

BiDBrF 1 *The Biographical Dictionary of British Feminists.* Volume One: 1800-1930. By Olive Banks. New York: New York University Press, 1985.

BiDD *Biographical Dictionary of Dance.* By Barbara Naomi Cohen-Stratyner. New York: Macmillan Publishing Co., Schirmer Books; London: Collier Macmillan Publishers, 1982.

BiDFedJ *Biographical Dictionary of the Federal Judiciary.* Compiled by Harold Chase, Samuel Krislov, Keith O. Boyum, and Jerry N. Clark. Detroit: Gale Research Co., 1976.

  The Addendum, indicated in this index by the code *A*, begins on page 319.

BiDFilm *A Biographical Dictionary of Film.* By David Thomson. First edition. New York: William Morrow & Co., 1976.

BiDInt *Biographical Dictionary of Internationalists.* Edited by Warren F. Kuehl. Westport, Connecticut: Greenwood Press, 1983.

BiDIrW *A Biographical Dictionary of Irish Writers.* By Anne M. Brady and Brian Cleeve. New York: St. Martin's Press, 1985.

  BiDIrW   The "Writers in English" section begins on page 1.
  BiDIrW A   The Addendum begins on page 254.
  BiDIrW B   The "Writers in Irish and Latin" section begins on page 255.

BiDJaL *Biographical Dictionary of Japanese Literature.* By Sen'ichi Hisamatsu. Tokyo: Kodansha International, 1976. Distributed by Harper & Row, New York, New York.

  Use the Index to locate biographies.

BiDJaz *Biographical Dictionary of Jazz.* By Charles Eugene Claghorn. Englewood Cliffs, New Jersey: Prentice-Hall, 1982.

  The "Index of Jazz and Various Small Groups" section, indicated in this index by the code *A*, begins on page 327.

BiDLA *A Biographical Dictionary of the Living Authors of Great Britain and Ireland.* Comprising literary memoirs and anecdotes of their lives; and a chronological register of their publications, with the number of editions printed; including notices of some foreign writers whose works have been occasionally published in England. London: Printed for Henry Colburn, Public Library, Hanover Square, 1816. Reprint. Detroit: Gale Research Co., 1966.

The "Supplement of Additions and Corrections," indicated in this index by the code *SUP*, begins on page 407.

BiDMarx   *Biographical Dictionary of Marxism.* Edited by Robert A. Gorman. Westport, Connecticut: Greenwood Press, 1986.

BiDMPL   *Biographical Dictionary of Modern Peace Leaders.* Edited by Harold Josephson. Westport, Connecticut: Greenwood Press, 1985.

BiDNeoM   *Biographical Dictionary of Neo-Marxism.* Edited by Robert A. Gorman. Westport, Connecticut: Greenwood Press, 1985.

BiDPara   *Biographical Dictionary of Parapsychology, with Directory and Glossary, 1964-1966.* Edited by Helene Pleasants. New York: Garrett Publications, Helix Press, 1964.

BiDPsy   *Biographical Dictionary of Psychology.* By Leonard Zusne. Westport, Connecticut: Greenwood Press, 1984. A continuation of *Names in the History of Psychology: A Biographical Sourcebook* (see below).

BiDRP&D   *A Biographical Dictionary of Renaissance Poets and Dramatists, 1520-1650.* By J.W. Saunders. Sussex, England: Harvester Press; Totowa, New Jersey: Barnes & Noble Books, 1983.

BiDSA   *Biographical Dictionary of Southern Authors.* Originally published as *Library of Southern Literature, Volume 15, Biographical Dictionary of Authors.* Compiled by Lucian Lamar Knight. Atlanta: Martin & Hoyt Co., 1929. Reprint. Detroit: Gale Research Co., 1978.

BiD&SB   *Biographical Dictionary and Synopsis of Books Ancient and Modern.* Edited by Charles Dudley Warner. Akron, Ohio: Werner Co., 1902. Reprint. Detroit: Gale Research Co., 1965.

BiDrACP 79   *Biographical Directory of the American College of Physicians, 1979.* Compiled by Jaques Cattell Press. New York: R.R. Bowker Co., 1979.

Use the Index, which begins on page 1789, to locate biographies.

BiDrAC   *Biographical Directory of the American Congress, 1774-1971.* The Continental Congress (September 5, 1774 to October 21, 1788) and the Congress of the United States (from the first through the ninety-first Congress March 4, 1789, to January 3, 1971, inclusive). Washington, D.C.: United States Government Printing Office, 1971.

Biographies begin on page 487.

BiDrAPH 79   *Biographical Directory of the American Public Health Association, 1979.* Compiled by Jaques Cattell Press. New York: R.R. Bowker Co., 1979.

BiDrAPA 77   *Biographical Directory of the Fellows and Members of the American Psychiatric Association.* Compiled by Jaques Cattell Press. New York: R.R. Bowker Co., 1977.

BiDrGov   *Biographical Directory of the Governors of the United States, 1789-1978.* Four volumes. Edited by Robert Sobel and John Raimo. Westport, Connecticut: Microform Review, Meckler Books, 1978.

Use the Index in each volume to locate biographies.

BiDrLUS 70   *A Biographical Directory of Librarians in the United States and Canada.* Fifth edition. Edited by Lee Ash. Chicago: American Library Association, 1970.

BiDrUSE   *Biographical Directory of the United States Executive Branch 1774-1971.* Edited by Robert Sobel. Westport, Connecticut: Greenwood Publishing Co., 1971.

BiESc   *A Biographical Encyclopedia of Scientists.* Two volumes. Edited by John Daintith, Sarah Mitchell, and Elizabeth Tootill. New York: Facts on File, 1981.

BiE&WWA   *The Biographical Encyclopaedia and Who's Who of the American Theatre.* Edited by Walter Rigdon. New York: James H. Heineman, 1966. Revised edition published as *Notable Names in the American Theatre* (see below).

            "Biographical Who's Who" begins on page 227.

BiHiMed   *A Biographical History of Medicine: Excerpts and Essays on the Men and Their Work.* By John H. Talbott. New York: Grune & Stratton, 1970.

            Use the "Name Index," which begins on page 1193, to locate biographies.

BioIn   *Biography Index.* A cumulative index to biographical material in books and magazines. New York: H.W. Wilson Co., 1949-1984.

BioIn 1	Volume 1: January, 1946-July, 1949; 1949
BioIn 2	Volume 2: August, 1949-August, 1952; 1953
BioIn 3	Volume 3: September, 1952-August, 1955; 1956
BioIn 4	Volume 4: September, 1955-August, 1958; 1960
BioIn 5	Volume 5: September, 1958-August, 1961; 1962
BioIn 6	Volume 6: September, 1961-August, 1964; 1965
BioIn 7	Volume 7: September, 1964-August, 1967; 1968
BioIn 8	Volume 8: September, 1967-August, 1970; 1971
BioIn 9	Volume 9: September, 1970-August, 1973; 1974
BioIn 10	Volume 10: September, 1973-August, 1976; 1977
BioIn 11	Volume 11: September, 1976-August, 1979; 1980
BioIn 12	Volume 12: September, 1979-August, 1982; 1983
BioIn 13	Volume 13: September, 1982-August, 1984; 1984

BioNews   *Biography News.* A compilation of news stories and feature articles from American news media covering personalities of national interest in all fields. Edited by Frank E. Bair. Detroit: Gale Research Co., 1974-1975.

BioNews 74	Volume 1, Numbers 1-12, 1974
BioNews 75	Volume 2, Number 1, January-February, 1975

BlkAWP   *Black American Writers Past and Present: A Biographical and Bibliographical Dictionary.* Two volumes. By Theressa Gunnels Rush, Carol Fairbanks Myers, and Esther Spring Arata. Metuchen, New Jersey: Scarecrow Press, 1975.

BlkWWr   *Black Women Writers (1950-1980): A Critical Evaluation.* Edited by Mari Evans. Garden City, New York: Anchor Press/Doubleday, 1984.

BlueB 76   *The Blue Book: Leaders of the English-Speaking World.* 1976 edition. London: St. James Press; New York: St. Martin's Press, 1976. Republished in two volumes by Gale Research Co., Detroit, Michigan, 1979.

            The Obituary section, indicated in this index by the code *N*, begins on page 1837.

BluesWW   *Blues Who's Who: A Biographical Dictionary of Blues Singers.* By Sheldon Harris. New Rochelle, New York: Arlington House Publishers, 1979.

BkC   *The Book of Catholic Authors: Informal Self-Portraits of Famous Modern Catholic Writers.* Edited by Walter Romig. Detroit: Walter Romig & Co., 1942-?

BkC 1		First series, 1942
BkC 2		Second series, 1943
BkC 3		Third series, 1945
BkC 4		Fourth series (n.d.)
BkC 5		Fifth series (n.d.)
BkC 6		Sixth series (n.d.)

BkCL   *A Book of Children's Literature.* Third edition. Edited by Lillian Hollowell. New York: Holt, Rinehart & Winston, 1966.

       Biographies begin on page 553.

BkIE   *Book Illustrators in Eighteenth-Century England.* By Hanns Hammelmann. Edited and completed by T.S.R. Boase. New Haven, Connecticut: Yale University Press (for The Paul Mellon Centre for Studies in British Art, London), 1975.

BkP   *Books Are by People: Interviews with 104 Authors and Illustrators of Books for Young Children.* By Lee Bennett Hopkins. New York: Citation Press, 1969.

BriB   *Brilliant Bylines.* A biographical anthology of notable newspaperwomen in America. By Barbara Belford. New York: Columbia University Press, 1986.

BnEnAmA   *The Britannica Encyclopedia of American Art.* Chicago: Encyclopaedia Britannica Educational Corp., 1973. Distributed by Simon & Schuster, New York, New York.

Br&AmS   *British and American Sporting Authors: Their Writings and Biographies.* By A. Henry Higginson. London: Hutchinson & Co., 1951.

       Use the Index to locate biographies.

BrAu   *British Authors before 1800: A Biographical Dictionary.* Edited by Stanley J. Kunitz and Howard Haycraft. New York: H.W. Wilson Co., 1952.

BrAu 19   *British Authors of the Nineteenth Century.* Edited by Stanley J. Kunitz. New York: H.W. Wilson Co., 1936.

BrCA   *British Children's Authors: Interviews at Home.* By Cornelia Jones and Olivia R. Way. Chicago: American Library Association, 1976.

BrWr   *British Writers.* Edited under the auspices of the British Council, Ian Scott-Kilvert, General Editor. New York: Charles Scribner's Sons, 1979-1984.

BrWr 1	Volume I: William Langland to The English Bible, 1979
BrWr 2	Volume II: Thomas Middleton to George Farquhar, 1979
BrWr 3	Volume III: Daniel Defoe to The Gothic Novel, 1980
BrWr 4	Volume IV: William Wordsworth to Robert Browning, 1981
BrWr 5	Volume V: Elizabeth Gaskell to Francis Thompson, 1982
BrWr 6	Volume VI: Thomas Hardy to Wilfred Owen, 1983
BrWr 7	Volume VII: Sean O'Casey to Poets of World War II, 1983

       Use the "List of Subjects" at the front of each volume to locate biographies.

BroadAu   *Broadside Authors and Artists: An Illustrated Biographical Directory.* Compiled and edited by Leaonead Pack Bailey. Detroit: Broadside Press, 1974.

BusPN   *Business People in the News.* A compilation of news stories and feature articles from American newspapers and magazines covering people in industry, finance, and labor. Volume 1. Edited by Barbara Nykoruk. Detroit: Gale Research Co., 1976.

Cald 1938   *Caldecott Medal Books: 1938-1957.* With the artist's acceptance papers & related material chiefly from the *Horn Book Magazine.* Horn Book Papers, Volume II. Edited by Bertha Mahony Miller and Elinor Whitney Field. Boston: Horn Book, 1957.

CaW   *Canada Writes!* The members' book of the Writers' Union of Canada. Edited by K.A. Hamilton. Toronto: Writers' Union of Canada, 1977.

    The "Additional Members" section, indicated in this index by the code *A*, begins on page 387.

CanNov   *Canadian Novelists, 1920-1945.* By Clara Thomas. Toronto: Longmans, Green & Co., 1946. Reprint. Folcroft, Pennsylvania: Folcroft Library Editions, 1970.

CanWW 70   *Canadian Who's Who.* A biographical dictionary of notable living men and women. Volume 12, 1970-1972. Toronto: Who's Who Canadian Publications, 1972.

CanWW   *Canadian Who's Who.* A biographical dictionary of notable living men and women. Edited by Kieran Simpson. Toronto: University of Toronto Press, 1979, 1980, 1981, 1983.

    CanWW 79   Volume XIV, 1979
    CanWW 80   Volume XV, 1980
    CanWW 81   Volume XVI, 1981
    CanWW 83   Volume XVIII, 1983

CanWr   *Canadian Writers: A Biographical Dictionary.* New edition, revised and enlarged. Edited by Guy Sylvestre, Brandon Conron, and Carl F. Klinck. Toronto: Ryerson Press, 1966.

CarSB   *The Carolyn Sherwin Bailey Historical Collection of Children's Books: A Catalogue.* Edited and compiled by Dorothy R. Davis. New Haven, Connecticut: Southern Connecticut State College, 1966.

    Not in strict alphabetic sequence.

CasWL   *Cassell's Encyclopaedia of World Literature.* Edited by S.H. Steinberg in two volumes. Revised and enlarged in three volumes by J. Buchanan-Brown. New York: William Morrow & Co., 1973.

    Biographies are found in Volumes 2 and 3.

CathA   *Catholic Authors: Contemporary Biographical Sketches.* Two volumes. Edited by Matthew Hoehn. Newark, New Jersey: St. Mary's Abbey, 1948, 1952. Reprint (first volume). Detroit: Gale Research Co., 1981.

    CathA 1930   First volume: 1930-1947, 1948
    CathA 1952   Second volume, 1952

CelCen   *Celebrities of the Century.* Being a dictionary of men and women of the nineteenth century. Two volumes. Edited by Lloyd C. Sanders. London: Cassell & Co.,, 1887. Reprint. Ann Arbor: Gryphon Books, 1971.

CelR   *Celebrity Register.* Third edition. Edited by Earl Blackwell. New York: Simon & Schuster, 1973.

Chambr   *Chambers's Cyclopaedia of English Literature.* A history critical and biographical of authors in the English tongue from the earliest times till the present day with specimens of their writings. Three volumes. Edited by David Patrick, revised by

J. Liddell Geddie. Philadelphia: J.B. Lippincott, Co., 1938. Reprint. Detroit: Gale
Research Co., 1978.

Chambr 1	Volume I: 7th-17th Century
Chambr 2	Volume II: 18th Century
Chambr 3	Volume III: 19th-20th Century

Use the Index in each volume to locate biographies.

ChiLit   *Chicano Literature.* A reference guide. Edited by Julio A. Martinez and Francisco A.
Lomeli. Westport, Connecticut: Greenwood Press, 1985.

"Appendix A," indicated in this index by the code *A*, begins on page 441.

ChiSch   *Chicano Scholars and Writers: A Bio-Bibliographical Directory.* Edited and compiled by
Julio A. Martinez. Metuchen, New Jersey: Scarecrow Press, 1979.

ChhPo   *Childhood in Poetry.* A catalogue, with biographical and critical annotations, of the
books of English and American poets comprising the Shaw Childhood in Poetry
Collection in the Library of the Florida State University. By John Mackay Shaw.
Detroit: Gale Research Co., 1967, 1972, 1976, 1980.

ChhPo	Original Volumes, 1967
ChhPo S1	First Supplement, 1972
ChhPo S2	Second Supplement, 1976
ChhPo S3	Third Supplement, 1980

ChlLR   *Children's Literature Review.* Excerpts from reviews, criticism, and commentary on
books for children and young people. Detroit: Gale Research Co., 1976-1986.

ChlLR 1	Volume 1, 1976
ChlLR 2	Volume 2, 1976
ChlLR 3	Volume 3, 1978
ChlLR 4	Volume 4, 1982
ChlLR 5	Volume 5, 1983
ChlLR 6	Volume 6, 1984
ChlLR 7	Volume 7, 1984
ChlLR 8	Volume 8, 1985
ChlLR 9	Volume 9, 1985
ChlLR 10	Volume 10, 1986
ChlLR 11	Volume 11, 1986
ChlLR 12	Volume 12, 1987
ChlLR 13	Volume 13, 1987

ChrP   *The Children's Poets: Analyses and Appraisals of the Greatest English and American
Poets for Children.* By Walter Barnes. Yonkers-on-Hudson, New York: World
Book Co., 1924.

ChsFB   *The Child's First Books: A Critical Study of Pictures and Texts.* By Donnarae MacCann
and Olga Richard. New York: H.W. Wilson Co., 1973.

ChsFB A	"Author Biographies" begin on page 96.
ChsFB I	"Illustrator Biographies" begin on page 47.

CivR 74   *Civil Rights: A Current Guide to the People, Organizations, and Events.* A CBS News
Reference Book. Second edition. By Joan Martin Burke. New York: R.R. Bowker
Co., 1974.

Biographies begin on page 21.

CivRSt   *The Civil Rights Struggle: Leaders in Profile.* By John D'Emilio. New York: Facts on
File, 1979.

CivWDc   *The Civil War Dictionary.* By Mark Mayo Boatner, III. New York: David McKay Co.,
1959.

ClDMEL   *Columbia Dictionary of Modern European Literature.* First edition. Edited by Horatio Smith. New York: Columbia University Press, 1947.

CmCal   *A Companion to California.* By James D. Hart. New York: Oxford University Press, 1978.

CmMov   *A Companion to the Movies: From 1903 to the Present Day.* A guide to the leading players, directors, screenwriters, composers, cameramen and other artistes who have worked in the English-speaking cinema over the last 70 years. By Roy Pickard. New York: Hippocrene Books, 1972.

        Use the "Who's Who Index" to locate biographies.

CmScLit   *Companion to Scottish Literature.* By Trevor Royle. Detroit: Gale Research, 1983.

CmpEPM   *The Complete Encyclopedia of Popular Music and Jazz, 1900-1950.* Three volumes. By Roger D. Kinkle. New Rochelle, New York: Arlington House Publishers, 1974.

        Biographies are located in Volumes 2 and 3.

CompSN SUP   *Composers since 1900: First Supplement.* A biographical and critical guide. Compiled and edited by David Ewen. New York: H.W. Wilson Co., 1981.

CpmDNM   *Composium Directory of New Music.* Annual index of contemporary compositions. Sedro Woolley, Washington: Crystal Musicworks: 1981, 1983.

        CpmDNM 81   1981 edition
        CpmDNM 82   1982/83 edition

CnDAL   *Concise Dictionary of American Literature.* Edited by Robert Fulton Richards. New York: Philosophical Library, 1955. Reprint. New York: Greenwood Press, 1969.

CnE&AP   *The Concise Encyclopedia of English and American Poets and Poetry.* Edited by Stephen Spender and Donald Hall. New York: Hawthorn Books, 1963.

CnMD   *The Concise Encyclopedia of Modern Drama.* By Siegfried Melchinger. Translated by George Wellwarth. Edited by Henry Popkin. New York: Horizon Press, 1964.

        Biographies begin on page 159. The "Additional Entries" section, indicated in this index by the code *SUP*, begins on page 287.

CnMWL   *The Concise Encyclopedia of Modern World Literature.* Second edition. Edited by Geoffrey Grigson. London: Hutchinson & Co., 1970.

        Biographies begin on page 29.

CnThe   *A Concise Encyclopedia of the Theatre.* By Robin May. Reading, England: Osprey Publishing, 1974.

        Use the Index to locate biographies.

CngDr   *Congressional Directory.* Washington, D.C.: United States Government Printing Office, 1974, 1977, 1978, 1979, 1981, 1983, 1985, 1987.

        CngDr 74   93rd Congress, 2nd Session, 1974
        CngDr 77   95th Congress, 1st Session, 1977
        CngDr 78   *Supplement,* 95th Congress, 2nd Session, 1978
        CngDr 79   96th Congress, 1st Session, 1979
        CngDr 81   97th Congress, 1981
        CngDr 83   98th Congress, 1983-1984; 1983
        CngDr 85   99th Congress, 1985-1986; 1985
        CngDr 87   100th Congress, 1987-1988; 1987

        Use the "Individual Index" in each volume to locate biographies.

ConAmA   *Contemporary American Authors: A Critical Survey and 219 Bio-Bibliographies.* By Fred B. Millett. New York: Harcourt, Brace & World, 1940. Reprint. New York: AMS Press, 1970.

         Biographies begin on page 207.

ConAmC   *Contemporary American Composers: A Biographical Dictionary.* Compiled by E. Ruth Anderson. Boston: G.K. Hall & Co., 1976, 1982.

ConAmC	First edition, 1976
ConAmC A	First edition, Addendum begins on page 495.
ConAmC 82	Second edition, 1982

ConAmL   *Contemporary American Literature: Bibliographies and Study Outlines.* By John Matthews Manly and Edith Rickert. Revised by Fred B. Millett. New York: Harcourt, Brace, 1929. Reprint. New York: Haskell House Publishers, 1974.

         Biographies begin on page 101.

ConAmTC   *Contemporary American Theater Critics: A Directory and Anthology of Their Works.* Compiled by M.E. Comtois and Lynn F. Miller. Metuchen, New Jersey: Scarecrow Press, 1977.

ConArch   *Contemporary Architects.* Edited by Muriel Emanuel. New York: St. Martin's Press, 1980.

         The "Notes on Advisors and Contributors" section, indicated in this index by the code *A*, begins on page 927.

ConArt   *Contemporary Artists.* Edited by Colin Naylor and Genesis P-Orridge. London: St. James Press; New York: St. Martin's Press, 1977.

ConArt 83   *Contemporary Artists.* Second edition. Edited by Muriel Emanuel et al. New York: St. Martin's Press, 1983.

ConAu   *Contemporary Authors.* A bio-bibliographical guide to current writers in fiction, general nonfiction, poetry, journalism, drama, motion pictures, television, and other fields. Detroit: Gale Research Co., 1967-1987.

ConAu 1R	Volumes 1-4, 1st revision, 1967
ConAu 5R	Volumes 5-8, 1st revision, 1969
ConAu 9R	Volumes 9-12, 1st revision, 1974
ConAu 13R	Volumes 13-16, 1st revision, 1975
ConAu 17R	Volumes 17-20, 1st revision, 1976
ConAu 21R	Volumes 21-24, 1st revision, 1977
ConAu 25R	Volumes 25-28, 1st revision, 1977
ConAu 29R	Volumes 29-32, 1st revision, 1978
ConAu 33R	Volumes 33-36, 1st revision, 1978
ConAu 37R	Volumes 37-40, 1st revision, 1979
ConAu 41R	Volumes 41-44, 1st revision, 1979
ConAu 45	Volumes 45-48, 1974
ConAu 49	Volumes 49-52, 1975
ConAu 53	Volumes 53-56, 1975
ConAu 57	Volumes 57-60, 1976
ConAu 61	Volumes 61-64, 1976
ConAu 65	Volumes 65-68, 1977
ConAu 69	Volumes 69-72, 1978
ConAu 73	Volumes 73-76, 1978
ConAu 77	Volumes 77-80, 1979
ConAu 81	Volumes 81-84, 1979
ConAu 85	Volumes 85-88, 1980
ConAu 89	Volumes 89-92, 1980
ConAu 93	Volumes 93-96, 1980
ConAu 97	Volumes 97-100, 1981

ConAu 101	Volume 101, 1981
ConAu 102	Volume 102, 1981
ConAu 103	Volume 103, 1982
ConAu 104	Volume 104, 1982
ConAu 105	Volume 105, 1982
ConAu 106	Volume 106, 1982
ConAu 107	Volume 107, 1983
ConAu 108	Volume 108, 1983
ConAu 109	Volume 109, 1983
ConAu 110	Volume 110, 1984
ConAu 111	Volume 111, 1984
ConAu 112	Volume 112, 1985
ConAu 113	Volume 113, 1985
ConAu 114	Volume 114, 1985
ConAu 115	Volume 115, 1985
ConAu 116	Volume 116, 1986
ConAu 117	Volume 117, 1986
ConAu 118	Volume 118, 1986
ConAu 119	Volume 119, 1987
ConAu 120	Volume 120, 1987

ConAu AS *Contemporary Authors, Autobiography Series.* Detroit: Gale Research Co., 1984-1988.

ConAu 1AS	Volume 1, 1984
ConAu 2AS	Volume 2, 1985
ConAu 3AS	Volume 3, 1986
ConAu 4AS	Volume 4, 1986
ConAu 5AS	Volume 5, 1987
ConAu 6AS	Volume 6, 1988

ConAu BS *Contemporary Authors, Bibliographical Series.* Detroit: Gale Research Co., 1986.

ConAu 1BS	Volume 1: *American Novelists.* Edited by James J. Martine, 1986.
ConAu 2BS	Volume 2: *American Poets.* Edited by Ronald Baughman, 1986.

ConAu NR *Contemporary Authors, New Revision Series.* A bio-bibliographical guide to current writers in fiction, general nonfiction, poetry, journalism, drama, motion pictures, television, and other fields. Detroit: Gale Research Co., 1981-1987.

ConAu 1NR	Volume 1, 1981
ConAu 2NR	Volume 2, 1981
ConAu 3NR	Volume 3, 1981
ConAu 4NR	Volume 4, 1981
ConAu 5NR	Volume 5, 1982
ConAu 6NR	Volume 6, 1982
ConAu 7NR	Volume 7, 1982
ConAu 8NR	Volume 8, 1983
ConAu 9NR	Volume 9, 1983
ConAu 10NR	Volume 10, 1983
ConAu 11NR	Volume 11, 1984
ConAu 12NR	Volume 12, 1984
ConAu 13NR	Volume 13, 1984
ConAu 14NR	Volume 14, 1985
ConAu 15NR	Volume 15, 1985
ConAu 16NR	Volume 16, 1986
ConAu 17NR	Volume 17, 1986
ConAu 18NR	Volume 18, 1986
ConAu 19NR	Volume 19, 1987
ConAu 20NR	Volume 20, 1987
ConAu 21NR	Volume 21, 1987

ConAu P-   *Contemporary Authors, Permanent Series.* A bio-bibliographical guide to current authors and their works. Detroit: Gale Research Co., 1975-1978.

ConAu P-1	Volume 1, 1975
ConAu P-2	Volume 2, 1978

ConAu X   This code refers to pseudonym entries which appear as cross-references in the cumulative index to *Contemporary Authors.*

ConDes   *Contemporary Designers.* Edited by Ann Lee Morgan. Detroit: Gale Research Co., 1984.

ConDr   *Contemporary Dramatists.* Edited by James Vinson. London: St. James Press; New York: St. Martin's Press, 1973, 1977, 1982.

ConDr 73	First edition, 1973
ConDr 77	Second edition, 1977, The "Contemporary Dramatists" section begins on page 9.
ConDr 77A	Second edition, The "Screen Writers" section begins on page 893.
ConDr 77B	Second edition, The "Radio Writers" section begins on page 903.
ConDr 77C	Second edition, The "Television Writers" section begins on page 915.
ConDr 77D	Second edition, The "Musical Librettists" section begins on page 925.
ConDr 77E	Second edition, "The Theatre of the Mixed Means" section begins on page 941.
ConDr 77F	Second edition, Appendix begins on page 969.
ConDr 82	Third edition, 1982, The "Contemporary Dramatists" section begins on page 9.
ConDr 82A	Third edition, The "Screen Writers" section begins on page 887.
ConDr 82B	Third edition, The "Radio Writers" section begins on page 899.
ConDr 82C	Third edition, The "Television Writers" section begins on page 911.
ConDr 82D	Third edition, The "Musical Librettists" section begins on page 921.
ConDr 82E	Third edition, Appendix begins on page 951.

ConFLW 84   *Contemporary Foreign Language Writers.* Edited by James Vinson and Daniel Kirkpatrick. New York: St. Martin's Press, 1984.

ConGrA 1   *Contemporary Graphic Artists.* A biographical, bibliographical, and critical guide to current illustrators, animators, cartoonists, designers, and other graphic artists. Edited by Maurice Horn. Detroit: Gale Research Co., 1986-1987.

ConGrA 1	Volume 1, 1986
ConGrA 2	Volume 2, 1987

ConICB   *Contemporary Illustrators of Children's Books.* Compiled by Bertha E. Mahony and Elinor Whitney. Boston: Bookshop for Boys and Girls, Women's Educational and Industrial Union, 1930. Reprint. Detroit: Gale Research Co., 1978.

ConIsC   *Contemporary Issues Criticism.* Excerpts from criticism of contemporary writings in sociology, economics, politics, psychology, anthropology, education, history, law, theology, and related fields. Detroit: Gale Research Co., 1982-1984.

ConIsC 1	Volume 1, 1982
ConIsC 2	Volume 2, 1984

ConLC	*Contemporary Literary Criticism.* Excerpts from criticism of the works of today's novelists, poets, playwrights, short story writers, scriptwriters, and other creative writers. Detroit: Gale Research Co., 1973-1987.	

ConLC 1	Volume 1, 1973
ConLC 2	Volume 2, 1974
ConLC 3	Volume 3, 1975
ConLC 4	Volume 4, 1975
ConLC 5	Volume 5, 1976
ConLC 6	Volume 6, 1976
ConLC 7	Volume 7, 1977
ConLC 8	Volume 8, 1978
ConLC 9	Volume 9, 1978
ConLC 10	Volume 10, 1979
ConLC 11	Volume 11, 1979
ConLC 12	Volume 12, 1980
ConLC 13	Volume 13, 1980
ConLC 14	Volume 14, 1980
ConLC 15	Volume 15, 1980
ConLC 16	Volume 16, 1981
ConLC 17	Volume 17, 1981
ConLC 18	Volume 18, 1981
ConLC 19	Volume 19, 1981
ConLC 20	Volume 20, 1982
ConLC 21	Volume 21, 1982
ConLC 22	Volume 22, 1982
ConLC 23	Volume 23, 1983
ConLC 24	Volume 24, 1983
ConLC 25	Volume 25, 1983
ConLC 26	Volume 26, 1983
ConLC 27	Volume 27, 1984
ConLC 28	Volume 28, 1984
ConLC 29	Volume 29, 1984
ConLC 30	Volume 30, 1984
ConLC 31	Volume 31, 1985
ConLC 32	Volume 32, 1985
ConLC 33	Volume 33, 1985
ConLC 34	Volume 34, Yearbook 1984; 1985
ConLC 35	Volume 35, 1985
ConLC 36	Volume 36, 1986
ConLC 37	Volume 37, 1986
ConLC 38	Volume 38, 1986
ConLC 39	Volume 39: Yearbook 1985, 1986
ConLC 40	Volume 40, 1986
ConLC 41	Volume 41, 1987
ConLC 42	Volume 42, 1987
ConLC 43	Volume 43, 1987
ConLC 44	Volume 44: Yearbook 1986, 1987

Use the Table of Contents to locate entries in the Yearbook, Volume 34.

ConLCrt	*Contemporary Literary Critics.* By Elmer Borklund. London: St. James Press; New York: St. Martin's Press, 1977.

ConLCrt 82	*Contemporary Literary Critics.* Second edition. By Elmer Borklund. Detroit: Gale Research Co., 1982.

ConNews   *Contemporary Newsmakers.* A biographical guide to people in the news in business, education, technology, social issues, politics, law, economics, international affairs, religion, entertainment, labor, sports, design, psychology, medicine, astronautics, ecology, and other fields. Detroit: Gale Research Co., 1985-1987.

ConNews 85-1	1985, Issue 1; 1985
ConNews 85-2	1985, Issue 2; 1985
ConNews 85-3	1985, Issue 3; 1986
ConNews 85-4	1985, Issue 4; 1986
ConNews 86-1	1986, Issue 1; 1986
ConNews 86-2	1986, Issue 2; 1986
ConNews 86-3	1986, Issue 3; 1987
ConNews 86-4	1986, Issue 4; 1987
ConNews 87-1	1987, Issue 1; 1987

ConNov   *Contemporary Novelists.* Edited by James Vinson. London: St. James Press; New York: St. Martin's Press, 1972, 1976, 1982, 1986.

ConNov 72	First edition, 1972
ConNov 76	Second edition, 1976
ConNov 82	Third edition, 1982
ConNov 86	Fourth edition, 1986

Deceased novelists are listed in the Appendix at the back of each volume.

ConPhot   *Contemporary Photographers.* Edited by George Walsh, Colin Naylor, and Michael Held. New York: St. Martin's Press, 1982.

ConP   *Contemporary Poets.* London: St. James Press; New York: St. Martin's Press, 1970, 1975, 1980, 1985.

ConP 70	First edition, edited by Rosalie Murphy, 1970.
ConP 75	Second edition, edited by James Vinson, 1975.
ConP 80	Third edition, edited by James Vinson, 1980.
ConP 85	Fourth edition, edited by James Vinson and D.L. Kirkpatrick, 1985.

Biographies in the Appendix, indicated in this index by the code *A*, are located at the back of the later editions.

ConSFA   *Contemporary Science Fiction Authors.* First edition. Compiled and edited by R. Reginald. New York: Arno Press, 1975. Previously published as *Stella Nova: The Contemporary Science Fiction Authors.* Los Angeles: Unicorn & Son, Publishers, 1970.

ConTFT   *Contemporary Theatre, Film, and Television.* A biographical guide featuring performers, directors, writers, producers, designers, managers, choreographers, technicians, composers, executives, dancers, and critics in the United States and Great Britain. Detroit: Gale Research Co., 1984-1986. A continuation of *Who's Who in the Theatre.*

ConTFT 1	Volume 1, 1984
ConTFT 2	Volume 2, 1986
ConTFT 3	Volume 3, 1986
ConTFT 4	Volume 4, 1987

Conv   *Conversations.* Conversations series. Detroit: Gale Research Co., 1977-1978.

Conv 1	Volume 1: *Conversations with Writers*, 1977
Conv 2	Volume 2: *Conversations with Jazz Musicians*, 1977
Conv 3	Volume 3: *Conversations with Writers II*, 1978

CorpD   *Corpus Delicti of Mystery Fiction: A Guide to the Body of the Case.* By Linda Herman and Beth Stiel. Metuchen, New Jersey: Scarecrow Press, 1974.

Biographies begin on page 31.

CreCan   *Creative Canada: A Biographical Dictionary of Twentieth-Century Creative and Performing Artists.* Compiled by the Reference Division, McPherson Library, University of Victoria, British Columbia. Toronto: University of Toronto Press, 1971, 1972.

> *CreCan 1*   Volume 1, 1971
> *CreCan 2*   Volume 2, 1972

CroCAP   *Crowell's Handbook of Contemporary American Poetry.* By Karl Malkoff. New York: Thomas Y. Crowell Co., 1973.

> Biographies begin on page 43.

CroCD   *Crowell's Handbook of Contemporary Drama.* By Michael Anderson, et al. New York: Thomas Y. Crowell Co., 1971.

CroE&S   *Crowell's Handbook of Elizabethan & Stuart Literature.* By James E. Ruoff. New York: Thomas Y. Crowell Co., 1975.

CrtT   *The Critical Temper: A Survey of Modern Criticism on English and American Literature from the Beginnings to the Twentieth Century.* Three volumes. Edited by Martin Tucker. A Library of Literary Criticism. New York: Frederick Ungar Publishing Co., 1969.

> *CrtT 1*   Volume I: From Old English to Shakespeare, 1969
> *CrtT 2*   Volume II: From Milton to Romantic Literature, 1969
> *CrtT 3*   Volume III: Victorian Literature and American Literature, 1969
> *CrtT 4*   Volume IV: Supplement, 1979

> Authors are listed alphabetically within each period or division of literature.

CurBio   *Current Biography Yearbook.* New York: H.W. Wilson Co., 1950-1987.

> Number after the source code indicates the year covered by the yearbook. Obituaries, located in the back of some volumes, are indicated in this index by the code *N.*

CyAG   *Cyclopedia of American Government.* Three volumes. Edited by Andrew C. McLaughlin and Albert Bushnell Hart. New York: D. Appleton & Co., 1914. Reprint. Gloucester, Massachusetts: Peter Smith, 1963.

CyAL   *Cyclopaedia of American Literature.* Embracing personal and critical notices of authors, and selections from their writings, from the earliest period to the present day; with portraits, autographs, and other illustrations. Two volumes. By Evert A. Duyckinck and George L. Duyckinck. Philadelphia: William Rutter & Co., 1875. Reprint. Detroit: Gale Research Co., 1965.

> Use the Index in Volume 2 to locate biographies.

CyEd   *A Cyclopedia of Education.* Five volumes. Edited by Paul Monroe. New York: Macmillan Co., 1911. Reprint. Detroit: Gale Research Co., 1968.

CyWA   *Cyclopedia of World Authors.* Edited by Frank N. Magill. New York: Harper & Row, Publishers, 1958. Also published as *Masterplots Cyclopedia of World Authors.*

DcAfL   *Dictionary of Afro-Latin American Civilization.* By Benjamin Nunez with the assistance of the African Bibliographic Center. Westport, Connecticut: Greenwood Press, 1980.

DcAmArt   *Dictionary of American Art.* By Matthew Baigell. New York: Harper & Row, Publishers, 1979.

DcAmAu   *A Dictionary of American Authors.* Fifth edition, revised and enlarged. By Oscar Fay
                Adams. New York: Houghton Mifflin Co., 1904. Reprint. Detroit: Gale Research
                Co., 1969.

> Biographies are found in the "Dictionary of American Authors" section which
> begins on page 1 and in the "Supplement" which begins on page 441.

DcAmB   *Dictionary of American Biography.* 20 volumes and seven supplements. Edited under
                the auspices of the American Council of Learned Societies. New York: Charles
                Scribner's Sons, 1928-1936, 1944, 1958, 1973, 1974, 1977, 1980, 1981.

DcAmB	Volumes 1-20, 1928-1936
DcAmB S1	Supplement 1, 1944
DcAmB S2	Supplement 2, 1958
DcAmB S3	Supplement 3, 1973
DcAmB S4	Supplement 4, 1974
DcAmB S5	Supplement 5, 1977
DcAmB S6	Supplement 6, 1980
DcAmB S7	Supplement 7, 1981

DcAmDH   *Dictionary of American Diplomatic History.* By John E. Findling. Westport,
                Connecticut: Greenwood Press, 1980.

DcAmLiB   *Dictionary of American Library Biography.* Edited by Bohdan S. Wynar. Littleton,
                Colorado: Libraries Unlimited, 1978.

DcAmMeB   *Dictionary of American Medical Biography.* Lives of eminent physicians of the United
                States and Canada, from the earliest times. By Howard A. Kelly and Walter L.
                Burrage. New York: D. Appleton & Co., 1928. Reprint. Road Town, Tortola,
                British Virgin Islands: Longwood Press, 1979.

DcAmMeB 84   *Dictionary of American Medical Biography.* Two volumes. Edited by Martin Kaufman,
                Stuart Galishoff, and Todd L. Savitt. Westport, Connecticut Greenwood Press,
                1984.

DcAmMiB   *Dictionary of American Military Biography.* Three volumes. Edited by Roger J. Spiller.
                Westport, Connecticut: Greenwood Press, 1984.

DcAmNB   *Dictionary of American Negro Biography.* Edited by Rayford W. Logan and Michael
                R. Winston. New York: W.W. Norton & Co., 1982.

DcAmReB   *Dictionary of American Religious Biography.* By Henry Warner Bowden. Westport,
                Connecticut: Greenwood Press, 1977.

DcAmSR   *A Dictionary of American Social Reform.* By Louis Filler. New York: Philosophical
                Library, 1963.

DcBiA   *A Dictionary of Biographies of Authors Represented in the Authors Digest Series.* With
                a supplemental list of later titles and a supplementary biographical section. Edited
                by Rossiter Johnson. New York: Authors Press, 1927. Reprint. Detroit: Gale
                Research Co., 1974.

> "Biographies of Authors" begins on page 3 and "Biographies of Authors
> Whose Works Are in Volume XVIII" begins on page 437.

DcBiPP   *A Dictionary of Biography, Past and Present.* Containing the chief events in the lives of
                eminent persons of all ages and nations. Preceded by the biographies and
                genealogies of the chief representatives of the royal houses of the world. Edited
                by Benjamin Vincent. Haydn Series. London: Ward, Lock, & Co., 1877. Reprint.
                Detroit: Gale Research Co., 1974.

> The Addenda, indicated in this index by the code *A*, begin on page 638.

DcBrAmW   *A Dictionary of British and American Women Writers 1660-1800.* Edited by Janet Todd. Totowa, New Jersey: Littlefield, Adams & Co., Rowman & Allanheld, 1985.

Biographies begin on page 27.

DcBrAr   *Dictionary of British Artists Working 1900-1950.* Two volumes. By Grant M. Waters. Eastbourne, England: Eastbourne Fine Art Publications, 1975, 1976.

DcBrA 1	Volume I, 1975
DcBrA 2	Volume II, 1976

DcBrBI   *The Dictionary of British Book Illustrators and Caricaturists, 1800-1914.* With introductory chapters on the rise and progress of the art. By Simon Houfe. Woodbridge, England: Antique Collectors' Club, 1978. Distributed by Gale Research Co., Detroit, Michigan.

Biographies begin on page 215.

DcBrWA   *The Dictionary of British Watercolour Artists up to 1920.* By H.L. Mallalieu. Woodbridge, England: Antique Collectors' Club, 1976. Distributed by Gale Research Co., Detroit, Michigan.

DcCanB   *Dictionary of Canadian Biography.* Toronto: University of Toronto Press, 1966-1985.

DcCanB 8	*Volume VIII: 1851-1860,* edited by Francess G. Halpenny, 1985.
DcCanB 8A	Volume VIII, Appendix begins on page 968.
DcCanB 9	*Volume IX: 1861 to 1870,* edited by Francess G. Halpenny, 1976.
DcCanB 11	*Volume XI: 1881 to 1890,* edited by Henri Pilon, 1982.

DcCathB   *Dictionary of Catholic Biography.* By John J. Delaney and James Edward Tobin. Garden City, New York: Doubleday & Co., 1961.

DcCAA   *A Dictionary of Contemporary American Artists.* By Paul Cummings. London: St. James Press; New York: St. Martin's Press, 1971, 1977.

DcCAA 71	Second edition, 1971
DcCAA 77	Third edition, 1977

DcCAr 81   *Dictionary of Contemporary Artists.* Edited by V. Babington Smith. Oxford: Clio Press, 1981.

DcCLAA   *A Dictionary of Contemporary Latin American Authors.* Compiled by David William Foster. Tempe, Arizona: Center for Latin American Studies, Arizona State University, 1975.

DcCM   *Dictionary of Contemporary Music.* Edited by John Vinton. New York: E.P. Dutton & Co., 1974.

This book ignores prefixes in filing surnames.

DcD&D   *Dictionary of Design & Decoration.* A Studio Book. New York: Viking Press, 1973.

DcEnA   *A Dictionary of English Authors, Biographical and Bibliographical.* Being a compendious account of the lives and writings of upwards of 800 British and American writers from the year 1400 to the present time. New edition, revised with an appendix bringing the whole up to date and including a large amount of new matter. By R. Farquharson Sharp. London: Kegan Paul, Trench, Trubner & Co., 1904. Reprint. Detroit: Gale Research Co., 1978.

The Appendix, indicated in this index by the code *AP*, begins on page 311.

DcEnL	*Dictionary of English Literature: Being a Comprehensive Guide to English Authors and Their Works.* Second edition. By W. Davenport Adams. London: Cassell Petter & Galpin (n.d.). Reprint. Detroit: Gale Research Co., 1966.
DcEuL	*A Dictionary of European Literature.* Designed as a companion to English studies. Second, revised edition. By Laurie Magnus. London: George Routledge & Sons; New York: E.P. Dutton & Co., 1927. Reprint. Detroit: Gale Research Co., 1974.

The Appendix begins on page 595.

DcFM	*Dictionary of Film Makers.* By Georges Sadoul. Translated, edited, and updated by Peter Morris. Berkeley and Los Angeles: University of California Press, 1972. Originally published as *Dictionnaire des Cineastes*, 1965.
DcInB	*Dictionary of Indian Biography.* By C.E. Buckland. London: Swan Sonnenschein & Co., 1906. Reprint. Detroit: Gale Research Co., 1968.

The Addenda, indicated in this index by the code *A*, begin on page 467.

DcInv	*Dictionary of Inventions & Discoveries.* Edited by E.F. Carter. Stevenage, England: Robin Clark, 1978.
DcIrB	*A Dictionary of Irish Biography.* By Henry Boylan. New York: Barnes & Noble Books, 1978.
DcIrL	*Dictionary of Irish Literature.* Edited by Robert Hogan. Westport, Connecticut: Greenwood Press, 1979. Also published as *The Macmillan Dictionary of Irish Literature.* London: Macmillan Press, 1980.
DcIrW	*Dictionary of Irish Writers.* By Brian Cleeve. Cork, Ireland: Mercier Press, 1967, 1969, 1971.

DcIrW 1	Volume 1: Fiction, 1967
DcIrW 2	Volume 2: Non-fiction, 1969
DcIrW 3	Volume 3: Writers in the Irish Language, 1971

DcItL	*Dictionary of Italian Literature.* Edited by Peter Bondanella and Julia Conaway Bondanella. Westport, Connecticut: Greenwood Press, 1979.
DcLB	*Dictionary of Literary Biography.* Detroit: Gale Research Co., 1978-1987.

DcLB 1	Volume 1: *The American Renaissance in New England.* Edited by Joel Myerson, 1978.
DcLB 2	Volume 2: *American Novelists since World War II.* Edited by Jeffrey Helterman and Richard Layman, 1978.
DcLB 3	Volume 3: *Antebellum Writers in New York and the South.* Edited by Joel Myerson, 1979.
DcLB 4	Volume 4: *American Writers in Paris, 1920-1939.* Edited by Karen Lane Rood, 1980.
DcLB 5	Volume 5: *American Poets since World War II.* Two parts. Edited by Donald J. Greiner, 1980.
DcLB 6	Volume 6: *American Novelists since World War II.* Second series. Edited by James E. Kibler, Jr., 1980.
DcLB 7	Volume 7: *Twentieth-Century American Dramatists.* Two parts. Edited by John MacNicholas, 1981.
DcLB 8	Volume 8: *Twentieth-Century American Science- Fiction Writers.* Two parts, Edited by David Cowart and Thomas L. Wymer, 1981.
DcLB 9	Volume 9: *American Novelists, 1910-1945.* Three parts. Edited by James J. Martine, 1981.
DcLB 10	Volume 10: *Modern British Dramatists, 1900-1945.* Two parts. Edited by Stanley Weintraub, 1982.

DcLB 38	Volume 38: *Afro-American Writers after 1955: Dramatists and Prose Writers.* Edited by Thadious M. Davis and Trudier Harris, 1985.
DcLB 39	Volume 39: *British Novelists, 1600-1800.* Two parts. Edited by Martin C. Battestin, 1985.
DcLB 40	Volume 40: *Poets of Great Britain and Ireland since 1960.* Two parts. Edited by Vincent B. Sherry, Jr., 1985.
DcLB 41	Volume 41: *Afro-American Poets since 1955.* Edited by Trudier Harris and Thadious M. Davis, 1985.
DcLB 42	Volume 42: *American Writers for Children before 1900.* Edited by Glenn E. Estes, 1985.
DcLB 43	Volume 43: *American Newspaper Journalists, 1690-1872.* Edited by Perry J. Ashley, 1985.
DcLB 44	Volume 44: *American Screenwriters.* Second series. Edited by Randall Clark, 1986.
DcLB 45	Volume 45: *American Poets, 1880-1945.* First series. Edited by Peter Quartermain, 1986.
DcLB 47	Volume 47: *American Historians, 1866-1912.* Edited by Clyde N. Wilson, 1986.
DcLB 48	Volume 48: *American Poets, 1880-1945.* Second series. Edited by Peter Quartermain, 1986.
DcLB 50	Volume 50: *Afro-American Writers before the Harlem Renaissance.* Edited by Trudier Harris, 1986.
DcLB 51	Volume 51: *Afro-American Writers from the Harlem Renaissance to 1940.* Edited by Trudier Harris, 1987.
DcLB 52	Volume 52: *American Writers for Children since 1960: Fiction.* Edited by Glenn E. Estes, 1986.
DcLB 53	Volume 53: *Canadian Writers since 1960.* First series. Edited by W.H. New, 1986.
DcLB 54	Volume 54: *American Poets, 1880-1945.* Two parts. Third series. Edited by Peter Quartermain, 1987.
DcLB 55	Volume 55: *Victorian Prose Writers before 1867.* Edited by William B. Thesing, 1987.
DcLB 56	Volume 56: *German Fiction Writers, 1914- 1945.* Edited by James Hardin, 1987.
DcLB 57	Volume 57: *Victorian Prose Writers after 1867.* Edited by William B. Thesing, 1987.
DcLB 58	Volume 58: *Jacobean and Caroline Dramatists.* Edited by Fredson Bowers, 1987.
DcLB 59	Volume 59: *American Literary Critics and Scholars, 1800-1850.* Edited by John W. Rathbun, 1987.

Use the Index to locate biographies.

DcLB DS	*Dictionary of Literary Biography Documentary Series: An Illustrated Chronicle.* Detroit, Gale Research Co., 1982-1984.
DcLB DS1	Volume 1, edited by Margaret A. Van Antwerp, 1982.
DcLB DS2	Volume 2, edited by Margaret A. Van Antwerp, 1982.
DcLB DS3	Volume 3, edited by Mary Bruccoli, 1983.
DcLB DS4	Volume 4, edited by Margaret A. Van Antwerp and Sally Johns, 1984.

DcLB Y-	*Dictionary of Literary Biography Yearbook.* Detroit: Gale Research Co., 1981-1986.
DcLB Y80A	Yearbook: 1980. Edited by Karen L. Rood, Jean W. Ross, and Richard Ziegfeld, 1981. The "Updated Entries" section begins on page 3.
DcLB Y80B	Yearbook: 1980. The "New Entries" section begins on page 127.
DcLB Y81A	Yearbook: 1981. Edited by Karen L. Rood, Jean W. Ross, and Richard Ziegfeld, 1982. The "Updated Entries" section begins on page 21.

DcLB Y81B	Yearbook: 1981. The "New Entries" section begins on page 139.
DcLB Y82A	Yearbook: 1982. Edited by Richard Ziegfeld, 1983. The "Updated Entries" section begins on page 121.
DcLB Y82B	Yearbook: 1982. The "New Entries" section begins on page 203.
DcLB Y83A	Yearbook: 1983. Edited by Mary Bruccoli and Jean W. Ross, 1984. The "Updated Entries" section begins on page 155.
DcLB Y83B	Yearbook: 1983. The "New Entries" section begins on page 175.
DcLB Y83N	Yearbook: 1983. The "Obituaries" section begins on page 103.
DcLB Y84A	Yearbook: 1984. Edited by Jean W. Ross, 1985. The "Updated Entry" section begins on page 219.
DcLB Y84B	Yearbook: 1984. The "New Entries" section begins on page 225.
DcLB Y84N	Yearbook: 1984. The "Obituaries" section begins on page 163.
DcLB Y85A	Yearbook: 1985. The "Updated Entries" section begins on page 279.
DcLB Y85B	Yearbook: 1985. The "New Entries" section begins on page 319.
DcLB Y85N	Yearbook: 1985. The "Obituaries" section begins on page 253.
DcLB Y86A	*Yearbook: 1986.* Edited by J.M. Brook, 1987. "Updated Entries" section begins on page 247.
DcLB Y86B	*Yearbook: 1986.* "New Entries" section begins on page 271.
DcLB Y86N	*Yearbook: 1986.* "Obituaries" section begins on page 199.

DcLEL   *A Dictionary of Literature in the English Language.* Compiled and edited by Robin Myers. Oxford: Pergamon Press, 1970, 1978.

DcLEL	*From Chaucer to 1940,* 1970
DcLEL 1940	*From 1940 to 1970,* 1978

DcNaB   *The Dictionary of National Biography: The Concise Dictionary.* Part 1, From the Beginnings to 1900. London: Oxford University Press, 1953.

DcNaB C	Corrigenda begin on page 1457.
DcNaB S1	First Supplement

This volume contains abstracts of the biographies found in the main volumes of *The Dictionary of National Biography* (21 volumes, New York: Macmillan Co.; London: Smith, Elder & Co., 1908) and the First Supplement (Volume 22, in three volumes, New York: Macmillan Co.; London: Smith, Elder & Co., 1908).

DcNaB S2   *The Dictionary of National Biography.* Second Supplement. Three volumes. Edited by Sir Sidney Lee. New York: Macmillan Co.; London: Smith, Elder & Co., 1912.

DcNaB 1912   *The Dictionary of National Biography, 1912-1921.* Edited by H.W.C. Davis and J.R.H. Weaver. London: Oxford University Press, 1927.

DcNaB 1922   *The Dictionary of National Biography, 1922-1930.* Edited by J.R.H. Weaver. London: Oxford University Press, 1937.

DcNaB 1931   *The Dictionary of National Biography, 1931-1940.* Edited by L.G. Wickham Legg. London: Oxford University Press, 1949.

DcNaB 1941   *The Dictionary of National Biography, 1941-1950.* Edited by L.G. Wickham Legg and E.T. Williams. London: Oxford University Press, 1959. Reprinted with corrections, 1967.

DcNaB 1951   *The Dictionary of National Biography, 1951-1960.* Edited by E.T. Williams and Helen M. Palmer. London: Oxford University Press, 1971.

DcNaB 1961   *The Dictionary of National Biography, 1961-1970.* Edited by E.T. Williams and C.S. Nicholls. London: Oxford University Press, 1981.

DcNaB 1971   *The Dictionary of National Biography, 1971-1980.* Edited by Lord Blake and C.S. Nicholls. Oxford: Oxford University Press, 1986.

DcNiCA   *Dictionary of 19th Century Antiques and Later Objets d'Art.* By George Savage. London: Barrie & Jenkins, 1978.

DcNAA   *A Dictionary of North American Authors Deceased before 1950.* Compiled by W. Stewart Wallace. Toronto: Ryerson Press, 1951. Reprint. Detroit: Gale Research Co., 1968.

DcOrL   *Dictionary of Oriental Literatures.* Three volumes. Jaroslav Prusek, general editor. New York: Basic Books, 1974.

DcOrL 1	Volume I: East Asia. Edited by Zbigniew Slupski.
DcOrL 2	Volume II: South and South-East Asia. Edited by Dusan Zbavitel.
DcOrL 3	Volume III: West Asia and North Africa, edited by Jiri Becka.

DcPol   *A Dictionary of Politics.* Revised edition. Edited by Walter Laqueur. New York: Macmillan Publishing Co., Free Press, 1974.

DcRusL   *Dictionary of Russian Literature.* By William E. Harkins. New York: Philosophical Library, 1956. Reprint. Westport, Connecticut: Greenwood Press, 1971.

DcScB   *Dictionary of Scientific Biography.* 14 volumes and supplement. Edited by Charles Coulston Gillispie. New York: Charles Scribner's Sons, 1970-1976, 1978.

DcSeaP   *Dictionary of Sea Painters.* By E.H.H. Archibald. Woodbridge, England: Antique Collectors' Club, 1980. Distributed by Gale Research Co., Detroit, Michigan.
Biographies begin on page 59.

DcSoc   *A Dictionary of Sociology.* Edited by G. Duncan Mitchell. Chicago: Aldine Publishing Co., 1968.

DcSpL   *Dictionary of Spanish Literature.* By Maxim Newmark. New York: Philosophical Library, 1956. Reprint. Totowa, New Jersey: Littlefield, Adams & Co., 1970.

DcVicP   *Dictionary of Victorian Painters.* By Christopher Wood. Suffolk, England: Baron Publishing (for The Antique Collectors' Club), 1971.

DrAP&F 85   *A Directory of American Poets and Fiction Writers.* Names and addresses of 6,020 contemporary poets and fiction writers whose work has been published in the United States. 1985-1986 edition. New York: Poets & Writers, 1985.
Use the Index to locate listings.

DrAS   *Directory of American Scholars.* Edited by Jaques Cattell Press. New York: R.R.
              Bowker Co., 1974, 1978, 1982.

DrAS 74H	Sixth edition, Volume 1: History
DrAS 74E	Sixth edition, Volume 2: English, Speech, & Drama
DrAS 74F	Sixth edition, Volume 3: Foreign Languages, Linguistics, & Philology
DrAS 74P	Sixth edition, Volume 4: Philosophy, Religion, & Law
DrAS 78H	Seventh edition, Volume 1: History
DrAS 78E	Seventh edition, Volume 2: English, Speech, & Drama
DrAS 78F	Seventh edition, Volume 3: Foreign Languages, Linguistics, & Philology
DrAS 78P	Seventh edition, Volume 4: Philosophy, Religion, & Law
DrAS 82H	Eighth edition, Volume 1: History
DrAS 82E	Eighth edition, Volume 2: English, Speech, & Drama
DrAS 82F	Eighth edition, Volume 3: Foreign Languages, Linguistics, & Philology
DrAS 82P	Eighth edition, Volume 4: Philosophy, Religion, & Law

DrBlPA   *Directory of Blacks in the Performing Arts.* By Edward Mapp. Metuchen, New Jersey:
              Scarecrow Press, 1978.

DrInf   *The Directory of Infamy: The Best of the Worst.* An illustrated compendium of over 600
              of the all-time great crooks. By Jonathon Green. London: Mills & Boon, 1980.

              Use the Index to locate biographies.

DrLC 69   *Directory of Library Consultants.* Edited by John N. Berry, III. New York: R.R.
              Bowker Co., 1969.

DrRegL 75   *Directory of Registered Lobbyists and Lobbyist Legislation.* Second edition. Chicago:
              Marquis Academic Media, 1975.

              Use the "Lobbyist Index," which begins on page 451, to locate listings.

Dis&D   *Disease and Destiny: A Bibliography of Medical References to the Famous.* By Judson
              Bennett Gilbert. Additions and introduction by Gordon E. Mestler. London:
              Dawsons of Pall Mall, 1962.

Drake   Drake, Francis S. *Dictionary of American Biography, including Men of the Time.*
              Containing nearly 10,000 notices of persons of both sexes, of native and foreign
              birth, who have been remarkable, or prominently connected with the arts, sciences,
              literature, politics, or history, of the American continent. Giving also the
              pronunciation of many of the foreign and peculiar American names, a key to the
              assumed names of writers, and a supplement. Boston: James R. Osgood & Co.,
              1872. Reprint. Detroit: Gale Research Co., 1974.

              The Supplement, indicated in this index by the code *SUP,* begins on page 1015.

DrmM 2   *Dream Makers Volume II: The Uncommon Men & Women Who Write Science Fiction.*
              Interviews by Charles Platt. New York: Berkley Books, 1983.

Dun&B   *Dun & Bradstreet Reference Book of Corporate Managements* . New York: Dun &
              Bradstreet, 1979.

Dun&B 79	13th edition, 1979

              Use the Index to locate biographies.

EarABI   *Early American Book Illustrators and Wood Engravers, 1670-1870.* A catalogue of a collection of American books illustrated for the most part with woodcuts and wood engravings in the Princeton University Library. By Sinclair Hamilton. Princeton, New Jersey: Princeton University Press, 1958, 1968.

EarABI	Volume I: Main Catalogue, 1958
EarABI SUP	Volume II: Supplement, 1968

Ebony   *The Ebony Success Library.* Three volumes. By the Editors of *Ebony.* Nashville: Southwestern Co., 1973.

Ebony 1	Volume I: 1,000 Successful Blacks

EncAAH   *Encyclopedia of American Agricultural History.* By Edward L. Schapsmeier and Frederick H. Schapsmeier. Westport, Connecticut: Greenwood Press, 1975.

EncAB-A   *Encyclopedia of American Biography.* New Series. 40 volumes. New York and West Palm Beach, Florida: The American Historical Society, 1934-1970.

  Number after the source code indicates volume number. Use the Index in each volume to locate biographies.

EncAB-H   *Encyclopedia of American Biography.* Edited by John A. Garraty. New York: Harper & Row, Publishers, 1974.

EncAJ   *The Encyclopedia of American Journalism.* By Donald Paneth. New York: Facts on File, 1983.

EncAR   *Encyclopedia of the American Revolution.* By Mark Mayo Boatner, III. New York: David McKay Co., 1966.

EncASM   *Encyclopedia of American Silver Manufacturers.* By Dorothy T. Rainwater. New York: Crown Publishers, 1975.

EncE 75   *Encyclopedia of Espionage.* New edition. By Ronald Seth. London: New English Library, 1975.

EncFCWM   *Encyclopedia of Folk, Country & Western Music.* By Irwin Stambler and Grelun Landon. New York: St. Martin's Press, 1969, 1983.

EncFCWM 69	First edition, 1969
EncFCWM 83	Second edition, 1983

EncFWF   *Encyclopedia of Frontier and Western Fiction.* Edited by Jon Tuska and Vicki Piekarski. New York: McGraw-Hill Book Co., 1983.

EncJzS 70   *The Encyclopedia of Jazz in the Seventies.* By Leonard Feather and Ira Gitler. New York: Horizon Press, 1976.

EncLatA   *Encyclopedia of Latin America.* Edited by Helen Delpar. New York: McGraw-Hill Book Co., 1974.

EncMT   *Encyclopaedia of the Musical Theatre.* By Stanley Green. New York: Dodd, Mead & Co., 1976.

EncMys   *Encyclopedia of Mystery and Detection.* By Chris Steinbrunner and Otto Penzler. New York: McGraw-Hill Book Co., 1976.

EncO&P   *Encyclopedia of Occultism & Parapsychology.* A compendium of information on the occult sciences, magic, demonology, superstitions, spiritism, mysticism, metaphysics, psychical science, and parapsychology, with biographical and bibliographical notes and comprehensive indexes. Edited by Leslie Shepard. Detroit: Gale Research Co., 1978, 1980, 1981, 1984-1985, 1987.

EncO&P 78	Main volumes, 1978
EncO&P 78S1	Occultism Update, Issue Number 1, 1978
EncO&P 80	Occultism Update, Issue Number 2, 1980
EncO&P 81	Occultism Update, Issue Numbers 3-4, 1981
EncO&P 2	Second edition, 1984-1985
EncO&P 2S1	Occultism Update, First Supplement to the second edition, 1987.

EncPR&S   *Encyclopedia of Pop, Rock, and Soul.* By Irwin Stambler. New York: St. Martin's Press; London: St. James, 1974, 1977.

EncPR&S	1974 edition
EncPR&S 77	1977 edition
EncPR&S 77S	"Supplement" begins on page xvii.

EncSF   *The Encyclopedia of Science Fiction: An Illustrated A to Z.* Edited by Peter Nicholls. London: Granada Publishing, 1979.

EncSoA   *Encyclopaedia of Southern Africa.* Sixth edition. Compiled and edited by Eric Rosenthal. London: Frederick Warne & Co., 1973.

EncSoB   *Encyclopedia of Southern Baptists.* Two volumes and supplement. Nashville: Broadman Press, 1958, 1971.

EncSoB	Two volumes, 1958
EncSoB SUP	Volume III, Supplement, 1971

EncSoH   *The Encyclopedia of Southern History.* Edited by David C. Roller and Robert W. Twyman. Baton Rouge: Louisiana State University Press, 1979.

EncTR   *Encyclopedia of the Third Reich.* By Louis L. Snyder. New York: McGraw-Hill Book Co., 1976.

EncTwCJ   *Encyclopedia of Twentieth-Century Journalists.* By William H. Taft. Garland Reference Library of the Humanities, vol. 493. New York: Garland Publishing, 1986.

EncUrb   *Encyclopedia of Urban Planning.* Edited by Arnold Whittick. New York: McGraw-Hill Book Co., 1974.

EncWL   *Encyclopedia of World Literature in the 20th Century.* Three volumes and supplement. Edited by Wolfgang Bernard Fleischmann. New York: Frederick Ungar Publishing Co., 1967, 1975. An enlarged and updated edition of the Herder *Lexikon der Weltliteratur im 20. Jahrhundert.*

EncWL	Three volumes, 1967
EncWL SUP	Supplement, 1975

EncWL 2   *Encyclopedia of World Literature in the 20th Century.* Revised edition. Four volumes. Edited by Leonard S. Klein. New York: Frederick Ungar Publishing Co., 1981-1984. Distributed by Gale Research Co., Detroit, Michigan.

EncWM   *The Encyclopedia of World Methodism.* Two volumes. Edited by Nolan B. Harmon. Nashville: United Methodist Publishing House, 1974.

EncWT   *The Encyclopedia of World Theater.* Translated by Estella Schmid, edited by Martin Esslin. New York: Charles Scribner's Sons, 1977. Based on *Friedrichs Theaterlexikon,* by Karl Groning and Werner Kliess.

Entr	*Entrepreneurs: The Men and Women behind Famous Brand Names and How They Made It.* By Joseph J. Fucini and Suzy Fucini. Boston: G.K. Hall & Co., 1985. Use the Index to locate biographies.
EuAu	*European Authors, 1000-1900: A Biographical Dictionary of European Literature.* Edited by Stanley J. Kunitz and Vineta Colby. New York: H.W. Wilson Co., 1967.
EuWr	*European Writers.* Volumes 1 to 4. New York: Charles Scribner's Sons, 1983-1984.

	EuWr 1	Volume 1: *The Middle Ages and the Renaissance.* Prudentius to medieval drama. Edited by William T.H. Jackson and George Stade, 1983.
	EuWr 2	Volume 2: *The Middle Ages and the Renaissance.* Petrarch to Renaissance short fiction. Edited by William T.H. Jackson and George Stade, 1983.
	EuWr 3	Volume 3: *The Age of Reason and the Enlightenment.* Rene Descartes to Montesquieu. Edited by George Stade, 1984.
	EuWr 4	Volume 4: *The Age of Reason and the Enlightenment.* Voltaire to Andre Chenier. Edited by George Stade, 1984.

EvEuW	*Everyman's Dictionary of European Writers.* By W.N. Hargreaves-Mawdsley. London: J.M. Dent & Sons; New York: E.P. Dutton & Co., 1968.
EvLB	*Everyman's Dictionary of Literary Biography, English and American.* Revised edition. Compiled after John W. Cousin by D.C. Browning. London: J.M. Dent & Sons; New York: E.P. Dutton & Co., 1960.
FamA&A	*Famous Actors and Actresses on the American Stage: Documents of American Theater History.* Two volumes. By William C. Young. New York: R.R. Bowker Co., 1975.
FamAIYP	*Famous Author-Illustrators for Young People.* By Norah Smaridge. New York: Dodd, Mead & Co., 1973.
FamAYP	*Famous Authors for Young People.* By Ramon P. Coffman and Nathan G. Goodman. New York: Dodd, Mead & Co., 1943.
FamMS	*Famous Modern Storytellers for Young People.* By Norah Smaridge. New York: Dodd, Mead & Co., 1969.
FamPYP	*Famous Poets for Young People.* By Laura Benet. New York: Dodd, Mead & Co., 1964.
FamSYP	*Famous Storytellers for Young People.* By Laura Benet. New York: Dodd, Mead & Co., 1968.
FarE&A	*The Far East and Australasia: A Survey and Directory of Asia and the Pacific.* London: Europa Publications, 1978, 1979, 1980, 1981. Distributed by Gale Research Co., Detroit, Michigan.

	FarE&A 78	1978-1979 edition
	FarE&A 79	1979-1980 edition
	FarE&A 79A	Wade-Giles/Pinyin spellings of Chinese names begin on page 1155.
	FarE&A 80	1980-1981 edition
	FarE&A 80A	Wade-Giles/Pinyin spellings of Chinese names begin on page 1174.
	FarE&A 81	1981-1982 edition

Biographies are found in the "Who's Who in the Far East and Australasia" section at the back of each volume.

FemPA	*The Female Poets of America.* With portraits, biographical notices, and specimens of their writings. Seventh edition, revised. By Thomas Buchanan Read. Philadelphia: E.H. Butler & Co., 1857. Reprint. Detroit: Gale Research Co., 1978.
FifBJA	*Fifth Book of Junior Authors & Illustrators.* Edited by Sally Holmes Holtze. New York: H.W. Wilson Co., 1983.
FifIDA	*Fifth International Directory of Anthropologists.* Current Anthropology Resource Series, edited by Sol Tax. Chicago: University of Chicago Press, 1975.
FifCWr	*Fifty Caribbean Writers: A Bio-Bibliographical Critical Sourcebook.* Edited by Daryl Cumber Dance. New York: Greenwood Press, 1986.
Film	*Filmarama.* Compiled by John Stewart. Metuchen, New Jersey: Scarecrow Press, 1975, 1977.

	Film 1	Volume I: *The Formidable Years, 1893-1919*, 1975
	Film 2	Volume II: *The Flaming Years, 1920-1929*, 1977

FilmgC	*The Filmgoer's Companion.* Fourth edition. By Leslie Halliwell. New York: Hill & Wang, 1974.
ForWC 70	*Foremost Women in Communications.* A biographical reference work on accomplished women in broadcasting, publishing, advertising, public relations, and allied professions. New York: Foremost Americans Publishing Corp., in association with R.R. Bowker Co., 1970.
ForIl	*Forty Illustrators and How They Work.* By Ernest W. Watson. Cincinnati: Watson-Guptil Publications, Inc., 1946. Reprint. Freeport, New York: Books for Libraries Press, 1970.
FourBJA	*Fourth Book of Junior Authors and Illustrators.* Edited by Doris De Montreville and Elizabeth D. Crawford. New York: H.W. Wilson Co., 1978.
Future	*The Future: A Guide to Information Sources.* Second edition. Edited by Edward S. Cornish. Washington, D.C.: World Future Society, 1979. Biographies begin on page 125.
GolEC	*Golombek's Encyclopedia of Chess.* Edited by Harry Golombek. New York: Crown Publishers, 1977.
GoodHs	*The Good Housekeeping Woman's Almanac.* Edited by Barbara McDowell and Hana Umlauf. New York: Newspaper Enterprise Association, 1977. Use the Index to locate biographies.
GrEconS	*Great Economists since Keynes: An Introduction to the Lives & Works of One Hundred Modern Economists.* By Mark Blaug. Totowa, New Jersey: Barnes & Noble Books, 1985.
GrFLW	*Great Foreign Language Writers.* Edited by James Vinson and Daniel Kirkpatrick. Great Writers Series. New York: St. Martin's Press, 1984.
GuPsyc	*A Guide to Psychologists and Their Concepts.* By Vernon J. Nordby and Calvin S. Hall. San Francisco: W.H. Freeman & Co., 1974.
HalFC 84	*Halliwell's Filmgoer's Companion.* Eighth edition. By Leslie Halliwell. New York: Charles Scribner's Sons, 1984.

HanRL   *Handbook of Russian Literature.* Edited by Victor Terras. New Haven: Yale University Press, 1985.

HarEnUS   *Harper's Encyclopaedia of United States History: From 458 A.D. to 1915.* New edition entirely revised and enlarged. 10 volumes. By Benson John Lossing. New York: Harper & Brothers Publishers, 1915. Reprint. Detroit: Gale Research Co., 1974.

HerW   *Her Way.* Biographies of women for young people. By Mary-Ellen Kulkin. Chicago: American Library Association, 1976.

HerW 84   *Her Way.* A guide to biographies of women for young people. Second edition. By Mary-Ellen Siegel. Chicago: American Library Association, 1984.

HisEWW   *The Historical Encyclopedia of World War II.* Edited by Marcel Baudot, et al. New York: Facts on File, 1980. Originally published as *Encyclopedie de la Guerre 1939-1945.* Paris: Editions Casterman, 1977.

HolP   *Hollywood Players.* Two volumes. New Rochelle, New York: Arlington House Publishers, 1976.

                HolP 40   *The Forties.* By James Robert Parish and Lennard DeCarl.

HsB&A   *The House of Beadle and Adams and Its Dime and Nickel Novels: The Story of a Vanished Literature.* Two volumes and supplement. By Albert Johannsen. Norman, Oklahoma: University of Oklahoma Press, 1950, 1962.

ICPEnP   *ICP Encyclopedia of Photography.* New York: Crown Publishers, 1984.

      The Appendix, indicated in this index by the code *A*, begins on page 576.

IlBEAAW   *The Illustrated Biographical Encyclopedia of Artists of the American West.* By Peggy Samuels and Harold Samuels. Garden City, New York: Doubleday & Co., 1976.

IlDcG   *An Illustrated Dictionary of Glass.* 2,442 entries, including definitions of wares, materials, processes, forms, and decorative styles, and entries on principal glass-makers, decorators, and designers, from antiquity to the present. By Harold Newman. London: Thames & Hudson, 1977.

IlEncJ   *The Illustrated Encyclopedia of Jazz.* By Brian Case and Stan Britt. New York: Harmony Books, 1978.

IlEncMy   *An Illustrated Encyclopaedia of Mysticism and the Mystery Religions.* By John Ferguson. London: Thames & Hudson, 1976.

IlEncRk   *The Illustrated Encyclopedia of Rock.* Compiled by Nick Logan and Bob Woffinden. London: Hamlyn Publishing Group Ltd., 1976; New York: Harmony Books, 1977.

IlrAm   *The Illustrator in America, 1900-1960's.* Compiled and edited by Walt Reed. New York: Reinhold Publishing Corp., 1966.

            IlrAm A   "The Decade: 1900-1910" begins on page 13.
            IlrAm B   "The Decade: 1910-1920" begins on page 43.
            IlrAm C   "The Decade: 1920-1930" begins on page 77.
            IlrAm D   "The Decade: 1930-1940" begins on page 113.
            IlrAm E   "The Decade: 1940-1950" begins on page 167.
            IlrAm F   "The Decade: 1950-1960" begins on page 211.
            IlrAm G   "The Decade: 1960's" begins on page 239.

IlrAm 1880	*The Illustrator in America, 1880-1980.* A century of illustration. By Walt Reed and Roger Reed. New York: Madison Square Press (for The Society of Illustrators), 1984. Distributed by Robert Silver Associates, New York, New York. Use the Index to locate biographies.
IlsBYP	*Illustrators of Books for Young People.* Second edition. By Martha E. Ward and Dorothy A. Marquardt. Metuchen, New Jersey: Scarecrow Press, 1975.
IlsCB	*Illustrators of Children's Books.* Boston: Horn Book, 1947, 1958, 1968, 1978.

    IlsCB 1744   *1744-1945.* Compiled by Bertha E. Mahony, Louise Payson Latimer, and Beulah Folmsbee, 1947.

    IlsCB 1946   *1946-1956.* Compiled by Ruth Hill Viguers, Marcia Dalphin, and Bertha Mahony Miller, 1958.

    IlsCB 1957   *1957-1966.* Compiled by Lee Kingman, Joanna Foster, and Ruth Giles Lontoft, 1968.

    IlsCB 1967   *1967-1976.* Compiled by Lee Kingman, Grace Allen Hogarth, and Harriet Quimby, 1978.

InB&W 80	*In Black and White.* A guide to magazine articles, newspaper articles, and books concerning more than 15,000 Black individuals and groups. Third edition. Two volumes. Edited by Mary Mace Spradling. Detroit: Gale Research Co., 1980.
InB&W 85	*In Black and White.* A guide to magazine articles, newspaper articles, and books concerning more than 6,700 Black individuals and groups. Third edition, Supplement. Edited by Mary Mace Spradling. Detroit: Gale Research Co., 1985.

    InB&W 85   Biographies

    InB&W 85A   "Performing Groups" section begins on page 440.

    InB&W 85   "Prominent Duos" section begins on page 451.

InSci	*Index to Scientists of the World from Ancient to Modern Times: Biographies and Portraits.* By Norma Olin Ireland. Boston: F.W. Faxon Co., 1962.
InWom	*Index to Women of the World from Ancient to Modern Times: Biographies and Portraits.* By Norma Olin Ireland. Westwood, Massachusetts: F.W. Faxon Co., 1970.
IndAu 1816	*Indiana Authors and Their Books, 1816-1916.* Biographical sketches of authors who published during the first century of Indiana statehood with lists of their books. Compiled by R.E. Banta. Crawfordsville, Indiana: Wabash College, 1949.
IndAu 1917	*Indiana Authors and Their Books, 1917-1966.* A continuation of *Indiana Authors and Their Books, 1816-1916*, and containing additional names from the earlier period. Compiled by Donald E. Thompson. Crawfordsville, Indiana: Wabash College, 1974.
IntAu&W 76	*The International Authors and Writers Who's Who.* Seventh edition. Edited by Ernest Kay. Cambridge, England: Melrose Press, 1976.

    IntAu&W 76   Biographical Section

    IntAu&W 76A   Addendum begins on page 641.

    IntAu&W 76X   "Pseudonyms of Included Authors" section begins on page 645.

IntAu&W	*The International Authors and Writers Who's Who.* Edited by Adrian Gaster. Cambridge, England: International Biographical Centre, 1977, 1982, 1986. 1982 edition is combined with *International Who's Who in Poetry* (see below).

    IntAu&W 77   Eighth edition, 1977, Biographical Section

    IntAu&W 77X   The "Pseudonyms of Included Authors" section begins on page 1131.

IntAu&W 82	Ninth edition, 1982, Biographical Section
IntAu&W 82X	The "Pseudonyms of Included Authors" section begins on page 719.
IntAu&W 86	10th edition, 1986, Biographical section
IntAu&W 86X	"Pseudonyms of Authors and Writers" section begins on page 796.

IntDcF 2   *The International Dictionary of Films and Filmmakers.* Volume II: *Directors/Filmmakers.* Edited by Christopher Lyon. Chicago: St. James Press, 1984. Distributed by Gale Research Co., Detroit, Michigan.

IntDcWB   *The International Dictionary of Women's Biography.* Compiled and edited by Jennifer S. Uglow. New York: Continuum Publishing Co., 1982.

IntEnSS 79   *International Encyclopedia of the Social Sciences.* Volume 18: Biographical Supplement. Edited by David L. Sills. New York: Macmillan Publishing Co., Free Press, 1979.

IntMed 80   *International Medical Who's Who: A Biographical Guide in Medical Research.* First edition. Two volumes. Harlow, United Kingdom: Longman Group, Francis Hodgson, 1980. Distributed by Gale Research Co., Detroit, Michigan.

IntMPA   *International Motion Picture Almanac.* Edited by Richard Gertner. New York: Quigley Publishing Co., 1975, 1976, 1977, 1978, 1979, 1981, 1982, 1984, 1986.

IntMPA 75	1975 edition
IntMPA 76	1976 edition
IntMPA 77	1977 edition
IntMPA 78	1978 edition
IntMPA 79	1979 edition
IntMPA 81	1981 edition
IntMPA 82	1982 edition
IntMPA 84	1984 edition
IntMPA 86	1986 edition

Biographies are found in the "Who's Who in Motion Pictures and Television" section in each volume. The listings are identical to those found in the *International Television Almanac.*

IntWW   *The International Who's Who.* London: Europa Publications, 1974, 1975, 1976, 1977, 1978, 1979, 1980, 1981, 1982, 1983. Distributed by Gale Research Co., Detroit, Michigan.

IntWW 74	38th edition, 1974-1975
IntWW 75	39th edition, 1975-1976
IntWW 76	40th edition, 1976-1977
IntWW 77	41st edition, 1977-1978
IntWW 78	42nd edition, 1978-1979
IntWW 79	43rd edition, 1979-1980
IntWW 80	44th edition, 1980-1981
IntWW 81	45th edition, 1981-1982
IntWW 82	46th edition, 1982-1983
IntWW 83	47th edition, 1983-1984

The Obituary section, indicated in this index by the code *N,* is located at the front of each volume.

IntWWE   *International Who's Who in Energy and Nuclear Sciences.* Compiled by the Longman Editorial Team. Harlow, United Kingdom: Longman Group, 1983. Distributed by Gale Research Co., Detroit, Michigan.

IntWWM	*International Who's Who in Music and Musicians' Directory.* Cambridge, England: International Who's Who in Music, 1977, 1984. Distributed by Gale Research Co., Detroit, Michigan. Earlier editions published as *Who's Who in Music and Musicians' International Directory* (see below).

IntWWM 77	Eighth edition, 1977
IntWWM 85	10th edition, 1984

IntWWP	*International Who's Who in Poetry.* Edited by Ernest Kay. Cambridge, England: International Biographical Centre, 1977, 1982. 1982 edition is combined with *The International Authors and Writers Who's Who* (see above).

IntWWP 77	Fifth edition, 1977, Biographical Section
IntWWP 77A	Addendum begins on page 470.
IntWWP 77X	The "Pseudonyms and Pen Names of Included Authors" section begins on page 702.
IntWWP 82	Sixth edition, 1982. Biographies begin on page 759.
IntWWP 82X	The "Pseudonyms of Included Poets" section begins on page 1035.

IntYB	*The International Year Book and Statesmen's Who's Who.* West Sussex, England: Kelly's Directories, 1978, 1979, 1980, 1981. Distributed by Gale Research Co., Detroit, Michigan.

IntYB 78	1978 edition
IntYB 79	1979 edition
IntYB 80	1980 edition
IntYB 81	1981 edition

Biographies are found in Part 3 of each volume.

IntYB 82	*The International Yearbook and Statesmen's Who's Who.* West Sussex, England: Thomas Skinner Directories, 1982. Distributed by Gale Research Co., Detroit, Michigan.

Biographies are found in Part 3.

JBA 34	*The Junior Book of Authors.* An introduction to the lives of writers and illustrators for younger readers from Lewis Carroll and Louisa Alcott to the present day. First edition. Edited by Stanley J. Kunitz and Howard Haycraft. New York: H.W. Wilson Co., 1934.

JBA 51	*The Junior Book of Authors.* Second edition, revised. Edited by Stanley J. Kunitz and Howard Haycraft. New York: H.W. Wilson Co., 1951.

Use the Index to locate biographies.

LEduc 74	*Leaders in Education.* Fifth edition. Edited by Jaques Cattell Press. New York: R.R. Bowker Co., 1974.

LElec	*Leaders in Electronics.* New York: McGraw-Hill Book Co., 1979.

Title page reads *McGraw-Hill's Leaders in Electronics.*

LesBEnT	*Les Brown's Encyclopedia of Television.* By Les Brown. New York: New York Zoetrope, 1982. Previous edition published as *The New York Times Encyclopedia of Television* (see below).

LibW	*Liberty's Women.* Edited by Robert McHenry. Springfield, Massachusetts: G. & C. Merriam Co., 1980.

LinLib L   *The Lincoln Library of Language Arts.* Third edition. Two volumes. Columbus, Ohio: Frontier Press Co., 1978.

> Biographies begin on page 345 of Volume 1 and are continued in Volume 2. The "Pen Names" section, indicated in this index by the code *LP*, begins on page 331.

LinLib S   *The Lincoln Library of Social Studies.* Eighth edition. Three volumes. Columbus, Ohio: Frontier Press Co., 1978.

> Biographies begin on page 865 of Volume 3.

LitC   *Literature Criticism from 1400 to 1800.* Excerpts from criticism of the works of fifteenth, sixteenth, seventeenth, and eighteenth-century novelists, poets, playwrights, philosophers, and other creative writers, from the first published critical appraisals to current evaluations. Detroit: Gale Research Co., 1984-1987.

LitC 1	Volume 1, 1984
LitC 2	Volume 2, 1985
LitC 3	Volume 3, 1986
LitC 4	Volume 4, 1986
LitC 5	Volume 5, 1987

LivgBAA   *Living Black American Authors: A Biographical Directory.* By Ann Allen Shockley and Sue P. Chandler. New York: R.R. Bowker Co., 1973.

LongCTC   *Longman Companion to Twentieth Century Literature.* By A.C. Ward. London: Longman Group, 1970.

LuthC 75   *Lutheran Cyclopedia.* Revised edition. Edited by Erwin L. Lueker. St. Louis: Concordia Publishing House, 1975.

MacBEP   *Macmillan Biographical Encyclopedia of Photographic Artists & Innovators.* By Turner Browne and Elaine Partnow. New York: Macmillan Publishing Co.; London: Collier Macmillan Publishers, 1983.

MacDCB 78   *The Macmillan Dictionary of Canadian Biography.* Edited by W. Stewart Wallace. Fourth edition, revised, enlarged, and updated by W.A. McKay. Toronto: Macmillan of Canada, 1978.

MacEA   *Macmillan Encyclopedia of Architects.* Four volumes. Edited by Adolf K. Placzek. New York: Macmillan Publishing Co., Free Press; London: Collier Macmillan Publishers, 1982.

> Use the "Index of Names," which begins on page 533 of Volume 4, to locate biographies.

MajMD 1   *Major Modern Dramatists.* A Library of Literary Criticism. New York: Frederick Ungar Publishing Co., 1984, 1986.

MajMD 1	Volume I, compiled and edited by Rita Stein and Friedhelm Rickert; 1984.
MajMD 2	Volume II, compiled and edited by Blandine M. Rickert, Debra Popkin, Michael Popkin, Leonard S. Klein, Marshall J. Schneider, and Leo D. Rudnytzky; 1986.

> Use the "Dramatists Included" list on page ix to locate biographies.

MakMC   *Makers of Modern Culture.* Edited by Justin Wintle. New York: Facts on File, 1981.

MarqDCG 84   *Marquis Who's Who Directory of Computer Graphics.* First edition. Chicago: Marquis Who's Who, 1984.

McGDA   *McGraw-Hill Dictionary of Art.* Five volumes. Edited by Bernard S. Myers. New York: McGraw-Hill Book Co., 1969.

McGEWB   *The McGraw-Hill Encyclopedia of World Biography.* An international reference work in 12 volumes including an index. New York: McGraw-Hill Book Co., 1973.

McGEWD   *McGraw-Hill Encyclopedia of World Drama.* New York: McGraw-Hill Book Co., 1972, 1984.

> **McGEWD**   First edition, an international reference work in four volumes, 1972.
>
> **McGEWD 84**   Second edition, an international reference work in five volumes, 1984.

McGMS 80   *McGraw-Hill Modern Scientists and Engineers.* Three volumes. New York: McGraw-Hill Book Co., 1980.

MedHR   *Medal of Honor Recipients, 1863-1978.* Prepared by the Committee on Veterans' Affairs, United States Senate. 96th Congress, 1st Session, Senate Committee Print No. 3. Washington, D.C.: United States Government Printing Office, 1979.

> Use the "Medal of Honor Alphabetical Index," which begins on page 1023, to locate biographies.

MemAm   *Memorable Americans, 1750-1950.* By Robert B. Downs, John T. Flanagan, and Harold W. Scott. Littleton, Colorado: Libraries Unlimited, 1983.

MnBBF   *The Men behind Boys' Fiction.* By W.O.G. Lofts and D.J. Adley. London: Howard Baker Publishers, 1970.

MGM   *The MGM Stock Company: The Golden Era.* By James Robert Parish and Ronald L. Bowers. New Rochelle, New York: Arlington House, 1973.

> The "Capsule Biographies of MGM Executives" section, indicated in this index by the code *A*, begins on page 796.

MichAu 80   *Michigan Authors.* Second edition. By the Michigan Association for Media in Education. Ann Arbor: Michigan Association for Media in Education, 1980.

> The Addendum, indicated in this index by the code *A*, begins on page 339.

MidE   *The Middle East and North Africa.* London: Europa Publications, 1978, 1979, 1980, 1981, 1982. Distributed by Gale Research Co., Detroit, Michigan.

> **MidE 78**   25th edition, 1978-1979
> **MidE 79**   26th edition, 1979-1980
> **MidE 80**   27th edition, 1980-1981
> **MidE 81**   28th edition, 1981-1982
> **MidE 82**   29th edition, 1982-1983
>
> Biographies are found in the "Who's Who in the Middle East and North Africa" section at the back of each volume.

MinnWr   *Minnesota Writers: A Collection of Autobiographical Stories by Minnesota Prose Writers.* Edited and annotated by Carmen Nelson Richards. Minneapolis: T.S. Denison & Co., 1961.

> Use the Table of Contents to locate biographies.

ModAL   *Modern American Literature.* Five volumes. A Library of Literary Criticism. New York: Frederick Ungar Publishing Co., 1969, 1976, 1985.

> **ModAL**   Fourth edition, volumes I-III. Compiled and edited by Dorothy Nyren Curley, Maurice Kramer, and Elaine Fialka Kramer, 1969.

	ModAL S1	Supplement to the fourth edition, Volume IV. Compiled and edited by Dorothy Nyren, Maurice Kramer, and Elaine Fialka Kramer, 1976.
	ModAL S2	Second Supplement to the fourth edition, Volume V. Compiled and edited by Paul Schlueter and June Schlueter, 1985.

ModAWP   *Modern American Women Poets.* By Jean Gould. New York: Dodd, Mead & Co., 1984. Use the Table of Contents to locate biographies.

ModBlW   *Modern Black Writers.* Compiled and edited by Michael Popkin. A Library of Literary Criticism. New York: Frederick Ungar Publishing Co., 1978.

ModBrL   *Modern British Literature.* Five volumes. A Library of Literary Criticism. New York: Frederick Ungar Publishing Co., 1966, 1975, 1985.

	ModBrL	Volumes I-III, compiled and edited by Ruth Z. Temple and Martin Tucker, 1966.
	ModBrL S1	Volume IV, Supplement, compiled and edited by Martin Tucker and Rita Stein, 1975.
	ModBrL S2	Volume V, Second Supplement, compiled and edited by Denis Lane and Rita Stein, 1985.

ModCmwL   *Modern Commonwealth Literature.* Compiled and edited by John H. Ferres and Martin Tucker. A Library of Literary Criticism. New York: Frederick Ungar Publishing Co., 1977.

ModFrL   *Modern French Literature.* Two volumes. Compiled and edited by Debra Popkin and Michael Popkin. A Library of Literary Criticism. New York: Frederick Ungar Publishing Co., 1977.

ModGL   *Modern German Literature.* Two volumes. Compiled and edited by Agnes Korner Domandi. A Library of Literary Criticism. New York: Frederick Ungar Publishing Co., 1972.

ModLAL   *Modern Latin American Literature.* Two volumes. Compiled and edited by David William Foster and Virginia Ramos Foster. A Library of Literary Criticism. New York: Frederick Ungar Publishing Co., 1975.

ModRL   *Modern Romance Literatures.* Compiled and edited by Dorothy Nyren Curley and Arthur Curley. A Library of Literary Criticism. New York: Frederick Ungar Publishing Co., 1967.

ModSL   *Modern Slavic Literatures.* Two volumes. A Library of Literary Criticism. New York: Frederick Ungar Publishing Co., 1972, 1976.

	ModSL 1	Volume I: Russian Literature, compiled and edited by Vasa D. Mihailovich, 1972.
	ModSL 2	Volume II: Bulgarian, Czechoslovak, Polish, Ukrainian and Yugoslav Literatures, compiled and edited by Vasa D. Mihailovich, et al., 1976.

Use the alphabetic listing of authors at the front of each volume to locate biographies.

ModWD   *Modern World Drama: An Encyclopedia.* By Myron Matlaw. New York: E.P. Dutton & Co., 1972.

MorBMP   *More Books by More People: Interviews with Sixty-Five Authors of Books for Children.* By Lee Bennett Hopkins. New York: Citation Press, 1974.

MorJA   *More Junior Authors.* Edited by Muriel Fuller. New York: H.W. Wilson Co., 1963.

MorMA   *More Memorable Americans, 1750-1950.* By Robert B. Downs, John T. Flanagan, and Harold W. Scott. Littleton, Colorado: Libraries Unlimited, 1985.

MotPP   *Motion Picture Performers: A Bibliography of Magazine and Periodical Articles, 1900-1969.* Compiled by Mel Schuster. Metuchen, New Jersey: Scarecrow Press, 1971.

MouLC   *Moulton's Library of Literary Criticism of English and American Authors through the Beginning of the Twentieth Century.* Four volumes. Abridged, revised, and with additions by Martin Tucker. New York: Frederick Ungar Publishing Co., 1966.

MouLC 1	Volume I: The Beginnings to the Seventeenth Century
MouLC 2	Volume II: Neo-Classicism to the Romantic Period
MouLC 3	Volume III: The Romantic Period to the Victorian Age
MouLC 4	Volume IV: The Mid-Nineteenth Century to Edwardianism

Use the alphabetic listings at the front of each volume to locate biographies.

MovMk   *The Movie Makers.* By Sol Chaneles and Albert Wolsky. Secaucus, New Jersey: Derbibooks, 1974.

The "Directors" section begins on page 506.

MugS   *Mug Shots: Who's Who in the New Earth.* By Jay Acton, Alan Le Mond, and Parker Hodges. New York: World Publishing Co., 1972.

MusSN   *Musicians since 1900: Performers in Concert and Opera.* Compiled and edited by David Ewen. New York: H.W. Wilson Co., 1978.

NamesHP   *Names in the History of Psychology: A Biographical Sourcebook.* By Leonard Zusne. Washington, D.C.: Hemisphere Publishing Corp., 1975. Distributed by John Wiley & Sons, Halstead Press, New York, New York. Continued by *Biographical Dictionary of Psychology* (see above).

Use the "Alphabetic List of Names," which begins on page ix, to locate biographies.

NatCAB   *The National Cyclopaedia of American Biography.* 63 volumes. New York and Clifton, New Jersey: James T. White & Co., 1892-1984. Reprint. Volumes 1-50. Ann Arbor: University Microfilms, 1967-1971.

Number after the source code indicates volume number. Use the Index in each volume to locate biographies.

NatLAC   *National Leaders of American Conservation.* Edited by Richard H. Stroud. Washington, D.C.: Smithsonian Institution Press, 1985.

NatPD   *National Playwrights Directory.* Edited by Phyllis Johnson Kaye. Waterford, Connecticut: The O'Neill Theater Center, 1977, 1981. Distributed by Gale Research Co., Detroit, Michigan.

NatPD	First edition, 1977
NatPD 81	Second edition, 1981

NegAl 76   *The Negro Almanac: A Reference Work on the Afro American.* Third edition. Edited by Harry A. Ploski and Warren Marr, II. New York: Bellwether Co., 1976.

Use the Index to locate biographies.

NegAl 83   *The Negro Almanac: A Reference Work on the Afro-American.* Fourth edition.
                    Compiled and edited by Harry A. Ploski and James Williams. New York: John
                    Wiley & Sons, 1983.

                         Use the Index to locate biographies.

NewC   *The New Century Handbook of English Literature.* Revised edition. Edited by Clarence
                    L. Barnhart with the assistance of William D. Halsey. New York:
                    Appleton-Century-Crofts, 1967.

NewCBMT   *New Complete Book of the American Musical Theater.* By David Ewen. New York:
                    Holt, Rinehart & Winston, 1970.

                         Biographies are found in the "Librettists, Lyricists and Composers" section
                         which begins on page 607.

NewCon   *The New Consciousness, 1941-1968.* Concise Dictionary of American Literary
                    Biography Series. Detroit: Gale Research Co., 1987.

NewEOp 71   *The New Encyclopedia of the Opera.* By David Ewen. New York: Hill & Wang, 1971.

NewOxM   *The New Oxford Companion to Music.* Two volumes. Edited by Denis Arnold. Oxford:
                    Oxford University Press, 1983.

NewRR83   *The New Rock 'n' Roll.* By Stuart Coupe and Glenn A. Baker. New York: St. Martin's
                    Press, 1983.

NewYHSD   *The New-York Historical Society's Dictionary of Artists in America, 1564-1860.* By
                    George C. Groce and David H. Wallace. New Haven, Connecticut: Yale
                    University Press, 1957.

NewYTBE   *The New York Times Biographical Edition: A Compilation of Current Biographical
                    Information of General Interest.* New York: Arno Press, 1970-1973. Continued by
                    The New York Times Biographical Service (see below).

                         NewYTBE 70   Volume 1, Numbers 1-12, 1970
                         NewYTBE 71   Volume 2, Numbers 1-12, 1971
                         NewYTBE 72   Volume 3, Numbers 1-12, 1972
                         NewYTBE 73   Volume 4, Numbers 1-12, 1973
                    Use the "Annual Index" to locate biographies.

NewYTBS   *The New York Times Biographical Service: A Compilation of Current Biographical
                    Information of General Interest.* New York: Arno Press, 1974-1981. A
                    continuation of *The New York Times Biographical Edition* (see above).

                         NewYTBS 74   Volume 5, Numbers 1-12, 1974
                         NewYTBS 75   Volume 6, Numbers 1-12, 1975
                         NewYTBS 76   Volume 7, Numbers 1-12, 1976
                         NewYTBS 77   Volume 8, Numbers 1-12, 1977
                         NewYTBS 78   Volume 9, Numbers 1-12, 1978
                         NewYTBS 79   Volume 10, Numbers 1-12, 1979
                         NewYTBS 80   Volume 11, Numbers 1-12, 1980
                         NewYTBS 81   Volume 12, Numbers 1-12, 1981
                    Use the "Annual Index" to locate biographies.

NewYTBS   *The New York Times Biographical Service: A Compilation of Current Biographical
                    Information of General Interest.* Sanford, North Carolina: Microfilming Corp. of
                    America, 1982-1983.

                         NewYTBS 82   Volume 13, Numbers 1-12, 1982
                         NewYTBS 83   Volume 14, Numbers 1-12, 1983
                    Use the "Annual Index" to locate biographies.

NewYTBS   *The New York Times Biographical Service. A compilation of current biographical information of general interest.* Ann Arbor, Michigan: University Microfilms International, 1984-1986.

NewYTBS 84	Volume 15, Numbers 1-12, 1984-1985
NewYTBS 85	Volume 16, Numbers 1-12, 1985-1986
NewYTBS 86	Volume 17, Numbers 1-12, 1986-1987

Use the "Annual Index" to locate biographies.

NewYTET   *The New York Times Encyclopedia of Television.* By Les Brown. New York: New York Times Book Co., 1977. Expanded edition published as *Les Brown's Encyclopedia of Television* (see above).

NewbC   *Newbery and Caldecott Medal Books.* With acceptance papers, biographies and related material chiefly from the *Horn Book Magazine.* Edited by Lee Kingman. Boston: Horn Book, 1965, 1975.

NewbC 1956	*1956-1965*, 1965
NewbC 1966	*1966-1975*, 1975

Newb 1922   *Newbery Medal Books, 1922-1955.* With their authors' acceptance papers and related material chiefly from the *Horn Book Magazine.* Horn Book Papers, Volume 1. Edited by Bertha Mahony Miller and Elinor Whitney Field. Boston: Horn Book, 1955.

NinCLC   *Nineteenth-Century Literature Criticism.* Excerpts from criticism of the works of novelists, poets, playwrights, short story writers, and other creative writers who died between 1800 and 1900, from the first published critical appraisals to current evaluations. Detroit: Gale Research Co., 1981-1986.

NinCLC 1	Volume 1, 1981
NinCLC 2	Volume 2, 1982
NinCLC 3	Volume 3, 1983
NinCLC 4	Volume 4, 1983
NinCLC 5	Volume 5, 1984
NinCLC 6	Volume 6, 1984
NinCLC 7	Volume 7, 1984
NinCLC 8	Volume 8, 1985
NinCLC 9	Volume 9, 1985
NinCLC 10	Volume 10, 1985
NinCLC 11	Volume 11, 1986
NinCLC 12	Volume 12, 1986
NinCLC 13	Volume 13, 1986
NinCLC 14	Volume 14, 1987
NinCLC 15	Volume 15, 1987

NotAW   *Notable American Women, 1607-1950: A Biographical Dictionary.* Three volumes. Edited by Edward T. James. Cambridge, Massachusetts: Harvard University Press, Belknap Press, 1971.

NotAW MOD   *Notable American Women: The Modern Period.* A biographical dictionary. Edited by Barbara Sicherman and Carol Hurd Green. Cambridge, Massachusetts: Harvard University Press, Belknap Press, 1980.

NotNAT   *Notable Names in the American Theatre.* Clifton, New Jersey: James T. White & Co., 1976. First edition published as *The Biographical Encyclopaedia and Who's Who of the American Theatre* (see above).

NotNAT	"Notable Names in the American Theatre" begins on page 489.
NotNAT A	"Biographical Bibliography" begins on page 309.
NotNAT B	"Necrology" begins on page 343.

This book often alphabetizes by titles of address, e.g.: Dr., Mrs., and Sir.

Novels   *Novels and Novelists: A Guide to the World of Fiction.* Edited by Martin Seymour-Smith. New York: St. Martin's Press, 1980.

Biographies are located in the "Novelists: An Alphabetical Guide" section which begins on page 87.

ObitOF 79   *Obituaries on File.* Two volumes. Compiled by Felice Levy. New York: Facts on File, 1979.

ObitT   *Obituaries from the Times.* Compiled by Frank C. Roberts. Reading, England: Newspaper Archive Developments, 1975, 1978, 1979. Distributed by Meckler Books, Westport, Connecticut.

ObitT 1951	*1951-1960*, 1979
ObitT 1961	*1961-1970*, 1975
ObitT 1971	*1971-1975*, 1978

ODwPR 79   *O'Dwyer's Directory of Public Relations Executives, 1979.* Edited by Jack O'Dwyer. New York: J.R. O'Dwyer Co., 1979.

OhA&B   *Ohio Authors and Their Books: Biographical Data and Selective Bibliographies for Ohio Authors, Native and Resident, 1796-1950.* Edited by William Coyle. Cleveland and New York: World Publishing Co., 1962.

OxAmH   *The Oxford Companion to American History.* By Thomas H. Johnson. New York: Oxford University Press, 1966.

OxAmL   *The Oxford Companion to American Literature.* By James D. Hart. New York and Oxford: Oxford University Press, 1965, 1983.

OxAmL	Fourth edition, 1965
OxAmL 83	Fifth edition, 1983

OxAmT 84   *The Oxford Companion to American Theatre.* By Gerald Bordman. New York: Oxford University Press, 1984.

OxArt   *The Oxford Companion to Art.* Edited by Harold Osborne. Oxford: Oxford University Press, Clarendon Press, 1970.

OxAusL   *The Oxford Companion to Australian Literature.* By William H. Wilde, Joy Hooton, and Barry Andrews. Melbourne: Oxford University Press, 1985.

OxCan   *The Oxford Companion to Canadian History and Literature.* Toronto: Oxford University Press, 1967, 1973.

OxCan	Original volume, by Norah Story, 1967, reprinted with corrections, 1968
OxCan SUP	Supplement, edited by William Toye, 1973

OxCanL   *The Oxford Companion to Canadian Literature.* Edited by William Toye. New York: Oxford University Press, 1983.

OxChess 84   *The Oxford Companion to Chess.* By David Hooper and Kenneth Whyld. Oxford: Oxford University Press, 1984.

OxChL   *The Oxford Companion to Children's Literature.* By Humphrey Carpenter and Mari Prichard. New York: Oxford University Press, 1984.

OxEng *The Oxford Companion to English Literature.* Compiled and edited by Sir Paul Harvey. Fourth edition, revised by Dorothy Eagle. New York and Oxford: Oxford University Press, 1967.

OxEng 85 *The Oxford Companion to English Literature.* Fifth edition. Edited by Margaret Drabble. New York: Oxford University Press, 1985.

OxFilm *The Oxford Companion to Film.* Edited by Liz-Anne Bawden. New York and London: Oxford University Press, 1976.

OxFr *The Oxford Companion to French Literature.* Compiled and edited by Sir Paul Harvey and J.E. Heseltine. Oxford: Oxford University Press, Clarendon Press, 1959. Reprinted with corrections, 1966.

OxGer *The Oxford Companion to German Literature.* By Henry Garland and Mary Garland. Oxford: Oxford University Press, Clarendon Press, 1976.

OxLaw *The Oxford Companion to Law.* By David M. Walker. Oxford: Oxford University Press, Clarendon Press, 1980.

OxLitW *The Oxford Companion to the Literature of Wales.* Compiled and edited by Meic Stephens. Oxford: Oxford University Press, 1986.

OxMed 86 *The Oxford Companion to Medicine.* Two volumes. Edited by John Walton, Paul B. Beeson, and Ronald Bodley Scott. Oxford: Oxford University Press, 1986.

OxMus *The Oxford Companion to Music.* By Percy A. Scholes. 10th edition (corrected). Edited by John Owen Ward. London: Oxford University Press, 1974.

OxShips *The Oxford Companion to Ships and the Sea.* Edited by Peter Kemp. London and New York: Oxford University Press, 1976.

OxSpan *The Oxford Companion to Spanish Literature.* Edited by Philip Ward. Oxford: Oxford University Press, Clarendon Press, 1978.

OxThe *The Oxford Companion to the Theatre.* Third edition. Edited by Phyllis Hartnoll. London: Oxford University Press, 1967.

OxThe *The Oxford Companion to the Theatre.* Fourth edition. Edited by Phyllis Hartnoll. New York and Oxford: Oxford University Press, 1983.

OxTwCA *The Oxford Companion to Twentieth-Century Art.* Edited by Harold Osborne. Oxford: Oxford University Press, 1981.

PenC *The Penguin Companion to World Literature.* New York: McGraw-Hill Book Co., 1969, 1971.

      PenC AM *The Penguin Companion to American Literature.* Edited by Malcolm Bradbury, Eric Mottram, and Jean Franco, 1971.

      PenC CL *The Penguin Companion to Classical, Oriental and African Literature.* Edited by D.M. Lang and D.R. Dudley, 1969.

      PenC ENG *The Penguin Companion to English Literature.* Edited by David Daiches, 1971.

      PenC EUR *The Penguin Companion to European Literature.* Edited by Anthony Thorlby, 1969.

PhDcTCA 77 *Phaidon Dictionary of Twentieth-Century Art.* Second edition. Oxford: Phaidon Press; New York: E.P. Dutton, 1977.

PiP   *The Pied Pipers: Interviews with the Influential Creators of Children's Literature.* By Justin Wintle and Emma Fisher. New York: Paddington Press, 1974.

Use the Table of Contents to locate biographies.

PlP&P   *Plays, Players, and Playwrights: An Illustrated History of the Theatre.* By Marion Geisinger. Updated by Peggy Marks. New York: Hart Publishing Co., 1975.

Use the Index, which begins on page 575, to locate biographies in the main section of the book. A Supplemental Index to the last chapter, "The Theatre of the Seventies," begins on page 797 and is indicated in this index by the code *A*.

PoChrch   *The Poets of the Church: A Series of Biographical Sketches of Hymn-Writers with Notes on Their Hymns.* By Edwin F. Hatfield. New York: Anson D.F. Randolph & Co., 1884. Reprint. Detroit: Gale Research Co., 1978.

PoIre   *The Poets of Ireland: A Biographical and Bibliographical Dictionary of Irish Writers of English Verse.* By D.J. O'Donoghue. Dublin: Hodges Figgis & Co.; London: Henry Frowde, Oxford University Press, 1912. Reprint. Detroit: Gale Research Co., 1968.

"The Poets of Ireland" begins on page 5. The Appendices begin on page 495.

PoLE   *The Poets Laureate of England.* Being a history of the office of poet laureate, biographical notices of its holders, and a collection of the satires, epigrams, and lampoons directed against them. By Walter Hamilton. London: Elliot Stock, 1879. Reprint. Detroit: Gale Research Co., 1968.

Use the Index to locate biographies.

Po&Wr 77   *The Poets & Writers 1977 Supplement.* A complete update to *A Directory of American Poets* (1975) and *A Directory of American Fiction Writers* (1976). New York: Poets & Writers, 1977.

Use the Index to locate listings.

PolProf   *Political Profiles.* New York: Facts on File, 1976-1979.

PolProf E		*The Eisenhower Years.* Edited by Eleanora W. Schoenebaum, 1977.
PolProf J	*The Johnson Years.* Edited by Nelson Lichtenstein, 1976.	
PolProf K	*The Kennedy Years.* Edited by Nelson Lichtenstein, 1976.	
PolProf NF		*The Nixon/Ford Years.* Edited by Eleanora W. Schoenebaum, 1979.
PolProf T	*The Truman Years.* Edited by Eleanora W. Schoenebaum, 1978.	

PolsAm 84   *Politics in America: Members of Congress in Washington and at Home.* Edited by Alan Ehrenhalt. Washington, D.C.: Congressional Quarterly, CQ Press, 1983.

Use the Index to locate biographies.

PostFic   *Postmodern Fiction: A Bio-Bibliographical Guide.* Edited by Larry McCaffery. Movements in the Arts. New York: Greenwood Press, 1986.

Biographies begin on page 247.

PrintW   *The Printworld Directory of Contemporary Prints & Prices.* Edited by Selma Smith. Bala Cynwyd, Pennsylvania: Printworld, 1983, 1985. Distributed by Gale Research Co., Detroit, Michigan.

PrintW 83	*1983/84*, second edition, 1983
PrintW 85	*1985/86*, third edition, 1985

Not in strict alphabetical order.

Profile   *Profiles.* Revised edition. Edited by Irma McDonough. Ottawa: Canadian Library
                     Association, 1975, 1982.

Profile 1	Revised edition, 1975
Profile 2	Authors and Illustrators, Children's Literature in Canada, 1982

                     Contains articles from *In Review: Canadian Books for Children,* published
                     quarterly by the Ontario Provinical Library Service.

PseudAu   *Pseudonyms of Authors; Including Anonyms and Initialisms.* By John Edward Haynes.
                     New York: John Edward Haynes, 1882. Reprint. Detroit: Gale Research Co.,
                     1969.

                     The Addenda, indicated in this index by the code *A,* begins on page 104.
                     Pseudonyms are given exactly as written by the author and are filed under the
                     first letter of the pseudonym including the articles "a," "an," and "the."

PueRA   *Puerto Rican Authors: A Biobibliographic Handbook.* By Marnesba D. Hill and Harold
                     B. Schleifer. Translation of entries into Spanish by Daniel Maratos. Metuchen,
                     New Jersey: Scarecrow Press, 1974.

RAdv 1   *The Reader's Adviser: A Layman's Guide to Literature.* 12th edition. Volume 1: *The Best
                     in American and British Fiction, Poetry, Essays, Literary Biography, Bibliography,
                     and Reference.* Edited by Sarah L. Prakken. New York: R.R. Bowker Co., 1974.

                     Use the "Author Index," which begins on page 741, to locate biographies and
                     bibliographies.

RComWL   *The Reader's Companion to World Literature.* Second edition. Revised and updated by
                     Lillian Herlands Hornstein, Leon Edel, and Horst Frenz. New York: New
                     American Library, 1973.

REn   *The Reader's Encyclopedia.* Second edition. By William Rose Benet. New York:
                     Thomas Y. Crowell Co., 1965.

REnAL   *The Reader's Encyclopedia of American Literature.* By Max J. Herzberg. New York:
                     Thomas Y. Crowell Co., 1962.

REnAW   *The Reader's Encyclopedia of the American West.* Edited by Howard R. Lamar. New
                     York: Thomas Y. Crowell Co., 1977.

REnWD   *The Reader's Encyclopedia of World Drama.* Edited by John Gassner and Edward
                     Quinn. New York: Thomas Y. Crowell Co., 1969.

RGAfL   *A Reader's Guide to African Literature.* Compiled and edited by Hans M. Zell and
                     Helene Silver. New York: Africana Publishing Corp., 1971.

                     Biographies begin on page 113.

RkOn   *Rock On: The Illustrated Encyclopedia of Rock n' Roll.* By Norm N. Nite. New York:
                     Thomas Y. Crowell Co., 1974, 1978, 1982, 1984.

RkOn 74	Volume 1: *The Solid Gold Years,* 1974
RkOn 78	Volume 2: *The Modern Years: 1964-Present,* 1978
RkOn 78A	Volume 2: Appendix begins on page 543.
RkOn 82	Volume 1: *The Solid Gold Years,* Updated Edition, 1982
RkOn 84	Volume 2: *The Years of Change: 1964-1978,* Updated Edition, 1984.

Rk100   *Rock 100.* By David Dalton and Lenny Kaye. New York: Grosset & Dunlap, 1977.

RolSEnR 83   *The Rolling Stone Encyclopedia of Rock & Roll.* Edited by Jon Pareles and Patricia Romanowski. New York: Rolling Stone Press/Summit Books, 1983.

ScF&FL   *Science Fiction and Fantasy Literature.* A checklist, 1700-1974, with *Contemporary Science Fiction Authors II.* By R. Reginald. Detroit: Gale Research Co., 1979.

ScF&FL 1	Volume 1: "Author Index" begins on page 3.
ScF&FL 1A	Volume 1: Addendum begins on page 581.
ScF&FL 2	Volume 2: *Contemporary Science Fiction Authors II.*

ScFSB   *The Science Fiction Source Book.* Edited by David Wingrove. New York: Van Nostrand Reinhold Co., 1984.

Listings are located in the "Science Fiction Writers: A Consumers' Guide" section, which begins on page 87.

SelBAAf   *Selected Black American, African, and Caribbean Authors.* A bio-bibliography. Compiled by James A. Page and Jae Min Roh. Littleton, Colorado: Libraries Unlimited, 1985.

SelBAAu   *Selected Black American Authors: An Illustrated Bio-Bibliography.* Compiled by James A. Page. Boston: G.K. Hall & Co., 1977.

SenS   *A Sense of Story: Essays on Contemporary Writers for Children.* By John Rowe Townsend. London: Longman Group, 1971.

SingR   *The Singing Roads: A Guide to Australian Children's Authors and Illustrators.* Edited by Hugh Anderson. Surry Hills, Australia: Wentworth Books, 1970, 1972.

SingR 1	Part 1, Fourth Edition, 1972
SingR 2	Part 2, 1970

SixAP   *Sixty American Poets, 1896-1944.* Revised edition. Selected, with preface and critical notes by Allen Tate. Washington, D.C.: Library of Congress, 1954. Reprint. Detroit: Gale Research Co., 1969.

SmATA   *Something about the Author.* Facts and pictures about authors and illustrators of books for young people. Edited by Anne Commire. Detroit: Gale Research Co., 1971-1987.

SmATA 1	Volume 1, 1971
SmATA 2	Volume 2, 1971
SmATA 3	Volume 3, 1972
SmATA 4	Volume 4, 1973
SmATA 5	Volume 5, 1973
SmATA 6	Volume 6, 1974
SmATA 7	Volume 7, 1975
SmATA 8	Volume 8, 1976
SmATA 9	Volume 9, 1976
SmATA 10	Volume 10, 1976
SmATA 11	Volume 11, 1977
SmATA 12	Volume 12, 1977
SmATA 13	Volume 13, 1978
SmATA 14	Volume 14, 1978
SmATA 15	Volume 15, 1979
SmATA 16	Volume 16, 1979
SmATA 17	Volume 17, 1979
SmATA 18	Volume 18, 1980
SmATA 19	Volume 19, 1980
SmATA 20	Volume 20, 1980
SmATA 20N	Volume 20, Obituary Notices
SmATA 21	Volume 21, 1980
SmATA 21N	Volume 21, Obituary Notices

SmATA 22	Volume 22, 1981
SmATA 22N	Volume 22, Obituary Notices
SmATA 23	Volume 23, 1981
SmATA 23N	Volume 23, Obituary Notices
SmATA 24	Volume 24, 1981
SmATA 24N	Volume 24, Obituary Notices
SmATA 25	Volume 25, 1981
SmATA 25N	Volume 25, Obituary Notices
SmATA 26	Volume 26, 1982
SmATA 26N	Volume 26, Obituary Notices
SmATA 27	Volume 27, 1982
SmATA 27N	Volume 27, Obituary Notices
SmATA 28	Volume 28, 1982
SmATA 28N	Volume 28, Obituary Notices
SmATA 29	Volume 29, 1982
SmATA 29N	Volume 29, Obituary Notices
SmATA 30	Volume 30, 1983
SmATA 30N	Volume 30, Obituary Notices
SmATA 31	Volume 31, 1983
SmATA 31N	Volume 31, Obituary Notices
SmATA 32	Volume 32, 1983
SmATA 32N	Volume 32, Obituary Notices
SmATA 33	Volume 33, 1983
SmATA 33N	Volume 33, Obituary Notices
SmATA 34	Volume 34, 1984
SmATA 34N	Volume 34, Obituary Notices
SmATA 35	Volume 35, 1984
SmATA 35N	Volume 35, Obituary Notices
SmATA 36	Volume 36, 1984
SmATA 36N	Volume 36, Obituary Notices
SmATA 37	Volume 37, 1985
SmATA 37N	Volume 37, Obituary Notices
SmATA 38	Volume 38, 1985
SmATA 38N	Volume 38, Obituary Notices
SmATA 39	Volume 39, 1985
SmATA 39N	Volume 39, Obituary Notices
SmATA 40	Volume 40, 1985
SmATA 40N	Volume 40, Obituary Notices
SmATA 41	Volume 41, 1985
SmATA 41N	Volume 41, Obituary Notices
SmATA 42	Volume 42, 1986
SmATA 42N	Volume 42, Obituary Notices
SmATA 43	Volume 43, 1986
SmATA 43N	Volume 43, Obituary Notices
SmATA 44	Volume 44, 1986
SmATA 44N	Volume 44, Obituary Notices
SmATA 45	Volume 45, 1986
SmATA 45N	Volume 45, Obituary Notices
SmATA 46	Volume 46, 1987
SmATA 46N	Volume 46, Obituary Notices
SmATA 47	Volume 47, 1987
SmATA 47N	Volume 47, Obituary Notices
SmATA 48	Volume 48, 1987
SmATA 48N	Volume 48, Obituary Notices

SmATA AS	*Something about the Author, Autobiography Series.* Detroit: Gale Research Co., 1987.	
	SmATA 1AS	Volume 1, 1986
	SmATA 2AS	Volume 2, 1986
	SmATA 3AS	Volume 3, 1987
	SmATA 4AS	Volume 4, 1987

SmATA X   This code refers to pseudonym entries which appear only as cross-references in the cumulative index to *Something about the Author.*

St&PR   *Standard & Poor's Register of Corporations, Directors and Executives.* New York: Standard & Poor's Corp., 1975

         St&PR 75   1975 edition, Volume 2: *Directors and Executives.*

Str&VC   *Story and Verse for Children.* Third edition. By Miriam Blanton Huber. New York: Macmillan Co., 1965.

     Biographies begin on page 793.

SupFW   *Supernatural Fiction Writers: Fantasy and Horror.* Two volumes. Edited by E.F. Bleiler. New York: Charles Scribner's Sons, 1985.

     Use the Index to locate biographies.

TelT   *Tellers of Tales: British Authors of Children's Books from 1800 to 1964.* Revised edition. By Roger Lancelyn Green. New York: Franklin Watts, Inc., 1964.

TexWr   *Texas Writers of Today.* By Florence Elberta Barns. Dallas: Tardy Publishing Co., 1935. Reprint. Ann Arbor: Gryphon Books, 1971.

ThFT   *They Had Faces Then: Super Stars, Stars and Starlets of the 1930's.* By John Springer and Jack Hamilton. Secaucus, New Jersey: Citadel Press, 1974.

ThrBJA   *Third Book of Junior Authors.* Edited by Doris De Montreville and Donna Hill. New York: H.W. Wilson Co., 1972.

ThrtnMM   *13 Mistresses of Murder.* By Elaine Budd. New York: Ungar Publishing Co., 1986.

     Use the Table of Contents to locate biographies.

TwCA   *Twentieth Century Authors: A Biographical Dictionary of Modern Literature.* New York: H.W. Wilson Co., 1942, 1955.

         TwCA   Original volume, edited by Stanley J. Kunitz and Howard Haycraft, 1942

         TwCA SUP   First Supplement, edited by Stanley J. Kunitz, 1955

TwCBDA   *The Twentieth Century Biographical Dictionary of Notable Americans.* Brief biographies of authors, administrators, clergymen, commanders, editors, engineers, jurists, merchants, officials, philanthropists, scientists, statesmen, and others who are making American history. 10 volumes. Edited by Rossiter Johnson. Boston: The Biographical Society, 1904. Reprint. Detroit: Gale Research Co., 1968.

TwCCW   *Twentieth-Century Children's Writers.* Edited by D.L. Kirkpatrick. New York: St. Martin's Press, 1978, 1983.

         TwCCW 78   "Twentieth-Century Children's Writers," 1st ed.
         TwCCW 78A   Appendix begins on page 1391.
         TwCCW 78B   "Children's Books in Translation" section begins on page 1481.
         TwCCW 83   "Twentieth-Century Children's Writers," 2nd ed.
         TwCCW 83A   Appendix begins on page 859.
         TwCCW 83B   "Foreign-Language Writers" section begins on page 893.

TwCCr&M   *Twentieth-Century Crime and Mystery Writers.* Edited by John M. Reilly. New York: St. Martin's Press, 1980, 1985.

         TwCCr&M 80   "Twentieth-Century Crime and Mystery Writers," 1st ed.
         TwCCr&M 80A   "Nineteenth-Century Writers" section begins on page 1525.

TwCCr&M 80B	"Foreign-Language Writers" section begins on page 1537.
TwCCr&M 85	"Twentieth-Century Crime and Mystery Writers," 2nd ed.
TwCCr&M 85A	"Nineteenth-Century Writers" section begins on page 931.
TwCCr&M 85B	"Foreign-Language Writers" section begins on page 939.

TwCLC   *Twentieth-Century Literary Criticism.* Excerpts from criticism of the works of novelists, poets, playwrights, short story writers, and other creative writers who died between 1900 and 1960, from the first published critical appraisals to current evaluations. Detroit: Gale Research Co., 1978-1987.

TwCLC 1	Volume 1, 1978
TwCLC 2	Volume 2, 1979
TwCLC 3	Volume 3, 1980
TwCLC 4	Volume 4, 1981
TwCLC 5	Volume 5, 1981
TwCLC 6	Volume 6, 1982
TwCLC 7	Volume 7, 1982
TwCLC 8	Volume 8, 1982
TwCLC 9	Volume 9, 1983
TwCLC 10	Volume 10, 1983
TwCLC 11	Volume 11, 1983
TwCLC 12	Volume 12, 1984
TwCLC 13	Volume 13, 1984
TwCLC 14	Volume 14, 1984
TwCLC 15	Volume 15, 1985
TwCLC 16	Volume 16, 1985
TwCLC 17	Volume 17, 1985
TwCLC 18	Volume 18, 1985
TwCLC 19	Volume 19, 1986
TwCLC 20	Volume 20, 1986
TwCLC 21	Volume 21, 1986
TwCLC 22	Volume 22, 1987
TwCLC 23	Volume 23, 1987
TwCLC 24	Volume 24, 1987

TwCSFW 86   *Twentieth-Century Science-Fiction Writers.* Second edition. Edited by Curtis C. Smith. Twentieth-Century Writers Series. Chicago: St. James Press, 1986.

TwCSFW 86	Twentieth-Century Science-Fiction Writers
TwCSFW 86A	"Foreign-Language Writers" section begins on page 837.
TwCSFW 86B	"Major Fantasy Writers" section begins on page 863.

TwCWr   *Twentieth Century Writing: A Reader's Guide to Contemporary Literature.* Edited by Kenneth Richardson. Levittown, New York: Transatlantic Arts, 1971.

TwYS   *Twenty Years of Silents, 1908-1928.* Compiled by John T. Weaver. Metuchen, New Jersey: Scarecrow Press, 1971.

TwYS	"The Players" begin on page 27.
TwYS A	"Directors" begin on page 407.

UFOEn   *The UFO Encyclopedia.* By Margaret Sachs. New York: G.P. Putnam's Sons, 1980.

USBiR 74   United States. Department of State. *The Biographic Register, July, 1974.* Washington, D.C.: United States Government Printing Office, 1974.

Ward   *1977 Ward's Who's Who among U.S. Motor Vehicle Manufacturers.* Detroit: Ward's Communications, 1977.

Ward 77F	"The Automotive Press" section begins on page 387.
Ward 77G	"Where Are They Now?" section begins on page 404.

WebAB   *Webster's American Biographies.* Edited by Charles Van Doren. Springfield, Massachusetts: G. & C. Merriam Co., 1974, 1979.

   WebAB   1974 edition
   WebAB 79   1979 edition

WebAMB   *Webster's American Military Biographies.* Springfield, Massachusetts: G. & C. Merriam Co., 1978.

WebE&AL   *Webster's New World Companion to English and American Literature.* Edited by Arthur Pollard. New York: World Publishing Co., 1973.

WhDW   *Who Did What.* The lives and achievements of the 5,000 men and women -- leaders of nations, saints and sinners, artists and scientists -- who shaped our world. Edited by Gerald Howat. New York: Crown Publishers, 1974.

WhAm HS   *Who Was Who in America, Historical Volume, 1607-1896.* A component volume of *Who's Who in American History.* Revised edition. Chicago: Marquis Who's Who, 1967.

   The Addendum, indicated in this index by the code *A,* begins on page 677.

WhAm 1   *Who Was Who in America, Volume I, 1897-1942.* A component volume of *Who's Who in American History.* Chicago: A.N. Marquis Co., 1943.

   The Corrigenda, indicated in this index by the code *C,* begins on page x.

WhAm 2   *Who Was Who in America, Volume II, 1943-1950.* A companion biographical reference work to *Who's Who in America.* Chicago: A.N. Marquis Co., 1963.

   WhAm 2A   Addendum begins on page 12.
   WhAm 2C   Corrigenda begins on page 5.

WhAm 3   *Who Was Who in America, Volume III, 1951-1960.* A component of *Who's Who in American History.* Chicago: Marquis Who's Who, 1966.

   The Addendum, indicated in this index by the code *A,* begins on page 952.

WhAm 4   *Who Was Who in America with World Notables, Volume IV, 1961-1968.* A component volume of *Who's Who in American History.* Chicago: Marquis-Who's Who, 1968.

   The Addendum, indicated in this index by the code *A,* begins on page 1049.

WhAm 5   *Who Was Who in America with World Notables, Volume V, 1969-1973.* Chicago: Marquis Who's Who, 1973.

WhAm 6   *Who Was Who in America with World Notables, Volume VI, 1974-1976.* Chicago: Marquis Who's Who, 1976.

WhAm 7   *Who Was Who in America with World Notables, Volume VII, 1977-1981.* Chicago: Marquis Who's Who, 1981.

WhAm 8   *Who Was Who in America with World Notables.* Volume VIII, 1982-1985. Chicago: Marquis Who's Who, 1985.

WhAmP   *Who Was Who in American Politics.* A biographical dictionary of over 4,000 men and women who contributed to the United States political scene from colonial days up to and including the immediate past. By Dan and Inez Morris. New York: Hawthorn Books, 1974.

WhE&EA   *Who Was Who among English and European Authors, 1931-1949.* Based on entries which first appeared in *The Author's and Writer's Who's Who and Reference Guide* originally compiled by Edward Martell and L.G. Pine, and in *Who's Who among*

Living Authors of Older Nations, originally compiled by Alberta Lawrence. Three volumes. Gale Composite Biographical Dictionary Series, Number 2. Detroit: Gale Research Co., 1978.

WhFla   *Who Was Who in Florida.* Written and compiled by Henry S. Marks. Huntsville, Alabama: Strode Publishers, 1973.

WhJnl   *Who Was Who in Journalism, 1925-1928.* A consolidation of all material appearing in the 1928 edition of *Who's Who in Journalism*, with unduplicated biographical entries from the 1925 edition of *Who's Who in Journalism*, originally compiled by M.N. Ask (1925 and 1928 editions) and S. Gershanek (1925 edition). Gale Composite Biographical Dictionary Series, Number 4. Detroit: Gale Research Co., 1978.

> The "1925 Supplement," indicated in this index by the code *SUP*, begins on page 639.

WhLit   *Who Was Who in Literature, 1906-1934.* Based on entries that first appeared in *Literary Yearbook* (1906-1913), *Literary Yearbook and Author's Who's Who* (1914-1917), *Literary Yearbook* (1920-1922), and *Who's Who in Literature* (1924-1934). Two volumes. Gale Composite Biographical Dictionary Series, Number 5. Detroit: Gale Research Co., 1979.

WhNAA   *Who Was Who among North American Authors, 1921-1939.* Compiled from *Who's Who among North American Authors*, Volumes 1-7, 1921-1939. Two volumes. Gale Composite Biographical Dictionary Series, Number 1. Detroit: Gale Research Co., 1976.

WhScrn   *Who Was Who on Screen.* By Evelyn Mack Truitt. New York: R.R. Bowker Co., 1974, 1977, 1983.

WhScrn 74	First edition, 1974
WhScrn 77	Second edition, 1977
WhScrn 83	Third edition, 1983

WhThe   *Who Was Who in the Theatre: 1912-1976.* A biographical dictionary of actors, actresses, directors, playwrights, and producers of the English-speaking theatre. Compiled from *Who's Who in the Theatre*, Volumes 1-15 (1912-1972). Four volumes. Gale Composite Biographical Dictionary Series, Number 3. Detroit: Gale Research Co., 1978.

WhWW-II   *Who Was Who in World War II.* Edited by John Keegan. London: Arms & Armour Press, 1978.

WhsNW   *Who's New Wave in Music.* An illustrated encyclopedia, 1976-1982 (the first wave). Edited by David Bianco. Ann Arbor, Michigan: Pierian Press, 1985.

Who   *Who's Who.* An annual biographical dictionary. New York: St. Martin's Press; London: Adam & Charles Black, 1974, 1982, 1983, 1985.

Who 74	126th Year of Issue, 1974-1975
Who 82	134th Year of Issue, 1982-1983
Who 83	135th Year of Issue, 1983-1984
Who 85	137th Year of Issue, 1985-1986

> Each volume contains an Obituary section, indicated in this index by the code *N*, "The Royal Family" section, indicated in this index by the code *R*, and a Supplement, indicated in this index by the code *S*. The Supplement may contain up to three parts: "Additions," "Members of Parliament," and "New Year Honours List."

WhoAdv 72   *Who's Who in Advertising.* Second edition. Edited by Robert S. Morgan. Rye, New York: Redfield Publishing Co., 1972.

> Biographies are found in "U.S. Advertising Executives," beginning on page 1; "Canadian Advertising Executives," beginning on page 585; and the Addendum beginning on page 637.

WhoAdv 80   *Who's Who in Advertising.* Third edition. Edited by Catherine Quinn Serie. Monroe, New York: Redfield Publishing Co., 1980.

WhoAm   *Who's Who in America.* Chicago: Marquis Who's Who, 1974, 1976, 1978, 1980, 1982, 1984, 1986.

WhoAm 74	38th edition, 1974-1975
WhoAm 76	39th edition, 1976-1977
WhoAm 78	40th edition, 1978-1979
WhoAm 80	41st edition, 1980-1981
WhoAm 82	42nd edition, 1982-1983
WhoAm 84	43rd edition, 1984-1985
WhoAm 86	44th edition, 1986-1987

WhoAmA   *Who's Who in American Art.* Edited by Jaques Cattell Press. New York: R.R. Bowker Co., 1973, 1976, 1978, 1980, 1982, 1984.

WhoAmA 73	1973 edition
WhoAmA 76	1976 edition
WhoAmA 78	1978 edition
WhoAmA 80	1980 edition
WhoAmA 82	1982 edition
WhoAmA 84	1984 edition

> The Necrology, indicated in this index by the code *N*, is located at the back of each volume.

WhoAmJ 80   *Who's Who in American Jewry.* Incorporating *The Directory of American Jewish Institutions.* 1980 edition. Los Angeles: Standard Who's Who, 1980.

WhoAmL   *Who's Who in American Law.* Chicago: Marquis Who's Who, 1978, 1979, 1983, 1985.

WhoAmL 78	First edition, 1978
WhoAmL 79	Second edition, 1979
WhoAmL 83	Third edition, 1983
WhoAmL 85	Fourth edition, 1985

WhoAmM 83   *Who's Who in American Music: Classical.* First edition. Edited by Jaques Cattell Press. New York: R.R. Bowker Co., 1983.

WhoAmP   *Who's Who in American Politics.* Edited by Jaques Cattell Press. New York: R.R. Bowker Co., 1973, 1975, 1977, 1979, 1981, 1983, 1985.

WhoAmP 73	Fourth edition, 1973-1974
WhoAmP 75	Fifth edition, 1975-1976
WhoAmP 77	Sixth edition, 1977-1978
WhoAmP 79	Seventh edition, 1979-1980
WhoAmP 81	Eighth edition, 1981-1982
WhoAmP 83	Ninth edition, 1983-1984
WhoAmP 85	10th edition, 1985-1986

> Biographies in the later editions are divided by geographical areas. Use the Index to locate biographies.

WhoAmW	*Who's Who of American Women.* Chicago: Marquis Who's Who, 1958, 1961, 1963, 1965, 1967, 1969, 1971, 1973,1975, 1978, 1979, 1981, 1983, 1984, 1986.	

WhoAmW 58	First edition, 1958-1959
WhoAmW 61	Second edition, 1961-1962
WhoAmW 64	Third edition, 1964-1965
WhoAmW 66	Fourth edition, 1966-1967
WhoAmW 68	Fifth edition, 1968-1969
WhoAmW 70	Sixth edition, 1970-1971
WhoAmW 72	Seventh edition, 1972-1973
WhoAmW 74	Eighth edition, 1974-1975
WhoAmW 75	Ninth edition, 1975-1976
WhoAmW 77	10th edition, 1977-1978
WhoAmW 79	11th edition, 1979-1980
WhoAmW 81	12th edition, 1981-1982
WhoAmW 83	13th edition, 1983-1984
WhoAmW 85	14th edition, 1985-1986
WhoAmW 87	15th edition, 1987-1988

Earlier editions have Addenda, indicated in this index by the code *A*.

WhoArab   *Who's Who in the Arab World.* Edited by Gabriel M. Bustros. Beirut, Lebanon: Publitec Publications, 1981.

Biographies are located in Part III.

WhoArt   *Who's Who in Art.* Biographies of leading men and women in the world of art today -- artists, designers, craftsmen, critics, writers, teachers and curators, with an appendix of signatures. Havant, England: Art Trade Press, 1980, 1982, 1984. Distributed by Gale Research Co., Detroit, Michigan.

WhoArt 80	19th edition, 1980
WhoArt 82	20th edition, 1982
WhoArt 84	21st edition, 1984

The Obituary section, indicated in this index by the code *N*, is located at the back of each volume.

WhoAtom 77   *Who's Who in Atoms.* Sixth edition. Edited by Ann Pernet. Guernsey, British Isles: Francis Hodgson, 1977.

WhoBbl 73   *Who's Who in Basketball.* By Ronald L. Mendell. New Rochelle, New York: Arlington House, 1973.

WhoBlA   *Who's Who among Black Americans.* Northbrook, Illinois: Who's Who among Black Americans, 1976, 1978, 1981.

WhoBlA 75	First edition, 1975-1976
WhoBlA 77	Second edition, 1977-1978
WhoBLA 80	Third edition, 1980-1981

WhoBlA 85   *Who's Who among Black Americans.* Fourth edition, 1985. Lake Forest, Illinois: Educational Communications, 1985.

WhoBox 74   *Who's Who in Boxing.* By Bob Burrill. New Rochelle, New York: Arlington House, 1974.

WhoBW&I   *Who's Who of Boys' Writers and Illustrators, 1964.* Edited by Brian Doyle. London: Published by the author, 1964.

WhoBW&IA	Author biographies begin on page 5.
WhoBW&II	Illustrator biographies begin on page 79.

WhoCan   *Who's Who in Canada.* An illustrated biographical record of men and women of the
               time in Canada. Toronto: International Press, 1973, 1975, 1977, 1980, 1982.

        WhoCan 73   1973-1974 edition
        WhoCan 75   1975-1976 edition
        WhoCan 77   1977-1978 edition
        WhoCan 80   1980-1981 edition
        WhoCan 82   1982-1983 edition

               Use the Index at the front of each volume to locate biographies.

WhoCan 84   *Who's Who in Canada.* An illustrated biographical record of Canada's leading men and
               women in business, government and academia. 1984-1985 edition. Agincourt,
               Ontario: Global Press, 1984.

WhoCanL 85 *Who's Who in Canadian Literature 1985-86.* By Gordon Ripley and Anne Mercer.
               Toronto: Reference Press, 1985.

WhoChL   *The Who's Who of Children's Literature.* Compiled and edited by Brian Doyle. New
               York: Schocken Books, 1968.

WhoColR   *Who's Who of the Colored Race.* A general biographical dictionary of men and women
               of African descent. Volume one. Edited by Frank Lincoln Mather. Chicago: 1915.
               Reprint. Detroit: Gale Research Co., 1976.

               The Addenda, indicated in this index by the code *A*, begins on page xxvi.

WhoCon 73   *Who's Who in Consulting.* A reference guide to professional personnel engaged in
               consultation for business, industry and government. Second edition. Edited by
               Paul Wasserman. Detroit: Gale Research Co., 1973.

WhoCtE 79   *Who's Who in Continuing Education: Human Resources in Continuing
               Library-Information-Media Education, 1979.* Compiled by CLENE (The
               Continuing Library Education Network and Exchange.) New York and London:
               K.G. Saur, 1979. Distributed by Gale Research Co., Detroit, Michigan.

WhoE   *Who's Who in the East.* Chicago: Marquis Who's Who, 1974, 1975, 1977, 1979, 1981,
               1983, 1984.

        WhoE 74   14th edition, 1974-1975
        WhoE 75   15th edition, 1975-1976
        WhoE 77   16th edition, 1977-1978
        WhoE 79   17th edition, 1979-1980
        WhoE 81   18th edition, 1981-1982
        WhoE 83   19th edition, 1983-1984
        WhoE 85   20th edition, 1985-1986
        WhoE 85A   20th edition, Addendum

WhoEc   *Who's Who in Economics: A Biographical Dictionary of Major Economists
               1700-1981.* Edited by Mark Blaug and Paul Sturges. Cambridge: Massachusetts:
               MIT Press, 1983.

WhoEc 86   *Who's Who in Economics.* A biographical dictionary of major economists 1700-1986.
               Second edition. Edited by Mark Blaug. Cambridge, Massachusetts: MIT Press,
               1986.

WhoEng 80   *Who's Who in Engineering.* Fourth edition. Edited by Jean Gregory. New York:
               American Association of Engineering Societies, 1980.

WhoF&I   *Who's Who in Finance and Industry.* Chicago: Marquis Who's Who, 1974, 1975, 1977, 1979, 1981, 1983, 1985.

WhoF&I 74	18th edition, 1974-1975
WhoF&I 75	19th edition, 1975-1976
WhoF&I 77	20th edition, 1977-1978
WhoF&I 79	21st edition, 1979-1980
WhoF&I 81	22nd edition, 1981-1982
WhoF&I 83	23rd edition, 1983-1984
WhoF&I 85	24th edition, 1985-1986

WhoFla   *Who's Who in Florida, 1973/74.* A composite of biographical sketches of outstanding men and women of the State of Florida. First edition. Lexington, Kentucky and Acworth, Georgia: Names of Distinction, 1974.

WhoFtbl 74   *Who's Who in Football.* By Ronald L. Mendell and Timothy B. Phares. New Rochelle, New York: Arlington House, 1974.

WhoFr 79   *Who's Who in France: Qui est Qui en France.* 14th edition, 1979-1980. Dictionnaire biographique de personnalites francaises vivant en France, dans les territoires d'Outre-Mer ou a l'etranger et de personnalites etrangeres residant en France. Paris: Editions Jacques Lafitte, 1979.

"Liste des Personnalites Decedees," indicated in this index by the code *N*, begins on page cviii.

WhoFrS   *Who's Who in Frontier Science and Technology.* First edition, 1984-1985. Chicago: Marquis Who's Who, 1984.

WhoGen 81   *Who's Who in Genealogy & Heraldry.* Volume 1. Edited by Mary Keysor Meyer and P. William Filby. Detroit: Gale Research Co., 1981.

The "Late Additions" section, indicated in this index by the code *A*, begins on page 231.

WhoGolf   *Who's Who in Golf.* By Len Elliott and Barbara Kelly. New Rochelle, New York: Arlington House Publishers, 1976.

WhoGov   *Who's Who in Government.* Chicago: Marquis Who's Who, 1972, 1975, 1977.

WhoGov 72	First edition, 1972-1973
WhoGov 75	Second edition, 1975-1976
WhoGov 77	Third edition, 1977

WhoGrA   *Who's Who in Graphic Art.* An illustrated book of reference to the world's leading graphic designers, illustrators, typographers and cartoonists. First edition. Edited by Walter Amstutz. Zurich: Amstutz & Herdeg Graphis Press, 1962. Distributed by Gale Research Co., Detroit, Michigan.

Use the "Index of Artists' Names," which begins on page 576, to locate biographies.

WhoGrA 82   *Who's Who in Graphic Art.* An illustrated world review of the leading contemporary graphic and typographic designers, illustrators and cartoonists. Volume Two. Edited and designed by Walter Amstutz. Dubendorf, Switzerland: De Clivo Press, 1982. Distributed by Gale Research Co., Detroit, Michigan.

Use the "Index of Artists' Names," which begins on page 886, to locate biographies.

WhoHcky 73   *Who's Who in Hockey.* By Harry C. Kariher. New Rochelle, New York: Arlington House, 1973.

WhoHol	*Who's Who in Hollywood, 1900-1976.* By David Ragan. New Rochelle, New York: Arlington House, 1976.

WhoHol A	"Living Players" begins on page 11.
WhoHol B	"Late Players (1900-1974)" begins on page 539.
WhoHol C	"Players Who Died in 1975 and 1976" begins on page 845.

WhoHr&F	*Who's Who in Horror and Fantasy Fiction.* By Mike Ashley. London: Elm Tree Books, 1977.

WhoIns	*Who's Who in Insurance.* Englewood, New Jersey: Underwriter Printing & Publishing Co., 1975, 1976, 1977, 1978, 1979, 1980, 1981, 1982, 1984

WhoIns 76	1976 edition
WhoIns 77	1977 edition
WhoIns 78	1978 edition
WhoIns 79	1979 edition
WhoIns 80	1980 edition
WhoIns 81	1981 edition
WhoIns 82	1982 edition
WhoIns 84	1984 edition

The Addenda, indicated in this index by the code *A*, are located at the back of each volume.

WhoJazz 72	*Who's Who of Jazz: Storyville to Swing Street.* By John Chilton. Philadelphia: Chilton Book Co., 1972.
WhoLab 76	*Who's Who in Labor.* New York: Arno Press, 1976.
WhoLib 54	*Who's Who in Librarianship.* Edited by Thomas Landau. Cambridge, England: Bowes & Bowes, 1954.
WhoLib 72	*Who's Who in Librarianship and Information Science.* Second edition. Edited by T. Landau. London and New York: Abelard-Schuman, 1972.
WhoLibI 82	*Who's Who in Library and Information Services.* Edited by Joel M. Lee. Chicago: American Library Association, 1982.
WhoLibS 55	*Who's Who in Library Service.* A biographical directory of professional librarians of the United States and Canada. Third edition. Edited by Dorothy Ethlyn Cole. New York: Grolier Society, 1955.
WhoLibS 66	*Who's Who in Library Service.* A biographical directory of professional librarians in the United States and Canada. Fourth edition. Edited by Lee Ash. Hamden, Connecticut: Shoe String Press, 1966.
WhoLA	*Who's Who among Living Authors of Older Nations.* Covering the literary activities of living authors and writers of all countries of the world except the United States of America, Canada, Mexico, Alaska, Hawaii, Newfoundland, the Philippine Islands, the West Indies, and Central America. These countries are covered by our *Who's Who among North American Authors.* Volume 1, 1931-1932. Edited by A. Lawrence. Los Angeles: Golden Syndicate Publishing Co., 1931. Reprint. Detroit: Gale Research Co., 1966.
WhoMW	*Who's Who in the Midwest.* Chicago: Marquis Who's Who, 1974, 1976, 1978, 1980, 1982, 1984, 1985.

WhoMW 74	14th edition, 1974-1975
WhoMW 76	15th edition, 1976-1977
WhoMW 78	16th edition, 1978-1979

WhoMW 80	17th edition, 1980-1981
WhoMW 82	18th edition, 1982-1983
WhoMW 84	19th edition, 1984-1985
WhoMW 86	20th edition, 1986-1987

WhoMilH 76   *Who's Who in Military History: From 1453 to the Present Day.* By John Keegan and Andrew Wheatcroft. New York: William Morrow & Co., 1976.

WhoMus 72   *Who's Who in Music and Musicians' International Directory.* Sixth edition. New York: Hafner Publishing Co., 1972. Later editions published as *International Who's Who in Music and Musicians' Directory* (see above).

WhoNob   *The Who's Who of Nobel Prize Winners.* Edited by Bernard S. Schlessinger and June H. Schlessinger. Phoenix: Oryx Press, 1986.

Use the "Name Index," which begins on page 195, to locate biographies.

WhoOcn 78   *Who's Who in Ocean and Freshwater Science.* First edition. Edited by Allen Varley. Essex, England: Longman Group, Francis Hodgson, 1978. Distributed by Gale Research Co., Detroit, Michigan.

WhoOp 76   *Who's Who in Opera.* An international biographical directory of singers, conductors, directors, designers, and administrators. Also including profiles of 101 opera companies. Edited by Maria F. Rich. New York: Arno Press, 1976.

WhoPNW   *Who's Who among Pacific Northwest Authors.* Second edition. Edited by Frances Valentine Wright. Missoula, Montana: Pacific Northwest Library Association, Reference Division, 1969.

Biographies are arranged alphabetically by state. Use the "Index of Authors" to locate listings.

WhoPRCh   *Who's Who in the People's Republic of China.* By Wolfgang Bartke. Armonk, New York: M.E. Sharpe, 1981

WhoPRCh 81		Biographies
WhoPRCh 81A	Wade-Giles/Pinyin Conversion Table begins on page 719.	
WhoPRCh 81B	"Biographies of Important Deceased and Purged Cadres" section begins on page 573.	

WhoPolA   *Who's Who in Polish America.* A biographical directory of Polish-American leaders and distinguished Poles resident in the Americas. Third edition. Edited by Francis Bolek. New York: Harbinger House, 1943. Reprint, The American Immigration Collection - Series II. New York: Arno Press and The New York Times, 1970.

WhoProB 73   *Who's Who in Professional Baseball.* By Gene Karst and Martin J. Jones, Jr. New Rochelle, New York: Arlington House, 1973.

WhoPubR   *Who's Who in Public Relations (International).* Edited by Adrian A. Paradis. Meriden, New Hampshire: PR Publishing Co., 1972, 1976.

WhoPubR 72	Fourth edition, 1972
WhoPubR 76	Fifth edition, 1976

WhoReal 83   *Who's Who in Real Estate: The Directory of the Real Estate Professions.* Boston: Warren, Gorham & Lamont, 1983.

WhoRel   *Who's Who in Religion.* Chicago: Marquis Who's Who, 1975, 1977, 1985.

WhoRel 75	First edition, 1975-1976
WhoRel 77	Second edition, 1977
WhoRel 85	Third edition, 1985

WhoRock 81   *Who's Who in Rock.* By Michael Bane. New York: Everest House, 1981.

WhoRocM 82   *Who's Who in Rock Music.* By William York. New York: Charles Scribner's Sons, 1982.

WhoSciF   *Who's Who in Science Fiction.* By Brian Ash. London: Elm Tree Books, 1976.

WhoSocC 78   *Who's Who in the Socialist Countries.* A biographical encyclopedia of 10,000 leading personalities in 16 communist countries. First edition. Edited by Borys Lewytzkyj and Juliusz Stroynowski. New York: K.G. Saur Publishing, 1978. Distributed by Gale Research Co., Detroit, Michigan.

The Appendix, indicated in this index by the code *A*, begins on page 713.

WhoS&SW   *Who's Who in the South and Southwest.* Chicago: Marquis Who's Who, 1973, 1975, 1976, 1978, 1980, 1982, 1984, 1986.

WhoS&SW 73	13th edition, 1973-1974
WhoS&SW 75	14th edition, 1975-1976
WhoS&SW 76	15th edition, 1976-1977
WhoS&SW 78	16th edition, 1978-1979
WhoS&SW 80	17th edition, 1980-1981
WhoS&SW 82	18th edition, 1982-1983
WhoS&SW 84	19th edition, 1984-1985
WhoS&SW 86	20th edition, 1986-1987

WhoSpyF   *Who's Who in Spy Fiction.* By Donald McCormick. London: Elm Tree Books, 1977.

WhoStg 1906   *Who's Who on the Stage.* The dramatic reference book and biographical dictionary of the theatre. Containing records of the careers of actors, actresses, managers and playwrights of the American stage. Edited by Walter Browne and F.A. Austin. New York: Walter Browne & F.A. Austin, 1906.

Some entries are not in alphabetic sequence.

WhoStg 1908   *Who's Who on the Stage, 1908.* The dramatic reference book and biographical dictionary of the theatre. Containing careers of actors, actresses, managers and playwrights of the American stage. Edited by Walter Browne and E. De Roy Koch. New York: B.W. Dodge & Co., 1908.

Some entries are not in alphabetic sequence.

WhoTech 82   *Who's Who in Technology Today.* Third edition. Four volumes. Edited by Jan W. Churchwell. Highland Park, Illinois: J. Dick & Co., 1982.

Use the "Index of Names," which begins on page 667 of Volume 4, to locate biographies.

WhoTech 84   *Who's Who in Technology Today.* Fourth edition. Five volumes. Edited by Barbara A. Tinucci. Lake Bluff, Illinois: Research Publications, J. Dick Publishing, 1984.

Use the "Index of Names," which begins on page 1125 of Volume 5, to locate biographies.

WhoThe   *Who's Who in the Theatre: A Biographical Record of the Contemporary Stage.* London: Pitman Publishing; Detroit: Gale Research Co., 1972, 1977, 1981.

WhoThe 72	15th edition, compiled by John Parker, 1972
WhoThe 77	16th edition, edited by Ian Herbert, 1977
WhoThe 81	17th edition, edited by Ian Herbert, 1981
WhoThe 81N	17th edition, Obituary section begins on page 743

WhoTr&F 73   *Who's Who in Track and Field.* By Reid M. Hanley. New Rochelle, New York: Arlington House, 1973.

WhoTran   *Who's Who in Translating and Interpreting.* Compiled by A. Flegon. London: Flegon Press, 1967.

          WhoTran ARB   Arabic section begins on page 5.
          WhoTran FRE   French section begins on page 32.

WhoTwCL   *Who's Who in Twentieth Century Literature.* By Martin Seymour-Smith. New York: Holt, Rinehart & Winston, 1976.

WhoUN 75   *Who's Who in the United Nations and Related Agencies.* New York: Arno Press, 1975.

WhoWest   *Who's Who in the West.* Chicago: Marquis Who's Who, 1974, 1976, 1978, 1980, 1982, 1983.

          WhoWest 74   14th edition, 1974-1975
          WhoWest 76   15th edition, 1976-1977
          WhoWest 78   16th edition, 1978-1979
          WhoWest 80   17th edition, 1980-1981
          WhoWest 82   18th edition, 1982-1983
          WhoWest 84   19th edition, 1984-1985

WhoWor   *Who's Who in the World.* Chicago: Marquis Who's Who, 1973, 1976, 1978, 1980, 1982, 1984, 1986.

          WhoWor 74   Second edition, 1974-1975
          WhoWor 76   Third edition, 1976-1977
          WhoWor 78   Fourth edition, 1978-1979
          WhoWor 80   Fifth edition, 1980-1981
          WhoWor 82   Sixth edition, 1982-1983
          WhoWor 84   Seventh edition, 1984-1985
          WhoWor 87   Eighth edition, 1987-1988

WhoWorJ 72   *Who's Who in World Jewry: A Biographical Dictionary of Outstanding Jews.* Edited by I.J. Carmin Karpman. New York: Pitman Publishing Corp., 1972.

WhoWorJ 78   *Who's Who in World Jewry: A Biographical Dictionary of Outstanding Jews.* Edited by I.J. Carmin Karpman. Tel-Aviv, Israel: Olive Books of Israel, 1978.

WisWr   *Wisconsin Writers: Sketches and Studies.* By William A. Titus. Chicago: 1930. Reprint. Detroit: Gale Research Co., 1974.

          Use the Table of Contents to locate biographies.

WomWWA 14   *Woman's Who's Who of America.* A biographical dictionary of contemporary women of the United States and Canada, 1914-1915. Edited by John William Leonard. New York: American Commonwealth Co., 1914. Reprint. Detroit: Gale Research Co., 1976.

          The "Addenda and Corrections" and "Deaths during Printing" sections, indicated in this index by the code *A*, begin on page 29.

WomArt   *Women Artists: An Historical, Contemporary and Feminist Bibliography.* By Donna G. Bachmann and Sherry Piland. Metuchen, New Jersey: Scarecrow Press, 1978.

          WomArt   Use the Table of Contents which begins on page 47 to locate biographies.
          WomArt A   The Addenda begin on page 322.

WomNov   *Women Novelists, 1891-1920.* An index to biographical and autobiographical sources. By Doris Robinson. Garland Reference Library of the Humanities, vol. 491. New York: Garland Publishing, 1984.

WomPO 76   *Women in Public Office: A Biographical Directory and Statistical Analysis.* Compiled by Center for the American Woman and Politics. New York and London: R.R. Bowker Co., 1976.

> Use the "Name Index" to locate listings.

WomPO 78   *Women in Public Office: A Biographical Directory and Statistical Analysis.* Second edition. Compiled by Center for the American Woman and Politics. Metuchen, New Jersey: Scarecrow Press, 1978.

> Use the "Name Index" to locate listings.

WomWMM   *Women Who Make Movies.* Cinema Study Series. By Sharon Smith. New York: Hopkinson & Blake, 1975.

WomWMM	"Overview" section. Use the Index, which begins on page 299, to locate biographies.
WomWMM A	"The New Filmmakers" begins on page 145.
WomWMM B	"Directory" begins on page 221.

WorAl   *The World Almanac Book of Who.* Edited by Hana Umlauf Lane. New York: World Almanac Publications, 1980.

WorArt   *World Artists, 1950-1980.* An H.W. Wilson biographical dictionary. By Claude Marks. New York: H.W. Wilson Co., 1984.

WorAu   *World Authors.* A volume in the Wilson Authors Series. New York: H.W. Wilson Co., 1975, 1980, 1985.

WorAu	1950-1970, edited by John Wakeman, 1975.
WorAu 1970	1970-1975, edited by John Wakeman, 1980.
WorAu 1975	1975-1980, edited by Vineta Colby, 1985.

WorDWW   *World Defence Who's Who.* Edited by Paul Martell and Grace P. Hayes. London: Macdonald & Jane's, 1974.

WorECar   *The World Encyclopedia of Cartoons.* Two volumes. Edited by Maurice Horn. Detroit: Gale Research Co. (in association with Chelsea House Publishers, New York), 1980.

> The "Notes on the Contributors" section, indicated in this index by the code *A*, begins on page 631.

WorECom   *The World Encyclopedia of Comics.* Two volumes. Edited by Maurice Horn. New York: Chelsea House Publishers, 1976.

> Biographies begin on page 65.

WorEFlm   *The World Encyclopedia of the Film.* Edited by John M. Smith and Tim Cawkwell. New York: A. & W. Visual Library, 1972.

WorFshn   *World of Fashion: People, Places, Resources.* By Eleanor Lambert. New York: R.R. Bowker Co., 1976.

> Use the "Name Index," which begins on page 35l, to locate biographies.

WrDr   *The Writers Directory.* London: St. James Press; New York: St. Martin's Press, 1976, 1979.

WrDr 76	1976-1978 edition
WrDr 80	1980-1982 edition

WrDr 82   *The Writers Directory.* 1982-1984 edition. Detroit: Gale Research Co., 1981.

WrDr	*The Writers Directory.* Chicago: St. James Press, 1983, 1986. Distributed by Gale Research Co., Detroit, Michigan.	
	WrDr 84	1984-1986 edition, 1983
	WrDr 86	1986-1988 edition, 1986
YABC	*Yesterday's Authors of Books for Children.* Facts and pictures about authors and illustrators of books for young people, from early times to 1960. Edited by Anne Commire. Detroit: Gale Research Co., 1977-1978.	
	YABC 1	Volume 1, 1977
	YABC 2	Volume 2, 1978
YABC X	This code refers to pseudonym entries which appear as cross-references in the cumulative index to *Yesterday's Authors of Books for Children.*	

Key to Source Codes

WRITERS FOR YOUNG ADULTS:

BIOGRAPHIES
MASTER INDEX

A

Aaron, Chester 1923- *BioIn 11,
ConAu 8NR, −21R, SmATA 9,
TwCChW 83, WhoWest 74*
Aaron, Hank *BioIn 13*
Aaron, Hank 1934- *BioIn 12,
BioNews 74, BlueB 76, CelR,
ConAu X, CurBio 58, NegAl 76[port],
−83[port]*
Aaron, Hank *see also* Aaron, Henry
Aaron, Henry 1934- *BioIn 4, −5, −6,
−7, −8, −9, −10, −11, −12, −13,
ConAu 104, CurBio 58, Ebony 1,
InB&W 80, NewYTBE 72, −73,
NewYTBS 74, −75, −76, WebAB, −79,
WhoAm 74, −76, −78, −80, −82, −84,
−86, WhoBlA 75, −77, −80,
WhoProB 73, WorAl*
Aaron, Henry *see also* Aaron, Hank
Aaseng, Nate *SmATA X*
Aaseng, Nate 1953- *ConAu X*
Aaseng, Nathan 1953- *ConAu 106,
SmATA 38*
Abbey, Edward *DrAP&F 85*
Abbey, Edward 1927- *BioIn 10, −11,
−12, ConAu 2NR, −45,
ConLC 36[port], EncFWF, WrDr 80,
−82, −84, −86*
Abbey, Lynn *ConAu X*
Abbott, Berenice 1898- *AmAu&B,
BioIn 1, −7, −9, −10, −11, −12, −13,
BriEAA, ConAu 106, ConPhot,
CurBio 42, GoodHs, ICPEnP,
InWom, IntDcWB, MacBEP,
NewYTBS 80[port], −83[port],
WhoAm 82, −84, −86, WhoAmW 58,
WomArt, WorAl*
Abbott, Edwin A 1838-1926 *ScFSB*
Abbott, Edwin Abbott 1838-1926
*Alli SUP, CelCen, DcNaB 1922,
EncSF, NewC, ScF&FL 1, WhLit*
Abbott, Frank Frost 1860-1924
AmLY, DcAmAu, DcNAA, WhAm 1
Abbott, Jack Henry 1944- *BioIn 12,
ConAu X, ConIsC 2[port]*
Abbott, R Tucker 1919- *ConAu 4NR,
−9R, IntAu&W 76, −77, WrDr 82,
−84, −86*
Abbott, Robert Tucker 1919-
*AmM&WS 73P, −76P, −79P,
AuBYP SUP, ConAu 9R, WhoAm 76,
−80, −82, −84, −86, WhoE 74,
WhoOcn 78, WhoTech 84, WrDr 76,
−80*
Abdul, Raoul 1929- *BioIn 11,
ChhPo S2, ConAu 29R, DrBlPA,
InB&W 80, SelBAAf, SelBAAu,
SmATA 12, WhoBlA 75, −77, −80,
−85, WhoE 77, −79, −81*
Abdul-Jabbar, Kareem
NewYTBS 84[port], −85[port]
Abdul-Jabbar, Kareem 1947- *BioIn 9,
−10, −11, −12, −13, CelR, CmCal,
Ebony 1, NegAl 76, −83[port],*

*NewYTBS 74, −76, −82[port],
WhoAm 74, −76, −78, −80, −82, −84,
−86, WhoBbl 73, WhoBlA 80, −85,
WorAl*
Abe, Kobo 1924- *BioIn 7, −10, −12,
CasWL, ConAu 65, ConFLW 84,
ConLC 8, −22[port], DcOrL 1,
EncSF, EncWL, −2, FarE&A 78, −79,
−80, −81, IntAu&W 76, −77,
IntWW 74, −75, −76, −77, −78, −79,
−80, −81, −82, −83, MakMC,
McGEWD 84, NewYTBS 74, −79,
ScF&FL 1, ScFSB, TwCSFW 86A,
WhoSciF, WhoWor 74, −76, −78, −82,
−84, −87, WorAu*
Abel, Elie 1920- *CanWW 70, −79, −80,
−81, −83, ConAu 8NR, −61,
EncTwCJ, LEduc 74, LesBEnT[port],
WhoAm 74, −76, −78, −80, −82, −84,
−86, WhoE 74, WhoWor 74, −76,
WhoWorJ 72*
Abell, George O 1927- *WrDr 86*
Abell, George O 1927-1983 *BioIn 13,
ConAu 111*
Abell, George Ogden 1927-
*AmM&WS 73P, −76P, −79P, −82P,
ConAu 3NR, −9R, WhoAm 74, −76,
−78, −80, −82, WhoWest 82, −84,
WhoWor 74, WrDr 76, −80, −82, −84*
Abell, George Ogden 1927-1983
WhAm 8
Abels, Jules 1913- *ConAu 61,
WhoAm 74, −76*
Abercrombie, Barbara 1939- *BioIn 12,
ConAu 81, SmATA 16*
Abernethy, Robert Gordon 1927-
*BioIn 10, ConAu 21R, SmATA 5,
WhoAm 74, −76, −78, −80, −82*
Abley, Mark 1955- *ConAu 120*
Abodaher, David J 1919- *AuBYP SUP,
BioIn 12, ConAu 10NR, −17R,
MichAu 80, SmATA 17*
Abrahams, Peter 1919- *AfrA,
Au&Wr 71, BioIn 3, −4, −8, −9, −10,
−12, CasWL, ConAu 57, ConLC 4,
ConNov 76, −82, −86, CurBio 57,
DcLEL 1940, EncWL 2, InB&W 80,
−85, IntAu&W 76, −77, ModBlW,
Novels, PenC ENG, RGAfL, SelBAAf,
TwCWr, WebE&AL, WhE&EA,
WhoWor 74, WorAu, WrDr 76, −80,
−82, −84, −86*
Abrahams, Robert David 1905-
*AmAu&B, AuBYP, BioIn 8, −9,
ConAu P-2, SmATA 4, WhE&EA,
WhoAm 74, −76, −78, −80, −82, −84,
−86, WhoAmL 83, WhoE 74,
WhoWor 76, −82, WhoWorJ 72, −78*
Abrahams, Roger D 1933- *WrDr 86*
Abrahams, Roger David 1933-
*ConAu 5NR, −9R, DrAS 74E, −78E,
−82E, FifIDA, IntAu&W 76, −77,
WhoAm 76, −78, −80, −82,
WhoWor 78, WrDr 76, −80, −82, −84*

Abramovitz, Anita Zeltner Brooks
1914- *ConAu 97, WhoAmW 74, −66,
−68, −70, −72, −79, −81, WhoE 81,
−83, −85, WhoWor 87*
Abrams, Joy 1941- *BioIn 12,
ConAu 77, SmATA 16*
Abrams, Lawrence F *SmATA 47*
Abse, Dannie 1923- *BioIn 13,
ConAu 1AS[port], ConLC 29[port],
ConPo 85, DcLB 27[port],
ModBrL S2, OxEng 85, OxLitW 86,
Who 85, WrDr 85*
Abzug, Robert H 1945- *ConAu 21NR*
Abzug, Robert Henry 1945-
ConAu 104, DrAS 78H, −82H
Achebe, Chinua 1930- *AfSS 78, −79,
−80, −81, −82, AfrA, Au&Wr 71,
BioIn 7, −8, −9, −10, −12, −13,
CasWL, ConAu 1R, −6NR, ConLC 1,
−3, −5, −7, −11, −26[port], ConNov 72,
−76, −82, −86, ConPo 75, −80, −85,
DcLEL 1940, EncWL, −2[port],
InB&W 80, −85, IntAu&W 76, −77,
−82, IntWW 74, −75, −76, −77, −78,
−79, −80, −81, −82, −83, LinLib L,
LongCTC, McGEWB, ModBlW,
ModCmwL, Novels, OxChL,
OxEng 85, PenC CL, −ENG, RGAfL,
SelBAAf, SmATA 38, −40[port],
TwCChW 83, TwCWr, WebE&AL,
Who 74, −82, −83, −85, WhoTwCL,
WhoWor 74, −80, −82, −84, −87,
WorAu, WrDr 76, −80, −82, −84, −86*
Acheson, Patricia Castles 1924-
AuBYP, BioIn 8, ConAu 1R
Ackart, Robert 1921- *ConAu 109*
Ackerley, J R 1896-1967 *OxEng 85*
Ackerman, Diane *DrAP&F 85*
Ackerman, Diane 1948- *ConAu 57,
ConPo 85, DrAS 82E, IntWWP 77,
−82, WhoE 83, −85, WrDr 86*
Ackley, Edith Flack *InWom*
Acton, Jay 1949- *ConAu 45, −X*
Adair, Margaret Weeks d1971
BioIn 1, ConAu P-1, SmATA 10
Adam, Helen *DrAP&F 85*
Adam, Helen 1909- *ChhPo S2,
ConAu 7NR, −17R, ConPo 70, −80,
−85, IntWWP 77, WhoAm 82, −84,
WrDr 82, −84, −86*
Adams, Alice *DrAP&F 85*
Adams, Alice 1926- *BioIn 7, −11, −13,
ConAu 81, ConLC 6, −13,
ConNov 86, DcLB Y86B[port],
OxAmL 83, WhoAm 80, −82, −84,
−86, WrDr 84, −86*
Adams, Andy 1859-1935 *AmAu&B,
AmLY, BiDSA, BioIn 2, −7, −8, −11,
CnDAL, DcAmAu, DcAmB S1,
DcLEL, DcNAA, EncAAH, EncFWF,
IndAu 1816, JBA 34, −51, OxAmH,
OxAmL, −83, REnAL, REnAW,
TexWr, WebAB, −79, WhAm 2,
WhNAA, YABC 1*

Adams, Ansel 1902-1984 *AnObit 1984,
AuNews 1, BioIn 4, −6, −7, −8, −10,
−11, −12, BioNews 74, BlueB 76,
BriEAA, CmCal, ConAu 10NR, −112,
−21R, ConPhot, CurBio 77, −84N,
DcAmArt, DcCAr 81, EncTwCJ,
ICPEnP, NatLAC,
NewYTBS 84[port], WebAB, −79,
WhAm 8, WhoAm 74, −76, −78, −80,
−82, WhoAmA 76, −78, −80, −82,
WorAl, WrDr 80, −82, −84*
Adams, Bryan *NewRR 83*
Adams, Bryan 1960?- *BioIn 13*
Adams, Charlotte 1899- *AuBYP SUP,
ConAu 107, WhoAm 58, −61, −64*
Adams, Douglas 1952?- *BioIn 13,
ConDr 82B, ScFSB[port],
TwCSFW 86, WrDr 86*
Adams, Douglas Noel 1952-
*ConAu 106, ConLC 27[port],
DcLB Y83B[port], WrDr 82, −84*
Adams, Glenda *DrAP&F 85*
Adams, Glenda 1940- *OxAusL*
Adams, Harriet S 1893?-1982
*AmAu&B, AmWomWr,
AnObit 1982[port], AuNews 2,
BioIn 12, ConAu 106, −17R, EncMys,
NewYTBS 82[port], SmATA 1, −29N,
WhoAm 78, −80, −82*
Adams, Harriet S *see also* Appleton,
Victor, II
Adams, Harriet S *see also* Dixon,
Franklin W
Adams, Harriet S *see also* Hope, Laura
Lee
Adams, Harriet S *see also* Keene,
Carolyn
Adams, Harriet Stratemeyer
1893?-1982 *WhAm 8*
Adams, Hazard 1926- *BioIn 10,
ConAu 9R, DrAS 74E, −78E, −82E,
IntAu&W 76, −77, IntWWP 77,
LEduc 74, ScF&FL 1, SmATA 6,
WhoAm 74, −76, −78, −80, −82,
WhoWest 74, −76, WrDr 76, −80,
−82, −84, −86*
Adams, Hazard Simeon 1926-
WhoAm 84, −86
Adams, Henry Brooks 1838-1918
*Alli SUP, AmAu, AmAu&B, AmBi,
AmWr, ApCAB, AtlBL, BbD,
BiDAmEd, BiD&SB, BioIn 1, −2, −3,
−4, −5, −6, −7, −8, −9, −10, −11, −12,
CasWL, CnDAL, ConAu 104, CyWA,
DcAmAu, DcAmB, DcAmSR, DcBiA,
DcLB 12[port], DcLEL, DcNAA,
EncAB-H, EncWL 2, EvLB,
HarEnUS, LinLib L, −S, LongCTC,
McGEWB, ModAL, −S1, NatCAB 11,
Novels, OxAmH, OxAmL,
OxEng, −85, PenC AM, RAdv 1,
RComWL, REn, REnAL, TwCBDA,
TwCLC 4[port], TwCWr,
WebAB, −79, WebE&AL, WhAm 1,*

−4A, −HSA, WhAmP, WhoTwCL,
WorAl
Adams, Jane 1940- *ConAu 116*
Adams, Laurie 1941- *ConAu 53,*
SmATA 33, WhoAmW 83, WrDr 76,
−80, −82, −84, −86
Adams, Richard 1920- *AuBYP SUP,*
AuNews 1, −2, BioIn 10, −11, −12,
ChhPo S2, ConAu 3NR, −49,
ConLC 4, −5, −18, ConNov 86,
CurBio 78, HalFC 84, IntAu&W 77,
IntWW 78, −79, −80, −81, −82, −83,
Novels[port], OxChL, PiP, ScF&FL 1,
−2, ScFSB, SmATA 7, TwCCW 78,
−83, Who 82, −83, WhoAm 80, −82,
WhoWor 82, WorAu 1970, WrDr 76,
−80, −82, −84, −86
Adamson, George 1906- *BioIn 13*
Adamson, Joe *ConAu X*
Adamson, Joseph, III 1945-
ConAu 1NR, −21NR, −45
Adamson, Joy 1910-1980
AnObit 1980[port], −1981,
Au&Wr 71, BioIn 7, −8, −9, −11, −12,
−13, ConAu 69, −93, ConLC 17,
CurBio 72, −80N, FourBJA, GoodHs,
HalFC 84, IntAu&W 76, −77,
IntDcWB, LinLib L,
NewYTBS 80[port], SmATA 11,
−22N, WhAm 7, Who 74, WhoAm 74,
−76, −78, WhoAmW 74
Adamson, Wendy Wriston 1942-
ConAu 53, SmATA 22[port]
Addams, Charles Samuel 1912-
AmAu&B, BioIn 2, −3, −6, −7, −8,
−10, BlueB 76, CelR, ConAu 61,
CurBio 54, EncTwCJ, IntWW 74,
−75, −76, −77, −78, −79, −80, −81,
−82, −83, LinLib L, WebAB, −79,
WhDW, WhoAm 74, −76, −78, −80,
−82, −84, −86, WhoAmA 73, −76, −78,
−80, −82, −84, WhoWor 74, −76, −78,
−80, −82, −84, −87, WorAl, WrDr 76,
−80, −82, −84, −86
Adelberg, Roy P 1928- *ConAu 17R*
Adelman, Janet Ann 1941- *ConAu 61,*
DrAS 74E, −78E, −82E
Adkins, Jan 1944- *AuBYP SUP,*
BioIn 11, −12, ChlLR 7[port],
ConAu 33R, FifBJA[port], SmATA 8,
WhoE 77
Adlard, Mark 1932- *ConAu 65, EncSF,*
IntAu&W 76, −77, ScF&FL 1, −2,
ScFSB, TwCSFW 86, WhoSciF,
WrDr 84, −86
Adler, Bill 1929- *BioIn 7, −13,*
ConAu X, WhoE 74
Adler, Bill *see also* Adler, William
Adler, C S *DrAP&F 85*
Adler, C S 1932- *ConAu 19NR, −89,*
ConLC 35[port], SmATA 26[port]
Adler, Freda 1934- *ConAu 11NR, −69,*
WhoAm 82, WhoAmW 77, −79, −81,
−83, WhoE 77, −79, −81
Adler, Freda Schaffer 1934-
WhoAm 84, −86, WhoWor 84, −87
Adler, Helmut E 1920-
AmM&WS 73S, −78S, ConAu 33R,
WhoE 83, WhoWorJ 72, WrDr 76,
−80, −82, −84, −86
Adler, Irene *AuBYP SUP, ConAu X,*
SmATA X
Adler, Irene *see also* Penzler, Otto M
Adler, Irene *see also* Storr, Catherine
Adler, Irving 1913- *AmAu&B,*
Au&Wr 71, AuBYP, BioIn 7, −9, −13,
ConAu 2NR, −5R, SmATA 1,
−29[port], ThrBJA, WhoFrS 84
Adler, Larry 1939- *ConAu 105,*
SmATA 36
Adler, Mortimer J 1902- *OxAmL 83,*
WrDr 86
Adler, Mortimer Jerome 1902-
AmAu&B, BioIn 2, −3, −4, −5, −11,
−12, −13, ConAu 7NR, −65,
CurBio 40, −52, DrAS 74P, −78P,
−82P, LinLib L, NewYTBS 82,
OxAmL, REnAL, TwCA SUP,
WebAB, −79, WhNAA, WhoAm 76,
−78, −80, −82, −84, −86, WhoWor 74,
−76, WrDr 82, −84
Adler, William 1929- *ConAu 7NR,*
−9R
Adler, William *see also* Adler, Bill

Adoff, Arnold 1935- *AuBYP,*
AuNews 1, BioIn 10, ChlLR 7[port],
ChhPo S1, −S2, −S3, ConAu 20NR,
−41R, FourBJA, MorBMP, SmATA 5,
TwCChW 83, WrDr 86
Adshead, Gladys L 1896- *AmAu&B,*
BioIn 2, −6, −9, ConAu 108,
SmATA 3, WhAm 7, WhoAmW 58,
−64, −66
Agassi, Joseph 1927- *ConAu 15NR,*
−41R, DrAS 74P, −78P, −82P,
WhoAm 74, −76, −78, −80, −82,
WhoAmJ 80, WhoE 83, WhoWorJ 78
Agee, James 1909-1955 *AmAu&B,*
AmWr, AuNews 1, BioIn 3, −4, −5,
−6, −7, −8, −9, −10, −12, −13,
BioNews 74, CasWL, ConAu 108,
DcAmB S5, DcLB 2, −26[port],
EncAAH, EncAJ, EncSoH,
EncWL, −2, FilmgC, HalFC 84,
LinLib L, −S, ModAL, −S1,
NatCAB 42, NewCon[port],
NewYTBS 81[port], Novels,
ObitOF 79, OxAmL, −83, OxEng 85,
OxFilm, PenC AM, RAdv 1, REn,
REnAL, SixAP, TwCA SUP,
TwCLC 1, −19[port], TwCWr,
WebAB, −79, WebE&AL, WhAm 4,
−HSA, WhScrn 83, WhoTwCL,
WorEFlm
Agee, Joel *DrAP&F 85*
Agee, Joel 1940- *BioIn 12, ConAu 105,*
NewYTBS 81[port]
Agel, Jerome *ScF&FL 1*
Agnelli, Susanna 1922- *BioIn 10, −13,*
ConAu 109, NewYTBS 75, −83[port]
Agonito, Rosemary 1937- *ConAu 112,*
DrAS 78P, −82P, WrDr 82, −84, −86
Ahern, James F 1932- *ConAu 41R,*
IntAu&W 77, NewYTBE 70,
WhoAm 74, −76, −78, −80,
WhoIns 76, −77, −78, −79, −80, −81,
−82, −84, WhoWor 76, −78, −80, −82
Ahern, James F 1932-1986 *ConAu 118,*
NewYTBS 86[port]
Ahern, James Francis 1932-
WhoAm 84, −86, WhoWor 84
Ahnstrom, Doris Newell *WhoE 85*
Ahnstrom, Doris Newell 1915-
AuBYP, BioIn 8, ConAu 5R,
IntAu&W 86, WhoAmW 61, −64,
−68, −70, −77, −79, −81, WhoE 81,
−83, WhoS&SW 76, −78
Aiken, Conrad Potter 1889-1973
AmAu&B, AmLY, −XR, AmWr,
AnCL, ApCAB X, AuBYP, BioIn 1,
−2, −3, −4, −5, −6, −7, −8, −9, −10,
−11, −12, −13, CasWL, Chambr 3,
ChhPo, −S1, −S2, −S3, CnDAL,
CnE&AP, CnMD, CnMWL,
ConAmA, ConAmL, ConAu 4NR,
−5R, −45, CasWL, −2, −3, −5, −10,
ConNov 72, ConPo 70, CurBio 70,
−73, −73N, DcLB 9[port], DcLEL,
EncWL, −2, EvLB, IntAu&W 76,
−77, −82, IntWWP 77, LinLib L, −S,
LongCTC, MakMC, ModAL, −S1,
ModWD, NewYTBE 73, Novels,
ObitOF 79, ObitT 1971, OxAmL,
OxEng, −85, PenC AM, RAdv 1,
REn, REnAL, SixAP, SmATA 3,
−30[port], TwCA, −SUP, TwCWr,
WebAB, −79, WebE&AL, WhDW,
WhAm 6, WhE&EA, WhNAA,
WhoAm 74, WhoE 74, WhoTwCL,
WhoWor 74, −76, WorAl
Aiken, Joan 1924- *Au&Wr 71, AuBYP,*
BioIn 8, −9, −10, −11, BritCA,
ChlLR 1, ChhPo S3, ConAu 4NR,
−9R, ConLC 35[port], IntAu&W 76,
−82, OxChL, PiP, ScF&FL 1, −1A,
−2, SenS, SmATA 2, −30[port],
SmATA 1AS[port], ThrBJA,
TwCCW 78, −83, TwCCr&M 80, −85,
Who 82, −83, WhoHr&F, WrDr 76,
−80, −82, −84, −86
Ainsworth, Ruth Gallard 1908-
Au&Wr 71, BioIn 8, −10,
ChhPo, −S1, ConAu X, ScF&FL 1,
−2, SmATA 7, TwCCW 78, −83,
WhoChL, WrDr 76, −80, −82, −84
Ainsworth, Ruth Gallard *see also*
Gilbert, Ruth Gallard Ainsworth
Aitmatov, Chingiz 1926- *BioIn 13*

Aitmatov, Chingiz 1928- *Au&Wr 71,*
BioIn 10, ConAu 103, FarE&A 78,
−79, −80, −81, HanRL, IntAu&W 76,
−77, IntWW 74, −75, −76, −77, −78,
−79, −80, −81, −82, −83,
TwCCW 78B, −83B, WhoSocC 78,
WhoWor 74, −82, WorAu 1975[port]
Ajar, Emile 1940?- *BioIn 11*
Akens, David S 1921- *ConAu 12NR,*
−25R, WhoAm 78, −80
Akers, Charles Wesley 1920-
ConAu 13R, DrAS 74H, −78H, −82H,
IndAu 1917
Akhmatova, Anna *BioIn 13*
Akhmatova, Anna 1888?-1966 *AtlBL,*
BioIn 1, −2, −7, −8, −9, −10, −11, −12,
CasWL, ClDMEL, ConAu 25R,
ConAu P-1, ConLC 11, −25[port],
DcRusL, EncWL, −2[port], EvEuW,
IntDcWB, LinLib L, LongCTC,
McGEWB, ModSL 1, ObitOF 79,
ObitT 1961, PenC EUR, REn,
TwCWr, WhDW, WhoTwCL, WorAl,
WorAu
Akhmatova, Anna 1889-1966 *GrFLW,*
OxEng 85
Alajalov, Constantin 1900- *BioIn 1,*
−2, −5, CurBio 42, ForIl, IlrAm 1880,
−D, IlsBYP, IlsCB 1744, −1946,
WhoAm 74, −76, −78, −80, −82, −84,
−86, WhoAmA 73, −76, −78, −80, −82,
−84, WorECar
Alarcon, Pedro Antonio De 1833-1891
NinCLC 1[port]
Albee, Edward 1928- *AmAu&B,*
AmWr, AuNews 1, BiDAmM,
BiE&WWA, BioIn 5, −6, −7, −8, −9,
−10, −11, −12, BlueB 76, CasWL,
CelR, CnMD, CnThe, ConAu 5R,
−8NR, ConDr 73, −77, −82, ConLC 1,
−2, −3, −5, −9, −11, −13, −25[port],
ConTFT 4, CroCD, DcLB 7[port],
DcLEL 1940, EncAB-H,
EncWL, −2[port], EncWT, FilmgC,
HalFC 84, IntAu&W 76, −77,
IntWW 74, −75, −76, −77, −78, −79,
−80, −81, −82, −83, LinLib L,
LongCTC, MajMD 1, MakMC,
McGEWD, −84[port], ModAL, −S2,
−S1, ModWD, NatPD, −81[port],
NewCon[port], NotNAT, −A,
OxAmL, −83, OxAmT 84, OxThe,
PenC AM, PIP&P, −A, RComWL,
REn, REnAL, REnWD, TwCWr,
WebAB, −79, WebE&AL, WhDW,
Who 74, −82, −83, −85, WhoAm 74,
−76, −78, −80, −82, WhoE 77, −79,
−81, −83, WhoThe 72, −77, −81,
WhoTwCL, WhoWor 74, −76, −78,
−82, WorAl, WorAu, WrDr 76, −80,
−82, −84, −86
Albert, Louise 1928- *ConAu 69*
Albert, Marvin H *AuBYP, BioIn 8,*
ConAu 73, HalFC 84, ScF&FL 1,
WrDr 84, −86
Albert, Marvin H 1924- *TwCCr&M 85*
Alberti, Rafael 1902- *ConFLW 84,*
OxThe 83
Albery, Nobuko *ConAu 81*
Albion, Robert G 1896-1983
AnObit 1983
Albion, Robert Greenhalgh 1896-1983
AmAu&B, BioIn 3, −10, −13,
BlueB 76, ConAu 1R, −3NR, −110,
CurBio 54, −83N, DrAS 74H, −78H,
IntYB 78, −79, −80, −81, −82,
NewYTBS 83, WhAm 8, WhE&EA,
WhoAm 74, −76, −78, −80, WrDr 76,
−80, −82, −84
Albrand, Martha *BiGAW*
Albrand, Martha 1914?-1981
AmAu&B, AmNov,
AnObit 1981[port], Au&Wr 71,
BioIn 1, −2, −4, −6, −7, −12,
ConAu 108, −11NR, −13R, EncMys,
InWom, IntAu&W 76, Novels,
TwCA SUP, TwCCr&M 80, −85,
WhAm 8, WhoAm 74, −76, −78, −80,
−82, WhoAmW 74, −58, −61, −64,
−66, −68, −70, −72, WhoE 74,
WhoSpyF, WhoWor 78, −80,
WrDr 82, −84
Albright, Horace Marden 1890-
NatLAC

Albritton, Claude Carroll, Jr. 1913-
AmM&WS 86P, WhoAm 84, −86
Alcock, Vivien 1924?- *ConAu 110,*
IntAu&W 86, SmATA 38, −45[port],
TwCChW 83
Alcock, Vivien 1926- *WrDr 86*
Alcorn, Robert Hayden 1909-
ConAu 5R, WhoE 75
Alcott, Louisa M 1832-1888
HalFC 84, OxEng 85
Alcott, Louisa May 1832-1888
Alli SUP, AmAu&B, AmAu&B, AmBi,
AmWom, AmWomWr, AmWr S1,
ApCAB, AtlBL, AuBYP, BbD,
BiD&SB, BioIn 1, −2, −3, −4, −5, −6,
−7, −8, −9, −10, −11, −12, CarSB,
CasWL, CelCen, Chambr 3,
ChlLR 1, ChhPo, −S3, CivWDc,
CnDAL, CrtT 3, −4, CyAL 2, CyWA,
DcAmAu, DcAmB, DcBiA, DcBiPP,
DcEnL, DcLB 1, −42[port], DcLEL,
DcNAA, EncAB-H, EvLB, FamAYP,
FilmgC, GoodHs, HarEnUS,
HerW, −84, InWom, IntDcWB,
JBA 34, LibW, LinLib L, −S,
McGEWB, MorMA, MouLC 4,
NatCAB 1, NinCLC 6[port], NotAW,
Novels, OxAmH, OxAmL, −83,
OxChL, OxEng, PenC AM, REn,
REnAL, Str&VC, TwCBDA,
TwCCW 78A, −83A, WebAB, −79,
WhAm HS, WhoChL, WorAl,
YABC 1
Aldan, Daisy *DrAP&F 85*
Aldan, Daisy 1923- *AmAu&B,*
ConAu 8NR, −13R, ForWC 70,
IntAu&W 86, WhoAmW 70,
WomWMM B
Alderman, Clifford Lindsey 1902-
AuBYP, BioIn 8, −9, ConAu 1R,
−3NR, IntAu&W 86, SmATA 3
Alderson, William Thomas 1926-
WhoAm 84, −86
Alderson, William Thomas, Jr. 1926-
BiDrLUS 70, ConAu 9R, DrAS 74H,
−78H, −82H, EncAB 32[port],
St&PR 75, WhoAm 74, −76, −78, −80,
−82, WhoE 83, WhoLibI 82,
WhoLibS 66, WhoS&SW 73
Aldiss, Brian 1925- *Au&Wr 71,*
BioIn 11, −12, −13, BlueB 76,
ConAu 5R, −5NR, ConLC 5, −14,
ConNov 72, −76, −82, −86, ConSFA,
DcLB 14[port], DcLEL 1940, EncSF,
IntAu&W 76, −77, −82, IntWW 74,
−75, −76, −77, −78, −79, −80, −81,
−82, −83, LinLib L, Novels,
ScF&FL 1, −2, SmATA 34[port],
TwCSFW 86, TwCWr, Who 74, −82,
−83, WhoSciF, WhoWor 74, −76, −78,
−82, WorAl, WorAu 1970, WrDr 76,
−80, −82, −84, −86
Aldiss, Brian W 1925-
ConAu 2AS[port], ConLC 40[port],
ScFSB
Aldiss, Brian Wilson 1925- *OxEng 85,*
Who 85, WhoWor 84, −87
Aldrich, Bess Streeter 1881-1954
AmAu&B, AmNov, AmWomWr,
BioIn 2, −3, −4, −6, DcAmB S5,
EncAB 6, InWom, LibW,
NatCAB 46, ObitOF 79,
OxAmL, −83, REn, REnAL,
TwCA, −SUP, WhAm 3, WhE&EA,
WhLit, WhNAA
Aldridge, James 1918- *Au&Wr 71,*
BioIn 2, −4, −6, −10, ConAu 13NR,
−61, ConNov 72, −76, −82, −86,
CurBio 43, IntAu&W 77, IntWW 83,
Novels, OxAusL, TwCA SUP,
Who 74, −82, −83, WrDr 76, −80,
−82, −84, −86
Aldrin, Edwin E, Jr. *Who 85*
Aldrin, Edwin Eugene, Jr. 1930-
AmM&WS 73P, BioIn 7, −8, −9, −10,
−12, BioNews 74, BlueB 76, CelR,
ConAu 89, IntWW 74, −75, −76, −77,
−78, −79, −80, −81, −82, −83,
LinLib S, NewYTBE 71, UFOEn,
Who 74, −82, −83, WhoAm 74, −76,
−78, −80, −82, −84, WhoWest 78, −80,
WhoWor 74, −78, WorAl

Ambler, Eric 1909- *AmAu&B,*
Au&Wr 71, BioIn 4, -5, -10, -12,
BlueB 76, CnMWL, ConAu 7NR,
-9R, ConLC 4, -6, -9, ConNov 72,
-76, -82, -86, CorpD, CurBio 75,
DcLEL, EncMys, FilmgC, HalFC 84,
IntAu&W 76, -82, IntWW 83,
LinLib L, LongCTC, NewC,
NewYTBS 81[port], Novels,
OxEng 85, OxFilm, REn, ScF&FL 1,
TwCA SUP, TwCCr&M 80, -85,
TwCWr, Who 74, -82, -83, -85,
WhoAm 86, WhoSpyF, WhoWor 74,
-76, -82, -84, WorAl, WrDr 76, -80,
-82, -84, -86

Ambrose, Stephen E 1936- *ConAu 1R,*
-3NR, DrAS 74H, -78H, -82H,
IntAu&W 76, SmATA 40[port]

Ambrus, Gyozo Laszlo 1935-
ConAu 11NR, -25R, IntAu&W 77

Ambrus, Gyozo Laszlo *see also*
Ambrus, Victor G

Ambrus, Victor G *SmATA X*

Ambrus, Victor G 1935- *BioIn 7, -8,*
-9, -11, -12, BritCA, ChhPo S1, -S2,
ConAu X, IlsBYP, IlsCB 1957, -1967,
IntAu&W 77X, OxChL, SmATA 1,
ThrBJA, WhoArt 80, -82, WhoChL

Ambrus, Victor G *see also* Ambrus,
Gyozo Laszlo

Ambrus, Victor Gyozo Laszio 1935-
WhoArt 84

America *BiDAmM, EncPR&S 74,*
IlEncRk, RkOn 78, RolSEnR 83,
WhoRock 81, WhoRocM 82

America *see also* Beckley, Gerry

America *see also* Bunnell, Dewey

America *see also* Peek, Dan

Amerman, Lockhart 1911-1969
AuBYP, BioIn 8, -9, ConAu P-2,
SmATA 3

Ames, Delano 1906- *Au&Wr 71,*
ConAu 107, MnBBF, OhA&B,
ScF&FL 1, WhLit

Ames, Evelyn 1908- *ConAu 57,*
SmATA 13, WhoAmW 58, -61

Ames, Lee J 1921- *ConAu 18NR*

Ames, Lee Judah 1921- *AuBYP,*
BioIn 5, -8, -9, ConAu 1R, -3NR,
IlsCB 1946, -1957, -1967, SmATA 3,
WhoAmA 73, -76, -78, -80, -82, -84

Ames, Mildred 1919- *BioIn 13,*
ConAu 11NR, -69, FifBJA[port],
SmATA 22[port]

Amis, Kingsley 1922- *Au&Wr 71,*
AuNews 2, BioIn 3, -4, -5, -6, -8, -9,
-10, -11, -12, -13, BlueB 76,
CasWL, ChhPo S3, CnMWL,
ConAu 8NR, -9R, ConLC 1, -2, -3,
-5, -8, -13, -40[port], -44[port],
ConNov 72, -76, -82, -86, ConPo 70,
-75, -80, -85, ConSFA, CurBio 58,
DcLB 15[port], -27[port], DcLEL,
DcLEL 1940, EncMys, EncSF,
EncWL, -2, FilmgC, HalFC 84,
IntAu&W 76, -77, IntWW 74, -75,
-76, -77, -78, -79, -80, -81, -82,
-83, IntWWP 77, LinLib L,
LongCEL, LongCTC, MakMC,
ModBrL, -S2, -S1, NewC,
Novels[port], OxEng 85, PenC ENG,
RAdv 1, REn, ScF&FL 1, -2, ScFSB,
TwCCr&M 80, TwCSFW 86,
TwCWr, WebE&AL, WhDW,
Who 74, -82, -83, -85, WhoAm 74,
-76, -78, -80, -82, -84, -86,
WhoSciF, WhoSpyF, WhoTwCL,
WorAu, WrDr 76, -80, -82, -84, -86

Ammerman, Gale Richard 1923-
AmM&WS 73P, ConAu 107,
IntAu&W 76, -77

Ammons, A R *DrAP&F 85*

Ammons, A R 1926- *AmAu&B,*
AuNews 1, BioIn 13, BlueB 76,
ConAu 6NR, -9R, ConLC 2, -3, -5,
-8, -9, -25[port], ConPo 70, -75, -80,
-85, CroCAP, CurBio 82[port],
DcLB 5[port], EncWL 2,
IntWWP 77, LinLib L, ModAL S2,
-S1, OxAmL, RAdv 1, WorAu,
WrDr 76, -80, -82, -84, -86

Amon, Aline 1928- *AuBYP SUP,*
BioIn 11, ConAu 8NR, -61,
SmATA 9

Amory, Cleveland 1917- *AmAu&B,*
AuNews 1, BioIn 2, -4, -5, -7, -10,
-11, -12, -13, BioNews 75, CelR,
ConAu 69, LinLib L, -S, REnAL,
TwCA SUP, WhoAm 74, -76, -78,
-80, -82, -84, -86, WhoWor 74,
WrDr 76, -80, -82, -84, -86

Amoss, Berthe 1920?- *BioIn 10,*
ConAu 21R, SmATA 5, WhoAmA 78,
-80, -82, -84, WhoAmW 74

Amoss, Berthe 1925- *ConAu 14NR*

Anaya, Rudolfo A 1937- *ChiSch,*
ConAu 1NR, -45, ConAu 4AS[port],
ConLC 23[port], ConNov 86

Anaya, Rudolfo Alfonso 1937- *ChiLit*

Anckarsvard, Karin 1915-1969
AuBYP, BioIn 7, -9, -10, ConAu 9R,
-103, SmATA 6, ThrBJA

Ancona, George 1929- *AuBYP SUP,*
BioIn 11, ConAu 4NR, -19NR, -53,
SmATA 12, WhoAm 76, -78, -80,
-82

Ancona, George Ephraim 1929-
WhoAm 84, -86

Andersen, Christopher P 1949-
ConAu 14NR

Andersen, Christopher Peter 1949-
WhoE 85, WhoWor 84, -87

Andersen, Yvonne 1932- *AuBYP SUP,*
BioIn 10, -13, ConAu 29R,
SmATA 27[port], WomWMM A, -B

Anderson, Alan H, Jr. 1943-
ConAu 69, WrDr 82, -84

Anderson, Bernard E *AmEA 74,*
AmM&WS 73S, -78S, WhoBlA 77,
-80, WhoCon 73

Anderson, Bernice G 1894-
ConAu 101, SmATA 33[port],
WhNAA

Anderson, Brad 1924- *AmAu&B,*
ConAu 106, SmATA 31, -33[port],
WhoAmA 73, -76, -78, -80, -82

Anderson, Brad J 1924- *WhoAmA 84*

Anderson, C W 1891-1971 *BkP,*
JBA 51, LinLib L, OxChL,
SmATA 11, Str&VC, ThrBJA,
TwCChW 83

Anderson, C W *see also* Anderson,
Clarence William

Anderson, Chester Grant 1923-
ConAu 25R, DrAS 74E, -78E, -82E,
WhoAm 80, -82, -84, -86

Anderson, Chuck 1933- *ConAu 49*

Anderson, Clarence William
1891-1971 *ArtsAmW 1, AuBYP,*
BioIn 1, -2, -5, -7, -8, -9, -11,
ConAu 29R, -73, IIBEAAW,
IlsCB 1744, -1946, -1957

Anderson, Clarence William *see also*
Anderson, C W

Anderson, Clary *NewYTBE 72*

Anderson, Dave 1929- *AuNews 2,*
ConAu X

Anderson, David Poole 1929-
BioIn 11, ConAu 89, IntAu&W 82,
WhoAm 76, -78, -80, -82, -84, -86,
WhoE 85

Anderson, Edna A *BioIn 6, MinnWr*

Anderson, Ella *IntAu&W 86X,*
WrDr 86

Anderson, Ella 1916- *IntAu&W 76X,*
-82X, SmATA X, WrDr 76, -80, -82

Anderson, Ella *see also* MacLeod, Ellen
Jane

Anderson, J R L 1911-1981
ConAu 104, -18NR, -25R,
SmATA 15, -27N

Anderson, J R L *see also* Anderson,
John Richard Lane

Anderson, Jack 1922- *EncAJ, WrDr 86*

Anderson, Jack Northman 1922-
AuNews 1, BioIn 6, -8, -9, -10, -11,
-12, -13, BlueB 76, CelR,
ConAu 6NR, -57, CurBio 72,
EncTwCJ, PolProf J, PolProf NF,
WhoAm 74, -76, -78, -80, -82, -84,
-86, WhoS&SW 73, -75, -76,
WhoWor 74, -76, WorAl, WrDr 76,
-80, -82, -84

Anderson, Jean 1930?- *AuBYP SUP,*
ConAu 41R, ForWC 70,
WhoAmW 77, -79, -81, -83,
WhoE 77, -79, -81, -83

Anderson, Jean 1931- *ConAu 14NR,*
WhoAm 86, WhoAmW 85, -87,
WhoE 85, WhoWor 84, -87

Anderson, Johannes Carl 1873-1959
DcLEL

Anderson, John Richard Lane
1911-1981 *Au&Wr 71, BioIn 12,*
-13, IntAu&W 76, -77, -82,
WhoWor 76, WrDr 76, -80, -82

Anderson, John Richard Lane *see also*
Anderson, J R L

Anderson, LaVere Francis 1907-
BioIn 13

Anderson, LaVere Francis Shoenfelt
1907- *ConAu 101, SmATA 27,*
WhoAmW 77, -79, -81,
WhoS&SW 76, -78, -80

Anderson, Madelyn Klein
ConAu 11NR, -69, SmATA 28

Anderson, Margaret J 1909-
ConAu 1R, -3NR, WhoAmW 81

Anderson, Margaret Jean 1931-
BioIn 13, FifBJA[port]

Anderson, Marian 1902- *AmWomWr,*
Baker 78, -84, BiDAfM, BiDAmM,
BioIn 3, -4, -5, -6, -7, -8, -9, -10,
-11, -12, -13, CelR, CurBio 40, -50,
DrBlPA, EncAB-H, GoodHs,
HerW, -84, InB&W 85, InWom,
IntDcWB, IntWW 74, -75, -76, -77,
-78, -79, -80, -81, -82, -83, LibW,
LinLib L, -S, McGEWB, MusSN,
NegAl 76, -83, NewEOp 71,
NewYTBE 72, REn, SelBAAf,
SelBAAu, WebAB, -79, Who 82, -83,
-85, WhoAm 74, -76, -78, -80, -82,
-84, WhoAmW 77, -81, -83, -85,
-87, WhoBlA 75, -77, -80, -85,
WhoGov 72, WhoMus 72,
WhoWor 74, -78, WorAl

Anderson, Mary 1939- *AuBYP SUP,*
BioIn 10, ConAu 1NR, -16NR, -49,
IntAu&W 76, -77, -82, SmATA 7

Anderson, Mary Desiree 1902-
Au&Wr 71, ConAu 9R

Anderson, Maxwell 1888-1959
AmAu&B, AmSCAP 66, BiDAmM,
BioIn 1, -2, -3, -4, -5, -6, -7, -8, -9,
-10, -11, -12, -13, CasWL,
CmpEPM, CnDAL, CnMD, CnThe,
ConAmA, ConAmL, ConAu 105,
CroCD, CurBio 42, -53, -59, CyWA,
DcAmB S6, DcLB 7[port], DcLEL,
EncAB-H, EncMT, EncWL, EncWT,
EvLB, FilmgC, HalFC 84, LinLib L,
-S, LongCTC, McGEWB,
McGEWD, -84[port], ModAL,
ModWD, NatCAB 60, NewCBMT,
NotNAT A, -B, ObitOF 79,
ObitT 1951, OxAmL, -83,
OxAmT 84, OxThe, -83, PenC AM,
PlP&P, REn, REnAL, REnWD,
TwCA, -SUP, TwCLC 2, TwCWr,
WebAB, -79, WebE&AL, WhDW,
WhAm 3, WhJnl, WhThe, WorAl,
WorEFlm

Anderson, Norman D 1928- *BioIn 13*

Anderson, Norman Dean 1928-
ConAu 15NR, -33R, LEduc 74,
SmATA 22[port]

Anderson, Patrick 1936- *AmAu&B,*
ConAu 33R

Anderson, Paul Lewis 1880-1956
BioIn 4, MacBEP, WhAm 3, WhNAA

Anderson, Peggy 1938- *ConAu 93,*
NewYTBS 79, WrDr 76, -80, -82,
-84, -86

Anderson, Poul *DrAP&F 85*

Anderson, Poul 1926- *AmAu&B,*
AuBYP SUP, BioIn 3, -10, -12, -13,
ConAu 1R, -2NR, -15NR,
ConAu 2AS[port], ConLC 15,
ConSFA, DcLB 8[port], DcLEL 1940,
DrmM 2[port], EncSF, IntAu&W 82,
LinLib L, Novels, ScF&FL 1, -2,
ScFSB[port], SmATA 39, SupFW,
TwCSFW 86, WhoAm 74, -76, -78,
-80, -82, WhoHr&F, WhoSciF,
WorAl, WorAu, WrDr 76, -80, -82,
-84, -86

Anderson, Poul William 1926-
IntAu&W 86, WhoAm 84, -86

Anderson, Rachel 1943- *ConAu 9NR,*
-21R, SmATA 34[port], WrDr 76,
-80, -82, -84, -86

Anderson, Robert 1917- *AmAu&B,*
AuNews 1, BiE&WWA, BioIn 2, -3,
-8, -10, -11, -12, BlueB 76, CelR,
CnMD, ConAu 21R, ConDr 73, -77,
-82, ConLC 23[port], CroCD,
DcLB 7[port], DcLEL 1940, EncWT,
HalFC 84, IntAu&W 76, -77, -82,
LinLib L, McGEWD, -84[port],
ModAL, ModWD, NatPD, -81[port],
NotNAT, OxAmL, OxAmT 84,
PenC AM, REn, REnAL, Who 74,
-82, -83, WhoAm 74, -76, -78, -80,
-82, WhoThe 72, -77, -81,
WhoWor 74, -76, WorAl, WorAu,
WrDr 76, -80, -82, -84, -86

Anderson, Sherwood 1876-1941
AmAu&B, AmWr, ApCAB X, AtlBL,
BioIn 1, -2, -3, -4, -5, -6, -7, -8, -9,
-10, -11, -12, -13, CasWL,
Chambr 3, CnDAL, CnMWL,
ConAmA, ConAmL, ConAu 104,
CurBio 41, CyWA, DcAmB S3,
DcLB 4, -9[port], -DS1[port],
DcLEL, DcNAA, EncAB 14[port],
EncWL, -2[port], EvLB, LinLib L,
-S, LongCTC, MakMC, McGEWB,
ModAL, -S1, NatCAB 36,
NotNAT B, Novels, ObitOF 79,
OhA&B, OxAmL, -83, OxEng, -85,
PenC AM, RAdv 1, REn, REnAL,
TwCA, -SUP, TwCLC 1, -10[port],
-24[port], TwCWr, WebAB, -79,
WebE&AL, WhDW, WhAm 1,
WhJnl, WhLit, WhNAA, WhoTwCL,
WorAl

Anderson, William C *DrAP&F 85*

Anderson, William C 1943-
WhoTech 84

Anderson, William Carl 1943-
WhoE 85, WhoF&I 81

Anderson, William Charles 1920-
ConAu 5R

Anderson, William Robert 1921-
BiDrAC, BioIn 5, -6, -9, BlueB 76,
ConAu 5R, IntWW 74, -75, -76, -77,
-78, -79, -80, -81, -82, -83,
WhoAm 74, -76, -78, -80, -82, -84,
-86, WhoAmP 73, -75, -77, -79,
WhoGov 72, -75, WhoS&SW 73

Andrew, Prudence 1924- *Au&Wr 71,*
ConAu X, -1NR, TwCCW 78, -83,
WrDr 76, -80, -82, -84, -86

Andrews, Allen 1913- *ConAu 1NR,*
-49, IntAu&W 77, -82, WrDr 76,
-80, -82, -84, -86

Andrews, Bart 1945- *ConAu 9NR, -65*

Andrews, F Emerson 1902-1978
AmAu&B, BioIn 11, -13, ConAu 1R,
-1NR, -81, NewYTBS 78, ScF&FL 1,
-2, SmATA 22[port], WhAm 7,
WhoAm 74, -76, -78

Andrews, Mary Raymond 1865?-1936
WomNov

Andrews, Mary Raymond Shipman
1865?-1936 *AmAu&B, AmWomWr,*
ChhPo, ConAmA, ConAmL, InWom,
JBA 34, NotAW, REnAL, TwCA,
WhAm 1, WhNAA

Andrews, Michael Frank 1916-
ConAu 49, IntAu&W 77, LEduc 74,
WhoAm 74, WhoAmA 76, -78, -80,
-82, -84, WhoWor 74

Andrews, V C *ConAu 97,*
NewYTBS 80[port]

Andrews, V C d1986 *ConAu 21NR,*
NewYTBS 86

Andrist, Ralph K 1914- *AuBYP SUP,*
ConAu 5NR, -9R, -20NR,
SmATA 45[port]

Anema, Durlynn Carol 1935-
WhoWest 84

Angel, Heather 1941- *ConAu 69,*
ICPEnP A, WrDr 80, -82, -84, -86

Angeli, Marguerite De 1889- *JBA 51*

Angeli, Marguerite De *see also*
DeAngeli, Marguerite Lofft

Angell, Judie 1937- *BioIn 13,*
ConAu 19NR, SmATA 22[port]

Angell, Madeline 1919- *BioIn 12,*
ConAu 10NR, -65, SmATA 18,
WhoMW 80, -82, -84, -86

Angell, Roger *DrAP&F 85*
Angell, Roger 1920- *BioIn 9, -11, -13,*
ConAu 13NR, -57, ConLC 26[port],
WhoAm 74, -76, -78, -80, -82, -84,
-86, WorAu 1975[port]
Angelou, Maya *DrAP&F 85*
Angelou, Maya 1928- *AmWomD,*
AmWomWr, BioIn 8, -9, -10, -11,
-12, -13, BlkWWr, BlkAWP,
ConAu 19NR, -65, ConLC 12,
-35[port], ConPo 85, CurBio 74,
DcLB 38[port], DrBlPA, Ebony 1,
HerW, InB&W 80, -85, LivgBAA,
ModAL S2, NegAl 83[port],
NewYTBE 72, NotNAT A,
OxAmL 83, SelBAAf, SelBAAu,
WhoAm 74, -76, -78, -80, -82, -84,
-86, WhoAmW 72, -79, -81, -83,
-85, WhoBlA 77, -80, -85,
WomWMM, WorAu 1975[port],
WrDr 76, -80, -82, -84, -86
Angelou, Maya 1929- *HerW 84*
Angier, Bradford *AuBYP SUP,*
BioIn 11, ConAu 5R, -7NR,
SmATA 12
Anglund, Joan Walsh 1926- *AmAu&B,*
Au&Wr 71, AuBYP, BioIn 6, -7, -8,
-9, -10, ChlLR 1, ChhPo S1, -S2,
-S3, ConAu 5R, -15NR, FamAIYP,
IlsCB 1957, LinLib L, OxChL,
SmATA 2, ThrBJA, TwCCW 78,
WhoAm 74, -76, -78, -80,
WhoAmW 74, -61, -64, -66, -68,
-70, -83, -85, WrDr 80, -82, -84,
-86
Angrist, Stanley W 1933-
AmM&WS 73P, -79P, -82P, -86P,
BioIn 9, ConAu 25R, SmATA 4
Angus, Douglas Ross 1909-
ConAu 1R, -3NR, DrAS 74E, -78E,
-82E
Angus, Sylvia 1921-1982
ConAu 10NR, -61, WrDr 84
Anka, Paul 1941- *AmPS, Baker 78,*
-84, BiDAmM, BioIn 5, -6, -7, -9,
-10, -12, -13, CanWW 70, -79, -80,
-81, -83, CelR, CreCan 2,
EncPR&S 77, FilmgC, HalFC 84,
MotPP, RkOn 74, -78, -82, -84,
RolSEnR 83, WhoAm 74, -76, -78,
-80, -82, -84, -86, WhoArab 81,
WhoHol A, WhoRock 81[port],
WhoRocM 82, WorAl
Annixter, Jane *AuBYP, BioIn 8, -9,*
ConAu X, ForWC 70, MichAu 80,
SmATA 1
Annixter, Jane *see also* Sturtzel, Jane
Levington
Annixter, Paul *BioIn 6, -9, ConAu X,*
SmATA X
Annixter, Paul *see also* Sturtzel,
Howard A
Anno, Mitsumasa 1920?- *BioIn 10,*
-12, ChlLR 2, ConAu 4NR, -49,
FourBJA, IlsBYP, IlsCB 1967,
IntAu&W 77, SmATA 5,
TwCChW 83B
Anno, Mitsumasa 1926- *OxChL,*
SmATA 38[port]
Anobile, Richard J 1947- *ConAu 5NR,*
-53
Anouilh, Jean 1910- *Au&Wr 71,*
BiE&WWA, BioIn 3, -4, -5, -6, -7,
-8, -9, -12, CasWL, CnMD,
CnMWL, CnThe, ConAu 17R,
ConFLW 84, ConLC 1, -3, -8, -13,
-40[port], CroCD, CurBio 54, CyWA,
DcFM, EncWL, -2[port], EncWT,
EvEuW, FilmgC, HalFC 84,
IntAu&W 76, -77, IntWW 74, -75,
-76, -77, -78, -79, -80, -81, -82,
-83, LinLib L, -S, LongCTC,
MajMD 2, MakMC, McGEWB,
McGEWD, -84[port], ModFrL,
ModRL, ModWD, NotNAT, -A,
OxAmT 84, OxEng, -85, OxFilm,
OxFr, OxThe, PenC EUR, PIP&P,
RComWL, REn, REnWD,
TwCA SUP, TwCWr, WhDW,
Who 74, -82, -83, -85, WhoFr 79,
WhoThe 72, -77, -81, WhoTwCL,
WhoWor 74, WorAl, WorEFlm
Anson, Jay 1921?-1980 *BioIn 12,*
ConAu 81, -97, NewYTBS 80

Anson, Robert Sam 1945- *ConAu 115*
Anthony, Earl 1941- *BlkAWP,*
CivR 74, InB&W 80, LivgBAA,
NatPD
Anthony, Evelyn 1928- *Au&Wr 71,*
ConAu X, IntAu&W 76, -77, -82,
Novels, TwCCr&M 80, -85, Who 82,
-83, -85, WhoSpyF, WorAl,
WrDr 76, -80, -82, -84, -86
Anthony, Evelyn *see also*
Ward-Thomas, Evelyn Bridget
Anthony, Piers *BioIn 13*
Anthony, Piers 1934- *AmAu&B,*
Au&Wr 71, BioIn 12, ConAu X,
ConLC 35[port], ConSFA,
DcLB 8[port], DrmM 2[port], EncSF,
Novels, ScF&FL 1, -2, ScFSB[port],
SupFW, TwCSFW 86, WhoSciF,
WrDr 76, -80, -82, -84, -86
Anthony, Piers *see also* Jacob, Piers A
D
Antoncich, Betty 1913- *AuBYP,*
BioIn 8, ConAu 13R
Apel, Willi 1893- *AmAu&B,*
AmCath 80, Au&Wr 71, Baker 78,
-84, BlueB 76, ConAu 1R, -2NR,
DrAS 74H, -78H, -82H, IntWW 74,
-75, -76, -77, -78, -79, -80, -81,
-82, -83, IntWWM 77, -85, OxMus,
REnAL, WhoAm 74, -76, -78, -80
Apfel, Necia H 1930- *ConAu 107,*
IntAu&W 86, SmATA 41
Appel, Benjamin 1907- *ScFSB*
Appel, Benjamin 1907-1977 *AmAu&B,*
AmNov, BioIn 1, -2, -4, -11, -12,
ConAu 6NR, -13R, -69, DcLEL,
EncSF, IntAu&W 77, NewYTBS 77,
OxAmL, ScF&FL 1, -2,
SmATA 21N, -39[port],
TwCA, -SUP, WhAm 7, WhoAm 74,
-76
Appel, Benjamin 1907-1979
OxAmL 83
Appel, Martin E 1948- *ConAu 15NR,*
-85, SmATA 45[port]
Appelfeld, Aharon 1932- *BioIn 12,*
-13, CasWL, ConAu 112,
ConLC 23[port], NewYTBS 80[port],
WorAu 1975[port]
Appiah, Peggy 1921- *Au&Wr 71,*
BioIn 12, ConAu 41R, IntAu&W 76,
OxChL, SmATA 15, TwCCW 78,
-83, WrDr 76, -80, -82, -84, -86
Apple, Max *DrAP&F 85*
Apple, Max 1941- *BioIn 12, -13,*
ConAu 19NR, -81, ConLC 9,
-33[port], DrAS 74E, -78E, -82E,
NewYTBS 81[port]
Apple, Max 1942- *PostFic*
Appleton, Victor *AmAu&B,*
ConAu P-2, ScF&FL 1, -1A,
SmATA 1, WebAB 79
Appleton, Victor, II *AmAu&B,*
ConAu 17R, -X, ScF&FL 1,
SmATA 1, -X
Appleton, Victor, II *see also* Adams,
Harriet S
Appleton, Victor, II *see also*
Stratemeyer, Edward L
Appleton, Victor *see also* Stratemeyer,
Edward L
Apsler, Alfred 1907- *AuBYP SUP,*
BioIn 11, ConAu 3NR, -5R,
IntAu&W 76, -77, SmATA 10,
WhoPNW, WrDr 76, -80, -82, -84
Aptheker, Herbert 1915- *AmAu&B,*
BioIn 10, ConAu 5R, -6NR,
DrAS 74H, -78H, -82H, EncAAH,
IntAu&W 76, WhoAm 74, -76, -78,
-80, -82, -84, -86, WhoWor 74,
WhoWorJ 72, -78
Aragones, Sergio 1937- *SmATA 39,*
-48[port], WhoAm 82, -84, -86,
WorECom
Arbeiter, Jean S *AuBYP SUP*
Arbib, Michael A 1940-
AmM&WS 73P, -76P, -79P, -82P,
-86P, WhoAm 74, -76, -78, -80, -82,
WhoTech 84
Arbib, Michael Anthony 1940-
WhoAm 84, -86
Arbuckle, Wanda Rector 1910-
ConAu 41R, WhoAmW 74, -72,
WhoWest 74, -76

Arbus, Diane 1923-1971 *BioIn 13,*
ICPEnP, MacBEP,
NewYTBS 84[port]
Archer, Jeffrey *NewYTBS 85[port]*
Archer, Jeffrey 1940- *BioIn 12,*
ConAu 77, ConLC 28[port],
IntAu&W 82, IntWW 83,
NewYTBS 80[port], Novels, Who 74,
-82, -83, WhoWor 80, WrDr 82, -84,
-86
Archer, Jules 1915- *AuBYP, BioIn 8,*
-9, ConAu 6NR, -9R, ConLC 12,
FifBJA[port], IntAu&W 76, -77,
SmATA 4, WrDr 80, -82, -84, -86
Archer, Myrtle 1926- *ConAu 102,*
IntWWP 77X, -82X
Archibald, Joe *ConAu X, SmATA X*
Archibald, Joe 1898- *AuBYP,*
ConAu X
Archibald, Joseph S 1898- *BioIn 7, -9,*
ConAu 5NR, -9R, SmATA 3
Archibald, Joseph S 1898-1986
ConAu 118, SmATA 47N
Arden, John 1930- *Au&Wr 71,*
BioIn 7, -8, -9, -10, -12, -13,
BlueB 76, CasWL, CnMD, CnThe,
ConAu 13R, ConAu 4AS[port],
ConDr 73, -77, -82, ConLC 6, -13,
-15, CroCD, DcLB 13[port],
DcLEL 1940, EncWL 2, EncWT,
IntAu&W 76, -77, IntWW 74, -75,
-76, -77, -78, -79, -80, -81, -82,
-83, LongCEL, LongCTC,
McGEWD, -84, ModBrL S2, -S1,
ModWD, NewC, NotNAT, OxEng 85,
OxThe, -83, PenC ENG, PIP&P,
REnWD, TwCWr, WebE&AL,
WhDW, Who 74, -82, -83, -85,
WhoThe 72, -77, -81, WhoTwCL,
WhoWor 74, -84, -87, WorAu,
WrDr 76, -80, -82, -84, -86
Arden, William *ConAu X, EncMys,*
SmATA X, TwCCr&M 80, -85,
WrDr 82, -84, -86
Arden, William *see also* Lynds, Dennis
Ardizzone, Edward 1900-1979 *ArtsCL,*
Au&ICB, Au&Wr 71, AuBYP,
BioIn 1, -4, -5, -6, -7, -8, -9, -10,
-11, -12, -13, BlueB 76, BritCA,
ChlLR 3, ChhPo, -S1, -S2, -S3,
ConArt 77, ConAu 5R, -8NR, -89,
CurBio 64, -80N, DcBrAr 1,
IlsCB 1744, -1946, -1957, -1967,
IntAu&W 76, IntWW 74, 75, 76,
-77, -78, -79, LinLib L, LongCTC,
MorJA, NewYTBS 79, OxChL,
PhDcTCA 77, PiP, SmATA 1, -21N,
-28[port], TwCCW 78, -83,
WhE&EA, Who 74, WhoAmA 80N,
-82N, -84N, WhoArt 80, -82N,
WhoChL, WhoWor 74, -76, -78,
WrDr 76
Ardley, Neil 1937- *ConAu 115,*
SmATA 43[port]
Ardrey, Robert 1907-1980 *HalFC 84*
Ardrey, Robert 1908-1980 *AmAu&B,*
AnObit 1980[port], BiE&WWA,
BioIn 4, -9, -10, -12, BioNews 74,
BlkAWP, CelR, CnMD, ConAu 33R,
-93, ConDr 73, -77, CurBio 73,
-80N, EncSF, LinLib L, ModWD,
NewYTBS 80, NotNAT, OxThe 83,
PIP&P, ScF&FL 1, -2, TwCA SUP,
WhDW, WhAm 7, WhThe,
WhoAm 74, -76, -78, -80,
WhoThe 81N, WhoWor 74, -76, -78,
WorEFlm, WrDr 76, -80
Arehart-Treichel, Joan 1942- *BioIn 13,*
ConAu 6NR, -57, SmATA 22[port]
Argenzio, Victor 1902- *ConAu 53*
Arkin, Frieda *DrAP&F 85*
Arkin, Frieda 1917- *ConAu 11NR, -65*
Arlen, Michael J 1930- *AmAu&B,*
ASpks, BioIn 8, -10, -11, -13,
ConAu 13NR, -61, DcLEL 1940,
EncTwCJ, WhoAm 74, -76, -78, -80,
-82, -84, -86, WhoE 74,
WorAu 1975[port], WrDr 80, -82,
-84, -86
Armah, Ayi Kwei 1938- *ConNov 86*
Armah, Ayi Kwei 1939- *AfrA, CasWL,*
ConAu 21NR, -61, ConLC 5,
-33[port], ConNov 72, -76, -82,

Arbus, Diane 1923-1971 *BioIn 13,*
DcLEL 1940, EncWL, -2,
InB&W 80, -85, IntAu&W 76, -77,
ModBlW, ModCmwL, RGAfL,
SelBAAf, WorAu 1975[port],
WrDr 76, -80, -82, -84, -86
Armer, Alberta Roller 1904- *BioIn 11,*
ConAu 5R, ForWC 70, IndAu 1917,
SmATA 9
Armer, Laura Adams 1874-
ArtsAmW 2
Armer, Laura Adams 1874-1963
AmAu&B, AuBYP, BioIn 1, -2, -4,
-6, -7, ConAmA, ConAu 65,
IlsCB 1744, InWom, JBA 34, -51,
Newb 1922, SmATA 13, TwCCHW 83
Armes, Roy 1937- *ConAu 13NR, -73,*
IntAu&W 82, WrDr 76, -80, -82,
-84, -86
Armour, Richard 1906- *AmAu&B,*
AnCL, Au&Wr 71, AuBYP, BioIn 2,
-5, -7, -8, -12, ChhPo, -S1, -S2,
-S3, ConAu 1R, -4NR, CurBio 58,
DrAS 74E, -78E, -82E, FifBJA[port],
IntAu&W 76, -77, -82, REnAL,
SmATA 14, TwCCW 78, WhE&EA,
WhoAm 74, -76, -78, -80, -82, -84,
-86, WhoWor 74, -76, -78, -80, -82,
-84, -87, WorAl, WrDr 76, -80, -82,
-84, -86
Armstrong, Charlotte 1905-1969
AmAu&B, AmWomWr, BioIn 1, -8,
-10, ConAu 1R, -3NR, -25R, CorpD,
CurBio 46, -69, EncMys, InWom,
Novels, ObitOF 79, TwCCr&M 80,
-85, WhAm 5, WhoAmW 58, -66,
-68, -70, WorAu
Armstrong, Diana 1943- *ConAu 107*
Armstrong, Karen *BioIn 12*
Armstrong, Louise *AuBYP SUP,*
ConAu 111, -117, SmATA 33, -43
Armstrong, Neil A 1930-
AmM&WS 73P, -79P, -82P, -86P,
AsBiEn, BioIn 7, -8, -9, -10, -12,
BlueB 76, CelR, CurBio 69,
IntWW 74, -75, -76, -77, -78, -79,
-80, -81, -82, -83, LinLib S,
McGEWB, PolProf NF, UFOEn,
WebAB, -79, WebAMB, WhDW,
Who 74, -82, -83, -85, WhoAm 74,
-76, -78, -80, -82, -84, -86,
WhoEng 80, WhoFrS 84, WhoGov 72,
WhoMW 74, -75, -78,
WhoS&SW 73, WhoWor 74, -78,
-80, -82, -84, -87, WorAl
Armstrong, Neil Alden 1930-
BioIn 13, NewYTBS 86
Armstrong, Richard 1903- *Au&Wr 71,*
AuBYP, BioIn 2, -8, -9, -11,
ConAu 77, OxChL, SmATA 11,
ThrBJA, TwCCW 78, -83, WhoChL,
WrDr 80, -82, -84, -86
Armstrong, William H *OxChL*
Armstrong, William H 1914- *WrDr 86*
Armstrong, William Howard 1914-
AuBYP, AuNews 1, BioIn 8, -9, -10,
BioNews 74, ChlLR 1, ConAu 9NR,
-17R, MorBMP, NewbC 1966,
SmATA 4, ThrBJA, TwCCW 78, -83,
WhoAm 74, -76, -78, -80, -82, -84,
-86, WhoE 74, WrDr 76, -80, -82,
-84
Arnason, H H 1909- *ConAu 13NR*
Arnason, H H 1909-1986 *ConAu 119*
Arnason, H Harvard d1986
NewYTBS 86
Arnason, H Harvard 1909- *ConAu 61,*
WhoAmA 73, -76, -78, -80, -82, -84
Arneson, D J 1935- *ConAu 106,*
ScF&FL 1, SmATA 37
Arnett, Caroline *BioIn 13*
Arnett, Caroline 1902- *BioIn 11,*
ConAu X, SmATA X
Arnett, Caroline *see also* Cole, Lois
Dwight
Arno, Enrico 1913-1981 *BioIn 4, -5,*
-8, -13, ChhPo S1, -S2, -S3,
FourBJA, IlsBYP, IlsCB 1946, -1957,
-1967, SmATA 28N, -43[port]
Arnold, Alan 1922- *ConAu 5R,*
WhE&EA
Arnold, Arnold 1921- *ChhPo S2,*
ConAu 10NR, -17R
Arnold, Caroline 1944- *ConAu 107,*
SmATA 34, -36

Arnold, Eddy 1918- *AmPS A, -B,
Baker 84, BioIn 1, -4, -7, -8, -9,
-10, -12, CelR, CmpEPM,
CurBio 70, EncFCWM 69, -83[port],
IntMPA 77, -75, -76, -78, -79, -81,
-82, -84, -86, RkOn 74, WhoAm 74,
-76, -78, -80, -82, -84, -86, WorAl*

Arnold, Edmund Clarence 1913-
*BlueB 76, ConAu 1R, -3NR,
MichAu 80, WhoCon 73, WhoWor 74,
WrDr 76, -80, -82, -84, -86*

Arnold, Elliott 1912- *EncFWF*

Arnold, Elliott 1912-1980 *AmAu&B,
AmNov, AnObit 1980[port],
Au&Wr 71, BioIn 2, -4, -8,
-10, -12, -13, BlueB 76, ConAu 17R,
-97, NewYTBS 80, SmATA 22N, -5,
TwCA SUP, WhAm 7, WhoAm 74,
-76, -78, -80, WhoWest 74, -76, -78,
-80, WhoWor 74, -76, -78, -80,
WrDr 76, -80*

Arnold, Emily *DrAP&F 85*

Arnold, Emily 1939- *ConAu 109*

Arnold, Eve 1913- *BioIn 10, -12,
ConAu 112, ConPhot, ICPEnP A,
MacBEP, WomWMM, -A, -B*

Arnold, Francena H 1888- *ConAu P-1*

Arnold, Harry L, Jr. 1912-
*AmM&WS 86P, BiDrACP 79,
BlueB 76, WhoAm 74, -76, -78, -80,
-82, WhoWor 74, -76, -78, -80, -82,
-84, -87, WrDr 76, -80, -82, -84*

Arnold, Harry Loren, Jr. 1912-
WhoAm 84, -86

Arnold, Lois B *ConAu 107*

Arnold, Margot *ConAu X,
IntAu&W 82X, -86X*

Arnold, Oren 1900- *BioIn 3, -9, -10,
ConAu 2NR, -5R, SmATA 4*

Arnold, Pauline 1894-1974 *ConAu 1R,
-2NR, InWom*

Arnold, Peter 1943- *ConAu 1NR, -49,
IntAu&W 77, WrDr 76, -80, -82,
-84, -86*

Arnold, Richard 1912- *Au&Wr 71,
ConAu 3NR, -9R*

Arnold, William Van 1941- *ConAu 110*

Arnold-Forster, Mark 1920-1981
ConAu 105, -65

Arnosky, Jim 1946- *BioIn 13,
ConAu 12NR, -69, FifBJA[port],
SmATA 22[port]*

Arnothy, Christine 1930- *Au&Wr 71,
ConAu 10NR, -65, IntAu&W 76,
-77, REn, ScF&FL 1, WhoFr 79*

Arnott, Kathleen 1914- *BioIn 12,
ConAu 57, SmATA 20*

Arnov, Boris, Jr. 1926- *AuBYP,
BioIn 7, -11, ConAu 1R, -3NR,
SmATA 12*

Arnow, Harriette 1908- *AmAu&B,
AmNov, AmWomWr, BioIn 2, -3, -4,
-10, -11, ConAu 9R, -14NR,
ConLC 2, -7, -18, ConNov 76, -82,
CurBio 54, DcLB 6[port], InWom,
IntAu&W 76, MichAu 80,
OxAmL 83, SmATA 42[port],
WhoAmW 66, WorAu, WrDr 76, -80,
-82, -84, -86*

Arnow, Harriette 1908-1986 *BioIn 13,
ConAu 118, ConNov 86*

Arnow, Harriette Simpson 1908-1986
CurBio 86N, SmATA 47N

Arntson, Herbert Edward 1911-
*BioIn 11, ConAu 17R, DrAS 74E,
-78E, -82E, SmATA 12, WhoPNW*

Arpel, Adrien 1941- *WhoAm 84, -86*

Arquette, Lois S 1934- *BioIn 9, -12,
ConAu X, SmATA 1*

Arquette, Lois S *see also* Cardozo, Lois
S

Arquette, Lois S *see also* Duncan, Lois

Arquette, Lois S *see also* Kerry, Lois

Arr, E H 1831-1881 *Alli SUP,
DcAmAu, DcNAA*

Arr, E H *see also* Rollins, Ellen
Chapman Hobbs

Arre, John 1926- *ConAu X*

Arre, John *see also* Holt, John Robert

Arthur, Robert *SmATA X*

Arthur, Robert 1909- *HalFC 84,
IntMPA 86*

Arthur, Robert 1909-1969
*AuBYP SUP, BioIn 8, ConAu X,
FilmgC, IntMPA 77, -75, -76, -78,
-79, -84, ScF&FL 1, WhoHr&F*

Arthur, Ruth M 1905-1979
*Au&Wr 71, AuBYP SUP, BioIn 10,
-11, -13, BritCA, ChhPo,
ConAu 4NR, -9R, -85, ConLC 12,
FifBJA[port], IntAu&W 76, -77,
OxChL, ScF&FL 1, -1A, -2,
SmATA 26N, -7, TwCCW 78, -83,
WrDr 80*

Artzybasheff, Boris 1899-1965
*AmAu&B, AmPB, AnCL, AuBYP,
BioIn 1, -2, -3, -5, -7, -8, -12,
ChhPo S2, ConICB, CurBio 45, -65,
DcAmB S7, EncAJ, ForII,
IlrAm 1880, -D, IlsCB 1744, JBA 34,
-51, LinLib L, SmATA 14, Str&VC,
WhAm 4, WhoAmA 78N, WhoGrA 62*

Arundel, Honor 1919-1973 *Au&Wr 71,
AuBYP SUP, BioIn 9, -10, -13,
ConAu 41R, ConAu P-2, ConLC 17,
FourBJA, OxChL, SmATA 24N, -4,
TwCCW 78, -83*

Arvio, Raymond Paavo 1930-
ConAu 77

Arvio, Raymond Paavo 1930-1986
ConAu 120

Ascher, Carol *DrAP&F 85*

Ash, Brian 1936- *ConAu 114, EncSF,
WrDr 80, -82, -84, -86*

Ashabranner, Brent 1921- *BioIn 9,
BlueB 76, ConAu 5R, -10NR,
SmATA 1, WhoAm 74, -76, -78, -80*

Ashbery, John *DrAP&F 85*

Ashbery, John 1927- *AmAu&B,
BioIn 8, -10, -11, -12, BlueB 76,
ChhPo S2, ConAu 5R, -9NR,
ConLC 2, -3, -4, -6, -9, -13, -15,
-25[port], -41[port], ConPo 70, -75,
-80, -85, CroCAP, CurBio 76,
DcLB 5[port], -Y81A[port],
DcLEL 1940, IntWWP 77, LinLib L, ModAL S2,
-S1, NewYTBS 82, OxAmL 83,
PenC AM, RAdv 1, WebE&AL,
WhoAm 74, -76, -78, -80, -82,
WhoAmA 78, -80, -82, WhoE 77,
-79, -81, -83, WhoWor 74, -76, -78,
WorAu, WrDr 76, -80, -82, -84, -86*

Ashe, Arthur *NewYTBS 85*

Ashe, Arthur 1943- *BioIn 6, -7, -8,
-9, -10, -11, -12, -13, BioNews 74,
BlueB 76, CelR, ConAu 18NR, -65,
CurBio 66, Ebony 1, InB&W 80,
IntWW 78, -79, -80, -81, -82, -83,
NegAl 76, -83[port], NewYTBS 77,
-79, WebAB, -79, WhoAm 74, -76,
-78, -80, -82, -84, -86, WhoBlA 75,
-77, -80, WhoS&SW 73, -75, -76,
WhoTech 82, WorAl*

Ashe, Geoffrey 1923- *ConAu 12NR*

Asher, Sandy 1942- *ConAu 105,
DcLB Y83B[port], IntAu&W 86,
SmATA 34, -36*

Ashford, Jeffrey *TwCCr&M 85,
WrDr 86*

Ashford, Jeffrey 1926- *Au&Wr 71,
AuBYP, BioIn 8, -9, ConAu 1R, -X,
EncMys, IntAu&W 76,
TwCCr&M 80, WrDr 76, -80, -82,
-84*

Ashford, Jeffrey *see also* Jeffries,
Roderic

Ashley, Bernard 1935- *ChlLR 4[port],
ConAu 93, IntAu&W 82, -86,
OxChL, SmATA 39, -47[port],
TwCCW 78, -83, WrDr 80, -82, -84,
-86*

Ashner, Sonie Shapiro 1938- *ConAu 57*

Ashton, Dore *WhoAm 84, -86,
WhoAmA 84, WhoAmW 85, -87,
WrDr 86*

Ashton, Dore 1928- *AmAu&B,
ConAu 2NR, -5R, IntAu&W 77, -82,
WhoAm 74, -76, -78, -80, -82,
WhoAmA 73, -76, -78, -80, -82,
WhoAmW 58, -61, -64, -66, -68,
-83, WhoE 75, -77, WrDr 76, -80,
-82, -84*

Ashton-Warner, Sylvia 1908-1984
*AnObit 1984, BioIn 8, -9, -10, -12,
-13, BlueB 76, ConAu 112, -69,
ConLC 19, ConNov 72, -76, -82,
DcLEL 1940, IntAu&W 76, -77,
IntDcWB, LongCTC, ModCmwL,
NewYTBS 84, Novels, PenC ENG,
RAdv 1, TwCWr, WorAu, WrDr 76,
-80, -82, -84*

Ashworth, Mae Hurley *IndAu 1917*

Asimov, Isaac *DrAP&F 85*

Asimov, Isaac 1920- *AmAu&B,
AmM&WS 73P, -76P, -79P, -82P,
-86P, AsBiEn, Au&Wr 71, AuBYP,
BioIn 3, -7, -8, -9, -10, -11, -12,
-13, BlueB 76, CasWL, CelR,
ChlLR 12[port], ConAu 1R, -2NR,
-19NR, ConLC 1, -3, -9, -19,
-26[port], ConNov 72, -76, -82, -86,
ConSFA, CurBio 53, -68,
DcLB 8[port], DcLEL 1940, EncMys,
EncSF, Future, IntAu&W 76, -77,
-82, -86, IntWW 74, -75, -76, -77,
-78, -79, -80, -81, -82, -83,
LinLib L, -S, LongCTC, MakMC,
Novels[port], OxAmL 83, PenC AM,
REn, REnAL, ScF&FL 1, -2,
ScFSB[port], SmATA 1, -26[port],
ThrBJA, TwCSFW 86, -85,
TwCSFW 86, TwCWr, WebAB, -79,
WebE&AL, Who 82, -83, -85,
WhoAm 74, -76, -78, -80, -82, -84,
-86, WhoAmJ 80, -WhoE 74, -81,
-83, WhoSciF, WhoWor 74, -76, -78,
-80, -82, -84, -87, WhoWorJ 78,
WorAl, WorAu, WrDr 76, -80, -82,
-84, -86*

Asinof, Eliot 1919- *ConAu 7NR, -9R,
SmATA 6, WrDr 76, -80, -82, -84,
-86*

Asprin, Robert 1946- *ConAu 85,
ScFSB, TwCSFW 86, WrDr 84, -86*

Astor, Gerald *WrDr 86*

Atkinson, Brooks d1984 *Who 85N*

Atkinson, Brooks 1894- *BiE&WWA,
BioIn 1, -4, -5, -6, -7, -10,
BlueB 76, CelR, ConAu 61,
CurBio 42, -61, EncWT,
IntAu&W 77, LinLib L, -S,
NewYTBE 73, NotNAT,
OxAmL, -83, OxThe, -83, REnAL,
TwCA, -SUP, WebAB, -79, WhNAA,
Who 74, -82, -83, WhoThe 81,
WorAl, WrDr 76, -80, -82*

Atkinson, Brooks 1894-1984
*AnObit 1984, BioIn 13, ConAu 111,
-14NR, CurBio 84N, EncTwCJ,
NewYTBS 84[port], OxAmT 84*

Atkinson, Margaret Fleming *AuBYP,
BioIn 8, -12, ConAu 73, SmATA 14*

Atmore, Anthony 1932- *ConAu 25R*

Attanasio, A A *ScFSB*

Attenborough, David Frederick 1926-
*Au&Wr 71, BioIn 12, -13, BlueB 76,
ConAu 1R, -6NR, CurBio 83[port],
IntAu&W 77, IntMPA 77, -75, -76,
-78, -79, -81, -82, -84, IntWW 75,
-76, -77, -78, -79, -80, -81, -82,
-83, Who 74, -82, -83, -85,
WhoWor 76, -78, -82, -84, WrDr 76,
-80, -82, -84*

Atticus *ConAu X, SmATA X*

Atticus *see also* Fleming, Ian

Atwater, Constance Elizabeth 1923-
ConAu 13R

Atwater, James D 1928- *WhoMW 86*

Atwater, James David 1928-
*ConAu 101, WhoAm 74, -76, -78,
-80, -82, -84, -86*

Atwood, Ann Margaret *IntAu&W 86*

Atwood, Ann Margaret 1913-
*AuBYP SUP, BioIn 10, ConAu 41R,
FourBJA, IntAu&W 82, SmATA 7,
WhoAm 74, -76, -78, -80, -82, -84,
-86, WhoAmW 74, WrDr 82, -84*

Atwood, Margaret *DrAP&F 85,
NewYTBS 86[port]*

Atwood, Margaret 1939-
*ConLC 44[port], ConNov 86,
ConPo 85, CurBio 84[port],
DcLB 53[port], IntAu&W 86,
OxCanL, OxEng 85, WhoCanL 85,
WrDr 86*

Atwood, Margaret Eleanor 1939-
*Au&Wr 71, BioIn 10, -11, -12, CaW,
CanWW 70, -79, -80, -81, -83,
ConAu 3NR, -49, ConLC 2, -3, -4,
-8, -13, -15, -25[port], ConNov 76,
-82, ConPo 70, -75, -80,
DcLEL 1940, EncWL 2,
IntAu&W 76, -77, -82, IntDcWB,
IntWWP 77, -82, ModCmwL,
NewYTBS 82[port], Novels,
OxCan, -SUP, WhoAm 74, -76, -78,
-80, -84, -86, WhoAmW 81, -83,
-85, -87, WhoWor 80, -82,
WorAu 1970, WrDr 76, -80, -82, -84*

Auchincloss, Louis *DrAP&F 85,
NewYTBS 85[port]*

Auchincloss, Louis 1917- *AmAu&B,
Au&Wr 71, BioIn 3, -4, -5, -6, -7,
-8, -10, -11, -12, -13, BlueB 76,
CelR, ConAu 1R, -6NR, ConLC 4,
-6, -9, -18, ConLCrt, -82,
ConNov 72, -76, -82, -86, CurBio 54,
-78, DcLB 2, -Y80A[port],
DcLEL 1940, IntAu&W 76, -77,
IntWW 74, -75, -76, -77, -78, -79,
-80, -81, -82, -83, LinLib L,
ModAL, -S2, -S1, NewYTBS 79,
Novels, OxAmL 83, PenC AM,
RAdv 1, REn, REnAL, TwCWr,
WebE&AL, Who 74, -82, -83,
WhoAm 74, -76, -78, -80, -82,
WhoAmL 78, -79, -83, WhoWor 74,
-78, -80, -82, WorAl, WorAu,
WrDr 76, -80, -82, -84, -86*

Auchincloss, Louis Stanton 1917-
*Who 85, WhoAm 84, -86, WhoE 85,
WhoWor 84, -87*

Auden, W H 1907-1973 *AmAu&B,
AmSCAP 66, AmWr S2, Au&Wr 71,
BiE&WWA, BritWr 7, CasWL, CelR,
Chambr 3, ChhPo, -S1, -S2,
CnE&AP, CnMD, CnMWL,
ConAu 5NR, -9R, -45, ConDr 73,
ConLC 1, -2, -3, -4, -6, -9, -11,
-14, -43[port], ConLCrt, -82,
ConPo 70, -75, -80A, CurBio 71, -73,
-73N, CyWA, DcLB 10[port],
-20[port], DcLEL, EncWL, -2[port],
EvLB, LinLib L, -S, LongCTC,
McGEWD, -84[port], ModAL, -S2,
-S1, ModBrL, -S2, -S1, ModWD,
NewC, NewEOp 71, NewYTBE 71,
-72, -73, ObitOF 79, ObitT 1971,
OxAmL, -83, OxEng, -85,
PenC ENG, PIP&P, RAdv 1,
RComWL, REn, REnAL,
TwCA, -SUP, TwCWr, WebE&AL,
WhThe, WhoThe 72, WhoTwCL,
WorAl*

Audubon, John James 1785-1851
*BioIn 13, MemAm, NatLAC,
OxAmL 83, OxEng 85*

Auel, Jean M 1936- *BioIn 12,
ConAu 103, -21NR, ConLC 31[port],
NewYTBS 80[port], WrDr 86*

Auerbach, Arnold 1917- *BioIn 6, -7,
-8, -9, -10, -11, -12, CelR,
CurBio 69, WhoAm 74, -76, -78,
-80, -82, WhoBbl 73, WhoE 74, -79,
-81, -83, -85*

Auerbach, Arnold *see also* Auerbach,
Red

Auerbach, Red *WhoAm 84, -86*

Auerbach, Red 1917- *BioIn 6, -7, -8,
-9, -10, -11, -12, CurBio 69*

Auerbach, Red *see also* Auerbach,
Arnold

Ault, Phil H 1914- *BioIn 1, ConAu X,
SmATA X*

Ault, Phillip H 1914- *AuBYP SUP,
BioIn 13, ConAu 101, -18NR,
IntYB 78, -79, -80, -81, -82,
SmATA 23[port], WhoAm 74, -76,
-78, -80, WhoMW 74, -76, -78*

Auslander, Joseph 1897-1965
*AmAu&B, BioIn 4, -5, -7,
ChhPo, -S1, CnDAL, ConAu 116,
ObitOF 79, OxAmL, REn,
REnAL, TwCA, -SUP, WhJnl,
WhNAA*

Austen, Jane *NewOxM*

Austen, Jane 1775-1817 *Alli, AtlBL, BbD, BiD&SB, BioIn 1, -2, -3, -4, -5, -6, -7, -8, -9, -10, -11, -12, -13, BritAu 19, BritWr 4, CelCen, Chambr 2, CrtT 2, -4, CyWA, DcBiA, DcBiPP, DcEnA, DcEnL, DcEuL, DcLEL, DcNaB, Dis&D, EvLB, GoodHs, HalFC 84, HerW, -84, InWom, IntDcWB[port], LinLib L, -S, LongCEL, McGEWB, MouLC 2, NewC, NinCLC 1[port], -13[port], Novels[port], OxEng, -85, PenC ENG, RAdv 1, RComWL, REn, WebE&AL, WhDW, WorAl*

Auster, Paul *DrAP&F 85*

Austin, Elizabeth S 1907- *AuBYP SUP, BioIn 10, ConAu P-2, IntAu&W 77, SmATA 5, WhoAmW 72*

Austin, Oliver Luther, Jr. 1903- *AmM&WS 73P, -76P, -79P, -82P, -86P, AuBYP SUP, BioIn 10, ConAu 49, SmATA 7, WhoS&SW 73*

Austin, Paul Britten *ChhPo S3*

Avallone, Michael 1924- *Au&Wr 71, BioIn 7, -11, ConAu 4NR, -5R,*

EncMys, EncSF, IntAu&W 76, -77, Novels, ScF&FL 1, -2, TwCCr&M 80, -85, WhoAm 82, WhoE 83, WhoHr&F, WrDr 76, -80, -82, -84, -86

Avallone, Michael Angelo 1924- *WhoAm 84, -86*

Avery, Gillian Elise 1926- *AuBYP, BioIn 8, -10, ConAu 4NR, -9R, FourBJA, IntAu&W 77, -82, -86, SmATA 7, TwCCW 78, -83, Who 82, -83, -85, WhoChL, WhoWor 80, WrDr 80, -82, -84*

Avery, Ira 1914- *ConAu 81, WhoE 81*

Avery, Lynn *AuBYP, BioIn 11, -13, ConAu X, SmATA X*

Avery, Lynn *see also* Cole, Lois Dwight

Avery, Virginia Turner 1912- *WhoAmW 81*

Avi *ConAu X, SmATA X*

Avi 1937- *FifBJA[port]*

Awad, Elias Michael 1934- *ConAu 11NR, -17R, WhoCon 73, WhoMW 74, -76*

Axelrod, Herbert Richard 1927- *Au&Wr 71, BioIn 7, ConAu 85*

Axtell, James Lewis 1941- *ConAu 108, DrAS 78H, -82H*

Axthelm, Pete 1943- *WhoAm 80, -82, -84, -86*

Ayars, Albert Lee 1917- *AmM&WS 73S, BlueB 76, ConAu 29R, IntAu&W 77, LEduc 74, WhoAm 74, -76, -78, -80, -82, -84, -86, WhoPubR 72, -76, WhoS&SW 80, -82, WhoWor 74, -76, WrDr 76, -80, -82, -84, -86*

Ayars, James Sterling 1898- *AuBYP, BioIn 8, -9, ConAu 2NR, -5R, IntAu&W 77, -82, MichAu 80, SmATA 4, WhoMW 74, -82, -84, WrDr 76, -80, -82, -84, -86*

Ayensu, Edward Solomon 1935- *BioIn 11, WhoBlA 75, -77, -80, -85, WhoGov 77, -75, WhoS&SW 73, -75, -76, WhoWor 78*

Ayer, Margaret *BioIn 5, -6, -12, ConAu 65, ForWC 70, IlsBYP,*

IlsCB 1946, MorJA, SmATA 15, WhoAmW 58, -61

Ayer, Margaret d1981 *ConAu 13NR*

Aylesworth, Thomas Gibbons 1927- *AmM&WS 73P, -76P, -79P, -82P, -86P, AuBYP SUP, BioIn 9, ChlLR 6[port], ConAu 10NR, -25R, IndAu 1917, LEduc 74, ScF&FL 1, -2, SmATA 4, WhoAm 84, -86, WhoE 74, -75, -77, -79, -81, -83, -85*

Ayling, Keith 1898-1976 *BioIn 11, ConAu 69, -73, NewYTBS 76*

Aymar, Brandt 1911- *BioIn 13, ConAu 1R, -16NR, SmATA 22[port], WhNAA*

Azuela, Mariano 1873-1952 *BioIn 1, -2, -3, -5, -9, -10, CasWL, ConAu 104, CyWA, DcSpL, EncLatA, EncWL, -2, LinLib L, McGEWB, ModLAL, ObitOF 79, OxSpan, PenC AM, REn, TwCLC 3, TwCWr, WhAm 5, WhE&EA, WhNAA, WorAu*

B

Baastad, Babbis Friis 1921-1970
ConAu X, SmATA X
Baastad, Babbis Friis *see also*
Friis-Baastad, Babbis Ellinor
Babbis, Eleanor 1921-1970
AuBYP SUP, ConAu X, SmATA X,
ThrBJA
Babbis, Eleanor *see also* Friis-Baastad,
Babbis Ellinor
Babbitt, Natalie *WrDr 86*
Babbitt, Natalie 1932- *AuBYP SUP,*
BioIn 10, -12, ChlLR 2, ChhPo S2,
-S3, ConAu 2NR, -19NR, -49,
DcLB 52[port], FourBJA, IlsCB 1967,
IntAu&W 77, MorBMP, OxChL,
SmATA 6, TwCCW 78, -83,
WhoAm 82, WrDr 76, -80, -82, -84
Babel, Isaac 1894-1941 *LinLib L, -S,*
McGEWB, TwCLC 13[port], WorAl
Babson, Marian *ConAu 102,*
IntAu&W 76, TwCCr&M 80, -85,
WrDr 80, -82, -84, -86
Bacall, Lauren 1924- *BiDFilm,*
BiE&WWA, BioIn 1, -3, -4, -5, -7,
-8, -9, -10, -11, -12, -13, BlueB 76,
CelR, CmMov, ConAu 93,
ConTFT 1[port], CurBio 70, EncMT,
FilmgC, GoodHs, HalFC 84, InWom,
IntDcWB, IntMPA 77, -75, -76, -78,
-79, -81, -82, -84, -86, IntWW 74,
-75, -76, -77, -78, -79, -80, -81,
-82, -83, MotPP, MovMk,
NewYTBE 70, NewYTBS 79,
-80[port], NotNAT, OxAmT 84,
OxFilm, WhoAm 74, -76, -78, -80,
-82, -84, -86, WhoAmJ 80,
WhoAmW 74, -58, -61, -64, -66,
-68, -70, -72, -79, -81, -83, -85,
WhoHol A, WhoThe 72, -77, -81,
WhoWor 74, -78, WorAl, WorEFlm,
WrDr 82, -84, -86
Bach, Alice 1942- *AuBYP SUP,*
ConAu 101, FifBJA[port], ForWC 70,
SmATA 27, -30[port]
Bach, Alice Hendricks 1942- *BioIn 13*
Bach, Mickey 1909- *WhoAmA 76, -78*
Bach, Richard *ConAu 18NR*
Bach, Richard 1936- *AuNews 1,*
BioIn 9, -10, -11, BioNews 74,
ConAu 9R, ConLC 14, CurBio 73,
EncO&P 2, -78S1, Novels, ScF&FL 1,
-2, SmATA 13, WhoAm 76, -78, -80,
WorAl, WrDr 76, -80, -82, -84, -86
Bacher, June Masters 1918-
ConAu 108
Backus, Richard Haven 1922-
AmM&WS 73P, -76P, -79P, -82P
Bacon, Margaret Hope 1921-
BioIn 10, ConAu 25R, SmATA 6,
WrDr 76
Bacon, Martha 1917-1981
AuBYP SUP, BioIn 12, ChlLR 3,
ChhPo S1, ConAu 104, -85,
ScF&FL 1, SmATA 18, -27N,
TwCCW 78, -83

Baen, James 1943- *EncSF*
Baen, James P 1943- *ConAu 112*
Baender, Margaret Woodruff 1921-
WhoWest 84
Baer, Edith R 1920- *ConAu 21NR*
Baer, Edith Ruth 1920- *Au&Wr 71,*
ConAu 104, IntAu&W 76, -77
Baer, Jean L 1926- *ConAu 9NR,*
-13R, WhoAmW 61, -64, -66, -68,
-70, -77, -79, -81, -83, WhoE 74
Baer, Jean Louise 1926- *WhoAmW 87*
Baez, Joan 1941- *Baker 78, -84,*
BiDAmM, BioIn 6, -7, -8, -9, -10,
-11, -12, -13, BioNews 74, BlueB 76,
CelR, ChiSch, CivR 74, CmCal,
ConAu 21R, CurBio 63,
EncFCWM 69, -83[port],
EncPR&S 77, GoodHs, InWom,
IntAu&W 76, IntDcWB, IntWW 76,
-77, -78, -79, -80, -81, -82, -83,
IntWWM 77, LibW, MugS,
NewYTBE 72, PolProf J, RkOn 78,
-84, RolSEnR 83, WebAB, -79,
WhoAm 74, -76, -78, -80, -82, -84,
-86, WhoAmW 74, -66, -68, -70,
-72, -81, -83, WhoRock 81,
WhoRocM 82, WhoWest 74, -76,
-78, WhoWor 74, -78, -80, -82, -84,
WorAl
Baez, Joan Chandos 1941-
WhoAmW 85, -87
Bagdikian, Ben H 1920- *EncAJ*
Bagdikian, Ben Haig 1920- *AmAu&B,*
BioIn 7, -11, -13, ConAu 6NR, -9R,
DrAS 78E, -82E, EncTwCJ,
IntAu&W 77, -82, WhoAm 74, -76,
-78, -80, -82, -84, -86,
WhoS&SW 73, WhoWor 74, -82,
WrDr 76, -80, -82, -84, -86
Baginski, Frank 1938- *ConAu 93*
Bagley, Desmond 1923- *WrDr 86*
Bagley, Desmond 1923-1983
AnObit 1983, Au&Wr 71, BioIn 13,
ConAu 109, -17R, DcLEL 1940,
IntAu&W 76, -77, Novels,
TwCCr&M 80, -85, Who 82, -83,
WhoWor 78, WrDr 76, -80, -82, -84
Bagley, John Joseph 1908- *Au&Wr 71,*
ConAu 5R, IntAu&W 76, -77, -82,
-86, WhoWor 76, WrDr 76, -80, -82,
-84, -86
Bagni, Gwen *ConAu X*
Bagnold, Enid *WomNov*
Bagnold, Enid 1889-1981
AnObit 1981[port], AuBYP,
BiE&WWA, BioIn 2, -4, -6, -7, -8,
-9, -10, -12, -13, BlueB 76,
ChhPo S2, CnMD, ConAu 5R, -5NR,
-103, ConDr 73, -77,
ConLC 25[port], ConNov 76,
CurBio 64, -81N, DcLB 13[port],
DcLEL, EncWT, EvLB, FourBJA,
InWom, IntAu&W 76, -77,
IntWW 78, -79, -80, -81, -81N,

LinLib L, LongCTC, ModWD,
NewC, NewYTBS 81[port],
NotNAT, -A, Novels, OxChL, OxEng,
OxThe 83, PIP&P, REn, SmATA 1,
-25[port], TwCA, -SUP,
TwCChW 83, TwCWr, WhAm 7,
WhE&EA, Who 74, -82N,
WhoAmW 74, -66, -68, -70, -72,
WhoChL, WhoThe 72, -77, -81,
WhoWor 74, -76, -78, WorAl,
WrDr 76, -80, -82
Bailey, Anthony 1933- *BioIn 12,*
ConAu 1R, -3NR, WrDr 86
Bailey, Bernadine Freeman 1901-
AuBYP, BioIn 7, ConAu 5R, -7NR,
ForWC 70, IntAu&W 76, -77,
SmATA 14, WhoAmW 74, -58, -68,
-72
Bailey, Charles Waldo 1929- *BioIn 13,*
WrDr 86
Bailey, Charles Waldo, II 1929-
BioIn 7, ConAu 1R, -1NR,
EncTwCJ, ScF&FL 1, -2,
WhoAm 74, -76, -78, -80, -82, -84,
-86, WrDr 76, -80, -82, -84
Bailey, F Lee 1933- *BioIn 7, -8, -9,*
-10, -11, CelR, ConAu 89,
CurBio 67, NewYTBE 70,
WebAB, -79, WhoAm 74, -76, -78,
-80, -82, WhoAmL 78, -79,
WhoE 74, WorAl
Bailey, Jane H 1916- *BioIn 11,*
ConAu 4NR, -53, SmATA 12,
WhoAmW 77
Bailey, Maralyn Collins 1941-
BioIn 11, ConAu 53, IntAu&W 77,
SmATA 12
Bailey, Maurice Charles 1932-
BioIn 11, ConAu 53, SmATA 12
Bailey, Pearl 1918- *AmPS B,*
AmSCAP 66, Baker 84, BiDAfM,
BiDAmM, BiDJaz, BiE&WWA,
BioIn 3, -4, -6, -8, -9, -10, -11, -12,
CelR, CmpEPM, ConAu 14NR, -61,
ConTFT 4, CurBio 55, -69, DrBlPA,
Ebony 1, EncJzS, EncMT, FilmgC,
HalFC 84, HerW, -84, InB&W 80,
InWom, IntMPA 77, -75, -76, -78,
-79, -81, -82, -84, -86, LivgBAA,
MotPP, MovMk, NegAl 76, -83[port],
NewYTBE 71, NotNAT, -A,
OxAmT 84, SelBAAu, WhoAm 74,
-76, -78, -80, -82, -84, -86,
WhoAmW 74, -58, -64, -66, -68,
-70, -72, -77, -83, -85, WhoBlA 75,
-77, -80, -85, WhoHol A,
WhoThe 72, -77, -81, WhoWor 74,
WorAl, WrDr 80, -82, -84, -86
Bailey, Pearl Mae 1918- *InB&W 85,*
SelBAAf
Bailey, Ralph Edgar 1893- *BioIn 11,*
ConAu P-1, SmATA 11
Baillie, Allan 1943- *ConAu 118*

Bainbridge, Beryl 1934- *ASpks,*
BioIn 10, -11, -12, -13, ConAu 21R,
ConLC 4, -5, -8, -10, -14, -18,
-22[port], ConNov 76, -82, -86,
DcLB 14[port], EncWL 2,
IntAu&W 76, IntWW 81, -82, -83,
ModBrL S2, NewYTBS 81[port],
Novels, OxEng 85, Who 82, -83,
WhoWor 84, -87, WorAu 1970,
WrDr 76, -80, -82, -84, -86
Baird, Bil 1904- *BiE&WWA, BioIn 1,*
-3, -5, -10, BioNews 74, CelR,
ChhPo S2, ConAu 106, CurBio 54,
NotNAT, SmATA 30[port],
WhoThe 81, WorAl
Baird, Eva-Lee *AuBYP SUP*
Baird, Marie-Terese 1918- *ConAu 57*
Baird, Thomas 1923- *Alli, AmAu&B,*
ConAu 4NR, -21NR, -53,
SmATA 39, WrDr 76, -80, -82, -84,
-86
Baird, Thomas P 1923-
SmATA 45[port]
Baity, Elizabeth Chesley 1907-
AmAu&B, AnCL, BioIn 3, -6, -9,
ConAu 29R, MorJA, SmATA 1
Bakeless, John Edwin 1894-1978
AmAu&B, Au&Wr 71, AuBYP,
BioIn 4, -7, -11, -13, ConAu 5R,
-5NR, DrAS 74E, IntAu&W 76,
NatCAB 61[port], REnAL, SmATA 9,
TwCA, -SUP, WhAm 7, WhE&EA,
WhNAA, WhoAm 74, -76, -78,
WhoWor 74, WrDr 76
Bakeless, Katherine Little 1895-
Au&Wr 71, BioIn 11, ConAu 5R,
IntAu&W 76, SmATA 9,
WhoAmW 64, -66, WhoE 74,
WrDr 76, -80, -82, -84
Baker, Betty 1928- *AmAu&B, AuBYP,*
BioIn 8, -9, -10, ConAu 1R, -2NR,
ScF&FL 1, -2, SmATA 5, ThrBJA,
TwCCW 78, -83, WhoAmW 74, -64,
-66, -68, -70, -72, WhoWest 74, -76,
WrDr 84, -86
Baker, Betty *see also* Venturo, Betty
Lou Baker
Baker, Carlos 1909- *AmAu&B, ASpks,*
BioIn 10, -11, BlueB 76, ChhPo, -S3,
ConAu 3NR, -5R, ConLCrt, -82,
DcLEL 1940, DrAS 74E, -78E, -82E,
IntAu&W 77, -82, IntWW 74, -75,
-76, -77, -78, -79, -80, -81, -82,
-83, LinLib L, REnAL, WhNAA,
WhoAm 74, -76, -78, -80,
WhoWor 74, WorAu, WrDr 76, -80,
-82, -84, -86
Baker, Charlotte 1910- *AuBYP,*
BioIn 5, -7, -9, ConAu 17R,
IlsCB 1946, IntAu&W 77X,
SmATA 2, WhoAmW 58, -61, -64,
-66

Baker, Elizabeth 1923- *AuBYP SUP, BioIn 10, ConAu 1R, −3NR, SmATA 7, WrDr 76, −80, −82, −84, −86*
Baker, Ivon Robert 1928- *ConAu 73, WhoWor 80*
Baker, Jeffrey John Wheeler 1931- *AmM&WS 73P, −76P, −79P, −82P, BioIn 10, ConAu 1NR, −49, SmATA 5, WhoE 83*
Baker, Jerry *AuNews 2, BioIn 11, BusPN, ConAu 105*
Baker, Jim *ConAu X, SmATA X*
Baker, Laura Nelson 1911- *Au&Wr 71, AuBYP, BioIn 6, −8, −9, ConAu 5R, −5NR, ForWC 70, MinnWr, SmATA 3, WrDr 76, −80, −84*
Baker, Leonard 1931- *Alli SUP, AmM&WS 79P, −86P, ConAu 21R, OxAmL 83, WhoAm 80, −82, WhoAmJ 80, WhoS&SW 73, −75, −76, WrDr 76, −80, −82, −84, −86*
Baker, Lucinda 1916- *ConAu 65, WhoAmW 77, −79, −81, WrDr 80, −82, −84, −86*
Baker, Marilyn 1929- *BioIn 10, BioNews 75, ConAu 111, EncTwCJ, WhoAm 76, −78, −80, −82, −84, WhoAmW 77, −79, WhoWor 78*
Baker, Nina 1888-1957 *AmAu&B, AuBYP, BioIn 1, −2, −4, −7, −12, CurBio 47, −57, InWom, JBA 51, ScF&FL 1A, SmATA 15*
Baker, Rachel 1903-1978 *BioIn 13*
Baker, Rachel 1904-1978 *AuBYP, BioIn 6, −7, −9, BkCL, ConAu 5R, −103, MorJA, SmATA 2, −26N*
Baker, Robert H 1883- *WhNAA*
Baker, Russell 1925- *AmAu&B, ASpks, BioIn 8, −9, −10, −11, −12, CelR, ConAu 11NR, −57, ConLC 31[port], CurBio 80[port], DcLEL 1940, EncAJ, NewYTBS 82[port], ScF&FL 1, −2, WhoAm 74, −76, −78, −80, −82, WhoS&SW 73, WorAl, WorAu 1970, WrDr 80, −82, −84, −86*
Baker, Russell *EncTwCJ*
Baker, Russell Wayne 1925- *BioIn 13, WhoAm 84, −86, WhoE 85*
Baker, Samm Sinclair 1909- *BioIn 11, ConAu 3NR, −5R, −21NR, IntAu&W 77, −86, NewYTBS 79, SmATA 12*
Baker, Scott *ScFSB*
Baker, Scott 1947- *ConAu 93*
Baker, Susan 1942- *BioIn 13*
Baker, William Joseph 1938- *ConAu 69, DrAS 74H, −78H, −82H*
Balaam *ConAu X, IntAu&W 76X, LongCEL, SmATA X, WrDr 76, −80, −82, −86*
Balaam *see also* Lamb, Geoffrey Frederick
Balch, Glenn 1902- *AmAu&B, AuBYP, BioIn 6, −7, −9, ConAu 1R, −3NR, MorJA, SmATA 3, WhE&EA, WhoAm 74, −76, −78, −80, −82, −84, −86, WhoPNW, WhoWest 74, −76, −78*
Balchen, Bernt 1899-1973 *BioIn 1, −2, −3, −4, −5, −10, ConAu 45, CurBio 49, −73, −73N, InSci, NewYTBE 73, ObitOF 79, WebAMB, WhAm 6, WhoAm 74, WhoWor 74, WorAl*
Balderson, Margaret *WrDr 86*
Balderson, Margaret 1935- *ConAu 25R, FourBJA, OxAusL, TwCCW 78, −83, WrDr 80, −82, −84*
Baldick, Robert 1927-1972 *Au&Wr 71, BioIn 10, ConAu 89, ObitT 1971, WhoTran FRE*
Balducci, Carolyn *DrAP&F 85*
Balducci, Carolyn 1946- *AuBYP SUP, BioIn 10, ConAu 33R, SmATA 5, WhoAmW 79, −81, −83*
Baldwin, Ed 1935- *ConAu 118*
Baldwin, Edward R 1935- *ConAu 21NR*
Baldwin, Edward Robinson 1935- *AmArch 70, ConAu 45, IntAu&W 76*

Baldwin, Gordon C 1908- *AuBYP SUP, BioIn 11, ConAu 1R, −3NR, SmATA 12, WrDr 84, −86*
Baldwin, James *DrAP&F 85*
Baldwin, James 1924- *AmAu&B, AmWr S1, BioIn 3, −5, −6, −7, −8, −9, −10, −11, −12, BlueB 76, BlkAWP, CasWL, CelR, CivR 74, CivRSt, ConAu 1R, −3NR, ConAu 1BS, ConDr 73, −77, −82, ConLC 1, −2, −3, −4, −5, −8, −13, −15, −17, −42[port], ConNov 72, −76, −82, −86, ConTFT 3, CroCD, CurBio 59, −64, DcLB 2, −7[port], −33[port], DcLEL 1940, Ebony 1, EncAB-H, EncAJ, EncWL, −2, EncWT, InB&W 80, IntAu&W 76, −77, IntWW 74, −75, −76, −77, −78, −79, −80, −81, −82, −83, LinLib L, −S, LivgBAA, LongCTC, MakMC, McGEWB, McGEWD, −84[port], ModAL, −S2, −S1, ModBlW, ModWD, NatPD 81[port], NegAl 76[port], −83[port], NewCon[port], NewYTBE 72, NotNAT, −A, Novels[port], OxAmL, −83, OxEng 85, PenC AM, PolProf J, PolProf K, RAdv 1, REn, REnAL, SelBAAf, SelBAAu, SmATA 9, TwCWr, WebAB, −79, WebE&AL, WhDW, Who 74, −82, −83, −85, WhoAm 74, −76, −78, −80, −82, −84, −86, WhoBlA 75, −77, −80, −85, WhoE 74, −75, WhoTwCL, WhoWor 74, −78, WorAl, WorAu, WrDr 76, −80, −82, −84, −86*
Baldwin, Ned *ConAu X*
Baldwin, Ned *see also* Baldwin, Edward Robinson
Baldwin, Stan 1929- *BioIn 13, ConAu 2NR, −17NR, −49, SmATA 28*
Baldwin, Stanley Conrad 1929- *WhoRel 75, −77*
Bales, Carol Ann 1940- *BioIn 13, ConAu 45, SmATA 29*
Bales, William Alan 1917- *BioIn 10, ConAu 5R*
Balfour, Michael 1908- *Au&Wr 71, ConAu 6NR, −9R, WrDr 84, −86*
Balin, Marty 1942- *Baker 84, BioIn 9, WhoAm 74, −80, −82, −84, −86, WhoRocM 82*
Balin, Marty 1943- *BioIn 13, WhoRock 81*
Balin, Marty *see also* Jefferson Airplane
Balio, Agaton Thomas 1937- *DrAS 74E, −78E, −82E*
Balis, Andrea F 1948- *ConAu 108*
Ball, Brian N 1932- *ConAu 33R, EncSF, ScF&FL 1, ScFSB, TwCSFW 86*
Ball, David Raphael 1937- *ConAu 65, DrAS 74F, −78F, −82F*
Ball, Doris Bell *WrDr 86*
Ball, Doris Bell 1897- *Au&Wr 71, BioIn 6, ConAu 1R, −2NR, −18NR, EncMys, WhE&EA, WrDr 82, −84*
Ball, John Dudley, Jr. 1911- *AmAu&B, Au&Wr 71, AuBYP, BioIn 8, BlueB 76, ConAu 3NR, −5R, ConSFA, EncMys, EncSF, IntAu&W 76, −77, −82, −86, Novels, ScF&FL 1, −2, TwCCr&M 80, WhoAm 74, −76, −78, −80, −82, −84, −86, WhoWest 74, −76, −78, WhoWor 76, −80, −82, −84, WorAl, WrDr 76, −80, −82, −84*
Ball, Zachary *AuBYP, BioIn 3, −7, −9, ConAu X, CurBio 53, FourBJA, SmATA 3*
Ball, Zachary *see also* Masters, Kelly Ray
Ballantine, William 1911- *ConAu 106*
Ballantyne, Sheila *DrAP&F 85*
Ballantyne, Sheila 1936- *ConAu 101*
Ballard, J G *DrAP&F 85*
Ballard, J G 1930- *Au&Wr 71, ConAu 1R, −15NR, ConLC 3, −6, −14, −36[port], ConNov 72, −76, −82, −86, ConSFA, DcLB 14[port], EncSF, IntAu&W 76, −77, −82, ModBrL S2, Novels, OxEng 85, PostFic, ScF&FL 1, −2, ScFSB[port],*

TwCSFW 86, WhoSciF, WorAu, WrDr 76, −80, −82, −84, −86
Ballard, Martin 1929- *Au&Wr 71, BioIn 9, ConAu 25R, SmATA 1, TwCCW 78, −83, WrDr 80, −82, −84, −86*
Ballard, Willis Todhunter 1903- *ConAu 13R, IntAu&W 77, OhA&B, TwCCr&M 80, WrDr 76, −80, −82*
Ballard, Willis Todhunter 1903-1980 *TwCCr&M 85*
Balliett, Whitney 1926- *AmAu&B, ConAu 13NR, −17R, DcLEL 1940, WhoAm 74, −76, −78, −80, −82, −84, −86, WrDr 76, −80, −82, −84, −86*
Ballou, Arthur W 1915- *ConAu 25R, ScF&FL 1, −2*
Ballou, Robert O 1892-1977 *AmAu&B, BioIn 11*
Balmer, Edwin 1883-1959 *AmAu&B, ConAu 13R, EncMys, EncSF, ObitOF 79, REnAL, ScF&FL 1, TwCCr&M 80, −85, WhAm 3, WhNAA*
Balsdon, John Percy Vyvian Dacre 1901-1977 *Au&Wr 71, BioIn 12, BlueB 76, ConAu 5R, −73, WhE&EA, Who 74, WhoWor 76*
Balukas, Jean 1959- *BioIn 11, −12, ConAu 111, GoodHs, WhoAm 80, −82, −84, −86, WorAl*
Balzac, Honore De 1799-1850 *AtlBL, BbD, BiD&SB, BioIn 1, −2, −3, −4, −5, −6, −7, −8, −9, −10, −11, −12, −13, CasWL, CelCen, ChhPo S2, CyWA, DcBiA, DcBiPP, DcEuL, Dis&D, EncMys, EncSF, EncWT, EuAu, EvEuW, GrFLW, LinLib L, −S, McGEWB, McGEWD, −84[port], NewC, NinCLC 5[port], NotNAT B, Novels[port], OxEng, −85, OxFr, OxThe, −83, PenC EUR, RComWL, REn, ScF&FL 1, SupFW, WhDW, WorAl*
Bambara, Toni Cade *BlkWWr, DrAP&F 85*
Bambara, Toni Cade 1931- *BioIn 13*
Bambara, Toni Cade 1939- *BlkAWP, ConAu 29R, ConLC 19, DcLB 38[port], InB&W 80, −85, LivgBAA, SelBAAf, SelBAAu, WhoBlA 75, −77, −80, −85, WorAu 1975[port]*
Bambara, Toni Cade *see also* Cade, Toni
Bamman, Henry A 1918- *BioIn 11, ConAu 5R, −7NR, LEduc 74, ScF&FL 1, −2, SmATA 12*
Bancroft, Anne 1923- *WrDr 86*
Bancroft, Griffing 1907- *AuBYP, AuNews 1, BioIn 10, ConAu 29R, SmATA 6*
Bane, Michael 1950- *ConAu 108*
Baner, Skulda Vanadis 1897-1964 *BioIn 11, ConAu P-1, SmATA 10*
Banister, Manly 1914- *ConAu 41R, EncSF, ScF&FL 1, −2*
Banks, Carolyn *DrAP&F 85*
Banks, Carolyn 1941- *ConAu 105*
Banks, Lynne Reid 1929- *BioIn 13, ConLC 23[port], ConNov 72, −76, −86, DcLEL 1940, IntAu&W 82, −86, Novels, OxChL, TwCChW 83, TwCWr, WhoWor 76*
Banks, Oliver 1941- *ConAu 107*
Banks, Oliver Talcott 1941- *IntAu&W 86*
Banner, Lois W 1939- *ConAu 1NR, −49, DrAS 74H, −78H, −82H*
Banning, Evelyn I 1903- *SmATA 36[port]*
Banning, Evelyn Irene 1903- *ConAu 73, SmATA 36, WhoAmW 79, WrDr 76, −80, −82, −84, −86*
Bannister, Roger 1929- *Au&Wr 71, BioIn 3, −4, −5, −6, −7, −9, −10, −12, BlueB 76, CurBio 56, InSci, IntWW 79, −80, −81, −82, −83, WhDW, Who 74, −82, −83, −85, −85S, WhoTr&F 73, WhoWor 74, −76, WorAl, WrDr 76, −80, −82, −84, −86*
Baraheni, Reza 1935- *ConAu 69, WhoE 79, WorAu 1975[port]*

Baraka, Amiri *BioIn 13, DrAP&F 85*
Baraka, Amiri 1934- *AmWr S2, BioIn 12, ConDr 82, ConLC 33[port], ConNov 82, ConPo 80, −85, DcLB 5[port], −7, −16[port], −38[port], EncWL 2, ModAL S2, ModBlW, NewCon[port], WebE&AL, WhoAm*
Baraka, Amiri *see also* Jones, LeRoi
Barbary, James *BioIn 11, ConAu X, SmATA X*
Barbary, James *see also* Baumann, Amy Beeching
Barbary, James *see also* Beeching, Jack
Barber, D F 1940- *ConAu 21NR, −61*
Barber, D F *see also* Fletcher, David
Barber, Elsie Oakes 1914- *AmAu&B, AmNov, BioIn 2, InWom, WhoAmW 58*
Barber, James David 1930- *AmM&WS 73S, −78S, BioIn 8, −12, BlueB 76, ConAu 6NR, −13R, WhoAm 74, −76, −78, −80, −82, −84, −86, WrDr 76, −80, −82, −84, −86*
Barber, Richard 1941- *ConAu 13NR, −33R, IntAu&W 82, SmATA 35, WrDr 80, −82, −84, −86*
Barclay, Glen St. John 1930- *ConAu 77*
Bardi, Pietro Maria 1900- *ConAu 19NR, −85, WhoWor 74, −76, −78, −80, −82, −84*
Barfield, Arthur Owen 1898- *Au&Wr 71, ConAu 5R, DcLEL, IntAu&W 76, WhE&EA, WrDr 76*
Bark, Joseph Paul 1946- *WhoS&SW 84, −86*
Barker, A J 1918-1981 *ConAu 7NR, −104, −13R*
Barker, Arthur James 1918-1981 *IntAu&W 76, −77, Who 74, −82N, WhoWor 76, −80*
Barker, Carol 1938- *BioIn 6, −8, ChhPo S1, ConAu 107, IlsBYP, IlsCB 1957, −1967, InWom, SmATA 31[port]*
Barker, Eric 1905-1973 *BioIn 9, −10, ConAu 1R, −41R, ConPo 70, IntWWP 77*
Barker, Mildred Joy 1900- *ForWC 70*
Barkley, James Edward 1941- *BioIn 10, −12, IlsBYP, IlsCB 1967, SmATA 6*
Barkow, Al 1932- *ConAu 4NR, −53, WrDr 76, −80, −82, −84, −86*
Barlow, Judith Ellen 1946- *ConAu 107, DrAS 82E*
Barnaby, Frank 1927- *ConAu 13NR, −33R*
Barnaby, Ralph S d1986 *NewYTBS 86*
Barnaby, Ralph S 1893- *AuBYP SUP, ConAu 61, SmATA 9*
Barnard, Charles Nelson 1924- *ConAu 1NR, −49, WhoAm 74, −76, −78, −80, −82, −84, −86*
Barnard, Robert 1936- *ConAu 20NR, −77, IntAu&W 82, TwCCr&M 85, WhoWor 80, WrDr 86*
Barne, Kitty *ConAu X*
Barne, Kitty 1883-1957 *AuBYP SUP, BioIn 2, −8, JBA 51, OxChL, TwCCW 78, −83, WhoChL*
Barnes, Ben E 1933- *InB&W 80*
Barnes, Clive 1927- *AmAu&B, AuNews 2, BioIn 7, −8, −9, −10, −11, BlueB 76, CelR, ConAmTC, ConAu 77, ConTFT 3, CurBio 72, IntAu&W 77, IntWW 74, −75, −76, −77, −78, −79, −80, −81, −82, −83, NotNAT, OxAmT 84, Who 82, −83, WhoAm 74, −76, −78, −80, −82, WhoE 74, WhoThe 77, −81, WhoWor 78, WrDr 80, −82, −84, −86*
Barnes, Clive Alexander 1927- *OxThe 83, Who 85, WhoAm 84, −86*
Barnes, Eric Wollencott 1907-1962 *AmAu&B, AuBYP, BioIn 6, −8, −13, SmATA 22[port], WhAm 4*
Barnes, Gregory Allen 1934- *ConAu 10NR, −25R*
Barnes, Jonathan 1942- *WrDr 86*
Barnes, Leola Christie 1889- *TexWr, WhE&EA*

Barnes, Margaret Campbell 1891-1962
*BioIn 3, -6, CurBio 53, InWom,
WhAm 4, WhE&EA*
Barness, Richard 1917- *ConAu 65*
Barnet, Sylvan 1926- *WhoAm 84, -86*
Barnett, Correlli 1927- *Au&Wr 71,
ConAu 13R, -15NR, IntAu&W 76,
-82, Who 82, -83, -85, WrDr 76,
-80, -82, -84, -86*
Barnett, Lincoln Kinnear 1909-1979
*AmAu&B, BioIn 10, -12, ConAu 102,
-89, NewYTBS 79, SmATA 36,
WhAm 7, WorAu*
Barnett, Samuel Anthony 1915-
*Au&Wr 71, ConAu 13R,
IntAu&W 76, -77, WrDr 76*
Barnhart, Clarence L 1900-
SmATA 48[port]
Barnhart, Clarence Lewis 1900-
*AmAu&B, BioIn 2, -3, -11,
BlueB 76, ConAu 13R, CurBio 54,
DrAS 74F, NewYTBS 77, WhoAm 74,
-76, -78, -80, -82, -84, -86,
WhoWor 74, WorAl*
Barnouw, Erik 1908- *AmAu&B,
ConAu 12NR, -13R, CurBio 40,
DrAS 74E, -78E, -82E, EncAJ,
LesBEnT[port], NewYTET,
WhoAm 74, -76, -78, -80, -82, -84,
-86, WrDr 84, -86*
Barnouw, Victor 1915-
*AmM&WS 73S, -76P, BioIn 13,
ConAu 85, FifIDA, SmATA 28,
-43[port], WhoAm 74, WhoWor 76*
Barnstone, Aliki *DrAP&F 85*
Barnstone, Aliki 1956- *ChhPo S1,
ConAu 105, IntWWP 82, Po&Wr 77*
Barnstone, Willis *DrAP&F 85*
Barnstone, Willis 1927- *BioIn 12,
ConAu 17R, DrAS 74F, -78F, -82F,
IntAu&W 86, IntWWP 82,
SmATA 20, WhoAm 78, -80, -82,
-84, -86*
Barnwell, William Curtis 1943-
ConAu 103, DrAS 78E
Baron, Richard Warren 1923-
WhoAm 74, -76, -78, -80, -82, -84
Baron, Robert Alex 1920-1980
*BiE&WWA, BioIn 12, ConAu 41R,
NotNAT, WhoE 77, -79*
Baron, Virginia Olsen 1931-
*AuBYP SUP, BioIn 13, ConAu 25R,
SmATA 28, -46*
Barr, Alfred Hamilton 1902-1981
BioIn 13
Barr, Alfred Hamilton, Jr.
WhoArt 84N
Barr, Alfred Hamilton, Jr. 1902-1981
*AmAu&B, AnObit 1981[port],
BioIn 3, -5, -6, -7, -8, -9, -12,
BlueB 76, ConAu 105, -49,
CurBio 61, -81N, IntWW 74, -75,
-76, -77, -78, -79, -80, -81, -82N,
LinLib L, NewYTBS 81[port],
OxAmH, WhAm 8, WhE&EA,
Who 74, -82N, WhoAm 74, -76, -78,
WhoAmA 73, -76, -78, -80, -82N,
-84N, WhoArt 80, -82*
Barr, Stephen 1904- *ConAu P-1*
Barraclough, Elmer Davies 1920-
DrAS 74E, -78E, -82E
Barraclough, Geoffrey 1908- *BioIn 10,
ConAu 101, Who 74, -82, -83, -85,
WhoAm 76, -78, WhoWor 74, -76,
WorAu, WrDr 80, -82, -84, -86*
Barraclough, Geoffrey 1908-1984
AnObit 1984, ConAu 114, WhAm 8
Barraclough, Geoffrey 1908-1985
NewYTBS 85
Barrett, Bob 1925- *ConAu 73*
Barrett, Eugene F 1921- *ConAu 57*
Barrett, Stephen Melvil 1865-
AmAu&B, WhAm 4, WhNAA
Barrett, William E d1986
NewYTBS 86
Barrett, William E 1900-1986
ConAu 120
Barrett, William Edmund 1900-
*AmAu&B, AmCath 80, Au&Wr 71,
BioIn 3, -4, BkC 5, CathA 1952,
ConAu 5R, -6NR, Novels,
IntAu&W 76, REnAL, ScF&FL 1,
-2, WhoAm 74, -76, WhoWor 74,
-76, -78*

Barrie, Alexander 1923- *Au&Wr 71,
ConAu 1R, -5NR, IntAu&W 76, -77,
-82, -86, WhoWor 76, -78, WrDr 76,
-80, -82, -84, -86*
Barrie, J M 1860-1937 *ConAu 104,
Novels, ScF&FL 1, SupFW,
TwCChW 83, TwCLC 2, WorAl*
Barrie, James M 1860-1937
OxAmT 84
Barrie, James Matthew 1860-1937
OxThe 83
Barrie, Sir J M 1860-1937 *CmScLit,
HalFC 84, OxChL[port], OxEng 85*
Barrie, Sir James Matthew 1860-1937
*Alli SUP, AtlBL, BbD, BiD&SB,
BioIn 1, -2, -3, -4, -5, -6, -8, -9,
-10, -11, -12, -13, CarSB, CasWL,
Chambr 3, ChhPo, -S1, -S2, -S3,
CnMD, CnThe, CyWA, DcBiA,
DcEnA, -AP, DcLB 10[port], DcLEL,
DcNaB 1931, Dis&D, EncWL, -2,
EncWT, EvLB, FamAYP, FilmgC,
JBA 34, LinLib L, -S, LongCEL,
LongCTC, McGEWB,
McGEWD, -84[port], ModBrL,
ModWD, NewC, NotNAT A, -B,
OxEng, OxThe, PenC ENG, PlP&P,
RAdv 1, REn, REnWD, TelT,
TwCA, -SUP, TwCCW 78, TwCWr,
WebE&AL, WhDW, WhE&EA,
WhLit, WhScrn 77, -83, WhThe,
WhoChL, WhoStg 1906, -1908,
WhoTwCL, YABC 1*
Barrio, Raymond *DrAP&F 85*
Barrio, Raymond 1921- *ChiLit,
ChiSch, ConAu 11NR, -25R,
WhoAm 74, -76, -78, -80, -82, -84,
-86, WhoAmA 76, -78, -80, -82, -84,
WrDr 76, -80, -82, -84, -86*
Barroll, Clare *BioIn 10*
Barron, Greg 1952- *ConAu 110*
Barrow, John V *ApCAB X*
Barrows, Marjorie d1983 *WhAm 8*
Barrows, Marjorie 1892?-1983
*AmAu&B, AuBYP, BioIn 2, -7,
ChhPo, -S1, -S3, ConAu 109,
ConAu P-2, ScF&FL 1, -2, WhJnl,
WhNAA, WhoAm 74, -76, -78, -80,
-82, WhoAmW 74, -58, -64, -66,
-68, -70, -72*
Barry, Anne Meredith 1932-
*WhoAmA 78, -80, -82, -84,
WhoAmW 77*
Barry, James P 1918- *BioIn 12,
ConAu 37R, IntAu&W 76, -77, -82,
-86, SmATA 14, WhoMW 76, -78,
-80, -82, -84, -86, WrDr 76, -80,
-82, -84, -86*
Barry, Jane 1925- *ConAu 5R,
EncFWF, ForWC 70, IntAu&W 76,
-77, -82, WrDr 76, -80, -82, -84,
-86*
Barry, Joseph 1917- *ConAu 14NR,
-57*
Barry, Joseph Amber 1917-
IntAu&W 86
Bart, Peter *IntMPA 86*
Bart, Peter 1932- *ConAu 19NR, -93,
ConTFT 2, IntMPA 77, -75, -76,
-78, -79, -81, -82, -84*
Barth, Alan 1906- *WrDr 86*
Barth, Alan 1906-1979 *AmAu&B,
Au&Wr 71, BioIn 12, BlueB 76,
ConAu 1R, -5NR, -104, EncAJ,
IntAu&W 76, IntYB 78, -79, -80,
-81, -82, NewYTBS 79, WhAm 7,
WhoAm 74, -76, -78, WhoS&SW 73,
WhoWor 74, WhoWorJ 72, WrDr 80,
-82, -84*
Barth, Edna 1914-1980 *BioIn 13*
Barth, John *DrAP&F 85*
Barth, John 1930- *AmAu&B, AmWr,
Au&Wr 71, AuNews 1, -2, BioIn 6,
-7, -8, -9, -10, -11, -12,
BioNews 74, BlueB 76, CasWL,
ConAu 1R, -5NR, ConAu 1BS,
ConLC 1, -2, -3, -5, -7, -9, -10,
-14, -27[port], ConNov 72, -76, -82,
-86, CurBio 69, DcLB 2,
DcLEL 1940, DrAS 74E, -78E, -82E,
EncSF, EncWL, -2[port],
IntAu&W 76, IntWW 74, -75, -76,
-77, -78, -79, -80, -81, -82, -83,
LinLib L, -S, ModAL, -S2, -S1,
NewYTBS 82[port], Novels[port],
OxAmL, -83, PenC AM, PostFic,
RAdv 1, ScF&FL 1, -2, ScFSB,
TwCWr, WebAB, -79, WebE&AL,
WhoAm 74, -76, -78, -80, -82,
WhoTwCL, WhoWor 74, -78, -80,
-82, -84, -86*

Barthelme, Donald *DrAP&F 85,
ScFSB*
Barthelme, Donald 1931- *AmArch 70,
AmAu&B, AuBYP SUP, BioIn 9, -10,
-11, -12, -13, BlueB 76, CelR,
ConAu 21R, ConLC 1, -2,
-3, -5, -6, -8, -13, -23[port],
ConNov 72, -76, -82, -86, CurBio 76,
DcLB 2, -Y80A[port], DcLEL 1940,
EncSF, EncWL 2, IntAu&W 76, -77,
ModAL S2, -S1, Novels, OxAmL 83,
PenC AM, PostFic, RAdv 1,
SmATA 7, WhoAm 74, -76, -78, -80,
-84, -86, WhoE 75, -77, WorAl,
WorAu, WrDr 76, -80, -82, -84, -86*
Bartholomew, Barbara 1941-
ConAu 118, SmATA 42
Bartlett, Irving Henry 1923-
*ConAu 9NR, -21R, DrAS 74H,
-78H, -82H, WhoAm 74, -76, -78,
-80, -82*
Bartos-Hoeppner, Barbara 1923-
*Au&Wr 71, BioIn 10, ConAu 10NR,
-25R, FourBJA, SmATA 5,
TwCCW 78B*
Baruch, Grace Kestenman 1936-
AmM&WS 73S, -78S
Bar-Zohar, Michael 1938-
ConAu 12NR
Bar-Zohar, Michael J 1938-
ConAu 21R, WhoWorJ 72, -78
Barzun, Jacques 1907- *AmAu&B,
Au&Wr 71, Baker 78, -84, BioIn 2,
-4, -7, -9, -11, BlueB 76, CelR,
ConAu 61, CurBio 64, DrAS 74H,
-78H, -82H, EncMys, IntAu&W 76A,
-77, IntWW 74, -75, -76, -77,
-78, -79, -80, -81, -82, -83,
LinLib L, -S, NewYTBS 75,
OxAmL, -83, RAdv 1, REn, REnAL,
TwCA, -SUP, WebAB, -79,
WhE&EA, Who 74, -82, -83, -85,
WhoAm 74, -76, -78, -80, -82, -84,
-86, WhoAmA 73, -76, -78, -80, -82,
-84, WhoMus 72, WhoWor 74, -78,
-80, -82, -84, -87, WrDr 76, -80,
-82, -84, -86*
Bascom, Willard 1916-
*AmM&WS 73P, -76P, -79P, -82P,
-86P, BioIn 6, -12, ConAu 1R,
-6NR, WhoOcn 78, WhoWest 74,
-76, -78*
Basinger, Jeanine 1936- *ConAu 18NR,
-97, ForWC 70*
Bass, Althea 1892- *ConAu P-2,
WhoAmW 58, -61, -64*
Bass, Ellen *DrAP&F 85*
Bass, Ellen 1947- *ConAu 2NR, -49,
IntAu&W 86, IntWWP 77*
Bass, George F 1932- *AmM&WS 86P*
Bass, George Fletcher 1932- *BioIn 8,
-9, DrAS 74H, -78H, -82H*
Bassani, Giorgio 1916- *BioIn 9, -10,
CasWL, ConAu 65, ConFLW 84,
DcItL, EncWL, -2,
EvEuW, IntAu&W 76, -77,
IntWW 74, -75, -76, -77, -78, -79,
-80, -81, -82, -83, ModRL, Novels,
OxEng 85, PenC EUR, REn,
TwCWr, WhoTwCL, WhoWor 74,
-76, -78, WorAu*
Bates, Betty *ConAu X*
Bates, Betty 1921- *BioIn 12, ConAu X,
SmATA 19*
Bates, Robert L 1912- *ConAu 116*
Bates, Robert Latimer 1912-
AmM&WS 86P
Bathgate, Andy 1932- *BioIn 6, -9,
CurBio 64, WhoHcky 73*
Battcock, Gregory 1938?-1980
*AnObit 1980, BioIn 12, BlueB 76,
ConAu 105, -11NR, -21R,
WhoAm 80, -82, WhoAmA 73, -76,
-78, -80, WhoE 74, WrDr 76, -80,
-82*

Batten, Mary 1937- *AuBYP SUP,
BioIn 10, ConAu 41R, SmATA 5*
Batterberry, Ariane Ruskin 1935-
*ConAu 13NR, -69, SmATA 13,
WhoAmW 77, -79*
Batterberry, Ariane Ruskin *see also*
Ruskin, Ariane
Batterberry, Michael Carver 1932-
AuBYP SUP, ConAu 77, SmATA 32
Baudouy, Michel-Aime 1909-
*ConAu P-2, IntAu&W 82, SmATA 7,
ThrBJA*
Bauer, Henry Hermann 1931-
AmM&WS 86P, WhoAm 84, -86
Bauer, Marion Dane 1938- *BioIn 12,
ConAu 11NR, -69, FifBJA[port],
SmATA 20*
Bauer, Steven *DrAP&F 85*
Bauer, William Waldo 1892-1967
*BioIn 4, -5, -8, -9, -10, ConAu 5R,
-7NR, NatCAB 53, -54, WhAm 4A,
WhE&EA*
Baughman, James L 1952- *ConAu 118*
Baum, Daniel 1934- *ConAu 6NR*
Baum, Patricia *AuBYP SUP*
Baumann, Amy Beeching 1922-
BioIn 11, ConAu 21R, SmATA 10
Baumann, Elwood D *AuBYP SUP,
ConAu 111, SmATA 33*
Baumann, Hans 1914- *Au&Wr 71,
BioIn 9, ConAu 3NR, -5R,
IntAu&W 77, OxChL,
SmATA 2, ThrBJA, TwCCW 78B,
-83B, WhoWor 74, WorDWW*
Baur, John Edward 1922- *ConAu 9R,
DrAS 74H, -78H, -82H, WrDr 76,
-80, -82, -84, -86*
Bawden, Nina 1925- *Au&Wr 71,
AuBYP SUP, BioIn 9, -10, -11, -13,
BritCA, ChlLR 2, ConAu X,
ConNov 72, -76, -82, -86,
DcLB 14[port], DcLEL 1940,
FourBJA, IntAu&W 76, -77, -82,
-86, Novels, OxChL, SmATA 4,
TwCCW 78, -83, TwCCr&M 80,
Who 74, -82, -83, WhoWor 78,
WrDr 76, -80, -82, -84, -86*
Bawden, Nina *see also* Kark, Nina
Mary
Baxter, Anne 1923- *BiDFilm,
BiE&WWA, BioIn 9, -10, -11, -13,
CelR, ConAu 111, -114, CurBio 72,
FilmgC, HalFC 84, InWom,
IntMPA 77, -75, -76, -78, -79, -81,
-82, -84, -86, MotPP, MovMk,
NewYTBS 82[port], NotNAT, OxAusL, WhoAm 74, -76,
-78, -80, -82, -84, WhoAmW 74,
-58, -64, -66, -68, -70, -72, -83,
WhoHol A, WhoThe 77, -81,
WomPO 78, WorAl, WorEFlm*
Baxter, Anne 1923-1985 *ConAu 118,
ConNews 86-1[port], ConTFT 3,
CurBio 86N, NewYTBS 85[port]*
Bayley, Barrington J 1937-
ConAu 14NR, ScFSB[port]
Bayley, Barrington John 1937-
*ConAu 37R, EncSF, IntAu&W 76,
-77, -82, -86, ScF&FL 1, -2,
TwCSFW 86, WhoSciF, WrDr 76,
-80, -82, -84, -86*
Baylor, Byrd 1924- *AuBYP SUP,
BioIn 12, ChlLR 3, ChhPo S3,
ConAu 81, FourBJA, SmATA 16*
Bayly, Joseph 1920- *ConAu 17R,
IntAu&W 77, St&PR 75, WrDr 76,
-80, -82, -84*
Baym, Nina 1936- *ConAu 112,
WhoAm 86, WhoAmW 85, -87*
Bayne-Jardine, C C 1932- *ConAu 25R*
Bayrd, Edwin 1944- *ConAu 97*
Beach, Edward L *DrAP&F 85*
Beach, Edward L 1918- *WrDr 86*
Beach, Edward Latimer 1918-
*Au&Wr 71, BioIn 3, -5, -6, -11, -13,
ConAu 5R, -6NR, Novels,
SmATA 12, WebAMB, WhoAmP 73,
-75, -77, WhoGov 77, -72, -75,
WrDr 76, -80, -82, -84*
Beach Boys, The *CmCal,
EncPR&S 74, _, IlEncRk,
RkOn 74, -82, RkOneH,
RolSEnr 83, WhoRock 81[port],
WorAl*

Bickham, Jack M 1930- *AmAu&B, AmCath 80, ConAu 5R, -8NR, EncFWF[port], IntAu&W 82, WhoAm 74, WrDr 76, -80, -82, -84, -86*

Biemiller, Carl L 1912-1979 *SmATA 40[port]*

Biemiller, Carl Ludwig 1912-1979 *AuBYP SUP, BioIn 12, ConAu 106, ScF&FL 1, -2, SmATA 21N*

Bierce, Ambrose 1842-1914? *AmAu, AmAu&B, AmBi, AmWr, ApCAB SUP, AtlBL, BioIn 1, -2, -3, -4, -5, -6, -7, -8, -9, -10, -11, -12, -13, CasWL, Chambr 3, ChhPo, -S1, -S3, CmCal, CnDAL, ConAu 104, CrtT 3, -4, CyWA, DcAmAu, DcAmB, DcLB 11[port], -12[port], -23[port], DcLEL, DcNAA, EncAB-H, EncMys, EncSF, EncTwCJ, EvLB, LinLib L, -S, LongCTC, McGEWB, ModAL, -S1, NatCAB 14, Novels, OhA&B, OxAmL, -83, OxEng, -85, PenC AM, RAdv 1, REn, REnAL, REnAW, ScF&FL 1, ScFSB, SupFW, TwCLC 1, -7[port], WebAB, -79, WebE&AL, WhDW, WhAm 4, -HSA, WhoHr&F, WhoSciF, WorAl*

Bierhorst, John 1936- *AuBYP SUP, BioIn 10, ConAu 13NR, -33R, FifBJA[port], IntAu&W 77, SmATA 6, WhoE 83, -85, WrDr 76, -80, -82, -84, -86*

Biggle, Lloyd, Jr. 1923- *BioIn 12, ConAu 5NR, -13R, -20NR, ConSFA, DcLB 8[port], EncSF, ScF&FL 1, -2, ScFSB, TwCSFW 86, WhoSciF, WrDr 84, -86*

Biko, Steve 1947-1977 *InB&W 80*

Bill, J Brent 1951- *ConAu 117*

Billings, Charlene W 1941- *SmATA 41*

Billings, Henry 1901- *AmAu&B, BioIn 1, -5, -6, IlsCB 1946, MorJA, WhoAmA 73, -76, -78, -80, -82, -84*

Billings, Peggy 1928- *ConAu 25R*

Billingsley, Andrew 1926- *ConAu 57, Ebony 1, InB&W 80, -85, LivgBAA, NegAl 76, -83, SelBAAf, SelBAAu, WhoBlA 75, -77, -80, -85*

Billington, Elizabeth T *ConAu 101, SmATA 43*

Bing, Rudolf 1902- *Baker 78, BiDAmM, BioIn 1, -2, -3, -4, -5, -6, -7, -8, -9, -10, BlueB 76, CelR, ConAu 89, CurBio 50, IntWW 74, -75, -76, -77, -78, -79, -80, -81, -82, -83, IntWWM 77, -85, LinLib S, NewEOp 71, NewYTBE 71, -72, -73, REn, WhoAm 74, -82, -83, WhoAm 74, -76, -78, -80, -82, WhoMus 72, WhoOp 76, WhoWor 74, -78, -80, -82*

Bing, Sir Rudolf 1902- *Baker 84, BioIn 13, Who 85, WhoAm 84, WhoWor 84*

Bingham, Caroline 1938- *ConAu 10NR, -57, IntAu&W 76, -77, -82, Who 82, -83, WrDr 76, -80, -82, -84, -86*

Bingham, Caroline Margery Conyers 1938- *Who 85*

Binns, Archie 1899-1971 *AmAu&B, AmNov, BioIn 2, -4, ConAu 73, EncFWF, LinLib L, OxAmL, -83, REnAL, TwCA, -SUP, WhAm 5, WhoPNW*

Bioy Casares, Adolfo 1914- *BioIn 12, ConAu 19NR, -29R, ConLC 4, -8, -13, DcCLAA, EncLatA, EncSF, EncWL 2, IntAu&W 77, -82, ModLAL, OxSpan, PenC AM, ScF&FL 1, -2, WhoWor 74, -76, WorAu 1975*

Birch, Cyril 1925- *ConAu 85, DrAS 74F, -78F, -82F*

Bird, Anthony Cole 1917- *Au&Wr 71, ConAu 13R*

Bird, Caroline 1915- *BioIn 10, -11, -13, ConAu 11NR, -17R, CurBio 76, ForWC 70, IntAu&W 77, WhoAm 76, -78, -80, -82, -84, -86, WhoAmW 74, -61, -64, -66, -68,*

-70, -72, -77, -79, WhoE 75, WrDr 76, -80, -82, -84, -86

Bird, Larry *NewYTBS 85[port]*

Bird, Larry 1956- *BioIn 13*

Birley, Anthony Richard 1937- *Au&Wr 71, IntAu&W 76*

Birmingham, John 1951- *ConAu 45*

Birnbach, Lisa *BioIn 12*

Birnbach, Lisa 1957?- *BioIn 13*

Bischoff, David F 1951- *ConAu 81, ScFSB, TwCSFW 86, WrDr 84, -86*

Bishop, Claire Huchet *AmPB, AmWomWr, AuBYP, BioIn 1, -2, -3, -7, -8, -12, BkP, CathA 1952, ConAu 73, FamMS, JBA 51, SmATA 14, TwCCW 78, -83, WhoAmW 58, -61, -64, WrDr 80, -82, -84, -86*

Bishop, Curtis Kent 1912-1967 *AuBYP, BioIn 7, -10, ConAu P-1, EncAB 39[port], SmATA 6*

Bishop, Elizabeth 1911-1979 *AmAu&B, AmWomWr, AmWr S1, Au&Wr 71, AuBYP SUP, BioIn 4, -7, -8, -10, -11, -12, -13, BlueB 76, CelR, ChhPo, -S1, -S3, CnE&AP, ConAu 5R, -89, ConAu 2BS, ConLC 1, -4, -9, -13, -15, -32[port], ConPo 70, -75, -80, CroCAP, CurBio 77, -79N, DcLB 5[port], DcLEL 1940, EncWL, -2, FourBJA, IntAu&W 77, IntDcWB, IntWW 74, -75, -76, -77, -78, -79, IntWWP 77, LibW, LinLib L, MakMC, ModAL, -S2, -S1, ModAWP[port], NewYTBS 79, OxAmL, -83, OxEng 85, PenC AM, RAdv 1, REn, REnAL, SmATA 24N, TwCA SUP, TwCWr, WebE&AL, WhAm 7, WhoAm 74, -78, WhoAmW 74, -58, -64, -66, -68, -70, -72, WhoE 74, WhoWor 74, WrDr 76, -80*

Bishop, James Alonzo 1907- *AuNews 1, BioIn 3, -4, -8, -10, BioNews 74, ConAu 17R*

Bishop, James Alonzo *see also* Bishop, Jim

Bishop, Jim 1907- *AmAu&B, AuNews 1, -2, BioIn 11, -12, CelR, ConAu X, CurBio 69, EncTwCJ, LinLib L, REnAL, WhoAm 74, -76, -78, -80, -82, -84, -86, WhoS&SW 73, -75, 76, WhoWor 74, -76, -78, WorAl*

Bishop, Jim *see also* Bishop, James Alonzo

Bishop, Michael 1945- *AuNews 2, BioIn 11, ConAu 9NR, -61, EncSF, IntAu&W 82, -86, ScFSB[port], TwCSFW 86, WrDr 84, -86*

Bishop, Morris Gilbert 1893?-1973 *AmAu&B, BioIn 4, -10, ChhPo, -S1, -S2, ConAu 1R, -6NR, -45, ObitOF 79, OxAmL, REnAL, ScF&FL 1, -2, TwCA SUP, WhAm 6, WhLit, WhoAm 74*

Bishop, W Arthur 1923- *ConAu 21R*

Bixby, William Courtney 1920- *AmAu&B, AuBYP, BioIn 8, -10, ConAu 1R, -6NR, SmATA 6, WhoAm 74*

Bjorklund, Karna L *AuBYP SUP*

Bjorn, Thyra Ferre 1905-1975 *AmAu&B, BioIn 3, -7, -10, ConAu 3NR, -5R, -57, WhoAmW 61, -64, -68, -72*

Black, Bonnie Lee 1945- *ConAu 107, WhoAmW 85, -87*

Black, Cyril Edwin 1915- *AmAu&B, ConAu 1R, -3NR, DrAS 74H, -78H, -82H, WhoAm 74, -76, -78, -80, -82, -84, -86, WhoE 74, WhoWor 74, -76*

Black, Hallie 1943- *ConAu 108*

Black, Hugo LaFayette 1886-1971 *BiDFedJ, BiDrAC, BioIn 1, -2, -4, -5, -6, -7, -8, -9, -10, -11, -12, -13, DcAmSR, EncAB-H, EncSoH, LinLib L, -S, McGEWB, NewYTBE 71, ObitOF 79, ObitT 1971, OxAmH, PolProf E, PolProf J, PolProf K, PolProf NF,*

PolProf T, WebAB, -79, WhAm 5, WhAmP, WorAl

Black, Hugo LaFayette, Jr. 1922- *WhoAm 80, -82, -84, -86, WhoAmL 78, -79, WhoWor 84*

Black, Laura *WrDr 84, -86*

Black, Max 1909- *AmAu&B, ConAu 61, DrAS 74P, -78P, -82P, WhoAm 74, -76, -78, -80, -82, -84, -86, WhoAmJ 80, WhoE 74, WhoWorJ 72, -78, WrDr 86*

Black, Susan Adams 1953- *ConAu 105, SmATA 40*

Blackbeard, Bill 1926- *ConAu 97, WhoWest 80, WorECar A*

Blackburn, Graham 1940- *ConAu 69*

Blackburn, Joyce Knight 1920- *BioIn 13, ConAu 17R, IndAu 1917, SmATA 29[port], WhoAmW 74*

Blacker, Irwin R 1919- *EncFWF*

Blacker, Irwin R 1919-1985 *ConAu 115*

Blackmore, Michael 1916- *WhE&EA*

Blackmore, Richard Doddridge 1825-1900 *Alli SUP, BbD, BiD&SB, BioIn 1, -2, -3, -4, -5, -10, -11, -12, -13, BritAu 19, CelCen, Chambr 3, ChhPo, -S1, -S2, -S3, CyWA, DcBiA, DcEnA, -AP, DcEnL, DcEuL, DcLEL, DcNaB S1, EvLB, JBA 34, LinLib L, -S, MouLC 4, NewC, OxEng, OxLitW 86, PenC ENG, REn, TelT, WebE&AL, WhDW*

Blackwell, Elizabeth 1821-1910 *Alli, -SUP, AmBi, AmRef[port], AmWom, AmWomWr, ApCAB, BiD&SB, BiHiMed, BioIn 1, -2, -3, -4, -5, -6, -7, -8, -9, -10, -11, -12, -13, CelCen, CivWDc, DcAmAu, DcAmB, DcAmMeB 84, DcAmMeB, DcBiPP, DcNaB S2, DcNAA, Drake, EncAB-H, GoodHs, HarEnUS, HerW, -84, InSci, InWom, IntDcWB, LibW, LinLib S, McGEWB, NatCAB 9, NotAW, OhA&B, OxAmH, OxMed 86, TwCBDA, WebAB, -79, WhDW, WhAm 1, WhLit, WorAl*

Blackwood, Alan 1932- *ConAu 110*

Blackwood, Alan William 1932- *IntAu&W 86*

Blackwood, Paul Everett 1913- *AmM&WS 73P, ConAu 102, LEduc 74, WhoGov 77, -72, -75*

Blair, Clay Drewry, Jr. 1925- *AmAu&B, AuNews 2, BioIn 4, -8, -10, -11, ConAu 77, IntAu&W 76, -77, IntWW 74, WhoAm 76, -78, -80, -82, -84*

Blair, Cynthia 1953- *ConAu 118*

Blair, Lucile *ConAu X*

Blair, Lucile *see also* Yeakley, Marjorie Hall

Blair, Walter 1900- *ConAu 18NR, WrDr 86*

Blair, William Robert 1928- *WhoAm 82, -84*

Blaise, Clark *DrAP&F 85*

Blaise, Clark 1940- *ConAu 3AS[port], ConLC 29[port], ConNov 86, DcLB 53[port], OxCanL, WhoCanL 85, WrDr 86*

Blake, Howard E 1922- *DrAS 74E, -78E, -82E, LEduc 74*

Blake, Peter Jost 1920- *AmArch 70, AmAu&B, BioIn 4, -10, -13, ConArch, ConAu 65, McGDA, WhoAm 80, -82, -84, -86, WhoAmA 73, -76, -78, -80, -82, -84, WhoE 74, WrDr 82, -84*

Blake, Walker E *AuBYP SUP, ConAu X*

Blake, Walker E *see also* Butterworth, W E

Blake, William 1757-1827 *Alli, AnCL, AntBDN B, AtlBL, AuBYP SUP, BbD, BiD&SB, BiDLA, BioIn 1, -2, -3, -4, -5, -6, -7, -8, -9, -10, -11, -12, -13, BkIE, BritAu 19, BritWr 3, CarSB, CasWL, CelCen, Chambr 2, ChrP, ChhPo, -S1, -S2, -S3, CnE&AP, CrtT 2, -4, CyWA, DcBiPP, DcBrBI, DcBrWA,*

Blakemore, Colin Brian 1944- *ConAu 85, IntWW 76, -77, -78, -79, -80, -81, -82, -83, Who 82, -83, -85, WhoWor 78, -84, -87*

Blaker, Charles William 1918- *WhoS&SW 82*

Blanco, Richard L 1926- *ConAu 57, DrAS 74H*

Blanpied, Pamela Wharton *DrAP&F 85*

Blanpied, Pamela Wharton 1937- *ConAu 102*

Blanton, Catherine 1907- *AuBYP, BioIn 8, ConAu 1R*

Blanzaco, Andre Charles 1934- *ConAu 29R, WhoE 79, -81*

Blassingame, John W 1940- *ConAu 49, ConIsC 1[port], DrAS 74H, -78H, -82H, InB&W 80, LivgBAA, NegAl 83, SelBAAf, WhoBlA 75, -77, -80, -85*

Blassingame, John Wesley 1941- *InB&W 85*

Blassingame, Wyatt Rainey 1909- *AuBYP, BioIn 8, -9, ConAu 1R, -3NR, IntAu&W 77, -82, SmATA 1, -34[port], WhoHr&F, WhoS&SW 76, WrDr 76, -80, -82, -84*

Blassingame, Wyatt Rainey 1909-1985 *ConAu 114, SmATA 41N*

Blatter, Dorothy 1901- *ConAu P-1*

Blatty, William Peter *IntMPA 84*

Blatty, William Peter 1928- *BioIn 8, -9, -10, -11, ConAu 5R, -9NR, ConLC 2, ConTFT 4, CurBio 74, FilmgC, HalFC 84, IntAu&W 76, -77, IntMPA 77, -75, -76, -78, -79, -81, -82, -84, ScF&FL 1, -2, WhoAm 74, -76, -78, -80, -82, -84, -86, WrDr 76, -80, -82, -84*

Blaushild, Babette 1927- *ConAu 29R, WhoAmP 73, -75*

Blaylock, James P 1950- *ConAu 110*

Bleeck, Oliver *ConAu X, EncMys, TwCCr&M 80, -85, WrDr 76, -80, -82, -84, -86*

Bleeck, Oliver *see also* Thomas, Ross Elmore

Bleich, Alan R 1913- *BiDrAPH 79, ConAu 13R*

Bleiler, E F 1920- *ChhPo S2, WhoSciF*

Bleiler, Everett Franklin 1920- *ScF&FL 1, WhoAm 76, -78, -80*

Bligh, William 1754-1817 *Alli, BiDLA, BioIn 2, -3, -4, -6, -7, -8, -9, -10, -11, CelCen, DcBiPP, DcNaB, McGEWB, NewC, OxShips, REn, WhDW, WorAl*

Blinn, William *LesBEnT, NewYTET*

Blish, James 1921-1975 *AmAu&B, Au&Wr 71, BioIn 10, -12, -13, ConAu 1R, -3NR, -57, ConLC 14, ConNov 76, ConSFA, DcLB 8[port], DcLEL 1940, EncSF, IntAu&W 76, LinLib L, NewYTBS 75, Novels, ObitT 1971, ScF&FL 1, -2, WhoSciF, WorAl, WrAu, WrDr 76*

Blishen, Edward 1920- *Au&Wr 71, BioIn 11, ChhPo, ConAu 11NR, -17R, IntAu&W 77, OxChL, ScF&FL 1, -2, SmATA 8, Who 82, -83, -85, WrDr 76, -80, -82, -84, -86*

Blitzer, Charles 1927- *WhoAm 74, -76, -78, -80, -82, -84, WhoGov 77, -72, -75*

Blixen, Karen Christentze 1885-1962 *OxEng 85*

Blixen, Karen Christentze Dinesen 1885-1962 *BioIn 12, CasWL, ConAu P-2, ConLC 10, EncWL, InWom, IntDcWB, LongCTC, Novels[port], ObitT 1961, PenC ENG,*

Bowles, Paul Frederick 1910-
IntWWM 85

Bowman, Bruce 1938- *ConAu 65,
WhoAmA 78, –80, –82, –84,
WhoWest 80, –82*

Bowman, Gerald d1967 *MnBBF,
WhoBW&I A*

Bowman, James Cloyd 1880-1961
*AmAu&B, AnCL, AuBYP, BioIn 2,
–6, –8, –13, ConAu 97, JBA 51,
OhA&B, SmATA 23[port], Str&VC,
WhAm 4, WhNAA*

Bowman, John S 1931- *Au&Wr 71,
AuBYP SUP, BioIn 12, ConAu 5NR,
–9R, –19NR, ScF&FL 1, –2,
SmATA 16*

Bowra, Sir Cecil Maurice 1898-1970?
*Au&Wr 71, BioIn 4, –7, ConAu 1R,
–29R, DcLEL, EvLB, LongCTC,
ModBrL, NewC, NewYTBE 71, REn,
TwCA SUP, WhAm 5, WhE&EA*

Bowskill, Derek 1928- *ConAu 13NR,
–77, IntAu&W 76, –77*

Boyarsky, Bill 1936- *ConAu 25R*

Boyd, James 1888-1944 *AmAu&B,
BioIn 2, –3, –4, –5, –9, –11, –12,
CnDAL, ConAmA, ConAmL,
CurBio 44, CyWA, DcAmB S3,
DcLB 9[port], DcLEL, DcNAA,
LinLib L, LongCTC, NatCAB 35,
Novels, ObitOF 79, OxAmL, –83,
PenC AM, REnAL, TwCA, –SUP,
WhAm 2, WhLit, WhNAA*

Boyd, Jessie Edna 1899- *BiDrLUS 70,
WhoLibS 55, –66*

Boyd, John 1919- *ConAu X, ConSFA,
DcLB 8[port], EncSF, ScF&FL 1, –2,
ScFSB, TwCSFW 86, WhoSciF,
WrDr 76, –80, –82, –84, –86*

Boyd, John see also Upchurch, Boyd

Boyd, Malcolm *IntWWM 85*

Boyd, Malcolm 1923- *AmAu&B,
ASpks, Au&Wr 71, BioIn 6, –7, –8,
–10, –11, BlueB 76, CelR,
ConAu 4NR, –5R, CurBio 68,
IntAu&W 76, –77, –82, –86,
IntWWM 77, ScF&FL 1, –2,
WhoAm 74, –76, –78, –80, –82, –84,
–86, WhoE 74, WhoRel 75, –77, –85,
WhoWor 74, –76, WorAl, WrDr 76,
–80, –82, –84, –86*

Boyd, Mildred 1921- *AuBYP SUP,
ConAu 17R, ForWC 70*

Boyd, Waldo T 1918- *AuBYP SUP,
BioIn 12, ConAu 12NR, –29R,
SmATA 18, WrDr 76, –80, –82, –84,
–86*

Boyd, William C 1903-1983
*AmM&WS 73P, –76P, –79P, AsBiEn,
BiESc, BioIn 1, ConAu 109,
McGMS 80[port], NewYTBS 83,
WhoAm 74, –76, –78, –80, –82*

Boyd, William Clouser 1903-1983
BioIn 13, WhAm 8

Boyer, Elizabeth 1913- *ConAu 81,
WhoAmW 61*

Boyer, Ernest Leroy 1928- *BioIn 13,
WhoAm 84, –86, WhoAmP 85*

Boyer, Paul S 1935- *ConAu 1NR, –49,
DrAS 74H, –78H, –82H*

Boyer, Paul Samuel 1935-
ConAu 18NR

Boyer, Robert E 1929-
*AmM&WS 73P, –76P, –79P, –82P,
BioIn 12, ConAu 41R, LEduc 74,
SmATA 22[port], WhoAm 76, –78,
–80, –82, WhoS&SW 82*

Boyer, Robert Ernst 1929-
*AmM&WS 86P, BioIn 13,
WhoAm 84, –86, WhoFrS 84*

Boyington, Gregory 1912- *AmAu&B,
BioIn 1, –5, –10, –12, MedHR,
WebAMB*

Boyle, Sarah Patton 1906- *ConAu P-1,
WhoAmW 66, –68*

Boylston, Helen Dore d1984
NewYTBS 84

Boylston, Helen Dore 1895-
*AmWomWr, AuBYP, BioIn 2, –7, –8,
–13, ConAu 73, ConPo 42, InWom,
JBA 51, OxChL, SmATA 23[port],
TwCCW 78, –83, WhoChL, WrDr 80,
–82, –84*

Boylston, Helen Dore 1895-1984
ConAu 113, –21NR, CurBio 84N

Boyne, Walter J 1929- *ConAu 107*

Boyne, Walter James 1929-
*IntAu&W 86, WhoAm 84, –86,
WhoE 85, WhoWor 87*

Bracegirdle, Cyril 1920- *Au&Wr 71,
ConAu 45, IntAu&W 76, WrDr 76,
–80*

Bracewell, Ronald N *WhoTech 84*

Bracewell, Ronald Newbold 1921-
*AmM&WS 76P, –79P, –86P,
ConAu 57, LElec, WhoAm 74, –76,
–78, –80, WhoTech 82*

Bracken, Peg 1918- *AmWomWr,
BioIn 11, –12, ConAu 1R, –6NR,
WhoAm 78, –80, –82, –84, –86,
WhoAmW 74, –58, –61, –68A, –70,
–72, –77, –83, –85, –87, WhoWest 74,
–76*

Brackett, Leigh 1915-1978 *BioIn 11,
–12, CmMov, ConAu 1R, –1NR, –77,
ConSFA, DcLB 8[port], –26[port],
EncSF, FilmgC, ForWC 70,
HalFC 84, Novels, OhA&B,
ScF&FL 1, –2, ScFSB, SupFW,
TwCCr&M 85, TwCSFW 86,
WhoSciF, WomWMM, WrDr 76*

Brackman, Arnold C 1923- *WrDr 86*

Brackman, Arnold C 1923-1983
ConAu 111

Brackman, Arnold Charles 1923-1983
BioIn 13

Bradbury, Bianca 1908- *AmAu&B,
AuBYP, BioIn 8, –9, ConAu 5NR,
–13R, ForWC 70, FourBJA,
SmATA 3, WhoAmA W 68, –70,
WhoE 75, –77, –79, –81*

Bradbury, Ray *DrAP&F 85*

Bradbury, Ray 1920- *AmAu&B,
Au&Wr 71, AuNews 1, –2, BioIn 2,
–3, –4, –7, –8, –10, –11, –12, –13,
BioNews 74, BlueB 76, CasWL, CelR,
CmCal, CmMov, CnMWL,
ConAu 1R, –2NR, ConLC 1, –3, –10,
–15, –42[port], ConNov 72, –76, –82,
–86, ConSFA, CurBio 53, –82[port],
DcLB 2, –8[port], DcLEL 1940,
EncSF, FilmgC, HalFC 84,
IntAu&W 76, –77, LinLib L,
LongCTC, Novels[port], OxAmL, –83,
PenC AM, REn, REnAL, ScF&FL 1,
–2, ScFSB[port], SmATA 11, SupFW,
TwCA SUP, TwCCr&M 80,
TwCSFW 86, TwCWr, WebAB, –79,
Who 74, –82, –83, WhoAm 74, –76,
–78, –80, –82, WhoHr&F, WhoSciF,
WhoWor 74, WorAl, WorEFlm,
WrDr 76, –80, –82, –84, –86*

Bradbury, Ray Douglas 1920-
Who 85, WhoAm 84, –86

Braden, Thomas Wardell 1918-
*BioIn 8, –10, WhoAm 74, –76, –78,
–80, –82, –84, –86*

Braden, Vic 1929?- *BioIn 10, –12*

Bradford, Karleen 1936- *ConAu 112,
IntAu&W 86, SmATA 48[port],
WhoCanL 85*

Bradford, Richard 1932- *BioIn 8,
ConAu 2NR, –49, WhoAm 74, –76,
–78, –80, –82, WhoHol A, WrDr 84,
–86*

Bradley, Bill *NewYTBS 84[port]*

Bradley, Bill 1943- *AlmAP 80,
–82[port], –84[port], BioIn 7, –8, –9,
–10, –11, –12, –13, CelR, CngDr 79,
–81, –83, –85, –87, ConAu X,
CurBio 82[port], NewYTBS 83[port],
PolsAm 84[port], WhoAm 80, –82,
–84, –86, WhoAmP 79, –81, –83, –85,
WhoBbl 73, WhoE 81, –83, –85,
WhoWor 80, –82, –84, –87, WorAl*

Bradley, David Henry, Jr. 1950-
*BioIn 12, ConAu 104,
ConLC 23[port], InB&W 80, –85,
NegAl 83, NewYTBS 81[port],
SelBAAf, WhoBlA 77, –80, –85*

Bradley, Duane *SmATA X*

Bradley, Duane 1914- *AuBYP,
BioIn 8, ConAu X*

Bradley, Duane see also Sanborn,
Duane

Bradley, James Howard, Jr. 1936-
WhoBlA 80, –85

Bradley, James Vandiver 1924-
*AmM&WS 73S, –78S, ConAu 37R,
WrDr 76, –80, –82, –84, –86*

Bradley, Marion Zimmer *DrAP&F 85*

Bradley, Marion Zimmer 1930-
*BioIn 12, –13, ConAu 7NR, –57,
ConLC 30[port], ConSFA,
DcLB 8[port], EncSF, ScF&FL 1, –2,
ScFSB[port], TwCSFW 86,
WhoAm 84, –86, WhoSciF,
WhoWest 84, WrDr 84, –86*

Bradley, Michael *ConAu X*

Bradley, Michael see also Blumberg,
Gary

Bradley, Virginia 1912- *BioIn 13,
ConAu 8NR, –61, SmATA 23[port],
WhoAm 78, –80, –82, –84*

Bradshaw, Gillian 1956- *ConAu 103*

Brady, Esther Wood 1905- *ConAu 93,
SmATA 31*

Brady, Irene 1943- *BioIn 9, –12,
ConAu 20NR, –33R, IlsCB 1967,
SmATA 4*

Brady, Joan *BioIn 12, –13*

Brady, Maxine L 1941- *AuBYP SUP,
ConAu 69*

Bragdon, Elspeth 1897- *BioIn 10,
ConAu 5R, –5NR, SmATA 6*

Brahs, Stuart J 1940- *ConAu 57*

Braider, Donald d1977 *WhoAmA 84N*

Braider, Donald 1923-1976 *BioIn 10,
ConAu 33R, –65, ConAu P-2,
NewYTBS 76, WhAm 7, WhoAm 74,
–76, WhoAmA 78N, –80N, –82N,
WrDr 76, –80, –82*

Brainerd, John W 1918-
*AmM&WS 73P, –76P, –79P, –82P,
ConAu 57*

Brainerd, John Whiting 1918-
AmM&WS 86P

Braithwaite, E R 1912?- *ConAu 106,
ConNov 72, SelBAAf, WrDr 76, –80,
–82, –84*

Braithwaite, Edward R 1912?-
BioIn 5, –7, –8, –9, –10

Braithwaite, Edward R 1921?-
WhoWor 74

Braly, Malcolm 1925-1980 *ASpks,
BioIn 8, –10, –11, –12, ConAu 12NR,
–17R, –97, NewYTBS 80*

Brancato, Robin F 1936-
*ConAu 11NR, –69, ConLC 35[port],
FifBJA[port], SmATA 23[port]*

Brand, Dionne 1953- *FifCWr*

Brand, Max *EncFWF*

Brand, Max 1892-1944 *AmAu&B,
BioIn 1, –3, –4, –8, CmCal,
ConAu X, CurBio 44, DcAmB S3,
DcLEL, DcNAA, EncMys, FilmgC,
HalFC 84, LongCTC, MnBBF,
ObitOF 79, OxAmL 83, REn,
REnAL, REnAW, ScF&FL 1,
TwCA, –SUP, TwCCr&M 80,
WebAB, –79, WhLit, WorAl*

Brand, Max see also Faust, Frederick

Brand, Millen 1906-1980 *AmAu&B,
AmNov, BioIn 2, –4, –10, –12,
ChhPo S3, ConAu 21R, –97,
ConLC 7, IntAu&W 76, IntWWP 77,
NewYTBS 80[port], REnAL,
TwCA, –SUP, WrDr 76, –80*

Brand, Oscar 1920- *AmAu&B,
AuBYP, Baker 84, BiDAmM,
BioIn 6, –8, BlueB 76, CanWW 70,
–79, –80, –81, –83, ConAu 1R, –4NR,
ConTFT 1, CurBio 62,
EncFCWM 69, –83, IntAu&W 77,
NatPD, –81[port], NotNAT,
WhoAm 74, –76, –78, –80, –82, –84,
–86, WhoWor 74, –76, WhoWorJ 72,
–78, WrDr 76, –80, –82, –84, –86*

Brand, Stewart *NewYTBS 84[port]*

Brand, Stewart 1938- *BioIn 13,
EncTwCJ, WhoAm 84, –86*

Branden, Nathaniel 1930- *ConAu 33R,
IntAu&W 76, –77, WhoWest 78, –82,
–84, WhoWor 82, –84, –86*

Brandis, Marianne 1938- *ConAu 117*

Brandner, Gary 1933- *ConAu 17NR*

Brandon, James R 1927-
*ConAu 11NR, –69, DrAS 74E, –78E,
–82E*

Brandon, Jay 1953- *ConAu 119*

Brandon, William 1914- *ConAu 77,
IndAu 1917*

Brandreth, Gyles 1948- *BioIn 13,
WrDr 86*

Brandreth, Gyles D 1948- *BioIn 9,
ConAu 65, IntAu&W 77, –82,
SmATA 28[port], Who 82, –83,
WhoWor 80, WrDr 76, –80, –82, –84*

Brandreth, Gyles Daubeney 1948-
Who 85

Brandt, Bill d1983 *NewYTBS 85*

Brandt, Bill 1904- *PrintW 85,
WhoWor 84, –87*

Brandt, Bill 1904-1983 *AnObit 1983,
BioIn 13, ConAu 111, CurBio 84N,
ICPEnP*

Brandt, Bill 1905- *MacBEP*

Brandys, Marian 1912- *ConAu 57,
WhoSocC 78, WhoWor 74, –76*

Branfield, John 1931- *Au&Wr 71,
AuBYP SUP, BioIn 11, ConAu 14NR,
–41R, IntAu&W 76, –77, –82,
SmATA 11, TwCChW 83, WrDr 76,
–80, –82, –84, –86*

Branley, Franklyn M 1915-
*AmM&WS 73P, –76P, –79P, –82P,
–86P, Au&Wr 71, AuBYP, BioIn 6,
–7, –9, BlueB 76, BkP,
ChlLR 13[port], ConAu 14NR, –33R,
ConLC 21[port], IntAu&W 76,
MorJA, ScF&FL 1, –2, SmATA 4,
WhoAm 74, –76, –78, –80*

Branscum, Robbie 1937- *BioIn 13,
ConAu 8NR, –61, FifBJA,
SmATA 23[port]*

Brant, Charles S 1919-
*AmM&WS 73S, –76P, ConAu 25R,
FifIDA*

Brant, Irving Newton 1885-1976
*AmAu&B, BioIn 2, –4, –11,
ConAu 9R, –69, EncTwCJ,
NewYTBS 76, REnAL, TwCA SUP,
WhAm 7, WhoAm 74, –76*

Brasch, Rudolph 1912- *Au&Wr 71,
ConAu 8NR, –21R, IntAu&W 76,
WhoWor 74, –76, WhoWorJ 72, –78,
WrDr 76, –80, –82, –84, –86*

Brashler, William 1947- *BioIn 11, –13,
ConAu 2NR, –45*

Brauer, Earle William 1918- *WhoE 74,
–75, –77*

Braun, Wernher Von 1912-1977
*AsBiEn, AuBYP, BiESc, BioIn 2, –3,
–4, –5, –6, –7, –8, –9, –10, –11, –12,
CurBio 52, EncTR, HisEWW, InSci,
IntAu&W 77, IntWW 74, –75, –76,
–78N, LinLib L, –S, NewYTBE 70,
NewYTBS 77, ScF&FL 1,
WebAB, –79, WebAMB, WhDW,
WhWW-II, WhoMilH 76, WorAl*

Braun, Wernher Von see also
VonBraun, Wernher

Brautigan, Richard d1984
NewYTBS 84

Brautigan, Richard 1933?-1984
AnObit 1984, ConPo 85

Brautigan, Richard 1935?- *AmAu&B,
BioIn 9, –10, –12, BlueB 76, CelR,
CmCal, ConAu 53, ConLC 1, –3, –5,
–9, –12, ConNov 72, –76, –82,
ConPo 70, –75, –80, DcLB 2, –5,
–Y80A[port], DcLEL 1940, EncSF,
IntAu&W 76, –77, IntWWP 77,
ModAL S1, MugS, Novels,
OxAmL 83, PenC AM, ScF&FL 1,
ScFSB, WhoAm 74, –76, –78, –80,
–82, –84, WorAu 1970, WrDr 76,
–80, –82, –84*

Brautigan, Richard 1935-1984
*ConAu 113, ConLC 34[port],
–42[port], DcLB Y84N[port], PostFic,
WhAm 8*

Bray, Warwick 1936- *ConAu 15NR,
–25R, FifIDA*

Braymer, Marjorie Elizabeth 1911-
*AnCL, AuBYP, ConAu 1R,
SmATA 6, WhoAm 74, –76, –78, –80,
WhoAmW 74, –64, –66, –68, –70,
–72, WhoWest 74*

Brecher, Edward Moritz 1911-
*ConAu 7NR, –13R, WhoAm 76, –78,
–80, –82, –84, –86*

Brecht, Bertolt 1898-1956 *AtlBL, BiGAW, BiDMarx, BioIn 1, -2, -3, -4, -5, -6, -7, -8, -9, -10, -11, -12, -13, CnMWL, CnThe, ConAu 104, CroCD, CyWA, DcFM, DcLB 56[port], EncTR, EncWL, -2[port], EncWT, EvEuW, FilmgC, GrFLW, HalFC 84, LinLib L, -S, LongCTC, MajMD 1, MakMC, McGEWB, McGEWD, -84[port], ModGL, ModWD, NewEOp 71, NotNAT A, -B, OxAmT 84, OxEng, -85, OxFilm, OxGer, OxMed 86, OxThe, -83, PenC EUR, PlP&P, RComWL, REn, REnWD, TwCA, -SUP, TwCLC 1, -6[port], -13[port], TwCWr, WhDW, WhAm 4, -HSA, WhoTwCL, WorAl, WorEFlm*

Breck, Vivian 1895- *AmAu&B, AuBYP, BioIn 6, -8, -9, ConAu X, MorJA, SmATA 1*

Breck, Vivian *see also* Breckenfeld, Vivian Gurney

Breckenfeld, Vivian Gurney 1895- *AmAu&B, AuBYP, BioIn 6, -8, -9, ConAu 5R, ForWC 70, SmATA 1*

Breckenfeld, Vivian Gurney *see also* Breck, Vivian

Breckler, Rosemary 1920- *ConAu 101*

Bredes, Don *DrAP&F 85*

Bredes, Don 1947- *ConAu 110*

Bree, Germaine 1907- *AmWomWr, BioIn 9, -10, BlueB 76, ConAu 1R, -4NR, DrAS 74F, -78F, -82F, IntAu&W 77, -82, -86, WhoAm 74, -76, -78, -80, -82, -84, -86, WhoAmW 74, -58, -61, -64, -66, -68, -70, -72, -85, WhoFr 79, WhoWor 74, WorAu, WrDr 76, -80, -82, -84, -86*

Breen, Jon L 1943- *ConAu 119, TwCCr&M 85, WrDr 86*

Breihan, Carl W 1916- *Au&Wr 71, ConAu 1R, -1NR*

Breisky, William J 1928- *BioIn 13, ConAu 53, SmATA 22*

Breitman, George 1916- *ConAu 7NR, -61*

Breitman, George 1916-1986 *ConAu 119*

Breland, Osmond Philip 1910 *AmM&WS 73P, -76P, -79P, ConAu 9R, IntAu&W 76, -82, WrDr 76, -80, -82, -84, -86*

Breman, Paul 1931- *BroadAu, ConAu 21R*

Brendon, Piers 1940- *WrDr 86*

Brennan, Joseph Lomas 1903- *BioIn 10, ConAu 2NR, -5R, IntAu&W 77, SmATA 6*

Brennan, Joseph Lomas *see also* Lomas, Steve

Brennan, Joseph Payne *DrAP&F 85*

Brennan, Joseph Payne 1918- *ChhPo S1, ConAu 1R, -4NR, -19NR, EncMys, IntAu&W 77, -82, -86, IntWWP 77, -82, Po&Wr 77, ScF&FL 1, -2, WhoE 77, -79, -83, WhoHr&F, WrDr 76, -80, -82, -84, -86*

Brennan, Louis A 1910?-1983 *BioIn 13*

Brennan, Louis A 1911-1983 *BioIn 3, ConAu 109, -17R, NewYTBS 83, WhoE 74*

Brenner, Barbara 1925- *AuBYP, BioIn 8, -9, ConAu 9R, -12NR, ForWC 70, FourBJA, SmATA 4, -42[port]*

Brent, Madeleine *WrDr 84, -86*

Brent, Peter *TwCCr&M 85*

Brent, Peter 1931- *ConAu 13NR, -65, IntAu&W 77, -82, WrDr 76, -80, -82, -84*

Brent, Peter 1931-1984 *ConAu 114*

Brent-Dyer, Elinor M 1895-1969 *OxChL*

Breslin, Herbert H 1924- *ConAu 53*

Breslin, James 1930- *ConAu 73*

Breslin, Jimmy 1929- *WhoAm 84, -86*

Breslin, Jimmy 1930- *AmAu&B, AuNews 1, BioIn 6, -7, -8, -10, -11, -13, CelR, ConAu 73, -X, ConLC 4, -43[port], CurBio 73, EncAJ, EncTwCJ, LinLib L, WhoAm 74, -76, -78, -80, -82, WhoE 74, WhoWor 74, WorAl, WrDr 76, -80, -82, -84, -86*

Bretnor, Reginald 1911- *ConAu 10NR, -65, EncSF, ScF&FL 1, -2, ScFSB, TwCSFW 86, WrDr 84, -86*

Brett, Bernard 1925- *BioIn 12, -13, ConAu 17NR, -97, IlsCB 1967, SmATA 22[port]*

Brett, Simon 1945- *ConAu 69, TwCCr&M 80, -85, WrDr 82, -84, -86*

Breuig, Charles 1920- *DrAS 74H, -78H, -82H*

Brewton, John Edmund 1898- *BioIn 10, BkP, ChhPo, -S1, -S2, -S3, ConAu 3NR, -5R, SmATA 5*

Brewton, Sara W *BkP*

Brian, Denis 1923- *BioIn 8, ConAu 25R*

Brick, John 1922-1973 *AmAu&B, AuBYP, BioIn 3, -7, -10, -11, ConAu 45, ConAu P-1, CurBio 53, -73, -73N, SmATA 10*

Bridenbaugh, Carl 1903- *AmAu&B, ConAu 4NR, -9R, DrAS 74H, -78H, -82H, WhoAm 74, -76, -78, -80, WhoWor 74*

Bridge, Raymond 1943- *ConAu 69*

Bridgeman, William Barton 1917?-1968 *BioIn 2, -3, -6, -8, -12, ConAu 9R*

Bridgers, Sue Ellen *DrAP&F 85*

Bridgers, Sue Ellen 1942- *BioIn 13, ConAu 11NR, -65, ConLC 26[port], DcLB 52[port], FifBJA[port], SmATA 22[port], SmATA 1AS[port]*

Bridges, William d1984 *NewYTBS 84*

Bridges, William 1901- *AmAu&B, AuBYP, BioIn 7, -10, ConAu 33R, IndAu 1917, IntAu&W 77, -82, SmATA 5, WhoAm 74, -76, -78, -80, -82, WrDr 76, -80, -82, -84, -86*

Bridges, William 1901-1984 *BioIn 13*

Briggs, Katharine M 1898-1980 *OxChL*

Briggs, Katharine Mary 1898-1980 *Au&Wr 71, BioIn 12, -13, ChhPo S2, ConAu 9R, -102, -12NR, EncO&P 78, IntAu&W 76, -82, SmATA 25N, TwCChW 83, WhoWor 76, -78, WrDr 76, -80, -82*

Briggs, Mitchell Pirie 1892- *AmAu&B*

Briggs, Peter 1921-1975 *BioIn 10, ConAu 57, ConAu P-2, NewYTBS 75, SmATA 31N, -39[port], WhoE 74*

Briggs, Raymond 1934- *Au&Wr 71, BioIn 6, -8, -9, -10, -12, -13, BkP, ChlLR 10[port], ChhPo, -S1, -S2, ConAu 73, IlsBYP, IlsCB 1957, OxChL, SmATA 23[port], ThrBJA, TwCChW 83, Who 82, -83, WrDr 82, -84, -86*

Brightfield, Richard 1927- *ConAu 118*

Brill, Steven *ConAu 85*

Brilliant, Moshe D 1915- *WhoWorJ 72, -78*

Brin, David *ScFSB*

Brin, David 1950- *ConAu 102, ConLC 34[port], TwCSFW 86, WhoAm 86*

Brin, Ruth F 1921- *ConAu 8NR, -17R, SmATA 22[port]*

Brindel, June Rachuy *DrAP&F 85*

Brindel, June Rachuy 1919- *AuBYP SUP, BioIn 10, ConAu 49, IntWWP 77, -82, SmATA 7*

Brindle, Reginald Smith 1917- *WrDr 86*

Brindze, Ruth 1903- *AuBYP, BioIn 6, -8, -13, ConAu 73, MorJA, SmATA 23[port]*

Brinkley, William 1917- *AmAu&B, Au&Wr 71, BioIn 4, ConAu 11NR, -21R, WhoAm 74, -76, -78, -80, -82, WhoWor 82*

Brinkley, William Clark 1917- *WhoAm 84, -86, WhoWor 87*

Brinley, Bertrand R 1917- *ConAu 29R*

Brinnin, John Malcolm *DrAP&F 85*

Brinnin, John Malcolm 1916- *AmAu&B, Au&Wr 71, BioIn 4, -10, -12, ChhPo, ConAu 1R, -1NR, ConPo 70, -75, -80, -85, DcLB 48[port], DcLEL 1940, DrAS 74E, -78E, -82E, IntWW 77, -78, -79, -80, -81, -82, -83, IntWWP 77, LinLib L, OxAmL, -83, PenC AM, REn, REnAL, TwCA SUP, WhoAm 74, -76, -78, -80, -82, -84, -86, WhoTwCL, WhoWor 74, -76, WrDr 76, -80, -82, -84, -86*

Brinsmead, H F 1922- *ConAu 10NR, -21R, ConLC 21[port], OxChL, SmATA 18, TwCCW 78, WrDr 82, -84, -86*

Brinsmead, Hesba Fay 1922- *BioIn 12, ConAu 21R, FourBJA, IntAu&W 77, SenS, SingR 2, TwCChW 83, WrDr 76, -80*

Brinton, Henry 1901-1977 *Au&Wr 71, ConAu 1R, -4NR, EncSF, ScF&FL 1, -2, WhE&EA*

Brisco, Patty *IntAu&W 86X, WrDr 86*

Brisco, Patty 1927- *ConAu 69, -X, SmATA X, WrDr 84*

Brisco, Patty *see also* Matthews, Patricia

Briskin, Jacqueline 1927- *ConAu 13NR, -29R, WhoAmW 83, WrDr 80, -82, -84, -86*

Brister, C W, Jr. 1926- *ConAu 7NR, -13R*

Bristow, Gwen 1903- *WrDr 86*

Bristow, Gwen 1903-1980 *AmAu&B, AmNov, AmWomWr, Au&Wr 71, BioIn 2, -4, ConAu 102, -12NR, -17R, CurBio 40, -84N, EncFWF[port], EncMys, ForWC 70, InWom, IntAu&W 77, REnAL, TwCA, -SUP, WhAm 7, WhNAA, WhoAm 74, -76, -78, -80, WhoAmW 74, -61, -64, -66, -70, -72, WhoWor 76, -78, -80, WrDr 76, -80, -82, -84*

Britt, Katrina *WrDr 84, -86*

Brittain, Bill *ConAu X, DrAP&F 85, WrDr 86*

Brittain, Bill 1930- *FifBJA[port]*

Britton, Dorothy *IntAu&W 86X*

Britton, Dorothy 1922- *ConAmC, ConAu 107*

Brock, Edwin 1927- *ConAu 119, ConPo 70, -75, -80, -85, DcLB 40[port], DcLEL 1940, IntWWP 77, WorAu 1970, WrDr 76, -80, -82, -84, -86*

Brock, Stanley E 1936?- *BioIn 9, ConAu 57*

Brockett, Oscar Gross 1923- *ConAu 7NR, -13R, DrAS 74E, -78E, -82E, IntAu&W 77, -82, -86, WhoAm 80, -82, -84, -86, WhoAmA 80, WhoMW 74, -76, WhoS&SW 84, -86, WhoThe 81, WrDr 76, -80, -82, -84, -86*

Brockman, C Frank 1902- *BioIn 13, ConAu 5R, SmATA 26*

Brockway, Edith 1914- *ConAu 17R, ForWC 70*

Broder, Bill *DrAP&F 85*

Broder, David Salzer 1929- *EncTwCJ, WhoAm 84, -86*

Broderick, Dorothy M 1929- *AuBYP, BiDrLUS 70, BioIn 8, -10, ConAu 13R, SmATA 5, WhoLibS 66*

Broderick, Richard L 1927- *ConAu 1NR, -45*

Brodeur, Paul 1931- *ConAu 5R, ConNov 72, -76, DcLEL 1940, IntAu&W 76, -77, WrDr 76, -80, -82, -84, -86*

Brodie, Fawn McKay 1915-1981 *AnObit 1981, Au&Wr 71, BioIn 1, -12, ConAu 102, -10NR, -17R, DrAS 74H, -78H, ForWC 70, NewYTBS 81, WhAm 7, WhoAm 78, -80, WhoAmW 74, -70, -72, -77*

Brodkin, Sylvia Z *ScF&FL 1*

Brodsky, Beverly *ConAu X, DrAP&F 85*

Brodsky, Beverly 1941- *FifBJA[port]*

Brodsky, Joseph 1940- *AmNews 1, BioIn 12, ConAu X, ConFLW 84, ConLC 4, -6, -13, -36[port], CurBio 82[port], EncWL 2, IntWW 77, -78, IntWWP 82, NewYTBS 80[port], WorAu*

Brody, Jane E 1941- *CurBio 86[port]*

Brody, Jane Ellen 1941?- *BioIn 7, -12, ConAu 102, NewYTBS 81[port], WhoAm 80, -82, -84, -86*

Brokhin, Yuri 1934- *ConAu 57*

Brokhin, Yuri 1938?-1982 *BioIn 13*

Bromige, Iris 1910- *Au&Wr 71, IntAu&W 76, WrDr 84, -86*

Bromley, Dudley 1948- *ConAu 77, IntAu&W 82*

Brommer, Gerald F 1927- *AmArt, BioIn 13, ConAu 105, -21NR, SmATA 28[port], WhoAmA 76, -78, -80, -82, -84, WhoWest 78, -84*

Brondfield, Jerome 1913- *BioIn 13, ConAu 73, IntMPA 77, -75, -76, -78, -79, -81, -82, -84, -86, SmATA 22[port]*

Brondfield, Jerry 1913- *ConAu X, SmATA X*

Brondfield, Jerry *see also* Brondfield, Jerome

Bronner, Stephen Eric 1949- *ConAu 113, IntAu&W 86*

Bronowski, Jacob 1908-1974 *AmAu&B, AnCL, AuBYP SUP, BioIn 2, -4, -5, -7, -10, -11, -12, -13, BlueB 76N, ConAu 1R, -3NR, -53, CurBio 74, DcLEL, DcNaB 1971, InSci, IntAu&W 76, IntWW 74, -75N, LinLib L, -S, NewYTBS 74, ObitOF 79, ObitT 1971, WhAm 6, Who 74, WhoAm 74, WhoWor 74, WorAl, WorAu*

Bronson, Wilfrid Swancourt 1894- *AmAu&B, AuBYP, BioIn 1, -2, -5, -7, ConAu 73, IlsCB 1744, -1946, JBA 34, -51, Str&VC*

Bronson, Wilfrid Swancourt 1894-1985 *ConAu 116, SmATA 43N*

Bronson, William Knox 1926-1976 *ConAu 41R, -65, WhoWest 74, -76*

Bronte, Charlotte 1816-1855 *Alli, AtlBL, BbD, BiD&SB, BioIn 1, -2, -3, -4, -5, -6, -7, -8, -9, -10, -11, -12, -13, BritAu 19, BritWr 5, CasWL, Chambr 3, ChhPo, -S1, -S2, -S3, CrtT 3, -4, CyWA, DcBiA, DcBiPP, DcEnA, -AP, DcEnL, DcEuL, DcLB 21[port], DcLEL, DcNaB, Dis&D, EvLB, FilmgC, GoodHs, HalFC 84, HerW, -84, HsB&A, InWom, IntDcWB[port], LinLib L, -S, LongCEL, McGEWB, MouLC 3, NinCLC 3[port], -8[port], NotNAT B, Novels[port], OxEng, -85, PenC ENG, RAdv 1, RComWL, ScF&FL 1, WebE&AL, WhDW, WorAl*

Bronte, Emily 1818-1848 *AtlBL, BbD, BiD&SB, BioIn 1, -2, -3, -4, -5, -6, -7, -8, -9, -10, -11, -12, BritAu 19, BritWr 5, CasWL, Chambr 3, ChhPo, -S1, -S2, -S3, CnE&AP, CrtT 3, -4, CyWA, DcBiA, DcBiPP, DcEnA, -AP, DcEnL, DcEuL, DcLB 21[port], -32[port], DcLEL, Dis&D, EvLB, FilmgC, GoodHs, HalFC 84, HerW, -84, InWom, IntDcWB[port], LinLib L, LongCEL, McGEWB, MouLC 3, Novels[port], OxEng, PenC ENG, RAdv 1, RComWL, WebE&AL, WhDW, WorAl*

Bronte, Emily Jane 1818-1848 *BioIn 13, DcNaB, OxEng 85*

Brook, George Leslie 1910-
*Au&Wr 71, IntAu&W 76, −77,
Who 74, −82, −83, −85, WrDr 76,
−80, −82, −84, −86*
Brooke, Joshua *ConAu X*
Brooke, Joshua *see also* Miller, Victor
Brookins, Dana 1931- *BioIn 13,
ConAu 69, SmATA 28[port]*
Brooks, Anne Tedlock 1905-
*ConAu 1R, −1NR, WhoAmW 58,
−61, −64, −68, −72*
Brooks, Charlotte K *AuBYP,
BioIn 13, ConAu 89, InB&W 80,
LivgBAA, SmATA 24, WhoBlA 77,
−80*
Brooks, Charlotte Kendrick
InB&W 85, WhoBlA 85
Brooks, David H 1929- *ConAu 61*
Brooks, Gwendolyn *DrAP&F 85,
WhoBlA 85*
Brooks, Gwendolyn 1917- *AmAu&B,
AmWomWr, AuNews 1, BioIn 2, −4,
−6, −7, −8, −9, −10, −11, −12, −13,
BioNews 74, BlueB 76, BkCL,
BlkAWP, BroadAu[port], CasWL,
CelR, ChhPo, −S1, −S2, −S3,
ConAu 1R, −1NR, ConLC 1, −2, −4,
−5, −15, ConPo 70, −75, −80, −85,
CroCAP, CurBio 50, −77,
DcLB 5[port], DcLEL 1940, Ebony 1,
EncAB-H, EncWL 2, FourBJA,
GoodHs, InWom, IntAu&W 77,
IntDcWB, IntWW 74, −75, −76, −77,
−78, −79, −80, −81, −82, −83,
IntWWP 77, LibW, LinLib L,
LivgBAA, ModAL, −S1,
ModAWP[port], ModBlW,
NegAl 76[port], −83[port],
NewCon[port], OxAmL, −83,
PenC AM, RAdv 1, REnAL,
SelBAAu, SmATA 6, TwCA SUP,
WebAB, −79, WhoAm 74, −76, −78,
−80, −82, −84, −86, WhoAmW 74,
−58, −64, −66, −68, −70, −72, −77,
−79, −81, −83, −85, −87, WhoBlA 75,
−77, −80, WhoMW 86, WhoWor 74,
−76, −78, −80, −82, −84, −87, WorAl,
WrDr 76, −80, −82, −84, −86*
Brooks, Gwendolyn Elizabeth 1917-
BlkWWr
Brooks, Janice Young 1943-
ConAu 9NR, −65
Brooks, Jerome 1931- *BioIn 13,
ConAu 2NR, −49, SmATA 23[port]*
Brooks, Lester 1924- *AuBYP SUP,
BioIn 10, ConAu 13NR, −33R,
SmATA 7, WhoPubR 72*
Brooks, Maurice Graham 1900-
WhoAm 74
Brooks, Mel *ConAu X, WhoAm 84,
−86*
Brooks, Mel 1926- *BiE&WWA,
BioIn 7, −8, −10, −11, −12, ConAu 65,
ConLC 12, ConTFT 1, CurBio 74,
DcLB 26[port], FilmgC, HalFC 84,
IntDcF 2, IntMPA 77, −75, −76, −78,
−79, −81, −82, −84, −86, IntWW 82,
−83, LesBEnT, MovMk,
NewYTBS 75, NewYTET, Who 82,
−83, −85, WhoAm 74, −76, −78, −80,
−82, WhoAmJ 80, WhoWest 78, −80,
−82, WorAl*
Brooks, Mel 1928- *BioIn 13*
Brooks, Paul 1909- *ConAu 7NR,
−13R, WhoAm 74, −76, −78, −80,
WhoE 74, WrDr 80, −82, −84, −86*
Brooks, Polly 1912- *BioIn 11,
ConAu 1R, SmATA 12*
Brooks, Stewart M 1923- *ConAu 9NR,
−17R, WhoE 74*
Brooks, Terry *DrAP&F 85, ScFSB*
Brooks, Terry 1944- *ConAu 14NR,
−77, IntAu&W 82, −86, WhoAm 78,
−80, −82, −84, −86, WhoMW 80*
Brooks, Tim 1942- *ConAu 102, −19NR*
Brooks, Van Wyck 1886-1963
*AmAu&B, AmLY, AmWr, AtlBL,
CasWL, Chambr 3, CnDAL,
ConAmA, ConAmL, ConAu 1R,
ConLCrt, −82, CurBio 41, −60, −63,
DcLEL, EvLB, LinLib L, LongCTC,
ModAL, ObitOF 79, OxAmL,
PenC AM, RAdv 1, REn, REnAL,*

*TwCA, −SUP, TwCWr, WebE&AL,
WhLit, WhNAA*
Brophy, Ann 1931- *ConAu 106*
Brophy, Brigid 1929- *Au&Wr 71,
BioIn 9, −10, −11, −13, BlueB 76,
CasWL, ConAu 5R,
ConAu 4AS[port], ConDr 73, −77,
ConLC 6, −11, −29[port], ConNov 72,
−76, −82, −86, DcLB 14[port],
DcLEL 1940, EncWL 2,
IntAu&W 76, −77, −82, −86,
IntWW 74, −75, −76, −77, −78, −79,
−80, −81, −82, −83, LinLib L,
LongCTC, ModBrL, −S2, −S1, NewC,
Novels, ScF&FL 1, TwCWr, Who 74,
−82, −83, −85, WhoAmW 74, −68,
−70, −70A, −72, WhoTwCL,
WhoWor 74, −76, −78, WorAu,
WrDr 76, −80, −82, −84, −86*
Brophy, Donald 1934- *AmCath 80,
ConAu 10NR, −21R*
Broughton, James *DrAP&F 85*
Broughton, James 1912- *IntDcF 2*
Broughton, James 1913- *AmAu&B,
BioIn 11, −12, ChhPo, CmCal,
ConAu 2NR, −49, ConPo 70, −75,
−80, −85, DcLB 5[port], DcLEL 1940,
IntAu&W 76, −77, −82, −86,
IntWWP 77, −82, OxAmL 83,
PenC AM, WhoAm 76, −78, −80, −82,
WorEFlm, WrDr 76, −80, −82, −84,
−86*
Broughton, T Alan *DrAP&F 85*
Broughton, T Alan 1936- *ConAu 2NR,
−45, ConLC 19, IntAu&W 86,
IntWWP 77, −82, WrDr 80, −82, −84,
−86*
Broun, Heywood 1888-1939 *AmAu&B,
AmBi, ApCAB X, AuBYP SUP,
BiDAmLL, BioIn 1, −2, −3, −4, −5,
−6, −10, CathA 1930, ConAmA,
CurBio 40, DcAmB S2, DcAmSR,
DcCathB, DcLB 29[port], DcLEL,
DcNAA, EncAJ, EncTwCJ, LinLib L,
−S, NatCAB 30, NotNAT B, OxAmH,
OxAmL, −83, OxAmT 84, PlP&P,
REn, REnAL, ScF&FL 1,
TwCA, −SUP, WebAB, −79, WhAm 1,
WhJnl, WhThe, WorAl*
Broun, Heywood Campbell 1888-1939
BiDAmL
Broun, Heywood Hale 1918-
*BiE&WWA, BioIn 1, −3, −7, −8, −10,
−12, −13, BioNews 74, ConAu 12NR,
−17R, ConTFT 1, NewYTBS 75,
NotNAT, −A, PlP&P, WhoAm 80,
−82, −84, −86*
Browder, Walter Everett 1939-
ConAu 53
Brower, David Ross 1912- *BioIn 7, −8,
−9, −10, −11, −12, −13, CelR, CmCal,
ConAu 9NR, −61, CurBio 73,
NatLAC, PolProf J, PolProf K,
PolProf NF, WhoAm 74, −76, −78,
−80, −82, −84, −86, WhoWest 82, −84,
WhoWor 74*
Brower, Kenneth 1944- *ConAu 10NR,
−25R*
Browin, Frances 1898- *AuBYP,
BioIn 8, −10, ConAu P-1, SmATA 5*
Brown, Beth *AmSCAP 66, ConAu P-2,
ScF&FL 1, −2, WhoAmW 72*
Brown, Bob *ConAu X*
Brown, Bob 1886-1959 *AmAu&B,
ConAu X, DcLB 4, −45[port],
SmATA X, WhNAA, WhoE 74*
Brown, Bob *see also* Brown, Robert
Joseph
Brown, Christy 1932-1981
*AnObit 1981, BiDIrW, BioIn 8, −9,
−10, −12, −13, ConAu 104, −105,
DcIrL, DcIrW 2, DcLB 14[port],
NewYTBE 70, −71,
NewYTBS 81[port], Novels, WrDr 76,
−80, −82, −84*
Brown, Claude *DrAP&F 85*
Brown, Claude 1937- *AmAu&B,
BioIn 7, −8, BlkAWP, CivR 74,
ConAu 73, ConLC 30[port],
CurBio 67, InB&W 85, LinLib L,
LivgBAA, SelBAAf, SelBAAu,
WhoAm 74*
Brown, Curtis F 1925- *ConAu 61*

Brown, David *BiNAW Sup, −SupB,
DcNaB*
Brown, David 1916- *BioIn 13,
ConAu 13R, ConTFT 3[port],
HalFC 84, IntMPA 77, −75, −76, −78,
−79, −81, −82, −84, −86, WhE&EA,
WhoAm 74, −76, −78, −80, −82, −84,
−86, WhoE 74, WhoF&I 74, −75, −77,
−79, −81, −83, −85, WhoWor 74, −76,
−78, −80, −82, −84, −87*
Brown, Dee 1908- *AuBYP SUP,
BiDrLUS 70, BioIn 10, −11, −12,
ConAu 11NR, −13R,
ConAu 6AS[port], ConLC 18,
CurBio 79, DcLB Y80B[port],
DrAS 78H, −82H, EncFWF,
NewYTBS 80[port], REnAW,
SmATA 5, WhoAm 74, −76, −78, −80,
−82, WhoLibS 66, WhoMW 74,
WorAu 1975[port], WrDr 76, −80,
−82, −84, −86*
Brown, Dee Alexander 1908-
WhoAm 84, −86
Brown, E K 1905-1951 *ConAu 107,
OxCanL*
Brown, Fern G 1918- *ConAu 17NR,
−97, SmATA 34[port]*
Brown, Fredric 1906-1972 *AmAu&B,
Au&Wr 71, BioIn 9, −10, −12,
ConSFA, EncMys, EncSF, ObitOF 79,
ScF&FL 1, −2, ScFSB,
TwCCr&M 80, −85, TwCSFW 86,
WhAm 5, WhoSciF, WorAu*
Brown, H Rap 1943- *BioIn 8, −9, −10,
−11, CivR 74, CivRSt, ConAu 112,
LivgBAA, NegAl 76, −83, PolProf J,
WhoBlA 77, −80*
Brown, H Rap *see also* Brown, Hubert
Rap
Brown, Harrison d1986
NewYTBS 86[port]
Brown, Harrison 1917- *AmAu&B,
AmM&WS 73P, −76P, −79P, −82P,
BioIn 1, −3, −4, BlueB 76, ConAu 69,
ConSFA, CurBio 55, EncSF, Future,
InSci, IntWW 74, −75, −76, −77, −78,
−79, −80, −81, −82, −83,
McGMS 80[port], ScF&FL 1, −2,
WhoAm 74, −78, −80, −82,
WhoGov 72, −75, WhoWor 74, −82,
WrDr 80, −82, −84, −86*
Brown, Harrison Scott 1917-
*AmM&WS 86P, WhoAm 84, −86,
WhoFrS 84*
Brown, Harry Peter McNab, Jr. 1917-
*AmAu&B, AmNov, BioIn 2, −4,
ChhPo S3, CmMov, ConAu 69,
DcLB 26, DcLEL 1940, FilmgC,
IntMPA 77, −75, −76, −78, −79, −81,
−82, −84, OxAmL, REnAL,
TwCA SUP, WhoAm 74, −76, −78,
−80, −82*
Brown, Himan 1910- *BioIn 10,
IntMPA 77, −75, −76, −78, −79, −81,
−82, WhoWorJ 72, −78*
Brown, Hubert Rap 1943- *AmAu&B*
Brown, Hubert Rap *see also* Brown, H
Rap
Brown, Ida Mae 1908- *ConAu P-2*
Brown, Irene Bennett 1932- *BioIn 9,
ConAu 12NR, −29R, SmATA 3*
Brown, Ivor John Carnegie 1891-1974
*Au&Wr 71, BiE&WWA, BioIn 2, −3,
−4, −10, −13, ConAu 9R, −49,
DcLEL, DcNaB 1971, EncWT,
EvLB, IntAu&W 76, −77, LongCTC,
ModBrL, NewC, NewYTBS 74,
ObitT 1971, OxThe, PenC ENG,
SmATA 26N, −5, TwCA SUP,
WhAm 6, WhE&EA, WhLit, WhThe,
Who 74, WhoThe 72, WhoWor 74*
Brown, J P S 1930- *ConAu 61,
EncFWF, WrDr 86*
Brown, Jamie 1945- *ConAu 101,
−20NR, WhoCanL 85*
Brown, Jim 1936- *BioNews 74, CelR,
CurBio 64, FilmgC, HalFC 84,
IntMPA 77, −75, −76, −78, −79, −81,
−82, −84, −86, MotPP, MovMk,
NegAl 83[port], NewYTBE 73,
WhoAm 74, −76, −78, −80, −82, −84,
−86, WhoBlA 75, −77, −80,
WhoHol A, WorAl*

Brown, Jimmy 1936- *BioIn 6, −7, −8,
−9, −10, −11, −12, −13, CurBio 64,
NegAl 76[port]*
Brown, Joe David 1915-1976
*AmAu&B, AmNov, BioIn 2, −10,
ConAu 13R, −65, NewYTBS 76,
SmATA 44[port]*
Brown, John Mason 1900-1969
*AmAu&B, BiE&WWA, BioIn 1, −2,
−3, −4, −5, −8, −9, −10, CnDAL,
ConAu 9R, −25R, ConTFT 42, −69,
EncAJ, EncO&P 78, LinLib L, −S,
LongCTC, NotNAT A, −B,
ObitOF 79, OxAmL, −83, OxAmT 84,
OxThe, PenC AM, PlP&P, REnAL,
TwCA, −SUP*
Brown, John Russell 1923-
*ConAu 11NR, −21R, Who 74, −82,
−83, −85, WhoThe 72, −77, −81,
WhoWor 74, −76, WrDr 76, −80, −82,
−84, −86*
Brown, Joseph E 1929- *ConAu 6NR,
−53*
Brown, LeRoy 1908- *ConAu P-1,
DrAS 74E, −78E, −82E, IndAu 1917*
Brown, LeRoy Chester 1908-
ConAu 13NR
Brown, Lester R 1934- *AmM&WS 86P*
Brown, Lester Russell 1934-
*AmM&WS 82P, BioIn 7, −10, −12,
Future, NatLAC, WhoAm 74, −76,
−78, −80, −82, −84, −86, WhoWor 74*
Brown, Lloyd Arnold 1907-1966
*AuBYP, BioIn 4, −7, ConAu P-1,
SmATA 36, WhAm 4*
Brown, Marian A 1911- *ConAu 73,
WhoAmW 83*
Brown, Marion Marsh 1908- *AuBYP,
BioIn 7, −10, ConAu 1R, −3NR,
DrAS 74E, −78E, −82E,
IntAu&W 76, −77, SmATA 6,
WhoAmW 58, −61*
Brown, Morna Doris 1907- *ConAu 5R,
−5NR, EncMys*
Brown, Norman D 1935- *ConAu 53,
DrAS 74H, −78H, −82H,
IntAu&W 77*
Brown, Norman O 1913- *AmAu&B,
BioIn 10, ConAu 21R, DrAS 74F,
−78F, −82F, IntAu&W 76, MugS,
OxAmL 83, PenC AM, WorAu*
Brown, Peter L *IntAu&W 86X*
Brown, Peter Lancaster 1927-
ConAu 4NR, −53
Brown, Ralph Adams 1908-
*ConAu 33R, DrAS 74H, −78H, −82H,
WhoE 79, WrDr 76, −80, −82, −84,
−86*
Brown, Richard C 1917- *ConAu 17NR*
Brown, Richard C 1919- *ConAu 2NR,
−5R, DrAS 74H, −78H, −82H*
Brown, Richard Maxwell 1927-
*ConAu 11NR, −17R, DrAS 74H,
−78H, −82H, WhoAm 76, −78*
Brown, Rita Mae *DrAP&F 85*
Brown, Rita Mae 1944- *AmWomWr,
BioIn 10, −11, −13, ConAu 2NR,
−11NR, −45, ConLC 43[port],
CurBio 86[port], ForWC 70,
IntAu&W 77, IntWWP 77,
NewYTBS 77, WhoAm 84, −86,
WhoAmW 83, −85, −87*
Brown, Robert Joseph 1907- *BioIn 12,
ConAu 13NR, ConAu P-1, SmATA 14*
Brown, Robert Joseph *see also* Brown,
Bob
Brown, Robert McAfee 1920-
*AmAu&B, BioIn 6, −7, −9, −10,
BlueB 76, ConAu 9NR, −13R,
CurBio 65, DrAS 74P, −78P, −82P,
WhoAm 74, −76, −78, −80, −82, −84,
−86, WhoRel 75, −77, −85,
WhoWest 74, −76, WhoWor 74,
WrDr 76, −80, −82, −84, −86*
Brown, Robin 1937- *ConAu 97,
IntAu&W 82*
Brown, Rosellen *DrAP&F 85*
Brown, Rosellen 1939- *BioIn 13,
ConAu 14NR, −77, ConLC 32[port],
WorAu 1975[port]*
Brown, Rosemary 1917?- *Baker 84,
ConAu 115, EncO&P 2, −78, −80,
IntDcWB*

Brown, Roy Allen 1921- *WhoE 74,*
–75, –77, –79
Brown, Roy Frederick 1921-1982
Au&Wr 71, ConAu 65, FourBJA,
IntAu&W 82, TwCCW 78, –83,
WrDr 80, –82, –84
Brown, Seyom 1933- *ConAu 17NR,*
–65, Future, WhoAm 84, –86
Brown, Sterling A *DrAP&F 85*
Brown, Sterling A 1901- *AmAu&B,*
BioIn 2, –10, –11, –12, BlkAWP,
BroadAu, ChhPo S3, ConAu 85,
ConLC 1, –23[port], ConPo 80, –85,
CurBio 82[port], DcLB 51[port],
InB&W 80, LinLib L, LivgBAA,
ModBlW, NegAl 76, –83, OxAmL 83,
REnAL, SelBAAu, WhoBlA 77, –80,
WorAu 1970, WrDr 82, –84
Brown, Sterling Allan 1901-1983
InB&W 85
Brown, Sterling Allen 1901- *BioIn 13,*
SelBAAf
Brown, Theo W 1934- *ConAu 8NR,*
–61
Brown, Vinson 1912- *AuBYP, BioIn 7,*
–12, ConAu 1R, –1NR, IntAu&W 76,
SmATA 19, WhoWest 74, –76, –78,
WrDr 82, –84, –86
Brown, Walter R 1929- *ConAu 2NR,*
–45, SmATA 19
Browne, Anthony 1946- *SmATA 44,*
–45[port]
Browne, Dik *ConGrA 1, SmATA X*
Browne, Dik 1917- *AuNews 1,*
BioIn 10, –11, EncTwCJ, WhoAm 76,
–78, –80, –82, –84, –86, WorECom
Browne, Gerald A *Novels, ScF&FL 1*
Browne, Jackson *WhoAm 84, –86*
Browne, Jackson 1948- *Baker 84,*
BioIn 9, –11, –12, ConAu 120,
ConLC 21, EncFCWM 83,
EncPR&S 77, RkOn 78, –84,
RolSEnR 83, WhoRock 81[port],
WhoRocM 82, WorAl
Browne, Jackson 1950- *BioIn 13*
Browne, Malcolm Wilde 1931-
ConAu 17R, EncTwCJ, WhoAm 74,
–76, –78, –80, –82, –84, –86
Browne, Rose Butler 1893?-
InB&W 80, WhoBlA 77, –80
Browning, Elizabeth Barrett 1806-1861
Alli, –SUP, AtlBL, BbD, BiD&SB,
BioIn 1, –2, –3, –4, –5, –6, –7, –8, –9,
–10, –11, –12, BritAu 19, BritWr 4,
CasWL, CelCen, Chambr 3,
ChhPo, S1, S2, S3, CnE&AP,
ConAu 57, CrtT 3, CyWA, DcBiPP,
DcEnA AP, DcEnL, DcEuL,
DcLB 32[port], DcLEL, DcNaB,
Dis&D, EvLB, GoodHs, HerW,
InWom, IntDcWB, LinLib L, –S,
LongCEL, LuthC 75, McGEWB,
MouLC 3, NewC, NinCLC 1[port],
OxEng, –85, PenC ENG, RAdv 1,
RComWL, REn, WebE&AL, WhDW,
WorAl
Browning, Elizabeth Barrett 1809-1861
HerW 84
Browning, Frank 1946- *ConAu 107*
Browning, Robert *OxChL*
Browning, Robert 1812-1889
Alli, –SUP, AnCL, AtlBL, BiD&SB,
BioIn 1, –2, –3, –4, –5, –6, –7, –8,
–10, –11, –12, –13, BritAu 19,
BritWr 4, CasWL, CelCen,
Chambr 3, ChhPo, –S1, –S2, –S3,
CnE&AP, CnThe, CrtT 3, –4, CyWA,
DcBiPP, DcEnA, –AP, DcEnL,
DcEuL, DcLB 32[port], DcLEL,
DcNaB C, –S1, Dis&D, EncO&P 2,
–78, EncWT, EvLB, IlEncMy,
LinLib L, –S, LongCEL, LuthC 75,
McGEWB, McGEWD, –84[port],
MouLC 4, NewC, OxEng, –85,
OxMus, OxThe, –83, PenC ENG,
PlP&P, RAdv 1, RComWL, REn,
REnWD, Str&VC, WebE&AL,
WhDW, WorAl, YABC 1
Brownlee, Walter 1930- *ConAu 57*
Brownlow, Kevin 1938- *Au&Wr 71,*
ConAu 12NR, –25R, FilmgC,
HalFC 84, IntAu&W 76, OxFilm,
Who 82, –83, –85, WhoWor 76,
WrDr 76, –80, –82, –84, –86

Brownmiller, Susan 1935- *BioIn 10,*
–11, –12, –13, ConAu 103, CurBio 78,
ForWC 70, GoodHs, WhoAm 78, –80,
–84, WhoAmW 79, –81, –83, –85,
WorAl, WrDr 86
Brownstein, Samuel C 1909-
ConAu 5R, WrDr 76, –80, –82
Brownstone, David M 1928-
ConAu 104, –21NR
Bruccoli, Matthew J 1931- *BioIn 11,*
ChhPo S1, –S3, ConAu 7NR, –9R,
DrAS 74E, –78E, –82E,
IntAu&W 77, NewYTBS 77,
WhoAm 80, –82, WhoS&SW 73, –75,
WrDr 76, –80, –82, –84, –86
Bruccoli, Matthew Joseph 1931-
WhoAm 84, –86
Bruce, Leo 1903-1979 *ConAu X,*
TwCCr&M 80, –85
Bruch, Hilde d1984 *WhAm 8*
Bruch, Hilde 1904- *AmM&WS 73P,*
–76P, –79P, AuNews 1, BiDrAPA 77,
BioIn 10, –11, ConAu 53, InWom,
WhoAm 74, –76, –78, –80, –82,
WhoAmJ 80, WhoAmW 74, –58, –61,
–68, –72, WhoWorJ 72, –78
Bruchac, Joseph 1942- *WrDr 86*
Bruchac, Joseph Edward, III 1942-
IntAu&W 86
Bruchac, Joseph, III *DrAP&F 85*
Bruchac, Joseph, III 1942-
ConAu 13NR, –33R, IntAu&W 82,
IntWWP 77, –82, SmATA 42[port],
WrDr 76, –80, –82, –84
Brucker, Roger Warren 1929-
ConAu 11NR, –65, IntAu&W 77,
WhoAdv 80, WhoF&I 75,
WhoMW 74, –76
Bruemmer, Fred 1929- *BioIn 12,*
CanWW 83, ConAu 102,
IntAu&W 77, OxCan SUP,
SmATA 47[port], WhoAm 82, –84,
–86, WrDr 76, –80, –82, –84, –86
Brumbaugh, Robert S 1918- *WrDr 86*
Brumbaugh, Robert Sherrick 1918-
ConAu 3NR, –5R, DrAS 74P, –78P,
–82P, WhoAm 74, –76, –78, –80, –82,
–84, –86, WrDr 76, –80, –82, –84
Bruner, Richard W 1926-
AuBYP SUP, ConAu 49, NatPD
Brunetti, Cledo 1910-1971 *BioIn 1,*
ConAu P-2
Brunhouse, Robert Levere 1908-
ConAu 2NR, –49, DrAS 74H, –78H
Bruning, Nancy P 1948- *ConAu 106*
Brunner, John 1934- *Au&Wr 71,*
BioIn 12, ConAu 1R, –2NR,
ConLC 8, –10, ConSFA, EncSF,
IntAu&W 76, –77, –82, LinLib L,
Novels, PostFic, ScF&FL 1, –2,
ScFSB[port], TwCSFW 86, WhoSciF,
WorAl, WorAu 1975[port], WrDr 76,
–80, –82, –84, –86
Brunvand, Jan Harold 1933-
ConAu 108, DrAS 74E, –78E, –82E
Brust, Steven *ScFSB*
Brustein, Robert *OxThe 83*
Brustein, Robert 1927- *EncAJ,*
OxAmT 84
Bruton, Eric Moore *IntAu&W 86*
Bruton, Eric Moore 1915- *Au&Wr 71,*
ConAu 5NR, –13R, IntAu&W 77,
–82, TwCCr&M 80, WhE&EA,
WrDr 76, –80, –82, –84
Bruun, Ruth Dowling 1937-
BiDrAPA 77, ConAu 108,
WhoAmW 74, –77, –79, WhoE 75,
–77, –79, –81
Bryan, C D B *DrAP&F 85*
Bryan, C D B 1936- *AmAu&B,*
ConAu 13NR, –73, ConLC 29[port]
Bryan, C D B see also Bryan,
Courtlandt Dixon Barnes
Bryan, Christopher 1935- *ConAu 104,*
–20NR
Bryan, Courtlandt Dixon Barnes 1936-
WhoAm 74, –76, –78, –80, –82, –84,
–86, WhoE 74
Bryan, Courtlandt Dixon Barnes see
also Bryan, C D B
Bryan, J, III 1904- *ConAu 11NR,*
IntAu&W 82, WhoAm 80, –82

Bryant, Anita 1940- *AmPS A, –B,*
AmWomWr, BiDAmM, BioIn 9, –10,
–11, –12, ConAu X, CurBio 75,
InWom, NewYTBS 78, RkOn 74,
WhoAm 74, –76, –78, –80, –82,
WhoAmW 74, –72, –79, –81, –83,
WhoRock 81, WorAl
Bryant, Dorothy 1930- *ConAu 4NR,*
–19NR, –53, WrDr 80, –82, –84, –86
Bryant, Edward *DrAP&F 85*
Bryant, Edward 1945- *ConAu 1NR,*
–45, EncSF, IntAu&W 76, –77,
ScF&FL 1, –2, TwCSFW 86,
WrDr 80, –82, –84, –86
Bryant, Paul 1913-1983 *AnObit 1983,*
BioIn 2, –6, –7, –9, –10, –11, –12,
BioNews 75, CelR, ConAu 108,
CurBio 80[port], –83N, NewYTBS 79,
–81[port], –82, –83[port], WhoAm 74,
–76, –78, –82, WhoFtbl 74,
WhoS&SW 73, WorAl
Bryson, Bernarda 1903?- *BioIn 4, –5,*
–8, –9, –11, ChhPo, ConAu 49,
IlsBYP, IlsCB 1946, –1957, –1967,
SmATA 9, ThrBJA
Buban, Peter, Sr. 1920- *LEduc 74,*
WhoMW 76
Buchan, John *OxCanL*
Buchan, John 1875-1940 *BioIn 1, –2,*
–3, –4, –5, –6, –7, –9, –10, –11, –12,
–13, CasWL, Chambr 3, ChhPo, –S1,
–S2, CmScLit, CnMWL,
ConAu 108, CorpD, CurBio 40,
CyWA, DcLB 34[port], DcLEL,
DcNaB 1931, EncMys, EncSoA,
EvLB, FilmgC, HalFC 84, JBA 34,
LinLib S, LongCTC, MacDCB 78,
MnBBF, ModBrL, NewC, Novels,
OxCan, OxChL, OxEng, –85,
PenC ENG, REn, ScF&FL 1, TelT,
TwCA, –SUP, TwCCr&M 80, –85,
TwCWr, WebE&AL, WhDW,
WhE&EA, WhLit, WhoBW&I A,
WhoHr&F, WhoSpyF, YABC 2
Buchan, Stuart 1942- *ConAu 57*
Buchanan, Bruce, II 1945-
WhoS&SW 86
Buchanan, William J 1926- *ConAu 73*
Buchenholz, Bruce 1916- *BiDrAPA 77*
Buchman, Dian Dincin 1922-
BiDrAPH 79, ConAu 8NR, –61,
IntAu&W 76
Buchsbaum, Ralph 1907-
AmM&WS 73P, –76P, –79P, –82P,
–86P, WhoAm 74, –76, –78, –80, –82,
–84, –86, WhoOcn 78
Buchwald, Ann 1921?- *AuBYP SUP,*
BioIn 12
Buchwald, Art 1925- *AmAu&B,*
AuBYP SUP, AuNews 1, BioIn 3, –4,
–5, –6, –7, –8, –9, –10, –11, –12, –13,
BioNews 74, BlueB 76, CelR,
ConAu 5R, –21NR, ConLC 33[port],
CurBio 60, EncAJ[port], EncTwCJ,
IntAu&W 77, –82, IntWW 74, –75,
–76, –77, –78, –79, –80, –81, –82,
–83, NewYTBE 72, NewYTBS 79,
PenC AM, SmATA 10, Who 74, –82,
–83, –85, WhoAm 74, –76, –78, –80,
–82, –84, –86, WhoS&SW 73, –75,
–76, WhoWor 74, –76, –78, –80, –82,
–84, –87, WorAl, WorAu, WrDr 76,
–80, –82, –84, –86
Buck, Pearl S 1892-1973 *AmAu&B,*
AmNov, AmWomWr, AmWr S2,
Au&Wr 71, AuBYP, AuNews 1,
BiE&WWA, BioIn 1, –2, –3, –4, –5,
–6, –7, –8, –9, –10, –11, –12, CasWL,
CnDAL, ConAmA, ConAu 1R, –1NR,
–41R, ConLC 7, –11, –18,
ConNov 72, CurBio 56, –73, –73N,
CyWA, DcLB 9[port], DcLEL,
EncWL, EvLB, FilmgC, GoodHs,
HerW, InWom, IntDcWB, LibW,
LinLib L, –S, LongCTC, McGEWB,
ModAL, MorMA, NewYTBE 73,
NotAW MOD, Novels[port],
ObitOF 79, ObitT 1971, OxAmH,
OxAmL, PenC AM, REn, REnAL,
SmATA 1, –25[port], TwCA, –SUP,
TwCWr, WebAB, –79, WhDW,
WhAm 5, WhE&EA, WhNAA,
WhoAmW 74, –58, –61, –64, –66,
–66A, –68, –70, –72, WorAl

Buck, Sir Peter Henry 1880-1951
BioIn 1, –2, –3, –9, DcNaB 1951,
ObitOF 79, ObitT 1951, WhAm 3
Buck, William Ray 1930- *AuBYP,*
ConAu 1R, WrDr 76, –80, –82, –84
Buckingham, James William 1932-
ConAu 29R
Buckingham, James William see also
Buckingham, Jamie
Buckingham, Jamie 1932- *Au&Wr 71,*
ConAu X
Buckingham, Jamie see also
Buckingham, James William
Buckler, William Earl 1924?-
AmCath 80, ConAu 1R, –5NR,
–20NR, DrAS 74E, –78E, –82E,
WhoAm 74, WhoE 83, –85
Buckley, Christopher *DrAP&F 85*
Buckley, Christopher 1952- *BioIn 13*
Buckley, Jerome Hamilton 1917-
AmAu&B, CanWW 70, –79, –80,
–81, –83, ChhPo, ConAu 1R, –3NR,
DrAS 74E, –78E, –82E, WhoAm 74,
–76, –78, –80, –82, –84, –86,
WhoWor 74, –76
Buckley, Shawn 1943- *ConAu 93,*
WhoTech 82
Buckley, William F, Jr. 1925-
AmAu&B, AmCath 80, AuNews 1,
BioIn 3, –5, –6, –7, –8, –9, –10, –11,
–12, BioNews 74, BlueB 76, CelR,
ConAu 1R, –1NR, ConIsC 1[port],
ConLC 7, –18, –37[port], CurBio 62,
–82[port], DcAmSR, DcBrWA,
DcLB Y80B[port], DcLEL 1940,
EncAJ, EncTwCJ, Film 2,
IntAu&W 76, –77, –82, IntWW 74,
–75, –76, –77, –78, –79, –80, –81,
–82, –83, LinLib L, –S,
NewYTBE 70, NewYTBS 80[port],
Novels, PolProf E, PolProf J,
PolProf K, PolProf NF, St&PR 75,
TwCCr&M 85, WebAB, –79,
WhoAm 74, –76, –78, –80, –82,
WhoAmP 73, –75, –77, –79, –81, –83,
WhoE 74, –75, –77, WhoF&I 74,
WhoGov 77, –72, –75, WhoWor 74,
–76, –78, –80, –82, WorAl, WorAu,
WrDr 76, –80, –82, –84, –86
Buckley, William Frank 1925-
BioIn 13
Buckley, William Frank, Jr. 1925-
WhoAm 84, –86, WhoAmP 85,
WhoWor 84, –87
Buckmaster, Henrietta *BioIn 13*
Buckmaster, Henrietta 1909-1983
AmAu&B, AmNov, AmWomWr,
Au&Wr 71, BioIn 1, –2, –10,
ConAu 69, –X, CurBio 46, –83N,
InWom, IntAu&W 76, –77,
NewYTBS 83, OhA&B, ScF&FL 1,
–2, SmATA 6, WhoAmW 77, WorAu
Buckmaster, Henrietta see also Henkle,
Henrietta
Buckmaster, Henrietta see also
Stephens, Henrietta Henkle
Bucknall, Barbara J 1933-
ConAu 14NR
Bucknall, Barbara Jane 1933-
ConAu 33R, DrAS 74F, –78F, –82F,
WrDr 76, –80, –82, –84, –86
Buckvar, Felice *DrAP&F 85*
Buckvar, Felice 1939- *ConAu 107*
Budbill, David *DrAP&F 85*
Budbill, David 1940- *ConAu 73,*
ConPo 80, IntWWP 77, –82,
Po&Wr 77, WrDr 86
Budd, Lillian 1897- *AuBYP, BioIn 7,*
–10, ConAu 1R, –4NR, IntAu&W 77,
–82, SmATA 7, WhoAmW 58, –61,
–68, WrDr 76, –80, –82, –84, –86
Budden, Julian 1924- *Baker 84,*
IntWWM 85
Budoff, Penny Wise 1939- *ConAu 110,*
IntAu&W 86, WhoAmW 70, –85, –87
Budrys, Algis *ConAu X*
Budrys, Algis 1931- *ConSFA, EncSF,*
Novels, ScF&FL 1, –2, ScFSB,
TwCSFW 86, WhoSciF, WrDr 76,
–82, –84, –86
Budzik, Richard Steven 1938-
WhoMW 76

Buehr, Walter Franklin 1897-1971 *ArtsAmW 3, AuBYP, BioIn 5, –7, –8, –9, ConAu 3NR, –5R, –33R, IlsCB 1946, –1957, SmATA 3, ThrBJA*

Buell, Frederick Henderson *DrAP&F 85*

Buell, Frederick Henderson 1942- *ConAu 33R, DrAS 78E, –82E, IntWWP 77, –82, WrDr 76, –80, –82, –84*

Buell, Harold G 1931- *AuBYP SUP, WhoAm 78, –80, –82*

Buell, Harold George 1931- *WhoAm 84*

Buell, John 1927- *Au&Wr 71, BioIn 11, ConAu 1R, ConLC 10, CreCan 1, DcLB 53[port], NewC, OxCan, –SUP, OxCanL, ScF&FL 1, WhoCanL 85*

Buell, Lawrence 1939- *ConAu 49, DrAS 74E, –78E, –82E*

Bugbee, Emma 1888?-1981 *AuBYP, BioIn 7, –10, –12, –13, BriBl[port], ConAu 105, EncAJ, InWom, NewYTBS 81, SmATA 29N*

Bugliosi, Vincent 1934- *BioIn 12, ConAu 13NR, –73, WhoAm 76, –78, –80, –82*

Bugliosi, Vincent T 1934- *WhoAm 84, –86*

Bulfinch, Thomas 1796-1867 *Alli, –SUP, AmAu, AmAu&B, AmBi, ApCAB, BiD&SB, BioIn 3, CarSB, ChhPo, –S3, DcAmAu, DcAmB, DcNAA, Drake, OxAmL, –83, REn, REnAL, SmATA 35, WebAB, –79, WhAm HS*

Bulgakov, Mikhail 1891-1940 *BioIn 1, –8, –9, –10, –11, CasWL, ClDMEL, CnMD, CnThe, ConAu 105, DcRusL, EncWL, –2, EncWT, EvEuW, GrFLW, MajMD 2, McGEWB, McGEWD, –84, ModSL 1, ModWD, NotNAT B, Novels, PenC EUR, REn, REnWD, ScF&FL 1, ScFSB, TwCLC 2, –16[port], TwCSFW 86A, TwCWr, WhDW, WhoTwCL, WorAl, WorAu*

Bull, Angela 1936- *ConAu 9NR, –21R, IntAu&W 82, SmATA 45[port], TwCCW 78, –83, WrDr 80, –82, –84, –86*

Bulla, Clyde Robert 1914- *Au&ICB, AuBYP, BioIn 6, –7, –9, BkP, ConAu 3NR, –5R, –18NR, MorJA, SmATA 2, –41[port], TwCCW 78, –83, WhoAm 84, –86, WhoWest 74, –76, WrDr 80, –82, –84, –86*

Bullard, Pamela 1948- *ConAu 106*

Bunin, Ivan 1870-1953 *BioIn 1, –2, –3, –4, –5, –8, –9, –12, CasWL, ClDMEL, CnMWL, ConAu 104, CyWA, DcRusL, EncWL, –2, EvEuW, LinLib L, –S, LongCTC, McGEWB, ModSL 1, Novels, ObitOF 79, ObitT 1951, PenC EUR, REn, TwCA, –SUP, TwCLC 6[port], TwCWr, WhDW, WhAm 3, WhE&EA, WhoLA, WhoTwCL, WorAl*

Bunnell, Dewey *WhoRocM 82*

Bunnell, Dewey *see* America

Bunting, A E *ConAu X, WrDr 86*

Bunting, A E 1928- *AuBYP SUP, ConAu X, SmATA X, TwCChW 83*

Bunting, Anne Evelyn 1928- *AuBYP SUP, BioIn 12, ConAu 5NR, –19NR, –53, SmATA 18, WhoAm 78, –80, –82, –84, –86, WhoWor 82*

Bunting, Eve *ConAu X, WhoAm 84, –86*

Bunting, Eve 1928- *AuBYP SUP, ConAu X, FifBJA[port], SmATA X, TwCChW 83, WrDr 86*

Bunting, Eve *see also* Bunting, A E

Bunting, Eve *see also* Bunting, Anne Evelyn

Bunting, Glenn 1957- *BioIn 13, SmATA 22*

Bunyan, John 1628-1688 *Alli, AtlBL, BbD, BiD&SB, BioIn 1, –2, –3, –4, –5, –6, –7, –8, –9, –10, –11, –12, –13,*

Burack, Abraham S 1908-1978 *AmAu&B, BioIn 4, –11, ConAu 4NR, –9R, –77, WhoAdv 72, WhoE 75, WhoWorJ 72, –78*

Buranelli, Vincent 1919- *ConAu 5NR, –9R, –20NR, DrAS 74H, –78H, –82H, IntAu&W 76, –77, WhoE 75, WrDr 76, –80, –82, –84, –86*

Burch, Gladys 1899- *AuBYP, BioIn 8*

Burch, Robert 1925- *AuBYP, BioIn 7, –8, –9, –10, ConAu 2NR, –5R, DcLB 52[port], IntAu&W 82, MorBMP, OxChL, SmATA 1, ThrBJA, TwCCW 78, –83, WrDr 76, –80, –82, –84, –86*

Burchard, Peter Duncan 1921- *Au&Wr 71, AuBYP, BioIn 5, –8, –9, –10, –12, ConAu 3NR, –5R, –18NR, IlsCB 1946, –1957, –1967, IntAu&W 86, SmATA 5, ThrBJA, WhoAmA 78, –80, –82, –84, WhoE 75, –77, WhoWest 80*

Burchard, S H *ConAu X*

Burchell, Mary *Au&Wr 71, WrDr 84, –86*

Burdick, Eugene 1918-1965 *AmAu&B, BioIn 5, –6, –7, –10, ConAu 5R, –25R, DcAmB S7, EncSF, ObitOF 79, SmATA 22[port], TwCWr, WhAm 4, WhoSciF, WorAl, WorAu*

Burford, Lolah 1931- *BioIn 9, ConAu 41R, ScF&FL 1, –2, WrDr 76, –80, –82, –84, –86*

Burgess, Alan 1915- *WhE&EA*

Burgess, Anthony *DrAP&F 85*

Burgess, Anthony 1917- *Alli, Au&Wr 71, AuNews 1, Baker 78, –84, BioIn 7, –8, –9, –10, –12, –13, BlueB 76, CasWL, CelR, ConAu 1R, –X, ConLC 1, –2, –4, –5, –8, –10, –13, –15, –22[port], –40[port], ConNov 72, –76, –82, –86, ConSFA, CurBio 72, DcLB 14[port], DcLEL 1940, EncSF, EncWL, –2, HalFC 84, IntAu&W 76, –77, –86, IntWW 74, –75, –76, –77, –78, –79, –80, –81, –82, –83, LinLib L, LongCTC, MakMC, ModBrL, –S2, –S1, NewC, Novels, OxEng 85, PenC ENG, RAdv 1, ScF&FL 1, –2, ScFSB[port], TwCSFW 86, TwCWr, WebE&AL, Who 74, –82, –83, –85, WhoFr 79, WhoSciF, WhoTwCL, WhoWor 74, –76, –78, –80, –82, –84, –87, WorAl, WorAu, WrDr 76, –80, –82, –84, –86*

Burgess, Anthony *see also* Wilson, John Burgess

Burgess, Linda Cannon 1911- *ConAu 73*

Burgess, Mary 1916- *BioIn 12, ConAu 61, SmATA 18*

Burgess, Robert F 1927- *AuBYP SUP, BioIn 9, ConAu 11NR, –25R, SmATA 4*

Burgess-Kohn, Jane *ConAu X*

Burgess-Kohn, Jane 1928- *ConAu 73*

Burgoyne, Arthur Gordon d1914 *DcNAA*

Burke, Alan Dennis 1949- *ConAu 106*

Burke, Carl F 1917- *ConAu 25R*

Burke, Fred George 1926- *AmAu&B, AmM&WS 73S, ConAu 13R, LEduc 74, WhoAm 78, –80, –82, WhoE 74, –79, –81, –83, –85, WhoGov 77, –75*

Burke, John 1915-1975 *ConAu X*

Burke, John 1922- *TwCCr&M 85, WrDr 86*

Burke, John Frederick 1922- *Au&Wr 71, ConAu 5R, –9NR, IntAu&W 80, –86, ScF&FL 1, –2, TwCCr&M 80, WhoHr&F, WhoSciF, WrDr 82, –84*

Burke, John *see also* O'Connor, Richard

Burkert, Nancy Ekholm 1933- *BioIn 8, –9, –11, –12, ChhPo S1, IlsBYP, IlsCB 1957, –1967, SmATA 24[port], ThrBJA*

Burkhart, Kathryn Watterson 1942- *BioIn 10, ConAu 45, WhoAm 76, –78, –80*

Burkholz, Herbert *DrAP&F 85*

Burkholz, Herbert 1932?- *Au&Wr 71, BioIn 8, –11, ConAu 11NR, –25R*

Burland, C A 1905- *ConAu X, EncO&P 78, SmATA 5*

Burland, C A 1905-1983 *EncO&P 2*

Burland, C A *see also* Burland, Cottie Arthur

Burland, Cottie A *WhoArt 84N*

Burland, Cottie Arthur 1905- *Au&Wr 71, AuBYP, BioIn 8, –9, –10, ConAu 5R, –5NR, FifIDA, IntAu&W 76, –77, –82, SmATA 5, WhoArt 80, –82*

Burland, Cottie Arthur *see also* Burland, C A

Burley, W J 1914- *ConAu 13NR, –33R, TwCCr&M 80, –85, WrDr 82, –84, –86*

Burlingame, Roger 1889-1967 *AmAu&B, AuBYP SUP, BioIn 4, –5, –7, –9, ConAu 5R, REn, REnAL, SmATA 2, TwCA, –SUP, WhAm 4*

Burman, Ben Lucien 1895- *AmAu&B, AmNov, Au&Wr 71, BioIn 2, –3, –4, –10, ConAu 5R, –8NR, IntAu&W 76, –77, –82, OxAmL, –83, REnAL, ScF&FL 1, –2, SmATA 6, TwCA, –SUP, TwCChW 83, WhE&EA, WhNAA, WhoAm 74, –76, –78, –84, WhoWor 74, –76, WrDr 76, –80, –82, –84*

Burman, Ben Lucien 1895-1984 *WhAm 8*

Burman, Ben Lucien 1896-1984 *ConAu 114, NewYTBS 84, SmATA 40N*

Burman, Tom 1913- *ConAu 61, DrAS 74E, –78E, –82E, WhoAm 78, –80, –82, –84, –86*

Burness, Tad *ConAu X*

Burness, Tad *see also* Burness, Wallace B

Burness, Wallace B 1933- *ConAu 11NR, –69*

Burnet, Sir Alastair *Who 85*

Burnett, Avis 1937- *ConAu 41R*

Burnett, Carol *ConTFT 1*

Burnett, Carol 1933- *HalFC 84*

Burnett, Carol 1934- *BioIn 13, HerW 84*

Burnett, Carol 1936- *IntMPA 86, WhoAm 84, –86, WhoAmW 85*

Burnett, Constance Buel 1893-1975 *AuBYP, BioIn 1, –8, ConAu 5R, SmATA 36*

Burnett, David 1931-1971 *ConAu 9R, –33R*

Burnett, Frances Hodgson *WomNov*

Burnett, Frances Hodgson 1849-1924 *Alli SUP, AmAu&B, AmBi, AmWom, AmWomWr, ApCAB, ApCAB X, AuBYP, BbD, BiD&SB, BiDSA, BioIn 1, –2, –7, –8, –10, –11, –12, CarSB, CelCen, Chambr 3, ChhPo, –S2, ConAmL, ConAu 108, DcAmAu, DcAmB, DcBiA, DcLB 42[port], DcLEL, DcNAA, EvLB, FamSYP, HalFC 84, HerW, –84, InWom, IntDcWB, JBA 34, LibW, LinLib L, –S, LongCTC, NatCAB 1, –20, NotAW, NotNAT B, OxAmL, –83, OxAmT 84, OxChL, OxEng, –85, PenC AM, –ENG, PIP&P, REn, REnAL, ScF&FL 1, TelT, TwCA, –SUP, TwCBDA, TwCCW 78, –83, WhAm 1, WhLit, WhoAmW 70, –72, WhoChL, WhoMW 74, –76, –78,*

Burnett, Hallie Southgate 1908- *AmAu&B, BioIn 3, ConAu 6NR, –13R, CurBio 54, InWom, IntAu&W 77, –82, ScF&FL 1, –2, TwCA SUP, WhoAm 74, –58, –61, –70, –72, WhoWor 74, –76, –78, WrDr 76, –80, –82, –84*

Burnett, Whit 1899-1973 *AmAu&B, BioIn 4, –9, –10, –13, ConAu 41R, ConAu P-2, CurBio 41, –73, –73N, EncAJ, NewYTBS 73, ObitOF 79, REnAL, ScF&FL 1, TwCA, –SUP, WhAm 5, WhE&EA, WhoAm 74*

Burnett, S D *SmATA X*

Burnford, S D 1918-1984 *ConAu X, SmATA X*

Burnford, S D *see also* Burnford, Sheila

Burnford, Sheila *OxChL*

Burnford, Sheila 1918- *Au&Wr 71*

Burnford, Sheila 1918-1984 *AuBYP, BioIn 7, –9, –10, –11, BkCL, ChlLR 2, ConAu 1R, –1NR, –112, CreCan 2, FourBJA, OxCan, Profile, ScF&FL 1, –2, SmATA 3, –38N, TwCCW 78, –83, WhoAm 74, –78, WhoCanL 85, WrDr 76, –80, –82, –84*

Burnham, Sophy 1936- *AuNews 1, BioIn 10, ConAu 41R, IntAu&W 82, –86, WhoAmW 72*

Burns, E Bradford 1932- *ConAu 17R, WhoAm 82, –84, –86, WhoWest 74, –76, –80*

Burns, George 1896- *BioIn 2, –3, –4, –5, –7, –8, –10, –11, –12, –13, CelR, ConAu 112, ConTFT 3, CurBio 76, Film 2, FilmgC, HalFC 84, IntMPA 77, –81, –82, –84, –86, IntWW 79, –80, –81, –82, –83, MotPP, MovMk, NewYTBS 81[port], NotNAT A, WhoAm 74, –76, –78, –80, –82, –84, –86, WhoHol A, WhoWor 74, WorAl*

Burns, James MacGregor 1918- *AmAu&B, AmM&WS 73S, –78S, Au&Wr 71, BioIn 4, –5, –6, –10, –11, –12, CelR, ConAu 5R, –19NR, CurBio 62, DcLEL 1940, DrAS 74H, LinLib L, PolProf K, WhoAm 74, –76, –78, –80, –82, –84, –86, WhoGov 72, WhoWor 74, WorAu, WrDr 82, –84, –86*

Burns, John Horne 1916-1953 *AmAu&B, AmNov, BioIn 1, –2, –3, –4, –10, ConAu 115, DcLB Y85B[port], EvLB, LinLib L, ModAL, Novels, ObitOF 79, OxAmL, –83, PenC AM, REn, REnAL, TwCA SUP, TwCWr, WebE&AL, WhAm 4*

Burns, Marilyn *SmATA 33*

Burns, Olive Ann 1924- *ConAu 120*

Burns, Rex 1935- *ConAu 13NR, –77, DrAS 74E, –78E, –82E, TwCCr&M 80, –85, WrDr 82, –84, –86*

Burns, Robert 1759-1796 *Alli, AtlBL, BiD&SB, BioIn 1, –2, –3, –4, –5, –6, –7, –8, –9, –10, –11, –12, –13, BritAu, BritWr 3, CasWL, ChhPo, –S1, –S2, –S3, CmScLit, CnE&AP, CrtT 2, –4, CyWA, DcBiPP, DcEnA, –AP, DcEnL, DcEuL, DcLEL, DcNaB, Dis&D, EvLB, FamAYP, LinLib L, –S, LitC 3[port], LongCEL, McGEWB, MouLC 2, NewC, OxEng, –85, OxMus, PenC ENG, RAdv 1, RComWL, REn, WebE&AL, WhDW, WorAl*

Burns, William A 1909- *AuBYP SUP, BioIn 10, ConAu 11NR, ConAu P-1, SmATA 5, Who 74, –82, –84, WhoAm 74, –76, –78, –80, –82, –84, –86, WhoWor 82*

Burow, Daniel Robert 1931- *ConAu 11NR, –29R, WhoMW 74, –76, WhoRel 75, –77*

Burr, Esther Edwards 1732-1758 *AmWrBE, DcBrAmW*

Burr, Lonnie 1943- *ConAu 103, SmATA 47[port]*
Burr, Samuel Engle, Jr. 1897- *WhoS&SW 73, -75, -76*
Burroughs, Edgar Rice 1875-1950 *AmAu&B, AmLY, ApCAB X, BioIn 1, -2, -4, -6, -7, -8, -10, -12, CmCal, ConAu 104, DcAmB S4, DcLB 8[port], EncFWF, EncSF, EvLB, FilmgC, HalFC 84, LinLib L, LongCTC, MnBBF, Novels, ObitOF 79, OxAmL, -83, OxChL, OxEng 85, PenC AM, REn, REnAL, ScF&FL 1, -2, ScFSB[port], SmATA 41[port], TwCA, -SUP, TwCLC 2, TwCSFW 86, TwCWr, WebAB, -79, WhAm 2A, WhE&EA, WhLit, WhoHr&F, WhoSciF, WorAl*
Burroughs, William S *DrAP&F 85, DrmM 2[port]*
Burroughs, William S 1914- *AmAu&B, Au&Wr 71, AuNews 2, BioIn 7, -8, -9, -10, -11, -12, BlueB 76, CasWL, CelR, ConAu 9R, -20NR, ConLC 1, -2, -5, -15, -22[port], -42[port], ConNov 72, -76, -82, -86, ConSFA, CurBio 71, DcLB 2, -8, -16[port], -Y81A[port], DcLEL 1940, EncSF, EncWL, -2, IntAu&W 76, -77, -82, IntWW 74, -75, -76, -77, -78, -79, -80, -81, -82, -83, LinLib L, MakMC, ModAL, -S2, -S1, Novels, OxAmL, -83, PenC AM, RAdv 1, REn, REnAL, ScF&FL 1, -2, ScFSB, TwCSFW 86, TwCWr, WebAB, -79, WebE&AL, WhDW, WhoAm 74, -76, -78, -80, -82, WhoSciF, WhoTwCL, WhoWor 74, WorAu, WrDr 76, -80, -82, -84, -86*
Burroughs, William Seward 1914- *BioIn 13, OxEng 85, WhoAm 84, -86*
Burrow, John W 1935- *ConAu 12NR, -21R*
Burt, Jesse Clifton 1921-1976 *BioIn 12, ConAu 4NR, -9R, SmATA 20N, -46*
Burt, Olive Woolley 1894- *AuBYP, BioIn 7, -9, ChhPo S2, ConAu 5R, -5NR, ForWC 70, IntAu&W 76, -77, SmATA 4, WhoAmW 58*
Burt, William Henry 1903- *AmM&WS 73P, -76P, -79P, ConAu 106, WhoAm 74, -76, -78, -80, WhoWor 76*
Burton, Anthony 1933- *ConAu 61*
Burton, Elizabeth 1908- *Au&Wr 71, AuBYP, BioIn 8, ConAu 15NR, -65, ScF&FL 1, WrDr 82, -84, -86*
Burton, Hester 1913- *Au&Wr 71, AuBYP SUP, BioIn 8, -9, -10,*

ChlLR 1, ConAu 9R, -10NR, IntAu&W 82, -86, OxChL, SmATA 7, ThrBJA, TwCCW 78, -83, WhoChL, WrDr 76, -80, -82, -84, -86
Burton, Maurice 1898- *Au&Wr 71, BioIn 13, BlueB 76, ConAu 9NR, -65, IntAu&W 76, -77, -82, -86, SmATA 23[port], Who 74, -82, -83, -85, WrDr 80, -82, -84, -86*
Burton, Robert 1941- *BioIn 13, ConAu 17NR*
Buscema, John 1927- *WorECom*
Busch, Frederick *DrAP&F 85*
Busch, Frederick 1941- *BioIn 13, ConAu 33R, ConAu 1AS[port], ConLC 7, -10, -18, ConNov 76, -82, -86, DcLB 6[port], DrAS 74E, -78E, -82E, IntAu&W 86, PostFic, WrDr 76, -80, -82, -84, -86*
Busch, Noel F 1906-1985 *ConAu 117*
Busch, Noel Fairchild d1985 *NewYTBS 85*
Busch, Noel Fairchild 1906- *AmAu&B, BlueB 76, ConAu 49, WhoAm 74, -76, -78, -80, -82, -84, WhoWor 74, -76, WrDr 80, -82, -84*
Busch, Phyllis S 1909- *ConAu 107, SmATA 30[port], WhoAmW 70*
Bush, Douglas 1896- *WrDr 86*
Bush, Douglas 1896-1983 *AmAu&B, BioIn 4, -13, BlueB 76, CanWr, ConAu 109, -37R, DcLEL, DrAS 74E, -78E, -82E, LongCTC, NewYTBS 83, RAdv 1, TwCA SUP, Who 74, -82, -83, -84, WrDr 76, -80, -82, -84*
Bush, George P 1892- *ConAu 17R*
Bush, Jim 1926- *ConAu 57*
Bushnell, Geoffrey Hext Sutherland 1903-1978 *Au&Wr 71, BioIn 12, -13, FifIDA, IntAu&W 76, -77, Who 74, WhoWor 74, -76, WrDr 76, -80*
Bushyager, Linda E 1947- *ConAu 93*
Busoni, Rafaello 1900-1962 *AmAu&B, AuBYP, BioIn 1, -2, -3, -5, -6, -7, -8, -12, ConAu 117, IlsCB 1744, -1946, -1957, JBA 51, SmATA 16*
Butkus, Dick 1942- *BioIn 8, -9, -10, CelR, NewYTBS 74, WhoAm 74, -76, -78, -80, -82, -84, -86, WhoFtbl 74, WhoWor 78, WorAl*
Butler, Beverly Kathleen 1932- *AuBYP, BioIn 7, -10, ChhPo S2, ConAu 1R, ForWC 70, SmATA 7, WhoAmW 58, -61*
Butler, Bonnie Marie 1941- *LEduc 74*
Butler, Gwendoline *TwCCr&M 85*
Butler, Gwendoline 1922- *Au&Wr 71, ConAu 6NR, -9R, DcLEL 1940,*

IntAu&W 76, -77, Novels, TwCCr&M 80, WrDr 76, -80, -82, -84, -86
Butler, Gwendoline *see also* Melville, Jennie
Butler, Hal 1913- *AuBYP, BioIn 8, ConAu 57, MichAu 80*
Butler, Mildred Allen 1897- *AuBYP SUP, ConAu 29R, ConAu P-2, WhoPNW*
Butler, Octavia 1947- *ScFSB*
Butler, Octavia E 1947?- *BioIn 13, ConAu 12NR, -73, ConLC 38, DcLB 33[port], InB&W 80, SelBAAf, TwCSFW 86, WhoBlA 85, WrDr 80, -82, -84, -86*
Butler, Octavia Estelle 1948- *InB&W 85*
Butler, Samuel *OxCanL*
Butler, Samuel 1835-1902 *Alli SUP, AtlBL, BbD, BioIn 1, -2, -3, -4, -5, -6, -7, -8, -9, -10, -11, -12, -13, BritAu 19, CasWL, CnMWL, ConAu 104, CrtT 3, CyWA, DcBrAr 2, DcEnA, -AP, DcEuL, DcLB 18[port], -57[port], DcLEL, DcNaB S2, DcVicP, EncSF, EvLB, LinLib L, -S, LongCEL, LongCTC, McGEWB, ModBrL, NewC, Novels[port], OxEng, -85, OxMus, PenC ENG, RAdv 1, REn, ScF&FL 1, ScFSB, TwCLC 1, TwCSFW 86, WebE&AL, WhDW, WorAl*
Butler, William 1929- *Au&Wr 71, AuBYP SUP, ConAu 107, EncSF, ScF&FL 1*
Butlin, Martin 1929- *ConAu 19NR, WrDr 86*
Butterfield, Roger Place 1907-1981 *AmAu&B, Au&Wr 71, BioIn 12, -13, ConAu 104, ConAu P-1, CurBio 48, LinLib L, REnAL*
Butters, Dorothy Gilman *WhoAm 84, -86, WrDr 86*
Butters, Dorothy Gilman 1923- *AmAu&B, AuBYP, BioIn 7, -8, -10, -12, ConAu 1R, -2NR, ForWC 70, SmATA 5, WhoAmW 66, -68, -70, WrDr 82, -84*
Butters, Dorothy Gilman *see also* Gilman, Dorothy
Butterworth, Emma Macalik 1928- *ConAu 105, SmATA 43*
Butterworth, Michael 1924?- *ConAu 10NR, 25R, WrDr 76, 80, -82, -84*
Butterworth, W E 1929- *ConAu 1R, -2NR, -18NR, FifBJA[port], IntAu&W 76, SmATA 5*

Butterworth, W E *see also* Beech, Webb
Butterworth, W E *see also* Blake, Walker E
Butterworth, W E *see also* Butterworth, William Edmund, III
Butterworth, W E *see also* Douglas, James McM
Butterworth, W E *see also* Scholefield, Edmund O
Butterworth, W E *see also* Williams, Patrick J
Butterworth, William Edmund, III 1929- *AuBYP SUP, WhoS&SW 73, -75, -76*
Butterworth, William Edmund, III *see also* Butterworth, W E
Butti, Ken 1950- *ConAu 104*
Buxbaum, Robert C 1930- *BiDrACP 79, BiDrAPH 79, ConAu 97*
Buzan, Tony 1942- *IntAu&W 77, IntWWP 82, WrDr 76, -80, -82, -84, -86*
Byars, Betsy 1928- *AuBYP, BioIn 8, -9, -10, -12, -13, ChlLR 1, ConAu 18NR, -33R, ConLC 35[port], DcLB 52[port], MorBMP, NewbC 1966, OxChL, SmATA 4, -46[port], SmATA 1AS[port], ThrBJA, TwCCW 78, -83, WrDr 80, -82, -84, -86*
Byck, Robert 1933- *AmM&WS 86P, WhoFrS 84*
Byers, Edward A 1939- *ConAu 119*
Bykov, Vasilii Vladimirovich 1924- *WhoSocC 78*
Byrd, Elizabeth 1912- *Au&Wr 71, BioIn 8, ConAu 5R, -5NR, SmATA 34[port], WhoAmW 58*
Byrd, Richard E 1888-1957 *MemAm*
Byrd, Richard Evelyn 1888-1957 *AmAu&B, BioIn 1, -2, -3, -4, -5, -6, -7, -8, -9, -11, -12, -13, CurBio 42, -56, -57, DcAmB S6, DcAmMiB, EncAB-H, InSci, LinLib L, -S, McGEWB, MedHR, NatCAB 46, ObitOF 79, OxAmH, OxAmL, -83, REn, REnAL, TwCA, -SUP, WebAB, -79, WebAMB, WhDW, WhAm 3, WhNAA, WorAl*
Byrne, Donn 1931- *AmM&WS 73S, -78S, BioIn 12, ConAu 5NR, -9R, -20NR, IntAu&W 77, -82, WhoAm 80, -82, WhoMW 78, WrDr 76, -80, -82, -84*

C

Cable, Mary *DrAP&F 85* Cable, Mary 1920- *BioIn 11, ConAu 11NR, -25R, SmATA 9, WhoAmW 74, -70, -72*

Cabral, Olga *DrAP&F 85*

Cabral, Olga 1909- *ConAu 10NR, -25R, SmATA 46[port]*

Cade, Toni 1939- *BlkAWP, ConAu X*

Cade, Toni *see also* Bambara, Toni Cade

Cadell, Elizabeth 1903- *Au&Wr 71, BioIn 2, ConAu 11NR, -57, CurBio 51, InWom, ScF&FL 1, -2, WrDr 76, -80, -82, -84, -86*

Cadwallader, Sharon 1936- *BioIn 10, ConAu 1NR, -17NR, -49, SmATA 7*

Cady, Edwin H 1917- *WrDr 86*

Cady, Edwin Harrison 1917- *AmAu&B, BlueB 76, ConAu 1R, -4NR, DrAS 74E, -78E, -82E, WhoAm 74, -76, -78, -80, -82, -84, -86, WhoWor 74, -76, -78, -80, -82, -84, -87, WrDr 80, -82, -84*

Cady, Steve 1927- *ConAu 45*

Caffrey, Kate *ConAu 1NR, -49, IntAu&W 76, -77, -82, WrDr 76, -80, -82, -84, -86*

Cagle, Malcolm W 1918- *ConAu 108, SmATA 32, WhoAm 74, WorDWW*

Cahill, James Francis 1926- *ConAu 1NR, -6NR, DrAS 74H, -78H, -82H, WhoAm 74, -76, -78, -80, -82, -84, WhoAmA 73, -76, -78, -80, -82, -84*

Cahill, Susan 1940- *BioIn 11, ConAu 37R*

Cahill, Thomas 1940- *ConAu 49*

Cahn, Edgar S 1935- *ConAu 29R, WhoS&SW 75, -76*

Cahn, Rhoda 1922- *ConAu 81, SmATA 37*

Cahn, William 1912-1976 *BioIn 11, ConAu 21R, -69, NewYTBS 76, SmATA 37, WhoAdv 72*

Caidin, Martin 1927- *AmAu&B, AuNews 2, BioIn 6, -10, -11, -12, ConAu 1R, -2NR, ConSFA, EncSF, LinLib L, ScF&FL 1, -2, ScFSB, TwCSFW 86, WhoSciF, WrDr 84, -86*

Cain, Arthur H 1913- *AuBYP SUP, BioIn 9, ConAu 1R, -4NR, SmATA 3*

Cain, Michael Peter 1941- *ConAu 93, WhoAmA 73, -76, -84*

Caine, Lynn *WhoAm 84, -86*

Caine, Lynn 1927?- *ASpks, BioIn 10, -11, WhoAm 78, -80*

Caird, Janet 1913- *Au&Wr 71, ConAu 1NR, -49, IntAu&W 76, -77, -82, ScF&FL 1, -2, TwCCr&M 80, WrDr 76, -80, -82, -84, -86*

Cairns, Trevor 1922- *BioIn 12, ConAu 33R, IntAu&W 77, -82, SmATA 14, WrDr 76, -80, -82, -84, -86*

Calahan, Harold Augustin 1889-1965 *BioIn 7, -8, NatCAB 50*

Calde, Mark A 1945- *ConAu 69*

Caldecott, Moyra 1927- *BioIn 13, ConAu 13NR, -77, IntAu&W 86, SmATA 22*

Calder, Jenni 1941- *ConAu 1NR, -45*

Calder, Nigel 1931- *Au&Wr 71, ConAu 11NR, -21R, CurBio 86[port], DcLEL 1940, Future, IntAu&W 76, -77, Who 74, -82, -83, WhoWor 76, -80, WorAu 1975[port], WrDr 76, -80, -82, -84, -86*

Calder, Nigel David Ritchie 1931- *Who 85*

Calder, Robert Lorin 1941- *ConAu 65, -69, DrAS 74E, -78E, -82E*

Calder-Marshall, Arthur 1908- *Au&Wr 71, BioIn 2, -10, BlueB 76, ChhPo S3, ConAu 61, ConNov 72, -76, -82, DcLEL, IntAu&W 76, -77, ScF&FL 1, -2, WhE&EA, Who 74, -82, -83, -85, WorAu, WrDr 76, -80, -82, -84, -86*

Calderone, Mary Steichen 1904- *AuNews 1, BiDAmEd, BioIn 8, -10, -11, -12, BioNews 74, ConAu 104, CurBio 67, InWom, LibW, WhoAm 74, -76, -78, -80, -82, -84, -86, WhoAmW 74, -58, -61, -66, -68, -70, -72, -75, -79, -81, -83, -85, -87, WhoWor 74*

Calderwood, James Dixon 1917- *AmEA 74, AmM&WS 73S, -78S, ConAu 3NR, -5R, IntAu&W 77, WhoCon 73*

Caldwell, Erskine *DrAP&F 85*

Caldwell, Erskine 1903- *BioIn 13, ConAu 1AS[port], ConNov 86, HalFC 84, IntAu&W 86, ModAL S2, OxAmL 83, Who 85, WhoAm 84, -86, WhoWor 84, -87, WrDr 86*

Caldwell, John 1928- *BioIn 12, ConAu 12NR, -73, WhoWor 74, -76*

Caldwell, John C 1913- *ConAu 13NR*

Caldwell, John Cope 1913- *AuBYP, BioIn 7, -10, ConAu 21R, SmATA 7*

Caldwell, Taylor 1900- *AmAu&B, AmCath 80, AmNov, AmWomWr, Au&Wr 71, BioIn 1, -2, -5, -6, -9, -11, -12, BlueB 76, CelR, ConAu 5R, -5NR, ConLC 2, -28[port], CurBio 40, EncSF, ForWC 70, InWom, IntAu&W 77, LibW, LinLib LP, LongCTC, NewYTBS 76, -81[port], Novels, OxAmL, -83, REn, REnAL, ScF&FL 1, -2, ScFSB, Who 74, -82, -83, -85, WhoAm 80, -82, WhoAmW 58, -58A, -64, -66, -68, -70, -72, -81, WhoWor 80, -82, WorAl, WrDr 76, -80, -82, -84, -86*

Caldwell, Taylor 1900-1985 *ConAu 116, ConLC 39, CurBio 85N, NewYTBS 85[port]*

Calhoun, Mary *ConAu X*

Calhoun, Mary 1926- *AuBYP, BioIn 7, -9, ConAu 5R, -X, ForWC 70, ScF&FL 1, -2, SmATA 2, ThrBJA*

Call, Hughie Florence 1890-1969 *BioIn 9, ConAu 5R, SmATA 1, WhoAmW 66, WhoPNW*

Callahan, Dorothy Louise 1920- *AuBYP, BioIn 8, WhoAmW 74, -58, -61, -64, -66, -68, -70, -75*

Callahan, Philip S 1923- *AmM&WS 73P, -76P, -79P, -82P, AuBYP SUP, BioIn 13, ConAu 102, SmATA 25[port]*

Callahan, Philip Serna 1923- *AmM&WS 86P*

Callahan, Steven 1952- *ConAu 120*

Callan, Jamie *DrAP&F 85*

Callan, Jamie 1954- *ConAu 109*

Callaway, Kathy *DrAP&F 85*

Callaway, Kathy 1943- *ConAu 107, SmATA 36*

Callen, Larry 1927- *ConAu X, FifBJA[port], SmATA X*

Callen, Larry *see also* Callen, Lawrence Willard, Jr.

Callen, Lawrence Willard, Jr. 1927- *BioIn 12, ConAu 12NR, -73, SmATA 19*

Callenbach, Ernest William, Jr. 1929- *ConAu 6NR, -57, WhoWest 74, -76, -78*

Calley, William L, Jr. 1943- *BioIn 8, -9, -10, -11, -12, NewYTBS 74, PolProf NF*

Callison, Brian 1934- *Au&Wr 71, ConAu 29R, WrDr 76, -80, -82, -84, -86*

Callum, Myles 1934- *ConAu 9R, WhoAm 74, -76, -78, -80, -82, -84, -86, WhoWor 78*

Calter, Paul 1934- *ConAu 14NR, -41R, WhoE 77, -79, -81*

Calvert, James Francis 1920- *AuBYP, BioIn 5, -6, -8, Dun&B 79, NatCAB 63N[port], WhoAm 74, -76, -78, -80, -82, -84, -86, WhoF&I 83, -85, WhoGov 72, WorDWW*

Calvert, Patricia 1931- *ConAu 105, -21NR, SmATA 45[port]*

Calvino, Italo 1923- *BioIn 10, -12, -13, CasWL, ConAu 85, ConFLW 84, ConLC 5, -8, -11, -22[port], -33[port], Novels, OxAmL, -83, DcItL, EncSF, EncWL, -2[port], IntAu&W 76, -77, -82, IntWW 74, -75, -76, -77, -78, -79, -80, -81, -82, -83, ModRL, NewYTBS 81, -83[port], Novels, OxEng 85, PenC EUR, ScF&FL 1, ScFSB[port], TwCWr, Who 83, -85, WhoTwCL, WhoWor 74, -76, -78, -82, -84, WorAu*

Calvino, Italo 1923-1985 *ConAu 116, ConLC 39[port], CurBio 85N, NewYTBS 85[port], PostFic, TwCSFW 86A*

Calvocoressi, Peter 1912- *BlueB 76, ConAu 65, IntAu&W 76, -77, -82, IntWW 74, -75, -76, -77, -78, -79, -80, -81, -82, -83, Who 74, -82, -83, -85, WrDr 80, -82, -84, -86*

Cameron, Anne *InWom*

Cameron, Betsy 1949?- *BioIn 12, ConAu 101*

Cameron, Eleanor 1912- *AuBYP, BioIn 6, -8, -9, -13, ChlLR 1, ChhPo, ConAu 1R, -2NR, DcLB 52[port], IntAu&W 82, OxChL, ScF&FL 1, -2, SmATA 1, -25[port], ThrBJA, TwCCW 78, -83, WhoAm 76, -78, -80, -82, WhoAmW 81, -83, WrDr 80, -82, -84, -86*

Cameron, Ian *SmATA X, WrDr 86*

Cameron, Ian 1924- *ConAu X, ConSFA, EncSF, IntAu&W 76X, -77X, -82X, ScF&FL 1, WrDr 76, -80, -82, -84*

Cameron, Ian *see also* Payne, Donald Gordon

Cameron, Kenneth Neill 1908- *ChhPo S2, ConAu 3NR, -9R, DrAS 74E, -78E, -82E, NatPD*

Camner, James 1950- *ConAu 108*

Camp, Walter Chauncey 1859-1925 *AmAu&B, AmBi, AmLY, BiD&SB, BioIn 2, -3, -5, -6, -9, -11, -12, ChhPo, DcAmAu, DcAmB, DcNAA, JBA 34, -51, LinLib S, NatCAB 21, OxAmH, REnAL, WebAB, -79, WhAm 1, WhNAA, WhoFtbl 74, WorAl, YABC 1*

Campanella, Roy 1921- *BioIn 1, -2, -3, -4, -5, -6, -7, -8, -9, -10, -11, -13, CelR, CurBio 53, InB&W 80, NegAl 76, -83, NewYTBS 77, WhoAm 74, -76, -78, WhoBlA 75, -77, -80, -85, WhoProB 73, WorAl*

Campanella, Roy, Sr. 1921- *InB&W 85*

Campbell, Ann R 1925- *BioIn 11, ConAu 21R, SmATA 11*

Campbell, Archibald Bruce 1881-1966 *BioIn 2, -3, -7, ConAu P-1*

Campbell, Bruce *AuBYP, ConAu X, MorJA, SmATA X*

Campbell, Bruce *see also* Epstein, Samuel

Campbell, Hannah *ConAu 9R*

Campbell, Hope *WhoAmW 85, -87*

Campbell, Hope 1925- *BioIn 12, ConAu 10NR, -61, SmATA 20, WhoAmW 83*

Campbell, Jane 1932- *ConAu X, SmATA X, WomWWA 14*

Campbell, Jane C *AmWomWr*

Campbell, Jane *see also* Edwards, Jane Campbell

Campbell, John W 1910-1971 *AmAu&B, BioIn 7, –9, –10, –12, ConAu 29R, ConAu P-2, ConSFA, DcLB 8[port], EncSF, LinLib L, NewYTBE 71, Novels, ObitOF 79, ScF&FL 1, –2, WhoSciF, WorAl, WorAu*

Campbell, John W, Jr. 1910-1971 *ConLC 32[port], ScFSB, TwCSFW 86*

Campbell, Joseph 1904- *AmAu&B, BioIn 4, –11, –12, –13, ConAu 1R, –3NR, CurBio 84[port], DrAS 74P, –78P, LinLib L, REnAL, TwCA SUP, WhoAm 74, –76, –78, –80, –82, –84, –86, WhoE 74*

Campbell, Judith *IntAu&W 86X*

Campbell, Judith 1914- *ConAu X, IntAu&W 82X, WrDr 76, –80, –82, –84, –86*

Campbell, Judith *see also* Pares, Marion Stapylton

Campbell, Patricia J 1930- *ConAu 103, SmATA 45[port]*

Campbell, Ramsey 1946- *ConAu 7NR, –57, ConLC 42[port], IntAu&W 77, –82, –86, ScF&FL 1, –2, SupFW, WhoHr&F, WhoWor 86, WrDr 86*

Campbell, Walter Stanley 1887-1957 *AmAu&B, BioIn 4, CnDAL, OxAmL, –83, REn, REnAL, RENnAW, TwCA, –SUP, WhAm 3, WhE&EA, WhNAA*

Campbell, Walter Stanley *see also* Vestal, Stanley

Campbell, Will 1924?- *BioIn 8, –9, –11, ConAu 5R, –7NR*

Campbell, Will D 1924?- *BioIn 13*

Campbell, William Edward March 1893-1954 *AmAu&B, AmNov X, BioIn 2, –3, –4, –5, –12, ConAmA, ConAu 108, DcAmB S5, ObitOF 79, REn, REnAL, TwCA SUP*

Campbell, William Edward March *see also* March, William

Campion, Nardi Reeder 1917- *AuBYP, BioIn 7, ConAu 1R, –6NR, SmATA 22[port], WhoAmW 58, –61*

Camus, Albert 1913-1960 *AtlBL, BioIn 1, –3, –4, –5, –6, –7, –8, –9, –10, –11, –12, –13, CasWL, CldMEL, CnMD, CnMWL, CnThe, ConAu 89, ConLC 1, –2, –4, –9, –11, –14, –32[port], CroCD, CyWA, EncWL, –2[port], EncWT, EvEuW, GrFLW, LinLib L, –S, LongCTC, MajMD 2, MakMC, McGEWB, McGEWD, –84[port], ModFrL, ModRL, ModWD, NotNAT A, –B, Novels[port], ObitOF 79, ObitT 1951, OxEng, –85, OxFr, OxThe, –83, PenC EUR, RComWL, REn, REnWD, TwCA SUP, TwCWr, WhDW, WhAm 3, WhoNob, WhoTwCL, WorAl*

Camuti, Louis J 1893-1981 *BioIn 12, –13, ConAu 101, –103, NewYTBS 81, WhoE 74, –75, –77, –79, –81*

Canada, Lena 1942- *ConAu 93*

Canaday, John E 1907- *AmAu&B, BioIn 6, –9, –10, ConAu 7NR, –13R, DrAS 74H, EncMys, TwCCr&M 80, WhoAm 74, –76, –78, –80, WhoAmA 73, –76, –78, –80, –82, WhoE 74, WorAu, WrDr 82, –84*

Canaday, John E 1907-1985 *ConAu 116*

Canaday, John Edwin 1907- *WhoAm 84, WhoAmA 84*

Canaday, John Edwin 1907-1985 *WhAm 8*

Canfield, Dorothy *ConAu X, WomNov*

Canfield, Dorothy 1879-1958 *AmAu&B, AmNov, BioIn 2, –3, –4, –11, –12, Chambr 3, CnDAL, ConAmA, ConAmL, DcBiA, DcLEL, JBA 34, LongCTC, NotAW MOD, OxAmL, –83, REn, REnAL, TwCA, –SUP, WhNAA*

Canfield, Kenneth French 1909- *ConAu P-1*

Canning, Victor 1911- *Au&Wr 71, BioIn 10, ConAu 6NR, –13R, EncMys, HalFC 84, IntAu&W 76, –77, LongCTC, MnBBF, Novels, ScF&FL 1, TwCCr&M 80, –85, WhE&EA, Who 74, –82, –83, –85, WhoSpyF, WorAu, WrDr 76, –80, –82, –84, –86*

Canning, Victor 1911-1986 *ConAu 118*

Cannon, Grant G 1911?-1969 *BioIn 8, WhAm 5*

Cannon, Grant Groesbeck 1911-1969 *ConAu 117*

Cannon, Jimmy 1909-1973 *ConAu 104, NewYTBE 73, ObitOF 79, REnAL, WhAm 6*

Cannon, Jimmy 1910-1973 *EncAJ*

Cannon, LeGrand, Jr. 1899-1979 *AmAu&B, AmNov, Au&Wr 71, BioIn 2, –4, CnDAL, ConAu 93, CurBio 43, NewYTBS 79, REnAL, TwCA SUP, WhAm 7, WhoAm 74, –76, –78*

Cannon, Robert L 1939- *WhoTech 84*

Cannon, Robert Laurence 1939- *AmM&WS 86P*

Cantor, Muriel G 1923- *ConAu 12NR, –33R, WhoAm 82, –84, –86, WhoAmW 85, –87, WhoE 81, –83, –85, WhoWor 84, –87*

Cantwell, Robert Emmett 1908-1978 *AmAu&B, Au&Wr 71, BioIn 4, –9, –10, –11, ConAmA, ConAu 4NR, –5R, –81, ConNov 72, –76, –82, DcLB 9, IntAu&W 76, –77, NewYTBS 78, Novels, OxAmL, REnAL, TwCA, –SUP, TwCWr, WhAm 7, WhE&EA, WhoAm 74, –76, –78, WhoE 74, WrDr 76, –82, –84*

Canutt, Yakima *ConAu X*

Canutt, Yakima 1895- *BioIn 7, –8, –12, CmMov, Film 2, FilmgC, HalFC 84, IntMPA 77, –75, –76, –78, –79, –81, –82, –84, –86, OxFilm, TwYS, WhoHol A, WorEFlm*

Canutt, Yakima 1896-1986 *NewYTBS 86*

Capek, Josef 1887-1945 *BioIn 1, CasWL, CldMEL, CnThe, EncSF, EncWT, NotNAT B, OxTwCA, PhDcTCA 77, REnWD, ScF&FL 1*

Capek, Karel 1890-1938 *BioIn 1, –5, –6, –7, –12, CasWL, CldMEL, CnMD, CnThe, ConAu 104, CyWA, EncSF, EncWL, –2[port], EncWT, EvEuW, GrFLW, LinLib L, LongCTC, MajMD 2, MakMC, McGEWB, McGEWD, –84[port], ModSL 2, ModWD, NotNAT B, OxEng 85, OxThe, –83, PenC EUR, REn, REnWD, ScF&FL 1, ScFSB, TwCA, –SUP, TwCLC 6[port], TwCSFW 86A, TwCWr, WhDW, WhE&EA, WhThe, WhoSciF, WhoTwCL, WorAl*

Capizzi, Michael 1941- *ConAu 41R*

Capote, Truman *OxAmT 84*

Capote, Truman d1984 *Who 85N*

Capote, Truman 1924- *OxAmL 83, WhoAm 84*

Capote, Truman 1924-1984 *AmAu&B, AmNov, AmSCAP 66, AnObit 1984, Au&Wr 71, BiE&WWA, BioIn 1, –2, –3, –4, –7, –8, –9, –10, –11, –12, –13, BlueB 76, CasWL, CelR, CnDAL, CnMD, ConAu 5R, –113, –18NR, ConDr 73, –77D, –82D, ConLC 1, –3, –8, –13, –19, –34[port], –38[port], ConNov 72, –76, –82, –86A, CurBio 51, –68&N, DcLB 2, –Y80A[port], –Y84N[port], DcLEL 1940, EncWL, –2, FilmgC, IntAu&W 76, –77, –82, IntWW 74, –75, –76, –77, –78, –79, –80, –81, –82, –83, LinLib L, LongCTC, MakMC, ModAL, –S2, –S1, ModWD, NewCon[port], NewYTBE 71, NewYTBS 78, –84[port], NotNAT, Novels[port], OxAmL, OxEng 85, OxFilm, PenC AM, RAdv 1, REn, REnAL, TwCA SUP, TwCWr, WebAB, –79, WebE&AL, WhDW,*

Who 74, –82, –83, WhoAm 74, –76, –78, –80, –82, WhoHol A, WhoTwCL, WhoWor 74, –78, WorAl, WrDr 76, –80, –82, –84

Capote, Truman 1925- *HalFC 84*

Capps, Benjamin 1922- *BioIn 11, –12, ConAu 5R, –7NR, SmATA 9, WhoAm 74, –76, –78, –80, WrDr 76, –80*

Capps, Benjamin Franklin 1922- *EncFWF[port]*

Capron, Jean F 1924- *ConAu 21R*

Caputo, Philip 1941- *BioIn 12, –13, ConAu 73, ConLC 32[port], NewYTBS 81[port], WhoAm 74, –76, –78, –80, –82, WhoWor 80, –82*

Caras, Roger A 1928- *AmAu&B, BioIn 11, ConAu 1R, –5NR, IntAu&W 76, –77, –82, ScF&FL 1, SmATA 12, WhoAm 74, –76, –78, –80, –82, WhoE 74, WhoWor 74, WhoWorJ 72, –78, WrDr 76, –80, –82, –84, –86*

Caras, Roger Andrew 1928- *IntAu&W 86, WhoAm 84, –86*

Carawan, Candie *ConAu X*

Carawan, Candie *see also* Carawan, Carolanne M

Carawan, Carolanne M 1939- *ConAu 17R*

Carawan, Guy 1927- *BiDAmM, ConAu 17R, EncFCWM 69*

Carbonnier, Jeanne 1894-1974 *BioIn 9, ConAu P-2, SmATA 3, –34N*

Card, Orson Scott 1951- *ConAu 102, ConLC 44[port], ScFSB, TwCSFW 86*

Cardenal, Ernesto 1925- *BioIn 8, –12, CasWL, ConAu 2NR, –49, ConFLW 84, ConLC 31[port], DcCLAA, OxSpan, PenC AM, WhoTwCL, WorAu 1970*

Cardozo, Lois S 1934- *AuBYP, ConAu 1R*

Cardozo, Lois S *see also* Arquette, Lois S

Cardozo, Peter 1916- *ConAu 61*

Cardwell, Paul *AuBYP SUP*

Carefoot, Thomas Henry 1938- *AmM&WS 73P*

Carew, Dorothy 1910?-1973 *BioIn 9, ConAu 41R, NewYTBE 73*

Carew, Rod *NewYTBS 86[port]*

Carew, Rod 1945- *BioIn 13*

Carey, Ernestine Gilbreth *WrDr 86*

Carey, Ernestine Gilbreth 1908- *Au&Wr 71, BioIn 2, –4, ConAu 5R, ConLC 17, CurBio 49, InWom, IntAu&W 77, ScF&FL 1, –2, SmATA 2, WhoAm 74, –76, –78, –80, –82, –84, –86, WhoAmW 74, –58, –61, –64, –66, –68, –70, –72, –79, –81, –83, –87, WhoWor 74, –82, –87, WorAl, WrDr 76, –80, –82, –84*

Carl, Lillian Stewart 1949- *ConAu 118*

Carliner, David 1918- *WhoAm 76, –78, –80, –82, –84, –86, WhoAmL 85, WhoS&SW 73, WhoWor 82*

Carlinsky, Dan 1944- *ConAu 8NR, –21R, IntAu&W 77, WhoE 74, –75*

Carlisle, Olga 1930- *SmATA 35[port]*

Carlisle, Olga Andreyev 1930- *AuBYP SUP, BioIn 12, ConAu 7NR, –13R, IntAu&W 77, SmATA 35*

Carlsen, G Robert 1917- *ConAu 8NR, –17R, IntAu&W 77, SmATA 30[port], WrDr 76, –80, –82, –84, –86*

Carlsen, Ruth C 1918- *ConAu 8NR*

Carlsen, Ruth Christoffer 1918- *AuBYP SUP, BioIn 9, ConAu 17R, IntAu&W 77, ScF&FL 1, –2, SmATA 2, WhoAmW 75, WrDr 76, –80, –82, –84, –86*

Carlson, Avis D 1896- *ConAu 73*

Carlson, Bernice Wells 1910- *AuBYP, BioIn 7, –11, ConAu 2NR, –5R, ForWC 70, IntAu&W 77, –82, MichAu 80, SmATA 8, WrDr 76, –80, –82, –84, –86*

Carlson, Dale 1935- *WhoE 85*

Carlson, Dale Bick 1935- *AuBYP SUP, BioIn 9, ConAu 3NR, –9R, IntAu&W 76, ScF&FL 1, –2,*

SmATA 1, WhoAmW 74, –72, –75, –77, –79, –81, –83, –85, –87, WhoE 74, –75, –77, –81, –83, WhoWor 84, –87

Carlson, Don 1929- *WhoAmP 85*

Carlyle, Thomas 1795-1881 *Alli, –SUP, AtlBL, BbD, BiD&SB, BioIn 1, –2, –3, –4, –5, –6, –7, –8, –9, –10, –11, –12, –13, BritAu 19, BritWr 4, CasWL, CelCen, Chambr 3, ChhPo, –S1, –S2, –S3, CmScLit, CrtT 3, –4, CyEd[port], CyWA, DcAmSR, DcBiPP, DcEnA, DcEnL, DcEuL, DcLB 55[port], DcLEL, DcNaB, Dis&D, EvLB, FamAYP, LinLib L, –S, LongCEL, LuthC 75, McGEWB, MouLC 3, NewC, OxEng, –85, OxMus, PenC ENG, RAdv 1, RComWL, REn, WebE&AL, WhDW, WorAl*

Carmer, Carl Lamson 1893-1976 *AmAu&B, Au&Wr 71, AuBYP, BioIn 2, –3, –4, –7, –11, ChhPo, –S1, –S2, –S3, ConAu 4NR, –5R, –69, LinLib L, –S, NewYTBS 76, OxAmL, REn, REnAL, ScF&FL 1, –2, SmATA 30N, Str&VC, TwCA, –SUP, WhAm 7, WhoAm 74, –76, WhoWor 74*

Carmichael, Joel 1915- *AuBYP SUP, ConAu 1R, –2NR, WrDr 86*

Caroli, Betty Boyd 1938- *ConAu 118*

Caroselli, Remus F 1916- *SmATA 36*

Caroselli, Remus Francis 1916- *AmM&WS 73P, –76P, –79P, –82P, –86P, ConAu 97, SmATA 36*

Carpenter, Frances 1890-1972 *AmAu&B, Au&Wr 71, AuBYP, BioIn 6, –8, –9, –13, ConAu 4NR, –5R, –37R, ForWC 70, MorJA, SmATA 27N, –3*

Carpenter, Humphrey 1946- *ChhPo S3, ConAu 13NR, –89, WrDr 84, –86*

Carpenter, Kenneth John 1923- *AmM&WS 86P*

Carpentier, Alejo 1904-1980 *AnObit 1980, BioIn 5, –7, –10, CasWL, ConAu 11NR, –65, –97, ConLC 8, –11, –38[port], DcAfL, DcCLAA, EncLatA, EncWL, –2, GrFLW, ModLAL, Novels, OxSpan, PenC AM, ScF&FL 1, TwCWr, WorAu*

Carpozi, George, Jr. 1920- *ConAu 11NR, –13R*

Carr, Albert Z 1902-1971 *AmAu&B, BioIn 9, ConAu 1R, –1NR, –33R, NewYTBE 71, WhAm 5*

Carr, Archie F 1909- *WhoAm 84*

Carr, Archie F, Jr. 1909- *AmM&WS 73P, –76P, –79P, –82P, BioIn 12, ConAu 13R, WhoAm 74, –76, –78, –80, –82, WhoWor 74*

Carr, Archie Fairly 1909- *BioIn 13*

Carr, Archie Fairly, Jr. 1909- *AmM&WS 86P*

Carr, John Dickson 1905?-1977 *AmAu&B, Au&Wr 71, BioIn 2, –4, –5, –11, ConAu 3NR, –49, –69, ConLC 3, CorpD, DcLEL, EncMys, EncSF, EvLB, HalFC 84, IntAu&W 76, –77, LongCTC, NewC, NewYTBS 77, Novels, ObitOF 79, PenC AM, REn, REnAL, ScF&FL 1, –2, TwCA, –SUP, TwCCr&M 80, TwCWr, WhAm 7, WhE&EA, Who 74, WhoAm 74, –76, WhoWor 74, WorAl*

Carr, John Dickson 1906-1977 *ScFSB, TwCCr&M 85*

Carr, Mary Jane 1899- *AmCath 80, AuBYP, BioIn 2, –3, –7, –9, BkC 1, CathA 1952, ChhPo S2, ConAu P-1, JBA 51, SmATA 2, WhoAmW 61, –64*

Carr, Philippa *TwCCr&M 85, Who 85, WrDr 86*

Carr, Philippa 1906- *ConAu X, IntAu&W 77X, NewYTBS 77, Novels, Who 74, –82, –83, WrDr 76, –80, –82, –84*

Carr, Philippa *see also* Hibbert, Eleanor

Carr, Rachel *AuBYP SUP*

Carr, Robyn *WrDr 86* **Carr,** Robyn 1951- *ConAu 115*

Carr, Terry 1937- *ConAu 81, ConSFA, EncSF, ScF&FL 1, -2, ScFSB, TwCSFW 86, WhoSciF, WrDr 84, -86*

Carra, Andrew Joseph 1943- *WhoAm 76, -78, -80, -82, -84, -86*

Carrick, Donald 1929- *BioIn 10, -12, ConAu 5NR, -20NR, -53, FourBJA, IlsBYP, IlsCB 1967, MichAu 80, SmATA 7*

Carrick, Donald F 1929- *WhoAmA 84*

Carrico, John P 1938- *AmM&WS 73P*

Carrier, Jean-Guy 1945- *ConAu 101, WhoCanL 85*

Carrier, Roch 1937?- *ConLC 13, CreCan 2, DcLB 53[port], ModCmwL, OxCan SUP, OxCanL, WhoCanL 85*

Carrighar, Sally *BioIn 13*

Carrighar, Sally 1905?- *AmWomWr, AnCL, BioIn 3, ConAu 93, OhA&B, SmATA 24[port], WhoAmW 58, -61*

Carrington, Richard 1921- *Au&Wr 71, ConAu 9R*

Carris, Joan Davenport 1938- *ConAu 106, SmATA 42, -44[port]*

Carrison, Daniel Jordan 1917- *ConAu 37R, WhoAmP 73, WhoGov 72, WhoS&SW 76*

Carroll, Gladys Hasty 1904- *AmAu&B, AmNov, AmWomWr, Au&Wr 71, BioIn 2, -4, -6, -12, BlueB 76, ConAu 1R, -5NR, DcLB 9, ForWC 70, InWom, LinLib L, OxAmL, -83, REnAL, ScF&FL 1, -2, TwCA, -SUP, WhE&EA, WhNAA, WhoAm 74, -76, -78, -80, -82, -84, -66, -68, -70, -72, WhoE 74, WhoWor 74, WrDr 76, -80, -82, -84, -86*

Carroll, James 1943- *ConLC 38[port], WhoAm 82, -84, -86, WrDr 82, -84, -86*

Carroll, Jim *DrAP&F 85*

Carroll, Jim 1950?- *BioIn 12, ConAu 45, NewRR 83, RolSEnR 83, WhoRocM 82*

Carroll, Jim 1951- *ConLC 35[port]*

Carroll, John 1925- *AmM&WS 73P, -79P, -82P, ConAu 5R, -8NR, WhoLibI 82, WhoMW 74*

Carroll, Jonathan 1949- *ConAu 105, -21NR*

Carroll, Joseph T 1935- *Au&Wr 71, ConAu 102*

Carroll, Lewis *MacBEP, OxEng 85*

Carroll, Lewis 1832-1898 *Alli SUP, AnCL, AtlBL, AuBYP, BbD, BiD&SB, BioIn 1, -2, -3, -4, -5, -6, -7, -8, -9, -10, -11, -12, -13, BritAu 19, BritWr 5, CasWL, CelCen, Chambr 3, ChlLR 2, ChrP, ChhPo, -S1, -S2, -S3, CnE&AP, CrtT 3, -4, CyWA, DcEnA, DcEnL, DcEuL, DcLB 18[port], DcLEL, DcNaB S1, EncSF, EvLB, FamAYP, FamPYP, FilmgC, HalFC 84, ICPEnP A, InSci, JBA 34, LinLib L, -LP, -S, LongCEL, McGEWB, NewC, NewYTBE 71, NinCLC 2[port], Novels[port], OxChL[port], OxEng, PenC ENG, RAdv 1, REn, ScF&FL 1, ScFSB[port], Str&VC, SupFW, TelT, TwCCW 78A, -83A, WebE&AL, WhDW, WhoChL, WorAl, YABC X*

Carroll, Lewis *see also* Dodgson, Charles Lutwidge

Carroll, Paul *DrAP&F 85*

Carroll, Paul 1927- *BioIn 13, ConAu 25R, ConPo 70, -75, -80, -85, CroCAP, DcLB 16[port], DcLEL 1940, IntAu&W 77, IntWWP 77, WrDr 76, -80, -82, -84, -86*

Carroll, Theodus 1928- *ConAu 69, WhoAmW 79, -81*

Carruth, Estelle 1910- *ConAu 9R*

Carruth, Hayden *DrAP&F 85*

Carruth, Hayden 1921- *AmAu&B, BioIn 12, -13, ConAu 4NR, -9R, ConLC 4, -7, -10, -18, ConPo 70, -75, -80, -85, DcLB 5[port], DcLEL 1940, IntAu&W 77, -82, IntWWP 77, LinLib L, OxAmL 83, RAdv 1, REnAL, SmATA 47[port], WhoAm 74, -76, -78, -80, -82, -84, -86, WhoE 74, WhoWor 74, -76, WorAu, WrDr 76, -80, -82, -84, -86*

Carse, Robert 1902-1971 *BioIn 9, -10, ConAu 1R, -1NR, -29R, NewYTBE 71, ObitOF 79, SmATA 5*

Carson, John F 1920- *AuBYP, BioIn 8, -9, ConAu 9R, -13R, IndAu 1917, MichAu 80, ScF&FL 1, -2, SmATA 1*

Carson, Josephine *DrAP&F 85*

Carson, Josephine 1919- *BioIn 4*

Carson, Julia M 1899- *AuBYP, BioIn 8, InB&W 80, OhA&B, WhoAmP 81, WhoAmW 58, -61*

Carson, Rachel Louise 1907-1964 *AmAu&B, AmRef[port], AmWomWr, AnCL, BioIn 2, -3, -4, -5, -6, -7, -8, -9, -10, -11, -12, -13, ConAu 77, ConIsC 2[port], CurBio 51, -64, DcAmB S7, EncAAH, EncAB-H, EvLB, GoodHs, HerW, InSci, InWom, IntDcWB, LibW, LinLib L, -S, LongCTC, McGEWB, NatCAB 51, NatLAC, NewYTBS 82[port], NotAW MOD, ObitOF 79, OxAmL, REn, SmATA 23[port], TwCA SUP, TwCWr, WebAB, -79, WhAm 4, WhoAmW 58, -61, -64*

Carson, Robert 1909-1983 *AmAu&B, AnObit 1983, Au&Wr 71, BioIn 3, -13, ConAu 108, -21R, IntMPA 77, -75, -76, -78, -79, -81, -82, WhAm 8, WhoAm 74, -76, -78, -80, -82, WhoHol A*

Carter, Anne 1905- *ConAu X*

Carter, Anne *see also* Brooks, Anne Tedlock

Carter, Bruce 1922- *AuBYP, BioIn 6, -12, ConAu X, OxChL, ScF&FL 1, -2, ScFSB, SmATA X, TwCCW 78, -83, Who 74, -82, -83, WrDr 80, -82, -84*

Carter, Bruce *see also* Hough, Richard Alexander

Carter, Dorothy Sharp 1921- *ConAu 49, IntAu&W 77, SmATA 8, WhoAmW 77, -79*

Carter, Ernest Frank 1899- *Au&Wr 71*

Carter, Ernestine Marie d1983 *Au&Wr 71, BlueB 76, ConAu 110, Who 74, -82, -83, WrDr 76, -80, -82, -84*

Carter, Forest Charles 1922- *WhoAm 74, -76, -78, -80, WhoE 74*

Carter, Forrest Bedford 1926?-1979 *BioIn 11, ConAu 107, SmATA 32[port]*

Carter, Gary *NewYTBS 84[port], -86[port]*

Carter, Gary 1954- *BioIn 13, ConNews 87-1[port]*

Carter, Howard 1874-1939 *BioIn 2, -4, -6, -8, -9, -11, -12, DcBrAr 1, DcNaB 1931, InSci, LongCTC, WhDW*

Carter, Joseph 1912- *ConAu 49*

Carter, Joseph 1912-1984 *ConAu 112*

Carter, Lin 1930- *BioIn 13, ConAu 41R, ConSFA, DcLB Y81B[port], EncSF, ScF&FL 1, -2, ScFSB, TwCSFW 86, WhoHr&F, WhoSciF, WrDr 84, -86*

Carter, Paul A 1926- *ConAu 13NR*

Carter, Paul Allen 1926- *ConAu 33R, DrAS 74H, -78H, -82H*

Carter, Peter 1929- *ConAu 69, OxChL, TwCCW 78, -83, WrDr 80, -82, -84, -86*

Carter, Richard 1918- *AmAu&B, ConAu 8NR, -61, WhoAm 74, -76, -78, -80, -82, -84, -86, WhoE 74*

Carter, Robert F 1930- *DrAS 74H, -78H, -82H*

Carter, Rubin *SelBAAf*

Carter, Rubin 1937- *BioIn 6, -7, -10, -11, -12, ConAu 113, InB&W 80, -85, NewYTBE 72, NewYTBS 74, PolProf NF, SelBAAu*

Carter, Samuel, III 1904- *ConAu 57, SmATA 37, WhoAm 76, -78, -80, -82, WrDr 80, -82, -84, -86*

Carter, William E 1926?-1983 *AmM&WS 73S, -76P, AuBYP, BioIn 8, -9, ConAu 110, -17R, FifIDA, SmATA 1, -35N, WhoFla, WhoS&SW 75, -76, -78*

Carter, William E 1927-1983 *SmATA 35N*

Cartey, Wilfred G *InB&W 85*

Cartey, Wilfred G 1931- *ConAu 73, InB&W 80, WhoAm 82, WhoBlA 80, WhoWor 82*

Cartey, Wilfred G O 1931- *WhoBlA 85*

Cartey, Wilfred George Onslow 1931- *WhoAm 84, -86*

Cartland, Barbara *IntAu&W 86, Who 85, WrDr 86*

Cartland, Barbara 1900?- *Au&Wr 71, BioIn 1, -5, -8, -9, -10, -11, -12, BlueB 76, ConAu 6NR, -9R, CurBio 79, IntAu&W 76, -77, -82, IntDcWB, LinLib L, LongCTC, NewYTBE 73, NewYTBS 81[port], Novels, TwCWr, WhE&EA, WhLit, Who 74, -82, -83, WhoAm 78, -80, -82, WhoAmW 79, -81, -83, WhoE 83, WhoWor 78, -80, -82, WorAl, WrDr 76, -80, -82, -84*

Cartland, Barbara 1901- *WhoAm 84, -86, WhoWor 84, -87*

Cartwright, Rosalind Dymond 1922- *AmM&WS 73S, -78S, ConAu 81, WhoAmW 74, -58, -68, -70, -72*

Caruso, John Anthony 1907- *ConAu 33R, WrDr 76, -80, -82, -84, -86*

Carver, Raymond *DrAP&F 85*

Carver, Raymond 1938- *BioIn 13, ConAu 17NR, IntAu&W 86, ModAL S2, PostFic, WhoAm 84, -86, WorAu 1975[port]*

Carver, Raymond 1939- *NewYTBS 84[port]*

Cary, Diana Serra 1918- *BioIn 7, ConAu 57, WhoAmW 77*

Cary, Joyce 1888-1957 *BiDIrW, BioIn 13, BritWr 7, ModBrL S2, OxEng 85*

Casady, Jack 1944- *BioIn 9, WhoRocM 82*

Casady, Jack *see also* Jefferson Airplane

Casals, Pablo 1876-1973 *AmSCAP 66, Baker 78, -84, BiDAmM, BioIn 1, -2, -3, -4, -5, -6, -7, -8, -9, -10, -11, -12, -13, CelR, ConAu X, CurBio 50, -64, -73, -73N, LinLib S, MusSN, NewYTBE 73, ObitOF 79, ObitT 1971, REn, WhDW, WhAm 6, WhScrn 77, -83, Who 74, WhoMus 72, WhoWor 74, WorAl*

Casals, Pablo Carlos Salvador Defillo De 1876-1973 *BiDInt*

Casals, Pau Carlos Salvador Defillo De 1876-1973 *ConAu 45, -93, OxMus, REn*

Case, Victoria 1897- *ConAu 5R, WhoAmW 58, -61, -64, -66, WhoPNW*

Casewit, Curtis 1922- *BioIn 9, ConAu 6NR, -13R, ConSFA, EncSF, ScF&FL 1, -2, SmATA 4, WhoWest 76, -78*

Casey, Warren 1935- *BioIn 12, ConAu 101, ConDr 82D, WhoAm 78, -80, -82*

Cash, Johnny 1932- *Baker 78, -84, BioIn 5, -8, -9, -10, -12, -13, CelR, ConAu 110, CurBio 69, EncFCWM 69, -83[port], FilmgC, HalFC 84, NewYTBE 73, RkOn 74, -82, RolSEnR 83, WebAB, -79, WhoAm 74, -76, -78, -80, -82, -84, -86, WhoHol A, WhoRock 81[port], WhoRocM 82, WhoS&SW 73, -75, WorAl*

Cash, June Carter 1929- *WhoAm 84, -86*

Cashin, Edward 1927- *ConAu 9NR, -21R, -X, DrAS 82H*

Cass, James 1915- *ConAu 101*

Cassatt, Mary 1844-1926 *MorMA*

Cassatt, Mary 1845-1926 *BioIn 13, HerW 84*

Cassedy, Sylvia 1930- *AuBYP SUP, BioIn 13, ChhPo S2, ConAu 105, SmATA 27[port]*

Cassel, Virginia Cunningham *ConAu 105*

Cassiday, Bruce 1920- *ConAu 1R, -4NR, -19NR, ScF&FL 1, -2*

Cassidy, Vincent H 1923- *ConAu 21R, DrAS 74H, -78H, -82H*

Cassill, Kay *DrAP&F 85, IntAu&W 86*

Cassill, Kay 1930- *ConAu 89, Po&Wr 77, WhoAmW 77, -79*

Casson, Lionel 1914- *Au&Wr 71, ConAu 3NR, -9R, DrAS 74H, -78H, -82H*

Castaneda, Carlos 1925?- *EncO&P 2, PostFic*

Castaneda, Carlos 1931- *BioIn 9, -10, -11, -12, ConAu 25R, ConLC 12, EncO&P 78, MakMC, NewYTBE 72, WhoAm 74, -76, -78, -80, -82, -84, -86, WorAl, WorAu 1970, WrDr 76, -80, -82, -84, -86*

Castex, Pierre-Georges 1915- *IntAu&W 76, -77, -82, WhoFr 79*

Castor, Henry 1909- *AuBYP, BioIn 8, ConAu 17R*

Castro, Antonio 1946- *ConAu 53*

Castro, Tony 1946- *ConAu X, WrDr 76, -80, -82, -84, -86*

Casty, Alan Howard 1929- *ConAu 1R, -4NR, IntAu&W 77, WhoWest 78, WrDr 76, -80, -82, -84, -86*

Catchpole, Clive E 1938- *AmM&WS 73P*

Cate, Dick 1932- *ConAu 73, -X, SmATA X*

Cather, Willa Sibert 1873-1947 *AmAu&B, AmWomWr, AmWr, ApCAB X, AtlBL, BioIn 1, -2, -3, -4, -5, -6, -7, -8, -9, -10, -11, -12, -13, CasWL, Chambr 3, ChhPo, -S1, -S3, CnDAL, ConAmA, ConAmL, ConAu 104, CyWA, DcAmB S4, DcBiA, DcLB 9[port], -DS1[port], DcLEL, DcNAA, EncAAH, EncAB-H, EncFWF[port], EncWL, -2, EvLB, GoodHs, HerW, InWom, IntDcWB, JBA 34, LibW, LinLib L, -S, LongCTC, McGEWB, ModAL, -S1, MorMA, NatCAB 44, NotAW, Novels, ObitOF 79, OxAmH, OxAmL, OxCan, OxEng, PenC AM, RAdv 1, RComWL, REn, REnAL, REnAW, SmATA 30[port], TwCA, -SUP, TwCLC 1, -11[port], TwCWr, WebAB, -79, WebE&AL, WhDW, WhAm 2, WhE&EA, WhNAA, WhoTwCL, WomNov, WomWWA 14, WorAl*

Cather, Willa Sibert 1876-1947 *OxEng 85*

Catherall, Arthur 1906- *OxChL*

Catherall, Arthur 1906-1980 *Au&Wr 71, AuBYP, BioIn 8, -9, ConAu 5R, IntAu&W 76, -77, -82, MnBBF, SmATA 3, TwCCW 78, -83, WrDr 76, -80*

Catto, Max 1907- *HalFC 84*

Catto, Max 1909- *Au&Wr 71, ConAu 105*

Catton, Bruce 1899-1978 *Alli SUP, AmAu&B, AuNews 1, BioIn 3, -4, -5, -6, -7, -8, -9, -10, -11, -12, -13, BioNews 74, BlueB 76, CelR, ConAu 5R, -7NR, -81, ConLC 35[port], CurBio 54, -78, -78N, DcLB 17[port], DcLEL 1940, EncSoH, IntAu&W 76, -77, IntWW 74, -75, -76, -77, -78, -79N, LinLib L, -S, MichAu 80, NewYTBS 78, ObitOF 79, OxAmL, -83, PenC AM, REn, REnAL, SmATA 2, -24N, TwCA SUP, WebAB, -79, WhAm 7, Who 74, WhoAm 74, -76, -78, WhoWor 74, -78, WorAl, WrDr 76*

Catton, William R, Jr. 1926-
ConAu 109

Caudill, Harry M 1922- *ConAu 14NR*

Caudill, Harry Monroe 1922-
*AmAu&B, BioIn 8, ConAu 33R,
WhoAm 78, –80*

Caudill, Rebecca 1899- *AmAu&B,
AuBYP, BioIn 2, –6, –7, –9, –10,
ChhPo S1, ConAu 2NR, –5R,
CurBio 50, ForWC 70, InWom,
MorJA, SmATA 1, TwCCW 78, –83,
WhoAm 74, –76, –78, –80, –82, –84,
WhoAmW 74, –58, –61, –64, –66,
–68, –70, –72, WrDr 76, –80, –82,
–84, –86*

Caudill, Rebecca 1899-1985
*ConAu 117, CurBio 86N,
SmATA 44N*

Cauman, Samuel 1909?-1971 *BioIn 9,
ConAu P-2, NewYTBE 71*

Cauman, Samuel 1910-1971
SmATA 48

Causley, Charles 1917- *Au&Wr 71,
AuBYP, BioIn 8, –9, –10, –12,
BlueB 76, ChhPo, –S1, –S2, –S3,
CnE&AP, ConAu 5NR, –9R,
ConLC 7, ConPo 70, –75, –80, –85,
DcLB 27[port], DcLEL 1940,
IntAu&W 76, –77, –82, IntWWP 77,
LongCTC, NewC, OxChL, OxEng 85,
SmATA 3, TwCCW 78, –83,
WebE&AL, WhDW, Who 74, –82,
–83, WhoWor 74, –76, WorAu,
WrDr 76, –80, –82, –84, –86*

Cavallaro, Ann 1918- *ConAu 5R*

Cavallo, Robert M 1932-
*ConAu 10NR, –65, WhoAmL 78, –79,
–83, WhoE 79*

Cavanagh, Helen 1939- *ConAu 104,
SmATA 37, –48[port]*

Cavanah, Frances 1899-1982 *AuBYP,
BioIn 2, –3, –6, –7, –9, ConAu 13R,
CurBio 54, ForWC 70, InWom,
IndAu 1917, IntAu&W 76, –77,
MorJA, SmATA 1, –31[port],
WhNAA, WhoAmW 74, –70, –72,
–75, WhoS&SW 73*

Cavanna, Betty 1909- *Au&Wr 71,
AuBYP, BioIn 2, –6, –7, –9,
ConAu 6NR, –9R, ConLC 12,
CurBio 50, InWom, IntAu&W 76,
–77, –82, MorJA, SmATA 1,
–30[port], SmATA 4AS[port],
TwCCW 78, –83, WhoAmW 58, –61,
WrDr 76, –80, –82, –84, –86*

Cavanna, Betty *see also* Allen, Betsy

Cavanna, Betty *see also* Harrison,
Elizabeth Cavanna

Cavanna, Betty *see also* Headley,
Elizabeth

Cave, Hugh Barnett 1910- *Au&Wr 71,
ConAu 2NR, –5R, WhNAA,
WhoHr&F*

Cavendish, Richard 1930-
*ConAu 5NR, –9R, –20NR,
IntAu&W 82, WrDr 80, –82, –84, –86*

Cavett, Dick 1936?- *BioIn 7, –8, –9,
–10, –11, –12, –13, BioNews 74,
BlueB 76, CelR, ConAu X,
ConTFT 1, CurBio 70, IntMPA 77,
–75, –76, –78, –79, –81, –82, –84,
LesBEnT[port], NewYTBS 77,
–81[port], NewYTET, WhoAm 74,
–76, –78, –80, –82, –84, –86,
WhoE 74, WorAl*

Cavett, Dick 1937- *IntMPA 86*

Cavin, Ruth 1918- *ConAu 8NR, –61,
SmATA 38*

Cazeau, Charles J 1931-
*AmM&WS 73P, –76P, –79P, –82P,
–86P, ConAu 104, WhoE 75, –77, –79*

Cazzola, Gus 1934- *ConAu 108*

Cebulash, Mel 1937- *BioIn 11,
ConAu 12NR, –29R, IntAu&W 77,
ScF&FL 1, –2, SmATA 10, WhoE 75,
WrDr 76, –80, –82, –84, –86*

Cepeda, Orlando 1937- *BioIn 4, –5,
–6, –8, –11, –13, CmCal, CurBio 68,
InB&W 80, NewYTBS 77,
WhoAm 74, WhoProB 73*

Ceram, C W 1915-1972 *AmAu&B,
BioIn 3, –4, –9, –10, ConAu X,
CurBio 57, –72, –72N, LinLib L,
NewYTBE 72, ObitOF 79, WorAu*

Ceram, C W *see also* Marek, Kurt W

Cerf, Bennett Alfred 1898-1971
*AmAu&B, Au&Wr 71, AuBYP,
BiE&WWA, BioIn 1, –2, –3, –4, –5,
–6, –7, –8, –9, –10, –11, –12, –13,
ConAu 29R, ConAu P-2, CurBio 41,
–58, –71, –71N, LinLib L, –S,
NewYTBE 71, ObitOF 79, PIP&P,
REn, REnAL, ScF&FL 1, –2,
SmATA 7, WebAB, –79, WhAm 5,
WhE&EA, WorAl*

Cerf, Christopher 1941- *BioIn 9,
ConAu 25R, ConSFA, ScF&FL 1, –2,
SmATA 2, WhoE 83*

Cermack, Laird S 1942- *ConAu 53*

Cervantes, Miguel De 1547-1616
*AtlBL, BbD, BiD&SB, CasWL,
ChhPo S2, CnThe, CyWA, DcBiA,
DcEuL, DcSpL, EuAu, EuWr 2,
EvEuW, GrFLW, HalFC 84,
McGEWD, –84[port], NewC,
NewEOp 71, Novels[port], OxEng,
PenC EUR, RComWL, REn,
REnWD*

Cervantes Saavedra, Miguel De
1547-1616 *AtlBL, BbD, BiD&SB,
BioIn 1, –2, –3, –4, –5, –6, –7, –8, –9,
–10, –11, –12, –13, CasWL, CyWA,
DcBiA, DcBiPP, DcCathB, DcEuL,
DcSpL, Dis&D, EncWT, EuAu,
EvEuW, LinLib L, –S, LongCEL,
McGEWB, NotNAT B, OxEng, –85,
OxSpan, OxThe, –83, PenC EUR,
RComWL, WorAl*

Cervon, Jacqueline 1924- *ConAu X,
SmATA 4*

Cervon, Jacqueline *see also* Moussard,
Jacqueline

Cetera, Peter 1944- *BioNews 74,
WhoRocM 82*

Cetera, Peter *see also* Chicago

Chaber, M E *ConAu X,
TwCCr&M 80, –85, WrDr 82, –84*

Chaber, M E *see also* Crossen, Kendell
Foster

Chadwick, Lee 1909- *Au&Wr 71,
ConAu 69*

Chadwick, William Owen 1916-
*Au&Wr 71, ConAu 1R, DcLEL 1940,
IntWW 74, –75, –76, –77, –78, –79,
Who 74, –82, –85, WhoWor 74, –76,
–78*

Chaikin, Miriam 1928- *BioIn 13,
ConAu 14NR, –81, ForWC 70,
SmATA 24[port]*

Chalk, Ocania 1927- *ConAu 1NR, –45,
LivgBAA, SelBAAf*

Chalker, Jack L 1944- *ConAu 73,
ConSFA, EncSF, IntAu&W 82,
ScF&FL 1, –2, TwCSFW 86,
WrDr 84, –86*

Chalker, Jack Laurence 1944- *ScFSB*

Challans, Mary *BioIn 13*

Challans, Mary 1905-1983 *BioIn 5, –6,
–8, –9, –10, ConAu 111, –81,
IntAu&W 76X, –77X, NewC,
SmATA 23[port], –36N, Who 74, –82,
–83, WorAu, WrDr 76, –80, –82, –84*

Challans, Mary *see also* Renault, Mary

Chamberlain, John 1903- *OxAmL 83*

Chamberlain, William 1878-1967
WhAm 4

Chamberlain, Wilt 1936- *BioIn 12,
–13, CelR, CmCal, ConAu 103,
CurBio 60, Ebony 1, NegAl 76[port],
–83, NewYTBE 72, –73,
NewYTBS 75, WebAB 79,
WhoBbl 73, WhoBlA 75, –77, –80,
WorAl*

Chamberlain, Wilt N 1936-
WhoBlA 85

Chamberlin, Eric Russell 1926-
Au&Wr 71, ConAu 97, IntAu&W 76

Chamberlin, Jo Hubbard *AuBYP,
BioIn 8*

Chamberlin, M Hope 1920-1974
ConAu 45, –49

Chambers, Aidan 1934- *Au&Wr 71,
BioIn 9, ChhPo S2, –S3,
ConAu 12NR, –25R, ConLC 35[port],
IntAu&W 76, –77, –82, –86, OxChL,
ScF&FL 1, –2, SmATA 1,
TwCChW 83, WrDr 84, –86*

Chambers, Bradford *AuBYP SUP*

Chambers, Bradford 1922-1984
*ConAu 113, NewYTBS 84,
SmATA 39N*

Chambers, Henry Alban 1902-
WhoMus 72

Chambers, Margaret Ada Eastwood
1911-1965 *BioIn 9, ConAu 9R,
Film 2, IntAu&W 76, –77, SmATA 2,
WhScrn 74, –77, WhoHol B*

Chambers, Margaret Ada Eastwood *see
also* Chambers, Peggy

Chambers, Peggy 1911-1965
*Au&Wr 71, ConAu X, IntAu&W 76X,
–77X, SmATA 2, WhE&EA*

Chambers, Peggy *see also* Chambers,
Margaret Ada Eastwood

Chambers, Robert Hunter, III 1939-
*DrAS 82E, LEduc 74, WhoAm 86,
WhoE 75, –77*

Chambers, Robert Warner 1924-
*AmM&WS 76P, –79P, –82P, –86P,
AuBYP, BioIn 8, WhoAm 76, –78,
–80, –82*

Chambers, Whittaker 1901-1961
BioIn 13, EncAJ

Chambliss, William C 1908?-1975
ConAu 57

Champion, Frances 1909-
WhoAmW 58, –61, –64, –68

Champlin, Tim *ConAu X*

Chance, Stephen *IntAu&W 86X,
WrDr 86*

Chance, Stephen 1925- *ConAu X,
IntAu&W 77X, –82X, TwCCW 78,
–83, WrDr 80, –82, –84*

Chance, Stephen *see also* Turner, Philip

Chancellor, John 1900-1971
*Au&Wr 71, AuNews 1, BioNews 74,
ConAu P-2, CurBio 62, MnBBF,
WhE&EA*

Chand, Meira 1942- *ConAu 106*

Chandler, A Bertram *OxAusL*

Chandler, A Bertram 1912-
*ConAu 21R, ConSFA, EncSF,
IntAu&W 82, ScF&FL 1, –2, ScFSB,
WhoSciF, WrDr 76, –80, –82, –84*

Chandler, A Bertram 1912-1984
ConAu 13NR, TwCSFW 86

Chandler, Anna Curtis 1890?-1969
BioIn 8, ChhPo, InWom, WhAm 5

Chandler, Caroline A 1906-1979
*AmAu&B, AmCath 80,
AmM&WS 73S, –78S, AuBYP,
BiDrAPA 77, BioIn 1, –8, BkC 4,
CathA 1930, ConAu 17R, –93,
SmATA 22N, –24, WhAm 7,
WhoAm 74, –76, –78, –80,
WhoAmW 74, –58, –64, –66, –68,
–70, –72*

Chandler, Caroline Augusta 1906-1979
BioIn 13

Chandler, David Geoffrey 1934-
*ConAu 11NR, IntAu&W 76, –77,
–82, WrDr 76, –80, –82, –84*

Chandler, David L *ConAu 16NR*

Chandler, David L 1937?-
*ConAu 1NR, –49, DrAS 74H, –78H,
–82H, WhoAm 82, –84*

Chandler, Edna Walker 1908-1982
*AuBYP, BioIn 8, –11, ConAu 1R,
–4NR, –108, SmATA 11, –31N,
WhoAmW 58, –75, –77*

Chandler, Raymond 1888-1959
*AmAu&B, BioIn 1, –4, –5, –6, –7, –9,
–10, –11, –12, –13, CasWL, CmCal,
CmMov, CnMWL, ConAu 104,
CorpD, CurBio 46, –59, DcAmB S6,
DcFM, DcLEL, EncMys, FilmgC,
HalFC 84, LinLib L, LongCTC,
MakMC, ModAL, –S2, –S1,
NewYTBE 73, Novels, ObitOF 79,
ObitT 1951, OxAmL, –83,
OxEng, –85, OxFilm, PenC AM,
REn, REnAL, TwCA SUP,
TwCCr&M 80, –85, TwCLC 1,
–7[port], TwCWr, WebAB, –79,
WebE&AL, WhAm 3, WhE&EA,
WhoTwCL, WorAl, WorEFlm*

Chaneles, Sol 1926- *AmM&WS 73S,
–78S, AuBYP SUP, ConAu 41R*

Chang, Diana *DrAP&F 85*

Chanover, Hyman 1920- *ConAu 2NR,
–49, IntAu&W 77, WhoAmJ 80,
WhoWorJ 72, –78*

Chant, Joy 1945- *ConAu X,
ScF&FL 1, –2, ScFSB*

Chapin, Harry 1942-1981
*AnObit 1981[port], Baker 84,
BioIn 11, –12, ConAu 104, –105,
EncFCWM 83, NewYTBS 81[port],
RkOn 78, –84, RolSEnR 83,
WhScrn 83, WhoAm 76, –78, –80,
WhoRock 81, WhoRocM 82*

Chapin, Henry 1893-1983 *Au&Wr 71,
AuBYP, BioIn 13, ConAu 110, –93*

Chapin, Kim 1942- *ConAu 9NR, –53,
MichAu 80*

Chaplin, Blondie *WhoRocM 82*

Chaplin, Blondie *see also* Beach Boys,
The

Chapman, Abraham 1915-1976
BioIn 11, ConAu 45, DrAS 74E

Chapman, Clark Russell 1945-
*AmM&WS 76P, –79P, –82P, –86P,
ConAu 110*

Chapman, Hester W 1899-1976
*Au&Wr 71, ConAu 9R, –9NR, –65,
WhE&EA, Who 74*

Chapman, Sydney 1888- *WhAm 8*

Chapman, Sydney 1888-1970 *BiESc,
BioIn 1, –2, –3, –4, –8, –9,
ConAu 106, CurBio 57, –70,
DcNaB 1961, InSci, McGEWB,
McGMS 80[port], NewYTBE 70,
ObitOF 79, ObitT 1961, WhE&EA,
WhoLA*

Chapman, Vera 1898- *ConAu 81,
SmATA 33[port]*

Chapman, Walker *ConAu X*

Chapman, Walker 1935- *DcLEL 1940,
SmATA X, ThrBJA, WorAu 1970*

Chapman, Walker *see also* Silverberg,
Robert

Chapple, Steve *DrAP&F 85*

Chapple, Steve 1949- *ConAu 77*

Charles, Sharon Ashenbrenner 1947-
WhoLibI 82

Charlip, Remy 1929- *BiDD, BioIn 13,
ChlLR 8[port], WrDr 86*

Charren, Peggy 1928- *BioIn 12,
LesBEnT, NewYTET, PolProf NF,
WhoAm 76, –78, –80, –82, –84, –86,
WhoAmW 79, –81*

Charriere, Henri 1906?-1973 *ASpks,
BioIn 8, –9, –10, –11, ConAu 101,
–45, NewYTBE 73, ObitOF 79,
ObitT 1971, WhScrn 77*

Charriere, Henri 1907-1973
WhScrn 83

Charry, Elias 1906- *ConAu 69,
WhoWorJ 72, –78*

Charters, Ann *WrDr 86*

Charters, Ann 1936- *ConAu 9NR,
–17R, WhoAm 84, –86,
WhoAmW 83, WrDr 76, –80, –82,
–84*

Charyn, Jerome *DrAP&F 85*

Charyn, Jerome 1937- *AmAu&B,
ConAu 5R, –7NR, ConAu 1AS[port],
ConLC 5, –8, –18, ConNov 72, –76,
–82, –86, DcLB Y83B[port],
DcLEL 1940, DrAS 74E, –78E, –82E,
IntAu&W 76, –77, –82, WhoAm 74,
–76, –78, –80, –82, –84,
WorAu 1975[port], WrDr 76, –80,
–82, –84, –86*

Chasan, Daniel Jack 1943- *ConAu 29R*

Chase, Alice Elizabeth 1906-
*Au&Wr 71, AuBYP, –SUP, BioIn 8,
–9, ConAu X, ConAu P-1, DrAS 74H,
–78H, –82H, ForWC 70,
IntAu&W 76, SmATA 4,
WhoAmA 73, –76, –78, –80, –82, –84,
WhoAmW 58, –61, –64, WomPO 76,
–78*

Chase, Alice Elizabeth *see also*
McHargue, Georgess

Chase, Chris *AuNews 1, BioIn 10, –12*

Chase, Emily *ConAu X*

Chase, Joan Barbara 1936- *LEduc 74,
WhoAmW 74, –77*

Chase, Mary Ellen 1887-1973
*AmAu&B, AmNov, AmWomWr,
AuBYP, BioIn 2, –3, –4, –5, –7,
–8, –10, –11, BlueB 76N, ChhPo,
ConAmA, ConAu 41R, ConAu P-1,
ConLC 2, CurBio 40, –45, –73, –73N,*

DcLEL, FourBJA, InWom, LibW,
LinLib L, LongCTC, NewYTBE 73,
Novels, ObitOF 79, OxAmL, –83,
PenC AM, REn, REnAL,
ScF&FL 1A, SmATA 10,
TwCA, –SUP, WhAm 5, WhLit,
WhNAA, Who 74, WhoAmW 74, –58,
–64, –66, –68, –70, –72
Chase, Naomi Feigelson *DrAP&F 85*
Chase, Naomi Feigelson 1932-
ConAu 104
Chase, Stuart 1888- *AmAu&B,*
BioIn 2, –3, –4, BlueB 76, ChhPo S2,
ConAmA, ConAu 65, CurBio 40,
DcAmSR, DcLEL, Future,
IntAu&W 77, –82, IntWW 74, –75,
–76, –77, –78, –79, –80, –81, –82,
–83, LinLib L, –S, LongCTC,
OxAmH, OxAmL, –83, REn,
REnAL, TwCA, –SUP, WebAB, –79,
WhNAA, Who 74, –82, –83, –85,
WhoAm 74, –76, –78, WhoWor 74
Chase, Stuart 1888-1985 *ConAu 117,*
CurBio 86N, NewYTBS 85
Chase-Riboud, Barbara *BioIn 13,*
SelBAAf, WhoAmA 84
Chase-Riboud, Barbara 1936-
DcLB 33[port], WhoBlA 85
Chase-Riboud, Barbara 1939- *AfroAA,*
BioIn 12, ConArt 77, ConAu 113,
WhoAm 78, –80, –82, WhoAmA 73,
–76, –78, –80, –82, WhoBlA 77, –80,
WhoWor 78
Chatwin, Bruce 1940- *BioIn 12, –13,*
ConAu 85, ConLC 28[port],
WorAu 1975[port]
Chaucer, Geoffrey 1340?-1400? *Alli,*
AnCL, AtlBL, BbD, BiD&SB,
BioIn 1, –2, –3, –4, –5, –6, –7, –8, –9,
–10, –11, –12, –13, BritAu, BritWr 1,
CasWL, Chambr 1, ChhPo, –S1, –S2,
–S3, CnE&AP, CrtT 1, –4, CyWA,
DcBiPP, DcCathB, DcEnA, DcEnL,
DcEuL, DcLEL, DcNaB, DcScB,
Dis&D, EvLB, LinLib L, –S,
LongCEL, LuthC 75, McGEWB,
MouLC 1, NewC, NewEOp 71,
OxChL, OxEng, OxMus, PenC ENG,
PoLE, RAdv 1, RComWL, REn,
WebE&AL, WhDW, WorAl
Chaucer, Geoffrey 1343?-1400
OxEng 85
Chayefsky, Paddy *ConAu X*
Chayefsky, Paddy 1923- *ScFSB*
Chayefsky, Paddy 1923-1981
AmAu&B, AmSCAP 66,
AnObit 1981[port], BiE&WWA,
BioIn 3, –4, –10, –11, –12, –13,
BlueB 76, CelR, CnMD, CnThe,
ConAu 9R, –104, ConDr 73, –77,
ConLC 23[port], ConTFT 1, CroCD,
CurBio 57, –81N, DcFM,
DcLB 7[port], –44[port], –Y81A[port],
DcLEL 1940, EncSF, EncWT,
IntAu&W 76, –77, –82, IntMPA 77,
–75, –76, –78, –79, –81, IntWW 74,
–75, –76, –77, –78, –79, –80, –81,
–82N, LesBEnT, LinLib L,
McGEWD, –84, ModWD,
NewYTBS 81[port], NotNAT,
OxAmL, –83, OxAmT 84, OxFilm,
PenC AM, PlP&P, REnAL,
WebAB, –79, WhAm 8, WhoAm 74, –76, –78,
–80, WhoE 74, WhoThe 72, –77, –81,
WhoTwCL, WhoWor 74, –78, –80,
WorAl, WorAu, WorEFlm, WrDr 76,
–80, –82
Chayefsky, Paddy 1923-1982 *WhAm 8*
Cheatham, K Follis *DrAP&F 85*
Cheatham, K Follis 1943- *ConAu 81*
Cheever, John 1912-1982 *AmAu&B,*
AmWr S1, AnObit 1982[port],
BioIn 3, –4, –5, –6, –8, –10, –11, –12,
–13, BlueB 76, CasWL, CelR,
ConAu 5R, –5NR, –106, ConAu 1BS,
ConLC 3, –7, –8, –11, –15, –25[port],
ConNov 72, –76, –82, –86A,
CurBio 75, –82N, DcLB 2,
–Y80A[port], –Y82A[port],
DcLEL 1940, EncWL, –2,
IntAu&W 76, –77, IntWW 74, –75,
–76, –77, –78, –79, –80, –81, –82,
–83N, LinLib L, ModAL, –S2, –S1,

NewCon[port], NewYTBS 78, –79,
–82[port], Novels, OxAmL, –83,
OxEng 85, PenC AM, Po&Wr 77,
RAdv 1, REn, REnAL, TwCWr,
WebE&AL, WhAm 8, Who 74, –82,
–83N, WhoAm 74, –76, –78, –80,
–82, WhoTwCL, WhoWor 74, –76,
–78, WorAl, WorAu, WrDr 76, –80,
–82
Chekhov, Anton 1860-1904 *GrFLW,*
HalFC 84, MajMD 2, OxAmT 84
Chekhov, Anton Pavlovich 1860-1904
AtlBL, BioIn 1, –2, –3, –4, –5, –6, –7,
–8, –9, –10, –11, –12, CasWL,
ClDMEL, CnMD, CnThe,
ConAu 104, CyWA, DcEuL, DcRusL,
Dis&D, EncWL, –2[port], EncWT,
EuAu, EvEuW, HanRL, InSci,
LinLib L, –S, LongCEL, LongCTC,
McGEWB, McGEWD, –84[port],
ModSL 1, ModWD, NewC,
NotNAT A, –B, Novels[port],
OxEng, –85, OxMed 86, OxThe, –83,
PenC EUR, PlP&P, –A, RComWL,
REn, REnWD, TwCLC 3, –10[port],
WhDW, WorAl
Chekhov, Anton Pavlovich *see also*
Tchekhov, Anton Pavlovich
Chen, Jack 1908- *BioIn 9,*
ConAu 15NR, –41R, IntAu&W 77,
–82, –86
Chen, Jo-Hsi 1938- *IntAu&W 77X,*
–82, –86, WorAu 1975[port]
Chen, Yuan-Tsung 1932- *BioIn 12,*
ConAu 106, NewYTBS 80[port]
Cheney, Cora 1916- *AuBYP, BioIn 8,*
–9, ConAu 1R, –4NR, SmATA 3,
WhoAmW 58, –61
Cheney, David M *ScF&FL 1*
Cheney, Glenn Alan 1951- *ConAu 109*
Cheney, Sheldon 1886-1980 *AmAu&B,*
AnObit 1980, Au&Wr 71,
BiE&WWA, BioIn 4, –12,
ConAu 102, IntAu&W 76,
NewYTBS 80, NotNAT, OxAmT 84,
REnAL, TwCA, –SUP, WhAm 7,
WhE&EA, WhThe, WhoAm 74, –76,
–78, WhoAmA 73, –76, –78, –80,
–82N, –84N, WhoWor 74, –76
Cheney, Theodore A Rees 1928-
IntAu&W 86
Chennault, Anna Chan 1925-
AmAu&B, BioIn 6, –11, –12,
BlueB 76, ConAu 61, ForWC 70,
IntAu&W 76, WhoAm 74, –76, –78,
–80, –82, –84, –86, WhoAmP 73, –75,
–77, –79, –81, –83, –85,
WhoAmW 74, –66, –68, –70, –72,
–75, –77, –79, –81, –83, –85, –87,
WhoS&SW 73, –75, –76,
WhoWor 80, –82, –84, –87
Cherryh, C J 1942- *BioIn 12,*
ConAu 65, –X, ConLC 35[port],
DcLB Y80B[port], EncSF,
ScFSB[port], TwCSFW 86,
WhoAm 86, WrDr 84, –86
Chesher, Richard 1940- *ConAu 106*
Cheshire, Maxine 1930- *BioIn 8, –9,*
–11, CelR, ConAu 108, GoodHs,
WhoAm 74, –76, –78, –80, –82, –84,
WhoAmW 74, –70A, –72, –75, –79,
–83, –85
Chesler, Phyllis 1940- *AmWomWr,*
BioIn 11, ConAu 4NR, –49
Chesney, Marion 1936- *ConAu 111,*
–115
Chesnut, Mary Boykin 1823-1886
AmWomWr, BioIn 2, –4, –10, –12,
–13, InWom, LibW, NotAW,
OxAmL, –83, REnAL
Chester, Deborah 1957- *ConAu 102,*
–18NR
Chester, Laura *DrAP&F 85*
Chester, Laura 1949- *ConAu 9NR,*
–65, IntWWP 77
Chester, Michael 1928- *AuBYP,*
BioIn 8, ConAu 1R, –1NR,
ScF&FL 1, –2
Chester, William L 1907- *EncSF,*
ScF&FL 1
Chesterton, G K 1874-1936
DcLB 34[port], HalFC 84,
ModBrL S2, OxEng 85, ScFSB,
SupFW, TwCCr&M 85

Chesterton, Gilbert Keith 1874-1936
AnCL, AtlBL, BioIn 1, –2, –3, –4, –5,
–6, –7, –8, –9, –10, –11, –12, –13,
BkC 6, CasWL, CathA 1930,
Chambr 3, ChhPo, –S1, –S2, –S3,
CorpD, DcBrBI, DcCathB, DcLEL,
DcNaB 1931, EvLB, LinLib L, –S,
LongCEL, LuthC 75, MakMC,
McGEWB, NewC, OxEng,
PenC ENG, TwCA, –SUP, TwCWr,
WhDW, WhE&EA, WhLit, WhoLA
Chetin, Helen 1922- *BioIn 10,*
ConAu 12NR, –29R, SmATA 6
Chevigny, Bell Gale 1936- *ConAu 57,*
WhoAmW 74, –72
Chew, Ruth 1920- *BioIn 10,*
ConAu 14NR, –41R, IntAu&W 82,
SmATA 7
Chicago *BiDAmM, BiDJaz A,*
BioNews 74, EncJzS, EncPR&S 74,
–77, IlEncRk, RkOn 78, –84,
RolSEnR 83, WhoRock 81,
WhoRocM 82
Chicago, Judy 1939- *AmArt, BioIn 9,*
–10, –12, –13, ConArt 77, –83,
DcCAr 81, IntDcWB, NewYTBS 79,
PrintW 83, –85, WhoAm 76, –78,
–80, –82, –84, –86, WhoAmA 73, –76,
–78, –80, –82, –84, WhoAmW 75,
–77, –79, –81, –83, –85, –87,
WomWMM B
Chicago *see also* Cetera, Peter
Chicago *see also* Kath, Terry
Chicago *see also* Lamm, Robert
Chicago *see also* Loughnane, Lee
Chicago *see also* Pankow, James
Chicago *see also* Parazaider, Walt
Chicago *see also* Seraphine, Dan
Chichester, Sir Francis 1901-1972
Au&Wr 71, BioIn 6, –7, –8, –9, –10,
ConAu 37R, ConAu P-1, CurBio 67,
–72, –72N, LinLib L, NewYTBE 72,
ObitOF 79, ObitT 1971, OxShips,
WhDW, WhAm 5, WhE&EA
Chidsey, Donald Barr 1902-1981
AmAu&B, AmNov, Au&Wr 71,
BioIn 2, –4, –9, –13, ConAu 2NR,
–5R, –103, REnAL, SmATA 27N, –3,
TwCA SUP
Chieger, Bob 1945- *ConAu 114,*
IntAu&W 86
Child, John 1922- *ConAu 93,*
WrDr 76, –80, –82, –84, –86
Childers, Erskine 1905-1974 *BioIn 10,*
–11, BlueB 76N, DclrB, IntWW 74,
–75N, NewYTBE 74, ObitT 1971,
Who 74, WhoWor 74
Childress, Alice *BlkWWr,*
DrAP&F 85, WhoBlA 85
Childress, Alice 1920- *AmWomD,*
AuBYP SUP, BioIn 10, –12,
BlkAWP, ConAu 3NR, –45,
ConDr 77, –82, ConLC 12, –15,
DcLB 7[port], –38[port], DrBlPA,
FifBJA[port], InB&W 80, –85,
LivgBAA, McGEWD 84, NegAl 83,
NotNAT, PlP&P A, SelBAAf,
SelBAAu, SmATA 48[port], –7,
WhoAm 74, –76, –82, –84, –86,
WhoAmW 74, –72, WhoBlA 75, –77,
–80, WorAu 1975[port], WrDr 80,
–82, –84, –86
Chilton, Irma 1930- *ConAu 103,*
–19NR, OxLitW 86, ScF&FL 1, –2
Chin, Richard 1932- *WhoAmP 73*
Chinery, Michael 1938- *BioIn 13,*
ConAu 103, –20NR, IntAu&W 77,
SmATA 26, WrDr 76, –80, –82, –84,
–86
Chinn, William G 1919- *ConAu 33R,*
LEduc 74, WhoWest 76, –78
Chipman, Bruce Lewis 1946-
ConAu 37R, WhoE 83, WrDr 76,
–80, –82, –84, –86
Chipperfield, Joseph E 1912-1976
OxChL
Chipperfield, Joseph Eugene
1912-1976 *Au&Wr 71, AuBYP,*
BioIn 6, –8, –9, ConAu 6NR, –9R,
IntAu&W 76, MorJA, SmATA 2,
TwCCW 78, –83, WrDr 80
Chipperfield, Joseph Eugene *see also*
Craig, John Eland

Chisholm, Shirley 1924- *AlmAP 78,*
–80, –82[port], AmAu&B,
AmPolW 80, –80A, BiDrAC, BioIn 8,
–9, –10, –11, –12, BlueB 76, CelR,
CivR 74, CngDr 74, –77, –79, –81,
ConAu 29R, CurBio 69, Ebony 1, GoodHs,
HerW, –84, InB&W 80, IntDcWB,
LibW, LinLib S, LivgBAA, NegAl 76,
–83[port], NewYTBE 70, PolProf NF,
SelBAAu, WhoAm 74, –76, –78, –80,
–82, WhoAmP 73, –75, –77, –79, –81,
–83, WhoAmW 66A, –68, –70, –72,
–75, –77, –79, –81, –83, WhoBlA 75,
–77, –80, WhoE 74, –75, –77, –79,
–81, –83, WhoGov 77, –72, –75,
WomPO 76, –78, WorAl, WrDr 76,
–80, –82, –84
Chisholm, Shirley Anita 1924-
AmWomM, BioIn 13, SelBAAf,
WhoAmP 85
Chisholm, Shirley Anita St. Hill 1924-
InB&W 85, WhoAm 84, –86,
WhoAmW 85, WhoBlA 85
Chissell, Joan Olive *IntWWM 85,*
WrDr 86
Chissell, Joan Olive 1919- *Au&Wr 71,*
ConAu 61, IntAu&W 76,
IntWWM 77, WhoMus 72,
WhoWor 78, WrDr 76, –80, –82, –84
Chittenden, Elizabeth F 1903-
BioIn 11, ConAu 61, SmATA 9
Chittum, Ida 1918- *AuBYP SUP,*
BioIn 10, ConAu 14NR, –37R,
IntAu&W 77, SmATA 7,
WhoAmW 81, WrDr 76, –80, –82,
–84, –86
Chopin, Kate 1850-1904 *OxEng 85*
Chopin, Kate 1851-1904 *AmAu,*
AmAu&B, AmWomWr, AmWr S1,
BbD, BiDSA, BioIn 8, –10, –12, –13,
CasWL, CnDAL, ConAu 104, CrtT 4,
DcAmAu, DcAmB, DcLB 12[port],
DcLEL, DcNAA, EncSoH, GoodHs,
IntDcWB, LibW, ModAL, –S1,
NatCAB 25, NotAW, Novels,
OxAmL, –83, PenC AM, REn,
REnAL, TwCLC 5[port], –14[port],
WebAB, –79, WhAm 1, WomNov,
WorAl
Choron, Jacques 1904-1972 *AuBYP,*
BioIn 8, –9, ConAu 33R, ConAu P-1,
NewYTBE 72, WhoAm 74
Chrisman, Harry E 1906- *ConAu 1R*
Christ, Henry I 1915- *ConAu 2NR,*
–5R, IntAu&W 76, WrDr 76, –80,
–82, –84, –86
Christensen, Jo I 1943- *ConAu 57, –X*
Christensen, Jo I *see also* Christensen,
Yolanda Maria Ippolito
Christensen, Yolanda Maria Ippolito
1943- *ConAu 7NR, WhoAmW 77,*
–79
Christensen, Yolanda Maria Ippolito
see also Christensen, Jo I
Christgau, Robert 1942- *BioIn 10, –11,*
ConAu 65, MugS, WhoE 81
Christian, Catherine 1901- *ScF&FL 1,*
WhE&EA
Christian, Mary Blount 1933-
BioIn 11, ConAu 1NR, –17NR, –45,
IntAu&W 77, SmATA 9,
WhoAmW 83, WrDr 76, –80, –82,
–84, –86
Christian, Samuel Terry 1937-
AmM&WS 73P, –76P, –79P, –82P,
–86P, AuBYP SUP
Christian, Shirley 1938- *ConAu 119*
Christie, Agatha *WomNov*
Christie, Agatha 1890?-1976
Au&Wr 71, AuBYP, AuNews 1, –2,
BiE&WWA, BioIn 1, –2, –4, –6, –7,
–8, –9, –11, –12, –13, BioNews 74,
BlueB 76, CasWL, CelR, CnThe,
ConAu 10NR, –17R, –61, ConDr 73,
–77, ConLC 1, –6, –8, –12,
ConNov 72, –76, CorpD, CurBio 40,
–64, –76, –76N, DcLB 13[port],
DcLEL, EncMys, EncWT, EvLB,
FilmgC, GoodHs, InWom,
IntAu&W 76X, IntDcWB,
IntWW 74, –75, –76N, LinLib L,
–LP, –S, LongCTC, MnBBF, NewC,

NewYTBS 76, Novels, ObitOF 79,
OxEng, –85, PenC ENG, PIP&P,
REn, ScF&FL 1, –2, SmATA 36,
TwCA, –SUP, TwCCr&M 80, –85,
TwCWr, WhAm 6, WhE&EA,
Who 74, WhoAmW 74, –61, –66, –68,
–70, –72, –75, WhoHr&F,
WhoThe 72, –77, –81N, WhoWor 74,
WorAl, WrDr 76
Christie, Agatha 1891-1976 *HalFC 84*
Christie, Ian R 1919- *ConAu 20NR*
Christie, Ian Ralph 1919- *Au&Wr 71,*
ConAu 2NR, –5R, IntAu&W 76, –77,
–82, –86, Who 82, –83, –85,
WhoWor 82, –84, WrDr 76, –80, –82,
–84
Christie, Trevor L 1905?-1969 *BioIn 8,*
ConAu P-2
Christman, Elizabeth *DrAP&F 85*
Christman, Elizabeth 1914- *ConAu 89*
Christopher, John *SmATA X*
Christopher, John 1922- *BioIn 4, –10,*
ChLR 2, ConAu 73, –77, –X,
ConSFA, DcLEL 1940, EncSF,
FourBJA, LElec, LinLib L, Novels,
OxChL, ScF&FL 1, –2, ScFSB, SenS,
SmATA X, TwCCW 78, –83,
TwCSFW 86, WhoSciF, WorAu,
WrDr 80, –82, –84, –86
Christopher, John *see also* Youd,
Samuel
Christopher, Matt *IntAu&W 86X*
Christopher, Matt 1917- *ConAu 1R,*
–5NR, FifBJA[port], IntAu&W 77X,
–82X, SmATA 2, –47[port]
Christopher, Matt F 1917- *WrDr 86*
Christopher, Matthew F 1917-
AuBYP, BioIn 8, –9, –10, ConAu 1R,
IntAu&W 77, –82, –86, MorBMP,
SmATA 2, WrDr 76, –80, –82, –84
Christopher, Milbourne *BioIn 5, –10,*
BioNews, ConAu 105, EncO&P 2,
–78
Christopher, Milbourne 1914?-1984
ConAu 113, EncO&P 2S1,
SmATA 46[port]
Chrystie, Frances Nicholson 1904-
AuBYP, BioIn 3, –7
Chu, Daniel 1933- *BioIn 11,*
ConAu 13R, SmATA 11
Chu, Louis H 1913?-1970 *BioIn 8,*
ConAu 13R
Chu, Samuel C 1929- *ConAu 69,*
DrAS 74H, –78H, –82H
Chubb, Thomas Caldecot 1899-1972
AmAu&B, Au&Wr 71, BioIn 9,
ChhPo, –S1, –S2, ConAu 1R, –6NR,
–33R, NewYTBE 72, REn, REnAL,
WhAm 5, WhE&EA, WhNAA
Chukovsky, Kornei 1882-1969
ConAu 4NR, –25R, ObitOF 79,
SmATA 34[port], TwCCW 78B, –83B
Chukovsky, Kornei 1882-1970 *OxChL*
Chukovsky, Kornei Ivanovich
1882-1969 *HanRL*
Church, Alfred John 1829-1912
Alli SUP, AuBYP, BioIn 2, –8,
ChhPo S2, JBA 34, –51, ScF&FL 1,
TelT, WhLit
Church, Carol Bauer *AuBYP SUP*
Church, Richard 1893-1972 *Alli,*
Au&Wr 71, BioIn 4, –6, –7, –8, –9,
ChhPo, –S1, –S2, –S3, ConAu 1R,
–3NR, –33R, ConNov 72, ConPo 70,
DcLEL, EvLB, LongCTC, ModBrL,
MorJA, NewC, NewYTBE 74, Novels,
ObitT 1971, OxChL, PenC ENG,
REn, ScF&FL 1, SmATA 3,
TwCA, –SUP, TwCCW 78, –83,
TwCWr, WhE&EA, WhLit, WhoChL
Church, Richard Thomas 1893-1972
OxEng 85
Churchill, E Richard 1937- *BioIn 11,*
ConAu 11NR, –17R, SmATA 11,
WrDr 76, –80, –82, –84, –86
Churchill, Linda R 1938-
ConAu 11NR, –17R, WhoAmW 74
Churchill, Winston 1871-1947
AmAu&B, AmLY, ApCAB SUP,
ApCAB X, BbD, BiD&SB, BiDSA,
BioIn 1, –2, –4, –5, –10, –12, CarSB,
CasWL, Chambr 3, CnDAL,
ConAmA, ConAmL, CurBio 40, –42,

–53, –65, CyWA, DcAmAu,
DcAmB S4, DcAmSR, DcBiA,
DcLEL, DcNAA, EvLB, JBA 34,
LinLib L, –S, LongCTC, McGEWB,
NatCAB 10, NotNAT B, Novels,
ObitOF 79, OxAmL, –83,
OxEng, –85, PenC AM, REn,
REnAL, TwCA SUP, TwCBDA,
TwCWr, WebE&AL, WhAm 2,
WhE&EA, WhLit, WhNAA, WhThe
Chute, B J *DrAP&F 85*
Chute, B J 1913- *AmAu&B,*
ConAu 1R, IntAu&W 77X, –82X,
MnBBF, MorJA, SmATA 2,
WhoAmW 74, –58, –61, –66, –68,
–70, –72, WrDr 76, –80, –82, –84,
–86
Chute, Beatrice Joy 1913- *AmWomWr,*
BioIn 1, –2, –6, –9, CurBio 50,
InWom, IntAu&W 77, –82
Chute, Marchette 1909- *AmAu&B,*
AmWomWr, Au&Wr 71, AuBYP,
BiE&WWA, BioIn 2, –3, –4, –5, –6,
–7, –9, BkCL, ChhPo, –S1, –S2,
ConAu 1R, –5NR, CurBio 50,
DrAS 74H, –78H, –82H, EvLB,
InWom, IntAu&W 76, –77, –82,
IntWWP 77, LinLib L, MinnWr,
MorJA, NotNAT, RAdv 1, REnAL,
SmATA 1, TwCA SUP, TwCCW 78,
–83, Who 74, –82, –83, –85,
WhoAm 74, –76, –78, –80, –82, –84,
–86, WhoAmW 74, –58, –64, –66,
–68, –70, –72, –83, –85, –87,
WrDr 76, –80, –82, –84, –86
Ciardi, John *DrAP&F 85*
Ciardi, John 1916- *AmAu&B, AuBYP,*
BioIn 2, –4, –5, –6, –7, –8, –9, –12,
–13, BlueB 76, BkCL, CasWL,
CelR, ChhPo, –S1, –S2, –S3, CnDAL,
ConAu 5R, –5NR, ConAu 2AS[port],
ConLC 10, ConPo 70, –75, –80, –85,
CurBio 67, DcLB 5[port],
DcLEL 1940, DrAS 74E, –78E, –82E,
IntWWP 77, LinLib L, ModAL,
OxAmL, –83, OxChL, PenC AM,
RAdv 1, REn, REnAL, SmATA 1,
Str&VC, ThrBJA, TwCA SUP,
TwCCW 78, –83, WebAB, –79,
WebE&AL, WhoAm 74, –76, –78,
–80, –82, –84, WhoE 74, WhoWor 74,
WorAl, WrDr 76, –80, –82, –84, –86
Ciardi, John 1916-1986 *ConAu 118,*
ConLC 40[port], –44[port],
CurBio 86N, DcLB Y86N[port],
NewYTBS 86[port], SmATA 46N
Cipriano, Anthony 1941- *ConAu 102*
Cirino, Robert 1937- *ConAu 61*
Citron, Samuel J 1908-1979 *BioIn 12,*
WhoWorJ 72, –78
Claflin, Edward 1949- *AuBYP SUP,*
ConAu 97
Clagett, John 1916- *AmAu&B,*
AuBYP, BioIn 3, –8, ConAu 5R,
–6NR, DrAS 74E, –78E, –82E
Claiborne, Robert 1919- *ConAu 12NR,*
–29NR, IntAu&W 77
Claire, Keith 1940- *Au&Wr 71,*
ConAu X, ScF&FL 1
Clampitt, Amy *ConAu 110,*
ConLC 32[port], DrAP&F 85
Clampitt, Amy 1920- *ConPo 85,*
WrDr 86
Clancy, Tom *NewYTBS 86[port]*
Clapp, Patricia 1912- *BioIn 9,*
ConAu 10NR, –25R, FifBJA[port],
IntAu&W 82, OxChL, ScF&FL 1, –2,
SmATA 4, SmATA 4AS[port],
TwCCW 78, –83, WhoE 83,
WrDr 76, –80, –82, –84, –86
Clapton, Eric 1945- *Baker 84, BioIn 8,*
–9, –10, –11, –12, –13, CelR,
EncPR&S 74, –77, IlEncRk,
RkOn 78, –84, RolSEnR 83,
WhoAm 74, –76, –78, –80, –82, –84,
–86, WhoRock 81, WhoRocM 82,
WhoWor 78, WorAl
Clare, George 1920- *WrDr 84, –86*
Clarens, Carlos 1936- *ConAu 21R,*
ScF&FL 1, –2
Clark, Ann Nolan *see Clark,* Ann Nolan
Clark, Ann Nolan 1896-
DcLB 52[port], OxChL, WrDr 86

Clark, Ann Nolan 1898- *AmAu&B,*
AmCath 80, AmPB, AmWomWr,
AnCL, Au&ICB, AuBYP, BioIn 2, –3,
–4, –6, –7, –9, –10, ChhPo,
ConAu 20NR, –5R, IntAu&W 76,
JBA 51, LinLib L, MorBMP,
Newb 1922, SmATA 4, Str&VC,
TwCCW 78, –83, WhoAm 74, –76,
–78, –80, –82, WhoAmW 74, –58,
–61, –64, –66, –68, –70, –72,
WrDr 80, –82, –84
Clark, Baron Kenneth MacKenzie
1903-1983 *BioIn 13*
Clark, Billy Curtis 1928- *BioIn 4, –8,*
ConAu 1R, WhoS&SW 73
Clark, Brian 1932- *ConAu 41R,*
ConDr 77C, –82, ConLC 29[port],
ConTFT 4, WhoThe 81, WrDr 84,
–86
Clark, Dick *ConAu X*
Clark, Dick 1928- *WhoAm 86*
Clark, Dick 1929- *AlmAP 78,*
Baker 84, BiDD, BioIn 5, –10, –11,
CmpEPM, CngDr 77, ConTFT 3,
CurBio 59, IntMPA 77, –75, –76,
–78, –79, –81, –82, –84, –86,
IntWW 74, –75, –76, –77, –78,
LesBEnT[port], NewYTET,
RolSEnR 83, WhoAm 74, –76, –78,
–80, –82, –84, WhoAmP 75,
WhoHol A, WhoRock 81
Clark, Dorothy Park 1899- *AmAu&B,*
AmNov X, BioIn 2, –4, ConAu 5R,
CurBio 57, InWom, WhoAmW 58
Clark, Eleanor *DrAP&F 85,*
IntAu&W 86, WhoAm 84, –86,
WhoAmW 85, –87
Clark, Eleanor 1913- *AmAu&B,*
AmWomWr, BioIn 2, –4, –11,
ConAu 9R, ConLC 5, –19,
ConNov 72, –76, –82, –86, CurBio 78,
DcLB 6[port], DcLEL 1940,
IntAu&W 76, –77, –82,
NewYTBS 77, OxAmL 83, REnAL,
TwCA SUP, WhoAm 74, –76, –78,
–80, –82, WhoAmW 58, –68,
WrDr 76, –80, –82, –84, –86
Clark, Eric 1911- *Au&Wr 71,*
ConAu 9NR, –13R, WhE&EA,
WhoWor 76, WrDr 76, –80, –82, –84,
–86
Clark, Eugenie 1922- *AmM&WS 73P,*
–76P, –79P, –82P, –86P, BioIn 2, –3,
–5, –7, –8, –9, –11, –12, –13,
ConAu 49, CurBio 53, HerW, –84,
InSci, InWom, WhoAm 76, –78, –80,
–82, –84, –86, WhoAmW 74, –66,
–66A, –68, –70, –72, –75, –77,
WhoS&SW 73, –75, WhoWor 74
Clark, Frank J 1922- *AmSCAP 66,*
AuBYP, BioIn 8, –12, ConAu 13R,
–17NR, SmATA 18
Clark, Joan *OxCanL*
Clark, Joan 1934- *BioIn 13*
Clark, Kenneth M 1903- *Au&Wr 71,*
BioIn 2, –3, –4, –6, –8, –9, –10, –11,
–12, BlueB 76, CasWL, ConAu 93,
CurBio 63, IntAu&W 77, IntMPA 75,
IntWW 75, –76, –77, –78, –79, –80,
–81, LinLib L, LongCTC,
NewYTBE 70, TwCA SUP, Who 74,
WhoWor 74, –76, –78, –82, WrDr 82
Clark, LaVerne Harrell *DrAP&F 85*
Clark, LaVerne Harrell 1929-
ConAu 11NR, –13R, ForWC 70,
IntAu&W 77, –82, IntWWP 77, –82,
WhoAmW 75, –77, –81, WrDr 76,
–80, –82, –84, –86
Clark, Lord Kenneth Mackenzie
1903-1983 *OxEng 85*
Clark, Lord Kenneth McKenzie
1903-1983 *WhAm 8*
Clark, Margaret Goff 1913- *AuBYP,*
BioIn 8, –11, ConAu 1R, –5NR,
–20NR, ForWC 70, IntAu&W 76,
SmATA 8, WhoAmW 75, –77
Clark, Mary Higgins *SmATA 46[port],*
ThrtnMM, WhoAmW 85, –87
Clark, Mary Higgins 1929?- *BioIn 11,*
–12, ConAu 81, IntAu&W 82,
TwCCr&M 85, WhoAm 82, –84, –86,
WrDr 82, –84, –86
Clark, Mary Higgins 1931-
ConAu 16NR

Clark, Mavis Thorpe *WrDr 86* **Clark,**
Mavis Thorpe 1912?- *BioIn 11,*
ConAu 8NR, –57, ConLC 12,
FourBJA, OxAusL, SingR 1,
SmATA 8, TwCCW 78, –83,
WrDr 80, –82, –84
Clark, Ramsey 1927- *AmAu&B,*
BioIn 5, –7, –8, –9, –10, –11, –12,
BioNews 74, BlueB 76, CelR,
ConAu 29R, CurBio 67, IntWW 74,
–75, –76, –77, –78, –79, –80, –81,
–82, –83, NewYTBS 74, PolProf J,
PolProf NF, Who 74, –82, –83, –85,
WhoAm 74, –76, –78, –80, –82, –84,
–86, WhoAmL 78, –79, –83, –85,
WhoAmP 73, –75, –77, –79, –81, –83,
–85, WhoWor 74, –78, –80, WorAl
Clark, Ronald William 1916-
Au&Wr 71, AuBYP, BioIn 7, –9,
ConAu 25R, ConSFA, ScF&FL 1, –2, SmATA 2
Clark, Sue C 1935- *ConAu 41R*
Clark, Walter VanTilburg 1909-1971
AmAu&B, AmNov, BioIn 1, –2, –4,
–5, –8, –9, –10, –11, –12, –13,
CmCal, CnDAL, ConAu 9R, –33R,
ConLC 28[port], ConNov 72, –76,
–82A, CyWA, DcLB 9[port],
DcLEL 1940, EncFWF, LinLib L,
ModAL, NatCAB 57, NewYTBE 71,
Novels, ObitOF 79, OxAmL, –83,
PenC AM, RAdv 1, REn, REnAL,
REnAW, SmATA 8, TwCA SUP,
WhAm 5, WorAl
Clarke, Anna 1919- *ConAu 18NR,*
IntAu&W 86, TwCCr&M 85,
WrDr 86
Clarke, Arthur C *DrmM 2[port]*
Clarke, Arthur C 1917-
ConLC 35[port], ConNov 86,
EncO&P 2S1, HalFC 84,
IntAu&W 86, OxEng 85,
ScFSB[port], TwCSFW 86, WrDr 86
Clarke, Arthur Charles 1917-
Au&Wr 71, AuBYP, BioIn 3, –4, –6,
–7, –8, –10, –11, –12, –13, BlueB 76,
CelR, ConAu 1R, –2NR, ConLC 1,
–4, –13, –18, ConNov 72, –76, –82,
ConSFA, CurBio 66, DcLEL 1940,
EncSF, EvLB, FourBJA, Future,
IntAu&W 76, –77, –82, IntWW 74,
–75, –76, –77, –78, –79, –80, –81,
–82, –83, LinLib L, LongCTC, NewC,
NewYTBS 83[port], Novels[port],
ScF&FL 1, –2, SmATA 13,
TwCA SUP, TwCWr, WebE&AL,
Who 74, –82, –83, –85, WhoAm 86,
WhoSciF, WhoWor 74, –76, –78, –82,
–84, –87, WorAl, WrDr 76, –80, –82,
–84
Clarke, James 1934- *Au&Wr 71*
Clarke, Joan 1921- *SmATA 42*
Clarke, Joan B 1921- *BioIn 13,*
ScF&FL 1, SmATA 27, TwCCW 78,
WrDr 76, –80, –82
Clarke, John 1907- *BioIn 10,*
ConAu X, IntAu&W 77X, SmATA 5
Clarke, John Henrik 1915- *AfroAA,*
AmAu&B, AuNews 1, BioIn 4, –5,
–10, BioNews 74, BlkAWP, CivR 74,
ConAu 53, Ebony 1, InB&W 80, –85,
LinLib L, LivgBAA, NegAl 76, –83,
SelBAAf, SelBAAu, WhoAm 74, –76,
WhoE 74, –75
Clarke, John *see also* Laklan, Virginia
Carli
Clarke, Mary Stetson 1911- *BioIn 10,*
ConAu 8NR, –21R, SmATA 5,
WhoAmW 74, –75, –77, WhoE 83,
–85, WrDr 76, –80, –82, –84, –86
Clarke, Robin Harwood 1937-
Au&Wr 71, ConAu 9NR, –13R,
IntAu&W 76
Clarke, Ron 1937- *BioIn 7, –8, –9,*
–10, –12, ConAu 107, CurBio 71,
WhoTr&F 73
Clarke, Thurston 1946- *ConAu 13NR,*
–77
Clarke, Tom E 1915- *ConAu 5R,*
WhoPNW
Clarkson, E Margaret 1915-
ConAu 1R, –5NR, –20NR,
IntAu&W 76, –77, SmATA 37,
WrDr 76, –80, –82, –84, –86

Cohen, Barbara 1932- *AuBYP SUP, BioIn 11, ConAu 4NR, –19NR, –53, CurBio 57, FifBJA[port], SmATA 10*
Cohen, Daniel 1936- *AuBYP SUP, BioIn 11, ChlLR 3, ConAu 1NR, –20NR, –45, IntAu&W 77, –82, SmATA 8, SmATA 4AS[port]*
Cohen, Florence Chanock 1927- *ConAu 5R, IntAu&W 76, WhoAmW 68*
Cohen, Hennig 1919- *WhoAmW 84, –86*
Cohen, Joel H *AuBYP SUP*
Cohen, Leonard 1934- *Baker 84, BioIn 8, –9, –10, –11, –12, BlueB 76, CanWW 79, –80, –81, –83, CanWr, CasWL, CelR, ChhPo S1, ConAu 14NR, –21R, ConLC 3, –38[port], ConNov 72, –76, –82, –86, ConPo 70, –75, –80, –85, CreCan 1, CurBio 69, DcLB 53[port], DcLEL 1940, EncFCWM 83, EncPR&S 77, EncWL 2, IntAu&W 76, –77, IntWWP 77, ModCmwL, OxCan, –SUP, OxCanL, RolSEnR 83, WebE&AL, WhoAm 74, –76, –78, –80, –82, –84, –86, WhoCanL 85, WhoRock 81, WorAl, WorAu 1970, WrDr 76, –80, –82, –84, –86*
Cohen, Matt 1942- *ConNov 86, DcLB 53[port], OxCanL, WhoCanL 85, WrDr 86*
Cohen, Miriam 1926- *BioIn 13, FifBJA[port]*
Cohen, Peter Zachary 1931- *BioIn 9, ConAu 12NR, –33R, IntAu&W 82, SmATA 4, WhoMW 84, WrDr 76, –80, –82, –84*
Cohen, Richard Murry 1938- *ConAu 103, –19NR*
Cohen, Steve 1951- *ConAu 114*
Cohen, Susan 1938- *ConAu 20NR*
Cohn, Angelo 1914- *BioIn 12, ConAu 4NR, –5R, IntAu&W 77, SmATA 19*
Cohn, Nik 1946- *Au&Wr 71, AuBYP SUP, ConAu 102*
Coit, Margaret Louise 1919?- *AmAu&B, AmWomWr, Au&Wr 71, AuBYP, BioIn 2, –3, –4, –7, –9, ConAu 1R, –5NR, CurBio 51, DrAS 74H, EncAAH, ForWC 70, InWom, IntAu&W 77, OxAmL, REnAL, SmATA 2, TwCA SUP, WhoAm 74, –76, –78, –80, –82, –84, –86, WhoAmW 74, –58, –64, –66, –68, –70, –72*
Coker, Jerry 1932- *BiDAmM, ConAu 6NR, –9R, IndAu 1917*
Colbert, Edwin H 1905- *WhoAm 84, –86, WhoFrS 84*
Colbert, Edwin Harris 1905- *AmM&WS 73P, –76P, –79P, –82P, –86P, BioIn 2, –3, –7, BlueB 76, ConAu 8NR, –61, CurBio 65, IntWW 74, –75, –76, –77, –78, –79, –80, –81, –82, –83, WhoAm 74, –76, –78, –80, –82, WrDr 76, –80, –82, –84, –86*
Colby, C B 1904-1977 *ConAu 1R, –6NR, IntAu&W 77, SmATA 3, –35*
Colby, Carroll Burleigh 1904-1977 *AuBYP, BioIn 6, –7, –9, ConAu 1R, MorJA, SmATA 3, WhAm 7, WhoAm 74, –76, –78*
Colby, Jean Poindexter 1909- *AuBYP SUP, BioIn 2, ChhPo S1, ConAu 1R, –5NR, ForWC 70, IntAu&W 77, SmATA 23[port], WhoAmW 74, –58, –61, –64, –70, –72, –75, WrDr 76, –80, –82, –84, –86*
Cole, Ernest *InB&W 80*
Cole, Ernest 1940- *ICPEnP A*
Cole, Joanna 1944- *ConAu 115, FifBJA[port], SmATA 37*
Cole, Lewis 1946- *ConAu 109*
Cole, Lois Dwight 1902?-1979 *AmAu&B, AuBYP, BioIn 8, –11, –13, ConAu 1R, –4NR, –104, SmATA 10, –26N, WhoAmW 58, –61, –68, –70, –72*
Cole, Lois Dwight *see also* Avery, Lynn

Cole, Lois Dwight *see also* Dudley, Nancy
Cole, Lois Dwight *see also* Dwight, Allan
Cole, Lois Dwight *see also* Eliot, Anne
Cole, Richard *DrAP&F 85*
Cole, Sheila R 1939- *ConAu 4NR, –53, SmATA 24[port], WrDr 76, –80, –82, –84, –86*
Cole, William *DrAP&F 85*
Cole, William 1919- *AuBYP, BioIn 8, –11, BkP, ChhPo, –S1, –S2, –S3, ConAu 7NR, –9R, FourBJA, IntWWP 77, SmATA 9, WrDr 76, –80, –82, –84, –86*
Coleman, Eleanor 1901- *WhoAmW 61, –64*
Coleman, John Royston 1921- *AmEA 74, AmM&WS 73S, –78S, AuNews 1, BioIn 9, –10, –13, CanWW 70, –79, –80, –81, ConAu 1R, –1NR, CurBio 74, LEduc 74, WhoAm 74, –76, –78, –80, –82, –84, –86, WhoE 74*
Coleman, Ken *BioIn 13*
Coleman, Lonnie 1920-1982 *AmAu&B, AmNov, BiE&WWA, BioIn 2, –4, –5, –13, ConAu 107, –77, CurBio 58, –82N, NewYTBS 82, NotNAT*
Coleman, Ronny Jack 1940- *WhoGov 77*
Colen, B D 1946- *ConAu 65*
Coleridge, Samuel Taylor 1771?-1834 *Alli, AtlBL, BbD, BiD&SB, BiDLA, BioIn 1, –2, –3, –4, –5, –6, –7, –8, –9, –10, –11, –12, BritAu 19, BritWr 4, CasWL, CelCen, Chambr 3, ChhPo, –S1, –S2, –S3, CnE&AP, CrtT 2, –4, CyWA, DcBiPP, DcEnA, DcEnL, DcEuL, DcLEL, Dis&D, EncO&P 78, EncWT, EvLB, LinLib L, –S, LongCEL, LuthC 75, McGEWB, MouLC 3, NewC, NotNAT B, OxEng, OxMus, OxThe, PenC ENG, RAdv 1, RComWL, REn, WebE&AL, WhDW, WorAl*
Coleridge, Samuel Taylor 1772-1834 *BiDPsy, BioIn 13, DcNaB, –C, EncO&P 2, NinCLC 9[port], OxEng 85, OxThe 83*
Coles, Robert 1929- *AmAu&B, AmM&WS 79P, –82P, –86P, Au&Wr 71, AuBYP SUP, BiDrAPA 77, BioIn 8, –9, –10, –11, –13, BlueB 76, CelR, ConAu 3NR, –45, CurBio 69, IntAu&W 76, NewYTBS 78, SmATA 23[port], WhoAm 74, –76, –82, –84, –86, WhoE 83, WorAu 1970, WrDr 80, –82, –84, –86*
Coles, Robert Traynham 1929- *WhoAm 84, –86, WhoBlA 85*
Colford, William E 1908-1971 *BioIn 9, –11, ConAu 5R, –33R, NatCAB 56, NewYTBE 71, WhAm 5*
Collett, Rosemary K 1931- *ConAu 69*
Collier, Christopher 1930- *AuBYP SUP, BioIn 11, –12, ConAu 13NR, –33R, ConLC 30[port], DrAS 74H, –78H, –82H, FifBJA[port], SmATA 16, WhoE 75*
Collier, James L 1928- *ConLC 30[port]*
Collier, James Lincoln 1928- *AuBYP SUP, BioIn 7, –11, ChlLR 3, ConAu 4NR, –9R, FifBJA[port], SmATA 8*
Collier, Jane *ConAu X, WrDr 86*
Collier, Jane *see also* Collier, Zena
Collier, John 1901-1980 *AnObit 1980, BioIn 2, –4, –11, –12, ConAu 10NR, –65, –97, ConNov 72, –76, DcLEL, EncMys, FilmgC, HalFC 84, IntAu&W 76, –77, LongCTC, NewC, NewYTBS 80, Novels, OxEng 85, PenC AM, REn, REnAL, ScF&FL 1, SupFW, TwCA, –SUP, TwCCr&M 80, –85, WhoHr&F, WrDr 76, –80*
Collier, Peter 1929?- *ConAu 65, WrDr 82, –84*
Collier, Peter 1939- *WrDr 86*

Collier, Richard 1924- *Au&Wr 71, BioIn 5, ConAu 1R, –5NR, IntAu&W 76, –77, –82, WhoWor 76, –78, WrDr 76, –80, –82, –84, –86*
Collier, Zena *ConAu X, DrAP&F 85*
Collier, Zena 1926- *BioIn 13, ConAu 3NR, –X, IntAu&W 77X, –82X, SmATA 23[port], WhoAm 80, WhoAmW 81, WrDr 76, –80, –82, –84, –86*
Collins, David R 1940- *AuBYP SUP, BioIn 10, ConAu 11NR, –29R, IntAu&W 76A, SmATA 7, WhoMW 74, –76, –78, –80, –82, WrDr 76, –80, –82, –84, –86*
Collins, David Raymond 1940- *WhoMW 84, –86*
Collins, Gary Ross 1934- *AmM&WS 73S, –78S, ConAu 7NR, –57, WhoMW 74, –76, –78*
Collins, Henry Hill 1907-1961 *AuBYP, BioIn 5, –8*
Collins, Jean E 1948- *ConAu 110*
Collins, Judy 1939- *Baker 84, BiDAmM, BioIn 7, –8, –10, –11, –12, CelR, ConAu 103, CurBio 69, EncFCWM 69, –83[port], EncPR&S 77, GoodHs, NewYTBS 76, RkOn 78, –84, RolSEnR 83, WhoAm 74, –76, –78, –80, –82, WhoAmW 74, –66, –68, –70, –72, –75, –77, –79, –81, –83, WhoRock 81[port], WhoRocM 82, WhoWor 74, WorAl*
Collins, Larry *ConAu X*
Collins, Larry 1929- *AmAu&B, BioIn 9, –12, CelR, ConAu 65, EncFCWM 69, NewYTBS 80[port], WhoAm 74, –76, –78, –80, –82, –84, –86, WhoWor 74, –76, –78*
Collins, Max Allan 1948- *TwCCr&M 85, WrDr 86*
Collins, Max, Jr. 1948- *ConAu 103*
Collins, Meghan 1926- *ConAu 101*
Collins, Michael *IntAu&W 86X, SmATA X, WrDr 86*
Collins, Michael 1924- *ConAu X, EncMys, ScF&FL 1, –2, TwCCr&M 80, –85, WrDr 82*
Collins, Michael 1930- *AmM&WS 73P, –79P, ASpks, BioIn 7, –8, –9, –10, –11, –12, BlueB 76, CelR, ConAu 5NR, –53, CurBio 75, EncSF, IntWW 74, –75, –76, –77, –78, –79, –80, –81, –82, –83, LinLib S, UFOEn, WebAMB, Who 74, –82, –83, –85, WhoAm 74, –76, –78, –80, –82, –86, WhoGov 77, –72, –75, WhoS&SW 73, –75, –76, WhoWor 74, –76, –78, –80, –82, –84, –87, WorAl*
Collins, Michael *see also* Lynds, Dennis
Collins, Wilkie 1824-1889 *AtlBL, BioIn 1, –2, –3, –4, –5, –7, –8, –9, –10, –11, BritAu 19, CyWA, DcLB 18[port], EncMys, HalFC 84, HsB&A, LongCEL, MnBBF, NewC, NinCLC 1[port], NotNAT B, Novels[port], OxEng 85, OxThe 83, PenC ENG, PlP&P, RAdv 1, REn, ScF&FL 1, SupFW, TwCCr&M 80A, –85A, WebE&AL, WhDW, WhoHr&F, WorAl*
Collinson, Roger 1936- *WrDr 86*
Colman, Hila *AuBYP, BioIn 8, –9, –10, ConAu 7NR, –13R, ForWC 70, MorBMP, SmATA 1, ThrBJA*
Colman, Hila *see also* Crayder, Teresa
Colorado, Antonio J 1903- *BioIn 13, ConAu X, PueRA, SmATA 23[port]*
Colorado Capella, Antonio Julio 1903- *ConAu 17R*
Colt, Martin *AuBYP, ConAu X, SmATA X*
Colt, Martin *see also* Epstein, Beryl Williams
Colt, Martin *see also* Epstein, Samuel
Colton, Helen 1918- *ConAu 57, WhoAmW 74, –75*

Colton, Joel 1918- *ConAu 1R, –2NR, DrAS 74H, –78H, –82H, IntAu&W 77, –82, –86, WhoAm 74, –76, –78, –80, –82, –84, –86, WhoWorJ 72, –78, WrDr 76, –80, –82, –84, –86*
Colum, Padraic 1881-1972 *AmAu&B, AmSCAP 66, AnCL, AuBYP, BiDIrW, BioIn 1, –2, –3, –4, –5, –7, –8, –9, –10, –12, –13, BkC 3, CarSB, CasWL, CathA 1930, ChhPo, –S1, –S2, –S3, CnMD, ConAu 33R, –73, ConLC 28[port], ConPo 70, DcIrB, DcIrL, DcIrW 1, –2, DcLB 19[port], DcLEL, EncWL, EvLB, FamSYP, JBA 34, –51, LinLib L, –S, LongCTC, McGEWB, McGEWD, –84[port], ModBrL, –S1, ModWD, NewC, NewYTBE 71, –72, NotNAT A, ObitT 1971, OxChL, OxEng 85, OxThe, –83, PenC ENG, PlP&P, RAdv 1, REn, REnWD, SmATA 15, Str&VC, TwCA, –SUP, TwCCW 78, –83, TwCWr, WebE&AL, WhDW, WhAm 5, –7*
Colver, Alice Ross 1892- *AmAu&B, AmNov, AuBYP, BioIn 2, –7, ConAu 69, InWom, WhNAA, WhoAmW 58, –64, –66, –68, –70*
Colwell, Eileen 1904- *BioIn 6, –8, –9, ChhPo S1, ConAu 12NR, –29R, CurBio 63, InWom, SmATA 2, WhoChL*
Combs, Joseph Franklin 1892- *IntAu&W 76, WhoS&SW 73, –75, –76, –78, –80, –82*
Comfort, Alex 1920- *BlueB 76, ConAu 1R, –1NR, ConLC 7, ConNov 82, –86, ConPo 80, –85, CurBio 74, IntWWP 77, –82, WorAl, WrDr 80, –82, –84, –86*
Commager, Henry Steele 1902- *AmAu&B, AuBYP, BiDAmEd, BioIn 1, –2, –4, –7, –10, –13, BioNews 74, BlueB 76, ChhPo S1, ConAu 21R, CurBio 46, DcLB 17[port], DcLEL, DrAS 74H, –78H, –82H, IntAu&W 76, –77, IntWW 74, –75, –76, –77, –78, –79, –80, –81, –82, –83, LinLib L, –S, OxAmH, OxAmL, –83, PenC AM, REn, REnAL, SmATA 23[port], TwCA SUP, WebAB, –79, WhE&EA, Who 74, –82, –83, –85, WhoAm 74, –76, –78, –80, –82, –86, WhoE 74, WhoWor 74, WorAl, WrDr 76, –80, –82, –84, –86*
Commager, Henry Steele 1902-1984 *WhAm 8*
Commoner, Barry 1917- *AmAu&B, AmM&WS 73P, –76P, –79P, –82P, –86P, BioIn 7, –8, –9, –10, –11, –12, BlueB 76, CelR, ConAu 65, ConIsC 1[port], CurBio 70, IntWW 74, –75, –76, –77, –78, –79, –80, –81, –82, –83, NewYTBS 76, WhDW, WhoAm 74, –76, –78, –80, –82, –84, –86, WhoWor 74, –82, –84, WorAl, WrDr 82, –84, –86*
Comparetti, Alice Pattee 1907- *ConAu 37R, DrAS 74E, –78E, WhoAmW 58, –61, –64, –66*
Compton, D G 1930- *Au&Wr 71, ConAu 17NR, –25R, ConSFA, EncSF, Novels, ScF&FL 1, –2, ScFSB, TwCSFW 86, WhoSciF, WrDr 84, –86*
Comstock, Anna Botsford 1854-1930 *AmBi, AmWomWr, ArtsAmW 3, BiDAmEd, BiDAmS, BioIn 1, –2, –3, –6, –9, –11, InSci, InWom, LibW, LinLib S, NatCAB 13, –22, NotAW, TwCBDA, WhAm 1, WhNAA, WomWWA 14*
Conan Doyle, Arthur *OxEng 85*
Conan Doyle, Arthur 1859-1930 *CorpD, EncMys, SmATA X*
Conan Doyle, Arthur *see also* Doyle, Sir Arthur Conan
Conant, James Bryant 1893-1978 *AmAu&B, AmM&WS 73P, –76P, –79P, BiDAmEd, BiESc, BioIn 1, –2,*

-3, -4, -5, -6, -7, -8, -9, -11, -12, -13, BlueB 76, ConAu 13R, -77, CurBio 41, -51, -78, -78N, DcAmDH, EncAB 2, EncAB-H, InSci, IntAu&W 77, IntWW 74, -75, -76, -77, -78N, LinLib L, -S, McGEWB, NewYTBS 78, ObitOF 79, OxAmH, OxAmL, -83, PolProf E, PolProf T, REnAL, WebAB, -79, WhAm 7, Who 74, WhoAm 74, -76, -78, WhoWor 74, WorAl

Conard, Howard Louis 1853-1925 OhA&B

Condon, Richard 1915- AmAu&B, Au&Wr 71, BioIn 2, -9, -10, -11, -12, -13, ConAu 1R, -2NR, ConAu 1AS[port], ConLC 4, -6, -8, -10, ConNov 72, -76, -82, -86, EncSF, IntAu&W 76, -77, ModAL, -S1, NewYTBS 79, Novels, PenC AM, ScF&FL 1, -2, ScFSB, TwCCr&M 80, -85, WhoAm 74, -76, -78, -80, -82, -84, -86, WhoSpyF, WhoWor 74, -76, -78, WorAl, WorAu, WrDr 76, -80, -82, -84, -86

Condry, William 1918- ConAu 103, IntAu&W 77, -82, WrDr 76, -80, -82, -84, -86

Cone, Molly 1918- AuBYP, BioIn 7, -9, -13, ConAu 1R, -1NR, ForWC 70, IntAu&W 76, -77, SmATA 1, -28[port], ThrBJA, WhoAmW 64, WrDr 76, -80, -82, -84, -86

Conford, Ellen 1942- AuBYP SUP, BioIn 10, ChlLR 10[port], ConAu 13NR, -33R, FifBJA[port], SmATA 6, TwCChW 83, WrDr 76, -80, -82, -84, -86

Conigliaro, Tony 1945- BioIn 13, CurBio 71, NewYTBE 71, NewYTBS 83[port], WhoProB 73

Conkin, Paul Keith 1929- WhoAm 84, -86

Conklin, Barbara P 1927- ConAu 109

Conklin, Gladys Plemon 1903- AuBYP, BiDrLUS 70, BioIn 8, -9, ConAu 1R, -4NR, ForWC 70, FourBJA, SmATA 2, WhoAmW 64, -66, -75, -77, WhoLibS 55, -66

Conklin, Groff 1904-1968 AmAu&B, BioIn 8, ConAu 1R, -3NR, EncSF, ScF&FL 1, -2, WhoSciF

Conly, Robert L BioIn 13

Conly, Robert L 1918-1973 AuBYP SUP, BioIn 9, ConAu 41R, -73, ScF&FL 1, SmATA 23[port]

Conly, Robert L see also O'Brien, Robert C

Conn, Frances G 1925- AuBYP SUP, ConAu 33R

Conn, Martha Orr 1935- ConAu 93

Connell, Evan S DrAP&F 85

Connell, Evan S 1924- ConAu 2AS[port]

Connell, Evan S, Jr. 1924- AmAu&B, Au&Wr 71, BioIn 12, CmCal, ConAu 1R, -2NR, ConLC 4, -6, ConNov 72, -76, -82, -86, DcLB 2, -Y81A[port], DcLEL 1940, IntAu&W 76, -77, LinLib L, ModAL S1, OxAmL, -83, PenC AM, RAdv 1, REnAL, WhoAm 74, -76, -78, -80, -82, WhoTwCL, WhoWor 74, WorAu, WrDr 76, -80, -82, -84, -86

Connell, Evan Shelby 1924- BioIn 13

Connell, Evan Shelby, Jr. 1924- WhoAm 84, -86

Connell, Richard 1893-1949 Alli, AmAu&B, BioIn 2, -4, DcNAA, EncMys, HalFC 84, LinLib L, NatCAB 36, ObitOF 79, REnAL, TwCA, -SUP, WhAm 2, WhE&EA, WhNAA

Connelly, John Peter 1926- WhoAm 84, WhoE 74, WhoFrS 84, WhoMW 74, -76, -78, -80, -82, -84

Connelly, Marcus Cook 1890- AmAu&B, BiE&WWA, Chambr 3, CnDAL, CnMD, CnThe, ConAmA, ConAmL, ConDr 73, CurBio 69, DcLEL, IntAu&W 76, IntWW 74,

LongCTC, McGEWD, ModAL, ModWD, OxAmL, PenC AM, REn, REnAL, REnWD, TwCA, -SUP, Who 74, WhoAm 74, WhoThe 72, WhoWor 74, WorAl

Conner, Dennis NewYTBS 86[port]

Conner, Patrick 1947- ConAu 106, WrDr 86

Conner, Patrick Roy Mountifort 1947- IntAu&W 86, WhoWor 87

Conners, Bernard F 1926- BioIn 9, ConAu 41R, IntAu&W 76, WhoE 75, -77

Connolly, Peter 1935- SmATA 47[port], WrDr 86

Connolly, Ray WrDr 86

Connolly, Ray 1940- ConAu 101, IntAu&W 77, -82, WrDr 76, -80, -82, -84

Connor, Ralph BioIn 13, DcNaB 1931, OxAmL 83, OxCanL

Connor, Ralph 1860-1937 BioIn 1, -2, -11, CanWr, CasWL, Chambr 3, ChhPo, ConAu X, CreCan 1, DcBiA, DcLEL, DcNAA, EvLB, LinLib LP, -S, LongCTC, MacDCB 78, NewC, OxAmL, OxCan, OxChL, REnAL, TwCA, -SUP, TwCCW 78, TwCWr, WhLit, WhNAA

Connor, Ralph see also Gordon, Charles William

Conot, Robert E 1929- AmAu&B, ConAu 2NR, -45, WrDr 76, -80, -82, -84

Conquest, Robert 1917- BioIn 8, -10, BlueB 76, ConAu 9NR, -13R, ConNov 72, ConPo 70, -75, -80, -85, ConSFA, DcLB 27[port], EncSF, IntAu&W 76, -77, -82, IntWWP 77, -82, LinLib 1, LongCTC, OxEng 85, RAdv 1, ScF&FL 1, -2, ScFSB, TwCWr, Who 74, -82, -83, -85, WhoSciF, WorAu, WrDr 76, -80, -82, -84, -86

Conrad, Joseph 1857-1924 AtlBL, BbD, BiD&SB, BioIn 1, -2, -3, -4, -5, -6, -7, -8, -9, -10, -11, -12, -13, BritWr 5, CasWL, Chambr 3, CnMD, CnMWL, ConAu 104, CyWA, DcEnA AP, DcEuL, DcLB 10[port], -34[port], DcLEL, DcNaB 1922, Dis&D, EncMys, EncSF, EncWL, -2[port], EvLB, FilmgC, HalFC 84, JBA 34, LinLib L, -S, LongCEL, LongCTC, MakMC, McGEWB, ModBrL, -S2, -S1, ModWD, NewC, Novels[port], OxAusL, OxEng, -85, OxShips, PenC ENG, RAdv 1, RComWL, REn, ScF&FL 1, SmATA 27[port], TwCA, -SUP, TwCLC 1, -6[port], -13[port], TwCWr, WebE&AL, WhDW, WhoSpyF, WhoTwCL, WorAl

Conrad, Sybil 1921- AuBYP, BioIn 8, ConAu 21R

Conroy, Frank 1936- AmAu&B, BioIn 8, -9, -11, ConAu 77, WhoAm 74

Conroy, Pat 1945?- AuNews 1, BioIn 9, -10, -12, BioNews 74, ConAu 85, ConLC 30[port], DcLB 6[port]

Considine, Bob 1906-1975 AmAu&B, AuNews 2, BioIn 1, -5, -7, -10, -11, CathA 1930, CelR, ConAu 61, -93, -X, CurBio 67, -75, -75N, NewYTBS 75, ObitOF 79, REnAL, WhAm 6, -7, WhoAm 74, -76, WhoWor 74, -76, WorAl

Constable, Trevor James 1925- ConAu 89, UFOEn[port]

Constant, Alberta Wilson 1908-1981 AuBYP SUP, BioIn 3, ConAu 1R, -4NR, -109, SmATA 22[port], -28N

Conze, Edward 1904- Au&Wr 71, BioIn 12, ConAu 13R, IntAu&W 76

Cook, Ann Turner GoodHs

Cook, Bob 1957?-1981 BioIn 12

Cook, Bruce 1932- ConAu 33R

Cook, Chris 1945- WrDr 86

Cook, David 1929- ConAu 107

Cook, Fred J 1911- EncAJ

Cook, Fred James 1911- AmAu&B, AuBYP, BioIn 4, -5, -7, -9, ConAu 3NR, -9R, DcAmAu, EncTwCJ, SmATA 2, WhoAm 74, -76, -78, -80, -82, -84, -86, WhoWor 74

Cook, Glen 1944- ScF&FL 1, -2, TwCSFW 86

Cook, James Gordon 1916- ConAu 9R

Cook, Lyn IntAu&W 86X, WrDr 86

Cook, Lyn 1918- WhoCanL 85

Cook, Marjorie 1920- ConAu 81

Cook, Paul H 1950- ConAu 106, IntWWP 77, -82

Cook, Robert William Arthur 1931- Au&Wr 71, ConAu 25R

Cook, Robert William Arthur see also Cook, Robin

Cook, Robin 1931- ConAu X, DcLEL 1940, ScF&FL 1, -2, WrDr 76, -80, -82, -84, -86

Cook, Robin 1940- BioIn 13, ConAu 111

Cook, Robin see also Cook, Robert William Arthur

Cook, Stephani 1944?- BioIn 12, ConAu 106

Cook, Terry 1942- ConAu 12NR, -73

Cooke, Alistair Who 85

Cooke, Alistair 1908- AmAu&B, AuNews 1, BioIn 2, -3, -4, -8, -9, -10, -11, -12, -13, BlueB 76, CelR, ConAu 9NR, -57, CurBio 52, -74, IntAu&W 77, IntMPA 77, -75, -76, -78, -79, -81, -82, -84, -86, IntWW 74, -75, -76, -77, -78, -79, -80, -81, -82, -83, LongCTC, NewYTET, OxAmL, -83, REnAL, TwCA SUP, Who 74, -82, -83, WorAl, WrDr 76, -80, -82, -84, -86

Cooke, Barbara 1913- AuBYP, BioIn 7, ConAu 57

Cooke, Barbara see also Alexander, Anna Barbara Cooke

Cooke, David Coxe 1917- AuBYP, BioIn 8, -9, ConAu 1R, -2NR, SmATA 2

Cooke, Donald Edwin 1916- ScF&FL 1

Cooke, Donald Ewin 1916- AuBYP, BioIn 7, -9, ConAu 1R, -4NR, SmATA 2, WhoAmA 73, -76, -78, -80, WhoE 75, -77

Cooke, Donald Ewin 1916-1985 ConAu 117, SmATA 45N

Cookson, Catherine 1906- Au&Wr 71, BioIn 8, -9, -10, -11, ConAu 9NR, -13R, IntAu&W 76, Novels, SmATA 9, Who 83, -85, WrDr 76, -80, -82, -84, -86

Cooley, Denton Arthur 1920- AmM&WS 86P, WhoAm 86

Coolidge, Olivia 1908- AuBYP, BioIn 6, -7, -9, -13, BkCL, ConAu 2NR, -5R, MorJA, ScF&FL 1, SmATA 1, -26[port], TwCCW 78, WhoAmW 61, -64, WrDr 76, -80, -82, -84, -86

Coombs, Charles I 1914- ConAu 19NR, SmATA 43[port]

Coombs, Charles Ira 1914- AuBYP, BioIn 7, -9, ConAu 4NR, -5R, ScF&FL 1, -2, SmATA 3

Coon, Carleton Stevens 1904-1981 AmAu&B, AmM&WS 73S, -76P, AnObit 1981[port], Au&Wr 71, BioIn 4, -5, -10, -12, -13, BlueB 76, ConAu 2NR, -5R, -104, CurBio 55, -81N, FifIDA, InSci, IntAu&W 76, -77, -82, IntWW 74, -75, -76, -77, -78, -79, -80, -81, -82N, McGMS 80[port], NewYTBS 81[port], WhAm 7, WhoAm 74, -76, -78, -80, WhoWor 74, -76, -78, WorAu

Cooney, Caroline B 1947- ConAu 97, SmATA 48[port]

Cooney, Timothy J 1929?- BioIn 12, ConAu 107, WhoE 74

Coontz, Otto 1946- ConAu 105, SmATA 33[port]

Cooper, Alice WhoRock 81[port]

Cooper, Alice 1945- RolSEnR 83[port]

Cooper, Alice 1948- Baker 84, BioIn 9, -10, -11, -12, BioNews 74, CelR, ConAu 106, EncPR&S 74, -77, IlEncRk, RkOn 78, -84, RkOneH, RolSEnR 83, WhoAm 74, -76, -78, -80, -82, WhoRocM 82, WorAl

Cooper, Alice see also Furnier, Vincent

Cooper, Darien B 1937- ConAu 1NR, -16NR, -49

Cooper, Elizabeth Keyser SmATA 47

Cooper, Elizabeth Keyser 1910?- ConAu 1R, -1NR, FourBJA, WhoAmW 61

Cooper, Gale S 1946- BiDrAPA 77

Cooper, Gordon 1932- AuBYP SUP, BioIn 13, ConAu 61, IntAu&W 77, SmATA 23[port], TwCCW 78, -83, WrDr 76, -80, -82, -84

Cooper, Harold Eugene 1928- AmM&WS 73P, -76P, -79P, ConAu 45

Cooper, Harold R 1910?-1978 BioIn 11, ConAu 77

Cooper, Henry S F, Jr. 1933- ConAu 13NR, WhoE 75, -77

Cooper, Henry Spotswood Fenimore, Jr. 1933- ConAu 69, WhoE 75, -77

Cooper, Irving S AmM&WS 86P

Cooper, Irving S 1922- WhoAm 84

Cooper, Irving S 1922-1985 CurBio 86N, NewYTBS 85[port]

Cooper, Irving Spencer 1922- AmM&WS 73P, -76P, -79P, -82P, BioIn 7, -10, -11, -12, ConAu 69, CurBio 74, WhoAm 74, -76, -78, -80, -82, WhoE 74, WhoWor 76, -78

Cooper, James Fenimore 1789-1851 Alli, AmAu, AmAu&B, AmBi, AmWr, ApCAB, AtlBL, AuBYP, BbD, BiD&SB, BioIn 1, -2, -3, -4, -5, -6, -7, -8, -9, -10, -11, -12, -13, CasWL, CelCen, Chambr 3, CnDAL, CrtT 3, -4, CyAL 1, CyWA, DcAmAu, DcAmB, DcBiA, DcBiPP, DcEnA, DcEnL, DcLB 3, DcLEL, DcNAA, Drake, EncAAH, EncAB-H, EncFWF[port], EvLB, FilmgC, HalFC 84, HarEnUS[port], HsB&A, LinLib L, -S, McGEWB, MemAm, MnBBF, MouLC 3, NatCAB 1, NinCLC 1[port], Novels[port], OxAmH, OxAmL, -83, OxChL, OxEng, -85, OxShips, PenC AM, RAdv 1, RComWL, REn, REnAL, REnAW, SmATA 19, TwCBDA, WebAB, -79, WebE&AL, WhDW, WhAm HS, WhoBW&I A, WhoChL, WhoSpyF, WorAl

Cooper, Jamie Lee ConAu 9R, IndAu 1917

Cooper, Lettice 1897- Au&Wr 71, ConAu 5NR, -9R, ConNov 72, -76, -82, -86, IntAu&W 76, -77, -82, -86, SmATA 35, TwCCW 78, -83, WhE&EA, WhLit, WrDr 76, -80, -82, -84, -86

Cooper, Louise ScFSB

Cooper, Louise Field 1905- AmAu&B, AmNov, BioIn 2, -4, ConAu 5NR, -4NR, -107, CurBio 50, InWom, REnAL, ScF&FL 1, -2, TwCA SUP, WhoAm 74, -76, -78, -80, -82, -84, -86, WhoAmW 74, -58, -66, -68, -70, -72, WhoHr&F

Cooper, Lynna 1911- ConAu X

Cooper, Margaret 1893- ChhPo S2, WhE&EA

Cooper, Paulette 1944?- ConAu 37R, IntAu&W 76, -77, WhoAmW 75, -83, WhoE 77, -79, -81, -83, WrDr 76, -80, -82, -84, -86

Cooper, Susan 1935- Au&Wr 71, AuBYP SUP, BioIn 9, -11, ChlLR 4[port], ConAu 15NR, -29R, ConTFT 2[port], EncSF, FourBJA, IntAu&W 82, OxChL, ScF&FL 1, -2, ScFSB, SmATA 4, TwCCW 78, -83, WhoAm 76, -78, -80, -82, WrDr 76, -80, -82, -84, -86

Coover, Robert DrAP&F 85

Coover, Robert 1932- AmAu&B, BioIn 10, -13, ConAu 3NR, -45, ConLC 3, -7, -15, -32[port],

ConNov 72, –76, –82, –86, DcLB 2,
–Y81A[port], DcLEL 1940, EncSF,
IntAu&W 76, –77, –82, ModAL S2,
–S1, Novels, OxAmL 83, PenC AM,
PostFic, RAdv 1, ScFSB, WhoAm 74,
–76, –78, –80, –82, WhoE 74, –75,
WorAu 1970, WrDr 76, –80, –82,
–84, –86
Cope, Myron 1929- ConAu 57,
WhoE 77
Coppel, Alfred DrAP&F 85
Coppel, Alfred 1921- ConAu 10NR,
–17R, ConSFA, DcLB Y83B[port],
EncSF, ScF&FL 1, –2, TwCSFW 86,
WhoAm 82, –84, –86, WhoSciF,
WhoWest 74, –76, –78, WrDr 76,
–80, –82, –84, –86
Coppel, Alfred see also Gilman, Robert
Cham
Copper, Basil ScFSB
Copper, Basil 1924- Au&Wr 71,
IntAu&W 76, ScF&FL 1, –2,
TwCCr&M 80, –85, WhoHr&F,
WrDr 76, –80, –82, –84, –86
Copper, Marcia S 1934- ConAu 53
Corbett, James Edward 1875-1955
AuBYP, BioIn 1, –3, –4, –8, –12,
CurBio 46, –55
Corbett, Scott 1913- Au&Wr 71,
AuBYP, BioIn 8, –9, ChlLR 1,
ConAu 1R, –1NR, FourBJA,
IntAu&W 76, –77, –82, ScF&FL 1,
–2, SmATA 2, –42[port],
SmATA 2AS[port], TwCCW 78, –83,
WhoAm 80, –82, –84, WrDr 80, –82,
–84, –86
Corbett, W J 1938- SmATA 44
Corbin, Richard 1911- ConAu 3NR,
–5R, DrAS 74E, –78E, –82E,
WhoE 75, –77
Corcoran, Barbara DrAP&F 85
Corcoran, Barbara 1911- AuBYP SUP,
BioIn 9, ConAu 11NR, –21R, –13R,
ConAu 2AS[port], ConLC 17,
DcLB 52[port], FifBJA[port],
IntAu&W 82, –86, SmATA 3,
WhoAm 78, –80, –82, WrDr 76, –80,
–82, –84, –86
Corcoran, Barbara see also Dixon,
Paige
Corcoran, Barbara see also Hamilton,
Gail
Cordwell, Miriam 1908- ConAu 89,
WhoAmW 74, –58, –61, –64, –66,
–68, –70, –72, –75, –77, –79,
WhoE 74, –79, –81
Cordwell, Miriam 1908-1986
ConAu 120
Corle, Edwin 1906-1956 AmAu&B,
BioIn 4, –6, –7, CmCal,
DcLB Y85B[port], EncFWF,
NatCAB 46, OxAmL, –83, REnAL,
TwCA SUP, WhAm 3, WhNAA
Corlett, William 1938- ConAu 103,
ConTFT 2, IntAu&W 86, SmATA 39,
–46[port], TwCCW 78, –83,
WhoS&SW 78, –78–80,
WhoTech 82, WrDr 80, –82, –84, –86
Corley, Edwin 1931-1981 BioIn 8, –12,
ConAu 105, –12NR, –25R, EncSF,
ScF&FL 1, –2, WhoAm 74
Corliss, William R 1926- ConAu 1NR,
–16NR, –45
Cormack, Margaret L 1912-
AmM&WS 73S, –78S, ConAu 1R
Cormack, Maribelle 1902- AuBYP,
BioIn 2, –7, JBA 51, ScF&FL 1,
WhoAmW 58, –61, –64, –66, –68,
–72
Cormier, Robert 1925- BioIn 11, –12,
ChlLR 12[port], ConAu 1R, –5NR,
ConLC 12, –30[port], DcLB 52[port],
FifBJA[port], OxChL, SmATA 10,
–45[port], TwCChW 83, WhoAm 82,
WrDr 84, –86
Cormier, Robert Edmund 1925-
BioIn 13, WhoAm 84, –86
Corn, Ira George 1921-1982 BioIn 13
Corn, Ira George, Jr. 1921- WhAm 8
Corn, Ira George, Jr. 1921-1982
BioIn 12, ConAu 106, –85,
Dun&B 79, NewYTBE 70,

NewYTBS 82[port], St&PR 75,
WhoAm 74, –76, –78, –80, –82,
WhoF&I 74, –75, –77, –79, –81,
WhoS&SW 78, –82, WhoWor 78, –80
Cornelisen, Ann 1926- BioIn 9,
ConAu 17NR, –25R
Cornelius, Temple H 1891-1964
BioIn 7, ConAu P-1
Cornell, James 1938- BioIn 13,
ConAu 11NR, –69, SmATA 27[port]
Cornell, Jean Gay 1920- BioIn 13,
ConAu 1NR, –45, SmATA 23,
WhoAmW 77
Cornell, William Ainsworth 1923-
WhoAm 76, –78
Corner, George Washington 1889-1981
AmM&WS 73P, –76P, –79P,
AnObit 1981[port], BioIn 3, –4, –12,
BlueB 76, ConAu 102, –104,
IntWW 74, –75, –76, –77, –78, –79,
–80, –81, –82N, McGMS 80[port],
NewYTBS 81[port], WhAm 8,
WhNAA, Who 74, –82N, WhoAm 74,
–76, –78, –80
Cornish, Samuel 1935- BlkAWP,
ChhPo S3, ConAu 41R, ConPo 70,
–75, –80, DcLEL 1940, IntWWP 77,
LivgBAA, SelBAAu, SmATA 23[port],
–X, WrDr 76, –80, –82, –84
Cornish, Samuel James 1935-
BioIn 13, InB&W 85
Cornwall, Ian Wolfran 1909-
Au&Wr 71, BioIn 5, ConAu 9R,
IntAu&W 76, –77, ScF&FL 1,
Who 74, –82, –83, –85
Cornwell, David John Moore WrDr 86
Cornwell, David John Moore 1931-
Au&Wr 71, BioIn 6, –7, –10, –11,
–12, –13, BlueB 76, ConAu 5R,
ConLC 9, –15, EncMys,
IntAu&W 76, –77, IntWW 74, –75,
–76, –77, –78, –79, –80, –81, –82,
–83, NewC, NewYTBS 74, Who 74,
–82, –83, –85, WhoAm 80, –82, –84,
WhoSpyF, WhoWor 74, –76, –78,
–82, –84, WorAu, WrDr 76, –80, –82,
–84
Cornwell, David John Moore see also
LeCarre, John
Correy, Lee WrDr 86
Correy, Lee 1928- BioIn 11,
ConAu 65, –X, EncSF, ScF&FL 1,
–2, ScFSB, SmATA X, TwCSFW 86,
WrDr 84
Correy, Lee see also Stine, George
Harry
Corrigan, Barbara 1922- BioIn 11,
ChhPo, ConAu 57, SmATA 8
Corrigan, Robert W 1927-
BiE&WWA, BlueB 76, ConAu 5R,
–6NR, DrAS 74E, –78E, –82E,
NotNAT, WhoAm 74, –76, –78, –80,
–82, WhoWor 74, WrDr 76, –80, –82,
–84, –86
Corrigan, Robert Willoughby 1927-
WhoAm 84
Corsaro, Maria C 1949- ConAu 107
Corsi, Lawrence ConAu X
Corwen, Leonard 1921- ConAu 15NR,
–93
Cosman, Madeleine Pelner 1937-
ConAu 105, DrAS 74E, –78E, –82E
Costain, Thomas B 1885-1965
ConLC 30[port], OxAmL 83,
OxCanL
Costain, Thomas Bertram 1885-1965
AmAu&B, AmNov, AuBYP, BioIn 2,
–3, –4, –7, –8, –12, CanWr,
ConAu 5R, –25R, CreCan 2,
CurBio 53, –65, DcAmB S7,
DcLB 9[port], DcLEL, –1940,
LinLib L, –S, LongCTC,
MacDCB 78, ObitOF 79, OxAmL,
OxCan, REn, REnAL, ScF&FL 1,
–2, TwCA SUP, TwCWr, WhAm 4,
WhJnl, WorAl
Costello, David 1904- AmM&WS 76P,
–79P, –82P, WhoPNW, WrDr 76
Costello, David F 1904-
AmM&WS 73P, BioIn 13,
ConAu 33R, SmATA 23[port],
WhoPNW, WrDr 80, –82, –84, –86
Costello, David Francis 1904-
AmM&WS 86P

Costello, John Edmond 1943-
ConAu 85, WhoE 81, –83, –85
Cott, Nancy Falik 1945- ConAu 81,
DrAS 78H, –82H, WhoAmW 79
Cotten, Sallie Southall 1846-1929
BiDSA, BioIn 3, ChhPo, –S1,
EncSoH, NotAW, WhAm 1,
WomWWA 14
Cotterell, Arthur George 1917-
WhoArt 80, –82, –84
Cottler, Joseph 1899- BioIn 13,
ConAu P-2, SmATA 22[port]
Cottrell, Leonard 1913-1974
Au&Wr 71, AuBYP, BioIn 8, –10,
–13, BlueB 76N, ConAu 4NR, –5R,
DcLEL 1940, FourBJA,
IntAu&W 76, –77, IntWW 74, –75,
SmATA 24[port], TwCWr, WhAm 6,
Who 74, WhoWor 74, WorAu,
WrDr 76
Couffer, Jack C 1924- Au&Wr 71,
ConAu 1R, –1NR, FilmgC
Cougar, John WhoRocM 82
Cougar, John 1951- RolSEnR 83
Cougar, John 1952?- BioIn 13
Coughlan, Robert 1914- AmAu&B,
ConAu 65, IndAu 1917, WhoAm 78,
–80, –82, –86, WrDr 76, –80, –82,
–84, –86
Coughlin, George G 1900- ConAu 107,
WhoE 74
Coulson, Juanita 1933- ConAu 9NR,
–25R, ConSFA, EncSF, IntAu&W 77,
–82, ScF&FL 1, –2, ScFSB,
TwCSFW 86, WhoHr&F, WhoSciF,
WrDr 76, –80, –82, –84, –86
Coulson, Juanita Ruth 1933-
WhoMW 84
Counsilman, James Edward 1920-
BioIn 10, –12, WhoAm 82, –84, –86
Couper, John Mill 1914- Au&Wr 71,
ConAu 45, ConPo 70, IntWWP 77
Courlander, Harold 1908- AnCL,
AuBYP, BioIn 6, –8, –10, –11, BkCL,
ConAu 3NR, –9R, –18NR,
IndAu 1917, IntAu&W 76, –77, –82,
–86, MichAu 80, MorJA, SmATA 6
Cournos, John 1881-1966 AmAu&B,
BioIn 4, –7, –11, ConAmL,
ConAu P-2, DcLB 54[port], DcLEL,
LongCTC, OxAmL, –83, REnAL,
ScF&FL 1, TwCA, –SUP, WhE&EA,
WhLit, WhoLA
Courter, Gay 1944- ConAu 7NR, –57,
WrDr 84, –86
Courter, Gay Eleanor 1944-
WhoAmW 87
Courthion, Pierre-Barthelemy 1902-
ConAu 81, IntAu&W 77, –82, –86,
IntWW 74, –75, –76, –77, –78, –79,
–80, –81, –82, –83, WhoFr 79,
WhoWor 74, –76, –78
Cousins, Norman 1912?- AmAu&B,
BioIn 3, –4, –8, –9, –10, –11, –12,
BlueB 76, CelR, ChhPo, ConAu 17R,
CurBio 43, –77, DcLEL 1940, EncAJ,
IntAu&W 76, –77, IntWW 74, –75,
–76, –77, –78, –79, –80, –81, –82,
–83, LinLib L, –S, NewYTBE 71,
NewYTBS 79, OxAmL, –83,
PolProf E, PolProf K, REn, REnAL,
TwCA SUP, WebAB, –79, Who 74,
–82, –83, WhoAm 74, –76, –78, –80,
–82, WhoE 74, –79, WhoF&I 74,
WhoWor 74, WorAl, WrDr 76, –80,
–82, –84
Cousins, Norman 1915- BioIn 13,
ConAu 13NR, EncTwCJ, Who 85,
WhoAm 84, –86, WrDr 86
Cousteau, Jacques-Yves 1910- AnCL,
AsBiEn, BiESc, BioIn 1, –2, –3, –4,
–5, –6, –7, –8, –9, –10, –11, –12, –13,
BioNews 74, CelR, ConAu 15NR,
–65, ConLC 30[port], CurBio 76,
DcFM, FilmgC, HalFC 84, InSci,
IntAu&W 77, –82, IntMPA 84, –86,
IntWW 74, –75, –76, –77, –78, –79,
–80, –81, –82, –83, LinLib L,
NewYTBE 72, OxFilm, OxShips,
REn, SmATA 38[port], WhDW,
Who 74, –82, –83, –85, WhoAm 80,
–82, –84, –86, WhoFr 79,
WhoOcn 78, WhoUN 75,

WhoWor 74, –76, –78, –80, –82, –84,
–87, WorAl, WorEFlm
Coville, Bruce 1950- ConAu 97,
SmATA 32[port]
Cowden, Jeanne 1918- ConAu 85
Cowell, Cyril 1888- ChhPo S2,
ConAu P-2
Cowell, Frank Richard 1897-
Au&Wr 71, AuBYP, BioIn 8,
ConAu 8NR, IntAu&W 76, –77,
WhE&EA, Who 74, WrDr 76, –80
Cowell, Frank Richard see also Cowell,
Richard
Cowell, Richard 1897- ConAu 53
Cowell, Richard see also Cowell, Frank
Richard
Cowen, Eve ConAu X, SmATA X
Cowie, Leonard W 1919- ConAu 9NR
Cowie, Leonard Wallace 1919-
Au&Wr 71, BioIn 9, ConAu 13R,
IntAu&W 76, –77, –82, SmATA 4,
WrDr 76, –80, –82, –84, –86
Cowles, Virginia 1903-1983
Au&Wr 71, BioIn 13, ConAu 110,
–12NR, –65, CurBio 42, –83N,
InWom, IntAu&W 76, –77, –82,
NewYTBS 83, Who 74, –82, –83
Cowley, Joy 1936- AuBYP SUP,
BioIn 9, ConAu 11NR, –25R,
SmATA 4
Cowley, Malcolm 1898- AmAu&B,
AmWr S2, Au&Wr 71, BioIn 1, –2,
–4, –6, –7, –10, –11, –12, –13,
BlueB 76, CelR, ChhPo, –S3,
CnDAL, ConAmA, ConAu 3NR, –5R,
ConLCrt, –82, ConPo 70, –75, –80,
–85, CurBio 79, DcLB 4, –48[port],
–Y81A[port], DcLEL, EncWL, –2,
IntAu&W 76, –77, –82, –86,
IntWW 74, –75, –76, –77, –78, –79,
–80, –81, –82, –83, IntWWP 77, –82,
LinLib L, –S, ModAL, –S2, –S1,
NewYTBS 77, OxAmL, –83,
PenC AM, RAdv 1, REn, REnAL,
SixAP, TwCA, –SUP, WebAB, –79,
WhNAA, WhoAm 74, –76, –78, –80,
–82, –84, –86, WhoE 83, –85,
WhoWor 74, WrDr 76, –80, –82, –84,
–86
Cowling, Elizabeth 1910- ConAu 110,
DrAS 74H, –78H, –82H,
WhoAmW 70, –72
Cowper, Richard WrDr 86
Cowper, Richard 1926- Au&Wr 71,
ConAu X, ConSFA, EncSF,
IntAu&W 76, –76X, –77, –82, Novels,
ScF&FL 1, –2, ScFSB, TwCSFW 86,
WhoSciF, WrDr 76, –80, –82, –84
Cox, Barry 1931- ConAu 103
Cox, Charles Brian 1928- Au&Wr 71,
ConAu 25R, IntAu&W 76, –77, –82,
–86, Who 82, –83, –85, WrDr 76,
–80, –82, –84, –86
Cox, Donald William 1921- BioIn 13,
ConAu 1R, –4NR, SmATA 23[port]
Cox, William R SmATA 46[port]
Cox, William R 1901- EncFWF,
TwCCr&M 85, WrDr 86
Cox, William Robert 1901- AuBYP,
ConAu 6NR, –9R, SmATA 31,
WrDr 84
Coxe, Louis O 1918- OxAmL 83
Coxe, Louis Osborne 1918- AmAu&B,
BiE&WWA, BioIn 6, –10, –12,
ChhPo, –S1, –S3, ConAu 13R,
ConPo 70, –75, –80, DcLB 5[port],
DcLEL 1940, IntWWP 77, –82,
McGEWD, –84, NotNAT, OxAmL,
WhoAm 74, –76, –78, –80, –82, –84,
–86, WhoWor 74, WorAu, WrDr 76,
–80, –82, –84
Coy, Harold 1902- AuBYP, BioIn 7,
–9, ConAu 4NR, –5R, IntAu&W 76,
–77, SmATA 3, WrDr 76, –80, –82,
–84
Coyle, David Cushman 1887-1969
ConAu 1R, –103, –15NR, WhAm 5
Coyne, John R, Jr. 1935- ConAu 37R
Cozzens, James Gould 1903-1978
AmAu&B, AmNov, AmWr, BioIn 1,
–2, –4, –5, –7, –8, –9, –10, –11, –12,
–13, BlueB 76, CasWL, CnDAL,
ConAmA, ConAu 9R, –19NR, –81,

ConLC 1, –4, –11, ConNov 72, –76,
CurBio 49, –78, –78N, CyWA,
DcLB 9[port], –DS2[port],
–Y84A[port], DcLEL, EncWL, –2,
IntAu&W 76, –77, IntWW 74, –75,
–76, –77, –78, –79N, LinLib L, –S,
LongCTC, ModAL, –S2, NatCAB 61,
NewCon[port], NewYTBS 78, Novels,
ObitOF 79, OxAmL, –83, PenC AM,
RAdv 1, REn, REnAL, ScF&FL 1,
–2, TwCA, –SUP, TwCWr,
WebAB, –79, WebE&AL, WhAm 7,
WhE&EA, Who 74, WhoAm 74, –76,
–78, WhoWor 74, WorAl, WrDr 76

Crabb, Cecil VanMeter, Jr. 1924-
AmM&WS 73S, –78S, ConAu 13R,
WhoAm 74, –76

Cragg, Kenneth *Who 85*

Cragg, Kenneth 1913- *ConAu 7NR,*
–17R, IntAu&W 76, –77, Who 74,
–82, –83, WrDr 76, –80, –82, –84,
–86

Craig, Eleanor 1929- *ConAu 93*

Craig, John Eland 1912-1980?
ConAu X, IntAu&W 76X, SmATA 2,
WrDr 80

Craig, John Eland *see also* Chipperfield,
Joseph Eugene

Craig, John Ernest 1921- *BioIn 13*

Craig, John Ernest 1921-1982
BioIn 10, CaW, ConAu 101,
SmATA 23[port], TwCCW 78, –83,
WhoAm 74, WrDr 80, –82, –84

Craig, Margaret Maze 1911-1964
BioIn 6, –7, –11, ConAu 1R, MorJA,
SmATA 9, WhoAmW 61, –64, –66,
–66A, –68

Craig, Mary Francis 1923- *BioIn 9,*
–10, –12, ConAu 1R, –4NR,
IntAu&W 77, –82, –86, SmATA 6,
ThrBJA, WhoAmW 74, –70, –72,
–75, –77, –79, WrDr 76, –80, –82,
–84, –86

Craig, Mary Francis *see also* Shura,
Mary Francis

Craig, Mary Francis Shura 1923-
WhoAm 84, –86

Craig, Robert Wallace 1924- *BioIn 12,*
WhoWest 80, –82, –84

Craighead, Frank Cooper, Jr. 1916-
ConAu 97, NatLAC, WhoAm 84, –86,
WhoWest 74, –76, –78

Cramer, Kathryn 1943- *ConAu 25R*

Crandall, Richard E 1947-
WhoTech 84

Crane, Caroline 1930- *AuBYP SUP,*
BioIn 11, ConAu 3NR, –9R, –19NR,
ForWC 70, SmATA 11, WhoE 83,
–85, WrDr 76, –80, –82, –84, –86

Crane, Milton 1917- *DrAS 74E, –78E,*
–82E

Crane, Milton 1917-1985 *ConAu 117*

Crane, Stephen 1871-1900 *AmAu,*
AmAu&B, AmBi, AmWr,
ApCAB SUP, AtlBL, BbD, BiD&SB,
BioIn 1, –2, –3, –4, –5, –6, –7, –8, –9,
–10, –11, –12, –13, CasWL,
Chambr 3, ChhPo, –S3, CnDAL,
CnE&AP, ConAu 109, CrtT 3, –4,
CyWA, DcAmAu, DcAmB,
DcLB 12[port], –54[port], DcLEL,
DcNAA, EncAAH, EncAB-H,
EncAJ[port], EncFWF[port], EvLB,
HalFC 84, HarEnUS, LinLib L,
LongCTC, McGEWB, ModAL,
NatCAB 10, Novels, OxAmL, –83,
OxEng, –85, PenC AM, RAdv 1,
RComWL, REn, REnAL, TwCBDA,
TwCLC 11[port], –17[port],
WebAB, –79, WebE&AL, WhDW,
WhAm 1, WhFla, WorAl, YABC 2

Crane, William B 1904-1981
ConAu 107, DrRegL 75

Crane, William D 1892- *BioIn 9,*
ConAu 5R, SmATA 1

Crary, Margaret Coleman 1906-
AuBYP, BioIn 8, –11, ConAu 5R,
ForWC 70, SmATA 9

Craven, Margaret 1901-1980
AmWomWr, BioIn 10, –12,
ConAu 103, ConLC 17, IntAu&W 76,
–77, WhAm 7, WhoAm 76, –78, –80,
WrDr 76, –80, –82

Craven, Thomas 1889-1969 *AmAu&B,*
AuBYP, BioIn 8, –13, ConAu 97,
CurBio 44, –69, ObitOF 79, REnAL,
SmATA 22[port], TwCA, –SUP,
WhAm 5

Craven, Wayne 1930- *WhoAmA 84*

Crawford, Alan 1953- *ConAu 101*

Crawford, Char 1935- *ConAu 57*

Crawford, Char *see also* Johnson,
Charlene

Crawford, Charles P 1945- *BioIn 13,*
ConAu 45, SmATA 28

Crawford, Deborah 1922- *BioIn 10,*
ConAu 49, IntAu&W 77, SmATA 6

Crawford, F Marion 1854-1909
ConAu 107, Novels, ScF&FL 1,
SupFW, TwCLC 10[port], WhLit,
WhoHr&F

Crawford, Joanna 1941- *ConAu 9R,*
WomWMM

Crawford, Joanna 1942- *ConTFT 4*

Crawford, Richard 1935- *ConAu 9NR,*
–57, DrAS 78H, –82H, IntWWM 85,
WhoAm 78, –80, –82, –84, –86,
WhoAmM 83

Crawford, Thomas Edgar 1867-1941
BioIn 6

Crawshaw, Alwyn 1934- *WhoArt 80,*
–82, –84, WhoWor 80, –82, –84, –87

Crayder, Dorothy 1906- *AuBYP SUP,*
BioIn 10, ConAu 33R, ScF&FL 1,
SmATA 7

Crayder, Teresa *ConAu X, SmATA 1*

Crayder, Teresa *see also* Colman, Hila

Creamer, Robert W 1922- *BioIn 10,*
ConAu 21R, WhoE 83, –85,
WrDr 76, –80, –82, –84, –86

Creasey, John 1908-1973 *Au&Wr 71,*
BioIn 4, –5, –6, –7, –8, –9, –10,
ConAu 5R, –8NR, –41R, ConLC 11,
CorpD, CurBio 63, –73, –73N,
EncMys, EncSF, HalFC 84,
LongCTC, MnBBF, NewYTBE 73,
Novels[port], ObitT 1971, REn,
ScF&FL 1, –1A, –2, TwCCr&M 80,
–85, TwCWr, WhAm 5, WhE&EA,
WhoBW&I A, WhoSpyF, WorAl,
WorAu

Credle, Ellis 1902- *AuBYP, BioIn 1,*
–2, –3, –4, –5, –7, –9, ConAu 9NR,
–13R, IlsCB 1744, –1946, InWom,
JBA 51, LinLib L, SmATA 1,
Str&VC

Creekmore, Hubert 1907-1966
AmAu&B, AmNov, BioIn 2, –4, –7,
REnAL, TwCA SUP

Creeley, Robert White 1926-
AmAu&B, Au&Wr 71, BioIn 8, –10,
–11, –12, –13, BlueB 76, CasWL,
ConAu 1R, ConLC 1, –2, –4, –8, –11,
–15, ConPo 70, –75, –80, CroCAP,
DcLB 5[port], –16[port],
DcLEL 1940, EncWL 2,
IntAu&W 76, –77, –82, IntWW 74,
–75, –76, –77, –78, –79, –80, –81,
–82, –83, IntWWP 77, LinLib L,
ModAL, –S1, Novels, PenC AM,
RAdv 1, REnAL, WebE&AL,
WhoAm 74, –76, –78, –80, –82, –84,
–86, WhoTwCL, WhoWor 74, –80,
–82, –84, WorAu, WrDr 76, –80, –82,
–84

Creighton, Luella Sanders Bruce 1901-
BioIn 2, –10, ConAu P-1, CreCan 2,
OxCan, –SUP, WhoAm 76, –78, –80

Crenshaw, Marshall *NewRR 83*

Crenshaw, Marshall 1954?- *BioIn 13*

Crenshaw, Mary Ann 1929-
ConAu 8NR, –57, WhoAmW 77, –79,
–81, WhoE 79, –81

Cresswell, Helen 1934- *OxChL,*
SmATA 48[port]

Cresswell, Helen 1936?- *Au&Wr 71,*
AuBYP, BioIn 9, ConAu 8NR, –17R,
FourBJA, IntAu&W 76, –77, –82,
ScF&FL 1, –2, SenS, SmATA 1,
TwCCW 78, –83, WrDr 76, –80, –82,
–84, –86

Crews, Frederick C 1933- *AmAu&B,*
ConAu 1R, –1NR, ConLCrt, –82,
DrAS 74E, –78E, –82E,
IntAu&W 82, WhoAm 78, –80, –82,
WrDr 80, –82, –84, –86

Crews, Frederick Campbell 1933-
IntAu&W 86, WhoAm 84, –86

Crews, Harry *DrAP&F 85*

Crews, Harry 1935- *AuNews 1,*
BioIn 8, –10, –11, –12, –13,
BioNews 74, ConAu 20NR, –25R,
ConLC 6, –23[port], ConNov 82, –86,
DcLB 6[port], NewYTBS 78, PostFic,
WhoAm 74, –76, –78, –80, –82,
WorAu 1970, WrDr 84, –86

Crichton, Michael *IntMPA 86*

Crichton, Michael 1942- *AmAu&B,*
Au&Wr 71, AuNews 2, BioIn 8, –9,
–10, –11, –12, –13, CelR,
ConAu 13NR, –25R, ConLC 2, –6,
ConNov 76, –82, CurBio 76,
DcLB Y81B[port], EncSF, FilmgC,
HalFC 84, IntMPA 77, –75, –76, –78,
–79, –81, –82, –84, LinLib L,
NewYTBE 70, NewYTBS 81[port],
Novels, ScF&FL 1, –2, ScFSB,
SmATA 9, TwCCr&M 80, –85,
TwCSFW 86, WhoSciF, WorAl,
WorAu 1970, WrDr 76, –80, –82,
–84, –86

Crichton, Robert 1925- *AuNews 1,*
BioIn 7, –8, –10, BioNews 74,
ConAu 17R, IntAu&W 76, WrDr 76,
–80, –82, –84, –86

Crick, Bernard R 1929- *Au&Wr 71,*
ConAu 1R, –5NR, IntAu&W 76, –77,
–82, Who 74, –82, –83, WrDr 76,
–80, –82, –84, –86

Crick, Francis Harry Compton 1916-
AsBiEn, BiESc, BioIn 5, –6, –8, –9,
–11, –12, –13, BlueB 76, CelR,
CurBio 83[port], IntWW 74, –75, –76,
–77, –78, –79, –80, –81, –82, –83,
McGEWB, McGMS 80[port], WhDW,
Who 74, –82, –83, –85, WhoAm 84,
–86, WhoFrS 84, WhoNob,
WhoWor 74, –78, –80, –82, –84, –87,
WorAl

Criner, Beatrice Hall 1915-
AuBYP SUP, WhoAmW 64, –66, –68,
–75, –77, WhoS&SW 78, –80, –82,
–84

Criner, Calvin *AuBYP SUP*

Crispin, Edmund 1921-1978
Au&Wr 71, BioIn 1, –2, –10,
ConAu X, ConLC 22[port], ConSFA,
CurBio 49, EncMys, EncSF, Novels,
ScF&FL 1, –2, TwCCr&M 80, –85,
WhoSciF, WorAl, WorAu

Crispin, Edmund *see also* Montgomery,
Robert Bruce

Crist, Judith 1922- *AmAu&B,*
AmWomWr, AuNews 1, BioIn 7, –8,
–9, –10, –12, BlueB 76, BriB[port],
CelR, ConAu 17NR, –81, ConTFT 1,
ForWC 70, IntMPA 77, –75, –76,
–78, –79, –81, –82, –84, –86,
WhoAm 74, –76, –78, –80, –82, –84,
–86, WhoAmW 74, –61, –64, –66,
–68, –70, –72, –75, –83, –85, –87,
WhoE 74, WhoWorJ 72, –78,
WrDr 76, –80, –82, –84, –86

Critchfield, Richard 1931-
ConAu 16NR, WrDr 86

Critchfield, Richard Patrick 1931-
BioIn 13, BlueB 76, ConAu 41R,
IntAu&W 82, WhoAm 74, –76, –78,
–80, –82, –86, WhoS&SW 73,
WhoWor 80, –82, –84, –87, WrDr 80,
–82, –84

Croce, Arlene Louise 1934-
ConAu 104, WhoAm 80, –82, –84,
–86, WhoAmW 81, –83, –85, –87

Croce, Jim 1942-1973 *EncFCWM 83,*
WhoRock 81

Croce, Jim 1943-1973 *BioIn 10, –11,*
–12, BioNews 74, EncPR&S 74, –77,
IlEncRk, ObitOF 79, RkOn 78, –84,
RolSEnR 83, WhoRocM 82, WorAl

Croft-Cooke, Rupert *TwCCr&M 85*

Croft-Cooke, Rupert 1903-1979
Au&Wr 71, BioIn 3, –4, –6, –7, –8,
–10, BlueB 76, CathA 1952,
ChhPo, –S1, ConAu 4NR, –9R, –89,
IntAu&W 76, –77, IntWW 74, –75,
–76, –77, –78, –79N, IntWWP 77,
LongCTC, NewC, TwCA, –SUP,
TwCCr&M 80, WhE&EA, WhLit,

Who 74, WhoWor 74, –76, –78,
WrDr 76, –80

Crofts, Dash *WhoAm 78, –80, –82,*
WhoRocM 82

Crofts, Dash *see also* Seals & Crofts

Crofts, Freeman Wills 1879-1957
BioIn 4, ConAu 113, DcIrB, DcLEL,
EncMys, EvLB, LongCTC, NewC,
Novels, ObitOF 79, PenC ENG, REn,
TwCA, –SUP, TwCCr&M 80, –85,
TwCWr, WhE&EA, WhLit, WorAl

Cromie, William Joseph 1930-
AuBYP SUP, BioIn 9, ConAu 13R,
SmATA 4, WhoAm 84

Crompton, Anne Eliot 1930-
AuBYP SUP, ConAu 13NR, –33R,
SmATA 23[port]

Crompton, John *ConAu X*

Crompton, John *see also* Lamburn,
John Battersby Crompton

Crone, Ruth 1919- *AuBYP, BioIn 9,*
ConAu 9R, ForWC 70, SmATA 4

Cronin, A J 1896-1981
AnObit 1981[port], Au&Wr 71,
BlueB 76, CasWL, CathA 1930,
Chambr 3, CmScLit, ConAu 1R,
–5NR, –102, ConLC 32[port],
ConNov 76, CurBio 42, –81N,
DcLEL, EncWL, EvLB, FilmgC,
HalFC 84, LinLib L, LongCTC,
ModBrL, NewC, NewYTBS 81[port],
Novels, OxEng 85, PenC ENG,
RAdv 1, REn, SmATA 25N,
–47[port], TwCA, –SUP, TwCWr,
WhNAA, WhoTw 74, –78, –80

Cronin, Archibald Joseph 1896-1981
BioIn 1, –2, –3, –4, –6, –7, –8, –12,
–13, InSci, IntAu&W 76, –77, –82,
IntWW 74, –75, –76, –77, –78, –79,
–80, –81N, OxMed 86, WhAm 7,
WhE&EA, WhLit, Who 74, –82N,
WhoWor 74, –76, –78

Cronin, Vincent 1924- *Au&Wr 71,*
ConAu 5NR, –9R, IntAu&W 76, –77,
LongCTC, Who 74, –82, –83,
WhoWor 80

Cronkite, Kathy *BioIn 12,*
NewYTBS 81[port], WhoHol A

Cronley, Jay 1943- *ConAu 81*

Cronyn, George William 1888-1969
AmAu&B, IndAu 1917, WhAm 5

Crook, Beverly Courtney *ConAu 115,*
SmATA 35, –38[port]

Crosbie, John S 1920- *ConAu 12NR*

Crosbie, John Shaver 1920- *BioIn 12,*
CanWW 79, –80, –81, 83,
ConAu 73, WhoCan 77, –80[port],
–82[port], –84[port]

Crosby, Alexander L 1906-1980
AuBYP, BioIn 7, –9, –10, –12, –13,
ConAu 29R, –93, MorBMP,
NewYTBS 80, SmATA 2, –23N

Crosby, Alfred W, Jr. 1931- *WrDr 86*

Crosby, Alfred Worcester 1931-
WhoAm 84, –86

Crosby, David 1941- *BiDAmM,*
BioIn 9, –13, IlEncRk, WhoAm 78,
–80, –82, –84, WhoRock 81,
WhoRocM 82

Crosby, David *see also* Crosby, Stills,
Nash & Young

Crosby, Stills, Nash & Young
EncPR&S 74, –77, IlEncRk,
RkOn 78, –84, RkOneH,
RolSEnR 83

Crosby, Stills, Nash & Young *see also*
Crosby, David

Crosby, Stills, Nash & Young *see also*
Nash, Graham

Crosby, Stills, Nash & Young *see also*
Stills, Stephen

Crosby, Stills, Nash & Young *see also*
Young, Neil

Cross, Amanda *ThrtnMM,*
WorAu 1975, WrDr 86

Cross, Amanda 1926- *BioIn 12,*
ConAu X, TwCCr&M 80, –85,
WrDr 82, –84

Cross, Amanda *see also* Heilbrun,
Carolyn

Cross, Christopher 1949- *WhoRock 81*

Cross, Christopher 1951?- *BioIn 12,*
–13, RolSEnR 83, WhoAm 84, –86,
WhoRocM 82

Cross, Gilbert B 1939- *ConAu 105, DrAS 74E, –78E, –82E*
Cross, Gillian 1945- *ConAu 111, OxChL, SmATA 38[port], TwCChW 83, WrDr 86*
Cross, Gillian Clare 1945- *IntAu&W 86*
Cross, Helen Reeder *ConAu X, SmATA X*
Cross, Milton 1897-1975 *AmAu&B, BioIn 4, –9, –10, CelR, ConAu 53, CurBio 40, –75N, NewEOp 71, NewYTBE 71, NewYTBS 75, ObitOF 79, WhAm 6, WhScrn 77, WhoAm 74, WorAl*
Cross, Milton J 1897-1975 *WhScrn 83*
Cross, Wilbur L 1918- *WrDr 86*
Cross, Wilbur Lucius, III 1918- *Au&Wr 71, BioIn 9, BlueB 76, ConAu 1R, –2NR, IntAu&W 76, SmATA 2, WhoE 74, WhoF&I 77, WrDr 76, –80, –82, –84*
Crossen, Kendell Foster 1910- *ConAu 1R, –4NR, EncSF, ScF&FL 1, –2*
Crossen, Kendell Foster *see also* Chaber, M E
Crossley-Holland, Kevin 1941- *AuBYP SUP, BioIn 10, ChhPo S1, –S3, ConAu 70, –75, –80, –85, DcLB 40[port], DcLEL 1940, FourBJA, IntAu&W 76, –77, –82, IntWWP 77, –82, OxChL, SmATA 5, TwCCW 78, –83, WrDr 76, –80, –82, –84, –86*
Crossman, Richard 1907-1974 *Au&Wr 71, BioIn 1, –4, –8, –9, –10, –11, –12, ConAu 49, –61, DcPol, ObitOF 79, ObitT 1971, REn, WhAm 6, WhE&EA, Who 74, WhoWor 74, WorAu*
Crouse, Russel *OxThe 83*
Crouse, Russel 1893-1966 *AmAu&B, AuBYP, BiE&WWA, BioIn 1, –2, –4, –5, –7, –8, –11, CnDAL, CnThe, ConAu 25R, –77, CurBio 41, –66, EncMT, EncWT, HalFC 84, LinLib L, –S, McGEWD, –84, ModWD, NewCBMT, NotNAT B, ObitOF 79, OhA&B, OxAmL, –83, OxAmT 84, REn, REnAL, TwCA SUP, WhAm 4, WhE&EA, WhThe, WorAl*
Crouse, William H 1911- *WrDr 86*
Crouse, William Harry 1907- *AmM&WS 73P, AuBYP, BioIn 7, ConAu 5R, –6NR, IndAu 1917, WhoF&I 83, WrDr 76, –80, –84*
Crow, John Armstrong 1906- *AmAu&B, ConAu 13R, DcSpL, DrAS 74P, –78F, –82F, WhoAm 74, –76, –78, –80, –82, –84, –86, WhoWest 74, –76, WhoWor 78*
Crowe, Bettina Lum 1911- *Au&Wr 71, AuBYP, BioIn 10, ConAu 9R, IntAu&W 76, –77, –82, SmATA 6, WhoAm 74, WhoAmW 74, –70A, –75, WrDr 76, –80, –82, –84*

Crowe, Bettina Lum *see also* Lum, Peter
Crowe, Cameron Macmillan 1931- *AmM&WS 73P, –79P, –82P, –86P, CanWW 83, WhoAm 74, –76, –78, –80, –82, –84, –86*
Crowe, John *SmATA X, TwCCr&M 85, WrDr 86*
Crowe, John *see also* Lynds, Dennis
Crowley, John 1942- *BioIn 13, ConAu 61, DcLB Y82B[port], EncSF, ScFSB[port], TwCSFW 86, WrDr 84, –86*
Crowther, Bosley d1981 *HalFC 84*
Crowther, Bosley 1905-1981 *AmAu&B, AnObit 1981[port], BioIn 4, –5, –8, –12, ConAu 57, –81N, EncTwCJ, IntMPA 77, –75, –76, –78, –79, –81, NewYTBS 81[port], WhAm 7, WhoWor 74, WorAl*
Crowther, James Gerald 1899- *AuBYP, BioIn 12, ConAu 73, SmATA 14, WrDr 76, –80, –82, –84*
Croy, Homer 1883-1965 *AmAu&B, AmNov, BioIn 2, –4, –7, –8, –10, –12, ConAu 103, –65, CurBio 57, DcLB 4, EncFWF, NatCAB 51, ObitOF 79, REnAL, REnAW, TwCA, –SUP, WhAm 4, –5, WhScrn 77, –83*
Cruise O'Brien, Conor 1917- *Au&Wr 71, IntAu&W 76*
Crume, Vic *ScF&FL 1*
Cruse, Heloise 1920?- *AmAu&B, BioIn 5, –6, –7, ForWC 70, WhoAmW 74, –68, –70*
Crutcher, Chris 1946- *ConAu 113*
Cruz, Nicky 1938- *BioIn 12, WhoRel 75*
Crystal, Billy *WhoAm 84, –86*
Crystal, Billy 1947- *ConNews 85-3[port], ConTFT 3[port], IntMPA 86*
Cuadra, Pablo Antonio 1912- *BioIn 8, –13, DcCLAA, OxSpan, PenC AM, WorAu 1975[port]*
Cudahy, Brian J 1936- *AmCath 80, ConAu 41R, DrAS 74P, WhoE 74, –75*
Culliney, John L 1942- *ConAu 65*
Cumming, Patricia Arenas 1932- *ConAu 11NR, –61, IntWWP 82, Po&Wr 77*
Cumming, Patricia Arens 1932- *ForWC 70, IntAu&W 77, –82, –86, IntWWP 77*
Cumming, Primrose Amy 1915- *Au&Wr 71, ConAu 33R, IntAu&W 76, SmATA 24, TwCChW 83, WhE&EA, WrDr 76, –80, –82, –84*
Cumming, Robert 1943- *BioIn 13*
Cumming, Robert 1945- *ConAu 106*
Cummings, Betty Sue 1918- *BioIn 12, ConAu 14NR, –73, FifBJA[port], SmATA 15*

Cummings, E E 1894-1962 *AmAu&B, AmWr, AnCL, AtlBL, AuBYP, CasWL, ChhPo, CnDAL, CnE&AP, CnMD, CnMWL, ConAmA, ConAmL, ConAu 73, ConLC 1, –3, –8, –12, –15, CyWA, DcAmB S7, DcLB 4, –48[port], DcLEL, EncWL, –2, EvLB, LinLib L, –S, LongCTC, McGEWD, –84[port], ModAL, –S2, –S1, ModWD, ObitT 1961, OxAmL, –83, OxEng, –85, PenC AM, RAdv 1, REn, REnAL, SixAP, TwCA, –SUP, TwCWr, WebE&AL, WhoTwCL, WorAl*
Cummings, Richard *AuBYP, BioIn 8, –13, ConAu X, SmATA X, WrDr 76, –80, –82*
Cummings, Richard *see also* Gardner, Richard M
Cuneo, John Robert 1911- *ConAu 53, WhoE 83*
Cunliffe, Marcus Falkner 1922- *AmAu&B, Au&Wr 71, BlueB 76, ConAu 10NR, –21R, IntAu&W 82, –86, SmATA 37, Who 74, –82, –83, –85, WrDr 76, –80, –82, –84*
Cunningham, Chet 1928- *BioIn 13, ConAu 4NR, –19NR, –49, IntAu&W 86, SmATA 23, WrDr 84, –86*
Cunningham, E V *BioIn 13, WrDr 86*
Cunningham, E V 1914- *AuBYP, BioIn 10, –11, ConAu X, ConNov 72, –76, –82, EncSF, IntAu&W 76X, –77X, Novels, SmATA 7, TwCCr&M 80, –85, WrDr 76, –80, –82, –84*
Cunningham, E V *see also* Fast, Howard
Cunningham, Glenn 1910- *BioIn 2, –3, –5, –6, –7, –9, –10, –12, WorAl*
Cunningham, John D 1933- *ConAu 111*
Cunningham, John Donoven 1933- *AmM&WS 73P, LEduc 74*
Cunningham, Julia W 1916- *WrDr 86*
Cunningham, Julia Woolfolk 1916- *AmAu&B, AuBYP, BioIn 7, –9, –10, –13, ConAu 4NR, –9R, ConLC 12, MorBMP, SmATA 1, –26[port], ThrBJA, TwCCW 78, –83, WhoAm 74, –76, –78, –80, –82, –84, –86, WhoAmW 74, –68, –70, –72, WrDr 80, –82, –84*
Curie, Eve 1904- *AmAu&B, AnCL, Au&Wr 71, BioIn 3, –6, –9, ConAu P-1, CurBio 40, InWom, IntAu&W 76, –77, IntWW 74, –75, –76, –77, –78, –79, –80, –81, –82, –83, LinLib L, –S, SmATA 1, WhE&EA, Who 74, –83, –85, WhoAm 74, –76, –78, –80, –82, –84, WhoAmW 74, –61, –64, –66, –68, –70, –72, –75, –79, –81, –83, –85, –87, WhoE 85, WhoFr 79, WhoWor 74, –76, –78, –80, –84, –87*
Curley, Daniel *DrAP&F 85*

Curley, Daniel 1918- *BioIn 13, ConAu 3NR, –9R, –18NR, IntAu&W 76, –82, SmATA 23[port], WrDr 76, –80, –82, –84, –86*
Currier, Richard L 1940- *ConAu 57*
Curry, Jane Louise 1932- *AuBYP, BioIn 8, –9, ConAu 7NR, –17R, FourBJA, IntAu&W 82, ScF&FL 1, –2, SmATA 1, TwCCW 78, –83, WhoAm 82, –84, WhoAmW 83, WrDr 80, –82, –84*
Curtis, Anthony 1926?- *ConAu 101, –18NR, IntAu&W 77, –82, WhoAm 74, –76, WhoWor 74, WrDr 76, –80, –82, –84, –86*
Curtis, Edward S 1868-1952 *AmAu&B, BioIn 3, –10, –11, –12, –13, CmCal, DcAmB S5, ObitOF 79, REnAW, WhAm 4*
Curtis, Edward Sheriff 1868-1952 *ICPEnP*
Curtis, Edward Sheriff 1868-1954 *MacBEP*
Curtis, Patricia 1921- *BioIn 13, ConAu 69, SmATA 23[port]*
Curtis, Patricia 1924- *ConAu 18NR*
Curtis, Richard 1937- *AuBYP SUP, BioIn 13, ConAu 106, ConSFA, EncSF, ScF&FL 1, –2, SmATA 29*
Curtis, Robert H *AuBYP SUP*
Curtis, Will *ConAu X, IntAu&W 76X, –82X, –86X, WrDr 76, –80, –82, –84, –86*
Curtis, Will *see also* Nunn, William Curtis
Curtiss, Ursula Reilly 1923- *AmAu&B, AmWomMr, Au&Wr 71, ConAu 1R, –5NR, EncMys, IntAu&W 76, –77, TwCCr&M 80, WhoAm 78, –80, –82, –84, WhoAmW 74, –66, –68, –70, –72, –75, –77, WrDr 82, –84*
Curtiss, Ursula Reilly 1923-1984 *ConAu 114, WhAm 8*
Cusack, Anne E *DrAP&F 85*
Cusack, Michael Joseph 1928- *ConAu 69, WhoAm 78, –80, –82*
Cussler, Clive 1931- *BioIn 12, ConAu 1NR, –22NR, NewYTBS 81[port], Novels, WhoAm 78, –80, –82, WhoF&I 75, WrDr 80, –82, –84, –86*
Cussler, Clive Eric 1931- *WhoAm 84, –86*
Custer, Elizabeth Bacon 1842?-1933 *Alli SUP, AmAu&B, AmBi, AmWom, AmWomWr, ApCAB, BiD&SB, BioIn 2, –6, –7, –10, –11, DcAmAu, DcNAA, HarEnUS, HerW, InWom, OxAmL 83, REnAL, WhAm 1*
Cuthbertson, Tom 1945- *ConAu 1NR, –45*
Cutler, Ebbitt 1923- *AuBYP SUP, ConAu 4NR, –49, IntAu&W 82, SmATA 9*
Cuyler, Margery S 1948- *ConAu 117, WhoAmW 77, WhoLibI 82*
Cuyler, Margery Stuyvesant 1948- *SmATA 39[port]*

D

Dace, Letitia 1941- *ConAu 106, DrAS 74E, –78E*
Dace, Wallace 1920- *ConAu 61, DrAS 74E, –78E, –82E, NatPD, –81[port]*
Dachs, David 1922-1980 *ConAu 11NR, –69*
DaCruz, Daniel 1921- *ConAu 3NR, –5R, IntAu&W 76, WrDr 76, –80, –82, –84*
DaCruz, Daniel, Jr. 1921- *ConAu 19NR*
Dade, George C 1912?- *BioIn 12*
Dadie, Bernard B 1916- *ConAu 17NR*
Dadie, Bernard Binlin 1916- *BioIn 13, OxThe 83*
Dahl, Borghild 1890-1984 *AuBYP, BioIn 6, –8, –9, –10, ConAu 1R, –2NR, IntAu&W 82, MinnWr, SmATA 37N, –7, ThrBJA, WhoAmW 58, –61, –64, –66, –68, –70, –72, WrDr 76, –80, –84*
Dahl, Roald *DrAP&F 85*
Dahl, Roald 1916- *Au&Wr 71, AuBYP, BioIn 5, –6, –8, –9, –10, –11, –12, –13, BioNews 74, ChlLR 1, –7[port], ConAu 1R, –6NR, ConLC 1, –6, –18, ConNov 72, –76, –82, –86, DcLEL 1940, EncSF, HalFC 84, IntAu&W 76, –77, –82, IntWW 82, –83, LinLib L, MorBMP, NewC, NewYTBS 77, Novels, OxChL, PiP, RAdv 1, REn, REnAL, ScF&FL 1, –2, ScFSB, SmATA 1, –26[port], ThrBJA, TwCCW 78, –83, TwCCr&M 80, WhE&EA, Who 82, –83, –85, WhoAm 74, –76, –78, –80, –82, –84, –86, WhoHr&F, WhoSciF, WhoWor 74, –76, –78, WorAl, WorAu, WrDr 76, –80, –82, –84, –86*
Daiches, David 1912- *Au&Wr 71, BioIn 4, BlueB 76, ChhPo S1, –S3, CmScLit, ConAu 5R, –7NR, ConLCrt, –82, DcLEL, EvLB, IntAu&W 76, –77, IntWW 74, –75, –76, –77, –78, –79, –80, –81, –82, –83, LinLib L, LongCTC, ModBrL, OxEng 85, RAdv 1, REn, TwCA SUP, Who 74, –82, –83, –85, WhoAm 74, –76, –78, WhoWor 74, –76, –78, –84, –87, WhoWorJ 78, WrDr 76, –80, –82, –84, –86*
Daigon, Arthur 1928- *ConAu 33R, LEduc 74, WhoE 85*
Dale, Margaret J Miller 1911- *Au&Wr 71, ConAu 3NR, –5R, –19NR, SmATA 39*
Dale, Margaret J Miller *see also* Miller, Margaret J
Dale, Margaret Jessy 1911- *Au&Wr 71, ConAu 5R, IntAu&W 76, –77, –82, –86*
Daley, Arthur 1904-1974 *AmAu&B, BioIn 4, –10, ConAu 45, ConAu P-2, CurBio 56, –74, –74N*

Daley, Brian *ScFSB* **Daley,** Robert *IntMPA 86*
Daley, Robert 1930- *ConAu 1R, –2NR, IntMPA 84, WhoAm 74, –76, –78, –80, WhoE 74, WrDr 80, –82, –84, –86*
Dalmas, John *ConAu X*
Dalrymple, Byron W 1910- *ConAu 6NR, –57*
Dalrymple, Byron William 1910- *IntAu&W 86*
Dalton, David 1944- *ConAu 97*
Dalton, Stephen 1937- *ICPEnP A*
Daltrey, Roger 1944- *BioIn 13, HalFC 84, WhoAm 80, –82, –84, –86, WhoHol A, WhoRock 81, WhoRocM 82*
Daltrey, Roger *see also* Who, The
Daly, Donald F 1904- *ConAu 69, WhoWest 80, –82, –84*
Daly, Elizabeth 1878-1967 *AmAu&B, BioIn 4, –8, ConAu P-2, DcLEL 1940, EncMys, Novels, REnAL, TwCA SUP, TwCCr&M 80, –85*
Daly, Jay 1946- *WhoE 83, –85, WhoLibI 82*
Daly, Maureen *WrDr 86*
Daly, Maureen 1921- *AmAu&B, AmNov, AuBYP, BioIn 1, –2, –6, –7, –9, BkC 4, CathA 1930, ConAu X, ConLC 17, CurBio 46, MorJA, REnAL, SmATA 2, SmATA 1AS[port], TwCCW 78, –83, WhoAmW 58, –61, WrDr 80, –82, –84*
Daly, Maureen *see also* McGivern, Maureen Daly
Daly, Sheila John 1927?- *AuBYP, BioIn 2, –3, –8, CathA 1952*
D'Amato, Alex 1919- *AuBYP SUP, BioIn 12, ConAu 18NR, –81, SmATA 20*
D'Amato, Janet Potter *WhoAmA 84*
D'Amato, Janet Potter 1925- *AuBYP SUP, BioIn 11, ConAu 1NR, –49, SmATA 9, WhoAmA 78, –80, –82*
D'Ambrosio, Richard A 1927- *ConAu 102, WhoE 74*
Damsker, Matt 1951- *ConAu 108*
Dana, Barbara 1940- *BioIn 13, ConAu 8NR, –17R, ForWC 70, SmATA 22[port], WhoHol A*
Dana, Richard Henry *OxChL*
Dana, Richard Henry 1815-1882 *BioIn 13, MorMA, OxEng 85*
Dana, Richard Henry, Jr. 1815-1882 *Alli, –SUP, AmAu&B, AmBi, AmRef[port], ApCAB, BbD, BiAUS SUP, BiD&SB, BioIn 1, –2, –3, –5, –6, –8, –9, –12, CarSB, CasWL, Chambr 3, CivWDc, CmCal, CnDAL, CrtT 3, CyAL 2, CyWA,*

DcAmAu, DcAmB, DcAmSR, DcBiPP, DcEnL, DcLB 1, DcLEL, DcNAA, Drake, EncAB-H, EvLB, HarEnUS, LinLib L, –S, McGEWB, MouLC 4, NatCAB 7, OxAmH, OxAmL, –83, OxEng, OxLaw, OxShips, PenC AM, REn, REnAL, REnAW, SmATA 26[port], TwCBDA, WebAB, –79, WebE&AL, WhDW, WhAm HS, WhAmP, WorAl
Danaher, Kevin 1913- *BiDIrW, BioIn 13, WrDr 86*
Dance, Stanley Frank 1910- *Au&Wr 71, ConAu 8NR, –17R, IntAu&W 76, –77, –82, WhoE 74, –75, WrDr 76, –80, –82, –84*
Dandrea, Don 1936- *ConAu 120*
Daniel, Anita 1893?-1978 *AuBYP, BioIn 8, –11, –13, ConAu 77, ForWC 70, SmATA 23, –24N*
Daniel, Pete 1938- *ConAu 14NR, WrDr 86*
Daniel, Ralph T 1921- *ConAu 53, IntWWM 77*
Daniels, Dorothy 1915- *AmWomWr, ConAu 15NR, –89, ScF&FL 1, WhoAmW 83, –85, –87, WrDr 82, –84, –86*
Daniels, Jonathan 1902- *OxAmL 83*
Daniels, Jonathan 1902-1981 *AmAu&B, AnObit 1981[port], Au&Wr 71, AuBYP, BioIn 2, –3, –4, –5, –7, –10, –12, –13, BlueB 76, CnDAL, ConAu 105, –49, CurBio 42, –82N, EncSoH, IntAu&W 76, IntYB 78, –79, –80, –81, –82, LinLib L, NewYTBS 81[port], OxAmL, REn, REnAL, ScF&FL 1, –2, TwCA, –SUP, WhoAm 74, –76, –78, –80, WhoAmP 73, –75, –77, –79, WhoS&SW 73, WhoWor 74, WrDr 80, –82*
Daniels, Jonathan Worth 1902-1981 *WhAm 8*
Daniels, Robert Vincent 1926- *WhoAm 84, –86, WhoAmP 85, WhoE 85*
Daniken, Erich Von 1935- *BioIn 10, –11, –12, ConAu 76, IntAu&W 82, UFOEn*
Dank, Milton 1920- *AmM&WS 73P, –76P, –79P, –82P, –86P, ConAu 11NR, –69, SmATA 31[port]*
Dann, Colin 1943- *ConAu 108, WrDr 82, –84, –86*
Dann, Jack *DrAP&F 85*
Dann, Jack 1945- *ConAu 2NR, –49, EncSF, IntAu&W 82, ScF&FL 1, –2, TwCSFW 86, WrDr 84, –86*
Dann, Jack 1949- *ScFSB*
Dannay, Frederic *TwCCr&M 85*
Dannay, Frederic d1982 *WhAm 8*

Dannay, Frederic 1905-1982 *AmAu&B, AnObit 1982[port], ASpks, AuBYP, BioIn 2, –3, –4, –8, –10, –11, –12, –13, ConAu 1R, –1NR, –107, ConLC 11, CurBio 40, –82N, DcLEL, EncMys, EvLB, IntAu&W 76, –77, IntWW 74, –75, –76, –77, –78, –79, –80, –81, –82, –83N, LongCTC, NewYTBS 82[port], PenC AM, REn, ScF&FL 1, TwCA, –SUP, TwCCr&M 80, WebAB, –79, Who 74, –82, –83N, WhoAm 74, –76, –78, –80, –82, WhoWor 74, WrDr 76, –80, –82*
Dannay, Frederic *see also* Queen, Ellery
Dannett, Sylvia G L 1909- *ConAu 1R, –4NR, WhoAmW 74, –72, –75, –77, –79, WhoWorJ 72, –78*
Danziger, James *BioIn 13*
Danziger, Paula 1944- *ConAu 112, –115, ConLC 21[port], FifBJA[port], SmATA 30, –36*
Darack, Arthur J 1918- *ConAu 115, Ward 77F, WhoAm 74, –76, –78, –80, –82, –84, –86*
Darby, Patricia *AuBYP, BioIn 12, ConAu 73, SmATA 14*
Darby, Ray 1912- *AmSCAP 66, AuBYP, BioIn 8, –10, ConAu 17R, SmATA 7, WhoWest 74, –76, –78*
Darcy, Clare *ConAu 102, Novels, WrDr 76, –80, –82, –84, –86*
Dardis, Tom 1926- *ConAu 9NR, –65*
Dareff, Hal 1920- *AmAu&B, AuBYP, BioIn 8, ConAu 65, WhoAm 74, –76, –78, –80, –82, –84, –86, WhoE 74*
Daringer, Helen Fern 1892- *BioIn 2, –6, –9, ConAu P-2, CurBio 51, InWom, MorJA, SmATA 1*
Darion, Joe *ConAu X*
Darion, Joe 1917- *EncMT, NewCBMT, WhoAm 74, –76, –78, –80, –82, –84, –86*
Darion, Joseph 1917- *AmSCAP 66, BioIn 10, –12, ConAu 113*
Darke, Marjorie 1929- *BioIn 12, ConAu 15NR, –81, IntAu&W 82, SmATA 16, TwCCW 78, –83, Who 82, –83, WrDr 80, –82, –84, –86*
Darling, Kathy 1943- *BioIn 11, ConAu X, SmATA X*
Darling, Lois MacIntyre 1917- *AmAu&B, AuBYP, BioIn 8, –9, –12, ConAu 3NR, –5R, IlsCB 1967, SmATA 3, WhoAm 74, –76, –78, –80, –82, –84, –86, WhoAmW 74, –66, –68, –70, –72, WhoE 74, –83, WrDr 76, –80, –82, –84*
Darling, Louis 1916-1970 *AmAu&B, AuBYP, BioIn 5, –6, –8, –9, –13, ConAu 3NR, –89, IlsCB 1946, –1957, –1967, MorJA, NewYTBE 70, SmATA 23N, –3, WhAm 5*
Darr, John C 1929- *ConAu 53*
Darrow, Whitney 1909- *ConAu 14NR*

NewYTBE 70, NewYTBS 78,
−80[port], −81[port], WhDW,
WhoMilH 76, WhoWor 74, −78, −80,
WhoWorJ 72, −78, WorAl, WorDWW

Day-Lewis, Cecil 1904-1972
Au&Wr 71, BioIn 3, −4, −5, −6, −8,
−9, −10, −12, −13, CasWL,
ChhPo, −S1, −S3, CnE&AP,
CnMWL, ConAu 33R, ConAu P-1,
ConLC 1, −6, −10, ConLCrt, −82,
ConNov 72, ConPo 70, −75,
CurBio 40, −69, −72, −72N, DcIrB,
DcIrL, DcIrW 1, DcLB 15[port],
−20[port], DcLEL, DcNaB 1971,
EncMys, EncWL, −2, LinLib L, −S,
LongCTC, LongCTC, ModBrL, −S1,
NewC, Novels, ObitOF 79,
ObitT 1971, OxEng, −85, PenC ENG,
RAdv 1, REn, ScF&FL 1,
TwCA, −SUP, TwCCW 78, −83,
TwCCr&M 80, TwCWr, WebE&AL,
WhDW, WhAm 5, WhoTwCL

Day-Lewis, Cecil 1905-1972 *BiDIrW*
Day-Lewis, Cecil *see also* Lewis, C Day
Day-Lewis, Cecil *see also* Lewis, Cecil
Day

Deal, Borden *DrAP&F 85*
Deal, Borden 1922- *AmAu&B,*
Au&Wr 71, BioIn 5, ConAu 1R,
−2NR, DcLB 6, IntAu&W 76, −77,
−82, REnAL, WrDr 76, −80, −82, −84
Deal, Borden 1922-1985 *ConAu 114*
Dean, Anabel 1915- *BioIn 11,*
ConAu 14NR, −37R, IntAu&W 77,
SmATA 12, WhoAmW 83, WrDr 76,
−80, −82, −84, −86
Dean, John Wesley 1938- *BioIn 13*
Dean, John Wesley, III 1938- *BioIn 9,*
−10, −11, −12, ConAu 105,
NewYTBE 73, PolProf NF,
WhoAm 74, −76, −78, −80,
WhoAmP 73, WhoGov 72, WorAl
Dean, Karen Strickler 1923-
ConAu 109
DeAndrea, William L 1952-
ConAu 20NR, −81, TwCCr&M 85,
WrDr 76
DeAngeli, Marguerite Lofft 1889-
AmAu&B, AmWomWr, Au&ICB,
Au&Wr 71, AuBYP, AuNews 2,
BioIn 1, −2, −3, −4, −5, −7, −8, −9,
−10, −11, −12, BkCL, ChlLR 1,
ChhPo, −S1, ConAu 3NR, −5R,
ConICB, CurBio 47, DcLB 22[port],
FamMS, HerW, IlsCB 1744, −1946,
−1957, −1967, InWom, JBA 51,
LinLib L, MichAu 80, MorBMP,
Newb 1922, SmATA 1, −27[port],
TwCCW 78, −83, WhoAm 74,
WhoAmA 73, −76, WhoAmW 74,
−58, −64, −66, −70, −72, WrDr 80,
−82, −84
DeAngeli, Marguerite Lofft *see also*
Angeli, Marguerite De
Deary, Terry 1946- *SmATA 41*
DeBeauvoir, Simone *ConAu X*
DeBeauvoir, Simone 1908- *Au&Wr 71,*
ConAu X, IntDcWB[port], ModRL,
ScF&FL 1, WhoWor 78, −80, −82
DeBeauvoir, Simone 1908-1986
NewYTBS 86[port]
DeBeauvoir, Simone *see also* Beauvoir,
Simone De
Debo, Angie 1890- *BioIn 4, ConAu 69,*
ConInsC 1[port], TexWr, WhAm 8,
WhoAm 74, −76, −78, WhoAmW 58,
WhoLibS 55
DeBorhegyi, Suzanne Sims 1926-
AuBYP, BioIn 8, ConAu 5R,
ForWC 70, WhoAmA 73, −78, −80,
WhoAmW 74, −70, −72, −75
Debray, Regis 1940- *BiDNeoM,*
BioIn 8, −9, −12, −13, ConAu 21R,
CurBio 82[port], EncLatA,
NewYTBE 70, WhoAm 74, −76
DeCamp, L Sprague 1907- *AuBYP,*
ConAu 1R, −1NR, −9NR, −20NR,
ConSFA, DcLB 8[port], EncSF,
IntAu&W 77, −82, LinLib L, Novels,
ScF&FL 1, −2, ScFSB[port],
SmATA 9, SupFW, TwCSFW 86,
WhoAm 78, −80, −82, −84, −86,
WhoHr&F, WhoSciF, WorAl, WorAu,
WrDr 76, −80, −82, −84, −86

DeCamp, L Sprague *see also* Lyon,
Lyman R
DeCamp, L Sprague *see also* Wells, J
Wellington
DeCamp, Lyon Sprague 1907- *BioIn 7,*
−8, −10, −11, −12, DrAS 74H, −78H,
−82H, WhoAm 76, WhoE 75, −77
Decker, Duane Walter 1910-1964
AuBYP, BioIn 2, −7, −10, ConAu 5R,
SmATA 5
Decker, William B 1926- *ASpks,*
BioIn 8, −11, WrDr 76
DeClements, Barthe 1920- *ConAu 105,*
SmATA 35
Dee, Ruby *ConAu X, WhoAm 84, −86*
Dee, Ruby 1923- *HalFC 84,*
WhoBlA 85
Dee, Ruby 1924?- *BiE&WWA,*
BioIn 5, −6, −9, −10, −12, −13,
BlkAWP, CelR, ChhPo S2, CivR 74,
ConTFT 1, CurBio 70, DrBlPA,
Ebony 1, FilmgC, InB&W 80,
IntMPA 82, −84, −86, MotPP,
MovMk, NegAl 76, −83,
NewYTBE 70, NotNAT, WhoAm 74,
−76, −78, −80, −82, WhoAmW 74,
−66, −68, −70, −72, −75, WhoBlA 75,
−77, −80, WhoHol A, WhoThe 72,
−77, −81, WomWMM, WorAl
Dee, Ruby Ann Wallace 1924-
InB&W 85
Deedy, John Gerard, Jr. 1923-
AmCath 80, ConAu 33R,
SmATA 24[port], WhoAm 74, −76,
−78, −80, −82, −84, −86, WhoE 74,
WhoF&I 74
Deegan, Paul Joseph 1937-
ConAu 102, SmATA 38, −48
DeFelitta, Frank Paul 1921-
ConAu 61, WhoAm 74, −76, −78, −80,
−82, −84, −86, WhoWest 74, −76, −78,
WhoWor 74
Defoe, Daniel 1660?-1731 *Alli, AtlBL,*
BbD, BiD&SB, BioIn 1, −2, −3, −4,
−5, −6, −7, −8, −9, −10, −11, −12, −13,
BritAu, BritWr 3, CarSB, CasWL,
Chambr 2, ChhPo S1, −S3, CrtT 2,
−4, CyEd[port], CyWA, DcBiA,
DcBiPP, DcEnA, DcEnL, DcEuL,
DcLB 39[port], DcLEL, Dis&D,
EncE 75, EncSF, EvLB, FilmgC,
HalFC 84, HsB&A, LinLib L, −S,
LitC 1[port], LongCEL, LuthC 75,
McGEWB, MnBBF, MouLC 2,
NewC, Novels[port], OxChL,
OxEng, −85, OxShips, PenC ENG,
RAdv 1, RComWL, REn, ScF&FL 1,
SmATA 22[port], WebE&AL,
WhDW, WhoChL, WhoHr&F, WorAl
Defoe, Daniel 1661?-1731 *DcNaB, −C*
Deford, Frank 1938- *BioIn 10, −13,*
ConAu 33R, WhoAm 86, WrDr 76,
−80, −82, −84, −86
Degani, Meir H 1909- *AmM&WS 73P,*
−76P, −79P, −82P, ConAu 102,
WhoAmJ 80, WhoWorJ 72, −78
Degani, Meir Hershtenkorn 1909-
AmM&WS 86P
Degler, Carl Neumann 1921-
ConAu 3NR, −5R, DrAS 74H, −78H,
−82H, WhoAm 74, −76, −78, −80,
−82, −84, −86
DeGraft-Johnson, John Coleman
1919- *ConAu 21R, IntAu&W 76A,*
WrDr 76
DeGramont, Sanche *WorAu 1975*
DeGramont, Sanche 1932- *AmAu&B,*
BioIn 9, ConAu 45, WhoSpyF
DeGramont, Sanche *see also* Morgan,
Ted
DeGregorio, William A 1946-
ConAu 117
DeGrummond, Lena Young *AuBYP,*
BiDrLUS 70, BioIn 8, −10,
ConAu 1R, −1NR, SmATA 6,
WhoAmW 66, WhoLibS 55, −66
Deighton, Len *ConAu X*
Deighton, Len 1929- *BioIn 6, −7, −9,*
−10, −12, ConAu 9R, ConLC 4, −7,
−22[port], ConNov 72, −76, −82, −86,
CorpD, CurBio 84[port],
DcLEL 1940, EncMys, EncSF,
HalFC 84, IntAu&W 76, −77,

IntMPA 77, −75, −76, −78, −79,
IntWW 74, −75, −76, −77, −78, −79,
−80, −81, −82, −83, NewC,
NewYTBS 81[port], Novels, ScFSB,
TwCCr&M 80, −85, TwCWr,
WhoSpyF, WhoWor 74, −78, −80,
−82, −84, −87, WorAl, WorAu,
WrDr 76, −80, −82, −84, −86
Deindorfer, Robert Graves 1922-1983
BioIn 13
Deindorfer, Robert Greene 1922-1983
ConAu 3NR, −9R, −109,
IntAu&W 76, −77, −82, WhoWor 76,
−78
DeJesus, Carolina Maria 1921-
BioIn 10, InB&W 80
DeJong, Dola 1911- *AuBYP, BioIn 1,*
−6, −7, −10, ConAu 5R, CurBio 47,
InWom, MorJA, SmATA 7
DeJong, Meindert 1906- *AnCL,*
Au&ICB, Au&Wr 71, AuBYP,
BioIn 2, −3, −4, −6, −7, −8, −9, −10,
BkCL, CasWL, ChlLR 1,
ConAu 13R, CurBio 52,
DcLB 52[port], FamMS, MichAu 80,
MorBMP, MorJA, Newb 1922,
OxChL, SenS, SmATA 2,
TwCCW 78, −83, WhAm 8,
WhoAm 74, −76, −78, −80, −82,
WrDr 80, −82, −84, −86
DeJonge, Alex 1938- *ConAu 5NR,*
−53, WrDr 80, −82, −84, −86
DeJongh, James Laurence 1942-
ConAu 85, IntAu&W 82, WhoE 79,
−81, −83, −85
DeKay, Ormonde, Jr. 1923- *BioIn 10,*
ChhPo S2, ConAu 49, WhoE 77, −79,
−81
Dekle, Bernard 1905- *ConAu 17R*
DeKruif, Paul 1890- *WhAm 8*
DeKruif, Paul 1890-1971 *AmAu&B,*
BiE&WWA, BioIn 1, −2, −4, −6, −9,
−10, ConAu 9R, −29R, CurBio 42,
−63, −71, −71N, InSci, JBA 34,
LinLib L, −S, LongCTC, MichAu 80,
OxAmL, −83, REn, REnAL,
SmATA 5, TwCA, −SUP, WhAm 5
DeKruif, Paul *see also* Kruif, Paul De
DeLaguna, Frederica Annis 1906-
AmM&WS 73S, −76P, BioIn 10,
ConAu 37R, IntAu&W 77, −82,
WhoAm 74, −76, −78, WhoAmW 74,
−58, −61, −64, −66, −68, −70, −72,
−75, −77, −81
DeLaMare, Walter 1873-1956 *AnCL,*
AtlBL, AuBYP, BioIn 1, −2, −3, −4,
−5, −6, −7, −8, −9, −10, −12, −13,
BkCL, CarSB, CasWL, Chambr 3,
ChrP, ChhPo, −S1, −S2, −S3,
CnE&AP, CnMWL, ConAu 110,
CyWA, DcLB 19[port], DcLEL,
EncWL, −2, EvLB, FamPYP, JBA 34,
−51, LinLib L, LongCEL, LongCTC,
ModBrL, NewC, Novels, ObitOF 79,
ObitT 1951, OxChL, OxEng, −85,
PenC ENG, RAdv 1, REn,
ScF&FL 1, SmATA 16, Str&VC,
SupFW, TelT, TwCA, −SUP,
TwCCW 78, −83, TwCLC 4[port],
TwCWr, WebE&AL, WhDW,
WhAm 3, WhE&EA, WhLit,
WhoChL, WhoHr&F, WhoTwCL,
WorAl
DeLaMare, Walter *see also* LaMare,
Walter De
DeLaMare, Walter *see also* Mare,
Walter DeLa
Delaney, Bud *see* Delaney, Francis, Jr.
Delaney, Francis, Jr. 1931- *ConAu 57*
Delaney, Joseph H 1932- *TwCSFW 86*
Delaney, Lolo M 1937- *ConAu 57*
Delano, Hugh 1933- *BioIn 12,*
ConAu 65, SmATA 20, WhoE 79,
−81, −83
Delany, Samuel R *DrAP&F 85*
Delany, Samuel R 1942- *BioIn 12,*
BlkAWP, ConAu 81, ConLC 8, −14,
−38[port], ConNov 76, −82, −86,
ConSFA, DcLB 8[port], −33[port],
EncSF, LivgBAA, NegAl 83, Novels,
PostFic, ScF&FL 1, −2, WhoAm 82,
WhoSciF, WorAl, WorAu 1970,
WrDr 80, −82, −84, −86

Delany, Samuel Ray 1942- *BioIn 13,*
InB&W 85, ScFSB[port], WhoBlA 85
Delany, Samuel Ray, Jr. 1942-
SelBAAf
DeLaRamee, Louise 1839-1908
BioIn 1, −2, −3, −4, −5, −11, −12, −13,
BritAu 19, CarSB, JBA 34,
SmATA 20, TelT
DeLaRamee, Louise *see also* LaRamee,
Louise De
DeLaRamee, Louise *see also* Ouida
DeLaRamee, Louise *see also* Ramee,
Louise DeLa
Delaune, Lynn *AuBYP, BioIn 8, −10,*
ConAu 1R, −21NR
DelCastillo, Michel 1933- *Au&Wr 71,*
BioIn 10, ConAu 109,
ConLC 38[port], ModRL, WorAu
Delderfield, Ronald Frederick
1912-1972 *Au&Wr 71, BioIn 2, −3,*
−8, −9, −10, −11, −12, ConAu 37R,
−73, DcLEL 1940, IntAu&W 76, −77,
WhE&EA, WhoChL
Delear, Frank J 1914- *AuBYP SUP,*
ConAu 9NR, −21R, WhoE 75,
WhoPubR 72, −76, WrDr 76, −80,
−82, −84, −86
DeLeeuw, Adele Louise 1899-
AmAu&B, AuBYP, BioIn 2, −7, −9,
−12, ChhPo S1, −S3, ConAu 1R,
−1NR, JBA 51, NewYTBS 75,
OhA&B, SmATA 1, −30[port],
WhNAA, WhoAmW 74, −58, −61,
−64, −66, −68, −70, −72, −75, −77,
WrDr 76, −80, −82, −84
DeLeeuw, Adele Louise *see also* Leeuw,
Adele De
Delgado, Abelardo 1931- *ChiLit,*
ChiSch
Delhaye, Jean 1921- *IntWW 74, −75,*
−76, −77, −78, −79, −80, −81, −82,
−83, WhoFr 79, WhoWor 76, −78
DeLillo, Don 1936- *BioIn 13,*
ConAu 21NR, −81, ConLC 8, −10,
−13, −27[port], −39[port], ConNov 82,
−86, DcLB 6, DrAP&F 85, EncSF,
PostFic, ScFSB, WhoAm 86,
WorAu 1975[port], WrDr 82, −84,
−86
Deloria, Vine, Jr. 1933- *AmAu&B,*
ASpks, BioIn 8, −9, −10, −11, −12,
CivR 74, ConAu 5NR, −20NR, −53,
ConLC 21[port], CurBio 74, MugS,
REnAW, SmATA 21[port],
WhoAm 74, −76, −78, −82,
WhoWest 78, WorAu 1975[port]
DelRey, Lester *TwCSFW 86*
DelRey, Lester 1915- *AmAu&B,*
AuBYP, BioIn 7, −9, −12, −13,
ConAu 17NR, −65, ConSFA,
DcLB 8[port], EncSF, LinLib L,
Novels, ScF&FL 1, −2, ScFSB,
SmATA 22[port], ThrBJA,
TwCSFW 86, WhoAm 76, −78, −80,
−82, −84, −86, WhoSciF, WorAl,
WrDr 84, −86
DelRey, Lester *see also* Rey, Lester Del
DelRey, Lester *see also* Saint John,
Philip
DelRey, Lester *see also* VanLhin, Erik
DelRey, Lester *see also* Wright,
Kenneth
DelRio, Eduardo 1934- *WorECar*
Delton, Jina 1961- *ConAu 106*
DeLuca, A Michael 1912- *ConAu 21R,*
DrAS 74F
DeLuca, A Michael 1912-1976
ConAu 120
Delving, Michael *SmATA X*
Delving, Michael 1914-1978 *AmAu&B,*
BioIn 11, ConAu X, IntAu&W 76X,
−77X, SmATA 3, −X, TwCCr&M 80,
−85, WorAu, WrDr 76
Delving, Michael *see also* Williams, Jay
DeMare, Eric S 1910- *Au&Wr 71,*
ConArch A, ConAu 6NR, −9R,
IntAu&W 76, −77
DeMarinis, Rick 1934- *BioIn 10,*
ConAu 9NR, −57
Demas, Vida 1927- *BioIn 11,*
ConAu 49, SmATA
DeMaupassant, Guy 1850-1893 *EuAu,*
FilmgC, HalFC 84, ScF&FL 1,
WhoHr&F

DeMaupassant, Guy see also
Maupassant, Guy De
DeMessieres, Nicole 1930-
ConAu 107, SmATA 39[port]
DeMille, Agnes WhoAm 84, -86,
WhoAmW 85
DeMille, Agnes 1905?- AmAu&B,
AmWomWr, BioIn 1,
-2, -3, -4, -5, -6, -7, -8, -9, -10,
-11, -12, BioNews 74, CelR,
ConAu X, ConTFT 3[port],
CurBio 43, -85[port], EncMT,
GoodHs, HerW, InWom, LibW,
NewYTBS 76, NotNAT, -A, OxAmH,
OxAmT 84, REnAL, WebAB, -79,
Who 74, -82, -83, WhoAm 74, -76,
-78, -80, -82, WhoAmW 74, -58,
-58A, -64, -64A, -66, -68, -70, -72,
-81, -83, WhoThe 72, -77, -81,
WhoWor 74, -78, WorAl,
WorAu 1975[port]
DeMille, Agnes 1908- BioIn 13,
HerW 84
DeMille, Agnes see also Prude, Agnes
George
DeMille, Nelson Richard 1943-
ConAu 6NR, -57, WhoE 77, -79,
-81, -83, -85, WhoWor 84
Deming, Richard 1915- AuBYP SUP,
BioIn 13, ConAu 3NR, -9R,
IntAu&W 76, -77, -82,
SmATA 24[port], TwCCr&M 80,
WrDr 76, -80, -82, -84
Deming, Richard 1915-1983
TwCCr&M 85
Dempsey, Hugh Aylmer 1929-
ConAu 11NR, -69, IntAu&W 86,
OxCan SUP
Demuth, Patricia Brennan 1948-
ConAu 118
Dengler, Dieter 1938- BioIn 7, -9,
ConAu 102
Dengler, Marianna 1935- ConAu 102
Denham, Bertie 1927- ConAu 93
Denisoff, R Serge 1939-
AmM&WS 73S, -78S, ConAu 33R,
WhoAm 84, WhoMW 84, WrDr 76,
-80, -82, -84, -86
Denker, Henry OxAmT 84
Denker, Henry 1912- AmAu&B,
AmNov, AuNews 1, BiE&WWA,
BioIn 2, -10, CnMD SUP,
ConAu 33R, NotNAT, WhoAm 74,
-76, -78, -80, -82, -84, -86,
WhoThe 81, WhoWor 82, WrDr 80,
-82, -84, -86
Dennis, Henry Charles 1918-
AmM&WS 73S, ConAu 41R,
WhoF&I 74, -75, -77, WhoWest 74,
-76, -78
Dennis, Patrick 1921-1976 AmAu&B,
BioIn 4, -5, -6, -7, -10, -11,
ConAu X, CurBio 59, -77N,
NewYTBS 76, ObitOF 79,
WhoAm 74, -76, WhoThe 81N,
WorAl, WorAu, WrDr 76
Dennis, Patrick see also Tanner,
Edward Everett, III
Dennis, Peggy 1909- BioIn 11,
ConAu 77
Dennys, Rodney Onslow 1911-
ConAu 65, Who 74, -82, -83, -85,
WhoGen 81
Densen-Gerber, Judianne 1934-
AuBYP SUP, BiDrAPA 77, BioIn 9,
-12, -13, ConAu 37R,
CurBio 83[port], NewYTBE 70,
WhoAm 76, -78, -80, -82, -84,
WhoAmL 83, -85, WhoAmW 74,
-70, -72, -75, -77, -79, -81, -83,
WhoE 74, -77, -79, -81, -83, -85,
WomPO 78, WrDr 76, -80, -82, -84,
-86
Denver, John 1943- Baker 84,
BioIn 10, -11, -12, BioNews 74,
ChhPo S2, CurBio 75,
EncFCWM 83[port], EncPR&S 74,
-77, HalFC 84, IlEncRk,
NewYTBE 73, RkOn 78, -84,
RolSEnR 83, WhoAm 76, -78, -80,
-82, -84, -86, WhoRock 81[port],
WhoRocM 82, WorAl
Denvir, Bernard 1917- ConAu 115

Denzel, Justin F 1917- ConAu 4NR,
-53, SmATA 38, -46[port]
DePauw, Linda Grant 1940-
AuBYP SUP, BioIn 13, ConAu 9NR,
-21R, DrAS 74H, -78H, -82H,
SmATA 24[port], WhoAm 84, -86,
WhoAmW 83, -85, -87, WhoE 83,
-85
Derby, Pat 1942- BioIn 10, ConAu 69
Derleth, August 1909-1971 AmAu&B,
AmNov, AuBYP, BioIn 2, -3, -4, -6,
-7, -8, -9, -10, -12, BkC 6,
ChhPo, -S2, CnDAL, ConAu 1R,
-4NR, -29R, ConLC 31[port],
ConNov 72, DcLB 9[port], DcLEL,
EncMys, EncSF, NewYTBE 71,
Novels, OxAmL, -83, REn, REnAL,
ScF&FL 1, -2, ScFSB, SmATA 5,
SupFW, TwCA, -SUP,
TwCCr&M 80, -85, TwCSFW 86,
WhAm 5, WhNAA, WhoHr&F,
WhoSciF
DeRopp, Robert Sylvester 1913-
Au&Wr 71, ConAu 17R
Desai, Anita 1937- CasWL, ConAu 81,
ConLC 19, -37[port], ConNov 72,
-76, -82, -86, DcLEL 1940,
IntAu&W 76, -77, -82, Novels,
OxEng 85, REn, WorAu 1975[port],
WrDr 76, -80, -82, -84, -86
DeSaint-Exupery, Antoine 1900-1944
ModRL, ObitOF 79, ScF&FL 1,
WhAm 2
DeSaint-Exupery, Antoine see also
Saint-Exupery, Antoine De
Desbarats, Peter 1933- CanWW 79,
-80, -81, -83, ConAu 10NR, -17R,
OxCan, SmATA 39[port]
Deschin, Celia Spalter 1903-
ConAu 104, WhoAmW 74, -72, -75
DeSchweinitz, Karl 1887-1975
AuBYP SUP, BioIn 10, ConAu 57,
-61, NatCAB 63[port], ObitOF 79,
WhAm 6
DeShields, James Thomas 1891-
TexWr
Desmond, Adrian J 1947-
ConAu 8NR, -61
Desmond, Alice Curtis 1897-
AmAu&B, AuBYP, BioIn 7, -11,
ConAu 1R, -2NR, SmATA 8,
WhoAm 74, -76, -84, -86,
WhoAmW 74, -58, -61, -64, -66,
-68, -70, -72, -75, -77, WhoE 74,
-75, -77
Desoutter, Denis Marcel 1919-
Au&Wr 71
DesPres, Terrence 1939- ConAu 73,
DrAS 82E
Dethier, Vincent G 1915- WrDr 86
Dethier, Vincent Gaston 1915-
AmM&WS 76P, -79P, -82P, -86P,
BlueB 76, ConAu 9NR, -65,
IntAu&W 76, -77, IntWW 74, -75,
-76, -77, -78, -79, -80, -81, -82,
-83, McGMS 80[port], WhoAm 74,
-76, -86, WhoE 74, WrDr 76, -80,
-82, -84
DeTocqueville, Alexis 1805-1859
OxAmL, REnAL, WhAm HS
DeTocqueville, Alexis see also
Tocqueville, Alexis, Comte De
DeToledano, Ralph DrAP&F 85
DeToledano, Ralph 1916- AmAu&B,
AuNews 1, BioIn 3, -5, -6, -10,
CurBio 62, ConAu 37R,
DeTrevino, Elizabeth Borton BioIn 13
DeTrevino, Elizabeth Borton 1904-
Au&ICB, BioIn 10, -11, ForWC 70,
MorBMP, OxChL, ScF&FL 1,
NewbC 1966, TwCCW 78, -83,
WrDr 80, -82, -84
DeTrevino, Elizabeth Borton see also
Trevino, Elizabeth B De
Detz, Joan WrDr 86
Detz, Joan 1951- ConAu 118
Deutsch, Babette 1895-1982 AmAu&B,
AmWomWr, AnObit 1982[port],
AnCL, Au&Wr 71, BioIn 4, -6, -9,
-12, -13, BlueB 76, ChhPo, -S1, -S2,
-S3, ConAmL, ConAu 1R, -4NR,
-108, ConLC 18, ConPo 70, -75, -80,
DcLB 45[port], DcLEL, DrAS 74E,

EvLB, IntAu&W 76, -77, -82,
IntWW 74, -75, -76, -77, -78, -79,
-80, -81, -82, -83N, IntWWP 77,
-82, LinLib L, LongCTC, MorJA,
NewYTBS 82, Novels, OxAmL, -83,
PenC AM, RAdv 1, REn, REnAL,
SmATA 1, -33N, TwCA, -SUP,
TwCWr, WhAm 8, WhE&EA,
WhNAA, WhoAm 74, -58, -64, -66, -68,
-70, WhoWor 74, WhoWorJ 72,
WrDr 76, -80, -82
Deutsch, Robert W 1924-
AmM&WS 86P
Deutsch, Robert William 1924-
WhoAm 84, -86
Deutsch, Ronald M 1928- ConAu 1R,
-4NR
DeValois, Ninette NewOxM
DeValois, Ninette 1898- Au&Wr 71,
BiDD, BioIn 1, -2, -3, -4, -5, -6, -8,
-9, -11, -13, BlueB 76, ConAu 115,
CurBio 49, InWom, IntDcWB,
IntWW 74, -75, -76, -77, -78, -79,
-80, -81, -82, -83, PlP&P, WhThe,
Who 74, -82, -83, -85, WhoAmW 74,
-68, -70, -72, WorAl
DeVeaux, Alexis ConAu 65,
DrAP&F 85, NatPD
Deveaux, Alexis 1948- BioIn 13,
DcLB 38[port], InB&W 85
Devereux, Frederick Leonard, Jr.
1914- BioIn 11, ConAu 1NR, -49,
SmATA 9, WhoE 77, -79, -81
Devi, Shakuntala 1932?- BioIn 2
Devine, D M 1920- ConAu 1NR,
TwCCr&M 80, WrDr 82
Devine, D M 1920-1980 TwCCr&M 85
Devine, D M see also Devine, Dominic
Devine, Dominic 1920- ConAu X,
EncMys, WrDr 76, -80
Devine, Dominic see also Devine, D M
Devlin, Bernadette Who 85
Devlin, Bernadette 1947- BioIn 8, -9,
-10, -11, -12, BlueB 76, CelR,
ConAu 105, CurBio 70, HerW,
Who 74, -82, -83, WhoAmW 74, -72,
WhoWor 74, WorAl
Devorkin, David Hyam 1944-
AmM&WS 86P
Devries, Peter DrAP&F 85
DeVries, Peter 1910- AmAu&B,
Au&Wr 71, BiE&WWA, BioIn 4, -5,
-6, -8, -10, -12, -13, BlueB 76,
CelR, CnDAL, ConAu 17R,
ConLC 1, -2, -3, -7, -10, -28[port],
ConNov 72, -76, -82, -86,
ConTFT 1, CurBio 59, DcLB 6,
-Y82A[port], DcLEL 1940, EncWL,
IntAu&W 76, -77, -82, IntWW 74,
-75, -76, -77, -78, -79, -80, -81,
-82, -83, LinLib L, ModAL, -S2,
-S1, NewYTBS 83[port], NotNAT,
Novels[port], OxAmL, -83, PenC AM,
REnAL, Who 74, -82, -83, -85,
WhoAm 74, -76, -78, -80, -82, -84,
-86, WhoTwCL, WhoWor 74,
WorAu, WrDr 76, -80, -82, -84, -86
DeWeese, Gene SmATA X
DeWeese, Gene 1934- ConAu X,
EncSF, ScFSB, TwCSFW 86,
WrDr 84, -86
Dewhurst, Keith 1931- BioIn 10,
ConAu 18NR, -61, ConDr 73, -77,
-82, WhoThe 81, WhoWor 76,
WrDr 76, -80, -82, -84, -86
Dewitz, Ludwig Richard Max 1916-
DrAS 74P, -78P, -82P
Dexter, Colin 1930- IntAu&W 86,
TwCCr&M 85, WrDr 86
Dexter, Pat Egan ConAu 81
Deyneka, Anita 1943- BioIn 13,
ConAu 11NR, -61, SmATA 24[port]
Dhondy, Farrukh 1944- OxChL,
TwCChW 83, WrDr 86
Diamond, Neil WhoAm 84
Diamond, Neil 1941- Baker 84,
BiDAmM, BioIn 8, -9, -10, -11, -12,
BioNews 74, CelR, ConAu 108,

ConLC 30[port], CurBio 81[port],
EncPR&S 74, -77, HalFC 84,
IlEncRk, IntMPA 84, NewYTBE 72,
RkOn 78, -84, RolSEnR 83,
WhoAm 74, -76, -78, -80, -82, -84,
-86, WhoRock 81, WhoRocM 82,
WorAl
Diamonstein, Barbaralee D
ConAu 15NR, -21R, IntAu&W 82,
WhoAm 76, -78, -80, -82,
WhoAmA 82, WhoAmW 68, -70,
-75, -77, WhoE 77
Diamonstein, Barbaralee Dworkin
WhoAm 84
DiBacco, Thomas Victor 1937-
WhoAm 84, -86, WhoE 85
Dibdin, Michael 1947- ConAu 77
Dibner, Bern 1897- BioIn 10, -11, -12,
ConAu 107, LElec, St&PR 75,
WhoAm 74, -76, -78, -80,
WhoEng 80, WhoTech 82, -84
DiCerto, J J 1933- ConAu 13NR,
-21R, WrDr 76, -80, -82, -84, -86
Dick, Philip K 1928-1982 AmAu&B,
AnObit 1982, BioIn 12, -13,
ConAu 2NR, -106, -16NR, -49,
ConLC 10, -30[port], ConNov 76,
-82, ConSFA, DcLB 8[port], EncSF,
LinLib L, Novels, PostFic, ScF&FL 1,
-2, ScFSB[port], TwCSFW 86,
WhoAm 80, WhoSciF, WorAl,
WrDr 76, -80, -82
Dick, Philip Kindred 1928-1982
WhAm 8
Dickens, Charles 1812-1870
Alli, -SUP, AtlBL, AuBYP, BbD,
BiD&SB, BioIn 1, -2, -3, -4, -5, -6,
-7, -8, -9, -10, -11, -12, -13,
BritAu 19, BritWr 5, CasWL, CelCen,
Chambr 3, ChhPo, -S1, -S2,
-S3, CrtT 3, -4, CyEd, CyWA,
DcAmSR, DcBiA, DcBiPP,
DcEnA, -AP, DcEnL, DcEuL,
DcLB 21[port], -55[port], DcLEL,
Dis&D, EncMys, EncO&P 2, -78,
EvLB, FamAYP, FilmgC, HalFC 84,
HsB&A, JBA 34, LinLib L, -S,
LongCEL, McGEWB, MnBBF,
MouLC 3, NewC, NewEOp 71,
NinCLC 3[port], -8[port], NotNAT B,
Novels[port], OxAmH, OxAmL, -83,
OxAusL, OxChL, OxEng, OxFilm,
OxMus, OxThe, PenC AM, -ENG,
PlP&P, RAdv 1, RComWL, REn,
ScF&FL 1, SmATA 15, Str&VC,
SupFW, TelT, TwCCr&M 80A, -85A,
WebE&AL, WhDW, WhAm HS,
WhoChL, WhoHr&F, WhoSpyF,
WorAl
Dickens, Monica 1915- ConNov 86,
WrDr 86
Dickens, Monica Enid 1915-
Au&Wr 71, AuBYP SUP, BioIn 1, -2,
-3, -4, -5, -6, -7, -9, -10, -11,
CathA 1930, ConAu 2NR, -5R,
ConNov 72, -76, -82, DcLEL, EvLB,
ForWC 70, IntAu&W 76, -77, -82,
IntWW 79, -78, -79, -80, -81, -82,
-83, LongCTC, NewC, NewYTBS 77,
Novels, PenC ENG, REn, SmATA 4,
TwCWr, WhE&EA, Who 74, -82,
-83, -85, WhoAmW 74, -58, -61,
-68, -70, -72, -75, WorAu, WrDr 76,
-80, -82, -84
Dicker, Eva Barash 1936- ConAu 107
Dickerson, Eric NewYTBS 84[port],
WhoBlA 85
Dickerson, Robert B, Jr. 1955-
ConAu 106
Dickerson, Roy Ernest 1886-1965
AmAu&B, Au&Wr 71, BioIn 13,
ConAu 5R, -103, CurBio 44,
IndAu 1917, OhA&B, SmATA 26N,
WhAm 4, -7, WhE&EA, WhLit,
WhNAA
Dickey, Glenn Ernest, Jr. 1936-
ConAu 4NR, -53, WhoAm 80, -82,
-84, -86, WhoWest 76, -78
Dickey, James DrAP&F 85
Dickey, James 1923- AmAu&B, AnCL,
AuNews 1, -2, BioIn 8, -9, -10, -11,
-12, -13, BlueB 76, CelR, ConAu 9R,

–85, WhoAmW 58, –61, WrDr 82, –84

Doming, Eric 1918- *ConAu 9R*

Donaldson, Frances 1907-
ConAu 12NR, –61, Who 82, –83, WrDr 76, –80, –82, –84, –86

Donaldson, Margaret 1926-
ConAu 103, –20NR

Donaldson, Sam 1934- *BioIn 13, ConAu 111, EncTwCJ*

Donaldson, Stephen R 1947- *BioIn 12, –13, ConAu 13NR, –89, SupFW, WhoAm 82, WrDr 84, –86*

Donaldson, Stephen Reeder 1947-
WhoAm 84, –86

Donleavy, J P *DrAP&F 85*

Donleavy, J P 1926- *AmAu&B, Au&Wr 71, AuNews 2, BlueB 76, CnMD, ConAu 9R, ConDr 73, –77, –82, ConLC 1, –4, –6, –10, ConNov 72, –76, –82, –86, CurBio 79, DcIrL, DcLB 6, IntAu&W 76, LinLib L, ModAL, ModWD, Novels, OxAmL, –83, OxEng 85, PenC AM, RAdv 1, TwCWr, WebE&AL, WhoThe 72, –77, –81, WhoTwCL, WorAl, WorAu, WrDr 76, –80, –82, –84, –86*

Donleavy, James Patrick 1926-
BiDIrW, BioIn 8, –9, –10, –11, –12, –13, DcLEL 1940, IntAu&W 77, –82, –86, IntWW 74, –75, –76, –77, –78, –79, –80, –81, –82, –83, Who 74, –82, –83, –85, WhoAm 74, –76, –78, –80, –82, –84, –86, WhoWor 74, –76, –78, –80, –82, –84, –87

Donnan, Marcia Jeanne 1932-
ConAu 104, WhoLab 76, WomPO 76

Donnelly, Elfie *TwCChW 83B*

Donovan 1946- *AntBDN M, BioIn 8, EncFCWM 69, –83, EncPR&S 74, –77, IlEncRk, RkOn 78, –84, RolSEnR 83, WhoHol A, WhoRock 81, WhoRocM 82, WorAl*

Donovan, Frank Robert 1906-1975
AuBYP, BioIn 8, –10, ConAu 1R, –6NR, –61, SmATA 30N

Donovan, Hedley 1914- *ConAu 115, EncTwCJ, Who 85*

Donovan, John 1928- *BioIn 13, ChlLR 3, ConAu 35, ConLC 35, FifBJA, OxChL, SmATA 29, TwCCW 78, –83, WrDr 84, –86*

Donovan, Robert J 1912-
ConAu 18NR

Donovan, Robert John 1912-
AmAu&B, Au&Wr 71, BioIn 9, BlueB 76, ConAu 1R, –2NR, WhoAm 74, –76, –78, –80, –82, –84, –86, WhoWor 74, –76

Doob, Leonard W 1909- *AmAu&B, AmM&WS 73S, –78S, AuBYP SUP, BioIn 11, BlueB 76, ConAu 2NR, –5R, IntWW 74, –75, –76, –77, –78, –79, –80, –81, –82, –83, SmATA 8, WhoAm 74, –76, –78, –80, –82, WhoWor 74, WrDr 76, –80, –82, –84, –86*

Doob, Leonard William 1909-
WhoAm 84, –86

Doody, Margaret Anne 1939-
ConAu 11NR, –69, DrAS 82E, WhoAm 84, –86, WhoAmW 79, –81, –83, –85, –87

Dooley, Thomas Anthony 1927-1961
AmAu&B, BioIn 4, –5, –6, –7, –8, –9, –10, –11, –12, ConAu 93, CurBio 57, –61, DcAmB S7, DcCathB, InSci, LinLib L, LuthC 75, ObitOF 79, WebAB, –79, WebAMB, WhAm 4A

Dooley, Thomas Anthony, III
1927-1961 *DcAmMeB 84*

Doone, Jice 1887-1964 *ConAu X*

Doone, Jice *see also* Marshall, James Vance

Doray, Maya 1922- *ConAu 45*

Dore, Ronald Philip 1925-
ConAu 15NR, –89, Who 82, –83, –85

Dorman, Michael 1932- *AuBYP SUP, BioIn 10, ConAu 5NR, –13R, IntAu&W 77, SmATA 7, WhoE 74, –75, WrDr 76, –80, –82, –84*

Dorman, Michael L 1932- *WrDr 86*

Dorman, N B 1927- *ConAu 106, SmATA 39*

Dorman, Sonya *DrAP&F 85*

Dorman, Sonya 1924- *ConAu 73, EncSF, ScFSB, TwCSFW 86, WhoSciF, WrDr 84, –86*

Dornberg, John Robert 1931-
AuBYP SUP, ConAu 1R, –1NR, IntAu&W 77, –82, WrDr 76, –80, –82, –84

Dorson, Richard M 1916-1981
BioIn 13, ConAu 105, –106, DrAS 74H, –78H, NewYTBS 81, SmATA 30[port], WhAm 8, WhoAm 76, –78, WhoWor 78, –80

Dorson, Richard Mercer 1916-1981
BioIn 13

DosPassos, John 1896-1970 *AmAu&B, AmNov, AmWr, AtlBL, Au&Wr 71, BiE&WWA, BioIn 1, –2, –3, –4, –5, –6, –7, –8, –9, –10, –11, –12, –13, CasWL, Chambr 3, CnDAL, CnMD, ConAmA, ConAmL, ConAu 3NR, –29R, ConLC 1, –4, –8, –11, –25[port], CurBio 40, –70, CyWA, DcAmSR, DcLB 4, –9[port], –DS1[port], DcLEL, EncAB-H, EncWL, –2[port], EvLB, LinLib L, –S, LongCTC, MakMC, McGEWB, ModAL, –S2, –S1, ModWD, NewYTBE 70, Novels[port], ObitOF 79, OxAmL, –83, OxEng, PenC AM, RAdv 1, REn, REnAL, TwCA, –SUP, TwCWr, WebAB, –79, WebE&AL, WhDW, WhAm 5, WhE&EA, WhNAA, WhoTwCL, WorAl*

DosPassos, John *see also* Passos, John Dos

Doss, Helen 1918?- *AuBYP, BioIn 8, –12, ConAu 6NR, –9R, SmATA 20, WhoAmW 61*

Doster, William Clark 1921-
ConAu 13R, DrAS 74E, –78E, –82E

Doster, William Ernst 1941-
WhoAmL 79

Dostoyevsky, Fyodor Mikhailovich
1821-1881 *AtlBL, AuBYP SUP, BbD, BiD&SB, CasWL, ClDMEL, CyWA, DcEuL, DcRusL, EncMys, EncSF, EncWT, EuAu, EvEuW, McGEWB, NewC, Novels[port], OxEng, PenC EUR, RComWL, REn, WhDW, WorAl*

Doty, Jean Slaughter 1929-
AuBYP SUP, BioIn 13, ConAu 2NR, –45, SmATA 28[port]

Doubtfire, Dianne Joan 1918-
Au&Wr 71, ConAu 1R, –1NR, IntAu&W 76, –77, –82, –86, SmATA 29[port], WhoWor 76, –78, WrDr 76, –80, –82, –84

Doughty, Wayne Dyre 1929-1968
IndAu 1917

Douglas, Arthur 1928- *WrDr 86*

Douglas, Carole Nelson 1944-
ConAu 107, IntAu&W 86

Douglas, James McM *ConAu X, SmATA 5*

Douglas, James McM *see also* Butterworth, W E

Douglas, John Scott 1905- *AuBYP, BioIn 8, WhNAA*

Douglas, Lloyd C *ConAu X*

Douglas, Lloyd C 1877-1951
HalFC 84, OxAmL 83

Douglas, Lloyd Cassel 1877-1951
AmAu&B, AmNov, BioIn 1, –2, –3, –4, –5, –10, ConAu 120, CyWA, DcAmB S5, EvLB, FilmgC, IndAu 1917, LinLib L, LongCTC, MichAu 80, Novels, ObitOF 79, OhA&B, OxAmL, PenC AM, REn, REnAL, TwCA, –SUP, TwCWr, WebAB, –79, WhAm 3, WhNAA, WorAl

Douglas, Martha Carol 1937-
WhoWest 84

Douglas, Mike 1925- *AmPS B, BioIn 7, –8, –9, –10, –11, –12, –13, BioNews 75, CelR, CmpEPM,*

ConAu 89, CurBio 68, IntMPA 79, –81, –82, –84, –86, LesBEnT, NewYTET, RkOn 78, WhoAm 74, –76, –78, –80, –82, WhoE 74, WhoHol A, WhoRocM 82, WorAl

Douglas, William O 1898-1980
ConAu 21NR, OxAmL 83

Douglas, William Orville 1898-1980
AmAu&B, AmBench 79, AnObit 1980[port], Au&Wr 71, AuBYP, BiDFedJ, BioIn 1, –2, –3, –4, –5, –6, –7, –8, –9, –10, –11, –12, –13, BlueB 76, CelR, CngDr 74, –77, –79, ConAu 9R, –93, ConIsC 1[port], CurBio 41, –50, –80N, DcAmSR, DcLEL 1940, DcPol, DrAS 74P, –78P, EncAAH, EncAB-H, IntAu&W 77, IntWW 74, –75, –76, –77, –78, –79, LinLib L, –S, McGEWB, MinnWr, NewYTBE 70, NewYTBS 75, –80[port], OxAmH, OxAmL, OxLaw, PolProf E, PolProf J, PolProf K, PolProf NF, PolProf T, REn, REnAL, TwCA SUP, WebAB, –79, WhAm 7, Who 74, WhoAm 74, –76, –78, WhoAmL 78, –79, WhoAmP 73, –75, –77, –79, WhoGov 77, –72, –75, WhoPNW, WhoS&SW 73, –75, WhoWest 74, –76, WhoWor 74, –78, WorAl, WrDr 76

Douglass, Frederick 1817-1895
Alli SUP, AmAu, AmAu&B, AmBi, AmRef[port], ApCAB, BbD, BiDAmL, BiD&SB, BiDSA, BioIn 1, –2, –3, –4, –5, –6, –7, –8, –9, –10, –11, –12, –13, BlkAWP, CelCen, Chambr 3, CivWDc, CyAG, DcAmAu, DcAmB, DcBiPP, –A, DcLB 1, –43[port], –50[port], DcNAA, Drake, EncAAH, EncAB-H, EncAJ[port], EncSoH, HarEnUS[port], InB&W 80, –85, LinLib L, –S, McGEWB, MemAm, NatCAB 2, NegAl 76[port], –83[port], NinCLC 7[port], OxAmH, OxAmL, –83, REn, REnAL, SelBAAf, SelBAAu, SmATA 29[port], TwCBDA, WebAB, –79, WebE&AL, WhAm HS, WhAm, WorAl

Douty, Esther M 1911-1978
AuBYP SUP, BioIn 11, ConAu 3NR, –5R, –85, SmATA 23N, –8

Douty, Esther Morris 1911-1978
BioIn 13

Dowd, David L 1918-1968 *WhAm 5*

Dowdell, Dorothy Florence Karns
1910- *BioIn 11, ConAu 5NR, –9R, ForWC 70, SmATA 12, WhoAmW 74, –68, –70, –72, –75, –77*

Dowden, Anne Ophelia 1907-
ConAu 18NR, FifBJA[port]

Dowden, Anne Ophelia Todd 1907-
AuBYP, BioIn 8, –10, –12, ConAu 3NR, –9R, IlsCB 1967, SmATA 7, WhoAmA 73, –76, –78, –80, –82, –84, WhoAmW 83, WrDr 76, –80, –82, –84, –86

Dowden, Anne Ophelia Todd *see also* Todd, Anne Ophelia

Dowdey, Clifford 1904- *AmAu&B, AmNov, BioIn 2, –4, ConAu 9R, EncSoH, REnAL, TwCA, –SUP, WhoAm 74, –76, –78, –80*

Dowdey, Clifford Shirley, Jr.
1904-1979 *WhAm 8*

Down, Goldie 1918- *ConAu 11NR, –25R*

Downer, Marion 1892?-1971 *AuBYP, BioIn 8, –9, –13, ConAu 33R, SmATA 25[port]*

Downey, Fairfax Davis 1893-
AmAu&B, AmSCAP 66, AuBYP, BioIn 1, –2, –8, –9, ChhPo, ConAu 1R, –1NR, CurBio 49, IntAu&W 76, –82, OxCan, REnAL, SmATA 3, WhE&EA, WhNAA, WhoAm 74, –76, –78, –80, WrDr 76, –80, –82, –84, –86

Downey, Glanville 1908- *ConAu 1R, –1NR, DrAS 74H, –78H, –82H, WhoAm 74, –76, –78, –80*

Downie, John *OxCanL*

Downie, John 1931- *AmM&WS 73P, –79P, –82P, –86P, ConAu 108, OxCan SUP*

Downie, Leonard, Jr. 1942-
ConAu 1NR, –49, WhoAm 84, –86, WrDr 76, –80, –82, –84, –86

Downie, Mary Alice *OxCanL*

Downie, Mary Alice 1934- *BioIn 13, CaW, CaNWW 83, ConAu 10NR, –25R, IntAu&W 76, –82, OxCan SUP, SmATA 13, TwCCW 78, –83, WhoCanL 85, WrDr 76, –80, –82, –84, –86*

Downie, Mary Alice Dawe 1934-
IntAu&W 86

Downs, Robert C S *DrAP&F 85*

Downs, Robert C S 1937-
ConAu 1NR, –45, WrDr 80, –82, –84

Downs, Robert Conrad Smith 1937-
IntAu&W 86

Doyle, Arthur Conan 1859-1930
OxEng 85, TwCCr&M 85, TwCSFW 86

Doyle, Brian 1935- *WhoCanL 85*

Doyle, Robert V 1916- *ConAu 9NR, –65*

Doyle, Sir Arthur Conan 1859-1930
Alli SUP, AtlBL, AuBYP, BbD, BiD&SB, BiDPara, BiHiMed, BioIn 1, –2, –3, –4, –5, –6, –7, –8, –9, –10, –11, –12, –13, CarSB, CasWL, Chambr 3, ChhPo, –S1, CmScLit, ConAu 104, CyWA, DcBiA, DcEnA AP, DcLB 18[port], DcLEL, DcNaB 1922, Dis&D, EncMys, EncO&P 2, –78, EncSF, EvLB, FilmgC, HalFC 84, JBA 34, LinLib L, –S, LongCEL, LongCTC, McGEWB, MnBBF, ModBrL, NewC, NotNAT B, Novels[port], OxChL, OxEng, OxMed 86, PenC ENG, PlP&P, PoIre, RAdv 1, REn, ScF&FL 1, ScFSB, SmATA 24[port], TelT, TwCA, –SUP, TwCCr&M 80, TwCLC 7[port], TwCWr, WebE&AL, WhDW, WhE&EA, WhLit, WhThe, WhoBW&I A, WhoChL, WhoHr&F, WhoSciF, WhoSpyF, WhoTwCL, WorAl

Doyle, Sir Arthur Conan *see also* Conan Doyle, Arthur

Dozois, Gardner R 1947- *ConAu 108, EncSF, ScF&FL 1, WhoSciF, WrDr 84*

Drabble, Margaret 1939- *Au&Wr 71, BioIn 10, –11, –12, –13, BlueB 76, ConAu 13R, –18NR, ConLC 2, –3, –5, –8, –10, –22[port], ConNov 72, –76, –82, –86, CurBio 81[port], DcLB 14[port], DcLEL 1940, EncWL 2, IntAu&W 76, –77, IntDcWB, IntWW 74, –75, –76, –77, –78, –79, –80, –81, –82, –83, LongCTC, ModBrL S2, –S1, NewYTBS 77, Novels, RAdv 1, SmATA 48[port], TwCWr, Who 74, –82, –83, –85, WhoAm 74, –76, –78, –82, –84, –86, WhoAmW 74, –70, –72, –75, WhoTwCL, WhoWor 78, –80, –82, –84, –87, WomWMM, WorAl, WorAu 1970, WrDr 76, –80, –82, –84, –86*

Drackett, Phil 1922- *Au&Wr 71, ConAu 3NR, –9R, IntAu&W 76, –77, WrDr 76, –80, –82, –84, –86*

Drago, Harry Sinclair 1888-1979
AmAu&B, BioIn 3, –12, ConAu 113, –89, NewYTBS 79, OhA&B, REnAW

Drago, Harry Sinclair 1888-1980
EncFWF

Dragonwagon, Crescent *DrAP&F 85*

Dragonwagon, Crescent 1952-
BioIn 11, –13, ConAu 12NR, –65, IntAu&W 86, SmATA 11, –41[port]

Drake, David 1945- *ConAu 17NR*

Drake, Elizabeth 1948- *ConAu 109*

Drake, George Randolph 1938-
ConAu 11NR, –69

Drake, Samuel Adams 1833-1905
Alli, –SUP, AmAu, AmAu&B, AmBi, ApCAB, BbD, BiD&SB, ChhPo S1, CyAL 2, DcAmAu, DcAmB, DcNAA, HarEnUS, NatCAB 25, TwCBDA, WhAm 1

Drane, John 1946- *ConAu 15NR*
Draper, Cena C 1907- *WrDr 86*
Draper, Cena Christopher 1907-
*ConAu 10NR, −17R, IntAu&W 77,
WrDr 76, −80, −82, −84*
Draper, R P 1928- *WrDr 86*
Dreifus, Claudia 1944- *BioIn 10,
ConAu 1NR, −45, ForWC 70, MugS,
WhoAmW 75, −77*
Dreiser, Theodore 1871-1945
*AmAu&B, AmLY, AmWr, ApCAB X,
AtlBL, BioIn 1, −2, −3, −4, −5, −6, −7,
−8, −9, −10, −11, −12, −13, CasWL,
Chambr 3, CnDAL, CnMD,
CnMWL, ConAmA, ConAmL,
ConAu 106, CurBio 46, CyWA,
DcAmAu, DcAmB S3, DcAmSR,
DcBiA, DcLB 9[port], −12[port],
−DS1[port], DcLEL, DcNAA,
EncAB-H, EncMys, EncWL, −2[port],
EvLB, FilmgC, HalFC 84,
IndAu 1816, LinLib L, −S, LongCTC,
MemAm, ModAL, −S2, −S1,
ModWD, NatCAB 15, −18, −34,
NotNAT B, Novels[port], ObitOF 79,
OxAmH, OxAmL, −83, OxEng,
PenC AM, RAdv 1, RComWL, REn,
REnAL, TwCA, −SUP,
TwCLC 10[port], −18[port], TwCWr,
WebAB, −79, WebE&AL, WhDW,
WhAm 2, WhE&EA, WhLit,
WhNAA, WhThe, WhoTwCL, WorAl*
Dresang, Eliza 1941- *BiDrLUS 70,
BioIn 12, ConAu 69, SmATA 19,
WhoLibI 82*
Drew, Elizabeth 1887-1965 *ChhPo,
ConAu 5R*
Drew, Wayland *CaW, OxCanL*
Dribben, Judith Strick 1923- *BioIn 9,
ConAu 37R*
Driggs, Howard Roscoe 1873-1963
*AmAu&B, EncAB 34, WhAm 4,
WhLit, WhNAA*
Driggs, Peter 1921-1975 *ConAu 25R*
Drimmer, Frederick 1916-
ConAu 7NR, −61
Drinkwater, John 1882-1937 *Alli,
BiDLA, BioIn 1, −2, −7, −9, −13,
CasWL, Chambr 3, ChhPo, −S1, −S2,
−S3, CnMD, CnThe, ConAu 109,
DcLB 10[port], −19[port], DcLEL,
DcNaB 1931, EncWT, EvLB, JBA 34,
LinLib L, −S, LongCTC,
McGEWD, −84[port], ModBrL,
ModWD, NewC, NotNAT A, −R,
OxEng, −85, OxMus, OxThe, −83,
PenC ENG, PlP&P, REn, Str&VC,
TwCA, −SUP, WebE&AL, WhE&EA,
WhLit, WhThe, WhoLA*
Driver, Tom Faw 1925- *BiE&WWA,
ConAu 1R, −1NR, DrAS 74P, −78P,
−82P, NotNAT, WhoAm 74, −76, −78,
−80, −82, −84, −86, WhoE 74,
WhoRel 75, −77, −85*
Droescher, Vitus B 1925- *ConAu 33R*
Drotning, Phillip Thomas 1920-
*ConAu 10NR, −25R, WhoF&I 85,
WhoMW 74, −76, −78, −80, −82, −84,
−86, WhoPubR 72, −76, WhoWor 87*
Drucker, Malka 1945- *BioIn 13,
ConAu 14NR, −81, SmATA 29,
−39[port]*
Drummond, Walter *ConAu X*
Drummond, Walter 1935- *AuBYP,
ConAu X, DcLEL 1940, SmATA X,
ThrBJA, WorAu 1970*
Drummond, Walter *see also* Silverberg,
Robert
Drury, Allen 1918- *AmAu&B, BioIn 5,
−10, BlueB 76, CelR, ConAu 18NR,
−57, ConLC 37[port], ConNov 72,
−76, −82, −86, DcLEL 1940, EncSF,
HalFC 84, IntAu&W 76, −77, −82,
IntWW 74, −75, −76, −77, −78, −79,
−80, −81, −82, −83, LinLib L, Novels,
OxAmL, −83, REnAL, ScF&L 1, −2,
ScFSB, TwCWr, Who 74, −82, −83,
WhoWor 74, −78, −80, −82, WorAl,
WorAu, WrDr 76, −80, −82, −84, −86*
Drury, John 1898-1972 *Au&Wr 71,
BioIn 9, ConAu 5R, −33R, WhAm 5*

Druxman, Michael B 1941-
*ConAu 1NR, −49, IntMPA 77, −75,
−76, −78, −79, −81, −82, −84, −86,
WhoWest 84*
Druxman, Michael Barnett 1941-
ConAu 16NR
Dryden, Ken *NewYTBS 84[port]*
Dryden, Ken 1947- *BioIn 9, −10, −11,
−12, ConAu 105, NewYTBE 71,
WhoE 74, −75, WhoHcky 73*
Dryden, Pamela *SmATA X, WrDr 86*
Dryden, Pamela *see also* Johnston,
Norma
Dryden, Spencer *WhoRocM 82*
Dryden, Spencer *see also* Jefferson
Airplane
Duane, Diane *TwCSFW 86*
Duane, Diane 1952- *SmATA 46*
Duane, Diane Elizabeth 1952-
WhoAmW 83, −85
Dubofsky, Melvyn 1934- *ConAu 16NR*
Dubois, Shirley Graham *BioIn 13*
DuBois, Shirley Graham 1907-1977
*AmWomD, BiDAfM, BioIn 11, −12,
BlkAWP, ConAu 69, −77, CurBio 77,
−77N, InB&W 80, IndAu 1917,
NewYTBS 77, ObitOF 79, ScF&FL 1,
SmATA 24[port], WrDr 76*
DuBois, Shirley Graham *see also*
Graham, Shirley
DuBois, W E B 1868-1963 *AmAu&B,
AmWr S2, ConAu 85, ConLC 1, −2,
−13, CurBio 40, −63, DcAmSR,
DcLB 47[port], −50[port], LinLib L,
MemAm, NegAl 76[port], −83[port],
ObitT 1961, OxAmL 83,
SmATA 42[port], WhLit, WorAl*
DuBois, William Edward Burghardt
1868-1962 *BiDNeoM*
DuBois, William Edward Burghardt
1868-1963 *AmRef[port], BiDAmEd,
BiDAmoPL, BiDSA, BioIn 1, −2, −3,
−4, −5, −6, −7, −8, −9, −10, −11, −12,
−13, BlkAWP, CasWL, ChhPo S3,
ConAmL, DcAmAu, DcAmB S7,
DcAmNB, DcLEL, EncAB-H, EncAJ,
EncSoH, HarEnUS, InB&W 80, −85,
LinLib S, LongCTC, LuthC 75,
McGEWB, NatCAB 13, Novels,
ObitOF 79, OxAmH, OxAmL,
OxEng 85, PenC AM, REn, REnAL,
SelBAAf, SelBAAu, TwCA, −SUP,
TwCBDA, WebAB, −79, WebE&AL,
WhAm 4, WhAmP, WhE&EA,
WhJnl, WhNAA, WhoColR*
Dubos, Rene J 1901-1982
WorAu 1975[port]
Dubos, Rene Jules 1901- *WhAm 8*
Dubos, Rene Jules 1901-1981
OxMed 86
Dubos, Rene Jules 1901-1982
*AmAu&B, AmM&WS 73P, −76P,
−79P, AnObit 1982[port], AsBiEn,
BiESc, BioIn 3, −5, −7, −9, −10, −12,
−13, BlueB 76, CelR, ConAu 5R,
−106, CurBio 52, −73, −82N, Future,
InSci, IntEnSS 79, IntWW 74, −75,
−76, −77, −78, −79, −80, −81, −82N,
McGEWB, McGMS 80[port],
NewYTBE 70, −71,
NewYTBS 82[port], WebAB, −79,
WhoAm 74, −76, −78, −80, −82,
WhoE 74, WhoWor 74, WrDr 80, −82*
Duboscq, Genevieve *BioIn 12*
Dubov, Paul d1979 *BioIn 12,
ConAu 89, −97, WhScrn 83*
DuBroff, Sidney 1929- *Au&Wr 71,
ConAu 9NR, −21R, IntAu&W 76*
Duckat, Walter Benjamin 1911-
ConAu 29R
Duckett, Alfred 1917?- *BlkAWP,
ConAu 45, InB&W 80, SelBAAu*
Duckett, Alfred A 1917?-1984
ConAu 114, NewYTBS 84
Dudley, Geoffrey A 1917- *WrDr 86*
Dudley, Geoffrey Arthur 1917-
*Au&Wr 71, ConAu 6NR, −13R,
IntAu&W 76, −77, −82, WhoWor 76,
−78, WrDr 76, −80, −82, −84*
Dudley, Nancy *BioIn 13*
Dudley, Nancy 1902- *AuBYP, BioIn 8,
−11, ConAu X, SmATA X,
WomPO 78*

Dudley, Nancy *see also* Cole, Lois
Dwight
Due, Linnea A 1948- *ConAu 105*
Duff, Annis *BioIn 5, ChhPo*
Duff, Annis 1904?-1986 *ConAu 120*
Duffy, Maureen 1933- *Au&Wr 71,
BioIn 10, −13, BlueB 76, ConAu 25R,
ConDr 73, −77, −82, ConLC 37[port],
ConNov 72, −76, −82, −86,
DcLB 14[port], DcLEL 1940,
IntAu&W 76, −77, −82, IntWWP 77,
−82, Novels, TwCWr, Who 82, −83,
WhoTwCL, WhoWor 80, WrDr 76,
−80, −82, −84, −86*
Dugan, James 1912-1967 *AnCL,
BioIn 7, ConAu 4NR, −5R,
ObitOF 79, WhAm 4*
Duggan, Alfred Leo 1903-1964 *AnCL,
AuBYP, BioIn 3, −4, −6, −7, −8, −13,
ConAu 73, FourBJA, LongCTC,
ModBrL, ObitOF 79,
SmATA 25[port], TwCA SUP,
TwCWr*
DuJardin, Rosamond Neal 1902-1963
*AmAu&B, AmWomWr, AuBYP SUP,
BioIn 2, −3, −6, −7, −9, ConAu 1R,
−103, CurBio 53, InWom, LinLib L,
MorJA, REnAL, SmATA 2, WhAm 4,
WhE&EA, WhoAmW 58, −61, −64*
Dukert, Joseph Michael 1929- *AuBYP,
BioIn 7, ConAu 3NR, −5R,
IntAu&W 77, WhoAmP 73, −75, −77,
−79, −81, −83, −85, WhoE 83,
WrDr 76, −80, −82, −84, −86*
Dulles, Allen Welsh 1893-1969
*AmAu&B, BioIn 1, −2, −3, −4, −5, −6,
−8, −9, −11, −12, ConAu P-2,
CurBio 49, −69, EncE 75, EncTR,
HisEWW, LinLib L, −S,
NatCAB 58[port], ObitOF 79,
ObitT 1961, PolProf E, PolProf K,
PolProf T, WhAm 5, WhE&EA,
WhWW-II, WorAl*
Dumas, Alexandre, Fils 1824-1895
*AtlBL, BbD, BiD&SB, BioIn 1, −2,
−4, −5, −6, −7, −9, −11, CasWL,
CelCen, CnThe, CyWA, DcBiA,
DcBiPP, DcEuL, DrBlPA, EncWT,
EuAu, EvEuW, FilmgC, HalFC 84,
HsB&A, InB&W 80, −85, LinLib L,
−S, McGEWD, −84[port], NewC,
NewEOp 71, NinCLC 9[port], OxFr,
OxThe, −83, PenC EUR, RComWL,
REn, REnWD, ScF&FL 1, WorAl*
Dumas, Alexandre, Pere 1802-1870
*AtlBL, BbD, BiD&SB, BioIn 1, −2,
−3, −4, −5, −6, −7, −9, −10, −11, −12,
−13, CarSB, CasWL, CelCen, CmCal,
CnThe, CyWA, DcBiPP, DcEuL,
Dis&D, EncWT, EuAu, EvEuW,
FilmgC, GrFLW, HalFC 84, HsB&A,
InB&W 80, LinLib L, −S, McGEWB,
McGEWD, DcBiA, NewC, MnBBF,
NewEOp 71, NinCLC 11[port],
NotNAT A, −B, Novels, OxChL,
OxEng, −85, OxFr, OxThe, −83,
PenC EUR, PlP&P, RComWL, REn,
REnWD, ScF&FL 1, SmATA 18,
WhDW, WhoChL, WhoHr&F, WorAl*
Dumas, Frederic 1913- *ConAu 69*
DuMaurier, Daphne 1907- *Au&Wr 71,
BiE&WWA, BioIn 1, −2, −4, −5, −8,
−9, −10, −11, BlueB 76, ConAu 5R,
−6NR, ConLC 6, −11, ConNov 72,
−76, −82, −86, CurBio 40, CyWA,
DcLEL, EncMys, EncSF, EncWT,
EvLB, FilmgC, HalFC 84, InWom,
IntAu&W 76, −77, −82, −86,
IntWW 74, −75, −76, −77, −78, −79,
−80, −81, −82, −83, LinLib L, −LP,
−S, LongCTC, ModBrL, NewC,
NotNAT, Novels[port], OxEng 85,
OxThe, PenC ENG, RAdv 1, REn,
ScF&FL 1, −2, SmATA 27[port],
TwCA, −SUP, TwCCr&M 80, −85,
TwCWr, WhE&EA, WhThe, Who 74,
−82, −83, −85, WhoAmW 74, −66,
−68, −70, −72, −75, WhoHr&F,
WhoWor 74, −76, −78, WorAl,
WrDr 76, −80, −82, −84, −86*
DuMaurier, Daphne *see also* Maurier,
Daphne Du

Dunaway, David King 1948-
ConAu 107, IntAu&W 86
Dunbar, Paul Laurence 1872-1906
*AmAu, AmAu&B, AmBi, AmWr S2,
ApCAB SUP, BiDAfM, BiDAmM,
BiD&SB, BioIn 1, −2, −3, −5, −6, −7,
−8, −9, −10, −11, −12, −13, BkCL,
BlkAWP, CasWL, Chambr 3,
ChhPo, −S1, −S2, −S3, CnDAL,
ConAu 104, DcAmAu, DcAmB,
DcAmNB, DcLB 50[port], −54[port],
DcNAA, Dis&D, InB&W 80, −85,
LinLib L, −S, McGEWB, ModBlW,
NatCAB 9, NegAl 76[port], −83[port],
OhA&B, OxAmL, −83, OxAmT 84,
PenC AM, RAdv 1, REn, REnAL,
SelBAAf, SelBAAu, SmATA 34[port],
TwCBDA, TwCLC 2, −12[port],
WebAB, −79, WebE&AL, WhAm 1,
WhFla, WorAl*
Dunbar, Robert E 1926- *ConAu 15NR,
−85, SmATA 32[port], WhoE 77, −79,
−81, WhoF&I 74, WhoMW 74*
Duncan, Frances *OxCanL*
Duncan, Frances 1942- *BioIn 13,
ConAu 17NR, −97, SmATA 48,
WhoCanL 85*
Duncan, Isadora 1878-1927 *AmAu&B,
AmBi, AmWomWr, BiDD, BioIn 1,
−2, −3, −4, −5, −6, −7, −8, −9, −10,
−11, −12, −13, CmCal, ConAu 118,
DcAmB, Dis&D, EncAB-H, GoodHs,
InWom, IntDcWB, LibW, LinLib L,
−S, McGEWB, NatCAB 22, NotAW,
NotNAT B, OxAmH, OxAmL, −83,
OxMus, REn, REnAL, WebAB, −79,
WhDW, WhAm 4, −HSA, WhThe,
WorAl*
Duncan, Lois 1934- *AuBYP, BioIn 8,
−9, −12, ConAu 2NR, −X,
ConLC 26[port], FifBJA[port],
IntAu&W 82, ScF&FL 1, −2,
SmATA 1, −36, SmATA 2AS[port],
TwCChW 83, WrDr 76, −80, −82,
−84, −86*
Duncan, Lois *see also* Arquette, Lois S
Duncan, Robert L *TwCCr&M 85*
Duncan, Robert L 1927- *ConAu 106,
ConAu 2AS[port], ScF&FL 1,
TwCCr&M 80, WrDr 82, −84, −86*
Duncan, Sylvia 1916- *Au&Wr 71*
Duncombe, Frances 1900- *BioIn 13,
ConAu 25R, SmATA 25*
Dunham, John L 1939- *BioIn 9,
ConAu 29R, EncASM, WhoBlA 75,
−77, −80, −85, WhoMW 74, −76, −78,
−80*
Dunham, Katherine
NewYTBS 86[port]
Dunham, Katherine 1910-
*AmSCAP 66, BiDAfM, BiE&WWA,
BioIn 1, −2, −3, −4, −5, −6, −8, −9,
−10, −11, −12, −13, BlkAWP,
ConAu 17NR, −65, CurBio 41,
DrBlPA, Ebony 1, GoodHs,
HerW, −84, InB&W 80, −85, InWom,
IntWW 74, −75, −76, −77, −78, −79,
−80, −81, −82, −83, LibW, LivgBAA,
NegAl 76, −83, NotNAT, −A,
OxAmT 84, REnAL, SelBAAf,
SelBAAu, WebAB, −79, WhDW,
WhoAm 74, −76, −78, WhoAmW 74,
−58, −64, −66, −68, −70, −72,
WhoBlA 75, −77, −80, −85, WhoE 74,
WhoHol A, WhoThe 72, −77, −81,
WhoWor 74, WomPO 76, WorAl*
Dunkling, Leslie Alan 1935-
ConAu 14NR, −81
Dunlap, Orrin Elmer, Jr. 1896-1970
*AmAu&B, BioIn 8, ConAu P-1,
NewYTBE 70, WhAm 5*
Dunlop, Agnes Mary Robinson d1982
*Au&Wr 71, AuBYP, BioIn 6, −8,
−9, BlueB 76, ConAu 9NR, −13R,
SmATA 3, Who 74, −82, WrDr 76,
−80, −82*
Dunlop, Agnes Mary Robinson *see also*
Kyle, Elisabeth
Dunlop, Eileen 1938- *BioIn 13,
ConAu 14NR, −73, SmATA 24[port],
WhoWor 80, WrDr 80, −82, −84*
Dunlop, Richard 1921- *ConAu 7NR,
−17R, WrDr 76, −80, −82, −84, −86*
Dunn, Judy *ConAu X*

Dunn, Judy 1942- *BioIn 10, ConAu X, SmATA 5*
Dunn, Judy *see also* Spangenburg, Judith Dunn
Dunn, Mary Lois 1930- *AuBYP SUP, BiDrLUS 70, BioIn 4, –10, ConAu 12NR, –61, SmATA 6, WhoLibS 66*
Dunn, Paul Harold 1924- *WhoRel 85, WhoWest 74*
Dunn, Stephen *DrAP&F 85*
Dunn, Stephen 1939- *ConAu 12NR, –33R, ConLC 36[port], ConPo 80, –85, IntAu&W 77, WrDr 76, –80, –82, –84, –86*
Dunnahoo, Terry *IntAu&W 86*
Dunnahoo, Terry 1927- *BioIn 10, ConAu 14NR, –41R, IntAu&W 77, –82, SmATA 7, WhoAm 74, –76, –78, –80, –82, –84, –86*
Dunne, John Gregory 1932- *AuNews 1, BioIn 9, –10, –12, –13, CmCal, ConLC 28[port], ConAu –25R, ConLC 28[port], CurBio 83[port], DcLB Y80B[port], OxAmL 83, TwCCr&M 80, WhoAm 84, –86, WorAl, WorAu 1975[port], WrDr 82, –84, –86*
Dunne, Mary Collins 1914- *AuBYP SUP, BioIn 11, ConAu 14NR, –41R, SmATA 11, WhoAmW 75, –77, –79*
Dunnett, Alastair MacTavish 1908- *Au&Wr 71, BlueB 76, ConAu 65, IntAu&W 76, –77, –82, IntWW 74, –75, –76, –77, –78, –79, –80, –81, –82, –83, IntYB 78, –79, –80, –81, –82, Who 74, –82, –83, –85, WhoWor 74, –76, –78*
Dunnett, Dorothy 1923- *Au&Wr 71, CmScLit, ConAu 1R, –3NR, IntAu&W 76, –77, –82, Novels, TwCCr&M 80, –85, WhoWor 76, –78, WrDr 76, –80, –82, –84, –86*
Dunnett, Margaret 1909- *ConAu 108*
Dunnett, Margaret 1909-1977 *SmATA 42[port]*
Dunning, Arthur Stephen 1924- *AuBYP SUP, DrAS 74E*
Dunning, Arthur Stephen *see also* Dunning, Stephen
Dunning, Stephen *DrAP&F 85*
Dunning, Stephen 1924- *ChhPo S1, ConAu 12NR, –25R, LEduc 74, MichAu 80*
Dunning, Stephen *see also* Dunning, Arthur Stephen
Dunsany, Baron Edward J M Drax Plunkett 1878-1957 *Alli SUP, AtlBL, BiDIrW, BioIn 1, –3, –4, –5, –9, –13, CasWL, ChhPo, –S1, –S2, –S3, CnMD, CnThe, ConAu 104, DcIrW 1, DcLB 10[port], DcLEL,*

EncMys, EvLB, JBA 34, LinLib L, –S, LongCTC, McGEWD, ModBrL, ModWD, NewC, OxEng, –85, OxThe, –83, PenC ENG, PIP&P, REn, REnWD, TwCA, –SUP, TwCWr, WhDW, WhE&EA, WhThe
Dunsheath, Percy 1886- *Au&Wr 71, BioIn 10, ConAu 107, IntAu&W 76, –77, IntWW 74, –75, –76, –77, –78, –79, WhE&EA, Who 74*
DuPlessis, Rachel Blau *DrAP&F 85*
Dupuy, R Ernest 1887-1975 *ConAu 1R, –6NR, –57, NewYTBS 75, ObitOF 79, WhAm 6, WhoWor 74*
Dupuy, Richard Ernest 1887-1975 *AmAu&B, BioIn 10, ConAu 1R, –57, DrAS 74H, WhoAm 74*
Dupuy, Trevor Nevitt 1916- *AuBYP, BioIn 8, –9, ConAu 1R, DrAS 74H, IntAu&W 77, SmATA 4, WhoAm 74, –76, –78, –80, –82, –84, –86, WhoWor 74, –84, –87, WrDr 76, –80, –82, –84, –86*
Durant, John 1902- *AmAu&B, AuBYP, BioIn 7, –13, ConAu 5NR, –9R, SmATA 27[port], WhoAm 74, –76, –78, –80, –82, WhoS&SW 73*
Durant, Will 1885-1981 *AmAu&B, AnObit 1981[port], ASpks, BlueB 76, CelR, ConAu 4NR, –9R, –105, CurBio 64, –82N, DcAmSR, DcLEL, EvLB, IntWW 74, –75, –76, –77, –78, –79, –80, –81, –82N, LinLib L, –S, LongCTC, NewYTBS 75, –81[port], OxAmL, –83, REn, REnAL, TwCA, –SUP, WebAB, –79, WhNAA, WhoWest 74, –76, WhoWor 74, –76, –78, –80*
Durer, Albrecht 1471-1528 *BioIn 13, OxEng 85*
Durfee, David A 1929- *WrDr 86*
Durfee, David Arthur 1929- *ConAu 29R, IntAu&W 77, WhoE 75, WrDr 76, –80, –82, –84*
Durgnat, Raymond Eric 1932- *Au&Wr 71, ConAu 17R, DcLEL 1940, IntAu&W 76, –77, WhoWor 76, WrDr 76, –80, –82, –84*
Durham, John 1925- *ConAu 107, DrAS 74E, –78E*
Durham, Marilyn *DrAP&F 85*
Durham, Marilyn 1930- *BioIn 9, –10, ConAu 49, EncFWF, WrDr 84, –86*
Durham, Philip 1912-1977 *ConAu 7NR, –9R, DrAS 74E, –78E, WhAm 7, WhoAm 76*
Durrell, Gerald Malcolm 1925- *Au&Wr 71, AuBYP, BioIn 5, –8, –9, –10, –11, –12, –13, BlueB 76, ConAu 4NR, –5R, DcLEL 1940, IntAu&W 76, –77, –82, IntWW 74, –75, –76, –77, –78, –79, –80, –81, –82, –83, LongCTC, NewC, REn,*

ScF&FL 1, –2, SmATA 8, TwCWr, Who 74, –82, –83, –85, WhoWor 74, –76, –78, –84, –87, WorAu, WrDr 76, –80, –82, –84
Durrell, Lawrence 1912- *ASpks, Au&Wr 71, BioIn 4, –5, –6, –7, –8, –9, –10, –11, –13, BlueB 76, CasWL, ChhPo, –S3, CnE&AP, CnMD, CnMWL, ConAu 9R, ConDr 73, –77, –82, ConLC 1, –4, –6, –8, –13, –27[port], –41[port], ConNov 72, –76, –82, –86, ConPo 70, –75, –80, –85, CurBio 63, DcLEL, EncSF, EncWL, –2[port], EvLB, IntAu&W 76, –77, IntWW 74, –75, –76, –77, –78, –79, –80, –81, –82, –83, IntWWP 77, LinLib L, –S, LongCEL, LongCTC, ModBrL, –S2, –S1, ModWD, NewC, Novels, OxEng, PenC ENG, RAdv 1, REn, ScF&FL 1, –2, ScFSB, TwCA SUP, TwCSFW 86, TwCWr, WebE&AL, WhDW, WhoAm 74, –82, –83, WhoFr 79, WhoTwCL, WhoWor 74, –78, –80, –82, WorAl, WrDr 76, –80, –82, –84, –86*
D'Urso, Joseph 1943- *BioIn 12*
Durst, Paul 1921- *Au&Wr 71, BioIn 11, ConAu 21R, IntAu&W 76, –77, –82, WrDr 84, –86*
Dutta, Reginald 1914- *ConAu 61*
Dutton, Mary 1922- *Au&Wr 71, ConAu 33R*
Duvall, Evelyn Millis 1906- *AmAu&B, AmM&WS 73S, –78S, BioIn 1, –11, ConAu 1R, –1NR, CurBio 47, ForWC 70, InWom, SmATA 9, WhoAm 74, –76, –78, WhoAmW 74, –58, –61, –64, –66, –68, –70, –72, WhoWor 74, WrDr 76, –80, –82, –84, –86*
Duvoison, Roger Antoine 1904-1968 *AmAu&B, AmPB, Au&ICB, Au&Wr 71, AuBYP, BkP, Cald 1938, ChhPo, –S1, –S2, ConAu 13R, FamAIYP, IlsBYP, IlsCB 1744, –1946, –1957, SmATA 2, Str&VC, WhoAmA 73, WhoChL, WhoGrA 62*
Dwiggins, Don 1913- *AuBYP SUP, BioIn 9, ConAu 8NR, –17R, SmATA 4*
Dwight, Allan *BioIn 13*
Dwight, Allan 1902?-1979 *BioIn 8, –11, ConAu X, SmATA X*
Dwight, Allan *see also* Cole, Lois Dwight
Dwyer-Joyce, Alice 1913- *Au&Wr 71, ConAu 4NR, –53, IntAu&W 76, –77, –82, WrDr 82, –84, –86*
Dybek, Stuart 1942- *ConAu 97, IntWWP 77, –82*
Dyer, T A *DrAP&F 85* **Dyer,** T A 1947- *ConAu 101*

Dygard, Thomas J 1931- *BioIn 13, ConAu 15NR, –85, SmATA 24[port], WhoAm 86*
Dygard, Thomas Jennings 1931- *WhoMW 84*
Dyke, Henry Van *DrAP&F 85*
Dyke, Henry Van 1852-1933 *Chambr 3, JBA 34, ScF&FL 1*
Dyke, Henry Van *see also* VanDyke, Henry
Dykeman, Wilma *WrDr 86*
Dykeman, Wilma 1920- *AmWomWr, BioIn 4, –7, ConAu 1NR, –X, DrAS 82H, ForWC 70, InWom, IntAu&W 77, WhoAmW 74, –58, –61, –75, –77, –83, –85, –87, WhoS&SW 75, –76, –78, WrDr 76, –80, –82, –84*
Dykeman, Wilma *see also* Stokely, Wilma Dykeman
Dykstra, Lenny *NewYTBS 86*
Dylan, Bob *NewYTBS 85[port]*
Dylan, Bob 1941- *AmAu&B, AmSCAP 66, Baker 78, –84, BiDAmM, BioIn 6, –7, –8, –9, –10, –11, –12, –13, BioNews 74, BlueB 76, CelR, ConAu 41R, –X, –6, –12, ConPo 70, –75, –80, –85, CurBio 65, DcLB 16[port], DcLEL 1940, EncFCWM 69, –83[port], EncPR&S 74, –77, IlEncRk, IntAu&W 76, –77, –82, –86, IntWW 74, –75, –76, –77, –78, –79, –80, –81, –82, –83, IntWWP 77, –82, LinLib L, MakMC, MugS, NewOxM, NewYTBE 71, –72, OxEng 85, PolProf J, RkOn 78, –84, RkOneH, RolSEnR 83, WebAB, –79, WhoAm 74, –76, –78, –80, –82, –84, –86, WhoE 74, –75, –77, WhoRock 81[port], WhoRocM 82, WhoWor 74, –76, –78, –80, –82, –84, WhoWorJ 78, WorAl, WrDr 76, –80, –82, –84, –86*
Dylan, Bob *see also* Zimmerman, Robert
Dyson, Freeman J 1923- *ConAu 17NR, WhoTech 84*
Dyson, Freeman John 1923- *AmM&WS 73P, –76P, –79P, –82P, –86P, BiEsc, BioIn 7, –11, –12, –13, BlueB 76, ConAu 89, CurBio 80[port], EncSF, IntWW 74, –75, –76, –77, –78, –79, –80, –81, –82, –83, McGMS 80[port], Who 74, –82, –83, –85, WhoAm 74, –76, –78, –80, –82, –84, –86, WhoE 74, WhoFrS 84, WhoTech 82, WrDr 82, –84*

Edwards, Frank 1908-1967 *BioIn 2,
-4, -7, -8, BluesWW, ConAu 1R,
-1NR, EncO&P 2, ObitOF 79,
UFOEn, WhAm 4*
Edwards, G B 1899-1976 *ConAu 110,
ConLC 25*
Edwards, Iorwerth Eiddon Stephen
1909- *Au&Wr 71, BlueB 76,
ConAu 13R, IntAu&W 76, -77, -82,
Who 74, -82, -83, -85, WhoArt 80,
-82, -84, WhoWor 74, -76, -82, -84,
WrDr 76, -80, -82, -84*
Edwards, Jane Campbell 1932-
*BioIn 11, ConAu 13R, ForWC 70,
SmATA 10*
Edwards, Jane Campbell *see also*
Campbell, Jane
Edwards, Ronald George 1930-
*IntAu&W 77, -86, WrDr 76, -80,
-82, -84, -86*
Effinger, George Alec 1947- *BioIn 12,
ConAu 37R, DcLB 8[port], EncSF,
ScF&FL 1, -2, TwCSFW 86,
WhoE 75, -77, -79, WhoSciF,
WhoS&SW 78, -80, -82, -84, -86,
WrDr 76, -80, -82, -84, -86*
Efron, Alexander 1897- *ConAu P-2*
Efron, Marshall *NewYTBE 71*
Efron, Marshall 1938?- *ConAu 112*
Ehrlich, Anne Howland 1933-
AmM&WS 86P
Ehrlich, Eugene 1922- *WrDr 86*
Ehrlich, Gretel *DrAP&F 85*
Ehrlich, Max 1909- *ConAu 1R, -1NR,
EncSF, IntAu&W 77, -82,
ScF&FL 1, -2, ScFSB, WrDr 76, -80,
-82, -84*
Ehrlich, Max 1909-1983 *ConAu 115,
TwCSFW 86*
Ehrlich, Paul Ralph 1932-
*AmM&WS 73P, -76P, -79P, -82P,
-86P, BioIn 9, -13, ConAu 8NR, -65,
CurBio 70, IntAu&W 77, IntWW 74,
-75, -76, -77, -78, -79, -80, -81,
-82, -83, NatLAC, WhoAm 74, -76,
-78, -80, -82, -84, -86, WhoFrS 84,
WhoWest 82, -84, WhoWor 74, -78,
-80, -82, -84, WrDr 76, -80, -82,
-84*
Eichenberg, Fritz 1901- *AnCL,
BioIn 1, -3, -4, -5, -6, -8, -10, -11,
-12, -13, ConAu 6NR, ConAu 6NR,
-57, IlsBYP, IlsCB 1744, -1946,
-1957, -1967, McGDA, MorJA,
SmATA 9, Str&VC, WhoAm 74, -76,
-78, -80, -82, -84, -86, WhoAmA 73,
-76, -78, -80, -82, -84, WhoGrA 62,
-82[port]*
Eichner, James A 1927- *BioIn 9,
ConAu 13R, SmATA 4, WhoAmL 83*
Eifert, Virginia S 1911-1966
ConAu 15NR
Eifert, Virginia Snider 1911-1966
*AmAu&B, Au&Wr 71, AuBYP,
BioIn 7, -9, ConAu 1R, SmATA 2,
WhAm 4, WhoAmW 58, -64, -66*
Eimerl, Sarel 1925- *ConAu 21R,
WhoWest 74*
Einstein, Charles 1926- *ConAu 65,
ConSFA, EncSF, ScF&FL 1, -2*
Eiseley, Loren Corey 1907-1977
*AmAu&B, AmM&WS 73S, -76P,
ASpks, Au&Wr 71, BioIn 1, -5, -6,
-7, -9, -10, -11, -13, BlueB 76,
CelR, ChhPo S3, ConAu 1R, -6NR,
-73, ConLC 7, CurBio 60, -77, -77N,
DcLEL 1940, FifIDA, InSci,
LinLib L, NewYTBS 77, ObitOF 79,
REnAL, WebAB, -79, WhAm 7,
WhoAm 74, -76, -78, WhoE 74,
WhoGov 77, -72, -75, WhoWor 74,
-76, WorAu, WrDr 80*
Eisenberg, Azriel 1903- *AuBYP,
BioIn 7, -11, ConAu 10NR, -49,
LEduc 74, SmATA 12, WhoAmJ 80,
WhoWorJ 72, -78*
Eisenberg, Dennis Harold 1929-
*ConAu 25R, IntAu&W 77,
WhoWor 76, WrDr 76, -80, -82, -84*
Eisenberg, Lisa 1949- *ConAu 110*
Eisenstein, Phyllis 1946-
*ConAu 16NR, -85, ScFSB,
TwCSFW 86, WrDr 84, -86*

Elbert, Virginie Fowler 1912-
AuBYP SUP, ConAu 8NR, -61
Elbert, Virginie Fowler *see also* Fowler,
Virginie
Elder, Lauren 1947?- *BioIn 11*
Elder, Lonne, III *SelBAAf*
Elder, Lonne, III 1931- *BioIn 10, -12,
BlkAWP, ConAu 81, ConDr 73, -77,
-82, DcLB 7[port], -38[port],
-44[port], DcLEL 1940, DrBlPA,
Ebony 1, InB&W 80, -85, LesBEnT,
LivgBAA, NatPD, NewYTBS 75,
NewYTET, NotNAT, PlP&P A,
SelBAAu, WhoAm 80, -82, -84,
WhoBlA 75, -77, -80, -85,
WhoThe 77, -81, WrDr 76, -80, -82,
-84, -86*
Eldredge, Niles *WhoFrS 84*
Eldredge, Niles 1943- *AmM&WS 86P*
Elfman, Blossom 1925- *BioIn 11,
ConAu 2NR, -17NR, -45, SmATA 8*
Elgin, Suzette Haden 1936-
*ConAu 8NR, -61, EncSF, ScF&FL 1,
-2, ScFSB, TwCSFW 86,
WhoWest 78, WrDr 84, -86*
Eliot, Anne *BioIn 13*
Eliot, Anne 1902?-1979 *BioIn 11,
ConAu X, SmATA X*
Eliot, Anne *see also* Cole, Lois Dwight
Eliot, George *DcNaB, NewOxM*
Eliot, George 1819-1880 *Alli SUP,
AtlBL, BbD, BiD&SB, BioIn 1, -2,
-3, -4, -5, -6, -7, -8, -9, -10, -11,
-12, -13, BritAu 19, BritWr 5,
CasWL, CelCen, Chambr 3,
ChhPo, -S2, -S3, CrtT 3, -4, CyWA,
DcBiA, DcEnA, -AP, DcEnL, DcEuL,
DcLB 21[port], -35[port], -55[port],
DcLEL, Dis&D, EvLB, GoodHs,
HerW, -84, HsB&A, InWom,
IntDcWB[port], LinLib L, -LP, -S,
LongCEL, McGEWB, MnBBF,
MouLC 3, NewC, NinCLC 4[port],
-13[port], Novels[port], OxEng, -85,
PenC ENG, RAdv 1, RComWL, REn,
WebE&AL, WhDW, WorAl*
Eliot, George *see also* Evans, Mary
Ann
Eliot, T S *OxChL*
Eliot, T S 1888-1965 *AmAu&B,
AmWr, AnCL, AtlBL, BiE&WWA,
BritWr 7, CasWL, Chambr 3,
ChhPo, -S1, -S2, CnDAL, CnE&AP,
CnMD, CnMWL, CnThe, ConAmL,
ConAu 5R, -25R, ConLC 1, -2, -3,
-6, -9, -10, -13, -15, -24[port],
-41[port], ConLCrt, -82, CroCD,
CyWA, DcAmB S7, DcLB 7[port],
-10[port], -45[port], DcLEL,
EncWL, -2[port], EvLB, HalFC 84,
LinLib L, LongCTC, MajMD 1,
McGEWD, ModAL, -S2, -S1,
ModBrL, -S2, -S1, ModWD, NewC,
NotNAT A, ObitOF 79, ObitT 1961,
OxAmH, OxAmL, -83, OxAmT 84,
OxEng, -85, OxThe 83, PenC AM,
-ENG, PlP&P, RAdv 1, RComWL,
REn, REnAL, REnWD, SixAP,
TwCA, -SUP, TwCWr, WebE&AL,
WhE&EA, WhNAA, WhThe,
WhoChL, WhoTwCL, WorAl*
Eliot, Thomas Stearns 1888-1963
DcNaB 1961
Eliot, Thomas Stearns 1888-1965
*BioIn 1, -2, -3, -4, -5, -6, -7, -8, -9,
-10, -11, -12, -13, ChhPo S3,
CnMD, CurBio 62, -65, EncWT,
LinLib S, LongCEL, LuthC 75,
MakMC, McGEWB,
McGEWD 84[port], NotNAT B,
OxThe, WebAB, -79, WhDW,
WhAm 4, WhLit, WhoNob*
Elkin, Stanley *DrAP&F 85*
Elkin, Stanley 1930- *AmAu&B,
BioIn 8, -10, -12, ConAu 8NR, -9R,
ConLC 4, -6, -9, -14, -27[port],
ConNov 72, -76, -82, -86, DcLB 2,
-28[port], -Y80A[port], DrAS 74E,
-78E, -82E, EncWL, IntAu&W 76,
-77, ModAL S2, Novels, OxAmL 83,
PenC AM, PostFic, WhoAm 74, -76,
-78, -80, -82, WorAu 1970,
WrDr 76, -80, -82, -84, -86*

Elkins, Dov Peretz 1937- *AuBYP,
BioIn 8, -10, ConAu 12NR, -29R,
SmATA 5, WhoAmJ 80,
WhoWorJ 78, WrDr 76, -80, -82,
-84, -86*
Elkon, Juliette *ConAu X*
Elkon-Hameleocourt, Juliette 1912-
ConAu 57
Ellacott, S E 1911- *ConAu 3NR, -5R,
SmATA 19, WrDr 82, -84*
Ellacott, Samuel Ernest 1911-
*Au&Wr 71, BioIn 12, ConAu 5R,
IntAu&W 76, -77, -82, WrDr 76, -80*
Ellington, Duke 1899-1974 *AmPS,
AmSCAP 66, BiE&WWA, BioIn 1,
-2, -3, -4, -5, -6, -7, -8, -9, -10,
-11, -12, -13, BioNews 74, CelR,
CmpEPM, ConAu 49, -X, CurBio 41,
-70, -74, -74N, DrBlPA, EncJzS,
FilmgC, HalFC 84, IlEncJ, MakMC,
NegAl 76[port], -83[port], NewOxM,
NewYTBE 72, NewYTBS 74,
NotNAT A, -B, ObitT 1971, OxAmH,
OxMus, WebAB, -79, WhScrn 77,
-83, WhoE 74, WhoGov 72,
WhoHol B, WhoMus 72, WhoWor 74,
WorAl*
Ellington, Duke *see also* Ellington,
Edward Kennedy
Ellington, Edward Kennedy *BioIn 13*
Ellington, Edward Kennedy 1899-1972
BiDD
Ellington, Edward Kennedy 1899-1974
*AmComp, Baker 78, -84, BiDAfM,
BiDAmM, BiDJaz, BioIn 1, -8, -9,
-10, -11, -12, ConAmC, -82,
ConAu 49, -97, Ebony 1, EncAB-H,
EncJzS, InB&W 80, -85, McGEWB,
MorMA, ObitOF 79, SelBAAf,
SelBAAu, WhDW, WhAm 6, Who 74,
WhoAm 74, WhoBlA 75, WhoJazz 72*
Ellington, Edward Kennedy *see also*
Ellington, Duke
Elliot, Ian Douglas 1925- *ConAu 69,
WhoE 79, -83, -85*
Elliott, Bob 1923- *BioIn 3, -4, -5, -9,
-10, -13, CelR, ConAu 109,
CurBio 57*
Elliott, Charles Newton 1906-
WhE&EA, WhoS&SW 76, -78
Elliott, David William 1939-
ConAu 45, WhoE 77, -79, -81
Elliott, Janice 1931- *BioIn 13,
ConAu 8NR, -13R, DcLB 14[port],
IntAu&W 76, -77, -82, -86,
WhoWor 78, WrDr 76, -80, -82, -84,
-86*
Elliott, Lawrence 1924- *ConAu 3NR,
-5R, -21NR, IntAu&W 86,
WhoAm 74, -76, -78, -80, -82, -84,
-86, WhoE 74*
Ellis, Ella T *WrDr 86*
Ellis, Ella Thorp *DrAP&F 85*
Ellis, Ella Thorp 1928- *AuBYP SUP,
BioIn 10, ConAu 2NR, -49,
FifBJA[port], IntAu&W 77, -82, -86,
SmATA 7, WhoAmW 77, -79,
WrDr 76, -80, -82, -84*
Ellis, Harry Bearse 1921- *AmAu&B,
AuBYP, BioIn 8, -11, BlueB 76,
ConAu 1R, -2NR, IntAu&W 77, -82,
SmATA 9, WhoAm 74, -76, -78, -80,
-82, -84, -86, WhoWor 74, -76,
WrDr 76, -80, -82, -84, -86*
Ellis, Melvin Richard 1912- *BioIn 10,
ConAu 13R, SmATA 7*
Ellis, Peter Berresford 1943-
ConAu 21NR, IntAu&W 86
Ellis, R Hobart, Jr. 1918-
AmM&WS 73P
Ellis, Richard 1938- *BioIn 12,
ConAu 104, WhoAmA 78, -80, -82,
-84*
Ellison, Harlan *DrAP&F 85*
Ellison, Harlan 1934- *BioIn 10, -12,
ConAu 5NR, ConLC 1, -13,
-42[port], ConSFA, DcLB 8[port],
EncSF, IntAu&W 76X, LinLib L,
Novels, ScF&FL 1, -2, ScFSB[port],
SupFW, TwCSFW 86, WhoAm 74,
-76, -78, -80, -82, WhoSciF, WorAl,
WorAu 1970, WrDr 76, -80, -82,
-84, -86*
Ellison, Ralph *DrAP&F 85*

Ellison, Ralph 1914- *AmAu&B,
AmWr S2, BioIn 2, -3, -4, -5, -6,
-7, -8, -9, -10, -11, -12, BlueB 76,
BlkAWP, CasWL, CivR 74, CnDAL,
ConAu 9R, ConLC 1, -3, -11,
ConNov 72, -76, -82, -86, CurBio 68,
DcAmSR, DcLB 2, DcLEL 1940,
Ebony 1, EncAB-H, EncSoH,
EncWL, -2, InB&W 80,
IntAu&W 76, -77, IntWW 74, -75,
-76, -77, -78, -79, -80, -81, -82,
-83, LinLib L, -S, LivgBAA,
McGEWB, ModAL, -S2, -S1,
ModBlW, NegAl 76[port], -83[port],
Novels, OxAmL, PenC AM,
RAdv 1, REn, REnAL, SelBAAu,
TwCWr, WebAB, -79, WebE&AL,
WhoAm 74, -76, -78, -80, -82, -84,
-86, WhoBlA 75, -77, -80, -85,
WhoE 74, WhoGov 72, -75,
WhoTwCL, WhoWor 74, -78, WorAl,
WorAu, WrDr 76, -80, -82, -84, -86*
Ellsberg, Daniel 1931- *BioIn 9, -10,
-12, -13, BioNews 74, ConAu 69,
CurBio 73, LinLib S, NewYTBE 71,
PolProf NF, WhoAm 74, -76, -78,
-80, -82, -84, WhoWor 80, -82, -84,
WorAl*
Ellsberg, Edward 1891-1983
*AmAu&B, AmNov, Au&Wr 71,
AuBYP, BioIn 2, -3, -4, -6, -7, -8,
-10, -13, ConAu 5R, CurBio 42,
JBA 34, -51, LinLib L,
NewYTBS 83, REnAL, SmATA 7,
TwCA, -SUP, WebAMB, WhAm 8,
WhE&EA, WhoAm 74, -76, -78, -80,
-82*
Elman, Robert 1930- *ConAu 3NR,
-45, WhoE 77, -79, -85*
Elmblad, Mary 1927- *ConAu 108*
Elmore, Patricia *DrAP&F 85*
Elmore, Patricia 1933- *ConAu 114,
SmATA 38, -38[port]*
Elting, Mary 1906- *AuBYP, BioIn 6,
-8, -9, ConAu 4NR, -9R, -19NR,
ForWC 70, MorJA, SmATA 2,
WhoAmW 79, -81*
Elwood, Roger 1943- *AuBYP SUP,
ConAu 10NR, -57, ConSFA, EncSF,
ScF&FL 1, -2, WhoSciF*
Emanuel, James A *DrAP&F 85*
Emanuel, James A 1921- *BioIn 10,
BlkAWP, BroadAu[port],
ConAu 12NR, -29R, ConPo 75, -80,
-85, CroCAP, DrAS 74E, -78E,
-82E, InB&W 80, IntAu&W 77,
IntWWP 77, LinLib L, LivgBAA,
SelBAAu, WrDr 76, -80, -82, -84,
-86*
Emanuel, James Andrew 1921-
*DcLB 41[port], InB&W 85,
IntAu&W 86, SelBAAf*
Embery, Joan 1949- *BioIn 12*
Emboden, William A, Jr. 1935-
ConAu 14NR
Emboden, William Allen, Jr. 1935-
*AmM&WS 73P, -76P, -79P, -82P,
-86P, ConAu 41R, IntAu&W 82*
Embry, Margaret Jacob 1919-1975
*AuBYP SUP, BioIn 10, ConAu 1R,
-3NR, ForWC 70, SmATA 5*
Emecheta, Buchi 1941?- *BioIn 13*
Emecheta, Buchi 1944- *BioIn 12,
ConAu 81, ConLC 14, ConNov 86,
InB&W 80, IntAu&W 82, SelBAAf,
Who 83, -85, WorAu 1975[port],
WrDr 76, -80, -82, -84, -86*
Emerson, Ralph Waldo 1803-1882
*Alli, -SUP, AmAu, AmAu&B, AmBi,
AmRef[port], AmWr, AnCL, ApCAB,
AtlBL, BbD, BiDAmM, BiD&SB,
BiDMoPL, BioIn 1, -2, -3, -4, -5,
-6, -7, -8, -9, -10, -11, -12, -13,
CasWL, CelCen, Chambr 3,
ChhPo, -S1, -S3, CnDAL, CnE&AP,
CrtT 3, -4, CyAL 2, CyEd, CyWA,
DcAmAu, DcAmB, DcAmReB,
DcEnL, DcLB 1, -59[port], DcLEL,
DcNAA, Dis&D, Drake, EncAAH,
EncAB-H, EvLB, HarEnUS[port],
LinLib L, -S, LuthC 75, McGEWB,
MemAm, MouLC 4, NatCAB 3,*

*NinCLC 1[port], OxAmH,
OxAmL, –83, OxEng, –85, PenC AM,
RAdv 1, RComWL, REn, REnAL,
Str&VC, TwCBDA, WebAB, –79,
WebE&AL, WhDW, WhAm HS,
WorAl*

Emery, Anne 1907- *AuBYP, BioIn 2,
–3, –6, –7, –9, ConAu 1R, –2NR,
CurBio 52, ForWC 70, InWom,
MorJA, SmATA 1, –33[port],
WhoAmW 58, –61, –64, –66, –68,
–70, –72*

Emmens, Carol Ann 1944-
*ConAu 106, SmATA 39,
WhoAmW 77, –79*

Emmet, Eric Revell 1909- *Au&Wr 71,
IntAu&W 76, –77, –82, WhoWor 78,
WrDr 76, –80*

Emmitt, Robert 1925- *ConAu 29R*

Emrich, Duncan 1908-197-?
*AuBYP SUP, –SUPA, BioIn 3, –4,
–11, ChhPo S1, –S2, ConAu 9NR,
–61, CurBio 55, SmATA 11,
WhAm 7, WhoAm 74, –76*

Endacott, M Violet 1915- *ConAu 9R*

Enderle, Judith 1941- *ConAu 106,
SmATA 38[port]*

Engdahl, Sylvia L 1933- *WrDr 86*

Engdahl, Sylvia Louise 1933-
*AuBYP SUP, BioIn 9, ChlLR 2,
ConAu 14NR, –29R, EncSF,
FourBJA, IntAu&W 76, –77,
ScF&FL 1, –2, SmATA 4,
TwCCW 78, –83, WrDr 76, –80, –82,
–84*

Engebrecht, P A 1935- *ConAu 57*

Engel, Howard *OxCanL*

Engel, Howard 1931- *ConAu 112,
IntAu&W 86, WhoCanL 85*

Engel, Lehman 1910- *ConAmC 82*

Engel, Lehman 1910-1982 *AmAu&B,
AnObit 1982[port], Baker 78, –84,
BiE&WWA, BioIn 1, –2, –4, –5, –10,
–13, ChhPo S3, ConAmC,
ConAu 107, –41R, DcCM,
IntWWM 77, NewYTBS 82[port],
NotNAT, –A, OxAmT 84, WhAm 8,
WhoAm 74, –76, –78, –80, –82,
WhoAmJ 80, WhoAmM 83,
WhoMus 72, WhoWor 74, –76, –78,
WhoWorJ 72, –78*

Engel, Lehman 1910-1985 *ConTFT 2*

Engel, Leonard 1916-1964 *AmAu&B,
BioIn 7, EncSF, ScF&FL 1*

Engel, Lyle Kenyon d1986
NewYTBS 86

Engel, Lyle Kenyon 1915- *BioIn 11,
–12, ConAu 85, EncSF, WhoAm 82,
–84, –86, WhoE 85*

Engel, Lyle Kenyon 1915-1986
ConAu 120

Engeman, John T 1901- *AuBYP,
BioIn 8*

Engle, Eloise *ConAu X, IntAu&W 86X*

Engle, Eloise 1923- *BioIn 11,
ConAu 1R, –2NR, ForWC 70,
IntAu&W 77, –82X, ScF&FL 1, –2,
SmATA 9, WhoAmW 74, –66, –68,
–70, –72, –75, –79, –81, WrDr 76,
–80, –82, –84, –86*

Engle, Paul *DrAP&F 85*

Engle, Paul 1908- *AmAu&B, BioIn 4,
–5, –7, –10, –12, BlueB 76,
ChhPo, –S1, –S2, CnDAL, ConAmA,
ConAu 1R, –5NR, ConPo 70, –75,
–80, –85, CurBio 42, DcLB 48[port],
DcLEL, DrAS 74E, –78E, –82E,
IntWWP 77, –82, LinLib L,
OxAmL, –83, REnAL, SixAP,
WhE&EA, WhoAm 74, –76, –78, –80,
–82, WhoWor 74, –76, WorAu,
WrDr 76, –80, –82, –84, –86*

Engle, Paul Hamilton 1908-
WhoAm 84, –86

Englebardt, Stanley L 1925-
IntAu&W 82

Englebert, Victor 1933- *BioIn 11,
ConAu 57, SmATA 8*

Engler, Larry 1949- *ConAu 53,
WhoE 77*

English, Urma Mae Peterson 1910-
WhoAmW 74, –66, –72

Enright, D J 1920- *BlueB 76,
ConAu 1NR, ConLC 8, –31[port],
ConLCrt, –82, ConPo 80, –85,
DcLB 27[port], EncWL 2,
IntWWP 77, –82, ModBrL S2,
Novels, OxEng 85, SmATA 25[port],
WrDr 80, –82, –84, –86*

Enright, John 1940- *ConAu 45,
SmATA 39*

Enright, Dennis Joseph 1920-
*Au&Wr 71, BioIn 8, –10, –13,
ChhPo S2, ConAu 1R, ConLC 4,
ConNov 72, –76, ConPo 70, –75,
DcLEL 1940, IntAu&W 76, –77, –82,
–86, IntWW 74, –75, –76, –77, –78,
–79, –80, –81, –82, –83, LongCTC,
ModBrL, –S1, NewC, PenC ENG,
TwCWr, Who 74, –82, –83, –85,
WhoTwCL, WhoWor 74, –76, –78,
–80, WorAu, WrDr 76*

Entwistle, John *WhoRock 81*

Entwistle, John 1944- *BioIn 11, –13,
WhoAm 80, –82, –84*

Entwistle, John *see also* Who, The

Epand, Len 1950- *ConAu 85*

Ephron, Delia 1944- *BioIn 11, –12,
ConAu 12NR, –97, NewYTBS 78*

Epp, Margaret A 1913- *BioIn 12,
ConAu 3NR, –9R, IntAu&W 77, –82,
SmATA 20, WhoAmW 74, –70, –72,
–75, –83, WhoWest 74, –76, –78,
WrDr 76, –80, –82, –84*

Epp, Margaret Agnes 1913- *WrDr 86*

Epstein, Anne Merrick 1931-
BioIn 12, ConAu 69, SmATA 20

Epstein, Beryl Williams 1910- *AuBYP,
BioIn 6, –7, –9, ConAu 2NR, –5R,
MorJA, OhA&B, SmATA 1, –31[port]*

Epstein, Cynthia Fuchs *WhoAm 84,
–86*

Epstein, Cynthia Fuchs 1933-
*AmM&WS 73S, –78S, ConAu 14NR,
–29R, IntAu&W 77, WrDr 76, –80,
–82, –84, –86*

Epstein, Daniel Mark *DrAP&F 85*

Epstein, Daniel Mark 1948- *BioIn 13,
WhoAm 84, –86*

Epstein, Edward Jay 1935- *BioIn 8,
–11, ConAu 13NR, –17R,
WhoWorJ 72, –78*

Epstein, Helen 1947- *ConAu 89,
WrDr 82, –84, –86*

Epstein, Jacob 1956?- *BioIn 12,
ConAu 114, ConLC 19*

Epstein, Joseph 1937- *ConAu 112,
–119, WhoAm 82, –84, –86*

Epstein, Leslie *DrAP&F 85*

Epstein, Leslie 1938- *BioIn 11, –13,
ConAu 73, ConLC 27[port],
WorAu 1975[port]*

Epstein, Morris 1921-1973 *BioIn 10,
ConAu 45, ConAu P-1, NewYTBE 73,
WhoWorJ 72*

Epstein, Perle S 1938- *AuBYP SUP,
BioIn 12, ConAu 9NR, –65,
SmATA 27[port]*

Epstein, Samuel 1909- *AuBYP,
BioIn 6, –7, –9, –13, ConAu 4NR,
–9R, –18NR, MorJA, SmATA 1,
–31[port], WhoWorJ 72, –78*

Erdman, Loula Grace d1976
*AmAu&B, AmNov, AuBYP, BioIn 2,
–6, –7, –9, ConAu 5R, –10NR,
DrAS 74E, ForWC 70, InWom,
MorJA, SmATA 1, TexWr,
WhoAmW 58, –61, –64, –66, –68,
–72*

Erdman, Loula Grace 1905?-1976
EncFWF[port]

Erdoes, Richard 1912- *BioIn 1, –3, –8,
–13, ConAu 77, IlsBYP, IlsCB 1957,
SmATA 28, –33[port]*

Erhard, Thomas A 1923-
*ConAu 13NR, –33R, DrAS 74E,
–78E, –82E, WrDr 76*

Erickson, Sabra R 1912-
SmATA 35[port]

Erickson, Sabra Rollins 1912-
*ConAu 5R, –5NR, SmATA 35,
WhoAmW 74, –72, –75, –77*

Erickson, Sabra Rollins *see also*
Holbrook, Sabra

Erlanger, Ellen 1950- *ConAu 15NR,
–85, WhoAmW 81*

Erlich, Lillian 1910- *AuBYP, BioIn 7,
–11, ConAu 1R, –5NR, ForWC 70,
SmATA 10, WhoAmW 74, –75*

Erno, Richard B 1923- *BioIn 3,
ConAu 13R, DrAS 74E, –78E, –82E,
MichAu 80, WrDr 80, –82, –84, –86*

Ernst, John 1940- *ConAu 45,
SmATA 39*

Ernst, Margaret 1894?-1964 *BioIn 7,
ConAu P-1*

Erskine, Albert Russel, Jr. 1911-
WhoAm 74, –76, –78

Erskine, Jim 1956- *ConAu 107*

Eshmeyer, R E 1898- *BioIn 13,
ConAu X, SmATA 29[port]*

Eskenazi, Gerald 1936- *ConAu 7NR,
–61, WhoAmJ 80, WhoE 79*

Esposito, Phil *NewYTBS 84[port],
–86[port]*

Esposito, Phil 1942- *BioIn 8, –9, –10,
–11, –12, ConAu 108, CurBio 73,
NewYTBS 79, –81[port],
WhoHcky 73, WorAl*

Esposito, Tony 1943- *BioIn 8, –9, –10,
–13, WhoAm 74, WhoHcky 73*

Espy, Willard R 1910- *BioIn 2, –11,
ConAu 2NR, –49, IntAu&W 76, –77,
SmATA 38[port], WhoAm 76, –78,
–80, –82, –84, –86, WhoWor 78, –80,
–82*

Esslin, Martin 1918- *BiE&WWA,
BlueB 76, ConAu 85, ConLCrt, –82,
DcLEL 1940, DrAS 82E, NotNAT,
Who 74, –82, –83, WhoThe 77, –81,
WhoWor 76, WorAu 1970, WrDr 80,
–82, –84, –86*

Esterow, Milton 1928- *ConAu 17R,
WhoAm 74, –76, –78, –80, –82, –84,
–86, WhoAmA 76, –78, –80, –82, –84,
WhoE 83*

Estes, Winston 1917- *ConAu 29R,
WhoS&SW 75, –76*

Estes, Winston M 1917- *BioIn 8,
ConAu 29R, IntAu&W 76, –77,
WrDr 76, –80, –82, –84, –86*

Estleman, Loren D 1952- *ConAu 85,
TwCCr&M 85, WrDr 84, –86*

Estoril, Jean *AuBYP, ConAu X,
IntAu&W 76X, –77X, –82X, OxChL,
SmATA X, TwCChW 83, WrDr 76,
–80, –82, –84, –86*

Estoril, Jean *see also* Allan, Mabel
Esther

Etchison, Birdie L 1937- *ConAu 106,
SmATA 38[port]*

Etchison, Dennis 1943- *ConAu 115,
–118*

Etter, Les 1904- *ConAu 25R*

Ettinger, Blanche 1922- *WhoE 81, –85*

Euller, John E 1926- *ConAu 9R*

Eulo, Ken 1939- *ConAu 109,
IntAu&W 76, NatPD*

Eunson, Roby *AuBYP SUP*

Eunson, Dale 1904- *AmAu&B,
AmNov, BiE&WWA, BioIn 2, –10,
ConAu 41R, IntAu&W 82, NotNAT,
SmATA 5*

Eustis, Helen 1916- *BioIn 3, –4,
CurBio 55, EncMys, InWom,
OhA&B, TwCCr&M 80, –85,
WrDr 82, –84, –86*

Evanoff, Vlad 1916- *ConAu 5R,
–6NR, IntAu&W 77, WrDr 76, –80,
–82, –84, –86*

Evans, Arthur L 1931- *WhoBlA 75,
–77, –80, –85*

Evans, Barbara Lloyd *ConAu X*

Evans, Bergen 1904-1978 *AmAu&B,
Au&Wr 71, BioIn 3, –4, –5, –11, –12,
CelR, ConAu 4NR, –5R, –77,
CurBio 55, –78, –78N, DcLEL 1940,
DrAS 74E, LesBEnT, LinLib L,
NatCAB 60[port], NewYTET,
ObitOF 79, OhA&B, WhAm 7,
WhoAm 74, –76, WhoWor 74, WorAl*

Evans, Christopher 1931-1979
*ConAu 102, EncO&P 2, –81,
IntAu&W 76, ScF&FL 1, –2*

Evans, David *DrAP&F 85*

Evans, David S 1916- *WhoTech 84*

Evans, David Stanley 1916-
*AmM&WS 86P, IntAu&W 86,
WhoAm 84, –86, WhoFrS 84,
WhoTech 84, WrDr 86*

Evans, Edna Hoffman 1913- *AuBYP,
BioIn 7, ForWC 70, WhoAmW 66,
–68, –70, –72*

Evans, Elizabeth *DrAP&F 85*

Evans, Elizabeth 1932- *ConAu 53*

Evans, Gareth Lloyd *ConAu X*

Evans, Gareth Lloyd 1923- *Au&Wr 71*

Evans, Gareth Lloyd 1923-1984
ConAu 115

Evans, Harold Matthew 1928-
*BioIn 10, –12, –13, BlueB 76,
ConAu 41R, IntAu&W 77, –82,
IntWW 75, –76, –77, –78, –79, –80,
–81, –82, –83, Who 74, –82, –83, –85,
WhoAm 86, WhoWor 74, –76, –78,
WrDr 76, –80, –82, –84, –86*

Evans, Howard Ensign 1919-
*AmM&WS 73P, –76P, –79P, –82P,
–86P, ConAu 5R, –6NR, WhoAm 74,
–76, –78, –80, –82, –84, –86*

Evans, Humphrey 1914- *ConAu 29R*

Evans, Idrisyn Oliver 1894-
*Au&Wr 71, ConAu 13R,
IntAu&W 76, –77, WhE&EA,
WrDr 76, –80, –82, –84*

Evans, Larry Melvyn 1932- *GolEC,
OxChess 84, WhoAm 74, –76, –78,
–80, –82, –84, –86*

Evans, Mari *BlkWWr, ConPo 85,
DrAP&F 85, WhoAm 84, –86,
WhoBlA 85, WhoE 85, WrDr 86*

Evans, Mari 1923- *AuBYP SUP,
BioIn 10, –11, BlkAWP,
BroadAu[port], ConAu 2NR, –49,
ConPo 75, –80, CroCAP,
DcLB 41[port], Ebony 1, InB&W 80,
LinLib L, LivgBAA, NegAl 76, –83,
SelBAAf, SelBAAu, SmATA 10,
WhoAm 76, –78, –80, –82,
WhoBlA 75, –77, –80, WrDr 76, –80,
–82, –84*

Evans, Mari E 1923- *InB&W 85*

Evans, Mary Ann 1819-1880 *BiD&SB,
BritAu 19, CarSB, DcLEL, Dis&D,
EvLB, GoodHs, InWom, IntDcWB,
LinLib S, NewC, OxEng, PenC ENG,
REn, WhDW*

Evans, Mary Ann *see also* Eliot, George

Evans, Max 1925- *Au&Wr 71,
ConAu 1R, –1NR, IntAu&W 76,
WrDr 84, –86*

Evans, Max 1926- *EncFWF*

Evans, Richard Jr 1921- *ConAu 106*

Evans, Rowland, Jr 1921- *BioIn 7,
CelR, ConAu 15NR, –21R, EncAJ,
EncTwCJ, WhoAm 74, –76, –78, –80,
–82, –84, –86, WhoS&SW 73,
WhoWor 74, WrDr 76, –80, –82, –84,
–86*

Evans, Shirlee 1931- *ConAu 61*

Evans, Sir Anthony 1922- *Au&Wr 71,
Who 74, –82, –83, –85*

Evans, Walker 1903-1975 *AmAu&B,
BioIn 1, –4, –7, –9, –10, –11, –12,
–13, BriEAA, ConAu 89, ConPhot,
CurBio 71, –75, –75N, DcAmArt,
EncAB-H, EncAJ, ICPEnP, MacBEP,
NewYTBS 75, ObitOF 79,
WebAB, –79, WhAm 6, WhoAm 74,
WhoWor 74*

Evans, William Eugene 1930-
AmM&WS 73P

Evarts, Hal G 1915- *AuBYP SUP,
BioIn 10, ConAu 2NR, –49, EncFWF,
SmATA 6, WhoWest 78, –80, –82,
–84, WrDr 84, –86*

Evelyn, John Michael 1916-
*ConAu 5R, IntAu&W 86, WrDr 82,
–84*

Everson, William K 1929- *AuBYP,
BioIn 8, –10, ConAu 1R, IntMPA 77,
–75, –76, –78, –79, –84, –86,
ScF&FL 1, –2, WhoAm 74, –76*

Every, George 1909- *WrDr 86*

Evslin, Bernard 1922- *AuBYP SUP,
BioIn 13, ConAu 9NR, –21R,
SmATA 28, –45[port]*

Ewart, William Dunlop 1923-
Au&Wr 71

Ewen, David 1907- *AmAu&B,
Au&Wr 71, AuBYP, Baker 84,
BiE&WWA, BioIn 8, –9, –10,*

ConAu 1R, –2NR, IntAu&W 77,
OxAmT 84, REnAL, SmATA 4,
WhE&EA, WhoAm 74, –76, –78, –80,
–82, –84, WhoMus 72,
WhoS&SW 73, WhoWor 74, –76,
WhoWorJ 72, –78, WrDr 76, –80,
–82, –84, –86
Ewen, David 1907-1985 ConAu 118,
SmATA 47N

Ewen, Robert B 1940- AmM&WS 73S,
ConAu 15NR, –37R, WhoS&SW 82
Ewen, Stuart Baer 1945-
AmM&WS 78S, ConAu 69,
DrAS 78H, –82H
Ewy, Donna 1934- ConAu 14NR
Eyerly, Jeanette Hyde 1908-
AuBYP SUP
Eyerly, Jeannette 1908- FifBJA[port]

Eyerly, Jeannette Hyde 1908-
AmCath 80, AuBYP SUP, BioIn 9,
ConAu 1R, –4NR, –19NR,
ForWC 70, SmATA 4, WhoAm 74,
–76, –78, –80, –82, –84, –86,
WhoAmW 74, –66, –68, –70, –72,
–75, –77, –79
Eyre, Katherine Wigmore 1901-1970
AmAu&B, BioIn 2, –4, –6, –8,

ConAu 104, CurBio 49, –57, InWom,
MorJA, ScF&FL 1, SmATA 26[port]
Eyre, Ronald 1929- BioIn 13,
ConAu 104, EncWT, IntAu&W 82,
Who 83, –85, WhoThe 72, –77, –81
Ezzell, Marilyn 1937- ConAu 109,
SmATA 38, –42

F

Faber, Doris 1924- *AuBYP, BioIn 7, -9, ConAu 8NR, -17R, ForWC 70, SmATA 3, WomPO 78*
Faber, Harold 1919- *AuBYP, BioIn 10, ConAu 8NR, -13R, SmATA 5*
Fabre, Jean Henri 1823-1915 *AnCL, BiDPsy, BiESc, BioIn 1, -2, -3, -4, -5, -6, -8, -9, -11, DcCathB, DcScB, Dis&D, InSci, JBA 34, -51, LinLib L, -S, LongCTC, NamesHP[port], OxFr, REn, SmATA 22[port], WhDW*
Fabre, Jean Henri Casimir 1823-1915 *BioIn 13*
Facklam, Margery 1927- *ConAu 21NR*
Facklam, Margery Metz 1927- *AuBYP SUP, BioIn 12, ConAu 5R, -6NR, SmATA 20, WhoAmW 68, -72*
Fader, Shirley Sloan *WhoAm 84, -86, WhoAmW 85, -87, WhoE 85*
Fader, Shirley Sloan 1931- *ConAu 14NR, -77, WhoAm 80, -82, WhoAmW 75, -77, -79, -81, -83, WhoE 77, -79, -81, -83, WhoWor 80, -82*
Fadiman, Clifton *WhoAm 84, -86*
Fadiman, Clifton 1904- *AmAu&B, BioIn 3, -4, -9, -10, -11, CelR, ChhPo S2, -S3, ConAu 9NR, -61, CurBio 41, -55, EncAJ, IntMPA 77, -75, -76, -78, -79, -81, -82, -84, -86, RAdv 1, REnAL, ScF&FL 1, -2, SmATA 11, TwCA, -SUP, WebAB, -79, WhoAm 74, -76, -78, -80, -82, WhoWest 74, -76, -78, WhoWor 74, WorAl, WrDr 86*
Faessler, Shirley *OxCanL, WhoCanL 85*
Faessler, Shirley 1921?- *ConAu 106, OxCan SUP*
Fagan, Brian Murray 1936- *AmM&WS 73S, BioIn 12, ConAu 14NR, -41R, FifIDA, WhoWest 74, -76, WhoWor 74, -76, WrDr 76, -80, -82, -84, -86*
Fager, Charles E 1942- *ConAu 21R*
Fahey, John *WhoPNW*
Fair, Ronald L 1932- *AmAu&B, BlkAWP, ConAu 69, ConLC 18, DcLB 33[port], InB&W 80, LivgBAA, NegAl 76, -83, SelBAAu, WhoAm 74, -76, WhoBlA 75, -77, -80, -85*
Fair, Sylvia 1933- *ConAu 69, SmATA 13*
Fairbairn, Ann 1901?-1972 *AmAu&B, BioIn 7, -9, ConAu X, NewYTBE 72, ObitOF 79*
Fairbairn, Ann *see also* Tait, Dorothy
Fairbairns, Zoe *OxAusL*
Fairbairns, Zoe 1948- *ConAu 21NR, ConLC 32[port], ConNov 86, TwCSFW 86, WrDr 84, -86*
Fairley, Peter 1930- *ConAu 29R, IntAu&W 76, -77, WhoWor 78*

Fairlie, Gerard 1889?-1983 *Au&Wr 71, BioIn 3, ConAu 109, EncMys, MnBBF, SmATA 34N, TwCCr&M 80, WhE&EA, WhLit, WhoSpyF, WrDr 82, -84*
Fairlie, Gerard 1899-1983 *TwCCr&M 85*
Falcon-Barker, Ted 1923- *Au&Wr 71, ConAu 25R*
Falk, Irving A 1921- *ConAu 21R*
Falk, Richard A 1930- *ConAu 12NR*
Falk, Richard Anderson 1930- *BlueB 76, ConAu 5R, ConIsC 1[port], Future, WhoAm 74, -76, -78, -80, -82, WhoE 74, -75*
Falkner, John Meade 1858-1932 *BioIn 2, -8, -9, -10, CnMWL, DcLEL, DcNaB 1931, EncSF, EvLB, LongCTC, REn, ScF&FL 1, WhDW, WhoChL, WhoHr&F, WorAu*
Falkner, Leonard 1900-1977 *BioIn 11, ConAu 21R, MnBBF, OhA&B, SmATA 12, WhAm 7, WhNAA, WhoE 74*
Fall, Thomas 1917- *Alli, AuBYP, BioIn 8, -12, ConAu X, FourBJA, SmATA X*
Fall, Thomas *see also* Snow, Donald Clifford
Fallows, James Mackenzie 1949- *BioIn 12, ConAu 2NR, -45, WhoAm 80, -82, -84, -86, WhoAmP 77, -79, -81, -83, WhoGov 77*
Falls, Cyril Bentham 1888-1971 *BiDIrW, ConAu P-1, DcIrW 2, DcNaB 1971, ObitT 1971, WhE&EA*
Falstein, Louis 1909- *SmATA 37, WhoAm 84, -86*
Falwell, Jerry 1933- *BioIn 13*
Fanning, Leonard M 1888-1967 *BioIn 10, ConAu 5R, SmATA 5*
Fanning, Robbie 1947- *ConAu 14NR, WhoAmA 84*
Fante, John 1911- *OxAmL 83*
Farago, Ladislas 1906-1980 *AmAu&B, BioIn 6, -9, -10, -12, BioNews 75, CelR, ConAu 102, -10NR, -65, NewYTBS 80[port], WhAm 7, WhoAm 74, -76, -78, -80, WhoWor 74, -78, WhoWorJ 72, -78*
Farb, Peter 1929-1980 *AmAu&B, AnObit 1980[port], Au&Wr 71, AuBYP SUP, BioIn 11, -12, -13, ConAu 12NR, -13R, -97, NewYTBS 80, SmATA 12, -22N, WhAm 7, WhoAm 74, -76, -78, -80, WhoE 74, WhoWor 74, -78, -80, WorAu 1970*
Farber, Norma 1909- *BioIn 13, FifBJA[port], WhoAmA 84, WrDr 86*
Farber, Norma 1909-1984 *AuBYP SUP, BioIn 12, ConAu 102, -112, SmATA 25[port], -38N,*

TwCChW 83, WhoAm 80, -82, WhoAmW 58, -61, -64, -77, -79, -81, -83
Fargo, Lucile Foster 1880-1962 *BioIn 7, DcAmLiB, WhAm 6, WhoAmW 58, WhoLibS 55*
Farhi, Moris 1935- *ConAu 13NR, -77, WrDr 80*
Farjeon, Annabel 1919- *BiDD, BioIn 11, ConAu 53, SmATA 11*
Farley, Carol 1936- *AuBYP SUP, BioIn 9, ConAu 10NR, -X, FifBJA[port], IntAu&W 77, MichAu 80, SmATA 4, WhoAmW 74, -75, WrDr 76, -80, -82, -84, -86*
Farley, Walter 1915?- *AuBYP, BioIn 1, -2, -7, -9, -10, ConAu 8NR, -17R, CurBio 49, DcLB 22[port], JBA 51, MorBMP, ScF&FL 1, -2, SmATA 2, TwCCW 78, -83, WhoAm 74, -76, -78, -80, -82, WrDr 80, -82, -84*
Farley, Walter 1920- *OxChL, SmATA 43[port], WrDr 86*
Farmer, Gene 1919-1972 *BioIn 9, ConAu 37R, NewYTBE 72, WhAm 5*
Farmer, John David 1939- *WhoAm 74, -76, -78, -80, -82, -84, -86, WhoAmA 76, -78, -80, -82, -84, WhoS&SW 78*
Farmer, Laurence 1895?-1976 *BioIn 10, ConAu 65, NewYTBS 76*
Farmer, Penelope 1939- *AuBYP, BioIn 7, -10, -11, BritCA, ChlLR 8[port], ConAu 9NR, -13R, FourBJA, OxChL, ScF&FL 1, -2, SmATA 39, -40[port], TwCCW 78, -83, WhoAmW 66, WrDr 76, -80, -82, -84, -86*
Farmer, Philip Jose *DrAP&F 85*
Farmer, Philip Jose 1918- *AmAu&B, BioIn 7, -12, ConAu 1R, -4NR, ConLC 1, -19, ConSFA, DcLB 8[port], EncSF, IndAu 1917, IntAu&W 77, LinLib L, Novels, ScF&FL 1, -2, ScFSB[port], TwCSFW 86, WhoAm 82, -84, -86, WhoSciF, WorAl, WorAu 1970, WrDr 84, -86*
Farmer, Robert Allen 1938- *ConAu 21R*
Farnsworth, Marjorie W 1921- *WhoTech 84*
Farnsworth, Marjorie Whyte 1921- *AmM&WS 73P, -76P, -79P, -82P, -86P, WhoAmW 61, -66, -68, -70, -72, WhoTech 82*
Farnworth, Warren 1935- *ConAu 93, WrDr 76, -80*
Farrar, Susan Clement 1917- *ConAu 101, SmATA 33[port]*
Farre, Rowena *Au&Wr 71*

Farrell, James T 1904-1979 *AmAu&B, AmNov, AmWr, ASpks, BioIn 1, -2, -3, -4, -5, -6, -7, -8, -9, -10, -11, -12, BlueB 76, CasWL, ChhPo S3, CnDAL, ConAmA, ConAu 5R, -9NR, -89, ConLC 1, -4, -8, -11, ConNov 72, -76, Conv 3, CurBio 42, -79N, CyWA, DcAmSR, DcLB 4, -9[port], -DS2[port], DcLEL, EncAB-H, EncWL, -2, EvLB, HalFC 84, IntAu&W 76, -77, IntWW 74, -75, -76, -77, -78, -79, IntWWP 77, LinLib L, -S, LongCTC, McGEWB, ModAL, -S2, NewYTBS 74, -79, OxAmL, -83, PenC AM, RAdv 1, REn, REnAL, TwCA, -SUP, TwCWr, WebAB, -79, WebE&AL, WhAm 7, Who 74, WhoAm 74, -76, -78, WhoTwCL, WhoWor 74, WorAl, WrDr 76, -80*
Farrell, James Thomas 1904-1979 *BioIn 13*
Farrington, Fielden 1909- *IndAu 1917*
Farris, Jack 1921- *BioIn 3, DrAS 74E, -78E, -82E*
Farris, John *ConAu 101, DrAP&F 85*
Fassi, Carlo 1929?- *BioIn 10*
Fast, Howard *TwCCr&M 85*
Fast, Howard 1914- *AmAu&B, AmNov, Au&Wr 71, AuBYP, BioIn 2, -3, -4, -5, -7, -8, -9, -10, -11, -12, BlueB 76, CnDAL, ConAu 1R, -1NR, ConLC 23[port], ConNov 72, -76, -82, -86, ConSFA, CurBio 43, DcLB 9[port], DcLEL, EncFWF, EncSF, HalFC 84, IntAu&W 76, -77, IntWW 74, -75, -76, -77, -78, -79, -80, -81, -82, -83, LinLib L, ModAL, NewYTBS 81[port], Novels, OxAmL, PenC AM, PolProf E, REn, REnAL, ScF&FL 1, -2, ScFSB, SmATA 7, TwCA SUP, TwCCr&M 80, TwCSFW 86, TwCWr, WebE&AL, WhoAm 74, -76, -78, -80, -82, -84, -86, WhoWor 74, -76, -78, -80, -82, -84, -87, WhoWorJ 72, WorAl, WrDr 76, -80, -82, -84, -86*
Fast, Howard *see also* Cunningham, E V
Fast, Julius 1919- *ConAu 25R, ScF&FL 1, -2, WhoAm 76, -78, -80, -82, -84, -86, WhoE 74, -75*
Fataar, Ricky *WhoRocM 82*
Fataar, Ricky *see also* Beach Boys, The
Fatchen, Max 1920- *Au&Wr 71, BioIn 12, ConAu 11NR, IntAu&W 76, SingR 2, SmATA 20, TwCCW 78, -83, WrDr 80, -82, -84, -86*
Fatchen, Max 1921- *OxAusL*
Faulk, John Henry 1913- *AmAu&B, BioIn 3, -6, -7, -8, -10, -11, ConAu 102, LesBEnT, NewYTET,*

WhoAm 74, –76, WhoHol A,
WhoS&SW 73
Faulkner, Anne Irvin 1906- *AuBYP,*
ConAu 1R, –2NR, ForWC 70,
IntAu&W 76, –77, SmATA 23[port]
Faulkner, Anne Irvin *see also* Faulkner,
Nancy
Faulkner, Nancy 1906- *Au&Wr 71,*
AuBYP, BioIn 4, –7, –13, ConAu X,
CurBio 56, FourBJA, InWom,
IntAu&W 76X, –77X, SmATA X
Faulkner, Nancy *see also* Faulkner,
Anne Irvin
Faulkner, Peter 1933- *Au&Wr 71,*
ConAu 3NR, –5R, –20NR,
IntAu&W 76, –77, –82
Faulkner, William 1897-1962
AmAu&B, AmWr, AtlBL,
AuNews 1, BioIn 1, –2, –3, –4, –5, –6,
–7, –8, –9, –10, –11, –12, –13,
BioNews 74, CasWL, Chambr 3,
CnDAL, CnMD, CnMWL, ConAmA,
ConAu 81, ConLC 1, –3, –6, –8, –9,
–11, –14, –18, –28[port], CroCD,
CurBio 51, –62, CyWA, DcAmB S7,
DcFM, DcLB 9[port], –11[port],
–44[port], –DS2[port], –Y86A[port],
DcLEL, EncAAH, EncAB-H,
EncMys, EncSoH, EncWL, –2[port],
EvLB, FilmgC, HalFC 84, LinLib L,
–S, LongCTC, MakMC, McGEWB,
MemAm, ModAL, –S2, –S1,
ModWD, NatCAB 57, NotNAT B,
Novels[port], ObitOF 79, ObitT 1961,
OxAmH, OxAmL, –83, OxEng,
OxFilm, PenC AM, RAdv 1,
RComWL, REn, REnAL,
TwCA, –SUP, TwCCr&M 80, –85,
TwCW, WebAB, –79, WebE&AL,
WhDW, WhAm 4, WhE&EA,
WhoTwCL, WorAl, WorEFlm
Faust, Frederick 1892-1944 *AmAu&B,*
BioIn 1, –3, –4, –8, ChhPo, CmCal,
ConAu 108, CurBio 44, DcAmB S3,
DcLEL, DcNAA, EncFWF[port],
EncMys, LongCTC, MnBBF,
NatCAB 33, ObitOF 79, REn,
REnAL, REnAW, ScF&FL 1,
TwCA, –SUP, WebAB, –79,
WhoBW&I 4, WhoHr&F
Faust, Frederick *see also* Brand, Max
Fawkes, Richard 1944- *ConAu 20NR*
Fax, Elton C 1909- *WhoBlA 85*
Fax, Elton Clay 1909- *AfroAA,*
BioIn 10, –13, ConAu 13R, –15NR,
IlsCB 1967, InB&W 80, –85,
LivgBAA, NegAl 76[port], –83[port],
SelBAAf, SmATA 25[port],
WhoAm 76, –78, –80, –82, –84, –86,
WhoAmA 73, –76, –78, –80, –82, –84,
WhoBlA 75, –77, –80, WhoWor 78
Fay, Frederic L 1890- *ConAu P-2*
Fay, Gordon S 1912- *ConAu 53*
Feagles, Anita M 1926- *AuBYP,*
BioIn 8, –11, ConAu 1R, –4NR,
ForWC 70, FourBJA, SmATA 9,
WhoAmW 64
Feagles, Elizabeth *ConAu X,*
SmATA X
Feagles, Elizabeth *see also* Day, Beth
Feagles
Feather, Leonard G 1914- *BiDJaz*
Feather, Leonard Geoffrey 1914-
AmAu&B, AmSCAP 66, Baker 78,
CmpEPM, ConAu 61, IntWWM 77,
WhoAm 74, –76, –78, –80, –82, –84,
WhoWor 74, –76
Featherstone, Helen 1944- *ConAu 102*
Fecher, Constance *ConAu X, WrDr 86*
Fecher, Constance 1911- *Au&Wr 71,*
AuBYP SUP, BioIn 10, ConAu 49,
–X, IntAu&W 77X, SmATA 7,
WrDr 76, –80, –82, –84
Fecher, Constance *see also* Heaven,
Constance
Fedder, Ruth 1907- *AmM&WS 73S,*
ConAu 2NR, –5R, LEduc 74,
WhoAmW 66, –68, –70, –72,
WhoWest 74
Feegel, John R 1932- *ConAu 9NR,*
–57
Feegel, John Richard 1932-
WhoAmL 85

Feelings, Thomas 1933- *ConAu 49,*
InB&W 80, –85, SmATA 8,
WhoBlA 77, –80, –85, WhoE 77, –79
Feelings, Tom *SelBAAf*
Feelings, Tom 1933- *AfroAA, BioIn 8,*
–9, –11, –12, BkP, ChlLR 5[port],
ConAu 49, IlsBYP, IlsCB 1967,
LivgBAA, SelBAAu, SmATA 8,
ThrBJA
Fehrenbach, T R 1925- *ConAu 1R,*
–1NR, IntAu&W 76, –77, –82, –86,
SmATA 33[port], WhoS&SW 73, –75,
–76, –84, –86, WhoWor 78, –80,
WrDr 82, –84, –86
Fehrenbacher, Don Edward 1920-
ConAu 1R, DrAS 74H, –78H,
–82H, WhoAm 74, –76, –78, –80,
–82, –84, –86, WrDr 76, –80, –82,
–84, –86
Feiblman, James Kern 1904-
AmAu&B, Au&Wr 71, AuNews 2,
BioIn 2, –4, –8, –11, BlueB 76,
ConAu 5R, –7NR, DrAS 74P, –78P,
–82P, IntAu&W 76, TwCA SUP,
WhoAm 74, –76, –78, –80, –82, –84,
–86, WhoS&SW 84, –86,
WhoWor 74, WhoWorJ 72, –78
Feifel, Herman 1915- *AmM&WS 73S,*
–78S, ConAu 101, WhoAm 80, –86,
WhoFrS 84, WhoWest 74, –76, –78,
–82
Feiffer, Jules *OxAmT 84*
Feiffer, Jules 1929- *AmAu&B, ArtCS,*
Au&Wr 71, BioIn 5, –6, –7, –8, –9,
–10, –11, –12, –13, BlueB 76, CelR,
CnThe, ConAu 17R, ConDr 73, –77,
–82, ConLC 2, –8, ConTFT 1,
CroCD, CurBio 61, DcLB 7[port],
–44[port], DcLEL 1940, EncAJ,
EncTwCJ, EncWT, FilmgC,
HalFC 84, IntAu&W 76, –77,
IntWW 74, –75, –76, –77, –78, –79,
–80, –81, –82, –83, LinLib L,
McGEWD, –84, NatPD 81[port],
NewYTBS 76, –81[port], NotNAT,
SmATA 8, WhoAm 74, –76, –78, –80,
–82, –84, –86, WhoAmA 76, –78, –80,
–82, –84, WhoAmJ 80, WhoThe 72,
–77, –81, WhoWor 74, –78,
WhoWorJ 72, –78, WorAl,
WorAu 1970, WorECom, WrDr 76,
–80, –82, –84, –86
Feil, Hila 1942- *BioIn 11, ConAu 37R,*
SmATA 12
Feinbloom, Deborah Heller 1940-
ConAu 65
Feingold, S Norman *WrDr 86*
Feingold, S Norman 1914-
AmM&WS 73S, –78S, ConAu 13NR,
–13R, LEduc 74, WhoAm 76, –78,
–80, –82, –84, –86, WhoAmJ 80,
WhoE 79, WhoS&SW 73, –75, –76,
WhoE 82, WhoWorJ 72, –78
Feininger, Andreas 1906- *AmAu&B,*
BioIn 2, –4, –12, –13, ConAu 20NR,
–85, ConPhot, CurBio 57, EncAJ,
EncTwCJ, ICPEnP, LinLib L,
WhoAm 74, –76, –78, –80, –82,
WhoWor 74, –76
Feininger, Andreas B L 1906- *AmArt,*
MacBEP, WhoAmA 84
Feininger, Andreas Bernhard Lyonel
1906- *WhoAm 84, –86*
Feinman, Jeffrey Paul 1943-
ConAu 10NR, –65, WhoAdv 72,
WhoCon 73, WhoE 83
Feirer, John Louis 1915- *LEduc 74,*
WhoAm 76, –78, –80, –82, –84, –86,
WhoMW 86
Fejes, Claire 1920- *ConAu 13NR,*
–21R, WhoAmA 82, –84,
WhoAmW 74, –75
Feldman, Annette Gerber 1913-
ConAu 69, WhoAmW 81
Feldman, Charles K 1904?-1968
BioIn 2, –8, FilmgC, HalFC 84,
NotNAT B, ObitOF 79, WhAm 5,
WorEFlm
Feldman, Edmund Burke 1924-
WhoAm 84, –86, WhoAmA 84,
WhoS&SW 84
Feldman, Ruth *DrAP&F 85*
Feldman, Ruth 1911- *IntAu&W 86*

Feldman, Samuel Nathan 1931-
BiDrAPA 77, ConAu 25R
Feldman, Silvia 1928- *ConAu 97*
Feldstein, Albert B 1925- *WhoAm 76,*
–78, –80, –82, –84, –86, WhoAmJ 80,
WhoWor 80, –82, WorECom
Felice, Cynthia *ScFSB*
Felice, Cynthia 1942- *ConAu 107,*
TwCSFW 86, WrDr 86
Feller, Bob *NewYTBS 86[port]*
Feller, Bob 1918- *BioIn 13, CurBio 41,*
NewYTBS 75
Feller, Robert William Andrew 1918-
AuBYP, BioIn 1, –2, –3, –4, –5, –6,
–7, –8, –9, –10, WebAB, –79,
WhoProB 73, WorAl
Fellini, Federico 1920- *BiDFilm,*
BioIn 4, –5, –6, –7, –8, –9, –10, –11,
–12, –13, BioNews 75, CelR,
ConAu 65, ConLC 16, ConTFT 1,
CurBio 57, –80[port], DcFM, FilmgC,
HalFC 84, IntDcF 2, IntMPA 77,
–75, –76, –78, –79, –81, –82, –84,
–86, IntWW 74, –75, –76, –77, –78,
–79, –80, –81, –82, –83, MakMC,
McGEWB, MovMk, OxFilm, REn,
WhDW, Who 74, –82, –83, –85,
WhoAm 80, –82, –84, –86,
WhoWor 74, –78, –80, –82, –84, –87,
WomWMM, WorAl, WorEFlm
Fellows, Lawrence Perry 1924-
ConAu 49, WhoE 77
Felsen, Henry Gregor 1916- *AuBYP,*
BioIn 2, –7, –9, ConAu 1R, –1NR,
ConLC 17, ScF&FL 1, –2, SmATA 1,
SmATA 2AS[port]
Felt, W Mark 1913- *BioIn 12,*
WhoAm 74, WhoGov 72,
WhoS&SW 73
Felton, Harold William 1902- *AuBYP,*
BioIn 6, –8, –9, ChhPo S2,
ConAu 1R, –1NR, MorJA, SmATA 1
Felton, Ronald Oliver 1909-1982
Au&Wr 71, BioIn 8, –9, ConAu 3NR,
–9R, IntAu&W 77, OxLitW 86,
SmATA 3, WrDr 82
Felton, Ronald Oliver *see also* Welch,
Ronald
Fenady, Andrew J 1928-
ConAu 13NR, –77, IntMPA 77, –75,
–76, –78, –79, –81, –82, –84, –86
Fendell, Bob 1925- *ConAu 57*
Fenderson, Lewis H 1907-1983
ConAu 106, –111, DrAS 74E,
SmATA 37N, –47[port]
Fenelon, Fania 1909-1983 *BioIn 13*
Fenelon, Fania 1918-1983
AnObit 1983, ConAu 111, –77,
NewYTBS 78, –83[port], WhoWor 80
Fenin, George N 1916- *ConAu 9R*
Fenner, Phyllis Reid 1899-1982
AuBYP, BioIn 3, –7, –9, –12, –13,
ConAu 2NR, –5R, –106, ForWC 70,
ScF&FL 1, –2, SmATA 1, –29N,
WhoAmW 74, –58, –61, –64, –66,
–68, –70, –72, –75, –77, WhoLibS 66
Fenten, Barbara D 1935- *BioIn 13,*
ConAu 5NR, –53, SmATA 26
Fenten, D X 1932- *AuBYP SUP,*
BioIn 9, ConAu 5NR, –33R,
SmATA 4, WhoE 75, –77, –79,
WrDr 76, –80, –82, –84, –86
Fenton, Carroll Lane 1900-1969
AmAu&B, AuBYP, BioIn 6, –7, –8,
–10, ConAu 1R, –6NR, –29R, MorJA,
NatCAB 55, SmATA 5, WhE&EA
Fenton, Edward 1917- *AuBYP,*
AuBYP, BioIn 9, –10, ConAu 9R,
–13NR, ScF&FL 1, SmATA 7,
ThrBJA, TwCCW 78, –83, WrDr 80,
–82, –84, –86
Fenton, Mildred Adams 1899-
Au&Wr 71, BioIn 6, –7, –12,
ConAu 77, MorJA, SmATA 21[port]
Fenwick, Elizabeth 1920- *Au&Wr 71,*
TwCCr&M 80, –85, WrDr 82, –84,
–86
Fenwick, Sheridan 1942- *ConAu 69*
Feola, Jose M 1926- *AmM&WS 79P,*
–82P, BiDPara, ConAu 69,
EncO&P 2, –78
Feola, Jose Maria 1926-
AmM&WS 86P
Ferber, Edna *OxThe 83*

Ferber, Edna 1885-1968
DcLB 28[port], EncFWF[port]
Ferber, Edna 1887-1968 *AmAu&B,*
AmNov, AmWomD, AmWomWr,
ApCAB X, AuNews 1, BiE&WWA,
BioIn 1, –2, –3, –4, –5, –6, –8, –9,
–10, –11, –12, Chambr 3, CnDAL,
CnMD, CnThe, ConAmA, ConAmL,
ConAu 5R, –25R, ConLC 18,
DcLB 9[port], DcLEL, EncWL,
EncWT, EvLB, FilmgC, GoodHs,
HalFC 84, InWom, LibW, LinLib L,
–S, LongCTC, McGEWB,
McGEWD, –84[port], ModAL,
ModWD, NatCAB 60, NotAW MOD,
NotNAT A, –B, Novels, ObitOF 79,
ObitT 1961, OxAmL, –83,
OxAmT 84, OxThe, PenC AM,
PIP&P, REn, REnAL, REnAW,
SmATA 7, TwCA, –SUP, TwCWr,
WebAB, –79, WhAm 5, WhE&EA,
WhNAA, WhThe, WhoAmW 58, –61,
–64, –66, –68, –70, WisWca, WomNov,
WorAl
Ferencz, Benjamin B 1920-
ConAu 19NR, –97, WhoAmJ 80,
WhoWorJ 72, –78
Ferencz, Benjamin Berell 1920-
WhoAmL 85
Ferguson, Annabelle Evelyn 1923-
ConAu 102, WhoAmW 74, –64, –66,
–68, –72, –75, –77, –79, WhoE 81
Ferguson, Bob *ConAu X, SmATA X*
Ferguson, Bob *see also* Ferguson,
Robert Bruce
Ferguson, Robert Bruce 1927-
BiDAmM, ConAu 69, SmATA 13
Fergusson, Erna 1888- *WhAm 8*
Fergusson, Erna 1888-1964 *AmAu&B,*
BioIn 3, –4, –7, –9, –10, ConAu P-1,
CurBio 55, InWom, SmATA 5,
WhE&EA
Fergusson, Harvey 1890- *WhAm 8*
Fergusson, Harvey 1890-1971
AmAu&B, AmNov, BioIn 2, –4, –8,
–9, –10, CmCal, CnDAL,
ConAu 33R, EncFWF[port],
OxAmL, –83, REnAL, REnAW,
TwCA, –SUP, WhLit, WhNAA
Ferlinghetti, Lawrence *DrAP&F 85,*
OxEng 85
Ferlinghetti, Lawrence 1919?-
AmAu&B, BioIn 8, –10, –12, –13,
BlueB 76, CasWL, CelR, ConLC,
ConAu 3NR, –5R, ConDr 73, –77,
–82, ConLC 2, –6, –10, –27[port],
ConPo 70, –75, –80, –85, CroCAP,
CroCD, DcLB 5, –16[port],
DcLEL 1940, IntAu&W 77,
IntWW 74, –75, –76, –77, –78, –79,
–80, –81, –82, –83, LinLib L,
ModAL, NewCon[port], OxAmL,
PenC AM, RAdv 1, REn, REnAL,
TwCWr, WebE&AL, WhoAm 74,
–76, –78, –80, –82, –86, WhoTwCL,
WhoWest 74, WhoWor 74, –78, –80,
–82, WorAl, WorAu, WrDr 76, –80,
–82, –84, –86
Ferlinghetti, Lawrence 1920-
OxAmL 83, WhoAm 84
Ferman, Edward L *DrmM 2[port]*
Ferman, Edward L 1937- *ConAu 106,*
ConSFA, EncSF, ScF&FL 1, –2,
WhoAm 82, WhoSciF
Fermi, Laura 1907-1977 *AmAu&B,*
AuBYP, BioIn 3, –4, –5, –7, –10, –11,
–13, BlueB 76, ConAu 1R, –6NR,
CurBio 58, InWom, IntAu&W 77,
SmATA 28N, –6, MorJA 7,
WhoAm 74, –76, –78, WhoAmW 74,
–58, –61, –64, –66, –68, –70, –72,
–75, WhoWor 74, WrDr 76, –80, –82,
–84
Ferrara, Peter J 1955- *WhoAmP 83,*
–85
Ferrara, Peter Joseph 1955-
WhoAm 84, –86
Ferrigno, Lou 1952?- *BioIn 12,*
NewYTBS 76
Ferris, Jean 1939- *ConAu 116*
Ferris, Paul 1929- *Au&Wr 71,*
BlueB 76, ConAu 3NR, –5R,
DcLEL 1940, IntAu&W 76, –77,

Flaubert, Gustave 1821-1880 *AtlBL,
BbD, BiD&SB, BioIn 1, -2, -3, -4,
-5, -6, -7, -8, -9, -10, -11, -12, -13,
CasWL, CelCen, ClDMEL, CyWA,
DcBiA, DcEuL, Dis&D, EncWT,
EuAu, EvEuW, GrFLW, LinLib L,
-S, LongCEL, McGEWB, NewC,
NewEOp 71, NinCLC 2[port],
-10[port], Novels[port], OxEng, -85,
OxFr, PenC EUR, RComWL, REn,
ScF&FL 1, WhDW, WorAl*

Flayderman, Phillip C 1930-1969
ConAu P-2

Fleetwood Mac *BioIn 11,
EncPR&S 74, -77, IlEncRk,
RkOn 78, -84, RolSEnR 83,
WhoRock 81[port], WhoRocM 82*

Fleetwood, Mick 1942- *BioIn 13*

Fleetwood, Mick 1947- *Baker 84,
BioIn 11, WhoAm 78, -80, -82, -84,
-86, WhoRocM 82*

Fleetwood, Mick *see also* Fleetwood
Mac

Fleetwood Mac *see also* Fleetwood,
Mick

Fleetwood Mac *see also* McVie,
Christine Perfect

Fleetwood Mac *see also* McVie, John

Fleetwood Mac *see also* Spencer,
Jeremy

Fleetwood Mac *see also* Welch, Bob

Fleischer, Leonore *BioIn 12,
ConAu 109*

Fleischer, Leonore 1934?- *SmATA 47*

Fleischman, Albert Sidney 1920-
*AuBYP, BioIn 8, -11, -13,
ConAu 1R, WhoAm 82, -84, -86*

Fleischman, Albert Sidney *see also*
Fleischman, Sid

Fleischman, Paul *SmATA 32*

Fleischman, Paul 1952- *ConAu 113,
FifBJA[port], SmATA 39[port]*

Fleischman, Sid *BioIn 13*

Fleischman, Sid 1920- *AnCL, BioIn 9,
ChlLR 1, ConAu 5NR, -X, OxChL,
SmATA 8, ThrBJA, TwCCW 78, -83,
WrDr 80, -82, -84, -86*

Fleischman, Sid *see also* Fleischman,
Albert Sidney

Fleischmann, Glen Harvey 1909-
*AuBYP SUP, BioIn 2, ConAu 33R,
WhoAm 74, -76, -78, -80, -82, -84,
-86, WhoE 74, WhoWor 74, -76, -78,
-80, -82, -84*

Fleissner, Else Mentz 1900-
DrAS 74F, WhoAmW 58

Fleming, Alice 1928- *WrDr 86*

Fleming, Alice Carew Mulcahey 1928-
*AuBYP, BioIn 8, -11, ConAu 1R,
-2NR, ForWC 70, SmATA 9,
WhoAmW 74, -66, -68, -70, -75,
-77, -79, -83, -87, WhoE 74, -79,
-81, WrDr 76, -80, -82, -84*

Fleming, Gordon Howard 1920-
DrAS 78E, -82E

Fleming, Ian *OxChL*

Fleming, Ian 1906-1964 *HalFC 84*

Fleming, Ian 1908-1964 *AuBYP,
BioIn 5, -6, -7, -8, -10, -11,
ConAu 5R, ConLC 3, -30[port],
CorpD, CurBio 64, DcLEL 1940,
EncMys, EncSF, FifBJA[port],
LinLib L, LongCTC, NewC,
Novels[port], ObitOF 79, ObitT 1961,
PenC ENG, REn, ScFSB, SmATA 9,
TwCA, TwCCr&M 80, -85, TwCWr,
WhDW, WhAm 4, WhoSpyF, WorAl,
WorAu*

Fleming, June 1935- *ConAu 110*

Fleming, Ronald Lee 1941-
WhoAm 86, WhoAmA 84

Fleming, Thomas J 1927-
ConLC 37[port]

Fleming, Thomas James 1927-
*AmAu&B, AuBYP SUP, BioIn 11,
ConAu 5R, -10NR, SmATA 8,
WhoAm 74, -76, -78, -80, -82, -84,
-86, WhoWor 74, -76*

Flender, Harold 1924- *AuBYP SUP,
ConAu 49*

Fles, Barthold 1902- *ScF&FL 1, -2*

Fletcher, Adele Whitely 1897?-
*BioIn 12, ConAu P-1, ForWC 70,
WhNAA*

Fletcher, Alan Mark 1928-
*AuBYP SUP, ConAu 73, WrDr 76,
-80, -82, -84, -86*

Fletcher, Charlie May Hogue
1897-1977 *AuBYP, BioIn 9, -11,
-12, ConAu 9R, SmATA 3*

Fletcher, Charlie May Hogue *see also*
Simon, Charlie May

Fletcher, Colin 1922- *AuNews 1,
BioIn 10, -12, -13, ConAu 11NR,
-13R, SmATA 28, WhoAm 74, -76,
-78, -80, -82, -84, -86, WrDr 76,
-80, -82, -84, -86*

Fletcher, David *ConAu X*

Fletcher, David 1940- *IntAu&W 82X,
WrDr 76, -80, -82, -84, -86*

Fletcher, David *see also* Barber, D F

Fletcher, Helen Jill 1911- *AuBYP,
BioIn 8, ConAu 9R, ForWC 70,
SmATA 13*

Flexner, Eleanor 1908- *AmWomWr,
BioIn 12, ConAu 45*

Flexner, James Thomas 1908-
*AmAu&B, Au&Wr 71, BioIn 1, -11,
-12, ConAu 1R, -2NR, IntAu&W 76,
NewYTBE 73, SmATA 9, WhNAA,
WhoAm 74, -76, -78, -80, -82, -84,
-86, WhoAmA 73, -76, -78, -80, -82,
-84, WhoE 74, WorAu 1970,
WrDr 76, -80, -82, -84, -86*

Flexner, Stuart B 1928- *ConAu 11NR,
-13R, DrAS 82F, WrDr 80, -82, -84,
-86*

Flexner, Stuart Berg 1928-
WhoAm 84, -86

Flink, James J 1932- *ConAu 112*

Flink, James John 1932- *DrAS 74H,
-78H, -82H*

Floethe, Louise Lee 1913- *AuBYP,
BioIn 9, ConAu 1R, -2NR,
ForWC 70, SmATA 4, WhoAmW 58*

Floherty, John Joseph 1882-1964
*AmAu&B, AuBYP, BioIn 2, -7, -13,
JBA 51, SmATA 25[port], WhAm 4*

Flood, Charles Bracelen 1929-
*AmAu&B, AmCath 80, ConAu 41R,
ScF&FL 1, -2, WhoAm 74, -76, -78,
WhoE 74, WrDr 80, -82, -84, -86*

Flood, Curt 1938- *AfroAA, ConAu 115,
NewYTBE 70, NewYTBS 81[port],
WorAl*

Flores, Angel 1900- *AmAu&B,
ConAu 103, -19NR, DcSpL,
DrAS 74F, -78F, -82F, ScF&FL 1,
WhoE 83*

Florescu, Radu R 1925- *ConAu 41R,
DrAS 74H, -78H, -82H*

Florman, Samuel C 1925- *WhoTech 84*

Flory, Jane Trescott 1917-
*AuBYP SUP, ConAu 3NR, -9R,
SmATA 22[port]*

Flower, Dean Scott 1938- *ConAu 21R,
DrAS 74E, -78E, -82E*

Flower, Desmond John Newman
1907- *Au&Wr 71, ChhPo, -S2,
ConAu 9R, IntAu&W 76, -77, -82,
IntYB 78, -79, -80, -81, -82,
WhE&EA, Who 74, -82, -83, -85*

Flower, Raymond 1921- *ConAu 108*

Flower, Raymond Charles 1921-
IntAu&W 86

Flumiani, Carlo M 1911- *ConAu 9NR,
-13R*

Flynn, Bethine *BioIn 12*

Flynn, James J 1911-1977
*AuBYP SUP, BioIn 11, ConAu 21R,
DrAS 74H, -78H, NewYTBS 77,
WhoE 74*

Flynn, Robert *DrAP&F 85*

Flynn, Robert 1932- *ConAu 29R,
EncFWF, WrDr 84, -86*

Fodor, Eugene 1905- *AmAu&B,
BioIn 5, ConAu 14NR, -21R,
CurBio 76, IntAu&W 76,
NewYTBS 74, WhoAm 74, -76, -78,
-80, -82, -84, -86, WhoWor 74*

Fogelberg, Dan 1951- *BioIn 13,
EncFCWM 83[port], RkOn 78, -84,
RolSEnR 83, WhoRock 81[port],
WhoRocM 82*

Foley, June 1944- *ConAu 109,
SmATA 44[port]*

Foley, Louise Munro 1933-
*AuBYP SUP, ConAu 37R,
IntAu&W 77X, SmATA 40, WrDr 76,
-80, -82, -84, -86*

Foley, Martha 1897-1977 *AmAu&B,
BioIn 11, ConAu 117, -73,
CurBio 41, -77, -77N, InWom,
NewYTBS 77, -79, ObitOF 79,
REnAL, WhoAmW 74, -58, -64, -66,
-68, -70, -72*

Foley, Rae *BioIn 13*

Foley, Rae 1900-1978 *ConAu X,
SmATA X, TwCCr&M 80, -85*

Foley, Scott *ConAu X*

Foley, Scott *see also* Dareff, Hal

Follett, James 1939- *ConAu 112,
EncSF*

Follett, Ken 1949- *BioIn 11, -13,
ConAu 13NR, -81, ConLC 18,
DcLB Y81B[port], Novels,
TwCCr&M 85, WrDr 86*

Folsom, Franklin Brewster 1907-
*AuBYP, BioIn 8, -10, ConAu 1R,
-2NR, IntAu&W 82, SmATA 5,
WhoAm 76, -78, -80, -82, -84, -86,
WrDr 76, -80, -82, -84, -86*

Fonarow, Jerry 1935- *ConAu 4NR,
-53*

Fon Eisen, Anthony 1917-
ConAu 13R, ScF&FL 2

Foner, Eric 1943- *ConAu 12NR, -29R,
DrAS 74H, -78H, -82H, WhoAm 82,
-84, -86, WrDr 76, -80, -82, -84,
-86*

Foner, Philip S 1910- *AmAu&B,
BlueB 76, ConAu 3NR, -9R,
DrAS 74H, -78H, -82H, IntYB 78,
-79, -80, -81, -82, WhoAm 76, -78,
-80, -82, -84, -86, WhoE 74, -79,
WhoWor 74, WrDr 80, -82, -84, -86*

Fontaine, Theodor 1819-1898 *BiD&SB,
BioIn 1, -3, -5, -7, -11, -12, -13,
CasWL, ChhPo S2, ClDMEL, CyWA,
EncWT, EuAu, EvEuW, GrFLW,
LinLib L, McGEWB, Novels,
OxEng 85, OxGer, PenC EUR, REn,
WhDW*

Fonteyn, Margot *ConAu X, Who 85,
WhoWor 84*

Fonteyn, Margot 1919- *BiDD, BioIn 1,
-2, -3, -4, -5, -6, -7, -8, -9, -10,
-11, -12, -13, BlueB 76, CelR,
ConAu X, CurBio 49, -72, GoodHs,
InWom, IntDcWB, IntWW 74, -75,
-76, -77, -78, -79, -80, -81, -82,
-83, LinLib S, NewYTBE 72,
NewYTBS 74, -80[port], WhDW,
WhThe, Who 74, -82, -83,
WhoAmW 75, WhoWor 74, WorAl*

Fooner, Michael *AuBYP SUP,
BioIn 13, ConAu 81, SmATA 22[port]*

Footman, David John 1895-
*Au&Wr 71, ConAu 97, IntAu&W 76,
-77, -82, ScF&FL 1, WhE&EA,
Who 74, -82, -83*

Forbes, Colin *WrDr 86*

Forbes, Colin 1923- *Au&Wr 71,
ConAu X, IntAu&W 76, WrDr 80,
-82, -84*

Forbes, Colin *see also* Sawkins,
Raymond

Forbes, Esther *OxChL*

Forbes, Esther 1891-1967 *OxAmL 83*

Forbes, Esther 1894?-1967 *AmAu&B,
AmNov, AmWomWr, AnCL, AuBYP,
BioIn 1, -2, -3, -4, -5, -6, -7, -8, -9,
-11, -12, ChhPo S2, ConAu 25R,
ConAu P-1, ConLC 12, CyWA,
DcLB 22[port], DcLEL, InWom,
MorJA, NatCAB 53, Newb 1922,
NotAW MOD, ObitOF 79, OxAmL,
REn, REnAL, ScF&FL 1, -2,
SmATA 2, TwCA, -SUP,
TwCCW 78, -83, WhAm 4,
WhoAmW 58, -64, -66, -68*

Forbes, Kathryn 1909-1966 *AmAu&B,
AmNov, BioIn 2, -4, CmCal,
ConAu X, CurBio 44, -66, InWom,
ObitOF 79, REn, REnAL, SmATA X,
WorAl*

Forbes, Kathryn *see also* McLean,
Kathryn

Forbis, William H 1918- *ConAu 15NR*

Forbis, William Hunt 1918-
*ConAu 37R, WhoAm 74, -76, -78,
-80, -82*

Ford, Adam 1940- *ConAu 111,
Who 85*

Ford, Barbara *ConAu 112, SmATA 34*

Ford, Betty *BioIn 13*

Ford, Betty 1918- *BioIn 12,
BioNews 74, ConAu X, CurBio 75,
HerW 84, NewYTBE 73,
NewYTBS 74, -75, -77, -78,
WhoAm 76, -78, -80, -82,
WhoWest 78, WhoWor 76, -78, -80,
-82*

Ford, Betty Bloomer 1918-
WhoAm 84, -86, WhoWor 84, -87

Ford, Brian J 1939- *ConAu 15NR,
-41R, IntAu&W 77, -82, -86,
WrDr 76, -80, -82, -84*

Ford, Brian John 1939- *WrDr 86*

Ford, Corey 1902-1969 *AmAu&B,
BioIn 5, -8, ConAu 25R,
DcLB 11[port], EncMys, ObitOF 79,
REnAL, WhAm 5, WhE&EA,
WhNAA*

Ford, Daniel 1931- *WhoE 85,
WrDr 86*

Ford, Jesse Hill 1928- *AmAu&B,
BioIn 5, -9, ConAu 1R, -1NR,
ConNov 72, -76, -82, -86,
DcLB 6[port], DcLEL 1940,
IntAu&W 76, -77, -86, OxAmL 83,
PenC AM, WhoAm 74, -76, -78, -80,
-82, -84, -86, WhoWor 82, WrDr 76,
-80, -82, -84, -86*

Ford, Paul Leicester 1865-1902
*Alli SUP, AmAu, AmAu&B, AmBi,
ApCAB, BbD, BiD&SB, BioIn 11,
CarSB, Chambr 3, ChhPo S1,
CnDAL, ConAu 25R, DcAmB, DcBiA,
DcLEL, DcNAA, EvLB, HarEnUS,
JBA 34, LinLib L, -S, McGEWB,
NatCAB 13, OxAmL, -83, REn,
REnAL, TwCBDA, WebAB, -79,
WhAm 1*

Ford, Richard *DrAP&F 85*

Ford, Richard 1944- *BioIn 13,
WrDr 86*

Forde-Johnston, James 1927-
*Au&Wr 71, ConAu 3NR, -9R,
IntAu&W 76, -77, -82, WhoWor 78,
WrDr 76, -80, -82, -84, -86*

Fordin, Hugh 1935- *BiE&WWA,
ConAu 57, ConTFT 1, NotNAT,
WrDr 76, -80, -82, -84, -86*

Forer, Lois G 1914- *WhoAmL 85*

Forer, Lois Goldstein 1914-
*AmBench 79, BioIn 3, ConAu 29R,
WhoAm 74, -76, WhoAmL 78, -79,
WhoAmW 74, -58, -68, -70, -72,
WomPO 76, -78*

Forest, Antonia *BioIn 13, ConAu 103,
OxChL, SmATA 29[port],
TwCCW 78, -83, WrDr 76, -80, -82,
-84, -86*

Forester, C S 1899-1966 *ConAu 25R,
-73, ConLC 35[port], EncSF, FilmgC,
HalFC 84, LinLib L, -S, Novels,
ObitOF 79, ObitT 1961, OxChL,
OxEng 85, ScF&FL 1, SmATA 13,
WhE&EA, WorAl*

Forester, Cecil Scott 1899-1966
*AmAu&B, BioIn 1, -2, -3, -4, -5, -7,
-8, -9, ConAu 25R, CyWA, DcLEL,
DcNaB 1961, EncMys, EvLB,
LongCTC, MnBBF, ModBrL,
NatCAB 53, NewC, OxShips, RAdv 1,
REn, REnAL, SmATA 13,
TwCA, -SUP, TwCWr, WebE&AL,
WhAm 4, WhLit, WhoChL*

Forkner, Benjamin Sands, III 1944-
WhoWor 82

Forman, Brenda 1936- *Au&Wr 71,
AuBYP, BioIn 8, -9, ConAu 6NR,
-9R, ForWC 70, SmATA 4,
WhoAmW 75*

Forman, James Douglas 1932- *AuBYP,
BioIn 8, -9, -11, ConAu 4NR, -9R,
-19NR, ConLC 21[port],
IntAu&W 76, -77, -82, SmATA 8,
ThrBJA*

Forrest, David *ConAu X,
IntAu&W 77X, -82X, ScF&FL 1,
WrDr 82, -84*

Forrest, Richard S 1932- *ConAu 9NR, -57*

Forrester, Helen *BioIn 13, ConAu X, IntAu&W 76X, -77X, -86X, WhoCanL 85, WrDr 76, -80, -82, -84, -86*

Forrester, Helen 1919- *SmATA 48[port]*

Forrester, Helen *see also* Bhatia, June

Forsee, Aylesa *AuBYP SUP, ConAu 1R, -1NR, InWom, IntAu&W 76, -77, -82, SmATA 1, WhoAm 74, -76, -78, -80, -82, -84, WhoAmW 74, -70A, -72, -75, WhoFrS 84, WrDr 76, -80, -82, -84, -86*

Forshay-Lunsford, Cin 1965- *ConAu 119*

Forster, E M 1879-1970 *AtlBL, BritWr 6, CasWL, Chambr 3, ChhPo S2, -S3, CnMWL, ConAu 25R, ConAu P-1, ConLC 1, -2, -3, -4, -9, -10, -13, -15, -22[port], ConLCrt, -82, CyWA, DcLB 34[port], DcLEL, EncSF, EncWL, -2[port], EvLB, LinLib L, -S, LongCEL, LongCTC, ModBrL, -S2, -S1, NewC, Novels[port], ObitOF 79, ObitT 1961, OxEng, -85, PenC ENG, RAdv 1, RComWL, REn, ScF&FL 1, ScFSB, SupFW, TwCA, -SUP, TwCWr, WebE&AL, WhAm 5, WhoTwCL, WorAl*

Forsyth, Frederick 1938- *BioIn 9, -11, -12, ConAu 85, ConLC 2, -5, -36[port], ConNov 82, -86, CurBio 86[port], HalFC 84, IntAu&W 76, -77, NewYTBS 80[port], Novels[port], TwCCr&M 80, -85, WhoAm 74, -76, -78, -80, WhoSpyF, WhoWor 84, -87, WorAl, WorAu 1975[port], WrDr 76, -80, -82, -84, -86*

Forsythe, George Elmer 1917-1972 *AmM&WS 73P, -76P, BioIn 9, NewYTBE 72, WhAm 5*

Forte, David F 1941- *ConAu 53*

Forten, Charlotte L *ConAu X*

Forten, Charlotte L 1837-1914 *DcAmNB, DcLB 50, InB&W 80, -85, NegAl 76, TwCLC 16[port]*

Forten, Charlotte L 1838-1914 *SelBAAf*

Forward, Robert L *ScFSB*

Forward, Robert L 1932- *AmM&WS 73P, -76P, -79P, -82P, -86P, ConAu 103, -20NR, TwCSFW 86, WhoAm 86, WhoTech 82, -84, WhoWest 84, WrDr 86*

Fosdick, Harry Emerson 1878-1969 *AmAu&B, ApCAB X, AuBYP, BiDAmM, BiDMoPL, BioIn 1, -2, -3, -4, -6, -7, -8, -9, -10, -11, ConAu 25R, CurBio 40, -69, DcAmReB, LinLib L, -S, LuthC 75, McGEWB, NatCAB 55, ObitOF 79, OxAmH, REnAL, TwCA SUP, WebAB, -79, WhLit, WhNAA, WorAl*

Foss, William O 1918- *AuBYP, BioIn 8, ConAu 17R*

Foster, Alan Dean 1946- *ConAu 5NR, -53, EncSF, IntAu&W 77, -82, ScF&FL 1, -2, ScFSB, TwCSFW 86, WrDr 84, -86*

Foster, F Blanche 1919- *BiDrLUS 70, BioIn 11, ConAu 61, SmATA 11, WhoAmW 83, -85, -87, WhoMW 78, -80, -82, -84*

Foster, G Allen 1907-1969 *BioIn 8, -13, ConAu 9R, SmATA 26*

Foster, Genevieve 1893-1979 *AmAu&B, AnCL, AuICB, AuBYP, BioIn 2, -5, -8, -9, -10, -12, -13, ChlLR 7[port], ConAu 4NR, -5R, -89, IlsCB 1946, -1957, -1967, JBA 51, MorBMP, NewYTBS 79, SmATA 2, -23N, WhoAmA 80N, -82N, -84N, WrDr 76, -80*

Foster, John T 1925- *AuBYP SUP, BioIn 11, ConAu 33R, SmATA 8*

Foster, M A 1939- *ConAu 9NR, -57, EncSF, ScFSB, TwCSFW 86*

Foster, Robert 1949- *ConAu 81, ScF&FL 1*

Foster, Robert Fitzroy 1949- *BiDIrW*

Foulds, Elfrida Vipont 1902- *BioIn 2, -8, ConAu 4NR, -53, IntAu&W 76, -77, -82, WrDr 76, -80, -82, -84, -86*

Foulds, Elfrida Vipont *see also* Vipont, Charles

Foulds, Elfrida Vipont *see also* Vipont, Elfrida

Fountaine, Margaret 1862-1940 *BioIn 12*

Fowke, Edith Margaret 1913- *BioIn 10, -12, CaW, CanWW 70, -79, -80, -81, -83, ChhPo S1, -S2, -S3, ConAu 37R, DrAS 74E, -78E, -82E, IntAu&W 76, -77, -82, -86, OxCan, -SUP, Profile, SmATA 14, WhoAm 80, -82, WhoAmW 75, -77, -79, -81, -83, WrDr 76, -80, -82, -84, -86*

Fowke, Edith Margaret Fulton 1913- *WhoAm 84, -86, WhoAmW 85, -87*

Fowler, Francis George 1870-1918 *DcLEL, LongCTC, OxEng 85, TwCA, -SUP*

Fowler, H W 1858-1933 *LinLib L, LongCTC, PenC ENG*

Fowler, Henry Watson 1858-1933 *BioIn 2, -3, -4, -7, DcLEL, DcNaB 1931, EncAJ, EvLB, NewC, OxEng 85, REn, TwCA, -SUP*

Fowler, Raymond E 1933- *ConAu 85, UFOEn[port]*

Fowler, Robert Howard 1926- *CanWW 79, ConAu 73, WhoAm 74, -76, -78, -80, -82, -84, -86, WhoE 74, WhoF&I 74, WhoWor 74*

Fowler, Virginia *BioIn 3, ConAu X*

Fowler, Virginie *see also* Elbert, Virginie Fowler

Fowles, John 1926- *ASpks, Au&Wr 71, AuBYP SUP, BioIn 7, -8, -10, -11, -12, -13, CelR, ConAu 5R, ConLC 1, -2, -3, -4, -6, -9, -10, -15, -33[port], ConNov 72, -76, -82, -86, CurBio 77, DcLB 14[port], DcLEL 1940, EncWL, -2, HalFC 84, IntAu&W 76, -77, IntWW 74, -75, -76, -77, -78, -79, -80, -81, -82, -83, IntWWP 77, LinLib L, ModBrL S2, -S1, NewC, NewYTBS 74, -77, Novels[port], PostFic, RAdv 1, SmATA 22[port], TwCWr, WebE&AL, Who 82, -83, -85, WhoAm 80, -82, -84, -86, WhoWor 74, -76, -78, -80, -82, -84, -87, WorAl, WorAu, WrDr 76, -80, -82, -84, -86*

Fox, Aileen 1907- *Au&Wr 71, ConAu 5R, -5NR, WrDr 76, -80, -82, -84, -86*

Fox, Anthony 1924- *ConAu X, WrDr 82, -84, -86*

Fox, Larry 1930- *WhoAm 86*

Fox, Larry 1942- *AuBYP SUP, ConAu 106, SmATA 30, WhoMW 74, -76, -78*

Fox, Mary Virginia 1919- *AuBYP, BioIn 7, ConAu 12NR, -29R, SmATA 39, -44[port]*

Fox, Michael W 1937- *ConAu 14NR*

Fox, Michael Wilson 1937- *AmM&WS 73S, -76P, -78S, -79P, -82P, -86P, AuBYP SUP, BioIn 12, -13, ConAu 73, CurBio 77, SmATA 15, WhoAm 78, -80, -82, -84, -86, WhoWor 82, WrDr 76, -80*

Fox, Paula *DrAP&F 85*

Fox, Paula 1923- *AmWomWr, AuBYP SUP, BioIn 10, -11, -12, -13, ChlLR 1, ConAu 20NR, -73, ConLC 2, -8, DcLB 52[port], FourBJA, IntAu&W 76, NewYTBS 81[port], OxChL, SenS, NewbC 1966, SmATA 17, TwCCW 78, -83, WhoAm 74, -76, -78, -80, -82, -84, -86, WhoAmW 87, WhoE 75, -77, WrDr 76, -80, -82, -84, -86*

Fox, Ray Errol 1941- *ConAu 85, IntAu&W 82, NatPD, -81[port]*

Fox, Robert J 1927- *AmCath 80, ConAu 1NR, -17NR, -45, SmATA 33[port]*

Fox, William Price 1926- *BioIn 11, -13, ConAu 11NR, -17R, ConLC 22[port], Conv 1, DcLB 2, -Y81A[port], OxAmL 83*

Foyt, Anthony Joseph 1935- *BioIn 6, -7, -8, -9, -10, -11, -13, BusPN, WebAB, -79*

Fradin, Dennis Brindell 1945- *BioIn 13*

Frame, Donald Murdoch 1911- *ConAu 17R, DrAS 74F, -78F, -82F, IntAu&W 76, -77, -82, WhoAm 74, -76, -78, -80, WhoE 74, WhoWor 78, WrDr 76, -80, -82, -84, -86*

Frame, Paul 1913- *BioIn 8, ConAu 111, IlsBYP, IlsCB 1957, -1967, SmATA 33*

Frampton, Peter 1950- *Baker 84, BioIn 10, -11, ConAu 117, CurBio 78, EncPR&S 74, -77S, IlEncRk, NewYTBS 76, RkOn 78, -84, RolSEnR 83, WhoAm 78, -80, -82, -84, -86, WhoRock 81[port], WhoRocM 82, WorAl*

France, Anatole 1844- *ScFSB*

France, Anatole 1844-1922 *OxEng 85*

France, Anatole 1844-1924 *AtlBL, BbD, BiD&SB, BioIn 1, -2, -4, -5, -6, -8, -9, -10, CasWL, ClDMEL, ConAu X, CyWA, DcBiA, DcEuL, Dis&D, EncSF, EncWL, -2[port], EvEuW, InWom, LinLib L, -LP, -S, LongCTC, McGEWB, ModFrL, ModRL, NewC, NewEOp 71, Novels, OxEng, OxFr, PenC EUR, PIP&P, RComWL, REn, ScF&FL 1, SupFW, TwCA, -SUP, TwCLC 9[port], TwCWr, WhDW, WhThe, WhoNob, WhoTwCL, WorAl*

Franchere, Ruth 1906- *BioIn 12, ConAu 73, FourBJA, SmATA 18, WhoPNW*

Francis, Clare 1946- *ConAu 15NR, -77, IntAu&W 86, IntDcWB, Who 82, -83, WhoWor 80, WrDr 84, -86*

Francis, Dick *NewYTBS 84[port]*

Francis, Dick 1920- *ASpks, Au&Wr 71, BioIn 8, -9, -10, -11, -12, -13, ConAu 5R, -9NR, ConLC 2, -22[port], -42[port], ConNov 76, -82, -86, CorpD, CurBio 81[port], EncMys, IntAu&W 76X, -77, NewYTBS 80[port], -82[port], Novels[port], TwCCr&M 80, -85, Who 74, -82, -83, -85, WhoAm 82, -84, -86, WorAl, WorAu 1970, WrDr 76, -80, -82, -84, -86*

Francis, Dorothy Brenner 1926- *BioIn 11, ConAu 9NR, -21R, SmATA 10, WhoAmW 74, -75, WomPO 76, -78, WrDr 76, -80, -82, -84, -86*

Francis, H E *DrAP&F 85*

Francis, H E 1924- *ConAu 10NR, WrDr 84*

Francis, H E, Jr. 1924- *WrDr 86*

Francis, Philip Sheridan 1918- *ConAu 17R*

Franck, Irene M 1941- *ConAu 21NR*

Franck, Irene Mary 1941- *WhoAmW 85, -87*

Francke, Linda Bird 1939- *ConAu 15NR, -85, WhoAm 78, -80, -82, -84, -86, WhoAmW 77*

Franco, Jean 1924- *ConAu 9NR, -21R, DrAS 74F, -78F, -82F, WhoAm 84, -86*

Franco, Johan 1908- *Baker 78, -84, BioIn 1, CpmDNM 82, ConAmC, -82, ConAu 97, DcCM, IntWWM 77, -85, WhoAm 74, -76, -78, -80, -82, -84, -86, WhoAmM 83, WhoMus 72, WhoS&SW 73, -75, -76*

Frank, Anne 1929-1945 *BioIn 2, -3, -4, -5, -7, -8, -10, -11, -12, -13, ConAu 113, DcAmSR, EncTR,*

GoodHs, HerW, -84, HisEWW, InWom, IntDcWB, LinLib L, REn, SmATA 42, TwCLC 17[port], TwCWr, WhWW-II, WorAl

Frank, Gerold 1907- *Au&Wr 71, BioIn 5, -7, -8, -9, ConAu 109, HalFC 84, IntAu&W 76, WhoAm 74, -76, -78, -80, -82, -84, -86, WhoWor 80, -82, -84, -87, WorAl*

Frank, Pat 1907-1964 *AmNov, BioIn 1, -2, -3, -5, -7, ConAu 5R, EncSF, ScF&FL 1, -2, ScFSB, TwCSFW 86, WhAm 4, WhoAmP 77, -79, WhoSciF*

Frank, Stuart Marshall 1948- *WhoE 85*

Franke, Herbert W 1927- *BioIn 11, ConAu 110, EncSF, ScF&FL 1, ScFSB, TwCSFW 86A, WhoSciF, WhoWor 78*

Frankel, Edward 1910- *AuBYP, BioIn 8, ConAu 65, LEduc 74, SmATA 44[port]*

Frankel, Haskel 1926- *ConAu 89*

Frankel, Sandor 1943- *ConAu 33R, IntAu&W 82, -86, WhoAm 74, -76, -78, -80, -82, -84, -86, WhoAmJ 80, WhoAmL 83, -85, WhoE 83, WrDr 76, -80, -82, -84, -86*

Frankenberg, Lloyd d1975 *ObitOF 79*

Frankenberg, Lloyd 1907-1975 *AmAu&B, BioIn 4, -10, ChhPo S1, -S3, ConAu 1R, -6NR, -57, NewYTBS 75, REnAL, TwCA SUP, WhAm 6, WhoAm 74*

Frankenberg, Robert Clinton 1911- *BioIn 5, -8, IlsBYP, IlsCB 1946, -1957, -1967, SmATA 22[port], WhoAmA 78, -80, -82, -84*

Frankenstein, Alfred 1906-1981 *AmAu&B, AnObit 1981, Baker 78, -84, BioIn 12, CmCal, ConAu 1R, -2NR, -104, DrAS 74H, -78H, NewYTBS 81[port], WhAm 8, WhoAm 74, -76, -78, -80, WhoAmA 73, -76, -78, -80, -82N, WhoMus 72, WhoWest 74, WhoWor 74, WrDr 82*

Franklin, Benjamin 1706-1790 *Alli, AmAu, AmAu&B, AmBi, AmWr, AmWrBE, ApCAB, AsBiEn, AtlBL, Baker 78, -84, BbD, BiAUS, BiDAmEd, BiDAmS, BiD&SB, BiDPsy, BiDrAC, BiESc, BioIn 1, -2, -3, -4, -5, -6, -7, -8, -9, -10, -11, -12, -13, BriEAA, CasWL, Chambr 3, ChhPo, -S1, -S2, -S3, CnDAL, CrtT 3, -4, CyAG, CyAL 1, CyEd[port], CyWA, DcAmAu, DcAmB, DcAmDH, DcAmLiB, DcAmMeB, DcAmSR, DcBiPP, DcEnL, DcInv, DcLB 24[port], -43[port], DcLEL, DcNAA, DcScB, Dis&D, Drake, EncAAH, EncAB-H, EncAJ, EncAR, EncO&P 2, -78S1, EvLB, GolEC, HarEnUS[port], InSci, LinLib L, -S, McGEWB, MemAm, MouLC 2, NamesHP[port], NatCAB 1, NewC, NewYHSD, OxAmH, OxAmL, -83, OxAmT 84, OxChess 84, OxEng, -85, OxMed 86, OxMus, PenC AM, RComWL, REn, REnAL, REnAW, TwCBDA, WebAB, -79, WebE&AL, WhDW, WhAm HS, WhAmP, WhoEc 81, -86, WorAl*

Franklin, H Bruce 1934- *BioIn 9, -11, ConAu 5NR, -9NR, ConSFA, DrAS 74E, -78E, -82E, EncSF, IntAu&W 77, -82, NewYTBE 72, ScF&FL 1, -2, WhE&EA, WhoE 77, WhoSciF*

Franklin, Harold 1920- *ConAu 29R, SmATA 13, WhoBlA 75, -77, -80*

Franklin, John H 1915- *WrDr 86*

Franklin, John Hope 1915- *AmAu&B, BioIn 5, -6, -8, -9, -11, -12, -13, BlueB 76, ConAu 1R, -1NR, -3NR, -5R, CurBio 63, DcLEL 1940, DrAS 74H, -78H, -82H, Ebony 1, EncAAH, EncSoH, InB&W 80, -85, IntAu&W 82, IntWW 83, LinLib L, -S, LivgBAA, NegAl 76[port].*

-83[port], SelBAAf, SelBAAu,
WebAB, -79, Who 83, WhoAm 74,
-76, -78, -80, -82, -84, -86,
WhoBlA 75, -77, -80, -85,
WhoWor 74, -78, -80, -82, -84, -87,
WorAu 1975[port], WrDr 76, -80,
-82, -84

Franklin, Jon Daniel 1942- BioIn 10,
ConAu 104, WhoAm 80, -82, -84,
-86

Franklin, Miles WomNov

Franklin, Miles 1879-1954 BioIn 1, -6,
-8, -9, -12, -13, CasWL, ConAu 104,
IntDcWB, McGEWB, ModCmwL,
OxAusL, TwCLC 7[port], TwCWr,
WorAu 1975

Franks, Arthur Henry 1907-
WhE&EA

Franks, Lucinda Laura 1946-
ConAu 53, WhoAm 74, -76, -78, -80,
-82, -84, -86, WhoAmW 74, -81

Franz, Barbara E 1946- ConAu 110

Franz, William S 1945- ConAu 110

Franzen, Nils-Olof 1916- BioIn 11,
ConAu 29R, IntAu&W 86,
SmATA 10

Fraser, Amy Stewart 1892-
ConAu 9NR, -49, IntAu&W 76, -77,
WrDr 76, -80, -82, -84, -86

Fraser, Antonia 1932-
ConLC 32[port], TwCCr&M 85,
Who 85, WrDr 86

Fraser, Conon 1930- Au&Wr 71,
ConAu P-1, IntAu&W 76, -77,
WrDr 76, -80, -82, -84, -86

Fraser, G S 1915-1980 AnObit 1980,
BioIn 10, -13, CmScLit, ConAu 105,
-85, ConLCrt, -82, ConPo 70, -75,
-80, DcLB 27[port], ModBrL,
PenC ENG, REn, WorAu

Fraser, Lady Antonia 1932- BioIn 8,
-10, -11, -12, -13, BlueB 76,
ChhPo S3, ConAu 85, CurBio 74,
DcLEL 1940, IntAu&W 76,
IntWW 74, -75, -76, -77, -78, -79,
-80, -81, -82, -83, NewYTBS 79,
-84[port], OxEng 85, SmATA 32,
ThrtnMM, TwCCr&M 80, Who 74,
-82, -83, WhoAmW 74, WhoWor 74,
-76, -78, WorAl, WorAu 1970,
WrDr 76, -80, -82, -84

Frassanito, William A 1946-
ConAu 9NR, -57

Frayn, Michael NewYTBS 85[port]

Frayn, Michael 1933- Au&Wr 71,
BioIn 10, -13, ConAu 5R, ConDr 73,
-77, -82, ConLC 7, -31[port],
ConNov 72, -76, -82, -86, ConSFA,
CurBio 85[port], DcLB 13[port],
-14[port], DcLEL 1940, EncSF,
IntAu&W 76, -77, -82, -86,
ModBrL S2, -S1, NewC, Novels,
OxEng 85, OxThe 83, ScF&FL 1, -2,
TwCSFW 86, Who 74, -82, -83, -85,
WhoThe 77, -81, WhoWor 76,
WorAl, WrDr 76, -80, -82, -84, -86

Frazer, Sir James George ConAu X

Frazer, Sir James George 1854-1941
Alli, -SUP, AtlBL, BioIn 1, -2, -3,
-5, -6, -9, -10, -11, CasWL,
Chambr 3, CmScLit, CurBio 41,
DcEnA AP, DcLEL, DcNaB 1941,
DcScB, DcSoc, EvLB, InSci,
LinLib L, -S, LongCEL, LongCTC,
LuthC 75, McGEWB, NewC,
ObitOF 79, OxEng, -85, PenC ENG,
REn, TwCA, -SUP, WebE&AL,
WhDW, WhE&EA, WhLit, WorAl

Frazier, Kendrick 1942- ConAu 17NR

Frazier, Kendrick Crosby 1942-
ConAu 101, WhoAm 78, -80, -82,
-84, WhoWest 82

Frazier, Neta Lohnes 1890- AuBYP,
BioIn 7, -10, ConAu 1R, -1NR,
ForWC 70, SmATA 7, WhoAmW 58,
-61, -64, -66, -70, -72, WhoPNW,
WrDr 76, -80, -82, -84

Frazier, Walt 1945- BioIn 8, -9, -10,
-11, -12, CelR, ConAu 103,
CurBio 73, NewYTBE 72, -73,
NewYTBS 74, -75, -76, -77, -78,
WhoAm 74, -76, -78, -80, -82,
WhoBbl 73, WhoBlA 75, -77, -80,
-85, WorAl

Freas, Frank Kelly 1922- ConAu 102,
-21NR, EncSF, WhoAm 78, -80, -82,
-84, -86, WhoSciF

Fredericks, Fred 1929- ArtCS

Frederikson, Edna DrAP&F 85

Frederikson, Edna 1904- ConAu 49

Freed, Alvyn M 1913-
AmM&WS 73S, -78S, BioIn 13,
ConAu 8NR, -61, SmATA 22[port]

Freedgood, Lillian 1911- ConAu 13R

Freedland, Michael 1934-
ConAu 11NR, -65, IntAu&W 77,
-82, -86, WhoWor 80, WrDr 76, -80,
-82, -84, -86

Freedley, George 1904-1967
AmAu&B, BiE&WWA, BioIn 1, -4,
-8, ConAu 4NR, -5R, CurBio 47,
-67, EncAJ, NotNAT B, OxAmT 84,
OxThe, WhAm 4, WhE&EA, WhThe,
WhoLibS 55

Freedman, Benedict 1919- AmAu&B,
AmNov, BioIn 1, -2, -3, -13,
ConAu 69, CurBio 47,
SmATA 27[port], WhoAm 74, -76

Freedman, Nancy 1920- AmAu&B,
AmNov, BioIn 1, -2, -3, -13,
ConAu 1NR, -19NR, -45, CurBio 47,
EncSF, ForWC 70, In Wom,
IntAu&W 86, ScF&FL 1, -2, ScFSB,
SmATA 27[port], TwCSFW 86,
WhoAm 74, -76, -78, -80,
WhoAmW 74, -64, -66, -68, -70,
-72, WrDr 80, 82, -84, -86

Freedman, Russell 1929- AuBYP,
BioIn 8, -12, ConAu 7NR, -17R,
ScF&FL 1, -2, SmATA 16, WhoE 74

Freehan, Bill 1941- WhoAm 74,
WhoProB 73

Freehof, Solomon B 1892- ConAu 93,
WhoWorJ 72

Freeling, Nicolas 1927- ASpks,
BioIn 7, -10, -11, ConAu 1NR,
-17NR, -49, ConLC 38[port],
ConNov 72, -76, -82, -86, EncMys,
IntAu&W 76, -82, -86, Novels,
TwCCr&M 80, -85, TwCWr,
Who 74, -82, -83, -85, WhoAm 74,
WorAl, WorAu, WrDr 76, -80, -82,
-84, -86

Freeman, Barbara C 1906- Au&Wr 71,
BioIn 13, ConAu 73, IntAu&W 76,
-77, SmATA 28, TwCCW 78, -83,
WrDr 76, -80, -82, -84, -86

Freeman, Bill BioIn 13, OxCanL,
SmATA X

Freeman, Don 1908-1978 AmPB,
AuBYP, BioIn 2, -3, -5, -6, -8, -11,
-12, BkP, ConAu 77, IlsCB 1946,
-1957, -1967, MorJA, NewYTBS 78,
SmATA 17, TwCCW 78, -83,
WhoAmA 78N, -80N, -82N

Freeman, Don 1909-1978
WhoAmA 84N

Freeman, Douglas Southall 1886-1953
AmAu&B, BioIn 1, -2, -3, -4, -5,
-11, -12, -13, ConAu 109, CyWA,
DcAmB S5, DcLB 17[port], EncSoH,
LinLib L, McGEWB,
NatCAB 58[port], ObitOF 79,
ObitT 1951, OxAmH, OxAmL, -83,
REn, REnAL, TwCA, -SUP,
TwCLC 11[port], WebAB, -79,
WhAm 3, WhJnl

Freeman, Ira M 1905- AmAu&B,
AmM&WS 73P, -76P, -79P, AuBYP,
BioIn 6, -7, -12, ConAu 73, MorJA,
SmATA 21[port]

Freeman, James Montague 1936-
AmM&WS 73S, ConAu 102

Freeman, Leslie Jane 1944-
ConAu 106, DrAS 78E, -82E

Freeman, Lucy IntAu&W 86,
ThrtnMM

Freeman, Lucy 1916- AmAu&B,
BioIn 2, -3, -12, -13, ConAu 3NR,
-5R, CurBio 53, ForWC 70, In Wom,
SmATA 24[port], WhoAm 74, -76,
-78, -80, -82, -84, -86, WhoAmJ 80,
WhoAmW 74, -58, -61, -64, -66,
-68, -70, -72, WhoWorJ 72, -78,
WrDr 76, -80, -82, -84, -86

Freeman, Mae 1907- BioIn 6, -8, -13,
ConAu 73, MorJA, SmATA 25[port],
WhoAmW 58, -61

Freeman, Mary E Wilkins 1852-1930
AmAu&B, AmBi, AmLY,
AmWomWr, BioIn 1, -4, -8, -9, -11,
-12, CarSB, CasWL, ChhPo, -S1,
-S2, CnDAL, ConAmL, ConAu 106,
DcAmAu, DcAmB, DcEnA AP,
DcLB 12[port], DcLEL, DcNAA,
HarEnUS, InWom, LibW, LinLib L,
-S, LongCTC, NotAW, Novels,
OxAmL, -83, OxEng, -85, PenC AM,
REn, REnAL, ScF&FL 1, TwCA,
TwCLC 9[port], WebAB, -79,
WhAm 1, WhoHr&F, WomWWA 14

Freeman, Mary Eleanor 1852-1930
BioIn 13, WomNov

Freeman, Warren Samuel 1911-
ConAu 5R, WhoAm 74, -76, -78,
-80, -82

Freemantle, Brian 1936-
TwCCr&M 80, -85, WrDr 82, -86

Freemantle, Brian Harry 1936-
ConAu 16NR

Freese, Arthur S 1917- ConAu 77

Fregosi, Claudia 1946- AuBYP SUP,
BioIn 13, ConAu 69, SmATA 24[port]

Freidel, Frank Burt, Jr. 1916-
AmAu&B, ConAu 1R, -5NR,
DrAS 78H, -82H, WhoAm 74, -76,
-78, -80, -82, -84, -86

Fremantle, Anne 1910- AmAu&B,
AmWomWr, BioIn 3, -4, -9, -12,
BkC 5, CathA 1952, ConAu 13R,
LongCTC, REnAL, TwCA SUP,
WhoAmW 58, -61, -64, WrDr 80,
-82, -84, -86

French, Allen 1870-1946 AmAu&B,
BioIn 1, -2, -11, CarSB, ChhPo,
DcAmAu, JBA 34, -51, MnBBF,
NatCAB 34, REnAL, WhAm 2,
YABC 1

French, Bevan M 1937- WhoTech 84

French, Bevan Meredith 1937-
AmM&WS 73P, -76P, -79P, -82P,
-86P, ConAu 97, WhoAm 78, -80,
-82, -84, -86, WhoTech 82

French, Dorothy Kayser 1926-
AuBYP, BioIn 8, -10, ConAu 3NR,
-9R, ForWC 70, IntAu&W 76, -77,
-82, -86, SmATA 5, WhoAm W 75,
-77, -79

French, Michael Raymond 1944-
ConAu 89, IntAu&W 82

Frese, Dolores Warwick 1936-
ConAu 5R, -9NR, DrAS 78E, -82E

Frewer, Glyn 1931- Au&Wr 71,
AuBYP, BioIn 8, -11, ConAu 10NR,
-13R, IntAu&W 76, -77, -82,
ScF&FL 1, -2, SmATA 11,
WhoWor 76, WrDr 76, -80, -82, -84,
-86

Frey, Glenn 1948- WhoAm 80, -82,
-84, -86, WhoRocM 82

Frey, Glenn see also Eagles, The

Frey, Shaney BioIn 8

Fribourg, Marjorie G 1920- AuBYP,
BioIn 8, ConAu 1R, -4NR

Frick, C H ConAu X, IntAu&W 77X,
-82X, SmATA 6, WrDr 76, -80, -82,
-84, -86

Frick, C H see also Irwin, Constance
Frick

Frick, Constance 1913- BioIn 3,
ConAu X, SmATA 6, WhoLibS 55

Frick, Constance see also Irwin,
Constance Frick

Friday, Nancy WrDr 86

Friday, Nancy 1937- BioIn 12,
ConAu 77, WhoAm 80, -82, -84, -86,
WrDr 82, -84

Fridell, Squire 1943- ConTFT 1

Fried, John J 1940- ConAu 12NR,
-33R

Fried, Joseph P 1939- ConAu 37R,
WhoE 75, WrDr 76, -80, -82, -84

Fried, Martha Nemes 1923-
WhoAmW 61

Friedan, Betty 1921- AmAu&B,
AmWomWr, BioIn 6, -9, -10, -11,
-12, -13, BlueB 76, CelR,
ConAu 18NR, -65, ConIsC 2[port],
CurBio 70, EncAB-H, ForWC 70,
GoodHs, IntDcWB, IntWW 74, -75,
-76, -77, -78, -79, -80, -81, -82,

-83, LibW, LinLib L, MakMC,
NewYTBE 70, -71, OxAmL 83,
PolProf J, PolProf NF, WebAB, -79,
WhoAm 74, -76, -78, -80, -82, -84,
-86, WhoAmJ 80, WhoAmW 74, -66,
-68, -72, -75, -77, -79, -81, -83,
-85, -87, WhoWor 78, -80, -82, -84,
-87, WorAl, WorAu 1975[port],
WrDr 76, -80, -82, -84, -86

Friedberg, Maurice 1929- ConAu 1R,
-5NR, DrAS 74F, -78F, -82F,
IntAu&W 76, -77, WhoAm 74, -76,
-78, -80, -82, -84, -86, WhoAmJ 80,
WhoMW 74, -76, -78, WhoWor 78,
WhoWorJ 72, -78, WrDr 76, -80,
-82, -84, -86

Friedland, Ronald Lloyd 1937-1975
BioIn 9, ConAu 57, ConAu P-2

Friedlander, Saul ConAu X

Friedlander, Saul 1932- BioIn 12,
WhoWorJ 72

Friedman, Albert B 1920-
ConAu 17NR

Friedman, Albert Barron 1920-
ConAu 1R, DrAS 74E, -78E, -82E,
LElec, WhoAm 74, -76, -78, -80,
-82, -84, -86, WhoWest 74,
WhoWorJ 72, -78

Friedman, Bruce Jay DrAP&F 85,
OxAmT 84

Friedman, Bruce Jay 1930- AmAu&B,
BioIn 7, -8, -9, -10, -11, ConAu 9R,
ConDr 73, -77, -82, ConLC 3, -5,
ConNov 72, -76, -82, -86,
ConTFT 1, -3, CurBio 72, DcLB 2,
-28[port], DcLEL 1940, EncSF,
IntAu&W 76, -77, LinLib L,
McGEWD, -84, ModAL, -S1,
NatPD, -81[port], Novels, OxAmL 83,
PenC AM, RAdv 1, WhoAm 74, -76,
-78, -80, WhoThe 81, WorAl,
WorAu, WrDr 76, -80, -82, -84, -86

Friedman, Estelle Ehrenwald 1920-
AuBYP, BioIn 8, -10, ConAu 5R,
ForWC 70, SmATA 7

Friedman, Ina R 1926- AuBYP SUP,
ConAu 53, SmATA 41

Friedman, Judi 1935- AuNews 2,
BioIn 11, ConAu 65

Friedman, Leon 1933- ConAu 81,
WhoAmL 78, -79, WhoWorJ 72, -78

Friedman, Marcia 1925- ConAu 57

Friedman, Michael J 1955- ConAu 119

Friedman, Milton 1912- BioIn 13,
GrEconS[port], Who 85, WhoAm 84,
-86, WhoEc 86, WhoNob,
WhoWor 84, -87, WrDr 86

Friedman, Milton 1912-1983
AmAu&B, AmEA 74,
AmM&WS 73S, -78S, Au&Wr 71,
BioIn 6, -7, -8, -9, -10, -11, -12,
BlueB 76, CelR, ConAu 1R, -1NR,
ConIsC 1[port], EncAB-H,
IntAu&W 76, -77, -82, IntWW 74,
-75, -76, -77, -78, -79, -80, -81,
-82, -83, LinLib L, MakMC,
NewYTBS 76, -80[port], -83,
PolProf J, PolProf NF, WebAB, -79,
Who 74, -82, -83, WhoAm 74, -76,
-78, -80, -82, WhoAmJ 80,
WhoEc 81, WhoF&I 79, -81, -83,
WhoWest 80, -82, -84, WhoWor 74,
-78, -80, -82, WhoWorJ 72, -78,
WorAl, WrDr 76, -80, -82, -84

Friedman, Myra BioIn 10, BioNews 74

Friedman, Paul 1899-1972 BioIn 9,
ConAu 37R

Friedman, Philip 1944- WhoE 83, -85,
WhoWor 84

Friedman, Rose BioIn 12, ConAu 101,
NewYTBS 80[port]

Friedman, Sara Ann 1935- ConAu 77

Friedman, Sonya 1936- WhoMW 84

Friedrich, Otto Alva 1929- AmAu&B,
AmPB, ConAu 3NR, -5R,
SmATA 33[port], WhoAm 74, -76,
-78, -80, -82, -84, -86

Friel, Brian 1929- Au&Wr 71,
BiDIrW, BioIn 10, -13, CnThe,
ConAu 21R, ConDr 73, -77, -82,
ConLC 5, -42[port], CurBio 74,
DcIrL, DcIrW 1, DcLB 13[port],
DcLEL 1940, IntAu&W 76, -77, -82,

55

G

Gaan, Margaret 1914- *ConAu 81, WrDr 86*

Gabriel, Roman 1940- *BioIn 8, –9, –10, –13, ConAu 107, CurBio 75, NewYTBS 83[port], WhoAm 74, –76, –78, WhoFtbl 74*

Gaddis, Vincent H 1913- *SmATA 35[port]*

Gaddis, Vincent Hayes 1913- *ConAu 13R, IntAu&W 77, SmATA 35, WrDr 76, –80, –82, –84, –86*

Gaddis, William *DrAP&F 85*

Gaddis, William 1922- *AmAu&B, BioIn 3, –8, –10, –12, ConAu 17R, –21NR, ConLC 1, –3, –6, –8, –10, –19, –43[port], ConNov 72, –76, –82, –86, DcLB 2, DcLEL 1940, EncWL 2, IntAu&W 76, –77, ModAL S2, –S1, Novels, OxAmL 83, PenC AM, PostFic, RAdv 1, WhoAm 74, –76, –78, –80, –82, –84, –86, WorAu, WrDr 76, –80, –82, –84, –86*

Gaeddert, Lou Ann 1931- *BioIn 12, BkP, ConAu 13NR, –73, SmATA 20*

Gaer, Joseph 1897-1969 *AmAu&B, AuBYP, BioIn 2, –6, –8, –10, ConAu 9R, CurBio 51, MorJA, NatCAB 55, WhoAm 74, –76, WhoWorJ 72, –78*

Gage, Edwin 1943- *ConAu 85*

Gage, Wilson *WrDr 86*

Gage, Wilson 1922- *AuBYP, BioIn 8, –9, –11, ConAu X, SmATA 3, ThrBJA, WrDr 76, –80, –82, –84*

Gage, Wilson *see also* Steele, Mary Quintard

Gaines, Charles Ellis 1924- *WhoAmP 81*

Gaines, Charles F 1944- *WhoBlA 80*

Gaines, Ernest J *DrAP&F 85, WhoAm 84, –86*

Gaines, Ernest J 1933- *AuBYP SUP, AuNews 1, BioIn 10, –11, –12, BlkAWP, CivR 74, CmCal, ConAu 6NR, –9R, ConLC 3, –11, –18, ConNov 72, –76, –82, –86, DcLB 2, –33[port], –Y80A[port], InB&W 80, IntAu&W 76, –77, –82, LivgBAA, ModAL S2, ModBlW, NegAl 76[port], –83[port], OxAmL 83, SelBAAf, SelBAAu, WhoAm 74, –76, –78, –80, –82, WhoBlA 75, –77, –80, –85, WorAu 1970, WrDr 76, –80, –82, –84, –86*

Gaines, Ernest J K 1933- *InB&W 85*

Gaines, William Maxwell 1922- *ConAu 108, EncTwCJ, WhoAm 76, –78, –80, –82, –84, –86, WhoWor 78, WorECom*

Gainham, Sarah 1922- *AmAu&B, ConAu X, DcLEL 1940, IntAu&W 76, –77, TwCCr&M 80,*

–85, *Who 74, –82, –83, WhoSpyF, WrDr 76, –80, –82, –84, –86*

Galanoy, Terry 1927- *ConAu 4NR, –45*

Galarza, Ernesto 1905- *BiDAmL, BiDAmLL, ChiSch*

Galarza, Ernesto 1905-1984 *ChiLit A, ConAu 113, NewYTBS 84*

Galbraith, John Kenneth 1908- *AmAu&B, AmEA 74, AmM&WS 73S, BioIn 5, –6, –7, –8, –9, –10, –11, –12, –13, CanWW 70, –79, –80, –81, –83, CelR, ConAu 21R, ConIsC 1[port], CurBio 59, –75, DcAmDH, EncAB-H, GrEconS[port], IntEnSS 79, LongCTC, MakMC, NewYTBE 73, NewYTBS 79, OxAmH, PolProf E, PolProf J, PolProf K, PolProf NF, PolProf T, REnAL, ScF&FL 1, –2, WebAB, –79, Who 74, –82, –83, –85, WhoAm 78, –80, –82, –84, –86, WhoAmP 81, –83, –85, WhoEc 81, –86, WhoF&I 83, WorAl, WorAu, WrDr 76, –84, –86*

Gale, Elizabeth *WhNAA*

Gallagher, Mary 1947- *ConAu 97, ConTFT 1, NatPD 81, WhoAmW 85*

Gallagher, Thomas *ConAu 1R, –5NR, IntAu&W 76*

Gallant, Mavis *DrAP&F 85, NewYTBS 85[port]*

Gallant, Mavis 1922- *BioIn 13, ConLC 38[port], ConNov 86, DcLB 53[port], OxCanL, WhoAm 84, –86, WhoCanL 85, WrDr 86*

Gallant, Roy A 1924- *AuBYP, BioIn 8, –9, ConAu 4NR, –5R, ConLC 17, FifBJA[port], SmATA 4, WrDr 76, –80, –82, –84*

Gallant, Roy Arthur 1924- *WhoE 85, WrDr 86*

Gallico, Paul 1897-1976 *AmAu&B, AmNov, ASpks, Au&Wr 71, AuBYP SUP, AuNews 1, BioIn 1, –2, –4, –6, –9, –10, –11, –12, BlueB 76, ConAu 5R, –65, –69, ConLC 2, ConNov 72, –76, –82, –86, –76N, DcLB 9[port], DcLEL, EncAJ, EncSF, EvLB, FilmgC, HalFC 84, IntAu&W 76, –77, IntWW 74, –75, –76, –77N, NatCAB 59[port], NewYTBS 76, Novels, ObitOF 79, OxChL, REnAL, ScF&FL 1, –1A, –2, ScFSB, SmATA 13, TwCA SUP, TwCWr, WhAm 7, WhE&EA, WhoAm 74, –76, WhoThe 81N, WhoWor 74, –76, WorAl, WrDr 76*

Galston, Arthur William 1920- *AmM&WS 73P, –76P, –79P, –82P, –86P, ConAu 102, McGMS 80[port], WhoAm 74, –76, –78, –80, –82, –84, –86, WhoAmJ 80, WhoE 74, WhoWor 74, WhoWorJ 72, –78*

Galsworthy, John 1867-1933 *AtlBL, BioIn 1, –2, –3, –4, –5, –6, –8, –9, –10, –11, –12, –13, BritWr 6, CasWL, Chambr 3, ChhPo, –S1, –S2, –S3, CnMD, CnMWL, CnThe, ConAu 104, CyWA, DcAmSR, DcBiA, DcLB 10[port], –34[port], DcLEL, DcNaB 1931, EncSoA, EncWL, –2, EncWT, EvLB, FilmgC, HalFC 84, LinLib L, –S, LongCEL, LongCTC, MajMD 1, MakMC, McGEWB, McGEWD, –84[port], ModBrL, –S2, –S1, ModWD, NewC, NotNAT A, –B, Novels[port], OxAmT 84, OxEng, –85, OxThe, –83, PenC ENG, PlP&P, RAdv 1, RComWL, REn, REnWD, TwCA, –SUP, TwCLC 1, TwCWr, WebE&AL, WhDW, WhE&EA, WhThe, WhoLA, WhoNob, WhoTwCL, WorAl*

Galvin, Brendan *DrAP&F 85*

Galvin, Brendan 1938- *BioIn 12, ConAu 1NR, –45, ConPo 85, DcLB 5[port], DrAS 74E, –78E, –82E, IntWWP 77, WrDr 86*

Gambaccini, Peter 1950- *ConAu 105*

Gammage, Allen Z 1917- *AmM&WS 73S, –78S, ConAu 5R, –11NR, IntAu&W 76, WhoWest 76, –78*

Gammage, William Leonard 1942- *ConAu 10NR, –57*

Gammond, Peter 1925- *ConAu 14NR, –81, IntAu&W 77, WhoMus 72*

Gamoran, Mamie G 1900- *ConAu 3NR, –5R, ForWC 70, IntAu&W 76, –77, –82, WhoAmW 74, –68, –70, –72*

Gamow, George 1904-1968 *AmAu&B, AsBiEn, BiEsc, BioIn 1, –2, –4, –8, ConAu 102, –93, CurBio 51, –68, DcScB, EncSF, InSci, McGMS 80[port], ObitOF 79, REnAL, ScF&FL 1, TwCA SUP, WebAB, –79, WhAm 5, WhE&EA, WorAl*

Gann, Ernest K 1910- *HalFC 84, OxAmL 83, WrDr 86*

Gann, Ernest Kellogg 1910- *AmAu&B, AmNov, AuNews 1, BioIn 2, –3, –4, –7, –8, –9, –10, –11, –12, BlueB 76, ConAu 1R, –1NR, ConLC 23[port], DcLEL 1940, LinLib L, NewYTBS 81[port], Novels, TwCWr, WhoAm 74, –76, –78, –80, –82, –84, –86, WhoPNW, WhoWest 74, WorAl, WorAu, WrDr 76, –80, –82, –84*

Gannett, Lewis Stiles 1891-1966 *AmAu&B, BioIn 1, –4, –7, ChhPo, ConAu 89, CurBio 41, –66, REnAL, TwCA, –SUP, WhAm 4, –4A*

Gannon, Robert Haines 1931- *BioIn 11, ConAu 4NR, –9R, IntAu&W 86, SmATA 8*

Ganz, David 1951?- *ConAu 105, DrAS 82F*

Garagiola, Joe *EncAJ*

Garagiola, Joe 1926- *BioNews 74, CelR, CurBio 76, LesBEnT, NewYTET, WhoAm 74, –76, –78, –80, –82, –84, –86, WhoE 74*

Garbedian, H Gordon 1905- *WhE&EA*

Garbo, Norman 1919- *ConAu 9NR, –17R, EncSF, ScF&FL 1, –2, WhoAm 74, –76, –78, –80, –82, –84, –86, WhoE 74, –75*

Garcia, Ann O'Neal 1939- *ConAu 108*

Gard, Wayne 1899- *AmAu&B, AnMV 1926, BioIn 9, ConAu 1R, REnAW, TexWr, WhJnl, WhNAA*

Gard, Wayne 1899-1986 *ConAu 120*

Gardam, Jane 1928- *AuBYP SUP, BioIn 13, ChlLR 12[port], ConAu 2NR, –18NR, –49, ConLC 43[port], DcLB 14[port], FifBJA[port], OxChL, SmATA 28, –39[port], TwCCW 78, –83, Who 82, –83, WrDr 80, –82, –84, –86*

Garden, Nancy *DrAP&F 85*

Garden, Nancy 1938- *AuBYP SUP, BioIn 11, ConAu 13NR, –33R, FifBJA[port], SmATA 12, WrDr 76, –80, –82, –84, –86*

Garden, Robert Hal 1937- *ConAu 69*

Gardner, Brian 1931- *Au&Wr 71, ChhPo S2, ConAu 13R, IntAu&W 82, WrDr 76, –80, –82, –84, –86*

Gardner, Erle Stanley 1889-1970 *AmAu&B, BioIn 1, –2, –4, –5, –6, –7, –8, –9, –10, –11, –12, –13, CmCal, ConAu 5R, –25R, CorpD, CurBio 44, –70, EncMys, EvLB, FilmgC, HalFC 84, LinLib L, –S, LongCTC, MnBBF, NatCAB 62[port], NewYTBE 70, ObitOF 79, ObitT 1961, OxAmL, –83, PenC AM, REn, REnAL, TwCA, –SUP, TwCCr&M 80, –85, TwCWr, WebAB, –79, WhAm 6, WhE&EA, WhNAA, WorAl*

Gardner, Gerald 1929- *ConAu 1R, –5NR*

Gardner, Herb *OxAmT 84*

Gardner, Herb 1934- *BiE&WWA, BioIn 6, ConLC 44[port], NatPD 81[port], NotNAT*

Gardner, John d1982 *NewYTBS 84[port]*

Gardner, John 1933-1982 *AnObit 1982[port], AuBYP SUP, AuNews 1, BioIn 7, –10, –11, –12, ConAu 107, –65, ConLC 2, –3, –5, –7, –8, –10, –18, –28[port], ConNov 76, –82, –86A, CurBio 78, –82N, DcLB 2, –Y82A[port], DcLEL 1940, EncSF, FifBJA[port], ModAL S2, –S1, NewYTBS 82[port], Novels, OxAmL 83, PostFic, RAdv 1,*

Gerassi, John 1931- *AuBYP SUP, ConAu 5R, -8NR*
Gerber, Dan *DrAP&F 85*
Gerber, Dan 1940- *ConAu 33R, IntWWP 77X, -82X, MichAu 80*
Gerber, Merrill Joan *DrAP&F 85*
Gerber, Merrill Joan 1938- *ConAu 10NR, IntAu&W 76, -77*
Gerber, William 1908- *ConAu 37R, DrAS 74P, -78P, -82P, WhoAm 74, -76, -78, -80, -82, -84, -86, WhoAmJ 80, WhoWorJ 72, -78, WrDr 76, -80, -82, -84, -86*
Gerlach, Larry Reuben 1941- *ConAu 109, DrAS 74H, -78H, -82H*
German, Tony 1924- *WhoCanL 85*
Germar, Herb 1911- *ConAu X*
Germar, Herb *see also* Germar, William H
Germar, William H 1911- *ConAu 21R*
Germond, Jack 1928- *BioIn 11, ConAu 108*
Geronimo 1829-1909 *AmBi, ApCAB, BioIn 1, -2, -3, -4, -5, -8, -9, -10, -11, -12, -13, DcAmB, DcAmMiB, EncAB-H, FilmgC, HalFC 84, HarEnUS[port], McGEWB, NatCAB 23, OxAmH, REn, REnAL, REnAW, WebAB, -79, WebAMB, WhDW, WhAm 4, -HSA, WorAl*
Gerrold, David 1944- *BioIn 12, ConAu 85, -93, DcLB 8[port], EncSF, ScF&FL 1, -2, ScFSB, TwCSFW 86, WhoSciF, WrDr 84, -86*
Gersh, Harry 1912- *BioIn 11, ConAu 1R, -1NR, NewYTBS 76, -77, WhoWorJ 72, -78*
Gerson, Corinne *DrAP&F 85, SmATA 37[port]*
Gerson, Corinne 1927- *ConAu 93, SmATA 37*
Gerson, Noel B 1914- *BioIn 13*
Gerson, Noel Bertram 1914- *AmAu&B, Au&Wr 71, AuBYP, BioIn 8, ConAu 81, IntAu&W 76, ScF&FL 1, SmATA 22[port], WhoAm 74, -76, -78, -80, -82, -84, -86, WhoE 74, -75, -77, -79, -81, -83, -85, WhoWor 74, -76, -78, -80, -82, -84, -87, WrDr 76, -80, -82, -84*
Gesch, Roy 1920- *ConAu 21R, IntAu&W 77, WrDr 76, -80, -82, -84, -86*
Gessner, Lynne 1919- *ConAu 10NR, -25R, IntAu&W 77, SmATA 16, WrDr 76, -80, -82, -84, -86*
Geyer, Georgie Anne 1935- *BioIn 7, -9, -13, BriB[port], ConAu 17NR, -29R, CurBio 86[port], ForWC 70, IntAu&W 77, -82, -86, WhoAm 74, -76, -78, -80, -82, -84, -86, WhoAmW 74, -68, -70, -72, -75, -77, -79, -81, -83, -85, -87, WhoMW 74, -76, WhoWor 74, -76*
Giannetti, Louis D 1937- *ConAu 33R, DrAS 82E*
Giannetti, Louis Daniel 1937- *WhoAm 86, WhoMW 84*
Giardina, Denise *DrAP&F 85*
Giardina, Denise 1951- *ConAu 119*
Gibb, Barry 1946- *BioIn 12, CurBio 81[port], WhoAm 80, -82, -84, -86, WhoRocM 82*
Gibb, Barry *see also* Bee Gees, The
Gibb, Jocelyn Easton 1907- *Au&Wr 71, ChhPo S1, IntAu&W 76, -77*
Gibb, Maurice 1949- *WhoAm 80, -82, -84, -86, WhoRocM 82*
Gibb, Maurice *see also* Bee Gees, The
Gibb, Robin 1949- *WhoAm 80, -82, -84, -86, WhoRocM 82*
Gibb, Robin *see also* Bee Gees, The
Gibbons, Bob *ConAu X*
Gibbons, Faye 1938- *ConAu 109*
Gibbons, Reginald *DrAP&F 85*
Gibbons, Reginald 1947- *ConAu 18NR, IntAu&W 86, WhoAm 86*
Gibbs, Alonzo 1915- *AuBYP, BioIn 8, -10, ConAu 5R, -5NR, IntAu&W 77, -82, SmATA 5, WhoE 83, WrDr 76, -80, -82, -84, -86*

Giblin, James C 1933- *ConAu 106, SmATA 33[port], WhoLibI 82*
Gibran, Kahlil 1883-1931 *AmAu&B, BioIn 1, -2, -3, -4, -5, -7, -9, -10, -13, CasWL, ChhPo S1, -S3, ConAu 104, DcNAA, EncO&P 2, -78, LinLib L, ScF&FL 1, TwCA, -SUP, TwCLC 1, -9[port], WorAl*
Gibson, Althea 1927- *BioIn 4, -5, -6, -7, -8, -9, -10, -11, -12, -13, CurBio 57, Ebony 1, GoodHs, HerW, -84, InB&W 80, -85, InWom, IntDcWB, LibW, NegAl 76, -83, NewYTBS 80, WebAB, -79, WhoAm 74, -76, -78, -80, -82, -84, -86, WhoAmW 74, -66, -68, -70, -72, -83, -85, -87, WhoBlA 75, -77, -80, -85, WorAl*
Gibson, Charles E 1916- *Au&Wr 71, ConAu 5R, IntAu&W 76, -77, WrDr 76, -80, -82, -84, -86*
Gibson, Donald B 1933- *ConAu 25R, DrAS 74E, -78E, -82E, SelBAAf*
Gibson, Evan Keith 1909- *ConAu 105, DrAS 74E, -78E, -82E, IntAu&W 86*
Gibson, Gwen 1927- *ForWC 70, WhoAmW 58, -61, -66*
Gibson, James 1919- *ConAu 117*
Gibson, Karon Rose 1946- *ConAu 105, WhoAmW 77, -81*
Gibson, Margaret 1948- *ConAu 103, OxCanL, Po&Wr 77, WhoCanL 85*
Gibson, Robert 1935- *BioIn 7, -8, -9, -10, -11, CurBio 68, InB&W 80, WhoAm 74, -76, -82, -84, -86, WhoBlA 75, -77, -80, -85, WhoCtE 79, WhoProB 73*
Gibson, Walker 1919- *AmAu&B, ChhPo S3, ConAu 1R, -1NR, DrAS 74E, -78E, -82E, LinLib L*
Gibson, Walter B 1897- *BioIn 7, ConAu 108, -110, EncMys, ScF&FL 1, TwCCr&M 80, -85, WhJnl, WhNAA, WrDr 82, -84, -86*
Gibson, Walter B 1897-1985 *ConAu 118*
Gibson, William *OxThe 83*
Gibson, William 1914- *BiE&WWA, BioIn 3, -4, -5, -10, -12, -13, ChhPo S2, CnMD, ConAu 9R, -9NR, ConDr 73, -77, -82, ConLC 23[port], ConTFT 2, CurBio 83[port], DcLB 7[port], DcLEL 1940, EncWT, IntAu&W 77, McGEWD, -84, ModAL, ModWD, NatPD, -81[port], OxAmT 84, PenC AM, PIP&P, RENAL, WhoAm 74, -76, -78, -80, -82, -84, -86, WhoE 74, WhoThe 72, -77, -81, WhoWor 74, WorAu, WrDr 76, -80, -82, -84, -86*
Gibson, William 1948- *ConLC 39[port], TwCSFW 86, WrDr 86*
Giddins, Gary 1948- *ConAu 13NR*
Gide, Andre 1860-1951 *OxEng 85*
Gide, Andre 1869-1951 *GrFLW, OxThe 83*
Gide, Andre 1870-1951 *WhScrn 83*
Gidley, M 1941- *ConAu 102*
Gielgud, John 1904- *ConAu 111, CurBio 84[port], OxAmT 84, OxThe 83, WrDr 86*
Gielgud, Sir John 1904- *BiDFilm, BiE&WWA, BioIn 1, -2, -3, -4, -5, -6, -7, -9, -10, -11, -12, -13, BlueB 76, CelR, CnThe, ConTFT 1, CurBio 84, EncWT, FamA&A, Film 2, FilmgC, HalFC 84, IntMPA 77, -75, -76, -78, -79, -81, -82, -84, -86, IntWW 74, -75, -76, -77, -78, -79, -80, -81, -82, -83, MotPP, MovMk, NewC, NewYTBE 70, NewYTBS 79, -80[port], -84[port], NotNAT, -A, OxFilm, OxThe, PIP&P, REn, WhDW, Who 74, -82, -83, -85, WhoHol A, WhoPolA, WhoThe 72, -77, -81, WorAl, WorEFlm, WrDr 80, -82, -84*
Gies, Frances 1915- *ConAu 9NR, -25R, WhoAmW 74, -75*
Gies, Joseph 1916- *ConAu 5R, -9NR*

Giff, Patricia Reilly 1935- *ConAu 101, -18NR, FifBJA[port], SmATA 33[port]*
Gifford, Denis 1927- *ConAu 101, -18NR, IntAu&W 82, ScF&FL 1, -2, ConAu 104, DcNAA, EncO&P 2, -78, WhoArt 80, -82, -84, WhoWor 78, WorECar A, WrDr 76, -80, -82, -84, -86*
Gifford, Frank 1930- *BioIn 4, -5, -6, -7, -8, -9, -11, -13, CelR, ConAu 109, CurBio 64, LesEnT[port], NewYTET, WhoAm 76, -78, -80, -82, WhoHol A, WorAl*
Gilbert, Anna 1916- *ConAu X, WrDr 82, -84, -86*
Gilbert, Anne Wieland 1927- *ConAu 7NR, -57, ForWC 70, WhoAm 78, -80, -82, -84, -86, WhoAmW 75, -77, -79, -81, WhoMW 78, -80, -82*
Gilbert, Bill 1931- *ConAu 105*
Gilbert, Doug 1938?-1979 *BioIn 12, ConAu 104*
Gilbert, Harriett 1948- *ConAu 9NR, SmATA 30[port], WrDr 80, -82, -84, -86*
Gilbert, Harry 1946- *ConAu 106*
Gilbert, Joan 1931- *ConAu 21R, SmATA 10, WhoAmW 77, -79*
Gilbert, Martin 1936- *IntAu&W 86, Who 85, WorAu 1975, WrDr 86*
Gilbert, Miriam *SmATA X*
Gilbert, Miriam 1919-1978 *BioIn 11, ConAu X, IntAu&W 77X, WhoAmW 74, -58, -61, -64, -66, -68, -72, -75, -77, WhoE 74, WrDr 76, -80, -82*
Gilbert, Miriam *see also* Presberg, Miriam Goldstein
Gilbert, Nan *WrDr 86*
Gilbert, Nan 1908- *BioIn 9, ConAu X, IntAu&W 76X, -77X, -82X, SmATA 2, WrDr 76, -80, -82, -84*
Gilbert, Nan *see also* Gilbertson, Mildred Geiger
Gilbert, Rod 1941- *BioIn 8, -10, -11, ConAu 109, CurBio 69, NewYTBS 77, WhoAm 78, -80, -82, WhoHcky 73*
Gilbert, Ruth Gallard Ainsworth 1908- *Au&Wr 71, ConAu 4NR, -9R, IntWWP 77X*
Gilbert, Ruth Gallard Ainsworth *see also* Ainsworth, Ruth Gallard
Gilbert, Sara 1943- *AuBYP SUP, BioIn 11, ConAu 6NR, -57, SmATA 11*
Gilbert, W S 1836-1911 *ConAu 104, FilmgC, HalFC 84, McGEWD 84[port], SmATA 36*
Gilbertson, Mildred Geiger 1908- *BioIn 9, ConAu 2NR, -5R, ForWC 70, IntAu&W 76, -77, -82, SmATA 2, WhoAm 83, WrDr 76, -80, -82, -84*
Gilbreath, Alice 1921- *BioIn 11, ConAu 10NR, -25R, SmATA 12*
Gilbreth, Frank Bunker, Jr. 1911- *AmAu&B, BioIn 11, ConAu 9R, ConLC 17, CurBio 49, SmATA 2, WhoAm 74, -76, -78, -80, -82, -84, -86, WhoS&SW 73, WhoWor 74*
Gilchrist, Ellen *DrAP&F 85*
Gilchrist, Ellen 1935- *ConAu 113, -116, ConNov 86, WhoAmW 87*
Gilchrist, Ellen 1939- *ConLC 34[port]*
Giles, Janice Holt 1909- *EncFWF*
Giles, Janice Holt 1909-1979 *AmAu&B, BioIn 4, -5, -12, ConAu 1R, -3NR, CurBio 58, InWom, WhoAmW 61*
Gilfond, Henry *BioIn 9, ConAu 9NR, -21R, NatPD, -81[port], SmATA 2*
Gill, Brendan *DrAP&F 85*
Gill, Brendan 1914- *AmAu&B, BiE&WWA, BioIn 2, -4, -10, -13, ConAmTC, ConAu 73, ConNov 72, -76, -82, -86, Conv 1, EncTwCJ, IntAu&W 76, -77, -82, NotNAT, -A, Novels, PenC AM, RENAL, TwCA SUP, WhoAm 74, -76, -78, -80, -82, -84, -86, WhoThe 72, -77, -81, WrDr 76, -80, -82, -84, -86*

Gill, Derek L T 1919- *BioIn 11, ConAu 4NR, -49, SmATA 9*
Gill, Elizabeth Standish 1903- *WhoAmW 64, -66, -68, -70, WomWMM B*
Gillespie, Dizzy *BioIn 13*
Gillespie, Dizzy 1917- *AmSCAP 66, BioIn 1, -2, -4, -5, -6, -7, -8, -9, -10, -11, -12, BioNews 74, CelR, CmpEPM, ConAu X, Conv 2, CurBio 57, DrBlPA, EncJzS, IlEncJ, NegAl 76[port], -83[port], NewYTBE 73, NewYTBS 78, WhoAm 84, -86, WorAl*
Gillespie, John T 1928- *BiDrLUS 70, BioIn 9, ConAu 13NR, -73, LEduc 74, WhoAm 82, WhoCon 73, WhoLibI 82, WhoLibS 66*
Gillespie, John Thomas 1928- *WhoAm 84, -86*
Gillette, J Michael 1939- *ConAu 113*
Gillette, William 1855-1937 *AmAu&B, AmBi, ApCAB, BbD, BiD&SB, BioIn 2, -3, -4, -5, -9, -12, Chambr 3, DcAmAu, DcAmB S2, DcLEL, DcNAA, EncWT, FamA&A, Film 1, FilmgC, HalFC 84, LinLib L, -S, McGEWD, OxAmT, ModWD, NatCAB 2, -28, NotNAT A, -B, OxAmL, -83, OxAmT 84, OxThe, -83, PIP&P, RENAL, TwCBDA, TwYS, WebAB, -79, WhAm 1, WhScrn 74, -77, WhThe, WhoHol B, WhoStg 1906, -1908*
Gillette, William 1856-1937 *WhScrn 83*
Gilliland, Hap 1918- *ConAu 5NR, -53*
Gillmor, Frances 1903- *AmAu&B, ArizL, ConAu P-2, DrAS 74E, -78E, -82E, FifIDA, ForWC 70, IntAu&W 77, WhNAA, WhoAm 76, -78, -80, WhoAmW 74, -58, -72, WhoWest 74, -76, WhoWor 78, WrDr 76, -80, -82, -84*
Gillon, Diana 1915- *Au&Wr 71, ConAu 13R, ConSFA, EncSF, ScF&FL 1, -2*
Gillon, Meir 1907- *Au&Wr 71, ConAu 13R, ConSFA, EncSF, ScF&FL 1, -2*
Gilman, Charlotte Perkins 1860-1935 *AmAu&B, AmBi, AmLY, AmWomWr, ApCAB X, BioIn 6, -9, -10, -11, -12, ChhPo, -S3, CmCal, ConAu 106, DcAmAu, DcAmB S1, DcAmSR, DcNAA, InWom, IntDcWB, LibW, LinLib L, -S, NatCAB 13, NotAW, TwCLC 9[port], WhAm 1, WhAmP, WhLit, WhNAA, WomWWA 14*
Gilman, Dorothy 1923- *Au&Wr 71, BioIn 7, -8, -10, -12, ConAu X, SmATA 5, TwCCr&M 80, -85, WhoAm 78, -80, -82, -84, -86, WorAl, WrDr 82, -84, -86*
Gilman, Dorothy *see also* Butters, Dorothy Gilman
Gilman, Robert Cham *TwCSFW 86, WrDr 86*
Gilman, Robert Cham 1921- *ConAu X, EncSF, ScF&FL 1, WrDr 76, -80, -82, -84*
Gilman, Robert Cham *see also* Coppel, Alfred
Gilmore, Gene 1920- *ConAu 33R*
Gilmore, Iris 1900- *BioIn 8, -13, ConAu 97, SmATA 22[port]*
Gilmour, Sir Ian 1926- *Who 85*
Gilot, Francoise 1921- *BioIn 2, -7, -8, -10, -12, ConAu 108, WhoAmW 74, -75, WhoFr 79, WhoWor 74*
Gilpin, Laura 1891-1979 *BioIn 13, ConAu 111, ICPEnP, MacBEP, NewYTBS 86[port], WhoAmA 84N*
Gilroy, Tom *ConAu X*
Gilson, Jamie *BioIn 13*
Gilson, Jamie 1933- *ConAu 111, SmATA 34, -37, WhoAmW 83*
Gilson, Jamie Marie 1933- *WhoAmW 85, -87*
Gimpel, Herbert J 1915- *ConAu 17R*
Gimpel, Jean 1918- *ConAu 69*
Gingher, Marianne *DrAP&F 85*
Ginns, Patsy M 1937- *ConAu 69*

Green, Martyn 1899-1975 *BiE&WWA,
BioIn 1, -2, -3, -5, -10, ConAu 57,
CurBio 50, -75N, -76, FilmgC,
HalFC 84, NewYTBS 75, NotNAT A,
-B, ObitOF 79, ObitT 1971,
WhScrn 77, -83, WhoHol C,
WhoThe 72, -77*

Green, Paul 1894- *WrDr 86*

Green, Paul 1894-1981 *AmAu&B,
AmSCAP 66, AnObit 1981[port],
Au&Wr 71, AuNews 1, BiE&WWA,
BioIn 2, -3, -4, -5, -8, -9, -10, -12,
-13, BlueB 76, CnDAL, CnMD,
CnThe, ConAmA, ConAmL,
ConAu 3NR, -5R, -103, ConDr 73,
-77, -82, ConLC 25[port],
DcLB 7[port], -9[port], -Y81A[port],
DcLEL, EncWL, EncWT,
IntAu&W 76, -77, -82, IntWW 74,
-75, -76, -77, -78, -79, -80, -81,
-81N, LongCTC, McGEWD, -84,
ModAL, ModWD,
NewYTBS 81[port], NotNAT, -A,
OxAmL, -83, OxAmT 84, OxThe,
PenC AM, PIP&P, REn, REnAL,
REnWD, TwCA, -SUP, WebAB, -79,
WebE&AL, WhAm 7, WhE&EA,
WhLit, WhNAA, Who 74, -82N,
WhoAm 74, -76, -78, -80,
WhoThe 72, -77, -81, WhoWor 74,
WrDr 76, -80, -82, -84*

Green, Peter *ConAu X, TwCSFW 86*

Green, Peter Morris 1924- *Au&Wr 71,
ChhPo, -S3, ConAu 4NR, -5R,
ConNov 72, -76, DcLEL 1940,
DrAS 78F, -82F, IntAu&W 76, -77,
-82, Who 74, -82, -83, -85,
WhoAm 84, -86, WhoS&SW 84, -86,
WrDr 76, -80, -82, -84, -86*

Green, Phyllis 1932- *BioIn 12,
ConAu 1NR, -17NR, -45,
MichAu 80, SmATA 20*

Green, Roger Curtis 1932-
*AmM&WS 73S, -76P, ConAu 45,
FifIDA*

Green, Roger Lancelyn 1918-
*Au&Wr 71, AuBYP, BioIn 8, -9,
ChhPo, -S1, -S2, -S3, ConAu 1R,
-2NR, IntAu&W 76, -77, OxChL,
ScF&FL 1, -2, SmATA 2, ThrBJA,
TwCCW 78, -83, WhE&EA, Who 82,
-83, WhoChL, WrDr 80, -82, -84,
-86*

Green, Roland 1944- *ConAu 77,
IntAu&W 77, ScF&FL 1, -2*

Green, Timothy 1936- *Au&Wr 71,
ConAu 5NR, -49, WrDr 76, -80, -82,
-84, -86*

Greenbank, Anthony Hunt 1933-
*ConAu 4NR, -19NR, -49,
SmATA 39[port]*

Greenberg, Alvin *DrAP&F 85*

Greenberg, Alvin 1932- *ConAu 33R,
DrAS 74E, -78E, -82E, IntWWP 77,
-82, WrDr 76, -80, -82, -84, -86*

Greenberg, Eliezer 1896?-1977
*BioIn 11, -12, CasWL, ConAu 69,
NewYTBS 77, WhoWorJ 72*

Greenberg, Harvey R 1935-
*BiDrAPA 77, BioIn 10, ConAu 33R,
SmATA 5*

Greenberg, Joanne *DrAP&F 85*

Greenberg, Joanne 1932- *AmAu&B,
AmWomM, BioIn 12, -13,
ConAu 5R, -14NR, ConLC 7,
-30[port], SmATA 25[port],
WhoAm 74, -76, -78, -80, -82, -84,
WhoAmJ 80, WhoAmW 74, -68, -70,
-72, WorAu 1975[port], WrDr 80,
-82, -84, -86*

Greenberg, Joanne see also Green,
Hannah

Greenberg, Martin Harry 1941-
*AmM&WS 73S, BiDrAPA 77,
ConAu 4NR, EncSF, IntAu&W 77,
ScF&FL 1, -2*

Greenberg, Saul Norman 1923-
WhoE 74

Greenberg, Sylvia S *AmM&WS 73P*

Greene, A C 1923- *ConAu 14NR,
-37R, IntAu&W 77, WhoAm 74, -76,
-78, -80, -82, WrDr 76, -80, -82,
-84, -86*

Greene, Bette *DrAP&F 85*

Greene, Bette 1934- *AuBYP SUP,
BioIn 11, ChlLR 2, ConAu 4NR, -53,
ConLC 30[port], FifBJA[port],
OxChL, SmATA 8, TwCCW 78, -83,
WhoAm 78, -80, -82, -84, -86,
WhoAmJ 80, WrDr 76, -80, -82, -84,
-86*

Greene, Bob *WhoAm 86*

Greene, Bob 1946?- *BioIn 10, -13,
ConAu X*

Greene, Constance C 1924-
*AuBYP SUP, BioIn 11, -12,
ConAu 8NR, -61, FourBJA,
SmATA 11, TwCCW 78, -83,
WrDr 80, -82, -84, -86*

Greene, Felix 1909- *Au&Wr 71,
ConAu 1R, -6NR, Who 82, -83, -85*

Greene, Felix 1909-1985 *ConAu 116*

Greene, Graham 1904- *Au&Wr 71,
AuBYP SUP, AuNews 2, BiE&WWA,
BioIn 1, -2, -3, -4, -5, -6, -7, -8, -9,
-10, -11, -12, -13, BioNews 74,
BlueB 76, CasWL, CathA 1930,
CelR, ChhPo S2, CnMD, CnMWL,
CnThe, ConAu 13R, ConDr 73, -77,
-82, ConLC 1, -3, -6, -9, -14, -18,
-27[port], -37[port], ConNov 72, -76,
-82, -86, CorpD, CroCD, CurBio 69,
CyWA, DcLB 13[port], -15[port],
-Y85A[port], EncMys,
EncWL, -2[port], EncWT, FilmgC,
HalFC 84, IntAu&W 76, -77,
IntWW 74, -75, -76, -77, -78, -79,
-80, -81, -82, -83, LinLib L, -S,
LongCTC, MakMC, McGEWB,
McGEWD, -84, ModBrL, -S2, -S1,
ModWD, NewC, NewYTBE 71,
NewYTBS 85[port], NotNAT, -A,
Novels[port], OxChL, OxEng, -85,
OxFilm, OxThe, -83, PenC ENG,
PIP&P, RAdv 1, REn, ScF&FL 1, -2,
SmATA 20, TwCA, -SUP,
TwCCW 78, TwCCr&M 80, -85,
TwCWr, WebE&AL, WhDW,
WhE&EA, Who 74, -82, -83, -85,
WhoAm 80, -82, -84, -86, WhoChL,
WhoFr 79, WhoSpyF, WhoThe 72,
-77, -81, WhoTwCL, WhoWor 74,
-76, -78, -80, -82, -84, -87, WorAl,
WorEFlm, WrDr 76, -80, -82, -84,
-86*

Greene, Howard Rodger 1937-
ConAu 61, WhoE 77, -79, -81

Greene, Hugh 1910- *WrDr 86*

Greene, Hugh Carleton 1910-
WhoWor 84, -87

Greene, Jack P 1931- *ConAu 18NR*

Greene, Jack Phillip 1931- *WhoAm 84,
-86*

Greene, Laura 1935- *ConAu 107,
SmATA 38[port]*

Greene, Sir Hugh 1910- *BioIn 6, -7,
-13, BlueB 76, ConAu 102,
CurBio 63, IntAu&W 77, -82, -86,
IntWW 74, -75, -76, -77, -78, -79,
-80, -81, -82, WhE&EA, Who 74,
-82, -83, -85, WhoAm 74, -76, -78,
WhoWor 74, -76, -78, WrDr 82, -84*

Greenebaum, Louise G 1919-
ConAu 69, WomPO 76

Greenfeld, Howard *AuBYP SUP,
BioIn 10, -12, ConAu 19NR, -81,
SmATA 19*

Greenfeld, Josh 1927?- *BioIn 12,
ConAu 116*

Greenfeld, Josh 1928- *ConTFT 2*

Greenfield, Eloise 1929- *BioIn 10, -12,
BlkAWP, ChlLR 4[port],
ConAu 1NR, -19NR, -49,
FifBJA[port], InB&W 80, -85,
IntAu&W 77, -82, LivgBAA,
SelBAAf, SelBAAu, SmATA 19,
TwCChW 83, WhoAm 78, -80, -82,
WhoBlA 77, -80, -85, WrDr 76, -80,
-82, -84, -86*

Greenfield, Jeff 1943- *BioIn 8, -10,
ConAu 19NR, EncTwCJ*

Greengrass, Mark 1949- *ConAu 118*

Greenleaf, Barbara Kaye 1942-
*BioIn 10, ConAu 29R, SmATA 6,
WhoAmW 75, -77, -79*

Greenleaf, Stephen 1942-
TwCCr&M 85, WrDr 86

Greenspan, Bud 1926?- *BioIn 10,
ConAu 103, LesBEnT, WhoAm 76,
-78*

Greenspan, Bud 1927- *BioIn 13*

Greenwald, Jerry 1923- *ConAu 57*

Greenwald, Sheila *ConAu X*

Greenwald, Sheila 1934- *BioIn 8, -11,
ChhPo, ConAu X, FifBJA[port],
IlsBYP, IlsCB 1957, SmATA 8,
WhoAmA 78, -80, -82, WhoAmW 75*

Greenwald, Sheila Ellen 1934-
WhoAmA 84

Greenway, James Cowan, Jr. 1903-
WhoAm 74

Greer, Germaine 1939- *ASpks,
AuNews 1, BioIn 9, -10, -11, -12,
-13, BioNews 75, BlueB 76, CelR,
ConAu 81, CurBio 71, DcLEL 1940,
IntAu&W 76, -77, -86, IntDcWB,
IntWW 74, -75, -76, -77, -78, -79,
-80, -81, -82, -83, MakMC,
NewYTBS 71, OxAusL, Who 82, -83,
-85, WhoAm 78, -80, -82, -84, -86,
WhoAmW 74, -75, -77, -81, -83,
WhoWor 74, -76, -78, WrDr 76, -80,
-82, -84, -86*

Greet, W Cabell *ConAu 37R,
NewYTBE 72*

Gregg, Charles T 1927-
*AmM&WS 73P, -76P, -79P, -82P,
ConAu 14NR, -81*

Gregg, Charles Thornton 1927-
AmM&WS 86P

Gregg, James R 1914- *AmM&WS 73P,
-76P, -79P, -82P, -86P, ConAu 21R*

Gregor, Arthur *DrAP&F 85*

Gregor, Arthur 1923- *BioIn 13,
ConAu 11NR, -25R, ConLC 9,
ConPo 70, -75, -80, -85,
IntAu&W 76, -77, IntWWP 77,
LinLib L, SmATA 36, WhoAm 74,
-76, -78, -80, -82, -84, -86,
WhoAmJ 80, WhoE 83, WrDr 76,
-80, -82, -84, -86*

Gregorian, Joyce Ballou 1946-
ConAu 107, SmATA 30[port]

Gregorich, Barbara 1943- *ConAu 117*

Gregory, Cynthia 1946- *BiDD,
BioIn 13*

Gregory, Diana 1933- *ConAu 97,
SmATA 42*

Gregory, Dick 1932- *AmAu&B,
BioIn 5, -6, -7, -8, -9, -10, -11, -12,
BioNews 74, BlueB 76, CelR,
CivR 74, CivRSt, ConAu 7NR, -45,
CurBio 62, DrBlPA, Ebony 1,
LivgBAA, NegAl 76[port], -83[port],
NotNAT A, PolProf J, UFOEn,
WhoAm 74, -76, -78, -80, -82, -84,
-86, WhoAmP 73, -75, -77, -79, -81,
-83, -85, WhoBlA 75, -77,
WhoHol A, WorAl, WrDr 76, -80,
-82, -84, -86*

Gregory, Horace 1898-1982 *AmAu&B,
AnObit 1982[port], BioIn 4, -5, -9,
-12, -13, BlueB 76, ChhPo, -S1, -S2,
CnDAL, ConAmA, ConAu 3NR, -5R,
-106, ConPo 70, -75, -80,
DcLB 48[port], DcLEL,
IntAu&W 77, IntWW 74, -75, -76,
-77, -78, -79, -80, -81, -82, -83N,
IntWWP 77, LinLib L, ModAL,
NewYTBS 82, OxAmL, -83,
PenC AM, RAdv 1, REn, REnAL,
SixAP, TwCA, -SUP, WhoAm 74,
-76, -78, -80, WhoE 74,
WhoWor 74, WrDr 76, -80, -82*

Gregory, Stephen *SmATA X*

Gregory, Stephen 1942- *ConAu X*

Gregory, Stephen see also Penzler, Otto
M

Greiner, James Duane 1933-
WhoWest 76, -78

Gresham, William Lindsay 1909-1962
*AmAu&B, BioIn 1, -2, -4, -6,
TwCA SUP*

Grey, Beryl 1927- *Au&Wr 71, BiDD,
BioIn 1, -2, -3, -4, -5, -7, -11, -12,
BlueB 76, ConAu 109, InWom,
IntAu&W 76, -77, -82, IntDcWB,
IntWW 74, -75, -76, -77, -78, -79,
-80, -81, -82, -83, WhThe, Who 74,
-82, -83, -85, WhoWor 74, -76, -78,*

–80, –82, WrDr 76, –80, –82, –84,
–86

Grey, Elizabeth 1917- *Au&Wr 71,
AuBYP, BioIn 8, ConAu X*

Grey, Elizabeth see also Hogg, Beth

Grey, Ian *WrDr 86*

Grey, Ian 1918- *Au&Wr 71,
ConAu 2NR, –5R, IntAu&W 76, –77,
–82, –86, WhoWor 76, WrDr 76, –80,
–82, –84*

Grey, Jerry 1926- *AmM&WS 73P,
–79P, –82P, –86P, BioIn 11,
ConAu 5NR, –20NR, –53, IntWWE,
SmATA 11, WhoAm 74, –76, –78,
–80, –82, –84, –86, WhoE 74, –83,
WhoTech 82, –84, WhoWor 74,
WrDr 82, –84, –86*

Grey, Zane 1872?-1939 *AmAu&B,
AmBi, ArizL, BioIn 1, –2, –3, –4, –5,
–6, –7, –8, –9, –10, –11, –12, –13,
CmCal, ConAu 104, DcAmB S2,
DcLB 9[port], DcLEL, DcNAA,
EncAAH, EncFWF[port], EvLB,
FilmgC, LinLib L, LongCTC,
MnBBF, Novels[port], OhA&B,
OxAmL, –83, OxAusL, PenC AM,
REn, REnAL, REnAW,
TwCA, –SUP, TwCLC 6[port],
TwCWr, WebAB, –79, WebE&AL,
WhAm 1, WhE&EA, WhLit,
WhNAA, WorAl*

Grey, Zane 1875-1939 *HalFC 84*

Grice, Frederick 1910- *Au&Wr 71,
BioIn 10, ConAu 3NR, –9R,
IntAu&W 77, –82, SmATA 6,
TwCCW 78, –83, WrDr 76, –80, –82,
–84, –86*

Gridley, Marion E 1906-1974
SmATA 35[port]

Gridley, Marion Eleanor 1906-1974
*AuBYP SUP, BioIn 2, –13,
ConAu 103, –45, ForWC 70,
SmATA 26N, –35, WhAm 6,
WhoAmW 68, –70, –75*

Grier, Rosey *ConAu X*

Grierson, John 1909-1977 *BioIn 11,
ConAu 69, ConAu P-2, IntAu&W 77,
NewYTBS 77, WhE&EA, WrDr 76*

Griffin, Alice 1924- *DrAS 74E, –78E,
–82E*

Griffin, Donald 1915- *AmM&WS 73P,
–76P, –79P, –82P, BlueB 76,
ConAu 15NR, –37R, IntAu&W 77,
–82, IntWW 74, –75, –76, –77, –78,
–79, –80, –81, –82, –83, WhoAm 74,
–80, –82, WhoE 83, WrDr 76, –80,
–82, –84*

Griffin, Donald R 1915- *WhoAm 84,
–86, WhoFrS 84, WrDr 86*

Griffin, Donald Redfield 1915-
AmM&WS 86P

Griffin, John Howard 1920-1980
*AmAu&B, AmCath 80,
AnObit 1980[port], Au&Wr 71,
AuNews 1, BioIn 3, –4, –5, –6, –9,
–10, –11, –12, –13, BlueB 76,
ConAu 1R, –2NR, –101, CurBio 60,
–80N, IntAu&W 76, LinLib L, –S,
NewYTBS 80, Novels, WhAm 7,
WhoAm 74, –76, –78, –80,
WhoRel 75, –77, WhoWor 74,
WorAu, WrDr 76, –80, –82*

Griffin, John Q 1948- *ConAu 77*

Griffin, Judith Berry *AuBYP SUP,
BioIn 13, BlkAWP, ConAu 108,
SmATA 34[port]*

Griffin, Susan *DrAP&F 85*

Griffin, Susan 1943- *AmWomWr,
BioIn 12, –13, ConAu 3NR, –49,
IntAu&W 77, –82, IntWWP 77, –82,
NatPD, –81[port]*

Griffith, A Kinney 1897- *ConAu 1R,
–17NR, WhNAA*

Griffith, Field *AuBYP SUP*

Griffiths, David 1938- *AmM&WS 86P*

Griffiths, G D 1910-1973 *ConAu P-2,
SmATA 20N, TwCCW 78, –83*

Griffiths, Gordon Douglas 1910-1973
Au&Wr 71, BioIn 12

Griffiths, Helen 1939- *AuBYP SUP,
ConAu 7NR, –17R, FourBJA,
IntAu&W 82, –86, SmATA 5,
TwCCW 78, WrDr 80, –82, –84,
–86*

Griffiths, John C 1934- *ConAu 108,*
Who 83
Griffiths, John Charles 1934- *Who 85*
Grigson, Geoffrey 1905- *Au&Wr 71,*
AuBYP, BioIn 2, –4, –8, –13,
BlueB 76, ChhPo, –S1, –S2,
ConAu 25R, ConLC 7, ConPo 70,
–75, –80, –85, DcLB 27[port],
DcLEL, EvLB, IntAu&W 76, –77,
IntWW 74, –75, –76, –77, –78, –79,
–80, –81, –82, –83, IntWWP 77, –82,
LongCTC, ModBrL, –S2, –S1, NewC,
PenC ENG, REn, TwCA SUP,
WhE&EA, Who 74, –82, –83, –85,
WhoTwCL, WhoWor 74, –78,
WrDr 76, –80, –82, –84, –86
Grigson, Geoffrey 1905-1985
ConAu 118, –20NR, ConLC 39[port]
Grigson, Jane 1928- *BioIn 13,*
ConAu 1NR, –20NR, –49,
IntAu&W 77, –82, –86, Who 82, –83,
–85, WrDr 80, –82, –84, –86
Grimble, Ian 1921- *ConAu 18NR,*
WrDr 86
Grimes, Martha *ConAu 113, –117*
Grimm, Jakob Ludwig Karl 1785-1863
AnCL, AtlBL, AuBYP, BbD,
BiD&SB, BioIn 1, –3, –6, –7, –8, –9,
–12, –13, CarSB, CasWL,
ChhPo, –S3, DcEuL, EuAu, EvEuW,
FamSYP, FilmgC, LinLib L, –S,
McGEWB, NewC, NewEOp 71,
NinCLC 3[port], OxEng, OxGer,
PenC EUR, REn, Str&VC, WhoChL
Grimm, Wilhelm Karl 1786-1859
AnCL, AtlBL, AuBYP, BiD&SB,
BioIn 1, –3, –6, –7, –8, –9, –12, –13,
CarSB, CasWL, ChhPo, –S2, –S3,
DcBiPP, DcEuL, Dis&D, EuAu,
EvEuW, FamSYP, FilmgC, LinLib L,
McGEWB, NinCLC 3[port], OxEng,
OxGer, PenC EUR, REn,
SmATA 22[port], Str&VC, WhDW,
WorAl
Grimm, William Carey 1907-
BioIn 12, ConAu 49, SmATA 14
Grinnell, George Bird 1849-1938
AmAu&B, AmBi, AmLY, BbD,
BiD&SB, BioIn 2, –4, –9, –12,
CarSB, DcAmAu, DcAmB S2,
DcNAA, EncAAH, JBA 34, –51,
NatCAB 13, –30, NatLAC,
OxAmL, –83, REnAL, REnAW,
SmATA 16, Str&VC, TwCBDA,
WebAB, –79, WhAm 1, WhLit,
WhNAA
Grinspoon, Lester 1928-
AmM&WS 79P, –82P, –86P, WhoE 81
Gripe, Maria 1923- *AuBYP SUP,*
BioIn 9, ChlLR 5[port],
ConAu 17NR, –29R, IntAu&W 76,
–77, –82, OxChL, ScF&FL 1,
SmATA 2, ThrBJA, TwCCW 78B,
–83B
Grissom, Virgil Ivan 1926-1967
BioIn 5, –6, –7, –8, –9, –10, –12, –13,
CurBio 65, –67, WhAm 4, WorAl
Griswold, Wesley S 1909- *ConAu 1R*
Groch, Judith 1929- *AuBYP, BioIn 8,*
–13, ConAu 9R, SmATA 25[port],
WhoAmW 74, –72, –75
Grohskopf, Bernice *DrAP&F 85,*
WrDr 86
Grohskopf, Bernice 1921-
AuBYP SUP, BioIn 10, ChhPo, –S3,
ConAu 3NR, –5R, ForWC 70,
IntAu&W 76, –77, –82, SmATA 7,
WrDr 76, –80, –82, –84
Gropman, Donald S 1936- *ConAu 101*
Groseclose, Elgin 1899- *WhoAm 84*
Groseclose, Elgin 1899-1983
AmAu&B, AmM&WS 73S, –78S,
AmNov, BioIn 2, BlueB 76,
ConAu 109, ConAu P-2,
IntAu&W 76, –77, –82,
NewYTBS 83, WhoAm 74, –76, –78,
–80, –82, WhoCon 73, WhoRel 75,
–77, WhoWor 74, –80, –82, WrDr 76,
–80, –82, –84

Groseclose, Elgin Earl 1899-1983
BioIn 13
Gross, Joel 1949?- *BioIn 9,*
ConAu 29R, WrDr 76, –80, –82, –84
Gross, Joel 1951- *ConAu 14NR,*
WrDr 86
Gross, Milton 1911?-1973 *BioIn 6, –9,*
ConAu 41R
Gross, Nathalie Friedland 1919-
WhoAdv 72, WhoAmW 72
Gross, Samuel Harry 1933- *ConAu 45*
Grosser, Morton 1931- *ConAu 17NR,*
–97, ScF&FL 1
Grossvogel, David I 1925- *ConTFT 1,*
WhoAm 84
Grosswirth, Marvin 1931- *ConAu 33R,*
WhoWorJ 72, –78
Grosswirth, Marvin 1931-1984
BioIn 13, ConAu 112
Groussard, Serge 1921- *ConAu 108,*
IntAu&W 76, –77, IntWW 74, –75,
–76, –77, –78, –79, –80, –81, –82,
–83, REn, WhoFr 79, WhoWor 74,
–76, –78
Grove, Fred 1913- *ConAu 1R, –2NR,*
–17NR, IntAu&W 76, –77, –82,
WrDr 84, –86
Groves, Ernest Rutherford 1877-1946
AmAu&B, BioIn 1, CurBio 43, –46,
DcNAA, WhAm 2, WhNAA
Groves, Paul 1930- *ConAu 17NR*
Grubb, Davis 1919-1980 *AmAu&B,*
Au&Wr 71, BioIn 6, –12, ConAu 1R,
–4NR, –101, DcLB 6,
NewYTBS 80[port], ScF&FL 2,
WhoHr&F, WorAu 1975[port]
Gruber, Gary R 1940-
AmM&WS 76P, –79P, ConAu 9NR,
–53
Gruber, Ruth *BioIn 1, –2,*
ConAu 12NR, –25R, ForWC 70,
WhoAmW 58, –61, –64, –66,
WhoWorJ 72, –78
Gruber, Terry 1953- *ConAu 97*
Grumbach, Doris *DrAP&F 85*
Grumbach, Doris 1918- *AmWomWr,*
BioIn 12, ConAu 5R, –9NR,
ConAu 2AS[port], ConLC 13,
–22[port], DrAS 74E, –78E, –82E,
ForWC 70, WhoAm 78, –80, –82,
–84, –86, WrDr 84, –86
Grun, Max Von Der 1926- *BioIn 12,*
OxGer
Grund, Josef Carl 1920- *ConAu 73*
Grzimek, Bernhard 1906?- *BioIn 9,*
–10, CurBio 73, IntAu&W 77
Guard, David 1934- *ConAu 77*
Guareschi, Giovanni 1908-1968
BioIn 3, –4, –7, –8, –9,
CathA 1952, ConAu 105, –25R,
EncWL, FilmgC, HalFC 84, ModRL,
ObitT 79, ScF&FL 1, TwCA SUP,
TwCWr, WhDW, WhAm 5, WorECar
Guerber, Helene Adeline 1859-1929
AmLY, BiD&SB, DcAmAu, DcNAA,
HarEnUS, WhAm 1, WhNAA,
WomWWA 14
Guess, Edward Preston 1925-
ConAu 73
Guest, Judith *DrAP&F 85*
Guest, Judith 1936- *BioIn 10, –11,*
–12, ConAu 15NR, –77, ConLC 8,
–30[port], MichAu 80, WhoAm 78,
–80, –82, WrDr 80, –82, –84, –86
Guffy, Ossie 1931- *BioIn 9,*
InB&W 80, –85
Gugliotta, Bobette 1918- *BioIn 10,*
ConAu 14NR, –41R, SmATA 7
Guild, Nicholas M 1944- *ConAu 93,*
ConLC 33[port]
Guillaume, Alfred 1888- *ConAu P-1,*
WhE&EA, WhLit, WhoLA
Guillaumin, Emile 1873-1951 *BioIn 2,*
–3, OxFr
Guillen, Jorge 1893- *BioIn 1, –4, –8,*
–10, –11, –12, CasWL, ClDMEL,

CnMWL, ConAu 89, ConLC 11,
DcSpL, EncWL, –2[port], EvEuW,
LinLib L, MakMC, ModRL, OxSpan,
PenC EUR, REn, TwCWr,
WhoTwCL, WorAu
Guillen, Jorge 1893-1984 *AnObit 1984,*
BioIn 13, ConAu 112, ConFLW 84,
WhAm 8
Guillen, Nicolas 1902- *ConAu 116,*
EncWL 2, IntWW 83, SelBAAf
Guillen, Nicolas 1904- *BioIn 13,*
InB&W 85
Guillot, Rene 1900-1969 *AuBYP,*
BioIn 6, –7, –8, –10, –11, ConAu 49,
MorJA, OxChL, ScF&FL 1, –2,
SmATA 7, TwCCW 78B, –83B,
WhoChL
Guisewite, Cathy Lee 1950- *BioIn 11,*
EncTwCJ, IntAu&W 86, WhoAm 80,
–82, –86, WhoAmW 81
Gulick, Bill *ConAu X*
Gulick, Bill *see also* Gulick, Grover C
Gulick, Grover C 1916- *ConAu 17NR,*
–33R, EncFWF[port], WhoPNW
Gulik, Robert Hans Van 1910-1967
BioIn 8, ConAu X, CorpD
Gulik, Robert Hans Van *see also* Van
Gulik, Robert H
Gummere, Richard M, Jr. 1912-
ConAu 45
Gunderson, Keith *DrAP&F 85*
Gunderson, Keith 1935- *ConAu 33R,*
DrAS 74P, –78P, –82P, WhoAm 74
Gunn, James E 1923- *BioIn 12,*
ConAu 5NR, –9R, ConSFA,
DcLB 8[port], EncSF, IntAu&W 76,
–82, –86, ScF&FL 1, –2, ScFSB[port],
SmATA 35, TwCSFW 86,
WhoMW 84, WhoSciF, WrDr 76,
–80, –82, –84, –86
Gunn, Thom *BioIn 13, DrAP&F 85*
Gunn, Thom 1929- *AmAu&B,*
Au&Wr 71, BioIn 10, –12, BlueB 76,
CasWL, ChhPo, –S1, –S2, CnE&AP,
ConAu 9NR, –17R, ConLC 3, –6,
–18, –32[port], ConPo 70, –75, –80,
–85, DcLB 27[port], IntAu&W 77,
–82, IntWW 74, –75, –76, –77, –78,
–79, –80, –81, –82, IntWWP 82X,
IntWWP 82X, LinLib L, LongCTC,
ModBrL, –S2, –S1, NewC, OxEng 85,
PenC ENG, RAdv 1, REn, TwCWr,
WebE&AL, WhoAm 74, –76, –78,
–80, –82, –84, –86, WhoTwCL,
WorAu, WrDr 76, –80, –82, –84, –86
Gunston, Bill *ConAu X*
Gunston, Bill 1927- *Au&Wr 71,*
BioIn 11, ConAu 49, –X,
IntAu&W 76, –77, –82, SmATA X,
WrDr 76, –80, –82, –84, –86
Gunston, Bill *see also* Gunston, William
Tudor
Gunston, David *Au&Wr 71,*
IntAu&W 76
Gunston, William Tudor 1927-
AuBYP SUP, BioIn 11, ConAu 3NR,
–19NR, –49, SmATA 9, WrDr 76,
–80
Gunston, William Tudor *see also*
Gunston, Bill
Gunther, John 1901-1970 *AmAu&B,*
AmNov, AuBYP, BioIn 1, –2, –3, –4,
–5, –6, –7, –8, –9, ConAu 9R, –25R,
CurBio 41, –61, –70, DcAmDH,
EncAJ, EvLB, LinLib L, –S,
LongCTC, NewYTBE 70, ObitOF 79,
ObitT 1961, OxAmL, –83, PenC AM,
REn, REnAL, ScF&FL 1, –2,
SmATA 2, TwCA, –SUP,
WebAB, –79, WhAm 6, WorAl
Gurko, Leo 1914- *BioIn 9, –11,*
ConAu 5R, –5NR, DrAS 74E, –78E,
–82E, SmATA 9, ThrBJA
Gurko, Miriam *BioIn 9, –11,*
ConAu 1R, SmATA 9, ThrBJA,
WrDr 76, –80, –82, –84, –86
Gurney, A R, Jr. *DrAP&F 85*
Gurney, A R, Jr. 1930- *ConAu 77,*
ConDr 77, –82, ConLC 32[port],

ConTFT 4, CurBio 86[port],
NatPD, –81[port], NewYTBS 82[port],
ScF&FL 1, WhoThe 81, WrDr 80,
–82, –84, –86
Gurney, Gene 1924- *ConAu 5R, –9NR*
Gustafson, Elton T *AuBYP, BioIn 8*
Gutcheon, Beth R 1945- *BioIn 12,*
ConAu 2NR, –49
Gutheim, Frederick 1908- *AmAu&B,*
BioIn 11, ConAu 9NR, –21R,
WhoAm 74, –76, –78, –80, –82, –84,
–86
Guthrie, A B, Jr. 1901- *CmMov,*
ConAu 57, ConLC 23[port],
ConNov 82, –86, ConAu 50, DcLB 6,
DrAP&F 85, EncFWF[port],
HalFC 84, IntAu&W 76, –77, Novels,
OxAmL 83, REnAW, WrDr 76, –80,
–82, –84, –86
Guthrie, Alfred Bertram, Jr. 1901-
AmAu&B, AmNov, BioIn 1, –2, –4,
–5, –7, –8, –10, CnDAL, ConAu 57,
ConNov 72, –76, CyWA,
DcLEL, –1940, IndAu 1917, ModAL,
OxAmL, REnAL, TwCA SUP,
WhoAm 74, –76, –78, –80, –82, –84,
–86, WhoPNW, WhoWest 74, –76,
WhoWor 74, WrDr 76
Guthrie, Anne 1890-1979 *AuBYP,*
BioIn 1, –13, ConAu 5R, SmATA 28,
WhoAmW 61, –64
Guthrie, Arlo 1947- *AmAu&B,*
BiDAmM, BioIn 7, –8, –9, –11, –12,
–13, CelR, ConAu 113,
CurBio 82[port], EncFCWM 69,
–83[port], HalFC 84, IlEncRk,
RkOn 78, RolSEnR 83, WhoAm 74,
–76, –78, –80, –82, WhoHol A,
WhoRock 81[port], WhoRocM 82,
WorAl
Guthrie, Sir Tyrone 1900-1971
BiE&WWA, BioIn 3, –4, –5, –6, –8,
–9, –10, –11, –12, CnThe,
ConAu 29R, CreCan 1, CurBio 54,
–71, –71N, DcIrB, DcNaB 1971,
EncWT, LinLib S, NewC,
NewYTBE 71, NotNAT A, –B,
ObitOF 79, ObitT 1971, OxThe,
PlP&P, WhScrn 83, WhThe,
WhoHol B, WhoThe 72, WorAl
Guthrie, Tyrone 1900-1971
OxAmT 84, OxThe 83
Guthrie, Woody *ConAu X*
Guthrie, Woody 1912-1967 *AmAu&B,*
Baker 78, –84, BioIn 6, –7, –8, –9,
–10, –11, –12, –13, CmpEPM,
ConAu X, ConLC 35[port],
CurBio 63, –67, EncFCWM 69,
–83[port], IlEncRk, ObitOF 79,
REnAW, RolSEnR 83, WebAB, –79,
WhAm 4, WhoRock 81,
WhoRocM 82, WorAl
Gutman, Bill *AuBYP SUP, SmATA 43*
Gutman, Herbert G d1985
NewYTBS 85[port]
Gutman, Herbert G 1928-1985
ConAu 116
Gutman, Herbert George 1928-
ConAu 65, DrAS 74H, –78H, –82H,
WhoAm 80, –82, –84
Gutman, Judith Mara 1928-
ConAu 21R, MacBEP, WhoAmW 74,
–75, –83, WrDr 76, –80, –82, –84,
–86
Gutnik, Martin J 1942- *ConAu 3NR,*
–49
Gutteridge, Lindsay 1923- *ConAu 49,*
EncSF, ScF&FL 1, –2, ScFSB,
TwCSFW 86, WrDr 80, –82, –84, –86
Guy, David 1948- *ConAu 105*
Guy, Rosa 1925- *DcLB 33[port]*
Guy, Rosa 1928- *BioIn 12, BlkAWP,*
ChlLR 13[port], ConAu 14NR, –17R,
ConLC 26[port], FifBJA[port],
InB&W 85, OxChL, SelBAAu,
SmATA 14, TwCCW 78, –83,
WrDr 80, –82, –84, –86
Gzowski, Peter 1934?- *BioIn 13,*
ConAu 106

H

Haar, Jaap Ter 1922- *BioIn 10,*
FourBJA
Haar, Jaap Ter *see also* Ter Haar, Jaap
Haas, Gerda 1922- *ConAu 110*
Haas, Kenneth B, Sr. 1898-
ConAu 6NR, –57
Habberton, William 1899- *AuBYP,*
BioIn 8
Habeeb, Virginia Thabet *WhoAm 84,*
–86
Habel, Norman C 1932- *ConAu 17R,*
DrAS 74P
Habeler, Peter 1942- *BioIn 11, –12*
Habenstreit, Barbara 1937-
AuBYP SUP, BioIn 10, ConAu 29R,
SmATA 5
Haber, Eitan 1940- *ConAu 104*
Haber, Louis 1910- *BioIn 11,*
ConAu 29R, SmATA 12, WhoE 75
Habig, Marion A 1901-1984
ConAu 114, –20NR
Habig, Marion Alphonse 1901-
AmCath 80, BioIn 1, BkC 2,
CathA 1930, ConAu 5R, –5NR,
DrAS 74H, –78H, –82H,
IntAu&W 77, WhoRel 75, –77,
WrDr 76, –80, –82, –84, –86
Hacker, Frederick J 1914-
BiDrAPA 77, ConAu 104
Hackett, Albert *OxAmT 84*
Hackett, Albert 1900- *AmAu&B,*
AuBYP, BiE&WWA, BioIn 4, –8,
–11, CmMov, CurBio 56,
DcLB 26[port], Film 1, –2, FilmgC,
HalFC 84, ModWD, NotNAT,
OxAmL, –83, REnAL, TwYS,
WhoAm 74, –76, –78, WorEFlm
Hadas, Moses 1900-1966 *AmAu&B,*
BioIn 5, –7, –9, –10, ConAu 1R,
–6NR, –25R, CurBio 60, –66,
LinLib 1, NatCAB 52, ObitOF 79,
PenC AM, REnAL, WhAm 4, WorAu
Haddix, Cecille 1937- *ConAu X*
Haddix, Cecille *see also*
Haddix-Kontos, Cecille P
Haddix-Kontos, Cecille P 1937-
ConAu 69
Hader, Berta 1890?-1976 *AmAu&B,*
AmPB, Au&ICB, AuBYP, BioIn 1,
–2, –4, –5, –7, –8, –10, –12, BkP,
Cald 1938, ConAu 65, –73, ConICB,
IlsBYP, IlsCB 1744, –1946, –1957,
–1967, InWom, JBA 34, –51, OxChL,
ScF&FL 1, SmATA 16, Str&VC,
TwCCW 78, –83, WhAm 6, –7,
WhE&EA, WhoAm 74,
WhoAmW 74, –58, –64, –66, –68,
–70, –72
Hader, Elmer Stanley 1889-
ArtsAmW 2
Hader, Elmer Stanley 1889-1973
AmAu&B, AmPB, Au&ICB, AuBYP,
BioIn 1, –2, –4, –5, –7, –8, –12, BkP,

Cald 1938, ConAu 73, ConICB,
IlsBYP, IlsCB 1744, –1946, –1957,
–1967, JBA 34, –51, ScF&FL 1,
SmATA 16, Str&VC, TwCCW 78,
–83, WhAm 7, WhE&EA,
WhoAm 74, WhoAmA 73, –76, –78N,
–80N, –82N
Hagberg, David J 1942- *ConAu 106*
Hageman, Howard Garberich 1921-
ConAu 1R, –5NR, DrAS 74P, –78P,
–82P, WhoAm 74, –76, –78, –80, –82,
–84, –86, WhoRel 75, WhoWor 78
Haggard, Sir Henry Rider 1856-1925
Alli SUP, BbD, BiD&SB, BioIn 1, –2,
–3, –5, –7, –8, –11, –12, –13,
Chambr 3, ConAu 108, CyWA,
DcBiA, DcEnA AP, DcEuL, DcLEL,
DcNaB 1922, EncSF, EncSoA, EvLB,
FilmgC, LinLib 1, –S, LongCTC,
MnBBF, ModBrL, NewC, Novels,
OxChL, OxEng, PenC ENG, REn,
ScF&FL 1, SmATA 16, TelT,
TwCA, –SUP, TwCLC 11[port],
WebE&AL, WhLit, WhoBW&I A,
WhoChL, WhoHr&F
Haggerty, James Joseph 1920-
BioIn 10, ConAu 41R, IntAu&W 77,
SmATA 5, WhoE 79, –81, –83, –85,
WhoS&SW 73, –75, –76,
WhoWor 84, –87
Hagon, Priscilla *ConAu X, WrDr 86*
Hagon, Priscilla 1915- *ConAu X,*
IntAu&W 76X, –77X, –82X,
SmATA 5, –X, TwCChW 83,
WrDr 76, –80, –82, –84
Hagon, Priscilla *see also* Allan, Mabel
Esther
Haher, Heinz 1913- *AuBYP,*
CurBio 52
Haher, Louis 1910- *ConAu 29R,*
SmATA 12
Hahn, Emily 1905- *AmAu&B,*
AmWomWr, AuBYP, BioIn 1, –2, –3,
–4, –7, –8, –9, –11, –12, –13,
ConAu 1R, –1NR, CurBio 42,
InWom, LongCTC, REnAL,
SmATA 3, TwCA SUP, WhNAA,
WhoAm 74, –76, –78, –80, –82, –84,
–86, WhoAmW 74, –58, –64, –66,
–68, –70, –72, –75, –77, –83, –85,
WhoE 74, WhoWor 74, –76,
WrDr 80, –82, –84, –86
Hahn, James 1947- *BioIn 11,*
ConAu 2NR, –17NR, –49, SmATA 9
Hahn, Lynn 1949- *BioIn 11,*
ConAu 2NR, –17NR, –49, SmATA 9
Hahn, Mary Downing 1937-
SmATA 44
Haig-Brown, Roderick Langmere
1908-1976 *Au&Wr 71, BioIn 1, –2,*
–6, –11, –12, –13, CanNov,
CanWW 70, CanWr, CasWL,
ConAu 4NR, –5R, –69,
ConLC 21[port], CreCan 1,

CurBio 50, IntAu&W 76, –77,
OxCan, REnAL, SmATA 12,
TwCCW 78, –83, WhAm 7,
WhoAm 74, –76, WhoCan 73, –75,
WhoWest 74, –76, WrDr 76
Hailey, Arthur 1920- *AmAu&B,*
Au&Wr 71, AuNews 2, BioIn 7, –9,
–10, –11, –13, BlueB 76, CanWW 70,
–83, CanWr, ConAu 1R, –2NR,
ConLC 5, ConNov 72, –76, –82, –86,
CreCan 2, CurBio 72,
DcLB Y82B[port], DcLEL 1940,
EncSF, HalFC 84, IntAu&W 76,
IntWW 74, –75, –76, –77, –78, –79,
–80, –81, –82, –83, LinLib 1,
NewYTBS 79, Novels[port], OxCan,
OxCanL, Who 82, –83, –85,
WhoAm 76, –78, –80, –82, –84, –86,
WhoCanL 85, WhoE 74, WhoWor 74,
–76, –78, –80, –82, –84, –87, WorAl,
WorAu 1970, WrDr 76, –80, –82,
–84, –86
Haines, Charles 1928- *AuBYP SUP,*
ConAu 41R, DrAS 74E, –78E, –82E,
IntAu&W 77
Haines, Gail Kay 1943- *AuBYP SUP,*
BioIn 11, ConAu 14NR, –37R,
SmATA 11, WhoAmW 83, WrDr 76,
–80, –82, –84, –86
Haines, John *DrAP&F 85*
Haines, John 1924- *ConAu 13NR,*
ConPo 85, WorAu 1975[port],
WrDr 86
Haining, Peter 1940- *BioIn 12,*
ConAu 1NR, –45, ConSFA,
EncO&P 2, –80, EncSF,
IntAu&W 76, –77, –82, ScF&FL 1,
–2, SmATA 14, WhoHr&F, WhoSciF,
WhoWor 76, WrDr 76, –80, –82, –84
Haining, Peter Alexander 1940-
WrDr 86
Halacy, D S, Jr. 1919- *ConAu 9NR,*
EncSF, FifBJA[port], ScF&FL 1, –2,
SmATA 36
Halacy, Daniel Stephen, Jr. 1919-
AuBYP, BioIn 8, ConAu 5R
Halberstam, David 1934- *AmAu&B,*
BioIn 9, –10, –11, –12, –13,
BlueB 76, CelR, ConAu 10NR, –69,
CurBio 73, DcLEL 1940, EncAJ,
EncTwCJ, NewYTBS 79, PolProf K,
WhoAm 74, –76, –78, –80, –82, –84,
–86, WhoWor 74, WorAu 1970,
WrDr 76, –80, –82, –84, –86
Halcomb, Ruth 1936- *ConAu 97*
Haldeman, Joe *DrAP&F 85*
Haldeman, Joe 1943- *BioIn 12,*
ConAu 6NR, –53, DcLB 8[port],
DrmM 2[port], EncSF, IntAu&W 82,
ScF&FL 1, –2, ScFSB[port],
TwCSFW 86, WhoAm 78, –80, –82,
WrDr 80, –82, –84, –86
Haldeman, Linda 1935- *ConAu 85*

CurBio 50, IntAu&W 76, –77,

Hale, Arlene 1924- *AuBYP, BioIn 8,*
ConAu 1R, –1NR, WhoAmW 74,
–66, –68, –70, –72, –75, –77
Hale, Edward Everett 1822-1909
Alli, –SUP, AmAu, AmAu&B, AmBi,
AmRef[port], ApCAB, BbD,
BiDAmM, BiD&SB, BioIn 1, –2, –3,
–4, –5, –7, –9, –12, CarSB,
Chambr 3, ChhPo, –S1, –S2, –S3,
CnDAL, ConAu 119, CyAL 2, CyWA,
DcAmAu, DcAmB, DcBiPP, DcEnL,
DcLB 1, –42[port], DcLEL, DcNAA,
Drake, EncSF, EvLB,
HarEnUS[port], JBA 34, LinLib 1,
–S, LuthC 75, McGEWB, NatCAB 1,
OxAmH, OxAmL, –83, OxChL,
PenC AM, REn, REnAL, ScF&FL 1,
SmATA 16, TwCBDA, WebAB, –79,
WhAm 1
Hale, Janet Campbell 1947-
AuBYP SUP, ChhPo, ConAu 49
Hale, John Rigby 1923- *Au&Wr 71,*
ConAu 102, –19NR, IntAu&W 76,
–77, IntWW 75, –76, –77, –78, –79,
–80, –81, –82, –83, Who 82, –83,
WhoWor 84, –87
Hale, Nancy *DrAP&F 85*
Hale, Nancy 1908- *AmAu&B,*
AmWomWr, Au&Wr 71, BioIn 1, –2,
–4, –7, –8, –12, ConAu 5R,
ConNov 72, –76, –82, –86,
DcLB Y80B[port], InWom,
IntAu&W 76, –77, LinLib 1,
OxAmL, –83, REn, REnAL,
SmATA 31[port], TwCA SUP,
WhoAm 74, –76, –78, –80, –82, –84,
–86, WhoAmW 74, –58, –61, –64,
–66, –68, –70, –72, WhoS&SW 73,
WhoWor 74, –76, WrDr 76, –80, –82,
–84, –86
Hale, Sir John Rigby 1923- *Who 85*
Hale, William Harlan 1910-1974
AmAu&B, BioIn 1, –10, –12,
ConAu 49, –93, EncTwCJ,
NatCAB 58[port], REnAL, WhAm 6,
WhoAm 74, WhoE 74
Haley, Alex 1921- *ASpks, BioIn 7, –9,*
–11, –13, ConAu 77, ConLC 8, –12,
CurBio 77, DcLB 38[port], Ebony 1,
LivgBAA, NegAl 83, OxAmL 83,
SelBAAf, SelBAAu, WhoAm 76, –78,
–80, –82, WhoWest 74, WhoWor 74,
–78, WorAl, WorAu 1975[port],
WrDr 80, –82, –84, –86
Haley, Neale *ConAu 41R*
Hall, Adam *TwCCr&M 85, Who 85,*
WrDr 86
Hall, Adam 1920- *ConAu X,*
DcLEL 1940, EncMys,
IntAu&W 76X, –77X, Novels,
SmATA X, TwCCr&M 80, Who 82,
–83, WrDr 76, –80, –82, –84
Hall, Adam *see also* Trevor, Elleston
Hall, Adele 1910- *AuBYP, BioIn 10,*
ConAu 1R, SmATA 7, WhoAmW 64

65

Hall, Carolyn Vosburg 1927-
*AuBYP SUP, ChhPo, ConAu 61,
MichAu 80*
Hall, Daryl 1948?- *BioIn 11, –12, –13,
WhoAm 82*
Hall, Daryl 1949- *WhoAm 84, –86*
Hall, Daryl *see also* Hall & Oates
Hall, Donald *DrAP&F 85*
Hall, Donald 1928- *AmAu&B,
AuBYP, BioIn 6, –8, –10, –12, –13,
ChhPo, SI, CnE&AP, ConAu 2NR,
–5R, ConLC 1, –37[port], ConPo 70,
–75, –80, –85, CurBio 84[port],
DcLB 5[port], DcLEL 1940,
FifBJA[port], NewYTBS 83[port],
OxAmL, –83, PenC AM, RAdv 1,
REn, REnAL, SmATA 23[port],
WhoAm 74, –76, –78, –80, –82, –84,
–86, WorAu, WrDr 76, –80, –82, –84,
–86*
Hall, Douglas Kent 1938- *BioIn 9,
ConAu 33R*
Hall, Edward Twitchell 1914-
*AmAu&B, AmM&WS 73S, –76P,
ConAu 65, FifJDA, WhoAm 74, –76,
–78, –80, –82, –84, –86*
Hall, Elizabeth 1929- *AuBYP SUP,
ConAu 14NR, –65, WhoAm 76, –78,
WhoAmW 79, –81*
Hall, Elvajean *WhoAmW 85,
WhoS&SW 84*
Hall, Elvajean 1910- *AuBYP,
BiDrLUS 70, BioIn 7, –10,
ConAu 8NR, –13R, DrLC 69,
ForWC 70, SmATA 6, WhoAmW 74,
–66, –68, –70, –72, –75, –77, –79,
–81, –83, WhoE 74, –75, –77,
WhoLibS 55, –66, WhoS&SW 78,
–80, –82*
Hall, Gordon Langley 1923?-
*Au&Wr 71, AuBYP, BioIn 8, –11,
ConAu 1R, –X*
Hall, Gordon Langley *see also*
Simmons, Dawn Langley
Hall, Grover C 1915-1971 *BioIn 13*
Hall, Grover C, Jr. 1915-1971 *BioIn 9,
NewYTBE 71, WhAm 5*
Hall, James Norman 1887-1951
*AmAu&B, AmNov, AuBYP, BioIn 1,
–2, –3, –4, –5, –7, –8, –9, –12,
CyWA, DcAmB S5, DcLEL, JBA 34,
LinLib L, –S, MnBBF, ObitOF 79,
OxAmL, –83, OxAusL, PenC AM,
REn, REnAL, SmATA 21[port],
TwCA, –SUP, TwCLC 23[port],
WhAm 3, WhLit, WhNAA, WorAl*
Hall, Lynn 1937- *AuBYP SUP,
BioIn 9, ConAu 9NR, –21R,
FifBJA[port], SmATA 2, –47[port],
SmATA 4AS[port], TwCChW 83,
WrDr 84, –86*
Hall, Malcolm 1945- *AuBYP SUP,
BioIn 10, ConAu 4NR, –49,
SmATA 7*
Hall, Marjory 1908- *AuBYP, BioIn 4,
–8, ConAu X, CurBio 57, ForWC 70,
InWom, IntAu&W 77X, –82X,
SmATA X, WhoAmW 74, –58, –61,
–64, –66, –68, –70, –72, –75, –77,
WhoE 74, WrDr 76, –80, –82, –84,
–86*
Hall, Marjory *see also* Yeakley,
Marjory Hall
Hall, Nancy Lee 1923- *ConAu 57,
WhoWest 78*
Hall, Oakley 1920- *CmCal,
ConAu 3NR, –9R, EncFWF,
OxAmL 83, WrDr 84, –86*
Hall & Oats *RkOn 84, RolSEnR 83*
Hall, Peter Geoffrey 1932-
IntAu&W 86, Who 85, WhoWor 87
Hall, Robert Anderson, Jr. 1911-
*AmAu&B, BioIn 11, ConAu 5NR,
–13R, DrAS 74F, –78F, –82F,
WhoAm 74, –76, –78, –80, –82, –84,
–86, WhoWor 78, –80, –82, –84, –87*
Hall, Roger 1919- *Au&Wr 71,
ConAu 29R*
Hall, Sandi *ScFSB*
Hallahan, William H *ConAu 109,
TwCCr&M 85, WrDr 86*
Haller, John S, Jr. 1940- *IntAu&W 86*
Haller, John Samuel, Jr. 1940-
ConAu 61, IntAu&W 82, WhoMW 78

Hallet, Jean-Pierre 1927- *BioIn 9,
ConAu 17R, IntAu&W 76,
WhoWest 74, –76, –78, WhoWor 74,
–76*
Halliburton, Richard 1900-1939
*AmAu&B, AmBi, BioIn 2, –5, –6, –7,
CnDAL, ConAu 114, DcNAA, EvLB,
LinLib L, –S, NatCAB 35,
OxAmL, –83, REnAL, TwCA, –SUP,
WhAm 1, –1C, WhE&EA, WhNAA*
Halliburton, Warren J 1924- *BioIn 12,
ConAu 33R, LivgBAA, SelBAAf,
SelBAAu, SmATA 19*
Halliday, Ernest Milton 1913-
ConAu 17R
Halliday, Frank Ernest 1903-1982
*Au&Wr 71, BioIn 5, ConAu 1R,
–2NR, –106, IntAu&W 77, –82,
Who 74, –82, –83N*
Halliday, William R 1926-
IntAu&W 86
Halliday, William Ross 1926-
*ConAu 49, IntAu&W 82, WhoAm 82,
–84, –86, WhoGov 77, WhoPNW,
WhoWest 74, –76, –78, –80, –82, –84,
WhoWor 82, –84, –87*
Hallman, Ruth 1929- *BioIn 13,
ConAu 15NR, –85, SmATA 28,
–43[port]*
Hall-Quest, Olga 1899- *Au&Wr 71,
AuBYP, BioIn 8, –11, ConAu 5R,
ForWC 70, SmATA 11, WhoAm 74,
–76, –78, WhoAmW 74*
Hall-Quest, Olga W 1899-1986
ConAu 118, SmATA 47N
Hallstead, William F 1924-
ConAu 21NR
Hallstead, William Finn, III 1924-
*AuBYP SUP, BioIn 11, ConAu 5R,
–6NR, SmATA 11, WhoE 74, –75,
–77, –79*
Halmi, Robert 1924- *WhoAm 82, –84,
–86*
Halperin, Morton H 1938-
WhoAm 84, –86
Halpern, Daniel *DrAP&F 85*
Halpern, Daniel 1945- *ConPo 85,
WhoAm 84, –86, WrDr 86*
Halsell, Grace 1923- *AuBYP,
AuNews 1, BioIn 8, –10,
ConAu 13NR, –21R, SmATA 13,
WhoAmW 74, –72, –75*
Halter, Jon C 1941- *AuBYP SUP,
BioIn 13, ConAu 13NR, –61,
SmATA 22[port]*
Hamalian, Leo 1920- *ConAu 2NR,
–5R, DrAS 74E, –78E, –82E,
SmATA 41[port], WhoE 75*
Hambleton, Ronald *OxCanL*
Hamblin, Dora Jane 1920- *AuBYP,
BioIn 6, ConAu 3R, ForWC 70,
SmATA 36, WhoAmW 74, –64, –66,
–68, –70, –72*
Hamerstrom, Frances 1907-
*AmM&WS 79P, –82P, –86P,
BioIn 12, –13, ConAu 69,
SmATA 24[port]*
Hamill, Pete *IntMPA 86*
Hamill, Pete 1935- *BioIn 8, –13, CelR,
ConAu 18NR, –25R, ConLC 10,
IntMPA 77, –75, –76, –78, –79, –81,
–82, –84, WhoAm 84, –86,
WomWMM*
Hamilton, Clive *BioIn 13*
Hamilton, Clive 1898-1963 *BioIn 1,
–3, –4, –6, –7, –8, –9, –10, –11, –12,
ConAu X, CurBio 44, –64, EvLB,
LongCTC, NewC, SmATA X,
TwCA SUP*
Hamilton, Clive *see also* Lewis, C S
Hamilton, Dorothy 1906-1983
*BioIn 11, ConAu 110, –33R,
SmATA 12, –35N, WhoAmW 75,
–77, –79, WomPO 76*
Hamilton, Edith 1867-1963 *AmAu&B,
AmWomM, AmWomWr, AnCL,
BioIn 3, –4, –5, –6, –7, –8, –9, –11,
–12, ConAu 77, CurBio 63,
DcAmB S7, EncAB-H, HerW, –84,
InWom, IntDcWB, LibW, LinLib L,
–S, NatCAB 52, NotAW MOD,
ObitOF 79, REn, REnAL,
SmATA 20, TwCA, –SUP,*

*WebAB, –79, WhAm 4, WhNAA,
WhoAmW 58, –64*
Hamilton, Edmond 1904-1977
*AmAu&B, BioIn 7, –11, –12,
ConAu 1R, –3NR, ConLC 1,
ConSFA, DcLB 8[port], EncSF,
LinLib L, OhA&B, ScF&FL 1, –2,
ScFSB, TwCSFW 86, WhoSciF*
Hamilton, Eleanor 1909-
*AmM&WS 73S, –78S, ConAu 1R,
–2NR, WhoAmW 58, –61, –64, –81,
–83*
Hamilton, Franklin W 1923-
*ConAu 33R, DrAS 74E, –78E, –82E,
MichAu 80, WrDr 76, –80, –82, –84,
–86*
Hamilton, Gail *AuBYP SUP,
ConAu X, DrAP&F 85,
IntAu&W 82X*
Hamilton, Gail *see also* Corcoran,
Barbara
Hamilton, Virginia 1936- *AmWomWr,
Au&ICB, AuBYP, AuNews 1,
BioIn 9, –10, –11, –12, BlkAWP,
ChlLR 1, –11[port], ChhPo S2,
ConAu 20NR, –25R, ConLC 26[port],
DcLB 33[port], –52[port], FourBJA,
InB&W 80, MorBMP, NewbC 1966,
OxChL, SelBAAu, SmATA 4,
TwCCW 78, –83, WhoAm 76, –78,
–80, –82, –84, –86, WhoAmW 74,
–77, –81, –83, –85, –87, WhoBlA 85,
WrDr 80, –82, –84, –86*
Hamilton, Virginia Esther 1936-
InB&W 85
Hamilton-Paterson, James Lee 1908-
AuBYP SUP, WhE&EA
Hamley, Dennis 1935- *ConAu 11NR,
–57, ScF&FL 1A, SmATA 39[port]*
Hamlisch, Marvin *IntMPA 86*
Hamlisch, Marvin 1944?-
*AmSCAP 66, Baker 78, –84,
BioIn 10, –11, –12, BioNews 74,
ConAmC 82, ConTFT 4, CurBio 76,
IntMPA 78, –79, –81, –82, –84,
OxAmT 84, RkOn 78, –82, –84, –86,
WhoAm 78, –80, –82, –84, –86,
WhoThe 81*
Hamlisch, Marvin 1945- *HalFC 84*
Hamm, Jack 1916- *BioIn 2,
ConAu 5R, –9NR*
Hammer, Richard 1928- *BioIn 10,
ConAu 11NR, –25R, SmATA 6*
Hammett, Dashiell 1894-1961
*AuNews 1, BioIn 2, –4, –6, –7, –8,
–10, –11, –12, –13, CasWL, CmCal,
CmMov, CnDAL, CnMWL,
ConAu 81, ConLC 3, –5, –10, –19,
CorpD, CyWA, DcFM, EncAB-H,
EncMys, FilmgC, HalFC 84,
LinLib L, LongCTC, ModAL, –S2,
–S1, Novels[port], ObitOF 79,
ObitT 1961, OxAmL, –83,
OxEng, –85, OxFilm, PenC AM,
PolProf T, REn, REnAL, ScF&FL 1,
TwCA, –SUP, TwCCr&M 80, –85,
TwCWr, WebAB, –79, WebE&AL,
WhoTwCL, WorAl, WorEFlm*
Hammond, Cleon E 1908-
AmSCAP 66
Hammond Innes, Ralph *ConNov 86*
Hammond Innes, Ralph 1913-
*Au&Wr 71, AuBYP, BioIn 3, –4, –5,
–8, –10, BlueB 76, ConAu 4NR, –5R,
CurBio 54, IntAu&W 76, –77, –82,
–86, IntWW 76, –77, –78, –79, –80,
–81, –82, –83, LongCTC, Who 74,
–82, –83, –85, WhoWor 74, –76, –78,
–84, –87, WrDr 76, –80, –82, –84,
–86*
Hammond Innes, Ralph *see also* Innes,
Hammond
Hammonds, Michael 1942- *ConAu 45*
Hamner, Earl Henry, Jr. 1923-
WhoAm 84, –86
Hamner, Earl, Jr. 1923- *AuNews 2,
BioIn 10, –11, ConAu 73, ConLC 12,
DcLB 6[port], LesBEnT, NewYTET,
WhoAm 76, –78, –80, –82*
Hamori, Laszlo Dezso 1911-
ConAu 9R
Hampden, John 1898-1974 *Au&Wr 71,
ConAu 109, ScF&FL 1, WhE&EA,
Who 74*

Hample, Stoo 1926- *ChhPo*
Hampshire, Susan 1938?- *BioIn 8,
–9, –10, –12, CelR, CurBio 74,
FilmgC, HalFC 84, IntMPA 77, –75,
–76, –78, –79, –81, –82, –84,
IntWW 82, –83, NewYTBE 70,
Who 82, –83, WhoAm 74, –76, –78,
–80, –82, WhoAmW 74, –83,
WhoHol A, WhoThe 72, –77, –81,
WhoWor 78, WorAl*
Hampshire, Susan 1941- *IntMPA 86*
Hampshire, Susan 1942- *BioIn 13,
ConAu 112, ConTFT 2, Who 85,
WhoAm 84, –86, WhoAmW 85, –87*
Hampson, Alfred Leete 1889?-1952
BioIn 2, –3, ChhPo
Hamre, Leif 1914- *Au&Wr 71,
BioIn 10, ConAu 4NR, –5R,
FourBJA, IntAu&W 76, –82,
SmATA 5, TwCCW 78B, –83B,
WrDr 76, –80, –82, –84, –86*
Hanaburgh, David Henry 1910-
WhoCon 73, WhoE 77
Hanchett, William 1922- *WhoAm 84*
Hanckel, Frances Stuart 1944-
BiDrAPH 79
Hancock, Carla *ConAu 89*
Hancock, Ian Francis 1942-
WhoAm 84, –86, WhoWor 84, –87
Hancock, Lyn *IntAu&W 86X*
Hancock, Lyn 1938- *BioIn 9, –13,
ConAu 77, WhoCanL 85*
Hancock, Niel Anderson 1941-
ConAu 21NR, –97
Hancock, Ralph Lowell 1903-
*AmAu&B, Au&Wr 71, ConAu P-1,
IndAu 1917, IntAu&W 76, –77,
WhoAm 74, –76, –78, –80, –82, –84,
–86*
Hand, Jackson 1913- *ConAu 10NR,
–61*
Hanenkrat, Frank Thomas 1939-
ConAu 93, DrAS 74E, –78E, –82E
Hanes, Frank Borden *DrAP&F 85*
Hanes, Frank Borden 1920- *AmAu&B,
BioIn 3, –4, ConAu 1R, WhoAm 76,
–78, –80, –82, –84, –86,
WhoS&SW 73, –75, –76,
WhoWor 82, WrDr 76, –80, –82, –84,
–86*
Haney, Lynn 1941- *BioIn 13,
ConAu 1NR, –49, SmATA 23[port]*
Hanff, Helene *BioIn 11, –12, –13,
ConAu 3NR, –9R, WhoAm 76,
NewYTBS 82[port], SmATA 11*
Hanley, Hope Anthony 1926-
ConAu 5NR, –9R
Hanlon, Emily *DrAP&F 85*
Hanlon, Emily 1945- *BioIn 12,
ConAu 77, SmATA 15*
Hanna, Mary Carr *DrAP&F 85*
Hanna, Mary Carr 1905- *ConAu 45*
Hannam, Charles Lewis *WrDr 86*
Hannam, Charles Lewis 1925-
*ConAu 11NR, –61, IntAu&W 77,
WrDr 76, –80, –82, –84*
Hannay, Allen 1946- *ConAu 109*
Hannay, Margaret Patterson 1944-
ConAu 104, –21NR, DrAS 78E, –82E
Hannum, Alberta Pierson 1906-
*AmAu&B, AmNov, BioIn 2, –3,
ConAu 65, InWom, OhA&B,
WhE&EA, WhoAm 74, –76,
WhoAmW 61, –77, –79, –81*
Hannum, Alberta Pierson 1906-1985
ConAu 115
Hannum, Sara *AuBYP, BioIn 8,
ChhPo S1*
Hano, Arnold 1922- *AuBYP, BioIn 8,
–11, ConAu 5NR, –9R, SmATA 12,
WhoWest 74, –76, –82*
Hanrahan, John D 1938-
ConAu 15NR
Hanrahan, John David 1938-
ConAu 77, IntAu&W 82
Hansberry, Lorraine *OxAmT 84*
Hansberry, Lorraine 1930-1965
*AmAu&B, AmWomD, AmWomWr,
AuNews 2, BiE&WWA, BioIn 5, –6,
–7, –8, –9, –10, –12, –13, BlkAWP,
CasWL, CnMD SUP, ConAu 109,
–25R, ConDr 77F, –82E, ConLC 17,
CroCD, DcAmB S7, DcLB 7[port],*

Harrison, William 1933- *BioIn 9,*
ConAu 9NR, –17R, DrAS 74E, –78E,
–82E, ScF&FL 1, –2, WhoAm 76,
–78, –80, –82
Harrison, William C 1919-
ConAu 25R
Harry, Debbie *WhsNW 85*
Harry, Debbie 1946?- *CurBio 81[port],*
NewYTBS 79
Harsanyi, Zsolt 1887-1943 *CurBio 44,*
ObitOF 79, PenC EUR
Hart, Bruce 1938- *AmSCAP 66,*
BioIn 12, ConAu 107, SmATA 39
Hart, Carole 1943?- *BioIn 12,*
ConAu 107, SmATA 39
Hart, Carolyn Gimpel 1936-
ConAu 13R, ForWC 70
Hart, Jeffrey *BioIn 13*
Hart, John 1948- *ConAu 11NR, –65,*
IntWWP 82
Hart, John Lewis 1931- *AmAu&B,*
BioIn 4, –5, –10, BlueB 76,
ConAu 4NR, –49, EncTwCJ,
WhoAm 74, –76, –78, –80, –82, –84,
–86, WhoAmA 76, –78, –80, –82, –84
Hart, John Lewis *see also* Hart, Johnny
Hart, Johnny 1931- *ArtCS, AuNews 1,*
BioNews 74, ConAu 49, –X,
IntAu&W 77, WorECom
Hart, Johnny *see also* Hart, John Lewis
Hart, Kitty *BioIn 12*
Hart, Kitty 1926- *BioIn 13,*
ConAu 117
Hart, Moss 1904-1961 *AmAu&B,*
BiDAmM, BioIn 1, –2, –4, –5, –6, –7,
–12, CasWL, CnDAL, CnMD,
CnThe, ConAu 109, –89, CurBio 40,
–60, –62, DcAmB S7, DcLB 7[port],
EncMT, EncWT, FilmgC, HalFC 84,
LongCTC, McGEWD, –84[port],
ModWD, NatCAB 46, NewCBMT,
NotNAT A, –B, ObitOF 79,
ObitT 1961, OxAmL, –83,
OxAmT 84, OxThe, –83, PenC AM,
PlP&P, REn, REnAL, REnWD,
TwCA, –SUP, WebAB, –79,
WebE&AL, WhAm 4, WhThe,
WorAl, WorEFlm
Harte, Bret *OxAmT 84*
Harte, Bret 1836?-1902 *AmAu,*
AmAu&B, AmWr S2, AtlBL, AuBYP,
BiD&SB, BioIn 1, –3, –4, –5, –6, –7,
–8, –9, –10, –11, –12, –13, CasWL,
CmCal, CnDAL, ConAu 104, CrtT 3,
–4, CyWA, DcAmAu, DcAmB,
DcAmSR, DcLB 12[port], DcNAA,
EncAAH, EncFWF[port], HalFC 84,
LinLib L, Novels[port], OxAmH,
OxAmL, –83, OxEng 85, PenC AM,
RAdv 1, REn, REnAL, REnAW,
SmATA 26[port], TwCBDA, TwCLC 1, WebAB, –79, WebE&AL,
WhDW, WhAm 1, WorAl
Hartland, Michael 1941- *WrDr 86*
Hartley, Fred Allan, III 1953-
ConAu 106, SmATA 41[port]
Hartley, L P 1895-1972 *ChhPo S3,*
ConAu 37R, ConLC 22[port],
DcLB 15[port], EncSF, EncWL 2,
LongCEL, ModBrL S2, Novels,
ObitOF 79, ObitT 1971, OxEng 85,
ScF&FL 1, –2, ScFSB, SupFW,
TwCSFW 86, WhoHr&F
Hartley, Leslie Poles 1895-1972
Au&Wr 71, BioIn 4, –6, –7, –9, –10,
–11, –13, CasWL, ConAu 37R, –45,
ConLC 2, ConNov 72, –76, DcLEL,
DcNaB 1971, EncWL, EvLB,
IntAu&W 76, –77, LongCTC,
ModBrL, –S1, NewC, PenC ENG,
RAdv 1, REn, TwCA SUP, TwCWr,
WebE&AL, WhAm 5, WhE&EA,
WhoTwCL
Hartman, Evert 1937- *ConAu 113,*
IntAu&W 86, SmATA 35, –38[port],
TwCChW 83B
Hartman, Gertrude 1876-1955
AmAu&B, BioIn 2, –3, –4, JBA 51,
ObitOF 79, WhAm 3
Hartman, Jane E 1928- *ConAu 105,*
SmATA 47[port]
Hartog, Jan De *OxThe 83*

Hartog, Jan De 1914- *BioIn 2, –3, –4,*
–7, –8, CasWL, EncWL, EncWT,
IntAu&W 77, IntWW 74, –75, –76,
–77, –78, –79, –80, –81, –82, –83,
TwCA SUP
Harvey, Harriet 1924- *ConAu 109*
Harvey, Virginia I 1917- *ConAu 57*
Harwood, Ronald *OxThe 83*
Harwood, Ronald 1934- *Au&Wr 71,*
BioIn 12, –13, ConAu 1R, –4NR,
ConDr 82, ConLC 32[port],
DcLB 13[port], IntAu&W 76,
IntMPA 77, –75, –76, –78, –79, –81,
–82, –84, –86, NewYTBS 81[port],
Novels, Who 82, –83, –85,
WhoThe 81, WhoWor 76, –78,
WrDr 76, –80, –82, –84, –86
Hasek, Jaroslav 1883-1923 *BioIn 1,*
–10, –11, –12, –13, CasWL,
CIDMEL, ConAu 104,
EncWL, –2[port], EncWT, EvEuW,
GrFLW, LongCTC, MakMC,
ModSL 2, Novels, PenC EUR, REn,
TwCA, –SUP, TwCLC 4[port],
TwCWr, WhDW, WhoTwCL, WorAl
Haseley, Dennis *SmATA 44*
Haskell, Molly *BioIn 13, WomWMM*
Haskins, James 1941- *AuBYP SUP,*
BioIn 11, ChlLR 3, ConAu 33R,
DrAS 82E, InB&W 80, IntAu&W 77,
NegAl 76, –83, SelBAAf, SelBAAu,
SmATA 9, WhoE 75
Haskins, Jim 1941- *AuBYP SUP,*
ChlLR 3, ConAu X, LivgBAA,
SmATA 9, SmATA 4AS[port],
WrDr 76, –80, –82, –84, –86
Haslam, Gerald William 1937-
ConAu 11NR, –29R, DrAS 74E,
–78E, –82E, IntAu&W 82,
Po&Wr 77, WhoWest 80, –82, –84,
WrDr 76, –80, –82, –84, –86
Hasler, Joan 1931- *BioIn 13,*
ConAu 29R, SmATA 28
Hass, Hans 1919- *Au&Wr 71, BioIn 4,*
–11, ConAu 108, CurBio 55, InSci
Hassler, Jon 1933- *BioIn 12,*
ConAu 21NR, –73, SmATA 19
Hastings, Max 1945- *ConAu 81,*
IntAu&W 82, WhoWor 80
Haston, Dougal 1940-1977 *BioIn 11,*
ConAu 105, WrDr 76
Haswell, Chetwynd John Drake 1919-
ConAu 41R, IntAu&W 76, –82,
WrDr 76, –80, –82, –84, –86
Haswell, Chetwynd John Drake *see also*
Haswell, Jock
Haswell, Jock *WrDr 86*
Haswell, Jock 1919- *Au&Wr 71,*
ConAu X, IntAu&W 76X, –82X,
WrDr 76, –80, –82, –84
Haswell, Jock *see also* Haswell,
Chetwynd John Drake
Hatch, Alden 1898-1975 *AmAu&B,*
Au&Wr 71, AuBYP, BioIn 8, –10,
ConAu 57, –65, NewYTBS 75,
ObitOF 79, WhAm 6, WhoAm 74
Hathaway, Donny 1945- *WhoRock 81*
Hathaway, Donny 1945-1979
Baker 84, BiDAfM, BioIn 11,
EncPR&S 77, InB&W 80, –85,
NewYTBS 79, RkOn 78, –84,
RolSEnR 83, WhoBlA 77
Hathaway, Nancy 1946- *ConAu 108*
Haugaard, Erik Christian 1923-
AuBYP, BioIn 8, –9, –12,
ChlLR 11[port], ConAu 3NR, –5R,
IntAu&W 76, –77, –82, SmATA 4,
ThrBJA, TwCCW 78, –83,
WhoWor 76, WrDr 76, –80, –82, –84
Haupt, Enid Annenberg 1906-
BioIn 5, ForWC 70, InWom,
NewYTBE 70, NewYTBS 82,
WhoAmW 74, –64, –66, –68, –70,
–72, –75
Hauptly, Denis J 1945- *ConAu 118*
Hauser, Thomas 1946- *ConAu 85*
Hausman, Gerald *DrAP&F 85*
Hausman, Gerald 1945- *ConAu 2NR,*
–17NR, –45, IntWWP 82, SmATA 13
Hautzig, Deborah 1956- *ConAu 89,*
FifBJA[port], SmATA 31[port]

Hautzig, Esther 1930- *AuBYP,*
BioIn 8, –9, –10, –11, ConAu 1R,
–5NR, ForWC 70, HerW, –84,
IntAu&W 77, –82, MorBMP, OxChL,
SmATA 4, ThrBJA, WhoAmW 83,
WrDr 76, –80, –82, –84, –86
Havens, Richie *WhoRock 81*
Havens, Richie 1941- *BioIn 8, –9,*
DrBlPA, EncFCWM 83,
EncPR&S 74, –77, IlEncRk,
InB&W 80, RkOn 78, –84,
RolSEnR 83, WhoRocM 82
Haverstock, Mary Sayre 1932-
AuBYP SUP, ConAu 81,
WhoAmW 75
Haviaras, Stratis *DrAP&F 85*
Haviaras, Stratis 1935- *ConAu X,*
ConLC 33[port], Po&Wr 77,
WorAu 1975[port], WrDr 82, –84,
–86
Havighurst, Walter 1901- *AmAu&B,*
AmNov, Au&Wr 71, AuBYP, BioIn 2,
–4, –6, –7, –9, CnDAL, ConAu 1R,
–1NR, DrAS 74E, –78E, –82E,
IntAu&W 76, –77, MichAu 80,
MorJA, OhA&B, OxAmL, –83,
REnAL, SmATA 1, TwCA SUP,
WhE&EA, WhoAm 74, –76,
WhoWor 78, WrDr 76, –80, –82, –84,
–86
Havrevold, Finn 1905- *AuBYP SUP,*
ConAu 109, IntAu&W 77,
IntWW 74, –75, –76, –77, –78, –79,
–80, –81, –82, –83, WhoWor 74, –76,
–78
Hawes, Charles Boardman 1889-1923
AmAu&B, AuBYP, BioIn 4, –7,
DcAmB, DcNAA, JBA 34,
Newb 1922, REnAL, TwCA,
TwCChW 83
Hawes, Evelyn Johnson *AuNews 1,*
BioIn 10, ConAu 13R, ForWC 70,
IntAu&W 82, WhoAmW 74, –70,
–72, –75, –77, –79, –81
Hawes, Gene R 1922- *ConAu 3NR,*
–5R, –18NR
Hawke, Simon *ConAu X*
Hawke, Simon *see also* Yermakov,
Nicholas
Hawkes, Jacquetta 1910- *Au&Wr 71,*
BioIn 3, –4, BlueB 76, ConAu 15NR,
–69, EncSF, IntAu&W 76, –77, –82,
IntWW 74, –75, –76, –77, –78, –79,
–80, –81, –82, –83, LongCTC,
OxEng 85, REn, ScF&FL 1, ScFSB,
TwCA SUP, Who 74, –82, –83, –85,
WhoWor 74, –76, –78, WrDr 76, –80,
–82, –84, –86
Hawkes, Terence 1932- *ConAu 17R*
Hawkesworth, Eric 1921-
AuBYP SUP, ConAu 29R,
SmATA 13, WrDr 76, –80, –82, –84,
–86
Hawkins, Anthony Hope *OxChL*
Hawkins, Arthur 1903- *BioIn 12,*
ConAu 8NR, –21R, IlsBYP,
SmATA 19, WhE&EA
Hawkins, Gerald Stanley 1928-
AmM&WS 73P, BiESc, ConAu 17R,
DrRegL 75, WhoE 74, WhoGov 77,
WhoWor 74, WrDr 76, –80, –82, –84,
–86
Hawkins, Jim 1944- *ConAu 73*
Hawkins, Paula *CngDr 85,*
WhoAm 84, –86, WhoS&SW 84, –86,
WhoWor 84, –87
Hawkins, Paula 1927?- *BioIn 13,*
CurBio 85[port], PolsAm 84[port],
WhoAmW 85, –87
Hawkins, Sir Anthony Hope
1863-1933 *BbD, BiD&SB, BioIn 2,*
–4, –5, –8, –12, Chambr 3,
DcEnA AP, DcLEL, DcNaB 1931,
EvLB, LinLib L, –S, LongCTC,
NewC, NotNAT B, OxEng, –85, REn,
TelT, TwCA, –SUP, WhoChL
Hawkins, Sir Anthony Hope *see also*
Hope, Anthony
Hawthorne, Nathaniel 1804-1864
Alli, –SUP, AmAu, AmAu&B, AmBi,
AmWr, ApCAB, AtlBL, AuBYP SUP,
BbD, BiAUS, BiD&SB, BioIn 1, –2,
–3, –4, –5, –6, –7, –8, –9, –10, –11,

–12, –13, CarSB, CasWL, CelCen,
Chambr 3, ChhPo S1, –S2, –S3,
CnDAL, CrtT 3, –4, CyAL 2, CyWA,
DcAmAu, DcAmB, DcAmSR, DcBiA,
DcBiPP, DcEnA, –AP, DcEnL,
Drake, EncAAH, EncAB-H, EncSF,
EvLB, FamAYP, FilmgC, HalFC 84,
HarEnUS[port], LinLib L, –S,
LuthC 75, McGEWB, MemAm,
MouLC 3, NatCAB 3, NewEOp 71,
NinCLC 2[port], –10[port],
Novels[port], OxAmH, OxAmL, –83,
OxChL, OxEng, –85, PenC AM,
RAdv 1, RComWL, REn, REnAL,
ScF&FL 1, ScFSB, Str&VC, SupFW,
TwCBDA, WebAB, –79, WebE&AL,
WhDW, WhAm HS, WhoChL,
WhoHr&F, WorAl, YABC 2
Hay, John 1915- *AmAu&B,*
ConAu 9NR, –65, EncSF,
IntWWP 77, –82, SmATA 13,
WhoAm 74, –76, –78, –80, –82
Hayakawa, S I 1906- *AlmAP 78, –80,*
–82[port], CelR, CmCal,
ConAu 20NR, CurBio 59, –77,
LinLib L, WhoWest 74, –76, –78,
–80, –82, WrDr 80, –82, –84
Hayakawa, Samuel Ichiye 1906-
AmAu&B, AmM&WS 73S, –78S,
BiDAmEd, BioIn 3, –4, –5, –8, –9,
–10, –11, –13, BlueB 76, CngDr 77,
–79, –81, ConAu 13R, DrAS 74F,
–78F, –82F, IntAu&W 77,
IntWW 74, –75, –76, –77, –78, –79,
–80, –81, –82, –83, IntYB 78, –79,
–80, –81, –82, LEduc 74, REn,
REnAL, TwCA SUP, WebAB, –79,
WhoAm 74, –76, –78, –80, –82, –84,
–86, WhoAmP 77, –79, –81, –83, –85,
WhoGov 77, WhoWor 78, –80, –82,
WorAl, WrDr 76
Haycraft, Howard 1905- *AmAu&B,*
AuBYP, BiDrLUS 70, BioIn 3, –7,
–8, –9, –10, ConAu 21R, CurBio 41,
–54, EncMys, IntAu&W 76, –77,
IntWW 74, –75, –76, –77, IntYB 78,
–80, –81, –82, –83, IntYB 78, –79,
–80, –81, –82, REnAL, SmATA 6,
WhoAm 74, –76, –78, –80,
WhoLibI 82, WhoLibS 55, –66
Haycraft, Molly 1911- *BioIn 10,*
ConAu 13R, SmATA 6
Hayden, Melissa 1923- *BiDD, BioIn 3,*
–4, –6, –7, –9, –10, –11, –13,
CanWW 70, –79, –80, –81, –83,
CurBio 55, InWom, LibW,
NewYTBE 73, WhoAm 74, –76, –78,
WhoAmW 74, –58, –61, –64, –66,
–70, –72, –75, WhoHol A,
WhoWor 74, –76, WorAl
Hayden, Robert C *SelBAAf*
Hayden, Robert C 1937- *BioIn 13,*
WrDr 86
Hayden, Robert C, Jr. 1937-
ConAu 69, SelBAAu, SmATA 28,
–47, WrDr 76, –80, –82, –84
Hayden, Robert E 1913-1980
AmAu&B, AnObit 1980,
AuBYP SUP, BioIn 4, –10, –11, –12,
–13, BlkAWP, BroadAu[port],
ChhPo S1, –S2, –S3, ConAu 69, –97,
ConLC 5, –9, –14, ConPo 70, –75,
–80, Conv 1, CroCAP, DcLB 5[port],
DcLEL 1940, InB&W 80, LinLib L,
LivgBAA, ModBlW, NegAl 76, –83,
NewYTBS 80[port], SelBAAf,
SelBAAu, SmATA 19, –26N,
WhAm 7, WhoAm 76, –78,
WorAu 1970, WrDr 76, –80, –82
Hayden, Robert Earl 1913-1980
InB&W 85
Hayden, Torey L 1951- *ConAu 103*
Hayes, Billy *AmSCAP 66, ConAu 97,*
NewYTBE 73
Hayes, Carlton Joseph Huntley
1882-1964 *AmAu&B, AmLY,*
BiDAmEd, BioIn 1, –2, –4, –7, –11,
–12, CathA 1930, ConAu 1R, –3NR,
CurBio 42, –64, DcAmB S7,
LongCTC, REnAL, SmATA 11,
TwCA SUP, WhAm 4, WhNAA
Hayes, Elvin *NewYTBS 84[port]*

Hayes, Elvin 1945- *BioIn 7, –8, –9, –11, –12, ConAu 111, InB&W 80, WhoAm 78, –80, –82, –84, –85, WorAl*
Hayes, Elvin 1947- *InB&W 85*
Hayes, John P 1949- *ConAu 15NR*
Hayes, Sheila 1937- *ConAu 106*
Haykal, Muhammad Husayn 1888-1956 *DcOrL 3*
Hayman, LeRoy 1916- *AuBYP SUP, ConAu 85*
Haynes, Betsy 1935- *SmATA 37*
Haynes, Betsy 1937- *ConAu 8NR, –57, SmATA 37, –48[port]*
Haynes, James 1932- *ConAu 110*
Haynes, Mary 1938- *ConAu 111*
Hays, Hoffman Reynolds 1904-1980 *AmAu&B, BioIn 4, –12, –13, ConPo 70, –75, TwCA SUP, WhoE 75, –77, –79, WrDr 76*
Hays, James D 1933- *AmM&WS 73P, –76P, –79P, –82P, –86P, BiESc, WhoAm 78, –80, –82*
Hays, James Douglas 1933- *WhoAm 84, –86*
Hays, Wilma P 1909- *SmATA 3AS[port]*
Hays, Wilma Pitchford 1909- *AuBYP, BioIn 8, –9, ConAu 1R, –5NR, ForWC 70, IntAu&W 77, SmATA 1, –28[port], ThrBJA, WhoAmW 74, –58, –61, –75, WrDr 76, –80, –82, –84, –86*
Hayward, Charles Harold 1898- *Au&Wr 71, ConAu 7NR, –9R, WhE&EA*
Haywood, Charles 1904- *Baker 78, BlueB 76, ConAu 1R, DrAS 74H, –78H, –82H, IntAu&W 76, –77, IntWWM 77, –85, OxCan, WhoAm 74, –76, –78, –80, –82, –84, –86, WhoAmJ 80, WhoAmM 83, WhoWor 74, WhoWorJ 72, –78, WrDr 76, –80, –82, –84, –86*
Haywood, Charles 1905- *Baker 84*
Hazelton, Elizabeth Baldwin *AuBYP SUP*
Hazen, Barbara Shook 1930- *BioIn 13, ConAu 105, SmATA 27[port]*
Hazlitt, Henry 1894- *IntAu&W 86, WhoAm 84, –86, WrDr 86*
Hazo, Samuel *DrAP&F 85*
Hazo, Samuel 1928- *ConAu 5R, –8NR, ConPo 70, –75, –80, –85, DrAS 74E, –78E, –82E, IntWWP 77, –82, WhoAm 76, –78, –80, WhoE 75, WrDr 82, –84, –86*
Hazzard, Shirley *DrAP&F 85*
Hazzard, Shirley 1931- *AmAu&B, Au&Wr 71, BioIn 12, –13, ConAu 4NR, –9R, ConLC 18, ConNov 72, –76, –82, –86, DcLB Y82B[port], DcLEL 1940, IntAu&W 76, –82, NewYTBS 76, –80[port], –82[port], Novels, OxAmL 83, OxAusL, WhoAm 74, –76, –78, –80, –82, –84, –86, WhoAmW 74, –70, –72, –75, –83, –85, –87, WorAu 1970, WrDr 76, –80, –82, –84, –86*
Head, Ann 1915- *ConAu X*
Head, Ann *see also* Morse, Anne Christensen
Head, Bessie 1937- *AfSS 79, –80, –81, –82, AfrA, ConAu 29R, ConLC 25[port], ConNov 72, –76, –82, –86, DcLEL 1940, IntAu&W 76, –77, –82, SelBAAf, WrDr 76, –80, –82, –84, –86*
Head, Bessie 1937?-1986 *ConAu 119*
Headington, Christopher 1930- *AuBYP SUP, Baker 78, –84, ConAu 106, IntWW 78, –79, –80, –81, –82, –83, IntWWM 77, WhoMus 72, WrDr 76, –80, –82, –84, –86*
Headley, Elizabeth 1909- *AuBYP, BioIn 2, –6, –7, –9, ConAu X, MorJA, SmATA 1, –X, TwCChW 83, WrDr 80*
Headley, Elizabeth *see also* Cavanna, Betty

Headstrom, Richard 1902- *AuBYP, ConAu 1R, –2NR, –13NR, –77, SmATA 8, WrDr 82, –84, –86*
Heal, Edith 1903- *BioIn 10, ConAu 1R, SmATA 7, WhoAmW 58, –61, –64, –66, –68, –70, –72, WhoE 74*
Heal, Edith *see also* Berrien, Edith Heal
Healey, Larry 1927- *ConAu 101, SmATA 42, –44[port]*
Healey, Robert C 1921- *ConAu 61*
Healy, John D 1921- *ConAu 93*
Heaney, Seamus 1939- *BioIn 10, –12, –13, ChhPo S2, ConAu 85, ConLC 5, –7, –14, –25[port], –37[port], ConPo 70, –75, –80, –85, CurBio 82[port], DcIrL, DcLB 40[port], DcLEL 1940, EncWL 2, IntWWP 77, ModBrL S2, –S1, NewYTBS 83[port], Who 82, –83, WhoWor 80, –82, WorAu 1970, WrDr 76, –80, –82, –84, –86*
Heaps, Willard A 1908?- *AuBYP, BioIn 8, ConAu 85, SmATA 26[port], WhoLibS 55, –66*
Heaps, Willard Allison 1908- *BioIn 13*
Hearn, Lafcadio 1850-1904 *Alli SUP, AmAu, AmAu&B, AmBi, AnCL, AtlBL, BbD, BiD&SB, BiDSA, BioIn 1, –2, –3, –4, –5, –6, –8, –9, –10, –11, –12, –13, CasWL, Chambr 3, ChhPo, –S3, CnDAL, ConAu 105, CrtT 3, CyWA, DcAmAu, DcAmB, DcBiA, DcEuL, DcLB 12[port], DcLEL, DcNAA, Dis&D, EncAB-H, EncO&P 78, EvLB, LinLib L, –S, McGEWB, ModAL, MorMA, NatCAB 1, NewC, Novels, OhA&B, OxAmH, OxAmL, –83, OxEng, –85, PenC AM, –ENG, PoIre, RAdv 1, REn, REnAL, ScF&FL 1, TwCLC 9[port], WebAB, –79, WhAm 1, WhLit, WhoHr&F*
Hearne, John 1926- *ConAu 116, ConNov 82, –86, FifCWr, Novels, SelBAAf, WrDr 82, –86*
Hearon, Shelby *DrAP&F 85*
Hearon, Shelby 1931- *AuNews 2, BioIn 11, –12, ConAu 18NR, –25R, WhoAmW 85, –87, WhoS&SW 73, –75, –76*
Hearst, James *DrAP&F 85*
Hearst, James 1900- *BioIn 12, –13, ChhPo, ConAu 85*
Hearst, James 1900-1983 *ConAu 15NR*
Heath, Caroline 1941- *WhoCanL 85*
Heath, Monroe 1899-1966 *AmAu&B, ConAu P-1*
Heatter, Maida *NewYTBS 81[port]*
Heaven, Constance 1911- *ConAu 2NR, –18NR, –49, IntAu&W 77, SmATA 7, WhoWor 76, WrDr 76, –80, –82, –84, –86*
Heaven, Constance *see also* Fecher, Constance
Hebblethwaite, Peter 1930- *Who 85, WhoWor 80, –87, WrDr 82, –86*
Hebden, Mark *ConAu X, IntAu&W 82X, –86X, WrDr 76, –80, –82, –84, –86*
Hebden, Mark 1916- *TwCCr&M 85*
Hebden, Mark *see also* Harris, John
Hebert, Ernest 1941- *ConAu 102*
Hechler, Ken 1914- *AmAu&B, BiDrAC, BioIn 5, –13, CngDr 74, ConAu 109, NewYTBS 75, WhoAm 74, –76, –78, –84, –86, WhoAmP 73, –75, –77, –79, –81, –83, –85, WhoE 74, –75, WhoGov 77, –72, –75, WhoS&SW 86*
Hecht, Anthony *DrAP&F 85*
Hecht, Anthony 1923- *ConAu 6NR, ConLC 19, ConPo 80, –85, CurBio 86[port], DcLB 5[port], DrAS 82E, IntWW 80, –81, –82, OxAmL 83, WhoAm 82, WrDr 82, –86*
Hecht, Anthony Evan 1923- *WhoAm 84, –86*

Heck, Bessie Holland 1911- *ConAu 5R, ForWC 70, SmATA 26[port]*
Heckel, Inge 1940- *WhoAm 82, –84, –86*
Heckler, Jonellen *DrAP&F 85*
Hedgecoe, John 1937- *Who 85*
Hedges, Elaine R 1927- *ConAu 7NR, DrAS 82E*
Heer, Friedrich 1916- *OxGer*
Heffron, Dorris 1944- *ConAu 49, WhoCanL 85, WrDr 80, –82, –84, –86*
Heffron, Dorris M 1944- *IntAu&W 86*
Hefley, James C 1930- *ConAu 7NR, –13R*
Hegarty, Walter 1922- *ConAu 65, WrDr 80, –82, –84, –86*
Hegner, Robert William 1880-1942 *BioIn 2, NatCAB 36, WhAm 2, WhNAA*
Heide, Florence Parry 1919- *AuBYP SUP, ChhPo S1, –S2, ConAu 19NR, –93, FourBJA, SmATA 32[port], TwCChW 83, WrDr 86*
Heidish, Marcy 1947- *BioIn 13, ConAu 101, DcLB Y82B[port]*
Heilbroner, Robert L *WhoAm 84, WrDr 86*
Heilbroner, Robert L 1919- *AmAu&B, AmEA 74, BioIn 9, –10, ConAu 1R, –4NR, –21NR, CurBio 75, Future, IntWW 79, –80, –81, –82, –83, WhoAm 74, –76, –78, –80, –82, –86, WhoE 74, –75, –83, WhoEc 81, WrDr 80, –82, –84*
Heilbroner, Robert Louis 1919- *BioIn 13, WhoEc 86*
Heilbrun, Carolyn G *TwCCr&M 85*
Heilbrun, Carolyn G 1926- *AmWomWr, BioIn 12, ConAu 1NR, –45, ConLC 25, DrAS 74E, –78E, –82E, TwCCr&M 80, WorAu 1975[port], WrDr 82, –84, –86*
Heilbrun, Carolyn G *see also* Cross, Amanda
Heilbrun, Carolyn Gold 1926- *WhoAm 84, –86, WhoAmW 85, –87*
Heilman, Henry 1919- *ConAu 53*
Heiman, Grover 1920- *ConAu 5R, –6NR, IntAu&W 76, –77, WhoAm 82*
Hein, Piet 1905- *BioIn 1, –7, CasWL, ConAu 4NR, –49, IntAu&W 77, PenC EUR, WhoWor 74, –76*
Heiney, Donald William 1921- *ConAu 1R, –3NR, ConLC 9, DrAS 74E, –78E, –82E*
Heiney, Donald William *see also* Harris, MacDonald
Heinlein, Robert A 1907- *AmAu&B, Au&Wr 71, AuBYP, BioIn 3, –4, –6, –7, –10, –11, –12, ConAu 1R, –1NR, –20NR, ConLC 1, –3, –8, –14, –26[port], ConNov 72, –76, –82, –86, ConSFA, CurBio 55, DcLB 8[port], EncSF, InSci, IntAu&W 76, LinLib L, MorJA, NewYTBS 80[port], Novels, OxAmL 83, PenC AM, REnAL, ScF&FL 1, –2, SmATA 9, TwCA SUP, TwCCW 78, –83, TwCSFW 86, TwCWr, WebAB, –79, WebE&AL, WhoAm 74, –76, –78, –80, –82, WhoSciF, WhoWor 76, –78, –80, –82, WorAl, WrDr 76, –80, –82, –84*
Heinlein, Robert Anson 1907- *BioIn 13, WhoAm 84, –86, WhoWor 84, –87*
Heintze, Carl 1922- *BioIn 13, ConAu 57, SmATA 26[port]*
Heinz, Hans Joachim 1904- *WhoAm 74, –76, –78*
Heinz, Hans Joachim 1904-1982 *BioIn 13*
Heinz, W C 1915- *ConAu 4NR, –5R, SmATA 26[port], WhoE 83, WrDr 76, –80, –82, –84, –86*
Heiser, Victor George 1873-1972 *AmAu&B, BioIn 1, –2, –3, –9, ConAu 33R, CurBio 42, –72, –72N,*

InSci, NewYTBE 72, WhAm 5, WhNAA
Heizer, Robert Fleming 1915-1979 *AmM&WS 73S, –76P, BioIn 12, –13, ConAu 102, NewYTBS 79, OxCan SUP, WhAm 7, WhoAm 74, –76, –78, WhoWor 74, –76*
Helfman, Elizabeth S 1911- *AuBYP, BioIn 8, –9, ConAu 5R, –5NR, ForWC 70, SmATA 3, WhoE 83, WrDr 76, –80, –82, –84, –86*
Helias, Pierre Jakez 1914- *BioIn 11, WhoFr 79*
Heller, David 1922-1968 *BioIn 8, ConAu P-1*
Heller, Deane 1924- *ConAu 9R, ForWC 70*
Heller, Joseph *DrAP&F 85, NewYTBS 86[port]*
Heller, Joseph 1923- *AmAu&B, AuNews 1, BioIn 8, –9, –10, –11, –12, –13, BioNews 74, BlueB 76, CasWL, ConAu 5R, –8NR, ConAu 1BS, ConDr 73, –77, –82, ConLC 1, –3, –5, –8, –11, –36[port], ConNov 72, –76, –82, –86, CurBio 73, DcLB 2, –28[port], –Y80A[port], DcLEL 1940, EncWL, –2, HalFC 84, IntAu&W 76, IntWW 83, LinLib L, ModAL, –S2, –S1, NewYTBS 79, NotNAT, Novels[port], OxAmL, –83, OxEng 85, PenC AM, RAdv 1, TwCWr, WebE&AL, WhoAm 74, –76, –78, –80, –82, –84, –86, WhoTwCL, WorAl, WorAu, WrDr 76, –80, –82, –84, –86*
Heller, Peter 1920- *ConAu 14NR, –41R, DrAS 74F, –78F, –82F, WhoAm 74, –76, –78*
Hellman, Hal 1927- *ConAu X, Future, IntAu&W 77X, –82X, SmATA 4, WrDr 76, –80, –82, –84, –86*
Hellman, Hal *see also* Hellman, Harold
Hellman, Harold 1927- *AuBYP SUP, BioIn 9, ConAu 10NR, –25R, IntAu&W 77, –82, SmATA 4*
Hellman, Harold *see also* Hellman, Hal
Hellman, Lillian 1905?-1984 *AmAu&B, AmWomD, AmWomWr, AmWr S1, AnObit 1984, Au&Wr 71, AuNews 1, –2, BiE&WWA, BioIn 1, –2, –4, –5, –7, –8, –9, –10, –11, –12, –13, BioNews 74, BlueB 76, CasWL, CelR, CnDAL, CnMD, CnThe, ConAu 112, –13R, ConDr 73, –77, –82, ConLC 2, –4, –8, –14, –18, –34[port], CroCD, CurBio 41, –60, –84N, CyWA, DcFM, DcLB 7[port], –Y84N[port], EncAB-H, EncSoH, EncWL, –2, EncWT, FilmgC, ForWC 70, GoodHs, HalFC 84, InWom, IntAu&W 76, –77, IntDcWB, IntMPA 77, –75, –76, –78, –79, –81, –82, –83, LibW, LinLib L, LongCTC, MajMD 1, McGEWB, McGEWD, –84[port], ModAL, –S2, –S1, ModWD, NatPD, –81[port], NewYTBE 73, NewYTBS 75, –84[port], –86, NotNAT, –A, OxAmL, –83, OxAmT 84, OxFilm, OxThe, –83, PenC AM, PIP&P, PolProf T, REn, REnAL, REnWD, TwCA, –SUP, WebAB, –79, WebE&AL, WhAm 8, WhE&EA, Who 74, –82, –83, –85N, WhoAm 74, –76, –78, –80, –82, WhoAmJ 80, WhoAmW 74, –58, –61, –64, –66, –68, –70, –72, –79, –81, –83, WhoE 74, WhoThe 72, –77, –81, WhoTwCL, WhoWor 74, –76, –78, –80, –82, WhoWorJ 72, –78, WomWMM, WorAl, WorEFlm, WrDr 76, –80, –82, –84*
Helm, June 1924- *AmM&WS 73S, FifIDA, WhoAm 86, WhoAmW 66, –68, –72, WhoMW 74*
Helm, Thomas 1919- *ConAu 5R, WhoS&SW 73*
Helprin, Mark *NewYTBS 84[port]*

Helprin, Mark 1947- *BioIn 12, –13, ConAu 81, ConLC 7, –10, –22[port], –32[port], DcLB Y85B[port], TwCSFW 86, WhoAm 82, –84, –86, WorAu 1975[port], WrDr 86*

Hemery, David 1944- *BioIn 9, –11, WhoTr&F 73*

Hemingway, Ernest *EncAJ*

Hemingway, Ernest d1961 *NewYTBS 85[port]*

Hemingway, Ernest 1899?-1961 *AmAu&B, AmNov, AmWr, ArizL, AuNews 2, BioIn 1, –2, –3, –4, –5, –6, –7, –8, –9, –10, –11, –12, –13, CasWL, Chambr 3, ChhPo S1, –S2, –S3, CnDAL, CnMD, CnMWL, ConAmA, ConAmL, ConAu 77, ConLC 1, –3, –8, –10, –13, –19, –30[port], –41[port], CyWA, DcAmB S7, DcLB 4, –9[port], –DS1[port], –Y81A[port], DcLEL, EncAB-H, EncTwCJ, EncWL, –2[port], EvLB, FilmgC, HalFC 84, LinLib L, –S, LongCTC, MakMC, McGEWB, MemAm, MichAu 80, ModAL, –S2, –S1, ModWD, NatCAB 57, NewYTBS 81[port], NotNAT B, Novels[port], ObitOF 79, ObitT 1961, OxAmH, OxAmL, –83, OxEng, OxFilm, PenC AM, RAdv 1, RComWL, REn, REnAL, TwCA, –SUP, TwCWr, WebAB, –79, WebE&AL, WhDW, WhAm 4, WhE&EA, WhFla, WhoTwCL, WorAl, WorEFlm*

Hemingway, Ernest Miller 1899-1961 *OxEng 85, WhoNob*

Hemingway, Gregory H 1931?- *BioIn 10, –12, ConAu 112, NewYTBS 76*

Hemingway, Joan 1950?- *BioIn 10*

Hemming, Roy 1928- *BioIn 11, ConAu 61, SmATA 11, WhoAm 78, –80, –82, WhoE 74*

Hemphill, Paul 1936?- *AuBYP SUP, AuNews 1, BioIn 9, –10, –11, ConAu 12NR, –49, WrDr 76, –80, –82, –84*

Hemphill, Paul 1938- *WrDr 86*

Henderson, Bill *DrAP&F 85*

Henderson, Bill 1941- *ConAu 33R, Po&Wr 77, ScF&FL 1*

Henderson, Harold Gould 1889-1974 *BioIn 10, ChhPo, –S1, ConAu 53, DrAS 74F, –78F, WhAm 6*

Henderson, Richard 1924- *ConAu 5NR, –13R, –20NR, IntAu&W 77, WrDr 76, –80, –82, –84, –86*

Henderson, Robert 1906- *ConAu 106, WhoE 75*

Henderson, Thomas *InB&W 85*

Henderson, Zenna 1917- *AmWomWr, BioIn 10, –12, ConAu 1R, –1NR, ConSFA, DcLB 8[port], EncSF, ForWC 70, ScF&FL 1, –2, SmATA 5, WhoSciF, WrDr 84, –86*

Henderson, Zenna 1917-1983 *ScF&FL, TwCSFW 86*

Hendin, David 1945- *ConAu 41R, IntAu&W 76, –77, WhoAm 74, –76, –78, –80, –82, WorAl*

Hendin, David Bruce 1945- *EncTwCJ, WhoAm 84, –86*

Hendrich, Paula Griffith 1928- *ConAu 1R, –1NR*

Hendry, James Findlay *OxEng 85*

Hendry, James Findlay 1912- *ChhPo S1, –S2, –S3, ConAu 29R, DrAS 74F, IntAu&W 77, –82, PenC ENG, WhE&EA, WhoCan 73, WhoWor 78, WrDr 76, –80, –82, –84, –86*

Henissart, Paul 1923- *ConAu 29R, IntAu&W 77, WhoSpyF, WrDr 76, –80, –82, –84, –86*

Henkle, Henrietta 1909-1983 *AmAu&B, BioIn 1, –2, –10, –13, ConAu 69, CurBio 46, InWom, OhA&B*

Henkle, Henrietta *see also* Buckmaster, Henrietta

Henkle, Henrietta *see also* Stephens, Henrietta Henkle

Henle, Faye d1972 *BioIn 9, ConAu 37R, NewYTBE 72*

Henley, Don 1946- *WhoRocM 82*

Henley, Don *see also* Eagles, The

Hennessy, Max *ConAu X, IntAu&W 82X, WrDr 80, –82, –84, –86*

Hennessy, Max *see also* Harris, John

Henningfield, Jack Edward 1952- *WhoFrS 84*

Henri, Adrian 1932- *ConAu 15NR, –25R, ConPo 70, –75, –80, –85, DcLEL 1940, IntWWP 77, –82, Who 82, –83, WhoArt 80, –82, –84, WhoWor 80, WrDr 76, –80, –82, –84, –86*

Henri, Florette d1985 *NewYTBS 85*

Henri, Florette 1908- *AmAu&B, ConAu 73*

Henri, Florette 1908-1985 *ConAu 117*

Henry, Marguerite *IntAu&W 86, OxChL, WhoAm 84, –86, WrDr 86*

Henry, Marguerite 1902- *AmAu&B, AmWomWr, Au&ICB, Au&Wr 71, AuBYP, BioIn 1, –2, –3, –4, –7, –8, –11, –12, BkCL, ChlLR 4[port], ConAu 9NR, –17R, CurBio 47, DcLB 22[port], FamMS, InWom, IntAu&W 77, –82, JBA 51, LinLib L, Newb 1922, SmATA 11, TwCCW 78, –83, WhoAm 74, –76, –78, –80, –82, WhoAmW 74, –58, –61, –66, –70, –72, –75, –77, WhoWor 74, –76, WrDr 76, –80, –82, –84*

Henry, O *BioIn 13, EncFWF, OxAmL 83*

Henry, O 1862-1910 *AmAu&B, AmBi, AmWr S2, AtlBL, BiDSA, BioIn 1, –2, –3, –4, –5, –6, –7, –8, –9, –10, –12, CasWL, Chambr 3, ChhPo, CnDAL, ConAu X, CyWA, DcAmB, DcAmSR, DcLEL, DcNAA, Dis&D, EncMys, EncWL, EvLB, FilmgC, HalFC 84, LinLib LP, LongCTC, McGEWB, ModAL, Novels, OxAmL, OxEng, –85, PenC AM, RAdv 1, REn, REnAL, TwCA, –SUP, TwCLC 1, –19[port], TwCWr, WebAB, –79, WebE&AL, WhDW, WhAm 1, WhoTwCL, WorAl, YABC X*

Henry, O *see also* Porter, William Sydney

Henry, Oliver *ConAu X, YABC X*

Henry, Oliver *see also* Porter, William Sydney

Henry, Robert Selph 1889-1970 *BioIn 10, –13, ConAu 1R, –103, –17NR, DcLB 17[port], NatCAB 55, NewYTBE 70, ObitOF 79, WhAm 5, WhNAA*

Henry, Sondra 1930- *ConAu 119*

Henry, Will *BioIn 13, EncFWF, WrDr 84*

Henry, Will 1912- *AmAu&B, AuBYP SUP, ConAu X, WrDr 84*

Henry, Will *see also* Allen, Henry Wilson

Hentoff, Nat *WrDr 86*

Hentoff, Nat 1925- *AuBYP, BioIn 13, ChlLR 1, ChhPo S2, ConAu 1R, –5NR, ConAu 6AS[port], ConLC 26[port], CurBio 86[port], IntAu&W 77, LinLib L, REnAL, SmATA 27, –42[port], ThrBJA, TwCCW 78, –83, WrDr 76, –80, –82, –84*

Hentoff, Nathan Irving 1925- *AmAu&B, BioIn 7, –8, –9, EncTwCJ, WhoAm 74, –76, –78, –80, –82, –84, –86, WhoE 74, WhoWor 74*

Henwood, James N J 1932- *ConAu 69, DrAS 74H, –78H, –82H*

Hepburn, Katharine *NewYTBS 85[port]*

Hepburn, Katharine 1907- *HalFC 84[port]*

Hepburn, Katharine 1909- *BioIn 13, IntMPA 86, Who 85, WhoAm 84, WhoAmW 85, –87, WhoWor 84, –87*

Hepler, Loren George 1928- *AmM&WS 73P, –76P, –79P, –82P, –86P*

Herald, Kathleen *ConAu 69, –X, IntAu&W 86X, ThrBJA, TwCChW 83*

Herald, Kathleen *see also* Peyton, Kathleen Wendy

Herber, Harold L 1929- *ConAu 108, DrAS 74E, –78E, –82E, WhoAm 86*

Herbert, Frank d1986 *NewYTBS 86[port]*

Herbert, Frank 1920- *AmAu&B, BioIn 10, –11, –12, –13, ConAu 5NR, –53, ConLC 12, –23[port], –35[port], ConSFA, DcLB 8[port], EncSF, IntAu&W 77, MnBBF, NewYTBS 81[port], Novels, ScF&FL 1, –2, ScFSB[port], SmATA 37, –9, WhoAm 74, –76, –78, –80, –82, WhoSciF, WorAl, WorAu 1970, WrDr 76, –80, –82, –84, –86*

Herbert, Frank 1920-1986 *ConAu 118, ConLC 44[port], SmATA 47N, TwCSFW 86*

Herbert, Wally *ConAu X*

Herbert, Wally 1934- *SmATA X, WhoWor 74, –76*

Herbert, Wally *see also* Herbert, Walter William

Herbert, Walter William 1934- *BioIn 13, ConAu 15NR, –69, SmATA 23, Who 74, –82, –83, –85*

Herbert, Walter William *see also* Herbert, Wally

Herda, D J 1946?- *IntAu&W 76, WhoMW 76*

Herge *BioIn 13*

Herge 1907-1983 *ChlLR 6[port], ConAu X, IntAu&W 77X, –82X, SmATA X, WorECom*

Herge *see also* Remi, Georges

Herkimer, L R 1925?- *ConAu 110, SmATA 42[port]*

Herlihy, James Leo *DrAP&F 85*

Herlihy, James Leo 1927- *AmAu&B, Au&Wr 71, BiE&WWA, BioIn 6, –7, –10, BlueB 76, CelR, ConAu 1R, –2NR, ConDr 73, –77, –82, ConLC 6, ConNov 72, –76, –82, –86, ConTFT 1, CurBio 61, DcLEL 1940, HalFC 84, IntAu&W 76, –77, LinLib L, NotNAT, Novels, OxAmL 83, WhoAm 74, –76, –78, –80, –82, –84, –86, WhoE 74, –75, WhoWor 74, –76, –78, –80, WorAl, WorAu, WrDr 76, –80, –82, –84, –86*

Herlin, Hans 1925- *ConAu 77*

Herman, Ben 1927- *ConAu 104*

Herman, Charlotte 1937- *BioIn 12, ConAu 15NR, –41R, SmATA 20*

Herman, Lewis 1905- *BiE&WWA, WhoAmL 78, –79*

Hermanns, William 1895- *BioIn 9, ConAu 15NR, –37R, WrDr 76*

Hermes, Patricia 1936- *ConAu 104, SmATA 31[port]*

Hermes, Patricia Mary 1936- *WhoAmW 85, –87*

Herndon, James Emmett 1925- *ConAu 89, WhoBlA 75, –77, –80, WhoRel 77*

Herold, Jean Christopher 1919-1964 *AmAu&B, BioIn 5, –7, ConAu P-1, CurBio 59, –65, WhAm 4*

Herrick, Robert 1591-1674 *Alli, AnCL, AtlBL, BbD, BiD&SB, BiDRP&D, BioIn 1, –2, –3, –4, –5, –6, –7, –10, –12, BritAu, BritWr 2, CasWL, Chambr 1, ChhPo, –S1, –S2, CnE&AP, CroE&S, CrtT 1, –4, CyWA, DcBiPP, DcEnA, DcEnL, DcEuL, DcLEL, DcNaB, Dis&D, EvLB, LinLib L, –S, LongCEL, LongCTC, McGEWB, MouLC 1, NewC, OxEng, –85, OxMus, PenC ENG, RAdv 1, REn, WebE&AL, WhDW, WorAl*

Herring, Reuben 1922- *ConAu 7NR, –17R, IntAu&W 86, WhoAm 86*

Herring, Robert H 1938- *ConAu 105, –21NR*

Herriot, James *SmATA X, Who 85, WrDr 86*

Herriot, James 1916- *BioIn 9, –10, –11, –12, ConAu X, ConLC 12, IntAu&W 76, –77, IntWW 82, –83, Who 82, –83, WhoWor 84, –87, WorAl, WorAu 1975[port], WrDr 76, –80, –82, –84*

Herriot, James *see also* Wight, James Alfred

Herrmanns, Ralph 1933- *AuBYP SUP, BioIn 11, SmATA 9, –18NR, IntAu&W 77, –82, SmATA 11, WrDr 76, –80, –82, –84, –86*

Herron, Edward A 1912- *BioIn 9, ConAu 5R, SmATA 4*

Hersey, John *DrAP&F 85*

Hersey, John 1914- *ConLC 40[port], ConNov 86, EncAJ, EncTwCJ, HalFC 84, OxAmL 83, ScFSB, TwCSFW 86, Who 85, WhoAm 84, –86, WhoWor 84, WrDr 86*

Hersey, John Richard 1914- *AmAu&B, AmNov, BioIn 1, –2, –4, –5, –7, –8, –9, –10, –12, –13, BlueB 76, CasWL, CelR, ChhPo S3, CnDAL, ConAu 17R, ConLC 1, –2, –7, –9, ConNov 72, –76, –82, CurBio 44, CyWA, DcLB 6[port], DcLEL 1940, DrAS 74E, –78E, –82E, EncSF, IntAu&W 76, –77, –82, IntWW 74, –75, –76, –77, –78, –79, –80, –81, –82, –83, LinLib L, –S, LongCTC, ModAL, Novels, OxAmL, PenC AM, RAdv 1, REn, REnAL, ScF&FL 1, –2, SmATA 25[port], TwCA SUP, WebAB, –79, Who 74, –82, –83, WhoAm 74, –76, –78, –80, –82, WhoE 74, WhoWor 74, –76, –78, –80, –82, WorAl, WrDr 76, –80, –82, –84*

Hersh, Seymour M 1936?- *AmAu&B, AuNews 1, BioIn 8, –9, –10, –11, ConAu 73, WhoAm 74, –76, –78, –80, –82, WhoS&SW 73, –75*

Hersh, Seymour M 1937- *BioIn 13, ConAu 15NR, EncAJ, WhoAm 84, –86*

Hershey, Edward Norman 1944- *WhoE 79, –81, –83*

Herst, Herman, Jr. 1909- *BioIn 5, –9, ConAu 1R, –2NR, WhoAm 84, –86, WhoS&SW 76, –78, –86*

Herz, Peggy 1936- *ConAu 37R*

Herz, Peggy *see also* Hudson, Peggy

Herzberg, Max J 1886-1958 *AmAu&B, REnAL, WhAm 3, WhNAA*

Herzberg, Max John 1886-1958 *BioIn 4*

Herzog, Arthur 1927- *WrDr 86*

Herzog, Arthur 1928- *ScFSB*

Herzog, Arthur, III 1927- *ConAu 9NR, –17R, EncSF, IntAu&W 77, ScF&FL 1, –2, WhoAm 76, –78, –80, –82, –84, –86, WhoE 74, WrDr 76, –80, –82, –84*

Herzog, Maurice 1919- *BioIn 3, –5, –9, CurBio 53, InSci, IntWW 74, –75, –76, –77, –78, –79, –80, –81, –82, –83, WhoFr 79, WhoWor 74, –76, –78*

Herzog, Whitey *NewYTBS 85[port], WhoAm 84, –86*

Herzog, Whitey 1931- *BioIn 13*

Hesse, Hermann 1877-1962 *AtlBL, BioIn 1, –2, –3, –4, –5, –6, –7, –8, –9, –10, –11, –12, –13, CasWL, ClDMEL, ConAu P-2, ConLC 1, –2, –3, –6, –11, –17, –25[port], CurBio 62, CyWA, EncO&P 2, –78, EncSF, EncWL, –2[port], EvEuW, GrFLW, LinLib L, –S, MakMC, McGEWB, ModGL, Novels[port], ObitOF 79, ObitT 1961, OxGer, OxGer PEUR, RComWL, REn, ScF&FL 1, ScFSB, TwCA, –SUP, TwCWr, WhDW, WhAm 4, WhoTwCL, WorAl*

Hettlinger, Richard F 1920- *ConAu 7NR, –17R, DrAS 74P, –78P, –82P*

Heuer, Kenneth John 1927- *ConAu 110, SmATA 44, WhoAm 76, –78, –80, –82, –84, –86*

Heuman, William 1912- · WrDr 86
Heuman, William 1912-1971
*AuBYP, BioIn 7, –8, –12, ConAu 5R,
–7NR, SmATA 21[port], WrDr 84*
Heward, William L 1949-
ConAu 4NR, –53, MichAu 80
Heward, William Lee 1949-
WhoFrS 84, WhoMW 84
Hewes, Agnes Danforth 1874-1963
*AmAu&B, AuBYP, BioIn 2, –8,
ConAu 113, JBA 34, –51, SmATA 35,
WhoAmW 58, –61*
Hewes, Henry 1917- *AmAu&B,
BiE&WWA, ConAmTC, ConAu 13R,
NotNAT, OxAmT 84, OxThe,
WhoAm 74, –76, –78, –80, –82, –84,
–86, WhoThe 72, –77, –81,
WhoWor 74, –76*
Hewitt, Geof *DrAP&F 85*
Hewitt, Geof 1943- *ConAu 33R,
ConPo 70, –75, –80, –85, WrDr 76,
–80, –82, –84, –86*
Hewitt, James 1928- *ConAu 21NR*
Hewitt, Paul G *BioIn 13*
Hewlett, Sylvia Ann 1946- *ConAu 118*
Hey, Nigel 1936- *BioIn 12,
ConAu 33R, IntAu&W 76,
SmATA 20, WhoWor 78, WrDr 76,
–80, –82, –84*
Heyer, Georgette 1902-1974
*Au&Wr 71, BioIn 4, –10, ConAu 49,
–93, CorpD, DcLEL, DcNaB 1971,
EncMys, LongCTC, NewC,
NewYTBS 74, Novels, ObitOF 79,
ObitT 1971, OxChL, OxEng 85, REn,
TwCA, –SUP, TwCCr&M 80, –85,
TwCWr, WhAm 6, WhE&EA, WhLit,
Who 74, WhoAm 74, WhoAmW 66,
–72, WhoWor 74, WorAl*
Heyer, Paul 1936- *WrDr 86*
Heyerdahl, Thor 1914- *Au&Wr 71,
BioIn 1, –2, –3, –4, –5, –6, –8, –9,
–10, –11, –12, CelR, ConAu 5R,
–5NR, ConLC 26[port], CurBio 47,
–72, InSci, IntAu&W 76, –77, –82,
IntWW 74, –75, –76, –77, –78, –79,
–80, –81, –82, –83, LinLib L, –S,
LongCTC, OxShips, SmATA 2,
TwCA SUP, TwCWr, UFOEn,
WhDW, Who, –82, –83, –85,
WhoAm 80, –82, –84, –86,
WhoWor 74, –76, –78, –82, –84, –87,
WorAl, WrDr 76, –80, –82, –84, –86*
Heyman, Abigail 1942- *ConAu 57,
ConPhot, ICPEnP A, WrDr 76, 80,
–82, –84, –86*
Heyn, Ernest V 1904- *ConAu 111,
WhoAm 74, –76, –78, –80, –82, –84,
–86, WhoWor 78*
Hibbert, Christopher 1924-
*Au&Wr 71, BioIn 9, BlueB 76,
ConAu 1R, –2NR, IntAu&W 76, –77,
–82, –86, LongCTC, OxCan,
SmATA 4, Who 74, –82, –83, –85,
WhoWor 76, –80, WorAu 1975[port],
WrDr 76, –80, –82, –84, –86*
Hibbert, Eleanor *Who 85*
Hibbert, Eleanor 1906- *BioIn 7, –9,
–10, –11, ConAu 9NR, –17R,
ConLC 7, EncMys, IntAu&W 76,
–77, NewYTBS 77, SmATA 2,
Who 74, –82, –83, WhoWor 84, –87,
WorAu, WrDr 76, –80, –82, –84*
Hibbert, Eleanor see also Carr, Philippa
Hibbert, Eleanor see also Holt, Victoria
Hibbert, Eleanor see also Plaidy, Jean
Hickel, Walter Joseph 1919-
*AmCath 80, BiDrGov, BiDrUSE,
BioIn 8, –9, –10, –11, –12, BlueB 76,
ConAu 41R, CurBio 69,
IntAu&W 77, IntWW 74, –75, –76,
–77, –78, –79, –80, –81, –82, –83,
PolProf NF, WhoAm 74, –76, –78,
–80, –82, –84, –86, WhoAmP 73, –75,
–77, –79, –81, –83, –85, WhoWor 74,
–76, –78*
Hicken, Victor 1921- *ConAu 21R,
DrAS 74H, –78H, –82H, WhoAm 74,
–76, –78, –80, –82, –84, –86,
WrDr 76, –80, –82, –84, –86*
Hickman, Janet 1940- *BioIn 11,
ConAu 10NR, –65, SmATA 12*

Hickok, Lorena A 1892?-1968
*AuBYP, BioIn 7, –8, –10, –12,
ConAu 73, InWom, NotAW MOD,
SmATA 20*
Hickok, Lorena A 1893-1968 *EncAJ*
Hicks, Clifford B 1920- *AmAu&B,
AuBYP, ConAu 9NR, ScF&FL 1, –2,
WhoAm 80*
Hicks, Clifford Byron 1920-
WhoAm 84, –86
Hicks, Granville 1901-1982 *AmAu&B,
AmNov, AnObit 1982[port], BioIn 1,
–2, –4, –6, –7, –12, –13, CnDAL,
ConAmA, ConAu 9R, –107, –13NR,
ConLCrt, –82, ConNov 72, –76, –82,
CurBio 42, –82N, DcLEL, DcLB 4[port],
IntAu&W 76, –77, IntWW 74, –75,
–76, –77, –78, –79, –80, –81, –82,
–83N, NewYTBS 82[port],
OxAmL, –83, PenC AM, RAdv 1,
REn, REnAL, ScF&FL 1,
TwCA, –SUP, WhAm 8, WhLit,
WhoAm 74, –76, –78, WhoWor 74,
–76, –78, WrDr 76, –80, –82*
Hiebert, Ray Eldon 1932- *AmAu&B,
ConAu 7NR, –17R, DrAS 74E, –78E,
SmATA 13, WhoAm 74, –76, –78,
–80, –82, –84, –86, WhoCon 73,
WhoE 74, –75, –77, –79, –81, –83,
–85, WhoPubR 72, –76, WhoWor 82*
Higbee, Kenneth Leo 1941-
*AmM&WS 73S, –78S, ConAu 101,
WhoWest 78*
Higdon, Hal 1931- *AuBYP SUP,
BioIn 9, –12, ConAu 3NR, –9R,
IntAu&W 86, ScF&FL 1, –2,
SmATA 4, WhoMW 84, WrDr 76,
–80, –82, –84, –86*
Higgins, Colin *HalFC 84*
Higgins, Colin 1941- *ConAu 33R,
ConTFT 1, DcLB 26[port],
IntMPA 79, –81, –82, –84, –86,
WhoAm 82, –84, –86, WrDr 76, –80*
Higgins, George V *DrAP&F 85*
Higgins, George V 1939- *BioIn 9, –10,
–12, –13, ConAu 17NR, –77,
ConAu 5AS[port], ConLC 4, –7, –10,
–18, ConNov 76, –82, –86, DcLB 2,
–Y81A[port], IntAu&W 77, Novels,
TwCCr&M 80, –85, WhoAm 76, –78,
–80, –82, WorAl, WorAu 1975[port],
WrDr 76, –80, –82, –84, –86*
Higgins, George Vincent 1939-
WhoAm 84, –86
Higgins, Jack *Who 85, WrDr 86*
Higgins, Jack 1929- *BioIn 12,
HalFC 84, NewYTBS 80[port],
TwCCr&M 80, –85, Who 82, –83,
WhoAm 78, –80, –82, –84, –86,
WhoWor 78, –80, –82, WorAl,
WrDr 76, –80, –82, –84*
Higgins, Jack see also Patterson, Henry
Higgins, Marguerite 1920-1966
*AmAu&B, AmWomWr, BioIn 2, –3,
–4, –5, –7, –8, –9, –12, –13,
BriB[port], ConAu 5R, –25R,
CurBio 51, –66, DcAmDH, EncAJ,
EncTwCJ, GoodHs, InWom,
NotAW MOD, ObitOF 79, WhAm 4,
WhoAmW 58, –64, –66*
Higgins, Reynold Alleyne 1916-
*ConAu 25R, IntAu&W 76, Who 74,
–82, –83, –85, WrDr 76, –80, –82,
–84, –86*
Higginson, Thomas Wentworth
1823-1911 *Alli, –SUP, AmAu,
AmAu&B, AmBi, ApCAB, BbD,
BiDAmM, BiD&SB, BioIn 3, –5, –6,
–8, –9, CasWL, Chambr 3,
ChhPo, –S1, –S2, CnDAL, CyAL 2,
DcAmAu, DcAmB, DcAmSR,
DcLB 1, DcLEL, DcNAA, Drake,
HarEnUS[port], LinLib L, –S,
McGEWB, NatCAB 1, OxAmL, –83,
REn, REnAL, TwCBDA,
WebAB, –79*
Higginson, Thomas Wentworth Storrow
1823-1911 *AmRef[port]*
Higham, Charles 1931- *Au&Wr 71,
ConAu 17NR, –33R, ConPo 70, –75,
–80, –85, DcLEL 1940, IntWWP 77,
OxAusL, ScF&FL 1, –2, WrDr 76,
–80, –82, –84, –86*

Highsmith, Patricia 1921- *AmWomWr,
Au&Wr 71, BioIn 10, –12,
BioNews 74, BlueB 76, ConAu 1R,
–1NR, –20NR, ConLC 2, –4, –14,
–42[port], ConNov 72, –76, –82, –86,
EncMys, HalFC 84, IntAu&W 76,
–77, –82, IntWW 82, –83,
Novels[port], OxEng 85,
TwCCr&M 80, –85, Who 74, –82,
–83, –85, WhoAmW 75, WhoHr&F,
WhoTwCL, WhoWor 76, WorAl,
WorAu, WrDr 76, –80, –82, –84, –86*
Hightower, Florence 1916-1981
*Au&Wr 71, AuBYP, BioIn 7, –9, –12,
–13, ConAu 1R, –103, SmATA 27N,
–4, ThrBJA, TwCCW 78, –83,
WhoAmW 74, –72, –75*
Highwater, Jamake *DrAP&F 85*
Highwater, Jamake 1942- *BioIn 11,
–12, ConAu 10NR, –65, ConLC 12,
DcLB 52[port], –Y85B[port],
FifBJA[port], IntAu&W 77, NatPD,
OxChL, SmATA 30, –32[port],
TwCChW 83, WhoAm 80, –82, –84,
–86, WhoAmA 78, –80, –82, –84,
WhoE 79, –81, –83, WhoWor 80,
WrDr 84, –86*
Highwater, Jamake see also Marks, J
Hilberry, Conrad Arthur 1928-
*ConAu 10NR, –25R, DrAS 74E,
–78E, –82E, IntAu&W 77, –82,
IntWWP 77, –82, MichAu 80,
WhoMW 84, WrDr 76, –80, –82, –84,
–86*
Hilburn, Robert 1939- *WhoAm 84*
Hildick, E W 1925- *AuBYP SUP,
BioIn 8, –9, ConAu X, FourBJA,
OxChL, ScFSB, SmATA 2,
TwCCW 78, –83, WhoChL, WrDr 80,
–82, –84, –86*
Hildick, Edmund Wallace 1925-
*Au&Wr 71, ConAu 25R,
IntAu&W 76, SmATA 2,
TwCCr&M 80*
Hill, Dave 1936- *ConAu X*
Hill, Donna Marie *BiDrLUS 70,
BioIn 13, ConAu 7NR, –13R,
SmATA 24[port], WhoAmW 77, –83,
WhoLibS 55, –66*
Hill, Douglas 1935- *Au&Wr 71,
BioIn 10, ConAu 4NR, –53,
ConPo 70, ConSFA, IntAu&W 76,
IntWWP 77, OxCan SUP, ScF&FL 1,
–2, ScFSB, SmATA 39, WrDr 76,
–80, –82, –84, –86*
Hill, Douglas Arthur 1935-
WhoCanL 85
Hill, Frank Ernest 1888-1969?
*AmAu&B, AuBYP, BioIn 4, –8,
ChhPo, ConAu 73, MedHR, REnAL,
TwCA, –SUP, WhAm 5*
Hill, Helen M 1915- *ChhPo S3,
ConAu 57, SmATA 27*
Hill, Helen Morey 1915- *BioIn 13*
Hill, Janet *AuBYP SUP*
Hill, Margaret 1915- *AuBYP, BioIn 1,
–8, ConAu 1R, –1NR, –16NR,
SmATA 36*
Hill, Phyllis Malie Sites 1923-
*BiDrLUS 70, WhoAmW 74, –68, –70,
–72, –75, –77, –79, –83, –85*
Hill, Ruth Livingston 1898- *BioIn 11,
ConAu X, SmATA X*
Hill, Ruth Livingston see also Munce,
Ruth Hill
Hillary, Edmund 1919- *ConAu 112,
WrDr 84*
Hillary, Sir Edmund 1919- *AsBiEn,
ASpks, Au&Wr 71, BioIn 3, –4, –5,
–6, –7, –8, –9, –10, –11, –12, –13,
BlueB 76, CurBio 54, FarE&A 78,
–79, –80, –81, IntAu&W 77,
IntWW 74, –75, –76, –77, –78, –79,
–80, –81, –82, –83, LinLib L, –S,
LongCTC, NewYTBE 70, WhDW,
Who 74, –82, –83, –85, WhoWor 74,
–82, WorAl, WrDr 76, –80, –82, –84*
Hillcourt, William 1900- *AmAu&B,
AuBYP, BioIn 7, –13, ConAu 93,
SmATA 27, WhoAm 74, –76, –78,
–80, –82, –84, –86*
Hiller, Carl E *AuBYP SUP*

Hillerman, Tony 1925- *BioIn 8, –10,
–12, ConAu 21NR, –29R, EncFWF,
SmATA 6, TwCCr&M 80, –85,
WrDr 82, –84, –86*
Hillesum, Etty 1914-1943 *BioIn 13*
Hilliard, Robert L 1925- *ConAu 107,
DrAS 74E, –78E, –82E,
IntAu&W 86, WhoGov 77, –72, –75*
Hillman, Howard 1934- *ConAu 20NR,
–41R*
Hillman, May *AuBYP, BioIn 8*
Hillocks, George, Jr. 1934- *ConAu 53,
LEduc 74*
Hills, C A R 1955- *ConAu 106,
SmATA 39[port]*
Hills, Patricia 1936- *WhoAmA 84*
Hilton, James 1900-1954 *Alli SUP,
BioIn 1, –2, –3, –4, –5, ChhPo S1,
ConAu 108, CurBio 42, –55, CyWA,
DcLB 34[port], DcLEL, DcNaB 1951,
EncMys, EncSF, EvLB, FilmgC,
HalFC 84, LongCTC, MnBBF,
ModBrL, NewC, NotNAT B, Novels,
ObitOF 79, ObitT 1951, OxEng 85,
PenC ENG, REn, REnAL,
ScF&FL 1, ScFSB, SmATA 34[port],
TwCA, –SUP, TwCCr&M 80,
TwCLC 21[port], TwCWr, WhAm 3,
WhE&EA, WhLit, WhoBW&I A,
WorAl*
Hilton, John Buxton 1921-
TwCCr&M 85, WrDr 86
Hilton, Ralph 1907- *BioIn 11,
ConAu 29R, SmATA 8,
WhoS&SW 76, –78, –80, –82*
Hilton, Suzanne 1922- *AuBYP SUP,
BioIn 9, ConAu 12NR, –29R,
IntAu&W 77, SmATA 4,
WhoAmW 75, WrDr 76, –80, –82,
–84, –86*
Himes, Chester *DrAP&F 85*
Himes, Chester 1909- *AmAu&B,
AmNov, BioIn 1, –2, –5, –9, –10, –11,
–12, BlkAWP, ConAu 25R, ConLC 2,
–4, –7, –18, ConNov 72, –76, –82,
DcLB 2, DcLEL 1940, EncWL, –2,
InB&W 80, IntAu&W 76, –77, –82,
LinLib L, LivgBAA, ModAL, –S1,
ModBlW, NegAl 76[port], –83,
Novels, OhA&B, OxAmL 83,
PenC AM, RAdv 1, SelBAAu,
TwCCr&M 80, WebE&AL,
WhoAm 74, –76, –78, –80, –82,
WhoBlA 75, –77, –80, WorAu,
WrDr 76, –80, –82, –84*
Himes, Chester 1909-1984
*AnObit 1984, ConAu 114, ModAL S2,
NewYTBS 84[port], TwCCr&M 85*
Hinckley, Helen *BioIn 13*
Hinckley, Helen 1903- *AuBYP,
BioIn 8, ConAu X, IntAu&W 76X,
–77X, –82X, SmATA X, WrDr 76,
–80, –82, –84, –86*
Hinckley, Helen see also Jones, Helen
Hinckley
Hinding, Andrea 1942- *WhoAm 86*
Hindle, Brooke 1918- *AmM&WS 86P,
WhoAm 84, –86*
Hindle, Lee J 1965- *ConAu 117*
Hindley, Geoffrey 1935- *Au&Wr 71,
ConAu 109*
Hine, Al 1915- *AuBYP, BioIn 8, –9,
ChhPo, –S1, ConAu 1R, –2NR,
ScF&FL 1, –2, ThrBJA*
Hine, Virginia H 1920- *ConAu 97*
Hines, Barry 1939- *ConAu 102,
ConNov 86, IntAu&W 76, –77, –82,
Novels, WhoWor 76, WrDr 76, –80,
–82, –84, –86*
Hingley, Ronald 1920- *Au&Wr 71,
ConAu 5R, EncSF, IntAu&W 77,
ScF&FL 1, –2, ScFSB*
Hingley, Ronald F 1920-
WorAu 1975[port]
Hinkemeyer, Michael T 1940-
ConAu 11NR, –69
Hinkemeyer, Michael Thomas
DrAP&F 85
Hinton, Nigel 1941- *ConAu 85*
Hinton, Phyllis 1900- *Au&Wr 71,
IntAu&W 76, –77, WhE&EA*
Hinton, S E *BioIn 13*
Hinton, S E 1948- *WhoAm 84, –86,
WrDr 86*

Hinton, S E 1950- *AuBYP SUP,
BioIn 8, –12, ChlLR 3, ConAu 81,
ConLC 30[port], FourBJA, OxChL,
SmATA 19, TwCCW 78, –83,
WhoAm 82, WrDr 80, –82, –84*
Hinton, Susie E 1950- *BioIn 8, –12*
Hintz, Martin 1945- *ConAu 12NR,
–65, SmATA 39, –47*
Hintze, Naomi 1909- *BioIn 8,
ConAu 1NR, –45, ScF&FL 1, –2,
WrDr 76, –80, –82, –84*
Hipple, Theodore W 1935-
ConAu 10NR, –65
Hiraoka, Kimitake 1925-1970 *BioIn 7,
–8, –9, –10, –12, ConAu 29R, –97,
ConLC 9, WorAu*
Hiraoka, Kimitake *see also* Mishima,
Yukio
Hirsch, Edward *DrAP&F 85*
Hirsch, Edward 1950- *ConAu 104,
–20NR, ConLC 31[port], DrAS 82E*
Hirsch, Phil 1926- *ConAu 102, –97,
SmATA 35*
Hirsch, S Carl 1913- *AnCL,
AuBYP SUP, BioIn 9, ConAu 2NR,
–5R, IntAu&W 76, –77, SmATA 2,
ThrBJA, WrDr 76, –80, –82, –84, –86*
Hirschfeld, Burt *AuBYP SUP*
Hirschfeld, Burt 1923- *ConAu 111,
ScF&FL 1*
Hirshberg, Albert Simon 1909-1973
*AuBYP, BioIn 7, –9, ConAu 1R,
–41R, WhAm 6, WhoE 74*
Hirst, Stephen Michael 1939-
ConAu 53
Hitchcock, Alfred 1899-1980
*AnObit 1980[port], Au&Wr 71,
BiDFilm, BioIn 1, –2, –3, –4, –5, –6,
–7, –8, –9, –10, –11, –12, –13,
BioNews 74, BlueB 76, CelR, CmCal,
CmMov, ConAu 97, ConLC 16,
ConTFT 1, CurBio 41, –60, –80N,
DcFM, EncMys, Film 2, FilmgC,
IntAu&W 77, IntDcF 2, IntMPA 77,
–75, –76, –78, –79, IntWW 74, –75,
–76, –77, –78, –79, –80, LesBEnT,
LinLib S, MakMC, McGEWB,
MovMk, NewC, NewYTBE 72,
NewYTBS 74, –80[port], NewYTET,
OxAmH, OxFilm, REnAL,
ScF&FL 1, SmATA 24N, –27[port],
WebAB, WhAm 7, WhDW, WhAm 7,
WhScrn 83, Who 74, WhoAm 74,
–76, –78, –80, WhoHr&F,
WhoWest 74, –76, WhoWor 74, –78,
WorAl, WorEFlm*
Hitchcock, Henry Russell 1903-
*WhoAm 84, –86, WhoAmA 84,
BioIn 3, –6, –9, –12, DcD&D,
IntAu&W 77, –82, –86, IntWW 74,
–75, –76, –77, –78, –79, –80, –81,
–82, –83, Who 74, –82, –83, –85,
WhoAm 74, –76, –78, –80, –82,
WhoAmA 73, –76, –78, –80, –82,
WhoWor 74, WrDr 82, –84, –86*
Hitchcock, Sir Alfred 1899-1980
HalFC 84
Hitchcock, Sir Alfred Joseph
1899-1980 *DcNaB 1971*
Hitchcock, Susan Tyler 1950-
ConAu 102, –18NR
Hitching, Francis 1933- *ConAu 103*
Hjortsberg, William *DrAP&F 85*
Hjortsberg, William 1941- *BioIn 9,
ConAu 33R, EncSF, IntAu&W 77,
–82, ScF&FL 1, –2, ScFSB,
WhoAm 80, –82, WrDr 76, –80, –82,
–84, –86*
Hoag, Edwin 1926- *AuBYP, BioIn 8,
ConAu 13R, WrDr 82, –84, –86*
Hoagland, Edward *DrAP&F 85*
Hoagland, Edward 1932- *AmAu&B,
BioIn 9, –10, –12, –13, ConAu 1R,
–2NR, ConLC 28[port], ConNov 72,
–76, –82, –86, CurBio 82[port],
DcLB 6[port], IntAu&W 76, –77, –86,
NewYTBS 81[port], OxAmL 83,
REnAL, WhoAm 86, WhoE 74, –75,
–77, WorAu 1970, WrDr 76, –80,
–82, –84, –86*
Hoagland, Edward Morley 1932-
WhoAm 84

Hoagland, Mahlon Bush 1921-
*AmM&WS 73P, –76P, –79P, –82P,
–86P, AsBiEn, BiESc, ConAu 85,
McGMS 80[port], WhoAm 74, –76,
–78, –80, –82, –84, –86,
WhoAtom 77, WhoE 83, WhoFrS 84,
WhoTech 82*
Hoare, Robert J 1921-1975 *Alli,
Au&Wr 71, BiDLA, ConAu 6NR,
–9R, IntAu&W 76, SmATA 38,
WrDr 76*
Hoban, Lillian 1925- *AmPB, AuBYP,
BioIn 8, –9, –12, –13, ChhPo S1,
ConAu 69, IlsCB 1957, –1967,
SmATA 22[port], ThrBJA*
Hoban, Russell 1925- *AuBYP, BioIn 6,
–8, –9, –10, –12, ChlLR 3, ChhPo S1,
–S2, ConAu 5R, ConLC 7, –25[port],
ConNov 86, DcLB 52[port], IlrAm G,
Novels, OxChL, PostFic, ScF&FL 1,
–1A, –2, ScFSB, SmATA 1, ThrBJA,
TwCCW 78, –83, TwCSFW 86,
Who 82, –83, WhoAm 82,
WorAu 1975[port], WrDr 76, –80,
–82, –84, –86*
Hobart, Lois *AuBYP, BioIn 6, –7, –10,
ConAu 5R, ForWC 70, MinnWr,
SmATA 7, WhoAmW 58, WrDr 76,
–80, –82, –84, –86*
Hobbs, David 1931- *WhoTech 84*
Hobsbawm, E J 1917- *IntAu&W 76,
–77, WorAu 1970*
Hobsbawm, Eric J 1917- *Au&Wr 71,
BiDMarx, ConAu 3NR, –5R,
Who 74, –82, –83, WhoWor 82,
WrDr 76, –80, –82, –84*
Hobsbawm, Eric John Ernest 1917-
Who 85, WhoWor 84, –87
Hobson, Burton 1933- *BioIn 13,
ConAu 2NR, –5R, SmATA 28,
WhoAm 74, –76, –78, –80, –82,
WhoE 75, –77*
Hobson, Burton Harold 1933-
WhoAm 84, –86
Hobson, Julius W 1922?-1977
*AuBYP SUP, BioIn 7, –8, –9, –11,
CivR 74, ConAu 102, InB&W 80,
LivgBAA, NewYTBS 77, ObitOF 79*
Hobson, Laura 1900- *AmAu&B,
AmNov, AmWomWr, Au&Wr 71,
BioIn 1, –2, –3, –4, –6, –12,
ConAu 17R, ConLC 7, –25[port],
ConNov 72, –76, –82, CurBio 47,
DcLEL 1940, InWom, IntAu&W 76,
–77, REn, REnAL, TwCA SUP,
WhoAm 74, –76, –78, –80, –82,
WhoAmW 74, –58, –61, –64, –66,
–68, –70, –72, –75, –77, –83,
WrDr 76, –80, –82, –84*
Hochschild, Adam 1942- *WhoAm 86*
Hochstein, Rolaine *ConAu 45,
DrAP&F 85, Po&Wr 77*
Hodge, Jane Aiken 1917- *Au&Wr 71,
AuBYP, BioIn 8, ConAu 3NR, –5R,
IntAu&W 76, –77, –82, –86, Novels,
WhoWor 76, WrDr 76, –80, –82, –84,
–86*
Hodge, Paul W 1934- *WhoTech 84*
Hodge, Paul William 1934-
*AmM&WS 73P, –76P, –79P, –82P,
–86P, BioIn 11, ConAu 33R,
IntAu&W 77, –82, WhoAm 74, –76,
–78, –80, –82, –84, –86, WhoTech 82,
WhoWest 76, WrDr 76, –80, –82,
–84, –86*
Hodgell, P C *ScFSB*
Hodgell, P C 1951- *ConAu 109,
SmATA 42[port]*
Hodges, C Walter 1909- *BioIn 1,
ConAu 5NR, –13R, IlsCB 1967,
IntAu&W 77, –82, –86, OxChL,
SmATA 2, TwCCW 78, –83, Who 82,
–83, –85, WrDr 76, –80, –82, –84,
WhoChL*
Hodges, Cyril Walter 1909- *AnCL,
Au&Wr 71, AuBYP, BioIn 4, –5, –7,
–8, –9, –12, ConAu 5R, IlsCB 1744,
–1946, –1957, SmATA 2, ThrBJA,
Who 74, WhoArt 80, –82, –84,
WhoChL*
Hodges, Gil 1924-1972 *BioIn 13,
ConAu 109, CurBio 62, –72, –72N,
NewYTBE 72, ObitOF 79,
WhScrn 83, WorAl*

Hodges, Gilbert Ray 1924-1972
*BioIn 2, –3, –4, –5, –6, –7, –8, –9,
–10, WhAm 5, WhoProB 73*
Hodges, Hollis *DrAP&F 85*
Hodges, Margaret 1911- *AuBYP SUP,
BiDrLUS 70, BioIn 9, ConAu 1R,
–2NR, DrAS 74E, –78E, –82E,
ForWC 70, FourBJA, IntAu&W 1917,
IntAu&W 77, –82, SmATA 1,
–33[port], WhoAm 74, –76, –78, –80,
–82, WhoAmW 74, –58, –61, –72,
–75, –77, –83, WhoLibS 66,
WrDr 76, –80, –82, –84, –86*
Hoehling, Adolph A *ConAu 1R*
Hoehling, Mary 1914- *AuBYP,
BioIn 7, ConAu 93*
Hoexter, Corinne 1927- *BioIn 10,
ConAu 49, SmATA 6, WhoAmW 77,
–79, WhoE 79, –81, –83*
Hoff, Rhoda *ChhPo S1*
Hoff, Syd 1912- *AmAu&B,
Au&Wr 71, AuBYP, ChhPo S1,
ConAu 4NR, –5R, ConGrA 1[port],
IlsCB 1957, –1967, SmATA 9,
SmATA 4AS[port], ThrBJA,
TwCCW 78, –83, WhoAm 74, –76,
–78, –82, –84, –86, WhoS&SW 84,
WhoWor 74, WhoWorJ 72, –78,
WorECar, WorAl 80, –82, –84, –86*
Hoff, Sydney 1912- *AuBYP, BioIn 7,
–8, –9, –11*
Hoffer, Eric 1902-1983 *AnObit 1983,
BioIn 2, –4, –6, –7, –8, –10, –11, –13,
CelR, CmCal, ConAu 109, –13R,
–18NR, ConISC 2[port], CurBio 65,
–83N, LinLib L, NewYTBS 83[port],
PolProf J, RAdv 1, WebAB, –79,
WhAm 8, WhoAm 74, –76, –78, –80,
–82, WorAl, WorAu, WrDr 76, –80,
–82, –84*
Hoffer, William 1943- *ConAu 65*
Hoffman, Alice 1952- *BioIn 13,
ConAu 77, ConNov 86*
Hoffman, Edwin D *ConAu 101*
Hoffman, Elizabeth 1921-
*BiDrLUS 70, ConAu 77,
WhoAmW 74, –70, –72, –75, –77,
–79, WhoE 74, –75*
Hoffman, Lee 1932- *ConAu 18NR,
–25R, ConSFA, EncFWF[port],
EncSF, ScF&FL 1, –2, ScFSB,
TwCSFW 86, WrDr 84, –86*
Hoffman, Marshall 1942- *ConAu 106*
Hoffman, Nancy Jo 1942- *ConAu 107*
Hoffman, Paul 1934- *ConAu 1NR, –45*
Hoffman, Paul 1934-1984 *BioIn 13,
ConAu 112*
Hoffmann, Banesh 1906-
*AmM&WS 73P, –79P, –82P, –86P,
BioIn 10, ConAu 3NR, –5R,
IntAu&W 77, WhoAmJ 80,
WhoWorJ 72, –78, WrDr 76, –80,
–82, –84, –86*
Hoffmann, Banesh 1906-1986
ConAu 119, NewYTBS 86[port]
Hoffmann, Margaret Jones 1910-
*AuBYP, BioIn 5, –7, ConAu 2NR,
–5R, SmATA 48[port]*
Hoffmann, Margaret Jones *see also*
Hoffmann, Peggy
Hoffmann, Peggy *SmATA X*
Hoffmann, Peggy 1910- *AuBYP,
ConAmC, –82, ConAu X, ForWC 70,
WrDr 76, –80, –82, –84, –86*
Hoffmann, Peggy *see also* Hoffmann,
Margaret Jones
Hofstadter, Richard 1916-1970
*AmAu&B, BioIn 4, –8, –9, –10, –11,
–13, ConAu 1R, –4NR, –29R,
CurBio 56, –70, DcLB 17[port],
EncAAH, EncAB-H, IntEnSS 79,
NewYTBE 70, ObitOF 79,
OxAmL, –83, PenC AM, PolProf E,
REn, REnAL, WebAB, –79,
WhAm 5, WorAl, WorAu*
Hogan, Bernice Harris 1929- *BioIn 11,
ChhPo, ConAu 7NR, –13R,
ForWC 70, SmATA 12*
Hogan, Desmond 1950- *BioIn 13,
ConAu 102, ConNov 86, DcIrL,
DcLB 14[port]*
Hogan, Desmond 1951- *BiDIrW*
Hogan, James Philip 1915-
WhoRel 75, –77, –85

Hodges, Gilbert Ray 1924-1972

Hogan, Ray 1908- *ConAu 9R,
EncFWF[port], WrDr 84, –86*
Hogarth, Grace 1905- *Au&Wr 71,
BlueB 76, ConAu 89, IntAu&W 76,
–77, TwCCW 78, –83, WhoAm 78,
–80, –82, WhoAmW 74, –72, –75,
–77, WrDr 80, –82, –84, –86*
Hogben, Lancelot 1895-1975 *BioIn 1,
–2, –4, –5, –10, –11, –12, BlueB 76N,
Chambr 3, ConAu 61, –73,
CurBio 41, –84N, EvLB, InSci,
IntWW 74, –75, –76N, LinLib L, –S,
LongCTC, NewC, NewYTBS 75,
ObitT 1971, TwCA, –SUP, WhAm 6,
–7, WhE&EA, Who 74*
Hogg, Beth 1917- *AuBYP, BioIn 8,
ConAu 5R, –X*
Hogg, Beth *see also* Grey, Elizabeth
Hogg, Garry 1902-1976 *Au&Wr 71,
BioIn 8, –9, ConAu 10NR, –21R,
IntAu&W 76, SmATA 2, WhoChL,
WrDr 76*
Hogner, Dorothy Childs *WrDr 86*
Hogner, Dorothy Childs 1904-
*AmAu&B, AuBYP, BioIn 2, –7, –9,
ConAu 33R, IntAu&W 77, JBA 51,
OxCan, SmATA 4, WhNAA,
WhoAmW 58, –81, WrDr 76, –80,
–82, –84*
Hogrefe, Pearl d1977 *ConAu P-1,
DrAS 74E, WhAm 7, WhoAm 74,
–76, –78, WhoAmW 74, –58, –64,
–66, –68, –70*
Hoh, Diane 1937- *ConAu 120,
SmATA 48*
Hoig, Stan 1924- *ConAu 1R, –1NR*
Hoke, Helen 1903- *AuBYP, BioIn 2,
–8, –12, ConAu 73, ScF&FL 1,
SmATA 15, WhoAmW 58*
Hoke, John Lindsay 1925- *BioIn 10,
ConAu 41R, SmATA 7*
Holbrook, Hal 1925- *BiE&WWA,
BioIn 5, –6, –7, –10, BioNews 74,
CelR, ConTFT 1[port], CurBio 61,
FilmgC, HalFC 84, IntMPA 77, –75,
–76, –78, –79, –81, –82, –84, –86,
MotPP, NewYTBE 73, NotNAT,
OxAmT 84, WhoAm 74, –76, –78,
–80, –82, –84, –86, WhoHol A,
WhoThe 72, –77, –81, WorAl*
Holbrook, Sabra *SmATA X*
Holbrook, Sabra 1912- *BioIn 1,
ConAu X, CurBio 48, InWom,
WhoAmW 58, –61, –64, –66*
Holbrook, Sabra *see also* Erickson,
Sabra Rollins
Holden, William Curry 1896?-
*AmAu&B, AmM&WS 73S,
Au&Wr 71, TexWr, WhNAA*
Holden, William Curry 1898?-
ConAu 117
Holder, William G 1937-
AuBYP SUP, ConAu 10NR, –25R
Holding, James 1907- *AuBYP,
BioIn 8, –9, ConAu 25R, SmATA 3,
TwCCr&M 80, –85*
Holdstock, Robert 1948- *ConLC 39,
EncSF, IntAu&W 82, ScFSB[port],
TwCSFW 86, WrDr 84, –86*
Holl, Kristi D 1951- *ConAu 114*
Holland, Barbara A *DrAP&F 85*
Holland, Barbara A 1925- *ConAu 57,
IntAu&W 76, –77, IntWWP 77, –82*
Holland, Cecelia *DrAP&F 85*
Holland, Cecelia 1943- *ASpks, BioIn 7,
–8, –9, –11, ConAu 9NR, –17R,
EncSF, TwCSFW 86, WhoAm 74,
–76, –78, WhoAmW 74,
WorAu 1975[port], WrDr 76, –80,
–82, –84, –86*
Holland, Isabelle 1920- *AuBYP SUP,
BioIn 11, ConAu 10NR, –21R,
ConLC 21[port], FifBJA[port],
IntAu&W 82, OxChL, SmATA 8,
TwCCW 78, –83, WhoAmW 58, –66,
WrDr 80, –82, –84, –86*
Holland, Isabelle Christian 1920-
IntAu&W 86
Holland, John L 1919- *ConAu 17NR*
Holland, John Lewis 1919-
*AmM&WS 73S, –78S, BioIn 12,
ConAu 25R, LEduc 74, SmATA 20*
Holland, Robert 1940- *ConAu 33R*
Hollander, John *DrAP&F 85*

Hollander, John 1929- *AmAu&B,*
AuBYP, BioIn 8, –10, –12, –13,
ChhPo, –S1, ConAu 1R, –1NR,
ConLC 2, –5, –8, –14, ConPo 70, –75,
–80, –85, DcLB 5[port], DcLEL 1940,
DrAS 74E, –78E, –82E,
IntAu&W 77, –82, –86, IntWW 78,
–79, –80, –81, –82, –83, IntWWP 77,
–82, LinLib L, ModAL S2,
OxAmL, –83, PenC AM, REnAL,
SmATA 13, WhoAm 74, –76, –78,
–80, –82, –84, –86, WhoE 74,
WhoTwCL, WorAu, WrDr 76, –80,
–82, –84, –86

Hollander, Phyllis 1928- *AuBYP SUP,*
ConAu 18NR, –97, SmATA 39

Hollander, Zander 1923- *AuBYP SUP,*
ConAu 18NR, –65

Hollon, William Eugene 1913-
AmAu&B, AuNews 1, ConAu 1R,
DrAS 74H, –78H, –82H, EncAAH,
REnAW, WhoAm 74, –76, –78, –80,
–82, –84, –86

Hollow, John Walter 1939-
ConAu 111, DrAS 74E, –78E, –82E

Holly, Buddy 1936?-1959 *AmPS A,*
Baker 84, BioIn 9, –10, –11, –12,
–13, EncPR&S 74, –77, IlEncRk,
RkOn 74, –82, RkOneH,
RolSEnR 83, WhoRock 81, WorAl

Holm, Anne 1922- *AnCL, BioIn 9,*
ConAu 17R, FourBJA, ScF&FL 1A,
SmATA 1, TwCCW 78B, –83B

Holman, Felice 1919- *AuBYP, BioIn 8,*
–10, ChhPo S2, –S3, ConAu 3NR,
–5R, –18NR, FourBJA, IntAu&W 77,
–82, OxChL, ScF&FL 1, SmATA 7,
TwCCW 78, –83, WhoAmW 75, –77,
–83, WrDr 76, –80, –82, –84, –86

Holme, Bryan 1913- *AuBYP, BioIn 8,*
–9, –14, ConAu 103,
SmATA 26[port], WhoE 75

Holmes, Burnham 1942- *ConAu 97*

Holmes, David Charles 1919-
ConAu 9R, WhoE 83

Holmes, Marjorie 1910- *AmAu&B,*
AmNov, Au&Wr 71, AuBYP,
AuNews 1, BioIn 2, –8, –10,
ConAu 1R, –5NR, ForWC 70,
InWom, IntAu&W 76, –77, –86,
SmATA 43[port], WhoAm 78, –80,
–82, WhoAmW 74, –58, –61, –72,
–75, –77, –79, WrDr 76, –80, –82,
–84, –86

Holmes, Martin 1905- *Au&Wr 71,*
ConAu 1NR, –49, MnBBF, WrDr 80,
–82, –84, –86

Holmes, Oliver Wendell 1809-1894
Alli, –SUP, AmAu, AmAu&B, AmBi,
AmWr S1, ApCAB, AsBiEn, AtlBL,
BbD, BiDAmM, BiD&SB, BiESc,
BiHiMed, BioIn 1, –2, –3, –4, –5, –6,
–7, –8, –9, –10, –11, –12, CasWL,
CelCen, Chambr 3, ChhPo, –S1, –S2,
–S3, CnDAL, CrtT 3, –4, CyAL 2,
CyWA, DcAmAu, DcAmB,
DcAmMeB 84, DcAmMeB, DcAmSR,
DcBiA, DcBiPP, DcEnA, DcEnL,
DcLB 1, DcLEL, DcNAA, Dis&D,
Drake, EncAB-H, EvLB, HarEnUS,
InSci, LinLib L, –S, McGEWB,
MorMA, MouLC 4, NatCAB 2,
NinCLC 14[port], Novels, OxAmH,
OxAmL, –83, OxEng, –85, OxMed 86, PenC AM, PoChrch,
RAdv 1, REn, REnAL, ScF&FL 1,
SmATA 34[port], Str&VC, TwCBDA,
WebAB, –79, WebE&AL, WhDW,
WhAm HS, WorAl

Holmes, W J 1900- *ConAu 29R*

Holst, Imogen 1907- *Baker 78,*
IntWWM 77, OxMus, Who 82, –83

Holst, Imogen 1907-1984
AnObit 1984, ConAu 112

Holst, Imogen Clare 1907-1984
Baker 84, IntWWM 85

Holt, John Caldwell 1923- *AmAu&B,*
BioIn 8, –11, –12, ConAu 69,
ConIsC 2[port], CurBio 81[port],
WhoAm 82

Holt, John Robert 1926-
ConAu 11NR, –25R, ScF&FL 1

Holt, Michael 1929- *Au&Wr 71,*
ConAu 5NR, –53, IntAu&W 76, –77,
SmATA 13, WrDr 76, –80, –82, –84,
–86

Holt, Rackham *ConAu X*

Holt, Rackham 1899-1963 *BioIn 6,*
CurBio 44, InWom, SmATA X,
WhAm 4

Holt, Victoria *Who 85, WhoAm 84,*
–86

Holt, Victoria 1906- *AmAu&B,*
Au&Wr 71, BioIn 7, –9, –10, –11,
ConAu X, CorpD, EncMys,
IntAu&W 77X, NewYTBS 77, Novels,
SmATA 2, TwCCr&M 85, Who 74,
–82, –83, WhoAm 74, –76, –78, –80,
–82, WhoAmW 74, –72, –75, –77,
–79, –81, –83, WorAl, WorAu,
WrDr 76, –80, –82, –84, –86

Holt, Victoria *see also* Hibbert, Eleanor

Holton, Leonard *ConAu X, SmATA X*

Holton, Leonard 1915- *AuBYP,*
ConAu X, EncMys, IntAu&W 76X,
–77X, –82X, SmATA 2,
TwCCr&M 80, WorAu, WrDr 80,
–82, –84

Holton, Leonard 1915-1983
TwCCr&M 85

Holton, Leonard *see also* Wibberley,
Leonard

Holtzman, Jerome 1926- *ConAu 4NR,*
–53, WhoAm 80, –82, –84, –86

Holz, Loretta 1943- *BioIn 12,*
ConAu 65, SmATA 17

Holzer, Hans *WhoAm 86*

Holzer, Hans 1920- *AmSCAP 66,*
BiDPara, ConAu 7NR, –13R,
EncO&P 78, ScF&FL 1, –2,
WhoAm 74, –76, –78, –80, –82, –84,
WhoE 74, WhoWor 82

Holzman, Red 1920- *ConAu X, WorAl*

Homze, Alma C 1932- *BioIn 12,*
ConAu 29R, SmATA 17

Hong, Edna H 1913- *ConAu 9NR,*
–21R, WhoAmW 74, –75, –77

Honig, Donald *DrAP&F 85*

Honig, Donald 1931- *BioIn 12,*
ConAu 9NR, –17R, IntAu&W 77,
SmATA 18

Honig, Edwin *DrAP&F 85*

Honig, Edwin 1919- *AmAu&B,*
Au&Wr 71, BiE&WWA, BioIn 10,
–12, BlueB 76, ConAu 4NR, –5R,
ConLC 33[port], ConPo 70, –75, –80,
–85, DcLB 5[port], DrAS 74E, –78E,
–82E, IntAu&W 76, –82, –86,
IntWWP 77, –82, LinLib L, NotNAT,
WhoAm 74, –76, –78, –80, –82, –84,
–86, WhoAmJ 80, WhoWor 74, –76,
WhoWorJ 72, –78, WorAu, WrDr 76,
–80, –82, –84, –86

Honness, Elizabeth H 1904- *AuBYP,*
BioIn 7, –9, ConAu 25R, SmATA 2,
WhoAmW 74

Honour, Alan Edward 1918-
Au&Wr 71

Hoobler, Dorothy *BioIn 13,*
ConAu 11NR, –69, SmATA 28[port]

Hoobler, Thomas *BioIn 13,*
ConAu 11NR, –69, SmATA 28[port]

Hood, Hugh 1928- *Au&Wr 71,*
CanWW 70, –79, –80, –81, –83,
CanWr, CasWL, ConAu 1NR, –49,
ConLC 15, –28[port], ConNov 72,
–76, –82, –86, CreCan 1,
DcLB 53[port], DcLEL 1940,
IntAu&W 76, –77, –82, –86,
OxCan, –SUP, OxCanL,
WhoCanL 85, WrDr 76, –80, –82,
–84, –86

Hook, Diana Ffarington 1918-
ConAu 61

Hook, Donald Dwight 1928-
ConAu 4NR, –53, DrAS 74F, –78F,
–82F

Hooke, Nina Warner 1907- *ConAu 73*

Hooker, Richard *BioIn 10, –13,*
ConAu X

Hooks, William H 1921- *BioIn 12,*
ConAu 19NR, –81, SmATA 16

Hooper, Meredith 1939- *BioIn 13*

Hooper, Meredith Jean 1939-
ConAu 106, IntAu&W 76, –77,
SmATA 28[port], WrDr 76, –80, –82,
–84, –86

Hooper, Walter 1931- *ChhPo S1, –S2,*
ConAu 7NR, –17R

Hoopes, Ned E 1932- *BioIn 12,*
ConAu 17R, DrAS 74E, –78E, –82E,
ScF&FL 1, –2, SmATA 21[port],
WrDr 76, –80, –82, –84

Hoopes, Roy 1922- *AuBYP SUP,*
BioIn 11, ConAu 15NR, –21R,
SmATA 11

Hoover, F Louis 1913- *AmArch 70,*
ConAu 41R

Hoover, H M *IntAu&W 86X, ScFSB*

Hoover, H M 1935- *ConAu 105,*
ScF&FL 1, SmATA 33, –44[port],
TwCSFW 86, WrDr 86

Hoover, Helen 1910- *Au&Wr 71,*
BioIn 9, –11, ConAu 21R, ForWC 70,
IntAu&W 76, –77, –82, SmATA 12,
WhoAm 74, –76, –78, –80, –82,
WhoAmW 74, –66, –68, –70, –72,
–75, –77, –79, WhoE 74, –75, –77,
WhoWest 78, –80, –82, WhoWor 80,
WrDr 76, –80, –82, –84

Hoover, Helen 1910-1984 *ConAu 113,*
SmATA 39N

Hoover, Helen D 1910- *WhoAm 84*

Hoover, Helen M 1910- *BioIn 13*

Hoover, J Edgar 1895-1972
AmRef 70, AmAu&B, ConAu 1R,
–2NR, –33R, CurBio 40, –50, –72,
–72N, EncAB 5[port], EncE 75,
HalFC 84, HisEWW, LinLib S,
McGEWB, NewYTBE 72, ObitOF 79,
ObitT 1971, PolProf E, PolProf J,
PolProf K, PolProf NF, PolProf T,
REnAL, WhAm 5, WhScrn 77, –83,
WorAl

Hoover, John Page 1910-
AmM&WS 73S, BioIn 2, ConAu 53,
WhoAm 74, –76, –78

Hope, Anthony *DcNaB 1931,*
OxEng 85

Hope, Anthony 1863-1933 *BiD&SB,*
BioIn 2, –4, –5, –8, –12, Chambr 3,
CyWA, DcBiA, DcEnA AP, DcLEL,
EvLB, FilmgC, HalFC 84,
LinLib LP, –S, LongCTC, ModBrL,
NewC, NotNAT B, Novels, OxChL,
OxEng, PenC ENG, REn,
TwCA, –SUP, TwCWr, WhLit,
WhThe, WhoChL

Hope, Anthony *see also* Hawkins, Sir
Anthony Hope

Hope, Christopher 1944- *ConAu 106,*
ConNov 86

Hope, Laura Lee *OxChL*

Hope, Laura Lee 1893?-1982 *BioIn 10,*
ConAu 118, –X, REnAL, SmATA 1,
–X, WebAB, –79, WhoChL

Hope, Laura Lee *see also* Adams,
Harriet S

Hope-Simpson, Jacynth 1930-
Au&Wr 71, BioIn 11, ConAu 7NR,
–13R, IntAu&W 76, –82, SmATA 12,
TwCCW 78, –83, WhoWor 76,
WrDr 76, –80, –82, –84, –86

Hopf, Alice L 1904- *AuBYP SUP,*
BioIn 10, ConAu 9NR, –17R,
ForWC 70, IntAu&W 76, –77, –82,
MichAu 80, SmATA 5, WhoAmW 74,
–72, –75, –77

Hopf, Alice L *see also* Lightner, A M

Hopke, William E 1918- *ConAu 21R*

Hopkins, Budd 1931- *PrintW 85,*
WhoAmA 84, WhoWor 87

Hopkins, Jack Walker 1930-
WhoAm 86, WhoAmP 85

Hopkins, Jerry 1935- *ConAu 18NR,*
–25R, LinLib L

Hopkins, Joseph G E 1909-
AmCath 80, BioIn 11, ConAu 1R,
–5NR, DrAS 74H, –78H, –82H,
SmATA 11, WhoAm 74, –76, –78

Hopkins, Lee Bennett 1938-
AuBYP SUP, BioIn 9, –13,
ChhPo S1, –S2, ConAu 25R,
FifBJA[port], IntAu&W 82,
SmATA 3, SmATA 4AS[port],
WhoBlA 75, –77, –80, WhoE 74, –75,
WrDr 76, –80, –82, –84, –86

Hopkins, Pauline Elizabeth 1856-1930
DcAmNB

Hopkins, Pauline Elizabeth 1859-1930
AmWomM, BioIn 12, BlkAWP,
DcLB 50[port], InB&W 80, SelBAAf,
WomNov

Hoppe, Joanne 1932- *ConAu 81,*
SmATA 42

Hopper, Nancy J 1937- *ConAu 115,*
SmATA 35, –38[port]

Horan, James D 1914-1981 *AmAu&B,*
AnObit 1981, BioIn 12, ConAu 9NR,
–105, –13R, NewYTBS 81,
WhoAm 74, –76, –78, –80, WhoE 74,
–75, –77, –79, –81, WrDr 80, –82

Horgan, Paul *DrAP&F 85*

Horgan, Paul 1903- *AmAu&B,*
AmCath 80, AmNov, Au&Wr 71,
AuBYP, BioIn 1, –2, –3, –4, –5, –6,
–7, –8, –9, –10, –13, BlueB 76,
CathA 1930, ChhPo, CnDAL,
ConAu 9NR, –13R, ConLC 9,
ConNov 72, –76, –82, –86, CurBio 71,
DcLB Y85B[port], DcLEL,
DrAS 74H, –78H, –82H, EncFWF,
IlsCB 1744, IntAu&W 76, –77, –82,
Novels, OxAmL, –83, REnAL,
REnAW, ScF&FL 1, –2, SmATA 13,
TwCA SUP, WhE&EA, WhNAA,
WhoAm 74, –76, –78, –80, –82, –84,
–86, WhoE 74, WhoGov 72,
WhoWor 74, –78, –80, –82, –84, –87,
WrDr 76, –80, –82, –84, –86

Horman, Richard Eliot 1945-
ConAu 29R, WhoE 75, –77, –83, –85,
WhoGov 77, –75

Horn, Daniel 1916- *AmM&WS 73S,*
WhoAm 74, –76, –78, WhoGov 77,
–72, –75

Horn, Daniel 1934- *ConAu 21R*

Horn, George F 1917- *ConAu 5R,*
–8NR

Horn, Pierre L 1942- *ConAu 119*

Hornby, Leslie 1949- *ConAu 103,*
CurBio 68, GoodHs, InWom,
NewYTBE 71, –72, WhoAm 74,
WhoAmW 74

Hornby, Leslie *see also* Twiggy

Horne, Alistair 1925- *Au&Wr 71,*
ConAu 5R, –9NR, IntAu&W 76, –82,
OxCan, Who 74, –82, –83,
WhoWor 74, –76, WrDr 76, –80, –82,
–84, –86

Horner, Dave 1934- *BioIn 11,*
ConAu 17R, SmATA 12

Horner, Joyce Mary 1903-1980
BioIn 12, ConAu 112, DrAS 74E,
WhoAmW 70

Horney, Karen 1885-1952 *AmAu&B,*
AmWomWr, BiDPsy, BioIn 3, –4, –7,
–10, –11, –12, –13, ConAu 114,
CurBio 41, –53, DcAmB S5,
DcAmMeB 84, EncTR, GoodHs,
GuPsyc[port], InSci, InWom,
IntDcWB, LibW, McGEWB,
NamesHP, NewYTBE 73,
NotAW MOD, ObitOF 79,
TwCA SUP, WhDW, WhAm 3,
WorAl

Hornig, Doug *DrAP&F 85*

Hornig, Doug 1943- *ConAu 117*

Hornik, Edith Lynn 1930- *ConAu 61,*
–X

Hornsby, Alton, Jr. 1940- *ConAu 37R,*
DrAS 74H, –78H, –82H, LivgBAA,
SelBAAf, WhoBlA 75, –77, –80, –85,
WhoS&SW 76, –78, WrDr 76, –80,
–82, –84, –86

Hornung, Clarence Pearson 1899-
ConAu 9NR, –17R, WhoAmA 73,
–76, –78, –80, –82, –84

Hornung, Ernest William 1866-1921
BbD, BiD&SB, BioIn 1, –2,
Chambr 3, CorpD, DcLEL, EncMys,
EvLB, LongCTC, MnBBF, NewC,
REn, TwCA, –SUP, TwCWr, WhLit

Horowitz, Edward 1904- *ConAu 1R,*
–4NR, WhoWorJ 72, –78

Horowitz, Israel Albert 1907-1973
ConAu 41R, GolEC, OxChess 84

Horowitz, Norman Harold 1915-
AmM&WS 86P, WhoAm 84, –86

Horton, Louise *DrAP&F 85*

Hyman, Dick 1904- *ConAu 7NR, –17R*

Hynd, Alan 1904?-1974 *BioIn 10, ConAu 45*

Hyndman, Jane Andrews 1912-1978 *AuBYP, BioIn 6, –9, –11, –13, ConAu 5NR, –89, –X, SmATA 1, –23N, –46[port]*

Hyndman, Jane Andrews *see also* Wyndham, Lee

Hynek, Joseph Allen *AmM&WS 86P*

Hynek, Joseph Allen 1910- *AmM&WS 73P, –76P, –79P, –82P, BioIn 7, CurBio 68, EncO&P 78S1, WhoAm 74, WhoWor 74*

I

Ian, Janis 1951- *BiDAmM, BioIn 7, –8, –10, –11, ChhPo, –S2, ConAu 105, ConLC 21[port], EncFCWM 83, EncPR&S 74, –77, GoodHs, IlEncRk, NewYTBS 77, RkOn 78, –84, RolSEnR 83, WhoAm 76, –78, –80, –82, –84, WhoAmW 74, –68, –70, –72, –81, WhoRock 81[port], WhoRocM 82, WorAl*

Iannuzzi, John N 1935- *ConAu 93, TwCCr&M 80, –85, WhoAmL 78, –79, WrDr 82, –84, –86*

Ibarruri, Dolores 1895- *BiDMarx, BioIn 6, –7, –8, –11, –13, CurBio 67, InWom, IntAu&W 86, IntDcWB[port], NewYTBS 77, –83[port], WhDW*

Ibsen, Henrik 1828-1906 *AtlBL, BbD, BiD&SB, BioIn 1, –2, –3, –4, –5, –6, –7, –8, –9, –10, –11, –12, CasWL, CelCen, ChhPo S3, ClDMEL, CnMD, CnThe, ConAu 104, CyWA, DcAmSR, DcEuL, Dis&D, EncWL, EncWT, EuAu, EvEuW, GrFLW, HalFC 84, LinLib L, –S, LongCEL, LongCTC, MajMD 2, McGEWB, McGEWD, –84[port], ModWD, NewC, NewEOp 71, NotNAT A, –B, OxAmT 84, OxEng, –85, OxGer, OxMus, OxThe, –83, PenC EUR, RComWL, REn, REnWD, TwCLC 2, –8[port], –16[port], WhDW, WhLit, WorAl*

Icenhower, Joseph Bryan 1913- *AuBYP, BioIn 8, ConAu 5R, –5NR*

Idyll, Clarence Purvis *AmM&WS 86P*

Idyll, Clarence Purvis 1916- *AmM&WS 73P, –76P, –79P, –82P, Au&Wr 71, ConAu 9R, WhoS&SW 73*

Ike, Chukwuemeka 1931- *WorAu 1975[port]*

Ilowite, Sheldon A 1931- *BioIn 13, ConAu 106, SmATA 27[port]*

Imbrie, John 1925- *AmM&WS 86P, WhoFrS 84*

Immel, Mary Blair 1930- *AuBYP, BioIn 13, ConAu 6NR, –13R, ForWC 70, SmATA 28[port], WhoAmW 77, –79, WrDr 76, –80, –82, –84*

Ind, Allison 1903-1974 *ConAu P-1*

Ing, Dean *ScFSB*

Ing, Dean 1931- *ConAu 106, TwCSFW 86*

Ing, Dean Charles 1931- *IntAu&W 86*

Ingalls, Robert Paul 1941- *ConAu 107, –110, DrAS 78H, –82H, WhoS&SW 84*

Ingraham, Leonard W 1913- *BioIn 9, ConAu 25R, SmATA 4*

Ingram, Tom 1924- *ChhPo, ConAu 49, –X, ScF&FL 1*

Innes, Hammond *Who 85, WrDr 86*

Innes, Hammond 1913- *AmAu&B, BioIn 3, –4, –5, –8, –10, ConAu X, ConNov 72, –76, –82, –86, CurBio 54, IntWW 74, –75, –76, –77, –78, –79, –80, –81, –82, –83, LinLib L, LongCTC, Novels, REn, TwCCr&M 80, –85, TwCWr, Who 74, –82, –83, WorAu, WrDr 76, –80, –82, –84*

Innes, Hammond *see also* Hammond Innes, Ralph

Innes, Jean *ConAu X, WrDr 86*

Innes, Jean 1932- *ConAu X, IntAu&W 82X, WrDr 76, –80, –82, –84*

Inouye, Daniel K 1924- *BioIn 13, PolsAm 84[port]*

Inouye, Daniel Ken 1924- *AlmAP 78, –80, –82[port], –84[port], BiDrAC, BioIn 5, –6, –8, –9, –10, –11, –12, BlueB 76, CelR, CngDr 74, –77, –79, –81, –83, –85, –87, ConAu 25R, CurBio 60, IntWW 74, –75, –76, –77, –78, –79, –80, –81, –82, –83, IntYB 80, –81, –82, NewYTBS 86[port], PolProf J, PolProf NF, WhoAm 74, –76, –78, –80, –82, –84, –86, WhoAmL 78, –79, WhoAmP 73, –75, –77, –79, –81, –83, –85, WhoGov 77, –72, –75, WhoWest 74, –76, –78, –80, –82, –84, WhoWor 74, –76, –78, –80, –82, –84, –87, WorAl*

Ioannou, Susan 1944- *IntAu&W 86, WhoCanL 85*

Ionesco, Eugene *OxEng 85*

Ionesco, Eugene 1912- *BiE&WWA, BioIn 5, –6, –7, –8, –9, –10, –11, –12, –13, CasWL, CelR, CnMD, CnMWL, CnThe, ConAu 9R, ConFLW 84, ConLC 1, –4, –6, –9, –11, –15, –41[port], ConTFT 4, CroCD, CurBio 59, EncWL, –2[port], EncWT, EvEuW, GrFLW, IntAu&W 76, –77, –82, IntWW 74, –75, –76, –77, –78, –79, –80, –81, –82, –83, LinLib L, LongCTC, MajMD 2, MakMC, McGEWB, McGEWD, –84[port], ModFrL, ModRL, ModWD, NewYTBE 70, NotNAT, –A, OxAmT 84, OxThe, –83, PenC EUR, PlP&P, RComWL, REn, REnWD, ScF&FL 1, –2, SmATA 7, TwCWr, WhDW, Who 74, –82, –85, WhoAm 74, –76, –78, –80, –82, –84, –86, WhoFr 79, WhoThe 72, –77, –81, WhoTwCL, WhoWor 74, –78, –82, –84, –87, WorAl, WorAu*

Ipcar, Dahlov 1917- *AuBYP, BioIn 5, –8, –9, –12, BkP, ChhPo S1, –S2, ConAu 9NR, –17R, IlsCB 1946, –1957, –1967, IntAu&W 77, –82,*

ScF&FL 1, –2, SmATA 1, ThrBJA, WhoAm 80, –82, –84, –86, WhoAmA 76, –78, –80, –82, –84, WhoAmW 74, –58, –61, –75, –77

Ipsen, D C 1921- *ConAu 33R, IntAu&W 77, –82, WhoWest 78, –80, –82, WrDr 76, –80, –82, –84, –86*

Ireland, Ann 1954- *WhoCanL 85*

Ireland, David 1927- *ConAu 25R, ConNov 76, –82, –86, IntAu&W 77, OxAusL, WrDr 76, –80, –82, –84, –86*

Ireson, Barbara 1927- *Au&Wr 71, ChhPo, –S1, –S3, ConAu 5R, –21NR, ScF&FL 1, –2*

Irvine, Lucy 1956- *ConAu 118*

Irving, Clifford 1930- *Au&Wr 71, AuNews 1, BioIn 9, –10, –11, BioNews 74, ConAu 1R, –2NR, DrInf[port], NewYTBE 72, WrDr 76, –80, –82, –84, –86*

Irving, Washington 1783-1859 *Alli, AmAu, AmAu&B, AmBi, AmWr, ApCAB, AtlBL, BbD, BiAUS, BiD&SB, BioIn 1, –2, –3, –4, –5, –6, –7, –8, –9, –10, –11, –12, –13, CarSB, CasWL, CelCen, Chambr 3, ChhPo, –S2, –S3, CnDAL, CrtT 3, –4, CyAL 1, CyWA, DcAmAu, DcAmB, DcAmDH, DcBiA, DcBiPP, DcEnA, DcEnL, DcLB 3, –11[port], –30[port], –59[port], DcLEL, DcNAA, DcSpL, Dis&D, Drake, EncAAH, EncAB-H, EncFWF, EvLB, FamAYP, HalFC 84, HarEnUS[port], LinLib L, –S, McGEWB, MemAm, MouLC 3, NatCAB 3, NewEOp 71, NewYHSD, NinCLC 2[port], NotNAT B, Novels[port], OxAmH, OxAmL, –83, OxAmT 84, OxCan, OxChL, OxEng, –85, OxSpan, OxThe, –83, PenC AM, PlP&P, RAdv 1, REn, REnAL, REnAW, ScF&FL 1, SupFW, TwCBDA, WebAB, –79, WebE&AL, WhDW, WhAm HS, WhoChL, WhoHr&F, WisWr, WorAl, YABC 2*

Irwin, Constance Frick 1913- *BioIn 10, ConAu 1R, –5NR, ForWC 70, IndAu 1917, IntAu&W 77, –82, SmATA 6, WhoAmW 58, –61, –64, –68, –83, WhoLibS 66, WrDr 76, –80, –82, –84*

Irwin, Constance Frick *see also* Frick, Constance

Irwin, Hadley *ConAu X, SmATA X, –X*

Irwin, Keith Gordon 1885-1964 *BioIn 11, ConAu 5R, SmATA 11*

Irwin, Vera Rushforth 1913- *ConAu 33R, DrAS 74E, –78E, WhoAmW 75, –77*

Isaacs, Neil D 1931- *ConAu 5R, –9NR, ConSFA, DrAS 74E, –78E, –82E, ScF&FL 1, –2*

Isaacson, Walter 1952- *ConAu 112*

Isenberg, Irwin M 1931-1979 *ConAu 11NR, –17R*

Isherwood, Christopher *DrAP&F 85*

Isherwood, Christopher 1904- *AmAu&B, Au&Wr 71, BioIn 1, –2, –3, –4, –7, –8, –9, –10, –11, –12, –13, BlueB 76, BritW 7, CasWL, CelR, CmCal, CnMD, CnMWL, ConAu 13R, ConDr 73, –77, –82, ConLC 1, –9, –11, –14, ConNov 72, –76, –82, CurBio 72, DcLB 15[port], DcLEL, EncWL, –2, EncWT, EvLB, HalFC 84, IntAu&W 77, IntWW 74, –75, –76, –77, –78, –79, –80, –81, –82, –83, IntWWP 77, LinLib L, LongCTC, MakMC, McGEWD, –84, ModBrL, –S2, –S1, ModWD, NewC, NewYTBE 72, –73, NewYTBS 79, Novels[port], OxAmL, –83, OxEng, PenC ENG, PlP&P, RAdv 1, REn, REnAL, TwCA, –SUP, TwCWr, WebE&AL, WhDW, WhE&EA, WhThe, Who 74, –82, –83, –85, WhoAm 74, –76, –78, –80, –82, –84, WhoTwCL, WhoWor 74, –76, –78, WorAl, WrDr 76, –80, –82, –84, –86*

Isherwood, Christopher 1904-1986 *ConAu 117, ConLC 44[port], CurBio 86N, DcLB Y86N[port], NewYTBS 86[port]*

Ishigo, Estelle 1899- *ConAu 61*

Ish-Kishor, Judith 1892-1972 *BioIn 11, ConAu 1R, –103, SmATA 11, WhoAmW 66*

Ish-Kishor, Sulamith 1896-1977 *FifBJA[port]*

Ish-Kishor, Sulamith 1897?-1977 *BioIn 8, –11, –12, ConAu 69, –73, NewYTBS 77, ScF&FL 1, SmATA 17, TwCCW 78, –83*

Ishmole, Jack 1924- *ConAu 49*

Iskander, Fazil 1929- *ConAu 102, IntWW 79, –80, –81, –82, –83, WhoSocC 78*

Israel, Fred L 1934- *ConAu 12NR*

Issawi, Charles 1916- *AmEA 74, AmM&WS 73S, –78S, Au&Wr 71, ConAu 4NR, –5R, IntAu&W 76, MidE 78, –79, –80, –81, –82, WhoAm 74, –76, –78, –80, –82, WhoArab 81, WhoE 74, –83, WhoWor 80*

Issawi, Charles Philip 1916- *ConAu 20NR, WhoAm 84, –86*

Issler, Anne Roller 1892- *ConAu 49, IndAu 1917, IntAu&W 76, WrDr 76*

Iverson, Lucille K 1925- *ConAu 61*

Izenberg, Jerry *AuBYP SUP*

J

Jablonski, Edward 1922- *AuBYP,*
ConAu 1R, –2NR, –18NR,
WhoAm 78, –80, –82, –84, –86,
WhoE 75, –77
Jacker, Corinne 1933- *AuBYP,*
ConAu 17R, ForWC 70,
NatPD, –81[port], WhoAm 80, –82,
WhoAmW 74, –68, –70, –72, –75,
–79, –81, –83, WhoThe 81, WrDr 76,
–80, –82, –84, –86
Jacks, Oliver *ConAu 69, –X,*
IntAu&W 77X, –82X, –86X,
TwCCr&M 80, –85, WhoSpyF,
WrDr 82, –84, –86
Jackson, Anne *WhoAm 84, –86*
Jackson, Anne 1924?- *BiE&WWA,*
BioIn 6, –8, –12, ConAu X,
CurBio 80[port], FilmgC, InWom,
MotPP, MovMk, NotNAT,
WhoAm 80, –82, WhoAmW 72, –75,
WhoHol A, WhoThe 72, –77, –81,
WorAl
Jackson, Anne 1925- *HalFC 84*
Jackson, Anne 1926- *ConTFT 1[port],*
HerW 84, IntMPA 86, OxAmT 84
Jackson, Basil 1920- *ConAu 8NR, –57*
Jackson, C Paul 1902 *AuBYP,*
ConAu 5R, –6NR, MichAu 80,
SmATA 6
Jackson, C Paul *see also* Jackson, O B
Jackson, C Paul *see also* Paulson, Jack
Jackson, Caary Paul 1902- *AuBYP,*
BioIn 7, –10, ConAu 5R, –X,
SmATA 6
Jackson, Donald Dale 1935-
ConAu 1NR, –19NR, –49, WhoE 77
Jackson, Helen Hunt 1830?-1885
Alli SUP, AmAu, AmAu&B, AmBi,
AmWom, AmWomWr, ApCAB, BbD,
BiD&SB, BioIn 1, –2, –8, –10, –11,
–12, CarSB, CasWL, ChhPo, –S1,
–S2, CmCal, CnDAL, DcAmAu,
DcAmB, DcAmSR, DcBiA,
DcLB 42[port], –47[port], DcLEL,
DcNAA, EncAAH, EncAB-H,
EncFWF, EvLB, HarEnUS, InWom,
IntDcWB, JBA 34, LibW, LinLib L,
–S, McGEWB, MouLC 4, NatCAB 1,
NotAW, OxAmH, OxAmL, –83,
OxChL, REn, REnAL, REnAW,
Str&VC, TwCBDA, WebAB, –79,
WhAm HS, WorAl
Jackson, Jacqueline 1928-
AuBYP SUP, BioIn 12, ConAu 45,
DrAS 74E, –78E, –82E, FourBJA,
WhoAm 74, –76, –78, –80, –82
Jackson, Jesse 1908- *SelBAAf*
Jackson, Jesse 1908-1983 *AuBYP,*
BioIn 8, –9, –11, –13, BlkAWP,
ConAu 109, –25R, ConLC 12,
InB&W 80, LinLib L, LivgBAA,
OhA&B, SelBAAu, SmATA 2,
–29[port], –48N, TwCCW 78, –83,
WrDr 80, –82, –84

Jackson, Joe *WhsNW 85, WhoAm 84,*
–86
Jackson, Joe 1954?- *BioIn 13*
Jackson, Joe 1955- *NewRR 83,*
RolSEnR 83, WhoRocM 82
Jackson, Joseph Henry 1894-1955
AmAu&B, BioIn 3, –4, CmCal,
DcAmB S5, REnAL, TwCA, –SUP,
WhAm 2, –3, WhNAA
Jackson, Livia E Bitton *BioIn 12*
Jackson, Livia Elvira Bitton
DrAS 78H
Jackson, Mahalia 1911-1972 *Baker 78,*
–84, BiDAfM, BiDAmM, BiDJaz,
BioIn 3, –4, –5, –6, –7, –8, –9, –10,
–11, –12, –13, CmpEPM,
ConAu 33R, CurBio 57, –72, –72N,
DrBlPA, EncJzS, GoodHs,
HerW, –84, InB&W 80, –85, InWom,
IntDcWB, LibW, LinLib S,
NegAl 76[port], –83, NewYTBE 72,
NotAW MOD, ObitOF 79,
ObitT 1971, RolSEnR 83,
WebAB, –79, WhAm 5, WhScrn 77,
–83, WhoAmW 58, –64, –66, –68,
–70, –72, WhoHol B, WorAl
Jackson, O B 1902 *AuBYP, BioIn 8,*
–10, ConAu X, SmATA 6
Jackson, O B *see also* Jackson, C Paul
Jackson, Robert 1911- *Au&Wr 71,*
ConAu 9R
Jackson, Robert Blake 1926- *AuBYP,*
BioIn 7, –11, ConAu 5R, SmATA 8,
WhoLibS 55, –66
Jackson, Shirley 1916-1965
OxAmL 83
Jackson, Shirley 1919-1965 *AmAu&B,*
AmNov, AmWomWr, BioIn 1, –2, –3,
–4, –6, –7, –8, –9, –10, –12,
ConAu 1R, –4NR, –25R, ConLC 11,
ConNov 76, –82A, DcAmB S7,
DcLB 6[port], DcLEL 1940, EncSF,
InWom, LongCTC, ModAL,
NewCon[port], Novels, ObitOF 79,
OxAmL, PenC AM, RAdv 1, REn,
REnAL, ScF&FL 1, –2, ScFSB,
SmATA 2, SupFW, TwCA SUP,
TwCCr&M 80, WhAm 4,
WhoAmW 58, –64, –66, WhoHr&F,
WorAl
Jacob, Piers Anthony 1934- *BioIn 12,*
ConAu 21R, ScF&FL 1, WhoAm 82,
WrDr 76, –80
Jacob, Piers Anthony Dillingham
1934- *BioIn 13, WhoAm 84, –86*
Jacob, Piers Anthony *see also* Anthony,
Piers
Jacobs, David Michael 1942-
ConAu 57
Jacobs, Francine 1935- *ConAu 1NR,*
–18NR, –49, SmATA 42, –43[port]
Jacobs, Frank 1929- *AuBYP, BioIn 8,*
ConAu 6NR, –13R, SmATA 30[port],
WrDr 76, –80, –82, –84

Jacobs, Helen Hull 1908- *AmAu&B,*
Au&Wr 71, AuBYP, BioIn 1, –7, –8,
–9, –11, –12, CmCal, ConAu 9R,
GoodHs, InWom, IntAu&W 76, –77,
–82, SmATA 12, WhE&EA,
WhoAm 74, –76, –78, –80, –82, –84,
–86, WhoAmW 74, –58, –64, –66,
–68, –70, –72, WorAl, WrDr 76, –80,
–82, –84, –86
Jacobs, Jane 1916- *AmAu&B,*
AmWomWr, BioIn 6, –8, –10, –11,
–12, ConAu 15NR, –21R, CurBio 77,
DcLEL 1940, PolProf K, WhoAm 74,
–76, –78, –80, –82, –84, –86,
WhoAmW 74, –66, –68, –70, –72,
–79, –87, WhoWor 74, –76,
WorAu 1975[port], WrDr 86
Jacobs, Jim 1942- *ConAu 97,*
ConDr 77D, –82D, ConLC 12,
ConTFT 1, NatPD, –81[port],
WhoAm 76, –78, –80, –82, –84, –86,
WhoMW 74, –76
Jacobs, John Kedzie 1918-
ConAu 21R, WhoAm 74, –76,
WhoS&SW 73
Jacobs, Karen Folger 1940-
AmM&WS 78S
Jacobs, Lewis 1906- *ConAu 77,*
OxFilm
Jacobs, Linda C 1943- *BioIn 12,*
ConAu 29R, SmATA 21[port]
Jacobs, Lou, Jr. 1921- *AuBYP SUP,*
BioIn 9, –11, ConAu 9NR, –21R,
IntAu&W 76, –77, SmATA 2,
WhoWest 74, –76, –78
Jacobs, Paul 1918-1978 *AmAu&B,*
BioIn 7, –9, –10, –11, BioNews 74,
ConAu 13R, –73, IntAu&W 76,
NewYTBS 74, –78, ObitOF 79,
WhAm 7, WhoAm 74, –76, –78,
WhoWest 74, –76, –78, WhoWor 74
Jacobs, Susan 1940- *ConAu X,*
SmATA 30
Jacobs, W W 1863-1943 *HalFC 84,*
Novels, ObitOF 79, OxEng 85,
SupFW, TwCLC 22[port], WhoHr&F
Jacobs, William Jay 1933- *BioIn 13,*
ConAu 7NR, –57, LEduc 74,
SmATA 28[port]
Jacobson, Dan 1929- *AfSS 78, –79,*
–80, –81, –82, Au&Wr 71, BioIn 10,
–13, CasWL, ConAu 1R, –2NR,
ConLC 4, –14, ConNov 72, –76, –82,
–86, DcLB 14[port], DcLEL 1940,
IntAu&W 76, –77, –82, –86,
IntWW 77, –78, –79, –80, –81, –82,
–83, ModBrL S1, ModCmwL, NewC,
Novels, PenC ENG, ScF&FL 1, –2,
TwCWr, WebE&AL, WhoAm 74,
–76, –78, –80, –82, –84, –86,
WhoWor 74, –78, –84, –87, WorAu,
WrDr 76, –80, –82, –84, –86

Jacobson, Daniel 1923-
AmM&WS 73S, –76P, AuBYP SUP,
BioIn 11, ConAu 53, MichAu 80,
SmATA 12, WhoMW 78
Jacobson, Michael F 1943-
AmM&WS 86P, ConAu 13NR
Jacobson, Michael Faraday 1943-
WhoAm 86
Jacobson, Michael Farraday 1943-
WhoAm 84
Jacobson, Morris K 1906- *BioIn 12,*
ConAu 3NR, –45, IntAu&W 77,
SmATA 21[port]
Jacoby, Susan *ConAu 108*
Jaffe, Bernard 1896- *ConAu 5R,*
REnAL, WhoWorJ 72
Jaffe, Leonard 1926- *WhoGov 72, –75,*
WhoWorJ 72, –78
Jaffe, Rona *WrDr 86*
Jaffe, Rona 1932?- *AmAu&B,*
AuNews 1, BioIn 5, –9, –10, –12,
BioNews 75, ConAu 73, InWom,
NewYTBS 79, Novels, WhoAm 80,
–82, –84, –86, WhoAmW 81, –83,
–85, –87, WhoWorJ 72, WrDr 76,
–80, –82, –84
Jaffee, Al 1921- *ConAu 116,*
SmATA 37
Jagendorf, Moritz 1888-1981
AnObit 1981, AnCL, AuBYP, BioIn 3,
–6, –8, –9, –12, ConAu 5R, –102,
CurBio 52, IntAu&W 77, –82,
MorJA, NewYTBS 81, SmATA 2,
–24N, WhNAA, WhoAm 78, –80,
WrDr 76, –80, –82
Jagger, Mick 1939?- *BioIn 7, –8, –9,*
–10, –11, –12, BioNews 75, BlueB 76,
CelR, ConLC 17, CurBio 72, FilmgC,
HalFC 84, IntMPA 84, IntWW 77,
–78, –79, –80, –81, –82, –83,
NewYTBS 83[port], WhoAm 74, –76,
–78, –80, –82, WhoHol A,
WhoRocM 82, WorAl
Jagger, Mick 1943- *BioIn 13,*
IntMPA 86, WhoAm 84, –86,
WhoWor 84, –87
Jagger, Mick 1944- *Baker 84*
Jagger, Mick *see also* Rolling Stones,
The
Jahn, Mike 1943?- *BioIn 8, –13,*
ConAu 49, –X, SmATA X
Jakes, John 1932- *AuBYP SUP,*
BioIn 11, ConAu 10NR, –57,
ConLC 29[port], ConSFA,
DcLB Y83B[port], EncSF,
IntAu&W 82, OxCan SUP,
ScF&FL 1, –2, ScFSB[port],
TwCSFW 86, WhoAm 78, –80, –82,
WhoHr&F, WrDr 82, –84, –86
Jakes, John William 1932-
WhoAm 84, –86
James, Bessie Rowland 1895-1974
AmAu&B, BioIn 10, ConAu 107,
WhNAA

James, Edward T 1917- *ConAu 33R, DrAS 74H, –78H, –82H*
James, Henry 1843-1916 *Alli SUP, AmAu, AmAu&B, AmBi, AmWr, ApCAB, AtlBL, BbD, BiD&SB, BioIn 1, –2, –3, –4, –5, –6, –7, –8, –9, –10, –11, –12, –13, BritWr 6, CasWL, CelCen, CnDAL, CnMD, CnMWL, CnThe, ConAu 104, CrtT 3, –4, CyWA, DcAmAu, DcAmB, DcBiA, DcEnA, –AP, DcEnL, DcEuL, DcLB 12[port], DcLEL, DcNaB 1912, DcNAA, Dis&D, EncAB-H, EncWL, EncWL, –2[port], EncWT, EvLB, HalFC 84, HarEnUS, LinLib L, –S, LongCEL, LongCTC, McGEWB, McGEWD, –84[port], MemAm, ModAL, –S1, ModBrL, –S2, –S1, ModWD, NatCAB 1, NewC, NewEOp 71, NotNAT B, Novels[port], OxAmH, OxAmL, OxAmT 84, OxEng, –85, OxThe, –83, PenC AM, –ENG, RAdv 1, RComWL, REn, REnAL, REnWD, ScF&FL 1, SupFW, TwCBDA, TwCLC 2, –11[port], –24[port], TwCWr, WebAB, –79, WebE&AL, WhDW, WhAm 1, –4A, –HSA, WhLit, WhoHr&F, WhoTwCL, WorAl*
James, Henry, Jr. 1843-1916 *OxAmL 83*
James, Janet Wilson 1918- *DrAS 74H, –78H, –82H, WhoAmW 74, –58, –61, –64, –66, –68, –70, –72, –75, –77*
James, John *ConAu 45*
James, M R 1862-1936 *HalFC 84, OxEng 85, SupFW*
James, Marquis 1891-1955 *AmAu&B, BioIn 1, –2, –4, –6, DcAmB S5, LinLib L, –S, NatCAB 44, OxAmL, –83, REnAL, TwCA, –SUP, WhAm 3, WhE&EA, WhNAA*
James, Michael 1922?-1981 *BioIn 12, ConAu 104, NewYTBS 81*
James, Naomi 1949- *BioIn 12, ConAu 102, Who 82, –83, –85*
James, P D *ConAu X*
James, P D 1920- *ASpks, BioIn 10, –11, –12, –13, ConAu 21R, ConLC 18, ConNov 86, CurBio 80[port], EncMys, NewYTBS 80[port], Novels, ThrtnMM, TwCCr&M 80, –85, WhoAm 84, –86, WorAl, WorAu 1975[port], WrDr 80, –82*
James, Rick *WhoBlA 85*
James, Rick 1952- *BioIn 12, –13, InB&W 85, NewRR 83, RolSEnR 83*
James, Will *EncFWF, OxChL*
James, Will 1892-1942 *ArtsAmW 1, AuBYP, BioIn 1, –2, –3, –4, –7, –8, –12, –13, CurBio 42, DcAmB S3, DcNAA, IlBEAAW, JBA 34, –51, LinLib L, NatCAB 35, Newb 1922, OxAmL, –83, REnAL, REnAW, SmATA 19, TwCA, –SUP, TwCCW 78, –83, WhAm 2, WhNAA*
Janes, Edward C 1908- *AuBYP, BioIn 8, –13, ConAu 93, SmATA 25[port]*
Janeway, Elizabeth *DrAP&F 85*
Janeway, Elizabeth 1913- *AmAu&B, AmNov, AmWomWr, Au&Wr 71, AuBYP, AuNews 1, BioIn 2, –3, –4, –8, –9, –10, –12, ChhPo, ConAu 2NR, –45, CurBio 44, DcLEL 1940, InWom, IntAu&W 76, IntWW 80, –81, –82, –83, NewYTBS 72, REnAL, SmATA 19, TwCA SUP, WhoAm 74, –76, –78, –80, –82, WhoAmW 74, –58, –64, –66, –68, –70, –72, –75, –77, –79, –81, –83, –85, –87, WhoE 74, WhoWor 74, –76, –78*
Janovy, John, Jr. 1937- *AmM&WS 82P, –86P, BioIn 12, ConAu 19NR, –97*
Janowitz, Tama *DrAP&F 85*
Janowitz, Tama 1957- *BioIn 12, ConAu 106, ConLC 43[port]*
Janson, Dora Jane 1916- *AuBYP, BioIn 8, ConAu 106, SmATA 31[port]*
Janson, H W 1913-1982 *ConAu 4NR, –107, NewYTBS 82[port]*

Janson, Horst Woldemar 1913- *AuBYP, BioIn 8, –10, –11, ConAu 1R, DrAS 74H, –78H, –82H, SmATA 9, WhoAm 74, –76, –78, –80, WhoAmA 73, –76, –78, –80, –82, WhoArt 80, –82, –84, WhoWor 74, –76, WrDr 76, –80, –82*
Janson, Horst Woldemar 1913-1982 *BioIn 13, WhAm 8, WhoAmA 84N*
Jansson, Tove *OxChL*
Jansson, Tove 1914- *Au&Wr 71, BioIn 6, –8, –9, –12, ChlLR 2, ConAu 17R, ConFLW 84, EncWL 2, IlsCB 1957, –1967, IntAu&W 76, –77, –82, SmATA 3, –41[port], ThrBJA, TwCCW 78B, –83B, WhoChL, WhoWor 78, –80, –82, –84, WorECom*
Jantzen, Steven L 1941- *ConAu 77*
Jardine, Alan 1942- *BioIn 11, –12*
Jardine, Alan *see also* Beach Boys, The
Jares, Joe 1937- *ConAu 12NR, –33R, WrDr 76, –80, –82, –84, –86*
Jarman, Thomas Leckie 1907- *Au&Wr 71, ConAu 4NR, –5R, IntAu&W 76, –77, –82, WhE&EA, WrDr 76, –80, –82, –84, –86*
Jarrell, Randall d1965 *WhoAmA 84N*
Jarrell, Randall 1914-1965 *AmAu&B, AmWr, AnCL, AuBYP, BioIn 3, –4, –5, –7, –8, –9, –10, –11, –12, –13, CasWL, ChlLR 6[port], ChhPo, –S1, –S3, CnDAL, CnE&AP, ConAu 5R, –6NR, –25R, ConAu 2BS, ConLC 1, –2, –6, –9, –13, ConLCrt, –82, ConPo 75, –80A, –85A, CroCAP, DcAmB S7, DcLB 48[port], –52[port], DcLEL 1940, EncWL, –2, LinLib L, ModAL, –S2, –S1, NewCon[port], Novels, ObitOF 79, OxAmL, –83, OxChL, OxEng 85, PenC AM, RAdv 1, REn, REnAL, ScF&FL 1, –2, SixAP, SmATA 7, ThrBJA, TwCA SUP, TwCCW 78, –83, TwCWr, WebAB, –79, WebE&AL, WhAm 4, WhoAmA 78N, –80N, –82N, WhoTwCL, WorAl*
Jaspersohn, William 1947- *ConAu 102*
Jastrow, Robert 1925- *AmM&WS 73P, –76P, –79P, –82P, –86P, BioIn 9, –10, –13, BlueB 76, ConAu 18NR, –21R, CurBio 73, IntAu&W 77, –82, IntWW 74, –75, –76, –77, –78, –79N, –80, –81, –82, –83, WhoAm 74, –76, –78, –80, –82, –84, –86, WhoFrS 74, WhoGov 77, –72, –75, WhoWor 74, WorAu 1975[port], WrDr 76, –80, –82, –84, –86*
Jauss, Anne Marie 1907- *AuBYP, BioIn 5, –8, –10, –11, ConAu 1R, –4NR, ForWC 70, FourBJA, IlsCB 1946, –1957, –1967, SmATA 10, WhoAmA 73, –76, –78, –80, –82, –84, WhoAmW 58, WrDr 76, –80, –82, –84, –86*
Jaworski, Irene D *AuBYP, BioIn 8*
Jay, Ruth I Johnson 1920- *ConAu X*
Jayne, Caroline Furness 1873-1909 *WhAm 1*
Jayne, Mitchell F *ScF&FL 1*
Jeffers, Harry Paul 1934- *AuBYP*
Jefferson Airplane *BiDAmM, BiDJaz A, CelR, EncPR&S 74, –77, IlEncRk, MugS, RkOn 78, –84, RkOneH, RolSEnR 83, WhoRock 81, WhoRocM 82*
Jefferson Starship *RkOn 78, RolSEnR 83, WhoRock 81[port], WhoRocM 82*
Jefferson Starship *see also* Jefferson Airplane&7E
Jefferson Airplane *see also* Balin, Marty
Jefferson Airplane *see also* Casady, Jack
Jefferson Airplane *see also* Dryden, Spencer
Jefferson Airplane *see also* Kaukomen, Jorma
Jefferson Airplane *see also* Slick, Grace
Jeffery, Gordon 1918- *Au&Wr 71*
Jeffreys-Jones, Rhodri 1942- *ConAu 13NR, –77*

Jeffries, Roderic 1926- *Au&Wr 71, AuBYP, BioIn 8, –9, ConAu 9NR, –17R, EncMys, SmATA 4, TwCCr&M 80, –85, WrDr 82, –84, –86*
Jeffries, Roderic *see also* Ashford, Jeffrey
Jencks, Charles 1939- *WrDr 86*
Jenkins, Alan C 1912?- *Au&Wr 71, IntAu&W 76, –77, –82, MnBBF*
Jenkins, Elizabeth *Who 85, WrDr 86*
Jenkins, Elizabeth 1905?- *BioIn 5, –10, ConAu 13NR, –73, DcLEL, InWom, IntWW 80, –81, –82, –83, Who 82, –83, WorAu, WrDr 82, –84*
Jenkins, Geoffrey 1920- *Au&Wr 71, ConAu 16NR, EncSoA, ScF&FL 1, –2*
Jenkins, Jerry B 1949- *ConAu 5NR, –20NR, –49, WhoAm 80, –82*
Jenkins, Marie Magdalen 1909- *AmM&WS 73P, –76P, –79P, –82P, –86P, AuBYP SUP, BioIn 10, ConAu 41R, SmATA 7, WhoAmW 74, –70, –72, –75*
Jenkins, Peter 1951?- *BioIn 13, ConAu 89*
Jenkins, Robin *BioIn 13, Who 85*
Jenkins, Robin 1912- *CasWL, CmScLit, ConAu 1NR, ConNov 72, –76, –82, –86, DcLB 14[port], WorAu, WrDr 76, –80, –82, –84, –86*
Jenner, Bruce 1949- *BioIn 11, –12, –13, ConAu 110, CurBio 77, NewYTBS 76, –77, –78, WhoAm 78, –80, –82, –84, –86, WorAl*
Jenner, Chrystie 1950- *BioIn 11, –12, ConAu 77*
Jenness, Aylette 1934- *ConAu 25R*
Jenness, Diamond *OxCanL*
Jenness, Diamond 1886-1969 *BioIn 5, –6, –9, MacDCB 78, OxCan, WhLit*
Jennings, Gary 1928- *AuBYP, BioIn 8, –11, –12, ConAu 5R, –9NR, IntAu&W 76, –77, –82, SmATA 9*
Jennings, Michael 1931- *ConAu 69, WhoE 79*
Jennings, Michael Glenn 1931- *WhoE 85, WhoWor 84, –87*
Jennings, William Dale 1917- *ConAu 25R, WhoAm 74, –76, –78, –80*
Jennison, Keith Warren 1911- *AmAu&B, AuBYP, BioIn 3, –4, –8, –12, ConAu 73, SmATA 14*
Jensen, Gordon D 1926- *AmM&WS 73P, –76P, –79P, –86P, BiDrAPA 77, ConAu 106*
Jensen, Joan Maria 1934- *DrAS 74H, –78H, –82H*
Jensen, Oliver 1914- *ConAu 25R, DrAS 74H, –78H, –82H, St&PR 75, WhoAm 74, –76, –78, –80, –82, WhoE 74, WhoWor 74, –76*
Jensen, Oliver Ormerod 1914- *WhoAm 84, –86*
Jeppson, Janet O 1926- *BiDrAPA 77, ConAu 19NR, –49, WhoAmW 70, WhoE 81, –83, WrDr 76, –82*
Jerome, Jerome K 1859-1927 *ConAu 119, DcLB 34[port], HalFC 84, OxEng 85, TwCLC 23[port]*
Jerome, Jerome Klapka 1859-1927 *Alli SUP, BbD, BiD&SB, BioIn 2, –5, –10, –12, –13, CasWL, Chambr 3, CyWA, DcBiA, DcEnA AP, DcLB 10[port], DcLEL, DcNaB 1922, EncWT, EvLB, LinLib L, –S, LongCTC, McGEWD, –84[port], MnBBF, ModBrL, ModWD, NewC, NotNAT A, –B, Novels, OxEng, OxThe, –83, PenC ENG, REn, ScF&FL 1, TwCA, TwCWr, WhDW, WhLit, WhThe, WhoBW&I A, WhoStg 1908*
Jerome, John 1932- *ConAu 2NR, –45, IntAu&W 76*
Jerome, Judson *DrAP&F 85*
Jerome, Judson 1927- *BioIn 7, ConAu 4NR, –9R, –22NR, ConPo 70, –75, –80, –85, DrAS 74E, IntAu&W 82, IntWWP 77, WhoS&SW 75, WrDr 76, –80, –82, –84, –86*

Jerome, Judson Blair 1927- *IntAu&W 86*
Jespersen, James 1934- *AmM&WS 79P, –82P, –86P, ConAu 103*
Jessel, Camilla 1937- *BioIn 13, ConAu 104, IntAu&W 77, SmATA 29[port], WhoWor 82*
Jeter, K W 1950- *TwCSFW 86, WrDr 86*
Jeune, Paul 1950- *ConAu 101*
Jewett, Sarah Orne 1849-1909 *Alli SUP, AmAu, AmAu&B, AmBi, AmWom, AmWomWr, AmWr, ApCAB, AtlBL, AuBYP, BbD, BiD&SB, BioIn 1, –2, –3, –4, –5, –6, –7, –8, –9, –11, –12, –13, CarSB, CasWL, Chambr 3, ChhPo, –S1, –S2, CnDAL, ConAu 108, CrtT 3, –4, CyWA, DcAmAu, DcAmB, DcBiA, DcLB 12[port], DcLEL, DcNAA, Dis&D, EncAAH, EvLB, HarEnUS, InWom, IntDcWB, JBA 34, LibW, LinLib L, –S, McGEWB, ModAL, NatCAB 1, NotAW, Novels, OxAmL, –83, OxEng, –85, PenC AM, RAdv 1, REn, REnAL, SmATA 15, TwCBDA, TwCLC 1, –22[port], WebAB, –79, WebE&AL, WhAm 1, WhLit, WomNov, WorAl*
Jhabvala, Ruth Prawer *DrAP&F 85, HalFC 84*
Jhabvala, Ruth Prawer 1927- *Au&Wr 71, BioIn 10, –11, –12, ConAu 1R, –2NR, ConLC 4, –8, –29[port], ConNov 72, –76, –82, –86, ConTFT 1, CurBio 77, DcLEL 1940, EncWL 2, IntAu&W 76, –82, IntWW 77, –78, –79, –80, –81, –82, –83, ModCmwL, NewYTBE 73, NewYTBS 76, –83[port], Novels, OxEng 85, TwCWr, Who 82, –83, –85, WhoWor 87, WorAu, WrDr 76*
Jhabvala, Ruth Prawer 1928- *WhoWor 84*
Jimenez, Juan Ramon 1881-1958 *GrFLW, WhoNob*
Jiminez, Janey 1953- *ConAu 77*
Jinks, William Howard, Jr. 1938- *ConAu 41R*
Joel, Billy *NewYTBS 86[port]*
Joel, Billy 1949- *Baker 84, BioIn 10, –11, –12, –13, BioNews 74, ConAu X, ConLC 26[port], CurBio 79, RkOn 78, –84, RolSEnR 83, WhoAm 80, –82, –84, –86, WhoRock 81[port], WhoRocM 82, WhoWor 80, –82, –87, WorAl*
Joffe, Joyce 1940- *Au&Wr 71, ConAu 77*
Johannesson, Olof 1908- *ConAu X, EncSF, ScF&FL 1, –2, ScFSB*
Johannesson, Olof *see also* Alfven, Hannes Olof Geosta
Johannis, Theodore B, Jr. 1914- *AmM&WS 73S, ConAu 33R*
Johanson, Donald C 1943- *BioIn 12, ConAu 107, ConIsC 1[port], CurBio 84[port], NewYTBS 79, WhoAm 82, WhoMW 76, –78*
Johanson, Donald Carl 1943- *BioIn 13, IntAu&W 86, WhoAm 84, –86*
John, Elton 1947- *Baker 78, –84, BioIn 9, –10, –11, –12, BioNews 74, CelR, CurBio 75, EncPR&S 74, –77, HalFC 84, IlEncRk, IntWW 77, –78, –79, –80, –81, –82, –83, NewYTBE 71, NewYTBS 74, RkOn 78, –84, RkOneH, RolSEnR 83, Who 83, WhoAm 76, –78, –80, –82, –84, –86, WhoHol A, WhoRock 81[port], WhoRocM 82, WhoWor 74, –76, –78, –80, –82, WorAl*
John, Otto 1909- *BioIn 3, –4, –5, –6, –9, EncE 75*
Johnsgard, Paul A 1931- *AmM&WS 73P, –76P, –79P, –82P, ConAu 1NR, –17NR, –49, IntAu&W 77, –82, WhoMW 76, WrDr 76, –80, –82, –84, –86*

EncPR&S 74, −77S, GoodHs,
IlEncRk, IntDcWB, NewYTBE 70,
NotAW MOD, ObitOF 79, RkOn 78,
−84, RkOneH, RolSEnR 83,
WhAm 5, WhScrn 77, −83,
WhoHol B, WhoRock 81,
WhoRocM 82, WorAl
Jordan, Archibald Campbell
1906-1968 *AfrA, PenC CL*
Jordan, Grace Edgington *ConAu 1R,*
ForWC 70, WhoAmW 74, −68, −70,
−72, −75, WhoPNW, WhoS&SW 73
Jordan, Hope D 1905- *BioIn 12,*
ConAu 77, SmATA 15
Jordan, Hope Dahle 1905-
ConAu 13NR
Jordan, June *DrAP&F 85*
Jordan, June 1936- *AuBYP SUP,*
BioIn 9, −12, −13, BlkAWP,
ChlLR 10[port], ChhPo S1, −S2,
ConAu 33R, ConLC 5, −11, −23[port],
ConPo 80, −85, DcLB 38[port],
FourBJA, InB&W 80, −85,
IntAu&W 77, IntWWP 77, −82,
LinLib L, LivgBAA, NegAl 83,
OxChL, SelBAAf, SelBAAu,
SmATA 4, TwCCW 78, −83,
WhoAmW 75, −77, WhoBlA 77, −80,
WorAu 1975[port], WrDr 76, −80,
−82, −84, −86
Jordan, Pat 1941?- *BioIn 9, −10, −12,*
ConAu 33R, ConLC 37[port]
Jordan, Ruth *BioIn 13, WrDr 86*
Jordan, Ruth 1926- *ConAu 7NR, −57,*
IntAu&W 77, −82, WrDr 76, −80,
−82, −84

Jorgenson, Ivar *AuBYP, ConAu X,*
DcLEL 1940, EncSF, ScF&FL 1,
SmATA X, ThrBJA, TwCSFW 86,
WorAu 1970
Jorgenson, Ivar *see also* Silverberg,
Robert
Joseph, Alexander 1907-1976
AmM&WS 73P, −76P, −79P, AuBYP,
BioIn 8, −11, ConAu 120, −13R,
NewYTBS 76
Joseph, James Herz 1924- *ConAu 1R,*
−2NR, IndAu 1917
Joseph, Joan 1937?- *ConAu 25R,*
SmATA 34[port], WhoAmW 74, −75,
−77, −79, −81, WhoE 75
Joseph, Joan 1939- *ConAu 17NR*
Joseph, Joan Judith 1937-
IntAu&W 86
Joseph, Joseph M 1903-1979 *BioIn 13,*
ConAu 5R, SmATA 22[port]
Joseph, Marie *ConAu 109*
Joseph, Stephen M 1938- *ConAu 25R,*
WhoE 75, WrDr 76, −80, −82, −84,
−86
Josephson, Hannah 1900-1976
BioIn 11, ConAu 69, ConAu P-2,
NewYTBS 76, WhoAmW 68
Josephy, Alvin M, Jr. 1915-
ConAu 8NR, −17R, OxCan SUP,
St&PR 75, WhoAm 74, −76, −78, −80,
−82, −84, −86, WhoE 74, WrDr 76,
−80, −82, −84, −86
Joslin, Sesyle 1929- *Au&Wr 71,*
AuBYP, BioIn 8, −9, ConAu X,

Joyce, James Avery 1902- *Au&Wr 71,*
BioIn 5, −11, CurBio 59,
IntAu&W 76, −77, −82, WhoAm 74,
−76, −82, −84, −86, WhoWor 74, −78,
−80, −82, −84
Judd, Denis 1938- *ConAu 13NR,*
−25R, IntAu&W 76, −77, −82,
SmATA 33[port], WhoWor 76,
WrDr 76, −80, −82, −84, −86
Judd, Frances K *ConAu P-2,*
SmATA 1
SmATA 2, ThrBJA, TwCCW 78,
WrDr 80, −82, −84, −86
Joyce, James 1882-1941 *AtlBL,*
AuBYP SUP, BiDIrW, BioIn 1, −2,
−3, −4, −5, −6, −7, −8, −9, −10, −11,
−12, −13, BritWr 7, CasWL,
Chambr 3, ChhPo, −S1, CnMD,
CnMWL, ConAu 104, CurBio 41,
CyWA, DcLB 10[port], −19[port], −36[port],
DcLEL, DcNaB 1941, Dis&D,
EncWL, −2[port], EncWT, EvLB,
LinLib L, −S, LongCEL, LongCTC,
MakMC, McGEWB,
McGEWD, −84[port], ModBrL, −S2,
−S1, ModWD, NewC, NewOxM,
NotNAT B, Novels[port], ObitOF 79,
OxEng, −85, OxThe 83, PenC ENG,
PoIre, RAdv 1, RComWL, REn,
TwCA, −SUP, TwCLC 3, −8[port],
−16[port], TwCWr, WebE&AL,
WhDW, WhE&EA, WhoHol A,
WhoTwCL, WorAl

Judson, Clara 1879-1960 *AmAu&B,*
Au&ICB, AuBYP, BioIn 1, −2, −3,
−5, −7, −13, CarSB, CurBio 48,
InWom, IndAu 1816, JBA 51,
LinLib L, OxCan, SmATA 27,
WhAm 4, WhE&EA, WhJnl, WhLit,
WhNAA, WhoAmW 58
Judson, Clara Ingram 1879-1960
SmATA 38[port]
Judson, Harry Pratt 1849-1927
Alli SUP, AmAu&B, BiDAmEd,
BiD&SB, DcAmB, DcNAA,
HarEnUS, LinLib L, NatCAB 11,
−20, TwCBDA, WhAm 1
Judson, William *ConAu X*
Judson, William *see also* Corley, Edwin
Judy, Stephen N *ConAu X*
Judy, Stephen N 1942- *ConAu 89,*
DrAS 82E
Judy, Susan J 1944- *ConAu 107*
Jungk, Robert 1913- *Au&Wr 71,*
BioIn 3, ConAu 85, Future,
IntAu&W 76, WhoWor 74
Jurgensen, Barbara 1928- *ConAu 17R,*
ForWC 70, IntAu&W 77, −82,
WhoAmW 75, WrDr 76, −80, −82,
−84
Just, Ward *DrAP&F 85*
Just, Ward 1935- *ConAu 25R,*
ConLC 4, −27[port], WhoAm 74, −76,
−78, −80, −82
Just, Ward Swift 1935- *WhoAm 84,*
−86

K

Kadesch, Robert R 1922-
*AmM&WS 73P, –76P, –79P, –82P,
–86P, AuBYP SUP, ConAu 57,
SmATA 31, WhoAm 74, –76, –78,
–80, WhoTech 82, –84*

Kael, Pauline 1919- *AmAu&B,
AmWomWr, Au&Wr 71, BioIn 7, –8,
–9, –10, –12, –13, BlueB 76, CelR,
CmCal, ConAu 6NR, –45,
ConTFT 3[port], CurBio 74, EncAJ,
EncTwCJ, ForWC 70, IntAu&W 76,
–77, –82, IntMPA 77, –75, –76, –78,
–79, –81, –82, –84, –86, LibW,
OxAmL 83, OxFilm, WhoAm 74,
–76, –78, –80, –82, –84, –86,
WhoAmW 74, –68A, –70, –72, –75,
–77, –81, –83, –85, –87, WhoE 85,
WomWMM, WorAu 1970, WrDr 76,
–80, –82, –84, –86*

Kafka, Franz 1883-1924 *AtlBL,
BioIn 1, –2, –3, –4, –5, –6, –7, –8, –9,
–10, –11, –12, –13, CasWL,
CIDMEL, CnMD, CnMWL,
ConAu 105, CyWA, Dis&D, EncSF,
EncWL, –2[port], EncWT, EvEuW,
GrFLW, HalFC 84, LinLib L, –S,
LongCTC, MakMC, McGEWB,
ModGL, NewEOp 71, Novels[port],
OxEng, –85, OxGer, PenC EUR,
RComWL, REn, ScF&FL 1, ScFSB,
TwCA, –SUP, TwCLC 2, –6[port],
–13[port], TwCWr, WhDW,
WhoHr&F, WhoTwCL, WorAl*

Kagan, Norman 1931- *AmM&WS 73S,
LEduc 74*

Kahn, Albert E 1912?-1979 *BioIn 12,
ConAu 118, –89, NewYTBS 79,
WhoWest 78*

Kahn, E J, Jr. 1916- *AmArch 70,
ConAu 65, WhoWorJ 72, –78*

Kahn, Ely Jacques, Jr. 1916-
*AmAu&B, Au&Wr 71, BioIn 2, –4,
–11, TwCA SUP, WhoAm 74, –76,
–78, –80, –82, –84, –86, WhoAmJ 80,
WhoE 74*

Kahn, James 1947- *ConAu 109,
TwCSFW 86, WrDr 86*

Kahn, James 1948?- *BioIn 13*

Kahn, Joan 1914- *AuBYP SUP,
BioIn 3, –8, ConAu 77, ScF&FL 1,
SmATA 48[port], WhoAm 84,
WhoAmW 58, –68*

Kahn, Kathy 1945- *BioIn 10,
ConAu 41R, WhoAm 76,
WhoAmW 87*

Kahn, Margaret 1949- *ConAu 101*

Kahn, Roger 1927- *AuBYP, BioIn 4,
–8, –9, –10, –11, –12, –13,
ConAu 25R, ConLC 30[port], Conv 3,
SmATA 37, WhoAm 84, –86,
WhoE 74*

Kain, John F 1935- *AmEA 74,
AmM&WS 73S, –78S, ConAu 29R,
IndAu 1917, IntAu&W 77,*

*WhoAm 74, –76, –78, –80, –82,
WhoE 74, WhoEc 81, –86, WrDr 76,
–80, –82, –84, –86*

Kain, John Forrest 1935- *WhoAm 84*

Kains, Maurice Grenville 1868-1946
*BioIn 1, –2, ChhPo, DcNAA,
NatCAB 36, ObitOF 79, WhAm 2,
WhLit, WhNAA*

Kaiser, Robert Greeley 1943-
*ConAu 65, EncTwCJ, WhoAm 76,
–78, –80, –82, –84, –86*

Kaku, Michio 1947- *AmM&WS 86P,
WhoTech 84*

Kalb, Bernard 1922- *BioIn 13,
NewYTBS 86*

Kalb, Bernard 1932?- *ASpks, BioIn 12,
ConAu 109, LesBEnT*

Kalb, Jonah 1926- *AuBYP SUP,
BioIn 13, ConAu 4NR, –53,
SmATA 23*

Kalb, Marvin *IntMPA 86*

Kalb, Marvin 1930- *AmAu&B, ASpks,
BioIn 13, ConAu 5R, EncTwCJ,
IntMPA 77, –75, –76, –78, –79, –81,
–82, –84, LesBEnT, WhoAm 74, –76,
–78, –82, WhoS&SW 73, WhoWor 74*

Kalb, Marvin Leonard 1930-
WhoAm 84

Kalb, S William 1897- *ConAu 33R,
WhoWorJ 72, –78*

Kallen, Lucille *ConAu 97,
TwCCr&M 85, WomWMM, WrDr 86*

Kals, W S 1910- *ConAu 45*

Kalter, Joanmarie 1951- *ConAu 102*

Kaminsky, Stuart M 1934- *ConAu 73,
DrAS 78E, –82E, TwCCr&M 85*

Kamm, Josephine 1905?- *Au&Wr 71,
BioIn 13, ConAu 5NR, –9R,
IntAu&W 76, –77, –82, OxChL,
SmATA 24[port], TwCCW 78, –83,
WhE&EA, WhoWor 80, WrDr 76,
–80, –82, –84*

Kamm, Josephine 1906- *WrDr 86*

Kammen, Michael 1936- *WhoAm 86,
WrDr 86*

Kane, Robert S 1925- *ConAu 7NR,
–9R*

Kanin, Garson 1912- *AmAu&B,
AmSCAP 66, AuNews 1, BiDFilm,
BiE&WWA, BioIn 1, –3, –8, –9, –10,
–11, –12, BioNews 75, BlueB 76,
CelR, CmMov, CnMD, CnThe,
ConAu 5R, –7NR, ConDr 73, –77,
–82, ConLC 22[port],
ConTFT 2[port], CurBio 41, –52,
DcFM, DcLB 7[port], EncWT,
FilmgC, HalFC 84, IntAu&W 76,
–77, –82, IntMPA 77, –75, –76, –78,
–79, –81, –82, –84, –86, IntWW 82,
–83, McGEWD 84, ModWD, MovMk,
NatPD, –81[port], NewYTBS 80[port],
NotNAT, –A, OxAmL, –83,
OxAmT 84, OxFilm, PenC AM,
REnAL, WhoAm 74, –76, –78, –80,*

*–82, –84, –86, WhoThe 72, –77, –81,
WhoWor 74, WorAl, WorAu,
WorEFlm, WrDr 76, –80, –82, –84,
–86*

Kantner, Paul 1941?- *BioIn 9, –12,
WhoAm 80, –82, –84, –86*

Kantner, Paul 1942- *Baker 84*

Kantner, Paul *see also* Jefferson
Airplane

Kantor, MacKinlay 1904-1977
*AmAu&B, AmNov, ASpks, AuBYP,
BioIn 1, –2, –3, –4, –7, –8, –9, –10,
–11, –12, ChhPo SI, CnDAL,
ConAmA, ConAu 61, –73, ConLC 7,
ConNov 72, –76, ConSFA,
DcLB 9[port], DcLEL, EncFWF,
EncMys, EncSF, FilmgC, HalFC 84,
IntAu&W 76, –77, LinLib L, –S,
ModAL, NewYTBS 77, Novels,
ObitOF 79, OxAmL, –83, PenC AM,
REn, REnAL, ScF&FL 1, –2, ScFSB,
TwCA, –SUP, TwCWr, WhAm 7,
WhScrn 83, WhoAm 74, –76, –78,
WrDr 76*

Kaplan, Albert A *AuBYP, BioIn 8*

Kaplan, Anne Bernays 1930-
ConAu 1R, –5NR, SmATA 32[port]

Kaplan, Anne Bernays *see also* Bernays,
Anne

Kaplan, Helen Singer 1929-
*AmM&WS 73P, –76P, –79P, –82P,
–86P, AuNews 1, BiDrAPA 77,
BioIn 10, –12, ConAu 102,
WhoAm 78, –80, –82, –84,
WhoAmJ 80, WhoAmW 74, –68, –70,
–72, –75, –77, –81, –83*

Kaplan, Janice Ellen 1955- *ConAu 117,
WhoAmW 79, –81*

Kaplan, Justin 1925- *AmAu&B,
Au&Wr 71, AuNews 1, BioIn 10, –12,
–13, BioNews 74, ConAu 8NR, –17R,
DrAS 74E, –78E, –82E,
IntAu&W 76, OxAmL 83,
WhoAm 74, –76, –78, –80, –82, –84,
–86, WhoAmJ 80, WhoE 74,
WorAu 1970, WrDr 76, –80, –82,
–84, –86*

Kaplan, Philip 1916- *ConAu 13R,
St&PR 75*

Kaplan, Richard 1929- *ConAu 73,
WhoAm 74, –76, –86*

Kapp, Colin 1928?- *ConSFA, EncSF,
ScF&FL 1, ScFSB, TwCSFW 86,
WhoSciF, WrDr 84, –86*

Kardish, Laurence 1945- *CanWW 70,
–79, –80, –81, –83, ConAu 49*

Karen, Ruth 1922- *AuBYP, BioIn 8,
–11, ConAu 11NR, –17R, SmATA 9,
WhoAmW 74, –75, –83, –85, –87,
WrDr 76, –80, –82, –84, –86*

Kark, Nina Mary *BioIn 13, Who 85*

Kark, Nina Mary 1925- *AuBYP SUP,
BioIn 9, –10, –11, ConAu 8NR,
–17R, SmATA 4, Who 74, –82, –83,
WhoAmW 74, –75*

Kark, Nina Mary *see also* Bawden,
Nina

Karl, Frederick R 1927- *Au&Wr 71,
BioIn 11, ConAu 3NR, –5R,
DrAS 74E, –78E, –82E*

Karl, Frederick Robert 1927- *WrDr 86*

Karl, Jean E 1927- *AuBYP SUP,
BioIn 11, ChhPo SI, ConAu 12NR,
–29R, FifBJA, ForWC 70,
SmATA 34[port], WhoAm 76, –78,
–80, –82, WhoAmW 74, –72, –75*

Karl, Jean Edna 1927- *WhoAm 84,
–86*

Karlin, Muriel S *ConAu X*

Karlin, Muriel Schoenbrun *ConAu 85,
WhoAmJ 80, WhoAmW 74, –72, –77,
–79, WhoE 75, –77, –79, –81*

Karp, Abraham J 1921- *ConAu 3NR,
–5R, –18NR, DrAS 74H, –78H,
–82H, IntAu&W 77, –82, WhoAm 74,
–76, –78, –80, –82, WhoAmJ 80,
WhoWorJ 72, –78, WrDr 76, –80,
–82, –84, –86*

Karp, Abraham Joseph 1921-
WhoAm 84, –86

Karp, David 1922- *AmAu&B.
Au&Wr 71, BioIn 4, BlueB 76,
ConAu 1R, BioIn 4, ConNov 72, –76,
–82, CurBio 57, DcLEL 1940, EncSF,
IntAu&W 76, –77, –82, –86,
IntWW 74, –75, –76, –77, –78, –79,
–80, –81, –82, –83, ScF&FL 1, –2,
TwCSFW 86, Who 74, –82, –83, –85,
WhoAm 74, –76, –78, –80, –82, –84,
WhoAmJ 80, WrDr 76, –80, –82, –84,
–86*

Karp, Walter *AuBYP SUP*

Karpf, Holly W 1946- *ConAu 37R*

Karr, Phyllis Ann 1944- *ConAu 101,
–18NR*

Karras, Alex 1935- *BioIn 7, –9, –10,
–11, –12, –13, BioNews 74,
ConAu 107, ConTFT 1, HalFC 84,
IntMPA 84, –86, WhoAm 74, –76,
–78, –80, –82, –84, –86, WhoHol A,
WorAl*

Karst, Gene 1906- *WhoProB 73*

Kastner, Erich 1899-1974 *AuBYP,
BiDMoPL, BioIn 1, –5, –6, –7, –8,
–9, –10, –12, CasWL, ChlLR 4[port],
CIDMEL, CnMD, CurBio 64, –74,
–74N, DcLB 56[port], EncWL, –2,
EncWT, EvEuW, HalFC 84,
IntAu&W 76, IntWW 74, LinLib L,
ModGL, ModWD, ObitT 1971,
OxChL, OxGer, PenC EUR,
SmATA 14, ThrBJA, TwCCW 78B,
–83B, WhDW, WhAm 6, WhE&EA,
Who 74, WhoChL, WhoWor 74,
WorAu*

Kastner, Jonathan 1937- *ConAu 25R*

Kastner, Joseph 1907- *WrDr 86*

Kastner, Marianna 1940- *ConAu 25R*

Katan, Norma-Jean 1936- *ConAu 113*

Kath, Terry 1945?-1978 *BioIn 11, BioNews 74, WhAm 7, WhoAm 76, -78, WhoRocM 82*

Kath, Terry *see also* Chicago

Katz, Fred 1938- *ConAu 49, SmATA 6*

Katz, Gloria *IntMPA 86, WhoAm 86*

Katz, Gloria 1943?- *BioIn 10, ConAu 107, IntMPA 81, -82, -84, WomWMM*

Katz, Jacqueline Hunt *AuBYP SUP*

Katz, Jane 1934- *ConAu 85, SmATA 33[port]*

Katz, Naomi Corrine *TexWr*

Katz, William Loren 1927- *AuBYP SUP, BioIn 11, BlueB 76, ConAu 49, -21R, IntAu&W 76, -77, SmATA 13, WhoAm 74, -76, -78, -80, -82, -84, -86, WhoE 74, WrDr 80, -82, -84, -86*

Katzman, David Manners 1941- *ConAu 5NR, -53, DrAS 74H, -78H, -82H, WhoAm 86*

Kauffmann, Stanley 1916- *Au&Wr 71, BioIn 2, -7, -10, -12, BlueB 76, ConAmTC, ConAu 5R, -6NR, LongCTC, Novels, PenC AM, WhoAm 74, -76, -78, -80, -82, WhoE 74, WhoWor 74, -76, WorAu, WrDr 76, -80, -82, -84, -86*

Kaufman, Bel *AmAu&B, BioIn 7, -12, BlueB 76, ConAu 13NR, -13R, DrAP&F 85, ForWC 70, IntAu&W 82, WhoAm 74, -76, -78, -80, -82, -84, -86, WhoAmJ 80, WhoAmW 74, -66, -68, -72, -75, -81, -83, -85, -87, WhoE 74, WhoWor 74, WrDr 76, -80, -82, -84, -86*

Kaufman, Mervyn D 1932- *BioIn 9, ConAu 5R, SmATA 4, WhoAm 82*

Kaufman, Mervyn Douglas 1932- *WhoAm 84, -86*

Kaufmann, Helen L 1887- *AuBYP SUP, Baker 78, ConAu 5R, -7NR, IntWWM 77, WhE&EA, WhoAmW 61, -64, WhoMus 72*

Kaufmann, Helen Loeb 1887- *WhAm 8*

Kaufmann, John 1931- *BioIn 8, -12, ConAu 81, IlsBYP, IlsCB 1957, -1967, SmATA 18*

Kaufmann, Walter 1921- *MacBEP*

Kaufmann, Walter 1921-1980 *AmAu&B, AnObit 1980, BioIn 6, ConAu 1R, -1NR, -101, DcLEL 1940, DrAS 74P, -78P, IntAu&W 76, -77, -82, IntWWP 77, -82, WhAm 7, WhoAm 74, -76, -78, -80, WhoAmJ 80, WhoE 74, -75, -77, -79, WhoWor 74, -76, WrDr 76, -80, -82*

Kaufmann, Walter 1933- *ConAu 61*

Kaukonen, Jorma 1941?- *BioIn 9, -12, WhoRocM 82*

Kaukonen, Jorma *see also* Jefferson Airplane

Kaula, Edna Mason 1906- *AuBYP, BioIn 8, -11, ConAu 5R, SmATA 13*

Kavaler, Lucy 1929?- *AuBYP, BioIn 8, ConAu 7NR, -57, IntAu&W 77, SmATA 23[port], WhoAmW 74, -72, -75, WhoE 75, -77*

Kavaler, Lucy 1930- *BioIn 13*

Kawabata, Yasunari 1899-1972 *BiDJaL, BioIn 8, -9, -10, -12, CasWL, CnMWL, ConAu 33R, -93, ConLC 2, -5, -9, -18, CurBio 69, -72, -72N, DcOrL 1, EncWL, -2[port], GrFLW, LinLib L, MakMC, McGEWB, NewYTBE 72, Novels, ObitOF 79, PenC CL, RComWL, REn, WhDW, WhAm 5, WhoNob, WhoTwCL, WorAl, WorAu*

Kay, Helen 1912- *AuBYP, BioIn 7, -10, ConAu X, ForWC 70, SmATA 6, WhoAmW 66, -68, -75, -77, WhoE 85*

Kay, Helen *see also* Goldfrank, Helen Colodny

Kay, Mara *BioIn 11, ConAu 2NR, -5R, ForWC 70, IntAu&W 76, -77, -82, -84, -86, SmATA 13, WhoAmW 68, WrDr 76, -80, -82, -84, -86*

Kay, Terry 1918- *ConAu X*

Kay, Terry Winter 1938- *ConAu 110*

Kaye, Geraldine 1925- *Au&Wr 71, BioIn 11, ConAu 7NR, -13R, IntAu&W 76, -77, -82, -86, SmATA 10, TwCCW 78, -83, WhoWor 76, -80, WrDr 76, -80, -82, -84, -86*

Kaye, M M 1908?- *ConAu 89, NewYTBS 78, Novels, WrDr 82*

Kaye, M M 1909?- *ConLC 28[port]*

Kaye, M M 1911- *WrDr 86*

Kaye, Marvin *DrAP&F 85*

Kaye, Marvin 1938- *ConAu 5NR, -19NR, -53, IntAu&W 77, WrDr 76, -80, -82, -84, -86*

Kaye, Marvin Nathan 1938- *IntAu&W 86*

Kayira, Legson Didimu 1940?- *AfrA, Au&Wr 71, BioIn 9, ConAu 17R, DcLEL 1940, InB&W 80, IntAu&W 76, RGAfL*

Kazan, Elia 1909- *ASpks, BiDFilm, BiE&WWA, BioIn 1, -2, -3, -4, -5, -6, -7, -8, -9, -10, -11, -12, BlueB 76, CelR, CnThe, ConAu 21R, ConLC 6, -16, ConTFT 3, CurBio 48, -72, DcFM, EncWT, FilmgC, HalFC 84, IntAu&W 77, IntDcF 2, IntMPA 77, -75, -76, -78, -79, -81, -82, -84, -86, IntWW 74, -75, -76, -77, -78, -79, -80, -81, -82, -83, MovMk, NewYTBE 72, NotNAT, -A, Novels, OxAmL, -83, OxAmT 84, OxFilm, OxThe, -83, PIP&P, PolProf T, REnAL, WebAB, -79, WhThe, Who 74, -82, -83, -85, WhoAm 74, -76, -78, -80, -82, -84, -86, WhoE 74, WhoHol A, WhoThe 72, WhoWor 74, -78, -80, -82, -84, -87, WorAl, WorEFlm, WrDr 76, -80, -82, -84, -86*

Kazimiroff, Theodore L 1941- *ConAu 109*

Kazin, Alfred 1915- *AmAu&B, Au&Wr 71, BioIn 2, -4, -6, -7, -9, -11, -13, BlueB 76, CasWL, CelR, ConAu 1R, -1NR, ConLC 38[port], ConLCrt, -82, CurBio 66, DcLEL 1940, DrAS 74E, -78E, -82E, IntAu&W 76, -77, IntWW 74, -75, -76, -77, -78, -79, -80, -81, -82, -83, LinLib L, OxAmL, -83, PenC AM, RAdv 1, REn, REnAL, TwCA SUP, WhoAm 74, -76, -78, -80, -82, -84, -86, WhoAmJ 80, WhoWor 74, -84, -87, WhoWorJ 72, -78, WorAl, WrDr 80, -82, -84, -86*

Keane, Bil 1922- *BioIn 9, ConAu 13NR, -33R, ConGrA 1[port], EncTwCJ, SmATA 4, WhoAm 78, -80, -82, -84, -86, WhoAmA 73, -76, -78, -80, -82, -84, -86, WhoWest 76, -78*

Keane, John 1945?- *BioIn 11*

Kearns, Martha 1945- *ConAu 57, WhoAmW 77, -79*

Keating, Bern 1915- *BioIn 11, ConAu X, SmATA X, WrDr 76, -80, -82, -84, -86*

Keating, Bern *see also* Keating, Leo Bernard

Keating, H R F 1926- *ConAu 18NR, -33R, Novels, TwCCr&M 80, -85, WhoSpyF, WorAu 1970, WrDr 80, -82, -84, -86*

Keating, Lawrence A 1903-1966 *AuBYP, BioIn 7, ConAu 5R, SmATA 23*

Keating, Lawrence Alfred 1903-1966 *BioIn 13*

Keating, Leo Bernard 1915- *BioIn 11, ConAu 29R, SmATA 10*

Keating, Leo Bernard *see also* Keating, Bern

Keats, Ezra Jack 1916- *OxChL, WhoAmA 84*

Keats, Ezra Jack 1916-1983 *AmPB, AnObit 1983, Au&ICB, AuBYP, AuNews 1, BioIn 5, -6, -7, -8, -9, -10, -12, -13, BioNews 74, BkP, ChlLR 1, ChhPo S1, -S2, ConAu 109, -77, IlsBYP, IlsCB 1946, -1957, -1967, LinLib L, MorJA, NewYTBS 83, NewbC 1956,*

NewbC 1956, SmATA 14, -34N, TwCCW 78, -83, WhAm 8, WhoAm 74, -76, -78, -80, -82, WhoAmA 76, -78, -80, -82, WrDr 76, -80, -82, -84

Keats, John 1795-1821 *Alli, AnCL, AtlBL, BiD&SB, BiHiMed, BioIn 1, -2, -3, -4, -5, -6, -7, -8, -9, -10, -11, -12, -13, BritAu 19, BritWr 4, CasWL, CelCen, Chambr 3, ChhPo, -S1, -S2, -S3, CnE&AP, CrtT 2, -4, CyWA, DcBiPP, DcEnA, DcEnL, DcEuL, DcLEL, DcNaB, Dis&D, EvLB, LinLib L, -S, LongCEL, McGEWB, MouLC 2, NewC, NinCLC 8[port], OxEng, -85, OxMed 86, PenC ENG, RAdv 1, RComWL, REn, Str&VC, WebE&AL, WhDW, WorAl*

Keats, John 1795-1821 *Alli, AnCL,* (cont.)

Keedy, Mervin L 1920- *WhoAm 86*

Keedy, Mervin Laverne 1920- *AmM&WS 86P*

Keefe, John Edwin 1942- *ConAu 107, DrAS 74F*

Keegan, Marcia 1942- *ICPEnP A, MacBEP*

Keegan, Marcia 1943- *AmAu&B, BioIn 11, ConAu 49, IntAu&W 77, SmATA 9, WhoAmW 75, -77, -79, WhoE 77, -79*

Keeley, Edmund *DrAP&F 85*

Keene, Carolyn *AmAu&B, BioIn 9, -10, -11, -12, -13, ConAu X, EncMys, OxChL, SmATA X, WebAB, -79*

Keene, Carolyn *see also* Adams, Harriet S

Keene, Carolyn *see also* Stratemeyer, Edward L

Keene, Donald 1922- *AmAu&B, BiE&WWA, BioIn 12, ConAu 1R, -5NR, DrAS 74F, -78F, -82F, NotNAT, WhoAm 74, -76, WrDr 86*

Keeping, Charles 1924- *OxChL, WrDr 86*

Keese, Parton 1926- *ConAu 109*

Keeton, Kathy 1939- *EncTwCJ, WhoAm 84, -86, WhoAmW 85*

Keil, Sally VanWagenen 1946- *ConAu 89*

Keillor, Garrison *ConAu X, DrAP&F 85*

Keillor, Garrison 1942- *BioIn 12, -13, ConAu 111, ConLC 40[port], CurBio 85[port], WhoMW 76*

Keillor, Garrison Edward 1942- *WhoAm 84, -86*

Keith, Agnes Newton 1901- *AmAu&B, AmWomWr, Au&Wr 71, BioIn 1, -2, -4, -12, CanWW 70, -79, -80, -81, ConAu 17R, IntAu&W 76, -77, -82, LinLib L, REnAL, TwCA SUP, WhoAmW 74, -58, -70, -72, WrDr 76, -80, -82, -84*

Keith, Harold 1903- *AmAu&B, AuBYP, BioIn 4, -5, -6, -7, -9, -10, ConAu 2NR, -5R, CurBio 58, LinLib L, MorBMP, MorJA, NewbC 1956, OxChL, SmATA 2, TwCCW 78, -83, WhNAA, WrDr 80, -82, -84, -86*

Keith, Sam 1921- *ConAu 65*

Keithley, George *DrAP&F 85*

Keithley, George 1935- *ConAu 37R, DrAS 74E, -78E, -82E, IntWWP 77, -82, WhoAm 74, -76, -78, -80, -82, WhoWest 74, -76*

Keithley, George Frederick 1935- *WhoAm 84, -86*

Keith-Lucas, Alan 1910- *ConAu 2NR, -5R, -20NR, WhoAm 74, -76, -78, -80*

Kelder, Diane M 1934- *ConAu 25R, WhoAm 80, WhoAmA 76, -78, -80, -82, -84*

Kelen, Emery 1896-1978 *AuBYP SUP, BioIn 1, -11, -13, ConAu 9R, -103, IlsCB 1744, SmATA 13, -26N*

Kelleher, Victor 1939- *OxAusL, WrDr 86*

Keller, Allan 1904- *ConAu 29R*

Keller, Beverly *ConAu 17NR*

Keller, Beverly L *AuBYP SUP, BioIn 11, ConAu 1NR, SmATA 13*

Keller, Charles 1942- *AuBYP SUP, BioIn 11, ConAu 2NR, -49, SmATA 8*

Keller, Helen 1880-1968 *AmAu&B, AmWomWr, ApCAB X, BiDSA, BioIn 1, -2, -3, -4, -5, -6, -7, -8, -9, -10, -11, -12, ChhPo S1, -S3, ConAu 101, -89, CurBio 42, -68, DcLEL, Dis&D, EncAB 6, EncSoH, GoodHs, HarEnUS, HerW, -84, InWom, IntDcWB[port], LibW, LinLib L, -S, LongCTC, LuthC 75, McGEWB, NatCAB 15, -57, NotAW MOD, ObitOF 79, ObitT 1961, OxAmH, OxAmL, -83, REn, REnAL, WebAB, -79, WhDW, WhAm 5, WhE&EA, WhNAA, WhoAmW 58, -61, -64, -66, -68, WhoHol B, WomWWA 14, WorAl*

Keller, Helen 1881-1968 *HalFC 84, WhScrn 83*

Kellerman, Jonathan 1949- *ConLC 44[port]*

Kelley, Leo P 1928- *ConAu 107, ConSFA, EncSF, ScF&FL 1, -2, ScFSB, SmATA 31, -32[port], TwCSFW 86, WrDr 84, -86*

Kellogg, Marjorie 1922- *AmAu&B, BioIn 8, ConAu 81, ConLC 2, WomWMM*

Kelly, Eric Philbrook 1884-1960 *AmAu&B, AnCL, AuBYP, BioIn 2, -4, -5, -6, -7, -11, ConAu 93, JBA 34, -51, NatCAB 44, Newb 1922, REnAL, TwCCW 78, -83, WhAm 3, WhNAA, YABC 1*

Kelly, Frank K 1914- *BioIn 1, -3, ConAu 1R, -1NR, -16NR, WhoSciF*

Kelly, Gary F 1943- *ConAu 89*

Kelly, Karen 1938- *ForWC 70*

Kelly, Robert *DrAP&F 85*

Kelly, Robert 1935- *Au&Wr 71, BioIn 10, -12, ConAu 17R, ConPo 70, -75, -80, -85, ConSFA, CroCAP, DcLB 5, EncSF, IntWWP 77, LinLib L, PenC AM, ScF&FL 1, -2, WhoAm 76, -78, -80, -82, -84, -86, WrDr 76, -80, -82, -84, -86*

Kelly, Walt 1913-1973 *AmAu&B, AmSCAP 66, ArtCS, BioIn 1, -2, -3, -4, -5, -6, -10, -12, CelR, ConAu 45, -73, CurBio 56, -73, -73N, EncAJ, IlsBYP, LinLib L, NewYTBE 73, ObitOF 79, REnAL, SmATA 18, WhAm 6, WhoAm 74, WorECom*

Kelsey, Joan Marshall 1907- *ConAu 5R*

Kelsey, Joan Marshall *see also* Grant, Joan

Kelton, Elmer *NewYTBS 86[port]*

Kelton, Elmer 1926- *ConAu 12NR, EncFWF[port], WrDr 86*

Kelty, Jean McClure 1926- *DrAS 74E, -78E, -82E, WhoAmW 66, -68, WhoMW 74, -76*

Kemal, Yashar 1922?- *BioIn 10, ConAu 89, ConLC 14, -29[port], IntWW 74, -75, -76, -77, -78, -79, -80, -81, -82, -83, TwCWr, WhoWor 74, WorAu*

Kemal, Yashar 1923- *ConFLW 84*

Kemelman, Harry 1908- *AmAu&B, ASpks, AuNews 1, BioIn 10, -11, ConAu 6NR, -9R, ConLC 2, DcLB 28[port], DcLEL 1940, EncMys, IntAu&W 76, -77, -82, -86, Novels, TwCCr&M 80, -85, WhoAm 74, -76, -78, -80, -82, -84, -86, WhoWorJ 72, -78, WorAl, WorAu 1970, WrDr 76, -80, -82, -84, -86*

Kemp, Gene 1926- *BioIn 13, ConAu 12NR, -69, IntAu&W 82, OxChL, SmATA 25[port], TwCChW 83, WrDr 76, -80, -82, -84, -86*

Kemp, Lysander 1920- *AmAu&B, ConAu 1NR, -45, WhoAm 76, -78, WhoS&SW 73, -75, -76*

Kemperman, Steve 1955- *ConAu 108*

Kendall, Carol 1917- *AuBYP, BioIn 7,*
-9, -11, ConAu 5R, -7NR,
ForWC 70, IntAu&W 76, -77, -82,
-86, OhA&B, OxChL, ScF&FL 1, -2,
SmATA 1, ThrBJA, TwCCW 78, -83,
WhoAmW 68, WrDr 80, -82, -84,
-86

Kendall, Lace *AmAu&B, ConAu X,*
IntWWP 77, SmATA 3, ThrBJA,
WhoAm 74, -76, -78, WrDr 82, -84,
-86

Kendall, Lace *see also* Stoutenburg,
Adrien

Keneally, Thomas 1935- *ASpks,*
BioIn 9, -10, -11, -13, BlueB 76,
CasWL, ConAu 10NR, -85,
ConLC 5, -8, -10, -14, -19,
-27[port], -43[port], ConNov 72, -76,
-82, -86, DcLEL 1940, FarE&A 78,
-79, -80, -81, IntAu&W 76, -77,
IntWW 78, -79, -80, -81, -82, -83,
ModCmwL, Novels, OxAusL,
ScF&FL 1, Who 82, -83,
WhoWor 78, -82, WorAu 1970,
WrDr 76, -80, -82, -84, -86

Keniston, Kenneth 1930- *AmAu&B,*
BioIn 9, ConAu 25R, WhoAm 74,
-76, -78, -80, -82, -84

Kennealy, Patricia 1946- *ConAu 120*

Kennedy, Adrienne 1931- *AmWomD,*
DcLB 38[port], InB&W 85, SelBAAf,
WrDr 86

Kennedy, David M 1941-
ConAu 13NR

Kennedy, David Michael 1941-
ConAu 29R, DrAS 74H, -78H,
IntAu&W 77, -82, -86, WhoAm 82,
-84, -86, WrDr 76, -80, -82, -86

Kennedy, John F 1917-1963 *AmAu&B,*
AnCL, BiDrAC, BiDrUSE, BioIn 1,
-2, -3, -4, -5, -6, -7, -8, -9, -10,
-11, -12, ChhPo, ConAu 1R, -1NR,
CurBio 50, -61, -64, DcAmB S7,
DcAmSR, DcPol, EncAAH,
EncAB-H, EncSoH, LinLib L, -S,
MakMC, McGEWB, NatCAB 52,
NewYTBE 72, ObitOF 79,
ObitT 1961, OxAmH, OxAmL, -83,
PolProf E, PolProf K, REn, REnAL,
SmATA 11, WebAB, -79, WhDW,
WhAm 4, WhAmP, WorAl

Kennedy, John Fitzgerald 1917-1963
BioIn 13

Kennedy, Ludovic 1919- *Au&Wr 71,*
BioIn 3, ConAu 65, IntAu&W 77,
IntWW 78, -79, -80, -81, -82, -83,
Who 74, -82, -83, WrDr 76, -80,
-82, -84, -86

Kennedy, Ludovic Henry Coverley
1919- *Who 85*

Kennedy, Malcolm Duncan 1895-
ConAu 9R, IntAu&W 76, -77,
WrDr 76, -80, -82, -84

Kennedy, Michael 1926- *Baker 84,*
ConAu 5NR, -13R, IntAu&W 77,
-86, IntWWM 77, -85, Who 74, -82,
-83, -85, WhoMus 72, WhoWor 76,
WrDr 76, -80, -82, -84, -86

Kennedy, Richard 1932- *BioIn 13,*
ConAu 7NR, FifBJA[port],
SmATA 22, WhoAm 82, WrDr 86

Kennedy, Richard Jerome 1932-
WhoAm 84

Kennedy, Robert Francis 1925-1968
AmAu&B, BiDrAC, BiDrUSE,
BioIn 4, -5, -6, -7, -8, -9, -10, -11,
-12, -13, ConAu 1R, -1NR,
CurBio 68, -68, DcPol, EncAB-H,
McGEWB, ObitOF 79, WebAB, -79,
WhAm 5, WhAmP, WorAl

Kennedy, Theodore R 1936-
ConAu 105, WhoBlA 80

Kennedy, Theodore Reginald 1936-
WhoBlA 85

Kennel, Arthur John 1929-
WhoMW 80, -82, -84

Kenner, Hugh 1923- *BiE&WWA,*
BlueB 76, ConAu 21R, ConLCrt, -82,
DrAS 74E, -78E, -82E, WorAu,
WrDr 80, -82, -84, -86

Kennerly, Karen 1940- *ConAu 33R*

Kenny, Kathryn *ConAu X,*
IntAu&W 76X, SmATA X

Kenny, Kathryn *see also* Sanderlin,
Owenita

Kenrick, Tony 1935- *Au&Wr 71,*
BioIn 9, ConAu 104, TwCCr&M 80,
-85, WrDr 82, -84, -86

Kent, Alexander *BioIn 13, WrDr 86*

Kent, Alexander 1924- *Au&Wr 71,*
ConAu X, DcLEL 1940,
IntAu&W 76, -76X, -77, -77X,
Novels, SmATA X, WrDr 76, -80,
-82, -84

Kent, Alexander *see also* Reeman,
Douglas Edward

Kent, Deborah Ann 1948- *ConAu 103,*
SmATA 41, -47[port]

Kenworthy, Leonard Stout 1912-
BioIn 10, -11, ConAu 1R, -1NR,
IndAu 1917, SmATA 6

Kenyon, Karen *DrAP&F 85*

Kenyon, Karen 1938- *ConAu 106*

Kenyon, Karen Beth 1938-
IntAu&W 86

Kenyon, Raymond G 1922- *AuBYP,*
BioIn 7

Keppel, Charlotte *TwCCr&M 85,*
WrDr 84, -86

Kerber, Linda K 1940- *ConAu 115*

Kerber, Linda Kaufman 1940-
DrAS 74H, -78H, -82H, WhoAm 84,
-86, WhoAmW 77, -85, -87,
WhoMW 82, -84

Kern, Gregory *ConAu X,*
TwCSFW 86, WrDr 86

Kern, Gregory 1919- *ConAu X,*
EncSF, ScF&FL 1, WrDr 84

Kern, Gregory *see also* Tubb, E C

Kern, Louis J 1909- *St&PR 75*

Kernan, Alvin Bernard 1923-
ConAu 49, DrAS 74E, -78E, -82E,
LEduc 74, WhoAm 74, -76, -78, -80,
-82, -84, -86, WhoE 74

Kerouac, Jack 1922-1969 *AmAu&B,*
AuNews 1, BioIn 4, -5, -7, -8, -9,
-10, -11, -12, -13, BioNews 75,
CasWL, CmCal, CnMWL, ConAu X,
ConLC 1, -2, -3, -5, -14, -29[port],
ConNov 76, -82A, -86A, ConPo 70,
CurBio 59, -69, DcLB 2, -16[port],
-DS3[port], DcLEL 1940, EncAB-H,
EncWL, -2, HalFC 84, LinLib L,
LongCTC, MakMC, ModAL, -S2,
-S1, NewCon[port], NewYTBS 79,
Novels[port], ObitOF 79, ObitT 1961,
OxAmL, -83, OxEng 85, PenC AM,
PolProf E, RAdv 1, REn, REnAL,
TwCWr, WebAB, -79, WebE&AL,
WhDW, WhAm 5, WhoHol B,
WhoTwCL, WorAl, WorAu

Kerouac, Jack *see also* Kerouac,
Jean-Louis Lebrid De

Kerouac, Jean-Louis Lebrid De
1922-1969 *AuNews 1, ConAu 5R,*
-25R

Kerouac, Jean-Louis Lebrid De *see also*
Kerouac, Jack

Kerouac, John 1922-1969 *ConAu X*

Kerouac, John *see also* Kerouac, Jack

Kerr, Jean 1923- *AmAu&B,*
AmCath 80, AmSCAP 66,
AmWomWr, BiE&WWA, BioIn 4,
-5, -6, -10, -12, BlueB 76, CelR,
ConAu 5R, -7NR, ConLC 22[port],
ConTFT 1, CurBio 58, DcLEL 1940,
HalFC 84, InWom, IntAu&W 77,
IntWW 74, -75, -76, -77, -78, -79,
-80, -81, -82, -83, LibW,
McGEWD 84, NatPD 81[port],
NewYTBE 73, NewYTBS 80,
NotNAT, OxAmL, -83, OxAmT 84,
FifIDA, IntAu&W 76, WhoAm 74, -76,
WhoAm 74, -76, -78, -80, -82, -84,
-86, WhoAmW 74, -64, -66, -68,
-70, -72, -81, -83, WhoThe 72, -77,
-81, WhoWor 74, -78, -80, -82, -84,
-87, WorAl, WorAu, WrDr 76, -80,
-82, -84, -86

Kerr, Jean 1924- *AmWomD*

Kerr, Jessica 1901- *AuBYP SUP,*
BioIn 11, ConAu P-2, SmATA 13

Kerr, Judith 1923- *AuBYP SUP,*
BioIn 13, ConAu 93, FifBJA[port],
SmATA 24[port], TwCCW 78, -83,
WrDr 80, -82, -84, -86

Kerr, M E 1927?- *AuBYP SUP,*
BioIn 10, -12, ConAu X, ConLC 12,
-35[port], FourBJA, SmATA X,
SmATA 1AS[port], TwCCW 78, -83,
WrDr 80, -82, -84

Kerr, M E 1932- *OxChL, WrDr 86*

Kerr, M E *see also* Meaker, Marijane

Kerry, Lois *SmATA X*

Kerry, Lois 1954- *ConAu X,*
IntAu&W 82X, SmATA 1

Kerry, Lois *see also* Arquette, Lois S

Kertesz, Andre 1894- *BioIn 13,*
ICPEnP, MacBEP, PrintW 85,
WhoAm 84, WhoWor 84

Kertesz, Andre 1894-1985 *ConAu 117,*
CurBio 85N, NewYTBS 85[port]

Ker Wilson, Barbara 1929-
Au&Wr 71, BioIn 12, ConAu 5R,
-7NR, FourBJA, SmATA 20

Ker Wilson, Barbara *see also* Wilson,
Barbara Ker

Kesey, Ken *DrAP&F 85*

Kesey, Ken 1935- *AmAu&B, BioIn 8,*
-10, -11, -12, -13, CasWL, CmCal,
ConAu 1R, ConLC 1, -3, -6, -11,
ConNov 72, -76, -82, -86, CurBio 76,
DcLB 2, -16[port], DcLEL 1940,
EncFWF, EncWL, -2, IntAu&W 76,
-77, -82, LinLib L, MakMC,
ModAL S1, MugS, Novels,
OxAmL 83, PenC AM, RAdv 1,
REnAW, WebE&AL, WhoAm 74,
-76, -78, -80, -82, -84, -86,
WhoTwCL, WorAl, WorAu 1970,
WrDr 76, -80, -82, -84, -86

Kesselman, Judi R 1934- *ConAu 61,*
-X

Kesselman-Turkel, Judi 1934-
ConAu X, IntAu&W 86

Kessner, Lawrence 1957- *ConAu 109*

Kessner, Thomas 1946- *ConAu 11NR,*
-69, DrAS 78H, -82H

Kesteven, G R *BioIn 12, ConAu 69,*
-X, SmATA X

Ketcham, Hank 1920- *ArtCS, BioIn 3,*
-4, -5, -11, -13, ConAu X,
CurBio 56, EncAJ, LinLib L,
SmATA X, WhoAmA 82, -84

Ketcham, Richard M 1922- *BioIn 10,*
-11, ConAu 25R, WhoAm 74, -76,
-78, -80, -82, WhoWor 74, WrDr 76,
-80, -82, -84, -86

Ketcham, Richard Malcolm 1922-
WhoAm 86

Ketcham, William C, Jr. 1931-
ConAu 12NR, IntAu&W 86,
WhoE 85, WrDr 86

Kett, Joseph Francis 1938-
ConAu 25R, DrAS 74H, -78H, -82H

Kettelkamp, Larry 1933-
ConAu 16NR, SmATA 3AS[port]

Kettelkamp, Larry Dale 1933- *AuBYP,*
BioIn 8, -9, -12, ConAu 29R,
ConLC 12, IlsCB 1957, -1967,
IntAu&W 77, -82, SmATA 2,
ThrBJA, WrDr 76, -80, -82, -84, -86

Kevles, Bettyann 1938- *BioIn 13,*
ConAu 11NR, -69, SmATA 23[port]

Kevles, Daniel J 1939- *WrDr 86*

Kevles, Daniel Jerome 1939-
AmM&WS 86P

Key, Alexander 1904-1979 *AuBYP,*
BioIn 8, -11, -12, ConAu 5R, -6NR,
-89, IntAu&W 77, ScF&FL 1, -2,
ScFSB, SmATA 23N, -8,
TwCSFW 86, WrDr 76, -80

Key, Alexander Hill 1904-1978
BioIn 13

Key, Mary Ritchie 1924- *ConAu 1NR,*
-16NR, -45, DrAS 74F, -78F, -82F,
WhoAm 82, -84, -86, WhoAmW 77,
-79, -81, -83, -85, -87, WhoWest 80,
-82, -84, WhoWor 82

Keyes, Daniel *DrAP&F 85*

Keyes, Daniel 1927- *BioIn 7,*
ConAu 10NR, -17R, ConSFA,
DrAS 74E, -78E, -82E, EncSF,
Novels, ScF&FL 1, -2, ScFSB,
SmATA 37, TwCSFW 86,
WhoAm 82, -84, -86, WhoHol A,
WhoMW 84, WhoSciF, WrDr 76,
-80, -82, -84, -86

Keyes, Fenton 1915- *AmM&WS 73S,*
-78S, ConAu 107, SmATA 34[port],
WhoAm 74, -76, -78, -80, -82, -84,
-86

Keyes, Frances Parkinson 1885-1970
AmAu&B, AmNov, AmWomWr,
BiCAW, BioIn 1, -2, -3, -4, -5, -7,
-9, -12, BkC 5, CathA 1930, CelR,
ConAu 5R, -7NR, -25R, EvLB,
InWom, LongCTC, Novels,
ObitOF 79, ObitT 1961, PenC AM,
REn, TwCA, -SUP, TwCWr,
WhAm 5, WhNAA, WhoAmW 58,
-64, -66, -68, -70, -72, WomNov

Keyes, Ralph 1945- *ConAu 3NR, -49*

Khan, Ismith 1925- *BioIn 9,*
ConNov 82, -86, FifCWr, WrDr 84,
-86

Khan, Jahangir 1963- *BioIn 13*

Khayyam, Omar 1048-1122 *HalFC 84*

Khayyam, Omar 1050?-1125? *BbD,*
BiD&SB, BioIn 4, -5, -8, -9, -10,
ChhPo S1, -S2, DcOrL 3, InSci,
NewC

Kherdian, David *DrAP&F 85*

Kherdian, David 1931- *BioIn 12,*
ChhPo S3, ConAu 21R,
ConAu 2AS[port], ConLC 6, -9,
FifBJA[port], IntAu&W 76, -77,
IntWWP 77, SmATA 16, WhoAm 82,
-84, -86, WrDr 76, -80, -82, -84,
-86

Kidd, Ronald 1948- *ConAu 116,*
SmATA 42[port]

Kidd, Virginia *DrAP&F 85*

Kidd, Virginia 1921- *ConAu 10NR,*
-65, IntAu&W 77, -82, -86,
ScF&FL 1, -2

Kiddell, John 1922- *Alli, Au&Wr 71,*
BioIn 9, ConAu 29R, SmATA 3

Kidder, Rushworth M 1944-
ConAu 77, DrAS 74E, -78E, -82E

Kidder, Tracy 1945- *BioIn 12, -13,*
ConAu 109, NewYTBS 81[port]

Kiefer, Irene 1926- *BioIn 12,*
ConAu 11NR, -69, SmATA 21[port]

Kiefer, Warren 1929?- *ConAu 77,*
IntAu&W 77, WrDr 76, -80, -82, -84

Kiefer, Warren 1930- *WrDr 86*

Kiely, Benedict 1919- *BioIn 13,*
ConLC 43[port], ConNov 86,
ModBrL S2, WrDr 86

Kienzle, William X 1928- *BioIn 12,*
ConAu 9NR, -93, ConLC 25[port],
TwCCr&M 85, WrDr 86

Kieran, John 1892-1981 *AmAu&B,*
AuBYP SUP, BioIn 1, -2, -3, -4, -5,
-7, -8, -9, -12, CathA 1930,
ChhPo S1, -S3, ConAu 101, -105,
CurBio 82N, EncAJ,
NewYTBS 81[port], REn, REnAL,
WhScrn 83, WhoAm 74, -76, -78,
WhoE 74

Kiesel, Stanley *DrAP&F 85*

Kiesel, Stanley 1925- *ConAu 104,*
SmATA 35

Kiev, Ari 1933- *BiDrAPA 77,*
BlueB 76, ConAu 3NR, -9R,
IntMed 80, WhoCon 73, WhoE 74,
-75, -77, -79, WrDr 76, -80, -82,
-84, -86

Kilby, Clyde Samuel 1902- *BioIn 11,*
ChhPo S1, ConAu 9NR, -13R,
DrAS 74E, -78E, -82E

Kilby, Clyde Samuel 1902-1986
ConAu 120

Kilgore, Al 1927- *WhoAm 74, -76,*
WhoAmA 76, -78, -80, -82, -84

Kilgore, Kathleen 1946- *ConAu 109,*
SmATA 42[port]

Kilian, Crawford 1941-
SmATA 35[port], TwCSFW 86,
WrDr 86

Killens, John Oliver *DrAP&F 85*

Killens, John Oliver 1916- *BlkAWP,*
ConAu 77, ConAu 2AS[port],
ConLC 10, ConNov 72, -76, -82, -86,
DcLB 33[port], DrBlPA, InB&W 80,
-85, IntAu&W 76, -77, LivgBAA,
ModBlW, NegAl 76[port], -83[port],
PenC AM, SelBAAf, SelBAAu,
WhoAm 74, -76, WhoBlA 75, -77,
-80, -85, WhoE 74, WorAu 1970,
WrDr 76, -80, -82, -84, -86

Killilea, Marie 1913- *BioIn 9,*
ConAu 5R, IntAu&W 76, SmATA 2,
WhoAmW 61, WhoE 74
Killough, Lee 1942- *ConAu 15NR,*
-89, ScFSB, TwCSFW 86, WrDr 84,
-86
Killy, Jean-Claude 1943- *BioIn 7, -8,*
-9, -10, -12, BioNews 74, CelR,
ConAu 115, CurBio 68, WhoFr 79,
WhoHol A, WhoWor 74, -76, WorAl
Kilworth, Garry 1941- *ScFSB,*
TwCSFW 86, WrDr 86
Kim, Richard E *DrAP&F 85*
Kim, Richard E 1932- *BioIn 6, -9,*
-12, ConAu 5R, ConNov 72, -76,
-82, -86, DcLEL 1940, IntAu&W 76,
-77, WhoAm 74, -76, -78, -80, -82,
-84, -86, WhoE 74, WhoWor 74,
WrDr 76, -80, -82, -84, -86
Kim, Yong-Ik 1920- *ConAu 17R*
Kimball, Dean 1912- *AuBYP SUP,*
ConAu 69
Kimbrell, Grady 1933- *ConAu 33R*
Kimbrough, Emily *OxAmL 83*
Kimbrough, Emily 1899- *AmAu&B,*
AmWomWr, Au&Wr 71, BioIn 1, -2,
-3, -4, -9, -10, -12, BlueB 76,
ConAu 17R, CurBio 44, InWom,
IndAu 1917, OxAmL, REnAL,
SmATA 2, WhoAm 74, -76, -78, -80,
-82, -84, -86, WhoAmW 74, -58,
-61, -64, -66, -68, -70, -72, -83,
-85, -87, WhoWor 74, -76, WorAu,
WrDr 76, -80, -82, -84, -86
Kimmel, Eric A 1946- *BioIn 11,*
ConAu 3NR, -49, IntAu&W 77,
SmATA 13, WrDr 76, -80, -82, -84,
-86
Kincaid, Jamaica 1949?-
ConLC 43[port], ConNov 86, FifCWr
Kinder, Gary 1946- *ConAu 109*
King, B B *BioIn 13*
King, B B 1925- *Baker 84, BiDAfM,*
BioIn 8, -9, -10, -11, -12,
BioNews 74, BluesWW, CurBio 70,
DrBlPA, Ebony 1, EncFCWM 83,
EncJzS, IlEncJ, NegAl 76[port],
-83[port], RkOn 74,
RolSEnR 83[port], WhoAm 74, -76,
-78, -80, -82, -84, -86, WhoBlA 75,
-77, -80, -85, WhoRock 81[port],
WhoRocM 82, WorAl
King, Billie Jean 1943- *BioIn 7, -8, -9,*
-10, -11, -12, -13, BioNews 74,
CelR, CmCal, ConAu 10NR, -53,
CurBio 67, GoodHs, HerW, -84,
InWom, IntDcWB, IntWW 76, -77,
-78, -79, -80, -81, -82, -83,
NewYTBE 70, NewYTBS 74, -75,
-76, -77, -80[port], -82[port],
-83[port], SmATA 12, WhDW,
Who 82, -83, -85, WhoAm 74, -76,
-78, -80, -82, WhoAmW 79, -81,
-83, WhoWor 78, WorAl, WrDr 80,
-82, -84, -86
King, Billie Jean Moffitt 1943-
WhoAm 84, -86, WhoAmW 85, -87
King, C Daly 1895-1963
TwCCr&M 80, -85, WhE&EA
King, Carole 1941- *Baker 84,*
BiDAmM, BioIn 9, -10, -12, -13,
CelR, CurBio 74, EncPR&S 77,
GoodHs, NewYTBE 70, RkOn 74,
-82, RolSEnR 83, WhoAm 74, -76,
-78, -80, -82, WhoAmW 74, -75,
-81, WhoRocM 82, WorAl
King, Carole 1942- *EncFCWM 83,*
RolSEnR 83, WhoAm 84, -86,
WhoRock 81
King, Charles 1844-1933 *Alli, -SUP,*
AmAu&B, AmBi, AmLY, ApCAB,
ArizL, BiD&SB, BioIn 5, -8, CarSB,
DcAmAu, DcNAA, EncFWF[port],
HarEnUS, NatCAB 5, -25,
OxAmL, -83, TwCBDA, WhAm 1,
WhNAA, WisWr
King, Charles Lester 1922- *ConAu 57,*
DrAS 74F, -78F, -82F
King, Clarence 1842-1901 *Alli SUP,*
AmAu, AmAu&B, AmBi, ApCAB,
BiDAmS, BiD&SB, BioIn 1, -2, -4,
-5, -8, -10, -12, -13, CmCal,
ConAu 110, DcAmAu, DcAmB,

DcLB 12[port], DcNAA, DcScB,
EncAAH, HarEnUS, InSci, LinLib L,
-S, McGEWB, NatCAB 13,
NewYTBS 74, OxAmH, OxAmL, -83,
REn, REnAL, TwCBDA,
WebAB, -79, WhDW, WhAm 1
King, Clarence 1884?-1974 *BioIn 10,*
ConAu 53
King, Clive 1924- *BioIn 13,*
ConAu 104, OxChL, SmATA 28,
TwCCW 78, -83, WrDr 82, -84, -86
King, Coretta 1927- *Au&Wr 71,*
BiDAfM, BioIn 7, -8, -9, -10, -11,
-12, -13, BlueB 76, CelR, CivR 74,
CivRSt, ConAu 29R, CurBio 69,
Ebony 1, GoodHs, HerW, InB&W 80,
IntAu&W 77, IntDcWB, IntWW 83,
LivgBAA, NegAl 76[port], -83[port],
NewYTBE 72, PolProf J, SelBAAu,
WhoAm 74, -76, -78, -80, -82,
WhoAmW 74, -70, -70A, -72, -75,
-77, -79, -81, -83, WhoBlA 75, -77,
-80, WhoRel 77, WhoS&SW 73, -75,
-76, WhoWor 74, -76, WorAl
King, Cynthia *DrAP&F 85*
King, Cynthia 1925- *BioIn 10,*
ConAu 29R, MichAu 80, ScF&FL 1A,
SmATA 7, WrDr 76, -80, -82, -84,
-86
King, Marian *AmAu&B, Au&Wr 71,*
BioIn 13, ConAu 2NR, -5R,
ForWC 70, SmATA 23[port],
WhoAm 74, -76, -78, -80, -82, -84,
WhoAmW 74, -58, -64, -66, -68,
-70, -72, -77, -79, WhoE 83,
-85, WhoS&SW 73, WrDr 76, -80,
-82, -84, -86
King, Marian 1900?-1986 *ConAu 118,*
SmATA 47N
King, Martin Luther 1929-1968
BioIn 13
King, Martin Luther, Jr. 1929-1968
AmAu&B, AmRef[port], BiDMoPL,
BioIn 4, -5, -6, -7, -8, -9, -10, -11,
-12, BlkAWP, CivRSt, ConAu P-2,
CurBio 57, -65, -68, DcAmNB,
DcAmReB, DcAmSR, DcPol,
EncAB-H, EncSoH, InB&W 80, -85,
LinLib L, -S, LuthC 75, MakMC,
McGEWB, NatCAB 54,
NegAl 76[port], -83[port],
NewYTBS 74, ObitOF 79,
ObitT 1961, OxAmH, OxAmL, -83,
PolProf E, PolProf J, PolProf K,
REnAL, SelBAAf, SelBAAu,
SmATA 14, WebAB, -79, WhDW,
WhAm 4A, WhAmP, WhoNob,
WorAl
King, Mary Louise 1911- *ConAu 21R*
King, Stephen *DrmM 2[port]*
King, Stephen 1940- *HalFC 84*
King, Stephen 1946- *WrDr 86*
King, Stephen 1947?- *BioIn 11, -12,*
-13, ConAu 1NR, -61, ConLC 12,
-26[port], -37[port], CurBio 81[port],
DcLB Y80B[port], EncSF,
NewYTBS 79, -81[port], Novels,
ScF&FL 1, -2, ScFSB, SmATA 9,
SupFW, WhoAm 78, -80, -82,
WhoHr&F, WrDr 82, -84
King, Woodie 1937- *SelBAAf*
King, Woodie, Jr. *WhoAm 84, -86*
King, Woodie, Jr. 1937- *BlkAWP,*
ConAu 103, DcLB 38[port], DrBlPA,
InB&W 80, -85, LivgBAA, SelBAAu,
WhoAm 74, -76, -78, -80, -82,
WhoBlA 75, -77, -80, -85,
WhoThe 81
King-Hall, Baron Stephen 1893-1966
DcNaB 1961
King-Hall, Stephen 1893-1966 *BioIn 3,*
-7, ChhPo S2, ConAu 5R, LongCTC,
ScF&FL 1, -2, WhE&EA, WhLit,
WhThe, WhoLA
Kingman, Lee 1919-
SmATA 3AS[port], WrDr 86
Kingman, Lee 1919-1978 *AuBYP,*
BioIn 1, -6, -8, ChhPo, -S1,
ConAu 5R, -X, ConLC 17,
ForWC 70, MorJA, ScF&FL 1,
SmATA 1, TwCCW 78, -83,
WhoAmW 58, -61, -64, WrDr 76,
-80, -82, -84

Kingman, Russ 1917- *ConAu 101,*
-17NR
Kingsley, Charles 1819-1875
Alli, -SUP, AnCL, AtlBL, AuBYP,
BbD, BiD&SB, BioIn 1, -2, -3, -4,
-5, -6, -8, -9, -10, -11, -12, BritAS,
BritAu 19, CarSB, CasWL, CelCen,
Chambr 3, ChhPo, -S1, -S2, -S3,
CrtT 3, CyEd, CyWA, DcAmSR,
DcBiA, DcBiPP, DcBrBI, DcEnA,
DcEnL, DcEuL, DcLB 21[port],
-32[port], DcLEL, DcNaB, Dis&D,
EvLB, FamPYP, JBA 34, LinLib L,
LongCEL, LuthC 75, McGEWB,
MouLC 3, NewC, Novels, OxChL,
OxEng, -85, PenC ENG, RAdv 1,
REn, TelT, TwCChW 83A,
WebE&AL, WhDW, WhoChL,
YABC 2
Kingston, Maxine 1940- *AmWomWr,*
BioIn 11, -12, -13, ConAu 69,
ConLC 12, -19, DcLB Y80B[port],
NewYTBS 77, -80[port], WhoAm 78,
-80, -82, WhoAmW 83, WrDr 80,
-82, -84, -86
Kinkead, Eugene 1906- *ConAu 1R,*
-1NR
Kinnell, Galway *DrAP&F 85*
Kinnell, Galway 1927- *AmAu&B,*
BioIn 6, -10, -12, -13, ConAu 9R,
-10NR, ConLC 1, -2, -3, -5, -13,
-29[port], ConPo 70, -75, -80, -85,
CroCAP, CurBio 86[port],
DcLB 5[port], DcLEL 1940,
EncWL 2, IntAu&W 82, -86,
IntWW 77, -78, -79, -80, -81, -82,
-83, IntWWP 77, -82, LinLib L,
ModAL S2, -S1, OxAmL, -83,
PenC AM, RAdv 1, WhoAm 74, -76,
-78, -80, -82, -84, -86, WhoE 85,
WhoTwCL, WhoWor 74, WorAu,
WrDr 76, -80, -82, -84, -86
Kinross, Lord Patrick 1904-1976
Au&Wr 71, ConAu 9R, -65
Kinsella, W P *DrAP&F 85*
Kinsella, W P 1935- *BioIn 12,*
ConAu 21NR, -97, ConLC 27[port],
-43[port], ConNov 86, OxCanL,
WrDr 82, -84, -86
Kinter, Judith 1928- *ConAu 109*
Kipling, Rudyard 1865-1936 *Alli SUP,*
AnCL, ApCAB SUP, AtlBL, AuBYP,
BbD, BiD&SB, BioIn 1, -2, -3, -4,
-5, -6, -7, -8, -9, -10, -11, -12, -13,
BritWr 6, CarSB, CasWL, Chambr 3,
ChhPo, -S1, -S2, -S3, CmCal,
CnE&AP, CnMWL, ConAu 105,
-120, CrtT 3, -4, CyWA, DcAmAu,
DcBiA, DcBrBI, DcEnA, -AP,
DcEuL, DcInB, DcLB 19[port],
-34[port], DcLEL, DcNaB 1931,
Dis&D, EncSF, EncWL, -2, EvLB,
FamAYP, FamSYP, FilmgC,
HalFC 84, JBA 34, LinLib L,
LongCEL, LongCTC, MnBBF,
ModBrL, -S1, -S2, NewC, NewC,
Novels[port], OxAmL, -83, OxCan,
OxChL, OxEng, -85, OxMus,
PenC ENG, RAdv 1, RComWL, REn,
ScF&FL 1, ScFSB, Str&VC, SupFW,
TelT, TwCA, -SUP, TwCCW 78, -83,
TwCLC 8[port], -17[port],
TwCSFW 86, TwCWr, WebE&AL,
WhDW, WhE&EA, WhLit,
WhoBW&I A, WhoChL, WhoHr&F,
WhoLA, WhoTwCL, WorAl, YABC 2
Kipnis, Claude 1938-1981
AnObit 1981, BioIn 12, ConAu 103,
-107, NewYTBS 81, WhoAm 78, -80
Kirk, Rhina *AuBYP SUP*
Kirk, Richard 1931- *ConAu 13R*
Kirk, Robert Warren 1922-
AmM&WS 73P, -76P, -79P, -82P,
-86P, WhoFrS 84
Kirk, Ruth 1925- *AuBYP, BioIn 8,*
-10, ConAu 9NR, -13R, ForWC 70,
SmATA 5, WhoAmW 75, WhoPNW
Kirkham, George L 1941- *BioIn 11,*
ConAu 77, WrDr 80, -82, -84, -86
Kirkup, James 1918?- *AntBDN Q,*
Au&Wr 71, BioIn 4, -5, -8, -10, -11,
BlueB 76, ChhPo, -S2, -S3,

ConAu 1R, -2NR, ConAu 4AS[port],
ConLC 1, ConPo 70, -75, -80,
DcLB 27[port], DcLEL 1940,
FarE&A 78, -79, -80, -81,
IntAu&W 76, -77, -82, IntWW 74,
-75, -76, -77, -78, -79, -80, -81,
-82, -83, IntWWP 77, -82,
LongCTC, NewC, PenC ENG, REn,
SmATA 12, Who 74, -82, -83,
WhoWor 74, -78, -82, WorAu,
WrDr 76, -80, -82, -84
Kirkup, James 1923- *ConPo 85,*
OxEng 85, Who 85, WrDr 86
Kirkwood, James 1930- *Au&Wr 71,*
AuNews 2, BioIn 11, ConAu 1R,
-6NR, ConLC 9, NatPD, -81[port],
NewYTBS 82[port], WhoAm 76, -78,
-80, -82, -84, -86, WhoThe 81,
WrDr 80, -82, -84, -86
Kirkwood, James 1931?- *BioIn 13*
Kirst, Hans Hellmut 1914- *ASpks,*
BioIn 6, -8, -10, -11, CasWL,
ConAu 104, EncSF, IntAu&W 76,
-77, IntWW 74, -75, -76, -77, -78,
-79, -80, -81, -82, -83, ModGL,
ScF&FL 1, TwCCr&M 80B, -85B,
TwCWr, WhoWor 74, -82, WorAu
Kirwan, Molly Morrow 1906-
Au&Wr 71, ConAu P-1
Kis, Danilo 1935- *CasWL, ConAu 109,*
-118, ConFLW 84, IntAu&W 76,
WhoSocC 78, WorAu 1975[port]
Kishon, Ephraim 1924- *Au&Wr 71,*
BioIn 13, ConAu 2NR, -49,
IntAu&W 77, -82, -86,
McGEWD 84, REnWD, WhoWor 76,
WhoWorJ 78
Kissin, Eva H 1923- *BioIn 11,*
ConAu 29R, SmATA 10
Kister, Kenneth F 1935- *BiDrLUS 70,*
ConAu 25R, WhoLibI 82,
WhoLibS 66
Kitano, Harry 1926?- *BioIn 13*
Kitman, Marvin 1929- *AmAu&B,*
BioIn 7, -8, ConAu 101, ScF&FL 1,
WhoAm 74, -76, -78, -80
Kitson, Harry Dexter 1886-1959
BiDAmEd, BioIn 1, -2, -5, -9,
CurBio 51, -59, InSci, IndAu 1816,
NatCAB 52, ObitOF 79, WhAm 3,
WhNAA
Kittredge, William *DrAP&F 85*
Kittredge, William 1932- *ConAu 111,*
DrAS 78E, -82E
Kjelgaard, James Arthur 1910-1959
AuBYP, BioIn 2, -3, -5, -7, -12,
ConAu 109, SmATA 17, Str&VC,
TwCCW 78
Kjelgaard, Jim 1910-1959 *ConAu X,*
JBA 51, OxChL, ScF&FL 1,
SmATA X, Str&VC, TwCChW 83
Klagsbrun, Francine Lifton
ConAu 21R, ForWC 70, SmATA 36,
WhoAmW 68, -70, -75, -77, -79,
-81
Klamkin, Lynn 1950- *ConAu 45*
Klaperman, Libby Mindlin 1921-1982
BioIn 12, ConAu 9R, -107,
SmATA 31N, -33
Klass, Morton 1927- *AmM&WS 73S,*
-76P, AuBYP SUP, BioIn 11,
ConAu 1R, -5NR, FifIDA,
SmATA 11, WhoAm 84, -86
Klass, Philip J 1919?- *BioIn 12,*
ConAu 25R, IntAu&W 76, LElec,
ScF&FL 1, UFOEn[port],
WhoEng 80, WhoS&SW 73, -75, -76,
WhoTech 82, WhoWorJ 72, -78,
WrDr 84
Klass, Sheila Solomon *DrAP&F 85*
Klass, Sheila Solomon 1927-
ConAu 13NR, -37R, IntAu&W 77,
SmATA 45[port], WhoAmW 83,
WrDr 76, -80, -82, -84, -86
Klaw, Spencer 1920- *ConAu 25R,*
WhoAm 82, -84, -86
Klebanow, Diana 1935- *DrAS 74H*
Kleeberg, Irene Cumming 1932-
ConAu 12NR
Klein, Aaron E 1930- *AmBench 79,*
AuBYP SUP, BioIn 13, ConAu 19NR,
-25R, SmATA 28, -45
Klein, Dave 1940- *ConAu 89*

Klein, David 1919- *AmM&WS 73S,
–78S, AuBYP, BioIn 8, –9,
ConAu 1R, –1NR, –18NR,
IntWW 83*
Klein, Deana Tarson 1925-
AmM&WS 73P, –76P, –79P, –86P
Klein, Elizabeth *DrAP&F 85*
Klein, Elizabeth 1939- *ConAu 110,
IntWWP 77, –77X, Po&Wr 77*
Klein, Gerard 1937- *ConAu 49,
EncSF, ScF&FL 1, –2, ScFSB,
TwCSFW 86A*
Klein, H Arthur *AuBYP, BioIn 11,
ConAu 13R, SmATA 8*
Klein, Joe 1946- *ConAu X*
Klein, Mina Cooper 1906- *BioIn 11,
ConAu 37R, IntAu&W 77, –82,
SmATA 8*
Klein, Norma *DrAP&F 85*
Klein, Norma 1938- *AuBYP SUP,
BioIn 10, ChlLR 2, ConAu 15NR,
–41R, ConLC 30[port], FifBJA[port],
IntAu&W 77, OxChL, SmATA 7,
SmATA 1AS[port], TwCCW 78, –83,
WhoAm 84, –86, WhoAmW 83,
WrDr 82, –84, –86*
Klein, Richard M 1923-
*AmM&WS 73P, –76P, –79P, –82P,
–86P, ConAu 108*
Klein, Robin 1936- *ConAu 116,
SmATA 45*
Kleinfield, Sonny 1950- *BioIn 12,
ConAu 97, WhoAm 82*
Klever, Anita *AuBYP SUP*
Kline, Morris 1908- *AmM&WS 73P,
–76P, –79P, –82P, –86P,
ConAu 2NR, –5R, IntAu&W 77, –82,
WhoAm 74, –76, –78, WhoAmJ 80,
WrDr 76, –80, –82, –84, –86*
Kline, Nancy Meadors 1946-
ConAu 57
Kline, Peter 1936- *ConAu 25R,
WhoE 75, WrDr 76, –80, –82, –84,
–86*
Klinkowitz, Jerome 1943-
*ConAu 1NR, –45, DrAS 78E, –82E,
IntAu&W 86, PostFic*
Kloepfer, Marguerite 1916- *ConAu 97,
IntAu&W 82*
Klots, Alexander Barrett 1903-
AmM&WS 73P, ConAu 107
Kluckhohn, Clyde 1905-1960
*AmAu&B, BioIn 1, –2, –3, –4, –5, –6,
CurBio 51, –60, DcSoc, InSci,
McGEWB, NamesHP, ObitOF 79,
REnAL, REnAW, TwCA SUP,
WhAm 4*
Kluckhohn, Clyde Kay Maben
1905-1960 *BiDPsy*
Kluge, P F 1942- *ConAu 16NR, –73*
Kluger, Ruth 1914?-1980 *AnObit 1981,
BioIn 10, ConAu 108, –116*
Knebel, Fletcher *DrAP&F 85*
Knebel, Fletcher 1911- *AmAu&B,
Au&Wr 71, AuNews 1, BioIn 7, –10,
–12, BioNews 75, ConAu 1R, –1NR,
ConAu 3AS[port], ConLC 14,
ConNov 72, –76, –82, –86,
DcLEL 1940, EncSF, IntAu&W 76,
–77, OxChL, SmATA 36,
WhoAm 74, –76, –78, –80, –82, –84,
–86, WhoE 74, WhoWor 74,
WorAu 1975[port], WrDr 76, –80,
–82, –84, –86*
Knight, Alanna *ConAu 15NR, –81,
IntAu&W 76, –77, –82, WhoWor 80,
WrDr 86*
Knight, Arthur *WhoAm 84, –86*
Knight, Arthur 1916- *BioIn 9,
ConAu 41R, IntMPA 77, –75, –76,
–78, –79, –81, –82, –84, –86, OxFilm,
WhoAm 74, –76, –78, –80, –82*
Knight, Bernard 1931- *Au&Wr 71,
ConAu 2NR, –49, IntAu&W 76,
IntMed 80, OxLitW 86, WrDr 76,
–80, –82, –84, –86*
Knight, Charles Robert 1874-1953
*BioIn 1, –3, –4, –5, –12, IlsCB 1946,
NatCAB 39, NewYHSD, WhAm 3*
Knight, Charles W 1891- *ConAu P-1*

Knight, Damon 1922- *BioIn 10, –11,
–12, ConAu 3NR, –17NR, –49,
ConSFA, DcLB 8[port], EncSF,
IntAu&W 76, LinLib L, Novels,
ScF&FL 1, –2, ScFSB, SmATA 9,
TwCSFW 86, WhoSciF, WorAu,
WrDr 76, –80, –82*
Knight, David C 1925- *AuBYP,
BioIn 8, –12, ConAu 73, SmATA 14*
Knight, Eric 1897-1943 *AuBYP,
BioIn 1, –3, –4, –5, –7, –8, –12,
CnDAL, CurBio 42, –43, CyWA,
FourBJA, HalFC 84, NatCAB 40,
OxChL, REn, REnAL, ScF&FL 1,
SmATA 18, TwCA, –SUP,
TwCChW 83, WhAm 2, WhoChL,
WorAl*
Knight, Franklin W 1942- *ConAu 101,
DrAS 82H, IntAu&W 82, WhoBlA 85*
Knight, Harold V 1907- *ConAu 21R*
Knight, Ruth Adams 1898-1974
*AuBYP, BioIn 3, –4, –6, –8,
ConAu 5R, –49, CurBio 43, –55,
ForWC 70, InWom, MorJA, OhA&B,
SmATA 20N, WhoAmW 58, –61*
Knoke, Heinz 1921- *BioIn 4*
Knott, Will C 1927- *ConAu X,
EncFWF[port]*
Knowles, Anne 1933- *ConAu 102,
SmATA 37, WrDr 80, –82, –84, –86*
Knowles, John *DrAP&F 85*
Knowles, John 1926- *AmAu&B,
Au&Wr 71, BioIn 7, –10, –11,
BlueB 76, CasWL, ConAu 17R,
ConLC 1, –4, –10, –26[port],
ConNov 72, –76, –82, –86, DcLB 6,
DcLEL 1940, IntAu&W 76, –77, –82,
LinLib L, Novels, OxAmL 83,
RAdv 1, SmATA 8, WhoAm 74, –76,
–78, –80, –82, –84, WhoWor 74,
WorAl, WorAu, WrDr 76, –80, –82,
–84, –86*
Knowlton, William H 1927-
*ConAu 17R, IntAu&W 77, WrDr 76,
–80, –82, –84*
Knox, Bill *WrDr 86*
Knox, Bill 1928- *TwCCr&M 85*
Knox, Calvin M *ConAu X,
TwCSFW 86*
Knox, Calvin M 1935- *AuBYP,
ConAu X, DcLEL 1940, EncSF,
ScF&FL 1, SmATA X, ThrBJA,
WorAu 1970, WrDr 84*
Knox, Calvin M *see also* Silverberg,
Robert
Knox, Donald E 1936- *ConAu 45*
Knox, Donald E 1936-1986
ConAu 119
Knox-Johnston, Robin 1939-
*Au&Wr 71, BioIn 8, ConAu 15NR,
–29R, IntAu&W 76, –77, –82, –86,
Who 82, –83, –85, WhoWor 76, –78,
WrDr 76, –80, –82, –84, –86*
Knudsen, James 1950- *ConAu 111,
SmATA 42*
Knudson, R R *ConAu X*
Knudson, R R 1932- *BioIn 10,
ConAu X, SmATA 7*
Knudson, Rozanne R 1932- *WrDr 86*
Knudson, Rozanne Ruth 1932-
*BioIn 10, ConAu 33R, ForWC 70,
SmATA 7, WhoAmW 74, WrDr 76,
–80, –82, –84*
Kobryn, A P 1949- *ConAu 93*
Koch, Claude F 1918- *AmCath 80,
BioIn 3, CathA 1952, ConAu 9R,
DrAS 74E, –78E, –82E,
IntAu&W 76, –77, –82, WrDr 76,
–80, –82, –84*
Koch, Claude Francis 1918-
IntAu&W 86
Koch, Eric 1919- *ConAu 69,
OxCan, –SUP, ScF&FL 1, WhoE 79*
Koch, Howard 1902- *AmAu&B,
ConAu 73, ConDr 73, –77A, –82A,
DcLB 26[port], FilmgC, HalFC 84,
IntMPA 77, –75, –76, –78, –79, –81,
–82, –84, WorEFlm*
Koch, Kenneth *DrAP&F 85*
Koch, Kenneth 1925- *AmAu&B,
BioIn 10, –11, –12, BlueB 76,
ChhPo S1, –S2, –S3, ConAu 1R,*

*–6NR, ConDr 73, –77, –82, ConLC 5,
–8, –44[port], ConPo 70, –75, –80,
–85, CroCAP, CurBio 78,
DcLB 5[port], DcLEL 1940,
DrAS 74E, –78E, –82E,
IntAu&W 77, IntWWP 77, LinLib L,
McGEWD 84, NewYTBE 70,
OxAmL 83, PenC AM, RAdv 1,
WebE&AL, WhoAm 74, –76, –78,
–80, –82, –84, WhoWor 74, –76,
WorAu, WrDr 76, –80, –82, –84, –86*
Kochan, Lionel 1922- *Au&Wr 71,
ConAu 105*
Kocher, Paul H 1907- *AmCath 80,
ConAu 65, DrAS 74E, –78E, –82E,
ScF&FL 1, WhoAm 74, –76, –78,
–80, –82*
Kocher, Paul Harold 1907-
WhoAm 84, –86
Koehn, Ilse *BioIn 11, ConAu X,
SmATA X*
Koehn, Ilse 1929- *BioIn 13,
FifBJA[port], HerW 84*
Koenig, Laird *BlkAWP, ConAu 29R*
Koenig, Laird Philip 1927- *WhoAm 74*
Koenig, Walter *IntMPA 86*
Koenig, Walter 1936- *ConAu 104*
Koestler, Arthur 1905-1983
*AnObit 1983, ASpks, Au&Wr 71,
BioIn 1, –2, –3, –4, –5, –6, –7, –8, –9,
–10, –11, –12, –13, BlueB 76,
CasWL, CnMWL, ConAu 1R, –1NR,
–109, ConLC 1, –3, –6, –8, –15,
–33[port], ConNov 72, –76, –82,
CurBio 43, –62, –83, CyWA,
DcAmSR, DcLB Y83N[port],
EncO&P 2, –2S1, EncSF,
EncWL, –2, IntAu&W 76, –77, –82,
IntWW 74, –75, –76, –77, –78, –79,
–80, –81, –82, –83N, LinLib L, –S,
LongCTC, MakMC, ModBrL, –S2,
NewC, NewYTBE 70,
NewYTBS 83[port], Novels[port],
OxEng, –85, PenC ENG, REn,
ScF&FL 1, ScFSB[port], TwCA SUP,
TwCWr, WebE&AL, WhDW,
WhAm 8, WhE&EA, Who 74, –82,
–83, WhoTwCL, WhoWor 74, –76,
–78, –82, WhoWorJ 72, –78, WorAl,
WrDr 76, –80, –82, –84*
Koff, Richard M 1926- *WhoTech 84,
WrDr 86*
Koff, Richard Myram 1926-
*ConAu 15NR, –89, WhoAm 74, –76,
–78, –80, –82, –84, –86, WrDr 82,
–84*
Kogawa, Joy 1935- *OxCanL,
WhoCanL 85*
Kohl, Herbert *WhoAm 86*
Kohl, Herbert 1937- *AmAu&B,
BioIn 10, –11, ConAu 14NR, –65,
NewYTBE 73, SmATA 47,
WhoAmP 75, –77, –79*
Kohn, Bernice *ConAu X*
Kohn, Bernice 1920- *AuBYP, BioIn 8,
–9, ConAu 9R, IntAu&W 77X,
SmATA 4, WorBio 74*
Kohn, Bernice *see also* Hunt, Bernice
Kohn
Kohout, Pavel 1928- *BioIn 9, –11, –12,
ConAu 3NR, –45, ConLC 13,
EncWT, IntAu&W 82, McGEWD 84,
NewYTBS 79, WhoSocC 78,
WorAu 1975*
Kolbas, Grace Holden 1914-
ConAu 93, IntAu&W 82
Kome, Penney 1948- *ConAu 116*
Komisar, Lucy 1942- *AuBYP SUP,
BioIn 11, ConAu 33R, ForWC 70,
IntAu&W 86, SmATA 9, WrDr 76,
–80, –82, –84*
Komroff, Manuel 1890-1974
*AmAu&B, AmNov, AuBYP, BioIn 2,
–3, –4, –7, –9, –10, –12, CnDAL,
ConAu 1R, –4NR, –53, DcLB 4,
NewYTBS 74, ObitOF 79,
OxAmL, –83, REnAL, ScF&FL 1, –2,
SmATA 2, –20N, TwCA, –SUP,
WhAm 6, WhE&EA, WhoAm 74,
WhoWor 74, WrDr 76*
Konecky, Edith *DrAP&F 85*
Konecky, Edith 1922- *ConAu 69*
Konigsberger, Hans 1912- *WrDr 86*

Konigsberger, Hans 1921- *AmAu&B,
Au&Wr 71, ConAu 1R, SmATA 5,
WhoWor 74, WorAu, WrDr 76, –80,
–82, –84*
Konigsberger, Hans *see also*
Koningsberger, Hans
Konigsburg, E L *SmATA 48[port]*
Konigsburg, E L 1930- *AmWomWr,
ConAu 17NR, –21R, DcLB 52[port],
OxChL, ScF&FL 1, TwCChW 83,
WrDr 80, –82, –84, –86*
Konigsburg, Elaine L 1930- *AnCL,
Au&ICB, AuBYP, BioIn 8, –9, –10,
–12, ChlLR 1, ConAu 81, MorBMP,
NewbC 1966, SmATA 4, ThrBJA,
TwCCW 78, WhoAm 74, –76, –78,
–80, –82, WhoAmW 74, –72,
WrDr 76*
Konigsburg, Elaine Lobl 1930-
WhoAm 84, –86
Koningsberger, Hans *DrAP&F 85,
IntAu&W 86X*
Koningsberger, Hans 1921- *AmAu&B,
Au&Wr 71, BioIn 10, BlueB 76,
ConAu 1R, –2NR, SmATA 5,
WhoWor 74, WorAu*
Koningsberger, Hans *see also*
Konigsberger, Hans
Konvitz, Jeffrey 1944- *BioIn 10,
ConAu 7NR, –53, ScF&FL 1, –2,
WrDr 80, –82, –84, –86*
Konwicki, Tadeusz 1926- *BioIn 10,
–12, –13, ConAu 101, ConFLW 84,
ConLC 8, –28[port], DcFM,
EncWL 2, IntWW 76, –77, –78, –79,
–80, –81, –82, –83, OxFilm,
WhoSocC 78, WhoWor 74, –82, –87*
Koob, Theodora 1918- *AuBYP,
ConAu 5R, SmATA 23[port]*
Koob, Theodora Johanna 1918-
BioIn 13
Koontz, Dean R 1945- *ConAu 19NR,
ScFSB, TwCCr&M 85, TwCSFW 86,
WrDr 86*
Kopal, Zdenek 1914- *AmM&WS 73P,
–76P, –79P, –82P, –86P, BioIn 2, –8,
BlueB 76, ConAu 93, CurBio 69,
IntAu&W 77, Who 74, –82, –83, –85,
WhoWor 74, WrDr 80, –82, –84, –86*
Kopit, Arthur 1937- *AmAu&B,
AuNews 1, BiE&WWA, BioIn 9, –10,
–12, –13, CasWL, ConAu 81,
ConDr 73, –77, –82, ConLC 1, –18,
–33[port], ConTFT 4, CroCD,
CurBio 72, DcLB 7[port],
DcLEL 1940, EncWT, LinLib L,
McGEWD, –84, ModAL S2,
NatPD, –81[port], NewYTBS 84[port],
NotNAT, OxAmL, OxAmT 84,
PenC AM, REn, WebE&AL,
WhoAm 74, –76, –78, –80, –82, –84,
–86, WhoThe 72, –77, –81, WorAu,
WrDr 76, –80, –82, –84, –86*
Kopit, Arthur 1938- *OxThe 83*
Kopper, Philip 1937- *ConAu 97*
Koppett, Leonard 1923- *ConAu 11NR,
–25R, WhoAm 80, –82, –84, –86,
WhoE 74, –75, WhoWorJ 72, –78*
Korchnoi, Viktor 1931- *BioIn 10, –11,
–12, GolEC*
Koren, Edward 1935- *BioIn 10, –12,
ConAu 11NR, –25R, SmATA 5,
WhoAm 80, –82, WhoAmA 76, –78,
–80, –82, WhoE 74,
WhoGrA 82[port], WorECar*
Korinetz, Yuri 1923- *BioIn 11,
ChlLR 4[port], ConAu 11NR, –61,
SmATA 9, TwCCW 78B, –83B*
Korman, Gordon *NewYTBS 85[port]*
Korman, Gordon 1963- *BioIn 13,
ConAu 112, IntAu&W 86,
SmATA 41, WhoCanL 85*
Kornbluth, C M 1923-1958
*ConAu 105, DcLB 8[port], EncSF,
ScF&FL 1, TwCLC 8[port],
TwCSFW 86, WhoSciF, WorAl*
Kornbluth, Cyril M 1923-1958
*BioIn 4, –10, –12, LinLib L, Novels,
ObitOF 79, ScFSB, WorAu*
Kornfeld, Anita Clay *DrAP&F 85*
Kornfeld, Anita Clay 1928- *BioIn 12,
ConAu 97*
Korschunow, Irina 1925- *IntAu&W 77,
–82*

Kosinski, Jerzy *DrAP&F 85* **Kosinski,** Jerzy 1933- *AmAu&B, ASpks, BioIn 7, -9, -10, -11, -12, ConAu 9NR, -17R, ConLC 1, -2, -3, -6, -10, -15, ConNov 72, -76, -82, -86, ConTFT 1[port], CurBio 74, DcLB 2, -Y82A[port], DcLEL 1940, EncSF, EncWL, -2, IntAu&W 76, ModAL S2, -S1, NewYTBS 79, -82[port], OxAmL 83, PostFic, RAdv 1, ScFSB[port], Who 82, -83, WhoAm 74, -76, -78, -80, -82, WhoE 74, -75, -77, -79, -81, -83, WhoWor 74, -76, -78, -80, -82, -84, -87, WorAl, WorAu, WrDr 76, -80, -82, -84, -86*

Kostelanetz, Richard *DrAP&F 85*
Kostelanetz, Richard 1940- *AmAu&B, BioIn 12, BlueB 76, ConAu 13R, ConLC 28[port], ConNov 86, ConPo 75, -80, -85, DrAS 74H, -78E, -82E, Future, IntAu&W 76, -77, -82, IntWWP 77, -82, PostFic, WhoAm 74, -76, -78, -80, -82, -84, -86, WhoWor 78, -82, WrDr 76, -80, -82, -84, -86*

Kotzwinkle, William *ScFSB*
Kotzwinkle, William 1938- *BioIn 13, ChlLR 6[port], ConAu 3NR, -45, ConLC 5, -14, -35[port], EncSF, SmATA 24[port], TwCSFW 86, WhoAm 82, -84, -86, WrDr 86*

Koufax, Sandy 1935- *BioIn 12, -13, CelR, CmCal, ConAu X, CurBio 64, NewYTBS 80[port], WorAl*
Koufax, Sanford 1935- *BioIn 4, -5, -6, -7, -8, -9, -10, -11, ConAu 89, WebAB, -79, WhoAm 74, -76, WhoProB 73*

Kouwenhoven, John A 1909- *AmAu&B, BioIn 3, -9, ConAu 1R, DrAS 74E, -78E, -82E, IntAu&W 77, WhoAm 74, -76, -78, -80, -82, WhoAmA 73, -76, -78, -80, -82, -84, WrDr 76, -80, -82, -84, -86*
Kouwenhoven, John Atlee 1909- *WhoAm 84, -86*

Kovic, Ron 1946- *BioIn 11, -13*
Kowet, Don 1937- *AuBYP SUP, ConAu 10NR, -57*
Kozelka, Paul 1909- *BiE&WWA, ConAu P-2, NotNAT*
Kozol, Jonathan 1936- *AmAu&B, BioIn 5, -8, -9, -10, CelR, ConAu 16NR, -61, ConLC 17, CurBio 86[port], WhoAm 74, -76, -78, -80, -82, -84, -86*
Kraft, Ken 1907- *ConAu 1R, -1NR*
Kraft, Stephanie 1944- *ConAu 105*
Kramer, Aaron *DrAP&F 85*
Kramer, Aaron 1921- *ConAu 12NR, -21R, DrAS 74E, -78E, -82E, IntAu&W 77, -82, -86, IntWWP 77, -82, WhoAm 76, -78, -80, -82, -84, WhoE 74, -75, -77, -79, WhoWorJ 72, -78, WrDr 76, -80, -82, -84, -86*
Kramer, Daniel Caleb 1934- *AmM&WS 73S, -78S, ConAu 53, WhoAmL 78, -79*
Kramer, Jane 1938- *ConAu 102, WhoAm 82, -84, -86, WhoAmW 87, WorAu 1975[port]*
Kramer, Mark 1944- *ConAu 17NR, -97*
Kramer, Paul 1914- *ConAu 21R*
Kramer, Samuel Noah 1897- *AmAu&B, ConAu 9R, DrAS 74H, WhoWorJ 72, -78*
Kramer, William A 1941- *WhoAmL 79*
Kramer, William Joseph 1939- *WhoAm 86, WhoAmL 78, -79, -83, -85*
Krantz, Hazel 1920- *BioIn 11, ConAu 1NR, ForWC 70, IntAu&W 77, SmATA 12, WhoAmW 75, WrDr 76, -80, -82, -84, -86*
Kraske, Robert *ConAu 116, SmATA 36*
Krauss, Robert G 1924- *ConAu 1R*

Krementz, Jill 1940- *AuNews 1, -2, BioIn 8, -10, -11, -12, -13, BioNews 75, ChlLR 5[port], ConAu 41R, EncTwCJ, FifBJA[port], ICPEnP A, MacBEP, NewYTBS 82[port], SmATA 17, WhoAm 74, -76, -78, -80, -82, -84, -86, WhoAmW 74, -70, -72, -83, -85, -87*
Krensky, Stephen 1953- *ConAu 13NR, -73, SmATA 41, -47[port]*
Krents, Harold 1944- *BioIn 8, -9, ConAu 37R, WhoAmL 78, -79*
Krepps, Robert Wilson 1919-1980 *Au&Wr 71, ConAu 1R, -1NR, IntAu&W 76, WhoE 74*
Krevitsky, Nathan I 1914- *ConAu 9R*
Krevitsky, Nathan I *see also* Krevitsky, Nik
Krevitsky, Nik 1914- *BioIn 7, ConAu X*
Krevitsky, Nik *see also* Krevitsky, Nathan I
Kriegel, Leonard *DrAP&F 85*
Kriegel, Leonard 1933- *BioIn 6, ConAu 12NR, -33R, DrAS 74E, -78E, -82E, IntAu&W 77, -82, WhoE 74, -75, WrDr 76, -80, -82, -84, -86*
Kristofferson, Kris 1936- *Baker 84, BioIn 9, -10, -11, -12, -13, BioNews 74, CelR, ConAu 104, ConLC 26[port], CurBio 74, EncPR&S 74, -77, HalFC 84, IlEncRk, IntMPA 78, -79, -81, -82, -84, -86, MovMk, NewYTBE 70, RkOn 78, -84, RolSEnR 83, WhoAm 76, -78, -80, -82, -84, -86, WhoHol A, WhoRock 81[port], WhoRocM 82, WorAl*
Kristofferson, Kris 1937- *EncFCWM 83, RolSEnR 83*
Kroeber, A L 1876-1960 *ConAu 110, CurBio 58, -60*
Kroeber, Theodora 1897-1979 *AmAu&B, AmWomWr, BioIn 9, -12, ConAu 5R, -5NR, -89, ForWC 70, SmATA 1, WhoAmW 64, WrDr 76*
Kroetsch, Robert 1927- *Au&Wr 71, BioIn 7, -12, CaW, CanWW 70, -79, -80, -81, -83, ConAu 8NR, -17R, ConLC 5, -23[port], ConNov 76, -82, -86, DcLB 53[port], DcLEL 1940, DrAS 74E, -78E, -82E, IntAu&W 82, OxCan SUP, OxCanL, WhoCanL 85, WrDr 76, -80, -82, -84, -86*
Kroll, Steven 1941- *BioIn 12, ConAu 9NR, -65, FifBJA[port], SmATA 19*
Kronenberger, Louis 1904-1980 *AmAu&B, AnObit 1980, Au&Wr 71, BiE&WWA, BioIn 2, -3, -4, -5, -9, -12, ChhPo, ConAu 1R, -2NR, -97, CurBio 44, -80N, DrAS 74E, -78E, EncAJ, LinLib L, -S, NewYTBS 80[port], NotNAT, OhA&B, OxAmL, -83, OxAmT 84, REnAL, TwCA SUP, WhAm 7, WhE&EA, WhoAm 74, -76, -78, -80, WhoThe 72, -77, -81N, WhoWor 74, WhoWorJ 72, WrDr 76, -80*
Kropp, Lloyd *WrDr 86*
Kropp, Paul 1948- *ConAu 112, SmATA 34, -38[port], WhoCanL 85*
Krosney, Mary Stewart 1939- *ConAu 17R*
Kruger, Rayne *Au&Wr 71, ConAu 5R*
Kruif, Paul De 1890-1971 *CurBio 42, -63, NewYTBE 71*
Kruif, Paul De *see also* DeKruif, Paul
Krumgold, Joseph 1908-1980 *AnObit 1980, AuBYP, BioIn 3, -4, -5, -6, -7, -8, -9, -12, -13, ConAu 7NR, -9R, -101, ConLC 12, EncMys, FamMS, LinLib L, MorJA, Newb 1922, NewbC 1956, OxChL, SmATA 1, -23N, -48[port], TwCCW 78, -83, WhAm 7, WrDr 80*
Krusch, Werner E 1927- *AuBYP, BioIn 7, ConAu 5R*

Krutch, Joseph Wood 1893-1970 *AmAu&B, Au&Wr 71, BiE&WWA, BioIn 1, -3, -4, -5, -6, -8, -9, -12, BlueB 76N, CnDAL, ConAmA, ConAmL, ConAu 1R, -4NR, -25R, ConLC 24[port], CurBio 59, -70, DcLEL, EncAAH, EncWT, EvLB, InSci, LinLib L, NewYTBE 70, NotNAT B, ObitOF 79, OxAmL, -83, OxAmT 84, OxThe, PenC AM, REn, REnAL, TwCA, -SUP, WebAB, -79, WhAm 5, WhJnl, WhNAA, WhThe*
Krythe, Maymie Richardson *ConAu 17R, WhoAmW 58, -61, -64, -66*
Kube-McDowell, Michael P 1954- *ConAu 119*
Kubie, Nora 1899- *AuBYP, BioIn 8, ConAu 5R, WhoAmW 74, -58, -61, -72*
Kubler-Ross, Elisabeth *EncO&P 2*
Kubler-Ross, Elisabeth 1926- *AmWomWr, BioIn 12, -13, ConIsC 2[port], CurBio 80[port], EncO&P 80, WhoAm 82, -84, -86, WorAl, WrDr 86*
Kublin, Hyman 1919- *AuBYP SUP, ConAu 9R, DrAS 74H, -78H, -82H, WhoE 75, WhoWorJ 72, -78*
Kubrick, Stanley 1928- *BiDFilm, BioIn 4, -5, -6, -7, -9, -10, -11, -12, -13, BlueB 76, CelR, ConAu 81, ConDr 73, -77A, -82A, ConLC 16, ConTFT 1, CurBio 63, -70, DcFM, DcLB 26[port], EncSF, FilmgC, HalFC 84, IntAu&W 76, -77, IntDcF 2, IntMPA 77, -75, -76, -78, -79, -81, -82, -84, -86, IntWW 74, -75, -76, -77, -78, -79, -80, -81, -82, -83, MovMk, NewYTBE 72, OxFilm, WebAB, -79, Who 74, -82, -83, -85, WhoAm 74, -76, -78, -80, -82, -84, -86, WhoAmJ 80, WhoSciF, WhoWor 74, -76, -78, -80, -82, -84, -87, WhoWorJ 78, WomWMM, WorAl, WorEFlm, WrDr 80, -82, -84, -86*
Kugel, James Lewis 1945- *WhoAm 84, -86*
Kugelmass, Joseph Alvin 1910-1972 *AmAu&B, AuBYP, BioIn 8, -9, ConAu 5R, -33R, WhNAA, WhoAm 74, -76*
Kuhn, Bowie 1926- *WhoAm 84, -86*
Kuhn, Ferdinand 1905-1978 *AmAu&B, BioIn 11, ConAu 5R, -57, -81, CurBio 74, IntWW 74, -75, -76, -77, -78, -79N, WhAm 7, WhE&EA, WhoAm 74, -76*
Kuhns, William *DrAP&F 85*
Kuhns, William 1943- *ConAu 21R, IntAu&W 76*
Kullman, Harry 1919-1982 *Au&Wr 71, ConAu 93, FifBJA[port], SmATA 35*
Kulski, Julian 1929- *AmArch 70, AmM&WS 73S, ConAu 14NR, -21R, WhoAm 80, -82, WhoF&I 74, WhoS&SW 73, WhoWor 80*
Kumin, Maxine *DrAP&F 85*
Kumin, Maxine 1925- *AmAu&B, AmWomWr, AnCL, AuBYP, AuNews 2, BioIn 8, -10, -11, -12, -13, ChhPo S1, ConAu 1R, -1NR, -21NR, ConLC 5, -13, -28[port], ConPo 75, -80, -85, DcLB 5[port], ForWC 70, IntAu&W 77, IntWWP 77, ModAWP[port], OxAmL 83, SmATA 12, WhoAm 74, -76, -78, -80, -82, WhoAmW 74, -58, -61, -68A, -70, -72, -75, -77, -81, -83, WorAl, WorAu 1970, WrDr 76, -80, -82, -84*
Kundera, Milan *NewYTBS 85[port]*
Kundera, Milan 1929- *BioIn 10, -11, -12, -13, CasWL, ConAu 19NR, -85, ConFLW 84, ConAu 14NR, -21R, -32[port], CurBio 83[port], EncWL 2, IntAu&W 76, -77, -86, IntWW 74, -75, -76, -77, -78, -79, -80, -81, -82, -83, IntWWP 77, McGEWD 84, ModSL 2, NewYTBS 82[port], OxEng 85, PenC EUR, PostFic, WhoFr 79, WhoSocC 78, WhoWor 84, -87, WorAu 1970*

Kunen, James Simon 1948- *BioIn 8, ConAu 25R, WhoE 74, -75*
Kuniczak, W S 1930- *BioIn 12, ConAu 85*
Kunitz, Stanley *DrAP&F 85*
Kunitz, Stanley 1905- *AmAu&B, BioIn 5, -6, -8, -12, BlueB 76, CnE&AP, ConAu 41R, ConLC 6, -11, -14, ConPo 70, -75, -80, -85, CurBio 43, -59, DcLB 48[port], DrAS 74E, -78E, -82E, IntAu&W 76, -77, IntWW 74, -75, -76, -77, -78, -79, -80, -81, -82, -83, IntWWP 77, LinLib L, ModAL, -S2, -S1, OxAmL, PenC AM, RAdv 1, REn, REnAL, WebE&AL, WhoAm 74, -76, -78, -80, -82, WhoTwCL, WhoWor 74, WhoWorJ 72, -78, WorAl, WorAu, WrDr 76, -80, -82, -84, -86*
Kunitz, Stanley J 1905- *OxAmL 83*
Kunitz, Stanley Jasspon 1905- *BioIn 13, WhoAm 84, -86*
Kuper, Jack 1932- *BioIn 12, ConAu 21R*
Kupfer, Fern 1946- *ConAu 106*
Kupferberg, Herbert 1918- *Baker 84, BioIn 12, ConAu 29R, SmATA 19, WhoAmJ 80, WhoE 75, WhoWorJ 72, -78, WrDr 76, -80, -82, -84, -86*
Kupferberg, Tuli *ConAu X*
Kupferberg, Tuli 1923- *AmAu&B, BioIn 10, -11, -13, ConAu X, DcLB 16[port], MugS, WhoRocM 82*
Kuralt, Charles *IntMPA 86*
Kuralt, Charles 1934- *BioIn 10, -11, -12, -13, ConAu 89, CurBio 81[port], EncAJ, IntMPA 82, -84, LesBEnT[port], WhoAm 74, -76, -78, -80, -82*
Kurland, Gerald 1942- *BioIn 11, ConAu 14NR, -41R, DrAS 74H, -78H, -82H, SmATA 13, WhoS&SW 80*
Kurland, Michael *DrAP&F 85*
Kurland, Michael 1938- *ConAu 11NR, -61, ConSFA, EncSF, ScF&FL 1, -2, ScFSB, SmATA 48[port], TwCSFW 86, WrDr 84, -86*
Kurland, Philip B 1921- *WhoAm 84, -86, WhoAmL 85*
Kursh, Harry 1919- *ConAu 9R, WhoE 75*
Kurshan, Barbara L 1948- *WhoTech 84*
Kurten, Bjorn 1924- *ConAu 20NR, -25R, FifIDA, WrDr 76, -80, -82, -84, -86*
Kurtz, Edwin Bernard 1926- *WhoS&SW 78*
Kurtz, Edwin Bernard, Jr. 1926- *AmM&WS 73P, -76P, -79P, -82P, -86P*
Kurtz, Katherine 1944- *ConAu 29R, EncSF, ScF&FL 1, -2, ScFSB, WhoAm 84, WhoHr&F, WrDr 76, -80, -82, -84, -86*
Kurtzman, Harvey 1924- *ConGrA 2[port]*
Kurzman, Dan 1927- *ConAu 14NR, -69, IntAu&W 76, WhoE 83, -85, WrDr 80, -82, -84*
Kurzman, Dan 1929- *WrDr 86*
Kusche, Larry 1940- *ConAu X*
Kusche, Lawrence David 1940- *BioIn 10, -11, ConAu 5NR, -53, EncO&P 2, -78*
Kushner, Donn 1927- *ConAu 113, WhoCanL 85*
Kushner, Harold S 1935- *ConAu 107, WhoAmJ 80, WrDr 84, -86*
Kuslan, Louis Isaac 1922- *AmM&WS 73P, -76P, -79P, -82P, -86P, ConAu 1NR, -45, LEduc 74, WhoAm 74, -76, -78, -80, -82, -84, -86*
Kusnick, Barry A 1910- *ConAu 53*
Kutner, Luis *WhoAmL 85*
Kutner, Luis 1908- *ConAu 109, WhoAm 74, -76, WhoAmL 79*

Kuttner, Henry 1914?-1958 *AmAu&B,
BioIn 4, −7, −12, ConAu 107,
DcLB 8[port], EncMys, EncSF,
LinLib L, Novels, ObitOF 79,
ScF&FL 1, −2, ScFSB[port],
TwCLC 10[port], WhoHr&F,
WhoSciF*

Kuttner, Henry 1915-1958
TwCSFW 86

Kwolek, Constance 1933- *ConAu X,
WrDr 76, −80, −82*

Kwolek, Constance *see also* Porcari,
Constance Kwolek

Kyle, David A 1912?- *EncSF*

Kyle, Duncan *ConAu X, WrDr 86*

Kyle, Duncan 1930- *ConAu 65, −X,
IntAu&W 76, −77X, −82X, Novels,
TwCCr&M 85, WrDr 76, −80, −82,
−84*

Kyle, Elisabeth d1982 *AuBYP,
BioIn 6, −7, −8, −9, BlueB 76,*

*ConAu X, IntAu&W 76, −77, MorJA,
SmATA 3, TwCCW 78, −83,
WhE&EA, Who 74, −82, −83N,
WhoChL, WrDr 76, −80, −82*

Kyle, Elisabeth *see also* Dunlop, Agnes
M R

L

LaBastille, Anne *BioIn 13 , –12,*

LaBastille, Anne 1938- *BioIn 10, –11 ConAu 8NR, –57, NewYTBS 77, WhoAmW 77, –79, –81, –83*

Lacaze, Andre 1918- *WhoFr 79*

Lacey, Robert 1944- *Au&Wr 71, BioIn 12, ConAu 16NR, –33R, IntAu&W 86, WhoWor 76, WrDr 76, –80, –82, –84, –86*

Lackmann, Ron 1934- *ConAu 13NR, –29R*

LaCroix, Mary 1937- *ConAu 106*

Lacy, Dan 1914- *BiDrLUS 70, BioIn 2, –3, –7, –11, ConAu 37R, CurBio 54, Dun&B 79, ODwPR 79, St&PR 75, WhoAm 74, –76, –78, –80, –82, WhoF&I 74, WhoLibI 82, WhoLibS 55*

Lacy, Dan Mabry 1914- *WhoAm 84, –86*

Lacy, Leslie Alexander 1937- *BioIn 8, –10, ConAu 33R, InB&W 80, LivgBAA, SelBAAf, SelBAAu, SmATA 6, WhoBlA 77, –80, –85*

Ladd, Veronica *ConAu X, IntAu&W 86X, SmATA X*

Ladd, Veronica *see also* Miner, Jane Claypool

Lader, Lawrence 1919- *AmAu&B, BioIn 10, ConAu 1R, –2NR, SmATA 6, WhoAm 74, –76, –78, –80, –82, –84, –86, WhoE 74*

LaFarge, Oliver 1901-1963 *AmAu&B, AmNov, AuBYP, BioIn 2, –3, –4, –5, –6, –7, –8, –9, –12, CnDAL, ConAmA, ConAu 81, CurBio 53, –63, DcAmB S7, DcLB 9[port], DcLEL, EncFWF[port], InSci, LongCTC, Novels, ObitOF 79, OxAmH, OxAmL, –83, PenC AM, REn, REnAL, REnAW, SmATA 19, TwCA, –SUP, WhAm 4, WhE&EA, WhNAA, WorAl*

Laffin, John 1922- *Au&Wr 71, AuBYP, ConAu 7NR, –53, IntAu&W 76, –77, –82, –86, SmATA 31[port], WhoWor 74, –76, –78, –80, –82, –84, WrDr 76, –80, –84, –86*

LaFountaine, George 1934- *ConAu 7NR, –57, WrDr 76, –80, –82, –84, –86*

Lagerkvist, Par 1891-1974 *BioIn 1, –2, –3, –4, –5, –8, –9, –10, –11, CasWL, ClDMEL, CnMD, CnThe, ConAu 49, ConLC 7, –10, –13, CurBio 52, –74N, CyWA, EncWL, –2[port], EncWT, EvEuW, GrFLW, IntWW 74, LinLib L, McGEWB, McGEWD, –84[port], ModWD, NewYTBS 74, Novels, ObitOF 79, ObitT 1971, OxThe, –83, PenC EUR, REn, REnWD, ScF&FL 1, TwCA SUP, TwCWr, WhDW,*

WhAm 6, WhE&EA, Who 74, WhoTwCL, WhoWor 74, WorAl

Lagerkvist, Par Fabian 1891-1974 *WhoNob*

Lahue, Kalton C 1934- *ConAu 7NR, –13R*

Laing, Frederick 1905- *BioIn 4, ConAu 105*

Laing, Martha *ConAu X, SmATA X*

Laird, Carobeth 1895-1983 *BioIn 11, ConAu 8NR, –110, –61, DcLB Y82B[port]*

Laird, Carobeth Harrington 1895-1983 *BioIn 13*

Laird, Charlton G 1901- *ConAu 13R, WhJnl*

Laird, Jean E 1930- *AmCath 80, ConAu 6NR, –9R, ForWC 70, SmATA 38[port], WhoAmW 74, –68, –70, –72, –75, –77, –79, –81, –83, WhoMW 74, –76, –78*

Laird, Jean Elouise Rydeski 1930- *WhoAmW 85, –87*

Laitin, Ken 1963- *ConAu 102*

Laitin, Steve 1965- *ConAu 102*

Lake, David J 1929- *ConAu 10NR, –65, EncSF, WrDr 84*

Lake, David John 1929- *WhoWor 87*

Laker, Rosalind *WrDr 86*

Laklan, Carli 1907- *AuBYP SUP, BioIn 10, ConAu 1NR, ForWC 70, IntAu&W 77, SmATA 5*

Laklan, Carli *see also* Clarke, John

Laliberte, Norman 1925- *AmAu&B, BioIn 8, ConAu 104, WhoAm 74, –76, WhoAmA 73, –76, –78, –80*

Lally, John Ronald 1939- *LEduc 74*

LaMare, Walter De 1873-1956 *JBA 51, ScF&FL 1, TwCA, –SUP*

LaMare, Walter De *see also* DeLaMare, Walter

Lamb, Beatrice Pitney 1904- *BioIn 12, ConAu 5R, IntAu&W 76, SmATA 21[port], WhoAmW 61, –64, –66, –68, –70*

Lamb, Charles 1775-1834 *Alli, AtlBL, BbD, BiD&SB, BiDLA, BioIn 1, –2, –3, –4, –5, –6, –7, –8, –9, –10, –11, –12, –13, BritAu 19, BritWr 4, CarSB, CasWL, CelCen, Chambr 3, ChhPo, –S1, –S2, –S3, CrtT 2, CyWA, DcBiPP, DcEnA, DcEnL, DcEuL, DcInB, DcLEL, DcNaB, Dis&D, EvLB, LinLib L, –S, LongCEL, McGEWB, MouLC 3, NewC, NinCLC 10[port], NotNAT B, OxAusL, OxChL, OxEng, –85, OxMus, OxThe, –83, PenC ENG, RAdv 1, RComWL, REn, SmATA 17, TelT, WebE&AL, WhDW, WhoChL, WhoHol A, WorAl*

Lamb, Eleanor 1917- *ConAu 69*

Lamb, G F *ConAu 4NR, –19NR, –53*

Lamb, G F *see also* Lamb, Geoffrey Frederick

Lamb, Geoffrey Frederick *Au&Wr 71, AuBYP SUP, BioIn 11, ConAu 53, IntAu&W 76, –77, –82, SmATA 10, WrDr 76, –80, –82, –84, –86*

Lamb, Geoffrey Frederick *see also* Balaam

Lamb, Geoffrey Frederick *see also* Lamb, G F

Lamb, Harold 1892-1962 *AmAu&B, AuBYP, BioIn 1, –2, –3, –4, –6, –7, –9, ChhPo S2, ConAu 101, –89, JBA 34, –51, NatCAB 52, ObitOF 79, OxAmL, –83, REn, REnAL, ScF&FL 1, TwCA, –SUP, WhAm 4, WhE&EA, WhNAA*

Lamb, Hugh 1946- *ConAu 1NR, –49, ScF&FL 1, –2, WhoHr&F*

Lamb, Mary Ann 1764-1847 *Alli, BioIn 1, –2, –6, –8, –9, –10, –11, –12, CarSB, ChhPo, –S2, –S3, DcEnA, DcEnL, DcLEL, DcNaB, Dis&D, NewC, OxEng, –85, SmATA 17, TelT, WhoChL*

Lamb, Mary Anne 1764-1847 *OxChL*

Lamb, Ruth S *ConAu 21NR*

Lamb, Ruth Stanton *ConAu 45, DrAS 74F, 78F, –82F, WhoAmW 74, –68, –70, –72, –75, –77*

Lambdin, William 1936- *ConAu 102*

Lambert, Gavin 1924- *BioIn 11, ConAu 1R, –1NR, DcLEL 1940, FilmgC, HalFC 84, IntAu&W 77, –82, TwCWr, WhoWor 76, WorEFlm, WrDr 76, –80, –82, –84, –86*

Lambert, Janet 1894-1973 *AuBYP, BioIn 3, –7, –9, –13, ConAu 41R, CurBio 54, InWom, IndAu 1917, REnAL, SmATA 25[port], ThrBJA, WhoAmW 58, –61*

Lamburn, John Battersby Crompton 1893- *ConAu P-1, ScF&FL 1*

Lame Deer 1895?-1976 *BioIn 9, –11, ConAu 69*

Lamm, Robert 1945- *BioNews 74, WhoAm 76, –78, –80, –82, WhoRocM 82*

Lamm, Robert *see also* Chicago

L'Amour, Louis 1908- *AuNews 1, –2, BioIn 10, –11, –12, CmCal, ConAu 1R, –3NR, ConLC 25[port], CurBio 80[port], DcLB Y80B[port], EncFWF[port], HalFC 84, NewYTBS 81[port], Novels, REnAW, WhoAm 74, –76, –78, –80, –82, WhoWest 76, –78, –80, –82, WhoWor 76, –78, WrDr 76, –80, –82, –84, –86*

Lampedusa, Giuseppe 1896-1957 *BioIn 5, –6, –10, CasWL, EncWL, –2, EvEuW, HalFC 84, ModRL, Novels, PenC EUR, REn, TwCWr, WhDW, WhoTwCL, WorAl, WorAu*

Lampell, Millard 1919- *AmAu&B, AmNov, BiE&WWA, BioIn 1, –2, ConAu 9R, EncFCWM 69, NotNAT, PIP&P, REnAL, WhoAm 74*

Lampman, Evelyn 1907-1980 *AnObit 1980, AuBYP, BioIn 6, –7, –9, –12, –13, ConAu 101, –11NR, –13R, MorJA, NewYTBS 80, ScF&FL 1, –1A, –2, SmATA 23N, –4, TwCCW 78, –83, WhoAmW 74, –58, –61, –64, –66, –68, –70, –72, –75, –77, WhoPNW, WrDr 80, –82*

Lamprey, Louise 1869-1951 *AmAu&B, BioIn 2, –12, CarSB, ChhPo, ConAu 117, JBA 34, –51, REnAL, WhAm 3, WhE&EA, WhLit, WhNAA, YABC 2*

Lampton, Christopher *SmATA 47*

Lamson, Peggy 1912- *ConAu 25R, OhA&B*

Lancaster, Bruce 1896-1963 *AmAu&B, AmNov, BioIn 1, –2, –4, –6, –7, –11, ConAu P-1, ConLC 36[port], NatCAB 48, ObitOF 79, SmATA 9, TwCA, –SUP, WhAm 4, WhE&EA*

Lancaster, Richard *ConAu 21R*

Lancour, Gene *ConAu X, EncSF, ScF&FL 1*

Land, Barbara 1923- *BioIn 12, ConAu 81, IntAu&W 76, –77, –82, SmATA 16, WhoAmW 61*

Landau, Elaine 1948- *AuBYP SUP, BioIn 11, ConAu 5NR, –53, IntAu&W 77, SmATA 10, WhoAmW 77, –79, –81*

Landau, Lev Davidovich 1908-1968 *AsBiEn, BiESc, BioIn 5, –6, –8, –11, –12, –13, ConAu 113, CurBio 63, –68, DcScB, McGEWB, McGMS 80[port], ObitOF 79, ObitT 1961, WhDW, WhAm 5, WhoNob, WorAl*

Lande, Nathaniel 1939- *BioIn 11, ConAu 104*

Landeck, Beatrice 1904- *AuBYP, BioIn 7, –12, ConAu 73, LEduc 74, SmATA 15*

Landers, Gunnard W 1944- *ConAu 93*

Landis, Paul H 1901- *AmM&WS 73S, ConAu 5R, –5NR, IntAu&W 76, –77, WhE&EA*

Landon, Margaret 1903- *AmAu&B, AmWomWr, BioIn 4, –12, ConAu 13R, ConAu P-1, CurBio 45, ForWC 70, InWom, PIP&P, TwCA SUP, WhoAmW 58*

Landorf, Joyce *AuNews 1, BioIn 9, –10*

Landry, Lionel 1919- *WhoAm 74, –76, –78, –80, –82, –84*

Landsburg, Alan 1933- *BioIn 12, ConAu 103, IntMPA 77, –75, –76, –78, –79, –81, –82, –84, –86, NewYTET, WhoWest 76, –78*

Landsman, Sandy *DrAP&F 85*

Lane, Arthur 1945- *WhoAmL 83,*
WhoReal 83
Lane, Burton 1912- *AmPS,*
AmSCAP 66, Baker 84, BiDAmM,
BiE&WWA, BioIn 5, -6, -7, -8, -9,
-10, -12, CmpEPM, CurBio 67,
EncMT, HalFC 84, NewCBMT,
NotNAT, OxAmT 84, PlP&P,
WhoAm 74, -76, -78, -80, -82, -84,
-86, WhoThe 72, -77, -81
Lane, Carolyn 1926- *AuBYP SUP,*
BioIn 11, ConAu 12NR, -29R,
SmATA 10, WhoAmW 75, -77, -79,
WhoE 77, -79, -81, WrDr 76, -80,
-82, -84, -86
Lane, Frank W 1908- *WrDr 86*
Lane, Frank Walter 1908-
IntAu&W 86
Lane, Peter 1925- *Au&Wr 71*
Lane, Rose Wilder 1886-1968
AmAu&B, AmWomWr, AuBYP SUP,
BioIn 4, -8, -10, -12, ConAu 102,
InWom, NatCAB 54, NotAW MOD,
REnAL, SmATA 28, -29[port],
TwCA, -SUP, WhAm 5, WhNAA,
WhoAmW 58A
Lane, Rose Wilder 1887-1968
EncFWF
Lane, Rose Wilder *see also* Wilder,
Rose
Lang, Daniel 1915-1981 *AmAu&B,*
AnObit 1981, BioIn 12, ConAu 4NR,
-5R, -105, NewYTBS 81[port],
WhoAm 74, -76, -78, -80,
WhoAmJ 80
Lang, H Jack 1904- *BioIn 5,*
ConAu 115, WhoAm 74, -76, -78,
-80, -82, -84, -86
Lang, Paul Henry 1901- *AmAu&B,*
Baker 78, -84, ConAu 103,
IntWW 74, -75, -76, IntWWM 77,
OxMus, REnAL, WhoMus 72
Lang, Robert 1912- *BiDrLUS 70,*
ConAu 41R, DrAS 74H, -78H,
WhoLibS 55, -66
Lange, Oliver *ScFSB*
Lange, Oliver 1927- *ConAu 103,*
EncSF, ScF&FL 1, WrDr 86
Lange, Suzanne 1945- *BioIn 10,*
ConAu 29R, SmATA 5
Langland, Joseph *DrAP&F 85*
Langland, Joseph 1917- *ConAu 5R,*
-8NR, ConPo 70, -75, -80, -85,
DrAS 74E, -78E, -82E, IntWWP 77,
-82, LinLib L, PenC AM,
WhoAm 78, -80, -82, WrDr 76, -80,
-82, -84, -86
Langley, Bob 1936?- *ConAu 85,*
WrDr 80, -82, -84
Langley, Bob 1938- *WrDr 86*
Langone, John 1929- *ConAu 1NR,*
-49, SmATA 38, -46
Langton, Jane 1922- *AuBYP, BioIn 9,*
-13, ConAu 1R, -18NR, -18NR,
FifBJA[port], ForWC 70,
IntAu&W 86, OxChL, ScF&FL 1A,
SmATA 3, TwCCW 78, -83,
TwCCr&M 85, WhoAmW 83,
WrDr 76, -80, -82, -84, -86
Lanham, Urless Norton 1918-
AmM&WS 73P, -76P, -79P, -82P,
-86P, WhoAm 82, -84, -86,
WhoWest 74, -76, -78, -80
Lanier, Sidney 1842-1881 *Alli SUP,*
AmAu, AmAu&B, AmBi, AmWr S1,
ApCAB, AtlBL, Baker 78, -84, BbD,
BiDAmM, BiD&SB, BiDSA, BioIn 1,
-2, -3, -4, -5, -6, -8, -9, -10, -11,
-12, CarSB, CasWL, Chambr 3,
ChhPo, -S1, -S2, -S3, CnDAL,
CnE&AP, CrtT 3, -4, CyWA,
DcAmAu, DcAmB, DcEnA AP,
DcLEL, DcNAA, DrAS 78E, -82E,
Dis&D, EncAAH, EncSoH, EvLB,
HarEnUS, LinLib L, -S, McGEWB,
MouLC 3, NatCAB 7,
NinCLC 6[port], OxAmL, -83,
OxChL, OxEng, -85, PenC AM,
RAdv 1, REn, REnAL, SmATA 18,
TwCBDA, WebAB, -79, WebE&AL,
WhAm HS, WhFla, WorAl

Lanier, Sterling E 1927- *AuBYP,*
ConAu 118, EncSF, ScF&FL 1, -2,
ScFSB, TwCSFW 86, WhoHr&F,
WrDr 84, -86
Lansdale, Joe R 1951- *ConAu 113*
Lansing, Alfred 1921-1975 *BioIn 10,*
ConAu 13R, -61, SmATA 35
Lansing, Elizabeth 1911- *AuBYP,*
ConAu 5R
Lantz, Fran *ConAu X, IntAu&W 86X*
Lao She 1899-1966 *CasWL, DcOrL 1,*
EncWL, PenC CL
Lapage, Geoffrey 1888-1971
Au&Wr 71, BioIn 9, ConAu P-1,
WhE&EA
Lapham, Lewis Henry 1935- *BioIn 13,*
WhoAm 84, -86
Lapierre, Dominique 1931- *BioIn 9,*
-12, CelR, ConAu 19NR, -69,
NewYTBS 80[port], WhoAm 76, -78,
-80, -82, -84, -86, WhoFr 79,
WhoWor 74, -76
Lapp, Ralph Eugene 1917- *AmAu&B,*
AmM&WS 73P, BioIn 3, -8,
ConAu 81, CurBio 55, InSci,
WhoAm 74, -76, WhoWor 74
Lappe, Frances Moore *BioIn 13*
Lappe, Frances Moore 1944-
ConAu 37R, IntAu&W 82,
WhoAm 84, -86, WhoAmW 83, -85,
-87, WrDr 76, -80, -82, -84, -86
Lapping, Brian 1937- *WrDr 86*
Laqueur, Walter 1921- *AmAu&B,*
BlueB 76, ConAu 5R, IntAu&W 77,
-86, IntWW 75, -76, -77, -78, -79,
-80, -81, -82, -83, Who 74, -82, -83,
-85, WhoAm 74, -76, -78, -80, -82,
-84, -86, WhoAmJ 80, WhoWor 74,
-78, -80, -82, -84, WhoWorJ 72,
-78, WorAu 1975[port], WrDr 76,
-80, -82, -84, -86
LaRamee, Louise De 1839-1908
BiD&SB, BritAu 19, DcEnA, JBA 34
LaRamee, Louise De *see also*
DeLaRamee, Louise
Lardner, Rex 1881-1941 *AmAu&B,*
AuBYP SUP, ObitOF 79, REnAL
Lardner, Ring 1885-1933 *AmAu&B,*
AmBi, AmSCAP 66, AmWr, AtlBL,
BioIn 1, -3, -4, -5, -6, -7, -9, -10,
-11, -12, CasWL, CnDAL, CnMWL,
ConAmA, ConAmL, ConAu 104,
CyWA, DcLB 11[port], -25[port],
DcLEL, EncAJ, EncWL, EncWT,
LinLib L, LongCTC, ModAL, -S1,
NatCAB 32, NotNAT B, Novels,
OxAmL, -83, OxAmT 84, PenC AM,
RAdv 1, REn, REnAL, TwCA, -SUP,
TwCLC 2, -14[port], TwCWr,
WebAB, -79, WebE&AL, WhAm 1,
WhNAA, WhoTwCL, WorAl
Largo, Michael 1950- *ConAu 73*
Larkin, Rochelle *NewYTBS 84[port]*
Larkin, Rochelle 1935- *BioIn 13,*
ConAu 13NR, -33R, IntAu&W 77,
WrDr 76, -80, -82, -84, -86
Larrabee, Harold A 1894-1979
AmAu&B, AuBYP, BioIn 1, -8, -11,
ConAu 85, ConAu P-1, NewYTBS 79,
WhAm 7, WhoAm 74, -76
Larrick, Nancy 1910- *AuBYP,*
BioIn 7, -9, -10, ChhPo, -S1, -S2,
-S3, ConAu 1R, -1NR, IntAu&W 86,
LEduc 74, MorBMP, SmATA 4,
WhoAmW 74, -58, -61, -64, -66,
-68, -72, -75, -77, -79, -81,
WrDr 76, -80, -82, -84, -86
Larsen, Carl *DrAP&F 85*
Larsen, Carl 1934- *BioIn 12,*
ConAu 77, NatPD
Larsen, Egon 1904- *Au&Wr 71,*
BioIn 12, ConAu 3NR, -9R,
IntAu&W 76, -77, -82, WhoWor 78,
ScF&FL 1, -2, SmATA 14, WrDr 76,
-80, -82, -84, -86
Larsen, Wendy Wilder 1940-
ConAu 120
Larson, Charles R *DrAP&F 85*
Larson, Charles R 1938- *BioIn 11,*
ConAu 33NR, -53, ConLC 31[port],
DrAS 78E, -82E, IntAu&W 77
Larson, E Richard 1944- *ConAu 105*
Larson, Gary *EncTwCJ*
Larson, Gary 1950- *ConAu 118*

Larson, George C 1942- *ConAu 9NR,*
-65
Larson, Peggy 1931- *ConAu 81*
Larson, Rodger 1934?- *BioIn 8*
Lartigue, Jacques Henri 1894-
MacBEP
Lartigue, Jacques Henri 1896-
BioIn 13
Lartigue, Jacques-Henri 1894-
ICPEnP
Lartigue, Jacques-Henri 1894-1986
ConAu 120, NewYTBS 86[port]
Larue, Gerald A 1916- *ConAu 21R,*
DrAS 74P, -78P, WhoRel 75, -77
Lash, Joseph P 1909- *BioIn 9, -11,*
ConAu 16NR, -17R, CurBio 72,
SmATA 43[port], WhoAm 74, -76,
-78, -80, -82, -84, -86, WhoE 74,
WorAu 1970, WrDr 80, -82, -84, -86
Laski, Marghanita *IntAu&W 86X*
Laski, Marghanita 1915- *Au&Wr 71,*
BioIn 2, -4, ConAu 105, CurBio 51,
DcLEL 1940, EncSF, InWom,
IntAu&W 76, -77, LongCTC,
ModBrL, REn, ScF&FL 1,
TwCA SUP, WhE&EA, Who 74, -82,
-83, -85, WrDr 82, -84, -86
Lasky, Kathryn 1944- *BioIn 11,*
ChlLR 11[port], ConAu 11NR, -69,
SmATA 13
Lasky, Victor 1918- *AmAu&B,*
AuNews 1, BioIn 8, -10, BioNews 75,
BlueB 76, CelR, ConAu 5R, -10NR,
IntAu&W 86, WhoAm 74, -76, -78,
-80, -82, -84, -86, WhoAmJ 80,
WhoE 74, WhoWorJ 72, -78,
WrDr 76, -80, -82, -84, -86
Lass, Abraham H 1907- *BioIn 2, -11,*
ConAu 9R, NewYTBE 71
Lassiter, Barbara B 1934-
NewYTBE 71, WhoAmW 70, -72
Lasson, Kenneth 1943- *ConAu 13NR,*
-33R, IntAu&W 77, WhoAmL 85,
WrDr 76, -80, -82, -84, -86
Lasson, Robert 1922- *AuBYP, BioIn 8*
Laszlo, John 1931- *AmM&WS 86P*
Latham, Aaron 1943- *BioIn 11,*
ConAu 33R
Latham, Frank B 1910- *AuBYP SUP,*
BioIn 10, ConAu 49, SmATA 6
Latham, Jean Lee 1902- *AmAu&B,*
AmWomWr, Au&Wr 71, AuBYP,
AuNews 1, BioIn 4, -6, -7, -8, -9,
-10, -12, ConAu 5R, -7NR,
ConLC 12, CurBio 56, InWom,
LinLib L, MorBMP, MorJA, OxChL,
SmATA 2, Str&VC, TwCCW 78, -83,
WhoAm 74, -76, -78, -80, -82, -84,
-86, WhoAmW 74, -58, -64, -66,
-68, -70, -72, WrDr 80, -82, -84,
-86
Latourette, Kenneth Scott 1884-1968
AmAu&B, BioIn 3, -4, -6, -8,
ConAu P-2, CurBio 53, -69,
DcAmReB, EncSoB SUP, LinLib L,
LuthC 75, OhA&B, TwCA SUP,
WhE&EA, WhNAA
Lattimore, Eleanor 1904- *AmAu&B,*
AuBYP, BioIn 1, -2, -5, -7, -8, -10,
ConAu 6NR, -9R, IlsCB 1744, -1946,
-1957, InWom, JBA 34, -51,
LinLib L, OxChL, SmATA 5, -7,
TwCCW 78, -83, WhoAmW 58, -61,
WrDr 80, -82, -84, -86
Lattimore, Owen 1900- *AmAu&B,*
AmM&WS 73S, BioIn 1, -2, -3, -4,
-5, -6, -7, -9, -11, BlueB 76,
ConAu 9R, CurBio 45, -64,
IntWW 74, -75, -76, -77, -78, -79,
-80, -81, -82, -83, OxAmL, -83,
PolProf T, REnAL, TwCA SUP,
WhE&EA, Who 74, -82, -83, -85,
WhoAm 74, -76, -78, -80, -82,
WhoWor 74, WrDr 86
Lattimore, Richmond d1984
NewYTBS 84[port]
Lattimore, Richmond 1906- *AmAu&B,*
BiE&WWA, BioIn 4, -6, BlueB 76,
ConAu 1NR, ConLC 3, ConPo 70,
-75, -80, DrAS 74F, IntAu&W 77,
-82, IntWWP 77, LinLib L,
ModAL, -S1, NotNAT, OxAmL, -83,
RAdv 1, REnAL, TwCA SUP,

Lattimore, Richmond 1906-1984
AnObit 1984, ConAu 112, WhAm 8
Lauber, Patricia 1924- *AuBYP,*
BioIn 7, -9, ConAu 6NR, -9R,
ForWC 70, SmATA 1, -33[port],
ThrBJA, WhoAmW 58
Laubin, Gladys *BioIn 1, -6,*
ConAu 111, WhoAmW 77, -79
Laufe, Abe 1906- *ConAu 17R,*
DrAS 74E, -78E
Laumer, Keith *DrmM 2[port]*
Laumer, Keith 1925- *AmAu&B,*
BioIn 12, ConAu 7NR, -9R, ConSFA,
DcLB 8[port], EncSF, ScF&FL 1, -2,
ScFSB, TwCSFW 86, WhoSciF,
WrDr 84, -86
Laure, Ettagale 1940- *ConAu 103*
Laure, Jason 1940- *ConAu 104,*
SmATA 44
Laurence, David Herbert 1885-1930
MakMC
Laurence, Margaret 1926- *Au&Wr 71,*
BioIn 8, -10, -11, -12, -13,
BlueB 76, CaW, CanWW 70, -79,
-80, -81, -83, CanWr, ConAu 5R,
ConLC 3, -6, -13, ConNov 72, -76,
-82, -86, CreCan 1, DcLB 53[port],
EncWL 2, IntAu&W 76, -77,
ModCmwL, Novels, OxCan, -SUP,
OxCanL, WhoAm 86, WhoAmW 68,
-70, -83, -87, WhoCanL 85,
WhoWor 74, WorAu 1970, WrDr 76,
-80, -82, -84, -86
Laurents, Arthur *IntMPA 86*
Laurents, Arthur 1918?- *AmAu&B,*
BiE&WWA, BioIn 4, -9, -10, -12,
BlueB 76, CnMD, ConAu 8NR,
-13R, ConDr 73, -77, -82,
ConTFT 2, CurBio 84[port],
DcLB 26[port], DcLEL 1940,
EncMT, EncWT, FilmgC, HalFC 84,
IntAu&W 76, IntMPA 77, -75, -76,
-78, -79, -81, -82,
McGEWD, -84[port], ModWD,
NewCBMT, NotNAT, OxAmL, -83,
OxAmT 84, PenC AM, PlP&P,
REnAL, TwCA SUP, WhoAm 74,
-76, -78, -80, -82, -84, -86,
WhoE 74, WhoThe 72, -77, -81,
WhoWor 74, -76, WrDr 76, -80, -82,
-84, -86
Laurie, Rona *ConAu 15NR, -85,*
IntAu&W 77, WhoWor 78, WrDr 76,
-80, -82, -84, -86
Laurie, Rona 1926- *IntAu&W 86*
Lauritzen, Jonreed 1902- *BioIn 3, -11,*
ConAu 5R, CurBio 52, SmATA 13,
WrDr 76, -80, -82, -84
Laury, Jean Ray 1928- *ConAu 77,*
WhoAmA 73, -76, -78, -80,
WhoAmW 74, -72, -75
Lavender, David 1910- *AuBYP,*
BioIn 8, -11, CmCal, ConAu 1R,
-2NR, -18NR, REnAW
Laver, James 1899-1975 *Au&Wr 71,*
BiE&WWA, BioIn 4, -6, -10,
BlueB 76N, ChhPo S3, ConAu 1R,
-3NR, -57, DcNaB 1971, EvLB,
IntWW 74, -75, -75N, LongCTC,
ModBrL, NewC, NewYTBS 75,
NotNAT A, ObitOF 79, ObitT 1971,
OxThe, PenC ENG, ScF&FL 1, -2,
TwCA, -SUP, WhE&EA, WhLit,
WhThe, Who 74, WhoWor 74, -76,
WorFshn
Lavine, Sigmund Arnold 1908-
AuBYP, BioIn 7, -9, ConAu 1R,
-4NR, -19NR, SmATA 3, WhoE 75,
-77, WrDr 76, -80, -82, -84, -86
Law, Janice *ConAu 65, -X*
Lawick-Goodall, Jane Van 1934-
BioIn 8, -9, -10, -11, -12, CurBio 67
Lawler, Donald L 1935- *ConAu 105,*
DrAS 82E
Lawrence, D H 1885-1930 *AtlBL,*
BritWr 7, CnE&AP, CnMWL,
CnThe, ConAu 104, CyWA,
DcLB 10[port], -19[port], -36[port],
EncFWF, EncWL 2[port], FilmgC,
HalFC 84, LongCTC, McGEWD 84,
ModBrL, -S2, -S1, ModWD, NewC,

Liddy, G Gordon 1930- *ConAu 114, CurBio 80[port], WorAl*

Lieberman, E James 1934- *BiDrAPA 77, BiDrAPH 79, ConAu 45*

Lieberman, Edwin James 1934- *AmM&WS 73S, -76P, -79P, -82P, -86P*

Lieberman, Jethro K 1943- *ConAu 10NR, -21R, WhoAmL 79, -83, WhoE 75, -77, WhoS&SW 73*

Lieberman, Jethro Koller 1943- *IntAu&W 86*

Lieberman, Mark 1942- *ConAu 29R*

Lieberman, Nancy 1958- *BioIn 11, -12, HerW 84, NewYTBS 80, -82[port]*

Lieberman, Robert 1941- *ConAu 10NR*

Liebers, Arthur 1913- *BioIn 11, ConAu 3NR, -5R, SmATA 12, WrDr 76, -80, -82, -84*

Liebman, Arthur 1926- *ConAu 6NR, -57*

Lief, Philip 1947- *ConAu 107*

Lifshin, Lyn *DrAP&F 85*

Lifshin, Lyn 1942- *BioIn 13, ConAu 8NR, -33R, ConPo 75, -80, -85, IntAu&W 82, WrDr 76, -80, -82, -84*

Lifshin, Lyn 1948- *WrDr 86*

Lifshin, Lyn 1949- *IntAu&W 86*

Lifton, Betty Jean *ConAu 12NR*

Lifton, Betty Jean 1926- *AuBYP, BioIn 8, -9, -10, ConAu 5R, ForWC 70, HerW 84, SmATA 6, ThrBJA, TwCCW 78, -83, WrDr 80, -82, -84, -86*

Lifton, Robert Jay 1926- *AmAu&B, AmM&WS 73S, -76P, -79P, -82P, -86P, BiDrAPA 77, BioIn 8, -10, -13, BlueB 76, ConAu 17R, CurBio 73, WhoAm 74, -76, -78, -80, -82, -86, WhoAmJ 80, WorAu 1970, WrDr 80, -82, -84, -86*

Lifton, Robert Jay 1929- *WhoAm 84*

Liggett, Clayton Eugene 1930- *ConAu 29R, IntAu&W 76, WhoWest 74, -76, -78, -80*

Light, Ivan 1941- *ConAu 73, WhoWest 84*

Light, Ken 1951- *ICPEnP A, MacBEP*

Lightfoot, Gordon 1938?- *AmSCAP 66, Baker 84, BioIn 8, -10, -11, -12, BioNews 74, CanWW 81, -83, ConAu 109, ConLC 26[port], CreCan 2, CurBio 78, EncFCWM 83[port], EncPR&S 74, -77, IlEncRk, RkOn 78, -84, RolSEnR 83, WhoAm 78, -80, -82, WhoRocM 82, WorAl*

Lightfoot, Gordon 1939?- *WhoRock 81*

Lightner, A M *AuBYP SUP, BioIn 10, ConAu X, IntAu&W 76X, -77X, -82X, MichAu 80, SmATA 5*

Lightner, A M *see also* Hopf, Alice L

Lightner, Robert P 1931- *ConAu 1NR, -16NR, -49, DrAS 74P, -78P, -82P, WhoRel 77*

Lilienfeld, Robert Henry 1927- *ConAu 1R, -1NR*

Lilienthal, David 1896?-1953 *BioIn 3*

Lilienthal, David E 1899-1981 *AmAu&B, AnObit 1981[port], BiDAmBL 83, BioIn 1, -2, -5, -7, -8, -9, -10, -11, -12, BlueB 76, CelR, ConAu 3NR, -5R, -102, CurBio 44, -81N, DcAmSR, EncAB-H, IntWW 74, -75, -76, -77, -78, -79, -80, -81N, IntYB 78, -79, -80, -81, LinLib S, McGEWB, NewYTBS 81[port], PolProf T, WebAB, -79, WhAm 7, WhoAm 74, -82N, WhoAm 74, -76, -78, -80, WhoWor 74, WhoWorJ 72, -78*

Lillington, Kenneth 1916- *SmATA 39[port]*

Lillington, Kenneth James 1916- *Au&Wr 71, ConAu 3NR, -5R, WrDr 76, -80, -82, -84, -86*

Liman, Ellen 1936- *AuBYP SUP, BioIn 13, ConAu 13NR, -61, SmATA 22*

Limburg, Peter R 1929- *BioIn 11, ConAu 33R, IntAu&W 77, -82, SmATA 13, WhoE 75, WrDr 76, -80, -82, -84, -86*

Lincoln, Abraham *OxAmT 84*

Lincoln, Abraham 1809-1865 *AmAu&B, AmBi, ApCAB, AtlBL, BbD, BiAUS, BiD&SB, BiDSA, BiDrAC, BiDrUSE, BioIn 1, -2, -3, -4, -5, -6, -7, -8, -9, -10, -11, -12, -13, CelCen, Chambr 3, ChhPo S2, -S3, CivWDc, CyAG, CyWA, DcAmAu, DcAmB, DcAmMiB, DcAmReB, DcAmSR, DcBiPP, DcLEL, DcNAA, Dis&D, Drake, EncAAH, EncAB-H, EncO&P 2, -78, EncSoH, EvLB, FilmgC, HalFC 84, HarEnUS[port], LinLib L, McGEWB, MemAm, NatCAB 2, OxAmH, OxAmL, -83, OxEng, -85, OxFilm, PenC AM, RComWL, REn, REnAL, REnAW, TwCBDA, WebAB, -79, WebE&AL, WhDW, WhAm HS, WhAmP, WorAl*

Lincoln, C Eric 1924- *AmAu&B, AmM&WS 73S, -78S, CivR 74, ConAu 1R, -1NR, DrAS 74P, -78P, -82P, Ebony 1, IntAu&W 82, LivgBAA, SmATA 5, WhoAm 74, -76, -78, -80, -82, -84, -86, WhoBlA 77, -80, -85, WhoRel 75, -77, -85, WhoWor 74, WrDr 76, -80, -82, -84, -86*

Lind, Levi Robert 1906- *ConAu 5R, DrAS 74F, -78F, -82F, IntAu&W 76, WhoAm 74, -76, -78, -80, -82, -84, -86, WrDr 76, -80, -82, -84, -86*

Lindberg, Richard 1953- *ConAu 110*

Lindberg, Richard C 1953- *IntAu&W 86*

Lindberg, Stanley W 1939- *ConAu 112*

Lindberg, Stanley William 1939- *WhoAm 84, -86*

Lindbergh, Anne *ConAu X, SmATA X*

Lindbergh, Anne 1906- *BioIn 13*

Lindbergh, Anne Moorow 1906- *BioIn 4, -5, -6, -8, -9, -10, -11, -12*

Lindbergh, Anne Morrow 1906- *AmAu&B, AmWomWr, AnCL, CelR, ChhPo, ConAu 16NR, -17R, CurBio 76, GoodHs, InScI, InWom, IntAu&W 76, -77, -82, LibW, LinLib L, -S, LongCTC, NewYTBS 80[port], OxAmH, OxAmL, -83, REn, REnAL, SmATA 33[port], TwCA, -SUP, Who 74, -82, -83, WhoAm 74, -76, -78, -80, -82, WhoAmW 74, -58, -61, -64, -66, -68, -70, -72, -75, -77, -79, -81, -83, WhoWor 74, WrDr 76, -80, -82, -84, -86*

Lindbergh, Charles A 1902-1974 *AmAu&B, AsBiEn, BioIn 1, -2, -3, -4, -5, -6, -7, -8, -9, -10, -11, -12, BioNews 74, BlueB 76, CelR, ConAu 16NR, -53, -93, CurBio 41, -54, -74, -74N, DcAmSR, EncAB-H, InScI, IntWW 74, -75N, LinLib L, -S, McGEWB, MedHR, NatCAB 60, NewYTBE 71, NewYTBS 74, ObitOF 79, ObitT 1971, OxAmH, OxAmL, -83, REn, REnAL, SmATA 33[port], WebAB, -79, WebAMB, WhDW, WhAm 6, WhNAA, Who 74, WhoAm 74, WhoWor 74, WorAl*

Lindbergh, Charles Augustus 1902-1974 *BioIn 13*

Lindbergh, Charles Augustus, Jr. 1902-1974 *MorMA*

Lindblom, Steven 1946- *ConAu 106, SmATA 39, -42*

Linden, Catherine 1939- *ConAu 110*

Lindenmeyer, Otto J 1936- *ConAu 77*

Linderman, Frank Bird 1868?-1938 *AmAu&B, BioIn 2, -4, -8, DcNAA, JBA 34, -51, NatCAB 40, OhA&B, OxAmL, REnAL, WhAm 1, WhNAA*

Linderman, Frank Bird 1869-1938 *OxAmL 83*

Lindop, Edmund 1925- *AuBYP SUP, BioIn 10, ConAu 2NR, -5R, -17NR, SmATA 5*

Lindquist, Willis 1908- *AuBYP, BioIn 6, -8, -12, ConAu 73, MorJA, SmATA 20*

Lindsay, Jeanne Warren 1929- *ConAu 106*

Lindsay, Merrill K d1985 *NewYTBS 85*

Lindsay, Merrill K 1915- *ConAu 73*

Lindsay, Merrill K 1915-1985 *ConAu 115*

Lindsay, Rachel *WrDr 84, -86*

Lindsey, Robert 1935- *ConAu 97*

Line, David *WrDr 86*

Line, David *see also* Davidson, Lionel

Line, Les 1935- *ConAu 73, SmATA 27[port]*

Lines, Kathleen *AuBYP SUP, ChhPo, -S1, OxChL*

Lineweaver, Thomas H, III 1926- *ConAu 73*

Lingard, Joan *ConAu 18NR, FifBJA[port], OxChL, WrDr 86*

Lingard, Joan 1932- *Au&Wr 71, AuBYP SUP, BioIn 11, ConAu 41R, IntAu&W 82, SmATA 8, TwCCW 78, -83, WrDr 76, -80, -82, -84*

Lingeman, Richard R 1931- *ConAu 11NR, -17R, IndAu 1917, WhoAm 80, -82*

Lingeman, Richard Roberts 1931- *WhoAm 84, -86*

Lingenfelter, Mary Rebecca 1893-1953 *BioIn 3, WhAm 3*

Linington, Elizabeth 1921- *AmWomWr, Au&Wr 71, ConAu 1R, -1NR, -20NR, EncMys, Novels, TwCCr&M 80, -85, WrDr 82, -84, -86*

Linn, Charles F 1930- *AuBYP SUP, ConAu 85*

Linneman, Robert E 1928- *AmM&WS 73S, -78S, ConAu 29R, WhoE 74, -75*

Linton, Ralph 1893-1953 *AmAu&B, BiDPsy, BioIn 3, -4, -5, -9, DcAmB S5, InScI, McGEWB, NamesHP, ObitOF 79, TwCA SUP, WebAB, -79, WhAm 3, WhE&EA, WhNAA*

Lipman, David 1931- *AuBYP SUP, BioIn 12, ConAu 21R, IntAu&W 77, -86, SmATA 21[port], WhoAm 74, -76, -78, -80, -82, -84, -86, WhoAmJ 80, WhoMW 74, -76, -84, -86, WhoWor 78, WrDr 76, -80, -82, -84, -86*

Lipman, Jean 1909- *ConAu 10NR, -21R, ForWC 70, WhoAmA 73, -76, -78, -82*

Lipp, Frederick J 1916- *BioIn 7, ConAu 106*

Lipp, Frederick John 1916- *IntAu&W 86*

Lippard, Lucy R *DrAP&F 85*

Lippard, Lucy R 1937- *ConAu 20NR*

Lippard, Lucy Rowland 1937- *ConAu 25R, IntAu&W 76, -77, -82, WhoAm 84, WhoAmA 73, -76, -78, -80, -82, -84, WhoAmW 74, -75*

Lippincott, David M 1925- *AmSCAP 66, ConAu 9NR, -61*

Lippincott, Joseph Wharton 1887-1976 *AmAu&B, AuBYP, BioIn 1, -3, -4, -6, -7, -11, -12, ConAu 69, -73, CurBio 55, -77, -77N, MorJA, NewYTBS 76, ObitOF 79, OxChL, REnAL, SmATA 17, TwCCW 78, -83, WhAm 7, WhE&EA, WhLit, WhNAA*

Lippincott, Sarah L *WhoTech 84*

Lippincott, Sarah Lee 1920- *AmM&WS 73P, -76P, -79P, -82P, -86P, BioIn 13, ConAu 17R, ForWC 70, SmATA 22[port], WhoAm 78, -80, -82, -84, -86, WhoAmW 74, -75, -77, WhoFrS 84, WhoTech 82*

Lipscomb, James 1926- *ConAu 85*

Lipsyte, Robert 1938- *AuBYP SUP, BioIn 10, -12, ConAu 8NR, -17R, ConLC 21[port], FifBJA[port], IntAu&W 77, SmATA 5*

Lipton, James 1926- *AmSCAP 66*

Lisca, Peter 1925- *ConAu 37R, DrAS 74E, -78E, -82E, IntAu&W 82*

Lisker, Sonia O 1933- *AuBYP SUP, ConAu 2NR, -49, SmATA 44[port]*

Lisle, Janet Taylor *SmATA 47*

Liss, Howard 1922- *AuBYP, BioIn 8, -9, ConAu 16NR, -25R, SmATA 4*

List, Albert, Jr. 1928- *AmM&WS 82P, -86P*

List, Ilka 1935- *BioIn 10, ConAu 37R, ForWC 70, SmATA 6, WrDr 80, -82, -84, -86*

Liston, Robert A 1927- *AuBYP, BioIn 8, -10, ConAu 12NR, -17R, SmATA 5*

Litowinsky, Olga *DrAP&F 85*

Litowinsky, Olga 1936- *ConAu 81, SmATA 26[port]*

Litowinsky, Olga Jean 1936- *BioIn 13*

Littell, Robert 1896-1963 *AmAu&B, BioIn 6, -8, ConAu 93, NatCAB 50, NotNAT B, WhAm 4, WhJnl, WhNAA, WhThe*

Littell, Robert 1935?- *ConAu 112, ConLC 42[port], TwCCr&M 85, WrDr 86*

Littell, Robert 1937- *AuBYP SUP*

Little, Charles Eugene 1931- *WhoAm 74, -76*

Little, Jean 1932- *AuBYP, BioIn 8, -9, -10, -12, CaW, ChlLR 4[port], ChhPo S2, ConAu 21R, FourBJA, OxCan SUP, OxCanL, Profile, SmATA 2, TwCCW 78, -83, WhoCanL 85, WrDr 80, -82, -84, -86*

Little, Lessie Jones 1906- *ConAu 101*

Little, Malcolm *BioIn 13*

Little, Malcolm 1925-1965 *AmAu&B, BioIn 9, -10, -11, -12, BlkAWP, ConAu 111, InB&W 80, ObitOF 79, SelBAAf, SelBAAu, WebAB 79*

Little, Malcolm *see also* Malcolm X

Little, Sara Pamela 1919- *WhoAmW 75, -77, WhoRel 75, -77*

Little, Stuart W 1921- *BiE&WWA, ConAu 1NR, -45, ConTFT 4, IntAu&W 86, NotNAT, WhoE 75, -77, WrDr 76, -80, -82, -84*

Little, Thomas Russell 1911- *Au&Wr 71, ConAu 13R, IntAu&W 76*

Littledale, Freya *WrDr 86*

Littledale, Freya 1929- *ConAu 10NR, -21R, IntAu&W 76, -77, -82, ScF&FL 1, -2, SmATA 2, WhoAmW 74, -68, -72, -75, -77, -81, -83, WhoE 75, -77, -81, -83, WrDr 76, -80, -82, -84*

Litwack, Leon F 1929- *ConAu 1R, -1NR, DrAS 74H, -78H, -82H, WhoAm 82, WrDr 82, -84*

Litwack, Leon Frank 1929- *WhoAm 84, -86*

Lively, Penelope 1933- *Au&Wr 71, AuBYP SUP, BioIn 10, -11, -13, ChlLR 7[port], ChhPo S2, ConAu 41R, ConLC 32[port], DcLB 14[port], FourBJA, IntAu&W 77, -82, Novels, OxChL, ScF&FL 1, -2, SmATA 7, TwCCW 78, -83, Who 82, -83, WrDr 76, -80, -82, -84, -86*

Liversidge, Douglas 1913- *BioIn 11, ConAu P-1, IntAu&W 76, -77, -82, -86, SmATA 8*

Liversidge, Douglas *see also* Liversidge, Henry Douglas

Liversidge, Henry Douglas 1913- *Au&Wr 71, BioIn 11, WhE&EA, WrDr 76, -80, -82, -84, -86*

Liversidge, Henry Douglas *see also* Liversidge, Douglas

Livingston, James T 1931- *DrAS 74E, -78E, -82E*

Livingston, Myra Cohn 1926- *AmAu&B, AmWomWr, AnCL, AuBYP SUP, BioIn 10, -12, BkCL, BkP, ChlLR 7[port], ChhPo, -S1, -S2, -S3, ConAu 1R, -1NR, FourBJA, IntAu&W 76, -77, -82, -86, IntWWP 77, -82, SmATA 5, SmATA 1AS[port], TwCCW 78, -83,*

WhoAm 82, –84, –86, WhoAmW 75, –77, –83, –85, –87, WhoWor 82, WrDr 80, –82, –84, –86
Livsey, Clara G 1924- *BiDrAPA 77, ConAu 107*
Llewellyn, Edward 1917-
Llewellyn, Edward 1917-1984 *TwCSFW 86*
Llewellyn, Richard *ConAu X, SmATA X*
Llewellyn, Richard d1983 *WhAm 8*
Llewellyn, Richard 1906-1983 *BioIn 2, –4, –5, –11, –13, ConAu X, ConLC 7, CurBio 40, –84N, CyWA, DcLB 15[port], DcLEL, EvLB, HalFC 84, IntAu&W 82X, LongCTC, NewC, NewYTBS 83[port], Novels, OxLitW 86, RAdv 1, REn, SmATA X, TwCA, –SUP, TwCWr, Who 74, –82, –83, WhoWor 74, WorAl, WrDr 76, –80, –82, –84*
Llewellyn, Richard 1907-1983 *AnObit 1983*
Llewellyn, Richard *see also* Llewellyn Lloyd, Richard D V
Llewellyn-Jones, Derek 1923- *ConAu 15NR, WrDr 86*
Llewellyn Lloyd, Richard D V 1906-1983 *ConAu 7NR, –111, –53, CurBio 40, SmATA 11, –37N, TwCA, –SUP*
Llewellyn Lloyd, Richard D V *see also* Llewellyn, Richard
Lloyd, Alan C 1915- *ConAu 1R, –1NR, LEduc 74, WhoE 75, –77*
Lloyd, Chris Evert *BioIn 12, NewYTBS 80[port], –85[port]*
Llywelyn, Morgan 1937- *ConAu 16NR, –81, WhoAmW 87, WhoE 85, WrDr 86*
Lo, Ruth Earnshaw 1910- *BioIn 12, ConAu 106*
Lobb, Charlotte 1935- *ConAu 15NR, –65*
Lobenz, Norman Mitchell 1919- *AmAu&B, ConAu 9R, SmATA 6*
Lobley, Robert John 1934- *Au&Wr 71, ConAu 29R, WrDr 76, –80, –82*
Locke, Charles O 1896?-1977 *BioIn 11, ConAu 69, NewYTBS 77*
Lockerbie, Jeanette W Honeyman *ConAu 9R*
Lockley, Ronald Mathias 1903- *Au&Wr 71, BioIn 12, ConAu 5NR, –9R, IntAu&W 76, –77, OxLitW 86, ScF&FL 1, –2, WhE&EA, Who 74, –82, –83, –85, WhoWor 76, WrDr 76, –80, –82, –84, –86*
Lockwood, Charles Andrews 1890-1967 *AmAu&B, BioIn 1, –2, –7, –9, ConAu 1R, EncAB 38[port], NatCAB 53, ObitOF 79, OxShips, WhAm 4*
Lockwood, Douglas 1918- *ConAu 21R, WhoWor 74, –78*
Lockwood, Douglas 1918-1980 *OxAusL*
Lockwood, Lee 1932- *ASpks, BioIn 7, –11, ConAu 37R, ICPEnP A, WhoAm 74, –76, –78, –80, WhoBlA 75, –77, –80*
Lockwood, Margo 1939- *ConAu 117*
Loeb, Robert H, Jr. 1917- *BioIn 12, ConAu 12NR, –29R, SmATA 21[port]*
Loebl, Suzanne *AuBYP SUP, ConAu 69, WhoAm 76, –78, –80, WhoAmW 74, –70, –72, –75, WhoE 74*
Loeper, John J 1929- *BioIn 11, ConAu 12NR, –29R, IntAu&W 77, –82, SmATA 10, WhoE 75, WrDr 76, –80, –82, –84, –86*
Loeper, John Joseph 1929- *IntAu&W 86*
Loescher, Ann Dull 1942- *BioIn 12, ConAu 9NR, –61, SmATA 20*
Loescher, Gil 1945- *BioIn 12, ConAu 9NR, –61, SmATA 20*
Loftis, Anne 1922- *ConAu 45*
Lofts, Norah 1904-1983 *Au&Wr 71, AuBYP SUP, AuNews 2, BioIn 3, –4, –9, –10, –11, –13, ConAu 5R, –6NR,*

–110, IntAu&W 76, –77, –82, LinLib L, LongCTC, Novels, ScF&FL 1, –2, SmATA 36N, –8, TwCA, –SUP, TwCCr&M 80, WhAm 8, WhE&EA, WhNAA, Who 74, –82, –83, WhoAm 74, WhoAmW 74, –64, –66, –68, –70, –72, –75, WhoWor 76, WrDr 76, –80, –82, –84
Logan, Rayford W 1897-1982 *AmAu&B, BioIn 5, –9, ConAu 1R, –1NR, –108, DrAS 74H, –78H, InB&W 80, NegAl 76, –83, NewYTBS 82, SelBAAu, WhAm 8, WhoAm 74, –76, –78, –80, –82, WhoBlA 75, WhoWor 74, –76, –78, –80, –82*
Logan, Rayford Whittingham 1897-1982 *BioIn 13, SelBAAf*
Logan, Rayford Whittingham 1897-1984 *InB&W 85*
Logan, Robert Kalman 1939- *AmM&WS 86P*
Loggins, Kenny 1947- *BioIn 11, –12, WhoAm 80, –82, –84, –86, WhoRocM 82, WorAl*
Loggins, Kenny 1948- *EncFCWM 83, RolSEnR 83*
Loggins, Kenny *see also* Loggins & Messina
Loggins & Messina *EncPR&S 74, –77, IllEncRk, RkOn 78, –84*
Loggins & Messina *see also* Loggins, Kenny
Loggins & Messina *see also* Messina, Jim
Logsdon, Richard H 1912- *AuBYP, BiDrLUS 70, BioIn 1, –8, ConAu 2NR, –5R, DrLC 69, WhoAm 74, –76, –78, –80, –82, WhoLibI 82, WhoLibS 55, –66, WhoWor 80, –82*
Logsdon, Richard Henry 1912- *WhoAm 84, –86*
Logue, Christopher 1926- *BioIn 13, ConPo 85, DcLB 82[port], OxEng 85, Who 85, WrDr 86*
Loh, Jules 1931- *ConAu 33R*
Loken, Newton 1919- *BioIn 13, ConAu 1R, SmATA 26[port]*
Lolli, Giorgio 1905-1979 *BioIn 11, –12, ConAu 1R, –2NR, –85*
Lomas, Steve *BioIn 10, ConAu X, SmATA 6*
Lomas, Steve *see also* Brennan, Joseph Lomas
Lomask, Milton 1909- *AuBYP, BioIn 8, –12, BkC 6, ConAu 1R, –1NR, DrAS 74H, SmATA 20, WhoS&SW 76, –80, –82*
Lomax, Alan 1915- *AmAu&B, Au&Wr 71, Baker 78, –84, BiDAmM, BioIn 2, –4, –5, BlueB 76, ConAu 1R, –1NR, CurBio 41, EncFCWM 69, –83, IntWW 74, –75, –76, –77, –78, –79, –80, –81, –82, –83, LinLib L, REnAL, TexWr, TwCA SUP, WebAB, –79, WhoAm 74, –76, –84, WhoWor 74*
Lomax, Bliss *ConAu X, EncFWF, OhA&B*
Lomax, Bliss *see also* Drago, Harry Sinclair
Lomax, John A 1872-1948 *OxAmL 83*
Lomax, John Avery 1867?-1948 *AmAu&B, Baker 78, –84, BiDAmM, BiDSA, BioIn 1, –2, –3, –4, –5, ChhPo, –S3, CnDAL, DcAmB S4, DcNAA, EncFCWM 69, LinLib L, NatCAB 38, ObitOF 79, OxAmL, OxMus, REn, REnAL, REnAW, Str&VC, TexWr, TwCA SUP, WebAB, –79, WhAm 2, WhNAA*
Lomax, John Avery 1875-1948 *EncFCWM 83*
Lomax, Louis E 1922-1970 *AmAu&B, BioIn 5, –7, –8, –9, ConAu P-2, InB&W 80, NewYTBS 70, SelBAAu, WhAm 5, WhScrn 77*
Lomax, Louis Emanuel 1922-1970 *SelBAAf*
Lombardi, Vince 1913-1970 *CurBio 63, –70, NewYTBE 70, ObitOF 79, WhScrn 83, WorAl*

Lombardi, Vincent Thomas 1913-1970 *BioIn 6, –8, –9, –10, –11, –12, WebAB, –79, WhAm 5, WhoFtbl 74*
London, Jack *ConAu X, OxCanL*
London, Jack 1876-1916 *AmAu&B, AmBi, AmRef[port], AmWr, ApCAB X, AtlBL, AuBYP, AuNews 2, BiD&SB, BioIn 1, –2, –3, –4, –5, –7, –8, –9, –10, –11, –12, –13, CarSB, CasWL, Chambr 3, CmCal, CnDAL, ConAmL, ConAu X, CyWA, DcAmAu, DcAmB, DcAmSR, DcBiA, DcLB 8[port], –12[port], DcLEL, DcNAA, Dis&D, EncAB-H, EncFWF[port], EncMys, EncSF, EncWL, –2, FamAYP, FilmgC, HalFC 84, JBA 34, LinLib L, –S, LongCTC, MakMC, McGEWB, MnBBF, ModAL, –S1, MorMA, NatCAB 13, –57, NotNAT B, Novels[port], OxAmH, OxAmL, –83, OxCan, OxChL, OxEng, PenC AM, RAdv 1, RComWL, REn, RENAL, ScF&FL 1, ScFSB, SmATA 18, Str&VC, TwCA, –SUP, TwCLC 9[port], –15[port], TwCSFW 86, TwCWr, WebAB, –79, WebE&AL, WhDW, WhAm 1, WhoBW&I A, WhoHr&F, WhoRocM 82, WhoTwCL, WorAl*
London, Mel 1923- *ConAu 107*
Long, Judy 1953- *ConAu 65, –X, SmATA X*
Longfellow, Henry Wadsworth *OxCanL*
Longfellow, Henry Wadsworth 1807-1882 *Alli, –SUP, AmAu, AmAu&B, AmBi, AmWr, AnCL, ApCAB, AtlBL, AuBYP, BbD, BiDAmM, BiD&SB, BioIn 1, –2, –3, –4, –5, –6, –7, –8, –9, –10, –11, –12, –13, CasWL, CelCen, Chambr 3, ChhPo, –S1, –S2, –S3, CnDAL, CnE&AP, CrtT 3, CyAL 2, CyEd, CyWA, DcAmAu, DcAmB, DcAmSR, DcBiA, DcBiPP, DcEnA, DcEnL, DcLB 1, –59[port], DcLEL, DcNAA, DcSpL, Drake, EncAAH, EncAB-H, EvLB, FamAYP, FamPYP, HarEnUS[port], LinLib L, –S, LuthC 75, McGEWB, MemAm, MouLC 4, NatCAB 2, NewEOp 71, NinCLC 2[port], OxAmH, OxAmL, –83, OxEng, –85, OxSpan, PcnC AM, RAdv 1, RComWL, REn, REnAL, SmATA 19, Str&VC, TwCBDA, WebAB, –79, WebE&AL, WhDW, WhAm HS, WorAl*
Longford, Elizabeth *Who 85*
Longford, Elizabeth 1906- *Au&Wr 71, BlueB 76, ConAu 5R, DcLEL 1940, IntAu&W 76, –77, –82, –86, IntWW 77, –81, Who 74, –82, –83, WhoAmW 74, –70, –72, WhoWor 74, –76, –78, WrDr 76, –80, –82, –84, –86*
Longland, Jean R 1913- *BiDrLUS 70, ConAu 10NR, –21R, IntWWP 77, –82, WhoAm 82, WhoAmW 58, –68, WhoLibI 82, WhoLibS 55, –66*
Longo, Lucas 1919- *ConAu 25R, WrDr 76, –80, –82, –84, –86*
Longstreet, Stephen 1907- *AmAu&B, BiE&WWA, BioIn 4, ConAu 7NR, –9R, ConDr 73, –77D, –82D, FilmgC, HalFC 84, IntAu&W 86, IntMPA 77, –75, –78, –79, –81, –82, –84, –86, NotNAT, Novels, REnAL, TwCA SUP, WhoAm 74, –76, –78, –80, –82, –84, –86, WhoAmA 73, –76, –78, –80, –82, –84, WhoWorJ 72, –78, WrDr 76, –80, –82, –84, –86*
Longstreth, Thomas Morris 1886-1975 *AmAu&B, Au&Wr 71, AuBYP, BioIn 2, –6, –7, ConAu 5R, CurBio 50, MorJA, OxCan, WhAm 7, WhoAm 74, –76*
Longsworth, Polly 1933- *AuBYP, BioIn 8, –13, ConAu 106, SmATA 28[port]*
Longsworth, Polly Ormsby 1933- *IntAu&W 86*
Longyear, Barry B *ScFSB*

Longyear, Barry B 1942- *ConAu 102, IntAu&W 82*
Loomis, Frederic Brewster 1873-1937 *AmLY, DcNAA, NatCAB 30, WhAm 1, WhNAA*
Loomis, Robert D *AuBYP, BioIn 7, –10, –11, ConAu 17R, SmATA 5*
Loomis, Robert Duane 1926- *WhoAm 84, –86*
Lopez, Barry *DrAP&F 85*
Lopez, Barry 1945- *ConAu 7NR, –65*
Lopez, Nancy *NewYTBS 84[port], –85[port]*
Lopez, Nancy 1957- *BioIn 13, ConAu 113, HerW 84, WhoAm 84, –86, WhoAmW 85, –87*
Lopez Y Fuentes, Gregorio 1897?-1966 *BioIn 7, CasWL, ConLC 32, DcSpL, EncLatA, EncWL 2, OxSpan, PenC AM, REn*
Lorayne, Harry 1926- *ConAu 41R, IntAu&W 76, –77*
Lord, Athena V *WomPO 78*
Lord, Athena V 1932- *ConAu 109, SmATA 39[port]*
Lord, Bette Bao 1938- *BioIn 12, ConAu 107, ConLC 23[port], NewYTBS 81[port], WhoAmW 83, –85, –87*
Lord, Gabrielle 1946- *ConAu 106*
Lord, Walter 1917- *AmAu&B, AmSCAP 66, BioIn 5, –9, –10, ConAu 1R, –5NR, CurBio 72, IntAu&W 76, –77, –82, –86, REnAL, SmATA 3, WhoAm 74, –76, –78, –80, –82, –84, –86, WorAu, WrDr 80, –82, –84, –86*
Lorde, Audre *DrAP&F 85*
Lorde, Audre 1934- *BioIn 13, BlkWWr, ConAu 16NR, ConPo 85, DcLB 41[port], ModAWP[port], SelBAAf, WorAu 1975[port], WrDr 86*
Lorde, Audre 1937- *InB&W 85*
Lorenz, Ellen Jane 1907- *AmSCAP 66, ConAmC, –82, InWom, IntWWM 77, –85, WhoAmM 83, WhoAmW 58, –61, –64, –66, WhoMW 84, WhoMus 72*
Lorenz, Konrad 1903- *AmAu&B, BiEsc, BioIn 2, –3, –4, –8, –10, –11, –12, ConAu 61, CurBio 55, –77, EncTR, InSci, IntAu&W 77, IntEnSS 79, IntWW 74, –75, –76, –77, –78, –79, LinLib L, MakMC, McGMS 80[port], NewYTBE 73, WhDW, Who 74, –82, –83, –85, WhoWor 76, –78, –80, –82, WorAl, WorAu 1970*
Lorenz, Konrad Zacharias 1903- *BioIn 13, WhoNob, WhoWor 84, –87*
Lorenzo, Carol Lee 1939- *ConAu 53*
Lorimer, Lawrence T 1941- *ConAu 6NR, –57*
Lorrah, Jean *ConAu 103, –19NR, DrAS 74E, –78E, –82E*
Lortz, Richard 1930-1980 *ConAu 102, –57*
Lose, M Phyllis 1925- *BioIn 12, ConAu 101, –18NR*
Lossing, Benson J 1813-1891 *DcLB 30[port]*
Lossing, Benson John 1813-1891 *Alli, –SUP, AmAu, AmAu&B, BbD, BiD&SB, ChhPo, CyAL 2, DcAmAu, DcNAA, EarABI, –SUP*
Lott, Milton 1919- *BioIn 3, ConAu 17R, WhoPNW, WrDr 84, –86*
Lottman, Eileen 1927- *ConAu 12NR, –57, IntAu&W 76, WhoAmW 68*
Lotz, Wolfgang 1912-1981 *BioIn 13*
Lotz, Wolfgang 1921- *BioIn 7, –9*
Loughnane, Lee 1946- *BioIn 13, WhoAm 78, –80, –82, WhoRocM 82, WhoWor 80*
Loughnane, Lee *see also* Chicago
Louis, Joe 1914- *WhoBlA 85*
Louis, Joe 1914-1981 *AnObit 1981[port], BioIn 1, –2, –3, –4, –5, –6, –7, –8, –9, –11, –12, –13, CelR, ConAu X, CurBio 40, –81N, Ebony 1, EncAB-H, InB&W 80, –85, McGEWB,*

NegAl 76, –83, NewYTBS 79,
–81[port], OxAmH, WebAB, –79,
WhDW, WhAm 7, WhScrn 83,
WhoAm 74, –76, –78, –80,
WhoBlA 75, –77, –80, WhoBox 74,
WorAl

Louis, Murray 1926- *BiDD, BioIn 8,
–9, –11, CurBio 68, WhoAm 78, –80,
–82, –84, –86, WhoE 83, –85*

Louria, Donald B 1928-
*AmM&WS 73P, –76P, –79P, –82P,
BiDrACP 79, ConAu 107, IntMed 80,
WhoAm 82, WhoE 75*

Louria, Donald Bruce 1928-
AmM&WS 86P, WhoWor 84

Louthworth, John 1904- *WrDr 80*

Love, Edmund 1912- *AmAu&B,
BioIn 7, ConAu 1R, –4NR,
NewYTBE 73, ScF&FL 1, –2*

Love, Mike 1941- *BioIn 11, –12,
WhoRocM 82*

Love, Mike *see also* Beach Boys, The

Love, Robert 1914-1948 *WhScrn 83*

Love, Sandra 1940- *BioIn 13,
ConAu 11NR, –69, SmATA 26[port]*

Lovecraft, H P 1890-1937 *EncO&P 2,
OxAmL 83, ScFSB[port], SupFW,
TwCLC 22[port], TwCSFW 86*

Lovejoy, Bahija F 1914- *AuBYP,
BioIn 8, ConAu 5R*

Lovejoy, Clarence Earle 1894-1974
*AmAu&B, Au&Wr 71, BioIn 6, –10,
ConAu 5R, –45, NewYTBS 74,
WhAm 6, WhJnl, WhNAA*

Lovejoy, Jack 1931- *WhoAmP 73*

Lovelace, Delos Wheeler 1894-1967
*AmAu&B, AuBYP, BioIn 4, –6, –7,
–10, ConAu 5R, –25R, MinnWr,
ScF&FL 1, –2, SmATA 7,
TwCA, –SUP, WhAm 4, WhE&EA,
WhNAA*

Lovelace, Maud 1892-1980 *AmAu&B,
Au&Wr 71, AuBYP, BioIn 2, –4, –5,
–6, –7, –9, –11, –13, ConAu 5R,
–104, JBA 51, MinnWr, REnAL,
SmATA 2, –23N, TwCA, –SUP,
TwCChW 83, WhE&EA, WhNAA,
WhoAmW 74, –58, –61, –64, –66,
–68, –70, –72*

Lovelace, Richard 1618-1658
BiDRP&D, DcNaB, OxEng 85

Lovell, Alfred Charles Bernard 1913-
*AsBiEn, BioIn 2, –5, DcLEL 1940,
IntAu&W 77, McGEWB, Who 82,
–83, WorAl*

Lovell, Alfred Charles Bernard *see also*
Lovell, Bernard

Lovell, Bernard 1913- *Au&Wr 71,
BiESc, BioIn 7, BlueB 76,
ConAu 6NR, –13R, CurBio 59, InSci,
IntAu&W 82, IntWW 74, –75, –76,
–77, –78, –79, –80, –81, –82, –83,
IntYB 78, –80, –81, –82, LinLib L,
–S, McGMS 80[port], WhDW,
Who 74, WhoPubR 76, WhoWor 74,
–76, –78, –82, WrDr 76, –80, –82,
–84, –86*

Lovell, Bernard *see also* Lovell, Alfred
Charles Bernard

Lovell, Marc *IntAu&W 86X,
TwCCr&M 85, WrDr 86*

Lovell, Marc *see also* McShane, Mark

Lovell, Sir Alfred Charles Bernard
1913- *BioIn 13, Who 85*

Lovell, Sir Bernard *BioIn 13*

Lovell, Sir Bernard 1913- *WhoWor 84,
–87*

Lovesey, Peter 1936- *Au&Wr 71,
BioIn 13, ConAu 41R, EncMys,
IntAu&W 77, –82, –86, Novels,
TwCCr&M 80, –85, WrDr 76, –80,
–82, –84, –86*

Lovett, Margaret 1915- *Au&Wr 71,
BioIn 13, ConAu 61, ScF&FL 1,
SmATA 22[port], WrDr 76, –80, –82,
–84*

Low, Alice 1926- *AuBYP SUP,
BioIn 11, ConAu 8NR, –61,
SmATA 11*

Lowell, Robert 1917-1977 *Alli,
AmAu&B, AmWr, BioIn 1, –3, –4,
–5, –6, –7, –8, –9, –10, –11, –12, –13,*

*BlueB 76, CelR, ChhPo, –S3,
CnDAL, CnE&AP, CnMWL, CnThe,
ConAu 9R, –73, ConAu 2BS,
ConDr 77, ConLC 1, –2, –3, –4, –5,
–8, –9, –11, –15, –37[port], ConPo 70,
–75, –80A, –85A, CroCAP, CroCD,
CurBio 47, –72, –77, –77N,
DcLB 5[port], DcLEL 1940,
EncAB-H, EncWL, –2[port], EncWT,
EvLB, IntAu&W 76, –77, IntWW 74,
–75, –76, –77, –78N, IntWWP 77,
LinLib L, MakMC, McGEWB,
ModAL, –S2, –S1, ModWD,
NewYTBS 77, NotNAT, ObitOF 79,
OxAmL, –83, PenC AM, PolProf J,
RAdv 1, RComWL, REn, REnAL,
ScF&FL 1, TwCA SUP, TwCWr,
WebAB, –79, WebE&AL, WhDW,
WhAm 7, Who 74, WhoAm 74, –76,
–78, WhoTwCL, WhoWor 74, WorAl,
WrDr 76*

Lowenfels, Walter 1897-1976
*AmAu&B, AuBYP SUP, BioIn 11,
–12, BlueB 76, ConAu 1R, –3NR,
–65, ConPo 70, –75, DcLB 4,
IntAu&W 76, IntWWP 77,
NewYTBS 76, PenC AM, RAdv 1,
WhAm 7, WhoAm 76, WrDr 76*

Lowery, Bruce Arlie 1931- *BioIn 5,
ConAu 1R, –1NR, WhoAm 74, –76,
–78, –80, –82, –84, –86, WhoE 74*

Lowery, Mike *DrAP&F 85*

Lownsbery, Eloise 1888- *BioIn 1, –2,
CurBio 47, InWom, JBA 51*

Lowrey, Janette Sebring 1892-
*AmAu&B, AuBYP, BioIn 1, –7,
ChhPo, ConAu 13R, SmATA 43,
TexWr, WhoAmW 58, –61*

Lowry, Bates 1923- *BioIn 7, –8,
BlueB 76, ConAu 1R, –1NR,
DrAS 74H, –78H, –82H, IntWW 74,
–75, –76, –77, –78, –79, –80, –81,
–82, –83, WhoAm 74, –76, –78, –80,
–82, WhoAmA 73, –76, –78, –80, –82,
–84*

Lowry, Beverly *DrAP&F 85*

Lowry, Beverly 1938- *ConAu 101*

Lowry, Goodrich 1912- *BioIn 7*

Lowry, Lois 1937- *AuBYP SUP,
BioIn 13, ChlLR 6[port],
ConAu 13NR, –69, DcLB 52[port],
FifBJA[port], SmATA 23[port],
SmATA 3AS[port]*

Lowry, Peter 1953- *AuBYP SUP,
BioIn 10, ConAu 49, SmATA 7*

Lozier, Herbert 1915- *BioIn 13,
ConAu 49, SmATA 26*

Luard, Nicholas 1937- *ConAu 85,
IntAu&W 76, Novels, TwCCr&M 85,
WhoSpyF, WrDr 86*

Lubin, Leonard B *ConAu 115,
IlsCB 1967, SmATA 37*

Lubin, Leonard B 1943- *SmATA 45*

Lubowe, Irwin I 1905- *ConAu 53*

Lucas, Alec 1913- *CanWW 70, –79,
–80, –81, –83, ConAu 101, DrAS 74E,
–78E, –82E, OxCan, –SUP,
WhoAm 84, –86, WhoCan 82*

Lucas, George *TwCSFW 86*

Lucas, George 1944?- *BiDrACP 79,
BioIn 9, –10, –11, –12, –13,
ConAu 77, ConLC 16, ConTFT 1, –4,
CurBio 78, DcVicP, EncSF, IntDcF 2,
IntMPA 77, –75, –76, –78, –79, –81,
–82, –84, IntWW 82, –83, MovMk,
NewYTBE 73, NewYTBS 81[port],
ScFSB, WhoAm 78, –80, –82, –84,
–86, WrDr 80, –82, –84, –86*

Lucas, George 1945- *HalFC 84,
IntMPA 86*

Lucas, John 1937- *ConAu 14NR,
WrDr 86*

Luce, Clare B *OxAmT 84*

Luce, Clare Boothe *EncTwCJ,
OxAmL 83, Who 85, WhoAm 84,
–86, WhoAmP 85, WhoAmW 85, –87,
WhoWor 84, –87*

Luce, Clare Boothe 1903- *AmAu&B,
AmCath 80, AmPolW 80, –80A,
–80C, AmWomD, AmWomM,
AmWomW, Au&Wr 71, BiDrAC,
BioIn 1, –2, –3, –4, –5, –9, –10, –11,
–12, BlueB 76, CathA 1930, CelR,*

*ConAu 45, CurBio 42, –53, GoodHs,
InWom, IntAu&W 76, –77,
IntWW 74, –75, –76, –77, –83,
IntYB 78, –79, –80, –81, –82, LibW,
LinLib L, –S, McGEWD,
NewYTBS 79, –81[port], –82[port],
NotNAT, –A, OxAmL, PolProf E,
PolProf T, REn, REnAL,
TwCA SUP, UFOEn, WebAB, –79,
WhE&EA, WhoAm 74, –76, –78, –80,
–82, WhoAmP 73, –75, –77, –79, –81,
–83, WhoAmW 64, –66, –68, –70,
–75, –77, –79, –81, –83, WhoWor 74,
–78, –80, –82, WomWMM, WorAl,
WrDr 80, –82, –84, –86*

Luce, William 1931- *AmSCAP 66,
ConAu 11NR, –65*

Luciano, Ron 1937- *BioIn 10, –11,
–12, –13, NewYTBS 77, –79*

Lucie-Smith, Edward *Who 85*

Lucie-Smith, Edward 1933- *BioIn 8,
–9, –10, BlueB 76, ChhPo, –S1, –S2,
–S3, ConAu 7NR, –13R, ConPo 70,
–75, –80, –85, DcLB 40[port], EncSF,
IntAu&W 77, –82, IntWWP 77,
LinLib L, Who 74, –82, –83, WorAu,
WrDr 76, –80, –82, –84, –86*

Ludlum, Robert 1927- *BiE&WWA,
BioIn 11, –12, –13, ConAu 33R,
ConLC 22[port], –43[port],
CurBio 82[port], DcLB Y82B[port],
IntAu&W 76, NotNAT, Novels[port],
TwCCr&M 80, –85, WhoAm 78, –80,
–82, –84, –86, WhoE 75, WorAl,
WrDr 76, –80, –82, –84, –86*

Ludlum, Robert *see also* Ryder,
Jonathan

Ludvigson, Susan *DrAP&F 85*

Ludwig, Charles Shelton 1918-
*ConAu 5NR, –9R, –20NR,
WhoRel 75, –77*

Ludwig, Emil 1881-1948 *BiGAW,
BioIn 1, –2, –4, EncTR, EvEuW,
LinLib L, –S, LongCTC, NotNAT B,
ObitOF 79, OxGer, TwCA, –SUP,
WhAm 2, WhE&EA, WhLit, WhoLA*

Lueders, Edward *DrAP&F 85*

Lueders, Edward 1923- *AuBYP SUP,
BioIn 12, ChhPo S1, ConAu 5NR,
–13R, DrAS 74E, –78E, –82E,
SmATA 14, WhoAm 74, –76, –78,
–80, –82*

Lueders, Edward George 1923-
WhoAm 84, –86

Luehrmann, Arthur Willett, Jr. 1931-
*AmM&WS 73P, –76P, –79P, –82P,
–86P, BioIn 9*

Luenn, Nancy 1954- *ConAu 116*

Luger, Harriett M 1914- *ConAu 1NR,
–45, SmATA 23[port]*

Luis, Earlene W 1929- *BioIn 11,
ConAu 61, SmATA 11*

Lukas, J Anthony 1933- *AmAu&B,
AuBYP SUP, BioIn 9, –10, –11, –13,
BlueB 76, ConAu 2NR, –19NR, –49,
WhoAm 74, –76, –78, –80, –82, –84,
–86*

Luke, Mary M 1919- *ConAu 14NR,
–21R, WhoAmW 75*

Luke, Thomas *WrDr 86*

Luke, Thomas 1946- *ConAu X,
WrDr 84*

Luke, Thomas *see also* Masterton,
Graham

Lum, Peter 1911- *AnCL, AuBYP,
BioIn 7, –8, –10, ConAu X,
IntAu&W 76X, –77X, –82X,
SmATA 6, WrDr 76, –80, –82, –84*

Lum, Peter *see also* Crowe, Bettina
Lum

Lund, Doris Herold 1919- *BioIn 11,
ChhPo S2, ConAu 17R, ForWC 70,
IndAu 1917, IntAu&W 77,
SmATA 12*

Lundquist, James Carl 1941-
ConAu 65, DrAS 74E, –78E, –82E

Lundwall, Sam J 1941- *ConAu 1NR,
–17NR, –49, EncSF, Novels,
ScF&FL 1, –2, ScFSB, TwCSFW 86,
WhoSciF*

Lunn, Janet *OxCanL*

Lunn, Janet 1928- *BioIn 9, –10, CaW,
ConAu 33R, OxCan SUP, ScF&FL 1,
SmATA 4, WhoAmW 75,
WhoCanL 85*

Lupoff, Richard A 1935- *ConAu 9NR,
–21R, ConSFA, EncSF, ScF&FL 1,
–2, ScFSB, TwCSFW 86, WhoSciF,
WrDr 84, –86*

Lurie, Alison *DrAP&F 85*

Lurie, Alison 1926- *BioIn 10, –12,
–13, BlueB 76, ConAu 1R, –2NR,
–17NR, ConLC 4, –5, –18, –39[port],
ConNov 72, –76, –82, –86,
CurBio 86[port], DcLB 2, DrAS 82E,
IntAu&W 76, –77, –82, –86,
NewYTBS 86[port], Novels[port],
OxAmL 83, OxEng 85,
SmATA 46[port], WhoAm 78, –80,
–82, –84, –86, WhoAmW 83, –87,
WorAu 1970, WrDr 76, –80, –82,
–84, –86*

Lustbader, Eric Van 1946- *BioIn 12,
ConAu 14NR, –85,
NewYTBS 80[port]*

Lustgarten, Karen 1944- *ConAu 85*

Lustig, Arnost 1926- *BioIn 11,
CasWL, ConAu 69, EncWL 2,
IntAu&W 76, –77, –82, IntWW 74,
–75, –76, –77, –78, –79, –80, –81,
–82, –83, ModSL 2, TwCWr,
WhoWor 74, –84, –87*

Luszki, Walter A 1914-
AmM&WS 73S, –78S, WhoS&SW 82

Lutyens, Mary 1908- *Au&Wr 71,
BioIn 5, ConAu 25R, IntAu&W 76,
–77, –82, –86, WhE&EA, Who 74,
–82, –83, –85, WhoWor 74, –76,
WrDr 76, –80, –82, –84, –86*

Lutz, Frank Eugene 1879-1943
*BioIn 5, –7, –9, CurBio 44,
DcAmB S3, DcNAA, InSci,
NatCAB 42, ObitOF 79, WhAm 2*

Lutz, John 1939- *ConAu 9NR, –65,
TwCCr&M 80, –85, WrDr 82, –84,
–86*

Lutz, John Thomas 1939-
*IntAu&W 86, WhoMW 84, –86,
WhoWor 84, –87*

Lutzker, Edythe 1904-
*AmM&WS 76P, –79P, –82P, –86P,
BioIn 10, ConAu 37R, DrAS 74H,
–78H, –82H, IntAu&W 77, –82, –86,
SmATA 5, WhoAmW 77, –79, –81,
–83, –85, –87, WhoE 85, WhoWor 87,
WrDr 76, –80, –82, –84, –86*

Lux, Donald Gregory 1924- *LEduc 74*

Lyall, Gavin 1932- *Au&Wr 71,
BioIn 7, ConAu 4NR, –9R,
DcLEL 1940, EncMys, IntAu&W 76,
–77, Novels, TwCCr&M 80, –85,
Who 74, –82, –83, WrDr 76, –80,
–82, –84, –86*

Lydecker, Beatrice 1938- *ConAu 106*

Lydon, Michael 1942- *BioIn 10, –11,
ConAu 85, MugS, SmATA 11*

Lyle, Katie Letcher *DrAP&F 85*

Lyle, Katie Letcher 1938- *BioIn 11,
ConAu 49, SmATA 8*

Lynds, Dennis *DrAP&F 85,
TwCCr&M 85*

Lynds, Dennis 1924- *Au&Wr 71,
ConAu 1R, –6NR, EncMys,
IntAu&W 86, ScF&FL 1, SmATA 37,
–47[port], TwCCr&M 80, WrDr 82,
–84, –86*

Lynds, Dennis *see also* Arden, William

Lynds, Dennis *see also* Collins, Michael

Lynes, Russell 1910- *BioIn 13,
OxAmL 83, WhoAm 84, –86,
WhoAmA 84, WrDr 86*

Lynn, Elizabeth A 1946- *BritAu 19,
ConAu 81, TwCSFW 86*

Lynn, Kenneth Schuyler 1923-
WhoAm 84, –86

Lynn, Loretta 1932- *Baker 84,
BiDAmM, BioIn 9, –10, –11, –12,
BioNews 74, CelR, ConAu 81,
CurBio 73, EncFCWM 69, GoodHs,
IntDcWB, NewYTBE 73,
RolSEnR 83, WhoAm 74, –76, –78,
–80, –82, WhoAmW 79, –81, –83,
WorAl*

Lynn, Loretta 1935- *BioIn 13,*
EncFCWM 83[port], HalFC 84,
HerW 84, RolSEnR 83, WhoRock 81
Lynne, James Broom 1920- *BioIn 10,*
ConAu 77, ConDr 73, WrDr 76, –80,
–82, –84, –86
Lynton, Harriet Ronken 1920-
ConAu 73
Lyon, Christopher 1949- *ConAu 118*
Lyon, Eugene 1929?- *BioIn 10, –11,*
ConAu 106
Lyon, Lyman R *ConAu X*

Lyon, Lyman R 1907- *BioIn 11, –12,*
ConAu X, EncSF, SmATA X
Lyon, Lyman R *see also* DeCamp, L
Sprague
Lyons, Augusta Wallace *ConAu 85,*
WhoAmW 74, –72, –75
Lyons, Barbara 1912- *ConAu 93*
Lyons, Dorothy Marawee 1907-
AmAu&B, BioIn 9, ConAu 1R,
ForWC 70, IntAu&W 82, SmATA 3,
WhoAmW 64, –66, –68, WrDr 76,
–80, –82, –84, –86

Lytle, Ruby 1917- *ConAu P-1,*
ForWC 70
Lyttelton, Humphrey 1921- *BioIn 3,*
–5, –10, CmpEPM, ConAu 118,
EncJzS, IlEncJ, IntAu&W 77,
IntWW 74, –75, –76, –77, –78, –79,
–80, –81, –82, –83, Who 82, –83,
WhoMus 72
Lyttelton, Humphrey Richard Adeane
1921- *Who 85, WhoWor 84, –87*
Lyttle, Richard B 1927- *AuBYP SUP,*
BioIn 13, ConAu 13NR, –33R,
SmATA 23[port]

Lytton, Baron Edward G E Lytton
Bulwer- 1803-1873 *Alli, –SUP,*
BiD&SB, BioIn 1, –2, –5, –9, –10,
–11, –12, –13, BritAu 19, CasWL,
CelCen, ChhPo, –S2, DcEnA, DcEuL,
DcLEL, DcNaB, –C, EvLB, HsB&A,
LinLib L, –S, LongCEL, MnBBF,
NewC, OxAmT 84, OxEng,
OxThe, –83, PenC ENG, REn,
ScF&FL 1, SmATA 23[port], TelT

M

Maas, Peter 1929- *AmAu&B,*
AmCath 80, BioIn 10, -13,
BioNews 74, ConAu 93,
ConLC 29[port], LinLib L,
WhoAm 74, -76, -78, -80, -82, -84,
-86, WrDr 76, -80, -82, -84, -86
MacArthur, D Wilson 1903-
ConAu 5NR, -9R, WhLit
MacArthur, D Wilson *see also* Wilson,
David
Macaulay, David 1946- *FifBJA[port],*
SmATA 46[port]
Macaulay, David A 1946-
AuBYP SUP, BioIn 11, -12,
ChlLR 3, ConAu 5NR, -53,
IlsCB 1967, SmATA 27, WhoAm 82,
WhoAmA 80, -82, WhoE 79, -81,
-83, WrDr 76, -80, -82, -84
Macaulay, David Alexander 1946-
BioIn 13, WhoAmA 84
Macauley, Robie *DrAP&F 85, ScFSB*
Macauley, Robie 1919- *ConNov 86,*
OxAmL 83, WrDr 86
MacBeth, George *DrAP&F 85*
MacBeth, George 1932- *AuBYP SUP,*
BioIn 8, -9, -10, ChhPo S2,
ConAu 25R, ConLC 2, -5, -9,
ConPo 70, -75, -80, -85,
DcLB 40[port], DcLEL 1940,
IntAu&W 76, -77, -82, IntWWP 77,
ModBrL S2, -S1, RAdv 1, SmATA 4,
Who 74, -82, -83, WhoWor 76,
WorAu, WrDr 76, -80, -82, -84, -86
MacClintock, Dorcas 1932-
AuBYP SUP, BioIn 11, ConAu 6NR,
-57, SmATA 8, WhoAmA 78, -80,
-82, -84
MacCloskey, Monro 1902-
ConAu 5NR, -9R
MacCracken, Mary 1926- *ConAu 49,*
WrDr 80, -82, -84, -86
MacDonald, Bernice 1930-
BiDrLUS 70, WhoLibS 55
MacDonald, Donald 1900- *Au&Wr 71*
MacDonald, George 1824-1905
Alli, -SUP, AuBYP, BbD, BiD&SB,
BioIn 1, -3, -4, -6, -7, -8, -9, -10,
-11, -12, -13, BritAu 19, CarSB,
CasWL, Chambr 3, ChhPo, -S1, -S2,
-S3, ConAu 106, DcBiA, DcBiPP,
DcEnA, -AP, DcEnL, DcEuL,
DcLB 18[port], DcLEL, DcNaB S2,
EncSF, EvLB, FamSYP, JBA 34,
LongCTC, NewC, Novels, OxChL,
OxEng, -85, PenC ENG, REn,
ScF&FL 1, -1A, ScFSB,
SmATA 33[port], SupFW, TelT,
TwCCW 78A, -83A, TwCLC 9[port],
WebE&AL, WhoChL, WhoHr&F
MacDonald, J Fred 1941- *ConAu 117*
MacDonald, John D 1916- *AmAu&B,*
ASpks, BioIn 3, -5, -7, -9, -10, -11,
-12, ConAu 1R, -1NR, -19NR,

ConLC 3, -27[port], CorpD,
CurBio 86[port], DcLB 8[port],
EncMys, EncSF, HalFC 84,
IntAu&W 82, Novels, OxAmL 83,
ScF&FL 1, -2, ScFSB,
TwCCr&M 80, -85, TwCSFW 86,
WhoAm 74, -76, -78, -80, -82,
WhoSpyF, WorAl, WorAu, WrDr 76,
-80, -82, -84, -86
MacDonald, John D 1916-1986
ConLC 44[port], DcLB Y86N[port],
NewYTBS 86
MacDonald, John Dann 1916-
WhoAm 84, -86
MacDonald, John *IntMPA 86*
MacDonald, Philip 1896?- *AmAu&B,*
BioIn 4, ConAu 81, EncMys, EvLB,
HalFC 84, IntMPA 77, -75, -76, -78,
-79, -84, LongCTC, NewC,
TwCA, -SUP, TwCCr&M 80,
WhE&EA, WhLit
MacDonald, Philip 1899-1981
TwCCr&M 85
Macdonald, Ross *BioIn 13, ConAu X*
Macdonald, Ross 1915- *OxAmL 83*
Macdonald, Ross 1915-1983
AnObit 1983, ASpks, BioIn 11, -12,
BlueB 78, CmCal, ConAu X,
ConLC 1, -2, -3, -14, -41[port],
ConNov 72, -76, -82, -86A, CorpD,
CurBio 53, -79, -83N, DcLEL 1940,
EncMys, HalFC 84, IntAu&W 76X,
IntWW 81, -82, -83, LinLib L,
ModAL, -S1, NewYTBS 83[port],
Novels, TwCCr&M 80, -85,
WhoAm 76, WorAl, WorAu,
WrDr 76, -80, -82, -84
Macdonald, Ross *see also* Millar,
Kenneth
MacDonald, Shelagh 1937- *BioIn 13,*
ConAu 97, SmATA 25[port],
WrDr 76, -80, -82, -84
Mace, Elisabeth 1933- *BioIn 13,*
ConAu 77, SmATA 27[port],
WrDr 80, -82, -84
MacFall, Russell P 1903-1983
ChhPo S2, ConAu 110, ConAu P-1,
IndAu 1917
MacGowan, Kenneth 1888-1963
AmAu&B, BioIn 6, -12, ConAu 93,
EncWT, FilmgC, HalFC 84,
LinLib L, -S, NotNAT B,
OxAmT 84, OxFilm, OxThe, -83,
PlP&P, REnAL, WhAm 4, WhE&EA,
WhNAA, WhThe, WorEFlm
MacGregor-Hastie, Roy 1929-
AuBYP, BioIn 7, -8, -9, ConAu 1R,
-2NR, -20NR, IntAu&W 76, -77,
IntWWP 77, SmATA 3, WhoWor 78,
-80, -82, WrDr 76, -80, -82, -84
Macgregor-Morris, Pamela 1925-
ConAu 29R
Mach, Elyse Janet *WhoAmM 83*
Mach, Elyse Janet 1942- *WhoMW 84,*
-86

Machado, Antonio 1875-1939
BioIn 10, -13, ClDMEL, CnMWL,
ConAu 104, EncWL 2,
McGEWD, -84[port], ModRL,
PenC EUR, REn, TwCLC 3, TwCWr,
WhDW, WhoTwCL, WorAu
Machetanz, Sara 1918- *ConAu 1R,*
ForWC 70, WhoAmW 58, -61, -70,
-72
Machiavelli, Niccolo 1469-1527
AtlBL, BiD&SB, BioIn 1, -3, -4, -5,
-6, -7, -8, -9, -10, -11, -12, -13,
CasWL, CnThe, CyWA, DcAmSR,
DcCathB, DcEuL, DcItL, Dis&D,
EncWT, EuAu, EuWr 2, EvEuW,
GrFLW, LinLib L, -S, LongCEL,
LuthC 75, McGEWB,
McGEWD, -84[port], NewC,
NewEOp 71, NotNAT B, OxEng, -85,
OxThe, PenC EUR, PlP&P,
RComWL, REn, REnWD, WhDW,
WorAl
Machlis, Joseph 1906- *Au&Wr 71,*
Baker 78, -84, BioIn 13, ConAu 1R,
-2NR, IntAu&W 76,
NewYTBS 82[port], WhoAmM 83
Machorton, Ian 1923- *BioIn 7,*
ConAu 8NR, -17R, IntAu&W 77,
-82
MacInnes, Helen d1985
NewYTBS 85[port]
MacInnes, Helen 1907- *AmAu&B,*
ASpks, Au&Wr 71, BioIn 1, -2, -4,
-8, -10, -11, -12, -13, BlueB 76,
ConAu 1R, -1NR, ConLC 27[port],
ConNov 72, -76, CorpD, CurBio 67,
EncMys, ForWC 70, InWom,
IntAu&W 76, -77, -82, IntWW 74,
-75, -76, -77, -78, -79, -80, -81,
-82, -83, LibW, LinLib L, NewC,
NewYTBS 78, Novels, REnAL,
SmATA 22[port], TwCA SUP,
TwCCr&M 80, -85, WhE&EA,
Who 74, -82, -83, WhoAm 74, -76,
-78, -80, -82, -84, WhoAmW 74,
-58, -64, -66, -68, -70, -72, -83,
-85, WhoE 74, WhoSpyF,
WhoWor 78, -80, -82, -84, WorAl,
WrDr 76, -80, -82, -84
MacInnes, Helen 1907-1985
ConAu 117, ConLC 39[port],
CurBio 85N, SmATA 44N
MacInnes, Helen Clark 1907- *Who 85*
MacIntyre, Donald George 1904-
Au&Wr 71, ConAu 5R, WrDr 76,
-82, -84
Mack, John Edward 1929-
BiDrAPA 77, ConAu 106, LEduc 74,
WhoAm 78, -80, -82, -84, WhoE 79,
-81, -83, -85
Mackal, Roy Paul 1925-
AmM&WS 73P, -76P, -79P, -86P,
BioIn 12, -13, ConAu 73,
WhoAm 74, -76, -78, -80, -84, -86,
WhoWor 74

Mackay, Claire 1930-
SmATA 40[port], WhoCanL 85
Mackay, David *AuBYP SUP,*
ChhPo S1
MacKaye, Percy 1875-1956 *AmAu&B,*
AnMV 1926, ApCAB X, BioIn 1, -2,
-4, -12, Chambr 3, ChhPo, -S1, -S2,
-S3, CnDAL, CnMD, CnThe,
ConAmA, ConAmL, ConAu 113,
DcAmB S6, DcLB 54[port], DcLEL,
EncWT, LinLib L, -S,
McGEWD, -84[port], ModAL,
ModWD, NatCAB 14, NotNAT B,
ObitOF 79, OxAmL, -83, OxAmT 84,
OxThe, PlP&P, REn, REnAL,
REnWD, SmATA 32[port], Str&VC,
TwCA, -SUP, WhAm 3, WhLit,
WhNAA, WhThe, WhoStg 1908
MacKellar, William 1914- *AuBYP,*
BioIn 7, -9, ConAu 13NR, -33R,
ScF&FL 1, SmATA 4
Macken, Walter 1915-1967
AuBYP SUP, BioIn 2, -4, -7, -10,
-13, CnMD, ConAu 25R, ConAu P-1,
DcIrB, DcIrL, DcIrW 1,
DcLB 13[port], NotNAT B,
ObitOF 79, OxChL, SmATA 36,
TwCCW 78, -83, WhAm 4,
WhScrn 77, -83, WhoHol B, WorAu
Macken, Walter 1916-1967 *BiDIrW*
MacKenzie, Christine Butchart 1917-
ConAu 13R
MacKenzie, Midge *BioIn 10,*
WomWMM B
MacKenzie, Rachel 1909-1980
BioIn 12, ConAu 102, -97,
NewYTBS 80[port]
Mackey, Mary *DrAP&F 85*
Mackey, Mary 1945- *ConAu 15NR,*
-77, DrAS 74E, -78E, -82E
MacKinnon, John 1947- *ConAu 103,*
WrDr 76, -80, -82, -84
Mackler, Bernard 1934-
AmM&WS 73S, ConAu 21R,
LEduc 74, WhoE 77
Mack Smith, Denis 1920- *Au&Wr 71,*
ConAu 17NR, -21R, IntAu&W 77,
Who 74, -82, -83, -85, WhoWor 84,
WrDr 80, -82, -84, -86
MacLachlan, Patricia *ConAu 118,*
SmATA 42
MacLaine, Shirley 1934- *AmWomWr,*
BiDD, BiDFilm, BioIn 3, -4, -5, -6,
-7, -8, -9, -10, -11, -12, -13,
BlueB 76, CelR, ConAu X,
ConTFT 1, -4[port], CurBio 59, -78,
FilmgC, ForWC 70, GoodHs,
HalFC 84, InWom, IntAu&W 77,
IntAu&W 77, IntMPA 77, -75, -76,
-78, -79, -81, -82, -84, -86,
IntWW 74, -75, -76, -77, -78, -79,
-80, -81, -82, -83, MotPP, MovMk,
NewYTBE 71, NewYTBS 84[port],
OxFilm, WhoAm 74, -76, -78, -80,

–82, –84, –86, WhoAmW 74, –61,
–64, –66, –68, –70, –72, –79, –81,
–83, –85, –87, WhoHol A,
WhoWor 74, WomWMM, WorAl,
WorEFlm, WrDr 80, –82, –84, –86
MacLean, Alistair *WhoWor 84, –87*
MacLean, Alistair 1922- *AuBYP SUP,*
BioIn 9, –10, –13, BlueB 76,
ConAu 57, ConLC 3, –13,
DcLEL 1940, FilmgC, HalFC 84,
IntAu&W 76, –77, IntWW 74, –75,
–76, –77, –78, –79, –80, –81, –82,
–83, Novels[port], SmATA 23[port],
TwCCr&M 80, Who 74, –82, –83,
–85, WhoAm 78, –80, –82, –84, –86,
WhoSpyF, WhoWor 76, –80, –82,
WorAl, WorAu, WrDr 76, –80, –82,
–84, –86
MacLean, Alistair 1923-
TwCCr&M 85
Maclean, Charles 1946- *ConAu 109*
Maclean, Fitzroy 1911- *ConAu 14NR,*
WrDr 86
MacLean, Katherine 1925- *BioIn 12,*
ConAu 33R, ConSFA, DcLB 8,
EncSF, IntAu&W 76, ScF&FL 1, –2,
ScFSB, TwCSFW 86, WhoSciF,
WrDr 76, –80, –82, –84, –86
Maclean, Norman Fitzroy 1902-
BioIn 11, –12, ConAu 102,
DrAS 74E, –78E, –82E, WhoAm 74,
–86
Maclean, Sir Fitzroy 1911-
Au&Wr 71, BioIn 2, –8, –12,
BlueB 76, ConAu 29R, IntAu&W 77,
–82, IntWW 74, –75, –76, –77, –78,
–79, –80, –81, –82, –83, IntYB 78,
–79, –80, –81, –82, WhWW-II,
Who 74, WhoWor 74, –78, –80, –82,
WrDr 76, –80, –82, –84
MacLeish, Archibald *OxAmT 84*
MacLeish, Archibald 1892-1982
AmAu&B, AmSCAP 66, AmWr,
AnObit 1982[port], BiDAmM,
BiE&WWA, BioIn 1, –2, –3, –4, –5,
–7, –8, –9, –10, –11, –12, –13,
CasWL, CelR, ChhPo S1, –S2, –S3,
CnDAL, CnE&AP, CnMD, CnMWL,
CnThe, ConAmA, ConAmL,
ConAu 9R, –106, ConDr 73, –77,
–82, ConLC 3, –8, –14, ConPo 70,
–75, –80, CroCD, CurBio 40, –59,
–82N, CyWA, DcAmDH, DcAmSR,
DcLB 4, –7[port], –45[port],
–Y82A[port], DcLEL, EncWL, –2,
EncWT, EvLB, IntAu&W 76, –77,
–82, IntWW 74, –75, –76, –77, –78,
–79, –80, –81, –82, –82N,
IntWWP 77, –82, LinLib L, –S,
LongCTC, McGEWB,
McGEWD, –84, ModAL, –S2, –S1,
ModWD, NewYTBS 82[port],
NotNAT, OxAmL, –83, OxEng, –85,
OxThe, PenC AM, PIP&P, RAdv 1,
REn, REnAL, SixAP, TwCA, –SUP,
TwCWr, WebAB, –79, WebE&AL,
WhDW, WhAm 8, WhNAA, Who 74,
–82, –83N, WhoAm 74, –76, –78,
–80, –82, WhoThe 72, –77, –81,
WhoWor 74, –78, –80, WorAl,
WrDr 76, –80, –82
MacLennan, Hugh 1907- *Au&Wr 71,*
BioIn 1, –3, –4, –9, –10, –11, –12,
BlueB 76, CaW, CanNov,
CanWr 70, –79, –80, –81, –83,
CanWr, CasWL, ConAu 5R,
ConLC 2, –14, ConNov 72, –76, –82,
–86, CreCan 2, CurBio 46,
EncWL, –2, IntAu&W 76, –77, –82,
IntWW 77, –78, –79, –80, –81, –82,
–83, LinLib L, LongCTC, McGEWB,
ModCmwL, NewC, Novels, OxAmL,
OxCan, –SUP, OxCanL, PenC ENG,
RAdv 1, REn, REnAL, TwCA SUP,
TwCWr, WebE&AL, WhDW,
WhE&WA, Who 74, –82, –83, –85,
WhoAm 74, –76, –78, –80, –82, –84,
WhoCan 73, –75, –77, WhoCanL 85,
WhoWor 74, WrDr 76, –80, –82, –84,
–86
MacLennan, Hugh *see also* MacLennan,
John Hugh
MacLennan, John Hugh 1907-
CreCan 2, DcLEL 1940

MacLennan, John Hugh *see also*
MacLennan, Hugh
MacLeod, Charlotte 1922- *BioIn 13,*
ConAu 18NR, –21R,
SmATA 28[port], TwCCr&M 85,
WrDr 84, –86
MacLeod, Ellen Jane *IntAu&W 86,*
WrDr 86
MacLeod, Ellen Jane 1916-
Au&Wr 71, BioIn 12, ConAu 3NR,
–5R, IntAu&W 76, –77, –82,
SmATA 14, WrDr 76, –80, –82, –84
MacLeod, Ellen Jane *see also*
Anderson, Ella
MacLeod, Jean S 1908- *WrDr 86*
MacLeod, Jean Sutherland 1908-
Au&Wr 71, ConAu 3NR, –9R,
IntAu&W 76, –77, –82, –86, WrDr 84
MacLeod, Mary d1914 *ChhPo, –S2,*
–S3, WhLit
MacManus, Yvonne 1931-
ConAu 11NR, –25R, IntAu&W 77,
–82, WhoAm 76, –78, –80, –82,
WhoCon 73
Macnamara, Ellen 1924- *ConAu 103,*
WrDr 76, –80, –82, –84
MacPeek, Walter G 1902-1973
AuBYP SUP, BioIn 9, –13,
ConAu 41R, ConAu P-2,
SmATA 25N, –4, WhNAA
MacPherson, Margaret 1908- *AuBYP,*
BioIn 7, –11, BritCA, ConAu 49,
FourBJA, SmATA 9,
SmATA 4AS[port], TwCCW 78, –83,
WrDr 80, –82, –84, –86
MacQuitty, William *ConAu 7NR,*
–17R, FilmgC, IntMPA 77, –75, –76,
–78, –79, –81, –82, –84, –86
Macquitty, William 1905- *HalFC 84*
Macrorie, Ken 1918- *BioIn 13,*
ConAu 65
MacShane, Frank 1927- *ConAu 3NR,*
–9R, DrAS 74E, –78E, –82E,
IntAu&W 77, –82, WrDr 76, –80,
–82, –84, –86
Macshane, Frank Sutherland 1927-
IntAu&W 86
Macvey, John W 1923- *ConAu 7NR,*
–17R, IntAu&W 79, –82,
ScF&FL 1A, WhoWor 76, WrDr 76,
–80, –82, –84
Macvey, John Wishart 1923- *WrDr 86*
Madden, David *DrAP&F 85*
Madden, David 1933- *BioIn 10, –13,*
ConAu 1R, –4NR, ConAu 3AS[port],
ConLC 5, –15, ConNov 82, –86,
DcLB 6[port], DrAS 78E, –82E,
IntAu&W 76, –77, –82, –86,
IntWWP 77, –82, LinLib L,
WhoAm 76, –78, –80, –82, –84, –86,
WrDr 76, –80, –82, –84, –86
Madden, John 1936- *CurBio 85[port],*
WhoAm 84, –86
Maddock, Reginald 1912- *Au&Wr 71,*
AuBYP SUP, BioIn 12, ConAu 81,
ScF&FL 1, SmATA 15, TwCCW 78
Maddox, John Royden 1925- *BioIn 12,*
–13, Who 74, –82, –83, –85,
WhoWor 74, –76, –80
Maddux, Rachel 1912- *BioIn 11,*
ConAu 1R, –5NR, EncSF, ForWC 70,
ScF&FL 1, –2
Madgett, Naomi Long *DrAP&F 85*
Madgett, Naomi Long 1923- *BlkAWP,*
BroadAu[port], ChhPo, ConAu 13NR,
–33R, InB&W 80, –85, IntAu&W 86,
IntWWP 77, –82, LivgBAA,
MichAu 80, SelBAAf, SelBAAu,
WhoAm 78, –80, –82, –84,
WhoAmW 75, –77, –79, –81,
WhoBlA 75, –77, –80, –85, WrDr 76,
–80, –82, –84, –86
Madison, Arnold 1937- *AuBYP SUP,*
BioIn 10, ConAu 9NR, –21R,
SmATA 6
Madison, Frank *ConAu X,*
IntAu&W 77X, –82X, WrDr 76, –80,
–82, –84, –86
Madison, Frank *see also* Hutchins,
Francis Gilman
Madison, Winifred *BioIn 10,*
ConAu 37R, SmATA 5

Madlee, Dorothy 1917-1980
AuBYP SUP, ConAu 10NR, –17R,
ForWC 70
Madruga, Lenor 1942- *BioIn 12,*
ConAu 102
Maeterlinck, Maurice 1862-1949
AtlBL, BbD, BiD&SB, BioIn 1, –2,
–3, –4, –5, –6, –8, –9, –10, –11, –12,
–13, CasWL, ChhPo, ClDMEL,
CnMD, CnThe, ConAu 104, CyWA,
Dis&D, EncO&P 2, –78,
EncWL, –2[port], EncWT, EvEuW,
GrFLW, HalFC 84, LinLib L, –S,
LongCTC, MajMD 2, McGEWB,
McGEWD, –84[port], ModFrL,
ModRL, ModWD, NewC,
NewEOp 71, NotNAT A, –B,
ObitOF 79, OxAmT 84, OxEng, –85,
OxFr, OxThe, –83, PenC EUR,
PIP&P, RComWL, REn, REnWD,
TwCA, –SUP, TwCLC 3, TwCWr,
WhDW, WhAm 2, WhE&EA, WhLit,
WhThe, WhoLA, WhoNob,
WhoTwCL, WorAl
Maffei, Paolo 1926- *ConAu 108,*
WhoWor 84, –87
Magary, Alan 1944- *ConAu 8NR, –61*
Magary, Kerstin Fraser 1947-
ConAu 12NR, –61
Maggin, Elliot S 1950- *ConAu 102*
Magnusson, Magnus 1929- *BioIn 12,*
ConAu 105, IntAu&W 76, –77, –82,
Who 82, –83, –85, WhoWor 80, –82,
–84, –87, WrDr 80, –82, –84, –86
Magruder, Jeb Stuart 1934- *BioIn 9,*
–10, –11, –12, ConAu 101,
NewYTBE 73, PolProf NF,
WhoAm 74, –76, WorAl
Magubane, Peter 1932- *ConPhot,*
ICPEnP A, InB&W 80, –85
Mahlmann, Lewis *AuBYP SUP*
Mahoney, Irene 1921- *ConAu 61,*
DrAS 74E, –78E, –82E
Mahony, Elizabeth Winthrop 1948-
BioIn 11, ConAu 41R, SmATA 8
Mahony, Elizabeth Winthrop *see also*
Winthrop, Elizabeth
Mahovlich, Frank 1938- *BioIn 6, –8,*
–9, WhoHcky 73
Mahy, Margaret 1936- *ChlLR 7[port],*
ConAu 13NR, OxChL, WrDr 86
Maier, Paul Luther 1930-
ConAu 2NR, –5R, DrAS 74H, –78H,
–82H, IntAu&W 76, –77, –82, –86,
WhoAm 82, –84, –86, WhoMW 74,
–76, –78, –82, –84, WrDr 76, –80,
–82, –84, –86
Mailer, Norman *DrAP&F 85*
Mailer, Norman 1923- *AmAu&B,*
AmNov, AmWr, ASpks, Au&Wr 71,
AuNews 2, BioIn 1, –2, –4, –5, –6, –7,
–8, –9, –10, –11, –12, –13,
BioNews 74, BlueB 76, CasWL, CelR,
CnDAL, ConAu 9R, ConAu 1BS,
ConLC 1, –2, –3, –4, –5, –8, –11,
–14, –28[port], ConNov 72, –76, –82,
–86, CurBio 48, –70, DcLB 2,
–16[port], –28[port], –DS3[port],
–Y80A[port], –Y83A[port],
DcLEL 1940, EncAB-H, EncAJ,
EncTwCJ, EncWL, –2[port], FilmgC,
HalFC 84, IntAu&W 76, –77,
IntWW 74, –75, –76, –77, –78, –79,
–80, –81, –82, –83, IntWWP 77,
LinLib L, –S, LongCTC, MakMC,
McGEWB, ModAL, –S2, –S1,
NewYTBS 82[port], Novels[port],
OxAmL, –83, OxEng 85, OxFilm,
PenC AM, PolProf J, PolProf K,
PolProf NF, RAdv 1, REn, REnAL,
TwCA SUP, TwCWr, WebAB, –79,
WebE&AL, WhDW, Who 74, –82,
–83, –85, WhoAm 74, –76, –78, –80,
–82, –84, –86, WhoAmJ 80,
WhoE 74, –85, WhoHol A,
WhoTwCL, WhoWor 74, –78,
WhoWorJ 72, –78, WorAl, WorEFlm,
WrDr 76, –80, –82, –84, –86
Maiorano, Robert 1946- *BiDD,*
ConAu 116, SmATA 43[port]
Maiorano, Robert 1947- *BioIn 9, –12*
Majerus, Janet 1936- *ConAu 65*
Major, Clarence *DrAP&F 85*

Major, Clarence 1936- *BlkAWP,*
BroadAu[port], ConAu 13NR, –21R,
ConAu 6AS[port], ConLC 3, –19,
ConNov 82, –86, ConPo 75, –80, –85,
DcLB 33[port], DrAS 78E, –82E,
InB&W 80, –85, IntAu&W 82, –86,
IntWWP 77, –82, LinLib L,
LivgBAA, NegAl 76, –83, SelBAAf,
SelBAAu, WhoAm 76, –78,
WhoBlA 75, –77, –80, –85, WhoE 75,
WorAu 1970, WrDr 76, –80, –82,
–84, –86
Major, Kevin *OxCanL*
Major, Kevin 1949- *BioIn 13,*
ChlLR 11[port], ConAu 21NR, –97,
ConLC 26[port], SmATA 32[port],
TwCChW 83, WhoAm 82,
WhoCanL 85, WrDr 86
Makeba, Miriam 1932- *AmSCAP 66,*
Baker 78, –84, BiDAfM, BioIn 5, –6,
–7, –8, –9, –11, –13, ConAu 104,
CurBio 65, DrBlPA, EncFCWM 69,
InB&W 80, –85, InWom,
WhoBlA 75, –77, –80, WhoE 74,
WorAl
Makeba, Miriam 1934- *WhoBlA 85*
Malamud, Bernard *DrAP&F 85*
Malamud, Bernard 1914- *AmAu&B,*
AmWr S1, Au&Wr 71, BioIn 5, –6,
–7, –8, –9, –10, –11, –12, –13,
BlueB 76, CasWL, CelR, CnMWL,
ConAu 5R, ConAu 1BS, ConLC 1,
–2, –3, –5, –8, –9, –11, –18,
–27[port], ConNov 72, –76, –82,
CurBio 58, –78, DcLB 2, –28[port],
–Y80A[port], DcLEL 1940,
EncWL, –2[port], IntAu&W 76, –77,
–82, IntWW 74, –75, –76, –77, –78,
–79, –80, –81, –82, –83, LinLib L,
–S, ModAL, –S2, –S1,
NewYTBS 80[port], –83[port],
Novels[port], OxAmL, –83, OxEng 85,
PenC AM, RAdv 1, REn, REnAL,
TwCWr, WebAB, –79, WebE&AL,
WhDW, Who 74, –82, –83, –85,
WhoAm 74, –76, –78, –80, –82, –84,
WhoE 74, WhoTwCL, WhoWor 74,
–80, –82, –84, WhoWorJ 72, –78,
WorAl, WorAu, WrDr 76, –80, –82,
–84, –86
Malamud, Bernard 1914-1986
ConAu 118, ConLC 44[port],
ConNov 86, CurBio 86N,
DcLB Y86N[port], NewCon[port],
NewYTBS 86[port]
Malcolm X *ConAu X, InB&W 85*
Malcolm X 1925-1965 *AmAu&B,*
AmRef[port], BioIn 6, –7, –8, –9, –10,
–11, –12, –13, BlkAWP, CivRSt,
DcAmB S7, DcAmNB, DcAmReB,
DcPol, EncAB-H, LinLib L, –S,
LuthC 75, MakMC, McGEWB,
NegAl 76[port], –83[port], ObitOF 79,
OxAmL 83, WebAB, –79, WhAm 4,
WhAmP, WorAl
Malcolmson, Anne 1910- *AnCL,*
AuBYP, BioIn 6, –8, –9, ChhPo S2,
ConAu X, ConAu X, MorJA,
SmATA 1
Malcolmson, Anne *see also* VonStorch,
Anne B
Malcolm X *see also* Little, Malcolm
Male, David Arthur 1928- *ConAu 57*
Malherbe, Abraham Johannes 1950-
WhoRel 85
Maling, Arthur 1923- *ConAu 3NR,*
–49, TwCCr&M 80, –85, WrDr 82,
–84, –86
Mallan, Lloyd 1914- *ConAu 5R*
Mallinson, Jeremy *WrDr 86*
Mallinson, Jeremy 1937- *ConAu 6NR,*
–57, IntAu&W 82, WrDr 76, –80,
–82, –84
Malo, John W 1911- *BioIn 9,*
ConAu 12NR, –33R, SmATA 4
Malocsay, Zoltan 1946- *ConAu 81*
Malone, Bill Charles 1934- *ConAu 65,*
DrAS 74H, –78H, –82H
Malone, Dorothy 1925?- *BiDFilm,*
BioIn 10, –12, FilmgC, HalFC 84,
HolP 40, IntMPA 77, –75, –76, –78,
–79, –81, –82, –84, –86, MotPP,
MovMk, WhoAm 74, WhoHol A,
WorAl, WorEFlm

Marlowe, Christopher 1564-1593 *Alli,
AtlBL, BiD&SB, BiDRP&D, BioIn 1,
-2, -3, -4, -5, -6, -7, -8, -9, -10,
-11, -12, -13, BritAu, BritWr 1,
CasWL, Chambr 1, ChhPo, -S1,
CnE&AP, CnThe, CroE&S, CrtT 1,
-4, CyWA, DcBiPP, DcEnA, DcEnL,
DcEuL, DcLEL, DcNaB, Dis&D,
EncE 75, EncWT, EvLB, LinLib L,
-S, LongCEL, McGEWB,
McGEWD, -84[port], MouLC 1,
NewC, NewEOp 71, NotNAT A, -B,
OxEng, -85, OxThe, -83, PenC ENG,
PlP&P, RComWL, REn, REnWD,
WebE&AL, WhoAl, WorAl*
Marlowe, Dan J 1914- *TwCCr&M 85,
WrDr 86*
Marney, Dean 1952- *ConAu 110*
Marquand, J P 1893-1960 *CurBio 42,
-60, EncWL 2, LinLib L, ObitOF 79,
OxAmL 83, WorAl*
Marquand, John P 1893-1960
HalFC 84, TwCCr&M 85
Marquand, John Phillips 1893-1960
*AmAu&B, AmNov, AmWr, BioIn 1,
-2, -3, -4, -5, -6, -7, -8, -9, -12,
CasWL, CnDAL, ConAu 85,
ConLC 2, -10, CyWA, DcAmB S6,
DcLB 9[port], DcLEL, EncMys,
EncWL, EvLB, FilmgC, LinLib S,
LongCTC, ModAL, NatCAB 47,
Novels, OxAmL, PenC AM, RAdv 1,
REn, REnAL, TwCA, -SUP,
TwCCr&M 80, TwCWr, WebAB, -79,
WebE&AL, WhAm 4*
Marquardt, Dorothy 1921-
*BiDrLUS 70, ConAu 13R, ForWC 70,
WhoAmW 75, WhoLibS 66*
Marquis, Arnold *ConAu 57,
WhoWest 78, -80, -82*
Marquis, Don *OxAmT 84*
Marquis, Don 1878-1937 *AmAu&B,
AmBi, AmLY, BiD&SB, BiDSA,
BioIn 1, -4, -5, -6, -8, -10, -12, -13,
CnDAL, CnE&AP, ConAmA,
ConAmL, ConAu 104, DcAmB S2,
DcLB 11[port], -25[port], DcNAA,
EncAJ, LinLib L, LongCTC, ModAL,
NatCAB 30, NotNAT A, Novels,
OxAmL, -83, PenC AM, RAdv 1,
REn, REnAL, ScF&FL 1, Str&VC,
TwCA, -SUP, TwCLC 7[port],
TwCWr, WhNAA, WhThe*
Marrin, Albert 1936- *ConAu 49,
SmATA 43*
Marriott, Alice Lee 1910- *AmAu&B,
AnCL, AuBYP, BioIn 2, -7, -8,
ConAu 57, CurBio 50, InSci, InWom,
SmATA 31[port]*
Marsden, Simon 1948- *ICPEnP A*
Marsh, Dave 1950- *BioIn 13,
ConAu 17NR, -97*
Marsh, John 1907- *Au&Wr 71,
ConAu P-1, IntAu&W 76, -77, -82,
ScF&FL 1, -2, WhE&EA,
WhoAmL 78, -79, WhoE 74, -75,
-77, WhoGov 77, -75, WrDr 76, -80,
-82*
Marsh, Ngaio 1899-1982
*AnObit 1982[port], Au&Wr 71,
AuBYP, BioIn 1, -4, -5, -7, -8, -11,
-12, BlueB 76, ConAu 6NR, -9R,
ConLC 7, ConNov 72, -76, -82,
CorpD, DcLEL, EncMys, EvLB,
FarE&A 78, -79, -80, -81, InWom,
IntAu&W 76, IntWW 74, -75, -76,
-77, -78, -79, -80, -81, -82N,
LongCTC, NewC, NewYTBS 82[port],
Novels, OxEng, REn, TwCA, -SUP,
TwCCr&M 80, -85, TwCWr,
WhE&EA, Who 74, -82, -83N,
WhoAmW 70, -72, -75, WhoWor 74,
-82, WorAl, WrDr 76, -80, -82*
Marshall, Alan *OxChL*
Marshall, Alan 1902- *Au&Wr 71,
BioIn 6, -9, -12, ConAu 85,
IntAu&W 76, -77, WhoWor 78, -80,
-82*
Marshall, Alan 1902-1984 *OxAusL*
Marshall, Anthony Dryden 1924-
*BioIn 12, ConAu 29R, SmATA 18,
WhoAm 74, -76, -78, WhoAmP 73,
-75, -77, -79, WhoGov 77, -72, -75,
WhoWor 74, -76*

Marshall, Catherine 1914-1983
*AmWomWr, AuBYP, BioIn 3, -4, -5,
-7, -9, -11, -12, -13, ConAu 8NR,
-109, -17R, CurBio 55, -83N,
LinLib L, -S, NewYTBS 83,
SmATA 2, -34N, WorAl, WrDr 76,
-80, -82, -84*
Marshall, Edison 1894-1967
*AmAu&B, AmNov, BioIn 1, -2, -3,
-4, -8, ConAu 29R, ConAu P-1,
EncSF, IndAu 1917, ObitOF 79,
REnAL, ScF&FL 1, -2, TwCA SUP,
WhAm 4, WhE&EA, WhLit,
WhoHr&F*
Marshall, James d1986 *NewYTBS 86*
Marshall, James 1942- *AuBYP SUP,
BioIn 10, -12, ConAu 41R, FourBJA,
IlsCB 1967, OxChL, SmATA 6,
TwCChW 83, WhoAm 76, -78, -80,
-82, WrDr 86*
Marshall, James Vance *ConAu X,
IntAu&W 76X, -77X, -82X, -86X,
SmATA X, WrDr 76, -82, -84, -86*
Marshall, James Vance 1887-1964
ConAu P-1, OxAusL
Marshall, James Vance see also Doone,
Jice
Marshall, James Vance see also Payne,
Donald
Marshall, John 1922- *Au&Wr 71,
ConAu 15NR, -89, IntAu&W 77,
Who 85, WrDr 76, -80, -82, -84, -86*
Marshall, Kathryn *DrAP&F 85*
Marshall, Mel 1911- *ConAu 12NR,
IntAu&W 86*
Marshall, Mel 1912- *ConAu 29R,
IntAu&W 82*
Marshall, Norman 1901-1980
*BlueB 76, CnThe, ConAu 108,
OxThe 83, Who 74, WhoThe 72, -77,
-81, WrDr 76, -80, -82, -84*
Marshall, Paule *BlkWWr, DrAP&F 85*
Marshall, Paule 1929- *AmAu&B,
AmWomWr, BioIn 13, BlkAWP,
ConAu 77, ConLC 27[port],
ConNov 72, -76, -82, DcLB 33[port],
DcLEL, InB&W 80, -85,
IntAu&W 76, -77, LivgBAA,
NegAl 76, -83, NewYTBS 83[port],
SelBAAf, SelBAAu, WhoAmW 66,
-68, -70, -72, WorAu 1970,
WrDr 76, -80, -82, -84, -86*
Marshall, Paule Burke 1929-
WhoBlA 85
Marshall, S L A 1900-1977 *ConAu 73,
-81, CurBio 53, -78, -78N,
NewYTBS 77, ObitOF 79,
SmATA 21[port]*
Marshall, Samuel Lyman Atwood
1900-1977 *AmAu&B, AuBYP,
BioIn 3, -5, -8, -10, -11, -12,
CurBio 53, DcAmMiB, WhAm 7,
WhoAm 74, -76, -78, WorAu*
Marshall, Shirley E 1925- *ChhPo S2,
ConAu 21R, WhoAmW 74,
WomPO 76, -78*
Martin, Albert *ConAu X*
Martin, Alfred 1916- *ConAu 117,
DrAS 74P, -78P, LEduc 74*
Martin, Alfred Manuel 1928- *BioIn 3,
-4, -5, -7, -8, -9, -10, -11,
ConAu 108, NewYTBS 77,
WhoAm 74, -76, -78, -80, -82, -84,
-86, WhoProB 73*
Martin, Alfred Manuel see also Martin,
Billy
Martin, Ann M 1955- *ConAu 111,
SmATA 41, -44[port]*
Martin, Billy *WhoAm 84, -86*
Martin, Billy 1928- *BioIn 3, -4, -5,
-7, -8, -10, -11, -12, -13, CmCal,
ConAu X, CurBio 76, NewYTBE 72,
-73, NewYTBS 74, -75, -77,
-83[port], -85[port], WorAl*
Martin, Billy see also Martin, Alfred
Manuel
Martin, Calvin 1948- *ConAu 113,
DrAS 78H, -82H*
Martin, David C 1943- *ConAu 102,
WhoAm 82*
Martin, David Clark 1943- *WhoAm 84*
Martin, Don 1931- *ConAu 101,
ConGrA 2[port], WhoAm 82,
WorECar*

Martin, Don Edward 1931-
WhoAm 84, -86
Martin, Donald Franklin 1944-
ConAu 65
Martin, Dorothy 1921- *ConAu 6NR,
-57, SmATA 47*
Martin, George R R 1948- *ConAu 81,
EncSF, ScFSB[port], TwCSFW 86,
WrDr 84, -86*
Martin, George Raymond Richard
1948- *WhoAm 78, -80, -82, -84,
-86*
Martin, Graham Dunstan 1932-
ConAu 106, IntAu&W 77, -82, -86
Martin, John Bartlow 1915-
*AmAu&B, Au&Wr 71, BioIn 3, -4,
-7, -11, BlueB 76, ConAu 8NR,
-13R, CurBio 56, EncAJ,
IntAu&W 76, IntWW 74, OhA&B,
PolProf K, WhoAm 78, -80, -82, -84*
Martin, Judith *EncTwCJ*
Martin, Judith 1938- *BioIn 13,
ConAu 12NR, CurBio 86[port],
WrDr 86*
Martin, Malachi 1921- *ASpks,
AuNews 1, BioIn 10, -11,
BioNews 75, ConAu 81*
Martin, Patricia Miles *WrDr 86*
Martin, Patricia Miles 1899- *AuBYP,
BioIn 7, -9, ConAu 1R, -2NR,
ForWC 70, IntAu&W 77, OxChL,
SmATA 1, -43[port], TwCCW 78,
-83, WhoAmW 74, -66, -68, -70,
-72, -75, WrDr 76, -80, -82, -84*
Martin, Patricia Miles 1899-1986
ConAu 119, SmATA 48N
Martin, Patricia Miles see also Miles,
Miska
Martin, Ralph G 1920- *AmAu&B,
ASpks, AuBYP, BioIn 5, -10, -11,
BlueB 76, ConAu 5R, IntAu&W 76,
-77, WhoAm 74, -76, -78, -80, -82,
WhoE 74, WhoWor 80, WrDr 76,
-80, -82, -84*
Martin, Ralph Guy 1920- *WhoAm 84,
-86, WhoWor 84, -87*
Martin, Robert Allen 1930-
*ConAu 110, DrAS 78E, -82E,
IntAu&W 86*
Martin, Vicky *BioIn 12, ConAu X,
IntAu&W 77X, SmATA X*
Martin, Vicky see also Storey, Victoria
Carolyn
Martin, William G *AuBYP SUP*
Martindale, Andrew Henry Robert
1932- *Au&Wr 71, WrDr 76, -80,
-82, -84, -86*
Martine-Barnes, Adrienne 1942-
ConAu 110
Martinez, Al 1929- *ConAu 57*
Martini, Teri 1930- *AuBYP, BioIn 7,
-9, ConAu 2NR, -5R, ForWC 70,
IntAu&W 76, SmATA 3,
WhoAmW 74, -66, -72, -75,
WrDr 76, -80, -82, -84, -86*
Martins, Peter 1946- *BiDD, BioIn 8,
-10, -11, -12, -13, ConAu 113,
CurBio 78, NewYTBS 75, -76, -79,
-80[port], -83[port], WhoAm 78, -80,
-82, -84, -86, WhoE 85*
Marton, Kati 1948?- *BioIn 13*
Marton, Kati Ilona 1947- *WhoAm 80*
Martyn, Norma Sydney 1927-
Au&Wr 71
Martz, William J 1928- *ConAu 9NR,
-21R, DrAS 74E, -78E, -82E*
Marvell, Andrew 1621-1678
*BiDRP&D, BioIn 13, DcNaB,
LitC 4[port], OxEng 85*
Marx, Groucho 1890?-1977 *AmAu&B,
AmPS B, BiE&WWA, BioIn 1, -2,
-3, -4, -5, -6, -7, -9, -10, -11, -12,
-13, BioNews 74, BlueB 76, CelR,
CmCal, ConAu 73, -81, -X,
CurBio 48, -73, -77, -77N, DcFM,
EncMT, FamA&A, Film 2,
HalFC 84[port], IntAu&W 77,
IntMPA 77, -75, -76, IntWW 74,
-75, -76, -77, -78N, LesBEnT,
MGM, MotPP, MovMk,
NewYTBE 72, NewYTBS 77,
NewYTET, ObitOF 79, OxFilm,
WebAB, -79, WhDW, WhScrn 83,*

Marx, Robert F 1936- *AuBYP,
BioIn 13, ConAu 6NR, -9R,
SmATA 24[port]*
Marx, Samuel 1902- *ConAu 103,
IntMPA 81, -82, -84, -86*
Marx, Wesley 1934- *ConAu 12NR,
-21R, IntAu&W 77, -82, WhoAm 74,
-76, -78, -80, -82, -84*
Marzan, Julio *DrAP&F 85*
Marzan, Julio 1946- *ConAu 113,
IntWWP 77*
Marzani, Carl 1912- *Au&Wr 71,
BioIn 1, -11, ConAu 61, SmATA 12,
WrDr 76, -80, -82, -86*
Marzollo, Jean 1942- *BioIn 13,
ChhPo S3, ConAu 15NR, -81,
SmATA 29[port]*
Mascaro, Juan *WhE&EA*
Masefield, John 1878-1967 *AnCL,
AuBYP, BioIn 1, -2, -3, -4, -5, -6,
-7, -8, -9, -10, -11, -12, -13,
BritAS, CasWL, Chambr 3,
ChhPo, -S1, -S2, -S3, CnE&AP,
CnMD, CnMWL, ConAu 25R,
ConAu P-2, ConLC 11,
DcLB 10[port], -19[port], DcLEL,
EncWL, -2, EvLB, LinLib L, -S,
LongCEL, LongCTC,
McGEWD, -84[port], MnBBF,
ModBrL, -S1, ModWD, NewC,
NotNAT B, Novels, ObitOF 79,
ObitT 1961, OxChL, OxEng,
OxShips, OxThe, -83, PenC ENG,
PlP&P, RAdv 1, REn, ScF&FL 1,
SmATA 19, Str&VC, TelT,
TwCA, -SUP, TwCCW 78, -83,
TwCWr, WebE&AL, WhDW,
WhAm 4, WhE&EA, WhLit, WhThe,
WhoBW&I A, WhoChL, WhoTwCL,
WorAl*
Maslach, Christina 1946-
*AmM&WS 73S, -78S, ConAu 111,
WhoAm 84, -86, WhoAmW 83,
WhoWest 84*
Mason, A E W 1865-1948 *HalFC 84,
Novels, OxChL, OxEng 85,
ScF&FL 1, TwCCr&M 80, -85,
WhoSpyF*
Mason, Alpheus Thomas 1899-
*AmAu&B, AmM&WS 73S, -78S,
BlueB 76, ConAu 1R, IntAu&W 77,
-82, IntYB 78, -79, -80, -81, -82,
REnAL, WhoAm 76, -78, -80, -82,
-84, -86, WhoE 74, WhoWor 74*
Mason, Douglas R *TwCSFW 86*
Mason, Douglas R 1918- *Au&Wr 71,
ConAu 1NR, -17NR, -49, ConSFA,
EncSF, IntAu&W 76, -77, -82,
ScF&FL 1, -2, WhoSciF,
WhoWor 78, WrDr 76, -80, -82, -84*
Mason, Douglas Rankine 1918-
WrDr 86
Mason, F VanWyck 1901-1978
*AmAu&B, AmNov, Au&Wr 71,
AuBYP, BioIn 11, BlueB 76,
ConAu 5R, -8NR, -81, LinLib L, -S,
ObitOF 79, REnAL, SmATA 26N, -3,
TwCCr&M 80, -85, WhE&EA,
WhoSpyF, WhoWor 74*
Mason, F VanWyck see also Coffin,
Geoffrey
Mason, F VanWyck see also Mason,
Francis VanWyck
Mason, F VanWyck see also Mason,
Frank W
Mason, F VanWyck see also Mason,
VanWyck
Mason, F VanWyck see also Weaver,
Ward
Mason, Francis Scarlett, Jr. 1921-
*WhoAm 82, -84, -86, WhoAmA 80,
-82, -84, WhoE 74, -75, -77, -79,
-81, -83, -85, WhoF&I 75,
WhoWor 82*
Mason, Francis VanWyck 1897-1978
BioIn 13
Mason, Francis VanWyck 1901-1978
*BioIn 9, -11, WhAm 7, WhoAm 74,
-76, -78*
Mason, Francis VanWyck see also
Mason, F VanWyck

Mason, Frank W 1901-1978 *AuBYP,*
BioIn 1, -2, -7, -9, ConAu X,
SmATA X, WhoSpyF
Mason, Frank W *see also* Mason, F
VanWyck
Mason, Herbert Molloy, Jr. 1927-
ConAu 6NR, -13R, WrDr 80, -82,
-84
Mason, Miriam E 1900-1973
ConAu 15NR
Mason, Miriam Evangeline 1899-1973
BioIn 13
Mason, Miriam Evangeline 1900-1973
AmAu&B, AuBYP, BioIn 6, -7, -9,
ConAu 1R, -103, IndAu 1917,
MorJA, SmATA 2, -26N, WhAm 6,
WhoAmW 74, -58, -70, -72
Mason, Philip *WrDr 86*
Mason, Philip 1906- *Au&Wr 71,*
BlueB 76, ChhPo S3, ConAu 3NR,
-9R, IntAu&W 76, -77, -82,
IntWW 74, -75, -76, -77, -78, -79,
-80, -81, -82, -83, WhE&EA,
Who 74, -82, -83, -85, WhoWor 74,
-78, WrDr 76, -80, -82, -84
Mason, VanWyck *BioIn 13*
Mason, VanWyck 1901-1978
ConAu X, EncMys, ScF&FL 1,
WhoAm 74, -76, -78
Mason, VanWyck *see also* Mason, F
VanWyck
Mason, Zane Allen 1919- *DrAS 74H,*
-78H, -82H
Masselink, Ben 1919- *ConAu 17R*
Masselman, George 1897-1971
BioIn 12, ConAu 9R, SmATA 19
Massie, Robert K 1929- *ASpks,*
BioIn 8, -10, -11, -12, ConAu 14NR,
-77, NewYTBS 80[port], WhoAm 76,
-78, -80, -82, WorAu 1975[port]
Massie, Robert Kinloch 1929-
WhoAm 84, -86
Mast, Gerald 1940- *ConAu 12NR,*
WhoAm 86, WrDr 86
Mast, Gerald J 1940- *ConAu 69,*
DrAS 74E, -78E, -82E
Masterman-Smith, Virginia 1937-
ConAu 110
Masteroff, Joe 1919- *AmAu&B,*
BiE&WWA, ConDr 73, -77D, -82D,
NotNAT, WhoAm 74, -76, -78, -80,
-82
Masters, Edgar Lee 1868-1950
DcLB 54[port], MorMA, OxAmL 83,
OxEng 85
Masters, Edgar Lee 1869?-1950
AmAu&B, AmLY, AmWr S1, AtlBL,
BioIn 1, -2, -3, -4, -5, -6, -8, -9,
-10, -11, -12, -13, CasWL,
Chambr 3, ChhPo, -S1, -S2, -S3,
CnDAL, CnE&AP, CnMWL,
ConAmA, ConAmL, ConAu 104,
CyWA, DcAmB S4, DcLEL,
EncAAH, EncWL, -2, EvLB,
LinLib L, -S, LongCTC, McGEWB,
ModAL, NatCAB 37, ObitOF 79,
OxAmL, OxEng, PenC AM, RAdv 1,
REn, REnAL, SixAP, TwCA, -SUP,
TwCLC 2, TwCWr, WebAB, -79,
WebE&AL, WhDW, WhAm 2, -2A,
WhoTwCL, WorAl
Masters, Kelly Ray 1897- *Au&Wr 71,*
AuBYP, BioIn 3, -7, -9, ConAu 1R,
CurBio 53, SmATA 3
Masters, Kelly Ray *see also* Ball,
Zachary
Masters, Nicholas A 1929-
AmM&WS 73S, ConAu 13R
Masterton, Graham 1946- *ConAu 105,*
IntAu&W 77, -86, WrDr 80, -82,
-84, -86
Maston, T B 1897- *ConAu 2NR, -5R,*
-18NR
Maston, Thomas Bufford 1897-
AmAu&B, Au&Wr 71, ConAu 5R,
IntAu&W 77, -82, WhoAm 74, -76,
WrDr 76, -80, -82, -84
Matchette, Katharine E 1941-
ConAu 53, SmATA 38[port]
Mather, Anne *WrDr 84, -86*
Matheson, Richard 1926- *BioIn 12,*
-13, CmMov, ConAu 97,
ConLC 37[port], ConSFA, ConTFT 1,

DcLB 8[port], -44[port], EncSF,
FilmgC, HalFC 84, NewYTET,
Novels, ScF&FL 1, -2, ScFSB,
SupFW, TwCSFW 86, WhoHr&F,
WhoSciF, WorEFlm, WrDr 84, -86
Mathews, Mitford M d1985
NewYTBS 85[port]
Mathews, Mitford M 1891-1985
ConAu 115
Mathews, Mitford McLeod, Sr. 1891-
AmAu&B
Mathews, Mitford McLeod, Sr.
1891-1985 *WhAm 8*
Mathewson, Christopher 1880-1925
BioIn 1, -2, -3, -4, -5, -6, -7, -8, -9,
-10, -11, -12, DcAmB, DcNAA,
Dis&D, WebAB, -79, WhAm 4,
-HSA, WhoProB 73
Mathewson, Christopher *see also*
Mathewson, Christy
Mathewson, Christy 1880-1925
BioIn 13, OxAmH, WhScrn 77, -83,
WorAl
Mathewson, Christy *see also*
Mathewson, Christopher
Mathiessen, Peter 1927- *IntAu&W 76*
Mathis, Sharon Bell *DrAP&F 85,*
InB&W 85
Mathis, Sharon Bell 1937-
AuBYP SUP, BioIn 10, BlkAWP,
ChlLR 3, ConAu 41R, DcLB 33,
FourBJA, InB&W 80, LivgBAA,
OxChL, SelBAAf, SelBAAu,
SmATA 7, SmATA 3AS[port],
TwCCW 78, -83, WhoAm 74, -76,
-78, -80, -82, -84, -86,
WhoAmW 74, WhoBlA 75, -77, -80,
-85, WrDr 76, -80, -82, -84, -86
Matson, Emerson N 1926- *BioIn 11,*
ConAu 45, IntAu&W 76, SmATA 12,
WhoAdv 80, WrDr 76, -80, -82, -84
Matsunaga, Spark M 1916-
PolsAm 84[port]
Matsunaga, Spark Masayuki 1916-
CngDr 85, -87, WhoAm 86, -86,
WhoAmP 85, WhoWor 87
Matthew, Eunice Sophia 1916-
AuBYP, BioIn 8, WhoAmW 66, -68
Matthews, Herbert L 1900-1977
EncAJ, EncTwCJ
Matthews, Herbert Lionel 1900-1977
AmAu&B, Au&Wr 71, AuBYP,
BioIn 1, -4, -8, -9, -10, -11, -13,
BlueB 76, ConAu 1R, -2NR, -73,
CurBio 43, -77, -77N, IntAu&W 77,
IntWW 74, -75, -76, -77, -78N,
ObitOF 79, REnAL, WhAm 7,
WhoAm 74, -76, -78, WhoWor 74,
WrDr 80, -82, -84
Matthews, L Harrison 1901- *Who 85,*
WrDr 82, -86
Matthews, Patricia 1927- *BioIn 11,*
-13, ConAu 9NR, -29R, -69,
SmATA 28[port], WhoAmW 79,
WrDr 84, -86
Matthews, Patricia *see also* Brisco,
Patty
Matthews, William *DrAP&F 85*
Matthews, William 1942- *BioIn 12,*
ConAu 12NR, ConLC 40[port],
ConPo 80, -85, DcLB 5[port],
IntAu&W 82, IntWWP 82, WrDr 82,
-84, -86
Matthews, William Henry 1919-
BioIn 13
Matthews, William Henry, III 1919-
AmM&WS 82P, -86P, AuBYP SUP,
ConAu 9R, SmATA 28, -45
Matthiessen, Peter *DrAP&F 85*
Matthiessen, Peter 1927- *AmAu&B,*
Au&Wr 71, BioIn 6, -9, -10, -13,
BlueB 76, ConAu 9R, -21NR,
ConLC 5, -7, -11, -32[port],
ConNov 72, -76, -82, -86, CurBio 75,
DcLB 6[port], DcLEL 1940,
IntAu&W 77, OxAmL 83,
SmATA 27[port], WhoAm 74, -76,
-78, -80, -82, -84, -86, WhoWor 74,
WorAu, WrDr 76, -80, -82, -84, -86
Mattingley, Christobel 1931-
ConAu 20NR, SmATA 37[port],
WrDr 86

Maugham, Robert Cecil Romer
1916-1981 *Alli, BioIn 4, -9, -10,*
-12, BlueB 76, ConAu 9R, -103,
DcLEL 1940, NewYTBS 81,
TwCA SUP, Who 74
Maugham, Robert Cecil Romer *see also*
Maugham, Robin
Maugham, Robin 1916- *IntAu&W 86*
Maugham, Robin 1916-1980 *HalFC 84*
Maugham, Robin 1916-1981
AnObit 1981[port], Au&Wr 71,
BioIn 4, -9, -10, -12, BlueB 76,
ConAu X, ConNov 72, -76,
DcLEL 1940, IntAu&W 76, -77, -82,
LongCTC, NewC, ScF&FL 1, -2,
TwCCr&M 80, WorAu 1970,
WrDr 76, -80, -82
Maugham, Robin *see also* Maugham,
Robert Cecil Romer
Maugham, W Somerset 1874-1965
BritWr 6, ConAu 25R, ConLC 11,
-15, DcLB 10[port], -36[port],
EncE 75, EncWL 2, FilmgC,
HalFC 84[port], LinLib L,
McGEWD 84[port], Novels[port],
ObitOF 79, OxEng 85, OxThe 83,
ScF&FL 1, -2, TwCCr&M 80, -85,
WhAm 4, WhScrn 77, -83, WhoSpyF,
WorAl
Maugham, William Somerset
1874-1965 *Alli, AtlBL, BiE&WWA,*
BiHiMed, BioIn 1, -2, -3, -4, -5, -6,
-7, -8, -9, -10, -11, -12, -13,
CasWL, Chambr 3, CnMD, CnMWL,
CnThe, ConAu SR, ConLC 1, CyWA,
DcBiA, DcLEL, DcNaB 1961, Dis&D,
EncMys, EncWL, EncWT, EvLB,
FilmgC, LinLib S, LongCEL,
LongCTC, MakMC, McGEWB,
McGEWD, ModBrL, -S1, ModWD,
NewC, NotNAT A, -B, OxEng,
OxMed 86, OxThe, PenC ENG,
PIP&P, RAdv 1, REn, REnWD,
TwCA, -SUP, TwCWr, WebE&AL,
WhE&EA, WhLit, WhScrn 77,
WhThe, WhoTwCL
Mauldin, Bill *BioIn 13, ConAu X*
Mauldin, Bill 1921- *BioIn 7, -9, -10,*
-11, CelR, CurBio 45, -64, EncAJ,
OxAmL, -83, REnAL, WhoAmA 73,
-76, -78, -80, -82, -84, WhoHol A
Mauldin, Bill *see also* Mauldin, William
H
Mauldin, William H 1921- *AmAu&B,*
BioIn 13, ConAu 111, EncTwCJ
Mauldin, William Henry 1921-
BioIn 13, ConAu 111, EncTwCJ
Maule, Hamilton Bee 1915- *AuBYP,*
BioIn 7, -9, -10, ConAu 1R, -3NR,
WhoAm 74, -76, -78, -80, -82, -84
Maule, Hamilton Bee *see also* Maule,
Tex
Maule, Henry Ramsay 1915-
Au&Wr 71, IntAu&W 77
Maule, Tex 1915- *BioIn 7, -9, -10,*
ConAu X
Maule, Tex *see also* Maule, Hamilton
Bee
Maunder, Leonard 1927- *Who 85*
Maupassant, Guy De 1850-1893
AtlBL, BiD&SB, BioIn 1, -2, -3, -4,
-5, -7, -8, -9, -10, -12, ClDMEL,
CyWA, DcEuL, Dis&D, EncWT,
EuAu, GrFLW, LinLib L, NewC,
NewEOp 71, NinCLC 1[port],
Novels[port], OxEng, -85, OxFr,
PenC EUR, RComWL, REn,
ScF&FL 1, SupFW, WhDW,
WhoHr&F, WorAl
Maupassant, Guy De *see also*
DeMaupassant, Guy
Maureen, Sister Mary 1924-
ConAu 21R
Maurier, Daphne Du 1907-
CurBio 40, InWom, LongCTC,
ScF&FL 1, TwCA, -SUP, WhLit

Maurier, Daphne Du *see also*
DuMaurier, Daphne
Maxey, Dale 1927- *ChhPo S1,*
IlsCB 1957, WhoRel 75
Maxon, Anne *BioIn 13*
Maxon, Anne 1892-1974 *BioIn 2, -5,*
-7, -9, ConAu X, ConAu X,
SmATA X
Maxon, Anne *see also* Best, Allena
Champlin
Maxwell, Ann *ScFSB*
Maxwell, Ann 1944- *ConAu 105*
Maxwell, Edith 1923- *AuBYP SUP,*
BioIn 10, ConAu 49, IntAu&W 77,
SmATA 7, WhoAmW 77
Maxwell, Gavin 1914-1969 *AuBYP,*
BioIn 7, -8, -9, -10, ConAu 5R,
-25R, DcLEL 1940, DcNaB 1961,
LongCTC, NewC, ObitOF 79,
OxEng 85, TwCWr, WhAm 5, WorAu
Maxwell, William *DrAP&F 85*
Maxwell, William 1908- *AmAu&B,*
AmNov, AuBYP, BioIn 2, -4, -7, -12,
-13, ConAu 93, ConLC 19,
ConNov 72, -76, -82, -86,
DcLB Y80B, IntAu&W 76, -77,
OxAmL, -83, REn, TwCA SUP,
WhoAm 74, -76, -78, -80, -82, -84,
-86, WhoWor 74, WrDr 76, -80, -82,
-84, -86
May, Charles Paul 1920- *AuBYP,*
BioIn 7, -8, -9, ConAu 1R, -5NR,
IntAu&W 76, -77, -82, SmATA 4
May, Julian 1931- *AuBYP, BioIn 11,*
ConAu 1R, -6NR, SmATA 11,
TwCSFW 86
May, Julian 1932- *ScFSB*
May, Rollo 1909- *AmAu&B, BioIn 8,*
-9, -10, BioNews 74, CelR,
ConAu 111, CurBio 73,
NewYTBE 71, WhoAm 74, -76, -78,
-80, -82, -84, -86, WhoE 74
May, Wynne *IntAu&W 82X,*
WrDr 84, -86
Mayall, R Newton 1904- *ConAu P-1*
Maybury, Anne *ConAu X, WrDr 84,*
-86
Mayer, Albert I 1906-1960 *BioIn 13*
Mayer, Albert Ignatius, Jr. 1906-1960
ConAu 109, OhA&B, SmATA 29N
Mayer, Debby *DrAP&F 85*
Mayer, Debby 1946- *ConAu X*
Mayer, Jean *NewYTBS 86*
Mayer, Jean 1920- *AmM&WS 73P,*
-76P, -79P, -82P, -86P, BioIn 8, 9,
-10, -11, -12, ConAu 117, CurBio 70,
IntMed 80, NewYTBS 76,
WhoAm 74, -76, -78, -80, -82, -84,
-86, WhoAmP 73, -75, -77, -79, -81,
-83, -85, WhoAmW 70, WhoE 74,
WhoWor 74, -76
Mayer, Joseph 1887-1975
AmM&WS 73S, WhAm 6, WhE&EA,
WhNAA, WhoAm 74
Mayer, Marianna 1945- *BioIn 12,*
ConAu 93, FourBJA, SmATA 32[port]
Mayer, Martin Prager 1928-
AmAu&B, Au&Wr 71, BioIn 3, -6,
-8, -10, ConAu 5R, IntAu&W 76,
-77, WhoAm 74, -76, -78, -80, -82,
-84, -86, WorAu
Mayer, Mercer 1943- *BioIn 12,*
ChLR 11[port], ChhPo S3,
ConAu 85, FourBJA, IlsBYP,
IlsCB 1967, SmATA 16, -32[port]
Mayerson, Charlotte Leon
ConAu 13R, ForWC 70, SmATA 36,
WhoAmW 68
Mayerson, Evelyn Wilde 1935-
ConAu 101
Mayhar, Ardath *ScFSB*
Mayhar, Ardath 1930- *ConAu 103,*
-19NR, IntAu&W 86, IntWWP 77,
SmATA 38[port], TwCSFW 86,
WrDr 76
Maynard, Joyce 1953- *BioIn 9, -10,*
ConAu 111, ConLC 23[port],
NewYTBE 72
Maynard, Olga 1920- *ConAu 114,*
SmATA 40[port], WhoAmW 77, -79,
-81
Maynard, Richard Allen 1942-
ConAu 33R

Mayne, William 1928- *AnCL, AuBYP, BioIn 6, -7, -8, -9, -10, ConAu 9R, ConLC 12, DcLEL 1940, IntAu&W 82, -86, OxChL, ScF&FL 1, -2, ScFSB, SenS, SmATA 6, ThrBJA, TwCCW 78, -83, Who 82, -83, -85, WhoAm 74, -76, -78, -80, -82, -84, WhoChL, WhoWor 74, WrDr 76, -80, -82, -84*

Mayne, William 1929- *WrDr 86*

Mayo, Margaret 1935- *ConAu 107, SmATA 38*

Mayo, Margaret Mary 1935- *IntAu&W 86*

Mays, Buddy 1943- *ConAu 12NR, -73, ICPEnP A*

Mays, Lucinda L 1924- *ConAu 101*

Mays, Victor 1927- *BioIn 10, ConAu 25R, FourBJA, SmATA 5, WhoAmA 78, -80, -82, -84*

Mays, Willie 1931- *BioIn 2, -3, -4, -5, -6, -7, -8, -9, -10, -11, -12, -13, BioNews 74, BlkAWP, CelR, CmCal, ConAu 105, CurBio 55, -66, Ebony 1, LinLib S, NegAl 76[port], -83[port], NewYTBE 70, -73, NewYTBS 74, -79, WebAB, -79, WhoAm 74, -76, -78, -80, WhoBlA 75, -77, -80, WhoProB 73, WorAl*

Mazer, Harry 1925- *ConAu 97, FifBJA[port], SmATA 31[port]*

Mazer, Norma Fox *DrAP&F 85*

Mazer, Norma Fox 1931- *ConAu 12NR, -69, ConLC 26[port], FifBJA[port], SmATA 24[port], SmATA 1AS[port], WhoAmW 87*

Mazo, Joseph H 1938- *ConAu 69*

Mazrui, Ali A 1933- *ConAu 13NR, Who 85, WhoWor 84, -87*

Mazrui, Ali Al'Amin 1933- *BioIn 13, WhoAm 86*

Mazzeo, Henry *ScF&FL 1*

McAleavy, Henry 1912-1968 *ConAu P-2*

McAleer, Neil 1942- *ConAu 119*

McBain, Gordon D, III 1946- *ConAu 106*

McBain, William Norseworthy 1918- *AmM&WS 73S, -78S*

McBeath, Marcia 1925- *WhoAmW 72, WhoWest 78*

McBride, Chris 1941?- *BioIn 11, ConAu 81*

McBurney, Laressa Cox 1883- *IntWWP 77, WhNAA*

McCabe, John C, III 1920- *ConAu 1R, -1NR, DrAS 74E, -78E, -82E, IntAu&W 76, -77, -82, WhoAm 74, -76, -78, -80, -82, WhoMW 74, -76, -78, WhoWor 78, WrDr 76, -80, -82, -84, -86*

McCabe, John Charles, III 1920- *WhoAm 84, -86, WhoMW 84*

McCabe, Joseph E 1912- *BlueB 76, ConAu 17R, IntAu&W 76, -77, LEduc 74, WhoAm 74, -76, -78, WhoMW 74, -76, -78*

McCaffrey, Anne 1926- *AmWomWr, AuNews 2, BioIn 10, -11, -12, -13, ConAu 15NR, -25R, ConLC 17, ConSFA, DcLB 8[port], EncSF, FifBJA[port], IntAu&W 77, -82, -86, LinLib L, ScF&FL 1, -2, ScFSB[port], SmATA 8, TwCSFW 86, WhoAm 74, -76, -78, -80, -82, WhoAmW 74, WhoSciF, WrDr 76, -80, -82, -84, -86*

McCague, James 1909-1977 *ConAu 1R, -2NR*

McCaleb, Walter Flavius 1873-1967 *AmAu&B, ConAu P-1, OhA&B, TexWr, WhAm 5, WhE&EA*

McCall, Dan Elliott 1940- *BioIn 8, -10, DrAS 74E*

McCall, Daniel Francis 1918- *AmM&WS 73S, -76P, ConAu 17R, FifIDA*

McCall, Virginia Nielsen 1909- *AuBYP SUP, BioIn 11, ConAu 1R, -1NR, -17NR, ForWC 70, SmATA 13, WhoAmW 74, -68, -70, -72, -75*

McCallum, John D 1924- *ConAu 4NR, -53, IntAu&W 77*

McCammon, Robert R 1952- *ConAu 81*

McCannon, Dindga *AfroAA, ConAu 114*

McCarry, Charles *DrAP&F 85*

McCarry, Charles 1930- *ConAu 103, Novels, TwCCr&M 80, -85, WhoSpyF, WrDr 80, -82, -84, -86*

McCarter, Neely Dixon 1929- *ConAu 109, SmATA 47[port], WhoRel 75, -77, -85*

McCarthy, Agnes 1933- *BioIn 9, ConAu 5R, -17R, SmATA 10, -4, WhoAmW 74, -68, -75, -77*

McCarthy, Dennis 1912- *WhoAm 84, -86, WhoAmL 85*

McCarthy, Eugene J 1916- *AmAu&B, AmCath 80, BiDrAC, BioIn 3, -4, -5, -6, -8, -9, -10, -11, -12, BlueB 76, ConAu 1R, -2NR, CurBio 55, DcPol, EncAB-H, IntAu&W 77, IntWW 74, -75, -76, -77, -78, -79, -80, -81, -82, -83, IntYB 78, -79, -80, -81, -82, McGEWB, MinnWr, NewYTBE 71, PolProf E, PolProf J, PolProf K, PolProf NF, WebAB, -79, Who 74, -82, -83, WhoAm 74, -76, -78, -80, -82, WhoAmP 73, -75, -77, -79, -81, -83, WhoWor 74, -78, -80, -82, WorAl, WrDr 76, -80, -82, -84*

McCarthy, Eugene Joseph 1916- *BioIn 13, Who 85, WhoAm 84, -86, WhoAmP 85*

McCarthy, Joe 1915-1980 *ConAu 1R, -97, -X*

McCarthy, Mary *DrAP&F 85*

McCarthy, Mary 1910- *ConTFT 1*

McCarthy, Mary 1912- *AmAu&B, AmWomWr, AmWr, ASpks, Au&Wr 71, BiE&WWA, BioIn 3, -4, -6, -7, -8, -9, -10, -11, -12, BlueB 76, CasWL, CelR, ConAu 5R, -16NR, ConLC 1, -3, -5, -14, -24[port], ConLCrt, -82, ConNov 72, -76, -82, -86, CurBio 55, -69, DcLB 2, -Y81A[port], DcLEL 1940, EncWL, -2, GoodHs, InWom, IntAu&W 76, -77, -82, -86, IntDcWB, IntWW 74, -75, -76, -77, -78, -79, -80, -82, -83, LibW, LongCTC, MakMC, ModAL, -S2, -S1, NewYTBS 79, NotNAT, Novels[port], OxAmL, -83, OxEng 85, PenC AM, PolProf J, RAdv 1, REn, REnAL, TwCA SUP, TwCWr, WebAB, -79, WebE&AL, Who 74, -82, -83, -85, WhoAm 74, -76, -78, -80, -82, -84, -86, WhoAmW 74, -58, -64, -66, -68, -70, -72, -85, -87, WhoTwCL, WhoWor 74, -80, -82, -84, -87, WorAl, WrDr 76, -80, -82, -84, -86*

McCartney, Linda 1941?- *BioIn 9, -10, -11, WhoRocM 82*

McCartney, Paul 1942- *BioIn 6, -7, -8, -9, -10, -11, -12, -13, BioNews 74, BlueB 76, CelR, ConLC 35[port], CurBio 66, -86[port], EncPR&S 74, -77, IlEncRk, IntWW 74, -75, -76, -77, -78, -79, -80, -81, -82, -83, IntWWM 77, MotPP, NewOxM, RkOn 78, -84, RolSEnR 83, Who 82, -83, -85, WhoHol A, WhoRocM 82, WhoWor 78, -80, -82, -84, -87, WorAl*

McCartney, Paul *see also* Beatles, The

McCartney, Paul *see also* Wings

McCaslin, Nellie 1914- *ConAu 33R, DrAS 74E, -78E, -82E, IntAu&W 77, -82, -86, SmATA 12, WhoAmW 74, -70, -72, -75, -77, WrDr 76, -80, -82, -84, -86*

McCaughrean, Geraldine *SmATA X*

McCaughrean, Geraldine 1951- *ConAu 117*

McClary, Jane Stevenson 1919- *ConAu 1R, -1NR, ForWC 70, WhoAmW 66, -68, -75, -77*

McClary, Jane Stevenson *see also* McIlvaine, Jane

McClean, Don 1945- *EncPR&S 74, IlEncRk*

McClendon, Edwin James 1921- *WhoAm 86, WhoMW 84*

McClendon, Sarah 1910?- *BioIn 4, -6, -10, -11, -12, CelR, ConAu 73, InWom, WhoAm 76, -78, -80, -82, WhoAmW 79, -81, -83*

McClendon, Sarah Newcomb 1910- *EncTwCJ, WhoAm 84, -86, WhoWor 84, -87*

McClory, Robert J 1932- *ConAu 13NR*

McClory, Robert Joseph 1932- *ConAu 77*

McCloskey, Robert 1914- *ChLR 7[port], OxChL, SmATA 39[port], WhoAm 84, -86, WhoAmA 84, WrDr 86*

McCloskey, William B, Jr. 1928- *ConAu 101*

McClung, Robert M 1916- *AuBYP, AuNews 2, BioIn 6, -7, -8, -9, -11, -12, ChLR 11[port], ConAu 6NR, -13R, -21NR, IlsCB 1957, -1967, MorJA, SmATA 2, WhoE 75, -77, WrDr 76, -80, -82, -84*

McClung, Robert Marshall 1916- *IntAu&W 86, WrDr 86*

McClure, Arthur F, II 1936- *ConAu 10NR, -65, DrAS 74H, -78H, -82H*

McClure, Arthur Frederick, II 1936- *WhoMW 84*

McClure, James 1939- *BioIn 13, TwCCr&M 85, WorAu 1975[port], WrDr 86*

McConnell, Frank DeMay 1942- *ConAu 104, DrAS 74E, -78E, -82E*

McConnell, James Douglas 1915- *SmATA 40[port]*

McConnell, James Douglas R 1915- *ConAu 6NR, -9R, EncMys, WrDr 76*

McConnell, James Douglas R *see also* Rutherford, Douglas

McCord, David 1897- *AmAu&B, AnCL, BioIn 6, -9, -11, -12, -13, BkCL, BkP, ChlLR 9[port], ChhPo, -S1, -S2, -S3, ConAu 73, OxAmL, -83, OxChL, REnAL, SmATA 18, Str&VC, ThrBJA, TwCCW 78, -83, WhE&EA, WhNAA, WhoAm 74, -76, -78, -80, -82, -84, -86, WhoWor 74, -76, -78, -80, -82, WrDr 80, -82, -84, -86*

McCord, Jean 1924- *ConAu 49, SmATA 34[port]*

McCormick, Donald 1911- *BioIn 12, ConAu 9R, -14NR, -73, IntAu&W 76X, -77X, -82X, -86, SmATA 14, WrDr 76, -80, -82, -84, -86*

McCormick, Jack 1929-1979 *AmM&WS 73P, -76P, -79P, ConAu 5NR, -9R, -85, IndAu 1917, WrDr 76, -80, -82, -84*

McCormick, Mona *ConAu 77, WhoLibI 82*

McCoy, Iola Fuller 1906- *BiDrLUS 70, ConAu 13R, InWom, MichAu 80, SmATA 3*

McCoy, Iola Fuller *see also* Fuller, Iola

McCoy, Jerome J 1917- *AuBYP, BioIn 8, -11, ConAu 6NR, -13R, SmATA 8*

McCoy, Kathy 1945- *ConAu X*

McCracken, Harold 1894- *AmAu&B, AuBYP, BioIn 2, -7, -8, ConAu 107, CurBio 49, JBA 51, WhAm 8, WhoAm 74, -76, -78, -80, -82, WhoAmA 73, -76, -78, -80, -82, -84, WhoWest 76, WhoWor 78*

McCrackin, Mark 1949- *ConAu 107*

McCready, Albert Lee 1918- *WhoAm 74, -76, -78, -80, -82, WhoWest 82*

McCrohan, Donna 1947- *ConAu 111*

McCullers, Carson 1917-1967 *AmAu&B, AmNov, AmWomD, AmWomWr, AmWr, BiE&WWA, BioIn 2, -4, -5, -6, -7, -8, -9, -10, -11, -12, -13, CasWL, CnDAL, CnMD, CnMWL, ConAu 5R, -18NR, -25R, ConAu 1BS, ConLC 1, -4, -10, -12, ConNov 76, -82A, -86A,*

CurBio 40, -67, CyWA, DcLB 2, -7[port], DcLEL 1940, EncSoH, EncWL, -2, EncWT, FilmgC, GoodHs, HalFC 84, InWom, IntDcWB, LibW, LinLib L, LongCTC, McGEWD, -84[port], ModAL, -S2, -S1, ModWD, NewCon[port], NotAW MOD, NotNAT B, Novels[port], ObitOF 79, ObitT 1961, OxAmL, -83, PenC AM, PlP&P, RAdv 1, REn, REnAL, SmATA 27[port], TwCA, -SUP, TwCWr, WebAB, -79, WebE&AL, WhDW, WhAm 4, WhoAmW 64, -66, -68, -70, WhoTwCL, WorAl

McCullough, Colleen 1937?- *BioIn 11, -12, -13, ConAu 81, ConLC 27[port], CurBio 82[port], NewYTBS 81[port], OxAusL, WorAl, WorAu 1975[port]*

McCullough, Colleen 1938?- *ConAu 17NR*

McCullough, David 1933- *BioIn 11, -12, ConAu 2NR, -49, NewYTBS 77, WhoAm 80, -82, -84, -86, WhoE 81*

McCullough, David G 1933- *BioIn 13*

McCullough, David William 1945- *WhoAmA 78, -80, -82, -84*

McCutchan, Philip 1920- *ScFSB, TwCCr&M 85, WrDr 86*

McDermott, Alice *DrAP&F 85*

McDermott, Gerald 1941- *AuNews 2, BioIn 10, -11, -12, ChlLR 9[port], ConAu 85, FifBJA[port], IlsBYP, IlsCB 1967, NewbC 1966, SmATA 16, WhoAm 76, -78, WhoAmA 80, -82, -84*

McDonagh, Don 1932- *ConAu 1NR, -49, IntAu&W 77X, -82X*

McDonald, Archie P 1935- *ConAu 15NR*

McDonald, Elvin 1937- *ConAu 5R, -8NR*

McDonald, Forrest 1927- *AuBYP SUP, BioIn 13, ConAu 5NR, -9R, DcLB 17[port], DrAS 74H, -78H, -82H, IntAu&W 77, -82, WrDr 76, -80, -82, -84, -86*

McDonald, Gerald D 1905-1970 *BiDrLUS 70, BioIn 1, -6, -8, -9, ChhPo, ConAu P-1, OhA&B, SmATA 3, WhoLibS 55, -66*

McDonald, Gregory 1937- *BioIn 13, BlueB 76, ConAu 3NR, -5R, TwCCr&M 80, -85, WhoAm 82, WrDr 82, -84, -86*

McDonald, Lucile Saunders 1898- *AuBYP, BioIn 7, -10, -11, ConAu 1R, -4NR, -18NR, ForWC 70, InWom, IntAu&W 76, -77, -82, SmATA 10, WhoAmW 74, -58, -61, -64, -66, -68, -70, -72, -75, -77, -79, -81, WhoPNW*

McDonnell, Virginia Bleecker *WhoAmW 85, WhoE 85, WhoWor 84*

McDonnell, Virginia Bleecker 1917- *AuBYP SUP, ConAu 8NR, -21R, IntAu&W 76, WhoAmW 75, -77, -79, -81, -83, WhoE 75, -77, -79, -83*

McDonough, Thomas Redmond *AmM&WS 86P*

McDonough, Thomas Redmond 1945- *WhoFrS 84*

McDougald, Gilbert James 1928- *BioIn 2, -3, -4, -5, St&PR 75, WhoProB 73*

McDowell, Bart 1923- *ConAu 25R*

McDowell, Josh *BioIn 13*

McDowell, Margaret B 1923- *ConAu 69*

McDowell, Michael 1950- *ConAu 93, WrDr 84, -86*

McElfresh, Adeline 1918- *ConAu 1R, WhoAmW 58, -61, WrDr 84, -86*

McEntee, Howard Garrett 1905- *AuBYP SUP*

McFadden, Dorothy Loa 1902- *AuBYP, BioIn 8, ConAu 17R, InWom, WhoAmW 58, -61*

McFall, Christie 1918- *BioIn 11, ConAu 5R, SmATA 12*

McFarland, Gerald Ward 1938- *WhoAm 84, -86*

Mendoza, George 1934- *AuBYP SUP, BioIn 9, -11, ConAu 73, SmATA 39, -41[port], ThrBJA*

Menen, Aubrey 1912- *BioIn 3, -4, -5, -9, BlueB 76, ConAu 1R, -2NR, ConNov 72, -76, -82, EncWL, IntAu&W 76, -77, IntWW 74, -75, -76, -77, -78, -79, -80, -81, -82, -83, LinLib L, LongCTC, ModBrL, ModCmwL, NewC, REn, ScF&FL 1, -2, TwCA SUP, WhoAm 74, -76, -78, -80, -82, WhoWor 74, -76, -78, WrDr 76, -80, -82, -84, -86*

Meng, Heinz Karl 1924- *AmM&WS 73P, -76P, -79P, -82P, -86P, BioIn 11, ConAu 69, SmATA 13*

Menke, Frank Grant 1885-1954 *BioIn 1, -3, ObitOF 79, OhA&B*

Menon, Bhaskar 1934- *St&PR 75, WhoF&I 75, -77*

Menuhin, Yehudi 1916- *Baker 78, -84, BiDAmM, BioIn 1, -2, -3, -4, -5, -6, -7, -8, -9, -10, -11, -12, -13, BlueB 76, CelR, CmCal, ConAu 2NR, -45, CurBio 41, -73, IntWW 74, -75, -76, -77, -78, -79, -80, -81, -82, -83, IntWWM 77, -85, LinLib S, MusSN, NewYTBS 76, -81[port], OxMus, SmATA 40[port], WebAB, -79, Who 74, -82, -83, -85, WhoAm 74, -76, -78, -80, -82, -84, -86, WhoAmJ 80, WhoAmM 83, WhoFr 79, WhoHol A, WhoMus 72, WhoWor 74, -78, -80, -82, -84, -87, WhoWorJ 78, WorAl, WrDr 80, -82, -84, -86*

Menville, Douglas 1935- *ConAu 57, EncSF, IntAu&W 77, ScF&FL 2, WhoWest 78*

Menzel, Donald Howard 1901-1976 *AmM&WS 73P, -76P, AsBiEn, BiESc, BioIn 3, -4, -11, -12, BlueB 76, ConAu 69, ConAu P-2, CurBio 56, -77, -77N, InSci, IntAu&W 77, IntWW 74, -75, -76, -77N, McGMS 80[port], NatCAB 59[port], NewYTBE 70, NewYTBS 76, ObitOF 79, UFOEn, WhAm 7, WhoAm 74, -76, WrDr 80*

Mercatante, Anthony Stephen 1940- *ConAu 41R, IntAu&W 76, -82*

Mercer, Charles 1917- *AmAu&B, AuBYP SUP, BioIn 12, ConAu 1R, -2NR, SmATA 16, WhoAm 74, -76, -78, -80, -82, -84, 86, WhoE 74*

Mercier, Vivian H 1919- *ConAu 81, DrAS 74E, -78E, -82E, WhoWest 78*

Meredith, Don *DrAP&F 85*

Meredith, Don 1938- *ConAu 102, ConTFT 1, NewYTBS 77, NewYTET, WhoAm 76, -78, -80, -82, -84, WorAl*

Meredith, Richard C 1937- *ConAu 85, EncSF, ScF&FL 1*

Meredith, Richard C 1937-1979 *ScFSB, TwCSFW 86*

Meredith, Scott 1923- *AmAu&B, BioIn 10, -13, ConAu 3NR, -9R, WhoAm 74, -76, -78, -80, -82, -84, -86, WhoE 74, -75, -77, -79, -81, WhoWor 84, -87, WrDr 76, -80, -82, -84, -86*

Meriwether, Louise *DrAP&F 85*

Meriwether, Louise 1923- *BlkAWP, ConAu 77, DcLB 33[port], Ebony 1, InB&W 80, LivgBAA, SelBAAf, SelBAAu, SmATA 31, WhoBlA 75, -77, -80, -85*

Merle, Robert 1908- *Au&Wr 71, ConAu 93, EncSF, IntAu&W 76, -77, ScF&FL 1, ScFSB, Who 74, -82, -83, -85, WhoFr 79*

Merne, Oscar James 1943- *ConAu 102, IntAu&W 77, WrDr 76, -80, -82, -84, -86*

Merriam, Eve *DrAP&F 85, WhoAm 86*

Merriam, Eve 1916- *AmAu&B, AmWomD, AuBYP, BioIn 1, -8, -9, -12, -13, BkP, ChhPo, -S1, -S2, -S3, ConAu 5R, ConTFT 1, ForWC 70, OxChL, SmATA 3, -40[port], ThrBJA, TwCCW 78, -83,*

WhoAm 74, -76, -78, -80, -82, -84, *WhoAmW 74, -66, -68, -70, -72, -75, -77, -81, WhoE 74, WrDr 80, -82, -84, -86*

Merril, Judith *OxCanL*

Merril, Judith 1923- *AmWomWr, BioIn 10, -12, CaW, ConAu 13R, -15NR, ConSFA, EncSF, IntAu&W 76, -77, LinLib L, Novels, ScF&FL 1, -2, ScFSB, TwCSFW 86, WhoAmW 58, -61, WhoCanL 85, WhoSciF, WorAu, WrDr 84, -86*

Merrill, John Nigel 1943- *Au&W 71, IntAu&W 76, -77, WrDr 76, -80*

Merritt, A *ConAu X*

Merritt, A 1884-1943 *EncSF, ScF&FL 1, SupFW, TwCSFW 86, WhoHr&F*

Mersand, Joseph 1907- *AmAu&B, ConAu 1R, -1NR, DrAS 74E, -78E, WhNAA, WhoE 74, -75, -77, -79, -81, WhoWorJ 78*

Merton, Thomas 1915-1968 *AmAu&B, BiDMoPL, BioIn 1, -2, -3, -4, -5, -8, -9, -10, -11, -12, -13, CathA 1930, ConAu 5R, -25R, ConLC 1, -3, -11, DcAmReB, DcLB 48[port], -Y81B[port], IlEncMy, LinLib L, -S, LongCTC, MakMC, ModAL, ObitOF 79, OxAmL, PenC AM, REnAL, TwCA SUP, WebAB, -79, WhAm 5*

Merton, Thomas 1915-1969 *OxAmL 83*

Mertz, Barbara G *TwCCr&M 85*

Mertz, Barbara Gross 1927- *Au&Wr 71, BioIn 11, ConAu 11NR, -21R, DrAS 74H, IntAu&W 86, ScF&FL 1, TwCCr&M 80, WrDr 76, -80, -82, -84*

Mertz, Barbara Gross see also Michaels, Barbara

Mertz, Barbara Gross see also Peters, Elizabeth

Merwin, W S *DrAP&F 85*

Merwin, W S 1927- *BioIn 11, BlueB 76, ConAu 15NR, ConLC 8, -13, -18, ConPo 80, -85, DcLB 5[port], EncWL 2, IntAu&W 77, ModAL S2, OxAmL 83, WhoWor 74, WrDr 80, -82, -84, -86*

Merwin, William Stanley 1927- *AmAu&B, BioIn 8, -10, -12, -13, CasWL, ChhPo S2, CnE&AP, ConAu 13R, ConLC 1, -2, -3, -5, ConPo 70, -75, CroCAP, DcLEL 1940, IntWWP 77, ModAL, -S1, OxAmL, PenC AM, RAdv 1, WebE&AL, WhoAm 74, -76, -78, -80, -82, -84, -86, WhoE 74, WhoTwCL, WorAu, WrDr 76*

Meserole, Harrison Talbot 1921- *DrAS 74E, -78E, -82E*

Messenger, Charles 1941- *ConAu 13NR*

Messer, Ronald Keith 1942- *ConAu 57*

Messina, Jim 1947- *WhoRocM 82, WorAl*

Messina, Jim see also Loggins & Messina

Messner, Reinhold 1944- *BioIn 11, ConAu 15NR, -81, CurBio 80[port], IntAu&W 77, -82*

Metcalf, George R *SelBAAf*

Metcalf, George R 1914- *ConAu 25R*

Metcalf, George Rich 1914- *WhoF&I 85*

Metcalf, Harlan Goldsbury 1899- *WhoE 77, -79, -81*

Metos, Thomas H 1932- *ConAu 93, LEduc 74, SmATA 37*

Metzger, Norman 1924- *ConAu 9NR, -53*

Metzker, Isaac 1901- *ConAu 45, WhoAmJ 80, WhoWorJ 72, -78*

Metzler, Paul 1914- *ConAu 6NR, -57*

Mewshaw, Michael 1943- *BioIn 9, -12, -13, ConAu 7NR, -53, ConLC 9, DcLB Y80B[port], IntAu&W 77, WrDr 76, -80, -82, -84, -86*

Meyer, Alfred W 1927- *DrAS 82P*

Meyer, Carolyn 1935- *AuBYP SUP, BioIn 11, ConAu 2NR, -49, FifBJA[port], SmATA 9*

Meyer, Edith Patterson 1895- *AuBYP, BioIn 1, -8, -10, ConAu 1R, -1NR, SmATA 5, WhoAmW 58, -61, -64, -75, -77, -79*

Meyer, Howard N 1914- *BioIn 10, ConAu 13R, WhoAmJ 80, WhoAmL 78, -79, WhoE 75, WhoWorJ 72, -78*

Meyer, Jerome Sydney 1895-1975 *Au&Wr 71, AuBYP, BioIn 7, -9, -10, -13, BlueB 76, ConAu 1R, -4NR, -57, SmATA 25N, -3, WhoWorJ 72*

Meyer, Karl Ernest 1928- *AmAu&B, BioIn 10, -11, ConAu 1R, -1NR, WhoAm 80, -82, -84, -86, WhoWor 74*

Meyer, Milton W 1923- *DrAS 74H, -78H, -82H*

Meyer, Nicholas 1945- *BioIn 10, -11, -12, ConAu 7NR, -49, ConTFT 1, HalFC 84, IntAu&W 76, -77, IntMPA 86, NewYTBS 82[port], TwCCr&M 80, -85, WhoAm 76, -78, -80, -82, -84, -86, WorAu 1975[port], WrDr 76, -80, -82, -84, -86*

Meyer, Nicholas 1946?- *BioIn 13*

Meyer, Susan E 1940- *ConAu 2NR, -19NR, -45, IntAu&W 77, WhoAm 74, -76, -78, -80, -82, -84, -86, WhoAmA 76, -78, -80, -82, -84, -86*

Meyerowitz, Joel 1938- *AmArt, BioIn 13, ICPEnP, MacBEP, PrintW 85, WhoAm 84, -86, WhoAmA 84, WhoWor 84, -87*

Meyers, Jeffrey 1939- *ConAu 73, DrAS 78E, -82E, WrDr 84, -86*

Meyers, Robert *DrAP&F 85*

Mezey, Robert 1935- *AmAu&B, BioIn 10, ConAu 7NR, -57, ConPo 70, -75, -80, -85, CroCAP, DrAS 74E, -78E, -82E, IntWWP 77, -82, PenC AM, SmATA 33, WorAu 1970, WrDr 76, -80, -82, -84, -86*

Michaels, Barbara *IntAu&W 86X, TwCCr&M 85*

Michaels, Barbara 1927- *BioIn 11, ConAu X, ScF&FL 1, -1A, -2, TwCCr&M 80, WrDr 76, -80, -82, -84, -86*

Michaels, Barbara see also Mertz, Barbara Gross

Michaels, Kristin *WrDr 80, -82, -84, -86*

Michaels, Leonard *DrAP&F 85*

Michaels, Leonard 1933- *BioIn 12, -13, ConAu 21NR, -61, ConLC 6, -25[port], ConNov 82, -86, DrAS 74E, -78E, -82E, NewYTBS 81[port], OxAmL 83, WhoAm 76, -78, -80, -82, -84, -86, WorAu 1975[port], WrDr 82, -84, -86*

Michell, John 1933- *ConAu 107*

Michelmore, Peter 1930- *ConAu 5R, -7NR, IntAu&W 86*

Michener, James A *NewYTBS 85[port]*

Michener, James A 1907- *BioIn 13, ConAu 21NR, ConNov 82, HalFC 84, OxAmL 83, WrDr 86*

Michener, James A 1908- *ConLC 29[port]*

Michener, James Albert 1907- *AmAu&B, AmNov, Au&Wr 71, AuNews 1, BioIn 1, -2, -3, -4, -5, -6, -7, -8, -9, -10, -11, -12, BioNews 74, BlueB 76, CelR, ConAu 5R, ConLC 1, -5, -11, ConNov 72, -76, -82, Conv 3, CurBio 48, -75, DcLB 6[port], DcLEL, -1940, FilmgC, IntAu&W 74, -77, IntWW 74, -75, -76, -77, -78, -79, -80, -81, -82, -83, LinLib L, -S, LongCTC, ModAL, NewYTBE 72, NewYTBS 78, -82, Novels[port], OxAmL, PenC AM, PIP&P, RAdv 1, REnAL, TwCA SUP, WebAB, -79, Who 74, -82, -83, -85, WhoAm 74, -76, -78, -80, -82, -84,*

-86, WhoWor 74, -78, WorAl, WrDr 76, -80, -82, -84

Michie, Allan Andrew 1915-1973 *AuBYP, BioIn 8, -10, -12, ConAu 45, CurBio 42, -52, -74, -74N, NatCAB 58[port], NewYTBE 73, WhE&EA*

Micoleau, Tyler *IlsBYP*

Middlebrook, Diane W 1939- *ConAu 81, DrAS 74E, -78E, -82E*

Middlebrook, Diane Wood 1939- *ConAu 15NR*

Middlekauff, Robert Lawrence 1929- *DrAS 74H, -78H, -82H, WhoAm 74, -76, -78, -84, -86*

Middleton, Robert Gordon 1908- *WhoWest 76, -78, -80, -82, -84*

Miers, Earl Schenck 1910-1972 *AmAu&B, AuBYP, BioIn 1, -2, -5, -7, -8, -9, -10, -13, ChhPo S2, ConAu 1R, -2NR, -37R, CurBio 49, -67, -73, -73N, NewYTBE 72, REnAL, SmATA 1, -26N, ThrBJA, WhAm 5, -7, WhoAm 74, -76*

Miesel, Sandra 1941- *IntAu&W 82, -86, ScF&FL 1, -2*

Mihaly, Mary E 1950- *ConAu 97, IntAu&W 82*

Miklowitz, Gloria D 1927- *AuBYP SUP, BioIn 9, ConAu 10NR, -25R, IntAu&W 82, SmATA 4, WhoAmW 79, -81, WrDr 76, -80, -82, -84, -86*

Milam, James Robert 1922- *AmM&WS 73S, -78S, WhoWest 76, -78*

Milcsik, Margie 1950- *ConAu 110*

Mild, Warren Paul 1922- *ConAu 8NR, -21R, DrAS 74E, -78E, -82E, WhoRel 75*

Mileck, Joseph 1922- *ConAu 107, DrAS 74F, -78F, -82F*

Miles, Bernard 1907- *OxThe 83*

Miles, Betty *DrAP&F 85*

Miles, Betty 1928- *AuBYP, BioIn 8, -11, ConAu 1R, -5NR, -20NR, FifBJA[port], ForWC 70, SmATA 8, WhoAmW 66, -68, -70, WomWMM B, WrDr 76, -80, -82, -84, -86*

Miles, Miska *ConAu X, OxChL, SmATA X, WrDr 86*

Miles, Miska 1899- *AuBYP, ChhPo S2, ConAu X, FourBJA, IntAu&W 77X, SmATA 1, TwCCW 78, -83, WrDr 76, -80, -82, -84*

Miles, Miska see also Martin, Patricia Miles

Miles, Patricia 1930- *AuBYP SUP, BioIn 13, ConAu 11NR, -69, SmATA 29[port]*

Miles, Sir Bernard 1907- *BioIn 5, CnThe, EncWT, FilmgC, HalFC 84, IntMPA 77, -75, -76, -78, -79, -80, -81, OxThe, PIP&P, Who 74, WhoAmP 75, WhoHol A, WhoThe 72, -77, -81*

Milford, Nancy 1938- *ConAu 29R, DrAS 78E, WrDr 76, -80, -82, -84, -86*

Milgram, Gail Gleason *IntAu&W 86*

Milgram, Gail Gleason 1942- *ConAu 29R, IntAu&W 76, WhoAmW 75, -77, -79, -83, WrDr 76, -80, -82, -84, -86*

Millar, Barbara F 1924- *BioIn 11, ConAu 25R, SmATA 12, WhoAmW 74*

Millar, Jeff 1942- *BioIn 10, ConAu 11NR, -69*

Millar, Kenneth *TwCCr&M 85*

Millar, Kenneth 1915-1983 *AmAu&B, AmNov, Au&Wr 71, BioIn 2, -3, -5, -8, -9, -10, -11, -12, -13, BlueB 76, ConAu 9R, -110, -16NR, ConLC 14, CurBio 53, -79, -83N, DcLB 2, -Y83N[port], DcLEL 1940, EncMys, IntAu&W 76, IntWW 81, -82, -83, Po&Pr 77, TwCCr&M 80, WhAm 8, WhoAm 74, -76, -78, -80, -82, WhoWest 76, -78, WhoWor 74, WorAu, WrDr 76, -80, -82, -84*

Millar, Kenneth *see also* Macdonald, Ross

Millar, Margaret Ellis 1915-
AmAu&B, AmNov, AmWomWr, Au&Wr 71, BioIn 1, –2, –5, –9, –10, –12, CanWW 70, –79, –80, –81, –83, ConAu 13R, ConNov 76, –82, CurBio 46, EncMys, InWom, IntAu&W 76, Novels, REnAL, TwCCr&M 80, WhoAm 74, –76, –78, –80, –82, –84, –86, WhoAmW 64, –66, –68, –70, –72, WhoWest 76, –78, WhoWor 74, –76, WorAu, WrDr 76, –80, –82, –84

Millar, Ronald 1919- *BioIn 10, ConAu 73, ConDr 73, –77, –82, DcLEL 1940, IntAu&W 77, –82, OxThe 83, Who 82, –83, WhoThe 72, –77, –81, WrDr 76, –80, –82, –84, –86*

Millar, Sir Ronald 1919- *Who 85*
Millard, Charles W 1932- *ConAu 115*
Millard, Charles Warren, III 1932-
WhoAm 80, –86, WhoAmA 76, –78, –80, –82, –84, WhoE 79, –83, –85
Millard, Reed *AuBYP SUP*
Millay, Edna St. Vincent 1892-1950
AmAu&B, AmSCAP 66, AmWomD, AmWomWr, AmWr, ApCAB X, AtlBL, BioIn 1, –2, –3, –4, –5, –6, –8, –9, –10, –11, –12, CasWL, Chambr 3, ChhPo, –S1, –S2, –S3, CnDAL, CnE&AP, CnMD, CnMWL, ConAmA, ConAmL, ConAu 104, CyWA, DcAmB S4, DcLB 45[port], DcLEL, EncWL, –2, EvLB, GoodHs, HerW, –84, InWom, IntDcWB, LibW, LinLib L, –S, LongCTC, McGEWB, McGEWD, ModAL, ModWD, NatCAB 38, NotAW, NotNAT B, OxAmL, –83, OxEng, –85, PenC AM, RAdv 1, REn, REnAL, SixAP, Str&VC, TwCA, –SUP, TwCLC 3, –4[port], TwCWr, WebAB, –79, WhDW, WhAm 3, WhNAA, WorAl

Miller, Albert G 1905-1982 *BioIn 11, –12, ConAu 1R, –1NR, –107, NewYTBS 82, SmATA 12, –31N*
Miller, Albert Griffith 1905-1982
BioIn 13
Miller, Alice Duer 1874-1942
AmAu&B, AmWomD, AmWomWr, ChhPo, –S1, CurBio 41, –42, DcAmAu, DcNAA, InWom, LibW, LongCTC, NotAW, NotNAT B, ObitOF 79, REn, REnAL, TwCA, –SUP, WhAm 2, WhLit, WhNAA, WhoHol B, WomWWA 14
Miller, Alice P *BioIn 13*
Miller, Alice Patricia McCarthy
Au&Wr 71, ConAu 9R, –29R, ForWC 70, SmATA 22[port], WhoAmW 74, –66, –68, –70, –72, –75, –77, WhoE 74
Miller, Arthur *DrAP&F 85, NewYTBS 84[port]*
Miller, Arthur 1915- *AmAu&B, AmNov, AmWr, Au&Wr 71, AuNews 1, BiE&WWA, BioIn 1, –2, –4, –5, –7, –8, –9, –10, –11, –12, –13, BioNews 74, BlueB 76, CasWL, CelR, CnDAL, CnMD, CnMWL, CnThe, ConAu 1R, –2NR, ConDr 73, –77, –82, ConLC 1, –2, –6, –10, –15, –26[port], ConTFT 1, CroCD, CurBio 47, –73, CyWA, DcFM, DcLB 7[port], DcLEL 1940, EncAB-H, EncWL, –2[port], EncWT, FilmgC, HalFC 84, IntAu&W 76, –77, IntMPA 84, –86, IntWW 74, –75, –76, –77, –78, –79, –80, –81, –82, –83, LinLib L, –S, LongCTC, MajMD 1, MakMC, McGEWB, McGEWD, –84[port], ModAL, –S2, –S1, ModWD, NatPD, –81[port], NewCon[port], NewEOp 71, NewYTBE 72, NewYTBS 80[port], NotNAT, –A, OxAmL, –83, OxAmT 84, OxEng, –85, OxFilm, OxThe, –83, PenC AM, PIP&P, PolProf E, PolProf T, RComWL, REn, REnAL, REnWD, TwCA SUP,*

TwCWr, WebAB, –79, WebE&AL, WhDW, Who 74, –82, –83, –85, WhoAm 74, –76, –78, –80, –82, –84, –86, WhoAmJ 80, WhoE 85, WhoThe 72, –77, –81, WhoTwCL, WhoWor 74, –78, –80, –82, –84, –87, WhoWorJ 72, –78, WorAl, WorEFlm, WrDr 76, –80, –82, –84, –86
Miller, Arthur R 1934- *ConAu 114*
Miller, Arthur Raphael 1934-
BioIn 12, WhoAm 74, –76, –78, –82, –84, –86, WhoAmL 83, –85
Miller, Casey 1919- *ConAu 69*
Miller, Casey Geddes 1919-
IntAu&W 86
Miller, Charles A 1937- *ConAu 29R, WrDr 76, –80, –82, –84, –86*
Miller, David William 1940-
ConAu 49, DrAS 74H, –78H, –82H, WhoMW 74
Miller, Douglas T *WrDr 86*
Miller, Douglas T 1937- *ConAu 21R, DrAS 74H, –78H, IntAu&W 77, WrDr 76, –80, –84*
Miller, Douglas Taylor 1937-
IntAu&W 86
Miller, Edwin Haviland 1918-
ConAu 110, DrAS 74E, –78E, –82E
Miller, Eugene 1925- *ConAu 101, Dun&B 79, ODwPR 79, SmATA 33[port], St&PR 75, WhoAm 74, –76, –78, –80, –82, –84, –86, WhoF&I 74, –75, –77, –79, –81, –83, –85, WhoMW 74, –76, –78, –80, –82, –84, –86, WhoPubR 72, –76*
Miller, Floyd C 1912- *ConAu 1R, –2NR, IndAu 1917*
Miller, Frances A 1937- *SmATA 46*
Miller, Helen Knapp 1899- *AuBYP*
Miller, Helen Knapp *see also* Miller, Helen Markley
Miller, Helen Markley 1899-
AmAu&B, AuBYP, BioIn 7, –10, ConAu 1R, –2NR, SmATA 5
Miller, Isabel *ConAu 49, MichAu 80*
Miller, Jason *OxAmT 84*
Miller, Jason 1932- *WrDr 86*
Miller, Jason 1939?- *AuNews 1, BioIn 9, –10, CelR, ConAu 73, ConDr 73, –77, –82, ConLC 2, ConTFT 4, CurBio 73, DcLB 7[port], HalFC 84, NotNAT, OxAmL 83, PIP&P A, WhoAm 74, –76, –78, –80, –82, –84, –86, WhoThe 77, –81, WorAl, WorAu 1970, WrDr 76, –80, –82*
Miller, Jason 1940- *IntMPA 84*
Miller, Jean Baker 1927- *BiDrAPA 77*
Miller, Jonathan *NewYTBS 84[port]*
Miller, Jonathan 1934- *BiE&WWA, BioIn 6, –7, –9, –11, –13, BlueB 76, ConAu 110, –115, CurBio 86[port], EncWT, FilmgC, IntWW 74, –75, –76, –77, –78, –79, –80, –81, –82, –83, NewYTBS 80[port], NotNAT, Who 74, –82, –83, WhoHol A, WhoOp 76, WhoThe 72, –77, –81, WorAl, WrDr 80, –82, –84, –86*
Miller, Jonathan 1936- *HalFC 84*
Miller, Katherine *AuBYP, BioIn 8*
Miller, Lillian Beresnack 1923-
ConAu 9NR, –21R, DrAS 74H, –78H, –82H, WhoGov 75
Miller, Mara 1944- *ConAu 97*
Miller, Margaret J *ConAu X, SmATA X*
Miller, Margaret J 1911- *Au&Wr 71, ConAu X, IntAu&W 76X, –77X*
Miller, Margaret J *see also* Dale, Margaret J Miller
Miller, Mary Beth 1942- *BioIn 11, ConAu 61, SmATA 9*
Miller, May *BlkAWP, DrAP&F 85, InB&W 80, SelBAAf, SelBAAu*
Miller, May 1899- *DcLB 41[port]*
Miller, Merle d1986
NewYTBS 86[port]
Miller, Merle 1919- *AmAu&B, AmNov, ASpks, Au&Wr 71, AuNews 1, BioIn 1, –2, –3, –9, –10, –11, –12, CelR, ConAu 4NR, –9R, CurBio 50, IntAu&W 76, –77, LinLib L, REn, REnAL, WhoAm 76,*

–78, –80, –82, –84, WhoWor 74, WorAu, WrDr 76, –80, –82, –84, –86
Miller, Merle 1919-1986 *ConAu 119, CurBio 86N*
Miller, Nathan 1927- *ConAu 4NR, –53, WhoAm 74, –76, –78, –80, –82, –84, –86, WhoS&SW 73, –75, –76*
Miller, Norman C 1934- *ConAu 37R, WhoAm 74, –76, –78, –80*
Miller, Norman Charles, Jr. 1934- *WhoAm 86*
Miller, Peter 1934- *ConAu 37R*
Miller, Robert T 1920- *WhoS&SW 86*
Miller, Ruth 1921- *ConAu 106, DrAS 82E, WhoAmW 83*
Miller, Sandy *ConAu X*
Miller, Sandy 1948- *SmATA 35, –41[port]*
Miller, Sigmund Stephen 1917- *ConAu 1R, –4NR*
Miller, Tom 1947- *ConAu 14NR*
Miller, Victor 1940- *ConAu 107*
Miller, Walter M 1922- *ScFSB*
Miller, Walter M, Jr. 1922- *TwCSFW 86, WrDr 86*
Miller, Walter M, Jr. 1923- *ConLC 30[port]*
Miller, Walter Michael, Jr. 1923- *AmAu&B, BioIn 4, BlueB 76, ConAu 85, ConLC 4, ConSFA, DcLB 8[port], EncSF, ScF&FL 1, –2, WhoAm 74, –76, –78, WhoSciF, WhoWor 74, WrDr 84*
Miller, Warren 1921-1966 *AmAu&B, AmM&WS 73S, –78S, BioIn 4, –5, –7, –10, BlueB 76, ConAu 11NR, –13R, –25R, EncSF, Novels, ObitOF 79, PenC AM, ScF&FL 1, WhoAm 80, –82, WhoMW 80, WhoWor 82, WorAu, WrDr 76, –80, –82, –84*
Miller, Wright W 1903- *Au&Wr 71, ConAu 17R*
Millhiser, Marlys 1938- *ConAu 53, IntAu&W 86, ScF&FL 1, –2, WrDr 76, –80, –82, –84, –86*
Milligan, Spike *BioIn 13*
Milligan, Spike 1918- *BioIn 9, –11, BlueB 76, ChhPo S1, –S2, ConAu X, DcIrL, EncWT, FilmgC, HalFC 84, IntAu&W 76X, –77X, IntWW 82, –83, OxChL, SmATA X, WhoHol A, WhoThe 72, –77, –81, WrDr 76, –80, –82, –84, –86*
Milligan, Spike *see also* Milligan, Terence Alan
Milligan, Terence Alan 1918- *Au&Wr 71, ConAu 4NR, –9R, IntAu&W 76, –77, SmATA 29[port], Who 74, –82, –83, –85*
Milligan, Terence Alan *see also* Milligan, Spike
Millington, Barry 1951- *ConAu 119*
Millington, Roger 1939- *ConAu 65, IntAu&W 77, WrDr 76, –80, –82, –84, –86*
Mills, Claudia 1954- *ConAu 109, IntAu&W 86, SmATA 41, –44[port]*
Mills, John FitzMaurice *WhoArt 84*
Mills, John FitzMaurice 1917- *Au&Wr 71, ConAu 103, WhoArt 82*
Mills, William *DrAP&F 85*
Mills, William 1935- *ConAu 118*
Millstead, Thomas E *ConAu 106, SmATA 30*
Milne, Christopher Robin 1920- *AuNews 2, BioIn 7, –10, –11, ChhPo S3, ConAu 11NR, –61, IntAu&W 82, WrDr 76, –80, –82, –84, –86*
Milne, Lorus J *ConAu 14NR, WhoTech 84, WrDr 86*
Milne, Lorus Johnson *AmM&WS 86P, WhoAm 84, –86*
Milne, Lorus Johnson 1912- *AmAu&B, AmM&WS 73P, –76P, –79P, –82P, Au&Wr 71, AuBYP, BioIn 7, –10, CanWW 70, –79, –80, –81, –83, ConAu 33R, IntAu&W 76, –77, –82, SmATA 5, WhoAm 74, –76, –78, –80, –82, WrDr 76, –80, –82, –84*
Milne, Margery *AmM&WS 86P, ConAu 14NR, WrDr 86*

Milne, Margery 1915- *AmAu&B, AmM&WS 73P, –76P, –79P, –82P, Au&Wr 71, BioIn 7, –10, ConAu 33R, ForWC 70, IntAu&W 76, SmATA 5, WhoAmW 74, –58, –61, –64, –66, –68, –70, –72, –75, –77, –79, –81, WhoE 74, WrDr 76, –80, –82, –84*
Milner, Ron 1938- *BioNews 75, ConAu 73, ConDr 77, –82, DcLB 38[port], PIP&P A, SelBAAf, WrDr 82, –84, –86*
Milner, Ronald *DrAP&F 85*
Milner, Ronald 1938- *AuNews 1, BioIn 10, BlkAWP, ConDr 73, DrBlPA, InB&W 80, –85, LivgBAA, SelBAAu, WrDr 76, –80*
Milosz, Czeslaw 1911- *BioIn 10, –11, –12, –13, CasWL, ConAu 81, ConFLW 84, ConLC 5, –11, –22[port], –31[port], CurBio 81[port], DrAS 74F, –78F, EncWL, –2[port], IntWW 81, –82, –83, IntWWP 77, ModSL 2, NewYTBS 80[port], –81[port], –82[port], OxAmL 83, OxEng 85, PenC EUR, Who 82, –83, –85, WhoAm 80, –82, –84, –86, WhoNob, WhoTwCL, WhoWest 82, –84, WhoWor 82, –84, –87, WorAl, WorAu*
Milsten, David Randolph 1903- *WhoAm 74, –76, –78, –80, –82, –84, –86, WhoAmJ 80, WhoAmJ 78, –79*
Milton, Hilary 1920- *BioIn 13, ConAu 6NR, –21NR, –57, SmATA 23[port]*
Milton, John *DcNaB*
Milton, John 1608-1674 *Alli, AtlBL, BbD, BiD&SB, BiDRP&D, BioIn 1, –2, –3, –4, –5, –6, –7, –8, –9, –10, –11, –12, –13, BritAu, BritWr 2, CasWL, Chambr 1, ChhPo, –S1, –S2, –S3, CnE&AP, CnThe, CroE&S, CrtT 2, –4, CyEd, CyWA, DcBiPP, DcEnA, –AP, DcEnL, DcEuL, DcLEL, DcNaB, Dis&D, EncWT, EvLB, HsB&A, LinLib L, –S, LongCEL, LuthC 75, McGEWB, MouLC 1, NewC, NewEOp 71, NotNAT B, OxEng, –85, OxMus, PenC ENG, PIP&P, PoChrch, RAdv 1, RComWL, REn, REnWD, WebE&AL, WhDW, WorAl*
Milton, Joyce *BioIn 13, DrAP&F 85*
Milton, Joyce 1946- *ConAu 106, SmATA 41*
Milts, Michael H *BioIn 10, –12*
Minahan, John 1933- *ConAu 2NR, –45, IntAu&W 76, WhoAm 78, –80, –82, WhoWor 80*
Miner, Jane Claypool 1933- *ConAu 109, SmATA 37, –38[port]*
Mines, Jeanette 1948- *ConAu 119*
Minnelli, Vincente 1913- *BiDFilm, BioIn 9, –10, –11, –12, CelR, CmMov, CurBio 75, DcFM, EncMT, FilmgC, IntMPA 77, –75, –76, –78, –79, –81, –82, –84, IntWW 74, –75, –76, –77, –78, –79, –80, –81, –82, –83, MovMk, NotNAT, –A, OxFilm, WhoAm 74, –76, –78, –80, –82, WhoWor 74, –78, WorAl, WorEFlm*
Minnelli, Vincente 1913?-1986 *BiDD, BioIn 13, ConAu 117, –119, ConTFT 1[port], CurBio 86N, HalFC 84, IntDcF 2, IntMPA 86, NewYTBS 86, OxAmT 84, WhoAm 84, –86*
Minton, Madge Rutherford 1920- *ConAu 45*
Minton, Robert 1918- *ConAu 57, WhoPubR 72*
Minton, Sherman Anthony 1919- *AmM&WS 73P, –76P, –79P, –82P, –86P, ConAu 45, IndAu 1917, WhoFrS 84*
Mintz, Lorelie Miller *AuBYP SUP*
Mintz, Morton Abner 1922- *ConAu 13R, EncTwCJ, WhoAm 74, –76, –78, –80, –82, –84, –86, WhoAmJ 80, WhoS&SW 73, –75, –76*
Mintz, Thomas 1931- *ConAu 108*
Mirvish, Robert F 1921- *WrDr 86*

Mirvish, Robert Franklin 1921-
*AmAu&B, Au&Wr 71, BioIn 3, –4,
–6, CanWW 70, –79, –80, –81, –83,
ConAu 1R, CurBio 57, IntAu&W 86,
WhoAm 74, –76, –78, –80, –82, –84,
–86, WhoWor 74, –76, WrDr 76, –80,
–82, –84*

Mishima, Yukio d1971 *WhScrn 83*

Mishima, Yukio 1925-1970
*Au&Wr 71, BiDJaL, BioIn 2, –5, –7,
–8, –9, –10, –12, CasWL, CnMD,
ConAu 29R, –X, ConLC 2, –4, –6,
–9, –27[port], DcOrL 1,
EncWL, –2[port], EncWT, GrFLW,
LinLib 1, ModWD, NewYTBE 70,
Novels[port], ObitOF 79, PenC CL,
RComWL, REn, WhDW, WhAm 5,
WhScrn 74, –77, WhoTwCL, WorAl,
WorAu*

Mishima, Yukio see also Hiraoka,
Kimitake

Misrach, Richard 1949- *ICPEnP A,
PrintW 85*

Mitchell, Don *DrAP&F 85,
IntAu&W 86X*

Mitchell, Don 1947- *ConAu 14NR,
–33R*

Mitchell, Gladys 1901-1983
*AnObit 1983, Au&Wr 71, BioIn 5,
ConAu 9R, –9NR, –110, EncMys,
IntAu&W 76, –77, –82, LongCTC,
Novels, SmATA 35N, –46,
TwCCr&M 80, –85, WhE&EA,
Who 74, –82, –83, WrDr 76, –80,
–82, –84*

Mitchell, Jerry 1905?-1972 *BioIn 9,
ConAu 33R*

Mitchell, Joni 1943- *Baker 84,
BioIn 8, –9, –10, –11, BioNews 74,
CanWW 81, CelR, ConAu 112,
ConLC 12, CurBio 76,
EncFCWM 83, EncPR&S 77,
GoodHs, RkOn 78, –84, RolSEnR 83,
WhoAm 74, –76, –78, –80, –82, –84,
–86, WhoAmW 70, –72, –75, –77,
–79, –81, –85, –87, WhoRock 81,
WorAl*

Mitchell, Joseph Brady 1915-
*ConAu 9R, DcLEL 1940,
WhoS&SW 73, –75, –76, –78, –80,
–82, –84, –86, WhoWor 84, –87*

Mitchell, Joyce Slayton 1933-
*ConAu 15NR, –65, SmATA 43,
–46[port], WhoAmW 72*

Mitchell, Margaret 1900-1949
*AmAu&B, AmWomWr, BioIn 1, –2,
–3, –4, –5, –6, –7, –8, –10, –11, –13,
CasWL, Chambr 3, CnDAL, CyWA,
DcAmB S4, DcLB 9[port], DcLEL,
DcNAA, EvLB, FilmgC, GoodHs,
HalFC 84, InWom, LibW, LinLib 1,
–S, LongCTC, ModAL, NatCAB 38,
NotAW, Novels[port], ObitOF 79,
OxAmL, –83, OxEng 85, PenC AM,
REn, REnAL, TwCA, –SUP,
TwCWr, WebAB, –79, WebE&AL,
WhAm 2, WhNAA, WorAl*

Mitchell, Ralph 1934- *AmM&WS 86P,
WhoAm 84, –86*

Mitchell, William Ormond 1914-
*BioIn 3, –13, CaW, CanWW 70, –79,
–80, –81, –83, CanWr, CasWL,
ConAu 77, ConNov 72, –76,
CreCan 1, DcLEL 1940, OxCan,
TwCWr, WhoCanL 85, WrDr 76*

Mitchison, Naomi 1897- *BioIn 13,
CmScLit, ConNov 86, OxChL,
ScFSB, TwCSFW 86, WrDr 86*

Mitchison, Naomi 1897-1964
*Au&Wr 71, BioIn 4, –8, –10, –12,
BlueB 76, CasWL, Chambr 3,
ChhPo, –S2, –S3, ConAu 77,
ConNov 72, –76, –82, ConSFA,
DcLEL, EncSF, EvLB, InWom,
IntAu&W 76, –77, –82, IntWW 74,
–75, –76, –77, –78, –79, –80, –81,
–82, –83, LongCTC, ModBrL, NewC,
Novels, PenC ENG, REn, ScF&FL 1,
–2, SmATA 24[port], TwCA, –SUP,
TwCCW 78, –83, WhE&EA, Who 74,
–82, –83, WhoChL, WhoLA,
WhoSciF, WhoWor 74, WrDr 76,
–80, –82, –84*

Mitford, Jessica 1917- *AmAu&B,
AmWomWr, ASpks, BioIn 8, –9, –10,
–11, –12, BlueB 76, ConAu 1R,
–1NR, CurBio 74, IntAu&W 76, –77,
IntDcWB, IntWW 74, –75, –76, –77,
–78, –79, –80, –81, –82, –83, NewC,
NewYTBS 77, Who 82, –83,
WhoAm 74, –76, –78, –80, –82, –84, –86,
WhoAmW 74, –66, –68, –70, –72,
–75, –83, –85, WhoWor 74, –76, –78,
WorAu, WrDr 76, –80, –82, –84, –86*

Mitgang, Herbert 1920- *AmAu&B,
BioIn 11, –12, ConAu 4NR, –9R,
IntAu&W 76, –77, ScF&FL 1, –2,
WhoAm 74, –76, –78, –80, –82, –84,
–86, WhoAmJ 80, WhoE 74,
WhoWor 74, –80, WhoWorJ 72,
WrDr 76, –80, –82, –84, –86*

Mitterrand, Francois
NewYTBS 86[port]

Mitterrand, Francois 1916- *BioIn 13*

Mitton, Jacqueline 1948- *ConAu 97*

Mitton, Simon 1946- *ConAu 97*

Mizener, Arthur 1907- *AmAu&B,
BioIn 2, –4, BlueB 76, ConAu 5R,
–5NR, DrAS 74E, –78E, –82E,
IntAu&W 76, –77, –82, IntWW 74,
–75, –76, –77, –78, –79, –80, –81,
–82, –83, REnAL, TwCA SUP,
WhoAm 74, –76, –78, –80, WhoE 74,
WhoWor 74, WrDr 76, –80, –82, –84,
–86*

Mizner, Elizabeth Howard 1907-
*AuBYP, BioIn 2, –13, ConAu 13R,
CurBio 51, InWom, IntAu&W 76,
–77, –82, SmATA 27[port],
WhoAmW 68, –70*

Mizner, Elizabeth Howard see also
Howard, Elizabeth

Mizumura, Kazue *AmPB, BioIn 8, –9,
–12, ChhPo S2, ConAu 85, IlsBYP,
IlsCB 1957, –1967, SmATA 18,
ThrBJA*

Moche, Dinah L 1936- *ConAu 89,
SmATA 40, –44[port]*

Modesitt, L E, Jr. *ScFSB*

Moe, Barbara 1937- *BioIn 12,
ConAu 69, SmATA 20*

Moeri, Louise 1924- *BioIn 13,
ConAu 9NR, –65, FifBJA[port],
SmATA 24[port]*

Moffat, Gwen 1924- *Au&Wr 71,
ConAu 10NR, –13R, IntAu&W 86,
TwCCr&M 80, –85, WrDr 82, –84,
86*

Moffat, Mary Jane 1933-
ConAu 17NR, –97

Mohr, Nicholasa 1935- *AfroAA,
AuBYP SUP, BioIn 11, ConAu 1NR,
–49, FifBJA[port], IntAu&W 77,
SmATA 8*

Mojtabai, A G 1937-
WorAu 1975[port]

Mojtabai, A G 1938- *AmWomWr,
ConAu 85, ConLC 5, –9, –15,
–29[port]*

Moldafsky, Annie 1930- *ConAu 61,
WhoAmW 79, –81, WhoMW 84*

Molden, Fritz P 1924- *BioIn 11, –12,
IntYB 78, –79, –80, –81, –82,
WhoWor 74, –76*

Mole, John 1941- *ConAu 18NR,
ConPo 85, SmATA 36[port], WrDr 86*

Moliere 1622-1673 *AtlBL, BbD,
BiD&SB, CasWL, ChhPo, CnThe,
CyWA, DcCathB, DcEnL, DcEuL,
Dis&D, EncWT, EuAu, EuWr 3,
EvEuW, GrFLW, LinLib 1, –S,
LongCEL, McGEWB,
McGEWD, –84[port], NewC,
NewEOp 71, NotNAT A, –B,
OxEng, –85, OxFr, OxMus,
OxThe, –83, PenC EUR, PlP&P, –A,
RComWL, REn, REnWD, WorAl*

Molloy, Anne Stearns 1907- *AuBYP,
BioIn 1, ConAu 13R, ForWC 70,
SmATA 32[port], WhoAmW 58*

Molloy, Paul 1920- *BioIn 6, –10,
ChhPo S2, ConAu 1R, SmATA 5,
WhoAm 74, –76, WhoMW 74*

Molloy, Paul 1924- *ConAu 17NR*

Momaday, N Scott *DrAP&F 85*

Momaday, N Scott 1934- *AmAu&B,
BioIn 9, –10, –11, –12, ChhPo S1,
CmCal, ConAu 14NR, –25R,
ConLC 2, –19, ConNov 76, –82, –86,
CurBio 75, EncFWF, ModAL S2,
OxAmL 83, REnAW, SmATA 30,
–48[port], WorAu 1975[port],
WrDr 76, –80, –82, –84, –86*

Momaday, Navarre Scott 1934-
*BioIn 9, –10, –11, –12, DrAS 74E,
–78E, –82E, WhoAm 74, –76, –78,
–80, –82, –84, –86*

Momiyama, Nanae *WhoAmA 84*

Momiyama, Nanae 1919?-
*WhoAmA 76, –78, –80, –82,
WhoAmW 75, –77, –79, –83*

Monaco, James 1942- *BioIn 13,
ConAu 15NR, –69, WrDr 86*

Monaghan, Patricia *DrAP&F 85*

Monaghan, Patricia 1946- *ConAu 107*

Mondale, Joan Adams 1930- *BioIn 10,
–11, –12, ConAu 41R,
CurBio 80[port], NewYTBS 76, –78,
WhoAm 78, –80, –82, –84, –86,
WhoAmA 78, –80, –82, –84,
WhoAmW 68, –70, –72, –77, –79,
–81, WhoE 77, –79, –81, –83*

Mondey, David 1917- *ConAu 93*

Monjo, F N 1924-1978 *AuBYP SUP,
ChlLR 2, ConAu 81, FifBJA, OxChL,
SmATA 16, TwCChW 83, WrDr 80*

Monjo, Ferdinand Nicholas 1924-1978
BioIn 11, –12, ChlLR 2, TwCCW 78

Monsarrat, Nicholas 1910-1979
*Au&Wr 71, BioIn 1, –2, –4, –7, –9,
–12, –13, BlueB 76, CanWW 70, –79,
CanWr, ConAu 1R, –3NR,
ConNov 72, –76, ConSFA, CurBio 50,
–79N, DcLB 15[port], DcLEL,
EncSF, EvLB, HalFC 84,
IntAu&W 76, –77, IntWW 74, –75,
–76, –77, –78, –79, LinLib L,
LongCTC, ModBrL, NewYTBS 79,
Novels, REn, ScF&FL 1, TwCA SUP,
TwCWr, WhAm 7, WhE&EA,
Who 74, WhoWor 74, –76, –78,
WrDr 76, –80*

Montagu, Ashley 1905- *AmAu&B,
AmM&WS 73S, –76P, –79P,
Au&Wr 71, BioIn 3, –4, –7, –8, –11,
BlueB 76, CelR, ConAu 5R, –5NR,
FifIDA, IntEnSS 79, TwCA SUP,
WebAB, –79, Who 74, –82, –83, –85,
WhoAm 74, –76, –78, –80, –82, –84,
–86, WhoAmJ 80, WhoE 74,
WhoWor 76, WhoWorJ 72, –78,
WorAl, WrDr 76, –80, –82, –84, –86*

Montagu, Ewen Edward Samuel 1901-
*Au&Wr 71, BioIn 3, –4, –8, –11,
BlueB 76, ConAu 77, CurBio 56,
IntAu&W 76, –77, –82, Who 74, –82,
–83, –85, WhoWor 76, WhoWorJ 72,
–78, WrDr 76, –80, –82, –84*

Monteleone, Thomas F 1946-
*ConAu 109, –113, EncSF,
IntAu&W 82, ScFSB, TwCSFW 86,
WrDr 84, –86*

Montgomerie, Norah Mary 1913-
*AuBYP, BioIn 5, –7, –8, –13,
ChhPo, –S1, –S2, ConAu 105,
IlsCB 1946, –1957, SmATA 26*

Montgomerie, William 1904-
*Au&Wr 71, ChhPo, CmScLit,
ConPo 70, IntAu&W 76, –77, –82,
–86, IntWWP 77*

Montgomery, Elizabeth Rider
ConAu X

Montgomery, Elizabeth Rider 1902-
*AuBYP, BioIn 2, –3, –7, –9,
ChhPo S1, –S2, –S3, ConAu 1R,
–3NR, CurBio 52, ForWC 70,
InWom, IntAu&W 76, –77, –82,
SmATA 3, –34[port], WhoAmW 74,
–58, –61, –64, –68, –70, –72, –75,
–77, –79, –81, WhoPNW,
WhoThe 72, –75?, –77, –81*

Montgomery, Elizabeth Rider
1902-1985 *SmATA 41N*

Montgomery, L M 1874-1942
*ChlLR 8[port], ConAu 108,
CurBio 42, ObitOF 79, OxCanL,
OxChL, TwCChW 83*

Montgomery, Lucy Maud *WomNov*

Montgomery, Lucy Maud 1874-1942
*BioIn 1, –3, –4, –6, –7, –10, –11, –12,
CanWr, CarSB, CasWL, Chambr 3,
ChhPo, –S1, –S2, –S3, CreCan 2,
DcLEL, DcNAA, EvLB, InWom,
JBA 34, LinLib L, LongCTC,
MacDCB 78, OxAmL, OxCan, REn,
REnAL, TwCA, TwCCW 78,
TwCWr, WhNAA, YABC 1*

Montgomery, Robert Bruce 1921-
*BioIn 1, –2, –10, CurBio 49,
ScF&FL 1, WhoWest 76, –78, WorAu*

Montgomery, Robert Bruce see also
Crispin, Edmund

Montgomery, Ruth Shick
ConAu 17NR, WhoAm 84, –86

Montgomery, Ruth Shick 1912-
*AmWomWr, BioIn 1, –4,
–9, –10, ConAu 1R, –2NR,
CurBio 57, ForWC 70, InWom,
IntAu&W 76, –77, –82, WhoAm 74,
–76, –78, –80, –82, WhoAmW 74,
–58, –61, –64, –66, –68, –70, –72,
–75, –77, WhoWor 74, –76, WrDr 76,
–80, –82, –84*

Montgomery, Rutherford George
1894- *AmAu&B, AuBYP, BioIn 6,
–7, –9, ConAu 9R, MorJA,
ScF&FL 1, –2, SmATA 3,
TwCCW 78, –83, WhNAA,
WhoAm 74, –76, –78, WrDr 76, –80,
–82, –84*

Montross, Lynn 1895-1961 *AmAu&B,
BioIn 5, ObitOF 79, WhE&EA,
WhNAA*

Moody, Anne 1940- *BioIn 8, –9, –11,
ConAu 65, HerW, –84, InB&W 80,
IntAu&W 77, LivgBAA, SelBAAu*

Moody, Anne 1940- *SelBAAf*

Moody, Ralph 1898- *AuBYP, BioIn 2,
–3, –4, –6, –7, –8, –9, –12,
ConAu P-1, CurBio 55, SmATA 1,
WhoAm 74, –76, –78*

Moody, Raymond Avery, Jr. 1944-
ConAu 93, WhoAm 78, –80, –82

Moon, Keith 1946-1978 *WhoRock 81*

Moon, Keith 1947-1978 *BioIn 11, –12,
–13, ObitOF 79, WhScrn 83,
WhoRocM 82*

Moon, Keith see also Who, The

Mooney, Michael M *ConAu X*

Mooney, Michael Macdonald
DrAP&F 85

Mooney, Michael Macdonald d1985
NewYTRS 85

Mooney, Michael Macdonald 1930-
ConAu 65, WrDr 82, –84, –86

Mooney, Michael Macdonald
1930-1985 *ConAu 117, –21NR*

Moorcock, Michael 1939- *BioIn 12,
ConAu 2NR, –17NR, –45,
ConAu 5AS[port], ConLC 5,
–27[port], ConSFA, DcLB 14[port],
EncSF, IntAu&W 76, –77, LinLib L,
MnBBF, Novels, OxEng 85,
ScF&FL 1, –2, ScFSB[port], SupFW,
TwCSFW 86, WhoHr&F, WhoSciF,
WorAu 1975[port], WrDr 76, –80,
–82, –84, –86*

Moorcock, Michael John 1939-
BioIn 13, WhoWor 84, –87

Moore, Alvin Edward 1904-
WhoS&SW 84, WhoWor 84, –87

Moore, Barbara 1934- *ConAu 53,
WhoAm 74, WrDr 76, –80, –82,
–84, –86*

Moore, Bob 1948- *ConAu 61*

Moore, Brian *DrAP&F 85*

Moore, Brian 1921- *ASpks,
Au&Wr 71, BiDIrW, BioIn 6, –8, –9,
–10, –11, –12, BlueB 76, CaW,
CanWW 70, –79, –80, –81, –83,
CanWr, CasWL, ConAu 1R, –1NR,
ConLC 1, –3, –5, –7, –8, –19,
–32[port], ConNov 72, –76, –82, –86,
CreCan 2, CurBio 86[port], DcIrL,
DcIrW 1, DcLEL 1940, DrInf,
EncSF, EncWL 2, IntAu&W 76, –77,
–82, –86, IntWW 76, –77, –78, –79,
–80, –81, –82, –83, ModBrL, –S1,
NewC, Novels, OxCan, –SUP,
OxCanL, OxEng 85, PenC ENG,
RAdv 1, REn, REnAL, ScF&FL 1,*

–2, ScFSB, TwCWr, WebE&AL,
Who 74, –82, –83, –85, WhoAm 78,
–80, –82, –84, –86, WhoCanL 85,
WhoE 75, WhoWor 84, –87, WorAl,
WorAu, WrDr 76, –80, –82, –84, –86
Moore, C L 1911- *ScFSB, SupFW,*
TwCSFW 86
Moore, C L 1911-1958 *ConAu 104,*
ConSFA, EncSF, Novels, ScF&FL 1,
–2, WhoHr&F, WhoSciF
Moore, Carman L 1936- *ConAmC 82*
Moore, Carman Leroy 1936-
Baker 78, BiDAfM, BioIn 10,
ConAmC, ConAu 61, DrBlPA,
InB&W 80, –85, IntAu&W 77, –82,
IntWWM 85, LivgBAA, WhoAm 76,
–78, –80, –82, –84, –86,
WhoAmM 83, WhoBlA 75, –77, –80,
–85, WhoE 75, WrDr 76, –80, –82,
–84
Moore, Frank Gardner 1865-1955
BioIn 4, –13, NatCAB 61[port],
WhAm 3, WhNAA
Moore, Gaylen *WomWMM B*
Moore, Honor *DrAP&F 85*
Moore, Honor 1945- *AmWomD,*
ConAu 85, IntWWP 77,
NatPD, –81[port]
Moore, Janet Gaylord 1905- *BioIn 12,*
ConAu 77, IlsBYP, SmATA 18,
WhoAmW 58, –61
Moore, John A 1915- *AmM&WS 73P,*
–76P, –79P, –82P, Au&Wr 71,
BioIn 11, BlueB 76, ConAu 45,
IntAu&W 82, IntWW 74, –75, –76,
–77, –78, –79, –80, –81, –82, –83,
McGMS 80[port], WhoAm 74, –76,
–78, –80, –82, WrDr 76, –80, –82,
–84, –86
Moore, John Alexander 1915-
AmM&WS 86P, WhoAm 84,
WhoFrS 84
Moore, John Newton 1920-
AmM&WS 73P, WhoAm 82, –84,
–86, WhoMW 76, –78, –80
Moore, Kenny 1943- *BioIn 9, –12,*
ConAu X
Moore, Lilian 1917-1967 *AuBYP,*
BioIn 7, –8, BkP, ChhPo S1, –S3,
ConAu 1R, –2NR, –103, FourBJA,
ObitOF 79, WhAm 4, WhoAmW 58,
–61, –64, –66, –68, –70, WhoLibS 55
Moore, Marianne Craig 1887-1972
AmAu&B, AmWomWr, AmWr,
AnCL, AnMV 1926, BioIn 1, –2, –3,
–4, –5, –6, –7, –8, –9, –10, –11, –12,
–13, CasWL, ChhPo S2, CnDAL,
CnE&AP, CnMWL, ConAmA,
ConAmL, ConAu 1R, –3NR, –33R,
ConLC 1, –2, –4, –8, –10, –13, –19,
ConPo 70, CurBio 52, –68, –72,
–72N, DcLEL, EncAB-H, EncWL,
EncWL, –2, EvLB, ForWC 70,
GoodHs, InWom, IntDcWB,
IntWWP 77, LibW, LinLib L, –S,
LongCTC, MakMC, McGEWB,
ModAL, –S1, NatCAB 57,
NewYTBE 72, NotAW MOD,
ObitOF 79, ObitT 1971, OxAmL,
OxEng, –85, PenC AM, RAdv 1,
REn, REnAL, SixAP, SmATA 20,
TwCA, –SUP, TwCWr, WebAB, –79,
WebE&AL, WhAm 5, WhE&EA,
WhoAmW 58, –61, –64,
–66, –68, –70, –72, WhoTwCL,
WorAl
Moore, Patrick 1923- *Au&Wr 71,*
AuBYP, BioIn 7, BlueB 76,
ConAu 8NR, –13R, DcLEL 1940,
EncSF, FourBJA, IntAu&W 77, –82,
ScF&FL 1, –2, ScFSB, SmATA 39,
TwCSFW 86, Who 74, WhoSciF,
WhoWor 76, WrDr 76, –80, –82, –84,
–86
Moore, Robert Lowell, Jr. 1925-
AmAu&B, AuNews 1, BioIn 10,
ConAu 13R, WhoAm 74, –76, –78,
–80, –82, –84, –86
Moore, Robert Lowell, Jr. *see also*
Moore, Robin
Moore, Robin *WhoAm 84, –86*
Moore, Robin 1925- *ArtCS, AuNews 1,*
BioIn 10, BioNews 74, CelR,
ConAu X, WorAl

Moore, Robin *see also* Moore, Robert
Lowell, Jr.
Moore, Ruth *BioIn 13, WhoAm 84*
Moore, Ruth 1908- *AmAu&B,*
Au&Wr 71, ConAu 1R, –6NR,
CurBio 54, IntAu&W 76, SmATA 23,
WhoAm 74, –76, –78, –80, –82,
WhoAmW 74, –58, –64, –66, –68,
–70, –72
Moore, Ruth Nulton 1923-
ConAu 15NR, –81, IntAu&W 82,
–86, SmATA 38[port]
Moore, S E *BioIn 13, ConAu 2NR,*
–49, SmATA 23
Moore, Silas *ScF&FL 1*
Moore, Susanna *BioIn 13*
Moore, Susanna 1948- *ConAu 109*
Moorehead, Alan 1910-1983
AnObit 1983, Au&Wr 71, BioIn 4, –6,
–9, –13, BlueB 76, ConAu 5R, –6NR,
–110, DcLEL 1940, FarE&A 78, –79,
–80, –81, IntAu&W 76, –77,
IntWW 74, –75, –76, –77, –78, –79,
–80, –81, –82, –83, LongCTC, NewC,
NewYTBS 83[port], OxAusL, PEn,
TwCA SUP, WhAm 8, WhE&EA,
Who 74, –82, –83, WhoWor 74,
WrDr 76, –80, –82, –84
Moorehead, Caroline 1944-
ConAu 101, –18NR, WrDr 82, –84,
–86
Moorhouse, Geoffrey 1931- *BioIn 10,*
ConAu 25R, IntAu&W 76, –77, –82,
–86, Who 82, –83, –85, WrDr 76,
–80, –82, –84, –86
Mooser, Stephen 1941- *BioIn 13,*
ConAu 15NR, –89, SmATA 28[port]
Moquin, Wayne 1930- *ChiSch,*
ConAu 33R
Mora, Joseph Jacinto 1876-1947
ArtsAmW 1, BioIn 1, ChhPo, DcNAA,
IlBEAAW, WhAm 2
Moraes, Frank 1907-1974 *BioIn 4,*
–10, ConAu 49, ConAu P-1,
CurBio 57, –74, –74N, NewYTBS 74,
ObitOF 79, WhE&EA, WhoWor 74
Moray Williams, Ursula 1911-
ConAu 111, FourBJA, IntAu&W 76,
TwCChW 83, WhE&EA, WrDr 76,
–80, –82, –84, –86
Moray Williams, Ursula *see also*
Williams, Ursula Moray
More, Sir Thomas 1477?-1535
OxEng 85
More, Sir Thomas 1478-1535 *Alli,*
AtlBL, BbD, BiDAmS, BiD&SB,
BioIn 1, –2, –3, –4, –5, –6, –7, –8, –9,
–10, –11, –12, –13, BritAu, CasWL,
Chambr 1, ChhPo, –S2, CroE&S,
CrtT 1, –4, CyEd, CyWA, DcAmSR,
DcBiPP, DcCathB, DcEnA, DcEnL,
DcEuL, DcLEL, DcNaB, –C, Dis&D,
EncSF, EncUrb[port], EvLB,
LinLib L, –S, LongCEL, LuthC 75,
McGEWB, MouLC 1, NewC, OxEng,
OxLaw, PenC ENG, RAdv 1, REn,
WebE&AL, WhDW, WorAl
Morehead, Albert Hodges 1909-1966
AmAu&B, AmSCAP 66, BioIn 3, –4,
–7, ConAu P-1, CurBio 55, –66,
ObitOF 79, WhAm 4
Morell, David L 1939- *WhoTech 84*
Morell, David Louis 1939- *WhoE 77,*
–79
Morey, Walt 1907- *Au&Wr 71,*
AuBYP, BioIn 8, –9, ConAu 29R,
OxChL, SmATA 3, ThrBJA,
TwCCW 78, –83, WrDr 80, –82, –84,
–86
Morey, Walter Nelson 1907-
WhoAm 74, –76, –78, –80, –82,
WhoPNW
Morgan, Alfred Powell 1889-1972
AuBYP, BioIn 6, –7, –9, ConAu 107,
MorJA, SmATA 33[port], WhAm 5,
WhNAA
Morgan, Alison 1930- *OxChL,*
OxLitW 86
Morgan, Alison M 1930- *WrDr 86*
Morgan, Alison Mary 1930-
ConAu 1NR, –18NR, –49,
SmATA 30[port], TwCCW 78, –83,
WrDr 76, –80, –82, –84

Morgan, Bryan Stanford 1923-1976
Au&Wr 71, AuBYP SUP, ConAu 5R,
–8NR, –9NR, IntAu&W 76, –77,
WhoWor 76, WrDr 76, –80
Morgan, Charles, Jr. 1930- *BioIn 6,*
–8, –11, –12, CivR 74, ConAu 13NR,
–17R, WhoAm 80, –82,
WhoS&SW 73, –75, –76
Morgan, Clifford Thomas 1915-1976
AmM&WS 73P, BiDPsy, BioIn 10,
–11, ConAu 1R, –4NR, –65,
WhAm 6, –7, WhoAm 74, –76
Morgan, Edmund S 1916- *BioIn 13*
Morgan, Edmund Sears 1916-
WhoAm 84, –86
Morgan, Edmund Sears 1916-1966
AmAu&B, Au&Wr 71, BlueB 76,
ConAu 4NR, –9R, DcLB 17[port],
DrAS 74H, –79H, –82H, WhoAm 74,
–76, –78, –80, –82
Morgan, Elizabeth 1947- *ConAu 108,*
WhoAm 82, –84, –86, WhoE 83, –85,
WhoS&SW 80
Morgan, Fred Troy 1926- *ConAu 89*
Morgan, Frederick *DrAP&F 85*
Morgan, Frederick 1922- *BioIn 10,*
ConAu 17R, –21NR, ConLC 23[port],
ConPo 75, –80, –85, IntWWP 77,
–82, OxAmL 83, WhoAm 84,
WhoF&I 74, –75, WrDr 76, –80, –82,
–84, –86
Morgan, Geoffrey 1916- *AuBYP SUP,*
ConAu 21R, MnBBF, SmATA 46
Morgan, Gwyneth *ConAu X*
Morgan, Jacqui 1939- *ConGrA 1[port],*
WhoAm 84
Morgan, James 1861-1955 *Alli, –SUP,*
AmAu&B, BioIn 3, –4, ObitOF 79,
WhAm 3, WhNAA
Morgan, Joe Leonard 1943- *BioIn 10,*
–11, –12, WhoAm 74, –78, –80, –82,
–84, –86, WhoBlA 77, –80, –85,
WhoProB 73, WorAl
Morgan, Lael 1936- *ConAu 5NR, –53,*
WrDr 76, –80, –82, –84, –86
Morgan, Lewis Henry 1818-1881
BioIn 13, OxAmL 83
Morgan, Murray 1916- *AmAu&B,*
AmNov, BioIn 2, ConAmTC,
ConAu 107, WhoPNW
Morgan, Roberta 1953- *ConAu 15NR,*
–93, IntAu&W 82
Morgan, Robin *DrAP&F 85*
Morgan, Robin 1941- *BioIn 10,*
ConAu 69, ConLC 2, WhoAmW 79,
–81, –83, –85, WhoHol A
Morgan, Speer *DrAP&F 85*
Morgan, Speer 1946- *ConAu 97*
Morgan, Ted 1932- *BioIn 11, –12,*
–13, ConAu 3NR, ConAu 4AS[port],
WorAu 1975[port], WrDr 86
Morgan, Ted *see also* DeGramont,
Sanche
Morgan-Grenville, Gerard Wyndham
1931- *ConAu 57, IntAu&W 77,*
WrDr 76, –80, –82, –84
Morgenroth, Barbara *ConAu 117,*
SmATA 36
Morgenthau, Hans Joachim 1904-1980
AmAu&B, AmM&WS 73S, –78S,
AnObit 1980[port], BiDInt, BioIn 4,
–6, –11, –12, –13, ConAu 9R, –101,
CurBio 63, –80N, IntEnSS 79,
NewYTBS 80, PolProf J, TwCA SUP,
WhAm 7, WhoAm 74, –76, –78, –80,
WhoAmJ 80, WhoWor 74,
WhoWorJ 72, –78
Moriarty, Florence Jarman
ConAu 104, WhoAm 74,
WhoAmW 74, –64, –66, –68, –70,
–72, –75, –79, –81, –83, –85,
WhoE 74
Morice, Anne *WrDr 86*
Morice, Anne 1918- *ConAu X,*
IntAu&W 76, TwCCr&M 80, –85,
WrDr 82, –84
Morison, Samuel Eliot 1887-1976
AmAu&B, AmWr S1, ASpks,
Au&Wr 71, AuBYP, BioIn 2, –3, –4,
–5, –6, –7, –8, –10, –11, –12, –13,
BlueB 76, CelR, ConAu 1R, –4NR,
–65, CurBio 51, –62, –76, –76N,
DcAmMiB, DcLB 17[port], DcLEL,

DrAS 74H, EncAB-H, IntAu&W 76,
–77, IntWW 74, –75, –76, –77N,
LinLib L, –S, LongCTC, McGEWB,
NatCAB 61, NewYTBE 71,
NewYTBS 76, ObitOF 79, OxAmH,
OxAmL, –83, OxCan SUP, OxShips,
PenC AM, REn, REnAL,
TwCA SUP, WebAB, –79, WebAMB,
WhAm 6, –7, WhLit, Who 74,
WhoAm 74, –76, WhoWor 74, WorAl,
WrDr 76
Morman, Jean Mary 1925- *ConAu 61*
Morowitz, Harold J *WrDr 86*
Morowitz, Harold J 1927-
WhoTech 84
Morowitz, Harold Joseph 1927-
AmM&WS 73P, –76P, –79P, –82P,
–86P, ConAu 104, WhoAm 74, –76,
–78, –80, –82, –84, –86, WhoTech 82,
WhoWorJ 72, –78, WrDr 84
Morrell, David *DrAP&F 85*
Morrell, David 1943- *ConAu 7NR,*
–57, IntAu&W 76, –77, –82, Novels,
WhoMW 78
Morressy, John *DrAP&F 85*
Morressy, John 1930- *AuBYP SUP,*
BioIn 7, –13, ConAu 8NR, –21R,
EncSF, IntAu&W 77, –86,
ScF&FL 1, –2, SmATA 23[port],
TwCSFW 86, WrDr 76, –80, –82,
–84, –86
Morris, Aldyth Vernon 1901-
ConAu 29R, NatPD, –81[port],
WhoAmW 58, –61, –75, –77
Morris, Desmond *WhoAm 84, –86*
Morris, Desmond 1928- *Au&Wr 71,*
BioIn 6, –8, –10, –11, –12, BlueB 76,
CelR, ConAu 2NR, –18NR, –45,
CurBio 74, DcLEL 1940,
IntAu&W 76, –77, –82, –86,
IntWW 74, –75, –76, –77, –78, –79,
–80, –81, –82, –83, LinLib L,
SmATA 14, Who 74, –82, –83,
WhoAm 74, –76, –78, –80, –82,
WhoWor 74, –76, –78, –82,
WorAu 1975[port], WrDr 76, –80,
–82, –84, –86
Morris, Edita 1902- *AmAu&B,*
AmNov, Au&Wr 71, BioIn 2, –12,
ConAu 1R, –1NR, InWom, WhE&EA
Morris, Edmund 1940- *BioIn 13,*
ConAu 89, WhoAm 82, –84,
WhoE 85, WrDr 82, –84, –86
Morris, Harry *DrAP&F 85*
Morris, Harry 1924- *ChhPo S2,*
ConAu 9R, DrAS 74E, –78E, –82E,
WrDr 76, –80, –82, –84, –86
Morris, Ivan 1925-1976 *Au&Wr 71,*
BioIn 11, ConAu 9R, –11NR, –65,
DrAS 74F, NewYTBS 76, WhAm 7,
WhoE 74, WorAu 1970
Morris, James *IntAu&W 86X,*
Who 85, WrDr 86
Morris, James 1926- *Au&Wr 71,*
BioIn 10, –11, ConAu 1R, –X,
CurBio 64, DcLEL 1940,
IntAu&W 76X, –77X, –82X,
IntWW 74, –75, –76, –77, –78, –79,
–80, –81, –82, –83, NewYTBS 74,
OxLitW 86, Who 74, –82, –83,
WhoWor 74, WorAu, WrDr 82, –84
Morris, James *see also* Morris, Jan
Morris, Jan 1926- *ASpks, BioIn 10,*
–11, BlueB 76, ConAu 1NR, –53,
CurBio 86[port], IntAu&W 76, –77,
–82, –86, IntWW 74, –75, –76, –77,
–78, –79, –80, –81, –82, –83,
NewYTBS 74, OxLitW 86, Who 74,
–82, –83, –85, WhoWor 84, –87,
WrDr 76, –80, –82, –84, –86
Morris, Jan *see also* Morris, James
Morris, Jean 1924- *ConAu 116*
Morris, Jeannie 1935?- *BioIn 9, –10*
Morris, Mary Elizabeth 1913-
ConAu 53, WhoAm 74, –76, –78, –80,
–82, –84, –86, WhoAmW 74
Morris, Michelle 1941- *ConAu 108*
Morris, Norval 1923- *BlueB 76,*
ConAu 37R, DrAS 74P, –78P, –82P,
WhoAm 76, –78, –80, –82, –84, –86,
WhoAmL 78, –79, –83, –85,
WhoWor 74, –76
Morris, Richard 1939- *ConAu 1NR,*
–18NR, –45

Morris, Richard Brandon 1904-
*AmAu&B, AuBYP, BioIn 7, –13,
ConAu 2NR, –49, DcLB 17[port],
DrAS 74H, –78H, –82H, WhoAm 74,
–76, –78, –80, –82*

Morris, Richard Knowles 1915-
*AmM&WS 73S, –76P, ConAu 21R,
LEduc 74, WhoE 74*

Morris, Taylor 1923- *ConAu 103*

Morris, Terry Lesser 1914- *ConAu 9R,
WhoAmW 74, –72, –75, –77,
WhoE 74, –75, –77, –79*

Morris, William 1913- *AmAu&B,
BioIn 13, BlueB 76, ConAu 12NR,
–17R, LinLib L, SmATA 29[port],
WhoAm 74, –76, –78, –80, –82, –84,
–86*

Morris, Willie 1934- *ASpks,
AuBYP SUP, AuNews 2, BioIn 7, –8,
–9, –10, –11, –12, –13, BlueB 76,
CelR, ConAu 13NR, –17R,
CurBio 76, DcLB Y80B[port], EncAJ,
EncTwCJ, IntAu&W 77, IntWW 74,
–75, –76, –77, –78, –79, –83,
WhoAm 74, –76, –78, –80, –82, –84,
–86, WhoE 74, WhoWor 74, WorAl,
WorAu 1975, WrDr 80, –82, –84, –86*

Morris, Wright *DrAP&F 85*

Morris, Wright 1910- *AmAu&B,
AmNov, AmWr, Au&Wr 71, BioIn 1,
–2, –4, –7, –8, –9, –10, –12, –13,
BlueB 76, CasWL, CmCal,
ConAu 9R, –21RN, ConLC 1, –3, –7,
–18, –37[port], ConNov 72, –76, –82,
–86, ConPhot, CurBio 82[port],
DcLB 2, –Y81A[port], DcLEL 1940,
EncWL, –2, ICPEnP, IntAu&W 76,
–77, –82, MacBEP, ModAL, –S2,
–S1, NewYTBS 82[port], Novels[port],
OxAmL, –83, PenC AM, RAdv 1,
REn, REnAL, TwCA SUP, TwCWr,
WebE&AL, WhoAm 74, –76, –78,
–80, –82, –84, WhoAmA 84,
WhoTwCL, WhoWest 76,
WhoWor 74, WrDr 76, –80, –82, –84,
–86*

Morrison, Carl V 1908- *BiDrAPA 77,
ConAu 93*

Morrison, Dorothy Nafus
ConAu 8NR, –61, SmATA 29[port]

Morrison, Lillian *DrAP&F 85*

Morrison, Lillian 1917- *AnCL,
BiDrLUS 70, BioIn 2, –9, BkP,
ChhPo, –S1, –S2, –S3, ConAu 7NR,
–9R, SmATA 3, WhoAmW 58,
WhoLibI 82, WhoLibS 55, –66*

Morrison, Lucile Phillips 1896-
*SmATA 77, WhNAA, WhoAmW 74,
–58, –61, –64, –66, –68, –70, –72,
–75, –77, –79, –81, –83, –85, –87,
WhoWest 74, –76, –78, –80, –82, –84*

Morrison, Philip 1915-
*AmM&WS 86P, BioIn 13,
WhoAm 84, –86, WhoFrS 84*

Morrison, Sean *ChhPo S1*

Morrison, Toni *BlkWWr, DrAP&F 85,
WhoAm 86*

Morrison, Toni 1931- *AmWomWr,
BioIn 11, –12, –13, BlkAWP,
ConAu 29R, ConLC 4, –10, –22[port],
ConNov 82, –86, CurBio 79,
DcLB 6[port], –33[port], –Y81A[port],
EncWL 2, InB&W 80, –85,
IntDcWB, LivgBAA, ModAL S2,
ModBlW, NegAl 83[port],
NewYTBS 77, –79, –81[port],
OxAmL 83, PostFic, SelBAAf,
SelBAAu, WhoAm 84, WhoBlA 85,
WorAu 1975[port], WrDr 84, –86*

Morrison, Van 1945- *Baker 84,
BioIn 11, –12, ConAu 116,
ConLC 21[port], EncPR&S 77,
RkOn 78, –84, RolSEnR 83,
WhoRock 81[port], WhoRocM 82*

Morriss, James E 1932- *AuBYP SUP,
BioIn 11, ConAu 57, SmATA 8,
WhoE 77*

Morrow, Charlotte *ConAu X*

Morrow, Charlotte see also Kirwan,
Molly Morrow

Morrow, Honore Willsie 1880-1940
*AmAu&B, AmWomWr, CurBio 40,
DcNAA, EncFWF, InWom,*

*NatCAB 29, OxAmL, –83, REnAL,
TwCA, WhAm 1, WisWr, WomNov*

Morrow, James *ScFSB*

Morrow, James 1947- *ConAu 108*

Morse, Anne Christensen 1915-
ConAu 1R

Morse, Carol *WrDr 86*

Morse, Carol 1908- *ConAu X,
CurBio 57, InWom, SmATA X,
WrDr 76, –80, –82, –84*

Morse, Carol see also Yeakley, Marjory
Hall

Morse, David 1940- *ChhPo S2,
ConAu 37R*

Morse, Flo 1921- *ConAu 106,
SmATA 30[port]*

Mortimer, John Clifford 1923-
*Au&Wr 71, BioIn 10, BlueB 76,
CnMD, CnThe, ConAu 13R,
ConDr 73, –77, –82, CroCD,
CurBio 83[port], DcLB 13[port],
DcLEL 1940, EncWT, FilmgC,
IntAu&W 76, –77, –86, IntWW 81,
–82, –83, LongCTC, McGEWD, –84,
ModWD, NewC, Novels, OxEng 85,
OxThe 83, REn, REnAL, TwCWr,
Who 74, –82, –83, –85, WhoThe 72,
–77, –81, WhoWor 74, WorAu,
WrDr 76, –80, –82, –84*

Mortimer, Penelope 1918- *Au&Wr 71,
BioIn 10, –12, BlueB 76, ConAu 57,
ConLC 5, ConNov 72, –76, –82, –86,
DcLEL 1940, IntAu&W 76, –77,
Novels, PenC ENG, TwCWr, Who 74,
–82, –83, –85, WhoAmW 74, –68,
–70, –72, WhoWor 74, WorAu,
WrDr 76, –80, –82, –84, –86*

Mortimer, Penelope Ruth 1918-
IntAu&W 86, OxEng 85

Morton, Alexander C 1936-
ConAu 12NR, –25R

Morton, Frederic *BiGAW*

Morton, Frederic 1924- *AmAu&B,
AmNov, Au&Wr 71, BioIn 2, –10,
ConAu 1R, –3NR, –20NR,
IntAu&W 86, ModAL, WhoAm 74,
–76, –78, –80, –82, –84, –86, WorAu*

Morton, Miriam 1918- *AuBYP SUP,
BioIn 11, ChhPo, –S1, –S2,
ConAu 2NR, –49, IntAu&W 76,
SmATA 9, WhoAmW 77, –79, –81,
–83*

Morton, Miriam 1918?-1985
ConAu 117, SmATA 46N

Moscati, Sabatino 1922- *Au&Wr 71,
ConAu 77, IntAu&W 76, –77, –82,
WhoWor 78*

Moseley, Elizabeth Robards
ForWC 70, WhoAmW 66, –68, –70

Moser, Don 1932- *ConAu 106,
SmATA X*

Mosesson, Gloria R *BioIn 13*

Mosesson, Gloria Rubin 1924-
*ConAu 41R, ForWC 70,
SmATA 24[port], WhoAmW 58, –61,
–64, –66, –68, –70, –72, –75, –77,
WhoWorJ 72, –78*

Moskin, Marietta D 1928-
ConAu 13NR, –73, SmATA 23[port]

Moskowitz, Sam 1920- *ConAu 4NR,
–5R, ConSFA, EncSF, IntAu&W 77,
–82, LinLib L, ScF&FL 1, –2,
WhoAm 76, –78, –80, –82, –84, –86,
WhoHr&F, WhoSciF, WhoWor 78,
–80, –82*

Mosley, Leonard 1913- *Au&Wr 71,
ConAu 108, –109, IntAu&W 76,
WrDr 76, –80, –82, –84, –86*

Moss, Howard *DrAP&F 85*

Moss, Howard 1922- *AmAu&B,
Au&Wr 71, BioIn 10, –12, ChhPo S3,
ConAu 1R, –1NR, ConLC 7, –14,
ConPo 70, –75, –80, –85, CroCAP,
DcLB 5[port], DcLEL 1940,
Dun&B 79, IntAu&W 76, –77, –82,
IntWWP 77, –82, LElec, LinLib L,
OxAmL 83, PenC AM, RAdv 1,
WhoAm 74, –76, –78, –80, –82, –84,
–86, WhoS&SW 75, –76, –78,
WhoWest 82, –84, WhoWor 74,
WorAu 1970, WrDr 76, –80, –82,
–84, –86*

Moss, Norman Bernard 1928-
*BiDrAPA 77, ConAu 49, WhoAm 76,
–78, –80, –82, –84, –86*

Mostert, Noel 1929- *ConAu 105,
IntAu&W 82, WrDr 76, –80, –82, –84*

Mothner, Ira S 1932- *ConAu 21R,
WhoE 74*

Motta, Dick 1931- *BioIn 9, –10, –11,
ConAu 111, WhoBbl 73*

Motz, Lloyd 1910- *AmM&WS 73P,
–76P, ConAu 1R, –79P, –82P, –86P, BioIn 12,
ConAu 4NR, –9R, IntAu&W 77, –82,
SmATA 20, WhoAm 74, –76, –78,
–80, –82, –84, WhoAmJ 80,
WhoWorJ 72, –78*

Moulton, Phillips Prentice 1909-
WhoAm 84, –86

Mountfort, Guy Reginald 1905-
*ConAu 17R, Who 74, –82, –83, –85,
WhoWor 76*

Moussard, Jacqueline 1924- *BioIn 13,
ConAu 8NR, –61, SmATA 24[port]*

Mowat, Farley 1921- *AmAu&B,
Au&Wr 71, AuBYP, BioIn 2, –4, –5,
–7, –9, –10, –11, –12, –13, BlueB 76,
CaW, CanWW 70, –79, –80, –81,
–83, CanWr, CasWL, ConAu 1R,
–4NR, ConLC 26[port], CreCan 2,
CurBio 86[port], DcLEL 1940,
IntAu&W 77, –82, IntWW 74,
–75, –76, –77, –78, –79, –80, –81,
–82, –83, LinLib L, OxCan, –SUP,
OxCanL, OxChL, SmATA 3,
ThrBJA, TwCCW 78, –83,
WhoAm 74, –76, –78, –80, –82,
WhoCan 73, –75, –77, –80, –82, –84,
WhoCanL 85, WhoE 74, WhoWor 82,
WorAu, WrDr 76, –80, –82, –84, –86*

Mowat, Farley McGill 1921-
*IntAu&W 86, WhoAm 84, –86,
WhoWor 84, –87*

Mowry, George E 1909-1984
ConAu 17NR

Mowry, George Edwin 1909-
*AmAu&B, ConAu 1R, DrAS 74H,
–78H, –82H, WhoAm 74, –76, –78,
–80, –82, –84, WhoWor 80, –82*

Mowry, George Edwin 1909-1984
WhAm 8

Moyers, Bill D 1934- *AuNews 1,
BioIn 6, –7, –8, –9, –10, –11, –12,
BlueB 76, ConAu 61, CurBio 66, –76,
EncAJ, IntAu&W 77, IntWW 74,
–75, –76, –77, –78, –79, –80, –81,
–82, –83, NewYTET, PolProf J,
Who 74, –82, –83, –85, WhoAm 74,
–76, –78, –80, –82, –84, –86,
WhoAmP 73, WhoWor 74, –78, –80,
–82, –84, WorAl*

Moyes, Patricia *ConAu X*

Moyes, Patricia 1923- *Au&Wr 71,
BiE&WWA, ConAu 17R, EncMys,
Novels, TwCCr&M 80, –85, WrDr 76,
–80, –82, –84, –86*

Moynihan, Daniel Patrick 1927-
*AlmAP 78, –80, –82[port], –84[port],
AmAu&B, AmCath 80,
AmM&WS 73S, BioIn 7, –8, –9, –10,
–11, –12, –13, BlueB 76, CelR,
CngEp 77, –79, –81, –83, –85, –87,
ConAu 5R, CurBio 68, –86[port],
DcAmDH, DcLEL 1940, IntWW 74,
–75, –76, –77, –78, –79, –80, –81,
–82, –83, IntYB 78, –79, –80, –81,
–82, LinLib S, NewYTBS 74, –75,
–76, –79, PolProf J, PolProf NF,
PolsAm 84[port], USBiR 74, Who 83,
–85, WhoAm 74, –76, –78, –80, –82,
–84, –86, WhoAmP 73, –75, –77, –79,
–81, –83, –85, WhoE 74, –77, –79,
–81, –83, –85, WhoGov 77, –72,
WhoWor 74, –76, –78, –80, –82, –84,
–87, WorAl, WrDr 80, –82, –84, –86*

Mphahlele, Ezekiel *DrAP&F 85*

Mphahlele, Ezekiel 1919- *AfSS 78,
–79, –80, –81, –82, AfrA, BioIn 7, –8,
–9, –11, CasWL, ConAu 81,
ConLC 25[port], ConNov 72, –76,
–82, DcLEL 1940, EncWL, –2,
InB&W 80, IntAu&W 76, –77,
IntWW 74, –75, –76, –77, –78, –79,
–80, –81, –82, –83, LongCTC,
ModBlW, ModCmwL, Novels,
PenC CL, –ENG, RGA/L, SelBAAf,
TwCWr, WhoTwCL, WhoWor 74,
WorAu 1970, WrDr 76, –80, –82,
–84, –86*

Mueller, Amelia 1911- *ConAu 57*

Mueller, Charles S 1929-
ConAu 5NR, –13R, –20NR

Mueller, Lisel *DrAP&F 85*

Mueller, Lisel 1924- *ConAu 93,
ConLC 13*

Muenchen, Al 1917- *ConAu 49,
IlrAm F*

Muenchen, Al 1917-1975 *IlrAm 1880*

Muhammad Ali 1942- *CelR, CivR 74,
WebAB*

Muhammad Ali see also Ali,
Muhammad

Muhlhausen, John Prague 1940-
ConAu 61, WhoF&I 83

Muhlhausen, John Praque 1940-
WhoS&SW 84, –86

Muir, Jean 1906-1973 *ConAu 29R,
–41R, ConAu P-2, ForWC 70,
WhoAmW 74, –66, –68, –70, –72,
WorFshn*

Muir, John 1838-1914 *AmAu&B,
AmBi, ApCAB SUP, ApCAB S,
BiDAmS, BiD&SB, BioIn 1, –2, –3,
–4, –5, –6, –7, –8, –9, –10, –11, –12,
–13, CmCal, DcAmAu, DcAmB,
DcLEL, DcNAA, EncAAH, EvLB,
HarEnUS[port], InSci, JBA 34,
LinLib L, –S, McGEWB, MorMA,
NatCAB 9, NatLAC, OxAmH,
OxAmL, –83, REn, REnAL,
REnAW, TwCA, –SUP, TwCBDA,
WebAB, –79, WhAm 1, WisWr,
WorAl*

Muir, Kenneth 1907- *IntAu&W 86,
OxEng 85, Who 85, WhoWor 84,
WrDr 86*

Muirden, James 1942- *Au&Wr 71,
ScF&FL 1*

Mukerji, Dhan Gopal 1890-1936
*AnCL, AuBYP, BioIn 4, –7, BkCL,
ChiLR 10[port], ConAu 119, JBA 34,
LongCTC, Newb 1922,
SmATA 40[port], TwCA, TwCCW 78,
–83, WhAm 1*

Mulac, Margaret Elizabeth 1912-
*ConAu 2NR, –5R, ForWC 70,
WhoAmW 74, –66, –68, –72, –75,
–77, –79*

Mulholland, Jim 1949- *ConAu 61*

Mulholland, John 1898-1970
*AmAu&B, BioIn 3, –8, ConAu 5R,
–89, REnAL, WhNAA 5, WhNAA*

Muller, Charles G 1897- *ConAu 1R,
–2NR, IntAu&W 77, –82, WhNAA,
WrDr 76, –80, –82, –84, –86*

Muller, Marcia 1944- *ConAu 81,
TwCCr&M 85, WrDr 86*

Munce, Ruth Hill 1898- *BioIn 11,
ConAu P-1, SmATA 12*

Muncy, Raymond Lee 1928-
ConAu 49

Mungo, Raymond 1946- *BioIn 9, –10,
–13, ConAu 2NR, –49*

Munro, Alice 1931- *AuNews 2,
BioIn 11, –13, CaW, CanWW 70,
–79, –80, –81, –83, CanWr 33,
ConLC 6, –10, –19, ConNov 72, –76,
–82, –86, CreCan 1, DcLB 53[port],
DcLEL 1940, IntAu&W 76, –77,
OxCan, –SUP, OxCanL,
SmATA 29[port], WhoAm 80, –82,
–86, WhoAmW 83, –85,
WhoCanL 85, WrDr 76, –80, –82,
–84, –86*

Munro, Eleanor C 1928- *AuBYP,
BioIn 7, ConAu 1R, SmATA 37,
WhoAmA 82, WhoAmW 81, –83*

Munro, George Colin 1907-
AmM&WS 73P

Munro, Hector Hugh 1870-1916
*Alli SUP, AtlBL, BioIn 1, –5, –9, –10,
–12, CasWL, ChhPo, ConAu 104,
DcLEL, DcNaB 1912, EncSF, EvLB,
LongCTC, ModBrL, NewC, Novels,
OxEng, PenC ENG, RAdv 1, REn,
ScF&FL 1, TwCA, –SUP, TwCLC 3,
WhoHr&F, WorAl*

Munro, Hector Hugh see also Saki

Munshower, Suzanne 1945- *ConAu 97*

Munson, Kenneth George 1929-
IntAu&W 77, –82, –86

Munson, Thurman 1947-1979
BioIn 11, -12, -13, ConAu 108, -89,
CurBio 77, -79N, NewYTBS 75, -79,
WhoAm 78, WhoBlA 77,
WhoProB 73, WorAl
Muntz, Hope 1907-1981 *BioIn 2,*
IntAu&W 76, -77, -82, Who 74,
-82N
Munves, James 1922- *ConAu 3NR,*
-5R, SmATA 30
Munz, Peter 1921- *ConAu 13R,*
IntAu&W 77, -82, -86, WhoWor 87,
WrDr 76, -80, -82, -84, -86
Munzer, Martha E 1899-
AuBYP SUP, ConAu 1R,
-4NR, IntAu&W 77, -82, -86,
SmATA 4, WrDr 76, -80, -82, -84,
-86
Murari, Timeri N 1941- *ConAu 102,*
IntAu&W 76, WhoWor 78
Murchie, Guy 1907- *AmAu&B,*
BioIn 3, ConAu 1R, IntAu&W 77,
LinLib L, WhE&EA, WhoAm 74,
-76, -78, -80, -82, -84, -86,
WrDr 76, -80, -82, -84, -86
Murdoch, Iris *Who 85*
Murdoch, Iris 1919- *BioIn 3, -4, -5,*
-7, -8, -10, -11, -12, -13, BlueB 76,
CasWL, ConAu 8NR, -13R,
ConDr 73, -77, -82, ConLC 1, -2,
-3, -4, -6, -8, -11, -15, -22[port],
-31[port], ConNov 72, -76, -82, -86,
CurBio 58, -80[port], DcIrW 1,
DcLB 14[port], EncWL, -2[port],
InWom, IntDcWB, IntWW 74, -75,
-76, -77, -78, -79, -80, -81, -82,
-83, LinLib L, LongCEL, LongCTC,
ModBrL, -S2, -S1, NewC,
Novels[port], PenC ENG, PIP&P,
RAdv 1, REn, TwCWr, WebE&AL,
Who 74, -82, -83, WhoAm 80, -82,
-84, -86, WhoAmW 74, -66, -68,
-70, -72, WhoTwCL, WhoWor 74,
-76, -78, -80, -82, -84, -87, WorAl,
WorAu, WrDr 76, -80, -82, -84, -86
Murdoch, Iris Jean 1919- *OxEng 85*
Muro, Diane P 1940- *BioIn 11,*
ConAu 65
Murphy, Arthur William 1922-
WhoAm 74, -76, -78, -80, -82, -84,
-86, WhoAtom 77
Murphy, Barbara Beasley *DrAP&F 85*
Murphy, Barbara Beasley 1933-
BioIn 10, ConAu 20NR, -41R,
SmATA 5

Murphy, Beatrice M 1908- *BlkAWP,*
BroadAu[port], ConAu 9NR, -53,
InB&W 80, LivgBAA, SelBAAu,
WhoBlA 75, -77, -80
Murphy, Brian 1931- *ConAu 13NR,*
-21R
Murphy, E Jefferson 1926-
AuBYP SUP, BioIn 9, ConAu 25R,
LEduc 74, SmATA 4, WrDr 76, -80,
-82, -84, -86
Murphy, E Jefferson *see also* Murphy,
Pat
Murphy, James Francis 1908-
WhoMW 74
Murphy, Jim 1947- *ConAu 111,*
SmATA 32, -37
Murphy, Pat *IntAu&W 86X*
Murphy, Pat 1926- *BioIn 9, ConAu X,*
SmATA 4
Murphy, Pat *see also* Murphy, E
Jefferson
Murphy, Patrick T 1939- *ConAu 108,*
WhoAmL 79
Murphy, Robert William 1902-1971
AuBYP SUP, BioIn 9,
ConAu 29R, ConAu P-1, ObitOF 79,
SmATA 10
Murphy, Sharon Margaret 1940-
ConAu 77, WhoAmW 75, -77, -83,
WhoMW 84
Murphy, Shirley R 1928- *WrDr 86*
Murphy, Shirley Rousseau 1928-
ConAu 13NR, -21R, SmATA 36,
WhoAmW 74, -75, -77, -79,
WrDr 76, -80, -82, -84
Murray, Albert *InB&W 85*
Murray, Albert 1916- *BioIn 9,*
BlkAWP, ConAu 49, InB&W 80,
LivgBAA, NegAl 83, SelBAAu,
WhoAm 74, -76, -78, WhoBlA 75,
-77, -80, WrDr 76, -80, -82, -84,
-86
Murray, Albert L 1916-
DcLB 38[port], SelBAAf, WhoAm 84,
-86, WhoBlA 85
Murray, Donald M 1924- *AmAu&B,*
AuBYP, ConAu 1R, -17NR,
WhoAm 74, -76, -78
Murray, Frances 1928- *WrDr 86*
Murray, Jim *ConAu X*
Murray, Jim 1919- *BioIn 10, -11,*
ConAu 65, IntAu&W 76

Murray, John 1923- *ConAu 4NR,*
-5R, -19NR, SmATA 39[port]
Murray, Marian *BioIn 10,*
ConAu 41R, SmATA 5
Murray, Michael V 1906- *ConAu 5R*
Murray, Michael William 1932-
WhoMW 80, -82
Murray, Michele 1933-1974
AuBYP SUP, BioIn 10, -13,
ConAu 49, NewYTBS 74, ObitOF 79,
SmATA 7
Murray, Pauli *InB&W 85*
Murray, Pauli d1985
NewYTBS 85[port]
Murray, Pauli 1910- *AmWomWr,*
BioIn 9, -11, -12, BlkAWP, Ebony 1,
InB&W 80, NewYTBS 74, SelBAAf,
SelBAAu, WhoAm 76, -78, -82, -84,
WhoAmW 58, -61, -64, -66, -72,
-77, WhoBlA 75, -77, -80, -85
Murray, Pauli 1910-1985 *ConAu 116,*
DcLB 41[port], WhAm 8
Murray, Robert Keith 1922-
ConAu 53, DrAS 74H, -78H, -82H,
IndAu 1917, WhoAm 74, -76, -78,
-80, -82, -84, -86
Murrell, Elsie Kathleen Seth-Smith
1883- *ConAu P-1*
Murrow, Edward R 1908-1965
BioIn 13, EncAJ[port], EncTwCJ,
WhScrn 83
Murrow, Edward Roscoe 1908-1965
BioIn 1, -2, -3, -4, -5, -6, -7, -8, -9,
-10, -11, -12, ConAu 103, -89,
CurBio 42, -53, -65, DcAmB S7,
DcAmDH, EncAB-H, LesBEnT[port],
LinLib L, -S, McGEWB,
NatCAB 52, NewYTET, ObitOF 79,
PolProf E, PolProf K, REnAL,
WebAB, -79, WhDW, WhAm 4,
WhScrn 74, -77, WhoHol B
Musciano, Walter A *AuBYP, BioIn 7*
Muse, Ken 1925- *ConAu 111*
Musgrave, Florence 1902- *AuBYP,*
BioIn 7, -9, ConAu P-1, SmATA 3
Myers, Alpha Blanche 1912-
BiDrLUS 70, WhoAmW 75, -77,
WhoLibS 55, -66
Myers, Arthur 1917- *IntAu&W 86,*
SmATA 35[port]
Myers, Arthur 1922- *ConAu 7NR,*
-17R

Myers, Bernard Samuel 1908-
Au&Wr 71, ConAu 65, IntAu&W 76,
-77, WhoAm 76, -78, -80, -82, -84,
WhoE 75, WhoWorJ 72, -78
Myers, Elisabeth P 1918-
SmATA 36[port], WrDr 86
Myers, Elisabeth Perkins 1918-
AuBYP SUP, ConAu 5R, ForWC 70,
SmATA 36, WhoAmW 74, WrDr 76
Myers, Gail Eldridge 1923-
ConAu 1NR, -49, DrAS 74E, -78E,
-82E, LEduc 74, WhoAm 78, -80,
-82, -84, -86, WhoS&SW 82
Myers, John Myers 1906- *AmAu&B,*
AmNov, BioIn 2, -4, ConAu 1R,
-1NR, IntAu&W 86, ScF&FL 1, -2,
TwCA SUP, WrDr 84, -86
Myers, Robert Manson 1921- *BioIn 9,*
ConAu 37R, DrAS 78E, -82E,
IntAu&W 76, -77, -82, -86,
NewYTBE 72, WhoAm 74, -76, -78,
-80, -82, -84, -86, WrDr 76, -80,
-82, -84, -86
Myers, Walter Dean *DrAP&F 85*
Myers, Walter Dean 1937-
AuBYP SUP, BioIn 13, BlkAWP,
ChlLR 4[port], ConAu 20NR, -33R,
ConLC 35[port], DcLB 33[port],
FifBJA[port], LivgBAA, SelBAAf,
SelBAAu, SmATA 27, -41[port],
SmATA 2AS[port], WhoAm 76
Myrdal, Alva 1902- *BioIn 2, -12, -13,*
ConAu 69, Future, InWom,
IntDcWB, IntWW 74, -75, -76, -77,
-78, -79, -80, -81, -82, -83,
IntYB 78, -80, -81, -82,
LadLa 86[port], NewYTBS 82,
Who 74, -82, -83, -85, WhoAmW 74,
-68, -70, -72, WhoWor 74, -76, -78,
-80, -82, -84
Myrdal, Alva 1902-1986 *CurBio 86N,*
NewYTBS 86[port]
Myrdal, Jan 1927- *ConAu 117,*
WhoWor 84, -87
Myres, Sandra Lynn 1933-
ConAu 14NR, -33R, DrAS 74H,
-78H, -82H, WhoAmW 75, -77
Myron, Robert 1926- *AuBYP SUP,*
ConAu 13R, DrAS 74H, -78H, -82H
Myrus, Donald 1927- *AuBYP,*
BioIn 8, -13, ConAu 1R, -4NR,
SmATA 23[port]

N

Nabokov, Peter 1940- *ConAu 9NR, −21R*
Nabokov, Vladimir 1899-1977
AmAu&B, AmNov, AmWr, Au&Wr 71, BioIn 1, −2, −4, −5, −6, −7, −8, −9, −10, −11, −12, −13, BlueB 76, CasWL, CelR, ClDMEL, CnMWL, ConAu 5R, −20NR, −69, ConLC 1, −2, −3, −6, −8, −11, −15, −23[port], ConNov 72, −76, ConPo 75, CurBio 66, −77, −77N, DcLB 2, −DS3[port], −Y80A[port], DcLEL, DcRusL, EncSF, EncWL, −2[port], EvEuW, HalFC 84, IntAu&W 76, −77, IntWW 74, −75, −76, −77, −78N, IntWWP 77, −82, LinLib L, LongCTC, MakMC, McGEWB, ModAL, −S2, −S1, ModSL 1, NewCon[port], NewYTBE 71, −72, NewYTBS 77, Novels, ObitOF 79, OxAmL, −83, OxEng, PenC AM, RComWL, REn, REnAL, ScF&FL 1, −2, ScFSB, TwCA SUP, TwCWr, WebAB, −79, WebE&AL, WhDW, WhAm 7, Who 74, WhoAm 74, −76, −78, WhoTwCL, WhoWor 74, WorAl, WrDr 76
Nader, Ralph 1934- *AmAu&B, BioIn 1, −8, −9, −10, −11, −12, −13, BlueB 76, CelR, ConAu 77, CurBio 68, −86[port], EncAB-H, IntAu&W 77, IntWW 74, −75, −76, −77, −78, −79, −80, −81, −82, −83, LinLib L, −S, MakMC, McGEWB, MugS, NewYTBS 76, PolProf J, PolProf NF, WebAB, −79, WhDW, Who 74, −82, −83, −85, WhoAm 74, −76, −78, −80, −82, −84, −86, WhoAmL 78, −79, WhoWor 74, −78, WorAl, WrDr 82, −84, −86*
Naether, Carl 1892- *ConAu 25R, WhLit*
Nagel, Shirley 1922- *ConAu 93*
Nagenda, Musa *ConAu X*
Nagorski, Andrew *BioIn 13*
Naha, Ed 1950- *ConAu 109, TwCSFW 86*
Naipaul, Shiva d1985
NewYTBS 85[port]
Naipaul, Shiva 1945- *ConAu 112, ConLC 32[port], ConNov 82, Novels, WrDr 82*
Naipaul, Shiva 1945-1985 *ConAu 116, ConLC 39[port], DcLB Y85N[port]*
Naipaul, V S 1932- *BioIn 13, BlueB 76, ConAu 1R, −1NR, ConLC 4, −7, −9, −13, −18, −37[port], ConNov 82, −86, CurBio 77, DcLB Y85B[port], EncWL 2[port], FifCWr, IntAu&W 82, IntWW 74, −75, −76, −77, −78, −79, −80, −81, −82, −83, LinLib L, ModCmwL, NewYTBS 80[port], Novels[port], OxEng 85, WhoWor 74, −76, −78,*

−80, −82, −84, −87, WorAl, WrDr 80, −82, −84, −86
Naismith, James 1861-1939 *BioIn 1, −3, −4, −5, −9, −10, ConAu 118, DcAmB S2, NatCAB 33, WebAB, −79, WhAm 1, WhoBbl 73, WorAl*
Najafi, Najmeh *BioIn 6, −7, ConAu 25R, InWom*
Nalty, Bernard Charles 1931-
ConAu 102, −18NR, DrAS 74H, −78H, −82H
Namath, Joe *NewYTBS 85[port]*
Namath, Joe 1943- *BioIn 7, −8, −9, −10, −11, −12, BioNews 74, BlueB 76, CelR, ConAu X, ConTFT 3, CurBio 66, FilmgC, HalFC 84, IntMPA 84, −86, NewYTBE 70, −71, −72, −73, NewYTBS 74, −75, −81[port], WhoAm 74, −76, WhoFtbl 74, WhoHol A, WorAl*
Namioka, Lensey 1929- *BioIn 13, ConAu 11NR, −69, SmATA 27[port]*
Napier, John Russell 1917- *FifIDA, WrDr 84, −86*
Narayan, R K 1906- *BioIn 1, ConAu 81, ConLC 7, −28[port], ConNov 82, −86, EncWL 2, LinLib L, McGEWB, ModCmwL, Novels, OxEng 85, Who 74, −82, −83, −85, WrDr 80, −82, −84*
Narayan, R K 1907- *WrDr 86*
Narayan, Rasipuram Krishnaswami 1906- *Au&Wr 71, BioIn 4, −6, −7, −9, −10, −11, −12, CasWL, ConNov 72, −76, DcLEL, DcOrL 2, EncWL, FarE&A 78, −79, −80, −81, IntAu&W 76, −77, IntWW 74, −75, −76, −77, −78, −79, −80, −81, −82, −83, LongCTC, NewC, PenC ENG, REn, TwCA SUP, WebE&AL, WhDW, WhoWor 74, WrDr 76*
Naremore, James 1941- *ConAu 11NR, −69*
Narramore, Clyde Maurice 1916-
WhoAm 78
Nasaw, Jonathan Lewis 1947-
ConAu 61
Nash, Graham 1942- *BioIn 11, −12, −13, IlEncRk, RkOn 78, WhoAm 78, −80, −82, WhoRock 81[port], WhoRocM 82, WorAl*
Nash, Graham *see also* Crosby, Stills, Nash & Young
Nash, Jay Robert, III 1937-
ConAu 21R, WhoAm 76, −78, −80, −82, −84, −86, WhoMW 82
Nash, Ogden 1902-1971 *AmAu&B, AmSCAP 66, AnCL, Au&Wr 71, AuBYP, BiE&WWA, BioIn 1, −2, −3, −4, −5, −6, −7, −8, −9, −10, −12, −13, BkCL, CasWL, ChhPo, −S1, −S2, −S3, CnDAL, CnE&AP, CnMWL, ConAmA, ConAu 29R, ConAu P-1,*

ConLC 23[port], ConPo 70, CurBio 41, −71, −71N, DcLB 11[port], DcLEL, EncMT, EncWL, FourBJA, LinLib L, LongCTC, ModAL, NewYTBE 71, NotNAT B, ObitOF 79, ObitT 1971, OxAmL, −83, OxAmT 84, OxChL, OxEng 85, PenC AM, RAdv 1, REn, REnAL, SmATA 2, −46[port], TwCA, −SUP, TwCWr, WebAB, −79, WebE&AL, WhDW, WhAm 5, WhoTwCL, WorAl
Naske, Claus-M 1935- *ConAu 13NR*
Naske, Claus-Michael 1935-
ConAu 77, DrAS 74H, −78H, −82H
Nathan, Robert 1894- *AmAu&B, AmNov, AmSCAP 66, Au&Wr 71, BioIn 1, −2, −4, −5, −6, −8, −10, −12, BlueB 76, ChhPo, −S1, −S3, CnDAL, ConAmA, ConAmC 82, −A, ConAmL, ConAu 6NR, −13R, ConNov 72, −76, −82, DcInB, DcLB 9[port], EncSF, IntAu&W 76, −77, −82, IntWW 74, −75, −76, −77, −78, −79, −80, −81, −82, −83, LinLib L, LongCTC, OxAmL, −83, REn, REnAL, ScF&FL 1, −2, SmATA 6, SupFW, TwCA, −SUP, WhE&EA, WhoAm 74, −76, −78, WhoAmJ 80, WhoWest 74, WhoWorJ 72, −78, WrDr 76, −80, −82, −84*
Nathan, Robert 1894-1985 *ConAu 116, NewYTBS 85[port], SmATA 43N, WhAm 8*
Navarra, John Gabriel 1927-
AmM&WS 73P, −76P, −79P, −82P, −86P, AuBYP SUP, BioIn 5, −11, ConAu 41R, IntAu&W 76, −77, SmATA 8, WhoE 74
Navasky, Victor Saul 1932- *BioIn 12, −13, ConAu 10NR, −21R, EncTwCJ, ScF&FL 1, −2, WhoAm 80, −82, −84, −86, WhoE 74*
Navratilova, Martina
NewYTBS 85[port], −86[port]
Navratilova, Martina 1956- *BioIn 13, HerW 84, WhoAm 84, −86, WhoAmW 85, −87, WhoWor 84, −87*
Naylor, Gloria *BioIn 13, DrAP&F 85, InB&W 85*
Naylor, Gloria 1950- *ConAu 107, ConLC 28[port], ConNov 86*
Naylor, Penelope 1941- *BioIn 11, ConAu 37R, IlsBYP, SmATA 10*
Naylor, Phyllis Reynolds *DrAP&F 85*
Naylor, Phyllis Reynolds 1933-
AuBYP SUP, BioIn 11, ConAu 8NR, −21R, FifBJA[port], IndAu 1917, IntAu&W 77, −82, SmATA 12, WhoAmW 74, −75, −87, WrDr 76, −80, −82, −84, −86
Neal, Harry Edward 1906- *AuBYP, BioIn 7, −10, ConAu 2NR, −5R, IntAu&W 76, −77, −82, −86,*

SmATA 5, WhoAm 76, −78, −80, −82, −84, −86, WrDr 76, −80, −82, −84, −86
Neame, Alan John 1924- *Au&Wr 71, ConAu 1R, −2NR, ConPo 70, WrDr 76, −80, −82, −84, −86*
Nebrensky, Alex *ConAu X*
Nee, Brett DeBary 1943- *ConAu 101*
Nee, Kay Bonner *BioIn 11, ConAu 2NR, −49, DrRegL 75, SmATA 10, WhoAmP 73, WhoAmW 77, WhoF&I 83, −85, WhoMW 80, −82*
Needleman, Jacob 1934- *BioIn 10, ConAu 12NR, −29R, DrAS 74P, −78P, −82P, SmATA 6, WhoRel 75, −77*
Neels, Betty *WrDr 84, −86*
Neely, Henry Mason 1942-
WhoBlA 75, −77, −80, −85, WhoGov 77, −75
Ne'eman, Yuval 1925- *BioIn 13, WhoWor 84*
Neeper, Cary *BioIn 10, ConAu 57*
Nef, Evelyn Stefansson 1913-
ConAu 20NR, −49, WhoAm 76, −78, −80, −82, −84, −86, WhoAmW 74, −72, −75, −77
Nef, Evelyn Stefansson *see also* Stefansson, Evelyn Baird
Neff, H Richard 1933- *ConAu 33R, WhoRel 77, WrDr 76, −80*
Neft, David S 1937- *AmM&WS 73S, ConAu 41R*
Neider, Charles 1915- *AmAu&B, BioIn 7, −10, ConAu 17R, WhoWest 80*
Neiderman, Andrew *DrAP&F 85*
Neiderman, Andrew 1940- *BioIn 9, ConAu 13NR, −33R*
Neier, Aryeh 1937- *BioIn 10, −11, ConAu 57, CurBio 78, WhoAm 74, −76, −78, −80, −82, −84, −86*
Neigoff, Mike 1920- *BioIn 11, ConAu 2NR, −5R, SmATA 13*
Neihardt, John G 1881-1973
ConLC 32[port], DcLB 54[port], EncFWF, EncO&P 2, OxAmL 83
Neihardt, John Gneisenau 1881-1973
AmAu&B, AmLY, AnMV 1926, BioIn 3, −4, −11, −12, ChhPo, −S2, −S3, CnDAL, ConAmA, ConAmL, ConAu P-1, DcLB 9[port], IntAu&W 76, −77, IntWW 74, −75, −76N, IntWWP 77, LinLib L, −S, OxAmL, REn, REnAL, REnAW, TwCA, −SUP, WebAB, −79, WhAm 6, WhLit, WhoMW 74
Neil, Randy *ConAu X*
Neilan, Sarah *ConAu 69, IntAu&W 86, WrDr 80, −82, −84, −86*
Neill, A S 1883-1973 *ConAu 101, CurBio 61, −73, −73N, NewYTBE 73, ObitOF 79, ObitT 1971, ScF&FL 1*

Neill, Alexander Sutherland 1883-1973
*BioIn 1, −5, −6, −8, −9, −10, −12, −13,
ConAu 45, DcNaB 1971, EvLB,
LongCTC, McGEWB, WhDW,
WhAm 6, WhE&EA, WhoWor 74*

Neimark, Anne E 1935- *BioIn 9,
ConAu 16NR, −29R, SmATA 4,
WhoAmW 75*

Neimark, Paul G 1934- *AuBYP SUP,
ConAu 115, SmATA 37*

Nelson, Carl Ellis 1916- *LEduc 74,
WhoAm 74*

Nelson, Cordner 1918- *BioIn 13,
ConAu 29R, IntAu&W 76,
SmATA 29, WhoWest 78, −80, −82,
WrDr 76, −80, −82, −84, −86*

Nelson, Edna *BioIn 6, ConAu 5R,
ForWC 70, MinnWr*

Nelson, Eugene Clifford 1911-
*ConAu 13R, DrAS 74P, −78P,
WhoRel 77*

Nelson, George 1908- *BioIn 12,
ConArch, ConAu 81, ConDes,
DcD&D, DrRegL 75, WhoAm 82, −84*

Nelson, George 1908-1986 *ConAu 118*

Nelson, Kent *DrAP&F 85*

Nelson, Kent 1943- *ConAu 77,
IntAu&W 86*

Nelson, Marg 1899- *AuBYP,
ConAu 1R, −2NR*

Nelson, Mary Carroll 1929-
*ConAu 1NR, −16NR, −49,
SmATA 23[port], WhoAmA 78, −80,
−82, −84, WhoAmW 79, −85, −87,
WhoWest 80, −82, −84*

Nelson, Ray Faraday *DrAP&F 85*

Nelson, Ray Faraday 1931- *ConAu 69,
IntAu&W 86, WrDr 84*

Nelson, Richard K 1941-
ConAu 12NR, −29R

Nelson, Roy Paul 1923- *ConAu 7NR,
−17R, DrAS 74E, −78E, −82E,
WhoWest 74, −76, −78, WrDr 76,
−80, −82, −84, −86*

Nelson, Russell Sage, Jr. 1927-
DrAS 74H, −78H, −82H

Nelson, Shirley *DrAP&F 85*

Nelson, Walter Henry 1928-
*AmAu&B, ConAu 7NR, −13R,
WhoAm 74, −76, −78, −80, −82,
WhoF&I 85, WhoWor 78, −80, −82,
−84, −87*

Nelson, Willie 1933- *Baker 84,
BiDAmM, BioIn 11, −12, −13,
ConAu 107, ConLC 17, CurBio 79,
EncFCWM 69, −83[port], HalFC 84,
IntMPA 84, −86, NewYTBS 78,
RolSEnR 83, WhoAm 78, −80, −82,
−84, −86, WhoRock 81[port],
WhoRocM 82*

Nemec, David *DrAP&F 85*

Nemerov, Howard *DrAP&F 85*

Nemerov, Howard 1920- *AmAu&B,
AmWr, Au&Wr 71, BioIn 4, −5, −7,
−8, −10, −12, BlueB 76, CasWL,
ChhPo S1, CnE&AP, ConAu 1R,
−1NR, ConAu 2BS, ConLC 2, −6, −9,
−36[port], ConNov 72, −76, −82,
ConPo 70, −75, −80, −85, CroCAP,
CurBio 64, DcLB 5[port], −6[port],
−Y83A, DcLEL 1940, EncWL 2,
IntAu&W 76, −82, IntWW 74, −75,
−76, −77, −78, −79, −80, −81, −82,
−83, IntWWP 77, −82, LinLib L,
ModAL, −S2, −S1, NatCAB 63N,
Novels, OxAmL, −83, PenC AM,
RAdv 1, REn, REnAL, TwCA SUP,
WhoAm 74, −76, −78, −80, −82, −84,
−86, WhoTwCL, WhoWor 74, −80,
−82, −84, WhoWorJ 72, −78, WorAl,
WrDr 76, −80, −82, −84, −86*

Nemiroff, Robert *AuNews 2,
ConAu 116, ConDr 77D, −82D,
NotNAT*

Neruda, Pablo 1904-1973 *BioIn 2, −4,
−7, −8, −9, −10, −11, −12, CasWL,
CelR, CnMWL, ConAu 45,
ConAu P-2, ConLC 1, −2, −5, −7, −9,
−28[port], CurBio 70, −73, −73N,
DcSpL, EncLatA, EncWL, −2[port],
GrFLW, LinLib L, −S, MakMC,
ModLAL, NewYTBE 71, −73,
ObitOF 79, ObitT 1971, OxEng 85,*

*OxSpan, PenC AM, REn,
TwCA SUP, TwCWr, WhDW,
WhAm 6, WhoNob, WhoTwCL,
WhoWor 74, −78, WorAl*

Neruda, Pablo *see also* Reyes Y
Basoalto, Ricardo E Neftali

Nesbitt, Cathleen 1888-1982
*AnObit 1982[port], BiE&WWA,
BioIn 4, −10, −11, −13, ConAu 107,
CurBio 56, −82N, FilmgC, HalFC 84,
MovMk, NewYTBS 82[port],
NotNAT, −A, OxAmT 84, OxThe 83,
Who 74, −82, WhoHol A,
WhoThe 72, −77, −81*

Ness, Evaline 1911- *AuBYP, BioIn 4,
−6, −7, −8, −9, −13, BkP,
ChlLR 6[port], ChhPo, −S1, −S2, −S3,
ConAu 5R, −5NR, IlsBYP,
IlsCB 1957, −1967, OxChL,
NewbC 1966, SmATA 1, −26[port],
SmATA 1AS[port], ThrBJA,
TwCCW 78, −83, WhoAm 74, −76,
−78, −80, −82, −84, −86, WhoAmA 76,
−78, −80, −82, −84, WhoAmW 74,
−66, −68, −70, −72, −75, WrDr 80,
−82, −84, −86*

Ness, Evaline 1911-1986 *ConAu 120*

Nestor, William P 1947- *ConAu 109*

Nettinga, James Zwemer 1912-
WhoRel 75

Neufeld, John 1938- *AuBYP, BioIn 10,
ConAu 11NR, −25R, ConLC 17,
ScF&FL 1, −2, SmATA 6,
SmATA 3AS[port]*

Nevell, Richard 1947- *ConAu 102*

Neville, Emily Cheney 1919-
*AmWomWr, AuBYP, BioIn 6, −7, −9,
−10, BkCL, ConAu 3NR, −5R,
ConLC 12, ForWC 70, LinLib L,
MorBMP, NewbC 1956, SmATA 1,
SmATA 2AS[port], ThrBJA,
TwCCW 78, −83, WhoAm 74, −76,
−78, −80, −82, −84, −86,
WhoAmW 74, −66, −68, −70, −72,
−75, WrDr 80, −82, −84, −86*

Nevins, Albert J 1915- *AmCath 80,
AuBYP, BioIn 3, −7, −12, BkC 6,
CathA 1952, ConAu 5R, −5NR,
−19NR, SmATA 20, WhoAm 74, −76,
−78, −80, −82, WhoRel 75, −77,
WhoWor 78*

Newbery, John 1713-1767 *Alli,
BioIn 3, −4, −7, −8, −9, −11, −12,
BritAu, ChhPo, −S1, DcLEL, DcNaB,
LinLib L, NewC, OxChL, OxEng 85,
REn, REnAL, SmATA 20, WhoChL*

Newby, Eric 1919- *Au&Wr 71,
BioIn 6, −8, −9, −13, ConAu 5R,
IntAu&W 76, −77, −82, −86, Who 74,
−82, −83, −85, WrDr 76, −80, −82,
−84, −86*

Newby, P H 1918- *BlueB 76,
ConAu 5R, ConLC 13, ConNov 82,
−86, CurBio 53, DcLB 15[port],
LinLib L, ModBrL S2, Novels,
ScF&FL 1, −2, WrDr 80, −82, −84,
−86*

Newby, Percy Howard 1918-
*Au&Wr 71, BioIn 3, −4, −9, −10, −13,
CasWL, ConAu 5R, ConLC 2,
ConNov 72, −76, DcLEL 1940,
IntAu&W 76, −77, −82, IntWW 74,
−75, −76, LongCTC, ModBrL, −S1,
NewC, RAdv 1, REn, TwCA SUP,
TwCWr, WebE&AL, WhoWor 74,
−78, −80, −82, −84, −87, WrDr 76*

Newcomb, Covelle 1908- *AmAu&B,
AuBYP, BioIn 1, −2, −7, BkC 1,
CathA 1930, ConAu P-2, JBA 51*

Newcomb, Kerry 1946- *ConAu 10NR,
−65*

Newcombe, Jack *AuBYP, BioIn 12,
ConAu 113, SmATA 33, −45*

Newell, Hope 1896-1965 *AmAu&B,
AuBYP, BioIn 6, −7, −13, ConAu 73,
LinLib L, MorJA, SmATA 24[port]*

Newell, Peter 1862-1924 *AmAu&B,
AmBi, CarSB, ChhPo, −S2, −S3,
DcAmAu, DcAmB, DcLB 42[port],
DcNAA, NatCAB 20, OxAmL, −83,
TwCBDA, WhAm 1, WorECar*

Newhall, Beaumont 1908- *BioIn 11,
−13, ConAu 9R, DcCAr 81, ICPEnP,
MacBEP, WhoAm 76, −78, −80, −82,
−84, −86, WhoAmA 73, −76, −78, −80,
−82, −84, WhoWor 80, −82, WrDr 86*

Newlon, Clarke 1905?-1982
*AuBYP SUP, BioIn 10, ConAu 108,
−10NR, −49, IntAu&W 76,
SmATA 33N, −6*

Newman, Andrea 1938- *Au&Wr 71,
ConAu 73, IntAu&W 77, −82, −86,
Novels, WrDr 76, −80, −82, −84, −86*

Newman, Arnold 1918- *BioIn 13,
ICPEnP, MacBEP, WhoAm 84, −86,
WhoAmA 84*

Newman, Bernard 1897-1968
*AuBYP SUP, BioIn 5, −8,
ConAu 25R, −97, ConSFA,
CurBio 59, −68, EncSF, LongCTC,
ScF&FL 1, TwCCr&M 80, −85,
WhAm 5, WhE&EA, WhoSpyF*

Newman, Daisy *WrDr 86*

Newman, Daisy 1904- *AuBYP SUP,
BioIn 13, ConAu 37R, IntAu&W 76,
−86, SmATA 27[port], WhoAmW 58,
−61, −66, WrDr 76, −80, −82, −84*

Newman, Edwin *IntMPA 86*

Newman, Edwin 1919- *BioIn 7, −8,
−10, −11, BioNews 74, CelR,
ChhPo S3, ConAu 5NR, −69,
ConLC 14, CurBio 67, EncAJ,
IntAu&W 82, IntMPA 78, −79, −81,
−82, IntWW 77, −78, −79, −80, −81,
−82, −83, NewYTET, WhoAm 74,
−76, −78, −80, −82, WhoE 74, −75,
WorAl*

Newman, Gerald 1931- *Dun&B 79,
WhoAm 74, −76, −78, −80, −82, −84,
−86, WhoAmJ 80, WhoF&I 74, −77,
−79, −85*

Newman, James Roy 1907-1966
*AmAu&B, BioIn 1, −4, −7, −9,
WhAm 4*

Newman, Lee Scott 1953-
ConAu 15NR, −65

Newman, Randy 1943- *Baker 84,
BiDAmM, BioIn 9, −10, −11, −12,
−13, CurBio 82[port], EncPR&S 74,
−77, IlEncRk, NewYTBE 71, −72,
RkOn 78, −84, RolSEnR 83,
WhoAm 78, −80, −82, −84, −86,
WhoRock 81[port], WhoRocM 82,
WorAl*

Newman, Randy 1944-
RolSEnR 83[port]

Newman, Robert 1909- *AuBYP,
BioIn 8, −9, ConAu 1R, −4NR,
−19NR, ScF&FL 1, −2, SmATA 4,
TwCChW 83, WrDr 86*

Newman, Sharan 1949- *ConAu 106*

Newman, Shirlee Petkin 1924-
*AuBYP SUP, BioIn 11, ConAu 5R,
ForWC 70, SmATA 10,
WhoAmW 74, −66, −68, −72, −75,
−77, WhoE 74*

Newman, Stephen Aaron 1946-
ConAu 97, WhoAmL 78, −79

Newman, Thelma R 1925-1978
*BioIn 11, ConAu 7NR, −13R, −81,
ForWC 70, LEduc 74*

Newman, William S 1912- *Baker 78,
−84, BlueB 76, ConAmC, −82,
ConAu 1R, −3NR, DrAS 74H, −78H,
−82H, IntWWM 85, WhoAm 74, −76,
−78, −80, −82, WhoAmM 83,
WhoMus 72, WhoWor 74, WrDr 76,
−80, −82, −84, −86*

Newman, William Stein 1912-
WhoAm 84, −86

Newton, Huey P 1942- *BioIn 8, −9,
−10, −11, −12, CelR, CivR 74,
CivRSt, CmCal, ConAu 114,
CurBio 73, Ebony 1, LivgBAA, MugS,
NegAl 76[port], −83[port],
NewYTBE 70, PolProf J, SelBAAu,
WhoBlA 75, −77, −80, −85*

Newton, Huey Percy 1942- *InB&W 85*

Newton, Suzanne *DrAP&F 85*

Newton, Suzanne 1936- *AuBYP SUP,
BioIn 10, ConAu 14NR, −41R,
ConLC 35[port], IntAu&W 77,
SmATA 5, WrDr 76, −80, −82, −84,
−86*

Ney, John 1923- *AuBYP SUP,
ConAu 115, FifBJA[port], SmATA 33,
−43[port]*

Nguyen-Dinh-Hoa 1924- *ConAu 21R*

Nguyen-Du 1765-1820 *CasWL,
DcOrL 2, PenC CL*

Niatum, Duane *DrAP&F 85*

Niatum, Duane 1938- *ConAu 21NR,
−X, IntWWP 77*

Niatum, Duane *see also* McGinnis,
Duane

Niccacci, Rufino *BioIn 7*

Nicholas, A X 1943- *BlkAWP*

Nicholls, Peter 1939- *ConAu 105,
EncSF, WhoSciF*

Nichols, John 1940- *BioIn 7, −12, −13,
ConAu 6NR, −9R, ConAu 2AS[port],
ConLC 38[port], DcLB Y82B[port],
WrDr 84, −86*

Nichols, John Treadwell 1940-
IntAu&W 86

Nichols, Nell Beaubien *AuBYP SUP,
WhoAmW 58, −61, −64*

Nichols, Ruth 1948- *Au&Wr 71,
AuBYP SUP, BioIn 10, −12,
ConAu 16NR, −25R, FourBJA,
IntAu&W 76, OxCan SUP, OxCanL,
OxChL, Profile, ScF&FL 1, −2,
SmATA 15, TwCCW 78, −83,
WhoCanL 85, WrDr 80, −82, −84,
−86*

Nicholson, Margaret Beda 1924-
*Au&Wr 71, ConAu 5R, IntAu&W 76,
WrDr 76, −82, −84*

Nickelsburg, Janet 1893- *BioIn 11,
ConAu 65, SmATA 11*

Nickson, Hilda 1912- *IntAu&W 76,
−77*

Nicole, Christopher *TwCCr&M 85*

Nicole, Christopher 1930- *Au&Wr 71,
BioIn 10, ConAu 13R, ConNov 72,
−76, −82, DcLEL 1940, IntAu&W 76,
−77, −82, SmATA 5, TwCCr&M 80,
WhoSpyF, WhoWor 76, −78, −80,
WrDr 76, −80, −82, −84, −86*

Niebling, Richard F *ChhPo S1,
WhoAmP 75, −77*

Nieburg, Herbert Alan 1946-
WhoE 79, −81, −85

Niehuis, Charles C *AuBYP, BioIn 7*

Nielsen, Virginia *ConAu X*

Nielsen, Virginia 1909- *SmATA X*

Nielsen, Virginia *see also* McCall,
Virginia Nielsen

Nierenberg, Gerard I 1923- *BioIn 12,
ConAu 25R, −61, IntAu&W 77,
WhoAmL 78, −79, WhoE 74,
WrDr 76, −80, −82, −84, −86*

Nies, Judith 1941- *ConAu 77,
WhoAmW 75*

Niggli, Josefina 1910- *BioIn 12,
ChiSch, ConAu P-2,
DcLB Y80B[port], DrAS 74E, −78E,
NatPD*

Niggli, Josephina 1910- *AmAu&B,
AmNov, AmWomWr, BioIn 1, −2, −3,
CurBio 49, InWom*

Nilsen, Alleen Pace 1936- *ConAu 112,
IntAu&W 86*

Nilsson, Harry 1941- *BiDAmM,
BioIn 9, EncPR&S 74, −77, IlEncRk,
RkOn 78, −84, RolSEnR 83, WhoAm 74,
−76, −78, −80, −82, −84, −86,
WhoHol A, WhoRock 81,
WhoRocM 82, WorAl*

Nilsson, Lennart 1922- *ConPhot,
ICPEnP, MacBEP*

Nisenson, Samuel 1905?-1968 *BioIn 8,
IlsBYP*

Nissenson, Hugh *DrAP&F 85*

Nissenson, Hugh 1933- *BioIn 10,
ConAu 17R, ConLC 4, −9,
DcLB 28[port], WhoAmJ 80,
WhoWorJ 72, −78, WrDr 76, −80,
−82, −84, −86*

Niven, David 1909-1983
HalFC 84[port]

Niven, David 1910-1983 *Alli,
AnObit 1983, ASpks, BioIn 4, −5, −7,
−8, −9, −10, −11, −13, BlueB 76,
CelR, ConAu 110, −77, ConTFT 1,
CurBio 57, −83N, FilmgC,
IntAu&W 76, −77, IntMPA 77, −75,*

-76, -78, -79, -81, -82, IntWW 74,
-75, -76, -77, -78, -79, -80, -81,
-82, -83, MotPP, MovMk,
NewYTBS 83[port], OxFilm,
WhAm 8, Who 74, -82, WhoAm 74,
-76, -78, -80, -82, WhoHol A,
WhoWor 74, WorAl, WorEFlm,
WrDr 76, -80, -82, -84

Niven, Larry ConAu X, DrAP&F 85,
DrmM 2[port], WhoAm 74

Niven, Larry 1938- BioIn 12,
ConAu X, ConLC 8, ConSFA,
DcLB 8[port], EncSF, IntAu&W 82,
Novels, ScF&FL 1, -2, ScFSB,
TwCSFW 86, WhoSciF, WrDr 80,
-82, -84, -86

Niven, Larry see also Niven, Laurence
VanCott

Niven, Laurence VanCott 1938-
BioIn 12, ConAu 14NR, -21R,
WhoAm 76, -78, -80, -82, -84, -86

Niven, Laurence VanCott see also
Niven, Larry

Niven, Laurence VonCott 1938-
WorAl

Nixon, Joan Lowery 1927-
AuBYP SUP, BioIn 11, -13,
ConAu 7NR, -9R, FifBJA[port],
IntAu&W 76, SmATA 44[port], -8

Nixon, Richard M 1913- Who 85

Nixon, Richard Milhous 1913-
AmAu&B, BiDrAC, BiDrUSE,
BioIn 1, -2, -3, -4, -5, -6, -7, -8, -9,
-10, -11, -12, -13, BioNews 74,
BlueB 76, CelR, CmCal, CngDr 74,
ConAu 73, CurBio 48, -58, -69,
DcAmSR, DcPol, EncAAH,
EncAB-H, EncSoH, IntWW 74, -75,
-76, -77, -78, -79, -80, -81, -82,
-83, IntYB 78, -79, -80, -81, -82,
LinLib L, -S, McGEWB,
NewYTBE 71, -72, -73,
NewYTBS 74, -75, PolProf E,
PolProf J, PolProf K, PolProf NF,
PolProf T, WebAB, -79, WhDW,
Who 74, -82, -83, WhoAm 74, -76,
-78, -80, -82, -84, -86, WhoAmP 73,
-75, -77, -79, -81, -83, WhoE 74,
-81, -83, -85, WhoGov 77, -72, -75,
WhoS&SW 73, WhoWest 74, -76,
-78, WhoWor 74, -78, -80, -82, -84,
-87, WorAl, WrDr 80, -82, -84

Nizer, Louis 1902- AmSCAP 66,
BiE&WWA, BioIn 4, -6, -9, -11,
-13, CelR, ConAu 53, CurBio 55,
IntMPA 77, -75, -76, -78, -79, -81,
-82, -84, -86, LinLib L,
NewYTBE 71, NewYTBS 77,
NotNAT, St&PR 75, WebAB, -79,
WhoAm 74, -76, -78, -80, -82,
WhoAmJ 80, WhoAmL 78, -79,
WhoE 74, WhoWor 74, -76,
WhoWorJ 72, -78, WorAl, WrDr 76,
-80, -82, -84, -86

Nketia, J H Kwabena 1921-
ConAu 7NR, -X, InB&W 80,
IntAu&W 76, WhoAmM 83

Noad, Frederick 1929- ConAu 4NR,
-9R

Nobile, Philip 1941- WhoE 74, -75,
-77

Noble, Iris 1922- AuBYP, BioIn 7,
-10, ConAu 1R, -2NR, SmATA 5,
WhoAmW 66

Noble, Iris 1922-1986 ConAu 120

Noble, Jeanne L 1926- ConAu 112,
SelBAAf

Noble, Jeanne Laveta 1926- BioIn 6,
InB&W 80, InWom, LivgBAA,
NegAl 76[port], -83[port],
WhoAmW 58, -68, -70

Noble, Mark d1827 Alli, BiDLA,
DcEnL

Noble, Mark 1754-1827 DcNaB

Nodset, Joan L AuBYP, BioIn 8, -9,
ConAu X, SmATA 1, -X,
TwCChW 83, WrDr 80, -82, -84, -86

Nodset, Joan L see also Lexau, Joan M

Noel, Ruth 1947- ConAu 69

Noel Hume, Ivor 1927- Au&Wr 71,
BlueB 76, ConAu 12NR, -13R,
DrAS 82H, IntAu&W 76, -77,
WhoAm 74, -76, -78, -80, -82, -84,
-86, WhoWor 74, -76, -80, -82,
WrDr 76, -80, -82, -84, -86

Nolan, Dennis 1945- ConAu 112,
SmATA 34, -42

Nolan, Jeannette Covert 1897?-1974
AmAu&B, Au&Wr 71, AuBYP,
BioIn 2, -7, -9, ConAu 4NR, -5R,
-53, ForWC 70, IndAu 1917,
IntAu&W 76, JBA 51, SmATA 2,
-27N, WhAm 6, WhE&EA,
WhoAm 74, WhoAmW 74, -58, -61,
-64, -66, -68, -70, -72, -75

Nolan, Paul T 1919- SmATA 48[port],
WrDr 86

Nolan, Paul Thomas 1919-
ConAu 2NR, -5R, DrAS 74E, -74P,
-78E, -78P, -82E, WhoAm 74, -76,
-78, -80, -82, -84, -86,
WhoS&SW 73, -75, -76, WrDr 76,
-80, -82, -84

Nolan, William F 1928- BioIn 9, -12,
-13, ConAu 1R, -1NR, ConSFA,
DcLB 8[port], EncMys, EncSF,
IntAu&W 76, ScF&FL 1, -2, ScFSB,
SmATA 28, St&PR 75,
TwCCr&M 80, -85, TwCSFW 86,
WhoAm 80, -82, WhoSciF,
WhoWest 74, WrDr 76, -80, -82,
-84, -86

Nolen, Barbara 1902- ChhPo S2,
ConAu 104, WhoAmW 74, -66, -68,
-70, -72, -75, -77, WhoE 74, -75,
-77

Noonan, Michael John 1921-
Au&Wr 71, ConAu 21R,
IntAu&W 76, WrDr 76, -80, -82, -84

Nordberg, Robert B 1921-
ConAu 13R, LEduc 74

Nordhoff, Charles Bernard 1887-1947
AmAu&B, AmNov, AuBYP, BioIn 1,
-2, -4, -5, -7, -8, -12, -13, CnDAL,
ConAu 108, CyWA, DcAmB S5,
DcLB 9[port], DcLEL, DcNAA,
JBA 34, LinLib L, LongCTC,
MnBBF, Novels, ObitOF 79,
OxAmL, -83, PenC AM, REn,
REnAL, SmATA 23[port],
TwCA, -SUP, WhAm 2, WorAl

Noren, Catherine 1938- ConAu 16NR,
-65, WhoAmW 79, -81

Noren, Catherine Hanf 1938- MacBEP

Norfleet, Barbara Pugh WhoAmA 84

Norfleet, Barbara Pugh 1926-
AmM&WS 78S, ConAu 107,
MacBEP, WhoAmA 78, -80, -82

Norman, Charles 1904- AmAu&B,
AuBYP, BioIn 4, -7, ChhPo S2,
ConAu 107, REnAL, SmATA 38,
TwCA SUP, WhoAm 74, -76

Norman, Geoffrey BioIn 13

Norman, James DrAP&F 85

Norman, James 1912- ConAu X,
ScF&FL 1, SmATA X,
TwCCr&M 80, -85, WhE&EA,
WrDr 82, -84

Norman, James see also Schmidt, James
Norman

Norman, John 1931- ConAu X, ScFSB,
TwCSFW 86, WrDr 84, -86

Norman, Lilith 1927- ConAu 1NR,
-45, OxAusL, TwCCW 78, -83,
WrDr 80, -82, -84, -86

Norman, Marsha WhoAmW 85, -87

Norman, Marsha 1947- BioIn 13,
ConLC 28[port], ConTFT 1,
CurBio 84[port], DcLB Y84B[port],
OxAmT 84, WhoE 85

Norman, Marsha 1948- AmWomD

Norris, Frank 1870-1902 AmAu&B,
AmBi, AmWr, AtlBL, BbD, BiD&SB,
BioIn 1, -2, -3, -4, -5, -6, -8, -9,
-10, -11, -12, -13, CasWL,
Chambr 3, CmCal, CnDAL, CrtT 3,

-4, CyWA, DcAmAu, DcAmB,
DcBiA, DcLB 12[port], DcLEL,
DcNAA, EncAAH, EvLB, HalFC 84,
LinLib L, LongCTC, ModAL,
NatCAB 14, -15, Novels, OxAmH,
-83, OxEng, -85, PenC AM,
RAdv 1, REn, REnAL, REnAW,
ScF&FL 1, TwCA, -SUP, TwCBDA,
TwCLC 24[port], TwCWr,
WebAB, -79, WebE&AL, WhDW,
WhAm 1, WhoHr&F, WorAl

Norris, Kenneth Stafford 1924-
AmM&WS 73P, -76P, -79P, -82P,
-86P, ConAu 77, WhoOcn 78,
WhoWest 80, -82, -84

Norris, Louanne 1930- ConAu 20NR,
-53

Norris, Marianna AuBYP SUP

North, Andrew SmATA X,
TwCSFW 86, WrDr 86

North, Andrew 1912- AmAu&B,
ConAu X, CurBio 57, EncSF,
IntAu&W 77X, ScF&FL 1,
SmATA 1, TwCChW 83, WorAu,
WrDr 84

North, Andrew see also Norton, Alice
Mary

North, Elizabeth 1932- WrDr 86

North, Joan Marian 1920- Au&Wr 71,
AuBYP SUP, BioIn 12, ConAu 13R,
IntAu&W 76, -77, -86, ScF&FL 1,
-2, SmATA 16, WhoAmW 70,
WrDr 76, -80, -82, -84, -86

North, Sterling 1906-1974 AmAu&B,
AmNov, Au&Wr 71, AuBYP, BioIn 2,
-4, -6, -7, -9, -10, -13, BlueB 76N,
ConAu 5R, -53, CurBio 43, -75,
-75N, LinLib L, -S, NewYTBS 74,
REnAL, ScF&FL 1, -2, SmATA 1,
-26N, -45[port], ThrBJA,
TwCA, -SUP, TwCCW 78, -83,
WhAm 6, WhE&EA, WhoAm 74,
WhoE 74

North, Wheeler J 1922- WhoTech 84

North, Wheeler James 1922-
AmM&WS 73P, -76P, -79P, -82P,
-86P, ConAu 101, WhoAm 76, -78,
-80, -82, -84, -86, WhoOcn 78,
WhoWest 74, -76, -78

Norton, Alden H 1903- ConAu 101,
ConSFA, ScF&FL 1, -2, WhoSciF

Norton, Alice Mary 1912- AmAu&B,
AuBYP, BioIn 4, -6, -9, -10, -12,
ConAu 1R, -2NR, CurBio 57,
OhA&B, SmATA 1, -43[port]

Norton, Alice Mary see also North,
Andrew

Norton, Alice Mary see also Norton,
Andre

Norton, Andre DrmM 2, OxChL,
SmATA X

Norton, Andre 1912- AuBYP, BioIn 4,
-6, -9, -10, -12, ConAu X,
ConLC 12, ConSFA, CurBio 57,
DcLB 8, -52[port], EncSF, InWom,
IntAu&W 76, -77, LinLib L, MorJA,
Novels, OhA&B, ScF&FL 1, -2,
ScFSB, SenS, SmATA 1, SupFW,
TwCCW 78, -83, TwCSFW 86,
WhoAm 80, -82, WhoAmW 58, -61,
WhoHr&F, WhoSciF, WorAu,
WrDr 76, -80, -82, -84, -86

Norton, Andre see also Norton, Alice
Mary

Norton, Browning ConAu X,
SmATA X

Norton, Browning see Norton, Frank R
B

Norton, Frank R B 1909- BioIn 11,
ConAu 61, SmATA 10

Norton, Joseph Louis 1918-
AmM&WS 73S, -78S, ConAu 29R,
LEduc 74, WhoE 75

Norton, Mary 1903- AnCL, Au&ICB,
Au&Wr 71, AuBYP, BioIn 5, -6, -8,
-9, -12, BkCL, CasWL,
ChlLR 6[port], ConAu 97, OxChL,
ScF&FL 1, SmATA 18, ThrBJA,

TwCCW 78, -83, Who 85, WrDr 76,
-80, -82, -84, -86

Norton, Olive WrDr 86

Norton, Olive 1913- Au&Wr 71,
ConAu 9R, WrDr 84

Norway, Kate 1913- ConAu X,
WrDr 84, -86

Norway, Kate see also Norton, Olive

Norwood, Warren DrAP&F 85

Norwood, Warren 1945- TwCSFW 86

Noshpitz, Joseph Dove 1922-
AmM&WS 73S, -76P, -79P, -82P,
-86P, BiDrAPA 77, WhoAm 82, -84,
-86

Nostlinger, Christine ConAu X

Nostlinger, Christine 1936-
ChlLR 12[port], FifBJA[port],
SmATA 37, TwCCW 78B, -83B

Nourse, Alan E 1928- Au&Wr 71,
AuBYP, BioIn 7, -12, ConAu 1R,
-3NR, -21NR, ConSFA,
DcLB 8[port], EncSF, LinLib L,
ScF&FL 1, -2, ScFSB,
SmATA 48[port], TwCSFW 86,
WhoPNW, WhoSciF, WrDr 84, -86

Nourse, James G 1947- ConAu 105

Novack, George 1905- BlueB 76,
ConAu 49, IntAu&W 77, WhoAm 74,
-76, -78, -80, -82, -84, -86,
WhoWor 74, WrDr 80, -82, -84, -86

Noverr, Douglas Arthur 1942-
ConAu 102, DrAS 78E, -82E

Noyes, Nell Braly 1921- ConAu 37R,
IntAu&W 77, WrDr 76, -80

Nugilak OxCan SUP

Null, Gary ConAu 17NR

Null, Gary 1945- ConAu 65

Nunn, William Curtis 1908-
ConAu 1NR, -1R, DrAS 74H, -78H,
-82H, IntAu&W 76, -82, -86,
WrDr 76, -80, -82, -84, -86

Nunn, William Curtis see also Curtis,
Will

Nunn, William Curtis see also Twist,
Ananias

Nurnberg, Maxwell d1984
NewYTBS 84

Nurnberg, Maxwell 1897- BioIn 13,
ChhPo S2, ConAu 2NR, -5R,
SmATA 27

Nurnberg, Maxwell 1897-1984
ConAu 114, SmATA 41N

Nutt, Grady 1934- ConAu 97

Nutt, Grady 1935?-1982 BioIn 13

Nuttall, Kenneth 1907- ConAu 17R,
IntAu&W 76

Nyad, Diana 1949?- BioIn 9, -10, -11,
-12, ConAu 111, CurBio 79,
NewYTBS 78, WhoAmW 85

Nyad, Diana 1950- HerW 84

Nye, Naomi Shihab DrAP&F 85

Nye, Robert 1939- Au&Wr 71,
BioIn 10, -13, ConAu 33R,
ConLC 13, -42[port], ConNov 72,
-76, -82, -86, ConPo 70, -75, -80,
-85, DcLB 14[port], IntAu&W 76,
-82, IntWWP 77, -82, Novels,
OxChL, SmATA 6, TwCCW 78, -83,
Who 82, -83, -85, WhoWor 76,
WorAu 1970, WrDr 76, -80, -82,
-84, -86

Nye, Russel Blaine 1913- AmAu&B,
Au&Wr 71, BioIn 4, BlueB 76,
ConAu 1R, -4NR, CurBio 45,
DrAS 74E, -78E, -82E, MichAu 80,
OxAmL, REnAL, TwCA SUP,
WhoAm 74, -76, -78, -80, -82, -84,
WrDr 76, -80, -82, -84

Nyro, Laura 1947- BiDAmM, BioIn 8,
-9, -10, CelR, ConLC 17,
EncFCWM 83, EncPR&S 74, -77,
IlEncRk, NewYTBS 76, RkOn 78,
-84, RolSEnR 83, WhoAm 74, -76,
-78, -80, -82, -84, WhoAmW 74,
-70, -72, -81, WhoRock 81[port],
WorAl

O

Oakes, Vanya 1909-1983 *BiDrLUS 70,*
BioIn 7, –10, ConAu 111, –33R,
SmATA 37N, –6, WhoAmW 74, –70,
–72, WhoWest 74, –76
Oakes, Vanya *see also* Oakes, Virginia
Oakes, Virginia 1909- *AuBYP,*
BioIn 7, –10, WhE&EA
Oakes, Virginia *see also* Oakes, Vanya
Oakley, Ann 1944- *ConAu 6NR, –57,*
IntAu&W 77, IntDcWB, WrDr 76,
–80, –82, –84, –86
Oakley, Graham 1929?-
ChLR 7[port], FifBJA[port], OxChL,
WrDr 86
Oakley, Mary Ann Bryant 1940-
ConAu 45, IntAu&W 76,
WhoAmW 77, –79, –87
Oaks, Dallin H 1932- *WrDr 86*
Oaks, Dallin Harris 1932- *BlueB 76,*
ConAu 25R, DrAS 74P, –78P, –82P,
IntAu&W 77, LEduc 74, WhoAm 74,
–76, –78, –80, –82, –84, –86,
WhoAmL 79, –83, –85, WhoRel 75,
–77, –85, WhoWest 74, –76, –78, –80,
–82, –84, WhoWor 74, –78, WrDr 82,
–84, –86
Oates, John 1948- *BioIn 11, –12,*
WhoAm 80, –82, WhoRocM 82
Oates, John 1949?- *BioIn 13*
Oates, John *see also* Hall & Oates
Oates, Joyce Carol *DrAP&F 85*
Oates, Joyce Carol 1938- *AmAu&B,*
AmWomD, AmWomWr, AmWr S2,
AuNews 1, BioIn 8, –9, –10, –11, –12,
–13, BioNews 74, BlueB 76, CelR,
ChhPo S3, ConAu 5R, ConLC 1, –2,
–3, –6, –9, –11, –15, –19, –33[port],
ConNov 72, –76, –82, –86, CurBio 70,
DcLB 2, –5[port], –Y81A[port],
DcLEL 1940, ForWC 70, IntAu&W 76,
IntAu&W 76, –77, –82, IntDcWB,
LibW, LinLib L, ModAL S2, –S1,
NewYTBS 80[port], –82[port], Novels,
OxAmL 83, OxEng 85, Po&Wr 77,
RAdv 1, WhoAm 74, –76, –78, –80,
–82, –84, –86, WhoAmW 74, –70,
–72, –81, –83, –85, –87, WhoWor 74,
–80, –82, WorAl, WorAu 1970,
WrDr 76, –80, –82, –84, –86
Oates, Stephen B 1936- *BioIn 13*
Oates, Stephen Baery 1936-
ConAu 4NR, –9R, DrAS 74H, –78H,
–82H, IntAu&W 77, –82, WhoAm 74,
–76, –78, –80, –82, –84, –86,
WrDr 76, –80, –82, –84, –86
Oatley, Keith 1939- *ConAu 45*
O'Ballance, Edgar 1918- *ConAu 5R,*
–7NR, IntAu&W 76, –77, –82, –86,
WrDr 76, –80, –82, –84, –86
Oberg, James Edward 1944-
ConAu 108, IntAu&W 86,
UFOEn[port]
O'Brien, Andrew William 1910-
ConAu 17NR, –25R
O'Brien, Andrew William *see also*
O'Brien, Andy

O'Brien, Andy *ConAu X*
O'Brien, Andy 1910- *Au&Wr 71,*
WrDr 76, –80, –82, –84
O'Brien, Andy *see also* O'Brien,
Andrew William
O'Brien, Esse Forrester 1895?-1975
ConAu 61, ForWC 70, SmATA 30N,
TexWr
O'Brien, Jack 1898-1938 *LinLib L,*
MorJA
O'Brien, Jack *see also* O'Brien, John
Sherman
O'Brien, John Sherman 1898-1938
AuBYP, BioIn 1, –6, –7, DcNAA
O'Brien, John Sherman *see also*
O'Brien, Jack
O'Brien, Justin 1906-1968 *Au&Wr 71,*
BioIn 1, –3, –8, ConAu 5R, –5NR,
NotNAT B, WhAm 5
O'Brien, Robert C 1917?-1973
BioIn 13
O'Brien, Robert C 1918-1973
AuBYP SUP, BioIn 9, ChlLR 2,
ConAu X, EncSF, FourBJA,
NewbC 1966, OxChL, ScF&FL 1,
SmATA X, TwCCW 78, –83
O'Brien, Robert C 1922?-1973 *ScFSB*
O'Brien, Robert C *see also* Conly,
Robert L
O'Brien, Tim 1946- *BioIn 12, –13,*
ConAu 85, ConLC 7, –19, –40[port],
DcLB Y80B[port], PostFic
Obukhova, Lydia *ScF&FL 1*
O'Casey, Sean 1880?-1964 *AtlBL,*
BiE&WWA, BioIn 1, –2, –3, –4, –5,
–6, –7, –8, –9, –10, –11, –12, –13,
BritWr 7, CasWL, Chambr 3, CnMD,
CnMWL, CnThe, ConAu 89,
ConLC 1, –5, –9, –11, –15, CroCD,
CurBio 62, –64, CyWA, DcIrB,
DcIrL, DcIrW 1, –2, DcLB 10[port],
DcLEL, DcNaB 1961,
EncWL, –2[port], EncWT, EvLB,
FilmgC, HalFC 84, LinLib L, –S,
LongCEL, LongCTC, MajMD 1,
MakMC, McGEWB,
McGEWD, –84[port], ModBrL, –S2,
–S1, ModWD, NewC, NewYTBE 72,
NotNAT A, –B, ObitOF 79,
ObitT 1961, OxAmT 84, OxEng, –85,
OxThe, –83, PenC ENG, PlP&P,
RComWL, REn, REnWD,
TwCA, –SUP, TwCWr, WebE&AL,
WhDW, WhAm 4, WhE&EA,
WhThe, WhoTwCL, WorAl
O'Casey, Sean 1884-1964 *BiDIrW*
Ochs, Phil 1940-1976 *AmSCAP 66,*
BioIn 8, –10, –11, ConAu 65,
ConLC 17, EncFCWM 69, –83[port],
NewYTBE 71, NewYTBS 76,
ObitOF 79, RolSEnR 83, WhAm 7,
WhoRock 81, WhoRocM 82
Ochs, Phil 1941-1976 *WhScrn 83*
O'Connell, Desmond Henry 1906-1973
WhAm 5, WhoF&I 74

O'Connell, Margaret F 1935-1977
BioIn 11, ConAu 73, NewYTBS 77,
SmATA 30N
O'Connor, Dick 1930- *ConAu 97*
O'Connor, Edwin 1918-1968
AmAu&B, BioIn 4, –5, –6, –7, –8,
–10, ConAu 25R, –93, ConLC 14,
CurBio 63, –68, DcLEL 1940,
LinLib L, ModAL, NotNAT B,
Novels, ObitOF 79, OxAmL, –83,
PenC AM, REnAL, WhAm 5, WorAl,
WorAu
O'Connor, Flannery 1925-1964
AmAu&B, AmWomWr, AmWr,
BioIn 2, –3, –4, –5, –6, –7, –8, –9,
–10, –11, –12, –13, ConAu 1R, –3NR,
ConLC 1, –2, –3, –6, –10, –13, –15,
–21[port], ConNov 76, –82A, –86A,
CurBio 58, –65, DcLB 2,
–Y80A[port], DcLEL 1940,
EncWL, –2[port], InWom, IntDcWB,
LibW, LinLib L, ModAL, –S2, –S1,
NatCAB 55, NewCon[port],
NotAW MOD, Novels, ObitOF 79,
OxAmL, –83, OxEng 85, PenC AM,
RAdv 1, REn, REnAL, TwCWr,
WebE&AL, WhAm 4, WhoAmW 58,
–61, –64, –66, WhoTwCL, WorAl,
WorAu
O'Connor, Frank 1903-1966
AmAu&B, AtlBL, BiDIrW, –B,
BioIn 2, –3, –4, –5, –7, –8, –11, –12,
–13, CasWL, CnMD, ConAu X,
ConLC 14, –23[port], DcIrB, DcIrL,
DcIrW 1, –2, –3, DcLEL, EncWL 2,
EvLB, LinLib L, LongCEL,
LongCTC, ModBrL, –S2, –S1, NewC,
NotNAT B, Novels, ObitOF 79,
ObitT 1961, OxEng, –85, PenC ENG,
RAdv 1, REn, TwCA SUP, WhDW,
WhAm 4, WhE&EA
O'Connor, Karen 1938-
SmATA 34[port]
O'Connor, Karen *see also* Sweeney,
Karen O'Connor
O'Connor, Patrick *ConAu X,*
SmATA X, WrDr 86
O'Connor, Patrick 1915-1983 *AuBYP,*
BbtC, ConAu X, EncMys,
IntAu&W 76X, –77X, –82X,
TwCChW 83, WrDr 80, –82, –84
O'Connor, Patrick *see also* Wibberley,
Leonard
O'Connor, Richard 1915-1975
AmAu&B, AuBYP SUP, BioIn 10,
–12, ConAu 57, –61, IndAu 1917,
NewYTBS 75, ObitOF 79,
SmATA 21N, TwCCr&M 80,
WhAm 6, WhoAm 74, WhoE 74
O'Connor, Rod 1934- *AmM&WS 73P,*
–76P, –79P, –82P, –86P, WhoAm 74,
–76, –78, –80, –82, –84, –86,
WhoTech 82, –84
O'Daniel, Janet *WrDr 86*

O'Daniel, Janet 1921- *BioIn 13,*
ConAu 29R, SmATA 24[port],
WrDr 76, –80, –82, –84
O'Dell, Scott 1897- *WrDr 86*
O'Dell, Scott 1898- *IntAu&W 86,*
WhoAm 86
O'Dell, Scott 1903?- *AmAu&B,*
AmNov, AnCL, Au&ICB, AuBYP,
BioIn 1, –2, –5, –6, –7, –9, –10, –11,
BkCL, ChlLR 1, ConAu 12NR, –61,
ConLC 30[port], DcLB 52[port],
LinLib L, MorJA, NewbC 1956,
OxChL, PiP, SenS, SmATA 12,
Str&VC, TwCCW 78, –83,
WhoAm 74, –76, –78, –80, –82, –84,
WhoWor 74, –78, WrDr 80, –82, –84
O'Donnell, Jim *ConAu X*
O'Donnell, Kevin, Jr. 1950-
ConAu 106, IntAu&W 86,
TwCSFW 86
O'Donnell, Lillian 1926- *AmWomWr,*
ConAu 3NR, –5R, TwCCr&M 80,
–85, WhoAmW 68, –70, WrDr 82,
–84, –86
O'Donoghue, Bryan 1921- *ConAu 77*
O'Faolain, Sean *Who 85*
O'Faolain, Sean 1900- *BiDIrW,*
BioIn 1, –3, –4, –5, –6, –7, –8, –11,
–13, BlueB 76, CasWL, CathA 1930,
ConAu 12NR, –61, ConLC 1, –7, –14,
–32[port], ConNov 72, –76, –82, –86,
CyWA, DcIrL, DcIrW 1, –2,
DcLB 15[port], DcLEL, EncWL,
EvLB, IntAu&W 76, –77, IntWW 74,
–75, –76, –77, –78, –79, –80, –81,
–82, –83, LinLib L, LongCEL,
LongCTC, ModBrL, –S2, –S1, NewC,
Novels, OxEng 85, PenC ENG,
RAdv 1, REn, TwCA, –SUP, TwCWr,
WhE&EA, WhLit, Who 74, –82, –83,
WhoAm 74, WhoWor 74, –76, –78,
–84, –87, WorAl, WrDr 76, –80, –82,
–84, –86
Ofek, Uriel 1926- *ConAu 101, –18NR,*
SmATA 36, WhoWorJ 72, –78
Offit, Sidney *DrAP&F 85*
Offit, Sidney 1928- *AuBYP SUP,*
BioIn 11, ConAu 1R, –1NR,
SmATA 10, WhoAm 74, –76, –78,
–80, –82, –84, –86, WhoE 74, –75,
–77, WhoWor 84, –87, WrDr 76, –80,
–82, –84
Offutt, Andrew J 1934?-
ConAu 15NR, –41R, EncSF,
ScF&FL 1, –2, ScFSB, TwCSFW 86,
WrDr 84
O'Flaherty, Liam d1984 *Who 85N*
O'Flaherty, Liam 1896- *Au&Wr 71,*
BioIn 4, –5, –9, –10, –11, CasWL,
Chambr 3, ConAu 101, ConLC 5,
ConNov 72, –76, –82, CyWA, DcIrL,
DcIrW 1, –3, DcLEL, EncWL, EvLB,
HalFC 84, IntAu&W 76, –77, –82,
IntWW 74, –75, –76, –77, –78, –79,

119

−80, −81, −82, −83, LinLib L,
LongCEL, LongCTC, ModBrL, −S1,
NewC, Novels, OxEng, PenC ENG,
REn, TwCA, −SUP, TwCWr, WhDW,
WhE&EA, Who 74, −82, −83,
WhoWor 74, WorAl, WrDr 76, −80,
−82, −84

O'Flaherty, Liam 1896-1984
AnObit 1984, ConAu 113,
ConLC 34[port], DcLB 36[port],
−Y84N[port], ModBrL S2

O'Flaherty, Liam 1897-1984
BiDIrW, −B, NewYTBS 84[port],
OxEng 85

Ogan, George F 1912- *AuBYP SUP,*
BioIn 11, ConAu 4NR, −9R,
SmATA 13

Ogan, Margaret E 1923-1979
AuBYP SUP, BioIn 11, ConAu 4NR,
−9R, SmATA 13

Ogburn, Charlton 1911- *WhoAm 84,*
−86, WrDr 86

Ogburn, Charlton, Jr. 1911- *AmAu&B,*
Au&Wr 71, BioIn 9, ConAu 3NR,
−5R, IntAu&W 82, SmATA 3,
WhoAm 74, −76, −78, −80, −82,
WhoS&SW 73, WrDr 80, −82, −84

Ogg, Oscar 1908-1971 *BioIn 9,*
ConAu 33R, ConAu P-1, LinLib L,
NewYTBE 71, WhoAmA 78N, −80N,
−82N, −84N, WhoGrA 62

Ogilvie, Elisabeth 1917- *AmAu&B,*
AmNov, AuBYP, BioIn 2, −4, −5, −8,
−13, ConAu 103, CurBio 51, InWom,
SmATA 29, TwCA SUP,
WhoAmW 74, −58, −61, −64, −66,
−68, −70, −72, −75, −77, WhoE 74,
WrDr 84, −86

Ogilvie, Elisabeth May 1917-
ConAu 19NR, SmATA 40[port]

Ogle, James Lawrence 1911-
ConAu 5R

Ogle, Jim *ConAu X*

Ogle, Jim *see also* Ogle, James
Lawrence

Oglesby, Carl 1935- *BioIn 11,*
PolProf J, WhoAm 74

O'Hanlon, Jacklyn *ConAu X,*
SmATA X

O'Hanlon, Jacklyn *see also* Meek,
Jacklyn O'Hanlon

O'Hara, Mary *BioIn 13, OxChL*

O'Hara, Mary 1885- *HalFC 84*

O'Hara, Mary 1885-1980 *AmAu&B,*
AmNov, AnObit 1980[port], BioIn 1,
−2, −3, −4, −7, −9, −12, CathA 1952,
ConAu X, CurBio 44, −81N, InWom,
LinLib L, REn, REnAL, SmATA 2,
−X, TwCA SUP, TwCCW 78, −83,
WhAm 7, WhoAm 74, −76, −78, −80,
WhoAmW 74, −58, −61, −66, −68,
−70, −72, WorAl, WrDr 86[port]

O'Hara, Mary *see also* Alsop, Mary
O'Hara

O'Hern, Elizabeth Moot 1913-
AmM&WS 86P, WhoE 85

O'Kane, Dick *AuBYP SUP*

O'Keeffe, Georgia 1887- *AmArt,*
ArtsAmW 1, −2, BioIn 1, −2, −4, −5,
−6, −7, −8, −9, −10, −11, −12, −13,
BriEAA, CelR, ConArt 83,
ConAu 110, CurBio 41, −64,
DcAmArt, DcCAA 71, −77, DcCAr 81,
EncAB-H, GoodHs, IntDcWB, LibW,
LinLib S, McGDA, McGEWB,
OxArt, OxTwCA, PhDcTCA 77, REn,
WebAB, −79, Who 74, −82, −83, −85,
WhoAm 74, −76, −78, −80, −82, −84,
WhoAmA 74, −76, −80, −82, −84,
WhoAmW 74, −58, −64, −66, −68,
−70, −83, −85, WhoWest 74,
WomArt, −A, WorAl, WorArt[port]

O'Keeffe, Georgia 1887-1986
ConAu 118, CurBio 86N,
NewYTBS 86[port]

Okimoto, Jean Davies 1942-
ConAu 16NR, −97, SmATA 34[port]

Okrent, Daniel 1948- *ConAu 105,*
WhoAm 74, −76

Okun, Lawrence E 1929- *ConAu 101*

Okun, Milton 1923?- *AmSCAP 66,*
EncFCWM 69, WhoE 79, −81

Okun, Milton Theodore 1923-
WhoAm 84

Olander, Joseph D *ScF&FL 1*

Olcheski, Bill 1925- *ConAu 8NR,*
−61

Olcott, Henry Steel 1832-1907
Alli, −SUP, AmAu&B, AmBi,
BiDPara, BioIn 4, −8, −9, ConAu 118,
DcAmB, DcAmReB, DcNAA,
EncO&P 2, −78, NatCAB 8, OhA&B,
WhAm 1, WorAl

Oldham, Mary 1944- *ConAu 109*

O'Leary, Liam 1910- *BiDIrW,*
ConAu 109, DcIrW 2, IntAu&W 77,
−86, WrDr 76, −80, −82, −84, −86

Oleksy, Walter 1930- *ConAu 1NR,*
−17NR, −45, SmATA 33[port]

Olenick, Richard Peter 1951-
AmM&WS 86P

Oles, Carole *DrAP&F 85*

Olesker, J Bradford *BioIn 10*

Olesky, Walter 1930- *SmATA X*

Olesky, Walter *see also* Oleksy, Walter

Olfson, Lewy 1937- *ConAu 93, NatPD*

Oliver, Anthony 1923- *ConAu 20NR,*
HalFC 84, IntAu&W 86

Oliver, Carl Russell 1941- *ConAu 106*

Oliver, Jane 1903-1970 *Au&Wr 71,*
AuBYP, BioIn 8, ChhPo, ConAu X

Oliver, Jane *see also* Rees, Helen
Christina Easson

Oliver, John E 1933- *WrDr 86*

Oliver, John Edward 1933-
AmM&WS 86P, IntAu&W 86,
WhoMW 86

Oliver, Mary *DrAP&F 85*

Oliver, Mary 1935- *BioIn 12,*
ChhPo S2, ConAu 9NR, −21R,
ConLC 19, −34, ConPo 85, DcLB 5,
IntAu&W 77, −82, IntWWP 77,
WhoAm 74, −76, −78, −80, −82, −84,
−86, WhoAmW 83, −87, WrDr 76,
−80, −82, −84, −86

Oliver, Roland 1923- *Au&Wr 71,*
BlueB 76, ConAu 73, IntAu&W 76,
−77, −82, IntWW 74, −75, −76, −77,
−78, −79, −80, −81, −82, −83, Who 74,
−82, −83, WhoWor 78, WrDr 76, −80,
−82, −84

Olivier, Laurence *NewYTBS 86[port]*

Olivier, Laurence 1907- *ConAu 111,*
HalFC 84[port], OxAmT 84

Olney, Ross Robert 1929- *AuBYP,*
BioIn 11, ConAu 7NR, −13R,
IntAu&W 77, −82, ScF&FL 1, −2,
SmATA 13, WhoWest 76, −78,
WrDr 76, −80, −82, −84, −86

Olsen, Alfa-Betty 1947- *ConAu 103*

Olsen, Eugene E 1936- *ConAu 33R*

Olsen, Jack 1925- *BioIn 13, ConAu X,*
WhoAm 74, −76, −78, −80, −82, −84,
−86, WhoWor 82, −87

Olsen, Jack *see also* Olsen, John
Edward

Olsen, John Edward 1925-
ConAu 9NR, −17R, IndAu 1917

Olsen, John Edward *see also* Olsen,
Jack

Olsen, Theodore Victor 1932-
ConAu 1R, IntAu&W 86,
WhoMW 84, WrDr 76

Olsen, Viggo Norskov 1916-
ConAu 53, DrAS 74P, −78P, −82P,
WhoAm 82, −84, WhoRel 75,
WhoWest 82, −84

Olsen, Violet 1922- *ConAu 113*

Olson, David F 1938- *ConAu 49*

Olson, Eric 1944- *ConAu 53*

Olson, Eugene E 1936- *ConAu 33R,*
ScF&FL 1, UFOEn

Olson, Eugene E *see also* Steiger, Brad

Olson, Gene 1922- *AuBYP, BioIn 7,*
ConAu 106, SmATA 32[port]

Olson, McKinley C 1931- *WrDr 82*

Olson, Sigurd F 1899-1982
AmM&WS 73P, BioIn 6, −7, −8, −12,
−13, BlueB 76, ConAu 1R, −1NR,
−105, IntAu&W 82[port], MinnWr,
NewYTBS 82[port], OxCan,
WhoAm 74, −76, −78, WhoMW 74,
−76, WrDr 80, −82, −84

Olson, Sigurd Ferdinand 1889-1982
WhAm 8

Olson, Sigurd Ferdinand 1899-1982
NatLAC

Olson, Toby *DrAP&F 85*

Olson, Toby 1937- *ConAu 9NR, −65,*
ConLC 28[port], ConPo 80, −85,
IntAu&W 86, WrDr 82, −84, −86

O'Meara, Walter Andrew 1897-
AmAu&B, Au&Wr 71, BioIn 1, −4,
−5, −6, −10, ConAu 13R, CurBio 58,
MinnWr, ScF&FL 1, −2, WhoAm 74,
−76

Oneal, Zibby *ConAu X, SmATA X*

Oneal, Zibby 1934- *ChlLR 13[port],*
ConLC 30[port]

O'Neil, Robert M 1934- *BioIn 12,*
ConAu 106, DrAS 82P, WhoAm 82

O'Neil, Robert Marchant 1934-
WhoAm 86, WhoAmL 85,
WhoMW 84, WhoWor 87

O'Neil, Terry 1949- *BioIn 13,*
ConAu 61

O'Neill, David P 1918- *ConAu 17R*

O'Neill, Eugene 1888-1953 *AmAu&B,*
AmWr, ApCAB X, AtlBL, AuNews 1,
BioIn 1, −2, −3, −4, −5, −6, −7, −8, −9,
−10, −11, −12, BioNews 74,
Chambr 3, CmCal, CnDAL, CnMD,
CnMWL, CnThe, ConAmA,
ConAmL, ConAu 110, CroCD,
CyWA, DcAmB S5, DcLB 7[port],
DcLEL, Dis&D, EncAB-H,
EncWL, −2[port], EncWT, EvLB,
FilmgC, HalFC 84, LinLib L, −S,
LongCTC, MajMD 1, MakMC,
McGEWB, McGEWD, −84[port],
MemAm, ModAL, −S2, −S1,
ModWD, NatCAB 55, NewEOp 71,
NotNAT A, −B, ObitOF 79,
ObitT 1951, OxAmH, OxAmL, −83,
OxAmT 84, OxEng, −85, OxThe,
PenC AM, PIP&P, −A, RComWL,
REn, REnAL, REnWD,
TwCA, −SUP, TwCLC 1, −6[port],
TwCWr, WebAB, −79, WebE&AL,
WhDW, WhAm 3, WhE&EA,
WhThe, WhoTwCL, WorAl

O'Neill, Eugene Gladstone 1888-1953
BioIn 13, OxThe 83, WhoNob

O'Neill, Gerard K 1927- *ConAu 21NR*

O'Neill, Gerard Kitchen 1927-
AmM&WS 76P, −79P, −82P, −86P,
BioIn 11, −12, −13, ConAu 93,
CurBio 79, Future, IntAu&W 82,
WhoAm 74, −76, −78, −80, −82, −84,
−86, WhoWor 80, −82, −84, −87

O'Neill, Tip *BioIn 13*

O'Neill, William L 1935-
ConAu 12NR, WrDr 86

O'Neill, William Lawrence 1935-
ConAu 21R, DcLEL 1940,
DrAS 74H, −78H, −82H,
IntAu&W 77, −82, WhoAm 80, −82,
−84, −86, WhoE 79, −81, −83,
WrDr 76, −80, −82, −84

Onoda, Hiroo 1922- *BioIn 10,*
ConAu 108, NewYTBS 74

Opdyke, John Baker 1878-1956
AmAu&B, ObitOF 79

Opie, Iona 1923- *AnCL, Au&Wr 71,*
BioIn 9, −13, ChhPo, −S1, −S2, −S3,
ConAu 61, IntAu&W 76, −77, −82,
OxChL, SmATA 3, Who 82, −83,
WrDr 76, −80, −82, −84, −86

Opie, Peter 1918-1982 *AnObit 1982,*
AnCL, Au&Wr 71, BioIn 9, −13,
ChhPo S3, ConAu 2NR, −5R, −106,
IntAu&W 76, −77, −82, OxChL,
SmATA 28N, −3, Who 82, −83N,
WhoWor 78, WrDr 76, −80, −82

Opie, Peter Mason 1918-1982
OxEng 85

Oppenheim, A Leo 1904-1974
ConAu 49

Oppenheim, Shulamith 1930-
ConAu 73

Oppenheimer, Joan L 1925- *BioIn 13,*
ConAu 17NR, −37R, IntAu&W 82,
SmATA 28[port]

Orbach, Susie 1946- *ConAu 19NR, −85*

Orben, Robert 1927- *BioIn 9, −10,*
−12, −13, ConAu 81, NewYTET,
WhoAm 82, −84, −86, WhoS&SW 80,
−82, −84

Orczy, Baroness Emmuska *WomNov*

Orczy, Baroness Emmuska 1865-1947
AuBYP, BioIn 1, −4, −5, −8,
ConAu X, DcLEL, EncMys, EvLB,
InWom, LongCTC, NewC,
NotNAT B, REn, SmATA 40[port],
TelT, TwCA, −SUP, TwCWr, WhThe,
WhoLA

Ordish, George 1906- *WrDr 86*

Ordish, George 1908?- *Au&Wr 71,*
ConAu 9NR, −61, IntAu&W 76, −77,
WrDr 76, −80, −82, −84

Ordway, Frederick I, III 1927-
ConAu 20NR, WrDr 86

Ordway, Frederick Ira, III 1927-
AmM&WS 73P, −79P, BioIn 12,
BlueB 76, ConAu 5R, −5NR,
WhoAm 74, −76, −78, −80, −82, −84,
−86, WhoWor 74, WrDr 80, −82, −84

Orgel, Doris 1929- *AuBYP, AuNews 1,*
BioIn 8, −10, ChhPo S3, ConAu 2NR,
−45, FourBJA, SmATA 7,
TwCCW 78, −83, WrDr 84, −86

Orkin, Ruth 1921- *ConPhot,*
ICPEnP A, MacBEP, WhoAmA 82,
−84

Orkin, Ruth 1921-1985 *ConAu 114,*
−119, NewYTBS 85[port]

Orlob, Helen Seaburg 1908-
AuBYP SUP, ConAu 5R, WhoPNW

Ormond, Clyde 1906- *ConAu 9R*

Ormond, Clyde 1906-1985 *ConAu 115*

O'Rourke, Frank 1916- *AmAu&B,*
ConAu 114, −118, ScF&FL 1,
WrDr 84, −86

O'Rourke, William *DrAP&F 85*

O'Rourke, William 1945- *ConAu 1NR,*
−45, WhoAm 76, −78, −80, −82,
WhoE 75, WrDr 76, −80, −82, −84,
−86

Orr, Bobby *ConAu X, WhoAm 84, −86*

Orr, Bobby 1948- *BioIn 7, −8, −9, −10,*
−11, −12, CelR, ConAu 69,
NewYTBE 71, WorAl

Orr, Jack *AuBYP SUP, ChhPo*

Orr, Robert Thomas 1908-
AmM&WS 73P, −76P, −79P, −82P,
−86P, ConAu 33R, WhoAm 74, −76,
−78, −80, −82, −84, −86, WhoWest 74,
−76

Orrmont, Arthur 1922- *AuBYP SUP,*
ConAu 1R, −4NR, WhoCon 73,
WhoE 77, −79

Ortego, Philip D *DrAP&F 85*

Ortego, Philip D 1926- *DrAS 74E*

Ortiz, Simon J *DrAP&F 85*

Ortiz, Simon J 1941- *ConPo 80, −85,*
WrDr 82, −84, −86

Ortiz, Victoria 1942- *ConAu 107*

Ortzen, Leonard Edwin 1912-
Au&Wr 71, ConAu 114,
IntAu&W 76, WhoWor 76

Ortzen, Leonard Edwin 1912-1979
ConAu 118

Orwell, George *DcNaB 1941*

Orwell, George 1903-1950 *AtlBL,*
BioIn 1, −2, −3, −4, −5, −6, −7, −8, −9,
−10, −11, −12, −13, BritWr 7, CasWL,
CnMWL, ConAu X, CyWA,
DcAmSR, DcLB 15[port], DcLEL,
EncSF, EncWL, −2[port], EvLB,
HalFC 84, LinLib L, −LP, LongCEL,
LongCTC, MakMC, McGEWB,
ModBrL, −S2, −S1, NewC,
NewYTBE 72, Novels[port],
ObitOF 79, OxEng, −85, PenC ENG,
RAdv 1, REn, ScF&FL 1,
ScFSB[port], SmATA X,
TwCA, −SUP, TwCLC 2, −6[port],
−15[port], TwCSFW 86, TwCWr,
WebE&AL, WhDW, WhAm 4,
WhoSciF, WhoTwCL, WorAl

Osborne, Adam 1938?- *BioIn 13*

Osborne, Adam 1939- *AmM&WS 73P,*
BioIn 12, ConAu 109, LElec,
WhoFrS 84, WhoTech 84

Osborne, Adam 1940- *WhoAm 84*

Osborne, Charles 1927- *ConAu 13NR,*
−13R, ConPo 70, DcLEL 1940,
IntAu&W 76, −77, −82, IntWWM 77,
IntWWP 77, WhoAm 80, −82, −83, −85,
WhoMus 72, WrDr 76, −80, −82, −84,
−86

Osborne, David *ConAu X,*
TwCSFW 86, WrDr 86

Osborne, David 1935- *AuBYP, ConAu X, SmATA X, ThrBJA, WrDr 84*

Osborne, David *see also* Silverberg, Robert

Osborne, John Franklin 1907-1981 *AnObit 1981, BioIn 8, –9, –12, ConAu 108, –10NR, –61, NewYTBS 81[port], WhAm 7, WhoAm 74, –76, –78, –80*

Osborne, John James 1929- *Au&Wr 71, BiE&WWA, BioIn 4, –5, –6, –7, –8, –9, –10, –11, –12, BlueB 76, CasWL, CelR, CnMD, CnMWL, CnThe, ConAu 13R, ConDr 73, –77, –82, ConLC 1, –2, –5, –11, CroCD, DcLB 13[port], DcLEL 1940, EncWL, –2[port], EncWT, FilmgC, IntAu&W 76, –77, –82, IntMPA 77, –75, –76, –78, –79, –81, –82, –84, IntWW 74, –75, –76, –77, –78, –79, –80, –81, –82, –83, LinLib L, LongCEL, LongCTC, MakMC, McGEWB, McGEWD, –84[port], ModBrL, –S1, ModWD, NewC, NotNAT, –A, OxEng, –85, OxFilm, OxThe, –83, PenC ENG, PIP&P, RComWL, REn, REnWD, TwCWr, WebE&AL, WhDW, Who 74, –83, WhoAm 74, –76, –78, –80, –82, –84, –86, WhoHol A, WhoThe 72, –77, –81, WhoTwCL, WhoWor 74, –76, –78,*

–80, –82, –84, –87, WorAl, WorAu, WorEFlm, WrDr 76, –80, –82, –84

Osborne, Mary Pope 1949- *ConAu 111, IntAu&W 86, SmATA 41*

Osgood, Charles 1933- *BioIn 12, –13, ConAu X, EncTwCJ, WhoAm 80, –82, –84, –86*

Osgood, William E 1926- *AuBYP, BiDrLUS 70, ConAu 33R, SmATA 37, WhoLibS 55, –66*

Osis, Karlis 1917- *AmM&WS 73S, –78S, BiDPara, ConAu 85, EncO&P 2, –78, WhoE 81, –83*

Osmond, Marie 1959- *BioIn 11, –12, –13, ConAu 112, EncFCWM 83, IntMPA 79, –81, –82, –84, –86, WhoAm 78, –80, –82, –84, –86, WorAl*

Otis, Raymond 1900-1938 *AmAu&B, DcNAA*

Ott, Virginia 1917- *ConAu 77*

Ottley, Reginald *Au&Wr 71, AuBYP SUP, ConAu 93, FourBJA, OxChL, SmATA 26[port], TwCCW 78, WrDr 80, –82, –84*

Otto, James Howard 1912?-1972 *IndAu 1917*

Oughton, Frederick 1923- *Au&Wr 71, ConAu 1R*

Ouida *BioIn 13, DcNaB S2, WomNov*

Ouida 1839-1908 *BbD, BiD&SB, BioIn 1, –2, –3, –4, –5, –11, –12, BritAu 19, CasWL, CelCen,*

Chambr 3, CyWA, DcBiA, DcEnA, –AP, DcEnL, DcEuL, DcLB 18[port], DcLEL, EvLB, HalFC 84, HsB&A, InWom, IntDcWB, JBA 34, LinLib LP, –S, LongCTC, NewC, Novels, OxChL, OxEng, –85, PenC ENG, PseudAu, SmATA X, TelT, WhLit

Ouida *see also* DeLaRamee, Louise

Oursler, Fulton *TwCCr&M 85*

Oursler, Fulton 1893-1952 *AmAu&B, AuBYP, BioIn 1, –2, –3, –4, –6, –7, –8, CathA 1930, ConAu 108, CurBio 42, –52, DcAmB S5, DcCathB, DcSpL, EncAJ, NatCAB 45, NotNAT B, REn, REnAL, ScF&FL 1, TwCA SUP, TwCCr&M 80, WhAm 3, WhNAA*

Ousmane, Sembene 1923- *ConAu 117, SelBAAf*

Outlar, Jesse 1923- *WhoS&SW 73*

Overholser, Stephen 1944- *ConAu 16NR, –97, WhoAm 78, –80*

Overstreet, Harry Allen 1875-1970 *AmAu&B, BioIn 2, –3, –4, –9, –10, ConAu 29R, ConAu P-1, CurBio 50, –70, NatCAB 55, NewYTBE 70, ObitOF 79, REnAL, TwCA –SUP, WhAm 5, WhNAA*

Overton, Jenny 1942- *Au&Wr 71, ConAu 57, IntAu&W 77, SmATA 36, TwCCW 78, –83, WrDr 76, –80, –82, –84, –86*

Ovington, Ray *AuBYP, BioIn 8*

Owen, Betty Meek 1913- *ForWC 70*

Owen, Guy 1925-1981 *AnObit 1981, BioIn 12, –13, ConAu 1R, –3NR, –104, ConNov 76, –82, DcLB 5[port], DrAS 74E, –78E, –82E, IntAu&W 82, WhoAm 82, WhoS&SW 73, –80, WrDr 76, –80, –82, –84*

Owen, Guy, Jr. 1925-1981 *WhAm 8*

Owen, Wilfred 1912- *AmM&WS 73S, ConAu 37R*

Owens, Bill 1938- *ConAu 73, ConPhot, ICPEnP A*

Owens, Jesse 1913-1980 *AnObit 1980[port], BioIn 3, –4, –5, –6, –7, –8, –9, –10, –11, –12, –13, BioNews 74, ConAu 110, CurBio 56, –80N, Ebony 1, InB&W 85, LinLib S, McGEWB, NegAl 76, –83, NewYTBS 80[port], SelBAAf, SelBAAu, St&PR 75, WebAB, –79, WhDW, WhAm 7, WhScrn 83, WhoAm 76, –78, –80, WhoBlA 75, –77, WorAl*

Oz, Amos 1939- *ASpks, BioIn 9, –10, –11, –13, CasWL, ConAu 53, ConLC 5, –8, –11, –27[port], –33[port], CurBio 83[port], EncWL 2, IntAu&W 77, –82, –86, Novels, WhoWor 84, –87, WhoWorJ 72, –78, WorAu 1970, WrDr 76, –80, –82, –84, –86*

P

Pace, Mildred Mastin 1907-
*AuBYP SUP, BioIn 13, ConAu 5R,
–5NR, SmATA 29, –46*
Pack, Robert *DrAP&F 85*
Pack, Robert 1929- *AmAu&B,
AuBYP, BioIn 8, –10, –12, –13,
ChhPo, ConAu 1R, –3NR, ConLC 13,
ConPo 70, –75, –80, –85,
DcLB 5[port], IntWWP 77, LinLib L,
OxAmL 83, PenC AM, REnAL,
WhoAm 82, WorAu, WrDr 76, –80,
–82, –84, –86*
Packard, Edward 1931- *ConAu 114,
SmATA 47[port]*
Packard, Jerrold M 1943- *ConAu 106,
IntAu&W 86*
Packard, Vance 1914- *AmAu&B,
ASpks, AuNews 1, BioIn 4, –5, –6, –7,
–8, –10, –11, BioNews 74, BlueB 76,
CelR, ConAu 7NR, –9R, CurBio 58,
DcLEL 1940, IntAu&W 76, –77, –82,
IntWW 74, –75, –76, –77, –78, –79,
–80, –81, –82, –83, LinLib L, –S,
LongCTC, PolProf E, REnAL,
Who 74, –82, –83, –85, WhoAm 74,
–76, –78, –80, –82, WhoE 74,
WhoWor 74, –78, –80, –82, WorAl,
WorAu, WrDr 76, –80, –82, –84, –86*
Packer, Joy 1905-1977 *Au&Wr 71,
AuBYP, BioIn 2, –8, –10, ConAu 1R,
–3NR, DcLEL 1940, EncSoA,
IntAu&W 76, –77, TwCWr, Who 74,
WrDr 76*
Paddock, Paul 1907-1975 *BioIn 10,
ConAu 61, ConAu P-2, NewYTBS 75*
Paddock, William 1921-
AmM&WS 73P, ConAu 21R, Future
Padovano, Anthony John 1933-
*AmArt, DcCAA 71, –77, DcCAr 81,
WhoAm 78, –80, WhoAmA 73, –76,
–78, –80, –82, –84, WhoE 75, –77*
Padover, Saul K 1905-1981 *AmAu&B,
AmM&WS 73S, –78S,
AnObit 1981[port], BioIn 3, –12,
ConAu 2NR, –103, –49, CurBio 52,
–81N, IntAu&W 77,
NewYTBS 81[port], REnAL,
WhAm 7, WhE&EA, WhNAA,
WhoAm 74, –76, –78, –80,
WhoWor 74, WhoWorJ 72, –78*
Page, Bruce 1936- *BioIn 13,
IntWW 80, –81, –82, –83, Who 82,
–83, –85*
Page, Emma *WrDr 86*
Page, Gerald W 1939- *ConAu 93,
WhoHr&F*
Page, Lou Williams 1912- *AuBYP,
ConAu 5R, –5NR, SmATA 38*
Page, Thomas 1942- *ConAu 81,
EncSF, ScF&FL 1, –2*
Page, Thornton L 1913- *WhoTech 84*
Page, Thornton Leigh 1913-
*AmM&WS 73P, –76P, –79P, –82P,
–86P, ConAu 2NR, –5R, UFOEn.*

*WhoAm 74, –76, –78, –80, –82, –84,
–86, WhoS&SW 73, –86, WhoWor 74*
Pagels, Elaine Hiesey 1943-
*ConAu 2NR, –45, DrAS 74P, –78P,
–82P, WhoAm 80, –82, –84,
WhoAmW 77, –79, –81, –83, –85,
–87, WhoRel 75, –77*
Pagnol, Marcel 1894-1974 *HalFC 84*
Pagnol, Marcel 1895-1974
*BiE&WWA, BioIn 1, –4, –5, –6, –9,
–10, –11, –12, CasWL, ClDMEL,
CnMD, ConAu 49, CurBio 56, –74,
–74N, DcFM, EncWL, –2, EncWT,
EvEuW, FilmgC, IntAu&W 76, –77,
IntDcF 2, McGEWD, –84[port],
ModFrL, ModWD, MovMk,
NewYTBS 74, NotNAT A, –B,
ObitOF 79, ObitT 1971, OxFilm,
OxFr, PenC EUR, REn, TwCWr,
WhAm 6, WhThe, Who 74,
WhoWor 74, WorAu, WorEFlm*
Paige, Harry W 1922- *ConAu 113,
SmATA 35, –41[port]*
Paine, Albert Bigelow 1861-1937
*AmAu&B, AmBi, AuBYP SUP,
BiD&SB, BioIn 4, CarSB,
ChhPo, S1, S2, ConAu 108, DcAmAu, DcAmB S2,
DcNAA, JBA 34, LinLib L,
NatCAB 13, –28, OxAmL, –83,
OxChL, REn, REnAL, ScF&FL 1,
TwCA, TwCBDA, WhAm 1, WhNAA*
Paine, Lauran 1916- *Au&Wr 71,
ConAu 19NR, –45, IntAu&W 76,
ScF&FL 1, –2*
Paine, Roberta M 1925- *AuBYP SUP,
BioIn 11, ConAu 33R, SmATA 13,
WhoAmW 75, –77, –79*
Painter, Charlotte *DrAP&F 85,
IntAu&W 86, WrDr 86*
Painter, Charlotte 1926- *BioIn 10,
ConAu 1R, –3NR, WhoAmW 75,
WrDr 82, –84*
Painter, Nell Irvin 1942-
*ConAu 19NR, DrAS 82H,
InB&W 80, SelBAAf, WhoBlA 80*
Paisley, Tom 1932- *BioIn 11,
ChlLR 3, ConAu 15NR, –61,
SmATA X*
Paisley, Tom *see also* Bethancourt, T
Ernesto
Palder, Edward L 1922- *BioIn 10,
SmATA 5*
Paley, Alan L 1943- *ConAu 69*
Paley, Grace *DrAP&F 85*
Paley, Grace 1922- *AmAu&B,
AmWomWr, AuNews 1, BioIn 5, –8,
–9, –10, –11, –13, BioNews 74,
ConAu 13NR, –25R, ConLC 4, –6,
–37[port], ConNov 76, –82, –86,
CurBio 86[port], DcLB 28[port],
DcLEL 1940, WhoAm 76, –78, –80,
–82, –84, –86, WhoAmW 74, –70,
–72, –81, –83, –85, –87, WhoE 85,*

*WorAu 1970, WrDr 76, –80, –82,
–84, –86*
Palgrave, Francis Turner 1824-1897
*Alli, –SUP, BiD&SB, BioIn 2, –6, –9,
BritAu 19, CasWL, CelCen,
Chambr 3, ChhPo, –S1, –S2, –S3,
DcBiPP, DcEnA, –AP, DcEnL,
DcEuL, DcLB 35[port], DcLEL,
DcNaB S1, EvLB, NewC,
OxEng, –85, PenC ENG, REn,
WebE&AL*
Palin, Michael *BioIn 13*
Palin, Michael 1943- *BioIn 10, –11,
ConAu 107, ConLC 21[port],
HalFC 84*
Pall, Ellen Jane 1952- *ConAu 93*
Pallas, Norvin 1918- *BioIn 13,
ConAu 1R, –3NR, SmATA 23[port],
WrDr 76, –80, –82, –84*
Pallenberg, Corrado 1912- *ConAu 13R*
Palmer, Bernard 1914- *BioIn 13,
ConAu 7NR, –12NR, –57, ScF&FL 1,
–2, SmATA 26[port]*
Palmer, Dave Richard 1934-
WhoAm 84, –86
Palmer, Joan Lilian 1934-
IntAu&W 76, –77
Palmer, Lilli 1914- *BioIn 2, –9, –10,
–11, ConAu X, CurBio 51, FilmgC,
HalFC 84, InWom, IntMPA 77, –75,
–76, –78, –79, –81, –82, –84, –86,
IntWW 83, MotPP, MovMk,
NotNAT A, OxFilm, OxThe 83,
WhoAm 74, –76, –78, –80, –82, –84,
WhoAmW 74, –58, –64, –66, –68,
–70, –72, –83, WhoHol A,
WhoThe 72, –77, –81, WhoWor 74,
–76, WorAl, WorEFlm*
Palmer, Lilli 1914-1986 *ConTFT 3,
CurBio 86N, NewYTBS 86[port]*
Palmer, Robert Franklin, Jr. 1945-
WhoAm 82, –84, –86
Palmer, Robin 1911- *AuBYP, BioIn 7,
ConAu 109, SmATA 43*
Palmer, Roy 1932- *ConAu 8NR, –61*
Panati, Charles 1943- *ConAu 81*
Panella, Vincent 1939- *ConAu 97*
Panger, Daniel 1926- *ConAu 93*
Pankow, James 1947- *WhoAm 76, –78,
–80, –82, WhoRocM 82*
Pankow, James *see also* Chicago
Panov, Valery 1938?- *BioIn 10, –11,
–12, –13, BioNews 74, ConAu 102,
CurBio 74, WhoAm 82*
Panov, Valery 1939- *WhoWor 84, –87*
Panshin, Alexei 1940- *BioIn 12,
ConAu 57, ConSFA, DcLB 8[port],
EncSF, ScF&FL 1, –2, ScFSB,
TwCSFW 86, WhoAm 74, –76, –78,
–80, –82, –84, –86, WhoSciF,
WrDr 84, –86*
Panter, Carol 1936- *AuBYP SUP,
BioIn 11, ConAu 49, SmATA 9*
Panzarella, Andrew 1940- *ConAu 25R*

Papanek, Ernst 1900-1973 *BioIn 10,
ConAu 1R, –4NR, WhAm 6,
WhoE 74*
Paperny, Myra *OxCanL*
Paperny, Myra 1932- *BioIn 13,
ConAu 69, SmATA 33, WhoCanL 85*
Paperny, Myra Green 1932-
WhoAm 78
Pappas, Lou Seibert 1930-
ConAu 8NR, –61
Paradis, Adrian A 1912- *ConAu 18NR*
Paradis, Adrian Alexis 1912- *AuBYP,
BioIn 6, –7, –9, ConAu 1R, –3NR,
IntAu&W 77, –86, MorJA, SmATA 1,
WhoPubR 72, –76, WrDr 76, –80,
–82, –84, –86*
Parazaider, Walt 1948- *BioNews 74*
Parazaider, Walt *see also* Chicago
Parcells, Bill 1941- *BioIn 13*
Paredes, Americo 1915- *ChiLit,
ChiSch, ConAu 37R, DrAS 74E,
–78E, –82E, IntAu&W 77, –82,
WhoAm 82, –84, –86*
Parent, Gail 1940- *BioIn 10, –11, –12,
ConAu 101, WomWMM*
Parent, Gail 1941- *WhoAmW 85*
Parenteau, Shirley Laurolyn 1935
*ConAu 15NR, –85, WhoAmW 75,
–77*
Parenti, Michael 1933- *ConAu 73*
Pares, Marion Stapylton 1914-
*Au&Wr 71, ConAu 17R,
IntAu&W 76, –82, –86*
Pares, Marion Stapylton *see also*
Campbell, Judith
Paretti, Sandra *Au&Wr 71,
ConAu 7NR, –53*
Pargeter, Edith Mary 1913-
*Au&Wr 71, BlueB 76, ConAu 1R,
–4NR, IntAu&W 76, –77,
LongCTC, Novels, ScF&FL 1, –1A,
–2, TwCCr&M 80, WhE&EA,
Who 74, –82, –83, WhoWor 76,
WorAu, WrDr 76, –80, –82, –84*
Pargeter, Edith Mary *see also* Peters,
Ellis
Paris, Jeanne 1918- *ConAu 1R,
WhoAm 74, –76, WhoAmW 74, –72,
–79, WhoE 74*
Parisi, Joseph 1944- *ConAu 93,
DrAS 78E, –82E, WhoAm 86*
Park, Brad 1948- *BioIn 9, –10, –11,
CurBio 76, WorAl*
Park, Ruth *BioIn 13, OxChL,
WrDr 86*
Park, Ruth 1920?- *Au&Wr 71,
BioIn 3, –6, CathA 1952, ConAu 105,
InWom, SingR 2, SmATA 25,
TwCCW 78, –83, TwCWr, WrDr 80,
–82, –84*
Park, Ruth 1923?- *OxAusL*
Parker, Barry 1935- *ConAu 112*
Parker, Brant Julian 1920-
*ConAu 114, EncTwCJ, WhoAm 78,
–80, –82, –84, –86, WorECom*

123

Payne, Donald Gordon *see also*
Marshall, James Vance
Payne, Robert 1911-1969 *AmAu&B,*
Au&Wr 71, BioIn 4, −5, −6, −7, −8,
−9, −11, ConAu 25R, CurBio 47,
ScF&FL 1, −2, WhoE 74,
WhoWor 74, −76
Paz, Octavio 1914- *BioIn 6, −9, −10,*
−12, −13, CasWL, CnMWL,
ConAu 73, ConFLW 84, ConLC 3,
−4, −6, −10, −19, CurBio 74,
DcCLAA, EncLatA, EncWL, −2[port],
GrFLW, IntAu&W 76, −77,
IntWW 74, −75, −76, −77, −78, −79,
−80, −81, −82, −83, IntWWP 77,
LinLib L, ModLAL, OxSpan,
PenC AM, TwCWr, Who 74, −82,
−83, −85, WhoAm 74, −76, −78,
WhoTwCL, WhoWor 74, −78, −80,
−82, −84, −87, WorAl, WorAu
Peake, Lilian *WrDr 86*
Peake, Lilian 1924- *ConAu 115,*
IntAu&W 76, −77X, −82X, WrDr 84
Pearce, Mary E 1932- *ConAu 69,*
IntAu&W 77, WrDr 76, −80, −82,
−84, −86
Pearce, Mary Emily 1932-
IntAu&W 86
Pearce, Philippa *IntAu&W 86X,*
ScFSB, Who 85, WrDr 86
Pearce, Philippa 1920- *AuBYP,*
ChlLR 9[port], ConAu 5R, −X,
ConLC 21[port], SenS, SmATA 1,
ThrBJA, Who 82, −83
Pearcy, George Etzel 1905-1980
AmM&WS 73S, ConAu 1R, −3NR,
IndAu 1917, WhAm 7, WhoAm 74,
−76, −78
Peare, Catherine Owens 1911-
Au&Wr 71, AuBYP, BioIn 5, −6, −7,
−11, ConAu 5R, CurBio 59, InWom,
MorJA, SmATA 9, WhoAmW 58,
−61, −64
Pearl, Bill 1931?- *BioIn 13*
Pearl, Jack 1923- *ConAu X*
Pearl, Jack *see also* Pearl, Jacques Bain
Pearl, Jacques Bain 1923- *ConAu 5R*
Pearl, Richard Maxwell 1913-1980
AmM&WS 73P, −76P, −79P, AuBYP,
BioIn 7, −12, ConAu 3NR, −9R,
WhAm 7, WhoAm 76, −78, −80,
WhoWor 80
Pearlman, Moshe 1911- *ConAu 5R,*
−X, IntAu&W 76, WhoWor 74, −76,
WhoWorJ 72, WrDr 76, −80, −82,
−84, −86
Pearsall, Ronald 1927- *ChhPo S2,*
ConAu 14NR, −21R, IntAu&W 77,
WhoWor 76, WrDr 76, −80, −82, −84,
−86
Pearson, Norman Holmes 1909-1975
AmAu&B, BioIn 10, ConAu 61,
ConAu P-1, DrAS 74E, NewYTBS 75,
WhAm 6, WhoAm 74, −76,
WhoGov 72, −75, WhoWor 74,
WrDr 76
Peary, Danny *ConAu X*
Peary, Robert Edwin 1856-1920
BioIn 13, MemAm
Pease, Howard 1894-1974 *AmAu&B,*
AuBYP, BioIn 1, −2, −7, −9, −10, −13,
ConAu 5R, −106, JBA 34, −51,
REnAL, SmATA 2, −25N,
TwCCW 78, −83, WhoAm 74, −76
Peattie, Donald Culross 1898-1964
AmAu&B, AuBYP, BioIn 2, −3, −4,
−7, ConAmA, ConAu 102, CurBio 40,
−65, DcAmB S7, DcLEL, InSci,
LinLib L, MnBBF, OxAmL, −83,
REnAL, TwCA, −SUP, WhAm 4,
WhE&EA, WhNAA
Peavy, Linda *DrAP&F 85*
Peavy, Linda 1943- *ConAu 109*
Peccei, Aurelio d1984
NewYTBS 84[port]
Peccei, Aurelio 1908- *BioIn 12,*
Future, IntWW 74, −75, −76, −77,
−78, −79, −80, −81, −82, −83,
WhoWor 74
Peccei, Aurelio 1908-1984
AnObit 1984, BioIn 13, ConAu 112

Peck, Anne Merriman 1884-
AmAu&B, ArtsAmW 3, AuBYP,
BioIn 1, −2, −5, −8, −12, ChhPo, −S1,
ConAu 77, IlsCB 1744, −1946,
InWom, JBA 34, −51, SmATA 18
Peck, Ira 1922- *ConAu 77*
Peck, Ralph H *ConAu 69*
Peck, Richard *DrAP&F 85*
Peck, Richard 1934- *BioIn 12, −13,*
ChhPo S2, ConAu 19NR, −85,
ConLC 21[port], FifBJA[port],
IntAu&W 82, OxChL, SmATA 18,
SmATA 2AS[port], TwCCW 78, −83,
WhoAm 80, −82, −84, −86, WrDr 80,
−82, −84, −86
Peck, Richard E 1936- *ConAu 81,*
DrAS 74E, −78E, −82E, EncSF,
ScFSB
Peck, Robert McCracken 1952-
ConAu 112, IntAu&W 86
Peck, Robert Newton *WrDr 86*
Peck, Robert Newton 1928-
AuBYP SUP, BioIn 12, ConAu 1R,
−81, ConLC 17, FifBJA[port],
SmATA 21[port], SmATA 1AS[port],
TwCCW 78, −83, WrDr 80, −82, −84
Pedersen, Elsa Kienitz 1915- *AuBYP,*
BioIn 8, ConAu 1R, −2NR,
ForWC 70
Peek, Dan *WhoRocM 82*
Peek, Dan *see also* America
Peek, Walter W 1922- *ConAu 45*
Peekner, Ray *DrAP&F 85, WrDr 82,*
−84, −86
Pei, Mario Andrew 1901-1978
AmAu&B, AmCath 80, BiDInt,
BioIn 3, −4, −8, −9, −11, −12,
ConAu 5R, −5NR, −77, CurBio 68,
−78, −78N, DrAS 74F, LinLib L,
NatCAB 60[port], ObitOF 79,
REnAL, ScF&FL 1, −2, TwCA SUP,
WhAm 7, WhoAm 74, −76, −78,
WhoWor 74, WrDr 76
Peirce, Neal R 1932- *ConAu 21NR,*
−25R, WhoAm 76, −78, −80, −82,
−84, −86, WhoS&SW 73,
WhoWor 80, −82, WrDr 76, −80, −82,
−84, −86
Peissel, Michel 1936?- *BioIn 13*
Peissel, Michel 1937- *ConAu 12NR,*
−25R
Pelissier, Roger 1924-1972
ConAu 37R, ConAu P-2
Pell, Arthur Robert 1920-
ConAu 11NR, −29R, WhoAm 74,
−76, −78, −80, −82, −84, WhoS&SW,
WhoE 74, WhoF&I 74, −75
Pell, Derek *DrAP&F 85*
Pell, Derek 1947- *ConAu 77,*
IntAu&W 82, IntWWP 82, WhoE 81
Pell, Eve 1937- *ConAu 33R*
Pelletier, Jean 1935- *AmCath 80,*
CanWW 83, WhoAm 80, −82, −84,
−86, WhoE 81, −83, −85, WhoFr 79,
WhoWor 82
Pelta, Kathy 1928- *BioIn 12,*
ConAu 85, SmATA 18
Peltier, Leslie Copus 1900-1980
AmM&WS 73P, −76P, −79P, BioIn 1,
−2, −7, −11, −12, ConAu 17R,
SmATA 13
Pelton, Robert W 1934- *ConAu 29R*
Penfield, Thomas 1903- *ConAu 5R*
Penner, Dick 1936- *DrAS 82E*
Pennington, Howard 1923- *ConAu 49*
Penrod, James Wilford 1934-
WhoAm 82, −84, −86, WhoWest 80
Pentecost, Hugh *ConAu X, WrDr 86*
Pentecost, Hugh 1903- *TwCCr&M 85*
Pentecost, Hugh *see also* Philips,
Judson P
Penzler, Otto M 1942- *ConAu 81,*
IntAu&W 86, −77
Penzler, Otto M *see also* Adler, Irene
Pepe, Phil 1935- *ConAu 18NR, −25R,*
SmATA 20
Peper, George Frederick 1950-
ConAu 108, IntAu&W 86,
WhoAm 80, −82, −84, −86, WhoE 83,
−86
Peple, Edward Henry 1869-1924
AmAu&B, DcNAA, ScF&FL 1,
WhAm 1
Percival, John 1927- *ConAu 33R*

Percy, Walker *DrAP&F 85*
Percy, Walker 1916- *AmAu&B,*
AmCath 80, BioIn 9, −10, −11, −12,
−13, ConAu 1R, −1NR, ConLC 2, −3,
−6, −8, −14, −18, ConNov 72, −76,
−82, −86, CurBio 76, DcLB 2,
−Y80A[port], DcLEL 1940, EncSoH,
EncWL, −2, IntAu&W 76, −77,
LinLib L, ModAL, −S2, −S1,
NewYTBS 80[port], Novels,
OxAmL, −83, RAdv 1, ScF&FL 1, −2,
TwCSFW 86, WebE&AL,
WhoAm 74, −76, −78, −80, −82, −84,
−86, WhoS&SW 73, −75,
WhoWor 74, WorAl, WorAu,
WrDr 76, −80, −82, −84, −86
Perelman, S J 1904-1979 *AmAu&B,*
Au&Wr 71, AuNews 1, −2,
BiE&WWA, BioNews 75, BlueB 76,
CelR, CnDAL, ConAu 18NR, −73,
−89, ConDr 73, −77, ConLC 3, −5,
−9, −15, −23[port], CurBio 71, −80N,
DcLB 11[port], −44[port], DcLEL,
FilmgC, HalFC 84, LongCTC,
McGEWD, −83, NewYTBE 70, −72,
NewYTBS 79, NotNAT, Novels,
OxAmL, −83, OxAmT 84, PenC AM,
RAdv 1, REn, REnAL, TwCA, −SUP,
TwCWr, WebE&AL, Who 74, WorAl,
WrDr 76, −80
Perelman, Sidney Joseph 1904-1979
BioIn 3, −4, −5, −6, −7, −8, −9, −10,
−11, −12, −13, IntAu&W 76, −77,
IntWW 74, −75, −76, −77, −78, −79,
WebAB, −79, WhDW, WhAm 7,
WhoAm 74, −76, −78, −80,
WhoWor 74, −78, WorECar
Peretz, Don 1922- *AmM&WS 73S,*
−78S, ConAu 4NR, −9R, −19NR,
IntAu&W 77, −82, WhoAmJ 80,
WhoWorJ 72, −78
Perez, Norah A *OxCan SUP*
Perkins, Charles Elliott 1881-1943
NatCAB 32, WhAm 2
Perkins, David 1928- *WhoAm 84, −86*
Perkins, Edwin Judson 1939-
ConAu 106, DrAS 74H, −78H, −82H
Perkins, Marlin 1905- *BioIn 3, −7,*
−12, −13, ConAu 103, LinLib L, −S,
SmATA 21[port], WebAB, −79,
WhoAm 74, −76, −78, −80
Perkins, Marlin 1905-1986
ConAu 119, SmATA 48N
Perl, Lila *AuBYP, BioIn 8, −10,*
ConAu 33R, SmATA 6
Perl, Teri 1926- *ConAu 19NR, −93*
Perlberg, Deborah 1948- *ConAu 118*
Perlman, Anne S *DrAP&F 85*
Pernoud, Regine 1909- *ConAu 102*
Perrault, Charles 1628-1703 *BioIn 13,*
DcBiPP, LitC 2[port], Novels, OxChL,
OxEng 85, SmATA 25[port]
Perrett, Geoffrey 1940- *ConAu 4NR,*
−53
Perrin, Blanche Chenery 1894?-1973
BioIn 9, −10, ConAu 5R, −41R
Perrin, Noel 1927- *AmAu&B,*
Au&Wr 71, ConAu 13R, DrAS 74E,
−78E, −82E, IntAu&W 76, −77,
WhoAm 84, −86, WhoE 75,
WorAu 1975[port]
Perry, George 1935- *BiDBrA,*
ConAu 103, IntAu&W 77, −82,
WrDr 76, −80, −82, −86
Perry, Jim 1942- *ConAu 53*
Perry, Richard 1909- *ConAu 41R,*
WhE&EA
Persico, Joseph E 1930- *ConAu 21NR,*
−93, IntAu&W 82, −86, WhoAm 80,
−82, −84, −86
Persico, Joseph Edward 1930-
WhoAm 84, −86
Perske, Robert 1927- *ConAu 106*
Pesek, Ludek 1919- *ConAu 29R,*
ScF&FL 1, −2
Peter, Laurence J 1919- *ConAu 17NR,*
DcLB 53[port]
Peter, Laurence Johnston 1919-
AmM&WS 73S, Au&Wr 71, BioIn 8,
−10, ConAu 17R, IntAu&W 76, −77,
−82, LEduc 74, WhoAm 74, −76, −78,
−80, −82, −84, −86, WrDr 80, −82,
−84

Peters, Charles 1926- *BioIn 13,*
DcAfL, WhoAm 82
Peters, Daniel 1948- *ConAu 15NR,*
−85
Peters, Donald Leslie 1925-
ConAu 21R, IntAu&W 76, −77,
WhoWest 74, −76
Peters, Elizabeth *WrDr 86*
Peters, Elizabeth 1927- *ConAu 57, −X,*
TwCCr&M 80, −85, WrDr 76, −82,
−84
Peters, Elizabeth *see also* Mertz,
Barbara Gross
Peters, Ellis *Who 85, WrDr 86*
Peters, Ellis 1913- *ConAu X,*
IntAu&W 76X, −77X, −82X, Novels,
TwCCr&M 80, −85, Who 82, −83,
WorAu, WrDr 76, −80, −82, −84
Peters, Ellis *see also* Pargeter, Edith
Mary
Peters, Ken 1929- *ConAu 17R*
Peters, Margaret Evelyn 1936-
ConAu 53
Peters, Mike 1943- *ConAu X,*
WorECar
Peters, S H 1862-1910 *ConAu X,*
YABC X
Peters, S H *see also* Porter, William
Sydney
Peters, William 1921- *ConAu 20NR,*
ConTFT 2, WhoAm 84, −86
Petersen, P J 1941- *ConAu 112,*
IntAu&W 86, SmATA 43, −48[port]
Peterson, Harold Leslie 1922-1978
BioIn 2, −11, ConAu 1R, −4NR,
DrAS 74H, EncAAH, SmATA 8,
WhoS&SW 76, WrDr 76
Peterson, Levi S 1933- *ConAu 109,*
DrAS 74E, −78E, −82E
Peterson, Levi Savage 1933-
IntAu&W 86
Peterson, Ottis 1907- *ConAu 21R*
Peterson, P J *WhoOcn 78*
Peterson, Robert W 1925?-
ConAu 33R, WhoAmP 83
Peterson, Roger Tory *AmM&WS 86P*
Peterson, Roger Tory 1908- *AmArt,*
AmAu&B, AmM&WS 76P, −79P,
−82P, BioIn 4, −5, −6, −7, −8, −10,
−11, −12, BlueB 76, CelR, ConAu 1R,
−1NR, CurBio 59, InSci,
IntAu&W 77, −82, IntWW 74, −75,
−76, −77, −78, −79, −80, −81, −82,
−83, LinLib L, NatLAC,
NewYTBS 74, −80[port], REnAL,
TwCA SUP, WebAB, −79,
WhoAm 74, −76, −78, −80, −82, −84,
−86, WhoAmA 76, −78, −80, −82, −84,
WhoWor 74
Petesch, Natalie L M *ConAu 6NR,*
−21NR, −57, DrAP&F 85,
IntAu&W 86
Petrakis, Harry Mark *DrAP&F 85*
Petrakis, Harry Mark 1923-
AmAu&B, BioIn 10, ConAu 4NR,
−9R, ConLC 3, ConNov 72, −76, −82,
−86, IntAu&W 76, −77, −82,
WhoAm 74, −76, −78, −80, −82, −84,
−86, WhoWor 74, WrDr 76, −80, −82,
−84, −86
Petrosky, Anthony *DrAP&F 85*
Petrovskaya, Kyra 1918- *BioIn 5, −11,*
ConAu X, −X, SmATA 8
Petrovskaya, Kyra *see also* Wayne,
Kyra Petrovskaya
Petry, Ann *DrAP&F 85, WhoBlA 85*
Petry, Ann 1908?- *AmNov,*
AmWomM, AnCL, AuBYP, BioIn 1,
−2, −3, −4, −6, −7, −9, −10, BlkAWP,
ChlLR 12[port], ConAu 4NR, −5R,
ConAu 6AS[port], ConLC 1, −7, −18,
ConNov 72, −76, −82, −86, CurBio 46,
DcLEL 1940, InB&W 80, InWom,
IntAu&W 76, −82, −86, LinLib L,
LivgBAA, NegAl 76, −83, OxChL,
REn, REnAL, SelBAAu, SmATA 5,
ThrBJA, TwCA SUP, TwCCW 78,
−83, WhoAmW 74, −58, −70, −72,
WhoBlA 77, −80, WrDr 76, −80, −82,
−84, −86
Petry, Ann 1911- *OxAmL 83*
Pettersson, Allan 1911-1980
AnObit 1980, WhoWor 80
Pettit, Florence H *AuBYP SUP*

ScF&FL 1, SmATA 21[port],
WhoAm 74
Platt, Rutherford 1894-1975 *BioIn 10,*
ConAu 61, NewYTBS 75, OhA&B,
WhAm 6
Player, Gary 1935- *BioIn 5, -6, -7,*
-8, -9, -10, -11, -12, -13,
BioNews 74, CelR, ConAu 101,
CurBio 61, EncSoA, IntWW 76, -77,
-78, -79, -80, -81, -82, -83,
NewYTBS 74, -78, -86[port],
Who 82, -83, -85, WhoAm 74, -76,
-78, -80, -82, WhoGolf, WhoWor 74,
-78, -80, -82, WorAl
Playfair, Guy Lyon 1935- *ConAu 106*
Pleasants, Henry 1910- *AmAu&B,*
Baker 84, ConAu 107, IntAu&W 77,
-82, -86, WhoAm 78, -80, -82, -84,
-86, WrDr 76, -80, -82, -84, -86
Plimpton, George 1927- *AuNews 1,*
BioIn 4, -6, -7, -8, -9, -10, -11, -12,
-13, BlueB 76, CelR, ConAu 21R,
ConLC 36[port], CurBio 69,
LinLib L, NewYTBE 70, SmATA 10,
WebAB, -79, WhoAm 74, -76, -78,
-80, -82, WhoHol A, WhoWor 74,
WrDr 80, -82, -84, -86
Plimpton, George Ames 1927-
EncTwCJ, WhoAm 84, -86
Plotz, Helen Ratnoff 1913-
ChhPo, -S1, ConAu 8NR, -9R,
WhoAmW 72
Plowden, Alison 1931- *ConAu 15NR,*
-33R, WrDr 76, -80, -82, -84, -86
Plowden, David 1932- *BioIn 11,*
ConAu 33R, ConPhot, ICPEnP A,
MacBEP
Plowman, Edward E 1931-
ConAu 37R, WhoRel 75, -77,
WrDr 76, -80, -82, -84, -86
Plowman, Stephanie *OxChL*
Plowman, Stephanie 1922- *BioIn 10,*
ConAu 5NR, -53, SmATA 6,
TwCCW 78, -83, WrDr 76, -80, -82,
-84, -86
Plumb, John Harold 1911- *Au&Wr 71,*
BioIn 10, ConAu 5R, DcLEL 1940,
IntAu&W 77, -82, -86, IntWW 74,
-75, -76, -77, -78, -79, -80, -81,
-82, -83, LongCTC, Who 74, -82,
-83, WhoWor 82, WorAu, WrDr 76,
-80, -82, -84
Plummer, Beverly J 1918- *ConAu 29R,*
WhoAmW 75, WrDr 76, -80, -82,
-84
Plumpp, Sterling D 1940-
DcLB 41[port]
Plumpp, Sterling Dominic 1940-
BlkAWP, BroadAu, ConAu 5R,
InB&W 80, IntAu&W 76, SelBAAf,
SelBAAu, WhoBlA 77, -80
Plumpp, Sterling Dominic 1941-
WhoBlA 85
Plunkett, Jim 1947- *BioIn 9, -10, -11,*
-12, -13, CelR, CmCal, CurBio 71,
-82[port], NewYTBE 70, -71,
NewYTBS 81[port], WhoAm 74,
WhoFtbl 74
Plunkett, Jim 1948-
NewYTBS 84[port]
Podlecki, Anthony Joseph 1936-
IntAu&W 86, WhoAm 84, -86
Poe, Charlsie 1909- *ConAu P-2*
Poe, Edgar Allan 1809-1849 *Alli,*
AmAu, AmAu&B, AmBi, AmWr,
AnCL, ApCAB, AtlBL, BbD,
BiD&SB, BiDSA, BioIn 1, -2, -3, -4,
-5, -6, -7, -8, -9, -10, -11, -12, -13,
CasWL, CelCen, Chambr 3,
ChhPo, -S1, -S2, -S3, CnDAL,
CnE&AP, CrtT 3, -4, CyAL 2,
CyWA, DcAmAu, DcAmB, DcBiA,
DcBiPP, DcEnA, DcEnL, DcLB 3,
-59[port], DcLEL, DcNAA, Dis&D,
Drake, EncAB-H, EncAJ, EncMys,
EncO&P 78, EncSF, EncSoH, EvLB,
FilmgC, HalFC 84, HarEnUS,
LinLib L, -S, McGEWB, MemAm,
MnBBF, MorMA, MouLC 3,
NatCAB 1, NewEOp 71,
NinCLC 1[port], NotNAT B,
Novels[port], OxAmH, OxAmL, -83,
OxAmT 84, OxEng, -85, PenC AM,

RAdv 1, RComWL, REn, REnAL,
ScF&FL 1, ScFSB[port],
SmATA 23[port], Str&VC, SupFW,
TwCBDA, TwCCr&M 80A, -85A,
WebAB, -79, WebE&AL, WhDW,
WhAm HS, WhoHr&F, WhoSciF,
WhoSpyF, WorAl
Pohl, Frederik *DrAP&F 85*
Pohl, Frederik 1919- *AmAu&B,*
BioIn 10, -11, -12, -13,
ConAu 11NR, -41, ConAu 1AS[port],
ConLC 18, ConNov 72, -76, -82, -86,
ConSFA, DcLB 8[port], EncSF,
Future, IntAu&W 76, -77, -82,
LinLib L, Novels, PenC AM,
ScF&FL 1, -2, ScFSB[port],
SmATA 24, TwCSFW 86,
WhoAm 74, -76, -78, -80, -86,
WhoSciF, WorAl, WorAu, WrDr 76,
-80, -82, -84, -86
Pohlmann, Lillian 1902- *AuBYP,*
BioIn 8, ConAu 9R, ForWC 70,
SmATA 11, -8, WrDr 76, -80, -82,
-84
Pointer, Larry 1940- *ConAu 101*
Poirier, Richard 1925- *AmAu&B,*
BlueB 76, ConAu 1R, -3NR,
ConLCrt, -82, DcLEL 1940,
DrAS 74E, -78E, -82E,
IntAu&W 86, WhoAm 74, -76, -78,
-80, -82, -84, -86, WhoE 74,
WorAu 1970, WrDr 76, -80, -82, -84, -86
Poitier, Sidney 1924?- *BiDFilm,*
BiE&WWA, BioIn 4, -5, -6, -7, -8,
-9, -10, -11, -12, BioNews 74,
BlueB 76, CelR, CivR 74,
ConLC 26[port], CurBio 59, DrBlPA,
Ebony 1, FilmgC, HalFC 84,
InB&W 80, -85, IntMPA 77, -75,
-76, -78, -79, -81, -82, -84, -86,
IntWW 74, -75, -76, -77, -78, -79,
-80, -81, -82, -83, LinLib L, MotPP,
MovMk, NegAl 76[port], -83[port],
NotNAT, OxFilm, Who 74, -82, -83,
WhoAm 74, -76, -78, -80, -82,
WhoBlA 75, -77, -80, WhoHol A,
WhoThe 72, -77, -81, WhoWor 74,
-78, WorAl
Poitier, Sidney 1927- *ConAu 117,*
ConTFT 2[port], SelBAAf, Who 85,
WhoAm 84, -86, WhoBlA 85
Polatnick, Florence 1923- *BioIn 10,*
ConAu 29R, SmATA 5
Polenberg, Richard 1937- *ConAu 21R,*
DrAS 74H, -78H, -82H, WhoAm 74,
-76, -78, -80, WhoAmJ 80,
WhoE 74, WrDr 82, 84, -86
Polgreen, John *IlsBYP*
Polk, Dora 1923- *ConAu 49*
Polking, Kirk *IntAu&W 86X*
Polking, Kirk 1925- *ConAu 12NR,*
WhoMW 84, WrDr 86
Pollack, Peter 1909-1978 *ICPEnP,*
MacBEP
Pollack, Peter 1911-1978 *BioIn 11,*
ConAu 77, -81, WhoAmA 73, -76,
-78, -80N, -82N, -84N
Polland, Madeleine A 1918- *AuBYP,*
BioIn 7, -9, -10, ConAu 3NR, -5R,
SmATA 6, ThrBJA, TwCCW 78, -83,
WrDr 80, -82, -84
Polland, Madeleine Angela 1918-
IntAu&W 86
Pollard, Jack 1926- *ConAu 29R*
Pollock, Bruce 1945- *ConAu 7NR,*
-57, SmATA 46
Pollowitz, Melinda 1944- *BioIn 13,*
ConAu 77, SmATA 26[port]
Polmar, Norman 1938- *Au&Wr 71,*
ConAu 49, IntAu&W 77
Polner, Murray 1928- *ConAu 5NR,*
-13R
Polvay, Marina 1928- *BioIn 12,*
IntAu&W 82, WhoAmW 83
Pomerance, Bernard 1940-
ConAu 101, ConDr 82, ConLC 13,
WrDr 84, -86
Pomeroy, Earl *WhoAmP 85*
Pomeroy, Earl 1915- *AmAu&B,*
CmCal, ConAu 17R, DrAS 74H,
-78H, -82H, RENAW, WhoAm 74,
-76, -78, -80, -82, -84, -86,
WhoAmP 81, WhoPNW
Pomeroy, Pete *SmATA X*

Pomeroy, Pete 1925- *AuBYP SUP,*
ConAu X, SmATA X
Pomeroy, Pete *see also* Roth, Arthur J
Pomeroy, Wardell Baxter 1913-
AmM&WS 73S, -78S, BioIn 10,
ConAu 1R, -1NR, CurBio 74,
IndAu 1917, WhoAm 74, -76, -78,
-80, -82, -84, -86
Pond, John Hamilton 1923-
WhoF&I 74, -75, -77
Ponsot, Marie B 1922- *ConAu 9R,*
ForWC 70, WhoAmW 70
Poole, Frederick King 1934- *BioIn 9,*
ConAu 25R
Poole, Gary Thomas 1931-
ConAu 107, WhoAm 74, WhoF&I 74
Poole, Gray Johnson 1906-
AuBYP, -SUP, BioIn 7, -9,
ConAu 5R, -6NR, IntAu&W 76,
SmATA 1
Poole, Josephine *IntAu&W 86X,*
ScF&FL 1A
Poole, Josephine 1933- *Au&Wr 71,*
BioIn 10, ConAu 10NR, -21R,
ConLC 17, IntAu&W 76, -77,
ScF&FL 1, -2, SmATA 5,
SmATA 2AS[port], TwCCW 78, -83,
WrDr 76, -80, -82, -84, -86
Poole, Lynn 1910-1969 *AmAu&B,*
AuBYP, -SUP, BioIn 3, -6, -7, -8,
-9, ConAu 5R, CurBio 54, -69,
MorJA, SmATA 1, WhAm 5
Poole, Victoria 1927- *ConAu 102*
Poortvliet, Rien 1933?- *BioIn 12,*
SmATA 37
Pope, Clifford Hillhouse 1899-1974
AmAu&B, AmM&WS 73P,
Au&Wr 71, AuBYP, BioIn 7,
ConAu 1R, -103, WhAm 6,
WhoAm 74
Pope, Dudley Bernard Egerton 1925-
Au&Wr 71, BioIn 10, ConAu 2NR,
-5R, DcLEL 1940, IntAu&W 76,
-77, -82, Who 74, -82, -83, -85,
WhoE 74, WhoWor 74, WorAu,
WrDr 76, -80, -82, -84
Pope, Elizabeth Marie 1917-
AuBYP SUP, ConAu 49, DrAS 74E,
-78E, -82E, FifBJA[port],
ScF&FL 1A, SmATA 36, -38,
WhoAmW 58, -68, -70
Pope-Hennessy, John 1913- *BioIn 12,*
IntWW 83, NewYTBS 85[port],
Who 83, WhoWor 82, WrDr 84, -86
Pope-Hennessy, John Wyndam 1913-
BioIn 13
Pope-Hennessy, John Wyndham 1913-
WhoAm 84, -86
Pope-Hennessy, Sir John 1913-
Who 85
Pope-Hennessy, Sir John Wyndham
1913- *WhoWor 87*
Popham, Estelle L 1906- *ConAu 1R,*
-5NR, ForWC 70, WhoAm 74,
WhoAmW 74, -66, -68, -70, -72
Popkin, Henry 1924- *DrAS 74E, -78E,*
-82E
Popkin, Zelda 1898-1983 *AmAu&B,*
AmNov, BioIn 2, -4, -13, ConAu 109,
-25R, CurBio 51, -83N, InWom,
NewYTBS 83, TwCCr&M 80,
WhoAmJ 80, WhoWorJ 72, -78,
WrDr 76, -80, -82, -84
Porcari, Constance Kwolek 1933-
ConAu 33R
Porcari, Constance Kwolek *see also*
Kwolek, Constance
Porges, Paul Peter 1927-
ConGrA 1[port], WorECar
Porte, Barbara Ann *DrAP&F 85,*
SmATA 45
Porter, David 1780-1843 *DcAmMiB,*
OxAmL 83
Porter, Eliot Furness 1901- *AmArt,*
BioIn 7, -8, -10, -11, -12, -13,
ConAu 5R, ConPhot, CurBio 76,
LinLib L, MacBEP, WhoAm 74, -76,
-78, -80, -82, -84, -86, WhoAmA 76
-78, -80, -82, -84
Porter, Jack Nusan 1944-
AmM&WS 73S, -78S, ConAu 20NR,
-41R, IntAu&W 82, WhoE 79, -81
Porter, James Armer, Jr. 1922-
AmM&WS 86P

Porter, Katherine Anne 1890-1980
AmAu&B, AmWomWr, AmWr,
AnObit 1980[port], AuNews 2,
BioIn 1, -3, -4, -5, -6, -7, -8, -9,
-10, -11, -12, -13, BlueB 76,
CasWL, CelR, CnDAL, CnMWL,
ConAmA, ConAu 1R, -1NR, -101,
ConLC 1, -3, -7, -10, -13, -15,
-27[port], ConNov 72, -76,
CurBio 40, -63, -80N, CyWA,
DcLB 4, -9[port], -Y80A[port],
DcLEL, EncFWF[port], EncSoH,
EncWL, -2[port], EvLB, ForWC 70,
GoodHs, HalFC 84, InWom,
IntAu&W 76, -77, IntDcWB,
IntWW 74, -75, -76, -77, -78, -79,
-80, -81N, LibW, LinLib L, -S,
LongCTC, MakMC, McGEWB,
ModAL, -S2, -S1, NewYTBE 70,
NewYTBS 80[port], Novels[port],
OxAmL, -83, OxEng, -85, PenC AM,
RAdv 1, REn, REnAL, SmATA 23N,
-39[port], TwCA, -SUP, TwCWr,
WebAB, -79, WebE&AL, WhDW,
WhAm 7, WhE&EA, Who 74,
WhoAm 74, -76, -78, -80,
WhoAmW 74, -58, -61, -64, -66,
-68, -70, -72, -75, -77, -79, -81,
WhoE 74, WhoTwCL, WhoWor 74,
-78, WorAl, WrDr 76, -80
Porter, Sheena 1935- *BioIn 7, -9, -13,*
ConAu 81, IntAu&W 82, OxChL,
SmATA 24[port], ThrBJA,
TwCCW 78, -83, WrDr 80, -82, -84,
-86
Porter, Sylvia 1913- *BioIn 13,*
EncTwCJ, WhoAm 84, -86, WrDr 86
Porter, William Sydney *OxEng 85*
Porter, William Sydney 1862-1910
AmAu&B, AmBi, AtlBL,
AuBYP SUP, BioIn 1, -2, -3, -4, -5,
-6, -7, -8, -9, -10, -11, -12, -13,
CasWL, CnDAL, ConAu 104,
DcAmB, DcLB 12[port], DcLEL,
DcNAA, Dis&D, EncFWF, EncMys,
EncSoH, EvLB, LinLib L, -S,
LongCTC, NatCAB 15, OhA&B,
OxAmL, -83, OxEng, PenC AM,
REn, REnAL, TwCA, -SUP,
WebAB, -79, WebE&AL, YABC 2
Porter, William Sydney *see also* Henry,
O
Porter, William Sydney *see also* Henry,
Oliver
Porter, William Sydney *see also* Peters,
S H
Portis, Charles 1933- *AmAu&B,*
ConAu 1NR, -45, DcLB 6, EncFWF,
WrDr 84, -86
Portisch, Hugo 1927- *ConAu 21R,*
WhoWor 74, -76
Posell, Elsa Z *AuBYP SUP, BioIn 9,*
ConAu 1R, -4NR, -20NR, SmATA 3,
WhoAmW 74, -66, -72, WhoLibS 66
Posner, Richard 1944- *ConAu 20NR,*
WrDr 86
Post, Elizabeth Lindley 1920-
BioIn 12, ConAu 49, WhoAm 76,
-78, -80, -82, -84, -86,
WhoAmW 74, -72, -75
Post, Robert Charles 1937- *DrAS 82H*
Potok, Chaim *DrAP&F 85*
Potok, Chaim 1929- *AmAu&B, ASpks,*
Au&Wr 71, AuNews 1, -2, BioIn 7,
-10, -11, -13, BioNews 74,
ConAu 17R, -19NR, ConLC 2, -7,
-14, -26[port], ConNov 86,
CurBio 83[port], DcLB 28[port],
IntAu&W 76, -77, -86, LinLib L,
Novels, SmATA 33[port], WhoAm 74,
-76, -78, -80, -82, -84, -86,
WhoAmJ 80, WhoE 74, WhoWor 74,
WhoWorJ 72, -78, WorAl,
WorAu 1975[port], WrDr 76, -80,
-82, -84, -86
Potter, David Morris 1910-1971
AmAu&B, BioIn 5, -9, -10, -13,
ConAu 108, DcLB 17[port],
EncAB-H, EncSoH, NewYTBE 71,
WhAm 5, WhoWor 1970
Potter, Lois 1941- *ConAu 15NR*
Potter, Marian 1915- *BioIn 11,*
ConAu 1NR, -49, SmATA 9,
WhoAmW 77, -79, -81

Q

Queen, Ellery *BioIn 13, OxAmL 83, TwCCr&M 85, WrDr 86*
Queen, Ellery 1905-1971 *AmAu&B, ASpks, AuBYP, BioIn 2, -3, -4, -8, -9, -10, -11, -12, CelR, ConAu X, ConLC 3, -11, CorpD, CurBio 40, DcLEL, EncMys, EvLB, IntAu&W 76X, -77X, IntWW 74, -75, -76, -77, -78, -79, -80, -81, -82, LinLib LP, LongCTC, Novels[port], OxAmL, PenC AM, REn, REnAL, ScF&FL 1, SmATA 3, TwCA, -SUP, TwCCr&M 80, TwCWr, WebAB, -79, Who 74, -82, WorAl, WrDr 76, -80, -82, -84*
Queen, Ellery *see also* Dannay, Frederic
Queen, Ellery *see also* Lee, Manfred B
Queneau, Raymond 1903-1976 *Au&Wr 71, BioIn 4, -7, -9, -11, -12, CasWL, CnMWL, ConAu 69, -77, ConLC 2, -5, -10, -42[port], DcFM, EncSF, EncWL, -2, EvEuW, GrFLW, IntWW 74, -75, -76, -77N,*

LinLib L, MakMC, ModFrL, ModRL, NewYTBS 76, Novels, OxFilm, OxFr, PenC EUR, REn, TwCA SUP, TwCWr, WhE&EA, WhoTwCL, WhoWor 74, -76, WorEFlm
Quennell, Charles Henry Bourne 1872-1935 *BioIn 6, DcBrBI, LongCTC, MorJA, TwCA, -SUP, WhE&EA*
Quennell, Marjorie 1884-1972 *BioIn 4, -6, -13, ConAu 73, DcBrAr 1, DcLEL, EvLB, JBA 34, LinLib L, LongCTC, MorJA, SmATA 29[port], TwCA, -SUP, WhE&EA*
Quentin, Dorothy 1911- *WhE&EA*
Quentin, Patrick *WrDr 86*
Quentin, Patrick 1912- *AmAu&B, Au&Wr 71, BioIn 10, BlueB 76, ConAu X, EncMys, IntAu&W 76X, TwCCr&M 80, -85, WorAu, WrDr 80, -82, -84*

Quilici, Folco 1930- *ConAu 105, DcFM, WhoWor 82, -87, WorEFlm*
Quiller-Couch, Arthur Thomas 1863-1944 *ConAu 118*
Quiller-Couch, Sir Arthur Thomas 1863-1944 *BbD, BiD&SB, BioIn 1, -4, -5, -12, CasWL, Chambr 3, ChhPo, -S1, -S2, -S3, CurBio 44, DcBiA, DcEnA, -AP, DcLEL, DcNaB 1941, EvLB, JBA 34, LinLib L, LongCTC, MnBBF, ModBrL, NewC, Novels, ObitOF 79, OxEng, -85, PenC ENG, RAdv 1, REn, TwCA, -SUP, TwCWr, WhAm 2, WhE&EA, WhLit, WhoHr&F*
Quimby, Myrtle 1891- *ConAu P-2*
Quin-Harkin, Janet 1941- *BioIn 12, ConAu 15NR, -81, IntAu&W 82, SmATA 18*
Quinlan, Joseph *BioIn 11, -12*
Quinlan, Julia *BioIn 11, -12*

Quinn, David B 1909- *ConAu 15NR*
Quinn, David Beers 1909- *Au&Wr 71, BlueB 76, ConAu 77, DrAS 78H, -82H, IntAu&W 82, -86, OxCan, -SUP, Who 74, -82, -83, -85, WhoAm 74, -76, -78, WrDr 80, -82, -84*
Quintero, Jose 1924- *BiDrAPA 77, BiE&WWA, BioIn 3, -4, -5, -9, -10, -11, CnThe, ConTFT 2, CurBio 54, EncWT, NewYTBS 74, -77, NotNAT, -A, OxAmT 84, PIP&P, -A, WhDW, WhoAm 74, -76, -78, -80, -82, WhoE 74, WhoThe 72, -77, -81, WhoWor 74*
Quirk, Randolph 1920- *BioIn 12, BlueB 76, ConAu 2NR, -5R, IntAu&W 82, IntWW 82, -83, WhoWor 76, -87, WrDr 76, -80, -82, -84, -86*
Quirk, Sir Randolph *Who 85S*

131

R

Raab, Lawrence *DrAP&F 85*
Raab, Robert Allen 1924- *ConAu 29R*
Rabalais, Maria 1921- *ConAu 61*
Raban, Jonathan 1942- *ConAu 17NR,
–61, ConDr 73, –77B, –82B,
IntAu&W 77, WorAu 1975[port],
WrDr 76, –80, –82, –84, –86*
Rabe, Berniece 1928- *BioIn 10,
ConAu 1NR, –49, FifBJA[port],
IntAu&W 82, SmATA 7, WrDr 80,
–82, –84, –86*
Rabinovitz, Rubin 1938- *ConAu 21R,
DrAS 74E, –78E, –82E,
IntAu&W 86, WrDr 76, –80, –82,
–84, –86*
Rabinow, Paul 1944- *BioIn 11,
ConAu 13NR, –61*
Rabinowich, Ellen 1946- *BioIn 13,
ConAu 106, SmATA 29[port]*
Rabkin, Brenda 1945- *ConAu 101*
Rabkin, Eric S 1946- *ConAu 4NR,
–49, DrAS 74E, –78E, –82E, EncSF,
WhoMW 78*
Rachleff, Owen S 1934- *ConAu 14NR*
Rachleff, Owen Spencer 1934-
*ConAu 21R, WhoAm 76, –78, –80,
–82, –84, –86, WhoE 74, –75, –77*
Rachlin, Carol King 1919-
*AmM&WS 73S, –76P, ConAu 57,
FifIDA, WhoAmW 74, –66, –68, –70,
–72, –75*
Rachlin, Harvey 1951- *ConAu 107,
SmATA 47[port], WhoE 79, –81, –83*
Rachlin, Nahid *ConAu 14NR, –81,
DrAP&F 85*
Radice, Betty 1912- *Au&Wr 71,
ConAu 12NR, –25R, IntAu&W 76,
–77, –82, WhoWor 76, WrDr 76, –80,
–82, –84, –86*
Radice, Betty 1912-1985 *ConAu 115*
Radin, Paul *IntMPA 86, OxCanL*
Radin, Paul 1883-1959 *BioIn 5,
ConAu 120, DcAmB S6, IntMPA 77,
–76, –78, –79, –81, –82, –84,
McGEWB, OxCan, WebAB, –79,
WhAm 3*
Radley, Gail 1951- *BioIn 13,
ConAu 16NR, –89, SmATA 25[port]*
Radley, Sheila *IntAu&W 86X,
WrDr 84, –86*
Rado, James 1932?- *ConAu 105,
ConDr 73, –77D, –82D, ConLC 17,
EncMT, NotNAT, PlP&P*
Raeburn, John Hay 1941- *ConAu 57,
DrAS 74E, –78E, –82E, WhoAm 86*
Raeburn, Michael 1940- *ConAu 107*
Raeff, Marc 1923- *BioIn 13,
WhoAm 84, –86, WrDr 86*
Ragni, Gerome 1942- *ConAu 105,
ConDr 73, –77D, –82D, ConLC 17,
EncMT, NotNAT, PlP&P*
Ragosta, Millie J 1931- *ConAu 12NR,
–73*

Rahn, Joan Elma 1929-
*AmM&WS 73P, –76P, –79P, –82P,
–86P, BioIn 13, ConAu 13NR, –37R,
SmATA 27[port], WhoFrS 84,
WhoMW 84*
Raht, John Milton 1928- *WhoF&I 81,
–83, WhoWest 78, –80, –82,
WhoWor 82*
Raiff, Stan 1930- *BioIn 11, ConAu 61,
SmATA 11*
Raines, Howell 1943- *ConAu 73*
Rainwater, Clarence Elmer 1884-1925?
DcNAA, NatCAB 21, WhAm 1
Ralbovsky, Martin Paul 1942-
ConAu 49
Ramati, Alexander 1921- *Au&Wr 71,
ConAu 7NR, –13R*
Ramee, Louise DeLa *BioIn 13*
Ramee, Louise DeLa 1839-1908
*BiD&SB, BioIn 1, –2, –3, –11,
BritAu 19, Chambr 3, DcEuL, EvLB,
HsB&A, JBA 34, LinLib L, –S*
Ramee, Louise DeLa see also
DeLaRamee, Louise
Ramke, Bin *DrAP&F 85*
Ramke, Bin 1947- *ConAu 14NR*
Rampa, T Lopsang 1911?- *EncO&P 78*
Rampa, T Lopsang 1911?-1981
EncO&P 2
Rampo, Edogawa 1894- *ScF&FL 1*
Ramsay, William M 1922-
*ConAu 12NR, –13R, WhoS&SW 75,
–76*
Ramsey, Jarold *DrAP&F 85*
Ramsey, Jarold 1937- *ConAu 33R,
DrAS 74E, –78E, –82E, IntWWP 77,
–82, WhoE 75, –77, WrDr 76, –80,
–82, –84, –86*
Rand, Ayn *OxAmT 84*
Rand, Ayn 1905-1982 *AmAu&B,
AmNov, AmWomWr,
AnObit 1982[port], BioIn 2, –4, –5,
–6, –7, –8, –10, –11, –12, –13,
CasWL, CelR, ConAu 105, –13R,
ConLC 3, –30[port], ConNov 72, –76,
–82, CurBio 82[port], EncSF,
ForWC 70, InWom, IntAu&W 76,
–77, LibW, NewYTBS 82[port],
Novels, OxAmL, –83, PenC AM,
PolProf E, REn, REnAL, ScF&FL 1,
–2, ScFSB, TwCA SUP, TwCSFW 86,
WebAB, –79, WebE&AL, WhAm 8,
WhoAm 74, –76, –78, –80, –82,
WhoAmW 74, –58, –66, –68, –70,
–72, –75, –77, –81, –83, WhoSciF,
WhoTwCL, WorAl, WrDr 76, –80,
–82*
Rand, Suzanne 1950- *BioIn 12*
Randall, Dudley *DrAP&F 85*
Randall, Dudley 1914- *BiDrLUS 70,
BioIn 10, BlkAWP, ConAu 25R,
ConAu 25R, ConLC 1, ConPo 70,
–75, –80, –85, DcLB 41[port],
DcLEL 1940, Ebony 1, InB&W 80,*

*IntAu&W 82, IntWWP 82, LinLib L,
LivgBAA, MichAu 80, SelBAAu,
WhoAm 76, –78, WhoBlA 75, –77,
–80, WhoF&I 75, WhoLibS 55, –66,
WhoMW 74, –76, –78, WrDr 76, –80,
–82, –84, –86*
Randall, Dudley F 1914- *WhoBlA 85*
Randall, Dudley Felker 1914-
InB&W 85, SelBAAf, WhoMW 84
Randall, Florence Engel 1917-
*AuBYP SUP, BioIn 10, BlkAWP,
ConAu 41R, IntAu&W 76, –77,
ScF&FL 1, –2, SmATA 5,
WhoAmW 77, –79, –81, WrDr 84,
–86*
Randall, Janet *AuBYP, BioIn 7, –9,
ConAu X, IntAu&W 76X, –77X,
–82X, PoIre, SmATA 3, WrDr 76,
–80, –82, –84, –86*
Randall, Janet see also Young, Janet
Randall
Randall, Janet see also Young, Robert
W
Randall, Marta 1948- *ConAu 107,
ScFSB, TwCSFW 86, WrDr 84, –86*
Randall, Robert *AuBYP, ConAu X,
OxCan, SmATA X, ThrBJA,
TwCSFW 86, WrDr 84, –86*
Randall, Robert see also Silverberg,
Robert
Randall, Rona *Au&Wr 71,
IntAu&W 76, –76X, –77, –86, –86X,
WrDr 76, –80, –82, –84, –86*
Randall, Ruth Elaine Painter
1892-1971 *AmAu&B, AmWomWr,
Au&Wr 71, AuBYP, BioIn 4, –7, –8,
–9, ConAu 1R, –103, CurBio 57,
InWom, SmATA 3, WhAm 5,
WhoAmW 58, –64, –66, –68, –70,
–72*
Randall, Willard Sterne 1942-
WhoE 85
Randi, James 1928?- *BioIn 12,
ConAu 117, EncO&P 2, –81,
WhoAm 84, –86, WhoE 85*
Randles, Jenny 1951- *EncO&P 2S1*
Randolph, David 1914- *AmAu&B,
Baker 84, BioIn 10, IntWWM 77,
WhoAm 74, –76, –78, –80, –82, –84,
–86, WhoE 83, –85, WhoWor 74*
Ranelagh, John *Who 83*
Raphael, Bertram 1936-
*AmM&WS 73P, –76P, –79P,
ConAu 97, WhoWest 74, –76, –78*
Raphael, Chaim *TwCCr&M 85*
Raphael, Chaim 1908- *BioIn 6,
ConAu 16NR, –85, CurBio 63,
Who 74, –82, –83, –85, WrDr 86*
Raphael, Rick 1919- *ConAu 10NR,
–21R, ConSFA, DrRegL 75, EncSF,
ScF&FL 1, –2, ScFSB, TwCSFW 86,
WhoMW 76, –78, –80, –82, WrDr 84,
–86*
Rapoport, Roger 1946- *ConAu 33R,
WrDr 76, –80, –82, –84, –86*

Rapp, Joel *AuNews 1, BioIn 10*
Rappoport, Ken 1935- *ConAu 4NR,
–20NR, –53*
Rasch, Sunna Cooper 1925-
ConAu 105, WhoAmW 70, WhoE 74
Rashke, Richard L 1936- *ConAu 107*
Rashkis, Harold A 1920- *BiDrAPA 77*
Raskin, Edith Lefkowitz 1908-
*AuBYP SUP, BioIn 11, ConAu 3NR,
–9R, ForWC 70, WhoAmW 9*
Raskin, Ellen *WhoAmA 84*
Raskin, Ellen 1928- *ALA 80, AmPB,
BioIn 8, –9, –10, –12, BkP, ChlLR 1,
ChhPo, –S1, –S2, ConAu 21R,
IlsBYP, IlsCB 1957, –1967,
IntAu&W 76, OxChL, SmATA 2,
ThrBJA, TwCCW 78, –83,
WhoAm 80, –82, –84, –86,
WhoAmA 80, –82, WrDr 80, –82, –84*
Raskin, Ellen 1928-1984
*ChlLR 12[port], ConAu 113,
DcLB 52[port], SmATA 38[port]*
Rathbone, Julian 1935- *ConAu 101,
ConLC 41[port], IntAu&W 82, –86,
TwCCr&M 80, –85, WrDr 80, –82,
–84, 86*
Rather, Dan *IntMPA 86*
Rather, Dan 1931- *AuNews 1,
BioIn 10, –11, –12, –13, BioNews 74,
ConAu 9NR, –53, CurBio 75, EncAJ,
EncTwCJ, IntMPA 79, –81, –82, –84,
IntWW 83, LesBEnT[port],
NewYTET, PolProf NF, WhoAm 76,
–78, –80, –82, –84, –86, WhoE 85*
Rau, Margaret 1913- *BioIn 11,
ChlLR 8[port], ConAu 8NR, –61,
IntAu&W 82, SmATA 9*
Rauch, Constance 1937- *BioIn 10,
ConAu 57*
Raucher, Herman 1928- *BioIn 11,
ConAu 29R, ConTFT 1, IntMPA 86,
Novels, ScF&FL 1, –2, SmATA 8,
WhoAm 80, –82, –84, –86, WhoE 77,
–79, –81, –83, WrDr 76, –80, –82,
–84, –86*
Ravielli, Anthony 1916- *Au&Wr 71,
AuBYP, BioIn 5, –7, –8, –9,
ConAu 11NR, –29R, IlsCB 1946,
–1957, –1967, SmATA 3, ThrBJA,
WhoE 74*
Ravin, Neil 1947- *ConAu 105*
Rawcliffe, Michael 1934- *ConAu 115*
Rawlings, Marjorie Kinnan *OxChL*
Rawlings, Marjorie Kinnan 1896-1953
*AmAu&B, AmNov, AmWomWr,
BioIn 1, –2, –3, –4, –5, –7, –8, –9,
–10, –11, –12, CnDAL, ConAu 104,
CurBio 42, –54, CyWA, DcAmB S5,
DcLB 9[port], –22[port], DcLEL,
EvLB, InWom, LibW, LinLib L,
LongCTC, ModAL, NotAW MOD,
Novels, ObitOF 79, OxAmL, –83,
PenC AM, REn, REnAL, ThrBJA,
TwCA, –SUP, TwCCW 78, –83,*

Remini, Robert Vincent 1921-
ConAu 3NR, –9R, DrAS 74H, –78H, –82H, IntAu&W 76, –77, WhoAm 74, –76, –78, –80, –82, –84, –86
Renard, Jules 1864-1910 *BioIn 1, –7, CasWL, CIDMEL, CnMD, ConAu 117, Dis&D, EncWL, EuAu, EvEuW, McGEWD, –84, ModWD, NotNAT B, OxFr, PenC EUR, TwCLC 17[port]*
Renaud, Bernadette 1945-
IntAu&W 86, WhoCanL 85
Renault, Mary *ConAu X, SmATA X*
Renault, Mary d1983 *Who 85N*
Renault, Mary 1905-1983
AnObit 1983, Au&Wr 71, AuBYP, BioIn 5, –6, –8, –9, –10, –11, –13, BlueB 76, ConAu X, ConLC 3, –11, –17, ConNov 72, –76, –82, CurBio 59, –84N, DcLB Y83N[port], EncSoA, InWom, IntAu&W 76, –77, IntWW 74, –75, –76, –77, –78, –79, –80, –81, –82, –83, LinLib L, –LP, LongCTC, ModBrL S2, –S1, ModCmwL, NewC, NewYTBS 79, –83[port], Novels[port], OxEng 85, RAdv 1, REn, SmATA X, TwCWr, WhAm 8, Who 74, –82, –83, WhoAmW 66, –68, –70, –72, WhoWor 74, –76, –78, WorAl, WorAu, WrDr 76, –80, –82, –84
Renault, Mary *see also* Challans, Mary
Rendell, Joan *Au&Wr 71, BioIn 13, ConAu 7NR, –61, IntAu&W 76, –77, –86, SmATA 28[port], WrDr 76, –80, –82, –84, –86*
Rendell, Ruth *ThrtnMM*
Rendell, Ruth 1930- *BioIn 12, –13, ConAu 109, ConLC 28[port], Novels, TwCCr&M 80, –85, WrDr 82, –84, –86*
Rendina, Laura Cooper 1902- *AuBYP, BioIn 6, –7, –11, ConAu 9R, MorJA, SmATA 10*
Rendon, Armando B *DrAP&F 85*
Rendon, Armando B 1939- *ChiSch, ConAu 37R, WrDr 76, –80, –82, –84, –86*
Renich, Jill 1916- *ConAu 25R, MichAu 80, WhoAmW 74, –75*
Rennert, Vincent P 1928- *ODwPR 79, WhoPubR 76*
Reno, Marie R *ConAu 10NR, –65*
Rentzel, T Lance 1943- *WhoFtbl 74*
Renvoize, Jean 1930- *Au&Wr 71, BioIn 10, ConAu 41R, IntAu&W 76, SmATA 5*
Resnick, Michael D 1942- *ConAu 107, ConSFA, EncSF, ScF&FL 1, –2, ScFSB, SmATA 38[port]*
Resnick, Mike *SmATA X*
Resnick, Mike 1942- *ConAu X, TwCSFW 86*
Resnick, Seymour 1920- *AuBYP, BioIn 8, –13, ConAu 73, DrAS 74F, –78F, –82F, SmATA 23*
Rethi, Lili 1894?-1969 *BioIn 8, IlsBYP*
Rettig, Jack Louis 1925-
AmM&WS 73S, –78S, ConAu 57, WhoCon 73
Retton, Mary Lou *NewYTBS 85[port]*
Retton, Mary Lou 1968?- *BioIn 13, ConNews 85-2[port], CurBio 86[port], NewYTBS 84[port]*
Reuben, David 1933- *Au&Wr 71, AuNews 1, BioIn 9, –10, BioNews 74, CelR, ConAu 41R, WhoAm 76, –78, –80, –82, WhoWest 74, WorAl, WrDr 76, –80, –82, –84, –86*
Reuter, Carol 1931- *BioIn 9, ConAu 21R, SmATA 2*
Revson, Peter 1939-1974 *BioIn 9, –10, –12, BioNews 74, CelR, ObitOF 79, ObitT 1971, WhScrn 83*
Rewald, John *NewYTBS 86[port]*
Rewald, John 1912- *IntAu&W 86, WhoAm 84, WhoAmA 84, WhoArt 84*
Rexroth, Kenneth 1905-1982
AmAu&B, AnObit 1982[port], BioIn 4, –7, –8, –9, –10, –12, –13, BlueB 76, CelR, ChhPo, –S3, CmCal, CnE&AP, ConAu 5R, –107, –14NR,

ConDr 73, –77, –82, ConLC 1, –2, –6, –11, –22[port], ConPo 70, –75, –80, CurBio 81[port], –82N, DcLB 16[port], DcLEL 1940, –Y82A[port], EncWL, –2, IndAu 1917, IntAu&W 76, –77, IntWW 74, –75, –76, –77, –78, –79, –80, –81, –82, –83N, IntWWP 77, LinLib L, ModAL, –S2, –S1, NewCon[port], NewYTBS 82, OxAmL, –83, PenC AM, RAdv 1, REn, REnAL, TwCA SUP, WebE&AL, WhAm 8, WhoAm 74, –76, –78, –80, –82, WhoTwCL, WhoWest 74, WhoWor 74, WrDr 76, –80, –82
Rey, H A *BioIn 13*
Rey, H A 1898-1977 *ChlLR 5[port], ChsFB A, ConAu 6NR, –73, DcLB 22[port], IlsCB 1967, OxChL, SmATA 26[port], TwCChW 83, WhoAmA 73, –76, –78, –80, –82N, –84N, WhoFr 79N*
Rey, Hans Augusto 1898-1977 *AmPB, Au&ICB, AuBYP, BioIn 1, –2, –5, –7, –8, –9, –10, –11, –12, –13, BkP, ChsFB A, ConAu 5R, FamAIYP, IlsCB 1744, –1946, –1957, JBA 51, SmATA 1, TwCChW 78, WhoAmA 73*
Rey, Lester Del 1915- *ScF&FL 1, ThrBJA*
Rey, Lester Del *see also* DelRey, Lester
Reyes Y Basoalto, Ricardo E Neftali 1904-1973 *ConAu X, ConLC 9*
Reyes Y Basoalto, Ricardo E Neftali *see also* Neruda, Pablo
Reynolds, Charles O 1921- *ConAu 9R*
Reynolds, Dallas McCord 1917-
BioIn 12, ConAu 5R, –9NR, ScF&FL 1
Reynolds, Dallas McCord *see also* Reynolds, Mack
Reynolds, David K 1940-
ConAu 9NR, –65
Reynolds, Mack 1917- *AuBYP SUP, BioIn 12, ConAu X, ConSFA, DcLB 8[port], EncSF, IntAu&W 76X, Novels, ScF&FL 1, –2, WhoSciF, WrDr 84*
Reynolds, Mack 1917-1983
ScFSB[port], TwCSFW 86
Reynolds, Mack *see also* Reynolds, Dallas McCord
Reynolds, Marjorie Harris 1903-
AuBYP, ConAu 5R, WhoAmW 66
Reynolds, Moira Davison 1915-
ConAu 105, –21NR, IntAu&W 86
Reynolds, Pamela 1923?- *ConAu 103, ScF&FL 1, –2, SmATA 34[port]*
Reynolds, Quentin 1902?-1965
AmAu&B, AuBYP, BioIn 2, –3, –4, –6, –7, –8, –9, BlueB 76, ConAu 73, CurBio 41, –65, DcAmB S7, EncAJ, EncTwCJ, IntWW 74, –75, –76, –77, –78, –79, LongCTC, ObitOF 79, ObitT 1961, REnAL, St&PR 75, TwCA SUP, WhAm 4, WhE&EA, WhScrn 77, WhoAm 74, –76, –78, WhoF&I, –75, WhoWest 74, –76, –78
Reynolds, Quentin 1903-1965
WhScrn 83
Rezmerski, John Calvin *DrAP&F 85*
Rezmerski, John Calvin 1942-
ConAu 29R, IntWWP 77, WhoMW 74, –76
Rhinehart, Luke *BioIn 9, ConAu X*
Rhodehamel, Josephine DeWitt 1901-
ConAu 61, WhoLibS 55, WhoWest 78
Rhodes, Eugene Manlove 1869-1934
AmAu&B, AmBi, AmLY, BioIn 1, –2, –3, –4, –6, –8, –11, –13, CmCal, DcAmB S1, DcLEL, DcNAA, EncAAH, EncFWF[port], NatCAB 45, OxAmL, –83, REnAL, REnAW, TwCA, –SUP, WhAm 1, WhNAA
Rhodes, Evan H 1929- *ConAu 10NR, –57*
Rhodes, John J 1916- *AlmAP 78, –80, –82[port], BiDrAC, BioIn 9, –10, –11, –12, BioNews 74, BlueB 76, CngDr 74, –77, –79, –81, ConAu 103, CurBio 76, IntWW 75, –76, –77, –78,*

–79, –80, –81, –82, –83, NewYTBE 72, –73, NewYTBS 76, –80[port], PolProf J, PolProf K, PolProf NF, WhoAm 74, –76, –78, –80, –82, WhoAmP 73, –75, –77, –79, –81, –83, –85, WhoGov 77, –72, –75, WhoWest 74, –76, –78, –80, –82, WorAl
Rhodes, John Jacob 1916- *WhoAm 84, –86*
Rhodes, Richard *DrAP&F 85*
Rhodes, Richard 1937- *BioIn 13, ConAu 20NR*
Ribner, Irving 1921-1972 *BiE&WWA, BioIn 9, ConAu 1R, –3NR, –37R, NewYTBE 72, NotNAT B, WhAm 5*
Ricci, Larry J 1948- *ConAu 109*
Ricciardi, Lorenzo 1930- *ConAu 109*
Ricciuti, Edward R 1938- *BioIn 11, ConAu 41R, IntAu&W 76, –77, SmATA 10*
Rice, Anne 1941- *ConAu 12NR, –65, ConLC 41[port], WrDr 80, –82, –84, –86*
Rice, Edward E 1918- *AuBYP SUP, ConAu 1NR, –49, SmATA 42*
Rice, Eve 1951- *AuBYP SUP, BioIn 12, ConAu 4NR, –53, FifBJA[port], IlsCB 1967, SmATA 34[port]*
Rice, Tamara *AuBYP SUP*
Rice, Tim *OxThe 83, WhoRock 81*
Rice, Tim 1944- *BioIn 9, ConAu 103, ConDr 73, –77D, –82D, ConLC 21[port], ConTFT 2, IntWW 80, –81, –82, –83, LinLib L, NewYTBE 71, WhoRocM 82, WhoThe 77, –81*
Rich, Adrienne *DrAP&F 85, InB&W 85*
Rich, Adrienne 1929- *AmWomWr, AmWr S1, BioIn 9, –10, –11, –12, –13, ChhPo S3, ConAu 9R, –20NR, ConLC 3, –6, –7, –11, –18, –36[port], ConPo 70, –75, –80, –85, CroCAP, CurBio 76, DcLB 5[port], DcLEL 1940, IntDcWB, IntWWP 77, LinLib L, ModAL, –S2, –S1, ModAWP[port], OxAmL, PenC AM, RAdv 1, WhoAm 76, –78, –80, –82, –84, –86, WhoAmW 58, –81, –83, WhoE 85, WorAu, WrDr 76, –80, –82, –84, –86*
Rich, Adrienne 1931- *OxAmL 83*
Rich, Josephine 1912- *AuBYP, BioIn 7, –11, ConAu 5R, SmATA 10*
Rich, Louise Dickinson 1903-
AmAu&B, AmWomWr, AuBYP, BioIn 1, –2, –3, –4, –7, ConAu 73, CurBio 43, InWom, REnAL, TwCA SUP, WhoAmW 58, –61, –64, –66, –68, –70, –72
Rich, Norman 1921- *ConAu 45, DrAS 74H, –78H, –82H*
Richard, Adrienne 1921- *AuBYP SUP, BioIn 10, ConAu 29R, FifBJA[port], SmATA 5, WhoAmW 75, WrDr 76, –80, –82, –84, –86*
Richard, Keith 1943- *Baker 84, BioIn 8, –10, –11, –12, –13, CelR, ConAu X, ConLC 17, WhoAm 74, –76, –78, –80, –82, –84, –86*
Richard, Keith *see also* Rolling Stones, The
Richards, Arlene Kramer 1935-
ConAu 11NR, –65, LEduc 74, WhoAmW 74, –75, –83
Richards, David Adams 1950- *CaW, ConAu 93, DcLB 53, OxCanL, WhoCanL 85*
Richards, Denis 1910- *IntAu&W 86*
Richards, Larry *ConAu X*
Richards, Larry 1931- *ConArch A, ConAu X*
Richards, Larry *see also* Richards, Lawrence O
Richards, Lawrence O 1931-
ConAu 17R, –20NR, –29R, WhoRel 75, WhoWest 74, –76
Richards, Lawrence O *see also* Richards, Larry
Richards, Stanley 1918- *InB&W 85*

Richards, Stanley 1918-1980
BiDrLUS 70, BioIn 12, ConAu 101, –25R, IntAu&W 76, –77, –82, IntMPA 77, –75, –76, –78, –79, –81, OxCan, WhoE, WhoLibS 66
Richardson, Frank Howard 1882-1970
AmAu&B, AuBYP SUP, BioIn 9, –13, ConAu 104, SmATA 27N, WhAm 6, WhE&EA, WhLit, WhNAA
Richardson, Grace Lee 1916-
ConAu X, IntAu&W 77X, SmATA 8
Richardson, Grace Lee *see also* Dickson, Naida
Richardson, Harry W 1938-
ConAu 29R, WrDr 80, –82, –84, –86
Richardson, Henry Handel *WomNov*
Richardson, Henry Handel 1870-1946
BioIn 1, –2, –3, –4, –5, –6, –8, –9, –10, –12, CasWL, ConAu X, CurBio 46, CyWA, DcLEL, DcNaB 1941, EncWL, –2, EvLB, IntDcWB, LinLib LP, LongCTC, McGEWB, ModCmwL, NewC, Novels, OxAusL, OxEng, –85, PenC ENG, REn, TwCA, –SUP, TwCLC 4[port], WhE&EA, WhLit, WhoTwCL
Richardson, Henry V M 1923-
WrDr 86
Richardson, Henry Vokes-Mackey 1923- *ConAu 25R, WhoPNW, WhoWest 74, –76, –78, –80, WrDr 82, –84*
Richardson, Jack 1935- *AmAu&B, BiE&WWA, BioIn 10, –12, CnMD, CnThe, ConAu 5R, ConDr 73, –77, –82, CroCD, DcLB 7[port], DcLEL 1940, McGEWD, –84, ModWD, NotNAT, OxAmL 83, PenC AM, PIP&P, RENAL, REnWD, WorAu, WrDr 76, –80, –82, –84, –86*
Richardson, Joanna *Au&Wr 71, BlueB 76, ConAu 10NR, –13R, IntAu&W 76, –77, –82, Who 74, –82, –83, –85, WhoWor 78, WrDr 76, –80, –82, –84, –86*
Richardson, John Adkins 1929-
ConAu 57, WhoAmA 82, –84, WhoMW 78, –80, –82
Richardson, Robert S *TwCSFW 86*
Richardson, Robert S 1902- *BioIn 8, –11, ConAu 49, IntAu&W 77, –82, ScF&FL 1, –2, SmATA 8, WrDr 84*
Richason, Benjamin 1922-
AmM&WS 73P, –76P, BioIn 11, ConAu 41R, WhoAm 74
Richelson, Geraldine 1922- *BioIn 13, ConAu 106, SmATA 29*
Richie, Donald 1924- *ConAu 8NR, –17R, WrDr 86*
Richler, Mordecai 1931- *Au&Wr 71, AuNews 1, BioIn 9, –10, –11, –12, –13, BioNews 75, BlueB 76, CaW, CanWW 70, –79, –80, –81, –83, CanWr, CasWL, ConAu 65, ConLC 3, –5, –9, –13, –18, ConNov 72, –76, –82, –86, CreCan 1, CurBio 75, DcLB 53[port], DcLEL 1940, EncWL, –2, HalFC 84, IntAu&W 76, –77, –86, IntWW 74, –75, –76, –77, –78, –79, –80, –81, –82, –83, ModCmwL, NewYTBS 80[port], –83[port], Novels, OxCan, –SUP, OxCanL, PenC ENG, RENAL, SmATA 27, –44[port], TwCWr, WebE&AL, Who 74, –82, –83, –85, WhoAm 76, –78, –80, –82, –84, –86, WhoCanL 85, WhoTwCL, WhoWor 74, –78, –80, –82, –84, –87, WorAl, WorAu, WrDr 76, –80, –82, –84, –86*
Richmond, Julius B 1916-
AmM&WS 73P, –76P, –79P, –82P, AuBYP SUP, ConAu 29R, WhoAm 74, –76, –78, –80, –82, WhoAmP 81, WhoE 74
Richmond, Julius Benjamin 1916-
AmM&WS 86P, WhoAm 84, –86, WhoFrS 84
Richmond, Leonard *WhE&EA*
Richmond, Leonard d1965 *ArtsAmW 3*
Richmond, Sandra 1948- *ConAu 117*
Richoux, Pat 1927- *BioIn 10, ConAu 25R*

Richoux, Pat *see also* Richoux, Patricia
Richoux, Patricia 1927- *SmATA 7*
Richoux, Patricia *see* Richoux, Pat
Richter, Conrad 1890-1968 *AmAu&B,
AmNov, AuBYP SUP, BioIn 1, –2,
–3, –4, –5, –7, –8, –9, –12, CnDAL,
ConAu 5R, –25R, ConLC 30[port],
CurBio 51, –68, CyWA,
DcLB 9[port], DcLEL,
EncFWF[port], LinLib L, McGEWB,
ModAL, Novels, ObitOF 79,
OxAmL, –83, PenC AM, RAdv 1,
REn, REnAL, REnAW, ScF&FL 1,
SmATA 3, TwCA, –SUP, WhAm 5,
WhE&EA, WhNAA*
Richter, Ed *AuBYP SUP*
Richter, Hans Peter 1925- *BioIn 9,
–10, ConAu 2NR, –45, FourBJA,
IntAu&W 76, –77, –82, –86,
SmATA 6, TwCCW 78B, –83B,
WhoWor 78*
Richter, Hans Peter 1926- *OxChL*
Rickenbacker, Edward Vernon
1890-1973 *AmAu&B, ApCAB X,
BiDAmBL 83, BioIn 1, –2, –3, –5, –6,
–7, –8, –9, –10, –11, –12, CelR,
ConAu 101, –41R, CurBio 40, –52,
–73, –73N, InSci, LinLib L, –S,
MedHR, NewYTBE 73, ObitOF 79,
OhA&B, WebAB, –79, WebAMB,
WhAm 5, WhoMilH 76, WorAl*
Rickett, Frances 1921- *ConAu 107*
Rickey, Don, Jr. 1925- *ConAu 5R,
–9NR*
Ricks, Christopher 1933- *WrDr 86*
Riddell, Charlotte Eliza Lawson
1832?-1906 *Alli SUP, BbD,
BiD&SB, BiDIrW, CelCen, DcEnL,
DcIrW 1, DcNaB S2, InWom, NewC,
WomNov*
Ride, Sally 1951- *BioIn 13, HerW 84*
Rider, John R 1923- *ConAu 25R,
DrAS 74E, –78E, –82E, WhoMW 74,
–76*
Ridge, Martin 1923- *DrAS 74H, –78H,
–82H, EncAAH, SmATA 43[port],
WhoAm 78, –80, –82, –84, –86*
Ridgeway, James Fowler 1936-
*AmAu&B, BioIn 7, ConAu 106,
WhoAm 74, –76, –78, –80, –82, –84,
–86*
Ridgeway, Rick 1949?- *BioIn 12,
ConAu 93*
Ridgway, John 1938- *BioIn 12,
ConAu 25R, IntAu&W 77, –82,
WrDr 76, –80, –82, –84, –86*
Ridle, Julia Brown 1923- *ConAu 1R*
Ridley, Anthony 1933- *Au&Wr 71,
ConAu 107, IntAu&W 77, –82,
WrDr 76, –80, –82, –84, –86*
Riedman, Sarah Regal 1902- *AuBYP,
BioIn 8, –9, ConAu 1R, –1NR,
ForWC 70, SmATA 1, WhoAmW 58,
–61, –64*
Rienow, Leona Train *AuBYP, BioIn 8,
ScF&FL 1, WhoAmW 74, –70, –72,
–75, –77, WhoE 74*
Rienow, Leona Train 1903?-1983
BioIn 13, ConAu 111
Rienow, Robert 1909- *AmM&WS 73S,
–78S, ConAu 21R, ScF&FL 1, –2*
Rieseberg, Harry E 1892- *BioIn 9,
ConAu 5R*
Riesenberg, Felix 1879-1939
*AmAu&B, AmLY, DcNAA,
NatCAB 29, OxAmL, –83, REnAL,
TwCA, WhAm 1, WhNAA*
Riesenberg, Felix 1913-1962 *BioIn 13*
Riesenberg, Felix, Jr. 1913-1962
*AuBYP, BioIn 4, –7, ConAu 101,
CurBio 57, SmATA 23*
Riesman, David 1909- *AmAu&B,
AmM&WS 73S, –78S, Au&Wr 71,
BiDAmEd, BioIn 3, –4, –5, –12,
BlueB 76, ConAu 5R, CurBio 55,
DcLEL 1940, EncAB-H,
IntAu&W 76, IntWW 74, –75, –76,
–77, –78, –79, –80, –81, –82, –83,
LinLib L, NewYTBS 80[port],
PenC AM, REnAL, TwCA SUP,
WebAB, –79, WhoAm 74, –78,
–80, –86, WhoE 74, WhoWor 74, –78,
–80, –82, –84, WhoWorJ 72, –78,
WrDr 80, –82, –84, –86*

Riessen, Clare 1941- *AuBYP SUP*
Riessen, Clare *see also* Riessen,
Martin Clare
Riessen, Martin Clare 1941-
ConAu 41R
Riessen, Martin Clare *see also* Riessen,
Clare
Riker, Tom L 1936- *ConAu 104*
Rikhoff, Jean *DrAP&F 85*
Rikhoff, Jean 1928- *AuBYP SUP,
BioIn 11, ConAu 61, IntAu&W 82,
SmATA 9*
Riley, Glenda 1938- *WhoAmW 87*
Riley, James Whitcomb 1849-1916
*Alli SUP, AmAu, AmAu&B, AmBi,
AmSCAP 66, ApCAB, ApCAB X,
BbD, BiD&SB, BioIn 1, –2, –3, –4,
–5, –6, –7, –8, –9, –10, –11, –12, –13,
BlkAWP, CarSB, CasWL, Chambr 3,
ChrP, ChhPo, –S1, –S2, –S3, CnDAL,
ConAu 118, DcAmAu, DcAmB,
DcEnA AP, DcLEL, DcNAA,
EncAAH, EvLB, IndAu 1816,
JBA 34, LinLib L, –S, LongCTC,
McGEWB, NatCAB 6, OxAmL, –83,
OxChL, PenC AM, RAdv 1, REn,
REnAL, SmATA 17, Str&VC,
TwCBDA, WebAB, –79, WhAm 1,
WhFla, WhLit, WhoC 74*
Riley, Jocelyn *DrAP&F 85*
Riley, Jocelyn 1949- *ConAu 115*
Rilke, Rainer Maria 1875-1926 *AtlBL,
BioIn 1, –2, –3, –4, –5, –6, –7, –8, –9,
–10, –11, –12, –13, CasWL,
ChhPo S3, ClDMEL, CnMWL,
ConAu 104, CyWA, Dis&D,
EncWL, –2[port], EvEuW, GrFLW,
IlEncMy, LinLib L, –S, LongCTC,
LuthC 75, MakMC, McGEWB,
ModGL, OxEng, –85, PenC EUR,
RComWL, REn, TwCA, –SUP,
TwCLC 1, –6[port], –19[port],
TwCWr, WhDW, WhAm 4A,
WhoTwCL, WorAl*
Rimland, Ingrid 1936- *ConAu 61*
Rinaldi, Ann 1934- *ConAu 111*
Rinehart, Mary Roberts 1876-1958
*AmAu&B, AmNov, AmWomD,
AmWomWr, ApCAB X, BioIn 1, –2,
–3, –4, –5, –11, –12, ConAmL,
ConAu 108, CorpD, DcAmB S6,
DcBiA, DcLEL, EncAB 2, EncMys,
EvLB, HalFC 84, InWom, LibW,
LinLib L, –S, LongCTC, ModWD,
NotAW MOD, NotNAT B, Novels,
ObitOF 79, ObitT 1951, OxAmL, –83,
OxAmT 84, PenC AM, REn, REnAL,
TwCA, –SUP, TwCCr&M 80, –85,
TwCWr, WebAB, –79, WhAm 3,
WhLit, WhNAA, WhThe,
WomWWA 14, WorAl*
Rink, Paul 1912- *AuBYP, BioIn 7*
Rinker, Rosalind Beatrice 1906-
ConAu 5R, –5NR
Rinkoff, Barbara Jean 1923-1975
*AuBYP, BioIn 8, –9, –10, ConAu 57,
ConAu P-2, IntAu&W 76, MorBMP,
SmATA 27N, –4, WhAm 6,
WhoAmW 75, WrDr 76*
Rintels, David W 1938?- *ConAu 73,
LesBEnT, NewYTET, WhoAm 78,
–80, –82*
Riordan, James 1936- *BioIn 13,
ConAu 11NR, –69, SmATA 28[port],
WrDr 82, –84, –86*
Rios, Tere 1917- *BioIn 9, ConAu X,
ForWC 70, ScF&FL 1, –2, SmATA 2*
Rios, Tere *see also* Versace, Marie
Teresa Rios
Ripley, Dillon *Who 85*
Ripley, Dillon 1913- *ConAu 57,
Who 83*
Ripley, Dillon *see also* Ripley, Sidney
Dillon
Ripley, Elizabeth 1906-1969 *AuBYP,
BioIn 4, –5, –7, –8, –10, ChhPo S2,
ConAu 1R, –3NR, CurBio 58,
InWom, SmATA 5*
Ripley, S Dillon 1913-
*AmM&WS 73P, BlueB 76, CelR,
CurBio 66, IntAu&W 74, –75, –76,
–82, IntWW 74, –75, –76, –77, –78,
–79, –80, –81, –82, –83, WhoGov 77,
–72, –75, WhoS&SW 73, –75, –76*

Ripley, Sidney Dillon 1913-
*AmM&WS 76P, –79P, –82P, BioIn 2,
–7, –9, –10, –11, Who 83, –85,
WhoAm 74, –76, –78, –80, –82,
WhoE 79, –81, WhoWor 74*
Ripley, Sidney Dillon, II 1913-
AmM&WS 86P, WhoAm 84, –86
Ripley, Sidney Dillon *see also* Ripley,
Dillon
Rischin, Moses 1925- *ConAu 3NR,
–9R, DrAS 74H, –78H, –82H,
IntAu&W 77, WhoRel 75, –77,
WhoWorJ 78, WrDr 76, –80, –82,
–84, –86*
Riser, Wayne H 1909-
*AmM&WS 73P, –76P, –79P, BioIn 4,
ConAu P-1*
Ritch, Ocee 1922- *WhoWest 74, –76,
–78, –80*
Ritchie, Barbara Gibbons 1943-
*AuBYP, BiDrLUS 70, BioIn 8, –12,
ConAu 73, SmATA 14*
Rittenhouse, Mignon 1904-
*ConAu 41R, WhoAmW 74, –58, –61,
–64, –66, –68, –70, –72, –75, –77,
–79, –81*
Ritter, Lawrence S 1922- *AmEA 74,
AmM&WS 73S, –78S, ConAu 21R,
WhoAm 74, –76, WhoE 74*
Rivera, Edith *AuBYP SUP*
Rivera, Edward *DrAP&F 85*
Rivera, Feliciano 1932- *ChiSch,
ConAu 45, DrAS 74H, –78H, –82H,
IntAu&W 79*
Rivera, Geraldo 1943- *AuBYP SUP,
BioIn 9, –10, –12, –13, BioNews 74,
CelR, ConAu 108, CurBio 75, EncAJ,
EncTwCJ, IntMPA 78, –79, –81, –82,
–84, –86, LesBEnT[port],
NewYTBE 71, NewYTET,
SmATA 28, WhoAm 78, –80, –82,
–84*
Rivers, Caryl 1937- *BioIn 10,
ConAu 4NR, –49*
Rivers-Coffey, Rachel 1943- *ConAu 73*
Riviere, Bill 1916- *ConAu X*
Riviere, Bill *see also* Riviere, William
Alexander
Riviere, William Alexander 1916-
ConAu 5R, –8NR
Roach, Marilynne K 1946- *BioIn 11,
ConAu 12NR, –57, SmATA 9*
Robbins, Chandler S 1918-
*AmM&WS 73P, –76P, –79P, –82P,
WhoE 83, –85, WhoWor 84*
Robbins, Chandler Seymour 1918-
AmM&WS 86P
Robbins, Harold *Who 85*
Robbins, Harold 1912?- *AmAu&B,
AmNov, BioIn 8, –9, –10, –12, CelR,
ConAu 73, ConLC 5, CurBio 70,
FilmgC, IntAu&W 76, –77,
IntWW 74, –75, –76, –77, –78, –79,
–80, –81, –82, –83, Novels[port],
TwCWr, Who 74, –82, –83,
WhoAm 74, –76, –78, –80, –82,
WhoWor 78, –80, –82, WorAl,
WrDr 76, –80, –82, –84, –86*
Robbins, Harold 1916- *HalFC 84,
WhoAm 84, –86, WhoWor 84, –87*
Robbins, Paul R 1930- *ConAu 114*
Robbins, Tom 1936- *BioIn 9, –11, –12,
–13, ConAu X, ConLC 9, –32[port],
ConNov 82, –86, DcLB Y80B[port],
NewYTBS 80[port], OxAmL 83,
PostFic, WhoAm 82, –84, –86,
WrDr 82, –84, –86*
Roberts, Cecil 1892-1976 *Au&Wr 71,
BioIn 3, –4, –7, –8, –9, –10, –11,
ChhPo, –S1, –S2, ConAu 69,
ConAu P-2, DcLEL, IntAu&W 76,
IntMed 80, LongCTC, NewC,
ScF&FL 1, –2, TwCA, –SUP,
WhAm 7, WhE&EA, WhLit,
WhNAA, Who 74, WrDr 76*
Roberts, Charles G D 1860-1943
*ApCAB, –SUP, ConAu 105, EncSF,
NatCAB 11, ScF&FL 1, SmATA 29,
TwCCW 78, –83, TwCLC 8[port],
WhAm 3, WhE&EA*
Roberts, David S 1943- *ConAu 33R*
Roberts, Elliott B 1899- *ConAu 1R,
WrDr 76, –80, –82, –84*

Roberts, Eric 1914- *Au&Wr 71,
ConAu 5R, IntAu&W 76, –86,
WrDr 76, –80, –82, –84, –86*
Roberts, Jane *ConAu X*
Roberts, Jane 1929- *AmWomWr,
ConAu 41R, ConSFA, EncO&P 2S1,
EncSF, ScF&FL 1, –2, ScFSB,
WrDr 76, –80, –82, –84*
Roberts, John G 1913- *BioIn 13,
ConAu 49, SmATA 27[port]*
Roberts, Keith *DrmM 2[port]*
Roberts, Keith 1935- *ConAu 25R,
ConLC 14, ConSFA, EncSF, Novels,
ScF&FL 1, –2, ScFSB, TwCSFW 86,
WhoSciF, WrDr 76, –80, –82, –84,
–86*
Roberts, Kenneth Lewis 1885-1957
*AmAu&B, AmNov, BioIn 1, –2, –4,
–5, –7, –12, CasWL, CnDAL,
ConAmA, ConAu 109, DcAmAu,
DcAmB S6, DcLB 9[port], DcLEL,
EvLB, LinLib L, –S, LongCTC,
ModAL, NatCAB 48, Novels,
ObitOF 79, ObitT 1951, OxAmL,
OxCan, PenC AM, REn, REnAL,
TwCA, –SUP, TwCWr, WhAm 3,
WhE&EA, WhLit, WhNAA, WorAl*
Roberts, Lawrence *WrDr 82*
Roberts, Nancy Correll 1924-
*AuBYP SUP, BioIn 13, ConAu 6NR,
–9R, ForWC 70, SmATA 28,
WhoAmW 74, –68, –70, –72, –75,
–77*
Roberts, Sir Charles G D 1860-1943
*Alli SUP, BbD, BiD&SB, BioIn 1, –4,
–5, –9, –10, CanNov, CanWr,
Chambr 3, ChhPo, –S1, –S2, –S3,
ConAmL, CreCan 2, CurBio 44,
DcAmAu, DcBiA, DcNAA, EvLB,
JBA 34, LinLib L, –S, LongCTC,
MacDCB 78, ObitOF 79, OxAmL,
OxCan, OxCanL, OxChL, OxEng,
PenC ENG, REn, REnAL,
TwCA, –SUP, WebE&AL, WhAm 3,
WhE&EA, WhLit*
Roberts, Sir Charles George Douglas
1860-1943 *BioIn 13, OxAmL 83*
Roberts, Thom 1940- *ConAu 15NR,
–81*
Roberts, Willo Davis 1928- *BioIn 12,
ConAu 3NR, –19NR, –49,
FifBJA[port], IntAu&W 86,
MichAu 80, SmATA 21[port],
TwCCr&M 85, WrDr 76, –80, –82,
–84, –86*
Robertson, Charles Patrick 1919-
WhoLib 75
Robertson, Don 1929- *BioIn 11,
ConAu 7NR, –9R, SmATA 8*
Robertson, Dougal 1924- *BioIn 10,
ConAu 61*
Robertson, James Oliver 1932-
*ConAu 106, –111, DrAS 74H, –78H,
–82H*
Robertson, Keith *OxChL*
Robertson, Keith 1914- *Au&Wr 71,
AuBYP, BioIn 6, –7, –9, –10,
ConAu 9R, MorBMP, MorJA,
SmATA 1, TwCCW 78, –83,
WhoRocM 82, WrDr 80, –82, –84,
–86*
Robertson, Martin *ConAu X*
Robertson, Mary Elsie *DrAP&F 85*
Robertson, Mary Elsie 1937- *BioIn 13,
ConAu 15NR, –81*
Robeson, Kenneth *ConAu X,
TwCCr&M 85, TwCSFW 86,
WrDr 86*
Robeson, Kenneth 1933- *ConAu X,
TwCCr&M 80, WrDr 82, –84*
Robeson, Kenneth *see also* Goulart,
Ron
Robichaud, Beryl 1919- *Dun&B 79,
ForWC 70, St&PR 75, WhoAm 74,
–76, –78, –82, WhoAmW 74, –70,
–72, –75, –77, WhoF&I 74, –75, –77*
Robins, Denise *Who 85*
Robins, Denise 1897- *BioIn 7,
ConAu 10NR, –65, IntAu&W 76,
–77, –82, Novels, WhE&EA, Who 74,
–82, –83, WrDr 76, –80, –82, –84*
Robins, Denise 1897?-1985
ConAu 116, –19NR
Robins, Elizabeth *OxEng 85, WomNov*

Robins, Elizabeth 1862?-1952
*AmAu&B, AmWomWr, BbD,
BiDBrF 1, BioIn 2, -4, -11, -12,
CnDAL, ConAu 116, InWom,
LongCTC, NotNAT A, -B,
ObitOF 79, ObitT 1951, OhA&B,
OxAmL, OxThe, -83, REn, REnAL,
TwCA, -SUP, WhThe*
Robins, Elizabeth 1865-1952
OxAmL 83
Robinson, Alice M 1920-1983
*ConAu 108, -109, WhoAmW 74, -75,
-77*
Robinson, Barbara Webb 1927-
*AuBYP SUP, BioIn 8, -11, ConAu 1R,
SmATA 8, WhoAmW 64*
Robinson, Bill *ConAu X*
Robinson, Chaille Howard Payne
ConAu 13R, WhoAmW 58
Robinson, Charles 1931- *BioIn 10,
-12, ConAu 49, IlsBYP, IlsCB 1967,
SmATA 6, WhoBW&I I*
Robinson, Charles Alexander, Jr.
1900-1965 *AmAu&B, AuBYP,
BioIn 1, -3, -7, ConAu 1R,
SmATA 36, WhAm 4, WhE&EA*
Robinson, David A 1925- *ConAu 17R,
WhoTech 82, -84*
Robinson, David Adair 1925-
AmM&WS 86P, WhoAm 84, -86
Robinson, Derek 1932- *AmEA 74,
BioIn 10, BlueB 76, ConAu 77,
IntAu&W 82, Who 74, -82, -85,
WrDr 76, -80, -82, -86*
Robinson, Donald 1913- *ConAu 25R,
IntAu&W 77*
Robinson, Frank 1935- *BioIn 6, -7,
-8, -9, -10, -11, -12, -13,
BioNews 74, CelR, CmCal,
CurBio 71, InB&W 80, -85,
NewYTBS 74, -75, WhoAm 74, -76,
-78, -80, -82, -84, -86, WhoBlA 75,
-77, -80, -85, WhoProB 73,
WhoWest 84, WorAl*
Robinson, Frank M 1926-
*ConAu 3NR, -19NR, -49, EncSF,
ScF&FL 1, -2, ScFSB, TwCSFW 86,
WhoSciF, WrDr 84, -86*
Robinson, Helen Caister 1899-
ConAu 16NR
Robinson, Jerry *MarqDCG 84*
Robinson, Jerry 1922- *ConAu 112,
IlsBYP, SmATA 34*
Robinson, Joan G *OxChL, WrDr 86*
Robinson, Joan G 1910- *Au&Wr 71,
AuBYP SUP, BioIn 8, -9, -10,
ConAu 5R, -5NR, IntAu&W 77,
-77X, -82, -82X, SmATA 7,
TwCCW 78, -83, WhoChL, WrDr 80,
-82, -84*
Robinson, Kathleen *ConAu X*
Robinson, Kathleen *see also* Robinson,
Chaille Howard Payne
Robinson, Kim Stanley *ConLC 34*
Robinson, Kim Stanley 1952-
TwCSFW 86
Robinson, Logan G 1949- *BioIn 12,
ConAu 108*
Robinson, Mabel Louise 1874-1962
*AmAu&B, AmNov, BioIn 1, -2, -6,
-7, ConAu 113, DcLB 22[port],
InWom, JBA 51, NatCAB 47,
WhAm 4, WhE&EA, WhLit,
WhNAA, WhoAmW 58*
Robinson, Margaret A *DrAP&F 85*
Robinson, Margaret A 1937-
ConAu 107
Robinson, Margaret King 1906-
WhoAmP 83, -85
Robinson, Marilynne *BioIn 13*
Robinson, Marilynne 1943- *ConNov 86*
Robinson, Marilynne 1944-
ConAu 116, ConLC 25[port]
Robinson, Nancy K 1942- *ConAu 106,
SmATA 31, -32[port]*
Robinson, Ray 1920- *AuBYP, BioIn 7,
-13, ConAu 77, SmATA 23*
Robinson, Richard 1945- *BioIn 10,
ConAu 13NR, -57, MugS*
Robinson, Sondra Till 1931-
ConAu 7NR, -53
Robinson, Spider *OxCanL*

Robinson, Spider 1948- *ConAu 11NR,
-65, EncSF, IntAu&W 82, ScFSB,
TwCSFW 86, WhoCanL 85,
WrDr 84, -86*
Robinson, Stuart 1936- *BiE&WWA*
Robinson, Veronica 1926-
*AuBYP SUP, ConAu 105,
SmATA 30[port]*
Robinson, Willard B 1935-
AmArch 70, ConAu 57
Robison, Nancy L 1934- *ConAu 93,
SmATA 32[port]*
Robotham, John Stanley 1924-
BiDrLUS 70, WhoLibS 55, -66
Robottom, John *WrDr 86*
Robottom, John 1934- *Au&Wr 71,
BioIn 10, ConAu 16NR, -29R,
IntAu&W 76, SmATA 7, WrDr 76,
-80, -82, -84*
Robson, Ernest *DrAP&F 85*
Robson, Lucia St. Clair 1942-
ConAu 108
Rock, Gail *AuBYP SUP, ConAu 111,
SmATA 32*
Rockne, Knute Kenneth 1888-1931
*AmBi, BioIn 1, -2, -3, -4, -5, -6, -7,
-8, -9, -10, -11, -12, DcAmB,
DcCathB, IndAu 1917, McGEWB,
NatCAB 25, OxAmH, WebAB, -79,
WhAm 1, WhoFtbl 74, WorAl*
Rockowitz, Murray 1920- *ConAu 25R,
WhoE 74*
Rocks, Lawrence 1933-
*AmM&WS 73P, -76P, -79P, -82P,
-86P, ConAu 85, WhoE 81, -83,
WhoTech 82, -84*
Rockwell, Anne 1934- *BioIn 12,
ChhPo S3, ConAu 21R, FifBJA[port],
IlsBYP, IlsCB 1967, SmATA 33[port]*
Rockwell, Frederick Frye 1884-1976
*BioIn 10, -13, ConAu 49,
NatCAB 61[port], NewYTBS 76,
WhAm 7*
Rockwell, Norman 1894-1978 *BioIn 1,
-2, -3, -4, -5, -6, -7, -9, -10, -11,
-12, -13, BlueB 76, CelR, ChhPo S2,
ConAu 81, -89, CurBio 45, -79N,
EncAJ, ForIl, IlBEAAW,
IlrAm 1880[port], -C, IlsBYP,
IlsCB 1744, LinLib S, NewYTBE 71,
NewYTBS 78, ObitOF 79, PrintW 83,
-85, REn, REnAL, SmATA 23[port],
WebAB, -79, WhAm 7, WhoAm 74,
-76, -78, WhoAmA 73, -76, -78,
-80N, -82N, -84N, WhoGrA 62,
WhoWor 74, WorAl, WorECar*
Rockwell, Thomas 1933- *BioIn 10,
ChlLR 6[port], ChhPo S1,
ConAu 29R, FifBJA[port],
IntAu&W 77, SmATA 7, WrDr 76,
-80, -82, -84, -86*
Rockwood, Joyce 1947- *ConAu 6NR,
-57, SmATA 39[port]*
Rockwood, Louis G 1925- *ConAu 45,
WhoMW 76*
Roddenberry, Gene *SmATA X*
Roddenberry, Gene 1921- *ConAu X,
ConLC 17, ConSFA, ConTFT 3[port],
FilmgC, HalFC 84, IntMPA 84, -86,
LesBEnT, NewYTET, ScF&FL 1, -2,
WhoSciF*
Roderus, Frank 1942- *ConAu 17NR,
-89, EncFWF, WrDr 86*
Rodgers, Bill 1947- *BioIn 11, -12, -13,
CurBio 82[port], NewYTBS 81[port],
WorAl*
Rodgers, Mary 1931- *AmSCAP 66,
AuBYP SUP, BiE&WWA, BioIn 5,
-11, ConAmC, -82, ConAu 8NR, -49,
ConLC 12, EncMT, FifBJA[port],
InWom, IntAu&W 77, NewCBMT,
NotNAT, ScF&FL 1, -2, SmATA 8,
TwCCW 78, -83, WhoAm 78, -80,
-82, -84, -86, WhoAmW 74, -61,
-70, -72, -75, WhoThe 81, WrDr 80,
-82, -84, -86*
Rodgers, Raboo 1945- *ConAu 119*
Rodinson, Maxime 1915- *ConAu 4NR,
-53, FifIDA, WhoFr 79*
Rodman, Bella 1903- *AuBYP SUP,
ConAu P-2*
Rodman, F Robert 1934- *ConAu 117*
Rodman, Maia *DrAP&F 85*

Rodman, Maia 1927- *ConAu X,
ForWC 70, SmATA 1, -X,
TwCChW 83*
Rodman, Maia *see also* Wojciechowska,
Maia
Rodman, Selden 1909- *AmAu&B,
AuBYP SUP, BioIn 4, -11,
ChhPo, -S1, ConAu 5R, -5NR,
LinLib L, OxAmL, -83, REn,
REnAL, SmATA 9, TwCA SUP,
WhoAm 74, -76, -78, WhoAmA 73,
-76, -78, -80, -82, -84, WhoWor 74*
Rodowsky, Colby 1932- *BioIn 12,
ConAu 69, SmATA 21*
Rodriguez, Richard 1944- *ConAu 110*
Rodriguez, Richard 1946?- *BioIn 13*
Roesch, Roberta F 1919- *ConAu 2NR,
-5R, IntAu&W 76, -82,
WhoAmW 68, -70*
Roessler, Carl 1933- *ConAu 117*
Roethke, Theodore 1908-1963
*AmAu&B, AmWr, AnCL, AtlBL,
BioIn 3, -4, -6, -7, -8, -9, -10, -11,
-12, -13, CasWL, ChhPo, -S1, -S2,
-S3, CnDAL, CnE&AP, ConAu 81,
ConAu 2BS, ConLC 1, -3, -8, -11,
-19, ConPo 75, -80A, -85A, CroCAP,
DcAmB S7, DcLB 5, DcLEL 1940,
EncWL, -2[port], LinLib L,
LongCTC, MakMC, McGEWB,
MichAu 80, ModAL, -S2, -S1,
NewCon[port], ObitOF 79,
ObitT 1961, OxAmL, -83, OxEng 85,
PenC AM, RAdv 1, REn, REnAL,
TwCA SUP, TwCWr, WebAB, -79,
WebE&AL, WhDW, WhAm 4,
WhoPNW, WhoTwCL, WorAl*
Rofes, Eric Edward 1954- *ConAu 106*
Rogers, Barbara Radcliffe 1939-
*WhoAmP 73, -75, -77, -79, -81, -83,
-85*
Rogers, Dale Evans 1912- *AmAu&B,
BioIn 3, -4, -9, -10, -12, ConAu 103,
CurBio 56, InWom, WhoAm 76, -78,
-80, -82*
Rogers, Frances 1888-1974 *BioIn 11,
ConAu 53, MichAu 80, SmATA 10*
Rogers, Isabel Wood 1924- *DrAS 74P,
-78P, -82P, WhoRel 75, -77*
Rogers, James Tracy 1921- *ConAu 45,
WhoAmP 73, WhoE 75, -77*
Rogers, Julia Ellen 1866- *AmAu&B,
WhAm 4, WomWWA 14*
Rogers, Katharine M 1932-
*AmWomWr, ConAu 8NR, -21R,
DrAS 74E, -78E, -82E,
WhoAmW 74, -70, -75, -79, -81,
-83, WrDr 76, -80, -84, -86*
Rogers, Katharine Munzer 1932-
WhoAmW 85, -87
Rogers, Kenny 1937-
EncFCWM 83[port]
Rogers, Kenny 1938?- *BioIn 11, -12,
-13, ConAu X, CurBio 81[port],
RkOn 78, WorAl*
Rogers, Kenny 1939- *Baker 84*
Rogers, Kenny 1941- *RolSEnR 83,
WhoRock 81[port]*
Rogers, Michael *DrAP&F 85*
Rogers, Michael 1950- *ConAu 1NR,
-49, ScF&FL 1, -2*
Rogers, Michael 1951- *ScFSB*
Rogers, Pamela 1927- *AuBYP SUP,
BioIn 11, ConAu 4NR, -49,
SmATA 9, WrDr 80, -82, -84, -86*
Rogers, Thomas 1927- *BioIn 8,
ConAu 89, IntAu&W 82, WhoAm 74,
-76, -78, WhoE 75, -77, WrDr 76,
-80, -82, -84, -86*
Rogers, Thomas Hunton 1927-
IntAu&W 86
Rogers, W G 1896-1978 *ConAu 77,
SmATA 23[port]*
Rogers, William Garland 1896-1978
*AmAu&B, AuBYP, BioIn 1, -8, -11,
-13, ConAu 9R, IntAu&W 77,
NewYTBS 78, WrDr 76*
Rohmer, Sax *EncO&P 2*
Rohmer, Sax 1883-1959 *BioIn 1, -4,
-5, -6, -9, -13, ConAu X, CorpD,
EncMys, EncO&P 78, EncSF, EvLB,
LinLib LP, LongCTC, MnBBF,
NewC, NotNAT B, Novels, ObitOF 79,*

*ObitT 1951, PenC ENG, ScF&FL 1,
SupFW, TwCA, -SUP,
TwCCr&M 80, -85, TwCWr,
WhE&EA, WhLit, WhThe,
WhoBW&I A, WhoHr&F, WhoLA,
WhoSpyF, WorAl*
Rohmer, Sax 1886-1959 *HalFC 84*
Rohmer, Sax *see also* Ward, Arthur
Sarsfield
Roland, Albert 1925- *BioIn 11,
ConAu 61, SmATA 11, USBiR 74,
WhoGov 77*
Roll, Winifred 1909- *BioIn 10,
ConAu 49, SmATA 6*
Rolling Stones, The *CelR,
EncPR&S 74, -77, IlEncRk,
MakMC, RkOn 78, -84, RkOneH,
RolSEnR 83, WhoRock 81[port]*
Rolling Stones, The *see also* Jagger,
Mick
Rolling Stones, The *see also* Jones,
Brian
Rolling Stones, The *see also* Richard,
Keith
Rolling Stones, The *see also* Taylor,
Mick
Rolling Stones, The *see also* Watts,
Charles
Rolling Stones, The *see also* Wyman,
Bill
Rollins, Charlemae Hill 1897-1979
*ALA 80N[port], AuBYP, BioIn 2, -3,
-7, BlkAWP, ChhPo S1, ConAu 9R,
-104, ForWC 70, InB&W 80, -85,
LivgBAA, MorBMP, SelBAAf,
SelBAAu, SmATA 26N, -3, WhAm 7,
WhoAm 76, WhoAmW 58, -61, -64,
-66, -68, -70, WhoLibS 55*
Rollins, Ellen Chapman Hobbs
1831-1881 *Alli SUP, ApCAB,
DcAmAu, DcNAA*
Rollins, Ellen Chapman Hobbs *see also*
Arr, E H
Rolston, Holmes, II 1932-
IntAu&W 86
Rolston, Holmes, III 1932-
*ConAu 113, DrAS 74P, -78P, -82P,
WhoRel 85, WhoWest 82*
Rolvaag, O E *ConAu X*
Rolvaag, O E 1876-1931 *DcLB 9[port],
EncFWF, OxAmL 83,
TwCLC 17[port], WorAl*
Rome, Margaret *WrDr 84, -86*
Rome, Margaret 1929- *IntAu&W 86*
Romulo, Carlos P 1899- *AmAu&B,
BiDrAC, BioIn 1, -2, -3, -4, -5, -6,
-8, -10, CathA 1930, ConAu 10NR,
-13R, CurBio 43, -57, FarE&A 78,
-79, -80, -81, IntAu&W 77, -82,
IntWW 74, -75, -76, -77, -78, -79,
-80, -81, -82, IntYB 78, -79,
-80, -81, -82, LinLib L, -S,
McGEWB, WhE&EA, WhNAA,
WhoUN 75, WhoWor 74, -76, -78,
-80, -82*
Romulo, Carlos P 1899?-1985
ConAu 118, NewYTBS 85[port]
Romulo, Carlos P 1901-1985
CurBio 86N
Ronan, Colin Alistair 1920-
*Au&Wr 71, ConAu 5R, -6NR,
IntAu&W 76, -77, -82, -86,
WhoWor 76, WrDr 76, -80, -82, -84,
-86*
Ronan, Margaret 1918- *ConAu 102,
WhoAmW 66*
Ronning, Chester A 1894- *BioIn 13,
CanWW 70*
Ronning, Chester A 1894-1984
ConAu 114, NewYTBS 85[port]
Rood, Robert Thomas 1942-
*AmM&WS 73P, -76P, -79P, -82P,
-86P, ConAu 107*
Rood, Ronald 1920- *BioIn 11,
ConAu 9NR, -21R, IntAu&W 86,
SmATA 12*
Rooke, Patrick John 1925- *Au&Wr 71*
Rooney, Andrew A 1919- *WrDr 86*
Rooney, Andrew Aitken *BioIn 13*
Rooney, Andrew Aitken 1919-
EncTwCJ, WhoAm 84, -86

Rounds, David 1930-1983 *BioIn 13, ConAu 111, NewYTBS 83[port], NotNAT, WhAm 8, WhoAm 82, WhoHol A*

Rounds, Glen H 1906- *AuBYP, BioIn 1, –2, –3, –5, –7, –8, –10, –11, –12, ChhPo S1, –S2, ConAu 7NR, –53, IlsCB 1744, –1946, –1957, –1967, JBA 51, REnAL, SmATA 8, TwCCW 78, –83, WrDr 80, –82, –84*

Rourke, Constance Mayfield 1885-1941 *AmAu&B, AmWomWr, AnCL, BioIn 1, –6, –11, –12, CnDAL, ConAmA, ConAu 107, CurBio 41, DcAmB S3, DcNAA, InWom, LibW, ModAL, MorJA, NatCAB 32, NotAW, OhA&B, OxAmL, PenC AM, REn, REnAL, TwCA, –SUP, TwCLC 12[port], WhAm 1, YABC 1*

Rouse, Parke Shepherd, Jr, 1915- *ConAu 17R*

Rouse, Parke Shepherd, Jr. 1915- *IntAu&W 77, –82, WhoGov 77, –75, WhoS&SW 73*

Rouse, Parke Shepherd, Jr, 1915- *WrDr 76*

Rouse, Parke Shepherd, Jr. 1915- *WrDr 80, –82, –84, –86*

Rouse, William Henry Denham 1863-1950 *BioIn 2, –5, DcInB, DcNaB 1941, WhE&EA, WhLit, WhoLA*

Rover, Constance Mary 1910- *ConAu 21R, WrDr 76, –80, –82, –84, –86*

Rovin, Jeff 1951- *ConAu 77*

Rowe, Jack F 1927- *WhoTech 84*

Rowe, Jack Field 1927- *Dun&B 79, WhoAm 74, –76, –78, –80, –82, –84, –86, WhoEng 80, WhoF&I 74, –77, –85, WhoTech 82*

Rowe, Jeanne A 1938- *ConAu 29R*

Rowe, Terry *AuNews 2, BioIn 11*

Rowell, Galen *BioIn 13*

Rowell, Galen 1940- *ConAu 18NR, –65, ICPEnP A*

Rowes, Barbara Gail *ConAu 101*

Rowland-Entwistle, Theodore 1925- *IntAu&W 76, –77, –86, IntWWM 77, SmATA 31[port]*

Rowlands, John *IntAu&W 82*

Rowlands, John 1938- *OxLitW 86*

Rowling, Marjorie Alice 1900- *Au&Wr 71, ConAu 5R, IntAu&W 77, WrDr 76, –80, –82, –84*

Rowse, Alfred Leslie *BioIn 13*

Rowse, Alfred Leslie 1903- *Au&Wr 71, BioIn 2, –4, –6, –7, –11, –12, BlueB 76, ChhPo, –S1, ConAu 1R, –1NR, ConPo 70, –75, –80, CurBio 79, IntAu&W 76, –77, –82, –86, IntWW 74, –75, –76, –77, –78, –79, –80, –81, –82, –83, IntWWP 77, –82, LinLib L, LongCTC, ModBrL, NewC, TwCA SUP, WhE&EA, Who 74, –82, –83, –85, WhoWor 74, –76, –78, –84, –87, WrDr 76, –80, –82, –84*

Rowsome, Frank, Jr. 1914-1983 *AmAu&B, ChhPo S3, ConAu 112, SmATA 36, WhoGov 77, –75, WhoS&SW 73*

Roy, Cal *ChhPo*

Roy, Rob 1933- *AmM&WS 86P*

Royce, Kenneth *ConAu X, IntAu&W 86X*

Royce, Kenneth 1920- *Au&Wr 71, ConAu 13NR, IntAu&W 77X, –82X, –86, TwCCr&M 85, WhoSpyF, WrDr 76, –80, –82, –84, –86*

Rozin, Skip 1941- *ConAu 89*

Ruark, Robert 1915-1965 *AmAu&B, BioIn 1, –2, –3, –4, –5, –6, –7, ConAu 25R, ConAu P-2, DcAmB S7, LinLib L, LongCTC, ObitOF 79, REn, REnAL, WhAm 4, WhScrn 77, WorAl*

Rubens, Bernice 192-?- *ConLC 31[port]*

Rubens, Bernice 1927?- *Au&Wr 71, ConAu 25R, ConLC 19, ConNov 72, –76, –82, DcLB 14[port],*

Rubens, Bernice 1928- *BioIn 13, ConNov 86, WrDr 86*

Rubens, Peter Paul 1577-1640 *AtlBL, BioIn 1, –2, –3, –4, –5, –6, –7, –8, –9, –10, –11, –12, ChhPo, DcBiPP, DcCathB, Dis&D, LinLib S, LuthC 75, McGDA, McGEWB, NewC, OxArt, OxEng 85, REn, WhDW, WorAl*

Rubens, Sir Peter Paul 1577-1640 *BioIn 13*

Rubenstein, Joshua 1949- *ConAu 103*

Rubin, Arnold P 1946- *ConAu 69, WhoE 79, –81*

Rubin, Barry 1950- *ConAu 108, DrAS 82H*

Rubin, Barry Mitchel 1950- *WhoAm 86*

Rubin, Charles J 1950- *ConAu 101*

Rubin, Jerry 1938- *AmAu&B, BioIn 8, –10, –11, –12, –13, ConAu 69, MugS, NewYTBS 76, PolProf J*

Rubin, Jonathan 1940?- *BioIn 10*

Rubin, Louis D, Jr. 1923- *ChhPo S1, –S3, ConAu X, –6NR, –21NR, DrAS 74E, –78E, –82E, WhoAm 74, –76, –78, –80, –82*

Rubin, Louis Decimus, Jr. 1923- *WhoAm 84, –86*

Rubin, Michael *DrAP&F 85*

Rubin, Michael 1935- *ConAu 1R, –1NR*

Rubin, Robert Jay 1932- *AmM&WS 73P, –76P, –79P, –86P*

Rubinstein, Erna F 1922- *ConAu 120*

Rubinstein, Morton Karl 1930- *WhoWest 74, –76*

Rubinstein, Robert E 1943- *ConAu 106*

Rublowsky, John M 1928- *AuBYP SUP, ConAu 17R, WhoE 74*

Ruby, Kathryn *DrAP&F 85*

Ruby, Kathryn 1947- *ConAu 65, IntWWP 82*

Ruby, Lois 1942- *ConAu 97, SmATA 34, –35, WhoLibI 82*

Ruchlis, Hyman 1913- *AuBYP, BioIn 7, –9, ConAu 1R, –2NR, SmATA 3*

Rucker, Rudy *ConAu X*

Rucker, Rudy 1946- *ScFSB, TwCSFW 86*

Ruckman, Ivy 1931- *ConAu 111, SmATA 37*

Rudley, Stephen 1946- *ConAu 106, SmATA 30*

Rudloe, Jack 1943- *ConAu 97*

Rudolph, Wilma 1940- *BioIn 5, –6, –7, –8, –9, –10, –11, –12, CurBio 61, GoodHs, HerW, –84, InB&W 80, InWom, IntDcWB, LibW, LinLib S, NegAl 76[port], –83[port], WhoBlA 77, –80, –85, WhoTr&F 73, WorAl*

Rudwick, Elliott 1927- *AmM&WS 78S, DrAS 74H*

Rue, Leonard Lee, III 1926- *AuBYP SUP, BioIn 12, ConAu 1R, –1NR, IntAu&W 76, –77, –82, –86, SmATA 37[port], WrDr 76, –80, –82, –84, –86*

Ruesch, Hans 1913- *Au&Wr 71, BioIn 5, ConAu 13R*

Ruffell, Ann 1941- *ConAu 107, SmATA 30[port]*

Ruggles, Eleanor 1916- *AmAu&B, Au&Wr 71, BioIn 3, –4, ConAu 5R, ForWC 70, REnAL, TwCA SUP, WhoAm 74, –76, –78, WhoAmW 74, –58, –61, –64, –66, –68, –70, –72*

Rugoff, Milton 1913- *ConAu 21R, DrAS 74E, –78E, –82E, SmATA 30[port], WhoAm 76, –78, –80, –82, –84, –86*

Ruhen, Olaf 1911- *Au&Wr 71, BioIn 6, –12, ConAu 1R, –5NR, –20NR, IntAu&W 76, –77, –82, –86, OxAusL, SingR 2, SmATA 17, WhoWor 76, WrDr 76, –80, –82, –84, –86*

Ruiz, Ramon Eduardo 1921- *ChiSch, ConAu 11NR, –25R, DrAS 74H, –78H, –82H, WhoAm 74, –76, –78, –80, –82, –84, –86*

Rukeyser, Muriel 1913-1980 *AmAu&B, AmWomWr, AnObit 1980[port], AuBYP, BioIn 4, –7, –8, –10, –11, –12, –13, BlueB 76, CasWL, ChhPo, –S1, CnDAL, ConAu 5R, –93, ConLC 6, –10, –15, –27[port], ConPo 70, –75, –80, CurBio 43, –80N, DcLB 48[port], DcLEL, DrAS 74E, –78E, ForWC 70, InWom, IntDcWB, IntWW 78, –79, IntWWP 77, –82, LibW, LinLib L, ModAL, –S2, –S1, NewYTBS 80[port], OxAmL, –83, PenC AM, RAdv 1, REn, REnAL, SixAP, SmATA 22N, TwCA, –SUP, TwCWr, WebE&AL, WhAm 7, WhoAm 74, –76, –78, –80, WhoAmW 74, –58, –61, –64, –66, –68, –70, –72, –83, WhoWor 74, –76, WorAl, WrDr 76, –80*

Rukeyser, Muriel 1914-1980 *ModAWP[port]*

Rulfo, Juan 1918- *BioIn 7, –13, CasWL, ConAu 85, ConFLW 84, ConLC 8, DcCLAA, EncLatA, EncWL, –2, ModLAL, Novels, OxSpan, PenC AM, TwCWr, WhoS&SW 73, WorAu 1970*

Rulfo, Juan 1918-1986 *ConAu 118, NewYTBS 86*

Rundgren, Todd 1948- *BioIn 11, –12, EncPR&S 74, –77, IlEncRk, RkOn 78, –84, RolSEnR 83, WhoAm 80, –82, –84, –86, WhoRock 81[port], WhoRocM 82, WorAl*

Rundle, Anne *ConAu 12NR, WrDr 86*

Runyon, Catherine 1947- *ConAu 61*

Runyon, Damon 1880-1946 *BioIn 13*

Runyon, Damon 1884?-1946 *AmAu&B, BioIn 1, –2, –3, –4, –5, –7, –11, –12, CasWL, CnDAL, CnMWL, ConAu 107, CurBio 47, DcAmB S4, DcLB 11[port], DcLEL, DcNAA, EncAJ, EncMys, Film 2, FilmgC, HalFC 84, LinLib L, LongCTC, ModAL, ModWD, NatCAB 39, NotNAT A, –B, Novels[port], ObitOF 79, OxAmL, –83, OxAmT 84, PenC AM, PlP&P, REn, REnAL, TwCA, –SUP, TwCLC 10[port], TwCWr, WebAb, –79, WebE&AL, WhDW, WhAm 2, WhScrn 77, –83, WhoHol B, WorAl*

Runyon, Richard Porter 1925- *AmM&WS 73S, –78S, ConAu 3NR, –45, WhoWest 82, –84*

Rus, Vladimir 1931- *ConAu 17R, IntAu&W 77*

Rush, Anne Kent 1945- *ConAu 8NR, –61, WhoAmW 83*

Rushdie, Salman *OxEng 85*

Rushdie, Salman 1947- *BioIn 13, ConAu 108, –111, ConLC 23[port], –31[port], ConNov 86, CurBio 86[port], EncSF, IntWW 82, –83, PostFic, ScFSB[port], Who 85, WhoWor 84, –87, WorAl 1975[port], WrDr 84, –86*

Rushforth, Peter 1945- *ConAu 101, ConLC 19*

Rushing, Jane Gilmore 1925- *ConAu 49, EncFWF, WhoAm 78, –80, –82, –84, –86, WrDr 84, –86*

Rushmore, Robert *DrAP&F 85*

Rushmore, Robert 1926- *BioIn 11, ConAu 25R, IntAu&W 77, SmATA 8*

Rushmore, Robert 1926-1986 *ConAu 120*

Rushton, William Faulkner 1947- *ConAu 101*

Rusk, Howard A 1901- *AmM&WS 73P, –76P, –79P, BioIn 1, –2, –3, –5, –7, –8, –9, –10, CelR, ConAu 103, CurBio 46, –67, InSci, WhoAm 74, –76, –78, –80, –82, WhoWor 74*

Ruskin, Ariane *ConAu X*

Ruskin, Ariane 1935- *AuBYP, BioIn 8, –10, ConAu 13R, SmATA 7*

Ruskin, Ariane *see also* Batterberry, Ariane Ruskin

Russ, Joanna 1937- *AmWomWr, Au&Wr 71, ConAu 11NR, –25R, ConLC 15, ConNov 86, ConSFA, DcLB 8[port], DrmM 2[port], EncSF, IntAu&W 76, ScF&FL 1, –2, ScFSB[port], TwCSFW 86, WhoAm 74, –76, –78, –80, –82, –84, –86, WhoAmW 74, –75, WhoSciF, WrDr 76, –80, –82, –84, –86*

Russ, Lavinia 1904- *AuBYP SUP, BioIn 9, ConAu 25R*

Russ, Martin 1931- *BioIn 4, ConAu 106*

Russell, Andrew J *BioIn 13*

Russell, Andrew J 1830-1902 *DcAmArt*

Russell, Andy 1915- *BioIn 9, ConAu 10NR, –21R, WhoHol A*

Russell, Bertrand 1872-1970 *AsBiEn, AtlBL, BiESc, BioIn 1, –2, –3, –4, –5, –6, –7, –8, –9, –10, –11, –12, CasWL, Chambr 3, ConAu 25R, ConAu P-1, CurBio 40, –51, –70, DcAmSR, DcLEL, DcScB, EncSF, EvLB, IlEncMy[port], InSci, IntEnSS 79, LinLib L, –S, LongCEL, LongCTC, LuthC 75, MakMC, McGEWB, ModBrL, NewC, NewYTBE 70, ObitOF 79, OxEng, PenC ENG, REn, ScF&FL 1, –2, ScFSB, TwCA, –SUP, TwCWr, WebE&AL, WhDW, WhAm 5, WhE&EA, WhLit, WhoLA, WorAl*

Russell, Bill 1934- *BioIn 10, –11, –12, CelR, CmCal, ConAu X, NegAl 76, –83, NewYTBE 73, WhoAm 74, –76, –80, –82, –84, –86, WhoBbl 73, WhoBlA 75, –77, –80, –85, WhoRocM 82, WorAl*

Russell, Cazzie 1944- *BioIn 7, –8, –12, InB&W 80, NewYTBE 70, NewYTBS 80[port], WhoBbl 73, WhoBlA 75, –77, –80, –85*

Russell, Franklin Alexander 1926- *AmAu&B, Au&Wr 71, AuBYP, BioIn 11, ConAu 11NR, –17R, OxCanan, SmATA 11, WhoAm 74, –76, –78, –80, –82, WrDr 76, –80, –82, –84*

Russell, Helen Ross *AmM&WS 86P*

Russell, Helen Ross 1915- *AmM&WS 73P, –76P, –79P, –82P, BioIn 11, ConAu 33R, SmATA 8, WhoAmW 61, –64, –66, –75, WrDr 76, –80, –82, –86*

Russell, Howard S 1887-1980 *ConAu 105*

Russell, Jeffrey Burton 1934- *ConAu 11NR, –25R, DrAS 74H, –78H, –82H, IntAu&W 76, WhoAm 80, –82, –84, –86, WhoWest 74, –76, –78, –80, –82, WhoWor 82*

Russell, John 1919- *Au&Wr 71, ConAu 13R, IntAu&W 77, Who 74, –82, –83, –85, WhoAm 78, –80, –82, –84, –86, WhoArt 80, –82, –84, WhoE 75, WorAu 1975, WrDr 86*

Russell, Mark 1932- *BioIn 8, –11, –12, ConAu 108, –113, CurBio 81[port], Who 83, WhoAm 80, –82, –84, –86*

Russell, Robert William 1923?- *ConAu 1R, DrAS 74E, –78E, –82E, WhoF&I 74, –75, WhoMW 74, –76*

Russell, Robert William 1924- *WhoAm 86*

Russell, Ross 1909- *ConAu 1R*

Rust, Claude 1916- *ConAu 109*

Ruth, Babe *BioIn 13, ConAu X, NewYTBS 85*

Ruth, Babe 1895-1948 *BioIn 1, –2, –3, –4, –5, –6, –7, –8, –9, –10, –11, –12, BioNews 74, CurBio 44, –48, Film 2, OxAmH, WhDW, WhScrn 74, –77, –83, WhoHol B*

Ruth, Babe *see also* Ruth, George Herman

Ruth, George Herman 1895-1948 *BioIn 1, –2, –3, –4, –5, –6, –7, –8, –9, –10, –11, –12, –13, ConAu 116,*

*CurBio 44, –48, DcAmB S4, DcCathB,
EncAB-H, LinLib S, McGEWB,
NewYTBE 73, ObitOF 79,
WebAB, –79, WhAm 2, WhoProB 73,
WorAl*

Ruth, George Herman *see* Ruth, Babe

Ruth, Rod 1912-   *BioIn 11, EncSF,
IlsBYP, SmATA 9*

Rutherford, Douglas   *SmATA X,
WrDr 86*

Rutherford, Douglas 1915-   *Au&Wr 71,
ConAu X, TwCCr&M 80, –85,
WrDr 76, –80, –82, –84*

Rutherford, Douglas *see also*
McConnell, James Douglas R

Rutland, Robert Allen 1922-
WhoAm 84, –86

Rutman, Leo 1935?-   *ConAu 45,
NatPD, –81[port], WhoE 75, –77*

Rutsala, Vern   *DrAP&F 85*

Rutsala, Vern 1934-   *AmAu&B,
ConAu 6NR, –9R, –20NR, ConPo 70,*

*–75, –80, –85, DcLEL 1940,
IntWWP 77, –82, LinLib L,
WrDr 76, –80*

Rutstrum, Calvin 1895-1982   *BioIn 6,
–12, ConAu 1R, –1NR, –106,
IndAu 1917, IntAu&W 77, MinnWr*

Ruxton, George Frederick 1820-1848
OxAmL 83

Ruxton, George Frederick Augustus
1820-1848   *Alli, ApCAB,
ArtsAmW 1, BioIn 2, –7, –10, –12,
Drake, OxAmH, OxAmL, REnAL*

Ryan, Alan 1940-   *ConAu 29R,
WrDr 80, –82, –84, –86*

Ryan, Betsy 1943-   *ConAu X,
SmATA X*

Ryan, Betsy *see also* Ryan, Elizabeth

Ryan, Bob 1946-   *ConAu 4NR, –49*

Ryan, Bob 1947?-   *BioIn 13*

Ryan, Cornelius 1920-1974   *BiDIrW,
BioIn 2, –7, –10, –11, –12, CelR,
ConAu 53, –69, ConLC 7, DcIrB,*

*DcIrW 2, IntAu&W 76,
NewYTBS 74, –79, ObitOF 79,
WhAm 6, Who 74, WhoAm 74,
WhoE 74, WhoWor 74, WorAl,
WorAu 1970*

Ryan, Desmond 1893-1964   *BiDIrW,
ConAu 113, DcIrB, DcIrW 2,
WhE&EA*

Ryan, Elizabeth 1943-   *ConAu 7NR,
–61, SmATA 30[port]*

Ryan, Mary P 1945-   *ConAu 113*

Ryan, Mary Patricia 1945-
WhoAmW 85

Ryan, Nolan 1947-   *BioIn 8, –9, –10,
–11, –12, –13, CmCal, CurBio 70,
NewYTBE 70, –73,
NewYTBS 83[port], WhoAm 74, –76,
–78, –80, –82, –84, –86,
WhoS&SW 86, WorAl*

Ryback, Eric 1952-   *ConAu 37R*

Ryckmans, Pierre 1891-1959   *BioIn 1,
–2, –5, –11, ObitOF 79, WhAm 3*

Rydberg, Ernest E 1901-   *BioIn 12,
ConAu 13R, SmATA 21[port]*

Rydberg, Ernie 1901-   *WrDr 76, –80,
–82, –84, –86*

Rydberg, Lou 1908-   *BioIn 13,
ConAu 69, SmATA 27*

Rydell, Wendy 1927-   *BioIn 9,
ConAu 33R, IntAu&W 82, SmATA 4,
WhoAmW 75, –77, –79, WrDr 76,
–80, –82, –84, –86*

Ryden, Hope   *BioIn 10, –11, –12,
ConAu 14NR, –33R, ForWC 70,
SmATA 8, WhoAmW 74, –64, –66,
–68, –72, WhoE 74, WomWMM A,
–B*

Ryder, Jonathan   *TwCCr&M 85,
WrDr 86*

Ryder, Jonathan 1927-   *ConAu X,
WrDr 76, –80, –82, –84*

Ryder, Jonathan *see also* Ludlum,
Robert

Rylant, Cynthia 1954-   *SmATA 44*

S

Sabatier, Robert 1923?- *ConAu 102, -18NR, IntAu&W 76, -77, IntWW 74, -75, -76, -77, -78, -79, -80, -81, -82, -83, WhoFr 79, WhoWor 82, -84, -87*

Sabatini, Rafael 1875-1950 *BioIn 2, -4, -11, DcBiA, DcLEL, EvLB, FilmgC, HalFC 84, LongCTC, MnBBF, NewC, NotNAT B, ObitOF 79, REn, TwCA, -SUP, TwCWr, WhAm 2, WhE&EA, WhLit, WhThe, WhoSpyF*

Saberhagen, Fred 1930- *BioIn 12, ConAu 7NR, -57, ConSFA, DcLB 8[port], EncSF, ScF&FL 1, -2, ScFSB, SmATA 37, TwCSFW 86, WhoSciF, WrDr 84, -86*

Sabin, Francene *BioIn 13, ConAu 11NR, -69, SmATA 27*

Sabin, Louis 1930- *BioIn 13, ConAu 11NR, -69, SmATA 27*

Sachar, Howard Morley 1928- *ConAu 5R, -6NR, DrAS 78H, -82H, WhoAm 80, -82, -84, -86, WhoAmJ 80, WhoE 79, -81, -83, WhoWorJ 72, -78*

Sachar, Louis 1954- *ConAu 15NR, -81*

Sachs, Marilyn 1927- *ConAu 13NR, ConLC 35[port], IntAu&W 86, OxChL, SmATA 2AS[port], WrDr 86*

Sachs, Marilyn Stickle 1927- *AmWomWr, BioIn 9, ChlLR 2, ConAu 17R, FourBJA, IntAu&W 77, -82, SmATA 3, TwCCW 78, -83, WhoAmW 75, WrDr 76, -80, -82, -84*

Sack, John 1930- *BioIn 7, ConAu 14NR, -21R, WhoE 74*

Sackett, Susan 1943- *ConAu 106*

Sackler, Howard *OxAmT 84, OxThe 83*

Sackler, Howard 1929-1982 *AnObit 1982, BioIn 10, -12, -13, ChhPo S2, ConAu 108, -61, ConDr 73, -77, -82, ConLC 14, DcLB 7[port], McGEWD, -84, NatPD 81, NewYTBS 82[port], NotNAT, OxAmL 83, PIP&P, WhAm 8, WhoAm 74, -76, -78, -80, -82, WorAl, WrDr 76, -80, -82*

Sacks, Oliver 1933- *CurBio 85[port]*

Sackson, Sid 1920- *BioIn 12, ConAu 12NR, -69, SmATA 16*

Sadat, Anwar 1918-1981 *AnObit 1981[port], BioIn 9, -10, -11, -12, BioNews 75, ConAu 101, -104, CurBio 71, -81N, IntYB 78, -79, -80, -81, LinLib S, NewYTBE 70, -72, NewYTBS 81[port], WhDW, WhoGov 72, WhoWor 74, -76, -78, -80, WorAl*

Sadler, Barry 1941- *RolSEnR 83, WhoRock 81*

Sadler, John 1934- *AmM&WS 86P*

Sadoul, Georges 1904-1967 *HalFC 84, OxFilm*

Saffell, David C 1941- *ConAu 11NR, -61*

Safire, William 1929- *BioIn 8, -9, -10, -11, -12, ConAu 17R, ConLC 10, CurBio 73, EncAJ, EncTwCJ, NewYTBE 73, PolProf NF, WhoAm 74, -76, -78, -80, -82, -84, -86, WhoE 79, -81, -83, -85, WhoGov 72, WhoS&SW 73, WorAl, WrDr 86*

Sagan, Carl 1934- *AmM&WS 73P, -76P, -79P, -82P, -86P, AsBiEn, BiESc, BioIn 6, -8, -10, -11, -12, -13, BlueB 76, ConAu 11NR, -25R, ConIsC 2[port], ConLC 30[port], CurBio 70, EncSF, IntAu&W 76, IntWW 76, -77, -78, -79, -80, -81, -82, -83, NewYTBS 79, -85[port], UFOEn, WhoAm 74, -76, -78, -80, -82, WhoE 74, -75, -77, -79, -81, -83, WhoWor 78, -80, -82, WorAl, WorAu 1975, WrDr 76, -80, -82, -84, -86*

Sagarin, Edward 1913- *AmM&WS 73S, -78S, ConAu 4NR, -5R*

Sager, Carole Bayer *WhoRock 81*

Sager, Carole Bayer 1945?- *BioIn 11, -12, RolSEnR 83, WhoAm 80, -82, WhoRocM 82*

Sager, Carole Bayer 1947?- *RolSEnR 83, WhoAm 84, -86*

Saggs, Henry 1920- *ConAu 5R, IntAu&W 82, WrDr 76, -80, -82, -84, -86*

Sagnier, Thierry 1946- *ConAu 53*

Sahakian, William S 1921- *AmM&WS 73S, -78S, BlueB 76, ConAu 8NR, -17R, DrAS 74P, -78P, -82P, IntAu&W 77, -82, WhoAm 74, -76, -78, -80, -82, -84, WhoE 85, WhoWor 74, -76, -82, WrDr 76, -80, -82, -84, -86*

Sahgal, Nayantara 1927- *BioIn 3, -6, ConAu 9R, -11NR, ConLC 41[port], ConNov 72, -76, -82, -86, FarE&A 78, IntAu&W 76, -77, -82, -86, IntWW 75, -76, -77, -78, -79, -80, -81, -82, -83, WhoWor 74, -76, -78, WrDr 76, -80, -82, -84, -86*

Sailor, Charles 1947- *ConAu 97*

Saint, Dora Jessie 1913- *Au&Wr 71, BioIn 5, -10, -11, ConAu 7NR, -13R, IntAu&W 76, -77, -82, -86, SmATA 10, WhoWor 78, WorAu, WrDr 76, -80, -82, -84, -86*

St. Aubyn, Giles 1925- *Au&Wr 71, ConAu 4NR, -5R, -19NR, IntAu&W 77, -82, -86, WhoWor 76, WrDr 76, -80, -82, -84, -86*

St. Clair, David 1932- *ConAu 33R*

St. Clair, David 1932- *EncO&P 2*

St. Clair, David 1932- *EncO&P 80, WhoWest 76*

Saint-Exupery, Antoine De *OxChL*

Saint-Exupery, Antoine De 1900-1944 *AnCL, AtlBL, BioIn 1, -2, -3, -4, -5, -7, -9, -10, -11, -12, -13, CasWL, ChlLR 10[port], ClDMEL, CnMWL, ConAu 108, CurBio 40, -45, CyWA, EncWL, -2[port], EvEuW, FourBJA, HalFC 84, InSci, LinLib L, LongCTC, McGEWB, ModFrL, ModRL, Novels, OxEng 85, OxFr, PenC EUR, REn, ScF&FL 1, SmATA 20, TwCA, -SUP, TwCCW 78B, -83B, TwCLC 2, TwCWr, WhDW, WhoTwCL, WorAl*

Saint-Exupery, Antoine De *see also* DeSaint-Exupery, Antoine

St. George, George 1904- *ConAu 25R*

St. George, Judith 1931- *BioIn 11, ConAu 14NR, -69, SmATA 13, WrDr 86*

St. John, Philip *ConAu X, TwCSFW 86, WrDr 86*

St. John, Philip 1915- *AuBYP, BioIn 7, ConAu 65, -X, EncSF, ScF&FL 1, WrDr 84*

St. John, Philip *see also* DelRey, Lester

St. John, Primus *DrAP&F 85*

St. John, Primus 1939- *BlkAWP, ConAu 113*

St. John, Robert 1902- *AmAu&B, Au&Wr 71, BioIn 1, -3, -4, -5, BlueB 76, ConAu 1R, -5NR, CurBio 42, EncAJ, IntAu&W 76, -82, WhoAm 74, -76, -78, -80, -82, -84, WhoWor 74, -82, WrDr 76, -80, -82, -84, -86*

St. John, Wylly Folk 1908- *AuBYP SUP, BioIn 11, ConAu 21R, ForWC 70, IntAu&W 76, -77, -82, SmATA 10, WhoAmW 74, -75, -77, -79, -81, WhoS&SW 75, -76, -78, -80, -82, WrDr 76, -80, -82, -84, -86*

St. John, Wylly Folk 1908-1985 *ConAu 117, SmATA 45N*

Saint-Phalle, Niki De *WorArt*

Saint-Phalle, Niki De 1930- *BioIn 13*

St. Vincent Millay, Edna d1950 *ObitOF 79*

Sakai, Saburo *BioIn 11*

Sakharov, Vladimir 1945- *BioIn 12*

Saki 1870-1916 *AtlBL, BioIn 1, -5, -9, -10, -12, CasWL, CnMWL, ConAu X, CyWA, DcLEL, EncSF, EvLB, LinLib LP, LongCTC, ModBrL, NewC, Novels, OxEng, -85, PenC ENG, REn, SupFW, TwCA, -SUP, TwCWr, WhDW, WhoHr&F, WhoTwCL*

Saki *see also* Munro, Hector Hugh

Salas, Floyd Francis 1931- *ChiSch*

Salassi, Otto R 1939- *ConAu 106*

Sale, Kirkpatrick 1937- *ConAu 10NR, -13R, IntAu&W 82*

Saletan, Alberta L 1917- *WrDr 76, -80, -82*

Salinas, Louis Omar *DrAP&F 85*

Salinger, J D *DrAP&F 85, OxChL*

Salinger, J D 1916- *EncWL 2*

Salinger, J D 1919- *AmAu&B, AmWr, Au&Wr 71, BlueB 76, CasWL, CelR, CnMWL, ConAu 5R, ConLC 1, -3, -8, -12, ConNov 72, -76, -82, -86, DcLB 2, EncWL, IntAu&W 76, -77, IntWW 74, -75, -76, -77, -78, -79, -80, -81, -82, -83, LinLib L, -S, LongCTC, ModAL, -S1, NewCon[port], Novels, OxAmL, -83, OxEng 85, PenC AM, RAdv 1, REn, REnAL, TwCA SUP, TwCWr, WebE&AL, WhoTwCL, WorAl, WrDr 76, -80, -82, -84, -86*

Salinger, Jerome David 1919- *BioIn 2, -4, -5, -6, -7, -8, -9, -10, -11, -12, -13, DcLEL 1940, DcLB 2, EncAB-H, MakMC, WebAB, -79, WhDW, Who 74, -82, -83, -85, WhoAm 74, -76, -78, -80, -82, -84, WhoWor 74, -84*

Salinger, Margaretta d1985 *NewYTBS 85*

Salinger, Margaretta 1908?-1985 *ConAu 115*

Salinger, Pierre 1925- *BiDrAC, BioIn 5, -6, -7, -8, -10, -11, -12, BlueB 76, CmCal, ConAu 14NR, -17R, -17R, CurBio 61, DcLEL 1940, IntAu&W 86, IntWW 74, -75, -76, -77, -78, -79, -80, -81, -82, -83, PolProf J, PolProf K, ScF&FL 1, Who 74, -82, -83, -85, WhoAm 74, -76, -78, -80, -82, WhoAmP 73, -75, -77, -79, -81, WhoFr 79, WhoS&SW 73, -75, WhoWor 74, WorAl, WrDr 80, -82, -84, -86*

Salisbury, Carola 1943- *ConAu 89, WrDr 84*

Salisbury, Harrison E 1908- *BioIn 13, EncAJ, EncTwCJ, WrDr 86*

Salisbury, Harrison Evans 1908- *AmAu&B, Au&Wr 71, BioIn 3, -4, -5, -6, -7, -10, -11, -12, BlueB 76, CelR, ConAu 1R, -3NR, CurBio 55, -82[port], IntAu&W 76, -77, -82, IntWW 74, -75, -76, -77, -78, -79, -80, -81, -82, -83, MinnWr, PolProf E, PolProf J, REnAL, Who 74, -82, -83, -85, WhoAm 74, -76, -78, -80, -82, -84, -86, WhoE 74, WhoWor 74, -78, WorAl, WorAu, WrDr 76, -80, -82, -84*

Salk, Lee 1926- *WhoAm 84, -86, WhoWor 82*

141

Salkey, Andrew 1928- *BioIn 9, –12, CasWL, ChhPo S2, ConAu 5R, –13NR, ConNov 72, –76, –82, –86, FifCWr, IntAu&W 76, –77, LongCTC, Novels, OxChL, PenC ENG, SelBAAf, SmATA 35, TwCCW 78, –83, WebE&AL, WorAu 1970, WrDr 76, –80, –82, –84, –86*

Saltykov, Mikhail 1826-1889 *BbD, BiD&SB, BioIn 1, –7, –11, CasWL, DcRusL, EuAu, EvEuW, PenC EUR, REn*

Salvadori, Mario 1907- *BioIn 8, –10, ConAu 108, SmATA 40[port], WhoAm 74, –76, –80, WhoCon 73, WhoEng 80*

Salvadori, Mario Giorgio 1907- *BioIn 13*

Salverson, Laura Goodman 1890- *Au&Wr 71, BioIn 1, –4, CanNov, CanWr, CreCan 1, CurBio 57, DcLEL, InWom, LinLib L, OxCan, WhLit*

Salverson, Laura Goodman 1890-1970 *OxCanL*

Salzman, Marian Lynn 1959- *WhoAmW 87*

Samachson, Dorothy 1914- *AuBYP, BioIn 7, –9, ConAu 9R, ForWC 70, SmATA 3*

Samachson, Joseph 1906-1980 *AmM&WS 73P, AuBYP, BioIn 7, –9, –12, ConAu 17R, ScF&FL 1, –2, SmATA 3*

Sammons, Martha Cragoe 1949- *DrAS 78E, –82E*

Sampson, Anthony 1926- *Au&Wr 71, BioIn 10, BlueB 76, ConAu 1R, –3NR, DcLEL 1940, IntAu&W 77, –82, IntWW 76, –77, –78, –79, –80, –81, –82, –83, Who 74, –82, –83, –85, WhoWor 74, –76, –78, WorAu, WrDr 76, –80, –82, –84, –86*

Sampson, Fay 1935- *ConAu 101, –18NR, SmATA 40, –42[port]*

Samson, John Gadsden 1922?- *ConAu 109, WhoAm 76, –78, –82*

Samuel, Helen Jo 1909- *SingR 1*

Samuel, Maurice 1895-1972 *AmAu&B, AmNov, BioIn 2, –4, –6, –9, –11, ConAu 102, –33R, NewYTBE 72, ObitOF 79, REnAL, ScF&FL 1, TwCA SUP, WhAm 5, WhoWorJ 72*

Samuels, Charles 1902-1982 *BioIn 11, –12, ConAu 1R, –5NR, –106, SmATA 12*

Samuels, Charles Thomas 1936-1974 *ConAu 41R, –49*

Samuels, Gertrude *AuBYP, BioIn 7, –12, ConAu 9R, –9R, ForWC 70, NatPD, –81[port], SmATA 17, WhoAmW 58, –61, –64, –66, –75, –77, –79, –81, WhoWorJ 72, –78*

Samuelson, Paul A 1915- *NewYTBS 86[port], Who 85*

Samuelson, Paul Anthony 1915- *AmAu&B, AmM&WS 73S, –78S, BioIn 5, –7, –9, –11, –12, BlueB 76, CelR, ConAu 5R, CurBio 65, EncAB-H, GrEconS[port], IndAu 1917, IntAu&W 77, –82, IntWW 74, –75, –76, –77, –78, –79, –80, –81, –82, –83, McGEWB, NewYTBE 70, –71, PolProf J, PolProf K, PolProf NF, WebAB, –79, Who 74, –82, –83, WhoAm 74, –76, –78, –80, –82, –84, –86, WhoE 74, –77, –79, –81, –83, –85, WhoFI 79, –81, –83, –85, WhoNob, WhoWor 74, –78, –80, –82, –84, –87, WorAl, WrDr 76, –80, –82, –84, –86*

Sanberg, Paul Ronald 1955- *WhoFrS 84*

Sanborn, Duane 1914- *AuBYP, ConAu 1R, –1NR, SmATA 38[port], WhoAm W 64, –66, –68*

Sanborn, Duane *see also* Bradley, Duane

Sanborn, Margaret 1915- *ConAu 4NR, –53, WrDr 76, –80, –82, –84, –86*

Sancha, Sheila 1924- *ConAu 11NR, –69, SmATA 38[port]*

Sanchez, Thomas *DrAP&F 85*

Sanchez, Thomas 1943?- *BioIn 9, ConAu 2NR, –45*

Sand, George 1804-1876 *AtlBL, BbD, BiD&SB, BioIn 1, –2, –3, –4, –5, –6, –7, –8, –9, –10, –11, –12, CasWL, CelCen, CyWA, DcAmSR, DcBiA, DcEnL, DcEuL, Dis&D, EuAu, EvEuW, GoodHs, GrFLW, HerW 84, IntDcWB[port], LinLib L, –LP, –S, McGEWB, NinCLC 2[port], NotNAT B, Novels[port], OxEng, –85, OxFr, PenC EUR, RComWL, REn, ScF&FL 1, WhDW, WorAl*

Sand, George X *AuBYP SUP, ConAu 13R*

Sandak, Cass R 1950- *SmATA 37*

Sandburg, Carl *OxChL*

Sandburg, Carl 1878-1967 *AmAu&B, AmSCAP 66, AmWr, AnCL, ApCAB X, AtlBL, AuBYP, BiDAmM, BioIn 1, –2, –3, –4, –5, –6, –7, –8, –9, –10, –11, –12, –13, CasWL, Chambr 3, ChhPo, –S1, –S2, –S3, CnDAL, CnE&AP, CnMWL, ConAmA, ConAmL, ConAu 5R, –25R, ConLC 1, –4, –10, –15, –35[port], CurBio 40, –63, –67, CyWA, DcLB 17[port], –54[port], DcLEL, EncAAH, EncAB-H, EncAJ, EncFCWM 69, EncWL, –2, EvLB, FamPYP, LinLib L, –S, LongCTC, MakMC, McGEWB, ModAL, –S2, –S1, MorMA, ObitOF 79, ObitT 1961, OxAmH, OxAmL, –83, OxEng, OxMus, PenC AM, RAdv 1, REn, REnAL, SixAP, SmATA 8, Str&VC, TwCA, –SUP, TwCWr, WebAB, –79, WebE&AL, WhDW, WhAm 4, WhE&EA, WhoTwCL, WisWr, WorAl*

Sandburg, Carl August 1878-1967 *OxEng 85*

Sande, Theodore Anton 1933- *AmArch 70, ConAu 12NR, –65, WhoAm 82, –84, –86, WhoE 74*

Sanderlin, George 1915- *BioIn 9, ConAu 13R, DrAS 74E, –78E, –82E, IntAu&W 76, –77, –82, SmATA 4, WrDr 76, –80, –82, –84, –86*

Sanderlin, Owenita 1916- *BioIn 11, ConAu 7NR, –17R, SmATA 11, WhoAmW 83, WhoWest 84, WrDr 76, –80, –82, –84, –86*

Sanders, Dennis 1949- *ConAu 108*

Sanders, Lawrence 1920- *ASpks, BioIn 8, –11, –12, ConAu 81, ConLC 41[port], EncSF, IntAu&W 76, –77, NewYTBS 80[port], Novels, ScFSB, TwCCr&M 80, –85, WhoAm 80, –82, –84, –86, WorAl, WrDr 82, –84, –86*

Sanders, Leonard 1929- *ConAu 9R, ScF&FL 1, WhoAm 74, –76, –78, –80*

Sanders, Leonard Marion, Jr. 1929- *WhoAm 84, –86*

Sanders, Marion K 1905-1977 *BioIn 11, ConAu 33R, –73, ForWC 70, NewYTBS 77, WhoAmW 58, –61*

Sanders, Thomas E 1926- *BioIn 10, ConAu 21R, NewYTBE 73, ScF&FL 1, –2*

Sanders, William B 1944- *ConAu 10NR, –65*

Sanderson, Derek 1946- *BioIn 9, –10, –11, CurBio 75, NewYTBE 70, –72, –73, NewYTBS 74, –78, –83[port], WhoAm 76, –78, WhoHcky 73*

Sanderson, Derek Michael 1946- *BioIn 13*

Sanderson, Ivan T 1911-1973 *AmAu&B, AmM&WS 73P, –76P, AuBYP, BioIn 1, –4, –5, –7, –9, –10, –11, ConAu 37R, –41R, EncO&P 2, –78S1, EncSF, IlsCB 1744, –1946, InSci, LinLib L, NatCAB 57, NewYTBE 73, REnAL, ScF&FL 1, SmATA 6, TwCA, –SUP, UFOEn[port]*

Sandman, Peter Mark 1945- *AmM&WS 73S, –78S, ConAu 25R, IntAu&W 77, WrDr 76, –80, –82, –84*

Sandoz, Mari 1896-1966 *ConAu 17NR, ConLC 28[port], EncFWF[port], OxAmL 83*

Sandoz, Mari 1901-1966 *AmAu&B, AmWomWr, AuBYP, BioIn 3, –4, –5, –7, –9, –10, –12, CnDAL, ConAu 1R, –25R, DcLB 9[port], EncAAH, InWom, LinLib L, NotAW MOD, ObitOF 79, OxAmL, REn, REnAL, REnAW, SmATA 5, ThrBJA, TwCA, –SUP, WhAm 4, WhNAA, WhoAmW 58*

Sands, Bill *AmAu&B*

Sands, Leo G 1912-1984 *ConAu 114*

Sands, Leo George 1912- *ConAu 17R, WhoAm 76, –78, –80*

Sandved, Kjell *BioIn 12*

Sandweiss, Martha A 1954- *WhoAmA 85, –87*

Sandweiss, Martha Ann 1954- *WhoAmA 84*

Sanford, Agnes Mary White 1898- *ConAu 17NR, WhoAmW 58, –61*

Sanger, Margaret 1879-1966 *BioIn 13, DcAmMeB 84*

Sanger, Margaret 1883-1966 *AmAu&B, AmWomWr, BioIn 2, –3, –4, –7, –8, –9, –10, –11, –12, ConAu 89, CurBio 44, –66, DcAmSR, EncAB-H, HerW, –84, InWom, IntDcWB, LibW, LinLib L, –S, LongCTC, LuthC 75, McGEWB, MemAm, NatCAB 52, NotAW MOD, ObitOF 79, ObitT 1961, OxAmL, –83, OxMed 86, WebAB, –79, WhAm 4, WorAl*

Sanger, Marjory Bartlett 1920- *AuBYP SUP, BioIn 11, ConAu 37R, IntAu&W 86, SmATA 8, WrDr 76, –80, –82, –84, –86*

Santalo, Lois *AuBYP, BioIn 8*

Santee, Ross 1888?-1965 *AmAu&B, ArizL, ArtsAmW 1, BioIn 2, –3, –4, –7, –8, ConAu 108, EncFWF, IlBEAAW, ObitOF 79, REnAL, REnAW, TwCA SUP*

Santesson, Hans Stefan 1914?-1975 *BioIn 10, ConAu 9R, –57, –93, ConSFA, EncSF, ScF&FL 1, –2, SmATA 30N*

Santiago, Danny 1911- *ConLC 33[port]*

Santoli, Al 1949- *ConAu 105*

Santos, Bienvenido N *DrAP&F 85*

Santos, Bienvenido N 1911- *ConAu 101, –19NR, ConLC 22[port], ConPo 70, WorAu 1975[port]*

Sargent, Pamela *BioIn 13, DrAP&F 85*

Sargent, Pamela 1948- *BioIn 12, ConAu 8NR, –61, DcLB 8, EncSF, ScF&FL 2, ScFSB, SmATA 29, TwCSFW 86, WrDr 84, –86*

Sargent, Sarah 1937- *ConAu 106, SmATA 41, –44[port]*

Sargent, Shirley 1927- *AuBYP, BioIn 7, –11, ConAu 1R, –2NR, ForWC 70, SmATA 11*

Sargent, William 1946- *ConAu 106*

Sarnoff, Jane 1937- *AuBYP SUP, BioIn 11, ConAu 9NR, –53, FifBJA[port], SmATA 10*

Sarnoff, Paul 1918- *ConAu 2NR, –5R, –18NR, NewYTBS 80[port]*

Saroyan, Aram 1943- *AmAu&B, BioIn 13, ConAu 21R, ConAu 5AS[port], ConPo 70, –75, –80, –85, DcLEL 1940, IntAu&W 86, IntWWP 77, WrDr 76, –80, –82, –84, –86*

Saroyan, William 1908-1981 *AmAu&B, AmNov, AnObit 1981[port], Au&Wr 71, BiE&WWA, BioIn 1, –2, –3, –4, –5, –6, –7, –8, –9, –10, –11, –12, –13, BlueB 76, CasWL, CelR, CmCal, CnDAL, CnMD, CnMWL, CnThe, ConAmA, ConAu 5R, –103, ConDr 73, –77, ConLC 1, –8, –10, –29[port], ConNov 72, –76, CurBio 40, –72, –81N, CyWA, DcLB 7[port], –9[port], –Y81A[port], DcLEL, EncWT, EvLB, FilmgC, HalFC 84, IntAu&W 76, –77, IntWW 74, –75, –77, –78, –79,*

–80, –81, –81N, LinLib L, –S, LongCTC, McGEWB, McGEWD, –84, ModAL, –S1, ModWD, NewYTBE 72, NewYTBS 75, –79, –81[port], NotNAT, OxAmL, –83, OxAmT 84, OxThe, –83, PenC AM, PIP&P, RAdv 1, REn, REnAL, REnWD, SmATA 23[port], –24N, TwCA, –SUP, TwCWr, WebAB, –79, WebE&AL, WhAm 7, WhE&EA, Who 74, –82N, WhoAm 74, –76, –78, –80, WhoThe 72, –77, –81, WhoTwCL, WhoWor 74, WorAl, WrDr 76, –80, –82

Sarris, Andrew 1928- *AmAu&B, BioIn 9, –10, –13, ConAu 21R, OxFilm, WhoAm 76, –78, –80, –82, WhoE 74, –75, WhoWor 78*

Sarton, May *DrAP&F 85*

Sarton, May 1912- *AmAu&B, AmWomWr, BioIn 4, –5, –8, –10, –11, –12, –13, BlueB 76, ConAu 1R, –1NR, ConLC 4, –14, ConNov 72, –76, –82, –86, ConPo 70, –75, –80, –85, CurBio 82[port], DcLB 48[port], –Y81B[port], DrAS 74E, –78E, –82E, EncWL 2, IntAu&W 76, –77, –86, IntWWP 77, ModAL, –S2, –S1, NewYTBS 83[port], Novels, OxAmL, –83, PenC AM, RAdv 1, REnAL, ScF&FL 1, SmATA 36, TwCA SUP, WhoAm 74, –76, –78, –80, –82, WhoAmW 58, –64, –66, –68, –70, –72, –81, –83, –85, –87, WhoWor 74, WrDr 76, –80, –82, –84, –86*

Sartre, Jean-Paul 1905-1980 *AnObit 1980[port], –1981, Au&Wr 71, BiDNeoM, BiDPsy, BiE&WWA, BioIn 1, –2, –3, –4, –5, –6, –7, –8, –9, –10, –11, –12, –13, CasWL, CelR, ClDMEL, CnMD, CnMWL, CnThe, ConAu 9R, –21NR, –97, ConLC 1, –4, –7, –9, –13, –18, –24[port], CroCD, CurBio 47, –71, –80N, CyWA, EncWL, –2[port], EncWT, EvEuW, FilmgC, GrFLW, HalFC 84, IntAu&W 76, –77, IntWW 74, –75, –76, –77, –78, –79, LinLib L, –S, LongCTC, LuthC 75, MajMD 2, MakMC, McGEWB, McGEWD, –84[port], ModFrL, ModRL, ModWD, NewYTBE 71, NewYTBS 80[port], NotNAT, –A, Novels, OxEng, –85, OxFr, OxThe, PenC EUR, PIP&P, RComWL, REn, REnWD, ScF&FL 1, –2, TwCA SUP, TwCWr, WhDW, WhAm 7, WhScrn 83, Who 74, WhoFr 79, WhoThe 72, –77, –81, –81N, WhoTwCL, WhoWor 74, –78, WorAl*

Sartre, Jean-Paul Charles Aymard 1905-1980 *WhoNob, OxThe 83*

Satchidananda, Swami 1914- *WhoRel 77*

Satterfield, Archie 1933- *BioIn 12, ConAu 14NR, –57*

Sattler, Helen Roney 1921- *AuBYP SUP, BioIn 9, ConAu 14NR, –33R, SmATA 4*

Sauer, Julia 1891-1983 *BioIn 6, ConAu 81, MorJA, ScF&FL 1, SmATA 32[port], –36N, TwCChW 83, WhoLibS 55*

Saul, John *ScFSB*

Saul, John 1942- *BioIn 13, ConAu 16NR, –81, WhoAm 82*

Saunders, Blanche 1906-1964 *Au&Wr 71, AuBYP, BioIn 2, –7, ConAu P-1*

Saunders, Keith 1910- *BioIn 11, ConAu 57, SmATA 12*

Saunders, Rubie Agnes 1929- *BioIn 12, ConAu 49, ForWC 70, SmATA 21, WhoAm 78, –80, –82, –84, –86, WhoAmW 74, –68, –75, –79, –81, –87*

Saunders, Susan 1945- *SmATA 41, –46*

Savage, Elizabeth 1918- *AmAu&B, AmWomWr, ConAu 1R, –1NR*

Savage, Katharine 1905- *Au&Wr 71, ConAu 13R, FourBJA*

Savage, William Woodrow, Jr. 1943-
ConAu 57, DrAS 74H, –78H, –82H
Saville, Malcolm 1901- *BioIn 13*
Saville, Malcolm 1901-1982 *OxChL*
Savitch, Jessica *WhoAmW 85*
Savitch, Jessica d1983 *WhAm 8*
Savitch, Jessica 1947-1983
*AnObit 1983, BioIn 11, –12, –13,
ConAu 108, –110, CurBio 83[port],
–84N, EncTwCJ, ForWC 70,
LesBEnT, NewYTBS 83[port],
WhoAm 80, –82, WhoAmW 83*
Savitt, Sam *ConAu 17NR,
WhoAmA 84, WrDr 86*
Savitt, Sam 1917- *AuBYP, BioIn 7,
–11, ChhPo S3, ConAu 1R, –1NR,
IlBEAAW, IntAu&W 77, SmATA 8,
WhoAmA 78, –80, –82, WhoAmJ 80,
WhoE 77, –79, WrDr 76, –80, –82,
–84*
Savitz, Harriet May 1933-
*AuBYP SUP, BioIn 10, ConAu 14NR,
–41R, FifBJA[port], SmATA 5,
WhoAmW 79, –81, –83, WhoE 83,
–85*
Sawkins, Raymond 1923- *Au&Wr 71,
ConAu 103*
Sawkins, Raymond *see also* Forbes,
Colin
Sawyer, Ruth 1880-1970 *AmAu&B,
AmLY, AmWomWr, AnCL, AuBYP,
BioIn 2, –4, –6, –7, –8, –9, –11, –12,
BkCL, CarSB, ChhPo, ConAu 73,
DcLB 22[port], HerW, JBA 51,
Newb 1922, NotAW MOD, OxChL,
SmATA 17, TwCA, –SUP,
TwCCW 78, –83, WhAm 5,
WhE&EA, WhNAA, WhoAmW 58,
–70, –72, WomNov*
Saxon, James Anthony 1912-
WhoWest 74, –76, –78, –80, –82
Saxton, Mark 1914- *AmAu&B,
AmNov, BioIn 2, ConAu 93,
WhoAm 76, –78, –80, –82, –84, –86,
WhoWor 80, –84, –87*
Say, Allen 1937- *BioIn 13,
ConAu 29R, SmATA 28[port]*
Sayer, Leo 1948?- *BioIn 11, RkOn 78,
RolSEnR 83, WhoRock 81,
WhoRocM 82*
Sayers, Charles Marshall 1892-1957
AuBYP, BioIn 7
Sayers, Dorothy L 1893-1957
*ConAu 119, DcLB 36[port],
HalFC 84, ModBrL S2, OxEng 85,
TwCCr&M 85, TwCLC 15[port]*
Sayers, Dorothy Leigh 1893-1957
*BioIn 1, –4, –5, –8, –10, –11, –12, –13,
CasWL, Chambr 3, CnMD,
ConAu 104, CorpD, DcLB 10[port],
DcLEL, DcNaB 1951, EncMys,
EncWL, EvLB, InWom,
IntDcWB[port], LinLib L, –LP, –S,
LongCTC, ModBrL, –S1, ModWD,
NewC, NotNAT B, Novels[port],
ObitOF 79, ObitT 1951, OxEng,
PenC ENG, REn, ScF&FL 1,
TwCA, –SUP, TwCCr&M 80,
TwCLC 2, TwCWr, WhAm 3,
WhE&EA, WhLit, WhThe,
WhoHr&F, WorAl*
Sayers, Gale 1943- *BioIn 7, –8, –9,
–10, –12, ConAu 73, Ebony 1,
InB&W 80, –85, NegAl 76, –83,
NewYTBE 70, –72, WhoAm 74, –76,
–78, –80, –82, –84, –86, WhoFtbl 74,
WorAl*
Sayre, Anne 1923?- *ConAu 61,
WhoE 79*
Sayre, Joel 1900-1979 *AmAu&B,
AmNov, BioIn 2, –12, ConAu 89,
NewYTBS 79*
Sayre, Joel 1901-1979 *EncAJ*
Scaduto, Anthony *ConAu 104*
Scagnetti, Jack 1924- *AuBYP SUP,
BioIn 10, ConAu 4NR, –49,
IntAu&W 86, MichAu 80, SmATA 7*
Scalzo, Joe 1941- *ConAu 49*
Scanlon, Marion Stephany d1977
*BioIn 6, –11, ConAu 5R, ForWC 70,
MichAu 80, MinnWr, SmATA 11,
WhoAmW 58, –61, –64, –66,
WrDr 76, –80*

Scarbrough, George 1915-
ConAu 16NR
Scarf, Maggie 1932- *BioIn 10, –12,
ConAu 29R, NewYTBS 80[port],
SmATA 5, WhoAmW 75, WrDr 84,
–86*
Scarne, John 1903- *BioIn 1, –4, –7,
CelR, IntAu&W 76, WhoAm 76, –78,
–80, –82, –84, –86*
Scarne, John 1903-1985 *ConAu 116*
Scarry, Richard 1919- *AuBYP,
BioIn 8, –9, –10, –12, ChLR 3,
ConAu 17R, –18NR, FamAIYP,
IlsCB 1957, –1967, IntAu&W 77,
–82, –86, NewYTBS 76, –80[port],
OxChL, PiP, SmATA 2, –35,
ThrBJA, TwCCW 78, –83,
WhoAm 78, –80, –82, WrDr 76, –80,
–82, –84, –86*
Schaap, Dick 1934- *ConAu X*
Schaap, Richard 1934- *AmAu&B,
BioIn 8, ConAu 5NR, –9R, WhoE 74*
Schaap, Richard Jay 1934-
WhoAm 84, –86
Schaefer, Jack Warner 1907-
*AmAu&B, Au&Wr 71, AuBYP,
BioIn 5, –8, –9, –11, ConAu 15NR,
–17R, ConAu P-1, IntMPA 77, –75,
–76, –78, –79, –81, –82, –84, OhA&B,
REnAW, ScF&FL 1, SmATA 3,
ThrBJA, TwCCW 78, –83,
WhoAm 74, –76, –78, –80, –82, –84,
–86, WhoWest 74*
Schaefer, Vincent J 1906- *ConAu 120,
WhoTech 84*
Schaefer, Vincent Joseph 1906-
*AmM&WS 73P, –76P, –79P, AsBiEn,
BiESc, BioIn 1, –2, –5, CurBio 48,
InSci, McGMS 80[port], WhoAm 74,
–76, –78, –80, –82, –84, WhoTech 82*
Schafer, William John 1937-
ConAu 49, DrAS 74E, –78E, –82E
Schaff, Louise E *AuBYP SUP*
Schaffer, Ulrich 1942- *ConAu 69*
Schaffner, Nicholas 1953-
ConAu 15NR, –85
Schaller, George B 1933-
*AuBYP SUP, BioIn 12, ConAu 5R,
–9NR, CurBio 85[port], FifIDA,
SmATA 30*
Schaller, George Beals 1933-
WhoAm 84, –86
Schapira, Joel Richard 1949-
WhoS&SW 76
Scharfenberg, Doris 1925- *ConAu 108*
Schary, Dore 1905-1980 *AmAu&B,
AnObit 1980[port], BiDFilm,
BiE&WWA, BioIn 1, –2, –3, –4, –5,
–6, –9, –10, –12, BlueB 76,
ConAu 1R, –1NR, –101, ConDr 73,
–77, CurBio 48, –80N, DcFM,
FilmgC, HalFC 84, IntAu&W 76,
IntMPA 77, –75, –76, –78, –79, –81,
–82, LinLib L, –S, MGM A,
ModWD, NatPD, NewYTBE 70,
NewYTBS 80[port], NotNAT,
OxFilm, REnAL, WhAm 7,
WhoAm 74, –76, –78, –80,
WhoAmJ 80, WhoE 74, –75, –77,
–79, –81, WhoThe 72, –77, –81,
WhoWor 74, –76, –78, –80,
WhoWorJ 72, –78, WorAl, WorAu,
WorEFlm, WrDr 76, –80*
Schatt, Stanley 1943- *ConAu 69*
Schechter, Betty 1921- *AuBYP,
BioIn 8, –10, ConAu 5R, FourBJA,
SmATA 5*
Schechter, William 1934- *ConAu 21R,
ODwPR 79, WhoPubR 76*
Scheffer, Victor B 1906-
*AmM&WS 86P, BioIn 10,
ConAu 11NR, –29R, IntAu&W 86,
SmATA 6, WhoAm 74, –76,
WrDr 80, –82, –84, –86*
Scheinfeld, Amram 1897-1979
*Au&Wr 71, BioIn 12, ConAu 17R,
–89, NewYTBS 79, WhoWorJ 72, –78*
Schell, Jessie *DrAP&F 85*
Schell, Jonathan 1943?- *BioIn 12, –13,
ConAu 12NR, –73, ConLC 35,
WrDr 84*
Schell, Jonathan Edward 1943-
WhoAm 84, –86, WrDr 86

Schell, Orville H 1940- *AuBYP SUP,
BioIn 11, –12, –13, ConAu 25R,
SmATA 10, WrDr 84*
Schell, Orville Hickok, III 1940-
IntAu&W 86
Schellie, Don 1932- *BioIn 13,
ConAu 101, SmATA 29[port]*
Schemm, Mildred Walker 1905-
*BioIn 12, ConAu 1R, –1NR,
DrAS 74E, InWom, SmATA 21,
WhoAm 74, –76*
Schemm, Mildred Walker *see also*
Walker, Mildred
Schenck, Hilbert VanNydeck, Jr.
1926- *AmM&WS 73P, –79P, –82P,
–86P, WhoE 74*
Scherer, Joanna Cohan 1942-
ConAu 107, WrDr 76, –80, –82, –84
Scherman, David E 1916- *ConAu 102,
REnAL*
Scherman, David Edward 1916-
MacBEP
Scherman, Katharine 1915- *AuBYP,
BioIn 4, –7, ConAu 5R, –11NR*
Schevill, James *DrAP&F 85*
Schevill, James 1920- *BioIn 10,
ConAu 5R, ConDr 73, –77, –82,
ConLC 7, ConPo 70, –75, –80, –85,
ConTFT 4[port], DcLEL 1940,
IntAu&W 77, IntWWP 77, –82,
NatPD, –81[port], PenC AM,
WhoAm 74, –76, –78, –80, –82,
WhoE 74, WorAu, WrDr 76, –80,
–82, –84, –86*
Schick, Alice 1946- *AuBYP SUP,
BioIn 13, ConAu 15NR, –81,
SmATA 27[port]*
Schickel, Richard 1933- *AuNews 1,
BioIn 10, BioNews 74, ConAu 1R,
–1NR, WhoAm 74, –76, –78, –80,
–82, –84, –86, WhoE 74, WrDr 76,
–80, –82, –84, –86*
Schiffer, Don 1919?-1964 *BioIn 7*
Schiffer, Michael 1948- *ConAu 106*
Schiller, Barbara 1928- *AuBYP,
BioIn 8, –12, ConAu 17R, SmATA 21*
Schimel, John L 1916- *BiDRAPA 77,
ConAu 25R*
Schlachter, Gail Ann 1943-
ConAu 14NR, WhoAmW 85, –87
Schlauch, Margaret d1986
NewYTBS 86
Schlauch, Margaret 1898- *BioIn 2,
ConAu P-1, CurBio 42, InWom,
IntAu&W 77, –82, IntWW 74, –75,
–76, –77, –/8, –79, –80, –81, –82,
–83, LinLib L, WhE&EA,
WhoAmW 58, WhoSocC 78,
WhoWor 74, WrDr 76, –80, –82, –84*
Schlauch, Margaret 1898-1986
ConAu 119, CurBio 86N
Schlee, Ann 1934- *ConAu 101,
ConLC 35[port], FifBJA[port],
SmATA 36, –44[port], TwCCW 78,
–83, WrDr 80, –82, –84, –86*
Schlegel, Alice 1934- *AmM&WS 73S,
–76P, FifIDA*
Schlein, Miriam *WhoAmW 85, –87,
WrDr 86*
Schlein, Miriam 1926- *AmPB, AuBYP,
BioIn 5, –6, –7, –9, ConAu 1R,
–2NR, CurBio 59, InWom, MorJA,
SmATA 2, TwCCW 78, –83,
WhoAmW 58, –61, –83, WrDr 80,
–82, –84*
Schlesinger, Arthur, Jr. 1917-
*AmAu&B, ASpks, Au&Wr 71,
AuNews 1, BioIn 1, –2, –3, –4, –5, –6,
–7, –8, –10, –11, –12, BioNews 74,
BlueB 76, CelR, ChhPo S3,
ConAu 1R, –1NR, CurBio 46, –79,
DcLB 17[port], DcLEL 1940,
DrAS 74H, –78H, –82H, EncAAH,
EncAB-H, IntAu&W 76, –77, –82,
IntWW 74, –75, –76, –77, –78, –79,
–80, –81, –82, –83, LinLib L, –S,
NewYTBS 79, OhA&B, OxAmH,
OxAmL, –83, PenC AM, PolProf E,
PolProf J, PolProf K, PolProf T, REn,
REnAL, TwCA SUP, WebAB, –79,
Who 74, –82, –83, –85, WhoAm 74,
–76, –78, –80, –82, –84, –86,
WhoGov 72, –75, WhoWor 74, –78,*

–80, –82, –84, –87, WorAl, WrDr 76,
–80, –82, –84, –86
Schlesinger, Arthur M 1917- *BioIn 13*
Schlissel, Lillian 1930- *ConAu 13NR,
–25R, DrAS 74E, –78E, –82E*
Schlossberg, Dan 1948- *ConAu 101,
–19NR, IntAu&W 86*
Schmidt, James Norman *DrAP&F 85*
Schmidt, James Norman 1912-
*BioIn 12, ConAu 1R, –1NR,
DrAS 74E, –78E, –82E, ScF&FL 1,
SmATA 21[port]*
Schmidt, James Norman *see also*
Norman, James
Schmidt, Michael Norton 1947-
*ConAu 2NR, –49, ConPo 75, –80,
IntWWP 77, WhoWor 76, WrDr 76,
–80, –82, –84*
Schmidt, Peggy Jeanne 1951-
ConAu 109, WhoAmW 79
Schmidt, Stanley 1944- *ConAu 8NR,
–61, EncSF, ScFSB, TwCSFW 86,
WrDr 84, –86*
Schmitt, Gladys 1909-1972 *AmAu&B,
AmNov, AmWomWr, Au&Wr 71,
BioIn 1, –2, –3, –4, –9, –12,
ConAu 1R, –2NR, –37R, CurBio 43,
–72, –72N, NewYTBE 72, ObitOF 79,
OxAmL, –83, REnAL, TwCA SUP,
WhAm 5, WhoAmW 74, –58, –64,
–66, –68, –70, –72*
Schmitt, Martin 1917-1978
*BiDrLUS 70, ConAu 9NR, –53,
WhoLibS 55, –66*
Schmitz, James H 1911- *BioIn 12,
ConAu 103, ConSFA, DcLB 8[port],
EncSF, ScF&FL 1, –2, TwCSFW 86,
WhoSciF, WrDr 84, –86*
Schmitz, Joseph William 1905-1966
ConAu 5R, WhAm 4
Schneider, Herman 1905- *AmPB,
Au&Wr 71, AuBYP, BioIn 6, –7, –10,
ConAu 16NR, –29R, IntAu&W 76,
–77, –82, MorJA, SmATA 7*
Schneider, Joyce Anne 1942-
ConAu 107
Schneider, Leo 1916- *ConAu 5R*
Schneider, Richard Coy 1913-
*AmM&WS 73P, –76P, –79P, –82P,
–86P, WhoAm 74, –76, –78, –80, –82,
–84, –86, WhoWor 82, –84, –87*
Schneider, Stephen H 1945-
ConAu 12NR, WhoTech 84
Schneider, Stephen Henry 1945-
*AmM&WS 73P, –76P, –79P, –82P,
–86P, ConAu 69, WhoAm 78, –80,
–82, –84, –86, WhoFrS 84,
WhoTech 82, WhoWest 80*
Schneir, Miriam 1933- *ConAu 77*
Schnurnberger, Lynn 1949-
PrintW 83, –85
Schoen, Barbara 1924- *BioIn 11,
ConAu 21R, IntAu&W 77, –86,
SmATA 13, WrDr 76, –80, –82, –84,
–86*
Schoen, Juliet P 1923- *ConAu 69*
Schoenbaum, Samuel 1927- *DrAS 74E,
–78E, –82E, OxEng 85, WhoAm 74,
–76, –78, –80, –82, –84, –86*
Schoffelmayer, Victor H *BioIn 2,
TexWr*
Scholefield, Alan 1931- *Au&Wr 71,
ConAu 97, IntAu&W 77, –82, –86,
WhoWor 76, WrDr 76, –80, –82, –84,
–86*
Scholefield, Edmund O *ConAu X*
Scholefield, Edmund O 1929-
SmATA 5
Scholefield, Edmund O *see also*
Butterworth, W E
Scholes, Percy A 1877-1958 *NewOxM*
Scholes, Percy Alfred 1877-1958
*Baker 78, –84, BioIn 4, –5,
DcNaB 1951, LongCTC, ObitOF 79,
ObitT 1951, OxMus, TwCA SUP,
WhE&EA, WhLit, WhoLA*
Schollander, Don 1946- *CmCal,
CurBio 65*
Scholz, Jackson Volney 1897- *AuBYP,
BioIn 6, –8, –13, ConAu 5R, MorJA,
WhoTr&F 73*
Scholz, Jackson Volney 1897-1986
ConAu 120
Schonborg, Virginia 1913- *ConAu 77*

Schoor, Gene 1921- *AuBYP, BioIn 7,
-9, ConAu 29R, SmATA 3*
Schotter, Roni *DrAP&F 85*
Schowalter, John E 1936- *ConAu 109*
Schowalter, John Erwin 1936-
WhoE 85A
Schraff, Anne E 1939- *AuBYP SUP,
BioIn 13, ConAu 1NR, -17NR, -49,
SmATA 27[port]*
Schram, Martin Jay 1942- *ConAu 69,
WhoAm 76, -78, -80, -82, -84, -86*
Schrank, Jeffrey 1944- *ConAu 29R,
IntAu&W 77, WrDr 76, -80, -82,
-84, -86*
Schreiber, Flora Rheta 1918-
*AuNews 1, BioIn 10, -11,
BioNews 74, BlueB 76, ConAu 11NR,
-53, DrAS 74E, -78E, -82E,
ForWC 70, WhoAm 78, -80, -82,
-84, -86, WhoAmW 74, -58, -61,
-64, -66, -68, -70, -72, -75, -77,
-79, -81, -85, -87, WhoE 77, -79,
WhoWor 80, -84, WhoWorJ 72, -78*
Schroeder, Henry Alfred 1906-1975
*AmM&WS 73P, -76P, BioIn 10,
ConAu P-2, NewYTBS 75, WhAm 6,
WhoE 74, -75*
Schroeder, Paul Clemens 1938-
*AmM&WS 73P, -76P, -79P, -82P,
-86P*
Schrotenboer, Kathryn 1952?-
BioIn 12
Schueler, Donald G 1929- *ConAu 106,
DrAS 74E, -78E, -82E*
Schulberg, Budd *DrAP&F 85*
Schulberg, Budd 1914- *AmAu&B,
AmNov, AmSCAP 66, BiE&WWA,
BioIn 1, -2, -3, -4, -7, -10, -12,
BlueB 76, CelR, CmCal, CnDAL,
ConAu 19NR, -25R, ConDr 73,
-77D, -82D, ConLC 7, ConNov 72,
-76, -82, -86, CurBio 41, -51,
DcFM, DcLB 6[port], -26[port],
-28[port], -Y81A[port], DcLEL 1940,
FilmgC, HalFC 84, IntAu&W 76,
-77, IntMPA 77, -75, -76, -78, -79,
-81, -82, -84, IntWW 74, -75, -76,
-77, -78, -79, -80, -81, -82, -83,
LinLib L, LongCTC, ModAL,
NewYTBE 72, NotNAT, Novels,
OxAmL, -83, OxFilm, PenC AM,
REn, REnAL, TwCA SUP,
WebE&AL, WhE&EA, WhoAm 74,
-76, -78, -80, -82, -84, -86,
WhoWor 74, WorEFlm, WrDr 76,
-80, -82, -84, -86*
Schulberg, Budd Wilson 1914-
BioIn 13, IntMPA 86
Schulian, John Nielsen 1945-
WhoAm 82, -84
Schulke, Flip Phelps Graeme 1930-
ConAu 105, WhoS&SW 73
Schullery, Paul 1948- *ConAu 111*
Schulman, Grace *ConAu 65,
DrAP&F 85, DrAS 74E, -78E, -82E,
IntAu&W 82, IntWWP 77, -82,
WhoAmW 75*
Schulman, Grace Jan *WhoAmW 77*
Schulman, L M 1934- *ConAu 12NR,
-33R, ScF&FL 1, -2, SmATA 13*
Schulman, Paul 1948- *WhoAdv 77*
Schulte, Elaine L 1934- *ConAu 12NR,
-73, SmATA 36*
Schultes, Richard Evans 1915-
*AmM&WS 73P, -76P, -79P, -82P,
-86P, BioIn 12, ConAu 108,
WhoAm 74, -76, -78, -80, -82, -84,
-86, WhoFrS 84, WhoRel 75, -77*
Schultz, Barbara 1923- *ConAu 21R*
Schultz, Duane P 1934-
AmM&WS 73S, ConAu 29R
Schultz, John *DrAP&F 85*
Schultz, John 1932- *ConAu 15NR,
-41R, WhoAm 74, -76*
Schultz, Pearle Henriksen 1918-
*BioIn 12, ConAu 1NR, -49,
SmATA 21[port]*
Schulz, Charles M 1922- *EncAJ,
EncTwCJ*
Schulz, Charles Monroe 1922-
*AmAu&B, ArtCS, AuBYP, BioIn 4,
-5, -6, -7, -8, -9, -10, -11, -12,*

*CelR, CmCal, ConAu 6NR, -9R,
ConLC 12, CurBio 60, IntWW 78,
-79, -80, -81, -82, -83, LesBEnT,
LinLib L, MinnWr, NewYTET,
SmATA 10, ThrBJA, WebAB, -79,
WhoAm 74, -76, -78, -80, -82, -84,
-86, WhoAmA 73, -76, -78, -80, -82,
-84, WhoWor 74, -84, -87, WorAl,
WorECom, WrDr 76, -80, -82, -84*
Schulz, David A 1933-
*AmM&WS 73S, -78S, ConAu 29R,
WhoE 74, -75, -77*
Schur, Edwin Michael 1930-
*ConAu 7NR, -13R, WhoE 77, -83,
-85*
Schuster, Edgar Howard 1930-
DrAS 74E
Schutz, Susan Polis 1944- *ConAu 105,
IntAu&W 86*
Schuyler, Pamela R 1948- *ConAu 106,
SmATA 30[port]*
Schwab, Gustav Benjamin 1792-1850
*BiD&SB, BioIn 7, CasWL, DcEuL,
EuAu, OxGer, REn*
Schwartz, Alvin 1927- *AuBYP SUP,
BioIn 9, ChlLR 3, ConAu 7NR,
-13R, FifBJA[port], SmATA 4,
WhoE 75, -77*
Schwartz, Barry 1942- *WrDr 86*
Schwartz, Bernard 1923- *BioIn 4, -10,
-11, ConAu 117, DrAS 74P, -78P,
-82P, PolProf E, WhoAm 74, -76,
-78, -80, -82, -84, -86, WhoAmL 78,
-79, -83, -85*
Schwartz, Charles Walsh 1914-
*AuBYP, BioIn 7, -11, ConAu 13R,
-73, SmATA 8*
Schwartz, Delmore 1913-1966
*AmAu&B, AmWr S2, AtlBL, BioIn 4,
-5, -7, -8, -10, -11, -12, -13,
CasWL, CnDAL, CnE&AP, CnMWL,
ConAu 25R, ConAu P-2, ConLC 2,
-4, -10, ConLCrt, -82, ConPo 75,
-80A, CurBio 60, -66, DcLB 28[port],
-48[port], EncWL, -2, LinLib L,
ModAL, -S2, -S1, ObitOF 79,
OxAmL, -83, PenC AM, RAdv 1,
REn, REnAL, SixAP, TwCA, -SUP,
TwCWr, WebE&AL, WhAm 4,
WhoTwCL, WorAl*
Schwartz, Elliott S 1936- *Baker 78,
CpmDNM 81, -82, ConAmC,
ConAu 13R, IntAu&W 77, -82,
WhoAmM 83, WhoE 75, -77,
WrDr 76, -80, -82, -84, -86*
Schwartz, Elliott Shelling 1936-
WhoAm 84, -86
Schwartz, George 1908-1974 *BioIn 6,
-10, ConAu 104*
Schwartz, Howard *DrAP&F 85*
Schwartz, Howard 1945- *ConAu 49*
Schwartz, Julius 1907- *AuBYP,
ConAu 109, SmATA 45*
Schwartz, Julius 1915- *WhoE 74, -75,
-77, WorECom*
Schwartz, Lynne Sharon *DrAP&F 85*
Schwartz, Lynne Sharon 1939-
*ConAu 103, ConLC 31[port],
WhoAm 76, -78, -80, -82, -84, -86,
WrDr 86*
Schwartz, Mischa *WhoTech 84*
Schwartz, Mischa 1926-
*AmM&WS 73P, -79P, -82P, -86P,
LElec, WhoAm 74, -76, -78, -80,
-82, -84, -86, WhoAmJ 80,
WhoEng 80, WhoTech 82,
WhoWor 74*
Schwartz, Sheila *DrAP&F 85*
Schwartz, Sheila 1929- *BioIn 13,
ConAu 11NR, -25R, DrAS 74E,
-78E, -82E, LEduc 74,
SmATA 27[port], WrDr 76, -80, -82,
-84*
Schwartzman, Arnold 1936- *BioIn 7,
-11*
Schwarz, Ted *ConAu 65, -X*
Schwarzenegger, Arnold 1947-
*BioIn 10, -11, -12, -13,
ConAu 21NR, -81, ConTFT 2, -4,
CurBio 79, HalFC 84, IntMPA 84,
-86, NewYTBS 76, -82[port]*

Schweitzer, Albert 1875-1965
*Baker 78, -84, BiDMoPL, BioIn 1,
-2, -3, -4, -5, -6, -7, -8, -9, -10,
-11, -12, -13, BioNews 74,
ConAu 93, CurBio 48, -65, InSci,
LinLib L, -S, LongCTC, LuthC 75,
McGEWB, MusSN, NewYTBS 75,
ObitOF 79, ObitT 1961, OxGer,
OxMed 86, OxMus, REn,
TwCA SUP, TwCWr, WhDW,
WhAm 4, WhE&EA, WhoNob,
WorAl*
Schweitzer, Darrell 1952- *ConAu 116*
Schwerin, Doris H 1922- *BioIn 10,
ConAu 9NR, -65*
Schwiebert, Ernest George 1895-
*ConAu P-1, DrAS 74H, -78H,
IntAu&W 76, -77, OhA&B*
Scithers, George H 1929- *ConAu 57,
EncSF, ScF&FL 1, -2*
Scoble, John *Who 83, -85*
Scoggin, Margaret C 1905-1968
SmATA 47[port]
Scoggin, Margaret Clara 1905-1968
*BioIn 1, -2, -3, -8, -13, CurBio 52,
-68, DcAmLiB, InWom, SmATA 28,
WhoAmW 58, -61, -64, -66*
Scoppettone, Sandra 1936-
*AuBYP SUP, BioIn 11, ConAu 5R,
ConLC 26[port], FifBJA[port],
NatPD, -81[port], SmATA 9,
WhoAm 80, -82*
Scoppettone, Sandra Valerie 1936-
WhoAm 84
Scortia, Thomas N 1926- *BioIn 11,
ConAu 1R, -6NR, EncSF, ScF&FL 1,
-2, ScFSB, TwCSFW 86, WhoSciF,
WrDr 84, -86*
Scortia, Thomas N 1926-1986
ConAu 119
Scott, Andrew 1955- *IntAu&W 86*
Scott, Ann Herbert 1926-
*AuBYP SUP, BioIn 13, BkP,
ConAu 21R, FourBJA, SmATA 29*
Scott, Anne Firor 1921- *ConAu 33R,
DrAS 74H, -78H, -82H, WhoAm 82,
WhoAmW 68, -68A, -81, -83*
Scott, Bill 1935- *DcCAr 81,
InB&W 80*
Scott, Dave *BioIn 13*
Scott, Dennis Daniel 1949-
WhoAmP 81, -83, -85
Scott, Elaine 1940- *BioIn 13,
ConAu 21NR, SmATA 36*
Scott, Frances V *ConAu X*
Scott, Frances V *see also* Wing, Frances
Scott
Scott, George A *MnBBF*
Scott, George Arthur 1911- *WhoE 85*
Scott, Herbert *DrAP&F 85*
Scott, Herbert 1931- *ConAu 6NR, -53,
MichAu 80*
Scott, Jack Denton 1915- *BioIn 8,
ConAu 108, SmATA 31*
Scott, Jay 1949- *WhoAm 86*
Scott, John 1912-1976 *AmAu&B,
Au&Wr 71, BioIn 11, -12,
ConAu 5R, -6NR, -69, IntAu&W 76,
-77, NewYTBS 76, SmATA 14,
WhAm 7, WhoAm 74*
Scott, John Anthony 1916-
*AuBYP SUP, BioIn 6, -13,
ConAu 6NR, -9R, DrAS 74H, -78H,
-82H, IntAu&W 77, -86,
SmATA 23[port], WrDr 76, -80, -82,
-84, -86*
Scott, John M 1913- *BioIn 11,
ConAu 10NR, -65, SmATA 12*
Scott, Joseph 1917- *AuBYP SUP,
ConAu 57*
Scott, Judith Unger 1916- *ConAu 5R,
ForWC 70*
Scott, Lalla 1893- *ConAu P-2*
Scott, Lenore *AuBYP SUP, ForWC 70*
Scott, Margaret 1922- *BiDD, Who 85*
Scott, Sheila 1927- *BioIn 7, -10,
BlueB 76, ConAu 53, CurBio 74,
GoodHs, IntAu&W 76, -77,
IntDcWB, Who 74, -83, -85,
WhoWor 78, WrDr 76, -80, -84, -86*
Scott, Sir Walter 1771-1832 *Alli,
AnCL, AtlBL, BbD, BiD&SB,
BiDLA, -SUP, BioIn 1, -2, -3, -4,*

*-5, -6, -7, -8, -9, -10, -11, -12, -13,
BritAu 19, BritWr 4, CarSB, CasWL,
CelCen, Chambr 3, ChhPo, -S1, -S2,
-S3, CmScLit, CnE&AP, CrtT 2, -4,
CyWA, DcBiA, DcBiPP, DcEnA, -AP,
DcEnL, DcEuL, DcLEL, DcNaB,
Dis&D, EvLB, FamAYP, HalFC 84,
HsB&A, LinLib L, -S, LongCEL,
LuthC 75, McGEWB, MnBBF,
MouLC 3, NewC, NewEOp 71,
NinCLC 15[port], Novels[port],
OxChL, OxEng, -85, OxMus,
OxThe 83, PenC ENG, PIP&P,
PoChrch, RAdv 1, RComWL, REn,
Str&VC, SupFW, WebE&AL,
WhDW, WhoChL, WhoHr&F,
WorAl, YABC 2*
Scott, Walter Decker 1915-
*IntMPA 77, -75, -76, NewYTET,
St&PR 75, WhoAm 74, -76, -78, -80,
-82, -84, -86, WhoE 74*
Scott, Winfiel Townley 1910-1968
OxAmL 83
Scott, Winfield Townley 1910-1968
*AmAu&B, BioIn 4, -8, -9, ChhPo S1,
ConAu 5R, -7NR, -25R,
ModAL, -S1, ObitOF 79, OxAmL,
PenC AM, REn, REnAL,
TwCA SUP, WhAm 5*
Scott-Giles, C W 1893-1982?
ConAu 106
Scott-Stokes, Henry J M *ConAu 117*
Scott Stokes, Henry J M 1918?-
WrDr 76, -80, -82, -84
Screen, Robert Martin *BlkAWP*
Scribner, Harvey B 1913?- *BioIn 9,
NewYTBE 70, -71, WhoE 74*
Scribner, Kimball J 1917?- *BioIn 8*
Scruton, Roger 1944- *ConAu 16NR,
IntAu&W 86, WhoWor 87, WrDr 86*
Scudder, Mildred Lee 1908-
ConAu 9R, ThrBJA
Scudder, Mildred Lee *see also* Lee,
Mildred
Seabrook, Jeremy 1939- *BioIn 12,
ConAu 108, ConDr 77, -82, WrDr 80,
-82, -84, -86*
Seabrooke, Brenda 1941- *ConAu 107,
SmATA 30[port]*
Seagrave, Sterling 1937?- *BioIn 12*
Seale, Bobby 1936?- *BioIn 8, -9, -10,
-11, -12, CelR, CivR 74, CivRSt,
CmCal, ConAu X, Ebony 1, LivgBAA,
MugS, NegAl 76[port], -83[port],
NewYTBE 70, PolProf J, PolProf NF,
WhoBlA 75, -77, -80, -85*
Seale, Bobby 1937- *SelBAAf*
Seals & Crofts *EncPR&S 74, -77,
IlEncRk, RkOn 78, -84, RolSEnR 83*
Seals & Crofts *see also* Crofts, Dash
Sealts, Merton M, Jr. 1915-
*ConAu 13R, DrAS 74E, -78E, -82E,
IntAu&W 86, WhoAm 74, -76, -78,
WrDr 76, -80, -82, -84, -86*
Searight, Mary W 1918- *BioIn 12,
ConAu 29R, SmATA 17,
WhoAmW 75, -77, -79, WhoWest 78,
-80, -82*
Searle, Ronald 1920- *Au&Wr 71,
BioIn 1, -2, -4, -5, -6, -12,
BlueB 76, ChhPo S2, ConAu 9R,
DcBrAr 1, DcLEL 1940, IlsBYP,
IlsCB 1946, IntWW 74, -75, -76,
-77, -78, -79, -80, -81, -82, -83,
NewC, OxChL, OxTwCA,
SmATA 42[port], WhDW, Who 74,
-82, -83, WhoAm 74, -76, -78, -80,
-82, -83, -86, WhoArt 80, -82, -84,
WhoGrA 62, -82[port], WhoWor 74,
-82, -84, -87, WorECar, WrDr 76,
-80, -82, -84, -86*
Searls, Hank *IntAu&W 86X*
Searls, Hank 1922- *BioIn 11,
ConAu X, EncSF, ScF&FL 1, -2,
ScFSB, TwCSFW 86, WrDr 84, -86*
Searls, Hank *see also* Searls, Henry
Hunt, Jr.
Searls, Henry H, Jr. 1922-
IntAu&W 86
Searls, Henry Hunt, Jr. 1922-
Au&Wr 71, ConAu 13R
Searls, Henry Hunt, Jr. *see also* Searls,
Hank

Shaara, Michael Joseph, Jr. 1929-
*AuNews 1, BioIn 8, −10, ConAu 102,
ConLC 15, DcLB Y83B[port],
DrAS 74E, −78E, −82E, WhoAm 76,
−78, −80, −82, −84, −86,
WhoS&SW 78, −80, −82, WrDr 76,
−80, −82, −84*

Shackley, Myra 1949- *ConAu 115*

Shaff, Albert L 1937- *ConAu 29R*

Shaffer, Anthony *TwCCr&M 85*

Shaffer, Anthony 1926- *BioIn 13,
ConAu 110, −116, HalFC 84,
WrDr 84, −86*

Shaffer, Peter *TwCCr&M 85*

Shaffer, Peter 1926- *Au&Wr 71,
BiE&WWA, BioIn 7, −8, −9, −10,
−11, −12, −13, BlueB 76, CnMD,
CnThe, ConAu 25R, ConDr 73, −77,
−82, ConLC 5, −14, −18, −37[port],
ConTFT 4, CroCD, CurBio 67,
DcLB 13[port], DcLEL 1940,
EncMys, EncWL 2, EncWT,
HalFC 84, IntAu&W 76, −77,
IntWW 74, −75, −76, −77, −78, −79,
−80, −81, −82, −83, McGEWD, −84,
ModBrL S2, −S1, ModWD, NewC,
NewYTBS 75, NotNAT, OxAmT 84,
PenC ENG, PlP&P, −A, REnWD,
TwCr&M 80, TwCW, Who 74,
−82, −83, WhoThe 72, −77, −81,
WhoWor 74, −76, −78, −82, WorAl,
WorAu, WrDr 76, −80, −82, −84, −86*

Shaffer, Peter Levin 1926- *OxEng 85,
OxThe 83, Who 85, WhoAm 86,
WhoWor 84, −87*

Shah, Diane K 1945- *ConAu 73*

Shah, Idries 1924- *BioIn 10, −12,
BlueB 76, ConAu 7NR, −17R,
CurBio 76, EncO&P 2, −78S1,
IntAu&W 76, −77, −82, −86,
IntWWP 77, −82, IntYB 78, −79, −80,
−81, −82, MakMC, MidE 78, −79,
−80, −81, −82, OxEng 85, WhoAm 76,
−78, WhoRel 77, WhoWor 74, −76,
WrDr 76, −80, −82, −84, −86*

Shah, Idries Abutahir 1924-
WhoRel 86

Shah, Krishna Bhogilal 1938-
ConAu 17R, WhoE 74, −75

Shahn, Ben 1898-1969 *AtlBL, BioIn 1,
−2, −3, −4, −5, −6, −7, −8, −9, −10,
−12, −13, BriEAA, ChhPo S1,
ConArt 77, −83, ConAu 89, ConPhot,
CurBio 54, −69, DcAmArt,
DcCAA 71, −77, EncAB-H,
ICPEnP A, IlsCB 1957, −1967,
MacBEP, McGDA, McGEWB,
ObitOF 79, ObitT 1961, OxAmL, −83,
OxArt, OxTwCA, PhDcTCA 77,
PrintW 83, −85, REn, SmATA 21N,
WhAm 5, WhoAmA 78N, −80,
−82N, −84N, WhoGrA 62, WorAl,
WorArt[port]*

Shakespeare, William 1564-1616 *Alli,
AnCL, AtlBL, BbD, BiD&SB,
BiDRP&D, BioIn 1, −2, −3, −4, −5,
−6, −7, −8, −9, −10, −11, −12, −13,
BritAu, BritWr 1, CarSB, CasWL,
Chambr 1, −2, −3, ChhPo, −S1, −S2,
−S3, CnE&AP, CnThe, CroE&S,
CrtT 1, −4, CyWA, DcBiPP,
DcEnA, −AP, DcEnL, DcEuL,
DcLEL, DcNaB, Dis&D, EncWT,
EvLB, FamAYP, FilmgC, HalFC 84,
LinLib L, −S, LongCEL, LuthC 75,
McGEWB, McGEWD, −84[port],
MouLC 1, NewC, NewEOp 71,
NotNAT A, −B, OxAmT 84,
OxEng, −85, OxFilm, OxFr, OxGer,
OxMus, OxThe, −83, PenC ENG,
PlP&P, −A, RComWL, REn,
REnWD, WebE&AL, WhDW, WorAl*

Shalit, Gene *WhoAm 84, −86*

Shalit, Gene 1932- *IntMPA 86*

Shange, Ntozake *DrAP&F 85,
WrDr 86*

Shange, Ntozake 1948- *AmWomD,
BioIn 11, −12, −13, ConAu 85,
ConDr 82, ConLC 8, −25[port],
−38[port], CurBio 78, DcLB 38[port],
DrBlPA, InB&W 80, −85,
NatPD, −81[port], NegAL 83,
NewYTBS 76, −77, Po&Wr 77,*

*SelBAAf, SelBAAu, WhoAm 80, −82,
−84, −86, WhoAmW 83, WhoBlA 77,
−80, −85, WhoThe 81, WorAl,
WorAu 1975[port], WrDr 84*

Shankar, Ravi 1920- *AuBYP SUP,
Baker 78, −84, BioIn 6, −7, −8, −9,
−11, −13, CelR, CurBio 68,
FarE&A 78, −79, −80, −81,
IntWW 74, −75, −76, −77, −78, −79,
−80, −81, −82, −83, IntWWM 77,
WhoHol A, WhoMus 72,
WhoRocM 82, WhoWor 74, −84, −87,
WorAl, WorEFlm*

Shanks, Ann Zane *WhoAm 84, −86*

Shanks, Ann Zane Kushner *BioIn 11,
ConAu 53, SmATA 10, WhoAm 78,
−80, −82, WhoAmW 74, −70, −72,
−75, −77, −79, WomWMM B*

Shannon, Doris 1924- *ConAu 8NR,
−61, ScF&FL 1, −2, WrDr 80, −82,
−84, −86*

Shapiro, Fred C 1931- *ConAu 17R*

Shapiro, Gilbert 1934- *AmM&WS 86P*

Shapiro, Harry L 1902- *AmAu&B,
AmM&WS 73S, −76P, −79P, −82P,
BioIn 3, −5, −12, BlueB 76,
ConAu 49, CurBio 52, FifIDA, InSci,
IntAu&W 77, −82, IntWW 74, −75,
−76, −77, −78, −79, −80, −81, −82,
−83, WhoAm 74, −76, −78, −80,
WhoAmJ 80, WhoWor 74,
WhoWorJ 72, WrDr 80, −82, −84,
−86*

Shapiro, Harry Lionel 1902-
AmM&WS 86P, WhoAm 86

Shapiro, Irwin 1911-1981 *AuBYP,
BioIn 2, −7, ChhPo S1, ConAu 81,
JBA 51, SmATA 32[port]*

Shapiro, James E 1946- *ConAu 108*

Shapiro, Karl Jay 1913- *AmAu&B,
AnCL, BioIn 1, −4, −5, −7, −8, −10,
−11, −12, BlueB 76, CasWL, CelR,
ChhPo, −S2, −S3, CnDAL, EncAP,
ConAu 1R, −1NR, ConLC 4, −8, −15,
ConLCrt, −82, ConPo 70, −75, −80,
CroCAP, CurBio 44, DcLEL,
DrAS 74E, −78E, −82E, EncWL,
EvLB, IntAu&W 77, IntWW 74, −75,
−76, −77, −78, −79, −80, −81, −82,
−83, IntWWP 77, LinLib L,
ModAL, −S1, OxAmL, PenC AM,
RAdv 1, REn, REnAL, SixAP,
TwCA SUP, TwCWr, WebAB, −79,
WebE&AL, WhE&EA, WhoAm 74,
−76, −78, −80, −82, −84, −86,
WhoTwCL, WhoWest 74,
WhoWor 74, WhoWorJ 72, −78,
WorAl, WrDr 76, −80, −82, −84*

Shapiro, Milton 1926- *AuBYP,
BioIn 7, ConAu 81, SmATA 32[port],
WhoAm 74, −76, −78, −80, −82, −84,
−86*

Shapiro, Rebecca *AuBYP, BioIn 8*

Shapiro, Stanley 1937-
*AmM&WS 86P, WhoAm 84, −86,
WhoF&I 83, WhoTech 82, −84*

Shapley, Harlow 1885-1972 *AmAu&B,
AmM&WS 73P, −76P, AsBiEn,
BiESc, BioIn 1, −3, −4, −7, −9, −10,
−11, −13, ConAu 37R, CurBio 41,
−52, −72, −72N, DcScB, EncAB-H,
InSci, LinLib L, −S, McGEWB,
McGMS 80[port], NewYTBE 72,
ObitOF 79, OxAmH, REnAL,
TwCA, −SUP, WebAB, −79, WhDW,
WhAm 5*

Sharmat, Marjorie Weinman 1928-
*AuBYP SUP, BioIn 9, ConAu 12NR,
−25R, FifBJA[port], IntAu&W 76,
−77, −82, −86, SmATA 33[port], −4,
TwCCW 78, −83, WhoAm 74, −75,
WrDr 76, −80, −82, −84, −86*

Sharp, Harold S 1909- *BiDrLUS 70,
ConAu 3NR, −9R, IntAu&W 76, −77,
−82, WhoLibS 66*

Sharp, Margery *Who 85, WhoWor 84,
−87*

Sharp, Margery 1905- *Au&Wr 71,
AuBYP, BioIn 1, −2, −4, −8, −9, −13,
BlueB 76, ConAu 18NR, −21R,
ConNov 72, −76, −82, −86, DcLEL,
EvLB, IntAu&W 76, −77, IntWW 74,
−75, −76, −77, −78, −79, −80, −81,*

*−82, −83, LongCTC, NewC, OxChL,
RAdv 1, REn, ScF&FL 1, −2,
SmATA 1, −29[port], ThrBJA,
TwCA, −SUP, TwCCW 78, −83,
WhLit, WhThe, Who 74, −82, −83,
WhoAmW 74, −68, −70, −72,
WhoWor 74, −76, −78, WrDr 76, −80,
−82, −84, −86*

Sharp, Marilyn 1941?- *BioIn 11*

Sharpe, Mitchell R 1924- *Au&Wr 71,
BioIn 11, ConAu 29R, SmATA 12,
WhoS&SW 75, −76, WrDr 76, −80,
−82, −84*

Sharpe, Roger Carter 1948- *ConAu 93*

Shattuck, Roger W *DrAP&F 85*

Shattuck, Roger Whitney 1923-
*AmAu&B, Au&Wr 71, BioIn 10,
BlueB 76, ConAu 5R, −7NR,
DrAS 74F, −78F, −82F, IntAu&W 76,
−77, −82, IntWWP 77, −82,
WhoAm 74, −76, −78, −80, −82, −84,
−86, WorAu, WrDr 76, −80, −82, −84*

Shavelson, Melville 1917- *CmMov,
ConAu 4NR, −53, ConTFT 1,
FilmgC, HalFC 84, IntMPA 77, −75,
−76, −78, −79, −81, −82, −84, −86,
WhoAm 74, −76, −78, −80, −82, −84,
−86, WorEFlm*

Shaw, Arnold 1909- *AmSCAP 66,
AuBYP SUP, Baker 78, −84, BioIn 3,
−9, CpmDNM 82, ConAmC, −82,
ConAu 1R, −1NR, IntWWM 85,
ScF&FL 1, SmATA 4, Who 74, −82,
−83, WhoAm 74, −76, −78, −80, −82,
−84, −86, WhoAmM 83, WhoE 74,
WhoWor 78*

Shaw, Bernard *BioIn 13*

Shaw, Bernard 1856-1950
*DcLB 57[port], MajMD 1,
ModBrL S2, NewOxM, OxEng 85,
TwCLC 21[port]*

Shaw, Bob 1931- *ConAu 1NR, −19NR,
−49, ConSFA, EncSF, IntAu&W 77,
−82, Novels, ScF&FL 1, −2,
ScFSB[port], TwCSFW 86, WhoSciF,
WrDr 76, −80, −82, −84, −86*

Shaw, David 1943- *ConAu 49*

Shaw, George Bernard 1856-1950
*Alli SUP, AtlBL, Baker 78, −84,
BiD&SB, BiDIrW, BioIn 1, −2, −3,
−4, −5, −6, −7, −8, −9, −10, −11, −12,
−13, BritWr 6, CasWL, Chambr 3,
ChhPo, −S2, −S3, CnMD, CnMWL,
CnThe, ConAu 104, DcAmB,
DcBiA, DcEnA AP, DcIrB, DcIrW 1,
−2, DcLEL, DcNaB 1941, Dis&D,
EncSF, EncWL, −2[port], EncWT,
EvLB, Film 2, FilmgC, HalFC 84,
LinLib L, −S, LongCEL, MakMC,
McGEWB, McGEWD, −84[port],
ModBrL, −S1, NewC, NewC,
NotNAT A, −B, Novels, ObitOF 79,
OxAmT 84, OxEng, OxMus,
OxThe, −83, PenC ENG, PlP&P,
RComWL, REn, REnWD,
ScF&FL 1, ScFSB, TwCA, −SUP,
TwCLC 3, TwCWr, WebE&AL,
WhDW, WhAm 3, WhE&EA, WhLit,
WhScrn 77, −83, WhoNob,
WhoStg 1906, −1908, WhoTwCL,
WorAl*

Shaw, Irwin d1984 *Who 85N*

Shaw, Irwin 1912-1984 *HalFC 84*

Shaw, Irwin 1913- *AmAu&B, AmNov,
Au&Wr 71, AuNews 1, BiE&WWA,
BioIn 1, −2, −4, −5, −6, −7, −8, −10,
−12, BlueB 76, CelR, CnDAL,
CnMD, CnThe, ConAu 13R,
ConDr 73, −77, ConLC 7,
−23[port], ConNov 72, −76, −82,
CurBio 42, DcLB 6[port], DcLEL,
EncWL, EncWT, FilmgC,
IntAu&W 76, −77, −82, IntWW 74,
−75, −76, −77, −78, −79, −80, −81,
−82, −83, LinLib L, LongCTC,
McGEWD, −84, ModAL, ModWD,
NewYTBS 80[port], −83[port],
NotNAT, Novels[port], OxAmL, −83,
PenC AM, PlP&P, RAdv 1, REn,
REnAL, TwCA, −SUP, TwCWr,
Who 74, −82, −83, WhoAm 74, −76,
−78, −80, −82, −84, −86, WhoThe 72,
−77, −81, WhoTwCL, WhoWor 74,*

*−78, −80, −82, WorAl, WorEFlm,
WrDr 76, −80, −82, −84*

Shaw, Irwin 1913-1984 *AnObit 1984,
BioIn 13, ConAu 112, −21NR,
ConLC 34[port], CurBio 84N,
DcLB Y84N[port], NewCon[port],
NewYTBS 84[port], OxAmT 84*

Shaw, Peter 1936- *ConAu 9NR, −65,
DrAS 74E, −78E, −82E*

Shaw, Richard 1923- *BioIn 11,
ChhPo S2, −S3, ConAu 37R,
SmATA 12, WrDr 76, −80, −82, −84,
−86*

Shaw, Robert 1925-1978 *WhScrn 83*

Shaw, Robert 1927-1978 *AuNews 1,
BiDrAPA 77, BiE&WWA, BioIn 4,
−6, −7, −8, −9, −10, −11, −13,
BlueB 76, CelR, ConAu 1R, −4NR,
−81, ConDr 73, −77, ConLC 5,
ConNov 72, −76, CroCD, CurBio 49,
−66, −68, −78, −78N, DcLB 13[port],
−14[port], DcLEL 1940, EncWT,
FilmgC, HalFC 84, IntAu&W 76,
−77, IntMPA 77, −75, McGEWD,
MovMk, NewYTBE 70, −72,
NewYTBS 78, −80[port], NotNAT,
ObitOF 79, PlP&P, −A, TwCWr,
WhAm 7, Who 74, WhoAdv 72,
WhoAm 76, −78, −82, WhoHol A,
WhoS&SW 80, −82, WhoThe 72, −77,
−81N, WhoWor 74, WorAl, WorAu,
WrDr 76*

Shaw, Robert Byers 1916-
*AmM&WS 73S, −78S, ConAu 37R,
DrAS 74H, −78H, −82H*

Shay, Arthur 1922- *BioIn 9,
ConAu 33R, SmATA 4, WhoAm 74,
−76, −78, WhoMW 74, −76*

Shcharansky, Avital 1951?- *BioIn 12*

Shea, Michael *EncSF, ScF&FL 1,
ScFSB*

Shea, Michael 1946- *ConAu 112*

Sheaks, Barclay *WhoAmA 84*

Shearer, John 1947- *BioIn 13,
SmATA 27, −43[port]*

Sheats, Mary Boney 1918-
ConAu 13R, DrAS 74P, −78P, −82P

Sheats, Mary Boney *see also* Boney,
Mary Lily

Shebar, Sharon Sigmond 1945-
*ConAu 103, −19NR, SmATA 36,
WhoE 83*

Sheckley, Robert 1928- *BioIn 12,
ConAu 1R, −2NR, ConSFA,
DcLB 8[port], EncSF, IntAu&W 77,
Novels, ScF&FL 1, −2, ScFSB[port],
TwCSFW 86, WhoSciF, WrDr 84,
−86*

Shecter, Ben *WrDr 86*

Shecter, Ben 1935- *AuBYP, BioIn 8,
−12, ChhPo S1, ConAu 81,
IlsCB 1957, −1967, ScF&FL 1,
SmATA 16, ThrBJA, WrDr 76, −80,
−82, −84*

Shedd, Charlie W 1915- *BioIn 10, −12,
ConAu 17R*

Shedley, Ethan I *ConAu X*

Sheean, Vincent 1899-1975 *AmAu&B,
AmNov, AuBYP SUP, BioIn 1, −2,
−3, −4, −5, −10, ConDAL, ConAmA,
ConAu 61, CurBio 41, −75, −75N,
EncAJ[port], IntAu&W 76, −77,
LinLib L, NewYTBS 74, −75,
ObitOF 79, OxAmL, −83, REn,
REnAL, ScF&FL 1, −2, TwCA, −SUP*

Sheed, Wilfrid *DrAP&F 85*

Sheed, Wilfrid 1930- *AmCath 80,
BioIn 8, −10, −11, −12, −13,
ConAu 65, ConLC 2, −4, −10,
ConNov 72, −76, −82, −86,
CurBio 81[port], DcLB 6[port],
IntAu&W 76, ModAL S1, NewC,
WhoAm 74, −76, −78, −80, −82,
WorAu, WrDr 76, −80, −82, −84, −86*

Sheehan, Susan 1937- *Au&Wr 71,
ConAu 12NR, −21R, WhoAm 86,
WhoAmW 74, −75, −77, −81, −83,
−87, WhoE 85, WrDr 76, −80, −82,
−84, −86*

Sheehy, Eugene Paul 1922-
WhoAm 84, −86

Sheehy, Gail *WrDr 86*

Sheffield, Charles *ScFSB,
TwCSFW 86*

Shefter, Harry 1910- *ConAu 9R*

Sheldon, Alice Hastings 1915-
BioIn 12, ConAu 108, WrDr 84

Sheldon, Alice Hastings *see also*
Tiptree, James, Jr.

Sheldon, Mary 1955?- *BioIn 12*

Sheldon, Walter J 1917- *AuBYP,
AuNews 1, BioIn 10, ConAu 10NR,
−25R*

Sheldon, Walter James 1917-
IntAu&W 86

Shellabarger, Samuel 1888-1954
*AmAu&B, AmNov, BioIn 1, −2, −3,
−4, −7, CnDAL, CurBio 45, −54,
DcAmB S5, NatCAB 40, −47,
ObitOF 79, OhA&B, REn, REnAL,
TwCA SUP, WhAm 3*

Shelley, Mary Wollstonecraft
1797-1851 *Alli, AtlBL, BbD,
BiD&SB, BioIn 1, −2, −3, −4, −5, −7,
−8, −9, −10, −11, −12, BritAu 19,
CasWL, Chambr 3, ChhPo, −S1, −S3,
CrtT 4, CyWA, DcBiA, DcBiPP,
DcEnA, DcEnL, DcEuL, DcLEL,
EncMys, EncSF, EvLB, FilmgC,
HerW, InWom, IntDcWB, LinLib L,
−S, MouLC 3, NewC, Novels[port],
OxEng, PenC ENG, RAdv 1, REn,
ScF&FL 1, SmATA 29[port],
WebE&AL, WhDW, WhoHr&F,
WhoSciF, WorAl*

Shelley, Mary Wollstonecraft *see also*
Wollstonecraft, Mary

Shelley, Percy Bysshe 1792-1822 *Alli,
AtlBL, BbD, BiD&SB, BioIn 1, −2,
−3, −4, −5, −6, −7, −8, −9, −10, −11,
−12, −13, BritAu 19, BritWr 4,
CasWL, CelCen, Chambr 3,
ChhPo, −S1, −S2, −S3, CnE&AP,
CnThe, CrtT 2, −4, CyWA, DcBiPP,
DcEnA, DcEnL, DcEuL, DcLEL,
DcNaB, −S, Dis&D, EncWT, EvLB,
IlEncMy, LinLib L, −S, LongCEL,
McGEWB, McGEWD, −84[port],
MouLC 2, NewC, NotNAT B,
OxEng, −85, OxThe, −83, PenC ENG,
RAdv 1, RComWL, REn, REnWD,
ScF&FL 1, WebE&AL, WhDW,
WorAl*

Shelnutt, Eve *DrAP&F 85*

Shelp, Earl E 1947- *ConAu 116*

Shelton, William Roy 1919-
*AuBYP SUP, AuNews 1,
BiDrAPA 77, BioIn 2, −10,
ConAu 5R, −11NR, IntAu&W 76,
−77, −82, −86, ScF&FL 1, −2,
SmATA 5, WhoS&SW 76, −78*

Shen, Tsʻung-Wen 1902?- *BioIn 9,
CasWL, DcOrL 1*

Shenton, Edward 1895- *AmAu&B,
BioIn 1, −2, −5, IlrAm E, IlsBYP,
IlsCB 1744, −1946*

Shenton, Edward 1895-1977
IlrAm 1880, SmATA 45[port]

Shenton, James Patrick 1925-
*AmAu&B, BlueB 76, ConAu 2NR,
−5R, DrAS 74H, −78H, −82H,
WhoAm 74, −76, −78, −80, −82, −84,
−86, WrDr 80, −82, −84*

Shepard, Jim *ConLC 36[port]*

Shepard, Leslie Alan 1917-
IntAu&W 86, WrDr 86

Shepard, Sam *NewYTBS 84[port],
−85[port]*

Shepard, Sam 1942?- *BioIn 10, −11,
−12, BioNews 74, ConAu 69,
ConDr 73, −77, −82, ConLC 4, −6,
−17, ConTFT 1, CroCD, CurBio 79,
DcLB 7[port], DcLEL 1940, EncWT,
IntMPA 81, −82, −84, McGEWD 84,
ModAL S1, NatPD, −81[port],
NewYTBS 80[port], NotNAT, PIP&P,
WhoAm 74, −76, −78, −80, −82,
WhoRocM 82, WhoThe 77, −81,
WorAu 1970, WrDr 76, −80, −82, −84*

Shepard, Sam 1943- *BioIn 13,
ConLC 34[port], −41[port], −44[port],
EncWL 2, HalFC 84, IntMPA 86,
ModAL S2, OxAmT 84, OxAmL 84,
OxThe 83, WhoAm 84, −86, WrDr 86*

Shepard, Thomas Rockwell, Jr. 1918-
*ConAu 105, St&PR 75, WhoAdv 72,
WhoAm 74, −76, −78, −80, −82, −84,*

*−86, WhoE 74, −75, −77, −79, −81,
WhoF&I 74, −75, −77, −79, −81*

Shephard, Esther 1891-1975 *BioIn 1,
−10, −13, ConAu 57, ConAu P-2,
DrAS 74E, SmATA 26N, −5,
WhoAmW 58*

Shepherd, Jean 1925?- *BioIn 13,
CurBio 84[port]*

Shepherd, Walter Bradley 1904-
Au&Wr 71, ConAu 105, WhE&EA

Shepherd, William Robert 1871-1934
*DcAmAu, DcAmB S1, DcNAA,
HarEnUS, WhAm 1*

Sheppard, Harold L 1922-
*AmM&WS 73S, ConAu 1NR, −45,
IntAu&W 76, WhoS&SW 76*

Sherburne, Zoa 1912- *AuBYP,
BioIn 8, −9, ConAu 1R, −3NR,
ConLC 30[port], EncSF, ForWC 70,
FourBJA, ScF&FL 1, −2, SmATA 3,
WhoAmW 66, −68, −70, −72,
WhoPNW*

Sheridan, Richard Brinsley 1751-1816
*Alli, AtlBL, BbD, BiD&SB, BiDIrW,
BiDLA, BioIn 1, −2, −3, −4, −5, −6,
−7, −8, −9, −10, −11, −12, BritAu,
BritWr 3, CasWL, CelCen,
Chambr 2, ChhPo, CnThe, CrtT 2,
−4, CyWA, DcBiPP, DcEnA, DcEnL,
DcEuL, DcInB, DcIrB, DcIrL,
DcIrW 1, DcLEL, DcNaB, EncWT,
EvLB, LinLib L, −S, LongCEL,
McGEWB, McGEWD, −84[port],
MouLC 2, NewC, NewEOp 71,
NinCLC 5[port], NotNAT A, −B,
OxAmT 84, OxEng, −85, OxThe, −83,
PenC ENG, PIP&P, PoIre, REn,
REnWD, WebE&AL, WhDW, WorAl*

Sherlock, John 1932- *ConAu 3NR,
−9R, IntAu&W 77*

Sherlock, Philip Manderson 1902-
*AnCL, Au&Wr 71, AuBYP, BioIn 7,
−9, BlueB 76, ConAu 5R, −6NR,
ConPo 70, DcAfL, IntAu&W 77,
Who 74, −82, −83, WhoWor 74, −76,
WrDr 80, −82, −84*

Sherman, D R 1934- *BioIn 13,
ConAu 8NR, −13R, SmATA 29, −48*

Sherman, Diane 1928- *BioIn 11,
ConAu 5NR, −9R, SmATA 12*

Sherman, Eileen Bluestone 1951-
ConAu 119

Sherman, Roger *WrDr 86*

Sherman, Roger 1930- *AmEA 74,
ConAu 37R, DrAS 74E, −78E,
IntAu&W 77, −82, −86, WhoAm 86,
WhoF&I 85, WhoS&SW 86,
WrDr 76, −80, −84*

Sherriff, Robert Cedric 1896-1975
*Au&Wr 71, BiE&WWA, BioIn 2, −4,
−5, −8, −10, −13, Chambr 3, CnMD,
CnThe, ConAu 61, ConDr 73, CroCD,
CyWA, DcLEL, IntAu&W 76,
EncWT, EvLB, IntAu&W 76,
IntMPA 75, IntWW 74, −75, −76N,
LongCTC, McGEWD, ModBrL,
ModWD, NewC, NewYTBS 75,
NotNAT A, −B, OxEng, OxThe,
PenC ENG, REn, TwCA, −SUP,
TwCWr, WhE&EA, WhThe, Who 74,
WhoThe 72, WhoWor 74*

Sherrill, Elizabeth 1928- *ConAu 110*

Sherrod, Jane *ConAu X, SmATA 4, −X*

Sherwin, Judith Johnson *DrAP&F 85*

Sherwin, Judith Johnson 1936-
*ConAu 25R, ConLC 7, −15,
ConPo 75, −80, −85, DcLEL 1940,
IntAu&W 76, −77, −82, IntWWP 77,
−82, WhoAm 76, −78, −80, −82, −84,
−86, WhoAmW 79, −81, −83,
WrDr 76, −80, −82, −84, −86*

Sherwin, Martin Jay 1937-
ConAu 110, DrAS 74H, −78H

Sherwood, Debbie *ConAu 25R,
WhoAmW 74, −75, WrDr 76, −80,
−82, −84*

Sherwood, Robert E 1896-1955
OxAmT 84

Sherwood, Robert Emmet 1896-1955
BioIn 13, OxThe 83

Sherwood, Robert Emmett 1896-1955
*AmAu&B, BioIn 1, −2, −4, −5, −6, −7,
−9, −12, CasWL, CnDAL, CnMD,*

*CnThe, ConAmA, ConAu 104,
CurBio 40, −56, CyWA, DcAmB S5,
DcLB 7[port], −26[port], DcLEL,
EncWL, EncWT, EvLB, FilmgC,
LinLib L, −S, LongCTC, McGEWB,
McGEWD, −84[port], ModAL,
ModWD, NotNAT A, −B, ObitOF 79,
ObitT 1951, OxAmL, OxThe,
PenC AM, PIP&P, REn, REnAL,
REnWD, TwCA, −SUP, TwCLC 3,
TwCWr, WebAB, −79, WebE&AL,
WhAm 3, WhE&EA, WhThe, WorAl*

Shetler, Stanwyn Gerald 1933-
AmM&WS 86P, WhoFrS 84

Shetterly, Will 1955- *ConAu 119*

Shevey, Sandra *WomWMM B*

Shields, Art 1888- *BioIn 13*

Shikes, Ralph E 1912- *ConAu 12NR*

Shikes, Ralph Edmund 1912-
*ConAu 29R, IntAu&W 77, −82,
WrDr 76, −80, −82, −84, −86*

Shimer, Dorothy Blair 1911-
*ConAu 45, DrAS 74E, −78E, −82E,
WhoAmW 74, −68, −70, −75, −77,
−79, WomPO 76*

Shipler, David K 1942- *ConAu 21NR,
WrDr 86*

Shipler, David Karr 1942- *ConAu 103,
WhoAm 76, −78, −80, −82, −84, −86*

Shipley, Joseph T 1893- *WhoAm 84,
−86*

Shipley, Joseph Twaddell 1893-
*AmAu&B, AnMV 1926, BioIn 2,
BlueB 76, ChhPo, −S1, ConAmTC,
ConAu 9NR, −13R, IntAu&W 76,
−82, NotNAT, REnAL, WhJnl,
WhNAA, WhoAm 74, −76, −78, −80,
−82, WhoThe 72, −77, −81, WrDr 76,
−80, −82, −84*

Shipley, Joseph Twadell 1893-
IntAu&W 86, WrDr 86

Shippen, Katherine Binney 1892-1980
*AnCL, AuBYP, BioIn 2, −3, −6, −7,
−9, −12, −13, ConAu 5R, −93,
CurBio 54, InWom, IntAu&W 76,
MorJA, SmATA 1, −23N, Str&VC*

Shirer, William L 1904- *EncAJ[port],
IntAu&W 86, NewYTBS 86[port],
OxAmL 83, SmATA 45[port],
WrDr 86*

Shirer, William Lawrence 1904-
*AmAu&B, Au&Wr 71, AuBYP,
BioIn 1, −2, −3, −4, −6, −7, −8, −11,
−12, −13, BlueB 76, ConAu 7NR,
−9R, CurBio 41, −62, DcLB 4,
EncTR, EncTwCJ, IntAu&W 76, −77,
−82, IntWW 74, −75, −76, −77, −78,
−79, −80, −81, −82, −83, LinLib L,
NewYTBS 82[port], OxAmL, REn,
REnAL, TwCA SUP, WebAB, −79,
WhE&EA, Who 74, −82, −83, −85,
WhoAm 74, −76, −78, −80, −82, −84,
−86, WhoWor 74, −78, WorAl,
WrDr 76, −80, −82, −84*

Shirley, John *ScFSB*

Shirley, John 1953- *TwCSFW 86*

Shirreffs, Gordon D 1914-
ConAu 21NR, EncFWF

Shirreffs, Gordon Donald 1914-
*AuBYP, BioIn 7, −11, ConAu 6NR,
−13R, IntAu&W 76, SmATA 11,
WrDr 76, −80, −82, −84, −86*

Shirts, Morris A 1922- *ConAu 73,
LEduc 74*

Shockley, Robert Joseph 1921-
LEduc 74

Sholl, Betsy *DrAP&F 85*

Sholokhov, Mikhail A d1984
NewYTBS 84[port]

Sholokhov, Mikhail A 1905-1984
CurBio 84N, SmATA 36N

Sholokhov, Mikhail Aleksandrovich
d1984 *Who 85N*

Sholokhov, Mikhail Aleksandrovich
1905-1984 *AuBYP SUP, BioIn 1, −4,
−5, −6, −7, −9, −10, −11, −12, −13,
CasWL, ClDMEL, CnMWL,
ConAu 101, ConLC 7, −15,
CurBio 42, −60, CyWA, DcRusL,
EncWL, EvEuW, HanRL,
IntAu&W 76, −77, IntWW 74, −75,
−76, −77, −78, −79, −80, −81, −82,
−83, LinLib L, −S, LongCTC,*

*MakMC, McGEWB, ModSL 1,
Novels, OxEng 85, PenC EUR, REn,
SmATA 36N, TwCA, −SUP, TwCWr,
Who 74, −82, −83, WhoSocC 78,
WhoTwCL, WhoWor 74, −82, WorAl*

Shook, Robert L 1938- *ConAu 8NR,
−61*

Shore, Jane *DrAP&F 85*

Shore, Jane 1947- *ConAu 77,
Po&Wr 77*

Shorris, Earl 1936- *ConAu 10NR, −65,
WhoF&I 85*

Short, Lester LeRoy, Jr. 1933-
*AmM&WS 73P, −76P, −79P, −82P,
−86P, WhoE 75*

Short, Robert Lester 1932- *ConAu 77,
WhoMW 74, −76*

Shorter, Edward 1941- *WrDr 86*

Shostak, Stanley 1938-
*AmM&WS 73P, −76P, −79P, −82P,
−86P, ConAu 117*

Shotwell, Louisa R 1902- *OxChL,
WrDr 86*

Shotwell, Louisa Rossiter 1902-
*AuBYP SUP, BioIn 3, −9, −10,
ConAu 1R, −4NR, MorBMP,
SmATA 3, ThrBJA, TwCCW 78, −83,
WhoAmW 58, WrDr 76, −80, −82,
−84*

Shoumatoff, Alex 1946- *ConAu 9NR,
−53*

Shrader, Robert Louis 1913-
WhoWest 74, −76

Shreve, Susan E 1952- *ConAmC, −82*

Shreve, Susan Richards *DrAP&F 85*

Shreve, Susan Richards 1939-
*ConAu 5NR, −49, ConAu 5AS[port],
ConLC 23[port], SmATA 41,
−46[port], WhoAmW 87, WrDr 76,
−80, −82, −84, −86*

Shriver, Donald Woods, Jr. 1927-
*ConAu 1NR, −45, DrAS 74P, −78P,
−82P, WhoAm 80, −82, −84, −86,
WhoE 81, −83, WhoRel 75, −85*

Shroyer, Frederick B 1916-1983
ConAu 13NR

Shroyer, Frederick Benjamin 1916-
*AmAu&B, ConAu 13R, DrAS 74E,
−78E, −82E, IndAu 1917, WhoAm 74,
−76, −78, −80, −82, WhoWest 74, −76,
WhoWor 78, −80, −82*

Shroyer, Frederick Benjamin
1916-1983 *WhAm 8*

Shu, Chʻing-Chʻin *WorAu 1975*

Shu, Chʻing-Chʻun 1897-1966 *BioIn 13*

Shu, Chʻing-chʻun 1898?-1966
*BioIn 10, ConAu 109, CurBio 45,
DcOrL 1, PenC CL*

Shulevitz, Uri 1935- *WhoAm 84, −86*

Shulman, Alix Kates *DrAP&F 85*

Shulman, Alix Kates 1932- *BioIn 10,
−13, ConAu 29R, ConLC 2, −10,
SmATA 7, WhoAmW 74, −75,
WorAu 1975[port]*

Shulman, Arthur 1927- *WhoAm 74,
−76, −78, −80, −82*

Shultz, Gladys Denny 1895-
*ConAu 49, WhoAmW 58, −61,
WhoWest 78, −80*

Shuman, James B 1932- *ConAu 61*

Shura, Mary Francis *IntAu&W 86X,
WrDr 86*

Shura, Mary Francis 1923- *BioIn 9,
−10, −12, ConAu X, ForWC 70,
IntAu&W 77X, −82X, SmATA 6,
ThrBJA, WrDr 76, −80, −82, −84*

Shura, Mary Francis *see also* Craig,
Mary Francis

Shurkin, Joel N 1938- *ConAu 14NR,
−69*

Shute, Nevil *DcNaB 1951*

Shute, Nevil 1899-1960 *BioIn 3, −4,
−5, −7, ConAu X, ConLC 30[port],
CurBio 42, −60, DcLEL, EncSF,
EvLB, FilmgC, HalFC 84, InSci,
LinLib LP, LongCTC, ModBrL,
NewC, Novels, ObitOF 79,
ObitT 1951, OxAusL, PenC ENG,
REn, ScF&FL 1, ScFSB,
TwCA, −SUP, TwCCr&M 80,
TwCSFW 86, TwCWr, WhAm 3, −4,
WhoTwCL, WorAl*

Smith, Anthony David 1938- *Who 85*
Smith, Beatrice S *BioIn 11,*
ConAu 10NR, –57, SmATA 12
Smith, Betty 1896-1972 *AmAu&B,*
AmNov, AmWomWr, BioIn 13,
CnDAL, ConAu 5R, –33R,
ConLC 19, CurBio 43, –72, CyWA,
DcLB Y82B[port], DcLEL 1940,
LongCTC, NewYTBE 72, NotNAT B,
ObitOF 79, OxAmL, PenC AM, REn,
REnAL, SmATA 6, TwCA SUP,
WhAm 5, WhE&EA, WhoAmW 61,
–66, –68, –70, –72
Smith, Betty 1904- *HalFC 84*
Smith, Betty 1904-1972 *OxAmL 83*
Smith, Bradley 1910- *BioIn 7,*
ConAu 2NR, –5R, –19NR, ICPEnP A
Smith, Bradley F 1931- *WrDr 86*
Smith, Charles Merrill *BioIn 10, –11*
Smith, Charles Merrill d1985
ConAu 115
Smith, Clark Ashton 1893-1961
BioIn 12, ChhPo, –S1, CmCal,
ConLC 43[port], EncSF, ScF&FL 1,
SupFW, TwCSFW 86, WhNAA,
WhoHr&F
Smith, Cordelia Titcomb 1902-
BiDrLUS 70, ConAu P-1, ConSFA,
ScF&FL 1, –2, WhoLibS 55, –66
Smith, Curt 1951- *ConAu 81*
Smith, Datus Clifford, Jr. 1907-
AuBYP SUP, BioIn 7, –11, BlueB 76,
ConAu 11NR, ConAu P-1,
SmATA 13, WhoAm 74, –76, –78,
–80, –82, –84, –86, WhoWor 74
Smith, Dave *DrAP&F 85,*
IntAu&W 86X
Smith, Dave 1942- *BioIn 13,*
ConAu X, ConLC 22[port], –42[port],
ConPo 80, –85, DcLB 5[port],
DrRegL 75, WrDr 82, –84, –86
Smith, Dave *see also* Smith, David
Jeddie
Smith, David Bruce 1923-
WhoF&I 85, WhoS&SW 82, –84
Smith, David Jeddie 1942- *BioIn 12,*
ConAu 1NR, –49, IntAu&W 86
Smith, David Jeddie *see also* Smith,
Dave
Smith, Dennis *DrAP&F 85*
Smith, Dennis 1940- *BioIn 12,*
ConAu 10NR, –61, WhoAm 82,
WhoE 79, WrDr 80, –82, –84, –86
Smith, Dian G 1946- *ConAu 120*
Smith, Dinitia *DrAP&F 85*
Smith, Dodie *BioIn 13, WrDr 86*
Smith, Dodie 1896- *Au&Wr 71,*
BiE&WWA, BioIn 12, Chambr 3,
ConAu 33R, ConDr 77, –82,
DcLB 10[port], DcLEL,
IntAu&W 82, IntWW 77, –78, –79,
–80, –81, –82, –83, LongCTC,
McGEWD, –84, NewC, NotNAT,
OxChL, PIP&P, REn, ScF&FL 1,
SmATA 4, TwCChW 83, WhE&EA,
Who 74, –82, –83, –85, WhoThe 72,
–77, –81, WhoWor 74, –76, –78,
WorAu, WrDr 76, –82, –84
Smith, Dodie Gladys 1896- *OxThe 83*
Smith, Doris Buchanan 1934-
AuBYP SUP, BioIn 13, ConAu 11NR,
–69, DcLB 52[port], FifBJA[port],
SmATA 28[port]
Smith, E E *ConAu X*
Smith, E E 1890-1965 *DcLB 8[port],*
EncSF, Novels, ScF&FL 1,
TwCSFW 86, WhoSciF
Smith, E E Doc *ConAu X*
Smith, E E Doc *see also* Smith, Edward
Elmer
Smith, E E *see also* Smith, Edward
Elmer
Smith, Edward E 1890-1965 *ScFSB*
Smith, Edward Elmer 1890-1965
BioIn 12, ConAu 118
Smith, Eleanor Touhey 1910-
BiDrLUS 70, ConAu 25R, ForWC 70,
WhoAmW 74, –64, –66, –68, –70,
–72, –75, –77, WhoLibI 82,
WhoLibS 55, –66
Smith, Elsdon Coles 1903- *AmAu&B,*
ConAu 1R, –6NR, DrAS 74E, –78F,
–82F, IntAu&W 77, –82, –86,

IntYB 78, –79, –80, –81, –82,
WhoAm 74, –76, –78, –80,
WhoS&SW 84, WrDr 76, –80, –82,
–84, –86
Smith, Emma 1923- *AuBYP, BioIn 8,*
ConAu 73, ConNov 72, –76, –82, –86,
DcLEL 1940, IntAu&W 76, –77, –82,
–86, LongCTC, SmATA 36,
TwCCW 78, –83, Who 74, –82, –83,
–85, WrDr 76, –80, –82, –84, –86
Smith, Ethel Sabin 1887- *ConAu P-1,*
IntAu&W 77, WhoAmW 58,
WrDr 76, –80, –82, –84
Smith, Frank Kingston 1919- *BioIn 5,*
–10, ConAu 102, –18NR
Smith, Gary Milton 1943- *ConAu 97*
Smith, Gary Richard 1932- *BioIn 12,*
ConAu 69, SmATA 14
Smith, George O 1911- *TwCSFW 86*
Smith, George O 1911-1981 *BioIn 12,*
ConAu 103, –97, DcLB 8[port],
EncSF, NewYTBS 81, ScF&FL 1, –2,
WhoSciF, WrDr 84
Smith, George O 1911-1982 *ScFSB*
Smith, Grahame J C 1942-
AmM&WS 73P, –76P, –79P, –82P,
–86P
Smith, Harry Allen 1907-1976
AmAu&B, BioIn 1, –3, –4, –6, –10,
–11, –12, –13, ChhPo, TwCA SUP,
WhE&EA
Smith, Hedrick 1933- *BlueB 76,*
ConAu 11NR, –65, IntAu&W 82,
WhoAm 76, –78, –80, –82,
WhoS&SW 73, WorAl, WrDr 80, –82,
–84, –86
Smith, Hedrick Laurence 1933-
EncTwCJ, WhoAm 84, –86
Smith, Hedrick Lawrence 1933-
IntAu&W 86
Smith, Henry Nash d1986
NewYTBS 86
Smith, Henry Nash 1906- *AmAu&B,*
BlueB 76, ConAu 1R, –2NR,
DrAS 74E, –78E, –82E,
IntAu&W 77, –82, IntWW 74, –75,
–76, –77, –78, –79, –80, –81, –82,
–83, REnAL, REnAW, WhoAm 74,
–76, –78
Smith, Henry Nash 1906-1986
ConAu 119
Smith, Howard E, Jr. 1927-
ConAu 21NR, –25R, SmATA 12,
WrDr 76, –80, –82, –84, –86
Smith, Howard Everett, Jr. 1927-
IntAu&W 86
Smith, Joan 1938- *WrDr 84, –86*
Smith, John M *Who 85*
Smith, Joseph Burkholder 1921-
BioIn 12, ConAu 65, WhoS&SW 80,
–82, –84
Smith, Julie 1944- *ConAu 112,*
IntAu&W 86
Smith, Kay Nolte 1932- *ConAu 101,*
–18NR, TwCCr&M 85, WrDr 86
Smith, Ken 1902- *ConAu 1NR, –45*
Smith, Lacey Baldwin 1922-
AmAu&B, ConAu 5R, –6NR,
DrAS 74E, –78H, –82H, WhoAm 74,
–76, –78, –80, –82, WrDr 76, –80,
–82, –84, –86
Smith, LeRoi 1934- *AuBYP SUP,*
ConAu 29R, WhoAm 82,
WhoWest 74
Smith, Lillian Eugenia 1897-1966
AmAu&B, AmNov, AmWomWr,
BioIn 2, –3, –4, –6, –7, –8, –9, –12,
–13, CnDAL, ConAu 25R,
ConAu P-2, CurBio 44, –66,
DcAmSR, EncSoH, InWom,
LinLib L, LongCTC, NotAW MOD,
ObitOF 79, OxAmL, REn, REnAL,
TwCA SUP, WhAm 4, WhE&EA,
WhoAmW 58, –64, –66
Smith, Lou 1918- *ConAu 73*
Smith, Michael Townsend 1935-
BioIn 10, ConAu 11NR, –21R,
ConDr 73, –77, –82, IntAu&W 86,
WhoAm 74, –76, –78, –80, –82, –84,
–86, WrDr 76, –80, –82, –84, –86
Smith, Nancy Covert 1935- *BioIn 11,*
ConAu 10NR, –57, SmATA 12
Smith, Norman F 1920- *BioIn 10,*
ConAu 29R, SmATA 5

Smith, Norman Frederick 1920-
WhoAmP 85
Smith, Norman Lewis 1941-
ConAu 77, WhoE 81, –83, –85
Smith, Page 1917- *AmAu&B,*
ConAu 1R, –2NR, DrAS 74H, –78H,
–82H, WhoAm 74, WrDr 80, –82,
–84, –86
Smith, Patrick J 1932- *Baker 84*
Smith, Patrick John 1932-
ConAu 41R, IntWWM 77,
WhoAmM 83
Smith, Patti *DrAP&F 85*
Smith, Patti 1946?- *BioIn 10, –11, –12,*
ConAu 93, ConLC 12, EncPR&S 77S,
NewRR 83, RolSEnR 83,
WhoRock 81[port], WhoRocM 82,
WorAl
Smith, Pauline C 1908- *ConAu 29R,*
SmATA 27[port]
Smith, Red *BioIn 13*
Smith, Red 1905- *WhAm 8*
Smith, Red 1905-1982
AnObit 1982[port], BioIn 1, –2, –3,
–4, –5, –6, –10, –11, –12, CelR,
ConAu 77, –X, ConAu 59, –82N,
DcLB 29[port], EncTwCJ,
NewYTBS 82[port], –86[port],
REnAL, WebAB, –79, WhoAm 76,
–78, –80, –82, WorAu 1975[port]
Smith, Red *see also* Smith, Walter
Wellesley
Smith, Rex Alan 1921- *ConAu 61,*
WhoF&I 77, –79, WhoS&SW 78,
WhoWor 80
Smith, Richard Harris 1946-
ConAu 41R
Smith, Robert Kimmel 1930-
BioIn 11, –13, ConAu 8NR, –61,
NatPD, –81[port], SmATA 12,
WhoE 81
Smith, Roger J 1938- *WhoLibI 82*
Smith, Ruth Leslie 1902- *BioIn 9,*
ConAu P-2, SmATA 2
Smith, Sally Liberman 1929- *BioIn 3,*
–12, ConAu 11NR, –21R
Smith, Sam 1937- *ConAu 73*
Smith, Stan 1943- *ConAu 120*
Smith, Stan 1946- *BioIn 8, CelR,*
ConAu 85, NewYTBE 73
Smith, Vian 1920-1969 *AuBYP SUP,*
BioIn 11, ConAu 1R, –3NR,
SmATA 11, TwCChW 83
Smith, Walter Wellesley 1905-1982
AmCath 80, BioIn 1, –2, –3, –4, –5,
–6, –10, –12, –13, ConAu 105, –77,
CurBio 59, REnAL, WebAB, –79,
WorAl
Smith, Walter Wellesley *see also* Smith,
Red
Smith, Wilbur Addison 1933-
Au&Wr 71, BioIn 12, ConAu 7NR,
–13R, EncSoA, NewYTBS 80[port],
Novels[port], ScF&FL 1, –2, Who 82,
–83, –85, WrDr 76, –80, –82, –84
Smith, William Jay *DrAP&F 85*
Smith, William Jay 1918-
AuBYP SUP, BioIn 6, –8, –9, –10,
–11, –12, BkCL, ChhPo, –S1, –S2,
–S3, CivWDc, ConAu 5R, ConLC 6,
ConPo 70, –75, –80, –85, CurBio 74,
DcLB 5[port], DcLEL 1940,
DrAS 74E, –78E, FifBJA[port],
IntAu&W 77, IntWWP 77,
OxAmL 83, PenC AM, SmATA 2,
TwCCW 78, –83, WhoAm 74, –76,
–78, –80, –82, –84, –86, WorAu,
WrDr 76, –80, –82, –84, –86
Smolan, Rick 1949- *ICPEnP A*
Smucker, Barbara *OxCanL*
Smucker, Barbara 1915- *BioIn 13,*
ChlLR 10[port], WhoCanL 85
Smucker, Barbara Claassen 1915-
ConAu 106, SmATA 29[port],
TwCChW 83, WhoAm 82, –84, –86,
WrDr 86
Smythe, Mabel M 1918- *AmWomM,*
WhoAmW 85
Smythe, Mabel Murphy *InB&W 85*
Smythe, Mabel Murphy 1918-
AmM&WS 73S, –78S, AmPolW 80B,
–80C, ConAu 37R, InB&W 80,

LivgBAA, SelBAAf, WhoAm 78, –80,
–82, –84, –86, WhoAmP 77, –79, –81,
–83, –85, WhoAmW 74, –64, –66,
–68, –70, –72, –75, –79, –81, –83,
WhoBlA 75, –77, –80, –85,
WhoWor 78, –80, –82, –84,
WomPO 78
Snedeker, Caroline Dale 1871-1956
WomNov
Snedeker, Caroline Dale Parke
1871-1956 *AmAu&B, AmWomWr,*
AnCL, AuBYP, BioIn 1, –2, –4, –8,
–12, IndAu 1816, JBA 34, –51,
OhA&B, TwCCW 78, –83, WhAm 3,
WhE&EA, WhNAA, WomWWA 14,
YABC 2
Sneider, Vern 1916-1981 *BioIn 3, –4,*
–12, ConAu 5R, –103, CurBio 56,
–81N, IntAu&W 76, –77, MichAu 80,
NewYTBS 81
Sneider, Vern John 1916-1981
ConAu 13NR
Snelling, Robert Orren 1932-
WhoF&I 85
Sneve, Virginia Driving Hawk 1933-
BioIn 11, ChlLR 2, ConAu 3NR, –49,
ScF&FL 1, –2, SmATA 8
Snider, Dee 1955- *ConNews 86-1[port]*
Snively, William Daniel, Jr. 1911-
ConAu 29R
Snodgrass, W D *DrAP&F 85*
Snodgrass, W D 1926- *Alli,*
ConAu 1R, –6NR, ConLC 2, –6, –10,
–18, ConPo 70, –75, –80, –85,
CroCAP, CurBio 60, DcLB 5[port],
DrAS 82E, LinLib L, ModAL, –S2,
–S1, OxAmL, –83, PenC AM,
RAdv 1, REn, REnAL, WebE&AL,
WhoAm 86, WhoTwCL, WhoWor 74,
WorAu, WrDr 76, –80, –82, –84, –86
Snodgrass, William DeWitt 1926-
BioIn 5, –6, –10, –11, –12, BlueB 76,
CasWL, ChhPo, –S1, CIDMEL,
DcLEL 1940, DrAS 74E, –78E,
IntAu&W 77, –82, IntWW 74, –75,
–76, –77, –78, –79, –80, –81, –82,
–83, IntWWP 77, –82, MichAu 80,
WhoAm 74, –76, –78, –80, –82,
WorAl
Snow, Baron Charles Percy 1905-1980
BioIn 13
Snow, C P 1905-1980
AnObit 1980[port], –1981, ASpks,
BlueB 76, BritWr 7, ConAu 5R, –101,
ConLC 1, –4, –6, –9, –13, –19,
ConNov 76, CurBio 54, –61, –80N,
DcLB 15[port], EncMys, EncWL 2,
IntAu&W 76, –77, LinLib L,
ModBrL, –S2, –S1, NewC,
NewYTBS 80[port], Novels[port],
OxEng 85, RAdv 1, REn, ScF&FL 1,
–2, TwCWr, WebE&AL, WhoTwCL,
WorAl, WrDr 76, –80
Snow, Charles Percy 1905-1980
Au&Wr 71, BioIn 3, –4, –5, –6, –7,
–8, –9, –10, –11, –12, CasWL,
ConNov 72, CurBio 54, –61, DcLEL,
DcNaB 1971, EncWL, EvLB, InSci,
IntWW 74, –75, –76, –77, –78, –79,
–80, LinLib S, LongCEL, LongCTC,
McGEWB, OxEng, PenC ENG,
TwCA SUP, WhE&EA, Who 74
Snow, Donald Clifford 1917- *BioIn 12,*
ConAu 85, FourBJA, SmATA 16
Snow, Donald Clifford *see also* Fall,
Thomas
Snow, Donald R 1931- *WhoTech 84*
Snow, Donald Ray 1931-
AmM&WS 86P, WhoAm 84, –86,
WhoWest 82
Snow, Dorothea J 1909- *BioIn 11,*
ConAu 1R, –3NR, SmATA 9
Snow, Edgar Parks 1905-1972
AmAu&B, Au&Wr 71, BioIn 4, –5,
–9, –10, –11, –12, ConAu 33R, –81,
CurBio 41, –72, –72N, NatCAB 60,
NewYTBE 72, ObitOF 79,
ObitT 1971, REn, REnAL,
TwCA, –SUP, WhAm 5, WhE&EA
Snow, Edward Rowe 1902-1982
Au&Wr 71, BioIn 5, BlueB 76,
ConAu 6NR, –9R, –106, CurBio 58
Snow, Richard F 1947- *ConAu 106,*
SmATA 37

Snyder, Anne 1922- *BioIn 9, ConAu 14NR, –37R, SmATA 4, WrDr 76, –80, –82, –84, –86*

Snyder, Carol 1941- *SmATA 35*

Snyder, Ernest Elwood, Jr. 1917- *AmM&WS 73P, –76P, –79P, LEduc 74*

Snyder, Gary *DrAP&F 85, OxEng 85*

Snyder, Gary 1930- *BioIn 13, ConLC 32[port], ConPo 85, ModAL S2, OxAmL 83, WrDr 86*

Snyder, Gary Sherman 1930- *AmAu&B, BioIn 8, –9, –10, –11, –12, CasWL, CmCal, ConAu 17R, ConLC 1, –2, –5, –9, ConPo 70, –75, –80, CroCAP, CurBio 78, DcLEL 1940, –16[port], DcLEL 1940, IntWWP 77, LinLib L, ModAL S1, MugS, PenC AM, RAdv 1, REn, REnAL, WebE&AL, WhoAm 74, –76, –78, –80, –82, –84, –86, WhoE 74, –77, –79, WhoWor 74, WorAu, WrDr 76, –80, –82, –84*

Snyder, Gerald S 1933- *ConAu 12NR, –61, SmATA 34, –48*

Snyder, Jerome 1916-1976 *ConAu 65, IlsBYP, IlsCB 1957, WhoGrA 62*

Snyder, Louis L 1907- *AuBYP, BioIn 8, BlueB 76, ConAu 1R, –2NR, DrAS 74H, –78H, –82H, IntAu&W 76, –77, WhoAm 74, –76, –78, WhoE 74, WhoWor 74, –76, WrDr 76, –80, –82, –84, –86*

Snyder, Louis Leo 1907- *WhoAm 84, –86*

Snyder, Zilpha Keatley 1927- *AmWomWr, AuBYP, BioIn 8, –9, –10, ConAu 9R, ConLC 17, MorBMP, ScF&FL 1, –1A, –2, SmATA 1, –28[port], SmATA 2AS[port], ThrBJA, TwCCW 78, –83, WhoAm 82, –84, WrDr 76, –80, –82, –84, –86*

Snyder, Zilpha Keatley 1928- *BioIn 13, OxChL*

Sobel, Robert 1931- *AmArch 70, ConAu 5R, –8NR, DrAS 74H, –78H, –82H, ScF&FL 1, –2*

Sobol, Donald J 1924- *AuBYP, BioIn 8, –9, ChlLR 4[port], ConAu 1R, –1NR, –18NR, FourBJA, SmATA 1, –31[port], TwCCW 78, –83, WhoAm 78, –80, –82, –84, –86, WhoAmJ 80, WhoWor 80, –82, –84, –87, WrDr 84, –86*

Sobol, Harriet Langsam 1936- *ConAu 69R, –61, SmATA 34, –47[port]*

Sobol, Rose 1931- *ConAu 101*

Sohn, David A 1929- *ConAu 6NR, –9R, IndAu 1917, ScF&FL 1, –2, WhoMW 74, –76*

Sokolov, Sasha 1943- *HanRL*

Sokolov, Sasha 1944?- *BioIn 11, ConAu 73, –X*

Solberg, Carl 1915- *ConAu 12NR, –73*

Solbert, Romaine G 1925- *BioIn 9, –12, ConAu 29R, SmATA 2*

Solbert, Romaine G *see also* Solbert, Ronni G

Solbert, Ronni G 1925- *BioIn 5, –8, –12, ChhPo S2, –S3, ConAu X, IlsBYP, IlsCB 1946, –1957, –1967, SmATA 2*

Solbert, Ronni G *see also* Solbert, Romaine G

Solensten, John M *DrAP&F 85*

Solensten, John M 1929- *ConAu 110, DrAS 74E*

Solomon, Barbara H 1936- *ConAu 13NR*

Solomon, Louis 1910?-1981 *AuBYP, BioIn 8, –12*

Solzhenitsyn, Aleksandr Isaevich 1918- *BioIn 13, EncWL 2, HanRL*

Solzhenitsyn, Aleksandr Isayevich 1918- *AuNews 1, BioIn 7, –8, –9, –10, –11, –12, BioNews 74, CasWL, ConAu 25R, –69, ConLC 1, –2, –4, –7, –9, –10, –18, –26[port], DcPol, EncWL, IntAu&W 76, –77, IntWW 74, –75, –76, –77, –78, –79, –80, –81, –82, –83, IntYB 78, –79,*

–80, –81, –82, LinLib L, –S, MakMC, McGEWB, ModSL 1, NewYTBE 70, –72, NewYTBS 74, –80[port], Novels[port], PenC EUR, RComWL, REn, TwCWr, WhDW, Who 74, –82, –83, WhoAm 76, –78, –80, –82, WhoTwCL, WhoWor 74, –78, –80, –82, WorAl, WorAu

Somer, John Laddie 1936- *ConAu 37R, DrAS 78E, –82E*

Somerlott, Robert 1928- *ConAu 105, ScF&FL 1A*

Somerville, Lee 1915- *ConAu 69*

Somma, Robert 1944- *BioIn 10, MugS*

Sommer, Elyse 1929- *AuBYP SUP, BioIn 10, ConAu 2NR, –49, SmATA 7*

Sommer, Scott 1951- *ConAu 106, ConLC 25[port]*

Sommerfelt, Aimee 1892- *AuBYP, ConAu 37R, SmATA 5, ThrBJA, TwCCW 78B, –83B*

Sommerfelt, Aimee 1892-1975 *OxChL*

Somtow, S P *ConAu X*

Somtow, S P *see also* Sucharitkul, Somtow

Sonnabend, Roger P 1925- *BioIn 8, St&PR 75, WhoAm 74, –76, –78, –80, WhoAmJ 80, WhoE 74, WhoWorJ 72, –78*

Sonnabend, Roger Philip 1925- *WhoAm 86, WhoS&SW 84*

Sootin, Harry *AuBYP, BioIn 7*

Soper, Tony *WrDr 86*

Soper, Tony 1939- *ConAu 105, WrDr 80, –82, –84*

Sorel, Julia *ConAu X, WrDr 86*

Sorell, Walter 1905- *BiGAW, ConAu 21R, WhoE 74*

Sorensen, Theodore Chaikin 1928- *AmAu&B, BioIn 5, –6, –7, –8, –11, BlueB 76, ConAu 2NR, –45, CurBio 61, IntAu&W 77, IntWW 74, –75, –76, –77, –78, –79, –80, –81, –82, –83, PolProf K, WhoAm 74, –76, –78, –80, –82, –84, –86, WhoAmL 85, WhoAmP 73, –75, –77, –79, –81, –83, –85, WhoWor 74, –78*

Sorensen, Virginia 1912- *AmAu&B, AmNov, Au&Wr 71, AuBYP, BioIn 2, –4, –6, –7, –9, –10, ConAu 13R, CurBio 50, EncFWF, InWom, MorBMP, MorJA, OxAmL 83, OxChL, NewbC 1956, SmATA 2, TwCA SUP, TwCCW 78, –83, WhoAm 74, –76, –78, –80, –82, –84, –86, WhoAmW 74, –58, –72, WhoWor 74, WrDr 76, –80, –82, –84, –86*

Sorrentino, Gilbert *DrAP&F 85*

Sorrentino, Gilbert 1929- *BioIn 7, –12, –13, ConAu 14NR, –77, ConLC 3, –7, –14, –22[port], –40[port], ConNov 82, –86, ConPo 70, –75, –80, –85, DcLB 5[port], –Y80B[port], IntAu&W 77, IntWWP 77, OxAmL 83, PenC AM, PostFic, RAdv 1, WhoAm 80, –82, –84, –86, WorAu 1975[port], WrDr 76, –80, –82, –84, –86*

Sorrentino, Joseph N 1937- *ConAu 3NR, –49, SmATA 6*

Soto, Gary *DrAP&F 85*

Soto, Gary 1952- *ChiLit, ChiSch, ConAu 119, ConLC 32[port], ConPo 85, WorAu 1975[port], WrDr 86*

Soto, Pedro Juan 1928- *BioIn 12, ConAu 114, DcCLAA, EncWL, –2, ModLAL, PueRA*

Soule, Gardner Bosworth 1913- *AuBYP SUP, BioIn 12, ConAu 2NR, –5R, SmATA 14, WhoAm 74, –76, –78, –80, –82, –84, –86, WhoWor 78*

Soulieres, Robert 1950- *WhoCanL 85*

South, Joe 1942?- *BioIn 8, EncPR&S 74, –77, IlEncRk, RkOn 74, –82, RolSEnR 83, WhoRock 81, WhoRocM 82*

South, Malcolm Hudson 1937- *ConAu 107, DrAS 74E, –78E, –82E*

South, Wesley W 1919- *WhoBlA 77, –80, –85*

Southall, Ivan 1921- *Au&Wr 71, AuBYP, BioIn 6, –8, –9, –10, ChlLR 2, ConAu 7NR, –9R, OxAusL, OxChL, ScF&FL 1, –2, SenS, SingR 1, SmATA 3, SmATA 3AS[port], ThrBJA, TwCCW 78, –83, WhoWor 74, –76, WrDr 76, –80, –82, –84, –86*

Southerland, Ellease *DrAP&F 85*

Southerland, Ellease 1943- *BlkAWP, ConAu 107, DcLB 33[port], InB&W 80, SelBAAf*

Southey, Robert *OxAusL*

Southey, Robert 1744-1843 *Alli, AtlBL, BbD, BiD&SB, BiDLA, BioIn 1, –2, –3, –5, –6, –7, –8, –9, –10, –11, –12, BritAu 19, BritWr 4, CasWL, CelCen, Chambr 3, ChhPo, –S1, –S2, –S3, CnE&AP, DcEnA, –AP, DcEnL, DcEuL, DcLEL, Dis&D, EvLB, LinLib L, –S, LongCEL, MouLC 3, NewC, OxEng, PenC ENG, PoLE, REn, WebE&AL, WhDW, WhoChL*

Southey, Robert 1774-1843 *BioIn 13, DcNaB, NinCLC 8[port], OxChL, OxEng 85*

Southworth, John VanDuyn 1904- *Au&Wr 71, BlueB 76, ConAu 5R, –6NR, IntAu&W 76, –77, WhNAA, WhoAm 74, –76, –78, WrDr 80, –82, –84*

Southworth, John VanDuyn 1904-1986 *ConAu 118*

Sowell, Thomas 1930- *BioIn 13, InB&W 85, SelBAAf, WhoAm 84, –86, WhoBlA 85*

Sowell, Thomas 1936- *WhoEc 86*

Soyinka, Wole *SelBAAf*

Soyinka, Wole 1934- *AfSS 78, –79, –80, –81, –82, BioIn 8, –9, –10, –12, –13, CasWL, CnThe, ConAu 13R, ConDr 73, –77, –82, ConLC 3, –5, –14, –36[port], –44[port], ConPo 70, –75, –80, –85, CurBio 74, DrBlPA, EncWL, –2[port], EncWT, InB&W 80, –85, IntAu&W 76, –77, IntWW 74, –75, –76, –77, –78, –79, –80, –81, –82, –83, IntWWP 77, McGEWB, McGEWD 84, ModBlW, ModCmwL, ModWD, Novels[port], OxEng 85, OxThe 83, PenC CL, –ENG, REnWD, RGAfL, TwCWr, WebE&AL, WhoTwCL, WhoWor 74, –82, –84, –87, WorAu, WrDr 76, –80, –82, –84, –86*

Spach, John Thom *DrAP&F 85*

Spach, John Thom 1928- *ConAu 29R, IntAu&W 77, WhoS&SW 75, –76, WrDr 76, –80*

Spache, George D 1909- *WrDr 86*

Spache, George Daniel 1909- *AmM&WS 73S, AuBYP, BioIn 8, ConAu 1R, –5R, –6NR, IntAu&W 77, WrDr 76, –80, –82, –84*

Spacks, Patricia Meyer 1929- *ConAu 1R, –1NR, DrAS 74E, –78E, –82E, IntAu&W 77, –86, WhoAm 86, WhoAmW 74, –72, –75, WrDr 76, –80, –82, –84, –86*

Spada, James 1950- *ConAu 7NR, –57, WhoWest 84*

Spangenburg, Judith Dunn 1942- *ConAu 29R, SmATA 5*

Spangenburg, Judith Dunn *see also* Dunn, Judy

Spark, Muriel *ConNov 86, ConPo 85, WrDr 86*

Spark, Muriel 1918- *BioIn 13, ConAu 12NR, ConLC 40[port], EncWL 2, HalFC 84, ModBrL S2, OxEng 85*

Spark, Muriel Sarah *IntAu&W 86, Who 85, WhoAm 84, –86, WhoAmW 85, WhoWor 84, –87*

Spark, Muriel Sarah 1918- *Au&Wr 71, BioIn 6, –7, –8, –9, –10, –12, CasWL, CmScLit, ConAu 5R, ConLC 2, –3, –5, –8, –13, –18, ConNov 72, –76, –82, ConPo 70, –75, –80, CurBio 75, DcLB 15[port], DcLEL 1940,*

EncWL, IntAu&W 76, –77, –82, IntWW 74, –75, –76, –77, –78, –79, –80, –81, –82, –83, IntWWP 77, –82, LinLib L, LongCEL, LongCTC, ModBrL, –S1, NewC, Novels[port], PenC ENG, RAdv 1, REn, ScF&FL 1, TwCWr, WebE&AL, Who 74, –82, –83, WhoAm 80, –82, WhoAmW 74, –68, –70, –72, –83, WhoTwCL, WhoWor 74, –78, –80, –82, WorAl, WorAu, WrDr 76, –80, –82, –84

Sparks, James Calvin, Jr. 1925- *AuBYP SUP, WhoE 74*

Speaight, Robert William 1904-1976 *Au&Wr 71, BioIn 1, –9, BlueB 76, BkC 4, CathA 1930, ChhPo, ConAu 13R, DcNaB 1971, IntAu&W 76, –77, IntWW 74, –75, –76, –77N, LongCTC, OxCan SUP, OxThe 83, PIP&P, ScF&FL 1, –2, WhE&EA, WhoThe 72, –77, –81N, WhoWor 74, –76, WrDr 76*

Spear, Hilda D 1926- *WrDr 86*

Speare, Elizabeth George 1908- *AmAu&B, AmWomWr, Au&Wr 71, AuBYP, BioIn 5, –6, –7, –10, ChlLR 8[port], ConAu 1R, CurBio 59, ForWC 70, InWom, IntAu&W 77, –82, LinLib L, MorBMP, MorJA, NewbC 1956, OxChL, SmATA 5, TwCCW 78, –83, WhoAm 74, –76, –78, –80, –82, –84, –86, WhoAmW 74, –64, –66, –68, –70, –72, WrDr 76, –80, –82, –84, –86*

Specht, Robert 1928- *ConAu 103*

Spector, Debra 1953- *ConAu 109*

Spector, Robert Melvyn 1926- *DrAS 74H, –78H, –82H, WhoAmL 78, –79*

Speicher, Helen Ross 1915- *BioIn 11, ConAu 4NR, –5R, ForWC 70, IndAu 1917, SmATA 8, WrDr 84, –86*

Spellman, Cathy Cash *BioIn 13*

Spellman, Cathy Cash 1942- *WhoAmW 83*

Spence, Eleanor 1928- *Au&Wr 71, BioIn 12, ConAu 3NR, –49, DcLEL 1940, IntAu&W 82, OxChL, SingR 1, SmATA 21[port], TwCCW 78, –83, WrDr 76, –80, –82, –84, –86*

Spence, Jonathan Dermot 1936- *ConAu 21R, DrAS 74H, –78H, –82H, WhoAm 78, –80, –82, –84, –86, WhoE 74, –75*

Spencer, Charles 1920- *ConAu 49, IntAu&W 82, WhoArt 80, –82, WhoWor 76, WrDr 76, –80, –82, –84, –86*

Spencer, Colin 1933- *ConAu 12NR, ConNov 86, WrDr 86*

Spencer, Cornelia 1899- *AmAu&B, AmNov, Au&Wr 71, AuBYP, ConAu X, JBA 51, SmATA 5*

Spencer, Cornelia *see also* Yaukey, Grace

Spencer, Donald D 1931- *ConAu 108, SmATA 41[port]*

Spencer, Helen A *WhoAmW 74, –72*

Spencer, Jeremy *WhoRocM 82*

Spencer, Jeremy *see also* Fleetwood Mac

Spencer, Lila 1928- *AuBYP SUP, ForWC 70, WhoAmW 72, –75, WhoPubR 72, –76*

Spencer, Ross 1921- *ConAu 101*

Spencer, Scott *BioIn 10, DrAP&F 85, ScF&FL 1, WrDr 82, –86*

Spencer, Scott 1945- *ConAu 113, ConLC 30[port], DcLB Y86B[port]*

Spencer, William 1922- *AuBYP, BioIn 11, ConAu 8NR, –17R, DrAS 74H, –78H, IntAu&W 76, –77, –82, –86, IntMed 80, SmATA 9, WhoFla, WrDr 76, –80, –82, –86*

Spencer, Zane A 1935- *ConAu 89, MichAu 80, SmATA 35*

Spender, Sir Stephen 1909- *OxEng 85, Who 85, WhoWor 84, –87*

Spender, Stephen 1909- *Au&Wr 71,
AuBYP SUP, BioIn 1, -2, -3, -4, -5,
-8, -9, -10, -11, -12, -13, BlueB 76,
CasWL, Chambr 3, ChhPo, -S2, -S3,
CnE&AP, CnMD, CnMWL,
ConAu 9R, ConLC 1, -2, -5, -10,
-41[port], ConLCrt, -82, ConPo 70,
-75, -80, -85, CurBio 40, -77,
CyWA, DcLB 20[port], DcLEL,
EncWL, -2, EvLB, IntAu&W 76,
-77, IntWW 74, -75, -76, -77, -78,
-79, -80, -81, -82, -83, IntWWP 77,
LinLib L, -S, LongCEL, LongCTC,
MakMC, ModBrL, -S2, -S1,
ModWD, NewC, OxEng, PenC ENG,
RAdv 1, REn, TwCA, -SUP, TwCWr,
WebE&AL, WhDW, WhE&EA,
Who 74, -82, -83, WhoAm 76,
WhoTwCL, WhoWor 74, -78, -80,
-82, WorAl, WrDr 76, -80, -82, -84,
-86*
Sperber, Murray A 1940-
ConAu 12NR, -61
Sperry, Armstrong W 1897-1976
*AmPB, AnCL, AuBYP, BioIn 1, -2,
-4, -5, -7, -9, -10, -13, ConAu 107,
ConAu P-1, CurBio 41, IlsCB 1744,
-1946, JBA 51, LinLib L, Newb 1922,
SmATA 1, -27N, Str&VC,
TwCCW 78, -83*
Spicer, Dorothy Gladys d1975
*AuBYP, BioIn 8, ConAu 1R, -4NR,
ForWC 70, SmATA 32,
WhoAmW 58, -61, -64*
Spicer, Keith 1934- *CanWW 79, -80,
-81, -83*
Spielberg, Nathan 1926-
AmM&WS 86P
Spielberg, Steven 1946- *HalFC 84*
Spielberg, Steven 1947- *BioIn 10, -11,
-12, -13, ConAu 77, ConLC 20,
ConTFT 1, CurBio 78, FilmgC,
IntDcF 2, IntMPA 77, -75, -76, -78,
-79, -81, -82, -84, -86, IntWW 83,
NewYTBS 82[port], ScFSB,
SmATA 32[port], WhoAm 78, -80,
-82, -84, -86*
Spies, Werner 1937- *ConAu 37R*
Spinelli, Jerry 1941- *ConAu 111,
SmATA 39[port]*
Spinner, Stephanie 1943- *ChhPo S2,
ConAu 45, SmATA 38*
Spinrad, Norman *DrAP&F 85*
Spinrad, Norman 1940- *Au&Wr 71,
BioIn 12, ConAu 20NR, -37R,
ConSFA, DcLB 8[port], EncSF,
IntAu&W 76, Novels, ScF&FL 1, -2,
ScFSB[port], TwCSFW 86, WhoSciF,
WhoWest 76, WrDr 76, -80, -82,
-84, -86*
Spires, Elizabeth *DrAP&F 85*
Spires, Elizabeth 1952- *ConAu 106,
IntAu&W 86, WhoAmW 87*
Splaver, Sarah 1921- *AuBYP SUP,
BioIn 13, ConAu 85, SmATA 28,
WhoAmJ 80, WhoAmW 74, -58, -61,
-64, -66, -68, -70, -72, -75, -77,
-79, -81, WhoE 74, -75, -77, -79,
-81, WhoWorJ 72, -78*
Spock, Benjamin 1903- *AmAu&B,
Au&Wr 71, AuNews 1, BioIn 3, -4,
-5, -6, -7, -8, -9, -10, -11, -12,
BioNews 74, BlueB 76, CelR,
ConAu 21R, CurBio 56, -69,
EncAB-H, InSci, IntWW 74, -75,
-76, -77, -78, -79, -80, -81, -82,
-83, LinLib L, MakMC, MugS,
NewYTBE 72, PolProf J, PolProf NF,
REnAL, WebAB, WhNAA, Who 74, -82,
-83, WhoAm 74, -76, -78, -80, -82,
WhoAmP 73, -75, -77, -79, -81, -83,
-85, WhoWor 74, -78, WorAl,
WrDr 76, -80, -82, -84, -86*
Sprague, Gretchen 1926- *AuBYP,
BioIn 8, -13, ConAu 13R,
SmATA 27[port]*
Sprague, Ken 1945- *ConAu 108*
Sprague, Marshall 1909- *ConAu 1R,
-1NR, DrAS 74H, -78H, -82H,
OhA&B*
Sprague, Rosemary 1922?-
*AmWomWr, AuBYP, BioIn 8,
ConAu 17R, DrAS 74E, -78E, -82E,
OhA&B, WhoAmW 74, -68, -72*

Spring, Norma 1917- *ConAu 61*
Springer, Marilyn Harris 1931-
ConAu 9NR, -21R, SmATA 47[port]
Springer, Marilyn Harris *see also*
Harris, Marilyn
Springer, Nancy *DrAP&F 85, ScFSB*
Springer, Nancy 1948- *ConAu 101,
-18NR*
Springfield, Rick *ConTFT 2*
Springfield, Rick 1949- *BioIn 12, -13,
RkOn 78, -84, RolSEnR 83,
WhoRocM 82*
Springsteen, Bruce *NewYTBS 85[port]*
Springsteen, Bruce 1949- *Baker 84,
BioIn 10, -11, -12, -13, BioNews 74,
ConAu 111, ConLC 17, CurBio 78,
EncPR&S 77S, IntWW 82, -83,
RkOn 78, -84, RolSEnR 83,
WhoAm 80, -82, -84, -86,
WhoRock 81[port], WhoRocM 82,
WorAl*
Springstubb, Tricia *DrAP&F 85*
Springstubb, Tricia 1950- *ConAu 105,
-21NR, SmATA 40, -46*
Sprunt, Alexander, Jr. 1898-1973
*BioIn 1, -9, ConAu 37R, EncAB 21,
WhAm 5*
Spyker, John Howland 1918-
ConAu 101
Spykman, Elizabeth Choate 1896-1965
*BioIn 6, -7, -11, MorJA, SmATA 10,
TwCCW 78*
Squire, Elizabeth 1919- *ConAu 13R*
Squires, Radcliffe 1917- *ConAu 1R,
-6NR, -21NR, ConPo 70, -75, -80,
-85, DrAS 74E, -78E, -82E,
IntWWP 77, WrDr 76, -80, -82, -84,
-86*
Stableford, Brian M 1948- *ConAu 57,
EncSF, IntAu&W 82, Novels,
ScF&FL 1, -2, ScFSB, TwCSFW 86,
WhoSciF, WrDr 76, -80, -82, -84,
-86*
Stachow, Hasso G 1924- *ConAu 109*
Stafford, Jean d1979
NewYTBS 84[port]
Stafford, Jean 1915-1979 *AmAu&B,
AmNov, AmWomWr, BioIn 2, -3, -4,
-7, -11, -12, -13, BlueB 76, CnDAL,
ConAu 1R, -3NR, -85, ConLC 4, -7,
-19, ConNov 72, -76, CurBio 51,
-79N, DcLB 2, DcLEL 1940,
EncWL, InWom, IntAu&W 76, -77,
LinLib L, ModAL, NewYTBS 79,
Novels, OxAmL, -83, PenC AM,
RAdv 1, REn, REnAL, SmATA 22N,
TwCA SUP, WhAm 7, WhoAm 74,
-76, -78, WhoAmW 74, -58, -64,
-66, -68, -70, -72, WhoE 74,
WhoTwCL, WhoWor 74, WorAl,
WrDr 76, -80*
Stafford, Kim R *DrAP&F 85*
Stafford, Kim R 1949- *ConAu 69,
IntWWP 77*
Stafford, William Edgar 1914-
*AmAu&B, BioIn 8, -10, -11, -12,
-13, BlueB 76, ChhPo, -S1, -S3,
ConAu 5R, -5NR, ConLC 4, -7,
ConPo 70, -75, -80, CroCAP,
DcLB 5[port], DcLEL 1940,
DrAS 74E, -78E, -82E, IntWWP 77,
LinLib L, ModAL S1, OxAmL,
PenC AM, RAdv 1, WhoAm 74, -76,
-78, -80, -82, -84, -86, WhoPNW,
WorAu, WrDr 76, -80, -82, -84*
Stahl, Ben 1910- *BioIn 1, -2, -7, -8,
-10, -11, -12, ConAu 29R,
IlsCB 1967, ScF&FL 1, -2,
WhoAm 74, -76, -78, -80, -82, -84,
-86, WhoAmA 73, -76, -78, -80, -82,
-84, WhoS&SW 73, -75, -76,
WhoWor 80, -82*
Staicar, Tom *ConAu X*
Stall, Sylvanus 1847-1915 *Alli SUP,
ApCAB, DcAmAu, DcNAA,
LuthC 75, WhAm 1*
Stallman, Robert Wooster 1911-1982
*AmAu&B, Au&Wr 71, BioIn 13,
ConAu 1R, -3NR, DrAS 74E, -78E,
-82E, NewYTBS 82, REnAL,
WhAm 8, WhoAm 74, -76, -78, -80,
-82, WhoE 74*

Stallone, Sylvester 1946- *BioIn 11,
-12, -13, ConAu 77, ConTFT 1,
CurBio 77, HalFC 84, IntMPA 78,
-79, -81, -82, -84, -86,
NewYTBS 76, WhoAm 78, -80, -82,
WorAl*
Stallone, Sylvester Enzio 1946-
WhoAm 84, -86
Stallworth, Anne Nall 1935-
ConAu 85, IntAu&W 82
Stallworthy, Jon 1935- *ConPo 85,
DcLB 40[port], WorAl 1975[port],
WrDr 86*
Stalvey, Lois Mark 1925- *BioIn 9,
-10, -12, ConAu 14NR, -29R,
WhoAmW 75, WrDr 76, -80, -82,
-84*
Stamaty, Mark Alan 1947- *BioIn 11,
-12, ConAu 15NR, -61, IlsCB 1967,
SmATA 12, WhoAm 86,
WhoGrA 82[port]*
Stamberg, Susan 1938- *BioIn 10, -12,
ConAu 103*
Stambler, Irwin 1924- *AuBYP,
BioIn 8, -10, ConAu 2NR, -5R,
IntAu&W 76, SmATA 5, WrDr 76,
-80, -82, -84, -86*
Stampp, Kenneth M 1912- *AmAu&B,
BioIn 13, ConAu 13R, DcLB 17[port],
DrAS 74H, -78H, -82H,
IntAu&W 77, -82, -86, WhoAm 74,
-76, -78, -80, -82, WhoWor 74,
WrDr 76, -80, -82, -84, -86*
Stampp, Kenneth Milton 1912-
WhoAm 84, -86
Stanbury, David 1933- *Au&Wr 71,
ConAu 104*
Standen, Michael Fred George 1937-
WhoWor 76
Standing Bear, Luther *BiNAW Sup,
-SupB*
Standing Bear, Luther 1868?-1939?
ConAu 113
Standing Bear, Luther 1868-1947
AmAu&B, DcNAA, REnAL, WhNAA
Standish, Carole *IntAu&W 82X*
Stands-In-Timber, John 1884-1967
BioIn 8, -9
Stanek, Carolyn 1951- *ConAu 107*
Stanford, Barbara 1943- *ConAu 37R,
IntAu&W 77, LEduc 74, WrDr 76,
-80, -82, -84, -86*
Stanford, Derek 1918- *Au&Wr 71,
ChhPo S2, ConAu 9R, ConPo 70,
DcLEL 1940, IntAu&W 77, -86,
IntWWP 77, -82, ModBrL, NewC,
WrDr 82, -84, -86*
Stanford, Don 1918- *ConAu 53*
Stanford, Gene 1944- *ConAu 37R,
LEduc 74*
Stankevich, Boris 1928- *BioIn 9,
ConAu 21R, SmATA 2*
Stanley, Carol *ConAu X*
Stanley, Henry Morton 1841-1904
OxLitW 86
Stanley, Sir Henry Morton 1841-1904
*Alli SUP, AmAu&B, AmBi, ApCAB,
BbD, BiD&SB, BioIn 1, -2, -3, -4,
-5, -6, -7, -8, -9, -10, -11, -12,
BritAu 19, CarSB, CelCen,
Chambr 3, DcAmAu, DcAmB,
DcBiPP, DcBrBI, DcEnA, -AP,
DcNaB S2, EvLB, HarEnUS[port],
LinLib L, -S, LuthC 75, McGEWB,
NatCAB 4, OxAmH, OxAmL, -83,
OxEng, -85, REn, REnAL,
WebAB, -79, WhDW, WhAm 1,
WorAl*
Stansbury, Donald Lloyd 1929-
*ConAu 37R, WhoWest 76, -78, -80,
-82*
Stanton, Stephen Sadler 1915-
DrAS 74E, -78E, -82E
Stapledon, Olaf *OxEng 85*
Stapledon, Olaf 1886-1950 *ConAu 111,
DcLB 15[port], EncSF, Novels,
ScF&FL 1, -2, ScFSB[port],
TwCLC 22[port], TwCSFW 86,
WhoSciF*
Stapler, Harry Bascom 1919-
*ConAu 61, WhoMW 74, -76, -78,
-80, -82, WhoS&SW 84, -86*

Starbird, Kaye 1916- *AuBYP,
BioIn 10, ChhPo, -S1, -S3,
ConAu 17R, SmATA 6*
Starkey, Marion L 1901- *BioIn 11,
ConAu 1R, -1NR, ForWC 70,
SmATA 13, -8, WhoAmW 58, -61,
-64, WorFDr 76, -80*
Starr, Bart 1934- *BioIn 7, -8, -9, -10,
-11, -12, BioNews 75, CurBio 68,
NewYTBS 81[port], WhoAm 84, -86,
WorAl*
Starr, Bart *see also* Starr, Byran B
Starr, Byran B 1934- *WhoFtbl 74*
Starr, Byran B *see also* Starr, Bart
Starr, Ringo 1940- *Baker 78, -84,
BioIn 6, -7, -8, -9, -10, -11, -12,
-13, BlueB 76, CelR, CurBio 65,
EncPR&S 74, -77, IlEncRk,
IntWW 74, -75, -76, -77, -78, -79,
-80, -81, -82, -83, MotPP, RkOn 78,
-84, RolSEnR 83, WhoAm 78, -80,
-82, -84, -86, WhoHol A,
WhoRock 81[port], WhoRocM 82,
WhoWor 74, -78, -80, -82, -84, -87,
WorAl*
Starr, Ringo *see also* Beatles, The
Stasheff, Christopher 1944-
*ConAu 10NR, -65, EncSF,
ScF&FL 1, ScFSB, TwCSFW 86,
WhoE 79, WrDr 86*
Stasheff, Edward 1909- *BiE&WWA,
ConAu 5R, DrAS 74E, -78E, -82E,
WhoAm 76, -78*
Statler, Oliver 1915- *Au&Wr 71,
ConAu 5R, IntAu&W 86, WrDr 76,
-80, -82, -84, -86*
Staubach, Roger *NewYTBS 84[port]*
Staubach, Roger 1942- *BioIn 6, -9,
-10, -11, -12, -13, CelR, ConAu 104,
CurBio 72, NewYTBE 71, -72,
WhoAm 74, -76, -78, -80, -82,
WhoFtbl 74, WorAl*
Stead, Christina 1902-1983
*AnObit 1983, Au&Wr 71, BioIn 1, -4,
-8, -9, -10, -11, -13, CasWL,
ConAu 109, -13R, ConLC 2, -5, -8,
-32[port], ConNov 72, -76, -82,
DcLEL, EncWL 2, EvLB,
FarE&A 78, -79, -80, -81, InWom,
IntAu&W 76, -77, IntDcWB,
IntWW 77, -78, -79, -80, -81, -82,
-83N, LongCTC, ModCmwL,
NewYTBS 83, Novels, OxAusL,
RAdv 1, ScF&FL 1, -2,
TwCA, -SUP, TwCWr, WhE&EA,
Who 74, -82, WhoAmW 74, -68,
-70, -72, -75, -77, WhoTwCL,
WhoWor 74, -76, WorAl, WrDr 76,
-80, -82, -84*
Stearn, Jess *ConAu 97, WrDr 76, -80,
-82, -84, -86*
Stearns, Marshall 1908-1966 *BioIn 7,
-8, ConAu 110, WhAm 4*
Stearns, Monroe 1913- *AuBYP SUP,
BioIn 10, ConAu 2NR, -5R,
IntAu&W 76, SmATA 5, WrDr 76,
-80, -82, -84, -86*
Stearns, Pamela Fujimoto 1935-
ConAu 65
Stebbins, Theodore Ellis, Jr. 1938-
*WhoAm 84, -86, WhoAmA 84,
WhoE 85*
Stedman, Raymond W 1930-
DrAS 74E, -78E, -82E
Stedwell, Paki 1945- *ConAu 103*
Steegmuller, Francis *DrAP&F 85*
Steegmuller, Francis 1906- *AmAu&B,
Au&Wr 71, BioIn 2, -4, -12, ChhPo,
ConAu 2NR, -49, ConNov 72, -76,
IntAu&W 76, -77, -82, -86,
NewYTBS 80[port], OxAmL 83,
REnAL, ScF&FL 1, TwCA SUP,
WhE&EA, Who 74, -82, -83, -85,
WhoAm 74, -76, -78, -80, -82, -84,
-86, WrDr 76, -80, -82, -84, -86*
Steel, Danielle *ConAu 19NR, WrDr 86*
Steel, Danielle 1947- *BioIn 11,
ConAu 81, IntAu&W 82,
WhoAmW 81, -83, WrDr 84*
Steele, George Peabody 1924-
*ConAu 5R, WhoF&I 79, -81, -83,
-85, WhoWor 80, -82, -84, -87,
WrDr 82, -84*
Steele, Mary Q 1922- *WrDr 86*

Steele, Mary Quintard 1922- *AuBYP,
BioIn 8, –9, –11, ConAu 1R, –6NR,
ScF&FL 1, –2, SmATA 3, ThrBJA,
TwCCW 78, –83, WrDr 76, –80, –82,
–84*
Steele, Mary Quintard *see also* Gage,
Wilson
Steele, Phillip W 1934- *ConAu 61*
Steele, William O 1917-1979 *OxChL*
Steele, William Owen 1917-1979
*AmAu&B, Au&Wr 71, AuBYP,
BioIn 6, –8, –9, –12, –13, BlueB 76,
BkCL, ConAu 1R, –2NR, –5R,
IntAu&W 77, LinLib L, MorJA,
SmATA 1, –27N, TwCCW 78, –83,
WhAm 7, WhoAm 74, –76, –78,
WrDr 76, –80*
Steelman, Robert J 1914-
*ConAu 11NR, –69, EncFWF,
WrDr 84, –86*
Stefansson, Evelyn Baird 1913-
*AuBYP, BioIn 8, ConAu 49,
WhoAmW 61, –64*
Stefansson, Evelyn Baird *see also* Nef,
Evelyn Stefansson
Stefansson, Thorsteinn 1912-
*ConAu 77, IntAu&W 77, –82, –86,
WhoWor 80*
Steffan, Alice Jack Kennedy 1907-
ConAu 5R, WhoAmW 68, WhoPNW
Steffan, Jack 1907- *ConAu X*
Steffan, Jack *see also* Steffan, Alice
Kennedy
Steffens, Lincoln 1866-1936 *AmAu&B,
AmBi, BioIn 1, –2, –3, –4, –5, –6, –8,
–9, –10, –11, –12, –13, CmCal,
ConAu 117, DcAmB S2, DcAmSR,
EncAJ, LinLib L, LongCTC,
McGEWB, MemAm, ModAL,
NatCAB 14, OxAmH, OxAmL, –83,
PenC AM, REn, REnAL, REnAW,
TwCA, –SUP, TwCLC 20[port],
WebAB, –79, WebE&AL, WhAm 1,
WorAl*
Stefferud, Alfred 1903- *AuBYP,
BioIn 8, ConAu P-1, IntYB 78, –79,
–80, –81, WhoAm 74, –76, –78,
WhoE 74, –75*
Stegner, Wallace Earle 1909-
*AmAu&B, AmNov, Au&Wr 71,
AuNews 1, BioIn 2, –3, –4, –9, –10,
–11, –12, BlueB 76, CmCal,
CnDAL, ConAu 1R, –1NR, ConLC 9,
ConNov 72, –76, –82, CurBio 77,
DcLB 9[port], DrAS 74E, –78E,
–82E, IntAu&W 76, –77, LinLib L,
ModAL, Novels, OxAmL, OxCan,
PenC AM, RAdv 1, REn, REnAL,
REnAW, TwCA, –SUP, WebE&AL,
WhNAA, WhoAm 74, –76, –78, –80,
–82, –84, –86, WhoWest 74, –76,
WrDr 76, –80, –82, –84*
Steiger, Brad 1936- *ConAu 21NR, –X,
EncO&P 2, –78S1, ScF&FL 1, –2,
UFOEn[port]*
Steiger, Brad *see also* Olsen, Eugene E
Stein, Aaron Marc 1906- *ConAu 6NR,
–9R, EncMys, IntAu&W 77, –82,
Novels, TwCCr&M 80, –85,
WhoAm 82, –84, WrDr 82, –84, –86*
Stein, Aaron Marc 1906-1985
ConAu 117
Stein, Joseph 1912- *BiE&WWA,
ConAu 13R, ConDr 73, –82D,
ConTFT 4, EncMT,
NatPD, –81[port], NewCBMT,
NotNAT, OxAmT 84, WhoAm 82,
–84, –86, WhoThe 77, –81*
Stein, Meyer Lewis 1920-
*AmM&WS 73S, AuBYP, BioIn 8,
–10, ConAu 17R, DrAS 74E, –78E,
–82E, IntAu&W 76, SmATA 6,
WhoE 74*
Stein, R Conrad 1937- *ConAu 41R,
SmATA 31*
Stein, Sol 1926- *AmEA 74, AuNews 1,
BioIn 8, –10, –12, BioNews 74,
ConAu 2NR, –49, IntAu&W 76, –77,
–82, NewYTBS 80[port], WhoAm 74,
–76, –78, –80, –82, –84, –86,
WrDr 76, –80, –82, –84, –86*
Stein, Stanley J 1920- *ConAu 108,
DrAS 74H, –78H, –82H*

Steinbeck, John 1902-1968 *AmAu&B,
AmNov, AmWr, AuBYP SUP,
BiE&WWA, BioIn 1, –2, –3, –4, –5,
–6, –7, –8, –9, –10, –11, –12, –13,
CasWL, CmCal, CnDAL, CnMD,
CnMWL, CnThe, ConAmA,
ConAu 1R, –1NR, –25R, ConLC 1,
–5, –9, –13, –21[port], CurBio 40,
–63, –69, CyWA, DcAmSR,
DcLB 7[port], –9[port], –DS2[port],
DcLEL, EncAAH, EncAB-H,
EncFWF[port], EncWL, –2[port],
EncWT, EvLB, FilmgC, HalFC 84,
LinLib L, –S, LongCTC, MakMC,
McGEWB, McGEWD, –84[port],
ModAL, –S2, ModWD,
NatCAB 61[port], NotNAT B,
Novels[port], ObitOF 79, ObitT 1961,
OxAmH, OxAmL, –83, OxAmT 84,
OxEng, OxFilm, OxThe, PenC AM,
RAdv 1, RComWL, REn, REnAL,
REnAW, ScF&FL 1, –2, SmATA 9,
TwCA, –SUP, TwCWr, WebAB, –79,
WebE&AL, WhDW, WhAm 5,
WhThe, WhoTwCL, WorAl*
Steinberg, Alfred 1917- *AuBYP,
BioIn 8, –11, ConAu 5R, –9NR,
SmATA 9*
Steinberg, David Joel 1937- *AmEA 74,
ConAu 25R, DrAS 74H, –78H, –82H*
Steinberg, Rafael Mark 1927-
*ConAu 9NR, –61, WhoAm 74, –76,
–78, –80, –82, WhoAmJ 80, WhoE 74*
Steinberg, Saul 1914- *AmArt,
AmAu&B, BioIn 1, –2, –3, –4, –5, –7,
–8, –9, –11, –12, –13, CelR,
ConArt 77, –83, ConAu 89,
CurBio 57, DcAmArt, DcCAA 71,
–77, IntWW 74, –75, –76, –77, –78,
–79, –80, –81, –82, –83, LinLib L,
McGDA, OxAmL, –83, OxTwCA,
PhDcTCA 77, REn, WebAB, –79,
WhoAm 74, –76, –78, –80, –82, –84,
–86, WhoAmA 78, –80, –82, –84,
WhoGrA 62, WhoWor 74,
WorArt[port], WorECar*
Steinbrunner, Chris 1933-
ConAu 1NR, –45, ScF&FL 1, –2
Steinem, Gloria 1934- *BioIn 13,
EncTwCJ, WhoAm 84, –86,
WhoAmW 85, –87*
Steinem, Gloria 1936?- *EncAJ*
Steiner, George 1929- *BioIn 8, –10,
–11, –13, BlueB 76, ConAu 73,
ConLC 24[port], ConLCrt, –82,
CurBio 83[port], DcLEL 1940,
EncWL, –2, IntAu&W 76, –77, –82,
IntWW 74, –75, –76, –77, –78, –79,
–80, –81, –82, –83, ModBrL S1,
OxEng 85, RAdv 1, REnAL, Who 74,
–82, –83, –85, WhoAm 74, –76, –78,
–86, WhoWor 74, –76, –78, –87,
WorAu, WrDr 76, –80, –82, –84, –86*
Steiner, Ralph d1986 *NewYTBS 86*
Steiner, Ralph 1899- *ConAu 113,
ICPEnP, MacBEP*
Steiner, Ralph 1899-1986 *ConAu 119*
Steiner, Stan *WhoAm 84, –86*
Steiner, Stan 1925- *ChiSch, ChhPo S1,
ConAu 1NR, –16NR, –45,
IntAu&W 77, SmATA 14,
WhoAm 74, –76, –78, –80, –82,
WrDr 80, –82, –84, –86*
Steiner, Stanley 1925- *AmAu&B,
BioIn 13, ConAu 45*
Steinhauer, Harry 1905- *ConAu 1R,
–1NR, DrAS 74F, –78F, –82F,
WhoAm 84*
Steinke, Ann E 1946- *IntAu&W 86*
Steinmark, Fred 1948?-1971 *BioIn 9,
–12, NewYTBE 71*
Steinmark, Freddie J 1948?-1971
ObitOF 79, WhoFtbl 74
Steneman, Shep 1945- *ConAu 107*
Stensland, Anna Lee 1922- *DrAS 74E,
–78E, –82E, WhoAm 80,
WhoAmW 79, –81*
Stephens, Eve *ConAu X*
Stephens, Eve *see also* Ward-Thomas,
Evelyn Bridget
Stephens, Henrietta Henkle 1909-1983
ConAu 6NR, –9R, –109, ScF&FL 1
Stephens, Henrietta Henkle *see also*
Buckmaster, Henrietta

Stephens, James 1880?-1950
DcNaB 1941, EncWL 2, ModBrL S2
Stephens, James 1882-1950 *AnCL,
AuBYP SUP, BiDIrW, BioIn 1, –2,
–3, –4, –5, –6, –7, –10, –11, –12, –13,
CarSB, CasWL, Chambr 3,
ChhPo, –S1, –S2, –S3, CnE&AP,
ConAu 104, CyWA, DcIrL, DcIrW 1,
DcLB 19[port], DcLEL, EncWL,
EvLB, LinLib L, LongCTC,
McGEWB, ModBrL, –S1, NewC,
Novels, OxEng, –85, PenC ENG,
PoIre, RAdv 1, REn, ScF&FL 1,
Str&VC, SupFW, TwCA, –SUP,
TwCLC 4[port], TwCWr, WhDW,
WhAm 3*
Stephens, Mary Jo 1935- *BioIn 11,
ConAu 37R, SmATA 8*
Stephens, Peggy *AuBYP SUP*
Stephens, William M 1925-
*AuBYP SUP, BioIn 12, ConAu 57,
SmATA 21[port]*
Stephenson, Andrew M 1946-
*ConAu 118, ScFSB, TwCSFW 86,
WrDr 84, –86*
Stephenson, Ralph 1910- *Au&Wr 71,
ConAu 17R, IntAu&W 77, –86,
WhoWor 76, WrDr 76, –80, –82, –84*
Steptoe, John Lewis 1950- *AfroAA,
BioIn 8, –11, –12, BlkAWP,
ChLR 2, ConAu 3NR, –49,
FourBJA, IlsBYP, IlsCB 1967,
InB&W 80, LivgBAA, SelBAAf,
SelBAAu, SmATA 8, TwCCW 78,
–83, WhoAm 74, –76, WrDr 80, –82,
–84*
Sterling, Bruce *ScFSB*
Sterling, Bruce 1954- *ConAu 119,
TwCSFW 86*
Sterling, Claire 1920?- *ConIsC 2[port],
NewYTBS 81[port]*
Sterling, Dorothy 1913- *AuBYP,
BioIn 5, –8, –9, –10, BkCL, ChlLR 1,
ConAu 5NR, –9R, ForWC 70,
MorBMP, SmATA 1,
SmATA 2AS[port], ThrBJA*
Sterling, Philip 1907- *BioIn 11,
ConAu 49, SmATA 8*
Stern, Ellen Norman 1927- *BioIn 13,
ConAu 14NR, –37R, IntAu&W 86,
–86X, SmATA 26[port], WrDr 76,
–80, –82, –84, –86*
Stern, Geraldine 1907- *ConAu 101*
Stern, Harold Phillip 1922-1977
*BioIn 11, ConAu 69, DrAS 74H,
NewYTBS 77, WhAm 7,
WhoAmA 73, –76, –78N, –80N,
–82N, –84N, WhoGov 77, –75*
Stern, Jane 1946- *ConAu 10NR, –61,
MacBEP*
Stern, Jane 1947?- *BioIn 13*
Stern, Michael 1910- *ConAu P-2,
IntAu&W 76, –77, –82, WhoWor 76,
–78, –80, –82, –84, –87,
WhoWorJ 72, –78*
Stern, Philip VanDoren d1984
NewYTBS 84
Stern, Philip VanDoren 1900-
*AmAu&B, AmNov, Au&Wr 71,
AuBYP SUP, BioIn 2, –4, –11,
ConAu 5R, –6NR, DrAS 74H, –78H,
REnAL, ScF&FL 1, –2, SmATA 13,
TwCA SUP, WhE&EA, WhNAA,
WhoAm 74, –76, –78, –80, –82*
Stern, Philip VanDoren 1900-1984
ConAu 113, SmATA 39N, WhAm 8
Stern, Richard Martin 1915-
*AmAu&B, Au&Wr 71, BioIn 1,
BlueB 76, ConAu 1R, –2NR, –18NR,
IntAu&W 86, TwCCr&M 80, –85,
WhoAm 74, –76, –78, –80, –82, –84,
–86, WrDr 76, –80, –82, –84, –86*
Stern, Susan 1943-1976 *BioIn 10, –11,
ConAu 65, NewYTBS 76, ObitOF 79*
Sterne, Emma Gelders 1894-1971
*AmAu&B, BioIn 4, –6, –10,
ConAu 5R, –5NR, MorJA, SmATA 6,
TwCA, –SUP, WhoAmW 58, –64,
–66, –68, –70, –72*
Stetson, Erlene *ConAu 108*
Steurt, Marjorie Rankin 1888-
*BioIn 11, ConAu 13R, SmATA 10,
WrDr 76, –80*
Stevens, Cat 1947- *RolSEnR 83[port]*

Stevens, Cat 1948- *BiDAmM, BioIn 9,
–10, –12, BioNews 74, ConAu X,
EncPR&S 74, –77, IlEncRk,
NewYTBE 71, RkOn 78, –84,
RolSEnR 83, WhoAm 74, –76, –78,
–80, –82, WhoRock 81, WhoRocM 82, WorAl*
Stevens, Franklin 1933- *BioIn 10,
ConAu 29R, SmATA 6*
Stevens, Gwendolyn 1944- *ConAu 104,
SmATA 33[port], WhoAmW 83*
Stevens, Gwendolyn Ruth 1944-
WhoAmW 85, –87, WhoFrS 84
Stevens, Leonard A 1920-
ConAu 12NR, –17R
Stevens, Patricia Bunning 1931-
BioIn 13, ConAu 53, SmATA 27
Stevens, William 1925- *AmAu&B,
ConAu 21R*
Stevens, William Oliver 1878-1955
*AmAu&B, AmLY, AuBYP, BiDPara,
BioIn 3, –8, ChhPo, EncAB 26,
EncO&P 2, –78, WhAm 3, WhE&EA,
WhNAA*
Stevenson, Anne *DrAP&F 85,
IntAu&W 76, WrDr 84, –86*
Stevenson, Anne 1933- *BioIn 13,
ConLC 33[port], ConPo 85,
DcLB 40[port], WorAu 1975[port],
WrDr 86*
Stevenson, Burton Egbert 1872-1962
*AmAu&B, BiD&SB, BioIn 4, –6, –13,
ChhPo, –S2, –S3, ConAu 102, –89,
DcAmAu, DcAmLiB, EvLB,
NatCAB 13, ObitOF 79, OhA&B,
REn, REnAL, ScF&FL 1,
SmATA 25, TwCA, –SUP, WhAm 4,
WhJnl, WhNAA*
Stevenson, David Lloyd 1910-1975
ConAu 57, ConAu P-2, WhAm 6
Stevenson, E Robert 1882-1978
WhAm 7, WhJnl
Stevenson, Gloria 1945- *ConAu 61*
Stevenson, Janet 1913- *AuBYP SUP,
BioIn 11, ConAu 13R, ForWC 70,
SmATA 8, WhoAmW 61, –66, –68,
–70*
Stevenson, Robert Louis 1850-1894
*Alli SUP, AnCL, ApCAB SUP,
AtlBL, AuBYP, BbD, BiD&SB,
BioIn 1, –2, –3, –4, –5, –6, –7, –8, –9,
–10, –11, –12, –13, BritAu 19,
BritWr 5, CarSB, CasWL, Chambr 3,
ChlLR 10[port], –11[port], ChrP,
ChhPo, –S1, –S2, –S3, CmCal,
CmScLit, CrtT 3, CyWA, DcBiA,
DcBrBI, DcEnA, –AP, DcEuL,
DcLB 18[port], –57[port], DcLEL,
DcNaB, –C, Dis&D, EncMys, EncSF,
EvLB, FamAYP, FamPYP, FilmgC,
HalFC 84, JBA 34, LinLib L,
McGEWB, MnBBF, MouLC 3,
NewC, NinCLC 5[port], –14[port],
Novels[port], OxAmL, –83, OxAusL,
OxChL, OxEng, OxMus, PenC ENG,
RAdv 1, REn, REnAL, ScF&FL 1,
–1A, ScFSB, Str&VC, SupFW, TelT,
TwCCW 78A, –83A, WebE&AL,
WhDW, WhoBW&I A, WhoChL,
WhoHr&F, YABC 2*
Stevenson, Robert Louis Balfour
1850-1894 *OxEng 85*
Stevenson, Robert Murrell 1916-
*DrAS 78H, –82H, IntAu&W 77, –82,
IntWWM 77, –85, WhoAm 74, –76,
–78, –80, –82, –84, –86, WhoRel 75,
–77, –85, WhoWest 82, WhoWor 76,
–78, –80, –84, –87*
Stevenson, William 1924?- *BioIn 12,
ConAu 13R, TwCCW 78, WhoAm 78,
WrDr 80, –84, –86*
Stewart, A C *AuBYP SUP, ConAu 77,
SmATA 15, TwCCW 78, –83,
WrDr 84, –86*
Stewart, Allan 1939- *ConAu 1R*
Stewart, Desmond 1924-1981
*AmAu&B, Au&Wr 71, ConAu 104,
–37R, DcLEL 1940, IntAu&W 76,
–77, –82, Who 74, –82N*
Stewart, Donald Ogden 1894-1980
*AmAu&B, AnObit 1980[port],
BiE&WWA,'BioIn 4, –10, –12, –13,*

*CarSB, ConAu 101, –81, Conv 1,
CurBio 41, –80N, DcLB 4, –11[port],
–26[port], DcLEL, FilmgC,
HalFC 84, NotNAT, OhA&B,
–83, PenC AM, REnAL,
TwCA, –SUP, WhAm 7, WhJnl,
WhNAA, WhScrn 83, WhThe,
WhoAm 74, WorEFlm*

Stewart, Fred Mustard 1936- *BioIn 8,
–12, ConAu 37R, NewYTBS 81[port],
ScF&FL 1, –2, WhoE 75, –77,
WrDr 76, –80, –82, –84, –86*

Stewart, George R 1895- *ScFSB*

Stewart, George R 1895-1980
OxAmL 83, TwCSFW 86

Stewart, George Rippey 1895-1980
*AmAu&B, AmNov, AnObit 1981,
Au&Wr 71, BioIn 1, –2, –4, –9, –12,
–13, CmCal, CnDAL, ConAu 1R,
–3NR, –101, CurBio 42, –80N,
DcLB 8[port], EncSF, IntAu&W 77,
NewYTBS 80, OxAmL, REnAL,
ScF&FL 1, –2, SmATA 23N, –3,
TwCA SUP, WhAm 7, WhE&EA,
WhNAA, WhoAm 74, WrDr 76, –80,
–82*

Stewart, Harold Frederick 1916-
*ConAu ConPo 70, –75, –80,
DcLEL 1940, IntAu&W 76, –82,
IntWWP 77, –82, TwCWr, WrDr 76,
–80, –82, –84*

Stewart, J I M *TwCCr&M 85*

Stewart, J I M 1906- *CmScLit,
ConAu 85, ConAu 3AS[port],
ConLC 7, –14, –32[port], ConNov 82,
–86, Novels, OxEng 85,
TwCCr&M 80, WrDr 80, –82, –84,
–86*

Stewart, Jackie *Who 85*

Stewart, Jackie 1939?- *BioIn 7, –8, –9,
–10, –11, –12, Who 74, –82, –83,
WorAl*

Stewart, John Craig 1915- *BioIn 2,
DrAS 74E, –78E, –82E,
WhoS&SW 73, –75, –76*

Stewart, John William 1920- *BioIn 12,
ConAu 33R, SmATA 14*

Stewart, Marjabelle 1930?- *BioIn 12*

Stewart, Mary 1916- *Au&Wr 71,
BioIn 5, –8, –9, –10, –11, –12,
ConAu 1R, –1NR, ConLC 7,
–35[port], CorpD, DcLEL 1940,
EncMys, IntAu&W 76, –77, –82,
LongCTC, NewYTBS 79,
Novels[port], OxChL, PoIre,
ScF&FL 1, –2, SmATA 12,
TwCCr&M 80, –85, TwCWr,
Who 74, –82, –83, –85, WhoAm 74,
–76, –78, –80, –82, WhoAmW 74,
–70, –72, –75, –77, WhoWor 74, –76,
WorAl, WorAu, WrDr 76, –80, –82,
–84, –86*

Stewart, Ora Pate 1910- *ForWC 70,
IntAu&W 76, –77, –82, IntWWP 77,
–82, WhoAmW 74, –61, –66, –68,
–70, –72, WhoWest 74*

Stewart, Ramona 1922- *ASpks,
ConAu 1R, –6NR, ForWC 70,
ScF&FL 1, –2*

Stewart, Rod 1945- *BioIn 10, –11,
–12, –13, CurBio 79, EncPR&S 74,
–77, IlEncRk, RkOneH, RkOn 78, –84,
RkOneH, RolSEnR 83,
WhoRock 81[port], WhoRocM 82,
WorAl*

Stickgold, Bob 1945- *ConAu 104*

Stiles, Martha Bennett *BioIn 10,
ConAu 37R, DrAP&F 85,
IntAu&W 82, MichAu 80, SmATA 6,
WhoAmW 75*

Still, C Henry 1920- *ConAu 9R,
WhoWest 74, –76, –78*

Stilley, Frank 1918- *BioIn 13,
ConAu 61, SmATA 29[port]*

Stillman, Myra Stephens 1915-
*AuBYP, BioIn 8, ConAu 5R, –6NR,
ForWC 70*

Stillman, Richard J 1917-
ConAu 14NR

Stillman, Richard Joseph 1917-
*ConAu 37R, IntAu&W 77, –82, –86,
WrDr 76, –80, –82, –86*

Stills, Stephen 1945- *BioIn 13,
EncPR&S 74, –77, IlEncRk,
WhoRocM 82, WorAl*

Stills, Stephen 1948-
WhoRock 81[port]

Stills, Stephen *see also* Crosby, Stills,
Nash & Young

Stine, G Harry *TwCSFW 86*

Stine, G Harry 1928- *ConAu 9NR,
–65, EncSF, ScF&FL 1, WrDr 84,
–86*

Stine, George Harry 1928- *AuBYP,
BioIn 8, –11, SmATA 10, WhoAm 82,
–84, –86, WhoWest 80, –82*

Stine, George Harry *see also* Correy,
Lee

Stine, Jovial Bob *ConAu X, SmATA X*

Stinetorf, Louise A 1900- *BioIn 11,
ConAu 9R, ForWC 70, SmATA 10*

Stinson, Robert William 1941-
ConAu 111, DrAS 74H, –78H, –82H

Stirling, Jessica *CmScLit, ConAu X,
IntAu&W 86X, WrDr 76, –80, –82,
–84, –86*

Stirling, Nora B *WrDr 86*

Stirling, Nora B 1900- *AuBYP,
BioIn 8, –9, ConAu 3NR, –5R,
SmATA 3, WrDr 76, –80, –82, –84*

Stobbs, William 1914- *ArtCS, BioIn 5,
–6, –8, –9, –12, ChhPo, –S2,
ConAu 81, IlsBYP, IlsCB 1946,
–1957, –1967, OxChL, SmATA 17,
ThrBJA, WhoChL*

Stockman, David A
NewYTBS 85[port]

Stockman, David Alan *WhoAmP 85*

Stockman, David Alan 1946- *BioIn 13*

Stockman, David Allen 1946-
WhoAm 84, –86, WhoF&I 85

Stockton, Frank R *SmATA X*

Stockton, Frank R 1834-1902 *Alli,
AmAu, AmAu&B, AuBYP, BbD,
BiD&SB, BioIn 1, –5, –6, –8, –12,
CarSB, CnDAL, ConAu X, CyAL 2,
DcAmB, DcLB 42[port], DcLEL,
EncMys, EncSF, EvLB, FamSYP,
JBA 34, LinLib L, OxAmL, –83,
OxChL, OxEng, RAdv 1, REn,
ScF&FL 1, ScFSB, SmATA 32,
SupFW, TwCCW 78A, –83A,
TwCSFW 86, WebAB, –79*

Stockton, Frank Richard 1834-1902
BioIn 13

Stoddard, Edward G 1923- *AuBYP,
BioIn 8, –11, ConAu 9R, SmATA 10,
WhoE 75, –77*

Stoddard, Hope 1900- *AuBYP,
BioIn 8, –10, ConAu 49, SmATA 6*

Stoddard, Sandol 1927- *BioIn 12,
ConAu 8NR, FourBJA, SmATA X*

Stoddard, Sandol *see also* Warburg,
Sandol Stoddard

Stohlman, Martha Lou Lemmon 1913-
ConAu 65

Stoiko, Michael 1919- *BioIn 12,
ConAu 9R, SmATA 14*

Stokely, Wilma Dykeman 1920-
ConAu 1R

Stokely, Wilma Dykeman *see also*
Dykeman, Wilma

Stoker, Bram 1847-1912 *Alli SUP,
BioIn 5, –6, –8, –10, –11, –12, –13,
ConAu X, CyWA, DcIrL,
DcLB 36[port], DcLEL, EncMys,
EncO&P 2, –78, EncSF, EvLB,
FilmgC, HalFC 84, LongCTC,
NotNAT B, Novels, OxEng 85,
PenC ENG, REn, ScF&FL 1,
SmATA X, SupFW, TwCA, –SUP,
TwCCr&M 80, TwCLC 8[port],
WhDW, WhLit, WhoChL,
WhoHr&F, WorAl*

Stokes, Geoffrey 1940- *ConAu 69*

Stokesbury, James L 1934-
ConAu 17NR

Stokesbury, James Lawton 1934-
ConAu 93, DrAS 74H, –78H, –82H

Stokley, James 1900- *AmAu&B,
AmM&WS 86P, WhJnl, WhoAm 74,
–76, –78*

Stolz, Mary 1920- *BioIn 13,
ConAu 13NR, OxChL,
SmATA 3AS[port], WrDr 86*

Stolz, Mary Slattery 1920- *AmAu&B,
Au&Wr 71, AuBYP, AuNews 1,
BioIn 3, –6, –7, –10, –11,
BioNews 74, ConAu 5R, ConLC 12,
CurBio 53, ForWC 70, InWom,
MorBMP, MorJA, REnAL,
SmATA 10, TwCCW 78, –83,
WhoAm 74, –76, –78, –80, –82,
WhoAmW 74, –58, –61, –64, –66,
–68, –70, –72, WrDr 80, –82, –84*

Stolzenberg, Mark 1950- *ConAu 102*

Stone, A Harris *AuBYP SUP*

Stone, George Kenneth *AuBYP,
BioIn 8*

Stone, Irving *NewYTBS 85[port]*

Stone, Irving 1903- *AmAu&B, AmNov,
Au&Wr 71, AuNews 1, BioIn 2, –4,
–5, –6, –7, –8, –9, –10, –12,
BlueB 76, CelR, CmCal, ConAu 1R,
–1NR, ConAu 3AS[port], ConLC 7,
ConNov 72, –76, –82, –86, CurBio 67,
DrAS 74E, –78E, –82E, HalFC 84,
IntAu&W 76, –77, IntWW 74, –75,
–76, –77, –78, –79, –80, –81, –82,
–83, LinLib L, LongCTC,
NewYTBS 80[port], Novels,
OxAmL 83, PenC AM, REn, REnAL,
SmATA 3, TwCA, –SUP, TwCWr,
WhE&EA, WhNAA, WhoAm 74, –76,
–78, –80, –82, –84, –86, WhoAmJ 80,
WhoWor 74, –78, WhoWorJ 72, –78,
WorAl, WrDr 76, –80, –82, –84, –86*

Stone, Josephine Rector 1936-
ConAu X, SmATA X

Stone, Josephine Rector *see also* Dixon,
Jeanne

Stone, Norman 1941- *Who 85*

Stone, Peter Bennet 1933- *WhoUN 75,
WhoWor 80*

Stone, Peter H 1930- *AmAu&B,
ConAu 7NR, –9R, ConDr 73, –82D,
IntAu&W 76, –82, –86, IntMPA 81,
–82, –84, WhoAm 74, –76, –78, –80,
–82, –84, –86, WhoThe 72, –81*

Stone, Ralph A 1934- *ConAu 37R,
WrDr 76, –80, –82, –84*

Stone, Robert Anthony 1937-
*BioIn 12, –13, ConLC 23[port],
WhoAm 76, –78, –80, –82, –84, –86*

Stone, Roger D 1934- *ConAu 119*

Stone, Roger David 1934- *WhoAm 84,
–86*

Stone, Scott C S 1932- *ConAu 18NR*

Stone, Scott Clinton Stuart 1932-
*ConAu 25R, WhoAm 74, –76, –78,
–80, WhoWor 80*

Stonehouse, Bernard 1926-
*Au&Wr 71, BioIn 11, ConAu 2NR,
–19NR, –49, IntAu&W 77, –82,
SmATA 13, WrDr 76, –80, –82, –84,
–86*

Stones, Rosemary *OxChL*

Stoppard, Miriam 1937- *ConAu 120,
Who 85, WrDr 86*

Stoppard, Tom 1937- *Au&Wr 71,
BioIn 8, –9, –10, –11, –12, –13,
BlueB 76, CnThe, ConAu 81,
ConDr 73, –77, –82, ConLC 1, –3,
–4, –5, –8, –15, –29[port], –34[port],
ConTFT 1, –4, CroCD, CurBio 74,
DcLB 13[port], –Y85A[port],
DcLEL 1940, EncWL, –2[port],
EncWT, IntAu&W 76, IntWW 74,
–75, –76, –77, –78, –79, –80, –81,
–82, –83, MajMD 1, MakMC,
McGEWD, –84[port], ModBrL S2,
–S1, ModWD, NewYTBE 72,
NewYTBS 74, –84[port], NotNAT,
OxAmT 84, OxEng 85, OxThe 83,
PlP&P A, WebE&AL, Who 74, –82,
–83, –85, WhoAm 80, –82, –84, –86,
WhoThe 72, –77, –81, WhoTwCL,
WhoWor 82, –84, –87, WorAl,
WorAu 1970, WrDr 76, –80, –82,
–84, –86*

Storer, Doug 1899- *ConAu 57*

Storer, Doug 1899-1985 *ConAu 118*

Storey, David Malcolm 1933-
*BioIn 12, ConDr 73, –82, ConLC 2,
–4, –5, ConNov 72, –76, –82,
DcLB 13[port], –14[port],
DcLEL 1940, IntWW 77, –78, –79,
–80, –81, –82, –83, LongCTC,*

*McGEWD 84, ModBrL S1, NewC,
Novels, OxEng 85, OxThe 83,
TwCWr, Who 74, –82, –83, –85,
WhoThe 81, WhoWor 74, –76, –78,
–80, –82, –84, –87, WorAu, WrDr 76,
–82, –84*

Storey, Graham 1920- *Who 85,
WrDr 86*

Storey, Margaret 1926- *BioIn 11,
ConAu 11NR, –49, ScF&FL 1,
SmATA 9, TwCCW 78, –83,
WrDr 80, –82, –84, –86*

Storey, Robert Gerald 1893-1981
*BioIn 2, –3, –4, –5, –7, BlueB 76,
CurBio 53, IntWW 74, –75, –76, –77,
–78, –79, –80, –81N, WhAm 7,
WhoAm 74, –76, –78, –80,
WhoS&SW 73, WhoWor 74, –76, –78*

Storey, Victoria Carolyn 1945-
*BioIn 12, ConAu 33R, IntAu&W 77,
SmATA 16*

Storme, Peter *AuBYP SUP, BioIn 2,
–4, –11, ConAu X, SmATA X*

Storme, Peter *see also* Stern, Philip
VanDoren

Storr, Catherine *WrDr 80*

Storr, Catherine 1913- *Au&Wr 71,
AuBYP SUP, BioIn 11, ConAu 13R,
EncSF, OxChL, SmATA 9,
TwCCW 78, –83, WrDr 76, –82, –84,
–86*

Storr, Catherine *see also* Adler, Irene

Story, Ronald Dean 1946-
*ConAu 11NR, –65, UFOEn,
WhoWest 80, –82*

Stott, William Merrell 1940-
ConAu 61, DrAS 74E, –78E, –82E

Stout, Rex Todhunter 1886-1975
*AmAu&B, AuNews 2, BioIn 1, –2, –3,
–4, –5, –7, –8, –9, –10, –11, –12,
BlueB 76N, CasWL, CelR, ConAu 61,
ConLC 3, ConNov 76, CorpD,
CurBio 46, –76, –76N, EncMys,
EncSF, EvLB, IndAu 1917, LinLib L,
LongCTC, NatCAB 59[port],
NewYTBE 71, NewYTBS 75,
Novels[port], ObitOF 79, ObitT 1971,
OxAmL, PenC AM, REn, REnAL,
ScF&FL 1, –2, TwCA, –SUP,
TwCCr&M 80, TwCWr, WhAm 6,
–7, WhoAm 74, –76, WorAl*

Stoutenburg, Adrien 1916- *AmAu&B,
Au&Wr 71, AuBYP, BioIn 6, –8, –9,
ChhPo S2, ConAu X, ConPo 70,
–75, –80, ForWC 70, IntWWP 77,
MinnWr, ScF&FL 1, –2, SmATA 3,
ThrBJA, WhoAm 74, –76, –78, –80,
–82, WhoAmW 74, –68, –70, –72,
WhoWest 74, WrDr 76, –80, –82,
–84, –86*

Stowe, Harriet Beecher 1811-1896
*Alli, –SUP, AmAu, AmAu&B, AmBi,
AmWom, AmWomWr, AmWr S1,
ApCAB, AtlBL, AuBYP SUP, BbD,
BiDAmM, BiD&SB, BioIn 1, –2, –3,
–4, –5, –6, –7, –8, –9, –10, –11, –12,
CarSB, CasWL, CelCen, Chambr 3,
ChhPo, –S1, –S2, CivWDc, CnDAL,
CrtT 3, –4, CyAL 2, CyWA,
DcAmAu, DcAmB, DcAmReB,
DcAmSR, DcBiA, DcBiPP, DcEnA,
DcEnL, DcLB 1, –12[port], –42[port],
DcLEL, DcNAA, Drake, EncAAH,
EncAB-H, EvLB, FilmgC, GoodHs,
HalFC 84, HarEnUS[port],
HerW, InWom, IntDcWB,
JBA 34, LibW, LinLib L, –S,
McGEWB, MemAm, MouLC 4,
NatCAB 1, NinCLC 3[port], NotAW,
NotNAT B, Novels, OhA&B, OxAmH,
OxAmL, –83, OxChL, OxEng,
PenC AM, PlP&P, RAdv 1, REn,
REnAL, TwCBDA, WebAB, –79,
WebE&AL, WhDW, WhAm HS,
WhAmP, WhFla, WhoChL, WorAl,
YABC 1*

Stowe, Leland 1899- *DcLB 29[port],
EncAJ, EncTwCJ, WhoAm 84, –86*

Strachan, Margaret Pitcairn 1908-
*BioIn 12, ConAu 5R, SmATA 14,
WhoPNW, WrDr 76, –80, –82, –84*

Strachey, Lytton *BioIn 13*

Sutcliff, Rosemary 1920- *Au&Wr 71,
AuBYP, BioIn 5, –6, –7, –8, –10, –11,
BlueB 76, BritCA, CasWL, ChlLR 1,
ChhPo, ConAu 5R, ConLC 26[port],
DcBrAr 1, DcLEL 1940, HerW,
IntAu&W 77, –82, –86, LinLib L,
MorJA, OxChL, PiP, ScF&FL 1, –2,
SenS, SmATA 44[port], –6, TelT,
TwCCW 78, –83, Who 74, –82, –83,
–85, WhoAmW 74, –66, –68, –72,
WhoChL, WhoWor 74, –76,
WrDr 76, –80, –82, –84, –86*

Sutherland, Audrey Margaret 1940-
WhoLib 72

Sutton, Ann 1923- *AuBYP, BioIn 8,
ConAu 5R, –10NR, SmATA 31[port]*

Sutton, Caroline 1953- *ConAu 106*

Sutton, David 1944- *ConAu 116*

Sutton, George Miksch
AmM&WS 86P

Sutton, George Miksch 1898-
ArtsAmW 3, WhAm 8

Sutton, George Miksch 1898-1982
WhoAmA 84N

Sutton, Jean 1916?- *AuBYP SUP,
ConSFA, EncSF, ScF&FL 1, –2,
TwCSFW 84, –86*

Sutton, Jeff 1913-1979 *AuBYP SUP,
ConAu X, ConSFA, EncSF,
ScF&FL 1, –2, ScFSB, TwCSFW 86,
WhoSciF*

Sutton, Jefferson H 1913-1979
ConAu 10NR, –21R

Sutton, Margaret 1903- *AuBYP,
BioIn 8, –9, ConAu 1R, ForWC 70,
IntAu&W 77, SmATA 1,
WhoAmW 58, –61*

Sutton, Margaret Rachel Irene 1903-
IntAu&W 86

Sutton, Myron Daniel 1925- *AuBYP,
BioIn 8, ConAu 107, SmATA 31[port]*

Svenson, Andrew E 1910-1975
*BioIn 9, –10, –13, ConAu 5R, –61,
NewYTBS 75, ObitOF 79, SmATA 2,
–26N, WhoE 74*

Svenson, Andrew E *see also* Dixon,
Franklin W

Svenson, Andrew E *see also* West, Jerry

Swados, Elizabeth 1951- *AmWomD,
BioIn 11, –12, –13, ConAu 97,
ConLC 12, CurBio 79, NewYTBS 77,
–78, WhoAm 78, –80, –82,
WhoAmW 81, WhoThe 81*

Swados, Harvey 1920-1972 *AmAu&B,
AuBYP SUP, BioIn 5, –6, –9, –10,
ConAu 5R, –6NR, –37R, ConLC 5,
ConNov 72, DcLB 2, DcLEL 1940,
IntAu&W 76, LinLib L, ModAL,
NewYTBE 72, Novels, OxAmL, –83,
PenC AM, REnAL, WhAm 5, WorAu*

Swain, Roger 1949- *ConAu 102*

Swallow, Norman 1921- *Au&Wr 71,
ConAu 21R, IntAu&W 77, –86,*

*IntMPA 77, –75, –76, –78, –79, –81,
–82, –84, –86, WrDr 76, –80, –82,
–84, –86*

Swanberg, William Andrew 1907-
*Au&Wr 71, BioIn 6, –10, ConAu 5R,
DcLEL 1940, MinnWr, WhoAm 74,
–76, –78, –80, –82, –84, –86, WorAu,
WrDr 76, –80*

Swann, Thomas Burnett 1928-1976
*ChhPo S1, ConAu 4NR, –5R,
ConSFA, EncSF, ScF&FL 1, –2,
ScFSB, SupFW, WhoHr&F*

Swansea, Charleen 1932- *BioIn 11,
ConAu 103, –16NR*

Swanwick, Michael 1950- *ConAu 119*

Swarthout, Glendon *DrAP&F 85*

Swarthout, Glendon 1918- *AuBYP,
BioIn 4, –11, ConAu 1R, –1NR,
ConLC 35[port], ConNov 72, –76,
–82, –86, DcLEL 1940, EncFWF,
FourBJA, IntAu&W 76, –77,
MichAu 80, Novels, SmATA 26[port],
WhoAm 80, –82, WhoWest 74, –76,
–78, WrDr 76, –80, –82, –84, –86*

Swarthout, Kathryn 1919- *AuBYP,
BioIn 10, ConAu 41R, FourBJA,
MichAu 80, SmATA 7*

Sweeney, James B 1910- *BioIn 12,
ConAu 12NR, –29R,
SmATA 21[port], WhoS&SW 75*

Sweeney, Joyce 1955- *ConAu 116*

Sweeney, Karen O'Connor 1938-
ConAu 89, SmATA X

Sweeney, Karen O'Connor *see also*
O'Connor, Karen

Sweet, Jeffrey 1950- *ConAu 81,
NatPD, –81[port], WhoMW 82*

Sweetkind, Morris 1898- *ChhPo S1,
ConAu 13R, DrAS 74E*

Swenson, May *DrAP&F 85*

Swenson, May 1913- *ModAWP[port]*

Swenson, May 1919- *AmAu&B,
AmWomWr, AnCL, AuBYP SUP,
BioIn 8, –9, –10, –12, ChhPo S1, –S2,
ConAu 5R, ConLC 4, –14, ConPo 70,
–75, –80, –85, CroCAP, DcLB 5[port],
DcLEL 1940, IntWWP 77, –82,
ModAL S2, PenC AM, RAdv 1,
SmATA 15, WhoAm 74, –76, –78,
–80, –82, –84, –86, WhoAmW 74,
–68, –70, –72, –75, –77, –81, –85,
–87, WhoWor 74, WorAu, WrDr 76,
–80, –82, –84, –86*

Swenson, May 1927- *OxAmL 83*

Swezey, Kenneth M 1905?-1972
BioIn 9, ConAu 33R

Swift, Benjamin *ConAu X*

Swift, Clive 1936- *WhoHol A,
WhoThe 72, –77, –81*

Swift, Hildegarde Hoyt 1890?-1977
*AuBYP, BioIn 2, –7, –11, –12,
ChhPo S2, ConAu 69, JBA 51,*

*NewYTBS 77, SmATA 20N,
WhoAmW 58, –61, –64, –66, –68*

Swift, Jonathan *OxChL*

Swift, Jonathan 1667-1745 *Alli, AtlBL,
BbD, BiD&SB, BiDIrW, BioIn 1, –2,
–3, –4, –5, –6, –7, –8, –9, –10, –11,
–12, –13, BritAu, BritWr 3, CarSB,
CasWL, Chambr 2, ChhPo, –S1, –S3,
CnE&AP, CrtT 2, –4, CyWA, DcBiA,
DcBiPP, DcEnA, –AP, DcEnL,
DcEuL, DcIrB, DcIrL, DcIrW 1, –2,
DcLB 39[port], DcLEL, DcNaB,
Dis&D, EncSF, EvLB, HalFC 84,
HsB&A, LinLib L, –S, LitC 1[port],
LongCEL, LuthC 75, McGEWB,
MouLC 2, NewC, Novels[port],
OxEng, –85, OxMus, PenC ENG,
PoIre, RAdv 1, RComWL, REn,
ScF&FL 1, ScFSB, SmATA 19,
UFOEn, WebE&AL, WhDW,
WhoChL, WorAl*

Swift, Kate 1923- *ConAu 69,
IntAu&W 86*

Swiger, Elinor Porter 1927-
*AuBYP SUP, BioIn 11, ConAu 37R,
SmATA 8, WhoAmL 79, –83,
WhoAmW 75, –77, –79*

Swinburne, Laurence 1924- *BioIn 11,
ConAu 15NR, –61, SmATA 9,
WhoE 79*

Swindell, Larry 1929- *ConAu 25R*

Swindells, Robert 1939- *ConAu 21NR*

Swindells, Robert E 1939- *ConAu 97,
SmATA 34*

Swindler, William F 1913- *WrDr 86*

Swindler, William F 1913-1984
ConAu 112

Swindler, William Finley 1913-
*Au&Wr 71, ConAu 13R, DrAS 74P,
–78P, –82P, WhAm 8, WhoAm 74,
–76, –78, –80, –82, –84, WhoAmL 78,
WrDr 76, –80, –82, –84*

Swinford, Betty 1927- *ConAu 5R,
–7NR, ForWC 70, IndAu 1917*

Switzer, Ellen 1923- *ConAu 2NR, –45,
SmATA 48*

Swope, Mary *DrAP&F 85*

Swortzell, Lowell Stanley 1930-
*ConAu 1NR, –49, DrAS 74E, –78E,
–82E, LEduc 74*

Sydenham, Michael John 1923-
*Au&Wr 71, ConAu 17R, DrAS 74H,
–78H, –82H, WrDr 76, –80, –82, –84,
–86*

Sykes, Pamela 1927- *Au&Wr 71,
AuBYP SUP, ScF&FL 1*

Sylvander, Carolyn W 1939-
ConAu 117

Sylvander, Carolyn Wedin 1939-
DrAS 78E, –82E, WhoAmW 83

Syme, Ronald 1910- *WrDr 86*

Syme, Ronald 1913- *Au&Wr 71,
AuBYP, BioIn 9, ConAu 6NR, –9R,
MorJA, SmATA 2, TwCCW 78*

Symonds, Pamela 1916- *Au&Wr 71,
WrDr 76, –80, –82, –84, –86*

Symons, Geraldine 1909- *ConAu 85,
OxChL, SmATA 33[port],
TwCCW 78, –83, WrDr 76, –80, –82,
–84, –86*

Symons, Julian Gustave 1912-
*Au&Wr 71, BioIn 4, –9, BlueB 76,
ConAu 3NR, –49, ConLC 2, –14,
ConNov 72, –76, –82, ConPo 70, –80,
DcLEL 1940, EncMys, IntAu&W 76,
–77, LongCTC, ModBrL, Novels,
TwCA SUP, TwCCr&M 80,
WhE&EA, Who 74, –82, –83, –85,
WhoAm 82, –84, –86, WhoSpyF,
WorAl, WrDr 76, –80, –82, –84*

Synge, John Millington 1871-1909
*AtlBL, BiDIrW, BioIn 1, –3, –4, –5,
–6, –7, –8, –9, –10, –11, –12, –13,
CasWL, Chambr 3, ChhPo S1,
CnMD, CnMWL, CnThe, CyWA,
DcEuL, DcIrB, DcIrL, DcIrW 1,
DcLB 10[port], –19[port], DcLEL,
DcNaB S2, Dis&D, EncWL, –2[port],
EncWT, EvLB, LinLib L, –S,
LongCEL, LongCTC, MajMD 1,
McGEWD, –84[port], ModBrL, –S2,
–S1, ModWD, NewC, NewEOp 71,
NotNAT A, –B, OxEng, –85,
OxThe, –83, PenC ENG, PIP&P,
PoIre, RComWL, REn, REnWD,
TwCA, TwCLC 6[port], TwCWr,
WebE&AL, WhDW, WhoTwCL,
WorAl*

Synge, Ursula 1930- *BioIn 11,
ConAu 1NR, –49, IntAu&W 77,
SmATA 9, WrDr 76, –80, –82, –84,
–86*

Syrett, Netta d1943 *ChhPo S2,
DcBrBI, ScF&FL 1, WhE&EA,
WhLit, WomNov*

Szasz, Suzanne 1915- *ConAu 18NR*

Szasz, Suzanne 1919- *AuBYP, BioIn 8,
–11, ConAu 3NR, –5R, ICPEnP A,
MacBEP, SmATA 13, WhoAmW 68,
–70*

Szulc, Tad 1926- *AmAu&B, BioIn 10,
–13, ConAu 4NR, –9R, EncTwCJ,
IntAu&W 76, SmATA 26[port],
WhoAm 74, –76, –78, –80, –82, –84,
–86, WhoWor 74, –80, –84, –87,
WrDr 76, –80, –82, –84, –86*

Szydlowski, Mary Vigliante
DrAP&F 85

Szydlowski, Mary Vigliante 1946-
ConAu 104

T

Taaffe, James Griffith 1932-
*ConAu 17R, DrAS 74E, −78E, −82E,
LEduc 74, WhoAm 74, −76, −78, −80,
−82, −84, −86*

Taber, Anthony Scott 1944-
ConAu 105

Tagliavia, Sheila 1936- *ConAu 104*

Tait, Dorothy 1902?-1972 *BioIn 9,
ConAu 33R, ObitOF 79*

Tait, Dorothy *see also* Fairbairn, Ann

Takashima, Shizuye 1928- *BioIn 11,
−13, ConAu 45, CreCan 2,
HerW, −84, IntAu&W 77,
OxCan SUP, SmATA 13,
WhoAmA 78, −80, −82*

Talbert, William Franklin 1918-
*Au&Wr 71, BioIn 3, −4, −5,
CurBio 57*

Talbot, Charlene Joy 1924?-
*AuBYP SUP, BioIn 11, ConAu 8NR,
−17R, ForWC 70, SmATA 10,
WrDr 76, −80, −82, −84, −86*

Talbot, Toby 1928- *AuBYP SUP,
BioIn 12, ConAu 21R, SmATA 14,
WomWMM B*

Talbot Rice, Tamara *ConAu X*

Talbot Rice, Tamara 1904-
IntAu&W 77, −82, −86

Talbot Rice, Tamara *see also* Rice,
Tamara

Talbott, Strobe 1946- *AuNews 1,
BioIn 10, ConAu 93, WhoAm 78,
−80, −82, −84*

Tall, Stephen 1908- *ScFSB, WrDr 84*

Tall, Stephen 1908-1981 *TwCSFW 86*

Tallcott, Emogene *BioIn 11,
ConAu 29R, SmATA 10*

Talmadge, Marian *AuBYP, BioIn 8,
−12, SmATA 14*

Tamarin, Alfred H 1913-1980
*BioIn 10, −11, −12, ConAu 4NR,
−102, −29R, FifBJA[port],
IntMPA 77, −75, −76, −78, −79,
MorBMP, NewYTBS 80, SmATA 13,
WrDr 80, −82, −84*

Tames, Richard Lawrence 1946-
*Au&Wr 71, ConAu 103, WrDr 76,
−80, −82, −84, −86*

Tanizaki, Jun'ichiro 1886-1965
*BiDJaL, BioIn 10, −12, −13, CasWL,
CnMWL, ConAu 25R, −93, ConLC 8,
−14, −28[port], DcOrL 1, EncWL, −2,
GrFLW, LinLib L, MakMC,
McGEWB, ModWD, ObitOF 79,
PenC CL, REn, WhAm 4,
WhoTwCL, WorAu*

Tannehill, Ivan Ray 1890-1959
AuBYP, BioIn 8, OhA&B

Tannen, Mary 1943- *ConAu 105,
IntAu&W 86, SmATA 37*

Tannenbaum, Beulah Goldstein 1916-
*AuBYP, BioIn 9, ConAu 5R, −7NR,
ForWC 70, SmATA 3, WhoAmW 68*

Tannenbaum, Frank 1893-1969
*AmAu&B, BioIn 2, −8, ConAu 9R,
IntEnSS 79, ObitOF 79, WhNAA*

Tanner, Chuck 1930- *WhoAm 74, −76,
WhoE 79, −81, −83*

Tanner, Edward Everett, III
1921-1976 *AmAu&B, BioIn 4, −5,
−6, −7, −10, −11, ConAu 69, −73,
CurBio 59, −77, −77N, WhAm 7,
WhoAm 74, −76, WorAu, WrDr 76*

Tanner, Edward Everett, III *see also*
Dennis, Patrick

Tanner, Helen Hornbeck 1916-
*ConAu 61, DrAS 74H, −78H, −82H,
WhoAm 86, WhoAmW 68, −70, −72,
−83, −85, −87, WhoMW 84*

Tanner, Louise S 1922- *AuBYP SUP,
BioIn 11, ConAu 69, SmATA 9*

Tapley, Caroline 1934- *AuBYP SUP,
ConAu 97*

Tappan, Eva March 1854-1930
*AmAu&B, AmLY, AmWomWr,
BiDAmEd, BiD&SB, CarSB,
ChhPo, −S1, DcAmAu, DcAmB,
DcNAA, JBA 34, NatCAB 22,
NotAW, REnAL, TwCA, TwCBDA,
WhAm 1, WhNAA, WomNov,
WomWWA 14*

Tardieu, Jean 1903- *BioIn 10, CnMD,
CnThe, ConAu 116, ConFLW 84,
EncWL, −2, EncWT, IntAu&W 76,
−77, IntWW 74, −75, −76, −77, −78,
−79, −80, −81, −82, −83,
McGEWD, −84, ModFrL, ModWD,
PenC EUR, REn, REnWD,
WhoFr 79, WhoWor 74, −76, −78,
WorAu*

Targan, Barry *DrAP&F 85*

Targan, Barry 1932- *ConAu 17NR,
−73*

Tarkenton, Fran 1940- *BioIn 12, −13,
CelR, ConAu 103, CurBio 69,
NewYTBE 71, −72, WorAl*

Tarkenton, Fran *see also* Tarkenton,
Francis Asbury

Tarkenton, Francis Asbury 1940-
*BioIn 6, −7, −8, −9, −10, −11,
NewYTBE 71, WhoAm 74, −76, −78,
−80, −82, −84, −86, WhoFtbl 74*

Tarkenton, Francis Asbury *see also*
Tarkenton, Fran

Tarkington, Booth *OxChL*

Tarkington, Booth 1869-1946
*AmAu&B, ApCAB X, AtlBL, BioIn 1,
−2, −3, −4, −5, −6, −8, −10, −11, −12,
−13, CarSB, ChhPo S2, CnDAL,
ConAmA, ConAmL, ConAu 110,
CurBio 46, CyWA, DcAmAu,
DcAmB S4, DcLB 9[port], DcLEL,
DcNAA, EncAB 36, FilmgC,
HalFC 84, JBA 34, LinLib L, −S,
LongCTC, McGEWD, −84, ModAL,
ModWD, MorMA, NatCAB 42,
Novels, ObitOF 79, OxAmL, −83,*

*OxAmT 84, OxEng, −85, OxThe, −83,
PenC AM, PIP&P, REn, REnAL,
SmATA 17, TwCA, −SUP,
TwCLC 9[port], TwCWr,
WebAB, −79, WebE&AL, WhAm 2,
WhLit, WhNAA, WhoChL, WorAl*

Tarkington, Booth *see also* Tarkington,
Newton Booth

Tarkington, Newton Booth 1869-1946
*BbD, BiD&SB, CasWL, Chambr 3,
DcBiA, EncAAH, EvLB, IndAu 1816,
McGEWB, MnBBF, NatCAB 4,
NotNAT B, TwCBDA, WhE&EA,
WhThe*

Tarkington, Newton Booth *see*
Tarkington, Booth

Tarr, Herbert *DrAP&F 85*

Tarr, Herbert 1929- *ConAu 13R*

Tarr, Judith 1955- *ConAu 120*

Tarrant, John J 1924- *ConAu 4NR,
−19NR, −53*

Tarry, Ellen *WhoBlA 85*

Tarry, Ellen 1906- *AmPB, AuBYP,
BioIn 3, −8, −9, −12, BkP, BlkAWP,
ConAu 73, InB&W 80, −85, LivgBAA,
NegAl 76, 83, SelBAAf, SelBAAu,
SmATA 16, WhoBlA 77, −80*

Tarshis, Barry *AuBYP SUP*

Tarshis, Jerome 1936- *BioIn 11,
ConAu 61, SmATA 9, WhoAmA 76,
−78, −80, −82, −84*

Taschdjian, Claire Louise 1914-
*AmM&WS 73P, −76P, −79P, −82P,
−86P, ConAu 73*

Tashjian, Levon Donald 1934-
BiDrAPA 77

Tate, Allen 1889-1979 *AmAu&B,
AmWr, Au&Wr 71, BioIn 3, −4, −5,
−7, −8, −9, −10, −11, −12, BlueB 76,
CasWL, CathA 1952, ChhPo, −S2,
−S3, CnDAL, CnE&AP, ConAmA,
ConAu 5R, −85, ConLC 2, −4, −6, −9,
−11, −14, −24[port], ConLCrt, −82,
ConNov 72, −76, ConPo 70, −75,
CurBio 40, −79N, DcLB 4,
DrAS 74E, −78E, −82E, EncWL,
IntAu&W 76, −77, IntWW 74, −75,
−76, −77, −78, −79N, IntWWP 77,
LinLib L, LongCTC, McGEWB,
ModAL, −S1, NewYTBS 79, OxAmL,
PenC AM, RAdv 1, REn, REnAL,
SixAP, TwCA, −SUP, TwCWr,
WebAB, −79, WebE&AL, WhAm 7,
WhE&EA, WhoAm 74, −76, −78,
WhoS&SW 73, −75, −76, WhoTwCL,
WhoWor 74, −76, −78, WorAl,
WrDr 76, −80*

Tate, Allen 1899-1979 *BioIn 13,
DcLB 45[port], EncWL 2,
ModAL S2, OxAmL 83, OxEng 85*

Tate, Eleanora E 1948-
SmATA 38[port]

Tate, Joan 1922- *BioIn 11,
ConAu 1NR, −49, IntAu&W 76, −77,
OxChL, SmATA 9, TwCCW 78, −83,
WrDr 76, −80, −82, −84, −86*

Tattersall, Jill 1931- *ConAu 10NR,
−25R, IntAu&W 77X, WrDr 76, −80,
−82, −84, −86*

Tatum, Jack 1948- *BioIn 10, −12,
ConAu X, NewYTBS 80[port],
WhoBlA 80, WhoFtbl 74*

Taupin, Bernie 1950- *BioIn 10, −11,
−12, EncPR&S 74, −77, IlEncRk,
WhoRocM 82*

Taylor, Alan John P *BioIn 13*

Taylor, Alan John Percivale 1906-
*Au&Wr 71, BioIn 4, −7, −10, −11,
ConAu 5R, IntAu&W 76, −77,
IntWW 74, −75, −76, −77, −78, −79,
−80, −81, −82, −83, LongCTC, NewC,
OxCan SUP, REn, WhDW,
WhE&EA, Who 74, −82, −83, −85,
WhoWor 74, −76, −78, −84, −87,
WorAu, WrDr 76*

Taylor, Alice L 1911- *ConAu 61,
ForWC 70, IntAu&W 77, −82,
WhoAmW 74, −58, −61A, −64, −66,
−68, −70, −72, −75, −77, WhoE 74,
−75, −77, WrDr 76, −80, −82, −84*

Taylor, Alice L 1911-1985 *ConAu 116*

Taylor, Andrew 1940- *ConAu 11NR,
−69, ConPo 80, −85, OxAusL,
WrDr 82, −84, −86*

Taylor, Bernard 1937- *ConAu 69*

Taylor, David 1900-1965 *BioIn 7, −11,
ConAu 1R, EncAB 36, SmATA 10*

Taylor, Dawson 1916- *AmSCAP 66,
ConAu 13R, MichAu 80*

Taylor, Duncan Burnett 1912-
*Au&Wr 71, ConAu 25R,
IntAu&W 76*

Taylor, Henry *DrAP&F 85*

Taylor, Henry 1942- *BioIn 9, −12,
−13, ConAu 33R, ConLC 44[port],
DcLB 5[port], DrAS 74E, −78E,
−82E, IntWWP 77, WhoAm 82,
WhoS&SW 73, −75, −76, WrDr 76,
−80, −82, −84, −86*

Taylor, Herb 1942- *BioIn 13,
ConAu 97, MacBEP, SmATA 22*

Taylor, James 1948- *BiDAmM,
BioIn 9, −11, −12, CelR, CurBio 72,
EncFCWM 83, EncPR&S 74, −77,
IlEncRk, NewYTBE 71, RkOn 78,
−84, RkOneH, RolSEnR 83,
WhoAm 74, −76, −78, −80, −82,
WhoHol A, WhoRock 81[port],
WhoRocM 82, WhoWest 74, WorAl*

Taylor, James Vernon 1948-
WhoAm 84, −86

Taylor, Joe Gray 1920- *ConAu 6NR,
−57, DrAS 74H, −78H, −82H*

Taylor, John G 1931- *Au&Wr 71,
ConAu 29R, EncO&P 78, −81,
Who 82, −83, WrDr 80, −82, −84*

157

Taylor, John Gerald 1931-
IntAu&W 86, Who 85

Taylor, John William Ransom 1922-
*Au&Wr 71, ConAu 49, IntAu&W 77,
–82, –86, Who 74, –82, –83, –85,
WhoWor 84, –87, WrDr 76, –80, –82,
–84, –86*

Taylor, Judy 1932- *BioIn 13, Who 85*

Taylor, Kamala Purnaiya 1924-
BioIn 14, ConAu 77, WorAu

Taylor, Kamala Purnaiya *see also*
Markandaya, Kamala

Taylor, Keith John 1946-
IntAu&W 82

Taylor, Kenneth Nathaniel 1917-
*Au&Wr 71, AuNews 2, BioIn 9, –10,
–11, –12, –13, ConAu 8NR, –17R,
IntAu&W 76, –77, SmATA 26[port],
WhoAm 74, –76, –78, –80, –82, –84,
–86, WhoF&I 85, WhoRel 75, –77,
–85*

Taylor, L A *IntAu&W 86X*

Taylor, L A 1939- *ConAu 111*

Taylor, L B 1932- *BioIn 13*

Taylor, L B, Jr. 1932- *ConAu 11NR,
–57*

Taylor, Lawrence 1942- *ConAu 105*

Taylor, Lawrence Eric 1942-
WhoAmL 85

Taylor, Lisa Suter 1933- *WhoAm 74,
–76, –78, –80, –82, –84, –86,
WhoAmA 78, –80, –82,
WhoAmW 75, –81, –85, –87,
WhoE 79, –81, –83, –85, WhoGov 77,
–72, –75, WhoWor 78, –82*

Taylor, Michael J H 1949-
ConAu 14NR

Taylor, Michael John Haddrick 1949-
*ConAu 77, IntAu&W 77, –82,
IntWWP 77*

Taylor, Mick 1948- *BioIn 8, –11,
WhoRocM 82*

Taylor, Mick *see also* Rolling Stones,
The

Taylor, Mildred D *AuBYP SUP,
BioIn 12, ChlLR 9[port], ConAu 85,
ConLC 21[port], FifBJA[port],
InB&W 80, –85, SmATA 15,
TwCChW 83, WrDr 86*

Taylor, Mildred D 1943-
DcLB 52[port]

Taylor, Paul 1930- *BiDD, BioIn 13,
WhoAm 84, –86, WhoWor 84, –87*

Taylor, Paula 1942- *ConAu 111,
SmATA 33, –48[port]*

Taylor, Peter Hillsman 1917-
*AmAu&B, BioIn 3, –4, –8, –9, –13,
BlueP 76, ConAu 9NR, –13R,
ConLC 1, –4, –18, ConNov 72, –76,
–82, DcLB Y81B[port], DcLEL 1940,
IntAu&W 76, –77, ModAL, –S1,
Novels, OhA&B, PenC AM, REnAL,
TwCA SUP, WhoAm 74, –76, –78,
–80, –84, WrDr 76, –80, –82, –84*

Taylor, Robert L 1899- *WhoAm 84,
–86, WhoAmL 85, WhoS&SW 84,
–86*

Taylor, Robert Lewis 1912- *AmAu&B,
Au&Wr 71, BioIn 1, –2, –5, –7, –8,
–10, –11, BlueB 76, ConAu 1R,
–3NR, ConLC 14, ConNov 72, –76,
CurBio 59, EncFWF, EncSF,
IntAu&W 76, –77, OxAmL, –83,
REnAL, ScF&FL 1, –2, SmATA 10,
WhoAm 74, –76, –78, –80, –82, –84,
–86, WhoE 74, –75, –77, WhoWor 74,
–76, –78, –80, –82, –84, WorAu,
WrDr 76, –80, –82, –84, –86*

Taylor, Sydney 1904?-1978 *AuBYP,
BioIn 6, –8, –9, –10, –11, –13, BkCL,
ConAu 4NR, –5R, –77, IntAu&W 76,
–77, MorBMP, MorJA, NewYTBS 78,
SmATA 1, –26N, –28[port],
TwCCW 78, –83, WrDr 76*

Taylor, Theodore *DrAP&F 85*

Taylor, Theodore 1921?- *AuBYP SUP,
BioIn 10, ConAu 9NR, –21R,
FourBJA, IntAu&W 77, OxChL,
SmATA 5, SmATA 4AS[port],
TwCCW 78, –83, WhoAm 74, –76,
–78, –80, –82, WrDr 76, –80, –84,
–86*

Tchekhov, Anton Pavlovich 1860-1904
CasWL, DcEuL, LongCTC, OxEng

Tchekhov, Anton Pavlovich *see also*
Chekhov, Anton Pavlovich

Teague, Bob *EncTwCJ, WhoAmP 85*

Teague, Bob 1929- *BlkAWP,
ConAu X, DrBlPA, LivgBAA,
NegAl 76, –83[port], SelBAAu,
SmATA X, WhoAmP 83*

Teague, Robert 1929- *AuBYP SUP,
BioIn 8, ConAu 106, InB&W 80,
SmATA 31, –32[port], WhoBlA 75,
–77, –80, –85*

Teale, Edwin Way 1899-1980
*AmAu&B, AnObit 1980[port],
Au&Wr 71, AuBYP, BioIn 1, –2, –3,
–4, –5, –6, –7, –8, –9, –10, –12, –13,
ConAu 1R, –2NR, –102, CurBio 61,
–81N, InSci, LinLib L, –S,
NewYTBS 80[port], OxAmL 83,
REnAL, SmATA 25N, –7, Str&VC,
ThrBJA, TwCA SUP, WhAm 7,
WhNAA, WhoAm 74, –76, –78, –80,
WhoWor 74, WrDr 76, –80, –82, –84*

Tebbel, John 1912- *AmAu&B, BioIn 3,
–13, ConAu 85, CurBio 53,
DrAS 74E, –78E, –82E,
SmATA 26[port], WhoAm 74, –76,
–78, –80, –82, –84, –86*

Tec, Nechama 1931- *ConAu 9R,
WhoAmW 68, –70, –72, –75*

Techter, David 1932- *BiDPara,
EncO&P 2, –78*

Tedeschi, Frank P 1938- *WhoEng 80*

Tedlock, Dennis 1939- *DrAS 82P,
FifIDA*

Tegner, Bruce 1928- *ConAu 8NR, –61,
IntAu&W 76*

Teissier DuCros, Janet 1906-
ConAu P-2, WrDr 76, –82

Teleki, Geza 1943- *ConAu 3NR,
–19NR, –49, SmATA 45[port]*

Telemaque, Eleanor Wong *DrAP&F 85*

Telemaque, Eleanor Wong 1934-
ConAu 104, SmATA 43

Teller, Edward 1908- *AmM&WS 86P,
BioIn 13, Who 85, WhoAm 84, –86,
WhoFrS 84, WhoTech 84,
WhoWor 84*

Temkin, Sara Anne 1912?- *AuBYP,
BiDrLUS 70, BioIn 8, –13,
ConAu 1R, ForWC 70,
SmATA 26[port], WhoAmW 66,
WhoLibI 82, WhoLibS 66*

TenBoom, Corrie 1892-1983 *BioIn 10,
–11, –12, –13, ConAu 109, –111*

Tene, Benjamin 1914- *IntAu&W 86,
IntWWP 77, –82, WhoWorJ 72, –78*

Tennenbaum, Silvia *DrAP&F 85*

Tennenbaum, Silvia 1928- *BioIn 11,
ConAu 21NR, –77*

Tennissen, Anthony C 1920-1982
ConAu 114

Tennissen, Anthony Cornelius 1920-
*AmM&WS 73P, –76P, –79P, –82P,
–86P*

Tennyson, Alfred 1809-1892
*Alli, –SUP, AnCL, AtlBL, AuBYP,
BbD, BiD&SB, BioIn 1, –2, –3, –4,
–5, –6, –7, –8, –9, –10, –11, –12,
BritAu 19, BritWr 4, CasWL, CelCen,
Chambr 3, ChhPo, –S1, –S2, –S3,
CnE&AP, CnThe, CrtT 3, –4, CyWA,
DcBiPP, DcEnA, –AP, DcEnL,
DcEuL, DcLB 32[port], DcLEL,
Dis&D, EvLB, IlEncMy, LinLib L,
–S, LongCEL, LuthC 75, McGEWB,
McGEWD, MouLC 4, NewC,
NewEOp 71, NotNAT B, OxEng, –85,
OxMus, OxThe, PenC ENG, PoLE,
RAdv 1, RComWL, REn, REnWD,
Str&VC, WebE&AL, WhDW, WorAl*

Tennyson, Baron Alfred 1809-1892
BioIn 13, DcNaB

Tennyson, Lord Alfred 1809-1892
OxThe 83

Tepper, Terri P 1942- *ConAu 107*

Tepper, Terri Patricia 1942-
WhoAm 84, –86

Ter Haar, Jaap 1922- *ConAu 37R,
IntAu&W 76, SmATA 6*

Ter Haar, Jaap *see also* Haar, Jaap Ter

Terhune, Albert Payson 1872-1942
*AmAu&B, AmLY, AuBYP, BiD&SB,
BioIn 2, –5, –7, –8, –9, –11, –12,*

*ChhPo, CnDAL, ConAu 111,
CurBio 42, DcAmAu, DcAmB S3,
DcLB 9[port], DcNAA, EvLB,
JBA 34, LinLib L, NatCAB 10, –34,
ObitOF 79, OxAmL, –83, OxChL,
REnAL, SmATA 15, TwCA, –SUP,
TwCBDA, WebAB, –79, WhAm 2, WhLit,
WhNAA, WorAl*

Terkel, Studs *ConAu X, WrDr 86*

Terkel, Studs 1912- *AmAu&B,
AuNews 1, BioIn 7, –10, –11, –12,
ConAu 57, ConLC 38[port],
CurBio 74, EncAJ, IntWW 83,
LinLib L, OxAmL 83, WhoAm 74,
–76, –78, –80, –82, WhoMW 74, –76,
–80, –82, WorAl, WrDr 76, –80, –82,
–84*

Terlouw, Jan 1931- *ConAu 108,
OxChL, SmATA 30[port],
WhoWor 82*

Terman, Douglas *BioIn 12*

Terman, Douglas 1933- *ConAu 112*

Terraine, John Alfred 1921-
*Au&Wr 71, ConAu 5R, IntAu&W 76,
–77, IntWW 77, –78, –79, –80, –81,
–82, –83, Who 74, –82, –83, –85,
WhoWor 84, –87, WrDr 76, –80, –82,
–84, –86*

Terrell, Donna McManus 1908-
ConAu 57

Terrell, John Upton 1900- *AmAu&B,
AmNov, AuBYP, BioIn 2, –8,
ConAu 29R, OxCan SUP,
WhoWest 74*

Terrell, Robert L 1943- *BlkAWP,
ConAu 17NR, –41R, WhoBlA 75,
–77, –80, –85*

Terres, John Kenneth 1905-
*AmAu&B, AmM&WS 73P, –76P,
–79P, Au&Wr 71, BioIn 5,
ConAu 5R, –5NR, WhoAm 74, –76,
–78, –80, –82, –84, WhoWor 78*

Terrien, Samuel 1911- *ConAu 81,
DrAS 74P, –78P, –82P, WhoAm 74,
–76, –78*

Terrill, Ross Gladwin *WhoAm 84, –86*

Terrill, Ross Gladwin 1938-
*AmM&WS 73S, –78S, BioIn 9,
ConAu 25R, IntAu&W 77, –82,
WhoAm 74, –76, –78, –80, –82,
WhoWor 82*

Terrill, Tom E 1935- *ConAu 41R,
DrAS 74H, –78H, –82H*

Terris, Susan *DrAP&F 85*

Terris, Susan 1937- *AuBYP SUP,
BioIn 9, ConAu 12NR, –29R,
FifBJA[port], IntAu&W 76, –77, –82,
SmATA 3, WhoAmW 75, WrDr 76,
–80, –82, –84, –86*

Terry, Luther L 1911-1985
*ConAu 115, CurBio 85N,
NewYTBS 85[port], SmATA 42N*

Terry, Luther Leonidas 1911-
*AmM&WS 73P, –76P, –79P, –82P,
BiDrACP 79, BiDrAPH 79, BioIn 5,
–6, –11, BlueB 76, ConAu P-2,
CurBio 61, InSci, IntWW 74, –75,
–76, –77, –78, –79, –80, –81, –82,
–83, PolProf J, PolProf K,
SmATA 11, WhAm 8, WhoAm 74,
–76, –78, –80, –82, –84, WhoE 85,
WhoWor 82*

Terry, Walter 1913-1982 *AmAu&B,
AnObit 1982[port], AuBYP, BioIn 8,
–12, –13, ConAu 9R, –10NR, –21R,
NewYTBS 82[port], SmATA 14,
WhAm 8, WhoAm 74, –76, –78, –80,
–82*

Terzian, James P 1915- *AuBYP SUP,
BioIn 12, ConAu 13R, SmATA 14*

Tesich, Steve *HalFC 84, IntMPA 86*

Tesich, Steve 1942- *WhoAm 84, –86,
WrDr 86*

Tesich, Steve 1943?- *ConAu 105,
ConDr 82, ConLC 40[port],
DcLB Y83B[port], IntMPA 82, –84,
NatPD 81, NewYTBS 80[port],
–82[port], WhoAm 82, WrDr 84*

Tevis, Walter *BioIn 13*

Tevis, Walter d1984 *NewYTBS 84*

Tevis, Walter 1928- *ConSFA, EncSF,
NewYTBS 83[port], ScF&FL 1,
ScFSB, WrDr 84*

Tevis, Walter 1928-1984 *ConAu 113,
ConLC 42[port], TwCSFW 86,
WorAu 1975[port]*

Tey, Josephine *BioIn 13*

Tey, Josephine 1896-1952 *HalFC 84*

Tey, Josephine 1897?-1952 *BioIn 2,
–3, –4, –12, ConAu X, CorpD,
DcLEL, EncMys, EvLB, LongCTC,
NewC, Novels, ObitOF 79,
ObitT 1951, PenC ENG, REn,
TwCA SUP, TwCCr&M 80, –85,
TwCLC 14, TwCWr, WorAl*

Thacher, Alida McKay 1951-
ConAu 11NR, –69

Thackeray, William Makepeace
1811-1863 *Alli, ArtsNiC, AtlBL,
BbD, BiD&SB, BioIn 1, –2, –3, –4,
–5, –6, –7, –8, –9, –10, –11, –12, –13,
BritAu 19, BritWr 5, CarSB, CasWL,
CelCen, Chambr 3, ChhPo, –S1, –S2,
–S3, CrtT 3, –4, CyWA, DcBiA,
DcBiPP, DcBrBI, DcBrWA,
DcEnA, –AP, DcEnL, DcEuL,
DcInB, DcLB 21[port], –55[port],
DcLEL, DcNaB, Dis&D, EncO&P 2,
EvLB, FamSYP, HsB&A, LinLib L,
–S, LongCEL, McGEWB, MouLC 3,
NewC, NinCLC 5[port], –14[port],
Novels[port], OxAmL, –83,
OxEng, –85, PenC ENG, RAdv 1,
RComWL, REn, ScF&FL 1, –1A,
SmATA 23[port], TelT, WebE&AL,
WhDW, WhoChL, WorAl*

Thackrah, John Richard 1947-
IntAu&W 86

Thaler, Susan 1939- *ConAu 21R*

Thane, Adele 1904- *AuBYP SUP,
BiE&WWA, ConAu 25R*

Thane, Elswyth 1900- *AmAu&B,
AmNov, AmWomWr, Au&Wr 71,
BioIn 2, –11, ConAu 5R, ForWC 70,
InWom, REnAL, ScF&FL 1, –2,
SmATA 32[port], WhE&EA, WhThe,
WhoAm 74, –76, –78, WhoAmW 74,
–58, –64, –66, –68, –70, –72,
WhoE 74, WrDr 84*

Tharp, Louise Hall 1898- *AmAu&B,
Au&Wr 71, AuBYP, BioIn 2, –3, –4,
–6, –8, –9, –10, ChhPo, ConAu 1R,
CurBio 55, ForWC 70, InWom,
MorJA, RAdv 1, SmATA 3,
WhoAm 74, –76, –78, WhoAmW 58,
–64, –66, –68, –70, –72, WorAu*

Thayer, Charles Wheeler 1910-1969
*BioIn 2, –4, –8, –11, ConAu 1R,
–103, NatCAB 56, ObitOF 79,
WhAm 5*

Thayer, Ernest Lawrence 1863-1940
ConAu 119

Thayer, James Stewart 1949-
ConAu 73

Thayer, Marjorie *BioIn 4, ConAu 116,
SmATA 37*

Theismann, Joe *NewYTBS 84[port]*

Theismann, Joe 1949- *BioIn 13*

Theroux, Paul *DrAP&F 85*

Theroux, Paul 1941- *Au&Wr 71,
BioIn 11, –12, –13, ConAu 20NR,
–33R, ConLC 5, –8, –11, –15,
–28[port], ConNov 72, –76, –82, –86,
ConPo 70, CurBio 78, DcLB 2,
IntAu&W 76, –77, –82, ModAL S2,
NewYTBS 76, –78, Novels[port],
OxAmL 83, SmATA 44[port],
Who 82, –83, WhoAm 78, –80, –82,
WhoE 74, WorAl, WorAu 1970,
WrDr 76, –80, –82, –84, –86*

Thiele, Colin 1920- *Au&Wr 71,
BioIn 12, ConAu 12NR, –29R,
ConLC 17, ConPo 70, –75,
DcLEL 1940, FifBJA[port],
IntWWP 77, OxAusL, OxChL,
SingR 1, SmATA 14,
SmATA 2AS[port], TwCCW 78, –83,
WrDr 76, –80, –82, –84, –86*

Thom, James Alexander *DrAP&F 85*

Thom, James Alexander 1933-
*BioIn 12, ConAu 119, –15NR, –77,
WhoAmW 80, –82, –84*

Thom, Robert 1929-1979 *BioIn 11,
–12, ConAu 21R, –85, NewYTBS 79,
ScF&FL 1, –2*

Thomas, Arline 1913- *ConAu 49,
NewYTBE 71*

Todd, Anne Ophelia *see also* Dowden, Anne Ophelia Todd

Todd, Karen Iris Rohne Pritchett 1936- *AmM&WS 73S, –78S, LEduc 74, WhoAmW 74, –72, –75*

Toepfer, Ray Grant 1923- *ConAu 21R*

Toffler, Alvin *DrmM 2[port]*

Toffler, Alvin 1928- *AmAu&B, BioIn 10, –12, –13, ConAu 13R, –15NR, ConIsC 1[port], CurBio 75, DcLEL 1940, EncSF, Future, NewYTBS 80, WhoAm 74, –76, –78, –80, –82, –84, –86, WhoE 75, WrDr 76, –80, –82, –84, –86*

Tolan, Stephanie S *DrAP&F 85*

Tolan, Stephanie S 1942- *ConAu 15NR, –77, Po&Wr 77, SmATA 38[port]*

Toland, John 1912- *SmATA 38[port], WrDr 86*

Toland, John Willard 1912- *Au&Wr 71, BioIn 10, ConAu 1R, –6NR, LinLib L, WhoAm 74, –76, –78, –80, –82, –84, –86, WhoWor 80, –82, –84, –87, WorAu, WrDr 76, –82, –84*

Tolchin, Martin 1928- *ConAu 120, WhoAm 84, –86, WhoE 74, –76*

Toliver, Raymond Frederick 1914- *ConAu 17R, IntAu&W 76, –77, WhoWest 74, –76, –78, –80, –82, WrDr 76, –80, –82, –84, –86*

Tolkien, J R R 1892-1973 *CelR, ConAu P-2, ConLC 8, –12, –38[port], CurBio 57, –67, –73, –73N, DcLB 15[port], EncSF, EncWL 2, HalFC 84, LinLib L, –S, ModBrL S2, NewYTBS 73, Novels[port], ObitOF 79, ObitT 1971, OxChL, OxEng 85, ScF&FL 1, –2, ScFSB[port], SmATA 24N, –32[port], SupFW, TwCCh W 83, TwCSFW 86B, WhoHr&F, WorAl*

Tolkien, John Ronald Reuel 1892-1973 *AnCL, Au&Wr 71, AuBYP, AuNews 1, BioIn 3, –4, –6, –7, –8, –9, –10, –11, –12, –13, CasWL, CelR, ChhPo, –S1, –S2, –S3, CnMWL, ConAu 45, ConAu P-2, ConLC 1, –2, –3, ConNov 72, –76, CurBio 57, –67, –73, DcLEL, DcNaB 1971, EncWL, LongCTC, MakMC, ModBrL, –S1, MorJA, NewC, OxEng, PenC ENG, RAdv 1, REn, SmATA 2, TelT, TwCCW 78, TwCWr, WebE&AL, WhDW, WhAm 6, WhLit, WhoChL, WhoTwCL, WhoWor 74, WorAu*

Toll, Robert Charles 1938- *ConAu 53, IntAu&W 86, WrDr 76, –80, –82, –84, –86*

Tolstoy, Leo 1828-1910 *GrFLW, HalFC 84, TwCLC 17[port]*

Tolstoy, Leo Nikolayevich 1828-1910 *AtlBL, BbD, BiD&SB, BioIn 1, –2, –3, –4, –5, –6, –7, –8, –9, –10, –11, –12, CasWL, CelCen, ClDMEL, CnMD, CnThe, ConAu 104, CyWA, DcAmSR, DcBiA, DcEuL, DcRusL, Dis&D, EncWT, EuAu, EvEuW, FilmgC, LinLib S, LongCEL, LongCTC, LuthC 75, McGEWB, McGEWD, –84[port], ModSL 1, ModWD, NewEOp 71, NotNAT B, Novels, OxChess 84, OxChL, OxEng, OxThe, –83, PenC EUR, PIP&P, RComWL, REn, REnWD, SmATA 26[port], TwCLC 4[port], –11[port], WhDW, WhoWol, WorAl*

Toma, David 1933- *ConAu 118*

Toma, David 1934?- *BioIn 9, –10, –12*

Tomalin, Nicholas 1931-1973 *Au&Wr 71, BioIn 10, ConAu 45, ObitT 1971*

Tombaugh, Clyde W 1906- *AmM&WS 86P*

Tombaugh, Clyde William 1906- *AmM&WS 73P, AsBiEn, BiESc, BioIn 4, –6, –10, –12, BlueB 76, InSci, IntWW 74, –75, –76, –77, –78, –79, –80, –81, –82, –83, UFOEn, WhDW, WhoAm 74, –76, WhoWest 74, –76, –78, WhoWor 74*

Tomerlin, John 1930- *AuBYP SUP*

Tomkins, Calvin 1925- *BioIn 2, ConAu 8NR, –13R, WhoAm 84, –86, WhoAmA 78, –80, –82, –84, WrDr 76, –80, –82, –84, –86*

Tomlinson, Gerald 1933- *ConAu 85*

Tompkins, Peter 1919- *ConAu 9R, –12NR*

Tonkin, Peter 1950- *ConAu 101*

Toole, John Kennedy 1937-1969 *BioIn 12, –13, ConAu 104, ConLC 19, DcLB Y81B[port], OxAmL 83, WorAu 1975[port]*

Toperoff, Sam 1933- *BioIn 8, ConAu 49*

Toppin, Edgar Allan 1928- *ConAu 21R, DrAS 74H, –78H, –82H, InB&W 80, LivgBAA, SelBAAf, SelBAAu, WhoBlA 75, –77, –80, –85*

Torbado, Jesus 1943- *BioIn 12, IntAu&W 76, –77, –82*

Torbet, Laura 1942- *ConAu 16NR, –69, WhoAmW 81, –83, –85, –87, WhoE 85, WhoWor 84*

Torgoff, Martin 1952- *ConAu 109*

Torok, Lou 1927- *BioIn 10, ConAu 49*

Torrey, Volta Wray 1905- *ConAu 69, WhoAm 74, –76, WhoGov 72, –75, WhoWor 74*

Tosches, Nick 1949- *ConAu 81*

Toth, Susan Erickson Allen 1940- *ConAu 105, DrAS 74E, –78E, –82E*

Tournier, Michel 1924- *BioIn 10, –13, ConAu 3NR, –49, ConFLW 84, ConLC 6, –23[port], –36[port], EncWL, –2, IntAu&W 76, –77, –82, IntWW 74, –75, –76, –77, –78, –79, –80, –81, –82, –83, ModFrL, PostFic, SmATA 23[port], TwCCW 78B, –83B, WhoFr 79, WhoWor 84, –87, WorAu 1975[port]*

Touster, Irwin *AuBYP SUP*

Tovey, Doreen Evelyn 1918- *Au&Wr 71, ConAu 104*

Tower, John 1925- *PolsAm 84[port]*

Towne, Mary *AuBYP SUP, BioIn 13, ConAu X, SmATA X*

Townsend, Doris Ann McFerran 1914- *ConAu 103, ForWC 70, WhoAmW 74, –66, –68, –70, –72, –75, WhoE 74, –75*

Townsend, Janet 1925- *AuBYP SUP, ConAu 107*

Townsend, John Rowe 1922- *Au&Wr 71, AuBYP SUP, ChlLR 2, ChhPo S2, –S3, ConAu 37R, DcLEL 1940, FourBJA, IntAu&W 76, –77, –82, –86, OxChL, PiP, ScFSB, SmATA 4, SmATA 2AS[port], TwCCW 78, –83, WhoWor 74, –76, –84, WrDr 76, –80, –82, –84, –86*

Townsend, Sue 1946- *ConAu 119, SmATA 48*

Townshend, Peter 1945- *BioIn 13, ConAu 107, ConLC 17, –42[port], CurBio 83[port], WhoAm 80, –82, –84, –86, WhoRock 81*

Townshend, Peter *see also* Who, The

Tracey, Hugh 1903-1977 *ConAu 77, ConAu P-2, OxMus*

Trachtenberg, Alan 1932- *DrAS 74E, –78E, –82E, WhoAm 80, WhoE 79, –81*

Trachtenberg, Marvin L 1939- *ConAu 65, DrAS 74H, –78H, –82H, WhoAm 80, –82, WhoE 79, –81*

Trachtenberg, Marvin Lawrence 1939- *WhoAm 84, –86*

Trahey, Jane 1923- *AmWomM, BioIn 8, ConAu 17NR, –17R, ForWC 70, SmATA 36, WhoAdv 72, WhoAmW 74, –58, –61, –64, –66, –68, –70, –72, –75, –79, –81, WhoE 74, WhoF&I 74*

Transtromer, Tomas 1931- *BioIn 9, CasWL, ConFLW 84, EncWL 2, IntWWP 77, WorAu 1970*

Transtromer, Tomas Gosta 1931- *IntAu&W 86*

Trapp, Maria Augusta Von 1905- *AmAu&B, BioIn 3, –6, –7, –8, –9, –10, –12, –13, CathA 1952,*

CurBio 68, GoodHs, InWom, SmATA 16, WhoAm 74, –76, –78, –80, –82, –84, –86, WhoAmW 74, –58, –61, –64, –66, –68, –70, –72, WhoE 74, WhoWor 74, –76, WorAl

Traven, B *BioIn 13, OxAmL 83*

Traven, B 1882?-1969? *DcLB 56[port], EncWL 2, HalFC 84, OxEng 85*

Traven, B 1890?-1969 *AmAu&B, BiDMoPL, BioIn 1, –2, –4, –5, –6, –7, –8, –9, –11, –12, ConAu 25R, ConAu P-2, ConLC 8, –11, DcLB 9[port], EncFWF, EncWL, ObitOF 79, OxAmL, OxGer, REnAL, ScF&FL 1, TwCA, –SUP, WebE&AL, WhAm 5*

Treadgold, Mary 1910- *Au&Wr 71, BioIn 8, ConAu 13R, IntAu&W 76, OxChL, TwCCW 78, –83, WhoChL, WrDr 76, –80, –82, –84, –86*

Trease, Geoffrey *Who 85*

Trease, Geoffrey 1909- *AuBYP, BioIn 6, –7, –8, –9, –10, ConAu 5R, –7NR, DcLEL, IntAu&W 86, MnBBF, MorJA, OxChL, SmATA 2, TelT, TwCCW 78, –83, Who 74, –82, –83, WhoBW&I A, WhoChL, WrDr 76, –80, –82, –84, –86*

Treat, Roger L 1905- *AuBYP, BioIn 7*

Treece, Henry *OxEng 85*

Treece, Henry 1911?-1966 *AuBYP, BioIn 4, –6, –7, –8, –9, CathA 1930, ConAu 1R, –6NR, –25R, DcLEL, EvLB, LongCTC, ModBrL, MorJA, NewC, ObitOF 79, OxChL, PenC ENG, REn, ScF&FL 1, –2, SmATA 2, TwCA SUP, TwCCW 78, –83, TwCWr, WhoChL*

Trefil, James S 1938- *AmM&WS 73P, –76P, –79P, –82P, –86P, ConAu 101, WhoTech 82, –84*

Tregaskis, Richard 1916-1973 *AmAu&B, Au&Wr 71, AuBYP, BioIn 7, –9, –10, –12, BlueB 76, ConAu 1R, –2NR, –45, CurBio 73, –73N, NatCAB 59[port], NewYTBE 73, ObitOF 79, SmATA 26N, –3, WebAMB, WhAm 6, WhoAm 74, WhoWor 74*

Tregaskis, Richard J 1916-1973 *EncAJ*

Tregaskis, Richard William 1916-1973 *BioIn 13*

Tregear, Thomas R 1897- *ConAu 21R, WrDr 76, –80, –82, –84, –86*

Trelease, Allen William 1928- *AuBYP SUP, ConAu 108, DrAS 74H, –78H, –82H, WhoAm 74, –76, –78, –80, –82, –84, –86*

Tremayne, Peter *ConAu X, IntAu&W 86X*

Tremayne, Peter *see also* Ellis, Peter Berresford

Tretyak, Vladislav 1952- *BioIn 11*

Trevanian *WhoAm 84, –86, WrDr 86*

Trevanian 1925?- *ConAu 108, ConLC 29[port], NewYTBS 79, Novels, TwCCr&M 80, –85, WhoAm 82, WhoSpyF, WrDr 82, –84*

Trever, John Cecil 1915- *BioIn 1, ConAu 17R, DrAS 74P, –78P, –82P, IntAu&W 77, –82, –86, WrDr 76, –80, –82, –84, –86*

Trevino, Elizabeth B De 1904- *AuBYP, BioIn 7, –8, –9, –10, –11, ConAu 9NR, –17R, NewbC 1966, ScF&FL 1, –2, SmATA 1, –29[port], ThrBJA, WhoAm 74, –76, –78, –80, –82, WhoAmW 74, –70, –72, WhoS&SW 73, –75, –76*

Trevino, Elizabeth B De *see also* DeTrevino, Elizabeth Borton

Trevino, Lee 1939- *BioIn 13, ConAu 113*

Trevor, Elleston *Who 85, WhoWor 84, –87, WrDr 86*

Trevor, Elleston 1920- *Au&Wr 71, BioIn 13, ConAu 5R, DcLEL 1940, EncMys, EncSF, IntAu&W 76, –77, MnBBF, Novels, ScF&FL 1, –2, ScFSB, SmATA 28[port], TwCCW 78,*

TwCCr&M 80, –85, Who 74, –82, –83, WhoAm 74, –76, –78, –80, –82, WhoWor 74, –82, WrDr 76, –80, –82, –84

Trevor, Meriol 1919- *Au&Wr 71, BioIn 11, ConAu 1R, –1NR, –16NR, IntAu&W 76, –77, –82, IntWWP 77, –82, ScF&FL 1, –2, SmATA 10, TwCCW 78, –83, Who 74, –82, –83, –85, WhoAmW 74, –68, –70, –72, –75, WhoWor 74, –76, WrDr 76, –80, –82, –84, –86*

Trevor, William 1928- *Alli, BiDIrW, BioIn 10, –13, BlueB 76, ConAu X, ConDr 73, –77, –82, ConLC 7, –9, –14, –25[port], ConNov 72, –76, –82, –86, CurBio 84[port], DcIrL, DcIrW 1, DcLB 14[port], DcLEL 1940, IntAu&W 76, –77, –82, –86, IntWW 81, –82, –83, ModBrL S2, –S1, NewC, Novels, OxEng 85, TwCWr, Who 74, –82, –83, –85, WhoWor 74, –76, –84, –87, WorAu, WrDr 76, –80, –82, –84, –86*

Trew, Antony 1906- *ConAu 2NR, –45, EncSoA, ScF&FL 1, –2, WhoSpyF, WrDr 80, –82, –84, –86*

Tribe, Laurence H 1941- *BioIn 13*

Tribe, Laurence Henry 1941- *WhoAm 84, –86, WhoAmL 85*

Tripp, Eleanor B 1936- *BioIn 9, ConAu 29R, SmATA 4*

Trivelpiece, Laurel *DrAP&F 85*

Trivelpiece, Laurel 1926- *SmATA 46*

Trogdon, William Oren 1920- *AmM&WS 73P, –76P, –79P, –82P, –86P, LEduc 74, NewYTBS 76, –78, –80, –82, WhoS&SW 73, –76*

Troise, Joe 1942- *ConAu 103*

Trojanski, John 1943- *ConAu 45*

Troop, Elizabeth 1931- *Au&Wr 71, BioIn 13, ConAu 116, ConDr 82B, DcLB 14[port]*

Tropp, Martin 1945- *ConAu 65*

Trotsky, Leon 1879-1940 *BiDMarx, BioIn 1, –2, –3, –4, –5, –6, –7, –8, –9, –10, –11, –12, –13, CasWL, ConAu 118, CurBio 40, DcAmSR, DcRusL, Film 1, HisEWW, LinLib L, –S, LongCTC, MakMC, McGEWB, REn, TwCLC 22[port], WhScrn 77, –83, WhoHol B, WorAl*

Trotter, Grace V 1900- *AuBYP, BioIn 7, –11, ConAu 1R, –1NR, SmATA 10*

Trotter, Grace V *see also* Paschal, Nancy

Troy, Simon *TwCCr&M 80, –85*

Troyat, Henri 1911- *Who 85, WhoWor 87*

Truax, Carol 1900- *ConAu 5R*

Trudeau, G B 1948- *ConAu 81, SmATA 35[port]*

Trudeau, Garry B *SmATA X*

Trudeau, Garry B 1948- *AuNews 2, ConAu X, ConLC 12, CurBio 75, SmATA 35, WhoAm 78, –80, –82, –84, –86, WhoAmA 84, WorECom, WrDr 76, –80, –82, –84*

Truman, Harry S 1884-1972 *AmAu&B, Au&Wr 71, BiDInt, BiDrAC, BiDrUSE, BioIn 1, –2, –3, –4, –5, –6, –7, –8, –9, –10, –11, –12, –13, ConAu 106, –37R, CurBio 42, –45, –73N, DcAmSR, DcPol, EncAAH, EncAB-H, EncSoH, HisEWW, LinLib L, –S, McGEWB, MemAm, NatCAB 57, NewYTBE 70, –72, ObitOF 79, ObitT 1971, OxAmH, OxAmL, –83, PolProf E, PolProf J, PolProf K, PolProf T, REn, REnAL, UFOEn, WebAB, –79, WhDW, WhAm 5, WhAmP, WhWW-II, WhoGov 72, WorAl*

Truman, Margaret 1924- *BioIn 12, BioNews 74, CelR, ConAu 105, CurBio 50, InWom, NewYTBS 80[port], WhoAm 74, –76, –78, –80, –82, –84, –86, WrDr 86*

Trumbo, Dalton 1905-1976 *AmAu&B, ASpks, BioIn 2, –4, –5, –9, –11, CmCal, ConAu 10NR, –21R, –69,*

ConDr 73, –77A, ConLC 19,
ConNov 72, –76, CurBio 41, –76,
–76N, DcFM, DcLB 26[port], FilmgC,
HalFC 84, IntAu&W 76, –77,
IntMPA 75, –76, NewYTBE 70,
NewYTBS 76, Novels, ObitOF 79,
OxFilm, PolProf T, REnAL,
ScF&FL 1, –2, TwCA, –SUP,
WhAm 7, WhE&EA, WhoAm 74,
–76, –78, WhoThe 81N, WhoWor 76,
WorEFlm, WrDr 76

Trumbull, Robert 1912- *AmAu&B,*
ConAu 5NR, –9R, WhoAm 74, –76,
–78, –80, –82, –84, –86, WhoWor 74,
–76, –78, –80

Trump, Fred 1924- *ConAu 13R*

Trupin, James E 1940- *ConAu 37R*

Truss, Jan 1925- *BioIn 13, ConAu 102,*
SmATA 35, TwCChW 83,
WhoCanL 85, WrDr 86

Tryon, Thomas 1926- *Alli, ASpks,*
AuNews 1, BioIn 10, –11,
BioNews 75, CelR, ConAu 29R,
ConLC 3, –11, Conv 1, CurBio 77,
IntAu&W 76, –77, Novels, ScF&FL 1,
–2, WhoAm 74, –76, –78, –80, –82,
–84, –86, WorAl, WrDr 76, –80, –82,
–84, –86

Tubb, E C 1919- *ConAu 101, –21NR,*
ConSFA, EncSF, IntAu&W 86,
MnBBF, ScF&FL 1, –2, ScFSB,
TwCSFW 86, WhoSciF, WrDr 84,
–86

Tubb, E C *see also* Kern, Gregory

Tuchman, Barbara 1912- *BioIn 13,*
IntAu&W 86, WrDr 86

Tuchman, Barbara W 1912-
OxAmL 83

Tuchman, Barbara Wertheim 1912-
AmAu&B, AmWomWr, Au&Wr 71,
BioIn 6, –10, –11, –12, BlueB 76,
CelR, ConAu 1R, –3NR,
ConIsC 1[port], CurBio 63,
DrAS 74H, –78H, –82H, InWom,
IntAu&W 76, –77, IntWW 74, –75,
–76, –77, –78, –79, –80, –81, –82,
–83, LibW, LinLib L, NewYTBS 78,
–79, OxAmL, WhoAm 74, –76, –78,
–80, –82, –84, –86, WhoAmJ 80,
WhoAmW 74, –58, –61, –64, –66,
–68, –70, –72, –75, –77, –81, –83,
–85, WhoE 74, WhoWor 74, –78, –80,
–82, –87, WhoWorJ 72, –78, WorAl,
WorAu, WrDr 76, –80, –82, –84

Tucker, Glenn 1892-1976 *AmAu&B,*
BioIn 14, ConAu 5R, –69,
IndAu 1917, IntAu&W 76, WhAm 7,
WhoAm 74, –76

Tucker, Wilson 1914- *ConAu 17R,*
ConSFA, IntAu&W 76, ScF&FL 1,
–2, ScFSB, TwCSFW 86, WhoSciF,
WrDr 84, –86

Tuffs, Jack Elsden 1922- *Au&Wr 71,*
ConAu 5R, WrDr 76

Tully, Andrew Frederick, Jr. 1914-
AmAu&B, ConAu 17R, IntAu&W 76,
WhoAm 74, –76, –78, –80, –82, –84,
–86, WrDr 76, –80, –82, –84, –86

Tully, John 1923- *ConAu 12NR*

Tunis, Edwin 1897-1973 *AuBYP,*
BioIn 5, –6, –8, –9, –10, –13,
ChlLR 2, ConAu 5R, –7NR, –45,
IlsCB 1946, –1957, –1967, MorJA,
SmATA 1, –24N, –28[port],
WhoAmA 73, –76N, –78N, –80N,
–82N, –84N

Tunis, John R 1889-1975 *Au&ICB,*
AuBYP, BioIn 4, –6, –7, –8, –10, –12,

ConAu 57, –61, ConLC 12,
DcLB 22[port], LinLib L, MorJA,
NatCAB 58[port], NewYTBS 75,
ObitOF 79, OxChL, REnAL,
SmATA 30, –37, TwCA, –SUP,
TwCCW 78, –83

Tunley, Roul 1912- *AmAu&B,*
ConAu 13R, IntAu&W 86,
WhoAm 74, –76, –78, –80, –82, –84,
–86, WrDr 76, –80, –82, –84

Tunnard, Christopher 1910-1979
AmAu&B, BioIn 5, –11, –12,
ConAu 5R, –6NR, –85, CurBio 59,
–79N, NewYTBS 79, WhAm 7,
WhoAm 74, –76, –78, WhoWor 74

Tuohy, William 1926- *WhoAm 86*

Turgenev, Ivan 1818-1883 *GrFLW*

Turgenev, Ivan S 1818-1883 *AtlBL,*
BbD, BiD&SB, BioIn 1, –2, –3, –4,
–5, –6, –7, –8, –9, –10, –11, –12,
CasWL, ClDMEL, CnThe, CyWA,
DcBiA, DcEuL, DcRusL, Dis&D,
EncWT, EuAu, EvEuW, LinLib L,
McGEWB, McGEWD, –84[port],
NewC, NewEOp 71, NotNAT A, –B,
Novels[port], OxEng, PenC EUR,
PIP&P, RComWL, REn, REnWD,
ScF&FL 1, WhDW, WhoHr&F,
WorAl

Turgenev, Ivan Sergeevich 1818-1883
BioIn 13, HanRL, OxEng 85,
OxThe 83

Turki, Fawaz 1940- *ConAu 41R*

Turley, William S 1943- *ConAu 21NR*

Turnage, Anne Shaw 1927- *ConAu 77*

Turnage, Mac N 1927- *ConAu 77*

Turnbull, Agnes 1888-1982 *AmAu&B,*
AmNov, AmWomWr,
AnObit 1982[port], Au&Wr 71,
AuBYP, BioIn 2, –4, –5, –7, –12,
ConAu 1R, –2NR, –105, InWom,
NewYTBS 82, REnAL, SmATA 14,
TwCA, –SUP, WhE&EA, WhNAA,
WhoAm 74, –76, –78, –80, –82,
WhoAmW 74, –58, –61, –64, –66,
–68, –70, –72

Turnbull, Andrew 1921-1970 *BioIn 8,*
–10, ChhPo S2, ConAu 1R, –3NR,
–25R, DcLEL 1940, DrAS 74H,
–78H, NatCAB 55, NewYTBE 70,
ObitOF 79, WhAm 5

Turnbull, Ann 1943- *BioIn 12,*
ConAu 65, NewYTBS 76, SmATA 18

Turnbull, Bob 1936- *BioIn 10,*
ConAu 14NR, –37R

Turnbull, Colin M 1924-
AmM&WS 73S, –76P, ASpks,
AuNews 1, BioIn 7, –9, –10, –11, –12,
ConAu 1R, –3NR, CurBio 80[port],
WhoAm 82, WorAu 1970

Turnbull, Colin Macmillan 1924-
WhoAm 84, –86

Turnbull, Stephen 1948- *ConAu 20NR,*
WrDr 86

Turner, Alice K 1940- *BioIn 11,*
ConAu 53, SmATA 10, WhoAm 76,
–78, –80, –82

Turner, Alice Kennedy *IntAu&W 86,*
WhoAm 84, –86

Turner, Ann *EncO&P 2*

Turner, Ann W 1945- *BioIn 12,*
ConAu 14NR, –69, SmATA 14

Turner, Darwin T 1931- *BlkAWP,*
ConAu 11NR, –21R, DrAS 74E,
–78E, –82E, InB&W 80, LinLib L,
LivgBAA, SelBAAf, SelBAAu,
WhoAm 74, –76, –78, –80, –82,
WhoBlA 75, –77, –80, –85,

WhoWor 78, WrDr 76, –80, –82, –84,
–86

Turner, Frederick W, III 1937-
ConAu 37R, DrAS 74E

Turner, George Eugene 1925-
ConAu 5NR, –53, WhoS&SW 76, –78

Turner, Kay 1932- *ConAu 69*

Turner, Kermit *DrAP&F 85*

Turner, Kermit 1936- *ConAu 104*

Turner, Philip 1925- *Au&Wr 71,*
BioIn 7, –11, ConAu 11NR, –25R,
FourBJA, IntAu&W 77, –82, OxChL,
SmATA 11, TwCCW 78, –83,
WrDr 80, –82, –84, –86

Turner, Philip *see also* Chance, Stephen

Turner, Richard E 1920- *BioIn 8,*
ConAu 29R

Turner, Susan 1952- *ConAu 106*

Turner, Tina 1938- *Baker 84,*
BioIn 13, WhoRock 81[port]

Turner, Tina 1939- *InB&W 85*

Turner, Tina 1940?- *CurBio 84[port]*

Turner, Tina 1941- *WhoAm 84, –86,*
WhoAmW 87, WhoBlA 85

Turner, William O 1914-
EncFWF[port]

Turner, William Oliver 1914-
Au&Wr 71, AuNews 1, BioIn 10,
BioNews 74, ConAu 1R, –3NR,
IntAu&W 76, –77, –82, WrDr 76

Turngren, Ellen d1964 *AuBYP,*
BioIn 6, –7, –9, ConAu 5R, MinnWr,
SmATA 3

Tusiani, Joseph 1924- *AmAu&B,*
AmCath 80, AuBYP, BkC 6,
ChhPo S2, ConAu 5NR, –9R, –20NR,
DrAS 74F, –82F, IntAu&W 76, –77,
–82, –86, IntWWP 77, ScF&FL 1, –2,
SmATA 45[port], WhoAm 74, –76,
–78, –80, –82, –84, –86

Tuska, Jon 1942- *ConAu 13NR, –73*

Tute, Warren 1914- *Au&Wr 71,*
ConAu 1R, –1NR, IntAu&W 77, –82,
Novels, Who 82, –83, WhoWor 76,
–78, WrDr 76, –80, –82, –84, –86

Tute, Warren Stanley 1914- *Who 85*

Tutko, Thomas Arthur 1931-
AmM&WS 73S, –78S, ConAu 69,
WhoWest 76

Tuttle, Lisa 1952- *ScFSB[port],*
TwCSFW 86, WrDr 86

Tutu, Desmond Mpilo *Who 85*

Tutu, Desmond Mpilo 1931- *AfSS 80,*
–81, –82, BioIn 12, –13, IntWW 81,
–82, –83, NewYTBS 82[port],
Who 82, –83, WhoNob, WhoWor 87

Tuve, George L 1896-1980
AmM&WS 73P, –79P, BioIn 4, –8,
–12, WhoEng 80

Twain, Mark *AmRef, BioIn 13,*
EncFWF, OxAmL 83, OxAmT 84

Twain, Mark 1835-1910 *Alli, –SUP,*
AmAu, AmAu&B, AmBi, AmWr,
AtlBL, AuBYP, BiD&SB, BiDPara,
BiDSA, BioIn 1, –2, –3, –4, –5, –6,
–7, –8, –9, –10, –11, –12, CasWL,
CelCen, Chambr 3, CmCal, CnDAL,
ConAu X, CrtT 3, –4, CyWA,
DcAmAu, DcAmB, DcAmSR,
DcBiPP, DcEnA, –AP, DcEnL,
DcLB 11[port], DcLEL, DcNAA,
Dis&D, EncAAH, EncAB-H, EncMys,
EncSF, EncSoA, EncSoH, EncWL,
EvLB, FamAYP, FilmgC, HalFC 84,
HarEnUS, JBA 34, LinLib LP, –S,
McGEWB, MemAm, ModAL, –S1,
NotNAT B, Novels[port], OxAmH,

OxAmL, OxAusL, OxChL,
OxEng, –85, OxMus, PenC AM,
RAdv 1, RComWL, REn, REnAL,
REnAW, ScF&FL 1, ScFSB[port],
SupFW, TwCCW 78A, –83A,
TwCLC 6[port], –12[port], –19[port],
TwCSFW 86, WebAB, –79,
WebE&AL, WhDW, WhLit,
WhoChL, WhoTwCL, WorAl,
YABC X

Twain, Mark *see also* Clemens, Samuel
Langhorne

Tweedie, Michael Willmer Forbes
1907- *Au&Wr 71*

Tweton, D Jerome 1933- *DrAS 74H,*
–78H, –82H, SmATA 48

Twichell, Chase *DrAP&F 85*

Twiggy 1949- *BioIn 7, –8, –9, –10,*
–11, –12, –13, CelR, ConAu X,
ConTFT 3, CurBio 68, FilmgC,
GoodHs, HalFC 84, InWom,
IntMPA 77, –75, –76, –78, –79, –81,
–82, –84, –86, NewYTBS 83[port],
Who 85, WhoAm 74, –76, –78, –80,
–84, –86, WhoHol A, WorAl

Twiggy *see also* Hornby, Leslie

Twist, Ananias *ConAu X,*
IntAu&W 76X, –82X, WrDr 76, –80,
–82, –84, –86

Twist, Ananias *see also* Nunn, William
Curtis

Twombly, Wells 1935-1977 *BioIn 11,*
ConAu 41R, –69, NewYTBS 77,
WhAm 7, WhoAm 76, WhoWest 74,
–76

Twyman, Gib 1943- *ConAu X*

Tydeman, William 1935- *ConAu 119,*
WrDr 86

Tyler, Anne *DrAP&F 85*

Tyler, Anne 1941- *AmWomWr,*
BioIn 10, –11, –12, –13, ConAu 9R,
ConLC 7, –11, –18, –28[port],
–44[port], ConNov 72, –76, –82, –86,
CurBio 81[port], DcLB 6,
–Y82A[port], DcLEL 1940,
IntAu&W 76, –77, ModAL S2,
NewYTBS 77, OxAmL 83, SmATA 7,
WhoAm 76, –78, –80, –82, –84, –86,
WhoAmW 74, –68, –70, –72, –75,
–79, –81, –83, –85, –87, WhoE 74,
–75, –77, WorAu 1970, WrDr 76,
–80, –82, –84, –86

Tyler, Hamilton A 1917- *ConAu 5NR,*
–9R

Tyler-Whittle, Michael 1927-
Au&Wr 71, ConAu 4NR, –5R,
IntAu&W 77, –86, WrDr 76, –80,
–82, –84, –86

Tyll, Al *AuBYP SUP*

Tynan, Kathleen 1940- *BioIn 8, –11,*
ConAu 97, IntAu&W 82

Tynan, Kenneth 1927-1980
AnObit 1980[port], BiE&WWA,
BioIn 3, –5, –6, –7, –8, –9, –10, –11,
–12, –13, BlueB 76, ConAu 101,
–13R, CroCD, CurBio 63, –80N,
DcLEL 1940, EncWT, IntAu&W 76,
–77, IntWW 74, –75, –76, –77, –78,
–79, –80, –81N, LinLib L, LongCTC,
ModBrL, NewC, NewYTBS 80[port],
NotNAT, OxAmT 84, PenC ENG,
WhAm 7, WhScrn 83, Who 74,
WhoThe 72, –77, –81, –81N,
WhoWor 74, –78, –80, WorAu,
WrDr 76, –80

Tynan, Kenneth Peacock 1927-1980
DcNaB 1971, OxEng 85, OxThe 83

U

Uttley, Alison 1884-1976 *Au&Wr 71,*
AuBYP, BioIn 3, −8, −10, −12,
ChhPo, ConAu 65, −X, DcLEL,
IntAu&W 76, LongCTC, OxChL,
OxEng 85, ScF&FL 1, SmATA 3, −X,
TelT, TwCCW 78, −83, WhE&EA,
Who 74, WhoChL, WrDr 76
Uttley, Alison *see also* Uttley, Alice
Jane

V

Vaeth, Joseph Gordon 1921- *BioIn 12, ConAu 5R, SmATA 17, WhoAm 74, –76, –78, –80, –82, –84, –86, WhoGov 72, –75, WhoS&SW 73, WhoWor 74*

Vaizey, John 1929- *Au&Wr 71, BioIn 6, –7, –10, ConAu 4NR, –5R, CurBio 64, DcLEL 1940, IntAu&W 77, –82, IntWW 74, –75, –76, –77, –78, –79, –80, –81, Who 74, WhoWor 74, WrDr 76, –80, –82, –84*

Vaizey, John 1929-1984 *ConAu 113*

Vaizey, Marina 1938- *ConAu 116, IntAu&W 82, –86, WhoArt 80, –82, –84, WrDr 86*

Valdes, Joan 1931- *ConAu 49*

Valdez, Luis 1940- *BioIn 10, –12, ChiSch, ConAu 101, ConDr 82, WhoThe 81, WrDr 84, –86*

Valencak, Hannelore *ConAu X, IntAu&W 77X, –82X, –86X*

Valencak, Hannelore 1929- *SmATA 42[port]*

Valens, Evans G *ConAu 14NR*

Valens, Evans G 1920- *AuBYP, BioIn 7, –9, ChhPo S2, ConAu 3NR, –5R, –81, SmATA 1, WhoAm 80, –82, WhoWest 76, –78*

Valens, Evans Gladstone 1920- *WhoAm 84, –86*

Valenti, Jack 1921- *BioIn 6, –7, –8, –10, –11, BlueB 76, BusPN, CelR, ConAu 73, CurBio 68, DrRegL 75, FilmgC, HalFC 84, IntMPA 77, –75, –76, –78, –79, –81, –82, –84, IntWW 74, –75, –76, –77, –78, –79, –80, –81, –82, –83, LesBEnT, NewYTBS 82[port], NewYTET, PolProf J, WhoAm 74, –76, –78, –80, –82, WhoGov 72, –75, WhoLab 76, WhoS&SW 73, WhoWor 74, –78, –80, –82, WorAl*

Valenti, Jack J 1921- *IntMPA 86*

Valenti, Jack Joseph 1921- *BioIn 13, WhoAm 84, –86, WhoE 85, WhoWor 84, –87*

Valentine, James Cheyne 1935- *ConAu 45*

Valentine, James Cheyne *see also* Valentine, Tom

Valentine, Tom 1935- *ConAu X*

Valentine, Tom *see also* Valentine, James Cheyne

Valeriani, Richard G 1932- *EncTwCJ*

Valeriani, Richard Gerard 1932- *ConAu 65, WhoAm 74, –76, –78, –80, –82, –84, –86, WhoS&SW 73*

Valette, Jean Paul 1937- *WhoE 85, WhoWor 87, DrAS 74F, –78F, –82F*

Valgardson, W D *DrAP&F 85*

Valgardson, W D 1939- *CaW, ConAu 41R, OxCanL*

Valin, Jonathan Louis 1948- *ConAu 101*

Valladares, Armando *NewYTBS 86[port]*

Valladares, Armando 1937?- *BioIn 13*

Vallee, Jacques F 1939- *ConAu 10NR, –17R, EncO&P 2, Future, UFOEn[port]*

VanAtta, Winfred 1910- *ConAu 1R, –1NR, IntAu&W 76*

VanBrunt, H L *DrAP&F 85*

VanBrunt, H L 1936- *ConAu 49, WhoE 77, –79*

VanBuren, Abigail *ConAu X*

VanBuren, Abigail 1918- *AmAu&B, BioIn 4, –5, –8, –12, CelR, ConAu X, CurBio 60, EncAJ, EncTwCJ, ForWC 70, GoodHs, InWom, LibW, WhoAm 74, –76, –78, –80, –82, –84, –86, WhoAmJ 80, WhoAmW 74, –58, –61, –64, –66, –68, –70, –72, –75, –77, –79, –81, –83, –85, WorAl*

Vance, Jack *ConAu X, DrmM 2, IntAu&W 86X*

Vance, Jack 1916?- *AmAu&B, BioIn 12, ConAu X, ConLC 35, ConSFA, DcLB 8, EncSF, IntAu&W 77, Novels, ScF&FL 1, –2, SupFW, TwCSFW 86, WhoHr&F, WhoSciF, WrDr 76, –80, –82, –84, –86*

Vance, Jack 1920- *ScFSB*

Vance, Jack *see also* Vance, John Holbrook

Vance, John Holbrook *WhoAm 84, –86, WrDr 86*

Vance, John Holbrook 1916?- *BioIn 12, ConAu 17NR, –29R, EncMys, IntAu&W 86, LinLib L, TwCCr&M 80, –85, WhoAm 82, WrDr 82, –84*

Vance, John Holbrook *see also* Vance, Jack

Vandenberg, Philipp 1941- *ConAu 8NR, –61*

VanDerPost, Laurens 1906- *Au&Wr 71, BioIn 4, –8, –9, –10, BlueB 76, CasWL, ConAu 5R, ConLC 5, ConNov 72, –76, –82, –86, DcLEL, EncSoA, IntAu&W 76, –77, –82, IntWW 74, –75, –76, –77, –78, –79, –80, –81, –82, –83, LinLib L, LongCTC, ModCmwL, Novels, PenC ENG, REn, TwCWr, Who 74, –82, –83, WhoAm 74, –76, –78, WhoWor 74, –76, –78, WorAu, WrDr 76, –80, –82, –84, –86*

VanDerPost, Sir Laurens 1906- *BioIn 13, Who 85*

VanDerPost, Sir Laurens Jan 1906- *OxEng 85*

VanDersal, William Richard 1907- *AmM&WS 73P, –76P, –79P, ConAu 77, IntAu&W 82, WhoGov 72*

VanDerVeer, Judy 1912-1982 *BioIn 9, –13, ChhPo, –S1, ConAu 108, –33R, SmATA 33N, –4, WhNAA*

Vandervelde, Marjorie 1908- *ConAu 10NR, –21R*

VanDeWater, Frederic F 1890-1968 *AmNov, BioIn 2, –4, –8, ConAu 110, REnAL, TwCA SUP, WhAm 5, WhNAA*

VanDeWetering, Janwillem 1931- *ConAu 4NR, –49, Novels, TwCCr&M 80B, –85*

Vandivert, Rita 1905- *BioIn 12, ConAu 5R, –6NR, SmATA 21[port], WhoAmW 74, –68, –70, –72, –75, WhoE 74, –75*

VanDoren, Mark 1894-1972 *AmAu&B, Au&Wr 71, BiDAmEd, BiE&WWA, BioIn 1, –3, –4, –5, –7, –8, –9, –10, –12, CasWL, ChhPo, –S1, –S2, –S3, CnDAL, CnE&AP, ConAmA, ConAu 1R, –3NR, –37R, ConLC 6, –10, ConNov 72, ConPo 70, CurBio 40, –73, –73N, DcLB 45[port], DcLEL, EvLB, IntAu&W 76, –77, LinLib L, LongCTC, ModAL, –S1, NewYTBE 72, Novels, ObitOF 79, OxAmL, –83, PenC AM, RAdv 1, REn, REnAL, ScF&FL 1, –2, SixAP, TwCA, –SUP, TwCWr, WebAB, –79, WhAm 5, WhE&EA, WhNAA, WorAl*

VanDuyn, Janet 1910- *BioIn 12, ConAu 69, SmATA 18*

VanDuyn, Mona *DrAP&F 85*

VanDuyn, Mona 1921- *AmAu&B, BioIn 12, ConAu 7NR, –9R, ConLC 3, –7, ConPo 70, –75, –80, –85, DcLB 5[port], IntWWP 77X, WhoAm 76, –78, –80, –82, WorAu 1970, WrDr 76, –80, –82, –84, –86*

VanDyke, Henry 1852-1933 *Alli SUP, AmAu&B, AmBi, ApCAB, ApCAB X, BbD, BiDAmM, BiD&SB, BioIn 1, –2, –5, –6, –11, Chambr 3, ChhPo, –S1, –S2, –S3, ConAmL, DcAmAu, DcAmB, DcAmReB, DcNAA, EvLB, HarEnUS, JBA 34, LinLib L, –S, LongCTC, NatCAB 7, –25, OxAmL 83, REnAL, ScF&FL 1, Str&VC, TwCA, –SUP, TwCBDA, WhAm 1, WhLit, WhNAA*

VanDyke, Henry *see also* Dyke, Henry Van

VanEvery, Dale 1896- *EncFWF*

VanEvery, Dale 1896-1976 *AmAu&B, AmNov, BioIn 2, –4, ConAu 1R, –3NR, REnAW, WhAm 7, WhoAm 74, –76*

VanGelder, Richard G 1928- *AmM&WS 73P, –76P, –79P, –82P, AuBYP SUP, ConAu 73, WhoAm 74, –76, –78, –80, –82, WhoWor 74*

VanGelder, Richard George 1928- *AmM&WS 86P, WhoAm 84, –86*

VanGulik, Robert H 1910-1967 *Au&Wr 71, ConAu 1R, –3NR, –25R, EncMys, ObitOF 79, TwCCr&M 80B, –85B*

VanGulik, Robert H *see also* Gulik, Robert Hans Van

VanIterson, S R *BioIn 13, ConAu 102, SmATA 26[port]*

VanLawick, Hugo 1937- *AuBYP SUP, ConAu 85, IntAu&W 77, WrDr 76, –80, –82, –84, –86*

VanLawick-Goodall, Jane 1934- *ASpks, BioIn 8, –9, –10, –11, –12, ConAu 45, –X, CurBio 67, InWom, LinLib L*

VanLawick-Goodall, Jane *see also* Goodall, Jane

VanLeeuwen, Jean 1937- *BioIn 10, ConAu 11NR, –25R, FifBJA[port], SmATA 6, WhoAmW 74, –75*

VanLhin, Erik *ConAu X*

VanLhin, Erik 1915- *EncSF, ScF&FL 1, SmATA X*

VanLhin, Erik *see also* DelRey, Lester

VanLoon, Hendrik Willem 1882-1944 *AmAu&B, AnCL, AuBYP, BioIn 1, –2, –3, –4, –7, –8, –9, –12, ChhPo S2, ConAmA, ConAmL, ConAu 117, CurBio 44, DcAmB S3, DcLEL, DcNAA, JBA 34, LinLib L, –S, LongCTC, NatCAB 33, Newb 1922, ObitOF 79, OxAmL, –83, REn, REnAL, ScF&FL 1, SmATA 18, TwCA, –SUP, WhAm 2, WhLit, WhNAA*

VanLustbader, Eric *EncSF*

VanNess, Bethann Faris 1902- *WhoAmW 66, –70, –72*

VanOrden, M D 1921- *AuBYP SUP, ConAu 37R, SmATA 4, WhoOcn 78*

VanOver, Raymond 1934- *ConAu 112, IntAu&W 76, –77, –82, –86*

VanRensselaer, Alexander 1892-1962 *AuBYP, BioIn 6, –8, –12, ConAu 73, EncAB 33, SmATA 14*

VanRjndt, Philippe 1950- *BioIn 11, ConAu 14NR, –65, WrDr 80, –82, –84, –86*

VanScyoc, Sydney J 1939- *ConAu 15NR, –89, EncSF, ScF&FL 1, –2, ScFSB, TwCSFW 86, WrDr 84*

VanSteenwyk, Elizabeth Ann 1928- *AuBYP SUP, ConAu 101, SmATA 34[port]*

VanTuyl, Barbara 1940- *BioIn 11, ConAu 53, SmATA 11*

VanVogt, A E *OxCanL*

VanVogt, A E 1912- *ConAu 21R, ConSFA, DcLB 8[port], EncSF, IntAu&W 76, –77, LinLib L, Novels, ScF&FL 1, –2, ScFSB[port], SmATA 14, TwCSFW 86, WhoSciF, WrDr 84, –86*

VanVogt, Alfred Elton 1912-
*AmAu&B, AmNov, Au&Wr 71,
BioIn 2, -4, -7, -10, -12,
CanWW 70, -79, -80, -81, -83,
CnMWL, ConAu 21R, ConLC 1,
IntAu&W 82, -86, REnAL,
TwCA SUP, WhoAm 82, -84, -86,
WhoWest 78, -80, -82, WorAl*

VanVoris, Jacqueline 1922- *ConAu 57*

VanWormer, Joe *SmATA X*

VanWormer, Joe 1913- *ConAu X,
IntAu&W 77X, SmATA 35*

Vardaman, James M 1921- *ConAu 104*

Varley, H Paul 1931- *ConAu 77*

Varley, John 1947- *BioIn 13,
ConAu 69, DcLB Y81B[port], EncSF,
PostFic, ScFSB, TwCSFW 86,
WhoAm 80, -82, WrDr 84, -86*

Vasquez, Richard *BioIn 8, ChiSch,
DrAP&F 85*

Vasquez, Richard 1928- *ChiLit*

Vaughan, Harold Cecil 1923-
*BioIn 12, ConAu 29R, SmATA 14,
WhoE 75*

Vaughn, Ruth 1935- *BioIn 12,
ConAu 15NR, -41R, IntAu&W 76,
-77, SmATA 14, WhoAmW 77,
WhoS&SW 78*

Vecsey, George 1939- *BioIn 11,
ConAu 10NR, -61, SmATA 9*

Veder, Bob 1940- *ConAu 104*

Veglahn, Nancy 1937- *AuBYP,
BioIn 8, -10, ConAu 7NR, -17R,
SmATA 5*

Velie, Lester 1907- *BioIn 1,
ConAu P-2, WhoAm 74, -76, -78,
-80, -82, -84, -86*

Vendler, Helen Hennessy 1933-
*AmWomWr, BioIn 12, ConAu 41R, DrAS 74E,
-78E, -82E, IntAu&W 77, -86,
WhoAm 74, -76, -78, -80, -82, -84,
-86, WhoAmW 83, -85, -87,
WrDr 82, -84*

Venturo, Betty Lou Baker 1928-
AuBYP, ConAu 1R, ThrBJA

Venturo, Betty Lou Baker *see also*
Baker, Betty

Verdick, Mary 1923- *ConAu 1R,
-4NR*

Vergara, William C 1923-
*AmM&WS 73P, -79P, -82P,
ConAu 1R, WhoE 77, -79,
WhoTech 82, -84*

Vergara, William Charles 1923-
AmM&WS 86P

Vermes, Hal G d1965 *AuBYP, BioIn 7*

Verne, Jules 1828-1905 *AtlBL,
AuBYP, BbD, BiD&SB, BioIn 1, -2,
-3, -4, -5, -6, -7, -8, -9, -10, -11,
-12, -13, CarSB, CasWL, CelCen,
ConAu 110, CyWA, DcBiA, DcBiPP,
DcCathB, DcEnL, DcEuL, Dis&D,
EncSF, EuAu, EvEuW, FilmgC,
HalFC 84, JBA 34, -51, LinLib L,
-LP, -S, LongCEL, LongCTC,
McGEWB, MnBBF, NewC, Novels,
OxChL, OxEng, -85, OxFr, OxShips,
PenC EUR, REn, ScF&FL 1,
ScFSB[port], SmATA 21[port],
TwCLC 6[port], TwCSFW 86A,
WhDW, WhoBW&I A, WhoChL,
WhoSciF, WorAl*

Vernon, John *DrAP&F 85*

Vernon, Louise A 1914- *BioIn 12,
ConAu 53, SmATA 14*

Versace, Marie Teresa Rios 1917-
ConAu 17R, SmATA 2

Versace, Marie Teresa Rios *see also*
Rios, Tere

Verschuur, Gerrit L 1937-
AmM&WS 86P

Veryan, Patricia *ConAu X,
IntAu&W 86X*

Veryan, Patricia 1923- *WrDr 84, -86*

Vestal, Stanley *OxAmL 83*

Vestal, Stanley 1887-1957 *AmAu&B,
BioIn 4, CnDAL, OxAmL, REn,
REnAL, REnAW, TwCA, -SUP,
WhE&EA, WhNAA*

Vestal, Stanley *see also* Campbell,
Walter Stanley

Vickers, Roy 1888?-1965 *Au&Wr 71,
EncMys, MnBBF, TwCCr&M 80,
WhE&EA*

Vickers, Roy C 1888?-1965
TwCCr&M 85

Victor, Joan Berg 1937- *BioIn 8,
ConAu 105, IlsBYP, IlsCB 1957,
-1967, SmATA 30[port]*

Vidal, Gore *DrAP&F 85,
TwCCr&M 85*

Vidal, Gore 1925- *AmAu&B, AmNov,
ASpks, AuNews 1, BiE&WWA,
BioIn 2, -3, -4, -5, -6, -7, -8, -9,
-10, -11, -12, -13, BioNews 74,
BlueB 76, CasWL, CelR, CnMD,
ConAu 5R, -13NR, ConDr 73, -77,
-82, ConLC 2, -4, -6, -8, -10,
-22[port], -33[port], ConNov 72, -76,
-82, -86, ConTFT 3, CroCD,
CurBio 65, -83[port], DcLB 6[port],
DcLEL 1940, EncMys, EncSF,
EncWL, -2, EncWT, IntAu&W 76,
-77, IntWW 74, -75, -76, -77, -78,
-79, -80, -81, -82, -83, LinLib L,
LongCTC, MakMC, McGEWD, -84,
ModAL S2, ModWD,
NatPD 81[port], NewYTBS 76,
NotNAT, -A, Novels[port],
OxAmL, -83, OxAmT 84, PenC AM,
RAdv 1, REn, REnAL, ScF&FL 1,
-2, ScFSB[port], TwCA SUP,
TwCCr&M 80, TwCSFW 86, TwCWr,
TwCWr, WebAB, -79, WebE&AL,
Who 74, -82, -83, -85, WhoAm 74,
-76, -78, -80, -82, -84, -86,
WhoSpyF, WhoTw 72, -77, -81,
WhoTwCL, WhoWor 74, WorAl,
WorEFlm, WrDr 76, -80, -82, -84,
-86*

Viertel, Joseph *DrAP&F 85*

Viertel, Joseph 1915- *BioIn 3,
ConAu 13R, IntAu&W 77, -86,
St&PR 75, WhoF&I 85,
WhoS&SW 75, -76, WrDr 76, -80,
-82, -84, -86*

Villarreal, Jose Antonio 1924- *ChiLit,
ChiSch*

Villas Boas, Claudio 1916-
*ConAu 117, IntWW 74, -75, -76,
-77, -78, -79, -80, -81, -82, -83*

Villas Boas, Orlando 1914-
*ConAu 117, IntWW 74, -75, -76,
-77, -78, -79, -80, -81, -82, -83*

Villet, Barbara 1931- *ConAu 85*

Villiard, Paul 1910-1974 *AuBYP SUP,
BioIn 10, -12, ConAu 10NR, -53,
ConAu P-2, SmATA 20N*

Villiers, Alan John 1903-1982
*Au&Wr 71, AuBYP, BioIn 1, -4, -7,
-10, -11, -13, BlueB 76, ConAu 1R,
-1NR, DcLEL, EvLB, IntAu&W 76,
-77, IntWW 74, -75, -76, -77, -78,
-79, -80, -81, -82N, LinLib L,
LongCTC, OxShips, SingR 1,
SmATA 10, TwCA, -SUP, TwCWr,
WhE&EA, WhNAA, Who 74, -82,
-83N, WhoAm 74, WhoWor 74, -76,
-78, WrDr 80, -82*

Vine, Louis L 1922- *ConAu 1R, -3NR,
IntAu&W 77*

Vinge, Joan D 1948- *ConAu 93,
ConLC 30[port], DrmM 2[port],
EncSF, SmATA 36, TwCSFW 86,
WrDr 84, -86*

Vinge, Vernor 1944- *ScFSB,
TwCSFW 86, WrDr 84, -86*

Vining, Elizabeth Gray 1902-
*AmAu&B, AmWomWr, AuBYP,
BioIn 1, -2, -3, -4, -5, -7, -10, -11,
ConAu 5R, -7NR, InWom,
IntAu&W 76, JBA 51, SmATA 6,
TwCCW 78, -83, WhoAm 74, -76,
-78, -80, -82, -84, -86,
WhoAmW 74, -58, -68, -70, -72,
-75, WrDr 80, -82, -84, -86*

Vining, Elizabeth Gray *see also* Gray,
Elizabeth Janet

Vinson, James 1933- *ConAu 118, -120*

Vinson, Kathryn 1911- *BioIn 12,
ConAu 5R, IntAu&W 77X,
SmATA 21[port], WrDr 76, -80, -82,
-84, -86*

Viola, Herman J 1938-
*AmM&WS 73S, -76P, ConAu 8NR,
-61, DrAS 74H, -78H, -82H,
IntAu&W 82, WhoAm 74, -76, -78,
-80, -82, WhoGov 77, WhoLibI 82*

Viola, Herman Joseph 1938-
WhoAm 84, -86

Viorst, Milton 1930- *BioIn 12,
ConAu 9R, IntAu&W 86, WhoAm 74,
-76, -78, -80, -82, -84, -86,
WhoS&SW 73, -75, -76, WrDr 82,
-84, -86*

Vipont, Charles *WrDr 86*

Vipont, Charles 1902- *ConAu X,
IntAu&W 76X, -77X, -82X,
WhoChL, WrDr 76, -80, -82, -84*

Vipont, Charles *see also* Foulds, Elfrida
Vipont

Vipont, Elfrida *WrDr 86*

Vipont, Elfrida 1902- *Au&Wr 71,
BioIn 2, -8, ChhPo S1, ConAu X,
IntAu&W 76X, -77X, -82X, OxChL,
TwCCW 78, -83, WhoChL, WrDr 76,
-80, -82, -84*

Vipont, Elfrida *see also* Foulds, Elfrida
Vipont

Virgines, George E 1920-
ConAu 12NR, -25R

Viscardi, Henry 1912- *BioIn 2, -3, -7,
-9, ConAu 5R, -5NR, CurBio 54,
-66, NewYTBE 72, WhoAm 74, -76,
-78, -80, WhoE 74*

Viscott, David S 1938- *AuNews 1,
BiDrAPA 77, BioIn 9, -10,
ConAu 29R, IntAu&W 76, -77,
WrDr 76, -80, -82, -84, -86*

Vizenor, Gerald 1934- *BioIn 12,
ConAu 5NR, -13R, IntWWP 77*

Vlahos, Olivia 1924- *ConAu 21R,
SmATA 31[port]*

Vliet, R G 1929- *ConAu 37R,
ConLC 22[port], ConPo 75, -80,
WrDr 76, -80, -82, -84, -86*

Vliet, R G 1929-1984 *BioIn 13,
ConAu 112, -18NR*

Voelker, John Donaldson 1903-
*AmAu&B, BioIn 4, -5, -10,
BlueB 76, ConAu 1R, IntAu&W 76X,
-77X, MichAu 80, WhoAm 74, -76,
-78, WorAu, WrDr 76, -80, -82, -84*

Vogel, Ezra F 1930- *AmM&WS 73S,
-78S, ConAu 13R, IntAu&W 76,
-78, -80, -82, -84, -86*

Vogel, John H 1950- *BioIn 12,
ConAu 77, SmATA 18*

Vogelman, Joyce 1936- *ConAu 106*

Vogelsang, Arthur *DrAP&F 85*

Vogelsang, Arthur 1942- *ConAu 49*

Vogelsinger, Hubert 1938-
ConAu 25R, WhoE 74, -75, -77

Vogt, Gregory *SmATA 45*

Voight, Virginia Frances 1909-
*AuBYP, BioIn 6, -8, -11,
ConAu 2NR, -5R, -18NR, MorJA,
SmATA 8*

Voigt, Cynthia 1942- *BioIn 13,
ChlLR 13[port], ConAu 106, -18NR,
ConLC 30[port], FifBJA[port],
SmATA 33, -48[port], WhoAm 84,
-86, WrDr 86*

Voinovich, Vladimir 1932?- *BioIn 10,
-11, -13, ConAu 81, ConFLW 84,
ConLC 10, IntWW 83, NewYTBS 77,
TwCWr*

Voinovich, Vladimir Nikolaevich 1932-
*HanRL, IntAu&W 86,
WorAu 1975[port]*

Volpe, Edmond L 1922- *BlueB 76,
ConAu 1R, -1NR, DrAS 74E, -78E,
-82E, LEduc 74, WhoAm 74, -76,
-78, -80, -82, WhoE 83, WrDr 76,
-80, -82, -84, -86*

Volpe, Edmond Loris 1922-
WhoAm 84, -86

Voltaire **1694-1778** *AsBiEn, AtlBL,
BiDPsy, CasWL, CnThe, DcEnL,
DcEuL, Dis&D, EncSF, EncWT,
EuWr 4, EvEuW, GrFLW,
LinLib LP, LongCEL, LuthC 75,
McGEWB, McGEWD, -84[port],
NamesHP, NewC, NewEOp 71,
Novels, OxEng, -85, OxMus,
OxThe, -83, PenC EUR, RComWL,
REn, REnWD, ScF&FL 1,
ScFSB[port]*

Voltaire, Francois Marie Arouet De
1694-1778 *BioIn 13, BbD, BiD&SB,
BioIn 1, -2, -3, -4, -5, -6, -7, -8, -9,*

-10, -11, -12, CyEd, CyWA, DcBiA,
DcBiPP, DcScB, EuAu, InSci,
NotNAT B, OxCan, OxFr, OxGer,
WhDW, WorAl*

VonAlmedingen, Martha Edith
ConAu X, SmATA 3

VonAlmedingen, Martha Edith *see also*
Almedingen, E M

VonBraun, Wernher 1912-1977
*AmAu&B, AmM&WS 73P, -76P,
-79P, BiESc, BioIn 2, -3, -4, -5, -6,
-7, -8, -9, -10, -11, -12, BlueB 76,
CelR, ConAu 5R, -9NR, -69,
CurBio 52, -77N, InSci, LinLib S,
McGEWB, McGMS 80[port],
ObitOF 79, PolProf E, PolProf K,
ScF&FL 1, -2, WebAB, -79,
WhAm 7, Who 74, WhoAm 74, -76,
WhoS&SW 73, WhoWor 74, WhoWor 76*

VonBraun, Wernher *see also* Braun,
Wernher Von

VonDaeniken, Erich 1935- *AuNews 1,
BioNews 75, ConAu 17NR, -37R*

VonDaeniken, Erich *see also*
VonDaniken, Erich

VonDamm, Helene A 1938-
*WhoAm 82, -84, WhoAmP 81, -83,
WhoAmW 83, WhoWor 84*

VonDaniken, Erich 1935-
*AuBYP SUP, AuNews 1, BioIn 10,
-11, -12, BioNews 75, ConAu X,
ConLC 30[port], CurBio 76,
EncO&P 2, -78S1, EncSF,
IntAu&W 77, UFOEn[port],
WhoSciF, WhoWor 82, WorAl*

VonDaniken, Erich *see also*
VonDaeniken, Erich

VonFrisch, Karl *ConAu X*

VonFrisch, Karl 1886- *WhoAm 84,
WhoWor 84, -87*

VonFrisch, Karl 1886-1982
*AnObit 1982[port], Au&Wr 71,
ConAu 107, CurBio 74, WhAm 7,
Who 82, -83N, WhoAm 76, -78, -80,
-82, WhoNob, WhoWor 74, -76, -78,
-80, -82*

VonFrisch, Otto 1929- *ConAu 101*

VonHagen, Victor Wolfgang 1908-
*AmAu&B, Au&Wr 71, AuBYP,
BioIn 3, -4, -5, -8, -13, ConAu 105,
CurBio 42, IntAu&W 77, REnAL,
SmATA 29[port], TwCA SUP,
WhE&EA, Who 74, -82, -83, -85,
WhoAm 74, -76, -78, WhoWor 74,
WrDr 76, -80, -82, -84, -86*

VonHoffman, Nicholas 1929-
*AmAu&B, BioIn 8, -10, CelR,
ConAu 81, EncAJ, EncTwCJ,
IntAu&W 82, WhoAm 74, -76, -78,
-80, -82, -84, -86, WhoS&SW 73,
-75, -76*

Vonnegut, Kurt *DrAP&F 85*

Vonnegut, Kurt 1922- *AmWr S2,
BioIn 13, ModAL S2, OxEng 85,
PostFic, ScFSB[port]*

Vonnegut, Kurt, Jr. 1922- *AmAu&B,
ASpks, Au&Wr 71, AuNews 1,
BioIn 2, -8, -9, -10, -11, -12,
BlueB 76, CasWL, CelR, ConAu X,
-1NR, ConDr 77, -82, ConLC 1, -2,
-3, -4, -5, -8, -12, -22[port],
-40[port], ConNov 72, -76, -82, -86,
ConSFA, CurBio 70, DcLB 2,
-8[port], -DS3[port], -Y80A[port],
DcLEL 1940, EncAB-H, EncSF,
EncWL, -2, IndAu 1917,
IntAu&W 76, -77, IntWW 74, -75,
-76, -77, -78, -79, -80, -81, -82,
-83, LinLib L, -S, MakMC,
ModAL S1, MugS, NatPD, -81[port],
NewYTBE 70, -71, Novels,
OxAmL 83, PenC AM, RAdv 1,
ScF&FL 1, -2, TwCSFW 86,
WebAB, -79, WebE&AL, Who 83,
-85, WhoAm 74, -76, -78, -80, -82,
-84, -86, WhoSciF, WhoSpyF,
WhoTwCL, WhoWor 74, -76, -78,
-80, -82, -84, -87, WorAl, WorAu,
WrDr 76, -80, -82, -84, -86*

Vonnegut, Mark 1947- *AuNews 2,
BioIn 10, -11, -12, ConAu 65*

VonStaden, Wendelgard 1925-
BioIn 12, ConAu 110

VonStorch, Anne B 1910- *BioIn 9,
ConAu 29R, ConAu P-2, SmATA 1*
VonStorch, Anne B *see also*
Malcolmson, Anne
Vorwald, Alan *AuBYP, BioIn 8*
Voss, Carl Hermann 1910- *AmAu&B,
BlueB 76, ConAu 10NR, –21R,
IntAu&W 76, –77, –82, –86,*

*WhoAm 74, –76, –78, –80, –82, –84,
–86, WhoWor 80*
Voss, Carroll A Schell 1899-
*ForWC 70, WhoAmW 74, –66, –68,
–70, –72, WhoMW 74*
Voyle, Mary *AuBYP, BioIn 11,
ConAu X, DcLEL 1940,*

*IntAu&W 76X, –77X, –82X,
SmATA X, WorAu*
Voyle, Mary *see also* Manning,
Rosemary
Vreeland, Herbert Harold, III 1920-
AmM&WS 73S, –76P
Vrettos, Theodore 1919- *ConAu 13R*

Vroman, Mary Elizabeth 1923-1967
*BioIn 7, BlkAWP, ConAu 109,
DcAfL, InB&W 80, SelBAAf,
SelBAAu*
Vroman, Mary Elizabeth 1924?-1967
DcLB 33[port]

W

Waddell, Martin 1941- *ConAu 113, IntAu&W 86, SmATA 43[port]*
Wade, Barrie 1939- *WhoWor 87*
Wade, Graham 1940- *ConAu 107, IntAu&W 86*
Wade, Henry William 1918- *WrDr 86*
Wade, Henry William Rawson 1918- *BlueB 76, ConAu 109, Who 74, –82, –83, –85, WhoWor 80, WrDr 80, –82, –84*
Wade, Henry William Rawson *see also* Wade, William
Wade, Nicholas 1942- *ConAu 16NR, –77*
Wade, William 1918- *ConAu 1R, –4NR*
Wade, William *see also* Wade, Henry William Rawson
Wade, Wyn Craig 1944- *ConAu 103*
Wagenheim, Kal 1935- *BioIn 12, ConAu 29R, SmATA 21*
Wagenknecht, Edward 1900- *AmAu&B, BioIn 4, BlueB 76, ConAu 1R, 6NR, DrAS 74E, –78E, –82E, IntAu&W 76, –77, –82, –86, REn, REnAL, ScF&FL 1, –2, TwCA SUP, WhE&EA, WhoAm 74, –76, –78, –80, –82, –84, –86, WrDr 76, –80, –82, –84, –86*
Wagenvoord, James 1937- *ConAu 41R*
Wagner, Frederick 1928- *AuBYP, BioIn 7, ConAu 5R*
Wagner, Sharon 1936- *BioIn 9, ConAu 10NR, –25R, IntAu&W 77, ScF&FL 1, WhoAmW 74, –75, WrDr 76, –80, –82, –84*
Wagoner, David *DrAP&F 85*
Wagoner, David 1926- *AmAu&B, BioIn 3, –10, –12, ConAu 1R, –2NR, ConAu 3AS[port], ConLC 3, –5, –15, ConNov 72, –76, –82, –86, ConPo 70, –75, –80, –85, CroCAP, DcLB 5, DcLEL 1940, DrAS 74E, –78E, –82E, IntAu&W 76, –77, IntWWP 77, LinLib L, OxAmL 83, SmATA 14, WhoAm 74, –76, –78, –80, –82, WhoPNW, WhoWor 78, WorAu, WrDr 76, –80, –82, –84, –86*
Wagoner, David Russell 1926- *WhoAm 84, –86*
Wahl, Jan 1933- *AuBYP, BioIn 8, –9, ConAu 12NR, –25R, SmATA 2, –34[port], SmATA 3AS[port], ThrBJA, TwCCW 78, –83, WhoAm 82, WrDr 80, –82, –84, –86*
Wahlgren, Erik 1911- *WhoAm 84, –86, WhoWor 84, –87*
Wahloo, Per 1926-1975 *BioIn 9, –10, ConAu 57, –61, ConLC 7, EncMys, EncSF, LinLib L, NewYTBE 71, NewYTBS 75, Novels, ObitOF 79, ScFSB, TwCCr&M 80B, –85B, WorAl, WorAu 1970*

Wain, John 1925- *Au&Wr 71, BioIn 3, –4, –5, –6, –8, –9, –10, –13, BlueB 76, CasWL, ConAu 5R, ConAu 4AS[port], ConLC 2, –11, –15, ConLCrt, –82, ConNov 72, –76, –82, –86, ConPo 70, –75, –80, –85, DcLB 15[port], –27[port], DcLEL 1940, EncWL, –2, IntAu&W 76, –77, IntWW 74, –75, –76, –77, –78, –79, –80, –81, –82, –83, IntWWP 77, LongCEL, LongCTC, ModBrL, –S2, –S1, NewC, Novels, PenC ENG, RAdv 1, REn, TwCWr, Who 74, –82, –83, WhoTwCL, WhoWor 74, WorAu, WrDr 76, –80, –82, –84, –86*
Wainwright, Gordon Ray 1937- *Au&Wr 71, ConAu 113, IntAu&W 76, –77, WhoWor 78, WrDr 76, –80, –82, –84, –86*
Waite, Helen Elmira 1903-1967 *BioIn 7, ConAu 1R*
Waitley, Douglas 1927- *ConAu 9NR, –21R, SmATA 30[port]*
Wakefield, Dan *DrAP&F 85*
Wakefield, Dan 1932- *AmAu&B, ASpks, BioIn 9, –10, –11, BlueB 76, ConAu 21R, ConLC 7, ConNov 86, DcLEL 1940, IndAu 1917, WhoAm 74, –76, –78, –80, –82, –84, –86, WrDr 76, –80, –82, –84, –86*
Wakefield, H Russell 1888-1964 *Novels, ScF&FL 1, –2, SupFW, WhoHr&F*
Wakin, Edward 1927- *ConAu 2NR, –5R, –17NR, SmATA 37, WhoE 74*
Wakoski, Diane *DrAP&F 85*
Wakoski, Diane 1937- *AmWomWr, BioIn 10, –11, –12, ConAu 9NR, –13R, ConAu 1AS[port], ConLC 2, –4, –7, –9, –11, –40[port], ConPo 70, –75, –80, –85, CroCAP, DcLB 5[port], DcLEL 1940, IntAu&W 86, IntWWP 77, ModAL S1, PenC AM, RAdv 1, WhoAm 80, –82, –84, –86, WorAu 1970, WrDr 76, –80, –82, –84, –86*
Walch, Timothy 1947- *ConAu 21NR*
Walcott, Derek *DrAP&F 85*
Walcott, Derek 1930- *BioIn 9, –10, –11, –12, CasWL, ConAu 89, ConDr 73, –77, –82, ConLC 2, –4, –9, –14, –25[port], –42[port], ConPo 70, –75, –80, –85, CurBio 84[port], DcAfL, DcLB Y81B[port], DcLEL 1940, DrBlPA, EncWL 2, FifCWr, InB&W 80, IntWWP 77, LongCTC, ModBlW, ModCmwL, NewYTBS 79, –82[port], PenC ENG, PlP&P A, WebE&AL, WhDW, WhoWor 82, WorAu, WrDr 82, –84, –86*
Walcott, Derek Alton 1930- *BioIn 13, OxEng 85, SelBAAf, WhoWor 84*

Walden, Amelia Elizabeth *WhoAm 84, –86, WhoAmW 85, –87, WhoWor 84, –87*
Walden, Amelia Elizabeth 1909- *AuBYP, BioIn 4, –6, –7, –9, ConAu 1R, –2NR, CurBio 56, ForWC 70, InWom, IntAu&W 77, –82, MorJA, SmATA 3, WhoAm 74, –76, –78, –80, –82, WhoAmW 74, –58, –61, –64, –68, –70, –72, –75, –77, –83, WhoE 74, –77, WhoWor 74, –76, –78, –80, –82, WrDr 76, –80, –82, –84*
Walden, Daniel 1922- *ConAu 25R, DrAS 74E, –78E, –82E*
Waldo, Anna Lee 1925- *BioIn 11, –12, ConAu 85, NewYTBS 79*
Waldo, Myra *BioIn 12, ConAu 93, ForWC 70, WhoAmW 58, –61*
Waldron, Ann 1924- *BioIn 12, ConAu 7NR, –13R, SmATA 16, WhoAm 74, –76*
Waldrop, Howard *ScFSB*
Waldrop, Howard 1946- *ConAu 118, TwCSFW 86*
Waldrop, W Earl 1910- *ConAu 5R*
Wales, Robert *OxAusL*
Wales, Robert 1923- *IntAu&W 86, WrDr 86*
Waley, Arthur 1889-1966 *BioIn 4, –7, –8, –9, –12, –13, CasWL, ChhPo, –S1, –S2, –S3, CnE&AP, CnMWL, ConAu 25R, –85, DcLEL, EvLB, LongCTC, MakMC, NewC, ObitT 1961, OxEng, PenC ENG, REn, TwCA, –SUP, TwCWr, WhDW, WhE&EA*
Walker, Alice *DrAP&F 85*
Walker, Alice 1944- *AmWomWr, ASpks, BioIn 11, –13, BlkWWr, BlkAWP, BroadAu, ConAu 9NR, –37R, ConLC 5, –6, –9, –19, –27[port], ConNov 86, CurBio 84[port], DcLB 6[port], –33[port], InB&W 80, IntAu&W 82, IntDcWB, LivgBAA, ModAL S2, ModBlW, NegAl 76, –83, NewYTBS 83[port], OxAmL 83, PostFic, SmATA 31[port], WhoAm 74, –76, –78, WhoAmW 74, –72, WhoBlA 75, –77, –80, –85, WomPO 76, –78, WorAu 1975[port], WrDr 86*
Walker, Barbara 1921- *AuBYP SUP, BioIn 9, ConAu 33R, SmATA 4*
Walker, Braz 1934- *ConAu 69*
Walker, Braz 1934-1983 *SmATA 45*
Walker, David 1911- *BioIn 6, –10, –11, CanWW 70, –79, –80, –81, –83, CanWr, CasWL, ConAu 1R, –1NR, ConLC 14, ConNov 72, –76, DcLEL 1940, EncSF, IntAu&W 76, –77, –82, LongCTC, OxCan, –SUP, OxCanL, Profile, REnAL, ScF&FL 1,*

–2, SmATA 8, TwCCW 78, –83, Who 74, –82, –83, WhoAm 76, –78, –80, –82, WhoCan 73, –75, –77, –80[port], –82[port], WhoCanL 85, WhoWor 80, WorAu, WrDr 76, –80, –82, –84, –86
Walker, Diana 1925- *AuBYP SUP, BioIn 11, –13, ConAu 4NR, –49, SmATA 9*
Walker, Greta 1927- *ConAu 77*
Walker, Irma Ruth 1921- *ConAu 5R, –6NR, –21NR*
Walker, Kathrine Sorley *AuBYP, BioIn 8*
Walker, Louise Jean 1891-1976 *ConAu 110, IntAu 80, SmATA 35N, WhoAmW 68*
Walker, Margaret *DrAP&F 85*
Walker, Margaret 1915- *AmWomWr, BioIn 7, –8, –9, –10, –13, BlkAWP, BroadAu, ChhPo S1, –S2, ConAu 73, ConLC 1, –6, ConNov 72, –76, –82, –86, ConPo 70, –75, –80, –85, CroCAP, CurBio 43, EncSoH, InWom, IntAu&W 76, –77, LivgBAA, ModBlW, NegAl 76, –83, WhoAm 74, –76, –78, WhoAmW 74, –58, –61, –68A, –72, WhoBlA 75, –77, –80, –85, WrDr 76, –80, –82, –84, –86*
Walker, Margaret Abigail 1915- *InB&W 85, SelBAAf*
Walker, Mary Alexander *DrAP&F 85*
Walker, Mary Alexander 1927- *ConAu 104, WhoAmW 85, –87*
Walker, Mildred 1905- *AmAu&B, AmNov, Au&Wr 71, BioIn 1, –2, –4, ConAu X, CurBio 47, InB&W 80, InWom, MichAu 80, REnAL, SmATA X, TwCA SUP, WhoAm 74, –76, WhoAmW 74, –58, –64, –66, –68, –70, –72, –75, WrDr 76, –80, –82, –84*
Walker, Mildred *see also* Schemm, Mildred Walker
Walker, Mort 1923- *BioIn 2, –8, –11, ConAu 3NR, –49, ConGrA 2[port], EncTwCJ, LinLib L, SmATA 8, WhoAm 74, –76, –78, –80, –82, –84, –86, WhoAmA 73, –76, –78, –80, –82, –84, WhoE 74, WhoWor 74*
Walker, Richard Louis 1922- *AmM&WS 73S, –78S, BioIn 13, ConAu 7NR, –9R, IntAu&W 77, –82, WhoAm 74, –76, –78, –80, –82, –84, –86, WhoWor 82, –84, –87*
Walker, Robert Harris 1924- *ConAu 7NR, –13R, DrAS 74E, –78E, –82H, WhoAm 80, –82, –84, –86, WhoE 79*
Walker, Robert W 1948- *ConAu 18NR*
Walker, Robert Wayne 1948- *ConAu 93, IntAu&W 82, –86*
Wall, Leonard Wong 1941- *AmM&WS 79P, –86P*

169

Washington, Booker T 1859-1915 *MemAm*

Washington, Booker Taliaferro 1856-1915 *BioIn 13, InB&W 85, SelBAAf*

Waskow, Arthur I 1933- *ConAu 4NR, -5R, DrAS 74H, -78H, -82P, Future, WhoAm 74, -76, -78, -80, -82*

Waskow, Arthur Irwin 1933- *WhoAm 84, -86*

Wason, Betty 1912- *ConAu X, CurBio 43, InWom, WhoAmW 64, -66, -68, -70, -72*

Wasserman, Dale 1917- *AmAu&B, BiDAmM, BiE&WWA, BlueB 76, ConAu 49, ConDr 73, -77D, -82D, EncMT, IntMPA 77, -75, -76, -78, -79, -81, -82, -84, -86, NatPD 81[port], NewYTET, NotNAT, WhoAm 74, -76, -78, -80, -82, -84, -86, WrDr 76, -80, -82, -84, -86*

Wassmer, Arthur C 1947- *ConAu 103, WhoWest 82*

Waterhouse, Keith *OxThe 83*

Waterhouse, Keith 1929- *BioIn 13, ConNov 82, HalFC 84, IntMPA 86, WrDr 86*

Waters, Frank *DrAP&F 85*

Waters, Frank 1902- *AmAu&B, AmNov, BioIn 2, -9, -10, -12, -13, CnDAL, ConAu 3NR, -5R, -18NR, DcLB Y86B[port], EncFWF[port], IntAu&W 76, -77, -82, REnAW, WhNAA, WhoAm 74, -76, -78, WhoWest 74, -76, WrDr 84, -86*

Waters, John F 1930- *AuBYP SUP, BioIn 9, ConAu 37R, IntAu&W 77, -82, SmATA 4, WhoE 75, -77, WrDr 76, -80, -82, -84*

Waters, John Frederick 1930- *IntAu&W 86, WrDr 86*

Waterton, Betty 1923- *ConAu 111, SmATA 37[port]*

Watkins, Peter 1934- *ConAu 109*

Watkins, William Jon *DrAP&F 85*

Watkins, William Jon 1942- *BioIn 9, ConAu 11NR, EncSF, IntAu&W 76, Po&Wr 77, ScF&FL 1, -2, ScFSB, TwCSFW 86, WrDr 84, -86*

Watson, Aldren A 1917- *SmATA 36, -42[port], WhoAmA 84*

Watson, Aldren Auld 1917- *BioIn 1, 5, -8, -12, ChhPo, -S2, -S3, ConAu 4NR, -81, ForIl, IlsBYP, IlsCB 1744, -1946, -1957, -1967, SmATA 36, WhoAmA 73, -76, -78, -80, -82*

Watson, Andrew Samuel 1920- *AmM&WS 73S, -76P, -79P, -82P, -86P, BiDrAPA 77, ConAu 45, DrAS 74P, -78P, -82P, WhoAmL 83, -85, WhoMW 80, -82*

Watson, Bryan 1942- *BioIn 7, WhoHcky 73*

Watson, Clyde 1947- *AuBYP SUP, BioIn 10, ChlLR 3, ChhPo S2, ConAu 4NR, -49, DrRegL 75, FourBJA, OxChL, SmATA 5, TwCCW 78, -83, WrDr 76, -80, -82, -84, -86*

Watson, Colin 1920-1982 *TwCCr&M 85*

Watson, Colin 1920-1983 *AnObit 1983, Au&Wr 71, ConAu 1R, -2NR, -108, EncMys, IntAu&W 76, Novels, TwCCr&M 80, WrDr 82, -84*

Watson, Ian 1943- *BioIn 13, ConAu 61, EncSF, IntAu&W 82, Novels, ScF&FL 1, -2, ScFSB[port], TwCSFW 86, WhoSciF, WrDr 84, -86*

Watson, J R 1934- *ConAu 18NR*

Watson, James 1936- *IntAu&W 86, WrDr 86*

Watson, James Dewey 1928- *AmAu&B, AmM&WS 73P, -76P, -79P, -82P, -86P, AsBiEn, BiESc, BioIn 5, -6, -7, -8, -9, -12, -13, BlueB 76, ConAu 25R, CurBio 63, EncAB-H, IntWW 74, -75, -76, -77, -78, -79, -80, -81, -82, -83, MakMC, McGEWB, McGMS 80[port], NewYTBE 70,*

NewYTBS 80[port], WebAB, -79, Who 74, -82, -83, -85, WhoAm 74, -76, -78, -80, -82, -84, -86, WhoE 81, -83, -85, WhoFrS 84, WhoNob, WhoWor 74, -76, -80, -82, -84, -87, WorAl

Watson, Jane Werner 1915- *AuBYP SUP, BioIn 9, ConAu 5R, -8NR, SmATA 3, WhoAmW 58, -61, -64, -68, -70*

Watson, Lyall 1939- *ConAu 8NR, -57, DcCAr 81, EncO&P 2, -78S1, WrDr 76, -80, -82, -84, -86*

Watson, Paul 1951?- *BioIn 12*

Watson, Sally 1924- *AuBYP SUP, BioIn 9, ConAu 3NR, -5R, FourBJA, IntAu&W 77, -82, SmATA 3*

Watson, Simon *EncSF, ScFSB*

Watson, Tom 1949- *BioIn 10, -11, -12, -13, CurBio 79, NewYTBS 79, -80, -82[port], WorAl*

Watt, Thomas 1935- *Alli, BioIn 9, ConAu 37R, SmATA 4, WhoE 79*

Wattenberg, Ben J 1933- *BioIn 8, BlueB 76, ConAu 57, CurBio 85[port], WhoAm 76, -78, -80, -82, -84, -86, WrDr 80, -82, -84, -86*

Watt-Evans, Lawrence 1954- *ConAu X*

Watts, Alan 1915-1973 *AmAu&B, BioIn 5, -6, -7, -9, -10, -11, -12, -13, CelR, ConAu 41R, -45, CurBio 62, -74, -74N, DcLB 16[port], EncO&P 2, -81, LinLib L, MugS, NewYTBE 73, ObitOF 79, OxAmL 83, WebAB, -79, WhAm 6, WhoAm 74, WhoWor 74, WomWMM, WorAl, WorAu*

Watts, Charles 1941- *BioIn 12, -13, WhoAm 80, -82*

Watts, Charles *see also* Rolling Stones, The

Watzlawick, Paul 1921- *ConAu 4NR, -9R, WhoFrS 84, WhoWest 82*

Waugh, Carol-Lynn Roessel 1947- *ConAu 107*

Waugh, Carol-Lynn Rossel 1947- *SmATA 41[port], WhoAmW 85, -87*

Waugh, Charles Gordon 1943- *ConAu 118*

Waugh, Evelyn 1903-1966 *AtlBL, BioIn 1, -2, -3, -4, -5, -6, -7, -8, -9, -10, -11, -12, -13, BritWr 7, CasWL, CathA 1930, CmCal, CnMWL, ConAu 25R, -85, ConLC 1, -3, -8, -13, -19, -27[port], CyWA, DcLB 15[port], DcLEL, EncSF, EncWL, -2[port], EvLB, LinLib L, -S, LongCEL, LongCTC, MakMC, McGEWB, ModBrL, -S2, -S1, NewC, NewYTBE 73, Novels[port], ObitOF 79, ObitT 1961, OxEng, PenC ENG, RAdv 1, REn, ScF&FL 1, ScFSB, TwCA, -SUP, TwCWr, WebE&AL, WhDW, WhAm 4, WhE&EA, WhoTwCL, WomWMM, WorAl*

Waugh, Hillary *IntAu&W 86*

Waugh, Hillary 1920- *Au&Wr 71, ConAu 1R, -2NR, EncMys, Novels, TwCCr&M 80, -85, WrDr 82, -84, -86*

Way, Margaret *WrDr 84, -86*

Way, Peter 1936- *ConAu 115, IntAu&W 76, ScF&FL 1, WrDr 80, -82, -84, -86*

Wayne, Jane Ellen 1936- *ConAu 20NR, WhoAmW 85, -87, WhoWor 84, -87*

Wayne, Kyra Petrovskaya 1918- *BioIn 11, ConAu 4NR, -X, SmATA 8, WhoAmW 66, -68, -70, -72, -87, WhoWest 76, -78, -80, -82, WhoWor 87*

Wayne, Kyra Petrovskaya *see also* Petrovskaya, Kyra

Weale, Anne 1929- *Au&Wr 71, IntAu&W 76, -77*

Weales, Gerald 1925- *AmAu&B, BiE&WWA, BioIn 11, ConAmTC, ConAu 3NR, -5R, DrAS 74E, -78E, -82E, IndAu 1917, SmATA 11, WrDr 80, -82, -84, -86*

Weaver, Earl S 1930- *BioIn 10, -12, ConAu 116, CurBio 83[port], WhoAm 74, -76, -78, -80, -82, WhoE 81, -83, -85, WhoFrS 84, WhoNob, WhoWor 74, -76, -80, -82, -84, -87, WorAl*

Weaver, Earl Sidney 1930- *BioIn 13, WhoAm 84, -86*

Weaver, Robert Glenn 1920- *DrAS 74E, -78E, -82E, IlsBYP*

Weaver, Ward *AmNov X, AuBYP, BioIn 1, -2, -9, ConAu X, SmATA X, WhoSpyF*

Weaver, Ward *see also* Mason, F VanWyck

Webb, Charles 1939- *BioIn 8, ConAu 25R, ConLC 7, DcLEL 1940, IntAu&W 76, -77, WhoAm 74, -76, -78, WrDr 76, -80, -82, -84, -86*

Webb, Christopher *ConAu X, SmATA X, WrDr 86*

Webb, Christopher 1915-1983 *ConAu X, EncMys, IntAu&W 76X, -77X, -82X, ScF&FL 1, SmATA 2, TwCChW 83, WrDr 80, -82, -84*

Webb, Christopher *see also* Wibberley, Leonard

Webb, Jean Francis 1910- *ConAu 5R, -6NR, -21NR, IntAu&W 77, ScF&FL 1, -2, SmATA 35, WrDr 76, -80, -82, -84, -86*

Webb, Jimmy 1946- *BioIn 8, -9, -11, -13, RolSEnR 83, WhoAm 74, -76, -78, -80, WhoRock 81, WhoRocM 82*

Webb, Kaye *OxChL, Who 85*

Webb, Nancy 1915- *ConAu 1R, -21NR, ForWC 70*

Webb, Robert N 1906- *AuBYP, BioIn 8*

Webb, Sharon *DrAP&F 85, ScFSB*

Webb, Sharon 1936- *ConAu 113, SmATA 41, TwCSFW 86*

Webb, Sheyann 1956- *SelBAAf*

Webb, Walter Prescott 1888-1963 *AmAu&B, BioIn 3, -4, -5, -6, -7, -8, -9, -10, -11, -13, ConAu 113, DcAmB S7, DcLB 17[port], EncAAH, EncAB 36[port], NatCAB 51, ObitOF 79, OxAmL, -83, REnAL, REnAW, TexMW, WhAm 4, WhE&EA*

Webb, William 1919- *Alli, BiDLA, BioIn 3, ConAu 25R*

Webber, Andrew Lloyd *BioIn 13, ConAu X*

Webber, Andrew Lloyd 1948- *BioIn 9, -12, ConLC 21, LinLib L, NewYTBE 71, OxAmT 84, WhoAm 82*

Weber, Bruce 1942- *ConAu 21NR, -97*

Weber, Dick *NewYTBS 85[port]*

Weber, Dick 1929- *BioIn 6, -7, -8, -9, -10, ConAu P-1, WhoAm 74, -76*

Weber, Eric 1942- *BioIn 12, ConAu 101, -15NR*

Weber, Lenora Mattingly 1895-1971 *AmAu&B, AuBYP, BioIn 2, -9, BkC 3, ConAu 29R, ConAu P-1, ConLC 12, MorJA, SmATA 2, -26N, WhoAmW 58, -61*

Weber, William John 1927- *BioIn 12, ConAu 69, SmATA 14*

Webster, Elizabeth 1918- *ConAu 117*

Webster, Jean *ConAu X, OxAmT 84, OxChL, WomNov*

Webster, Jean 1876-1916 *AmAu&B, AmWomWr, BioIn 8, -12, CarSB, ChhPo, -S3, CnDAL, DcAmB, DcNAA, EvLB, JBA 34, LibW, LongCTC, NotAW, NotNAT B, OxAmL, -83, REn, REnAL, SmATA X, TwCA, TwCChW 83, TwCWr, WhAm 1, WhoChL, WomWWA 14*

Wechsberg, Joseph 1907- *BiGAW, EncAJ*

Wechsberg, Joseph 1907-1983 *AmAu&B, Au&Wr 71, BioIn 1, -3, -4, -9, -10, -12, -13, BlueB 76, ConAu 105, -109, CurBio 55, -83N, EncTwCJ, NewYTBS 83, OxAmL, -83, REnAL, WhAm 8, WhE&EA, WhoAm 74, -76, -78, -80, -82, WhoMus 72, WhoWor 74, -76, -80, -82, WhoWor 74, -76, -80, -82*

Wechsler, James 1915-1983 *AmAu&B, BioIn 1, -3, -6, -9, -11, BlueB 76, CelR, ConAu 101, -110, IntWW 74, -75, -76, -78, -83, NewYTBS 83[port], PolProf T, WhoAm 82, WhoE 74, WhoWor 74, WhoWorJ 72, -78*

Wechsler, James A 1915-1983 *AnObit 1983*

Wechsler, James Arthur 1915-1983 *BioIn 13, WhAm 8*

Wechter, Nell Wise 1913- *BioIn 5, ConAu 57, ScF&FL 1, -2, WhoAmW 77, -79, -81, WhoS&SW 78*

Wedel, Leonard E 1909- *ConAu 21R*

Wedgwood, Cicely Veronica 1910- *BioIn 4, DcLEL, IntAu&W 76, -77, IntWW 74, -75, -78, -83, LongCTC, ModBrL, REn, WhE&EA, Who 74, -82, -83, -85, WhoAm 74, WhoAmW 68, -70, -72, WhoWor 74, -76, -78, WrDr 76*

Weekley, Ernest 1865-1954 *BioIn 4, DcLEL, EvLB, LongCTC, ObitT 1951, REn, TwCA, -SUP, WhE&EA, WhLit*

Weesner, Theodore 1935- *ConAu 105, MichAu 80*

Wegner, Fritz 1924- *BioIn 5, -12, ChhPo S2, IlsBYP, IlsCB 1946, -1967, SmATA 20, WhoArt 80, -82, -84*

Wehen, Joy DeWeese 1926?- *AuBYP, BioIn 8, ConAu 3NR, -5R, WrDr 76, -80, -82, -84*

Wehen, Joy DeWeese 1936- *WrDr 86*

Weider, Joe *BioIn 8*

Weidman, John 1946- *ConAu 109, NatPD, -81[port]*

Weil, Gordon L 1937- *ConAu 12NR*

Weil, Gordon Lee 1937- *BioIn 9, ConAu 73, WhoAmP 75, -77, -79, -83, -85, WhoE 83, -85*

Weilerstein, Sadie Rose 1894- *BioIn 9, ConAu 5R, SmATA 3, WhoAmW 66, -68, WhoWorJ 72*

Weiman, Eiveen 1925- *ConAu 108*

Weinbaum, Eleanor Perlstein *IntAu&W 76, -77, -82, IntWWP 77, -82, WhoAmW 77, -79, -81, -83, WhoS&SW 80, -82, -84, -86*

Weinbaum, Stanley G 1900-1935 *ScFSB*

Weinbaum, Stanley G 1902-1935 *BioIn 7, -10, -12, ConAu 110, DcLB 8[port], DcNAA, EncSF, ScF&FL 1, TwCSFW 86, WhoSciF, WorAu*

Weinberg, Larry *SmATA X, WhoAmP 77, -79, -81*

Weingartner, Charles 1922- *BioIn 10, ConAu 49, DrAS 74E, -78E, -82E, Future, LEduc 74, SmATA 5*

Weingast, David E 1912- *AuBYP, BioIn 8, ConAu 5R*

Weinstein, Grace W *IntAu&W 86*

Weinstein, Grace W 1935- *ConAu 10NR, -61, ForWC 70, WhoAmW 81, -83*

Weinstein, Howard 1954- *ConAu 107*

Weinstein, Nathan Wallenstein 1903?-1940 *ConAu 104, LongCTC, ScF&FL 1, TwCA, -SUP, WebAB, -79*

Weinstein, Nathan Wallenstein *see also* West, Nathanael

Weinstein, Robert A 1914- *ConAu 29R, WhoWest 80, -82*

Weir, LaVada *BioIn 9, ConAu 9NR, -21R, SmATA 2, WrDr 76, -80, -82, -84, -86*

Weir, Rosemary 1905- *Au&Wr 71, AuBYP, BioIn 8, -12, ConAu 10NR, -13R, SmATA 21[port], TwCCW 78, -83, WrDr 80, -82, -84, -86*

Weis, Margaret 1948- *ConAu 111, SmATA 38*

Weisberger, Bernard A 1922- *BioIn 12, ConAu 5R, -7NR, DrAS 74H, -78H, -82H, SmATA 21[port]*

Weisenfeld, Murray 1923- *ConAu 104*

Weisman, John 1942- *ConAu 1NR, -45*

Weiss, Ann E 1943- *ConAu 1NR,*
–11NR, –45, SmATA 30
Weiss, Carol *AuBYP SUP*
Weiss, Ehrich *DcAmB, DcNAA,*
WebAB, –79, WhDW
Weiss, Harvey 1922- *AuBYP, BioIn 5,*
–8, –9, –13, ChLR 4[port],
ConAu 5R, –6NR, IlsCB 1946, –1957,
–1967, SmATA 1, –27[port], ThrBJA,
WhoAmA 73, –76, –78, –80, –82, –84,
WhoE 75, –77
Weiss, Karl 1926- *OxGer, WhoAm 74*
Weiss, Louise 1893-1983 *AnObit 1983,*
BioIn 10, –13, ConAu 109,
NewYTBS 83, WhoFr 79,
WhoWor 78, –80, –82
Weiss, Malcolm E 1928- *BioIn 9,*
ConAu 11NR, –25R, SmATA 3,
WhoE 74, –75, –77
Weiss, Morton Jerome 1926-
ConAu 9NR, –17R
Weiss, Morton Jerry 1926- *ConAu X,*
DrAS 74E, –78E, –82E
Weiss, Peter 1916-1982
AnObit 1982[port], AuBYP SUP,
CnThe, ConAu 3NR, –106, –45,
ConLC 3, –15, CroCD, CurBio 68,
–82N, EncWL, –2[port], EncWT,
GrFLW, IntAu&W 76, –77,
IntWW 74, –75, –76, –77, –78, –79,
–80, –81, –82, –82N, LinLib L,
MajMD 1, McGEWD, –84[port],
ModGL, ModWD,
NewYTBS 82[port], NotNAT, –A,
OxFilm, OxGer, PenC EUR,
PIP&P, –A, REnWD, TwCWr,
Who 74, –82, –83N, WhoThe 72, –77,
–81, WhoWor 74, WorAl, WorAu,
WorEFlm
Weiss, Peter 1925- *WhoAmP 73*
Weiss, Sol 1913- *AmM&WS 86P*
Weissler, Paul W 1936- *Ward 77F*
Weissman, Dick 1935- *ConAu X*
Weitz, Joseph Leonard 1922-
AmM&WS 73P, –76P, –79P, –82P,
–86P
Weitzman, David 1898- *IntYB 78,*
–79, –80, –81, –82, Who 74, –82, –83,
–85
Welburn, Ron *DrAP&F 85*
Welburn, Ron 1944- *BlkAWP,*
ConAu 1NR, –17NR, –45,
IntAu&W 77, –82, –86, IntWWP 77,
–82
Welch, Bob 1946- *BioIn 11,*
NewYTBS 80[port], RkOn 78,
WhoRock 81, WhoRocM 82
Welch, Bob *see also* Fleetwood Mac
Welch, James *DrAP&F 85*
Welch, James 1940- *BioIn 10, –12,*
ConAu 85, ConLC 6, –14, ConPo 75,
–80, –85, EncFWF, WrDr 76, –80,
–82, –84, –86
Welch, Lew 1926-1971 *BioIn 12, –13,*
ConAu 113, ConPo 70, DcLB 16[port]
Welch, Mary Scott *IntAu&W 86*
Welch, Mary Scott 1914?- *ConAu 104,*
IntAu&W 76, –77, –82,
WhoAmW 74, –72, –75, –77, –83,
WhoE 79, –81, –83
Welch, Mary-Scott *WhoAmW 85, –87,*
WhoE 85, WhoWor 84, –87
Welch, Ronald 1909-1982 *BioIn 8, –9,*
ConAu X, IntAu&W 77X, OxChL,
OxLitW 86, SmATA 3, TwCCW 78,
–83, WhoChL, WrDr 82
Welch, Ronald *see also* Felton, Ronald
Oliver
Weld, Philip S 1914-1984 *ConAu 114*
Weld, Philip S 1915?- *BioIn 13*
Weld, Philip Saltonstall 1914-
WhoAm 74, –76, –78
Weldon, Fay *WrDr 86*
Weldon, Fay 1931?- *Au&Wr 71,*
BioIn 9, –13, ConAu 21R, ConDr 73,
–77C, –82C, ConLC 6, –9, –11, –19,
ConNov 82, –86, DcLB 14[port],
IntAu&W 77, –86, IntWW 83,
Novels, WhoAm 82, –83, –85, WrDr 76,
–80, –82, –84
Weldon, Fay 1933- *ConAu 16NR,*
ConLC 36[port], OxEng 85,
WorAu 1975[port]

Wellard, James Howard 1909-
Au&Wr 71, BioIn 2, ConAu 3NR,
–5R, IntAu&W 76, –77, –82, –86,
ScF&FL 1, –2, WrDr 76, –80, –82,
–84, –86
Welles, Orson 1915- *AmAu&B,*
BiDFilm, BiE&WWA, BioIn 1, –2,
–3, –4, –5, –6, –7, –8, –9, –10, –11,
–12, –13, BlueB 76, CelR, CmCal,
CmMov, CnThe, ConAu 93,
ConDr 73, –77A, –82A, ConLC 20,
CurBio 41, –65, DcAmSR, DcFM,
EncAB-H, EncMT, EncWT,
FamA&A, FilmgC, HalFC 84[port],
IntMPA 77, –75, –76, –78, –79, –81,
–82, –84, –86, IntWW 74, –75, –76,
–77, –78, –79, –80, –81, –82, –83,
LinLib L, –S, MotPP, MovMk,
NewYTBE 72, NotNAT, –A, OxAmH,
OxAmT 84, OxFilm, OxThe, –83,
PIP&P, REn, REnAL, ScF&FL 1,
UFOEnc, WebAB, –79, WhDW,
WhThe, Who 74, –82, –83, –85,
WhoAm 74, –76, –78, –80, –82, –84,
WhoHol A, WhoThe 72, WhoWor 74,
WorAl, WorEFlm, WrDr 80, –82, –84
Welles, Orson 1915-1985 *ConAu 117,*
ConTFT 3, CurBio 85N,
NewYTBS 85[port]
Welles, Orson 1916- *IntDcF 2*
Wellman, Henry Q 1945- *ConAu 37R*
Wellman, Manly Wade 1903- *AuBYP,*
BioIn 3, –4, –5, –6, –8, –10,
ConAu 1R, –6NR, –16NR, ConSFA,
CurBio 55, EncMys, EncSF, MorJA,
ScF&FL 1, –2, SmATA 6, SupFW,
TwCSFW 86, WhoHr&F, WhoSciF,
WrDr 84, –86
Wellman, Manly Wade 1903-1986
ConAu 118, SmATA 47N
Wellman, Paul 1928- *CurBio 49,*
WhoE 75, WhoEng 80
Wellman, Paul I 1898-1966
ConAu 16NR, EncFWF
Wellman, Paul Iselin 1898-1966
AmAu&B, AmNov, Au&Wr 71,
AuBYP, BioIn 1, –2, –4, –7, –8, –9,
ConAu 1R, –25R, ObitOF 79, REn,
REnAL, REnAW, SmATA 3,
TwCA SUP, WhAm 4, WhE&EA
Wells, Evelyn *ConAu 53,*
WhoAmW 58, –61, –64, –66, –68,
–70, –72
Wells, H G 1866-1946 *AtlBL, BbD,*
BiD&SB, BritWr 6, CnMWL,
ConAu 110, CyWA, DcLB 34[port],
EncMys, EncSF, EncUrb,
EncWL 2[port], FilmgC, HalFC 84,
LinLib L, LongCTC, ModBrL, –S2,
–S1, NewC, Novels[port], OxChL,
OxEng 85, PenC ENG, PIP&P,
RAdv 1, RComWL, REn, ScF&FL 1,
ScFSB[port], SmATA 20, SupFW,
TwCLC 6[port], –12[port], –19[port],
TwCSFW 86, TwCWr, WebE&AL,
WhScrn 74, –77, –83, WhoHol B,
WhoHr&F, WhoSciF, WhoTwCL,
WorAl
Wells, H G *see also* Wells, Herbert
George
Wells, Helen 1910?- *AuBYP, BioIn 2,*
–8, –9, ConAu 29R, ForWC 70,
IntAu&W 77, –82, SmATA 2,
WhoAmW 74, –58, –61, –64, –66,
–68, –70, –72, –75, WrDr 76, –80,
–82, –84
Wells, Helen 1910-1986 *IntAu&W 86*
Wells, Helen 1915- *WrDr 86*
Wells, Herbert George 1866-1946
BiDInt, BioIn 1, –2, –3, –4, –5, –6,
–7, –8, –9, –10, –11, –12, –13,
CasWL, Chambr 3, CurBio 46,
DcAmSR, DcBiA, DcEnA AP,
DcLEL, DcNaB 1941, EncWL,
EvLB, LinLib S, LongCEL, MakMC,
McGEWB, MnBBF, NotNAT B,
ObitOF 79, OxEng, TwCA, –SUP,
WhDW, WhAm 2, WhE&EA, WhLit,
WhoBW&I A, WhoLA
Wells, Herbert George *see also* Wells,
H G
Wells, J Wellington *ConAu X*
Wells, J Wellington 1907- *BioIn 11,*
–12, ConAu X, SmATA X

Wells, J Wellington *see also* DeCamp,
L Sprague
Wells, Robert L 1913- *AuBYP,*
BioIn 7
Wells, Robert Lynn 1942-
WhoS&SW 86
Wells, Rosemary 1943- *BioIn 12,*
ChhPo S1, –S2, ConAu 85,
ConLC 12, FourBJA, IlsBYP,
IlsCB 1967, SmATA 18,
SmATA 1AS[port], TwCChW 83,
WrDr 86
Wels, Byron G 1924- *ConAu 8NR,*
–61, SmATA 9
Welsch, Roger L 1936- *ConAu 9NR,*
–21R
Weltfish, Gene 1902-1980
AmM&WS 73S, BioIn 3, –12,
NewYTBS 80[port]
Weltner, Linda R 1938- *ConAu 105,*
SmATA 38[port]
Welty, Eudora *DrAP&F 85, Who 85,*
WhoAm 84, –86, WhoAmW 85, –87,
WhoWor 84, –87
Welty, Eudora 1909- *AmAu&B,*
AmNov, AmWomWr, AmWr,
BioIn 1, –2, –3, –4, –5, –6, –7, –8, –9,
–10, –11, –12, –13, BlueB 76,
CasWL, CelR, ChhPo, DcLAL,
ConAu 9R, ConAu 1BS, ConLC 1,
–2, –5, –14, –22[port], –33[port],
ConNov 72, –76, –82, –86, Conv 3,
CurBio 42, –75, CyWA, DcLB 2,
DcLEL 1940, EncSoH, EncWL, –2,
ICPEnP A, InWom, IntAu&W 76,
–77, IntDcWB, IntWW 74, –75, –76,
–77, –78, –79, –80, –81, –82, –83,
LibW, LinLib L, –S, LongCTC,
MacBEP, ModAL, –S2, –S1,
NewCon[port], NewYTBS 80[port],
–83[port], Novels, OxAmL, –83,
PenC AM, RAdv 1, REn, REnAL,
TwCA SUP, WebAB, –79,
WetE&AL, WhDW, WhE&EA,
Who 74, –82, –83, WhoAm 74, –76,
–78, –80, –82, WhoAmW 74, –58,
–61, –64, –66, –68, –70, –72, –81,
–83, WhoS&SW 76, –78, WhoTwCL,
WhoWor 74, –76, –78, –80, –82,
WorAl, WrDr 76, –80, –82, –84, –86
Wendel, Tim 1956- *ConAu 105*
Wendt, Albert 1939- *ConAu 57,*
ConNov 82, –86, IntAu&W 77, –82,
–86, WrDr 82, –84, –86
Wenkam, Robert 1920- *ConAu 4NR,*
–53, IntAu&W 82
Wenner, Jann S 1946- *BioIn 9, –10,*
–11, –12, ConAu 101,
CurBio 80[port], MugS, WhoAm 76,
–78, –80, –82, –84, –86, WhoE 83,
–85
Wenner, Jann S 1947- *EncAJ*
Went, Frits W 1903- *AmM&WS 76P,*
–79P, –82P, BlueB 76, IntWW 74,
–75, –76, –77, –78, –79, –80, –81,
–82, –83, McGMS 80[port]
Went, Frits Warmolt 1903-
AmM&WS 86P
Wentworth, Harold 1904- *ConAu P-1*
Wepman, Dennis 1933- *ConAu 120*
Werfel, Franz 1890-1945 *BiGAW,*
BiDAmM, BioIn 1, –2, –3, –4, –5, –7,
CasWL, ClDMEL, CmCal, CnMD,
CnThe, ConAu 104, CurBio 40, –45,
CyWA, DcNAA, EncSF, EncTR,
EncWL, –2[port], EncWT, EvEuW,
LinLib L, –S, LongCTC, LuthC 75,
McGEWB, McGEWD, –84[port],
ModGL, ModWD, NewEOp 71,
NotNAT B, Novels, ObitOF 79,
OxGer, OxThe, –83, PenC EUR,
PIP&P, REn, REnWD, ScF&FL 1,
ScFSB, TwCA, –SUP,
TwCLC 8[port], TwCSFW 86A,
TwCWr, WhAm 2, WhE&EA
Werfel, Franz V 1890-1945 *BioIn 10,*
–13
Wernecke, Herbert Henry 1895-
AuBYP, BioIn 8, ConAu 5R
Werner, Alfred 1911-1979 *Au&Wr 71,*
BioIn 7, –12, ConAu 89, –97N,
Who 74, –82, –83, WhoAm 74, –76,
–78, –80, WhoAmA 73, –76, –78,
–80N, –82N, –84N, WhoWorJ 72, –78

Werner, Vivian 1921- *AuBYP SUP,*
ConAu 105
Wernick, Robert 1918- *ConAu 97*
Wersba, Barbara 1932- *AuBYP,*
BioIn 8, –9, –11, ChLR 3,
ConAu 16NR, –29R, ConLC 30[port],
DcLB 52[port], OxChL, SmATA 1,
SmATA 2AS[port], ThrBJA,
TwCCW 78, –83, WrDr 80, –82, –84,
–86
Werstein, Irving 1914-1971 *AuBYP,*
BioIn 7, –9, –12, ConAu 29R, –73,
FourBJA, NewYTBE 71, SmATA 14
Wertenbaker, Lael Tucker 1909-
Au&Wr 71, ConAu 3NR, –5R,
ForWC 70, IntAu&W 77, –82,
WhoAmW 74, –68, –70, –72, –75,
WhoE 74, WrDr 76, –80, –82, –84,
–86
Wertheimer, Barbara M 1926-1983
AnObit 1983
Wertheimer, Barbara Mayer
1926?-1983 *BioIn 13*
Wesker, Arnold 1932- *Au&Wr 71,*
BiE&WWA, BioIn 6, –7, –8, –9, –10,
–11, –12, –13, BlueB 76, CasWL,
CnMD, CnThe, ConAu 1R, –1NR,
ConDr 73, –77, –82, ConLC 3, –5,
–42[port], CroCD, CurBio 62,
DcLB 13[port], DcLEL 1940,
EncWL, –2, EncWT, IntAu&W 76,
–77, –82, –86, IntWW 74, –75, –76,
–77, –78, –79, –80, –81, –82, –83,
LinLib L, LongCEL, LongCTC,
MajMD 1, MakMC, McGEWD, –84,
ModBrL, –S2, –S1, ModWD, NewC,
NotNAT, –A, OxEng 85, OxThe, –83,
PenC ENG, PIP&P, REnWD,
TwCWr, WebE&AL, Who 74, –82,
–83, –85, WhoThe 72, –77, –81,
WhoTwCL, WhoWor 74, –76, –78,
–84, –87, WorAu, WrDr 76, –80, –82,
–84, –86
Weslager, C A 1909- *ConAu 9NR,*
–21R
Weslager, Clinton Alfred 1909-
DrAS 74H, –78H, –82H, WhoAm 74,
–76, –78, –80, –82, –84, –86,
WhoE 74, –75, –77, –79, –81, –83,
–85, WhoWor 78, –80, –82, –84, –87
Wesolowski, Wayne Edward 1945-
AmM&WS 79P, –86P
Wessel, Thomas Roger 1937-
DrAS 78H
West, Anna 1938- *ConAu 106,*
SmATA 40[port]
West, Anthony 1914- *AmAu&B,*
Au&Wr 71, BioIn 2, –4, –13,
ConAu 3NR, –19NR, –45,
ConNov 72, –76, –82, –86, DcIrW 1,
DcLB 15, EncSF, IntAu&W 76, –77,
LongCTC, ModBrL, NewC, REn,
ScF&FL 1, –2, TwCA SUP, Who 82,
–83, WhoAm 74, –76, –78, –80,
WhoWor 74, WrDr 76, –80, –82, –84,
–86
West, Jerry *BioIn 9, –10, –13,*
ConAu X, ConAu X, SmATA 2
West, Jerry Alan 1938- *BioIn 5, –6,*
–8, –9, –10, –11, –12, CelR, CmCal,
NewYTBS 74, WhoAm 74, –78, –80,
–84, –86, WhoBbl 73, WhoWest 84,
WorAl
West, Jerry *see also* Stratemeyer,
Edward L
West, Jerry *see also* Svenson, Andrew E
West, Jessamyn *DrAP&F 85*
West, Jessamyn 1902- *EncFWF*
West, Jessamyn 1902-1984
AnObit 1984, BioIn 13, ConAu 112,
CurBio 84N, DcLB Y84N[port],
NewYTBS 84[port], WhAm 8
West, Jessamyn 1907- *OxAmL 83*
West, Jessamyn 1907-1984
AmWomWr, ASpks, BioIn 2, –3, –4,
–5, –8, –9, –10, –11, –12, ChhPo,
CmCal, ConAu 9R, ConLC 7, –17,
ConNov 72, –76, –82, CurBio 77,
DcLB 6[port], DcLEL 1940, InWom,
IndAu 1917, IntAu&W 77,
LibW, LinLib LP, OxAmL, REnAL,
ScF&FL 1, –2, SmATA 37N,
TwCA SUP, WhoAm 74, –76, –78,

White, William Anthony Parker 1911-1968 *AmAu&B, BioIn 1, -4, -6, -8, -12, ConAu 25R, ConAu P-1, EncMys, ObitOF 79, ScF&FL 1, TwCA SUP*

White, William Anthony Parker *see also* Boucher, Anthony

White, William, Jr. 1934- *BioIn 12, ConAu 14NR, -37R, DrAS 74H, -78H, -82H, IntAu&W 77, -82, MarqDCG 84, SmATA 16, WhoCon 73, WhoE 81, -83, -85, WrDr 76, -80, -82, -84, -86*

Whiteford, Andrew Hunter 1913- *AmM&WS 73S, -76P, ConAu 45, FifIDA, WhoAm 74, -76, -78, -82, -84, -86*

Whitehead, Alfred North 1861-1947 *AmAu&B, AsBiEn, BiDPsy, BiESc, BioIn 1, -2, -3, -4, -5, -6, -8, -9, -10, -12, -13, Chambr 3, ConAu 117, DcAmB S4, DcLEL, DcNaB 1941, DcNAA, DcScB, EncAB-H, InSci, LinLib L, -S, LongCTC, LuthC 75, MakMC, McGEWB, NamesHP, NatCAB 37, NewC, ObitOF 79, OxAmH, OxAmL, -83, OxEng, REn, REnAL, TwCA, -SUP, WebAB, -79, WhDW, WhAm 2*

Whitehill, Walter Muir 1905-1978 *ConAu 6NR, WhoAmA 84N*

Whitehouse, Arch *BioIn 13*

Whitehouse, Arch 1895-1979 *AuBYP, BioIn 7, -8, -12, ConAu X, MnBBF, SmATA X*

Whitehouse, Arch *see also* Whitehouse, Arthur George

Whitehouse, Arthur George 1895-1979 *AuBYP, BioIn 7, -8, -12, ConAu 4NR, SmATA 14, -23N*

Whitehouse, Arthur George Joseph 1895-1979 *BioIn 13*

Whitehouse, Arthur George *see also* Whitehouse, Arch

Whiteley, Opal Stanley 1899- *BioIn 3, -6, -11, REnAL*

Whiteside, Thomas 1918?- *ConAu 109*

Whitfield, Stephen E *ConSFA, EncSF*

Whitfield, Stephen J 1942- *ConAu 61, DrAS 78H, -82H, WhoAmJ 80, WhoWorJ 78*

Whitinger, R D *ConAu X*

Whitinger, R D 1910- *AuBYP, ConAu X, SmATA 3*

Whitinger, R D *see also* Place, Marian Templeton

Whitley, Mary Ann *ConAu X*

Whitlock, Herbert Percy 1868-1948 *AmAu&B, BioIn 7, -12, DcNAA, InSci, NatCAB 36, WhAm 2*

Whitlock, Ralph 1914- *Au&Wr 71, ConAu 101, -20NR, IntAu&W 76, -77, -82, -86, SmATA 35, WhoWor 76, WrDr 76, -80, -82, -84, -86*

Whitman, Alden 1913- *BioIn 7, -8, -9, -12, ConAu 17R, IntAu&W 76, -77, WhoE 74, -75, -77*

Whitman, Edmund Spurr 1900- *ConAu 17R, WhoAm 74, -76, -78*

Whitman, John 1944- *ConAu 11NR, -61*

Whitman, Walt *OxCanL*

Whitman, Walt 1819-1892 *Alli, -SUP, AmAu, AmAu&B, AmBi, AmRef[port], AmWr, AnCL, ApCAB, AtlBL, BbD, BiDAmM, BiD&SB, BioIn 1, -2, -3, -4, -5, -6, -7, -8, -9, -10, -11, -12, -13, CasWL, CelCen, Chambr 3, ChhPo, -S1, -S3, CnDAL, CnE&AP, CrtT 3, -4, CyWA, DcAmAu, DcAmB, DcAmSR, DcEnA, -AP, DcEnL, DcLB 3, DcLEL, DcNAA, Dis&D, EncAAH, EncAB-H, EvLB, HarEnUS, IlEncMy[port], LinLib L, -S, McGEWB, MemAm, MouLC 4, NinCLC 4[port], OxAmH, OxAmL, -83, OxAusL, OxCan, OxEng, -85, PenC AM, RAdv 1, RComWL, REn, REnAL, SmATA 20, Str&VC, WebAB, -79, WebE&AL, WhDW, WorAl*

Whitnell, Barbara *ConAu X*

Whitney, Alex 1922- *ConAu 53, SmATA 14*

Whitney, Charles Allen 1929- *AmM&WS 73P, -76P, -79P, -82P, -86P, ConAu 81, WhoAm 74, -76, -78, -80, -82, -84, -86, WhoE 75, -77, WhoGov 77, -72, -75*

Whitney, Leon Fradley 1894-1973 *AmAu&B, AuBYP, BioIn 7, ConAu 5R, -5NR, WhAm 6, WhNAA, WhoAm 74*

Whitney, Phyllis A *ThrtnMM*

Whitney, Phyllis A 1903- *ConLC 42[port], TwCCr&M 85, WrDr 86*

Whitney, Phyllis Ayame 1903- *AmAu&B, AmWomWr, AuBYP, AuNews 2, BioIn 1, -2, -7, -9, -11, -12, ConAu 1R, -3NR, CurBio 48, EncMys, ForWC 70, InWom, JBA 51, LibW, Novels, SmATA 1, -30[port], TwCCW 78, -83, TwCCr&M 80, WhoAm 74, -76, -78, -80, -82, -84, -86, WhoAmW 74, -58, -61, -64, -66, -68, -70, -72, -75, WorAl, WrDr 76, -80, -82, -84*

Whitney, Thomas Porter 1917- *AuBYP SUP, BioIn 10, -13, ConAu 104, SmATA 25[port], WhoAm 74, -76, WhoE 74, -75, -77, -79, -81, -83, -85, WhoWor 74, -76, -78, -80, -82, -84*

Whitridge, Arnold 1891- *AmAu&B, Au&Wr 71, ConAu 9R, DrAS 74H, WhE&EA, WhoAm 74, -76, -78*

Whittier, John Greenleaf 1807-1892 *Alli, -SUP, AmAu, AmAu&B, AmBi, AmRef[port], AmWr S1, AnCL, ApCAB, AtlBL, BbD, BiDAmM, BiD&SB, BiDMoPL, BioIn 1, -2, -3, -4, -5, -6, -7, -8, -9, -10, -11, -12, -13, CarSB, CasWL, CelCen, Chambr 3, ChhPo, -S1, -S2, -S3, CnDAL, CrtT 3, -4, CyAL 2, CyWA, DcAmAu, DcAmB, DcAmSR, DcBiPP, DcEnA, DcEnL, DcLB 1, DcLEL, DcNAA, Dis&D, Drake, EncAAH, EncAB-H, EvLB, HarEnUS[port], LinLib L, -S, McGEWB, MouLC 4, NatCAB 1, NinCLC 8[port], OxAmH, OxAmL, -83, OxChL, OxEng, -85, PenC AM, RAdv 1, REn, REnAL, Str&VC, TwCBDA, WebAB, -79, WebE&AL, WhDW, WhAm HS, WorAl*

Who, The *EncPR&S 74, -77, IlEncRk, RkOn 78, -84, RkOneH, RolSEnR 83, WhoRock 81[port]*

Who, The *see also* Daltrey, Roger

Who, The *see also* Entwistle, John

Who, The *see also* Moon, Keith

Who, The *see also* Townshend, Peter

Whyte, William Hollingsworth 1917- *AmAu&B, Au&Wr 71, BioIn 5, -8, BlueB 76, CelR, ConAu 9R, CurBio 59, DcLB 1940, IntAu&W 76, -77, -82, IntWW 74, -75, -76, -77, -78, -79, -80, -81, -82, -83, NatLAC, REnAL, WhoAm 74, -76, -78, -80, -82, -84, -86, WhoWor 74, -76, -78*

Wibberley, Leonard *TwCCr&M 85*

Wibberley, Leonard 1915- *OxChL, ScFSB, WrDr 86*

Wibberley, Leonard 1915-1983 *AnObit 1983, AuBYP, BioIn 5, -6, -7, -9, -10, -13, ChlLR 3, ChhPo, ConAu 3NR, -5R, EncMys, EncSF, IntAu&W 76, -77, -82, MorJA, NewYTBS 83, REn, ScF&FL 1, -2, SmATA 2, -36N, -45[port], TwCCW 78, -83, TwCCr&M 80, TwCSFW 86, WhoAm 76, -78, -80, -82, WorAu, WrDr 76, -80, -82, -84*

Wibberley, Leonard *see also* Holton, Leonard

Wibberley, Leonard *see also* O'Connor, Patrick

Wibberley, Leonard *see also* Webb, Christopher

Wickenden, Dan 1913- *AmAu&B, AmNov, BioIn 2, -4, CurBio 51, REnAL, TwCA SUP*

Wicker, Thomas Grey 1926- *AmAu&B, ASpks, BioIn 8, -9, -10, -11, ConAu 21NR, -65, EncTwCJ, WhoAm 74, -76, -78, -80, -82, -84, -86, WhoS&SW 73, WhoWor 74, WorAl*

Wicker, Tom *ConAu X*

Wicker, Tom 1926- *BioIn 3, -4, -13, BlueB 76, CelR, ConAu 65, -X, ConLC 7, CurBio 73, WrDr 76, -80, -82, -84, -86*

Wicker, Tom *see also* Wicker, Thomas Grey

Wickett, William Harold, Jr. 1919- *ConAu 108, WhoWest 74, -76, -78, -80, -82*

Wicklein, John Frederick 1924- *ConAu 106, IntAu&W 86, WhoAm 78, -80, -82, -84, -86*

Widder, Arthur 1928- *ConAu 5R*

Widder, Arthur *see also* Widder, John Arthur, Jr.

Widder, John Arthur, Jr. 1928- *WhoE 74*

Widder, John Arthur, Jr. *see also* Widder, Arthur

Wideman, John E 1941- *BioIn 6, BlkAWP, ConAu 85, ConLC 5, InB&W 80, LivgBAA, NegAl 76, -83, SelBAAu, WhoAm 76, WhoBlA 75, -77, -80, -85*

Wideman, John Edgar 1941- *ConAu 14NR, ConLC 34[port], -36[port], ConNov 86, DcLB 33[port], InB&W 85, SelBAAf, WhoAm 86*

Wiener, Harvey Shelby 1940- *ConAu 102, DrAS 74E, -78E, -82E*

Wier, Ester 1910- *BioIn 6, -7, -9, ConAu 9R, DcLB 52[port], LinLib L, SmATA 3, ThrBJA, TwCCW 78, -83, WhoAmW 74, -75, WrDr 84, -86*

Wiese, Kurt 1887-1974 *AmAu&B, AmPB, AuBYP, BioIn 1, -2, -4, -5, -7, -8, -9, -10, -13, ChhPo, ConAu 9R, -49, ConICB, IlsCB 1744, -1946, -1957, -1967, JBA 34, -51, LinLib L, OxChL, REnAL, SmATA 24N, -3, -36, TwCCW 78*

Wiesel, Elie *DrAP&F 85*

Wiesel, Elie 1928- *AmAu&B, Au&Wr 71, AuNews 1, BioIn 8, -9, -10, -11, -12, -13, ConAu 8NR, ConAu 4AS[port], ConIsC 1[port], ConLC 3, -5, -11, -37[port], CurBio 70, -86[port], EncWL, LinLib L, NewYTBE 73, NewYTBS 81[port], -83[port], WhoAm 74, -76, -78, -80, -82, -84, -86, WhoAmJ 80, WhoE 74, WhoWorJ 72, -78, WorAl, WorAu, WrDr 86*

Wiesenthal, Simon 1908- *BioIn 6, -7, -9, -10, -11, -12, -13, ConAu 13NR, -21R, CurBio 75, EncTR, IntAu&W 77, IntWW 77, -78, -79, -80, -81, -82, -83, WhoWor 74, -76, -78, -80, -82, -84, -87, WhoWorJ 78*

Wiggin, Kate Douglas *WomNov*

Wiggin, Kate Douglas 1856-1923 *Alli SUP, AmAu&B, AmBi, AmWom, AmWomWr, ApCAB X, AuBYP SUP, BbD, BiDAmEd, BiD&SB, BioIn 1, -2, -3, -4, -6, -8, -10, -11, -12, CarSB, Chambr 3, ChhPo, -S1, -S2, -S3, CmCal, CnDAL, ConAmL, ConAu 111, DcAmAu, DcAmB, DcLB 42[port], DcLEL, DcNAA, EvLB, FamAYP, FamSYP, HerW, -84, InWom, JBA 34, LibW, LinLib L, -LP, -S, LongCTC, NatCAB 16, NotAW, OxAmL, -83, OxChL, REn, REnAL, TwCA, -SUP, TwCBDA, TwCCW 78, -83, WebAB, -79, WhAm 1, WhLit, WhoChL, WomWWA 14, WorAl, YABC 1*

Wiggin, Maurice 1912- *Au&Wr 71, BioIn 8, -9, ConAu 5NR, -9R*

Wigginton, Eliot 1942?- *AuNews 1, BioIn 10, -12, BioNews 74, ConAu 101*

Wight, James Alfred 1916- *BioIn 10, -11, -12, ConAu 77, SmATA 44, Who 82, -83, -85, WrDr 76, -80, -82, -84*

Wight, James Alfred *see also* Herriot, James

Wilber, Donald N 1907- *SmATA 35[port]*

Wilber, Donald Newton 1907- *AuBYP, BioIn 7, ConAu 2NR, -5R, IntAu&W 77, -82, SmATA 35, WhoE 75, -77, WrDr 76, -80, -82, -84, -86*

Wilbur, Richard *DrAP&F 85*

Wilbur, Richard 1921- *AmAu&B, Au&Wr 71, AuBYP SUP, BiE&WWA, BioIn 3, -4, -7, -8, -9, -10, -11, -12, -13, BlueB 76, CasWL, ChhPo S1, -S2, -S3, CnDAL, CnE&AP, CnMWL, ConAu 1R, -2NR, ConAu 2BS, ConLC 3, -6, -9, -14, ConPo 70, -75, -80, -85, ConTFT 3[port], CroCAP, CurBio 66, DcLB 5[port], DcLEL 1940, DrAS 74E, -78E, -82E, EncWL, -2, IntAu&W 77, -82, -86, IntWW 74, -75, -76, -77, -78, -79, -80, -81, -82, -83, IntWWP 77, -82, LinLib L, ModAL, -S2, -S1, NotNAT, OxAmL, -83, PenC AM, PIP&P, RAdv 1, REn, REnAL, SmATA 9, TwCA SUP, TwCWr, WebE&AL, WhoAm 74, -76, -78, -80, -82, WhoE 74, WhoThe 72, -77, -81, WhoTwCL, WhoWor 74, WorAl, WrDr 76, -80, -82, -84, -86*

Wilcox, Collin 1924- *ConAu 14NR, -21R, ScF&FL 1, TwCCr&M 80, -85, WhoAm 82, WrDr 82, -84, -86*

Wilcox, Preston 1923- *InB&W 80, -85, WhoBlA 75, -77, -80, -85*

Wilcox, Robert Kalleen 1943- *ConAu 77*

Wilde, Oscar 1854?-1900 *Alli SUP, AtlBL, BbD, BiD&SB, BioIn 1, -2, -3, -4, -5, -6, -7, -8, -9, -10, -11, -12, -13, BritAu 19, BritWr 5, CarSB, CasWL, Chambr 3, ChhPo, -S2, -S3, CnE&AP, CnMD, CnThe, ConAu 104, -119, CrtT 3, -4, CyWA, DcAmSR, DcBiA, DcCathB, DcEnA AP, DcEuL, DcIrB, DcIrL, DcIrW 1, DcLB 10[port], -19[port], -34[port], -57[port], DcLEL, Dis&D, EncWL, EncWT, EvLB, FilmgC, HalFC 84, LinLib L, -S, LongCEL, LongCTC, MajMD 1, McGEWB, McGEWD, -84[port], ModWD, MouLC 4, NewC, NewEOp 71, NotNAT A, -B, OxAmT 84, OxEng, OxFilm, OxFr, OxThe, PenC ENG, PIP&P, PoIre, RAdv 1, RComWL, REn, REnWB, ScF&FL 1, SmATA 24[port], SupFW, TelT, TwCLC 1, -8[port], -23[port], WebE&AL, WhDW, WhoChL, WhoHr&F, WorAl*

Wilder, Cherry *SmATA X*

Wilder, Cherry 1930- *ConAu X, EncSF, ScFSB, TwCSFW 86, WrDr 84, -86*

Wilder, Laura Ingalls 1867-1957 *AmWomWr, AnCL, AuBYP, BioIn 1, -2, -3, -4, -5, -7, -8, -9, -10, -11, -12, BkCL, CasWL, ChlLR 2, ChhPo S1, InWom, JBA 51, LibW, NotAW MOD, ObitOF 79, OxAmL 83, OxChL, REnAL, REnAW, SmATA 15, -29[port], Str&VC, TwCCW 78, -83, WhAm 3, WhE&EA, WhoChL, WorAl*

Wilder, Rose 1887-1968 *AmAu&B, WhNAA*

Wilder, Rose *see also* Lane, Rose Wilder

Wilder, Thornton 1897-1975 *AmAu&B, AmNov, AmWr, Au&Wr 71, AuNews 2, BiDAmM, BiE&WWA, BioIn 1, -2, -3, -4, -5, -6, -7, -8, -9, -10, -11, -12, -13,*

*BlueB 76, CasWL, CelR, Chambr 3,
CnDAL, CnMD, CnMWL, CnThe,
ConAmA, ConAmL, ConAu 13R, –61,
ConDr 73, –77, ConLC 1, –5, –6,
–10, –15, –35[port], ConNov 72,
CroCD, CurBio 43, –71, –76N,
CyWA, DcLB 4, –7[port], –9[port],
DcLEL, EncAB-H, EncWL, –2[port],
EncWT, EvLB, FilmgC, HalFC 84,
IntAu&W 76, IntWW 74, –75, –76N,
LinLib L, –S, LongCTC, MajMD 1,
McGEWB, McGEWD 84[port],
MemAm, ModAL, –S2, –S1,
ModWD, NewEOp 71, NewYTBS 75,
NotNAT A, –B, Novels[port],
ObitOF 79, ObitT 1971, OxAmL, –83,
OxAmT 84, OxEng, OxThe,
PenC AM, PiP, PlP&P, RAdv 1,
RComWL, REn, REnAL, REnWD,
TwCA, –SUP, TwCWr, WebAB, –79,
WebE&AL, WhDW, WhAm 6,
WhE&EA, WhLit, WhNAA, WhThe,
Who 74, WhoAm 74, WhoThe 72,
WhoTwCL, WhoWor 74, WisWr,
WorAl, WorEFlm, WrDr 76*
Wildman, Eugene *DrAP&F 85*
Wildman, Eugene 1938- *ConAu 25R*
Wiley, Farida A d1986
NewYTBS 86[port]
Wiley, Farida Anna 1887- *OhA&B*
Wiley, Jack 1936- *ConAu 8NR, –61*
Wilford, John Noble 1933-
ConAu 15NR, IntAu&W 86
Wilford, John Noble, Jr. 1933-
*AuBYP SUP, ConAu 29R,
IntAu&W 76, –77, –82, WhoAm 76,
–78, –80, –82, –84, –86, WhoE 74,
–75, –77, –85*
Wilhelm, Kate *ConAu X*
Wilhelm, Kate 1928- *AmWomWr,
BioIn 12, ConAu 37R,
ConAu 5AS[port], ConLC 7, ConSFA,
DcLB 8[port], EncSF, IntAu&W 77,
ScF&FL 1, –2, ScFSB, TwCSFW 86,
WhoAmW 70, –72, WhoSciF,
WrDr 76, –80, –82, –84, –86*
Wilhelm, Steve 1905-1967 *AmAu&B*
Wilhelmsen, Frederick D 1923-
*AmCath 80, BioIn 3, –13, ConAu 1R,
–3NR*
Wilk, Max *DrAP&F 85*
Wilk, Max 1920- *BioIn 10, ConAu 1R,
–1NR, –16NR*
Wilkerson, David Ray 1931-
Au&Wr 71, ConAu 41R
Wilkerson, Margaret B 1936- *BioIn 13*
Wilkerson, Margaret Buford 1938-
WhoBlA 85
Wilkie, Katharine E 1904-1980
*AuBYP, BioIn 7, ConAu 21R,
ForWC 70, SmATA 31[port],
WhoAmW 61, –64, –66, –68, –70*
Wilkins, Frances 1923- *AuBYP SUP,
BioIn 12, ConAu 73, SmATA 14*
Wilkins, Hugh Percival 1896-1960
AuBYP, BioIn 5, –7
Wilkins, Roy 1901-1981 *AmRef[port],
AnObit 1981[port], BioIn 2, –5, –6,
–7, –8, –9, –10, –11, –12, –13,
BlueB 76, CelR, CivR 74, CivRSt,
ConAu 104, CurBio 50, –64, –81N,
Ebony 1, EncAB-H, EncSoH,
InB&W 80, –85, IntWW 74, –75,
–76, –77, –78, –79, –80, –81, –82N,
McGEWB, NegAl 76[port], –83[port],
NewYTBS 1981[port], PolProf E,
PolProf J, PolProf K, PolProf NF,
SelBAAf, WebAB, –79, WhAm 8,
WhoAm 74, –76, –78, –80,
WhoAmP 73, –75, –77, –79,
WhoBlA 75, –77, –80, WhoWor 74,
–76, WorAl*
Wilkinson, Alec 1952- *ConAu 109*
Wilkinson, Brenda 1946- *BioIn 12,
BlkAWP, ConAu 69, FifBJA[port],
InB&W 80, SmATA 14*
Wilkinson, Burke 1913- *AuBYP,
BioIn 8, –9, ConAu 9R, SmATA 4,
WrDr 76, –82, –84, –86*
Wilkinson, Frederick 1891- *Who 74*
Wilkinson, James Harvie, III 1944-
*ConAu 101, DrAS 74P, –78P, –82P,
WhoAm 80, –82, –84, WhoAmL 79*

Wilks, Mike *IntAu&W 86X,
SmATA X*
Wilks, Mike 1947- *ConAu X*
Will, George F 1941- *BioIn 10, –12,
ConAu 77, CurBio 81[port],
EncAJ[port], EncTwCJ, WhoAm 76,
–78, –80, –82, –84, –86*
Will, George Frederick 1941- *BioIn 13*
Willard, Barbara 1909- *ConAu 15NR,
OxChL, WrDr 86*
Willard, Barbara Mary 1909-
*Au&Wr 71, BioIn 11, –12, BritCA,
ChlLR 2, ConAu 81, FourBJA,
SmATA 17, TwCCW 78, –83,
WhE&EA, WrDr 76, –80, –82, –84*
Willard, Charlotte 1914-1977
*BioIn 11, ConAu 73, –81, WhAm 7,
WhoAm 74, –76, –78, WhoAmA 73,
–76, –78, WhoAmW 74, –68A, –70,
–72, WomWWA 14*
Willard, Nancy *DrAP&F 85*
Willard, Nancy 1936- *AmAu&B,
BioIn 12, –13, ChlLR 5[port],
ConAu 10NR, –89, ConLC 7,
–37[port], ConPo 75, –80, –85,
DcLB 5, –52[port], FifBJA[port],
SmATA 30, –37, TwCChW 83,
WhoAmW 75, –77, WrDr 76, –80,
–82, –84, –86*
Willensky, Elliot 1933- *AmArch 70,
ConAu 29R, WhoE 74, –75, –77,
WrDr 76, –80, –82, –84, –86*
Willerding, Margaret F 1919-
*AmM&WS 73P, –76P, –79P,
ConAu 57, WhoAm 78, –80, –82,
WhoAmW 74, –58, –61, –64, –66,
–68, –75, –77, WhoWest 74, –76*
Willerding, Margaret Frances 1919-
WhoAm 84, –86
Willetts, R F 1915- *ConAu 2NR, –5R*
Willetts, Ronald Frederick 1915-
*ConAu 5R, IntAu&W 76, –77, –82,
IntWWP 77, –82, WhoWor 76, –78,
WrDr 76, –80, –82, –84, –86*
Willey, Margaret *DrAP&F 85*
Willey, Margaret 1950- *ConAu 117*
Williams, Barbara 1925- *AuBYP SUP,
BioIn 11, –13, ConAu 1NR, –17NR,
–49, SmATA 11*
Williams, Barry 1932- *ConAu 29R,
WrDr 76, –80, –82, –84, –86*
Williams, Deryl *ConAu X*
Williams, Beryl 1910- *OhA&B,
SmATA 1, –X, WhoAmW 58, –61*
Williams, Beryl *see also* Epstein, Beryl
Williams
Williams, Brad 1918- *ConAu 1R,
–1NR*
Williams, Byron 1934- *ConAu 29R*
Williams, Charles 1928- *BioIn 11, –7,
ConAu X, SmATA 8*
Williams, Charles *see also* Collier,
James Lincoln
Williams, Clayton Wheat 1895-
*WhoF&I 75, –77, –79, WhoS&SW 73,
–75, –76, –78*
Williams, David Ricardo 1923-
IntAu&W 86
Williams, Dorian 1914- *Au&Wr 71,
BioIn 9, –12, ConAu 3NR, –9R,
IntAu&W 76, –77, Who 74, –82, –83,
–85*
Williams, E N 1917- *ConAu 9R*
Williams, E N *see also* Williams, Ernest
Neville
Williams, Edward Bennett 1920-
*BioIn 4, –5, –6, –7, –10, –11, –13,
CelR, ConAu 1R, CurBio 65,
NewYTBS 75, –83[port],
WebAB, –79, WhoAm 74, –76, –78,
–80, –82, –84, –86, WhoAmL 78, –79,
WhoAmP 75, –77, –79, WhoE 79,
–81, –83, –85, WhoF&I 74,
WhoS&SW 73, –75, –76, WorAl*
Williams, Emlyn 1905- *BioIn 13,
HalFC 84, OxAmT 84, OxLitW 86,
OxThe 83, Who 85, WhoAm 84, –86,
WrDr 86*
Williams, Emlyn 1905-1974
*Au&Wr 71, BiE&WWA, BioIn 1, –2,
–3, –4, –5, –6, –8, –10, –12,
BlueB 76, CasWL, CnMD, CnThe,
ConAu 104, –93, ConDr 73, –77, –82,*

*ConLC 15, CroCD, CurBio 41, –52,
DcLB 10[port], EncMys, EncWT,
EvLB, FamA&A, FilmgC,
IntAu&W 76, –77, IntWW 74, –75,
–76, –77, –78, –79, –80, –81, –82,
–83, LongCTC, McGEWD, –84[port],
ModBrL, ModWD, MotPP, MovMk,
NewC, NewYTBS 81[port],
NotNAT, –A, OxThe, PenC ENG,
PlP&P, REn, TwCA, –SUP, TwCWr,
Who 74, –82, –83, WhoAm 74, –76,
–78, –80, –82, WhoHol A,
WhoThe 72, –77, –81, WhoWor 74,
–76, –78, WorAl, WorEFlm,
WrDr 76, –80, –82, –84*
Williams, Emmett *DrAP&F 85*
Williams, Emmett 1925- *ConAu 2NR,
–45, ConPo 75, –80, –85, WrDr 76,
–80, –82, –84, –86*
Williams, Eric d1983 *Who 85N*
Williams, Eric 1911-1983 *Au&Wr 71,
AuBYP, BioIn 7, –12, BioNews 75,
ConAu 9R, –111, CurBio 66,
DcLEL 1940, IntAu&W 76, –77, –82,
IntYB 78, –79, SmATA 14, –37N,
–38N, WhE&EA, Who 74, –82, –83,
WrDr 76, –80, –82, –84*
Williams, Eric Eustace 1911-1981
BioIn 13, InB&W 85, SelBAAf
Williams, Ernest Neville 1917-
Au&Wr 71, ConAu 9R, IntAu&W 77
Williams, Frances Leigh 1909-
ConAu 13R, WhoAmW 68, –70, –72
Williams, Gordon *TwCCr&M 85*
Williams, Gordon 1934- *CmScLit,
ConAu 116, WrDr 86*
Williams, Gordon 1939- *Novels,
WrDr 76, –80, –82*
Williams, Gurney, III 1941- *ConAu 69*
Williams, Guy R 1920- *AmBench 79,
Au&Wr 71, BioIn 11, ConAu 13R,
DcBrAr 1, IntAu&W 77, –82,
SmATA 11, WhoArt 80, –82,
WhoWor 76, WrDr 76, –80, –82, –84,
–86*
Williams, Guy R O 1920- *WhoArt 84*
Williams, Guy Richard 1920-
IntAu&W 86
Williams, Hank, Jr. 1949- *BioIn 11,
–12, ConAu 117, EncFCWM 69,
–83[port], RolSEnR 83, WhoAm 82,
–84, –86, WhoHol A, WhoRock 81*
Williams, Jay *ScFSB, TwCCr&M 85*
Williams, Jay 1914-1978 *AuBYP SUP,
BioIn 4, –7, –9, –10, –11, –13,
ChlLR 8[port], ConAu 1R, –2NR,
–81, CurBio 55, –78, –78N, FourBJA,
IntAu&W 76, –77, NatCAB 61[port],
NewYTBS 78, ObitOF 79, ScF&FL 1,
–2, SmATA 24N, –3, –41[port],
TwCCW 78, –83, TwCCr&M 80,
WhScrn 83, WorAu, WrDr 76*
Williams, Jay *see also* Delving, Michael
Williams, Jerome 1926-
*AmM&WS 73P, –76P, –79P, –82P,
–86P, ConAu 1NR, –49, WhoE 74,
–75, –77*
Williams, Kim d1986
NewYTBS 86[port]
Williams, Kim 1924?-1986 *ConAu 120*
Williams, Kit 1946?- *BioIn 12, –13,
ChlLR 4, ConAu 107,
NewYTBS 80[port], –81[port],
SmATA 44[port], WrDr 82, –84*
Williams, Margery *WomNov*
Williams, Margery 1881- *JBA 34,
TwCChW 83*
Williams, Martin 1924- *ConAu 49,
IntWWM 85, WhoAm 74, –76, –78,
–80, –82, –84*
Williams, Mason 1938- *BiDAmM,
BioIn 8, ConAu 25R, RkOn 78,
WhoAm 74, –76, –78, –80, –82,
WhoRock 81*
Williams, Miller *DrAP&F 85,
IntAu&W 86*
Williams, Miller 1930- *BioIn 13,
ConAu 13R, ConPo 70, –75, –80, –85,
DrAS 74E, –78E, –82E,
IntAu&W 77, –82, IntWWP 77, –82,
WhoAm 74, –76, –78, –80, –82, –84,
WhoS&SW 82, –84, –86,
WhoWor 80, –82, –84, –87, WrDr 76,
–80, –82, –84, –86*

Williams, Ned 1909- *ConAu 13R*
Williams, Ned *see also* Harbin,
Robert
Williams, Oliver F 1939- *ConAu 114*
Williams, Oscar 1900-1964 *AmAu&B,
BioIn 4, –7, ChhPo, –S1, –S3,
ConAu 1R, –6NR, LinLib L,
LongCTC, REn, REnAL,
TwCA, –SUP*
Williams, Patrick J *ConAu X,
SmATA 5*
Williams, Patrick J *see also*
Butterworth, W E
Williams, Paul *IntMPA 86*
Williams, Paul 1940- *BioIn 12, –13,
ConTFT 3, –4[port], CurBio 83[port],
EncFCWM 83, HalFC 84, IlEncRk,
IntMPA 77, –75, –76, –78, –79, –81,
–82, –84, –86, RkOn 78,
RolSEnR 83, WhoHol A,
WhoRock 81*
Williams, Paul Hamilton 1940-
WhoAm 84, –86
Williams, Paul O *DrAP&F 85*
Williams, Paul O 1935- *ConAu 106,
DrAS 74E, –78E, –82E, TwCSFW 86*
Williams, Rosemary 1920-
*BiDrLUS 70, WhoLibS 66,
WhoMW 82*
Williams, Rosemary McDonald 1920-
WhoMW 84
Williams, Selma R 1925- *BioIn 12,
ConAu 1NR, –49, SmATA 14*
Williams, Sherley Anne *DrAP&F 85*
Williams, Sherley Anne 1944-
*BioIn 13, BlkAWP, ConAu 73,
DcLB 41[port], InB&W 85, LivgBAA,
SelBAAf, WhoAmW 79*
Williams, Ted *NewYTBS 85[port]*
Williams, Ted 1918- *BioIn 12, –13,
CelR, CmCal, CurBio 47,
NewYTBE 70, NewYTBS 74,
–82[port], WebAB, –79, WhoAm 76,
–78, –80, –82, –84, –86, WhoHol A,
WhoS&SW 73, WorAl*
Williams, Tennessee 1911?-1983
*AmAu&B, AmSCAP 66, AmWr,
AnObit 1983, Au&Wr 71, AuNews 1,
–2, BiE&WWA, BioIn 1, –2, –3, –4,
–5, –6, –7, –8, –9, –10, –11, –12, –13,
BioNews 74, BlueB 76, CasWL, CelR,
CnDAL, CnMD, CnMWL, CnThe,
ConAu 5R, –108, ConDr 73, –77,
–82, ConLC 1, –2, –5, –7, –8, –11,
–15, –19, –30[port], ConNov 72, –76,
–82, ConTFT 1, CroCD, CurBio 46,
–72, –83N, CyWA, DcLB 7[port],
–DS4[port], –Y83N[port],
DcLEL 1940, EncAB-H, EncSoH,
EncWL, –2[port], EncWT, EvLB,
FilmgC, HalFC 84, IntAu&W 76,
–77, –82, IntMPA 77, –75, –76, –78,
–79, –81, –82, IntWW 74, –75, –76,
–77, –78, –79, –80, –81, –82, –83N,
LinLib L, –S, LongCTC, MajMD 1,
MakMC, McGEWB,
McGEWD, –84[port], ModAL, –S2,
–S1, ModWD, NatPD, –81[port],
NewCon[port], NewYTBE 70, –72,
NewYTBS 75, –83[port],
NotNAT, –A, Novels, OxAmH,
OxAmL, –83, OxAmT 84, OxEng,
OxEng, –85, OxFilm, OxThe, –83,
PenC AM, PlP&P, RComWL, REn,
REnAL, REnWD, ScF&FL 1, –2,
TwCA SUP, TwCWr, WebAB, –79,
WebE&AL, WhDW, Who 74, –82,
–83, WhoAm 74, –76, –78, –80, –82,
WhoThe 72, –77, –81, WhoTwCL,
WhoWor 74, –76, –78, –80, WorAl,
WorEFlm, WrDr 76, –80, –82*
Williams, Thomas *DcNaB,
DrAP&F 85*
Williams, Thomas 1926- *BioIn 3,
ConAu 1R, –2NR, ConLC 14,
EncWM, IntAu&W 82, –86,
WhoAm 76, –78, –80, –82, –84,
WrDr 76, –80, –82, –84, –86*
Williams, Trevor Illtyd 1921- *BioIn 9,
BlueB 76, ConAu 109, IntAu&W 82,
Who 74, –82, –83, –85, WhoWor 76,
–78, –80, WrDr 76, –80, –82, –84,
–86*

Williams, Ursula Moray *ConAu X, IntAu&W 86X, WrDr 86*

Williams, Ursula Moray 1911-
Au&Wr 71, AuBYP SUP, BioIn 8, –9, ConAu 10NR, –13R, FourBJA, IntAu&W 76, –77, –82, –86, IntWWP 77, OxChL, ScF&FL 1, –1A, –2, SmATA 3, TwCCW 78, –83, WhoChL, WhoWor 76, WrDr 76, –80, –82, –84

Williams, Ursula Moray *see also* Moray Williams, Ursula

Williams, William Carlos 1883-1963
AmAu&B, AmWr, AtlBL, BiDAmM, BioIn 1, –2, –4, –5, –6, –7, –8, –9, –10, –11, –12, –13, CasWL, ChhPo, CnDAL, CnE&AP, CnMD, CnMWL, ConAmA, ConAmL, ConAu 89, ConLC 1, –2, –5, –9, –13, –22[port], –42[port], CyWA, DcAmB S7, DcAmMeB 84, DcLB 4, –16[port], –54[port], DcLEL, EncWL, –2[port], EvLB, InSci, LinLib L, –S, LongCTC, MakMC, McGEWB, ModAL, –S2, –S1, ModWD, Novels, ObitOF 79, OxAmL, –83, OxEng, –85, PenC AM, PIP&P, RAdv 1, REn, REnAL, SixAP, TwCA, –SUP, TwCWr, WebAB, –79, WebE&AL, WhDW, WhAm 4, WhLit, WhNAA, WhoTwCL, WorAl

Williamson, Henry Darvall 1907-
ConAu 65

Williamson, J N *ConAu X, DrAP&F 85*

Williamson, Jack 1908- *BioIn 7, –12, –13, ConAu X, ConLC 29[port], ConSFA, DcLB 8[port], EncSF, LinLib L, MnBBF, Novels, ScF&FL 1, –2, ScFSB[port], TwCSFW 86, WhNAA, WhoSciF, WrDr 76, –80, –82, –84, –86*

Williamson, Jack *see also* Williamson, John Stewart

Williamson, Joanne Small 1926-
AuBYP, BioIn 8, –9, ConAu 13R, ForWC 70, SmATA 3, ThrBJA, WhoAmW 66, –68

Williamson, John Stewart *BioIn 13*

Williamson, John Stewart 1908-
AmAu&B, BioIn 7, –12, ConAu 17R, DrAS 74E, –78E, –82E, WhoWest 74, –76, WorAl

Williamson, John Stewart *see also* Williamson, Jack

Williamson, Robin 1943- *DrAP&F 85, WrDr 86*

Willig, George 1949- *BioIn 11, ConAu 102, NewYTBS 77*

Willis, Connie 1945- *ConAu 114, TwCSFW 86*

Willis, Irene 1929- *ConAu 10NR, –65*

Willis, Jerry Weldon 1943-
AmM&WS 73S, ConAu 85, LEduc 74, WhoS&SW 84, –86, WhoWor 87

Willis, Meredith Sue *DrAP&F 85*

Willis, Meredith Sue 1946-
ConAu 16NR, –85

Willison, George Findlay 1896-1972
AmAu&B, Au&Wr 71, BioIn 1, –4, –9, ConAu 37R, ConAu P-1, CurBio 46, NewYTBE 72, ObitOF 79, REnAL, TwCA SUP, WhAm 5

Willson, Robina Beckles *ConAu X*

Willson, Robina Beckles 1930-
BioIn 13, ConAu 5NR, –13R, SmATA 27[port]

Willwerth, James 1943- *ConAu 57, WhoWest 80*

Wilmut, Roger 1942- *ConAu 19NR*

Wilson, A N 1950- *BioIn 13, ConAu 112, ConLC 33[port], ConNov 86*

Wilson, Barbara Ker 1929- *ConAu X, SingR 2, TwCCW 78, –83, WrDr 76, –80, –82, –84, –86*

Wilson, Barbara Ker *see also* Ker Wilson, Barbara

Wilson, Brian 1942- *Baker 84, BiDAmM, BioIn 11, –12, BlueB 76, ConLC 12, WhoAm 78, –80, –82, WhoRock 81, WhoRocM 82*

Wilson, Brian *see also* Beach Boys, The

Wilson, Carl 1946- *BioIn 11, –12, WhoAm 76, –78, –80, –82, WhoRock 81, WhoRocM 82*

Wilson, Carl *see also* Beach Boys, The

Wilson, Charles L 1932-
AmM&WS 73P, –76P, –79P, ConAu 65

Wilson, Charles Lindsay 1932-
WhoFrS 84

Wilson, Charles Morrow 1905-1977
AmAu&B, Au&Wr 71, AuBYP, BioIn 4, –8, ConAu 4NR, –5R, IntAu&W 77, REnAL, SmATA 30[port], TwCA SUP, WhE&EA, WhoAm 74, –76, –78, WrDr 76, –80

Wilson, Colin 1931- *Au&Wr 71, BioIn 4, –5, –6, –8, –9, –10, –13, BlueB 76, CasWL, ConAu 1R, –1NR, ConAu 5AS[port], ConLC 3, –14, ConNov 72, –76, –82, –86, CurBio 63, DcLB 14[port], DcLEL 1940, EncO&P 2, –78S1, EncSF, IntAu&W 76, –77, –82, IntWW 74, –75, –76, –77, –78, –79, –80, –81, –82, –83, LinLib L, LongCTC, ModBrL, –S1, NewC, Novels, RAdv 1, REn, ScF&FL 1, –2, ScFSB, TwCCr&M 80, –85, TwCSFW 86, TwCWr, Who 74, –82, –83, WhoAm 82, WhoHr&F, WhoSciF, WhoWor 74, –76, –78, WorAu, WrDr 76, –80, –82, –84, –86*

Wilson, David 1903- *ConAu X, IntAu&W 76X, WrDr 76, –80, –82*

Wilson, David *see also* MacArthur, D Wilson

Wilson, Dennis 1944- *WhoRock 81*

Wilson, Dennis 1944-1983
AnObit 1983, BioIn 11, –12, –13, NewYTBS 83[port], WhoRocM 82

Wilson, Dennis *see also* Beach Boys, The

Wilson, Dorothy Clarke 1904-
AmAu&B, AmNov, Au&Wr 71, BioIn 2, –12, ConAu 1R, –6NR, CurBio 51, ForWC 70, InWom, IntAu&W 76, –77, –82, –86, SmATA 16, WhoAm 74, –76, –78, –80, –82, –84, –86, WhoAmW 74, –58, –64, –66, –68, –70, –72, WrDr 76, –80, –82, –84, –86

Wilson, Ellen d1976 *AuBYP SUP, BioIn 11, –13, ConAu 103, –49, SmATA 26N, –9, WhoAmW 74, –75*

Wilson, Eric H 1940- *ConAu 101, SmATA 32, –34[port]*

Wilson, Erica *ConAu 7NR, –53, NewYTBE 71*

Wilson, F Paul 1946- *EncSF, ScFSB, TwCSFW 86*

Wilson, Forrest 1918- *AmArch 70, BioIn 13, ConAu 7NR, –53, SmATA 27[port], WhoMW 74*

Wilson, Gahan *PrintW 85*

Wilson, Gahan 1930- *BioIn 12, –13, ConAu 19NR, –25R, ConGrA 2[port], IlsBYP, PrintW 83, SmATA 27, –35, WhoAm 78, –80, –82, –84, –86, WhoHr&F, WorECar*

Wilson, Gina *IntAu&W 86X*

Wilson, Gina 1943- *ConAu 106, IntAu&W 86, SmATA 34, –36, TwCChW 83, WrDr 86*

Wilson, Ian 1941- *ConAu 85*

Wilson, Jacqueline 1945-
ConAu 17NR, TwCCr&M 85, WrDr 86

Wilson, James Q *WhoAm 84, –86*

Wilson, James Q 1931-
AmM&WS 73S, –78S, BioIn 10, BlueB 76, ConAu 116, WhoAm 74, –76, –78, –80, –82, WrDr 80, –82, –84

Wilson, James Quinn 1931- *WrDr 86*

Wilson, John Burgess *WrDr 86*

Wilson, John Burgess 1917- *BioIn 7, –8, –9, –10, –12, ConAu 2NR, –X, ConLC 8, –10, –13, DcLEL 1940, IntAu&W 76X, –77X, PenC ENG, ScF&FL 1, WebE&AL, WorAu, WrDr 76, –80, –82, –84*

Wilson, John Burgess *see also* Burgess, Anthony

Wilson, Joyce M *BioIn 12, ConAu 12NR, –17R, SmATA 21[port], WrDr 80, –82, –84*

Wilson, Joyce M *see also* Stranger, Joyce

Wilson, Lanford *OxThe 83*

Wilson, Lanford 1937- *BioIn 10, –11, –12, –13, ConAu 17R, ConDr 73, –77, –82, ConLC 7, –14, –36[port], ConTFT 1, –3, CurBio 79, DcLB 7[port], McGEWD 84, ModAL S2, NatPD, –81[port], NewYTBS 80[port], NotNAT, OxAmL 83, OxAmT 84, WhoAm 74, –76, –78, –80, –82, –84, –86, WhoE 74, –75, WhoThe 72, –77, –81, WorAu 1975[port], WrDr 76, –80, –82, –84, –86*

Wilson, Mitchell 1913-1973 *AmAu&B, AmNov, Au&Wr 71, BioIn 2, –5, –6, –9, ConAu 1R, –3NR, –41R, ConNov 72, DcLEL 1940, IntAu&W 76, –77, NewYTBE 72, –73, ObitOF 79, OxAmL, –83*

Wilson, Neill C 1889- *BioIn 6, ConAu 5R, MinnWr*

Wilson, Robert Alfred 1922-
WhoE 77, –79, –81

Wilson, Robley, Jr. *DrAP&F 85*

Wilson, Robley, Jr. 1930-
ConAu 14NR, –77, DrAS 74E, –78E, –82E

Wilson, Sloan 1920- *AmAu&B, BioIn 4, –5, –7, –10, –11, ConAu 1R, –1NR, ConLC 32[port], ConNov 72, –76, –82, –86, DcLEL 1940, IntAu&W 76, –77, Novels, PenC AM, PolProf E, REnAL, WhoAm 74, –76, –78, –80, –82, –84, –86, WorAl, WorAu, WrDr 76, –80, –82, –84, –86*

Wilson, Tom 1931- *ConAu 106, SmATA 30, –33[port], WhoAm 74, –76, –78, –80, –82, –84, –86*

Wilton, Elizabeth 1937- *BioIn 12, ConAu 69, SingR 2, SmATA 14*

Wimmer, Helmut Karl 1925- *BioIn 8, IlsCB 1957*

Wimp, Jet *DrAP&F 85*

Windeler, Robert 1944- *ConAu 102, IntAu&W 76*

Windham, Basil *ConAu X, MnBBF, SmATA X, WhoBW&I A*

Windham, Basil *see also* Wodehouse, Pelham Grenville

Windham, Kathryn T 1918- *BioIn 12, ConAu 11NR, –69, SmATA 14*

Windsor, Patricia 1938- *ConAu 4NR, –19NR, –49, FifBJA[port], SmATA 30[port], WhoAmW 83, WhoE 77, –79, WrDr 80, –82, –84, –86*

Wing, Frances Scott 1907- *ConAu P-1, WhoAmW 74*

Wings *RkOn 78, WhoRock 81, WhoRocM 82*

Wings *see also* McCartney, Paul

Winn, Janet B *DrAP&F 85*

Winn, Janet Bruce 1928- *ConAu 105, SmATA 43[port]*

Winogrand, Garry d1984
NewYTBS 84

Winogrand, Garry 1928- *BioIn 7, –9, –11, –12, BriEAA, ConPhot, DcCAr 81, MacBEP, WhoAm 82, WhoAmA 78, –80, –82, –84*

Winogrand, Garry 1928-1984
AnObit 1984, BioIn 13, ICPEnP, WhAm 8

Winship, Elizabeth C 1921- *BioIn 10, ConAu 41R, WhoAmW 77, –79, –81*

Winslow, Pauline Glen *ConAu 101, –18NR, TwCCr&M 85, WrDr 86*

Winsor, Kathleen *WhoAm 84, –86*

Winsor, Kathleen 1919- *AmAu&B, AmNov, BioIn 1, –2, –3, –7, ConAu 97, LongCTC, Novels, REn, REnAL, TwCWr, WhoAm 74, –76, –78, –80, –82, WhoAmW 74, –58, –68, –70, –72, WrDr 84, –86*

Winston, Richard 1917-1979
AuBYP SUP, BioIn 12, ConAu 25R, –93, NewYTBS 80, WhAm 8, WhoAm 80

Winstone, H V F 1926- *ConAu 21NR*

Wint, Guy 1910-1969 *ConAu 1R, –3NR*

Winter, Charles A 1902-
AmM&WS 73P

Winter, Douglas E 1950- *ConAu 118*

Winter, Elmer Louis 1912- *BioIn 7, –9, BlueB 76, ConAu 13R, IntYB 78, –79, –80, –81, –82, WhoAm 74, –76, –78, –80, WhoF&I 74, –85, WhoWorJ 78, WrDr 80, –82, –84*

Winter, Ruth Grosman 1930-
ConAu 37R, EncTwCJ, ForWC 70, IntAu&W 76, WhoAm 76, –78, –80, –82, –84, –86, WhoAmW 74, –66, –68, –72, –75, WhoE 74, –75, –77

Winter, William John 1912- *AuBYP*

Winterbotham, Frederick William 1897- *BioIn 12, ConAu 57, Who 74, –82, –83, –85, WrDr 76, –80, –82, –84, –86*

Winterfeld, Henry 1901- *ConAu 77, ScF&FL 1, ThrBJA*

Winters, Jon *ConAu X*

Winterton, Paul 1908- *BioIn 10, ConAu 5R, –6NR, EncMys, WhE&EA, WorAu, WrDr 80, –82, –84*

Winterton, Paul *see also* Garve, Andrew

Winther, Barbara 1926- *ConAu 17NR, –97*

Winthrop, Elizabeth *BioIn 11, ConAu X, DrAP&F 85, SmATA 8*

Winthrop, Elizabeth 1948-
FifBJA[port]

Winthrop, Elizabeth *see also* Mahony, Elizabeth Winthrop

Winton, John *ConAu X, IntAu&W 76X*

Winton, John *see also* Pratt, John

Winward, Walter 1938- *Au&Wr 71, ConAu 105, IntAu&W 76*

Wirt, Sherwood Eliot 1911-
ConAu 15NR

Wise, David 1930- *AmAu&B, ConAu 1R, –2NR, EncAJ, WhoAm 74, –76, –78, –80, –82, –84, –86, WrDr 76, –80, –82, –84, –86*

Wise, William 1923- *AuBYP, BioIn 7, –9, ChhPo, ConAu 6NR, –13R, SmATA 4*

Wise, Winifred E *WrDr 86*

Wise, Winifred E 1906- *AuBYP, BioIn 7, –9, ConAu 25R, ForWC 70, SmATA 2, WrDr 76, –80, –82, –84*

Wiseman, Bernard 1922- *AuBYP SUP, BioIn 9, ConAu 5R, IntAu&W 77, SmATA 4, WhoE 75, –77, WhoS&SW 78, –80, –82, –84, WrDr 76, –80, –82, –84, –86*

Wiseman, David 1916- *FifBJA[port], IntAu&W 86, SmATA 40, –43[port]*

Wiseman, Thomas 1931- *Au&Wr 71, ConAu 25R, Novels*

Wisler, G Clifton 1950- *SmATA 46, WrDr 82, –84, –86*

Wisner, Bill 1914?-1983 *ConAu X, SmATA X*

Wisner, William L 1914?-1983
AuBYP, BioIn 8, –13, ConAu 110, –111, SmATA 42

Wissmann, Ruth H Leslie 1914-
AuBYP, BioIn 7, ConAu 2NR, –5R, IntAu&W 77, WhoAmW 75

Wister, Owen *OxAmT 84*

Wister, Owen 1860-1938 *Alli SUP, AmAu&B, AmBi, AmLY, ApCAB SUP, ArizL, BiD&SB, BioIn 1, –3, –4, –5, –7, –9, –10, –12, –13, CarSB, CasWL, Chambr 3, ChhPo, –S2, CnDAL, ConAmA, ConAmL, ConAu 108, CyWA, DcAmAu, DcAmB, DcLB 9[port], DcLEL, DcNAA, EncAAH, EncAB-H, EncFWF[port], HalFC 84, HarEnUS, LinLib L, –S, LongCTC, MemAm, NatCAB 13, Novels, OxAmL, –83, PenC AM, RAdv 1, REn, REnAL, REnAW, ScF&FL 1, TwCA, –SUP, TwCLC 21[port], WebAB, –79, WebE&AL, WhAm 1, WhE&EA, WhLit, WhNAA, WorAl*

Witcover, Jules 1927- *AmAu&B, ConAu 25R, EncTwCJ*

Witheridge, Elizabeth P 1907-
*AuBYP SUP, BioIn 6, ConAu 97,
IntAu&W 82, MinnWr*

Withey, Lynne Elizabeth 1948-
DrAS 78H, -82H

Witt, Shirley Hill 1934-
*AmM&WS 73S, -76P, BioIn 12,
ConAu 5NR, -53, FifIDA,
SmATA 17, WhoAmW 77, -79, -81,
WhoWest 80, -82, -84*

Witton, Dorothy *AuBYP, BioIn 7,
ConAu 73, MichAu 80*

Wodehouse, P G *OxThe 83*

Wodehouse, P G 1881-1975 *AmAu&B,
AmPS, AmSCAP 66, BiDAmM,
BiE&WWA, BlueB 76N, CelR,
CmpEPM, ConAu 3NR, -45, -57,
ConDr 73, ConLC 2, -5, -10,
-22[port], ConNov 72, -76,
CurBio 71, -75, -75N,
DcLB 34[port], EncMT, EncSF,
EncWL 2, EncWT, HalFC 84,
LinLib L, LongCTC, McGEWD, -84,
ModBrL, -S2, -S1, NewC,
NewCBMT, NewYTBS 75, Novels,
ObitOF 79, OxAmT 84, PenC ENG,
PlP&P, RAdv 1, REn, ScF&FL 1, -2,
SmATA 22[port], TwCWr,
WebE&AL, WhoTwCL, WorAl*

Wodehouse, Pelham Grenville
1881-1975 *AmSCAP 66, Au&Wr 71,
AuNews 2, BioIn 1, -2, -3, -4, -5, -6,
-7, -8, -9, -10, -11, -12, CasWL,
Chambr 3, DcLEL, EncWL, EvLB,
IntWW 74, -75N, LinLib S, MakMC,
MnBBF, NotNAT A, ObitT 1971,
OxEng, TwCA, -SUP, WhDW,
WhAm 6, WhE&EA, WhLit, WhThe,
Who 74, WhoAm 74, WhoBW&I A,
WhoChL, WhoWor 74*

Wodehouse, Sir P G 1881-1975
OxChL, OxEng 85

Wodehouse, Sir Pelham Grenville
1881-1975 *BioIn 13, DcNaB 1971*

Wofsy, Leon 1921- *AmM&WS 86P,
WhoAm 84, -86*

Wohlrabe, Raymond A 1900-1977
*AuBYP, BioIn 7, -9, ConAu 1R,
-3NR, SmATA 4, WhoPNW,
WhoWest 74, WrDr 76, -80, -82, -84*

Woiwode, Larry *DrAP&F 85*

Woiwode, Larry 1941- *BioIn 8, -10,
ConAu 16NR, -73, ConLC 6, -10,
ConNov 82, -86, DcLB 6[port],
OxAmL 83, WhoAm 74, -76, -78,
-80, WrdrW Au 1975[port], WrDr 80,
-82, -84, -86*

Wojciechowska, Maia *DrAP&F 85*

Wojciechowska, Maia 1927- *AmAu&B,
AmCath 80, Au&ICB, AuBYP,
BioIn 7, -8, -9, -10, -11, -13,
ChlLR 1, ConAu 4NR, -9R,
ConLC 26[port], CurBio 76,
HerW, -84, MorBMP, NewbC 1956,
OxChL, PiP, SmATA 1, -28[port],
SmATA 1AS[port], ThrBJA,
TwCCW 78, -83, WhoAm 74, -76,
-78, WhoAmW 74, -66, -68, -70,
-72, -75, WrDr 80, -82, -84, -86*

Wojciechowska, Maia *see also* Rodman,
Maia

Wold, JoAnne 1938- *ConAu 61*

Wolf, Bernard 1930- *ConAu 115,
FifBJA[port], SmATA 37*

Wolf, Harold Arthur 1923- *AmEA 74,
AmM&WS 73S, -78S, ConAu 13R,
WhoAm 80, -82, -84, -86,
WhoS&SW 86*

Wolf, Jacqueline 1928- *ConAu 109*

Wolf, Jacqueline Glicenstein 1928-
HerW 84

Wolf, Marguerite Hurrey 1914-
BioIn 11, ConAu 53, WhoAmW 72

Wolfe, Burton H 1932- *BioIn 10,
ConAu 25R, DcAmSR, IntAu&W 77,
-82, SmATA 5, WhoWest 74, -76,
-78, WrDr 76, -80, -82, -84, -86*

Wolfe, Gene *DrAP&F 85*

Wolfe, Gene 1931- *BioIn 12,
ConAu 6NR, -14R, ConLC 25[port],
DcLB 8, EncSF, IntAu&W 76,
PostFic, ScF&FL 1, -2, ScFSB[port],
TwCSFW 86, WhoMW 80, -82,
WrDr 84, -86*

Wolfe, Jean Elizabeth 1925-
*WhoAmW 74, -68, -72, -75, -77,
-79, -81, -83, -85, -87, WhoE 74,
-75, -77, -79, -81, -83, -85*

Wolfe, Louis 1905- *AuBYP, BioIn 7,
-11, ConAu 3NR, -5R, ScF&FL 1,
-2, SmATA 8*

Wolfe, Thomas Clayton 1900-1938
*AmAu&B, AmBi, AmSCAP 66,
AmWr, AtlBL, BioIn 1, -2, -3, -4,
-5, -6, -7, -8, -9, -10, -11, -12,
CasWL, CnDAL, CnMD, CnMWL,
ConAmA, ConAu 104, CyWA,
DcAmB S2, DcLB 9[port],
-DS2[port], DcLEL, DcNAA,
EncAB-H, EncSoH, EncWL, EncWT,
EvLB, LinLib L, -S, LongCTC,
MakMC, McGEWB, ModAL,
ModWD, Novels, OxAmH, OxAmL,
OxEng, -85, PenC AM, PlP&P,
RAdv 1, REn, REnAL, TwCA, -SUP,
TwCLC 4[port], TwCWr,
WebAB, -79, WebE&AL, WhDW,
WhAm 1, WhoTwCL, WorAl*

Wolfe, Thomas K *BioIn 13*

Wolfe, Thomas Kennerly, Jr. 1931-
*AmAu&B, BioIn 12, BlueB 76,
ConAu 9NR, -13R, DcLEL 1940,
IntAu&W 82, WhoAm 74, -76, -78,
-80, -82, -84, -86, WhoWor 74*

Wolfe, Tom 1930- *WrDr 86*

Wolfe, Tom 1931- *AuNews 2, BioIn 7,
-8, -9, -10, -11, -12, -13, CelR,
CmCal, ConAu X, ConLC 1, -2, -9,
-15, -35[port], CurBio 71, EncAJ,
EncTwCJ, MakMC,
NewYTBS 81[port], OxAmL 83,
PenC AM, PostFic, WebE&AL,
WhoTwCL, WorAl, WorAu 1970,
WrDr 76, -80, -82, -84*

Wolff, Ruth 1909?-1972 *BioIn 9,
ConAu 37R*

Wolff, Virginia Euwer 1937-
ConAu 107

Wolfson, Victor 1910- *BiE&WWA,
BioIn 1, -4, ConAu 33R, NotNAT,
TwCA SUP, WhoWorJ 72, -78*

Wolitzer, Hilma *DrAP&F 85*

Wolitzer, Hilma 1930- *BioIn 11,
ConAu 18NR, -65, ConLC 17,
FifBJA[port], SmATA 31[port],
WhoAm 82, -84, 86, WrDr 76, -80,
-82, -84, -86*

Wolitzer, Meg *DrAP&F 85*

Wolitzer, Meg 1959- *ConAu 18NR*

Wolk, Allan 1936- *ConAu 77*

Wolkoff, Judie *ConAu 115, SmATA 37*

Wollheim, Donald A *DrmM 2[port]*

Wollheim, Donald A 1914- *AuBYP,
BioIn 7, ConAu 1R, -1NR, -19NR,
ConSFA, EncSF, ScF&FL 1, -2,
ScFSB, TwCSFW 86, WhoAm 78,
-80, -82, WhoE 74, -75, -77, -79,
WhoHr&F, WhoSciF, WhoWor 80,
WrDr 76, -80, -82, -84, -86*

Wollheim, Donald Allen 1914-
WhoAm 84, -86

Wollstonecraft, Mary *BioIn 13*

Wollstonecraft, Mary 1759-1797
*DcBrAmW, DcLB 39[port], DcNaB,
HerW 84, LitC 5[port], OxChL,
OxEng 85*

Wollstonecraft, Mary 1797-1851 *Alli,
AtlBL, BbD, BiD&SB, BioIn 1, -2,
-3, -7, -8, -9, -10, -11, -12, BritAu,
CasWL, CelCen, Chambr 3, CrtT 4,
CyEd, DcEnA, DcEnL, DcLEL,
Dis&D, GoodHs, HerW, InWom,
IntDcWB[port], NewC, OxEng,
PenC ENG, REn*

Wollstonecraft, Mary *see also* Shelley,
Mary Wollstonecraft

Wolters, Richard A 1920- *BioIn 8,
-12, ConAu 3NR, -5R, -18NR,
SmATA 35, WrDr 76, -80, -82, -84,
-86*

Womack, John, Jr. 1937- *ConAu 45,
WhoAm 74, -76, -78, -80*

Wonder, Stevie *ConAu X,
NewYTBS 85[port]*

Wonder, Stevie 1950?- *Baker 78, -84,
BiDAfM, BiDAmM, BioIn 9, -10,
-11, -12, -13, BioNews 74,*

ConLC 12, CurBio 75, DrBlPA,
Ebony 1, EncJzS, EncPR&S 74, -77,
IlEncRk, InB&W 80, -85,
IntWW 78, -79, -80, -81, -82, -83,
NegAl 83[port], NewYTBE 70,
NewYTBS 75, RkOn 74, -78, -82,
-84, RolSEnR 83, WhoAm 76, -78,
-80, -82, -84, -86, WhoBlA 75, -77,
-80, -85, WhoRock 81,
WhoRocM 82, Who Wor 84, -87,
WorAl*

Wonder, Stevie 1951- *BiDJaz*

Wong, Jade Snow 1922- *BioIn 2, -4,
-10, -13, ConAu 109, ConLC 17,
WhoAmW 58, -61, -64*

Wood, Barbara 1947- *ConAu 15NR,
-85*

Wood, Clement 1888-1950 *AmAu&B,
AmSCAP 66, AnMV 1926, BioIn 2,
-4, ChhPo, -S1, -S2, ObitOF 79,
REn, REnAL, TwCA, -SUP,
WhAm 3, WhE&EA, WhLit, WhNAA*

Wood, Clement Biddle 1925-
ConAu 21R

Wood, James Playsted 1905-
*AmAu&B, Au&Wr 71, AuBYP,
BioIn 9, ChhPo S2, ConAu 3NR,
-9R, FourBJA, IntAu&W 77, -82,
ScF&FL 1, SmATA 1, WhAm 8,
WhoAm 74, -76, -78, -80, -82,
WrDr 76, -80, -82, -84*

Wood, Kenneth 1922- *ConAu 11NR,
-69*

Wood, Laura N 1911- *AuBYP,
BioIn 7, ConAu 57, SmATA X,
WrDr 76, -80, -82, -84*

Wood, Laura N *see also* Roper, Laura
Wood

Wood, Laura Newbold *WrDr 86*

Wood, Michael 1936- *ConAu 37R*

Wood, Nancy 1936- *BioIn 10,
ConAu 9NR, -21R, MacBEP,
SmATA 6, WhoAmW 74, -75*

Wood, Paul W 1922- *ConAu 61,
WhoE 79*

Wood, Phyllis Anderson 1923-
*AuBYP SUP, ConAu 14NR, -37R,
IntAu&W 77, SmATA 30, -33[port],
WrDr 76, -80, -82, -84, -86*

Wood-Allen, Mary 1841-1908
DcAmAu, DcNAA, OhA&B, WhAm 1

Woodburn, John Henry 1914-
*AuBYP SUP, BioIn 11, ConAu 1R,
-4NR, LEduc 74, SmATA 11*

Woodcock, George 1912- *Au&Wr 71,
BioIn 13, CaW, CanWW 70, -79,
-80, -81, -83, CanWr, CasWL,
ConAu 1R, -1NR, ConAu 6AS[port],
ConDr 82B, ConPo 70, -75, -80, -85,
DcLEL 1940, IntAu&W 76, -77, -82,
IntWW 79, -80, -81, -82, -83,
IntWWP 77, ModBrL, OxCan, -SUP,
OxCanL, WhE&EA, Who 74, -82,
-83, -85, WhoAm 74, -76, -78, -80,
-82, -84, -86, WhoCanL 85,
WhoWor 84, -87, WorAu 1970,
WrDr 76, -80, -82, -84, -86*

Wooden, John R 1910- *BioIn 6, -9,
-10, -11, -12, CelR, CmCal,
CurBio 76, NewYTBE 73,
WhoAm 76, -78, -80, -82, WorAl*

Wooden, John Robert 1910-
WhoAm 84, -86

Woodford, Peggy 1937- *BioIn 13,
ConAu 104, SmATA 25[port],
WrDr 80, -82, -84, -86*

Woodham-Smith, Cecil 1896-1977
*Au&Wr 71, BioIn 2, -3, -4, -11,
ConAu 69, -77, CurBio 55, -77,
-77N, InWom, IntAu&W 76,
IntWW 74, -75, -76, -77N,
LongCTC, NewYTBS 77, ObitOF 79,
REn, TwCA SUP, Who 74,
WhoAmW 68, -70, -72, WhoWor 74,
WrDr 76*

Woodham-Smith, Cecil Blanche
1896-1977 *DcNaB 1971*

Woodman, James Monroe 1931-
ConAu 17R

Woodman, Jim 1931- *ConAu X*

Woodman, Jim *see also* Woodman,
James Monroe

Woodress, James 1916- *WrDr 86*

Woodress, James Leslie, Jr. 1916-
*ConAu 3NR, -5R, DrAS 74E, -78E,
-82E, WhoAm 74, -76, -78, -80, -82,
-84, -86, WrDr 80, -82, -84*

Woods, Donald 1933- *BioIn 12, -13,
ConAu 114, CurBio 82[port]*

Woods, George A 1926- *AuBYP SUP,
ConAu 29R, SmATA 30[port]*

Woods, Geraldine 1948- *ConAu 97,
SmATA 42, WhoBlA 80*

Woods, Harold 1945- *ConAu 97,
SmATA 42*

Woods, Stuart 1938- *BioIn 12,
ConAu 93, IntAu&W 82*

Woodward, Bob 1943- *AuNews 1,
BioIn 9, -12, BioNews 74, ConAu 69,
-X, CurBio 76, EncAJ,
NewYTBS 80[port], WrDr 80, -82,
-84, -86*

Woodward, Robert U 1943- *EncTwCJ*

Woodward, Robert Upshur 1943-
*AuNews 1, BioIn 10, -11, -12, -13,
ConAu 69, WhoAm 74, -76, -78, -80,
-82, -84, -86, WorAl*

Woody, Regina J 1894- *AuBYP,
BioIn 6, -7, -9, ConAu 3NR, -5R,
ForWC 70, IntAu&W 77, MorJA,
SmATA 3, WhoAmW 74, -61, -64,
-66, -68, -70, -72, -75, WhoE 74,
WrDr 76, -80, -82, -84*

Woody, Robert Henley 1936-
BiDrAPH 79, ConAu 93

Woodyard, George W 1934-
ConAu 81, DrAS 74F, -78F, -82F

Woolf, Virginia 1882-1941 *AtlBL,
BioIn 1, -2, -3, -4, -5, -6, -7, -8, -9,
-10, -11, -12, -13, BritWr 7, CasWL,
Chambr 3, CnMWL, ConAu 104,
ConLCrt, -2[port], CurBio 41, CyWA,
DcLB 36[port], DcLEL, DcNaB 1941,
EncSF, EncWL, -2[port], EvLB,
GoodHs, HalFC 84, InWom,
IntDcWB[port], LinLib L, -S,
LongCEL, LongCTC, McGEWB,
ModBrL, -S2, -S1, NewC,
Novels[port], ObitOF 79, OxEng, -85,
PenC ENG, RAdv 1, RComWL, REn,
ScF&FL 1, ScFSB, TwCA, -SUP,
TwCLC 1, -5[port], -20[port],
TwCWr, WebE&AL, WhDW,
WhE&EA, WhoTwCL, WorAl*

Woolley, Bryan *DrAP&F 85*

Woolley, Bryan 1937- *ConAu 4NR,
-49*

Woolsey, Janette 1904- *AuBYP,
BioIn 7, -9, ConAu 1R, -2NR,
ForWC 70, ScF&FL 1, SmATA 3,
WhoAmW 68, WhoLibS 55*

Wootten, Morgan 1931- *AmCath 80,
BioIn 11, -12, ConAu 101*

Worboys, Anne *ConAu 9NR, -65,
WrDr 76, -80, -82, -84, -86*

Worcester, Donald E 1915-
ConAu 19NR, WrDr 86

Worcester, Donald Emmet 1915-
WhoAm 84, -86

Worcester, Donald Emmett 1915-
*AmAu&B, AuBYP, BioIn 7, -12,
BlueB 76, ConAu 1R, -4NR,
DrAS 74H, -78H, -82H,
IntAu&W 76, -77, -82, SmATA 18,
WhoAm 74, -76, -78, -80, -82,
WhoS&SW 73, WhoWor 78,
WrDr 76, -80, -82, -84*

Wordsworth, William 1770-1850 *Alli,
AnCL, AtlBL, BbD, BiD&SB,
BiDLA, BioIn 1, -2, -3, -4, -5, -6,
-7, -8, -9, -10, -11, -12, -13,
BritAu 19, BritWr 4, CasWL, CelCen,
Chambr 3, ChhPo, -S1, -S2, -S3,
CnE&AP, CrtT 2, -4, CyEd, CyWA,
DcBiPP, DcEnA, DcEnL, DcEuL,
DcLEL, DcNaB, Dis&D, EvLB,
IlEncMy[port], LinLib L, -S,
LongCEL, LuthC 75, McGEWB,
MouLC 3, NewC, NinCLC 12[port],
OxEng, -85, OxMus, PenC ENG,
PoLE, RAdv 1, RComWL, REn,
Str&VC, WebE&AL, WhDW, WorAl*

Worrell, Estelle *AuBYP SUP*

Worster, Donald E 1941-
ConAu 12NR

Worster, Donald Eugene 1941-
ConAu 57, DrAS 74H, -78H, -82H

Worth, Douglas *DrAP&F 85* **Worth,**
Douglas 1940- *ConAu 9NR, –65,*
IntWWP 82
Worth, Douglas Grey 1940-
IntAu&W 86
Worth, Fred L 1943- *ConAu 97*
Worth, Richard *SmATA 46*
Worth, Richard 1945- *IntAu&W 86*
Worth, Valerie *ConAu X*
Worth, Valerie 1933- *FifBJA[port]*
Worthy, William 1921- *EncAJ,*
InB&W 80, WhoBlA 77, –80, –85
Worton, Stanley Nelson 1923-
ConAu 57, DrAS 74H, –78H, –82H
Wosmek, Frances 1917- *BioIn 13,*
ConAu 11NR, –29R,
SmATA 29[port], WrDr 80, –82, –84
Wouk, Herman 1915- *AmAu&B,*
AmNov, Au&Wr 71, BiE&WWA,
BioIn 1, –2, –3, –4, –5, –8, –9, –13,
BlueB 76, CnMD, ConAu 5R, –6NR,
ConLC 1, –9, –38[port], ConNov 72,
–76, –82, –86, ConTFT 1, CroCD,
CurBio 52, DcLB Y82B[port],
DcLEL 1940, EncSF, EncWL,
EncWT, FilmgC, HalFC 84,
IntAu&W 76, –77, IntWW 74,
–75, –76, –77, –78, –79, –80, –81,
–82, –83, LinLib L, LongCTC,
ModAL, ModWD, NatPD 81[port],
NotNAT, Novels, OxAmL, –83,
PenC AM, REn, REnAL, ScF&FL 1,
ScFSB, TwCA SUP, TwCWr,
WebAB, –79, Who 74, –82, –83, –85,
WhoAm 74, –76, –78, –80, –82, –84,
–86, WhoAmJ 80, WhoE 83,
WhoWor 74, –76, –78, –80, –82, –84,
–87, WhoWorJ 72, –78, WorAl,
WrDr 76, –80, –82, –84, –86
Wren, Percival C 1885-1941 *BioIn 1,*
CurBio 42, DcLEL, EvLB, LongCTC,
MnBBF, NewC, ObitOF 79, OxEng,
PenC ENG, REn, ScF&FL 1, TwCA,
TwCWr, WhE&EA, WhLit
Wright, Betty Ren *SmATA 48*
Wright, Constance 1897- *Au&Wr 71,*
ConAu 13R, WrDr 76, –80, –82, –84
Wright, Gary 1943- *IlEncRk,*
RkOn 78, RolSEnR 83, WhoRock 81,
WhoRocM 82
Wright, Helen 1914- *AmAu&B,*
BioIn 4, ConAu 9R, CurBio 56, InSci,
InWom, ScF&FL 1, –2, WhoAm 74,
–76, –78, –80, –82, –84, –86,
WhoAmW 74, –58, –61, –64, –66,
–68, –70, –72

Wright, James Arlington 1927-1980
AmAu&B, AnObit 1980[port],
AuNews 2, BioIn 9, –10, –11, –12,
–13, ChhPo, –S1, CnE&AP,
ConAu 4NR, –49, –97, ConLC 3, –5,
–10, ConPo 70, –75, –80, CroCAP,
DcLB 5[port], DcLEL 1940,
IntWWP 77, ModAL, –S1,
NewYTBS 80[port], PenC AM,
RAdv 1, WebE&AL, WhAm 7,
WhoTwCL, WorAu, WrDr 76, –80
Wright, John Stafford 1905-
Au&Wr 71, ConAu 57, WhoWor 76,
–78, WrDr 76, –80, –84, –86
Wright, Kenneth *ConAu X,*
TwCSFW 86, Who 85, WrDr 86
Wright, Kenneth 1915- *ConAu 65, –X,*
SmATA X, WrDr 84
Wright, Kenneth *see also* DelRey,
Lester
Wright, Lawrence 1947- *ConAu 93*
Wright, Louis B 1899-1984
CurBio 84N
Wright, Louis Booker d1984
Who 85N
Wright, Louis Booker 1899- *AmAu&B,*
Au&Wr 71, BlueB 76, ChhPo S1, –S3,
ConAu 1R, –1NR, CurBio 50,
DcLB 17[port], DrAS 74H, –78H,
–82H, IntAu&W 77, –82, IntWW 74,
–75, –76, –77, –78, –79, –80, –81,
–82, –83, NotNAT, REnAL,
WhAm 8, WhE&EA, Who 74, –82,
–83, WhoAm 74, –76, –78, –80, –82,
WrDr 76, –80, –82, –84
Wright, Louis Booker 1899-1984
AnObit 1984, BioIn 13, ConAu 112
Wright, Nancy Means *ConAu 104,*
DrAP&F 85, IntAu&W 82,
SmATA 38[port]
Wright, Nathan, Jr. 1923- *BioIn 9,*
BlkAWP, ConAu 37R, DrAS 74H,
Ebony 1, InB&W 80, –85, LivgBAA,
NegAl 76, –83, SelBAAf, SelBAAu,
WhoBlA 75, –77, –80, WhoE 74, –75,
–77
Wright, Richard 1908-1960 *AmAu&B,*
AmNov, AmWr, BioIn 1, –2, –3, –4,
–5, –6, –7, –8, –9, –10, –11, –12, –13,
BlkAWP, CasWL, CnDAL,
ConAu 108, ConLC 1, –3, –4, –9,
–14, –21[port], ConNov 76,
CurBio 40, –61, CyWA, DcAmB S6,
DcAmNB, DcAmSR,

DcLB DS2[port], DcLEL, DrBlPA,
Dis&D, EncAB-H, EncSoH,
EncWL, –2[port], EvLB, InB&W 80,
LinLib L, LongCTC, McGEWB,
ModAL, –S2, –S1, ModBlW,
NegAl 76[port], –83[port], NotNAT A,
–B, Novels[port], ObitOF 79,
ObitT 1951, OxAmL, –83, OxEng 85,
PenC AM, PlP&P, RAdv 1, REn,
REnAL, SelBAAf, SelBAAu,
TwCA, –SUP, TwCWr, WebAB, –79,
WebE&AL, WhDW, WhAm 4,
WhoTwCL, WorAl
Wright, Shannon 1956?- *BioIn 12*
Wright, T M 1947- *ConAu 120*
Wright, Theon 1904- *ConAu 109,*
WhNAA
Wrightson, Patricia 1921- *AuBYP,*
BioIn 8, –11, ChlLR 4[port],
ConAu 3NR, –19NR, –45, FourBJA,
OxAusL, OxChL, ScF&FL 1, –2,
SenS, SingR 1, SmATA 8,
SmATA 4AS[port], TwCCW 78, –83,
WrDr 80, –82, –84, –86
Wrigley, Denis *ChhPo S1, –S2, –S3*
Wrigley, Robert *DrAP&F 85*
Wrone, David R 1933- *ConAu 6NR,*
–57, WhoMW 78
Wrone, David Roger 1933-
WhoMW 84
Wroth, Lawrence Counselman
1884-1970 *AmAu&B, BioIn 1, –9,*
–10, ChhPo S3, ConAu 29R,
DcAmLiB, NewYTBE 70, OxAmL,
REnAL, WhNAA
Wulffson, Don L 1943- *ConAu 19NR*
Wunsch, Josephine 1914-
ConAu 15NR
Wunsch, Josephine M 1914- *AuBYP,*
BioIn 8, ConAu 1R, ForWC 70,
MichAu 80, WrDr 76, –80, –82, –84,
–86
Wunsch, Josephine McLean 1914-
WhoMW 84
Wuorio, Eva-Lis 1918- *AuBYP SUP,*
BioIn 9, –13, ConAu 77, CreCan 1,
SmATA 28, –34[port], ThrBJA
Wyatt, John 1925- *ConAu 105*
Wyatt-Brown, Bertram 1932-
ConAu 21NR, –25R, DrAS 74H,
–78H, –82H, WhoAm 76, –78, –80,
–82, –84, –86
Wyeth, N C 1882-1945 *AntBDN B,*
ArtsAmW 1, CurBio 45, ForIl,
OxChL, SmATA 17

Wyeth, Newell Convers 1882-1945
AmAu&B, ArtsAmW 3, BioIn 1, –2,
–4, –5, –7, –8, –9, –10, –12, –13,
ChhPo, –S2, –S3, ConICB,
DcAmB S3, IlBEAAW, IlrAm 1880,
–B, IlsBYP, JBA 34, –51, ObitOF 79,
OxAmH, REnAL, WebAB, –79,
WhAm 2
Wyler, Rose 1909- *AuBYP, BioIn 7,*
–9, –12, BkP, ConAu 93, SmATA 18,
ThrBJA, WhoAmW 58, –61, –64
Wylie, Philip *TwCCr&M 85*
Wylie, Philip 1902-1971 *AmAu&B,*
AmNov, BioIn 1, –2, –3, –4, –5, –7
–9, –12, ChhPo S2, CnDAL,
ConAu 33R, ConAu P-2,
ConLC 43[port], ConNov 72,
DcLB 9[port], EncMys, EncSF, EvLB,
LinLib L, –S, NewYTBE 71,
ObitOF 79, REn, REnAL, ScF&FL 1,
–2, ScFSB, TwCA, –SUP,
TwCSFW 86, TwCWr, WebAB, –79,
WhAm 5, WhFla, WhoSciF
Wyman, Bill 1941- *BioIn 12, –13,*
CelR
Wyman, Bill *see also* Rolling Stones,
The
Wymer, Norman George 1911-
Au&Wr 71, AuBYP, BioIn 7, –13,
ConAu 104, SmATA 25, WhE&EA,
WrDr 76, –80, –82, –84
Wyndham, John 1903-1969 *BioIn 7,*
–8, –10, –12, ConAu X, ConLC 19,
DcLEL 1940, DcNaB 1961, EncSF,
FilmgC, HalFC 84, LinLib L,
LongCTC, Novels, ObitOF 79,
OxEng 85, REn, ScF&FL 1, –2,
ScFSB[port], TwCSFW 86, TwCWr,
WebE&AL, WhoSciF, WorAl, WorAu
Wyndham, John *see also* Harris, John
Benyon
Wyndham, Lee *BioIn 13, SmATA X*
Wyndham, Lee 1912-1978 *AuBYP,*
BioIn 6, –7, –9, –11, ConAu 5R, –X,
ForWC 70, IntAu&W 76, –77, –82,
MorJA, SmATA 1, –X, TwCCW 78,
WhoAmW 58, –61, –66, –68,
WhoE 74, WrDr 76
Wyndham, Lee *see also* Hyndman, Jane
Andrews
Wyss, Johann David 1743-1818
AuBYP SUP, BioIn 1, –3, –8, –13,
CarSB, CasWL, NinCLC 10[port],
OxGer, SmATA 27, –29, Str&VC,
WhoChL

X

Ximenes, Ben Cuellar, Jr. 1911-
 ConAu 5R

Y

Yacowar, Maurice 1942- *CanWW 83, ConAu 41R, DrAS 74E, -78E, -82E*

Yannella, Donald 1934- *ConAu 8NR, -57, DrAS 78E, -82E*

Yarborough, Cale 1939- *BioIn 13*

Yarbro, Chelsea Quinn 1942- *ConAu 9NR, -65, EncSF, ScF&FL 1, -2, ScFSB, TwCSFW 86, WrDr 84, -86*

Yarrow, Philip John 1917- *Au&Wr 71, ConAu 13R, WhoWor 84, WrDr 76, -80, -82, -84, -86*

Yarwood, Doreen 1918- *ConAu 18NR, IntAu&W 86, WrDr 86*

Yastrzemski, Carl *NewYTBS 86[port]*

Yastrzemski, Carl 1939- *BioIn 5, -6, -8, -9, -10, -11, -12, -13, CelR, ConAu 104, CurBio 68, NewYTBE 70, -72, NewYTBS 75, -79, -82[port], -83[port], WhoAm 74, -76, -78, -80, -82, WhoProB 73, WorAl*

Yastrzemski, Carl Michael 1939- *WhoAm 84, -86*

Yates, Brock Wendel 1933- *AuBYP, BioIn 7, -9, ConAu 9R, Ward 77F*

Yates, Elizabeth 1905- *AmAu&B, AmNov, AmWomWr, Au&ICB, Au&Wr 71, AuBYP, BioIn 1, -2, -3, -4, -5, -7, -9, -10, -12, ChhPo, ConAu 1R, -6NR, -13R, -21NR, CurBio 48, HerW 84, InWom, IntAu&W 77, JBA 51, MorBMP, Newb 1922, OxChL, REnAL, SmATA 4, TwCA SUP, TwCCW 78, -83, WhoAm 74, -76, -78, -80, -82, -84, -86, WhoAmW 74, -58, -61, -64, -66, -68, -70, -72, WrDr 80, -82, -84, -86*

Yates, Madeleine 1937- *ConAu 109*

Yates, Raymond Francis 1895-1966 *Au&Wr 71, AuBYP, BioIn 6, -7, ConAu 110, EncAB 38[port], MorJA, SmATA 31[port], WhAm 4, WhE&EA, WhLit, WhNAA*

Yates, Richard *DrAP&F 85*

Yates, Richard 1926- *AmAu&B, BioIn 5, -10, -13, ConAu 5R, -10NR, ConLC 7, -8, -23[port], ConNov 72, -76, -82, -86, DcLB 2, -Y81A[port], DcLEL 1940, IntAu&W 76, -77, LinLib L, WorAu, WrDr 76, -80, -82, -84*

Yau, John *DrAP&F 85*

Yau, John 1950- *ConPo 85*

Yaukey, Grace S 1899- *AmAu&B, AmNov X, AuBYP, BioIn 2, -8, -10, ConAu 1R, -1NR, InWom, JBA 51, SmATA 5*

Yaukey, Grace S *see also* Spencer, Cornelia

Yeakley, Marjory Hall 1908- *BioIn 12, ConAu 1R, -2NR, CurBio 57, InWom, IntAu&W 77, -82, SmATA 21[port]*

Yeakley, Marjory Hall *see also* Hall, Marjory

Yeakley, Marjory Hall *see also* Morse, Carol

Yeats, William Butler 1865-1939 *Alli SUP, AnCL, ArizL, BbD, BiD&SB, BiDIrW, BioIn 1, -2, -3, -4, -5, -6, -7, -8, -9, -10, -11, -12, -13, BritWr 6, CasWL, Chambr 3, ChhPo, -S1, -S2, -S3, CnE&AP, CnMD, CnMWL, CnThe, ConAu 104, CyWA, DcEnA, -AP, DcIrB, DcIrL, DcIrW 1, DcLB 10[port], -19[port], DcLEL, DcNaB 1931, Dis&D, EncWL, -2[port], EncWT, EvLB, LinLib L, -S, LongCTC, MajMD 1, MakMC, McGEWB, McGEWD, -84[port], ModBrL, -S2, -S1, ModWD, NewC, NewEOp 71, NotNAT A, -B, OxEng, -85, OxThe, -83, PenC ENG, PIP&P, PoIre, RAdv 1, RComWL, REn, REnWD, TwCA, -SUP, TwCLC 1, -11[port], -18[port], TwCWr, WebE&AL, WhDW, WhE&EA, WhThe, WhoNob, WhoTwCL, WorAl*

Yee, Min S 1938- *ConAu 101, WrDr 76, -80, -82, -84, -86*

Yefremov, Ivan 1907-1972 *EncSF, ScF&FL 1, TwCSFW 86A, WhoSciF*

Yeo, Wilma 1918- *BioIn 13, ConAu 25R, SmATA 24[port]*

Yep, Laurence 1948- *ConLC 35[port], DcLB 52[port], FifBJA[port], ScFSB, TwCSFW 86, WrDr 84*

Yep, Laurence Michael 1948- *BioIn 10, ChlLR 3, ConAu 1NR, -49, EncSF, ScF&FL 1, -2, SmATA 7, TwCCh 83, WhoAm 78, -80, -82, -84, -86, WrDr 84*

Yerby, Frank 1916- *AmAu&B, AmNov, Au&Wr 71, BioIn 1, -2, -3, -4, -5, -7, -9, -12, BlueB 76, BlkAWP, CivR 74, ConAu 9R, ConLC 1, -7, -22[port], ConNov 72, -82, -86, CurBio 46, DcLEL 1940, EncSoH, InB&W 80, IntAu&W 76, -77, -82, IntWW 74, -75, -76, -77, -78, -79, -80, -81, LinLib L, LivgBAA, LongCTC, NegAl 76, -83, Novels[port], OxAmL 83, PenC AM, SelBAAf, SelBAAu, TwCA SUP, WebAB, -79, Who 74, -82, -83, WhoAm 74, -76, -78, -80, -82, -84, -86, WhoBlA 75, -77, -80, -85, WorAl, WrDr 76, -80, -82, -84, -86*

Yerkow, Charles *AuBYP SUP*

Yermakov, Nicholas *DrAP&F 85, ScFSB*

Yermakov, Nicholas 1951- *ConAu 118, TwCSFW 86*

Yevtushenko, Yevgeny *ConFLW 84, NewYTBS 86[port]*

Yevtushenko, Yevgeny 1933- *BioIn 6, -7, -8, -9, -10, -11, -12, ConAu 81, ConLC 1, -26[port], CurBio 63, EvEuW, IntAu&W 77, IntWW 76, LinLib L, MakMC, McGEWB, NewYTBE 71, -72, -73, PenC EUR, RComWL, TwCWr, WhoTwCL, WhoWor 74, WorAl, WorAu*

Yezierska, Anzia 1885-1970 *AmAu&B, AmWomWr, BioIn 2, -4, -7, -9, -12, ConAu 89, DcLB 28[port], InWom, LinLib L, NotAW MOD, OxAmL, -83, REnAL, TwCA, -SUP, WhAm 7, WomNov*

Yezzo, Dominick 1947- *ConAu 53*

Yglesias, Helen *DrAP&F 85*

Yglesias, Helen 1915- *BioIn 9, -10, -12, ConAu 15NR, -37R, ConLC 7, -22[port], ConNov 86, NewYTBS 81[port], WhoAm 76, -78, -80, -82, WhoE 74, -75, -77, WorAu 1975[port], WrDr 84, -86*

Yglesias, Rafael *DrAP&F 85*

Yglesias, Rafael 1954- *BioIn 9, -10, ConAu 37R, NewYTBE 72*

Yolen, Jane 1939- *AuBYP, BioIn 8, -9, -13, ChlLR 4[port], ChhPo S2, ConAu 11NR, -13R, DcLB 52[port], EncSF, ForWC 70, FourBJA, ScF&FL 1, -2, ScFSB, SmATA 4, SmATA 1AS[port], TwCCW 78, -83, WhoAm 78, -80, -82, WhoAmW 83, WrDr 80, -82, -84, -86*

Yorinks, Arthur 1953- *IntAu&W 86*

York, Carol Beach 1928- *AuBYP SUP, BioIn 10, ConAu 1R, -6NR, FifBJA[port], ForWC 70, SmATA 6, WhoAmW 64, -66*

York, William 1950- *ConAu 107, IntAu&W 86*

Yorke, Margaret *ConAu X*

Yorke, Margaret 1924- *Au&Wr 71, ConAu 2NR, IntAu&W 76, -77, -82, Novels, TwCCr&M 80, -85, WhoWor 80, WrDr 76, -80, -82, -84, -86*

Yoshida, Jim 1921- *BioIn 9, ConAu 41R*

Youd, Samuel 1922- *BioIn 10, ConAu 77, SmATA 30, -47[port], WorAu*

Youd, Samuel *see also* Christopher, John

Youman, Roger Jacob 1932- *ConAu 65, WhoAm 76, -78, -80, -82, -84, -86, WhoE&I 85*

Young, Al *DrAP&F 85*

Young, Al 1939- *BioIn 8, BlkAWP, ConAu 29R, ConLC 19, ConNov 76, -82, -86, ConPo 70, -75, -80, -85, DcLB 33[port], LivgBAA, NegAl 83, OxAmL 83, RAdv 1, SelBAAf, SelBAAu, WhoAm 76, 78, -80, -82, WrDr 76, -80, -82, -84, -86*

Young, Bob 1916-1969 *BioIn 7, ConAu X, SmATA 3*

Young, Bob *see also* Young, Robert W

Young, Carrie *IntAu&W 86X*

Young, Carrie 1923- *ConAu X*

Young, Chesley Virginia 1919- *AmSCAP 66, ConAu 33R, IntAu&W 76, -77, WhoAmW 74, -72, -75, -77, -79, -81, WhoE 74, -75, -77, -79, -81, WrDr 76, -80, -82, -84, -86*

Young, Dean Wayne 1938- *WhoAm 78, -80, -82*

Young, Dorothea Bennett 1924- *ConAu 13NR, -13R, SmATA 31*

Young, Edward 1910-1964 *AuBYP, ConAu X, SmATA 3*

Young, Edward *see also* Reinfeld, Fred

Young, James V 1936- *ConAu 69*

Young, Jan 1919- *AuBYP, BioIn 7, -9, ConAu X, IntAu&W 76X, -77X, SmATA 3, WrDr 76, -80, -82, -84*

Young, Jan *see also* Young, Janet Randall

Young, Janet Randall 1919- *AuBYP, BioIn 9, ConAu 5R, -5NR, ForWC 70, IntAu&W 76, -77, -82, SmATA 3, WhoAmW 75, WrDr 76, -80, -82, -84, -86*

Young, Janet Randall *see also* Randall, Janet

Young, John Richard *AuBYP*

Young, Leontine R 1910- *ConAu P-1, ForWC 70*

Young, Louise B 1919- *ConAu 10NR, -25R, IntAu&W 76, -77, WrDr 76, -80, -82, -84, -86*

Young, Louise Buchwalter 1919- *WhoMW 84*

Young, Margaret B 1922- *BkP, ConAu 21R, InB&W 80, SelBAAu, SmATA 2, WhoAmW 74, -68, -70, -72, -75, -83, WhoBlA 75, -77, -80, WhoE 74, -75, -77, -79, -81*

Young, Margaret Buckner *WhoBlA 85, WhoE 85, WhoWor 87*

Young, Margaret Buckner 1922- *InB&W 85, SelBAAf*

Young, Miriam 1913-1974 *AuBYP, BioIn 7, -10, ConAu 37R, -53, ScF&FL 1, -2, SmATA 7, WrDr 76, -80*

Young, Morris N 1909- *AmM&WS 73P, -76P, -79P, -82P, BioIn 8, ConAu 33R, IntMPA 78, WhoE 77, -79, WrDr 76, -80, -82, -84, -86*

Young, Morris Nathan 1909- *AmM&WS 86P*

Young, Neil 1945- *Baker 84, BioIn 11, -12, -13, ConAu 110, ConLC 17, CurBio 80[port], EncFCWM 83, EncPR&S 74, -77, IlEncRk, RkOn 78, RolSEnR 83, WhoAm 78,*

181

–80, –82, –84, –86, WhoHol A,
WhoRock 81[port], WhoRocM 82,
WorAl

Young, Neil *see also* Crosby, Stills,
Nash & Young

Young, Otis E, Jr. 1925- *ConAu 53,
DrAS 74H, –78H, –82H, IndAu 1917*

Young, Patrick 1937- *AuBYP, BioIn 8,
–11, –13, ConAu 69, SmATA 22[port]*

Young, Percy M 1912- *Au&Wr 71,
AuBYP, Baker 78, BioIn 8,
ConAu 13R, IntWWM 77, OxMus,
SmATA 31, WhoMus 72*

Young, Percy Marshall 1912- *Baker 84*

Young, Peter 1915- *Au&Wr 71,
ConAu 13R, IntAu&W 76, –77, –82,
Who 74, –82, –83, –85, WhoWor 78*

Young, Robert F 1915- *ConSFA,
EncSF, ScF&FL 1, –2, ScFSB,
TwCSFW 86, WhoSciF, WrDr 86*

Young, Robert W 1916-1969 *AuBYP,
ConAu 5R, SmATA 3*

Young, Robert W *see also* Randall,
Janet

Young, Robert W *see also* Young, Bob

Young, Scott 1918- *BioIn 10, CaW,
CanWW 79, –80, –81, –83,
ConAu 5NR, –9R, OxCan, –SUP,
SmATA 5, TwCCW 78, WhoAm 74,
–76, –78, –80, –82, WhoCanL 85,
WrDr 80, –82, –84, –86*

Young, Stanley 1906-1975 *AmAu&B,
Au&Wr 71, BiE&WWA, BioIn 2, –7,
–10, CathA 1930, ChhPo, ConAu 57,
CurBio 75N, DrAS 74E, IndAu 1917,
IntAu&W 76, NatCAB 63[port],
NewYTBS 75, NotNAT, WhAm 6,
WhE&EA, WhoAm 74*

Young, Whitney M 1921-1971 *BioIn 6,
–7, –8, –9, –10, –11, –12, CivRSt,
ConAu P-1, CurBio 65, –71, –71N,
EncAB-H, EncSoH, InB&W 80,
LinLib L, –S, McGEWB,
NatCAB 57, NegAl 76[port],
–83[port], NewYTBE 70, –71,
ObitOF 79, ObitT 1971, PolProf J,
PolProf K, SelBAAu, WebAB, –79,
WhAm 5, WorAl*

Young, Whitney Moore, Jr. 1921-1971
AmRef[port], InB&W 85, SelBAAf

Yourcenar, Marguerite 1903-
*Au&Wr 71, BioIn 3, –10, –11, –12,
–13, BlueB 76, ConAu 69,
ConFLW 84, ConLC 19, –38[port],*
CurBio 82[port], EncWL, –2,
ForWC 70, InWom, IntAu&W 76,
–77, –82, IntDcWB, IntWW 74, –75,
–76, –77, –78, –79, –80, –81, –82,
–83, LinLib L, ModFrL,
NewYTBS 79, –81[port], REn,
WhoAm 74, –76, –78, –82, –84, –86,
WhoAmW 74, –61, –68, –70, –72,
–75, –81, WhoFr 79, WhoWor 74,
–82, –84, –87, WorAu

Yurchenco, Henrietta 1916-
*AuBYP SUP, ConAu 37R, ForWC 70,
WhoAm 74, –76, –78, –80, –82,
WhoAmW 74*

Yurchenco, Henrietta Weiss 1916-
IntWWM 85, WhoAm 84, –86

Z

Zacharis, John C 1936- *ConAu 73*
Zachary, Hugh *TwCSFW 86*
Zachary, Hugh 1928- *ConAu 13NR, -21R, IntAu&W 77, ScF&FL 1, WhoS&SW 73, -75, -76, WrDr 76, -80, -82, -84, -86*
Zagoren, Ruby 1922-1974 *AuBYP, ConAu P-1, ForWC 70, WhoAmW 74*
Zaharias, Babe 1911?-1956 *BioIn 1, -2, -3, -4, -5, -6, -7, -8, -9, -10, -11, -12, CurBio 47, -56, WhAm HSA, WhFla, WorAl*
Zahn, Timothy 1951- *TwCSFW 86*
Zaidenberg, Arthur 1903?- *AmAu&B, AuBYP, -SUP, BioIn 7, ConAu 108, SmATA 34[port], WhoAm 74, -76, -78, -80, -82, WhoAmA 76, -78, -80, -82*
Zaidenberg, Arthur 1908- *WhoAm 84*
Zalben, Jane B 1950- *BioIn 10, ConAu 4NR, -49, SmATA 7, WrDr 76, -80, -82, -84*
Zalben, Jane Breskin *DrAP&F 85, WrDr 86*
Zalben, Jane Breskin 1950- *FifBJA[port]*
Zamyatin, Yevgeni 1884-1937 *CasWL, ClDMEL, CnMD, CnMWL, DcRusL, EncWL, EvEuW, McGEWD 84, ModSL 1, ModWD, Novels, PenC EUR, REn, TwCA, -SUP, TwCLC 8[port], TwCWr, WhoTwCL, WorAl*
Zappler, Lisbeth 1930- *AuBYP SUP, BioIn 11, ConAu 4NR, -49, SmATA 10*
Zarchy, Harry 1912- *AuBYP, BioIn 6, -7, ConAu 1R, -2NR, MorJA, SmATA 34[port]*
Zarem, Lewis *AuBYP, BioIn 7, EncSF, ScF&FL 1*
Zaslavsky, Claudia 1917- *ConAu 1NR, -49, SmATA 36*
Zassenhaus, Hiltgunt 1916- *AuNews 1, BioIn 10, -11, ConAu 49, WhoAm 78, -80, -82*
Zaturenska, Marya 1902-1982 *AmWomWr, AnObit 1982, BioIn 4, -11, -12, ChhPo, -S3, CnDAL, ConAu 105, -13R, ConLC 6, -11, ConPo 70, -75, -80, ForWC 70,*
NewYTBS 82, OxAmL, -83, PenC AM, REn, REnAL, SixAP, TwCA, -SUP, WhAm 8, WhoAm 74, -76, -78, -80, WhoAmW 74, -68, -70, -72, -75, -77, WhoPolA, WrDr 76, -80, -82
Zebrowski, George *DrAP&F 85*
Zebrowski, George 1945- *ScFSB, TwCSFW 86, WrDr 86*
Zechlin, Ruth Hedwig Conradine 1899- *Au&Wr 71*
Zei, Alki *BioIn 13*
Zei, Alki 1928- *AuBYP, ChlLR 6[port], ConAu 77, FourBJA, SmATA 24[port], TwCCW 78B, -83B*
Zelazny, Roger *DrAP&F 85*
Zelazny, Roger 1937- *Au&Wr 71, BioIn 12, ConAu 21R, ConLC 21[port], ConSFA, DcLB 8[port], EncSF, IntAu&W 76, -77, -82, LinLib L, Novels, PostFic, ScF&FL 1, -2, ScFSB, SmATA 39, SupFW, TwCSFW 86, WhoAm 82, WhoHr&F, WhoSciF, WorAl, WrDr 76, -80, -82, -84*
Zerman, Melvyn Bernard 1930- *ConAu 14NR, -77, IntAu&W 82, -86, SmATA 46[port]*
Ziemian, Joseph 1922-1971 *ConAu 65*
Ziff, Gil 1938- *ConAu 106*
Zim, Herbert 1909- *AmAu&B, AmPB, Au&Wr 71, AuBYP, BioIn 2, -3, -4, -7, -9, BlueB 76, BkP, ChlLR 2, ChhPo S3, ConAu 13R, CurBio 56, JBA 51, LinLib L, SmATA 1, -30[port], WhoAm 74, -76, -78, -80, -82, WrDr 76, -80, -82, -84*
Zimbardo, Philip 1933- *AmM&WS 73S, -78S, BioIn 10, -11, ConAu 85, WhoAm 80, -82, WrDr 80, -82, -84, -86*
Zimbardo, Philip George 1933- *WhoAm 84, -86*
Zimmerman, Paul L 1932- *ConAu 10NR, -25R*
Zimmerman, Robert 1941- *AmAu&B, ConAu X, IntWWP 82X, WebAB, -79*
Zimmerman, Robert *see also* Dylan, Bob
Zimring, Franklin E 1942- *WhoAmL 85*

Zindel, Bonnie 1943- *ConAu 105, SmATA 34[port], WhoAmW 85, -87, WhoWor 87*
Zindel, Paul *OxAmT 84*
Zindel, Paul 1936- *AuBYP, BioIn 9, -10, -11, -12, CelR, ChlLR 3, CnThe, ConAu 73, ConDr 73, -77, -82, ConLC 6, -26[port], ConTFT 3[port], CurBio 73, DcLB 7[port], -52[port], DcLEL 1940, FifBJA[port], McGEWD, -84, NatPD, -81[port], NotNAT, OxAmL 83, OxChL, SmATA 16, TwCCW 78, -83, WhoAm 74, -76, -78, -80, -82, -84, -86, WhoThe 72, -77, -81, WorAl, WorAu 1970, WrDr 76, -80, -82, -84, -86*
Ziner, Feenie *DrAP&F 85*
Ziner, Feenie 1921- *BioIn 7, -10, ConAu X, ForWC 70, SmATA 5*
Zinkin, Taya 1918- *ConAu 1R, -2NR, IntAu&W 77, -82, WhoWor 76, -78, WrDr 76, -80, -82, -84, -86*
Zinn, Howard 1922- *AmAu&B, AmM&WS 73S, BioIn 10, -11, ConAu 1R, -2NR, DrAS 74H, -78H, -82H, MugS, PolProf J, WhoAm 74, -76, -78, -80, -82, -84, -86, WhoWor 74, WrDr 76, -80, -82, -84, -86*
Zinner, Stephen H 1939- *ConAu 119*
Zinner, Stephen Harvey 1939- *AmM&WS 86P*
Zinsser, Hans 1878-1940 *AmAu&B, BiHiMed, BioIn 1, -2, -3, -4, -5, -7, -9, CurBio 40, DcAmB S2, DcAmMeB 84, DcNAA, DcScB, InSci, LongCTC, NatCAB 36, OxMed 86, REnAL, TwCA, -SUP, WebAB, -79, WhAm 1*
Zisfein, Melvin Bernard 1926- *ConAu 108, WhoAm 74, -76, -78, -80, -82, -84, -86, WhoE 75, -77, WhoGov 77, -75, WhoS&SW 75, -76, WhoWor 82*
Zistel, Era *ConAu 19NR, -25R*
Zizmor, Jonathan 1946?- *BioIn 12*
Zochert, Donald 1938- *ConAu 81, IntAu&W 82*

Zoffer, Gerald R 1926?-1982 *BioIn 13, ConAu 107*
Zola, Emile 1840-1902 *AtlBL, BbD, BiD&SB, BioIn 1, -2, -3, -4, -5, -6, -7, -8, -9, -10, -11, -12, -13, CasWL, CelCen, ClDMEL, CnThe, ConAu 104, CyWA, DcAmSR, DcBiA, DcEuL, Dis&D, EncWL, EncWT, EuAu, EvEuW, FilmgC, GrFLW, HalFC 84, LinLib L, -S, LongCEL, McGEWB, McGEWD, -84, ModWD, NewC, NewEOp 71, NotNAT A, -B, Novels[port], OxEng, -85, OxFr, OxThe, PenC EUR, RComWL, REn, REnWD, TwCLC 1, -6[port], -21[port], WhDW, WhoTwCL, WorAl*
Zolotow, Charlotte 1915- *AmPB, AmWomWr, AuBYP, BioIn 6, -7, -9, -10, -13, BkP, ChlLR 2, ConAu 3NR, -5R, DcLB 52[port], Dun&B 79, ForWC 70, IntAu&W 76, -77, LinLib L, MichAu 80, MorJA, OxChL, PiP, SmATA 1, -35, TwCCW 78, -83, WhoAm 76, -78, -80, -82, WhoAmW 74, -66, -68, -70, -72, -75, -77, -79, -81, -83, -85, -87, WrDr 76, -80, -82, -84, -86*
Zolotow, Maurice 1913- *AmAu&B, Au&Wr 71, BioIn 2, -4, ConAu 1R, -1NR, CurBio 57, REnAL, WhoAm 74, -76, -78, -80, -82, -84, -86, WhoWor 72, -78, WrDr 76, -80, -82, -84, -86*
Zolynas, Al *DrAP&F 85*
Zolynas, Al 1945- *ConAu 105, IntWWP 82*
Zuker-Bujanowska, Liliana 1928?- *BioIn 12*
Zulli, Floyd 1922-1980 *BioIn 4, -5, -12, ConAu 108, -37R, CurBio 58, -81N, DrAS 74F, -78F, WhoE 75*
Zumwalt, Eva 1936- *ConAu 9NR, -65*
Zweig, Stefan 1881-1942 *BiDMoPL, BioIn 13, ConAu 112, EncWL 2[port], OxThe 83, TwCLC 17[port]*
Zwinger, Ann 1925- *BioIn 13, ConAu 13NR, -33R, SmATA 46[port], WrDr 82, -84*

KEY TO SOURCE CODES

MorMA	More Memorable Americans, 1750-1950
MotPP	Motion Picture Performers
MouLC	Moulton's Library of Literary Criticism
MovMk	The Movie Makers
MugS	Mug Shots
MusSN	Musicians since 1900
NamesHP	Names in the History of Psychology
NatCAB	The National Cyclopedia of American Biography
NatLAC	National Leaders of American Conservation
NatPD	National Playwrights Directory
NegAl	The Negro Almanac
NewC	The New Century Handbook of English Literature
NewCBMT	New Complete Book of the American Musical Theater
NewCon	The New Consciousness, 1941-1968
NewEOp	The New Encyclopedia of the Opera
NewOxM	The New Oxford Companion to Music
NewRR83	The New Rock 'n' Roll
NewYHSD	The New-York Historical Society's Dictionary of Artists in America
NewYTBE	The New York Times Biographical Edition
NewYTBS	The New York Times Biographical Service
NewYTET	The New York Times Encyclopedia of Television
NewbC	Newbery and Caldecott Medal Books
Newb	Newbery Medal Books
NinCLC	Nineteenth-Century Literature Criticism
NotAW	Notable American Women
NotNAT	Notable Names in the American Theatre
Novels	Novels and Novelists
ObitOF	Obituaries on File
ObitT	Obituaries from the Times
ODwPR	O'Dwyer's Directory of Public Relations Executives
OhA&B	Ohio Authors and Their Books
OxAmH	The Oxford Companion to American History
OxAmL	The Oxford Companion to American Literature
OxAmT	The Oxford Companion to American Theatre
OxArt	The Oxford Companion to Art
OxAusL	The Oxford Companion to Australian Literature
OxCan	The Oxford Companion to Canadian History and Literature
OxCanL	The Oxford Companion to Canadian Literature
OxChess	The Oxford Companion to Chess
OxChL	The Oxford Companion to Children's Literature
OxEng	The Oxford Companion to English Literature
OxFilm	The Oxford Companion to Film
OxFr	The Oxford Companion to French Literature
OxGer	The Oxford Companion to German Literature
OxLaw	The Oxford Companion to Law
OxLitW	The Oxford Companion to the Literature of Wales
OxMed	The Oxford Companion to Medicine
OxMus	The Oxford Companion to Music
OxShips	The Oxford Companion to Ships and the Sea
OxSpan	The Oxford Companion to Spanish Literature
OxThe	The Oxford Companion to the Theatre
OxTwCA	The Oxford Companion to Twentieth-Century Art
PenC AM	The Penguin Companion to American Literature
PenC CL	The Penguin Companion to Classical, Oriental, and African Literature
PenC ENG	The Penguin Companion to English Literature
PenC EUR	The Penguin Companion to European Literature
PhDcTCA	Phaidon Dictionary of Twentieth-Century Art
PiP	The Pied Pipers
PlP&P	Plays, Players, and Playwrights
PoChrch	The Poets of the Church
PoIre	The Poets of Ireland
PoLE	The Poets Laureate of England
Po&Wr	The Poets & Writers, Inc. 1977 Supplement
PolProf	Political Profiles
PolsAm	Politics in America
PostFic	Postmodern Fiction

PrintW	The Printworld Directory
Profile	Profiles
PseudAu	Pseudonyms of Authors
PueRA	Puerto Rican Authors
RAdv	The Reader's Adviser
RComWL	The Reader's Companion to World Literature
REn	The Reader's Encyclopedia
REnAL	The Reader's Encyclopedia of American Literature
REnAW	The Reader's Encyclopedia of the American West
REnWD	The Reader's Encyclopedia of World Drama
RGAfL	A Reader's Guide to African Literature
RkOn	Rock On
Rk100	Rock 100
RolSEnR	The Rolling Stone Encyclopedia of Rock & Roll
ScF&FL	Science Fiction and Fantasy Literature
ScFSB	The Science Fiction Source Book
SelBAAf	Selected Black American, African, and Caribbean Authors
SelBAAu	Selected Black American Authors
SenS	A Sense of Story
SingR	The Singing Roads
SixAP	Sixty American Poets, 1896-1944
SmATA	Something about the Author
St&PR	Standard & Poor's Register of Corporations, Directors and Executives
Str&VC	Story and Verse for Children
SupFW	Supernatural Fiction Writers
TelT	Tellers of Tales
TexWr	Texas Writers of Today
ThFT	They Had Faces Then
ThrBJA	Third Book of Junior Authors
ThrtnMM	13 Mistresses of Murder
TwCA	Twentieth Century Authors
TwCBDA	The Twentieth Century Biographical Dictionary of Notable Americans
TwCCW	Twentieth-Century Children's Writers
TwCCr&M	Twentieth-Century Crime and Mystery Writers
TwCLC	Twentieth-Century Literary Criticism
TwCSFW	Twentieth-Century Science-Fiction Writers
TwCWr	Twentieth Century Writing
TwYS	Twenty Years of Silents
UFOEn	The UFO Encyclopedia
USBiR	United States. Department of State: The Biographic Register
Ward	1977 Ward's Who's Who among U.S. Motor Vehicle Manufacturers
WebAB	Webster's American Biographies
WebAMB	Webster's American Military Biographies
WebE&AL	Webster's New World Companion to English and American Literature
WhDW	Who Did What
WhAm	Who Was Who in America
WhAmP	Who Was Who in American Politics
WhE&EA	Who Was Who among English and European Authors
WhFla	Who Was Who in Florida
WhJnl	Who Was Who in Journalism
WhLit	Who Was Who in Literature
WhNAA	Who Was Who among North American Authors
WhScrn	Who Was Who on Screen
WhThe	Who Was Who in the Theatre
WhWW-II	Who Was Who in World War II
WhsNW	Who's New Wave in Music
Who	Who's Who
WhoAdv	Who's Who in Advertising
WhoAm	Who's Who in America
WhoAmA	Who's Who in American Art
WhoAmJ	Who's Who in American Jewry
WhoAmL	Who's Who in American Law
WhoAmM	Who's Who in American Music
WhoAmP	Who's Who in American Politics
WhoAmW	Who's Who of American Women